THE ROYAL & ANCIENT

GOLFER'S HANDBOOK

1990

87TH YEAR OF PUBLICATION

JOINT EDITORS:
MARK WILSON AND LAURENCE VINEY

MACMILLAN

Contents

Foreword   6
Michael Attenborough, R&A Captain, 1990   10

Part I: 1989 Season

The Professional Golf Year, Michael Williams   12
The Amateurs, Raymond Jacobs   16
The World of Women's Golf, Lewine Mair   20
Outstanding Moments of the Year   22
The Major Championships, Mitchell Platts   29
1989 Tournament Results   39
The Golf Foundation 1989, Chris Plumridge   140
Awards   145
1990 Programme of Events   148

Part II: Past Tournament Results

The Major Championships   156
Ladies' Major Championships   168
British and Irish National Championships   170
Overseas National Championships   186
PGA European Tour   204
Professional Men's Internationals   213
Men's Amateur   224
Ladies' Amateur   246
Juniors: Boys, Girls, Youths   258
County and District Championships   270
Royal & Ancient Tournaments   307

Part III: Who's Who in Golf *(compiled by Alan Elliott)*

British Players   310
Overseas Players   343
British International Players, Men   358
British International Players, Women   379
Association of Golf Writers   391
British Association of Golf Course Architects   394

Golfing Hotel Compendium
Buyer's Guide
Index of Advertisers

Golfing Hotel Compendium 397
Buyer's Guide 430
Index of Advertisers 442

Part IV: Clubs and Courses in the UK and Europe *(Compiled by Jan Bennett)*

1990 Centenary Clubs 444
Explanation of details and abbreviations 460
Great Britain and Ireland: Indexes and Maps 462
Courses and Clubs:
   England 492
   Ireland 583
   Scotland 599
   Wales 628
Driving Ranges in Great Britain and Ireland 636
France sets the pace for new courses, Michael Gedye 643
Maps: Northern France; Mediterranean Coast and Algarve 645
Continental Clubs and Courses 647

Part V: The Government of the Game

The Royal & Ancient Golf Club 704
Statement of Functions of the Royal & Ancient Golf Club 706
Rules of Golf 711
Standard Scratch Score and Handicapping Scheme: Men 770
LGU Handicapping System 788
Governing Bodies 799
Championship Conditions 805
International Match Conditions 807
Golf Associations 810
Addresses of British and Overseas Golfing Organisations 813

Part VI: Golf History

Origin of Golf 828
Evolution of the Rules of Golf 832
The Championships of Great Britain 834
Royal Golf Clubs 838
Famous Players of the Past 840

Part VII: Interesting Facts and Record Scoring

Interesting Facts and Unusual Incidents 852
Record Scoring 888

Index 895

Foreword: The Problems of Success

The year 1989 served the interests of golf in Europe remarkably well. Both the amateur and professional games enjoyed successes at the highest international levels – uniquely so in the case of the match for the Walker Cup at the Peachtree Club, Atlanta, Georgia, where the Great Britain and Ireland team won for the first time in the United States after a final day of near unbearable tension and excitement. It was an occasion that strengthened greatly the reputation of amateur golf as the epitome of true sportsmanship, and it also produced the ultimate reward for all the administrative effort that has gone into coaching programmes to raise playing standards throughout the British Isles. The same benefits were seen at Royal Birkdale during the Amateur Championship which attracted a widespread wealth of young, fresh talent. It all promises so much for the future, nowhere more so than in Wales, with Stephen Dodd becoming the fourth challenger from the Principality to win the Amateur title in the space of a decade.

Professional golf reached new peaks with the PGA European Tour staging its longest, richest season ever. And again it was a team contest that created the most memorable and meaningful moments. The tie at The Belfry that kept the Ryder Cup in Europe after two successive victories over the United States was compelling enough to command seven million TV spectators, and the subsequent New Year Honours award of the CBE to Tony Jacklin rightly recognised his exceptional powers of leadership. Once again, however, there was nothing quite comparable to the last minutes of the Open Championship for dramatic impact. The championship has now reached such levels of organisation and quality of play that each year is faced with the same, seemingly impossible, task of at least equalling the last. Somehow, the challenge is always mastered, and the 1989 route taken at Royal Troon was an historic, four-hole, three-way play-off from which America's Mark Calcavecchia emerged as the champion with a birdie on the last extra hole. Any venue other than the Old Course at St Andrews this year might have had a problem to keep pace with that excitement.

The brave pioneering that has gone into the Women's Professional Golfers European Tour deserved the progress achieved last season, sufficient to encourage its administrators into opening talks with their counterparts in America about an international series along Ryder Cup lines. Ambition and optimism are always to be applauded, but professional golf for women in Europe is still in its infancy and it would serve no purpose to create an uneven match. They have strived long and hard to gain respect, and now having earned it they need to protect it. Challenging the vastly more experienced women of the US Tour could have its dangers.

The amateur scene in women's golf also had much to admire and applaud. Helen Dobson's collection of championship wins set records that will stand for years, if not for ever. Helen, like Ronan

Rafferty who was the leading money winner on the men's European Tour, is a product of the Golf Foundation, and the overall flourishing state of junior golf in Britain is a fair testimony to the magnificent work being done by the Foundation's coaching scheme.

Invariably, however, success brings its problems, and especially so when it is enjoyed to the degree golf is experiencing. The popularity of the game has meant ever-lengthening queues of newcomers at too few courses. Radical changes in our attitude towards the need for new facilities will have to be accepted if we are to maintain golf's proud history. The full enormity of the task ahead was made clear in the two intriguing and invaluable surveys published late last year by the Royal & Ancient Golf Club of St Andrews, the government of the game. In *The Demand For Golf* it was proved that 691 more courses need to be built in Britain by the year 2000 to meet the full demand. Sadly, unless there are major changes in outlook, only a fraction of this number is likely to materialise, fewer even than the 159 completed in France over the past five years (with another 134 under construction). The R&A survey urges action in numerous directions, and recommends the formation of a National Golf Development Council to encourage an unprecedented increase in Britain's facilities. Hopefully, no time will be wasted in taking this first, vital step.

Along with the demand for new courses there is also a serious need to look after those in existence, declares the Royal & Ancient in *The Way Forward.* In this publication the R&A's Greenkeeping Panel examines almost every aspect of course management in Britain. It pulls no punches in condemning British golf's attitude to greenkeeping in many cases and, in marked contrast to America, as being disorganised, penny-pinching and arrogant.

Most clubs' greens committee members, it regrets, serve for three to five years, and then step down by rotation just as they are ready to make a serious contribution. The Panel urges greatly increasing the present levy for the training of greenkeepers. The Panel stresses that the production of year-round courses with firm, fast, true greens and firm, mud-free fairways is essential for the future of British golf. 'If the game is to survive in the form we know and cherish then failure to tackle greenkeeping problems cannot be contemplated.'

The urgent needs of the game detailed by the R&A documents form a disturbing catalogue. There can be no doubt now that British golf's record of progress is at serious risk. A decade of challenge lies ahead if the warnings are to be heeded. And they must be, whatever the cost or changes of attitude involved.

On this subject of change, *The Golfer's Handbook*, in its 87th year of publication, is proud to welcome formally the Royal & Ancient Golf Club of St Andrews as its new patron. The result is a uniquely authoritative partnership between the government of golf and the game's premier work of reference. *The Royal & Ancient Golfer's Handbook* now looks forward with confidence to the many challenges of the future.

Mark Wilson
Sunningdale, January 1990

The Ford Amateur Golf Tournament first teed-off in 1966. Since then it has grown into Britain's premier amateur golf event. Last year, for instance, over 138,000 club players competed for the opportunity to represent their country at the Belfry. For this Ford would like to pass on their congratulations to all the golf clubs, Ford dealers and of course competitors whose enthusiasm has made the tournament what it is today.

For 25 years Ford have been encouraging better driving.

1966 La Moye

More recently, Ford's involvement in Golf, and in particular this tournament, has raised over £170,000 for The Golf Foundation; a scheme whereby junior players can receive the coaching they need to become tomorrow's top stars.

Combine with this Ford's sponsorship of the increasingly competitive Ford Ladies' Classic, and you can see why they are proud to have been the driving force on Britain's fairways as well as its roads over the past 25 years.

1990 The Belfry

Ford in Golf
Twenty-five year anniversary

In 1966, Ford Motor Company Limited set up a national golf tournament for amateur club golfers all over the United Kingdom. The tournament, originally run in conjunction with Slazenger, soon grew in size and popularity to become the Ford Amateur Golf Tournament. The event grew to such a degree that it even merited an entry in the Guinness Book of Records as the largest participation amateur golf event in the world. Over the years, many famous golfing personalities have been involved with the event, such as Peter Alliss, Max Faulkner, Bernard Gallagher, Bernard Hunt and Patrick 'Teach' Tallack.

Twenty-five years on, the Ford Amateur Golf Tournament is still as popular as ever, with over 1100 golf clubs and some 130,000 club golfers playing for the chance to represent their country.

The tournament is open from 17 March to all UK golf clubs and male club golfers over 18. Each preliminary round is sponsored by the Local Ford Dealer. Following the National Team Trials in each of the four home nations, 12 golfers from each country qualify for the prestigious Ford Home International Final, staged at The Belfry at the end of August. The 48 finalists are guaranteed the golfing chance of a lifetime, playing in true Ryder-Cup style over three days of competitive play. Coached and captained by some of the game's top professionals, the 12-man teams from England, Northern Ireland, Scotland and Wales will gain invaluable experience throughout the event, and enjoy Ford's memorable hospitality. This year, the four professionals are: Tommy Horton for England, David Jones for Northern Ireland, George Will for Scotland and David Llewellyn for Wales.

The Golf Foundation has also benefited from the Ford Amateur Golf Tournament. A national prize draw, open to all-comers, generates substantial funds for the Golf Foundation. In fact, over £170,000 has been raised to date to assist in the development of junior golf.

Ford Motor Company have also supported the WPGET for many years through the Ford Ladies Classic, staged on the beautiful Duchess Course at Woburn Golf and Country Club. The 9th Ford Ladies Golf Classic, held this year between 25 and 28 April, with substantial prize money of £65,000, attracts the very top lady professional golfers from all over the world.

So why not join Ford in Golf during 1990 at the Ford Amateur Golf Tournament or go along to the Ford Ladies Golf Classic at Woburn? Whether you play, or just enjoy watching, the twenty-fifth anniversary of Ford's involvement in golf is sure to be a memorable one.

Introducing Michael Attenborough, Captain of the Royal & Ancient Golf Club of St Andrews

© David Miles ProColour Ltd

Michael Attenborough was born in Britford, near Salisbury, in October 1939 and later moved to Kent where he became a member of Chislehurst Golf Club and after that Royal St George's, Sandwich, where he was Captain in 1982/83.

He was educated at Rugby School, for which he still plays in the Halford-Hewitt, and is a Past President of the Public Schools Golfing Society. At Oxford he won his Blue for golf in 1959–60–61.

In 1957 he played for the England Boys Team, following which he had a number of major successes: the Hampshire Hog 1960, County Champion of Champions 1964, the Duncan Putter 1966, the Prince of Wales Challenge Cup 1969. He was also Scandinavian Amateur Champion in 1965 and Kent Amateur Champion in 1963, 1964 and 1965. He was a member of the Walker Cup team in 1967, and in 1966 and 1968 played for Great Britain and Ireland. He also played for England in 1964, 1966, 1967 and 1968.

His international golfing career was shortened by his increasing business responsibilities in the publishing company of Hodder and Stoughton, where he holds the position of Joint Managing Director.

Part I
The Season

The Professional Golf Year

Michael Williams

Just as 1988 was the year of Sandy Lyle, so 1989 was the year of his greatest rival, Nick Faldo. The latter has dogged the former's footsteps throughout his career and Faldo did it again, following Lyle's victories 12 months earlier not only in the United States Masters but also in the Dunhill Masters and then in the Suntory world match play.

There have been other occasions when Faldo had proved what Lyle could do, he could do, too. Lyle won the Open in 1985; Faldo won it two years later. Lyle was Europe's leading money winner first in 1979, Faldo's turn came four years later. Even their dates of birth are close, though in this instance Faldo comes first, born in July 1957 whereas Lyle arrived in February 1958.

In a golfing sense they are much closer to being twins, though the marked difference between them in 1989 was that Lyle had the worst year of his career, 53rd in the European money list and in such doldrums that when Tony Jacklin came to nominate his three selections for the Ryder Cup team, Lyle (who had nowhere near enough points to get in automatically) insisted that he be left out. This would have been unthinkable at the beginning of the year after he had started quite well in America and it has to

© Phil Sheldon

Nick Faldo completed his best season ever by giving his £100,000 victory prize to children's charities.

© Matthew Harris

Fellow professionals credit Severiano Ballesteros with the best swing in golf.

go down as probably the most callous, as well as one of the saddest decisions ever made by a sportsman, let alone a golfer.

Faldo, by comparison, stood head and shoulders above everyone, his finest hour being when he won the Masters in circumstances that were just about as gripping as in 1988 when Lyle had pulled the fat out of the fire with that historic seven iron from the fairway bunker at Augusta's 18th hole and followed it by sinking a birdie putt to beat Mark Calcavecchia. Similarly it was a birdie by Faldo that beat Scott Hoch, though this time it was at the second extra hole after they had tied on 283, five under par. After rain had interrupted play on the Saturday, Faldo had completed his third round with a seemingly irretrievable 77 to stand four strokes behind Ben Crenshaw. What followed was not the lowest final round by the ultimate champion for in 1978 Gary Player had had a 64; but Faldo's 65 matched Jack Nicklaus's score in 1986 and it has to go down as one of the finest pressure rounds in a major championship.

When Faldo came back home he promptly won the Volvo PGA championship at Wentworth and then the Dunhill British Masters at Woburn. After the intervention of the United States Open, in which he finished 18th, Faldo then won the French Open at Chantilly, making it three out of three in Europe.

Much later Faldo was to admit how much it had all taken out of him and there were times when one tended to think that he had become too wrapped up in the mechanics of the game, almost hypnotised by the guidance of his 'guru', David Leadbetter. However, this year was to end on an emphatic note when he won the Suntory world match play with a standard of golf that had never before been seen at Wentworth. He was approximately 38 under par for his three games and 105 holes and his last nine holes of 30 when he came back from three down to beat Ian Woosnam with an eagle at the last was something those who saw it will never forget. Immediately afterwards Faldo announced that he was to donate the whole of his winning cheque of £100,000, the first six-figure cheque ever to have been at stake in Europe, to charities for sick children. The esteem in which he is held has never been higher.

Despite the finest season he has ever had, Faldo was only fourth in the Volvo order of merit, the leading money winner being Ronan Rafferty, the first Irishman to finish at the top of the list since the great Christy O'Connor in 1962.

At 25, Rafferty represents the first of the new breed. Something of a child prodigy, playing indeed for the full Irish team when still a boy, his progress in his eight years as a professional has been one of steady improvement.

It was not until this year that he broke through with his first victory in Europe, in the Italian Open. The floodgates opened. He then won the Scandinavian Open and in 26 tournaments he did not once miss a cut. However it was in the last event of the season, the Volvo Masters at Valderrama, that Rafferty truly came of age with his third and certainly his best win of the year.

There could not have been a better last act, with less than £2000 between José-Maria Olazabal, who was then leading the money list, and Rafferty. The two of them fought it out shot for shot until they were tied for the lead with nine holes to play. It was only then that Olazabal, who at 23 is two years younger than Rafferty, finally buckled. Rafferty nevertheless had to re-double his efforts in the face of a brilliant late thrust from Faldo.

Altogether Rafferty's earnings for the year reached £400,311 but it is worth recalling that Olazabal, second with £336,239, had played in seven fewer tournaments and morally had the better record. His turn will surely come.

The curious coincidence was that the American season had an equally dramatic finish. In the Nabisco at Hilton Head, Tom Kite also overtook Payne Stewart at the head of the money list at the last gasp, winning at the second extra hole of a play-off. Kite's winnings for the season of $1,395,278 took his career earnings beyond $5million. He is now the game's biggest all-time money winner.

Yet a major championship continues to elude him. In the 1989 United States Open at Oak Hill, Rochester, he held a three-stroke lead with 15 holes to play. However at the fourth he took seven and Curtis Strange stepped in to win his second successive title, a stroke ahead of Ian Woosnam who, in tying with Chip Beck and Mark McCumber, enjoyed his best finish in a major championship.

No one since Ben Hogan in 1950–51 had won consecutive US Opens and Strange joins therefore one of the game's most revered figures. Desperate for a so-called 'superstar', the Americans have grabbed hold of him with both hands and hoisted him shoulder high. There were signs elsewhere that United States golf is again on the march; a tied Ryder Cup match, victory in the Dunhill Cup at St Andrews a week later and then in the Four Tours championship in Tokyo at the very end of the season. It is a pity that this Four Tours event between America, Europe, Australasia and Japan has seemingly taken root under the land of the rising sun for it is the third time it has been held there. The concept seems to me to be good and I would like to see each of the tours in turn hosting it.

What will have given the Americans particular satisfaction was the victory by Mark

Calcavecchia in the Open at Royal Troon in the first abbreviated version of a play-off. He beat Greg Norman and Wayne Grady, two Australians, over four holes. There had not been a play-off since Tom Watson beat Jack Newton at Carnoustie in 1975 but that was over 18 holes. A few years ago the Royal and Ancient decided that an extra day was better avoided, particularly in the interests of spectators, and they introduced a shortened version. With ties in both the Masters and US PGA decided by sudden death, the American Open is consequently the one remaining major championship that calls the players back for another 18 holes.

After a number of years of decidedly inclement weather, the Ayrshire coast was bathed in hot sunshine all week and the final afternoon was one of the most enthralling for many moons, largely made by a wonderful late thrust from Norman, who is so often so near and yet so far. Calcavecchia appeared late on the scene with a birdie at the last. The play-off was at once full of excitement as Norman resumed where he had left off with birdies at each of the first two holes. The American matched the second of them – in fact he holed out first – but it was the three strokes it took Norman to get down from the fringe of the third (17th) hole that opened wide the door.

Payne Stewart, another 'nearly' man, at last crossed that elusive threshold by winning the US PGA at Kemper Lakes, Chicago, though the memory will also be of the three-stroke lead the normally reliable Mike Reid lost with three holes to play.

However the focal point of the season was the Ryder Cup at The Belfry in September. It was billed as being the 'match of the century' and it was not far off it either, Europe and the United States tying 14–14. It was the second time the two sides had finished deadlocked, the other being at Royal Birkdale in 1969 though then it was a purely British team. By incorporating players from the continent, Europe has made a much better contest of it, the score since 1979, the year of the change, being America 3 1/2 Europe 2 1/2. This was Tony Jacklin's fourth and last term as captain and since he retires with only one defeat, in 1983, he will prove a most difficult man to follow.

With Europe gaining a slender two-point lead over the first two days, it was a predictably close finish, though at one stage on that breathtaking final afternoon the Americans had one point already in the bag from Kite, led in six other matches and were down in only one.

Gradually, however, Europe came fighting back, led by Olazabal, whose five and a half points out of six played a huge part in the Cup being retained after victories in 1985 and 1987.

Indeed when Christy O'Connor junior, with the 'two iron of his life' to beat Fred Couples, and José-Maria Canizares, with a wonderfully judged long putt close to the hole to beat Ken Green, gained their points, Europe could no longer be beaten.

The European Ryder Cup team survived last-day alarms to follow two victories with a dramatic tie at The Belfry.

© Matthew Harris

But three games were still left and America won them all, Mark McCumber, Lanny Wadkins and Curtis Strange. Indeed, the last hole with water to be carried both off the tee and with the second shot, caused enough drama to last a lifetime. On a golf course that has in its time taken its share of criticism, it is now only fair to say that I cannot think of a better finishing hole in the world.

In some ways it was disappointing that Rafferty was the only newcomer in the European team, too many of the next generation failing to take the opportunity that was there during the season. With signs that Severiano Ballesteros, despite three victories, and Bernhard Langer might be on the wane and Faldo, Lyle and Woosnam all of much the same age, opportunity not only beckons but must be taken if the progress that was made in the eighties is to be continued into the nineties.

Of the 29 players who earned more than £100,000, 10 of them did so without winning a tournament. The all-exempt tour in America is said to be at the root of their inability to find the same stars they did a decade or more ago. Now we have an all-exempt tour in Europe as well. For the time being all is still well and it may well remain so.

However there are interminable days in the middle of the season as over-large fields grind their way round at a snail's pace when one aches to give everybody a hearty kick up the backside. Golf, as we are reminded by the professionals, is not a race but, as they sometimes call it, 'just another day at the office'. By the look of some of them as they wait another 10 minutes on the tee they do not know how lucky they are to be doing what they are doing.

EVERYTHING JUST COMES TOGETHER.

Admittedly conditions were perfect (and the King's Course one of the world's finest) but the 13th, Braid's Brawest, is as hard a hole as they come.

I was playing it like a dream.

After a few days of complete relaxation in one of the world's greatest hotels something strange seems to happen to my game.

Distinctions between ball, club and action seem to blur. The swing is sweeter, the drives truer, the putting more assured.

There is a perfect balance between the demands of the fairways, the subtleties of the greens, the richness of the scenery and a wonderful stillness.

This is golf at its best. The least my game can do is rise to the occasion.

THE GLENEAGLES HOTEL

For full details of the Gleneagles Golfing Experience please write to the Leisure Manager,
THE GLENEAGLES HOTEL, AUCHTERARDER, PERTHSHIRE, SCOTLAND PH3 1NF
OR TELEPHONE 0764 62231. TELEX 76105.

one of The Leading Hotels of the World ®

The Amateurs

Raymond Jacobs

The victory of Britain and Ireland over the United States in the Walker Cup match at the Peachtree Club, Atlanta, stood so far above all other achievements in amateur golf in 1989 as to make them puny by comparison. Something similar was seen in 1938 and 1971, when the combined side won on both occasions at St Andrews, and in 1965 at Baltimore in the only tied match. To triumph on American soil for the first time in 16 attempts was as bewilderingly unexpected as it was joyously unique, as desperately fraught as it was ultimately deserved at the end of a hot and humid afternoon of prolonged turmoil.

Great Britain and Ireland's first Walker Cup Team to enjoy victory in the United States.

© Phil Sheldon

The crescendo of events which led towards a climax of unprecedented tension took on an almost dream-like quality. Britain took the opening series of foursomes and singles by 2 $^1/_2$–1 $^1/_2$ and 5–3 respectively to lead by 7 $^1/_2$–4 $^1/_2$ after the first day. When they again won the foursomes, by 3 $^1/_2$–$^1/_2$, to accumulate an 11–5 margin, a straightforward mopping-up operation seemed in prospect. Britain and

Ireland, after all, now needed only 1 $^1/_2$ points from the last eight singles, whereas the United States required 7 if they were to halve the match and retain the cup and another half point still if they were to win outright for the 29th time in 32 encounters – an order not so much tall but as good as invisible to the naked eye.

One of the most ill-timed and unprophetic remarks was then made by a British player. Returning to the clubhouse, part of which was occupied by General Sherman during his punitive march through Georgia in the Civil War, he said of the Americans: 'Their heads are really down. They could be in for a proper thrashing.' The British captain, Geoffrey Marks, and his counterpart, Fred Ridley, took views as sharply in contrast as the situation their teams were in, the former measuring level-headed caution against legitimate expectation, the latter trying to rally his beleaguered troops with a defiant cry. Marks cautioned each of his players: 'Don't make the false assumption that if you lose it won't matter. Be sure you win your point. Don't leave it to others.' Ridley said to his men: 'You've been written off. Now you've got a chance to make history.'

In mid-afternoon a state-of-the-matches board suggested the most miraculous resurrection since that of Lazarus. The Americans led in all eight singles. This was not a pretty sight to supporters expecting a short, sharp and painless advance towards inevitable success, and the suspicion that the road to victory would not be smooth was aroused when, in the lead single, Robert Gamez made a putt of some 30 feet from short of the home green for a birdie 3 to beat Stephen Dodd by one hole. The knock-on effect of that telling shot was to spread renewed hope and confidence through the American ranks, not an unkown phenomenon in team golf, however individualistic a game it remains.

In rapid succession Russell Claydon, Peter McEvoy, Neil Roderick and Craig Cassells went down. For something like an hour Marks listened in vain to his radio for one of his team to win a hole. A glimmer of light was kindled when Andrew Hare, two down and two to play to David Martin, won both holes with superb shots to the heart of the green and Eoghan O'Connell was deprived of providing the winning point only when Phil Mickelson holed from some 10 feet at the last for the half. Just half a point more needed, but impending doom seemed about to be confirmed when Jim Milligan, two down to Jay Sigel with four to play, had to hole a substantial putt on the 15th green to avoid letting the vastly experienced American become dormie three and almost certainly grant the United States the redemption of a halved match to retain the cup.

The ensuing half-hour was certainly not for the faint-hearted, neither players nor spectators. In essence, Milligan halved his game and won the match because the short, but clinging, fringe grass round the last three greens subverted Sigel's chipping. The Bermuda rough cost the American the long 16th and the 17th, where Milligan in succession chipped dead for a winning birdie and then, having miscued his own first effort, holed out down a slick and sharply breaking slope from 30 feet to square the game. Again at the last the fringe snagged Sigel, whose seventh appearance was proving to be a match too far. Milligan had two putts from 10 feet to immortalise himself and his compatriots – and he used them.

The theories surrounding Britain and Ireland's unheralded victory were as intriguing and complex as the result itself. A core of solidity was formed by the four players who a year before had won the Eisenhower Trophy, McEvoy, Garth McGimpsey, O'Connell and Milligan, but otherwise the team seemed no more, or less, capable of succeeding where their predecessors had failed. However, morale was high, the preparations were sensible, and the exaggerated expectations which had conspired towards a collective collapse two years before at Sunningdale were thankfully absent. Marks, an uncertain captain then, was a more assured, knowledgeable and articulate leader now.

Since the United States do not take kindly to defeat, as their reactions to Ryder Cup setbacks and the successes of European professionals on the US Tour have shown, a spirited response can be expected in 1991 when the match is played in Ireland for the first time. Whatever the USGA elect to do remains to be seen. Coincidentally, however, the reigning US champion, Eric Meeks, turned professional immediately after the match instead of defending his title at Merion. Sure enough, the championship was won by a college player, Chris Patton, who played 55 holes in six days, including two qualifying rounds, before he beat Danny Green 3 and 2 in the final – a considerable achievement by one who weighed in at more than 21 stone.

Chris Patton, 21 stone giant, revealed a delicate touch to become the US Amateur champion.

© Robert Walker

However, domestically, too, the urge to turn professional reached new levels, less so in Scotland and Ireland than in England and Wales. The six-man English side which beat Scotland in the final of the European championship at Royal Porthcawl in June had lost four of its members by the time of the Home Internationals at Ganton in September, not to mention Steve Richardson, winner of the English title only a few weeks before. Nevertheless, England's resources enabled them to retain the Raymond Trophy by beating the three other countries for the second successive year. McEvoy, aged 36 and after some 140 games for England since 1976, responded to the occasion by staying unbeaten with 4 $\frac{1}{2}$ points from five games to take his total contribution past a century.

Milligan, the hero of the hour at Atlanta, also performed yeoman service for Scotland in both team championships, twice playing in all six games and taking 9 $\frac{1}{2}$ points from them. Scotland's disregarded side, at one time apparently in danger of not qualifying even for the leading match play section, surprised everyone by beating Wales 4–3 and Ireland 4 $\frac{1}{2}$–2 $\frac{1}{2}$ before they bowed 5 – 2 to England. England's seventh victory, and their fourth by beating Scotland in the final, was counter-balanced by the disappointments suffered by Ireland and Wales both in that event and in the Home Internationals, in which Wales, despite individual successes during the season, were again the whipping boys, and Ireland, from whom much was hoped despite eight of their side being under 24, lost twice.

Taking performances in amateur golf over the four homes countries as a whole, precedence had to be given to Stephen Dodd. He began the season by winning the Welsh stroke play title, continued by taking the Amateur Championship at Royal Birkdale, and completed a unique treble for his country by later capturing the native match play title. When he beat the English Internationalist, Craig Cassells, by 5 and 4 in the final of the Amateur, Dodd became the fourth Welsh player to win the championship in the 1980s (in the footsteps of Duncan Evans, Philip Parkin and Paul Mayo), a remarkable feat, given that no one from The Principality had done so in in the 84 championships since the first, in 1885, and that no Scot since Reid Jack in 1957 has prevailed. Elsewhere, Neil Roderick, twice winner of the Welsh stroke play title, won the Duncan Putter and tied with a South African, Craig Rivett, for the Brabazon Trophy. Then he and two other Welsh Internationalists, Keith Jones and Phil Price, became professionals.

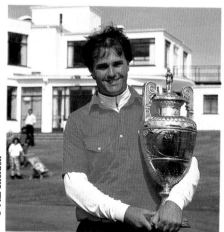

Stephen Dodd, the fourth Welshman to win the Amateur Championship in the 1980s.

© Phil Sheldon

The outstanding achievement in Scotland was the success, all the more appreciated for having been so long delayed and so many times narrowly missed, of Allan Thomson in the national championship at Lossiemouth. Thomson had been once a losing quarter-finalist, twice a

beaten semi-finalist and twice runner-up for the title in the previous eight years and for equity to be seen to be done his defeat of Alan Tait, a fellow-Ayrshireman and himself a semi-finalist two years before, by one hole in the final seemed no more than natural justice. Ironically, though, Thomson won his fourth-round match without having to play it, since his opponent was disqualified when he mistook his starting time and arrived too late on the first tee to be granted absolution.

If Thomson deserved to be the most elated Scottish golfer of the year, with the possible exception of Milligan, then the most deflated had to be Andrew Coltart. The runner-up at 18 to Milligan in the 1988 national championship, Coltart seemed assured of the British youths' title at Ashburnham when he held a lead of six strokes with nine holes of the final round to play and was still four ahead with three holes left. But Coltart lost even that advantage and paid the price when he succumbed at the first hole of a sudden-death play-off to Mike Smith, an English youth Internationalist, who must have been as agreeably surprised at such an unexpected turn of fortune as Coltart was inconsolably disbelieving.

Distribution of the spoils among the Irish was, to say the least, equitable since the four titles identifiable by the principal points of the compass, as well as the overall championship, were won by five different players, the last by Paul McGinley, another product of American college golf. The upshot was a situation sublimely in keeping with the paradoxical nature of the Irish character. The International team had the youngest average age, but the player recognised as being their best, Eoghan O'Connell, won nothing because of the allegiance to his American college which also did not allow him to play in the Home International matches. When a Scot, Alan Mathers, won the Irish youths' championship salt was rubbed more strongly into the wound.

Altogether, then, the last year of the decade proved to be its most memorable. The victory in the Walker Cup, following the nine-point defeat two years before, obviously was the summit of achievement and it led Charlie Yates, a member of the Peachtree Club and winner of the Amateur Championship at Troon in 1938, when Britain and Ireland won the match for the first time, to make the following wry, but courtly, observation to this correspondent: 'I have the record of being present at all three of your victories – 1938, 1971 and 1989. Can anyone tie me on this?' It might be a good idea if the R and A and the Golfing Union of Ireland ensure that Charlie Yates resumes his role as talisman when the defence of the cup is undertaken in 1991 at Portmarnock.

State-of-the-art cutting precision

means there's not a blade out of place

Perfection. That's what every green should be. And Ransomes GT (Greens Triple) is the greens mower that helps you achieve it.

The GT is the flagship of Ransomes' range. At its heart is an electronic control system that delivers precise cutting unit operation through a whole range of innovative features. Driven by an economical and reliable diesel engine, Ransomes GT has power to cover the course fast.

Hydrostatic transmission and steering gives effortless, precise control. Units can be removed without tools, ensuring ease of maintenance. Contact your dealer for a demonstration if you're not prepared to settle for a single blade being out of place.

The Ransomes GT. Now with new Greens Unit with Verti-Groom.

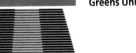

RANSOMES

No.1 in caring for courses

RANSOMES SIMS & JEFFERIES, RANSOMES WAY, IPSWICH IP3 9QG. TEL: (0473) 270000 TELEX: 98174 FAX: (0473) 270032

The World of Women's Golf

Lewine Mair

It does not necessarily take an Open to throw up the most arresting figures in golf. In 1989, the most eye-catching scoring sequence in the women's game occurred in the British Women's Senior championship at Wrexham when Wendy Russell, the most unassuming of golfers, notched two aces in the space of her first nine holes. Mrs Russell, who has since had congratulatory letters from all corners of the golfing globe, was none too proud of the first ace, that at the 127 yards fourth, for the ball had dived into the hole via a greenside tree. Ace number two, however, was the perfect specimen. Opting for a leisurely eight iron, she took aim on the right hand bank above the eighth green. She watched in mingled astonishment and disbelief as her ball rolled into the hole for a second time.

There was, as one wrote at the time, something of a misunderstanding when Mrs Russell, having had her husband summoned to the phone from his doctor's surgery in Bournemouth, proudly announced that she had had 'two holes in two'. 'What's so special about that?' said Dr Russell, before his wife made herself clear. With the British Women's Senior championship a strictly amateur affair, Mrs Russell did not find herself in the difficult position of having to drive home a couple of Mercedes. But, as she stole the headlines from the professionals, so one was reminded of the words of the late Sir Henry Cotton. Namely, that just about the finest thing about golf is the way it can bring pleasure to all ages, all standards and both sexes.

In terms of making money rather than history, Betsy King was the leading money-winner in women's golf in 1989, with her earnings on the US LPGA Tour totalling $654,132. A born-again Christian who chooses her words as carefully as her clubs, Miss King had her most memorable week at the US Women's Open at Indianwood, with scores of 67, 71, 72 and 68 to finish four ahead of that most charismatic woman golfer of them all, Nancy Lopez.

Britain's Laura Davies' stated aim at the start of 1989 was to win on both sides of the Atlantic. This she did, first fulfilling the American half of her ambition with a win in the Lady Keystone Open at Hershey. At home, she won the Laing Classic at Stoke Poges in the week when her holing of the more awkward putts was as watchable as her booming tee shots. As many as 16 under par in victory, the former Curtis Cup golfer put down her win to a Ben Sayers blade putter which she had picked up for less than £20.

That Miss Davies was not going to win again the title she most wanted, the British Open, was apparent from the moment she played her first practice round at Ferndown. Charming venue though it is, Ferndown in the middle of so dry a summer was no place for Miss Davies to let rip with her driver, even if it was a warning shade of luminous pink. The title went to the relentlessly straight Jane Geddes, the American doing the status of the championship no

Laura Davies won both sides of the Atlantic.

© *Mark Newcombe*

© Phil Sheldon

Jane Geddes took a 'relentlessly straight' route to Open title.

ohot in a semi-final match against Sweden's Helen Alfredsson which she lost at the sixteenth.

As luck would have it, the Tour's next stop was in Biarritz, her home town. Though medical opinion said she should not play, Mrs de Lorenzi did not want to let down followers who had known her since she was a child. She kept them enthralled with an opening 69, but dropped out half way through the second round as the pain became too much to take.

Her title went to Dennise Hutton, a 31-year-old Australian teaching professional who is seen as Australia's answer to Vivien Saunders. Miss Hutton, vice-president of the Australian Women's Professional Association, has a degree in psychology in education, but has only recently managed to practise what she preaches in terms of how to handle pressure. In the week prior to Biarritz, she won the Woolmark Match Play title in Barcelona. 'For the first time ever,' she said, 'I didn't allow my mind to interfere with my swing.'

Alison Nicholas, who intends to follow Laura Davies' example in playing a goodly section of both the American and the European tours in 1990, finished second on the Woolmark money list with £56,528. Her third win of the season came in the Qualitair Classic at La Manga, the final event in the most encouraging year the European Women's tour has had so far.

Though there was panic in some quarters when four early-season tournaments were called off, 21 tournaments took place. What is more, the girls played for £1.63 million, a figure not far short of the £1.85 million for which the men played only eight years ago.

It augurs well for the future of the European circuit that there are so many good amateurs waiting in the wings. Amateurs such as Sandrine Mendiburu, the 17-year-old French youngster who finished third among the professionals in Biarritz, and Helen Dobson, the English player who had a year in Britain which may never be matched. She won the English championship, the English Girls', the British Match Play championship and the British Stroke Play. On the team front, she was a member of the England side which reached the finals of the European Amateur Team championships in Spain before cleaning up in the Home Internationals at Westport. She also played in the Great Britain and Ireland side which, in September, defeated the Continent of Europe in the Vagliano Trophy match in Venice.

harm when, in describing her feelings as she came down the stretch, said that the golf she had played would have been good enough to have had her winning anywhere in the world. 'The nerves I felt coming down the stretch,' she added, 'were precisely the same as those which hit me when I was winning my US Open title.'

Marie-Laure de Lorenzi of France headed the European women's money list with £77,534. This magnificent striker of a ball would doubtless have become the first player to top the £100,000 mark had not a bad case of tendonitis forced her to cut down on tournament appearances towards the end of the season.

The injury really caught up with her in Barcelona, where she was defending her title in the Woolmark Match Play championship. At the start of the week, her caddie, Jimmy Finch, said that the pain showed only in her face but it ultimately affected her every shot. 'It's almost as if she is having to run away from the ball' said Florence Descampe as she watched the French player back off every

Nick Faldo celebrates
his US Masters victory
at Augusta.

Photo: Calvin Cruce

© Phil Sheldon

And golf is fun? Jack Nicklaus shows what he feels
about the rain at the US Masters.

Nick Faldo breaks golf's high jump record on
winning the Suntory World Match Play Championship at Wentworth.

© Matthew Harris

© Phil Sheldon

© Matthew Harris

Happiness is winning a vital Ryder Cup game – and Christy O'Connor is swamped by emotion.

© Matthew Harris

© Matthew Harris

The vast riches of professional golf can cause problems. Robert Lee uses a spare moment during a tournament to read The Financial Times.

Grief is finding trouble in the Swilcan Burn on the Old Course at St Andrews – and Christy O'Connor is swamped again during the Dunhill Cup.

Agony is losing the Walker Cup – and the moment of defeat is too painful for the US team to watch.

© Phil Sheldon

Drama is holing a chip shot at a crucial moment – an action sequence of Scotland's Jim Milligan in the final hour of the Walker Cup.

© Phil Sheldon

© Phil Sheldon

Showering sand and a destroyed dream – Australian Greg Norman bows to defeat in a bunker on the fourth extra hole of the Open Championship play-off at Royal Troon.

So far and so near – Ian Woosnam, who took the Concorde to the US Open at Rochester, New York, and finished tied second. Above, action in a bunker and, above right, celebrating a successful putt with his caddie.

It's ours, all ours – Europe's team captain Tony Jacklin hugs the Ryder Cup.

© Matthew Harris

©Matthew Harris

History at the US Masters: 1988 winner Sandy Lyle of Scotland obliges with the traditional ceremony of putting the Green Jacket on the new champion, Nick Faldo of England.

© *Phil Sheldon*

Water, water everywhere . . . Seve Ballesteros, below, takes a soaking trying to play out of trouble at the US Masters, and Payne Stewart, below right suffers the same fate during the Ryder Cup match at The Belfry.

© *Phil Sheldon*

© *Phil Sheldon*

Enhancing the future for clubs and players alike

International Golfers Club is working with clubs across Europe and beyond who are preparing now for the increasing demands of the future, enabling them to manage their facilities more effectively and more rewardingly, to everyone's advantage.

Perfected over seven years, the International Golfers Club system incorporates Tee-off reservations, membership, competitions, handicaps and accounts. It also enables golf to be booked throughout the network through your own home club.

INTERNATIONAL
GOLFERS CLUB

49 Queen Victoria Street, London EC4N 4SA. Tel: 01-248 4435. Fax: 01-236 6779.

The Majors

Mitchell Platts   golf correspondent of *The Times*

The Open
at Royal Troon

Not since Tom Watson, in 1983, had an American won the Open Championship and the prospect of Mark Calcavecchia so doing appeared remote halfway through a four holes play-off with the Australians Wayne Grady and Greg Norman.

They stood together on the tee at the first hole at Royal Troon following an intoxicating contest. It mattered not to the spectators, who gathered in their thousands on these historic links, that the likes of Severiano Ballesteros and Sandy Lyle, Curtis Strange and Ian Woosnam, were out of contention, for what they witnessed was a final day of pure theatre when the emotions of the players twisted and turned amongst the sand dunes.

Grady was an incongruous figure standing next to Calcavecchia and Norman, two of the most gregarious golfers in the game. He had led the way into that final day and indeed, had taken the lead at the halfway stage following a first round when a 28-year-old Channel Islander, competing in his first Open, had hoisted himself ahead of the finest golfers in the world. Wayne Stephens notched six birdies in a near flawless 66, a record for the lengthened Royal Troon course, and that equalled the lowest score of his career. He did not falter until the 11th hole the following day when he drove into thick gorse and took seven. It was Grady, with a 67, who moved ahead. He had a halfway score of 135 and a two strokes lead from Payne Stewart (who reset the course record with a sparkling 65) and Tom Watson. The halfway cut came at two over par which was the lowest in Open Championship history.

Grady did not falter in the third round, compiling a 69, but Watson, four of whose Open Championship triumphs have come in Scotland, edged to within one stroke with a 68. Watson had won in 1982 when last the Open had been played at Royal Troon but he had not won a tournament of any description since the Nabisco Championships of Golf in 1987. He

had the support of the spectators but the frailty of his putting stroke placed him in the high-risk category even if the bookmakers, with whom he was 80-1 at the start of the week, now rated him as the favourite.

The presence of Watson naturally heightened the drama. He, however, sabotaged his own prospects by taking three putts from 15 feet at the seventh hole and then Norman exploded out of the pack.

Norman erupted with six successive birdies from the first, completed a record 64 and set the target at 275 which is 13 under par. Calcavecchia's spirits had soared from the moment he holed with a wedge at the most unlikely of positions for a birdie at the 12th. It gave him the momentum to extract two more birdies – hitting two drivers on to the 16th and then at the last an eight iron of 161 yards to four feet – for a 68 and now all the pressure was on Grady. He was not blessed with the best of

The Open Championship's first play-off for 24 years ended with American Mark Calcavecchia as the winner.

fortune because he dropped a shot at each of the short holes, the 14th and 17th, coming home and a 71 left him level with Calcavecchia and Norman.

Grady had done his best but his best was not good enough. He must have known the gods were against him when at the first extra hole Norman made a birdie and when at the next both Calcavecchia and Norman birdied. There seemed to be no holding Norman but there was to be a twist in the tail. He missed the green at the 17th, a par three, and took three

to get down. Then at the last he smoked a huge drive which, to his horror, rolled 310 yards into a fairway bunker. Calcavecchia took the bull by the horns and struck a majestic five iron to within six feet of the flag. Norman had no answer. He could move the ball forward only 90 yards and it finished in another bunker. The Australian had no option but to try to hole out . He hit the ball long and out of bounds. Calcavecchia had three putts from six feet for the Championship. An American was back on top.

Mitchell Platts

The Results

Pos	Name	Score	Prize £
1	M Calcavecchia	71-68-68-68–275	80000
2	W Grady	68-67-69-71–275	55000
(Calcavecchia won 4-hole play-off)			
	G Norman	69-70-72-64–275	55000
	T Watson	69-68-68-72–277	40000
5	J Mudd	73-67-68-70–278	30000
6	F Couples	68-71-68-72–279	26000
	D Feherty	71-67-69-72–279	26000
8	E Romero	68-70-75-67–280	21000
	P Azinger	68-73-67-72–280	21000
	P Stewart	72-65-69-74–280	21000
11	N Faldo	71-71-70-69–281	17000
	M McNulty	75-70-70-66–281	17000
13	P Walton	69-74-69-70–282	13000
	H Clark	72-68-72-70–282	13000
	S Pate	69-70-70-73–282	13000
	R Chapman	76-68-67-71–282	13000
	M James	69-70-71-72–282	13000
	C Stadler	73-69-69-71–282	13000
19	L Mize	71-74-66-72–283	8575
	D Cooper	69-70-76-68–283	8575
	T Kite	70-74-67-72–283	8575
	D Pooley	73-70-69-71–283	8575
23	V Singh	71-73-69-71–284	6733
	D Love III	72-70-73-69–284	6733
	J-M Olazabal	68-72-69-75–284	6733
26	S Bennett	75-69-68-73–285	5800
	L Wadkins	72-70-69-74–285	5800
	C Beck	75-69-68-73–285	5800
	S Simpson	73-66-72-74–285	5800
30	J Hawkes	75-67-69-75–286	4711
	G Koch	72-71-74-69–286	4711
	J Nicklaus	74-71-71-70–286	4711
	P Jacobsen	71-74-71-70–286	4711
	B Marchbank	69-74-73-70–286	4711
	M A Martin	68-73-73-72–286	4711
	I Baker-Finch	72-69-70-75–286	4711
	M Ozaki	71-73-70-72–286	4711
	M Davis	77-68-67-74–286	4711
39	M Harwood	71-72-72-72–287	4100
	T Armour III	70-71-72-74–287	4100
	J Woodland	74-67-75-71–287	4100
42	M O'Meara	72-74-69-73–288	3725
	L Trevino	68-73-73-74–288	3725
	R Floyd	73-68-73-74–288	3725
	J Rivero	71-75-72-70–288	3725
46	M McCumber	71-68-70-80–289	3550
	A W B Lyle	73-73-71-72–289	3550
	N Ozaki	71-71-69-78–289	3550

Pos	Name	Score	Prize
49	J Miller	72-69-76-73–290	3400
	I Woosnam	74-72-73-71–290	3400
	C O'Connor Jr	71-73-72-74–290	3400
52	B Ogle	74-70-76-71–291	3100
	M Roe	74-71-73-73–291	3100
	T Ozaki	75-71-73-72–291	3100
	M Allen	74-67-76-74–291	3100
	T Johnstone	71-71-74-75–291	3100
	E Dussart	76-68-73-74–291	3100
	R Boxall	74-68-73-76–291	3100
	G Sauers	70-73-72-76–291	3100
	B Crenshaw	73-73-74-71–291	3100
61	C Strange	70-74-74-74–292	2675
	D Graham	74-72-69-77–292	2675
	K Green	75 71 68 78 292	2675
	P Hoad	72-71-77-72–292	2675
	B Tway	76-70-71-75–292	2675
	R Rafferty	70-72-74-76–292	2675
	M Reid	74-72-73-73–292	2675
	W Stephens	66-72-76-78–292	2675
69	L Carbonetti	71-72-74-76–293	2425
	AR Stephen	71-74-71-77–293	2425
	R Claydon (Am)	70-74-74-75–293	
71	C Gillies	72-74-74-74–294	2400
72	B Faxon	72-72-75-76–295	2400
	P Teravainen	72-73-72-78–295	2400
74	E Aubrey	72-73-73-78–296	2400
75	M Sludds	72-74-73-78–297	2400
76	S Ballesteros	72-73-76-78–299	2400
	R Karlsson (Am)	75-70-76-78–299	
77	G Levenson	69-76-77-79–301	2400
78	B Langer	71-73-83-82–309	2400

(The following players missed the cut)

Pos	Name	Score			Prize
79	S Hamill	74-73	–	147	500
	N Hansen	73-74	–	147	500
	P Affleck	72-75	–	147	500
	N Briggs	77-70	–	147	500
	B Lane	74-73	–	147	500
	P Senior	74-73	–	147	500
	D Smyth	78-69	–	147	500
	T Weiskopf	74-73	–	147	500
	J Bland	72-75	–	147	500
	BE Smith	70-77	–	147	500
	D Ray	73-74	–	147	500
	M Smith	76-71	–	147	500
	S Field	76-71	–	147	500
	S Torrance	70-77	–	147	500
	N Price	74-73	–	147	500
	L Nelson	73-74	–	147	500
	M Poxon	71-76	–	147	500
96	A Bean	73-75	–	148	500
	P Mayo	75-73	–	148	500
	B Barnes	73-75	–	148	500
	G Brand Jr	76-72	–	148	500
	M Clayton	74-74	–	148	500
	F Zoeller	73-75	–	148	500
	E Els (Am)	72-76	–	148	
103	C Bolling Jr	73-76	–	149	500
	W Henry	76-73	–	149	500
	D Durnian	75-74	–	149	500
	P Baker	74-75	–	149	500
	G Evans (Am)	73-76	–	149	
108	S Tinning	78-72	–	150	500
	P Parkin	73-77	–	150	500
	R McFarlane	73-77	–	150	500
	P Carrigill	78-72	–	150	500
	A Sorensen	74-76	–	150	500
	K Waters	74-76	–	150	500
	P Mitchell	75-75	–	150	500
	D Llewellyn	78-72	–	150	500
	S Jones	73-77	–	150	500
	L Rinker	75-75	–	150	500
	J Sewell	78-72	–	150	500
	G Emerson	75-75	–	150	500
	A Stubbs	72-78	–	150	500
121	V Fernandez	75-76	–	151	500
	J Sluman	78-73	–	151	500
	GJ Brand	78-73	–	151	500
	P Carman	76-75	–	151	500
125	B Hiskey	75-77	–	152	500
	M Mouland	77-75	–	152	500
	K Brown	74-78	–	152	500
	E Darcy	75-77	–	152	500
	G Player	79-73	–	152	500
	D Williams	77-75	–	152	500
131	D Lozano	79-74	–	153	500
	W Riley	76-77	–	153	500
	P Eales	74-79	–	153	500
	J Price	80-73	–	153	500
135	D Frost	75-79	–	154	500
	C Moody	81-73	–	154	500
	S Dodd (Am)	79-75	–	154	
	G Milne (Am)	79-75	–	154	
139	P Cowen	81-74	–	155	500
	P Harrison	79-76	–	155	500
	A Hare (Am)	73-82	–	155	
	J Oshea (Am)	80-75	–	155	
143	G Townhill	79-77	–	156	500
144	P Broadhurst	73-84	–	157	500
	R Davis	78-79	–	157	500
	T Jacklin	80-77	–	157	500
	N Serizawa	79-78	–	157	500
	P Kent	78-79	–	157	500
149	DJ Russell	80-78	–	158	500
	J Rystrom	79-79	–	158	500
	J Noon (Am)	81-77	–	158	
152	J Garner	78-81	–	159	500
153	E Meeks (Am)	81-80	–	161	
154	A Palmer	82-82	–	164	500

US Open
at Oak Hill, Rochester, New York

The French supposedly coined the expression 'Never two without three'. I have not the slightest notion if Curtis Strange has even a modicum of Gallic blood in him although I suspect that following his successful defence of the US Open in 1989, he will have no hesitation in giving that old adage more than a thought or two.

Strange won at Oak Hill because he possessed the strength of character to stay firm to the cause whereas others around him, notably Tom Kite, Scott Simpson and the Japanese challenger Masashi Ozaki, withered and died in the heat of the battle. In so doing, he became the sixth golfer in history and the first since Ben Hogan in 1951/52, to win successive US Opens.

A first round of 71 left Strange trailing by five strokes. His was by no means an exceptional round with which to start his defence since no fewer than 21 players broke the par of 70. That constituted a new US Open record. Such a little slice of history, however, paled in comparison to what was to take place the following morning. Doug Weaver, a relatively unknown golfer from Hilton Head Island, South Carolina, holed in one at precisely 8.15.

Weaver's ace would have ranked low in the events of the day had not Mark Wiebe, Jerry Pate and then Nick Price all emulated his achievement. Four holes-in-one in the space of two hours and each one of them at the sixth hole! Strange did not follow suit but he did equal the course record with a near-flawless round of 64. Bernhard Langer, Jay Don Blake and Payne Stewart, the first round leaders, had slipped a notch or two and Strange, with a halfway score of 135, led by one from Kite.

The scene was set for a wonderful weekend until officials of the United States Golf Association arrived at the course at 7.00 am on Saturday. What they saw resembled a reservoir. More than two inches of rain had fallen overnight, Allen's Creek had burst its banks and the local fire brigade had to be called in to pump the water from the fairways.

That play took place at all was little short of a miracle. But it did, under clearing skies, and Kite took command. He put together a typically workmanlike 69 for a score of 205 which gave him a one stroke lead over Scott Simpson. Strange slipped to a 73, finishing three strokes behind Kite, and the prospect of Ian Woosnam becoming the first British winner of the US Open since Tony Jacklin (1970) weakened as he, too, took 73. The

Welshman began the final round six strokes adrift.

For Kite the final round was again a case of déjà vu. With a birdie at the third to Simpson's bogey, he swept three clear. The bespectacled Texan had, at the age of 39, that elusive first major championship in his sights. Then came a look of utter disbelief at the fifth as he blocked his drive into the creek. A penalty drop, a chip, a pitch and three putts made for a seven.

Kite dropped another shot at the eighth, where Simpson marked a six on his card, so that Strange, who was collecting pars with metronomic efficiency, drew level as did Ozaki with a birdie at the 10th where Kite once again faltered.

Ozaki allowed the rather docile 14th hole to get the better of him at which point Strange sensed the US Open trophy was going back to Virginia. His confidence swelled when he holed from 15 feet at the 16th, his first birdie in 35 holes, with Kite, Ozaki and Simpson all back-pedalling. It was evidence again that the winning of major championships on the most exacting of courses so often hinges on the theory that par is a virtue.

Strange did drop a shot at the 18th but he was round in 70 for a score of 278, one under par. It was left for Chip Beck, Mark McCumber and Woosnam, who extracted a birdie from two of the last four holes, to share second place as Strange followed Willie Anderson, John McDermott, Bobby Jones, Ralph Guldahl and Ben Hogan into the record books by winning the US Open twice in a row.

Mitchell Platts

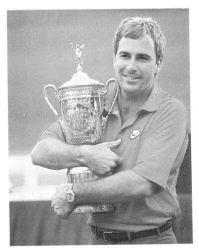

Curtis Strange successfully defended his US Open title to emulate the feat of legendary Ben Hogan.

© *Phil Sheldon*

The Results

Pos	Name	Score	Prize $
1	C Strange	71-64-73-70–278	200000
2	I Woosnam	70-68-73-68–279	67823
	M McCumber	70-68-72-69–279	67823
	C Beck	71-69-71-68–279	67823
5	B Claar	71-72-68-69–280	34345
6	S Simpson	67-70-69-75–281	28220
	J Ozaki	70-71-68-72–281	28220
8	P Jacobsen	71-70-71-70–282	24307
9	J-M Olazabal	69-72-70-72–283	19968
	T Kite	67-69-69-78–283	19968
	H Green	69-72-74-68–283	19968
	P Azinger	71-72-70-70–283	19968
13	L Nelson	68-73-68-75–284	15634
	P Stewart	66-75-72-71–284	15634
	T Pernice Jr	67-75-68-74–284	15634
	S Hoch	70-72-70-72–284	15634
	M Lye	71-69-72-72–284	15634
18	D Frost	73-72-70-70–285	13013
	N Faldo	68-72-73-72–285	13013
	JD Blake	66-71-72-76–285	13013
21	DA Weibring	70-74-73-69–286	11306
	N Henke	75-69-72-70–286	11306
	B Glasson	73-70-70-73–286	11306
	F Couples	74-71-67-74–286	11306
	S Elkington	70-70-78-68–286	11306
26	D Pooley	74-69-71-73–287	9983
	R Floyd	68-74-74-71–287	9983
	R Wrenn	74-71-73-69–287	9983
29	D Pohl	71-71-73-73–288	9006
	H Sutton	69-75-72-72–288	9006
	S Taylor	69-71-76-72–288	9006
	E Aubrey	69-73-73-73–288	9006
33	M Wiebe	69-71-72-77–289	7576
	J Sindelar	67-77-74-71–289	7576
	E Kirby	70-70-73-76–289	7576
	B Mayfair	72-69-76-72–289	7576
	L Mize	72-72-71-74–289	7576
	D Love III	71-74-73-71–289	7576
	G Norman	72-68-73-76–289	7576
	I Aoki	70-70-75-74–289	7576
	B Faxon	73-70-75-71–289	7576
	D Forsman	70-70-76-73–289	7576
43	J Nicklaus	67-74-74-75–290	6281
	S Ballesteros	75-70-76-69–290	6281
	C Dennis	72-72-72-74–290	6281
46	R Zokol	71-69-76-75–291	5485
	T Watson	76-69-73-73–291	5485
	S Jones	69-75-77-70–291	5485
	J Mahaffey	77-68-74-72–291	5485
	K Green	73-72-71-75–291	5485
51	S Pate	74-69-73-76–292	4690
	T Sieckmann	73-71-74-74–292	4690
	J Mudd	73-71-74-74–292	4690
54	C Perry	76-67-72-78–293	4299
	H Irwin	74-70-79-70–293	4299
	D Ogrin	73-72-73-75–293	4299
	W Heintzelman	72-70-75-76–293	4299
	R Black	71-74-76-72–293	4299
59	C Rose	70-75-73-76–294	4120
	B Langer	66-78-77-73–294	4120
61	D Graham	73-72-77-73–295	4099
	M Calcavecchia	74-70-74-77–295	4099
63	T Sills	72-72-71-81–296	4099
	D Halldorson	72-70-76-78–296	4099
	G Lesher (Am)	70-72-76-78–296	
66	B Wadkins	73-72-75-77–297	4099
67	D Pruitt	68-74-81-75–298	4099
	E Humenik	73-72-76-77–298	4099

US Masters

at Augusta National GC, Augusta, Georgia

The putt measured a little more than 25 feet. He had during his career holed many of a similar length. Yet as the ball disappeared into the sanctuary of the cup one could appreciate why he stood, impervious to the leaden skies and with his arms raised in a V-for-Victory salute, gaping in complete astonishment.

For this was the moment when the lad from the backwaters of Welwyn Garden City fulfilled a teenage dream. He had been hooked from the moment in 1971 when he saw Jack Nicklaus on TV playing in the Masters at Augusta. He was captivated by the charm of the setting and the challenge of the game. And he was consumed by an insatiable appetite to be the best.

Now Nick Faldo was the Master golfer.

An outstanding year for Britain's Nick Faldo began with his US Masters victory at August, Georgia, in April

The scenario which led to Faldo's famous win can never be repeated. He started with a 68 which was one stroke too many to enable him to capture the lead which went to the evergreen Lee Trevino. In practice Trevino had struck 2000 golf balls each day for three days. He had so often in the past given the Masters a derisory wave; he was now serious.

What strait-jackets Trevino is bad weather. His back reacts against wind and rain. So as the temperature plunged to 50° on the second day, he could have been forgiven for retreating. That he did not do. He remained at the head of affairs although Faldo, with a 73 against the average score that day of 75.87, moved alongside him with a three under par aggregate of 141. Seve Ballesteros and the Americans Ben Crenshaw, Ken Green, Scott Hoch and Mike Reid were all two strokes adrift.

There were only two previous Masters' champions amongst the top seven names on the leader board when the third round began. Ballesteros was one, although he seemed less than happy with his short game, and Crenshaw the other. It was Crenshaw, the winner in 1984, who pressed the accelerator. He drew four strokes clear in the third round before play, following a two hour suspension because of lightning, was brought to a halt.

Crenshaw was on the 14th hole when he was forced to quit. He completed his third round, as did the other players, on Sunday morning. The situation was no longer clear cut. Crenshaw's advantage had narrowed to one and no fewer than 22 players were separated by seven strokes. Faldo, having ballooned to a 77, was five behind. His was an Herculean task and the prospect of Faldo following Sandy Lyle into the record books appeared remote.

A European victory, however, seemed on the cards. Ballesteros, out in 31, was one ahead of Hoch and Reid. The Spaniard seemed on the threshold of repeating his wins of 1980 and 1983. The tenth, however, cost Ballesteros a stroke and Reid, pressed by Crenshaw, Faldo, Hoch and the charging Greg Norman, took the lead and then lost it with three putts at the 14th and a wedge into the water at the next. Ballesteros met his Waterloo with a six iron into the lake at the 16th.

Hoch grasped the baton but took three to get down at the 17th. Now Crenshaw, Faldo and Norman could all tie with Hoch but only Faldo did. Even then it seemed a wasted effort with Hoch standing over a two foot putt for victory at the first extra hole. It is now history that he missed. It is also history that on the very next green, Hoch met his Nemesis as Faldo completed another enthralling chapter in the history of the Masters.

Mitchell Platts

© Matthew Harris

The Results

Pos	Name	Score	Prize $
1	N Faldo	68-73-77-65–283	200000
2	S Hoch	69-74-71-69–283	120000

(Faldo won play-off at 2nd hole)

Pos	Name	Score	Prize $
3	G Norman	74-75-68-67–284	64450
	B Crenshaw	71-72-70-71–284	64450
5	S Ballesteros	71-72-73-69–285	44400
6	M Reid	72-71-71-72–286	40000
7	J Mudd	73-76-72-66–287	37200
8	J Sluman	74-72-74-68–288	32200
	J-M Olazabal	77-73-70-68–288	32200
	C Beck	74-76-70-68–288	32200
11	M O'Meara	74-71-72-72–289	25567
	F Couples	72-76-74-67–289	25567
	K Green	74-69-73-73–289	25567
14	T Watson	72-73-74-71–290	19450
	D Pooley	70-77-76-67–290	19450
	I Woosnam	74-76-71-69–290	19450
	P Azinger	75-75-69-71–290	19450
18	J Nicklaus	73-74-73-71–291	14000
	C Strange	74-71-74-72–291	14000
	J Ozaki	71-75-73-72–291	14000
	L Trevino	67-74-81-69–291	14000
	D Frost	76-72-73-70–291	14000
	T Kite	72-72-72-75–291	14000
24	P Stewart	73-75-74-70–292	10250
	T Purtzer	71-76-73-72–292	10250
26	S Pate	76-75-74-68–293	8240
	F Zoeller	76-74-69-74–293	8240
	L Wadkins	76-71-73-73–293	8240
	L Mize	72-77-69-75–293	8240
	B Langer	74-75-71-73–293	8240
31	D Rummells	74-74-75-71–294	6900
	M Calcavecchia	74-72-74-74–294	6900
	S Jones	74-73-80-67–294	6900
34	B Lietzke	74-75-79-68–296	6000
	H Green	74-75-76-71–296	6000
	P Jacobsen	74-73-78-71–296	6000
37	B Gilder	75-74-77-71–297	5400
38	S Simpson	72-77-72-77–298	4900
	T Aaron	76-74-72-76–298	4900
	C Coody	76-74-76-72–298	4900
	R Floyd	76-75-73-74–298	4900
42	D Pohl	72-74-78-75–299	4300
43	G Twiggs	75-76-79-70–300	3900
	G Archer	75-75-75-75–300	3900
	M McCumber	72-75-81-72–300	3900
46	DA Weibring	72-79-74-76–301	3125
	M Sullivan	76-74-73-78–301	3125
	J Haas	73-77-79-72–301	3125
	B Lohr	75-76-77-73–301	3125
50	C Pavin	74-74-78-76–302	2800
51	A Bean	70-80-77-77–304	2700
52	TC Chen	71-75-76-84–306	2600

(The following players missed the cut)

Name	Score		Name	Score		Name	Score	
T Simpson	75-77	– 152	L Nelson	77-76	– 153	PD Yates III	81-77	– 158
M Wiebe	77-75	– 152	B Tway	77-77	– 154	D Tewell	77-81	– 158
A North	77-75	– 152	T Sieckmann	79-75	– 154	N Price	76-82	– 158
G Player	76-77	– 153	H Sutton	72-82	– 154	S Verplank	79-79	– 158
A Magee	73-80	– 153	B Glasson	77-77	– 154	M Hatalsky	78-81	– 159
B McCallister	76-77	– 153	M Brooks	77-78	– 155	A Palmer	81-80	– 161
B Casper	75-78	– 153	M McNulty	80-75	– 155	E Meeks	83-79	– 162
J Sindelar	75-78	– 153	R Howe III	77-79	– 156	D Eger	84-78	– 162
AWB Lyle	77-76	– 153	G Koch	76-80	– 156	D Ford	81-82	– 163
C Stadler	74-79	– 153	J Benepe	82-75	– 157	C Hardin	85-85	– 170
G Sauers	74-79	– 153	T Nakajima	76-81	– 157	G Brewer	83	– 83

USPGA Championship

at Kemper Lakes, Illinois

Mike Reid scored 66 in the first round of the USPGA Championship at Kemper Lakes, on the outskirts of Chicago, to tie the lead with Leonard Thompson. Reid would lead through to the 71st hole of the Championship, at which point he would be the victim of misfortune, but on that first day no one took too much notice of the slim Mormon from Provo, Utah.

For the first day of the 1989 USPGA Championship was all about nostalgia. Tom Watson, one month short of his 40th birthday, finished on 67. Arnold Palmer, one month away from his 60th birthday, and Jack Nicklaus, five months short of being 50, were both on 68. 'Isn't that great,' Palmer said. 'When I saw Tom and Jack's names up there with mine I thought here are three guys, three generations apart, still competing with the best. That's the great thing about golf. History seems to repeat itself.'

In fact Palmer might have led. He dropped a stroke at each of the last two holes, so forfeiting that prospect. His second round of 74 put him back in the pack as Reid took charge with a 67 for a total of 133. He led by two from Craig Stadler and Thompson with Watson one stroke further adrift. Nicklaus, who scored 72 for 140, confessed to being 'flabbergasted' by the low scoring on this public course. The generous greens, however, were receptive targets and the course, laid out on gently undulating land, was a credit to the greenkeeping staff.

There was a suspension on Friday afternoon because of a thunderstorm, and eight threesomes were compelled to return early on Saturday to complete their second rounds. Another storm on Saturday curtailed play and Reid returned on Sunday morning to complete a 70, for a score of 203. With this he took a three stroke lead, ahead of Dave Rummells. Scott Hoch, Chris Perry and Stadler were each one stroke further adrift. Payne Stewart was six strokes behind following a 69 but Watson, Nicklaus and Palmer had all retreated.

Victory for Reid seemed a formality when with four holes to play he was left nursing a three strokes lead. He would most certainly have won had it not been that this was a major championship. The special pressures associated with winning such titles can consume even the steadiest of golfers and so it proved with Reid. He inexplicably drove into the water at the 16th.

That *faux pas* would not alone have destroyed Reid but the knowledge that Stewart, ahead of him, had in some style covered the inward half in 31 to complete a 67 for a 12 under par aggregate of 276, placed an additional burden on his shoulders. If Reid dropped another stroke then he would be forced to take part in a sudden death play-off. That did not occur because Reid dropped two.

Disaster for Mike Reid left Payne Stewart celebrating victory at the USPGA Championship.

© Phil Sheldon

The 17th hole at Kemper Lakes is a testing one, especially at such a critical point in a championship, but Reid turned it into a horror story. His tee shot left the ball in the fringe. His chip was woefully short. His first putt from 15 feet raced almost three feet past. His next missed. Reid marked a five on his card and walked to the 18th tee. He now needed a birdie to be in that play-off.

Stewart had come from nowhere and he was now the champion elect. He had shot the best back nine of the tournament and he deserved to be in the position that he was. Reid, however, did not deserve to be stood alone in the middle of the 18th fairway with a five iron in his hand. He hit that shot to seven feet and from there he might have salvaged everything. Reid, however, missed and Stewart was champion by one stroke. Andy Bean and Curtis Strange eventually shared second place with Reid. Stewart said: 'This is a dream I've worked at for a long time.' Reid said: 'Where can you go around here to have a good cry?'

Mitchell Platts

The Results

Pos	Name	Score	Prize $
1	P Stewart	74-66-69-67–276	200000
2	A Bean	70-67-74-66–277	83333
	M Reid	66-67-70-74–277	83333
	C Strange	70-68-70-69–277	83333
5	D Rummells	68-69-69-72–278	45000
6	I Woosnam	68-70-70-71–279	40000
7	C Stadler	71-64-72-73–280	36250
	S Hoch	69-69-69-73–280	36250
9	T Watson	67-69-74-71–281	30000
	E Fiori	70-67-75-69–281	30000
	N Faldo	70-73-69-69–281	30000
12	M Wiebe	71-70-69-72–282	21900
	M Sullivan	76-66-67-73–282	21900
	G Norman	74-71-67-70–282	21900
	J Gallagher Jr	73-69-68-72–282	21900
	S Ballesteros	72-70-66-74–282	21900
17	C Perry	67-70-70-76–283	15000
	L Mize	73-71-68-71–283	15000
	B McCallister	71-72-70-70–283	15000
	D Love III	73-69-72-69–283	15000
	B Gardner	72-71-70-70–283	15000
	I Aoki	72-71-65-75–283	15000
	B Crenshaw	68-72-72-71–283	15000
24	D Pohl	71-69-74-70–284	10000
	J Sluman	75-70-69-70–284	10000
	T Armour	70-69-73-72–284	10000
27	H Twitty	72-71-68-74–285	7535
	J Nicklaus	68-72-73-72–285	7535
	M Hulbert	70-71-72-72–285	7535
	T Simpson	69-70-73-73–285	7535
	B Tennyson	71-69-72-73–285	7535
	D Frost	70-74-69-72–285	7535
	P Jacobsen	70-70-73-72–285	7535
34	L Thompson	66-69-73-78–286	5750
	L Roberts	69-71-72-74–286	5750
	D Pooley	70-71-72-73–286	5750
	B Gilder	72-72-74-68–286	5750
	T Kite	67-73-72-74–286	5750
	I Baker-Finch	74-68-70-74–286	5750
	C Beck	73-71-69-73–286	5750
41	S Pate	70-72-74-71–287	4260
	B Lohr	75-69-69-74–287	4260
	B Britton	75-67-71-74–287	4260
	D Edwards	69-72-72-74–287	4260
	S Elkington	69-75-71-72–287	4260
46	N Price	70-72-72-74–288	3220
	L Nelson	71-74-68-75–288	3220
	W Grady	70-75-72-71–288	3220
	B Lietzke	70-72-73-73–288	3220
	R Floyd	73-71-70-74–288	3220
51	K Perry	71-74-70-74–289	2750
	S Jones	71-74-71-73–289	2750
53	S Simpson	70-74-75-71–290	2490
	D Tewell	73-69-72-76–290	2490
	T Purtzer	69-73-74-74–290	2490
	C Rose	74-71-72-73–290	2490
	P Blackmar	68-75-75-72–290	2490
58	G Sauers	76-68-75-72–291	2380
	A North	69-75-77-70–291	2380
	B Bryant	70-70-72-79–291	2380
61	B Langer	74-71-75-72–292	2330
	G Koch	71-72-77-72–292	2330
63	A Palmer	68-74-81-70–293	2290
	G Twiggs	71-73-74-75–293	2290
65	M McCumber	70-73-74-77–294	2260
66	H Green	69-73-76-77–295	2240
67	J Mudd	71-70-80-75–296	2220
68	D Stockton	76-69-75-77–297	2200
69	R Black	73-70-74-82–299	2180
70	C Byrum	73-71-76-87–307	2170

1989 Results

Johnnie Walker Ryder Cup
at The Belfry, Sutton Coldfield, September 22-24, 1989

First Day – Foursomes

USA	Matches	GB and Europe	Matches
T Kite and C Strange	½	N Faldo and I Woosnam	½
L Wadkins and P Stewart (1 hole)	1	H Clark and M James	0
T Watson and C Beck	½	S Ballesteros and J-M Olazabal	½
M Calcavecchia and K Green (2 and 1)	1	B Langer and R Rafferty	0
	3		1

Four-Ball

C Strange and P Azinger	0	S Torrance and G Brand Jr (1 hole)	1
F Couples and L Wadkins	0	H Clark and M James (3 and 2)	1
M Calcavecchia and M McCumber	0	N Faldo and I Woosnam (2 holes)	1
T Watson and M O'Meara	0	S Ballesteros and J-M Olazabal (6 and 5)	1
	0		4

Second-Day – Foursomes

L Wadkins and P Stewart	0	I Woosnam and N Faldo (3 and 2)	1
C Beck and P Azinger (4 and 3)	1	G Brand Jr and S Torrance	0
M Calcavecchia and K Green (3 and 2)	1	C O'Connor Jr and R Rafferty	0
T Kite and C Strange	0	S Ballesteros and J-M Olazabal (1 hole)	1
	2		2

Four-Ball

C Beck and P Azinger (2 and 1)	1	N Faldo and I Woosnam	0
T Kite and M McCumber (2 and 1)	1	B Langer and J-M Canizares	0
P Stewart and C Strange	0	H Clark and M James (1 hole)	1
M Calcavecchia and K Green	0	S Ballesteros and J-M Olazabal (4 and 2)	1
	2		2

Third Day – Singles

P Azinger (1 hole)	1	S Ballesteros	0
C Beck (3 and 2)	1	B Langer	0
P Stewart	0	J-M Olazabal (1 hole)	1
M Calcavecchia	0	R Rafferty (1 hole)	1
T Kite (8 and 7)	1	H Clark	0
M O'Meara	0	M James (3 and 2)	1
F Couples	0	C O'Connor Jr (1 hole)	1

K Green	0	J-M Canizares (1 hole)	1
M McCumber (1 hole)	1	G Brand Jr	0
T Watson (3 and 2)	1	S Torrance	0
L Wadkins (1 hole)	1	N Faldo	0
C Strange (2 holes)	1	I Woosnam	0
	—		—
	7		5

Match Aggregate: Europe 13; USA 13; halved 2.
Non-playing Captains: A Jacklin, Europe; R Floyd, USA.

Asahi Glass Four Tours World Championship
(formerly Nissan Cup and Kirin Cup)
at Yomiuri CC, Tokyo

Pos
1   USPGA Tour
2   PGA European Tour
3   PGA Japan Tour
4   Australia/New Zealand Tour

Championship Match

European Tour	Points	United States PGA Tour	Points
M James (74)	0	M Calcavecchia (68)	2
R Rafferty (66)	2	K Green (70)	0
G Brand Jr (69)	2	P Stewart (70)	0
B Langer (68)	0	C Beck (62)	2
I Woosnam (71)	0	T Kite (65)	2
J-M Olazabal (68)	2	C Strange (69)	0
	—		—
	6		6

Winners: United States PGA Tour on tie-break rule with 404 total strokes to Europe's 416 in final match.

World Cup
at Las Brisas, Spain

Pos		Score	Prize £ (each)
1	Australia (P Fowler 137, W Grady 141)	278	75,853
2	Spain (J-M Olazabal 143, J-M Canizares 138)	281	37,926
3	Sweden (M Lanner 142, O Sellberg 145)	287	24,020
	USA (P Azinger 141, M McCumber 146)	287	24,020

The 1989 Volvo Order of Merit

1989 Official Money List

Pos	Name	Official Prize Money £	Pos	Name	Official Prize Money £
1	R Rafferty (N Ire)	400,311.32	51	C Mason (Eng)	52,904.86
2	J-M Olazabal (Sp)	336,239.44	52	D Gilford (Eng)	52,337.79
3	C Parry (Aus)	277,321.86	53	A W B Lyle (Scot)	49,408.34
4	N Faldo (Eng)	261,552.68	54	J Bland (SA)	44,818.55
5	M James (Eng)	245,916.99	55	P Parkin (Wal)	44,201.38
6	I Woosnam (Wal)	210,100.97	56	P O'Malley (Aus)	43,914.59
7	B Langer (W Ger)	205,194.52	57	J Haas (USA)	43,841.21
8	S Ballesteros (Sp)	202,762.89	58	P Mitchell (Eng)	43,387.06
9	M McNulty (Zim)	179,693.60	59	P Carrigill (Eng)	42,588.35
10	D Feherty (N Ire)	178,167.17	60	V Fernandez (Arg)	42,577.35
11	S Torrance (Scot)	170,650.31	61	J van de Velde (Fr)	41,076.47
12	G Brand Jr (Scot)	169,890.37	62	G Turner (Eng)	40,757.31
13	E Romero (Arg)	168,558.15	63	M Poxon (Eng)	39,488.27
14	M Harwood (Aus)	165,059.60	64	A Sherborne (Eng)	39,356.80
15	M Allen (USA)	157,644.43	65	H Baiocchi (SA)	39,277.18
16	P Senior (Aus)	143,954.72	66	L Carbonetti (Arg)	38,624.62
17	P Walton (Ire)	135,195.33	67	E Dussart (Fr)	38,282.54
18	J-M Canizares (Sp)	133,289.42	68	P Teravainen (USA)	36,915.11
19	D Cooper (Eng)	123,776.88	69	B Longmuir (Scot)	36,792.12
20	H Clark (Eng)	123,566.34	70	B Norton (USA)	36,427.41
21	C O'Connor Jr (Ire)	122,797.41	71	K Brown (Scot)	36,338.41
22	P Fowler (Aus)	119,237.16	72	M Pinero (Sp)	36,250.64
23	D Durnian (Eng)	113,191.03	73	N Hansen (Eng)	35,104.47
24	V Singh (Fij)	109,612.24	74	M Moreno (Sp)	34,484.58
25	C Montgomerie (Scot)	109,084.21	75	G Levenson (SA)	34,438.92
26	M Roe (Eng)	107,647.95	76	M A Martin (Sp)	34,434.06
27	B Ogle (Aus)	106,002.38	77	K Dickens (Eng)	34,332.53
28	A Murray (Eng)	101,612.19	78	K Waters (Eng)	34,057.42
29	O Sellberg (Swe)	101,575.80	79	R Hartmann (SA)	33,695.48
30	G J Brand (Eng)	98,914.46	80	A Binaghi (It)	32,632.76
31	R Chapman (Eng)	95,698.07	81	J Rystrom (Swe)	32,285.52
32	M Lanner (Swe)	95,330.67	82	J Heggarty (N Ire)	31,161.02
33	B Lane (Eng)	87,144.44	83	M Clayton (Aus)	29,855.14
34	J Rivero (Sp)	85,981.37	84	B Marchbank (Scot)	29,833.12
35	E Darcy (Ire)	85,041.86	85	M A Jimenez (Sp)	29,348.86
36	F Nobilo (NZ)	79,325.12	86	R Lee (Eng)	29,147.21
37	D Smyth (Ire)	79,313.71	87	R Drummond (Scot)	28,585.76
38	M Persson (Swe)	75,087.60	88	B Malley (USA)	28,550.06
39	M Mouland (Wal)	74,829.46	89	B Gallacher (Scot)	28,258.12
40	R Boxall (Eng)	71,093.67	90	T Johnstone (Zim)	27,666.82
41	S Bennett (Eng)	70,553.38	91	D Jones (N Ire)	27,149.31
42	P Broadhurst (Eng)	67,103.80	92	D A Russell (Eng)	25,563.84
43	J Hawkes (SA)	64,850.22	93	O Moore (Aus)	25,425.35
44	R Davis (Aus)	63,396.04	94	A Garrido (Sp)	25,226.79
45	M Davis (Eng)	61,362.96	95	J Howell (USA)	23,880.34
46	M Smith (USA)	60,457.11	96	R McFarlane (Eng)	23,699.04
47	T Charnley (Eng)	57,417.56	97	P Curry (Eng)	23,544.90
48	M Mackenzie (Eng)	57,238.69	98	S McAllister (Scot)	23,403.33
49	D Williams (Eng)	55,773.43	99	J Quiros (Sp)	23,230.84
50	J Parnevik (Swe)	55,537.57	100	M Farry (Fr)	23,130.18

PGA European Tour 1989

AGF Open
at La Grande Motte, Montpellier, France

Name	Score	Prize £
M James	69-67-69-72–277	22909
M Mouland	72-73-70-65–280	15266
B Norton	70-70-70-71–281	8604
V Singh	73-68-73-68–282	5408
R Stelten	65-68-72-77–282	5408
S Torrance	68-67-73-74–282	5408
G Turner	73-73-65-71–282	5408
J Howell	70-75-70-68–283	3257
A Sherborne	72-70-70-71–283	3257
M Aparicio	74-72-73-65–284	2327
S Bennett	70-71-71-72–284	2327
M Besanceney	72-72-70-70–284	2327
J Quiros	69-69-72-74–284	2327
G Ralph	72-71-67-74–284	2327
D J Russell	74-73-66-71–284	2327

Baleares Open
at Santa Ponsa, Majorca

Name	Score	Prize £
O Sellberg	68-71-69-71–279	37500
M McNulty	69-70-71-71–281	16773
J-M Olazabal	71-75-68-67–281	16773
P Parkin	71-71-69-70–281	16773
D Durnian	71-72-69-70–282	6523
J Howell	68-74-70-70–282	6523
B Malley	69-70-70-73–282	6523
B Ogle	70-70-71-71–282	6523
J Quiros	71-70-71-70–282	6523
R Rafferty	72-69-69-72–282	6523

Barcelona Open
at Club Golf de Pals

Name	Score	Prize £
M Roe	69-70-69-71–279	33330
G Brand Jr	73-67-70-70–280	14906

Name	Score	Prize
C Montgomerie	73-68-72-67–280	14906
J-M Olazabal	70-71-68-71–280	14906
D Durnian	73-68-71-69–281	8470
H Clark	72-68-70-72–282	6000
P O'Malley	72-69-69-72–282	6000
G Turner	73-66-70-73–282	6000
M Calero	68-76-69-71–284	4480
D Ecob	68-72-75-70–285	3840
M Persson	72-72-71-70–285	3840

Bell's Scottish Open
at King's Course, Gleneagles

Name	Score	Prize £
M Allen	73-66-70-63-272	50000
J-M Olazabal	67-70-68-69–274	26040
I Woosnam	65-70-71-68–274	26040
R Rafferty	69-67-70-70–276	13850
D Feherty	71-67-69-69–276	13850
M McNulty	69-71-67-70–277	9750
E Romero	72-66-70-69–277	9750
R Chapman	69-70-70-69–278	7110
L Rinker	73-66 68-71–278	7110
AWB Lyle	70-66-72-71–279	5085
M Poxon	68-70-71-70–279	5085
D Smyth	67-72-74-66–279	5085
P Fowler	72-69-68-70–279	5085
R Boxall	72-69-69-69–279	5085
P Senior	71-66-68-74–279	5085

The Benson and Hedges
International Open
at Fulford, York

Name	Score	Prize £
G Brand Jr	64-72-72-64–272	50000
D Cooper	67-66-68-72–273	33300
M Mackenzie	66-68-71-69–274	18780
J-M Canizares	65-72-70-69–276	15000
C Parry	68-72-67-70–277	9925
H Clark	69-67-69-72–277	9925
I Mosey	69-67-69-72–277	9925
J Bland	67-68-70-72-277	9925
P Fowler	69-71-70-68–278	6360
B Hughes	62-71-71-74–278	6360

Benson & Hedges Trophy
at Aloha GC, Marbella, Spain

Name	Score	Prize £
MA Jimenez and X Wunsch-Ruiz	70-68-71-72–281	23,400
C Mason and G Stewart	67-69-71-76–283	17,300
GJ Brand F Descampe	69-71-72-72–284	13,400

B M W International Open
at Golfplatz München, Nord-Eichenried

Name	Score	Prize £
D Feherty	62-66-68-73–269	45820
F Couples	68-69-67-70–274	30540
P Walton	67-70-68-70–275	17210
E Darcy	70-69-70-67–276	13750
M Mouland	70-70-68-69–277	10645
M Harwood	70-71-66-70–277	10645
GJ Brand	68-68-70-72–278	7500
T Purtzer	69-69-69-71–278	7500
D Love III	65-73-70-71–279	5750
O Sellberg	66-71-70-72–279	5750

Carrolls Irish Open Championship
at Portmarnock, Dublin

Name	Score	Prize £
I Woosnam*	70-67-71-70–278	43782
P Walton	68-69-69-72–278	29159
B Ogle	69-69-74-70–282	13566
R Rafferty	67-71-72-72–282	13566
M McNulty	71-67-71-73–282	13566
S Torrance	71-70-72-70–283	7381
J-M Olazabal	69-70-73-71–283	7381
M Davis	73-71-66-73–283	7381
P McWhinney	70-68-73-72–283	7381
E Darcy	71-70-69-74–284	5253
BE Smith	69-71-73-72–285	4527
C O'Connor Jr	68-71-71-75–285	4527
P Senior	68-70-76-71–285	4527
M Roe	73-72-70-71–286	4019

Winner after play-off

Cepsa Madrid Open
at Puerta de Hierro, Madrid

Name	Score	Prize £
S Ballesteros	67-67-69-69–272	37500
H Clark	65-68-70-70–273	25000
P Walton	70-67-70-68–275	14070
M Lanner	70-70-68-68–276	11250
D Cooper	67-72-67-71–277	9500
T Charnley	70-69-70-69–278	7850
R Davis	69-72-70-68–279	6150
M Persson	64-70-75-70–279	6150
E Dussart	69-71-68-72–280	4370
C Mason	70-68-71-71–280	4370
M James	70-68-68-74–280	4370
M Smith	69-72-69-70–280	4370

Credit Lyonnais Cannes Open
at Cannes Mougins

Name	Score	Prize £
P Broadhurst	65-70-72–207	34851
J Heggarty	69-72-67–208	15588
B Ogle	71-68-69–208	15588
P Senior	70-66-72–208	15588
R Rafferty	72-67-70–209	8829
J van de Velde	71-69-70–210	5845
T Charnley	71-68-71–210	5845
M McNulty	71-70-69–210	5845
D Cooper	73-64-73–210	5845
D Smyth	70-72-69–211	3671
J Rivero	72-68-71–211	3671
M Calero	70-66-75–211	3671
P Walton	74-71-66–211	3671
M Persson	68-68-75–211	3671

Dunhill British Masters
at Woburn G & CC

Name	Score	Prize £
N Faldo	71-65-65-66–267	50000
R Rafferty	70-65-67-69–271	33300
C O'Connor Jr	69-66-73-68–276	15493
O Sellberg	71-66-70-69–276	15493
M Harwood	69-70-66-71–276	15493
I Woosnam	71-70-70-66–277	9000
R Hartmann	70-69-71-67–277	9000
M Smith	71-69-66-71–277	9000
M James	69-68-70-71–278	6080
P Senior	74-66-66-72–278	6080

Name	Score	Prize £
P Mitchell	67-73-64-74–278	6080
J-M Olazabal	69-71-71-68–279	4860
J-M Canizares	69-67-71-72–279	4860
J Hawkes	73-65-69-72–279	4860
G Brand Jr	72-73-67-68–280	4320
J Rivero	69-70-71-70–280	4320
I Mosey	70-73-69-69–281	3810
M Clayton	72-70-70-69–281	3810
B Shearer	72-71-69-69–281	3810
R McFarlane	72-73-65-71–281	3810

Dunhill Cup
at The Old Course, St Andrews

Semi-Finals:

USA 2; IRELAND 1

M Calcavecchia beat P Walton 69-71
T Kite beat C O'Connor Jr 71-71 on the 1st
    play-off hole
C Strange lost to R Rafferty 72-71

JAPAN 2; ENGLAND 1

N Ozaki beat D Durnian 70-72
K Suzuki beat H Clark 66-70
H Meshiai lost to M James 73-71

Play-off for 3rd and 4th places:

ENGLAND 2; IRELAND 1

D Durnian lost to P Walton 72-71
H Clark beat R Rafferty 72-75
M James beat C O'Connor Jr 69-76

(Ireland received £16,526 each and
England received £22,724 each)

Final:

USA 3½; JAPAN 2½

M Calcavecchia beat H Meshiai 67-68
T Kite halved with N Ozaki 68
C Strange beat K Suzuki 72-75

M Calcavecchia beat H Meshiai 66-68
T Kite lost to K Suzuki 74-71
C Strange lost to N Ozaki 71-69

(Japan received £30,988 each and
USA received £61,977 each)

Ebel European Masters Swiss Open
at Crans-Sur-Sierre, Switzerland

Name	Score	Prize £
S Ballesteros	65-68-66-67–266	69024
C Parry	66-69-66-67–268	45988
S Bennett	65-67-66-71–269	25935
J Rivero	66-64-67-73–270	19141
P Quirici	72-67-66-65–270	19141

Name	Score	Prize £
B Lane	67-65-67-72–271	14500
C Montgomerie	68-66-67-71–272	12429
G Levenson	68-66-71-68–273	9308
M Lanner	65-72-65-71–273	9308
J-M Olazabal	69-70-69-65–273	9308

Epson Grand Prix of Europe
at St Pierre G & CC Chepstow, Gwent

Quarter Finals:

S Ballesteros beat M Mouland 2 holes
M Harwood beat I Woosnam 1 hole
D Smyth beat J-M Olazabal 1 hole
D Durnian beat K Brown 3 and 2

(Quarter final losers received £9900)

Semi-Finals:

S Ballesteros beat M Harwood 6 and 5
D Durnian beat D Smyth 4 and 3

Play-off for 3rd and 4th place:

D Smyth beat M Harwood 1 hole
(Smyth won £18370 and Harwood won £14750)

Final:

S Ballesteros beat D Durnian 4 and 3
(Ballesteros won £50000 and Durnian won £32000)

The Equity & Law Challenge
at Royal Mid-Surrey, Richmond

Name	Birdies	Eagles	Points	Par	Prize £
B Ogle	23	1	25	24	22570
C Montgomerie	21		21	31	11285
D Feherty	20		20	29	7335
R Boxall	20		20	24	4850
P Senior	15	2	19	31	3665
C Mason	19		19	27	2935
M Harwood	16	1	18	37	2370
T Charnley	18		18	27	2030

German Masters
at Stuttgarter GC, Monsheim

Name	Score	Prize £
B Langer	67-71-70-68–276	55302
P Stewart	69-67-70-71–277	28813
J-M Olazabal	73-66-69-69–277	28813
B Ogle	73-68-71-68–280	15336
F Couples	69-72-73-66–280	15336
D Cooper	70-72-71-68–281	11618
S Bennett	72-70-70-70–282	8564
B Gallacher	73-71-70-68–282	8564
N Faldo	69-66-74-73–282	8564
R Davis	68-69-72-74–283	6639

German Open Championship
at Frankfurter Golf Club, Frankfurt

Name	Score	Prize £
C Parry*	66-70-66-64–266	54222
M James	65-66-65-70–266	36126
M Allen	68-66-64-69–267	20374
M Harwood	65-65-68-70–268	16273
J-M Canizares	66-72-62-69–269	10772
J Haas	66-69-64-70–269	10772
G Brand Jr	71-66-67-65–269	10772
B Langer	68-69-67-65–269	10772

Jersey European Airways Open
at La Moye, Jersey

Name	Score	Prize £
C O'Connor Jr*	73-70-66-72–281	24490
D Durnian	70-71-67-73–281	16315
M Lanner	71-69-70-72–282	8275
P Broadhurst	73-69-71-69–282	8275
D Smyth	74-69-71-69–283	4552
C Montgomerie	69-75-68-71–283	4552
B Gallacher	71-70-70-72–283	4552
S Torrance	72-70-69-72–283	4552
R Rafferty	74-69-68-72–283	4552

The Karl Litten Desert Classic
at Emirates GC, Dubai

Name	Score	Prize £
M James*	69-68-72-68–277	41660
P O'Malley	71-68-68-70–277	27760
P Broadhurst	72-66-70-72–280	15650
B Ogle	77-69-67-69–282	12500
M Persson	67-72-72-72–283	10600
E Dussart	71-71-72-70–284	6620
B Lane	71-73-73-67–284	6620
M Miller	72-74-67-71–284	6620
J Rutledge	73-70-70-71–284	6620
S Torrance	70-71-71-72–284	6620

* Winner after play-off

KLM Dutch Open
at Kennemer G & CC

Name	Score	Prize £
J-M Olazabal*	67-66-68-76–277	45830
R Chapman	70-67-71-69–277	23875
R Rafferty	72-66-66-73–277	23875
J Parnevik	69-67-72-70–278	13750
G Brand Jr	65-68-74-72–279	11665
S Torrance	69-70-72-69–280	8937
C Parry	69-65-70-76–280	8937

Lancia Italian Open
at Monticello

Name	Score	Prize £
R Rafferty	71-69-68-65–273	12589
S Torrance	69-70-65-70–274	28371
M Persson	66-72-69-68–275	15995
R Lee	66-73-69-69–277	12772
P Carman	70-69-67-72–278	9885
A Sherborne	72-70-65-71–278	9885
D Feherty	65-72-69-73–279	5915
S Ballesteros	71-69-68-71–279	5915
L Carbonetti	76-68-67-68–279	5915
F Nobilo	71-70-71-67–279	5915
N Hansen	71-72-71-65–279	5915

Lancôme Trophy
at St Nom La Breteche, Versailles

Name	Score	Prize £
E Romero	69-65-66-66–266	68330
B Langer	69-68-66-65–267	35585
J-M Olazabal	67-70-65-65–267	35585
P Fowler	66-64-68-70–268	20600
D Feherty	68-69-67-65–269	17400
V Singh	70-71-66-67–274	12320
H Clark	69 74 67 64–274	12320
C Parry	68-69-68-69–274	12320
S Torrance	72-68-69-66–275	8306
A Murray	64-78-68-65–275	8306
M Lanner	72-74-62-67–275	8306

Winner after play-off

Motorola Classic
at Burnham & Berrow GC, Burnham-on-Sea

Name	Score	Prize £
D Llewellyn	64-69-72-67–272	10500
D Williams	70-68-67-71–276	7100
R Weir	70-67-71-69–277	5100
P Carrigill	71-71-71-65–278	4100
D Prosser	71-69-69-70–279	3450
R Stelten	70-69-72-69–280	2700
B Barnes	73-66-68-73–280	2700
S Richardson	71-70-69-71–281	2100
P Teravainen	71-68-72-71–282	1800
D Jagger	69-70-73-71–283	1600

Murphy's Cup
(Stableford Points Format)
at St Pierre G&CC, Chepstow

Name	Score	Prize £
H Baiocchi	35-40-39-42–156	33000
J Hawkes	36-39-37-42–154	17500
J Bland	38-37-39-40–154	17500
M McNulty	38-38-37-39–152	9200
AR Stephen	37-38-37-39–151	7500
C Peete	35-42-35-37–149	5800
C Mason	38-38-36-37–149	5800
B Longmuir	31-36-39-42–148	3700
S Hoch	35-34-40-39–148	3700
B Barnes	32-38-41-37–148	3700

NM English Open Championship
at The Belfry G&CC (Brabazon Course)

Name	Score	Prize £
M James	72-70-69-68–279	41660
E Darcy	70-71-67-72–280	18636
C Parry	66-74-73-67–280	18636
S Torrance	66-73-70-71–280	18636
B Norton	74-70-67-71–282	9675
J Bland	69-70-70-73–282	9675
M Poxon	69-72-69-73–283	6450
P Teravainen	71-75-69-68–283	6450
C O'Connor Jr	71-73-68-71–283	6450
J Davila	68-75-73-68–284	4235
R Rafferty	72-67-73-72–284	4235
M Lanner	72-71-69-72–284	4235
J Hawkes	67-71-73-73–284	4235
R Chapman	73-72-73-66–284	4235
S Tinning	66-78-71-69–284	4235
R Claydon (Am)	72-71-71-70–284	

Panasonic European Open
at Walton Heath GC, Surrey

Name	Score	Prize £
A Murray	66-68-71-72–277	58330
F Nobilo	70-69-69-70–278	38860
S Torrance	70-71-69-70–280	21910
C Parry	73-72-70-66–218	16165
I Woosnam	71-68-70-72–281	16165
R Claydon	70-68-71-74–283	11375
R Drummond	70-69-71-73–283	11375
AWB Lyle	69-74-71-70–284	7863
R Davis	69-73-72-70–284	7863
D Feherty	72-71-71-70–284	7863
M James	70-73-75-67–285	6230
S Hoch	69-69-77-70–285	6230
P Fowler	67-72-79-68–286	4947
M Poxon	70-71-72-73–286	4947
M Allen	74-69-76-67–286	4947
V Singh	74-70-73-69–286	4947
D Cooper	72-69-70-75–286	4947
J Bland	73-73-71-69–286	4947
P Senior	70-68-71-77–286	4947

Peugeot French Open
at Chantilly, Paris

Name	Score	Prize £
N Faldo	70-70-64-69–273	52233
H Baiocchi	69-67-68-70–274	23359
M Roe	69-68-67-70–274	23359
B Langer	70-67-71-66–274	23359
M James	70-70-66-69–275	10368
I Woosnam	67-70-69-69–275	10368
M Harwood	68-68-69-70–275	10368
P Parkin	71-68-72-64–275	10368
R Rafferty	69-67-66-74–276	6351
M McNulty	70-70-70-66–276	6351
G Brand Jr	69-67-69-71–276	6351

Peugeot Spanish Open
at El Saler, Valencia

Name	Score	Prize £
B Langer	70-72-67-72–281	41660
J-M Canizares	72-72-70-70–284	21705
P Carrigill	70-69-72-73–284	21705
J-M Olazabal	70-72-70-73–285	12500
M Lanner	71-72-71-72–286	10600
G Brand Jr	71-73-69-74–287	8125
B Lane	72-69-75-71–287	8125
D Feherty	70-70-74-74–288	6250
S Ballesteros	75-68-74-72–289	5300
J Rystrom	72-73-72-72–289	5300

PLM Open
at Bokskogen, Malmo, Sweden

Name	Score	Prize £
M Harwood	66-70-67-68–271	50000
P Senior	68-67-65-72–272	33300
S Torrance	71-67-65-70–273	18780
M Lanner	70-68-69-67–274	13850
B Langer	68-66-69-71–274	13850
R Rafferty	69-69-66-72–276	9750
P Walton	67-72-66-71–276	9750
O Sellberg	69-73-65-70–277	7100
L Hederstrom	71-66-70-70–277	7100
M Moreno	68-68-73-69–278	6000

Portuguese Open
at Quinta do Lago

Name	Score	Prize £
C Montgomerie	67-65-69-63–264	45825
M Smith	70-69-66-70–275	20498
M Moreno	71-69-69-66–275	20498
R Davis	66-72-69-68–275	20498
M Pinero	68-70-72-66–276	10640
C O'Connor Jr	69-68-71-68–276	10640
S Stephen	71-69-68-69–277	6095
D Feherty	70-71-67-69–277	6095
GJ Brand	70-71-67-69–277	6095
P Senior	73-65-71-68–277	6095
A Garrido	69-71-67-70–277	6095
P Fowler	69-68-73-67–277	6095

Rolex Pro Am
at Golf Club de Genève

Name	Score	Prize £
R Stelten	69-66-70-75–280	6502
C Tucker	71-67-68-75–281	2608
J Bennett	72-70-70-69–281	2608
HP Thuel	77-71-67-66–281	2608

Scandinavian Enterprise Open
at Drottningholm, Stockholm

Name	Score	Prize £
R Rafferty	70-69-64-65–268	55810
M Allen	67-71-67-65–270	37180
P Senior	64-70-73-67–274	20970
G Brand Jr	70-70-66-69–275	15475
V Singh	69-70-67-69–275	15475
B Ogle	68-70-70-68–276	10887
D Cooper	70-70-69-67–276	10887
D Whelan	68-73-72-64–277	7526
M Mouland	70-71-67-69–277	7526
J Haas	71-68-68-70–277	2726

Suntory World Match-Play Championship
at Wentworth Club (West Course), Surrey

First Round:
R Rafferty beat M Reid 3 and 2
J-M Olazabal beat S Hoch 4 and 2
C Beck beat A Omachi 8 and 6
D Frost beat I Baker-Finch 4 and 3
(Each loser received £12500)

Second Round:
R Rafferty beat AWB Lyle 1 hole
I Woosnam beat J-M Olazabal 3 and 2
S Ballesteros beat C Beck 9 and 8
N Faldo beat D Frost at 38th
(Each loser received £17500)

Semi-Finals:
I Woosnam beat R Rafferty 2 and 1
N Faldo beat S Ballesteros 6 and 5

Play-off for 3rd and 4th places:
S Ballesteros beat R Rafferty 5 and 3
(Ballesteros received £30000 and Rafferty received £20000)

Final:
N Faldo beat I Woosnam 1 hole
(Faldo won £100000 and Woosnam £60000)

Tenerife Open
at Golf del Sur, Tenerife

Name	Score	Prize £
J-M Olazabal	69-68-68-70-275	33330
D Gilford	72-70-69-67–278	17360
J-M Canizares	70-66-70-72–278	17360
M King	74-70-69-67–280	7867
P Walton	70-70-68-72–280	7867
J Quiros	70-73-69-68–280	7867
J Rystrom	72-72-68-68–280	7867
J Rivero	70-72-68-71–281	4290
M Roe	68-69-69-75–281	4290
D Smyth	66-75-68-72–281	4290
R Chapman	74-70-67-70–281	4290

UAP Under 25's European Open Championship
at Golf du Prieure, France

Name	Score	Prize £
S Hamill	70-73-68-71–282	12973
S Bottomley	69-73-72-69–283	8652
MA Jimenez	66-77-73-69–285	4866
A Cotton	74-73-72-67–286	3892
N Briggs	71-73-74-70–288	3017
J Lomas	73-75-71-69–288	3017
M Davis	68-72-79-70–289	2011
E Giraud	75-72-72-70–289	2011
I Spencer	78-72-68-71–289	2011

Torras Monte Carlo Golf Open
at Mont Agel, Monte Carlo

Name	Score	Prize £
M McNulty	68-64-64-65–261	48285
J Hawkes	64-72-67-64–267	25147
J-M Canizares	68-66-65-68–267	25147
P Senior	66-66-67-69–268	14485
R Lee	68-70-69-64–271	11202
P Mitchell	65-68-67-71–271	11202
P Fowler	66-72-70-64–272	7967
L Carbonetti	68-66-71-67–272	7967
G Levenson	70-70-67-66–273	5452
M Allen	71-67-70-65–273	5452
B Langer	66-68-71-68–273	5452
J Rivero	67-71-67-68–273	5452
MA Jimenez	72-64-68-69–273	5452

Volvo Belgian Open
at Royal Waterloo GC, Brussels

Name	Score	Prize £
GJ Brand	67-69-68-69–273	33330
K Dickens	70-67-67-73–277	22200
M Davis	68-73-70-67–278	12520
J Parnevik	74-70-67-68–279	10000
R Boxall	69-70-66-75–280	6190
M Farry	69-69-71-71–280	6190
R Rafferty	70-73-67-70–280	6190
M Mackenzie	70-72-71-67–280	6190
D Cooper	71-71-71-67–280	6190
E Darcy	68-72-72-69–281	3480
A Murray	72-71-69-69–281	3480
D Williams	71-70-72-68–281	3480
G Turner	74-70-70-67–281	3480
P Walton	75-69-70-67–281	3480

Volvo Masters
at Valderrama, Spain

Name	Score	Prize £
R Rafferty	72-69-70-71–282	66660
N Faldo	74-68-72-69–283	44425
J-M Olazabal	69-70-74-74–287	25040
A W B Lyle	70-76-69-74–289	20000
P Fowler	75-72-69-74–290	14316
M James	77-70-71-72–290	14316
H Clarke	73-70-74-73–290	14316
C Parry	73-68-75-75–291	10000
V Fernandez	75-73-73-71–292	8106
E Romero	73-73-74-72–292	8106
O Sellberg	75-74-73-70–292	8106
A Murray	75-71-72-75–293	6190
R Chapman	73-72-77-71–293	6190
P Senior	73-78-68-74–293	6190
I Woosnam	71-69-75-78–293	6190
J-M Canizares	75-73-75-79–293	6190

Volvo Open
at Is Molas, Sardinia

Name	Score	Prize £
V Singh	72-68-68-68–276	33330
P Fowler	71-69-71-68–279	22200
G J Brand	69-72-70-72–283	11260
B Longmuir	71-69-72-71–283	11260
C Bolling Jr	68-72-71-73–284	7735
C O'Connor Jr	70-72-69-73–284	7735
M Mannelli	73-72-71-69–285	4870
P O'Malley	72-70-68-75–285	4870
R Rafferty	72-68-71-74–285	4870
D Williams	73-72-72-68–285	4870

Volvo PGA Championship
at Wentworth Club (West Course), Surrey

Name	Score	Prize £
N Faldo	67-69-69-67–272	58330
I Woosnam	67-72-68-67–274	38860
C Parry	68-68-69-71–276	21910
S Ballesteros	73-74-65-66–278	14860
M McNulty	70-69-69-70–278	14860
C O'Connor Jr	71-68-74-65–278	14860
D Durnian	73-68-69-69–279	10900
V Singh	71-70-71-68–280	7863
M James	71-75-68-66–280	7863
G J Brand	74-72-65-69–280	7863
J Hawkes	75-70-66-70–281	5860
J-M Olazabal	72 74-69-66–281	5860
G Levenson	70-69-69-73–281	5860
N Hansen	69-70-72-70–281	5860
R Rafferty	72-69-71-70–282	5140
J Parnevik	72-70-67-74–283	4930
P Fowler	71-70-74-69–284	4526
P Curry	68-72-73-71–284	4526
E Darcy	72-71-71-70–284	4526

Volvo Seniors British Open
at Ailsa Course, Turnberry

Name	Score	Prize £
B Charles	70-68-65-66—269	25000
B Casper	67-69-65-75—276	16400
B Hiskey	71-71-65-72—279	9150
G Player	74-68-69-71—282	6750
D Butler	72-74-67-69—282	6750
N Coles	70-74-70-69—283	5100
C O'Connor	76-70-70-68—284	4340
A Palmer	74-72-70-70—286	3610
A Grubb	73-72-70-73—288	3235
B Yancey	75-68-71-75—289	2716
L Mancour	72-68-73-76—289	2716
D Dalziel	72-76-71 70 380	2716

Wang Four Stars National Pro-Celebrity
at Moor Park, Rickmansworth

Name	Score	Prize £
C Parry	67-71-66-69—273	32000
I Woosnam	67-72-68-66—273	21900
D Gilford	71-69-65-69—274	11150
M Harwood	66-72-67-69—274	11150
B Lane	72-68-68-68—276	7650
G Brand Jr	72-67-72-65—276	7650
J Anderson	70-69-69-69—277	5800
B Marchbank	73-69-67-69—278	3818
P Senior	72-67-68-71—278	3818
B Shearer	69-72-65-72—278	3818
J Hawkes	71-70-66-71—278	3818
R McFarlane	68-74-67-69—278	3818

PGA European Tour Qualifying School
at La Manga, Spain

Pos	Name	Score
1	H P Thuel (W Ger)	68-70-68-72-67-66–411
2	D Ray (Eng)	70-70-70-66-69-69–414
3	B Hughes (Aus)	70-70-70-71-68-66–415
4	C Williams (Eng)	73-66-68-66-72-70–415
5	S Bowman (USA)	70-69-72-66-68-71–415
6	J Davila (Sp)	72-76-72-64-68-66–418
7	M McLean (Eng)	70-71-72-68-70-68–419
8	F Gemmel (Swe)	73-67-72-66-74-70–419
9	M Krantz (Swe)	74-67-69-69-73-69–421
10	T Giedeon (W Ger)	70-67-74-70-66-74–421
11	D R Jones (Eng)	70-73-72-69-70-68–422
12	C Platts (Eng)	68-66-76-70-73-69–422
13	M Calfro (Sp)	66-71-68-74-74-69–422
14	J Tumba (Swe)	73-71-73-67-67-71–422
15	G Turner (NZ)	71-72-73-69-70-68–423
16	M Aparicio (Sp)	69-72-70-69-74-69–423
17	R Huff (USA)	73-68-71-69-71-71–423
18	W Stephens (Eng)	71-71-68-72-67-74–423
19	M Jonsson (Swe)	72-71-72-71-68-69–424
20	J M Buendia (Sp)	71-71-70-73-70-69–424
21	J Hawksworth (Eng)	73-72-72-68-69-70–424
22	J Haeggman (Swe)	74-68-75-68-69-70–424
23	P Kent (Eng)	68-69-74-67-75-71–424
24	J Pinsent (Eng)	72-68-70-69-72-73–424
25	D J Russell (Eng)	70-72-72-71-71-69–425
26	J Spence (Eng)	72-71-74-65-74-69–425
27	S Hammill (N Ire)	70-74-67-67-75-72–425
28	M Sunesson (Swe)	70-76-71-72-69-68–425
29	P Hall (Eng)	75-69-74-70-70-68–426
30	R Stelton (USA)	72-70-76-70-69-69–426
31	G Ralph (Eng)	74-69-75-69-70-69–426
32	R Claydon (Eng)	73-75-66-72-71-69–426
33	D James (Scot)	70-74-70-71-71-70–426
34	A Cotton (Eng)	68-74-75-69-69-71–426
35	P Hedblom (Swe)	72-70-74-70-71-70–427
36	S Richardson (Eng)	72-70-72-72-71-70–427
37	S Bottomley (Eng)	76-70-72-69-69-71–427
38	G Krause (Eng)	74-71-74-70-66-72–427
39	W Grant (Eng)	69-74-73-73-66-72–427
40	I Higby (Eng)	75-72-71-72-70-68–428
41	M Sludds (Ire)	76-67-74-68-73-70–428
42	C Maltman (Scot)	70-74-72-69-72-71–428
43	W Henry (Eng)	73-73-72-70-68-72–428
44	J Berendt (Arg)	73-68-74-72-68-73–428
45	M Stokes (Eng)	72-67-75-73-68-73–428
46	C Cookson (USA)	73-70-67-72-71-75–428
47	E Rodriguez (Sp)	75-71-68-71-67-75–428
48	E Bolognesi (It)	74-70-70-65-72-77–428
49	S Luna (Sp)	71-72-75-71-71-69–429
50	J Rozadilla (Sp)	73-72-74-66-73-71–429

PGA Final Statistics, 1989

(Provided by Philips Radio Communications Systems)

Driving Distance

		Yds
1	E Romero	276
2T	M Davis	275
	S Torrance	275
4	E Darcy	273
5T	D Cooper	271
	M Mouland	271
	I Woosnam	271
8T	H Clark	270
	R Drummond	270
	P Senior	270
	P Walton	270

Putts per Round

		Avg
1	J-M Olazabal	28.75
2	R Rafferty	29.38
3	R Boxall	29.42
4T	M Davis	29.47
	V Singh	29.47
6	R Chapman	29.50
7T	J-M Canizares	29.56
	S Torrance	29.56
9T	GJ Brand	29.63
	M Allen	29.63

Fairways Hit

		%
1	M James	70.2
2	K Brown	69.5
3	S McAllister	69
4	J Rivero	68
5	S Bennett	67
6T	J-M Canizares	65
	E Romero	65
	D Smyth	65
	G Turner	65
10T	R Boxall	64
	E Darcy	64
	M Lanner	64
	J-M Olazabal	64

Sand-Saves

		%
1	R Chapman	68
2	R Drummond	64
3T	C O'Connor Jr	63
	J van de Velde	63
5T	M McNulty	62
	B Ogle	62
7T	V Fernandez	61
	P Fowler	61
9T	A Murray	57
	J-M Olazabal	57

Greens in Regulation

		%
1	R Rafferty	74
2T	M James	73
	I Woosnam	73
4	E Romero	72
5T	G Brand Jr	71
	C O'Connor Jr	71
7T	H Clark	70
	D Cooper	70
	M Lanner	70
	J Rivero	70
	S Torrance	70

Stroke Averages

		Avg
1	N Faldo	69.64
2	J-M Olazabal	69.83
3	C Parry	69.86
4	B Langer	70.14
5	R Rafferty	70.26
6	M James	70.44
7	S Ballesteros	70.50
8	M McNulty	70.52
9	P Senior	70.55
10	J Hawkes	70.65
11	J-M Canizares	70.70
12	M Harwood	70.72
13	H Clark	70.79
14	I Woosnam	70.81
15	P Fowler	70.90
16T	R Davis	71.02
	J Rivero	71.02
18	E Romero	71.10
19	S Torrance	71.12
20	R Chapman	71.13

PGA European Satellite Tour and Others

Barnham Broom Satellite
at Barnham Broom G & CC

Name	Score	Prize £
N Godin	74-70-66-68–278	2500
C Platts	73 72 69-69–283	1650
S Bottomley	78-72-62-72–284	961
K Dickins	74-70-70-70-284	961
J Higgins	72-72-69-71–284	961
F George	74-69-71-70–284	961
A Clapp	77-70-69-69–285	650
P Harrison	77-70-72-67–286	575
J Spence	75-67-70-74–286	575
J Robinson	76-70-73-67–286	575

Old Links Satellite
at Old Links, Bolton

Name	Score	Prize £
J Robinson	67-68-74–209	2500
A Hunter	67-74-69–210	1650
N Godin	71-69-72–212	1033
W Grant	67-71-74–212	1033
D Wills	69-72-71–212	1033
P Hall	75-68-70–213	668
G Walker	70-72-71–213	668
J Pinsent	68-72-73–213	668
M Archer	72-69-73–214	540
D Wood	71-75-68–214	540
P Eales	69-73-72–214	540

Prince's Satellite Tournament
at Prince's, Sandwich (Shore & Dunes Courses)

Name	Score	Prize £
J Higgins	68-65-71-73–277	2500
I Spencer	71-69-70-71–281	1650
D Wood	70-69-73-73–285	1250
J Bennett	71-73-70-72–286	925
J Robinson	72-73-71-70–286	925

Name	Score	Prize £
A Hunter	71-73-71-72–287	697
N Godin	71-69-73-74–287	697
A Cotton	73-72-75-68–288	610
C Platts	70-74-71-74–289	575

Belgian Classic
at Brussels

Name	Score
J Sluman	66-71-71–208
S Simpson	72-70-70–212
A Bean	72-73-71–216
L Mize	69-77-71–217
C Beck	72-71-77–220
G Norman	72-75-73–220

British Coal Manx Classic
at Castletown Golf Links

Name	Score
D Dunk	74-68-65–207
DJ Clare	67-75-67–209
S Smith	70-73-69–212
J Hawksworth	73-71-68–212
MJ Slater	74-69-70–213
GW Townhill	71-73-69–213
P Tupling	71-72-70–213

Dunbar Professional Championship
at Dunbar

Name	Score
R Weir	64-70-72-71–277
A Dickson	72-72-70-69–283
C Brooks	69-71-70-74–284
A Oldcorn	72-72-68-73–285
E Murray	69-73-69-74–285
C Innes	72-69-69-75–285

Glenmuir Scottish Assistant's Match-Play Championship
at Dalmahoy

Semi-Finals:

C Gillies beat K Walker 1 hole

C Brooks beat P Lawrie 2 and 1

Finals:

C Gillies beat C Brooks 2 holes

Irish Professional Championship
at Castle, Dublin

Name	Score
P Walton	67-65-69-65–266
D Smyth	71-66-69-69–275
E Darcy	71-69-67-70–277
B Todd	69-69-74-67–279
D Jones	67-71-70-71–279
M Sludds	70-68-69-72-279
A O'Connor	70-68-75-68–281
P Townsend	72-72-66-73–283
L Higgins	68-69-71-75–283

Paris Open
at Versailles

Name	Score
B Tway	66-64-67-72–269
F Lindgren	70-67-70-69–276
S Jones	74-69-66-68–277
B Crenshaw	70-68-71-68–277
P Azinger	65-73-67-73–278
F Couples	64-72-68-74–278

Peugeot PGA Assistant's Championship
at Hillside

Name	Score
C Brooks	76-67-75-73–291
P Eales	73-75-76-73–297
M McLaren	77-72-76-72–297
M Witchelow	74-71-78-74–297

Ram Classic
at Royal Aberdeen

Name	Score
C Maltman	72-72-67-70–281
P Terras	70-71-71-72–284
K Walker	70-77-67-71–285
A Webster	71-74-69-71–285

Ryder Scottish Assistants' Championship
at Windyhill

Name	Score
C Brooks	73-73-68-68–282
C Innes	70-70-73-70–283
W Guy	74-70-72-71–287
G Collinson	73-75-67-73–288
J White	76-70-69-73–288

Scottish Under-25 Championship
at Deer Park, Livingston

Name	Score
C Brooks	65-69-70-71–275
G Collinson	68-69-69-70–276
C Gillies	67-72-68-70–277
M McLaren	70-71-70-73–284
P Girvan	75-69-68-73–285

Sunderland Masters
at Drumpellier

Name	Score
C Maltman	67-65-65-67–264
A Webster	72-69-65-67–273
R Gregan	69-70-66-69–274
J Chillas	65-71-68-70–274

Surrey PGA Championship
at Cuddington

Name	Score
G Smith*	141
R Wynn	141
H Stott	142
W Grant	144
G Torbett	144
D Butler	144

Wilson Club Professionals' Championship
at Prince's

Name	Score
B Barnes	72-70-71-67–280
D Scott	77-66-71-70–284
G Stafford	77-69-66-72–284
R Weir	76-72-70-67–285
N Job	75-68-73-69–285
W McColl	72-73-71-70–286
J Harrison	78-69-70-70–287
M Gray	80-69-68-70–287

Winner after play-off

USPGA Tour Official Money List, 1989

Place	Name	Official Money $	Place	Name	Official Money $
1	T Kite	1,395,278	51	R Black	264,988
2	P Stewart	1,201,301	52	L Thompson	261,397
3	P Azinger	951,649	53	I Baker-Finch (Aus)	253,309
4	G Norman (Aus)	835,096	54	J Haas	248,831
5	M Calcavecchia	807,741	55	R Wrenn	243,638
6	T Simpson	761,597	56	M Lye	242,884
7	C Strange	752,587	57	D Edwards	238,908
8	S Jones	745,578	58	A Bean	236,097
9	C Beck	694,087	59	D Ogrin	234,196
10	S Hoch	670,680	60	L Wadkins	233,363
11	F Couples	653,944	61	S Elkington	231,062
12	D Frost (SA)	620,430	62	K Knox	230,012
13	M O'Meara	615,804	63	B Faxon	222,076
14	M McCumber	546,587	64	C Byrum	221,702
15	B McCallister	523,891	65	F Zoeller	217,742
16	W Levi	499,292	66	D Pooley	214,662
17	B Tway	488,340	67	C Perry	206,932
18	M Hulbert	477,621	68	J Huston	203,207
19	B Glasson	474,511	69	B Andrade	202,242
20	D Hammond	458,741	70	K Perry	202,099
21	B Crenshaw	443,095	71	JD Blake	200,499
22	M Donald	430,232	72	J Sindelar	196,092
23	H Sutton	422,703	73	B Langer (WGer)	195,973
24	D Rummells	419,979	74	D Pohl	195,789
25	C Stadler	409,419	75	D Barr (Can)	190,480
26	J Mudd	404,860	76	B Tennyson	189,345
27	W Grady (Aus)	402,364	77	E Fiori	188,637
28	M Reid	401,665	78	B Gilder	187,910
29	J Mahaffey	400,467	79	L Nelson	186,869
30	T Schulz	391,855	80	T Watson	185,398
31	N Faldo (GB)	327,981	81	T Armour	185,018
32	T Byrum	320,939	82	C Pavin	177,084
33	J Carter	319,719	83	D Tewell	174,607
34	B Britton	307,978	84	Brad Bryant	174,393
35	S Pate	306,554	85	BR Brown	162,964
36	B Lietzke	305,987	86	H Green	161,190
37	K Green	304,754	87	J Hallet	155,658
38	G Sauers	303,669	88	T Purtzer	154,868
39	G Morgan	300,395	89	J Sluman	154,507
40	S Simpson	298,920	90	G Twiggs	154,302
41	M Wiebe	296,269	91	B Wadkins	152,184
42	N Price (SA)	296,170	92	L Hinkle	151,828
43	AWB Lyle (GB)	292,293	93	H Irwin	150,977
44	D Love III	278,760	94	D Waldorf	149,945
45	L Mize	278,388	95	G Hallberg	146,833
46	L Roberts	275,882	96	LT Broeck	146,568
47	M Sullivan	273,962	97	I Woosnam (GB)	146,323
48	P Jacobsen	267,241	98	B Lohr	144,242
49	C Rose	267,141	99	D Forsman	141,174
50	J Gallagher Jr	265,809	100	P Blackmar	140,949

USPGA Tour 1989

Anheuser-Busch Golf Classic
at Kingsmill GC, Williamsburg, Virginia

Name	Score	Prize $
M Donald*	67-66-70-65–268	153000
H Sutton	64-71-65-68–268	74800
T Simpson	64-70-67-67–268	74800
M Hulbert	65-66-68-70–269	40800
T Byrum	70-70-64-66–270	34000
R Maltbie	72-63-67-69–271	28475
B McCallister	67-70-66-68–271	28475
B Tennyson	67-71-67-66–271	28475
C Perry	65-73-65-69–272	22950
R Streck	68-67-69-68–272	22950
J Mahaffey	69-67-69-67–272	22950

AT & T Pebble Beach National Pro-Am
at Pebble Beach GC, Spyglass Hill GC and Cypress Point GC

Name	Score	Prize $
M O'Meara	66-68-73-70–277	180000
T Kite	67-70-72-69–278	108000
N Price	66-74-67-73–280	52000
AWB Lyle	68-72-72-68–280	52000
J Carter	70-72-69-69–280	52000
L Wadkins	73-69-72-67–281	32375
S Pate	72-72-66-71–281	32375
H Sutton	70-73-70-68–281	32375
S Jones	71-69-71-70–281	32375
L Roberts	67-72-76-67–282	26000
D Stockton	65-70-78-69–282	26000

* Winner after play-off

Bank of Boston Classic
at Pleasant Valley CC, Sutton, Massachusetts

Name	Score	Prize $
B McCallister	67-67-71-66–271	126000
B Faxon	66-67-70-69–272	75600
D Pooley	66-65-72-70–273	36400
C Perry	68-69-70-66–273	36400
M Calcavecchia	67-68-69-69–273	36400
N Price	70-68-74-62–274	22662
F Zoeller	68-67-70-69–274	22662
M Lye	68-71-66-69–274	22662
S Jones	68-70-71-65–274	22662
W Grady	69-70-71-65–275	18200
W Heintzelman	68-69-69-69–275	18200

BC Open
at En-Joie GC, Endicott, New York

Name	Score	Prize $
M Hulbert*	69-66-68-65–268	90000
B Estes	66-68-66-68–268	54000
S Elkington	68-72-67-62–269	34000
F Zoeller	69-67-66-69–271	22000
D Eichelberger	67-67-67-70–271	22000
W Levi	69-73-64-66–272	18000
G Morgan	67-67-71-68–273	16750
N Henke	69-67-73-65–274	15500

Beatrice Western Open
at Butler National GC, Oak Brook, Illinois

Name	Score	Prize $
M McCumber*	68-67-71-69–275	180000
P Jacobsen	69-69-69-68–275	108000
P Azinger	67-68-72-69–276	68000
J Gallagher Jr	71-72-70-66–279	48000
LT Broeck	68-71-72-69–280	38000
L Trevino	73-71-67-69–280	38000
J Mudd	69-73-72-67–281	30125
J Sindelar	71-71-70-69–281	30125
L Mize	69-70-67-75–281	30125
C Beck	65-71-75-70–281	30125

Winner after play-off

Bell South Atlanta Golf Classic
at Atlanta CC, Marietta, Georgia

Name	Score	Prize $
S Simpson*	72-68-71-67–278	162000
B Tway	70-70-71-67–278	97200
D Love III	71-69-69-70–279	52200
JD Blake	66-71-70-72–279	52200
D Peoples	70-71-70-69–280	34200
D Canipe	71 70 70-69–280	34200
R Stewart	69-68-75-69–281	28050
W Levi	72-70-72-67–281	28050
W Grady	70-66-75-70–281	28050

Bob Hope Chrysler Classic
at Bermuda Dunes, PGA West, Indian Wells CC and La Quinta CC

Name	Score	Prize $
S Jones*	76-68-67-63-69–343	180000
AWB Lyle	70-68-68-68-69–343	88000
P Azinger	69-68-70-67-69–343	88000
L Wadkins	68-70-68-70-68–344	39375
K Knox	68-71-69 67-69–344	39375
M Calcavecchia	71-67-67-67-72–344	39375
F Couples	65-71-71-68-69–344	39375
B Langer	70-68-68-69-70–345	29000
H Green	73-70-65-68-69–345	29000
T Kite	68-69-68-69-71–345	29000

Buick Open
at Warwick Hills G & CC, Grand Blanc, Michigan

Name	Score	Prize $
L Thompson	65-71-69-68–273	180000
D Tewell	69-66-70-69–274	74666
B Andrade	67-71-69-67–274	74666
P Stewart	71-67-64-72–274	74666
H Sutton	67-68-68-72–275	36500
M O'Meara	66-70-71-68–275	36500
B Eastwood	73-66-66-70–275	36500
T Kite	69-70-71-66–276	29000
G Morgan	71-70-67-68–276	29000
W Grady	67-69-72-68–276	29000

Winner after play-off

Canadian Open
at Glen Abbey GC, Oakville, Ontario

Name	Score	Prize $
S Jones	67-64-70-70–271	162000
M Hulbert	71-66-72-64–273	67200
C Burroughs	69-66-64-74–273	67200
M Calcavecchia	67-69-68-69–273	67200
J Sindelar	69-72-65-68–274	32850
M McCumber	69-69-69-67–274	32850
M Brooks	67-73-68-66–274	32850
J Gallagher Jr	64-68-71-72–275	27000
D Barr	69-69-69-68–275	27000
C Pavin	70-70-69-67–276	18675
D Ogrin	68-69-68-71–276	18675
J Nicklaus	68 60 60 70–270	18675
B Sander	67-69-70-70–276	18675
L Hinkle	69-68-66-73–276	18675
D Halldorson	68-70-67-71–276	18675
J Adams	70-70-69-67–276	18675
F Couples	73-67-69-67–276	18675

Canon Greater Hartford Open
at TPC of Connecticut, Cromwell, Connecticut

Name	Score	Prize $
P Azinger	65-70-67-65–267	180000
W Levi	69-68-64-67–268	108000
D Rummells	70-67-67-66–270	68000
J Carter	66-68-71-66–271	41333
L Trevino	70-64-70-67–271	41333
M Calcavecchia	67-68-67-69–271	41333
H Sutton	67-71-68-66–272	29100
R Maltbie	66-69-69-68–272	29100
B McCallister	69-69-67-67–272	29100
D Shirey Jr	70-67-68-67–272	29100
C Burroughs	66-67-70-69–272	29100

Centel Classic
at Killearn G & CC, Tallahassee, Florida

Name	Score	Prize $
B Britton	71-66-63–200	135000
R Black	67-67-70–204	81000
G Hallberg	68-71-66–205	51000
M Reid	69-68-69–206	31000
T Pernice Jr	68-65-73–206	31000
B Buttner	69-66-71–206	31000
L Thompson	72-70-65–207	20303
T Simpson	68-69-70–207	20303
T Norris	70-68-69–207	20303
K Knox	69-69-69–207	20303
H Irwin	67-73-67–207	20303
P Jacobsen	69-69-69–207	20303
T Byrum	68-69-70–207	20303

Chattanooga Classic
at Valleybrook G & CC, Chattanooga, Tennessee

Name	Score	Prize $
S Utley	69-66-64-64–263	90000
R Stewart	71-63-67-63–264	54000
B Wadkins	67-67-65-66–265	29000
D Shirey Jr	65-65-68-67–265	29000
R Zokol	68-67-65-66–266	17562
J Inman	66-68-67-65–266	17562
B Estes	69-65-66-66–266	17562
R Cochran	66-67-67-66–266	17562
T Schulz	66-63-70-68–267	12500
S Lowery	66-69-67-65–267	12500
K Perry	70-67-66-64–267	12500
F Funk	68-64-67-68–267	12500
L Clements	70-65-67-65–267	12500

Deposit Guaranty Golf Classic
at Hattiesburg CC, Hattiesburg, Mississippi

Name	Score	Prize $
J Booros*	64-69-66–199	36000
M Donald	68-65-66–199	21600
R Thompson	65-71-65–201	9600
LT Broeck	69-65-67–201	9600
F Funk	71-65-65–201	9600
D Peoples	68-68-65–201	9600
PH Horgan III	69-69-64–202	6233
B Wolcott	70-66-66–202	6233
S Lowery	68-69-65–202	6233
P Arthur	69-68-67–204	5400

Doral Ryder Open
at Doral CC, Miami, Florida

Name	Score	Prize $
B Glasson	71-65-67-72–275	234000
F Couples	69-69-70-68–276	140400
C Strange	73-67-69-69–278	67600
B Lietzke	68-71-68-71–278	67600
M Calcavecchia	65-73-66-74–278	67600
D Pohl	69-71-73-66–279	43550
W Levi	68-69-73-69–279	43550
J Huston	69-69-70-71–279	43550
B Gardner	70-68-69-74–281	35100
P Azinger	73-71-66-71–281	35100
B Crenshaw	67-72-72-70–281	35100

Winner after play-off

Federal Express St Jude Classic
at TPC at Southwind, Germantown, Tennessee

Name	Score	Prize $
J Mahaffey	70-71-66-65–272	180000
B Tway	66-72-68-69–275	66000
B Langer	67-69-68-71–275	66000
H Green	70-69-73-63–275	66000
B Gilder	68-66-70-71–275	66000
J Haas	70-70-68-69–277	32375
R Fehr	71-71-69-66–277	32375
J Hallet	70-70-71-66–277	32375
M Donald	70-67-69-71–277	32375
B Lohr	69-73-72-64–278	27000

Greater Milwaukee Open
at Tuckaway CC, Franklin, Wisconsin

Name	Score	Prize $
G Norman	64-69-66-70–269	144000
A Bean	70-69-67-66–272	86400
T Schulz	68-69-68-68–273	46400
M Lye	67-66-72-68–273	46400
T Purtzer	72-67-66-69–274	30400
W Levi	69-66-68-71–274	30400
S Pate	65-71-70-69–275	21657
J Sluman	70-71-66-68–275	21657
D Waldorf	68-67-69-71–275	21657
J Sindelar	70-69-67-69–275	21657
L Roberts	69-67-68-71–275	21657
L Mize	68-67-70-70–275	21657
D Frost	67-67-70-71–275	21657

GTE Byron Nelson Golf Classic
at TPC at Las Colinas, Irving, Texas

Name	Score	Prize $
J Mudd*	68-66-66-65–265	180000
L Nelson	63-68-67-67–265	108000
M O'Meara	67-68-65-66–266	68000
L Roberts	65-68-66-68–267	48000
W Levi	62-67-68-71–268	36500
C Perry	65-65-70-68–268	36500
L Mize	67-67-63-71–268	36500
D Rummells	64-68-67-70–269	29000
P Stewart	64-70-68-67–269	29000
T Schulz	69-66-66-68–269	29000

Hardee's Golf Classic
at Oakwood CC, Coal Valley, Illinois

Name	Score	Prize $
C Byrum	66-67-69-66–268	126000
B Tennyson	69-69-67-64–269	61600
B Britton	70-65-69-65–269	61600
J Gallagher Jr	69-68-69-65–271	30800
B Jaeckel	70-71-67-63–271	30800
D Forsman	74-65-68-65–272	24325
J Adams	67-68-67-70–272	24325
A Magee	71-69-67-66–273	19600
T Sieckmann	69-68-69-67–273	19600
J Haas	72-68-67-66–273	19600
G Ladehoff	69-65-69-70–273	19600

Hawaiian Open
at Waialae CC, Honolulu, Hawaii

Name	Score	Prize $
G Sauers	65-67-65–197	135000
D Ogrin	65-67-66–198	81000
D Rummells	70-65-64–199	51000
J Carter	64-66-70–200	36000
D Reese	69-69-64–202	28500
C Beck	69-64-69–202	28500
R Caldwell	69-67-67–203	25125
K Takahashi	70-67-67–204	21000
B Glasson	67-67-70–204	21000
L Hinkle	66-70-68–204	21000
P Azinger	68-70-66–204	21000

Honda Classic
at TPC at Eagle Trace, Coral Springs, Florida

Name	Score	Prize $
B McCallister	70-67-65-64–266	144000
P Stewart	68-65-70-67–270	86400
S Pate	70-67-64-70–271	46400
C Strange	68-71-67-65–271	46400
D Pohl	66-62-75-69–272	32000
P Azinger	67-66-72-68–273	27800
T Byrum	65-69-70-69–273	27800
F Zoeller	70-66-70-68–274	24800
N Price	69-66-69-71–275	20800
G Koch	69-68-68-70–275	20800
M Hulbert	71-67-67-70–275	20800
D Love III	70-67-68-70–275	20800

*Winner after play-off

Independent Insurance Agent Open
at TPC at The Woodlands, Texas

Name	Score	Prize $
M Sullivan	76-71-68-65–280	144000
C Stadler	72-71-68-70–281	86400
M Reid	72-69-71-70–282	41600
M Donald	67-67-74-74–282	41600
S Ballesteros	69-69-72-72–282	41600
H Sutton	74-69-68-72–283	26800
C Strange	69-70-72-72–283	26800
D Frost	70-74-70-69–283	26800
G Morgan	70-77-69-68–284	21600
B Glider	70-71-71-72–284	21600
M Hulbert	68-76-71-69–284	21600

The International
at Castle Pines GC, Castle Rock, Colorado

(Modified Stableford with points awarded as follows: double eagle +8; eagle +5; birdie +2; par 0; bogey −1; double bogey or worse −3)

Name	Score	Prize $
G Norman	+13	180000
C Rose	+11	108000
C Beck	+ 9	68000
M Lye	+ 8	44000
B Andrade	+ 8	44000
D Frost	+ 7	36000
J Carter	+ 6	32250
D Forsman	+ 6	32250
J Nicklaus	+ 5	29000
M O'Grady	+ 4	26000
R Stewart	+ 4	26000

Kemper Open
at TPC at Avenel, Potomac, Maryland

Name	Score	Prize $
T Byrum	66-69-65-68–268	162000
J Thorpe	70-69-67-67–273	67200
T Armour	68-70-64-71–273	67200
BR Brown	69-67-70-67–273	67200
G Morgan	70-71-68-66–275	36000
M McCumber	69-69-66-72–276	31275
A Magee	73-69-65-69–276	31275
L Hinkle	68-70-68-71–277	26100
M Hulbert	68-72-67-70–277	26100
JD Blake	68-64-75-70–277	26100

K-Mart Greater Greensboro Open
at Forest Oaks CC, Greensboro, North Carolina

Name	Score	Prize $
K Green	73-66-66-72–277	180000
J Huston	71-69-67-72–279	108000
E Fiori	70-71-73-67–281	68000
D Eichelberger	72-67-72-71–282	48000
M Sullivan	70-74-70-69–283	36500
G Norman	73-72-70-68–283	36500
J Booros	69-70-72-72–283	36500
M Wiebe	72-69-71-72–284	30000
K Perry	70-70-72-72–284	30000
D Barr	71-69-73-73–286	27000

Manufacturers Hanover Westchester Classic
at Westchester CC, Rye, New York

Name	Score	Prize $
W Grady*	69-65-71-72–277	180000
R Black	69-71-69-68–277	108000
T Watson	71-69-70-68–278	58000
C Rose	72-69-67-70–278	58000
JC Snead	67-68-70-74–279	35125
T Kite	70-67-72-70–279	35125
B Andrade	69-69-70-71–279	35125
F Couples	66-72-70-71–279	35125
N Price	74-67-69-70–280	27000
M Reid	69-72-68-71–280	27000
M Lye	66-70-71-73–280	27000

MCI Heritage Classic
at Harbour Town GL, Hilton Head Is, South Carolina

Name	Score	Prize $
P Stewart	65-67-67-69–268	144000
K Perry	65-67-70-71–273	86400
B Langer	69-70-67-71–277	46400
F Couples	71-72-69-65–277	46400
L Wadkins	72-69-70-67–278	29200
C Stadler	70-70-70-68–278	29200
K Knox	69-70-67-72–278	29200
T Simpson	75-68-68-68–279	23200
M McCumber	71-64-69-75–279	23200
T Kite	72-67-70-70–279	23200

* Winner after play-off

Memorial Tournament
at Muirfield Village GC, Dublin, Ohio

Name	Score	Prize $
B Tway	71-69-68-69–277	160000
F Zoeller	69-66-72-72–279	96000
P Stewart	70-73-73-65–281	60440
B Lietzke	73-70-69-71–283	40835
M Calcavecchia	72-68-73-70–283	40835
S Verplank	72-73-69-70–284	32610
M O'Meara	75-68-72-69–284	32610
L Nelson	72-72-72-69–285	26610
S Hoch	72-76-69-68–285	26610
R Floyd	73-67-73-72–285	26610
D Frost	75-71-72-67–285	26610

Mony Tournament of Champions
at La Quinta, California

Name	Score	Prize $
S Jones	69-69-72-69–279	135000
D Frost	72-70-72-68–282	67000
J Haas	75-67-72-68–282	67000
G Norman	71-72-72-68–283	37000
C Beck	69-70-74-71–284	31000
M Hatalsky	74-74-70-67–285	26500
J Sluman	70-71-73-71–285	26500
L Wadkins	71-70-71-73–285	26500
B Glasson	75-73-67-71–286	23000
B Crenshaw	70-72-70-75–287	20000
B Lohr	70-74-70-73–287	20000
AWB Lyle	71-71-71-74–287	20000
C Strange	77-70-69-71–287	20000

Nabisco Championships
at Harbour Town GL, Hilton Head Is, South Carolina

Name	Score	Prize $
T Kite	69-65-74-68–276	450000
P Stewart	69-70-71-66–276	270000
P Azinger	71-73-67-67–278	146250
W Levi	71-72-63-72–278	146250
D Hammond	65-73-69 72–279	10000
M O'Meara	67-71-71-71–280	90000
S Hoch	71-71-68-71–281	82500
F Couples	68-74-67-72–281	82500
M Calcavecchia	70-75-68-70–283	73000
C Beck	71-68-73-71–283	73000

NEC World Series of Golf
at Firestone CC, Akron, Ohio

Name	Score	Prize $
D Frost*	70-68-69-69–276	180000
B Crenshaw	64-72-72-68–276	108000
P Stewart	72-67-68-71–278	68000
G Norman	73-65-70-71–279	48000
L Mize	73-66-70-71–280	38000
M Reid	68-71-70-71–280	38000
P Azinger	72-68-67-74–281	33500
M Calcavecchia	71-67-74-70–282	29166
B Glasson	69-74-73-66–282	29166
S Jones	76-63-69-74–282	29166
C Pavin	71-70-68-75–284	25000
B Claar	70-69-72-74–285	22000
S Hoch	74-69-70-72–285	22000
J Mahaffey	69-72-71-74–286	19000
P Blackmar	75-73-73-67–288	16000
S Simpson	75-73-68-72–288	16000
T Kite	76-70-73-69–288	16000
B McCallister	70-70-77-71–288	16000
M O'Meara	72-70-75-71–288	16000

The Nestle Invitational
at Bay Hill Club and Lodge, Orlando, Florida

Name	Score	Prize $
T Kite*	68-72-67-71–278	144000
D Love III	72-67-66-73–278	86400
C Strange	73-72-69-65–279	54400
P Stewart	76-69-65-70–280	33066
D Pooley	69-73-68-70–280	33066
L Roberts	66-73-69-72–280	33066
D Pohl	70-70-71-70–281	26800
L Rinker	72-68-68-74–282	24000
N Price	67-77-71-67–282	24000

Nissan Los Angeles Open
at Riviera CC, Pacific Palisades, California

Name	Score	Prize $
M Calcavecchia	68-66-70-68–272	180000
A WB Lyle	68-66-68-71–273	108000
H Irwin	70-67-69-68–274	68000
G Sauers	67-70-72-67–276	41333
S Pate	67-71-68-70–276	41333
P Blackmar	68-72-67-69–276	41333
F Couples	69-68-69-71–277	33500
T Kite	73-70-66-69–278	31000
T Purtzer	71-66-73-70–280	25000
M Reid	68-69-73-70–280	25000
J Miller	71-70-70-69–280	25000
D Hammond	68-73-68-71–280	25000
B Crenshaw	70-71-70-69–280	25000

Winner after play-off

Phoenix Open
at TPC of Scottsdale, Arizona

Name	Score	Prize $
M Calcavecchia	66-68-65-64–263	126000
C Beck	67-70-66-67–270	75600
S Hoch	64-70-69-68–271	36400
B Glasson	65-68-73-65–271	36400
P Azinger	68-68-68-67–271	36400
M McCumber	64-69-69-70–272	25200
T Schulz	64-70-71-68–273	21087
L Mize	70-69-67-67–273	21087
J Carter	68-68-70-67–273	21087
S Elkington	66-73-64-70–273	21087

Shearson Lehman Hutton Open
at Torrey Pines GC, La Jolla, California

Name	Score	Prize $
G Twiggs	68-70-64-69–271	126000
M Wiebe	68-65-70-70–273	46200
M O'Meara	68-67-72-66–273	46200
B Faxon	67-69-69-68–273	46200
S Elkington	70-63-67-73–273	46200
J McComish	68-69-67-70–274	23450
S Randolph	71-69-66-68–274	23450
D Forsman	73-64-70-67–274	23450
D Waldorf	68-69-69-69–275	18900
P Blackmar	69-68-70-68–275	18900
J Cook	70-68-69-68–275	18900

Southern Open
at Green Island CC, Columbus, Georgia

Name	Score	Prize $
T Schulz	66-66-68-66–266	72000
T Simpson	66-73-65-63–267	35200
J Haas	68-67-64-68–267	35200
B Tway	69-69-65-67–270	16533
LT Broeck	70-66-65-69–270	16533
L Rinker	70-68-64-68–270	16533
S Pate	64-68-70-69–271	12466
A Magee	66-70-66-69 271	12466
K Knox	65-68-67-71–271	12466
D Rummells	68-64-67-73–272	10400
M Donald	68-70-66-68–272	10400

Southwestern Bell Colonial
at Colonial Club, Fort Worth, Texas

Name	Score	Prize $
I Baker-Finch	65-70-65-70–270	180000
D Edwards	72-69-68-65–274	108000
T Simpson	71-71-66-68–276	58000
D Frost	70-66-71-69–276	58000
C Strange	74-71-66-66–277	36500
N Price	70-66-68-73–277	36500
L Hinkle	74-69-66-68–277	36500
P Stewart	70-70-70-68–278	28000
S Simpson	71-67-70-70–278	28000
I Aoki	66-74-66-72–278	28000
P Azinger	70-74-69-65–278	28000

Texas Open
at Oak Hills CC, San Antonio, Texas

Name	Score	Prize $
D Hammond	65-64-65-64–258	108000
P Azinger	64-62-70-69–265	64800
B Lohr	66-64-66-71–267	31200
D Waldorf	67-63-66-71–267	31200
M Wiebe	62-68-70-67–267	31200
JD Blake	67-65 68 68 268	20100
B Britton	67-65-67-69–268	20100
L Wadkins	62-68-68-70–268	20100

USF&G Classic
at English Turn G & CC, New Orleans, Louisiana

Name	Score	Prize $
T Simpson	68-67-70-69–274	135000
G Norman	68-68-68-72–276	66000
H Sutton	71-68-67-70–276	66000
M Hayes	72-71-67-68–278	36000
B Sander	68-71-70-70–279	26343
P Stewart	70-69-69-71–279	26343
M O'Meara	72-67-72-68–279	26343
PH Horgan III	70-70-67-72–279	26343
L Wadkins	72-70-67-71–280	18750
D Forsman	66-69-71-74–280	18750
D Edwards	72-68-72-68–280	18750
P McGowan	68-70-71-71–280	18750
C Beck	74-67-68-71–280	18750

The US Tournament Players Championship
at TPC at Sawgrass at Ponte Vedra, Florida

Name	Score	Prize $
T Kite	69-70-69-71–279	243000
C Beck	71-68-68-73–280	145800
B Lietzke	66-69-74-72–281	91800
G Norman	74-67-69-72–282	59400
F Couples	68-70-71-73–282	59400
M McCumber	69-70-70-74–283	46912
G Morgan	71-69-70-73–283	46912
D Frost	66-71-75-72–284	39150
G Koch	70-69 70 76–284	39150
A Bean	68-76-69-71–284	39150
T Watson	71-73-71-70–285	31050
R Mediate	73-71-69-72–285	31050
B Crenshaw	67-72-70-76–285	31050

Las Vegas Invitational
at Las Vegas CC, Desert Inn CC and Spanish Trail

Name	Score	Prize $
S Hoch*	69-64-68-65-70–336	225000
R Wrenn	69-66-66-69-66–336	135000
C Stadler	69-67-65-69-67–337	72500
G Morgan	70-63-73-64-67–337	72500
M Wiebe	71-67-66-68-66–338	43906
D Pohl	69-66-64-68-71–338	43906
B Bryant	67-68-69-70-64–338	43906
R Cochran	70-70-66-64-68–338	43906
T Sills	67-69-69-68-67–340	33750
G Sauers	65-69-72-66-68–340	33750
J Carter	70-67-65-67-71–340	33750

Walt Disney World Oldsmobile Classic
at Magnolia, Palm & Buena Vista Golf Courses, Lake Buena Vista, Florida

Name	Score	Prize $
T Simpson	65-67-70-70–272	144000
D Hammond	72-65 65 71–273	86400
P Azinger	65-70-71-68–274	41600
F Couples	70-65-69-70–274	41600
K Knox	70-65-71-68–274	41600
J Haas	71-66-70-68–275	27800
T Schultz	65-69-72-69–275	27800
B Gilder	70-65 69-72–276	24000
C Strange	72-66-72-66–276	24000

Winner after play-off

USPGA Tour Official Statistics

Scoring Leaders

		Avg
1T	G Norman	69.49
	P Stewart	69.49
3	T Kite	69.57
4T	P Azinger	69.69
	C Strange	69.69
6	F Couples	69.71
7	C Beck	69.77
8	T Simpson	69.84
9	M Calcavecchia	69.97
10	M McCumber	70.10

Greens in Regulation

		%
1	B Lietzke	.726
2	J Gallagher Jr	.710
3	D Barr	.703
4	J Mahaffey	.700
5	JC Snead	.698
6	D Shirey Jr.	.695
7T	W Levi	.694
	G Morgan	.694
	D Rummells	.694
	H Sutton	.694

Putting Leaders

		%
1	S Jones	1.734
2	D Hammond	1.736
3T	K Knox	1.738
	D Pooley	1.738
5	C Beck	1.742
6	J Huston	1.744
7	D Rummells	1.745
8	W Levi	1.747
9T	R Fehr	1.748
	J Sluman	1.748

Driving Distance

		Yds
1	E Humenik	280.9
2	D Jackson	280.7
3	D Waldorf	280.0
4T	K Perry	276.9
	B Sander	276.9
6	T Dodds	276.2
7	D Weaver	276.0
8	L Hinkle	275.5
9	J Mudd	274.6
10	P Blackmar	274.4

Driving Accuracy

		%
1	C Peete	.826
2	M Reid	.789
3	D Edwards	.782
4	B Lietzke	.763
5T	N Faldo	.761
	C Strange	.761
7T	F Allem	.756
	L Nelson	.756
9T	H Irwin	.752
	T Norris	.752

Sand Saves

		%
1	M Sullivan	.660
2	G Sauers	.658
3	T Simpson	.632
4	T Pernice Jr.	.625
5	D Edwards	.623
6	J Sluman	.615
7	N Price	.614
8	J Mahaffey	.608
9	G Archer	.607
10	B Mayfair	.601

Senior US PGA Tour Money List, 1989

Place	Name	Official Money $	Place	Name	Official Money $
1	B Charles	725887	51	K Still	81458
2	O Moody	647985	52	J O'Hern	78717
3	A Geiberger	527033	53	P Moran	77654
4	G Player	514116	54	A Kelley	76824
5	D Hill	488541	55	D Simon	69084
6	H Henning	453163	56	A Chandler	64216
7	B Crampton	443582	57	R Terry	63412
8	D Bies	421769	58	D January	59813
9	M Hill	412104	59	D Morgan	55753
10	C Coody	403880	60	T Aaron	51800
11	M Barber	370229	61	B Maxwell	51248
12	J Dent	337691	62	J King	47967
13	L Mowry	322788	63	R Botts	47006
14	D Douglass	313275	64	M Fetchick	46029
15	W Zembriski	291861	65	G Jones	44460
16	T Shaw	281393	66	J Barber	43333
17	CC Rodriguez	275414	67	B Yancey	42202
18	R McBee	258487	68	D Sanders	39954
19	G Littler	250516	69	R De Vicenzo	37613
20	L Graham	240027	70	J Brodie	37471
21	B Baird	234963	71	C Owens	34301
22	B Nichols	210097	72	R Beallo	33672
23	B Casper	198754	73	D Ford	29829
24	J Ferree	194992	74	J Cochran	29456
25	F Beard	189655	75	B Johnston	26573
26	J Powell	178888	76	B Collins	25060
27	J Jimenez	177753	77	J Fleck	23844
28	H Blancas	174332	78	R Rawlins	22491
29	G Brewer	152130	79	G Dickinson	20993
30	JP Cain	146763	80	B Goalby	20943
31	D Hendrickson	144739	81	P Thomson	20604
32	B Brue	140743	82	H Johnson	19092
33	D Massengale	134297	83	F Hawkins	18513
34	B Smith	133920	84	R Thompson	17300
35	L Ziegler	133339	85	J Whittenton	17283
36	Q Gray	125038	86	C Mehok	16513
37	B Devlin	121585	87	G Bayer	13575
38	A Palmer	119907	88	R Stafford	11831
39	B Erickson	116851	89	G Waldespuhl	11596
40	G Lanning	111373	90	B Hiskey	10358
41	R Rhyan	109933	91	B Toski	9895
42	P Rodgers	107361	92	A Bardha	9341
43	C Evans	105206	93	L Trevino	9258
44	L Elder	103170	94	D Wysong	9121
45	G Archer	98063	95	J Schlee	7250
46	R Boldt	96803	96	S Thirsk	7000
47	C Sifford	96340	97	L Garrison	6425
48	D Dalziel	96138	98	J Lopez	5938
49	JC Goosie	94200	99	F Haas	5888
50	T Dill	82332	100	M Joyce	5705

US Senior PGA Tour, 1989

Aetna Challenge
at Pelican Bay Club, Naples, Florida

Name	Score	Prize $
G Littler	70-70-69–209	45000
H Henning	70-70-71–211	26000
M Barber	70-73-71–214	21500
B Charles	74-69-72–215	16250
L Graham	75-69-71–215	16250

Ameritech Senior Open
at Canterbury GC, Cleveland, Ohio

Name	Score	Prize $
B Crampton	70-67-68–205	75000
O Moody	71-68-67–206	40500
J Ferree	70-72-64–206	40500
M Hill	69-70-68–207	31000
L Mowry	68-71-69–208	21000
C Coody	67-71-70–208	21000
H Henning	67-68-73–208	21000

Bell Atlantic St Christopher's Classic
at Chester Valley GC, Malvern, Pennsylvania

Name	Score	Prize $
D Hill*	76-66-68–206	60000
CC Rodriguez	67-72-67–206	35000
H Henning	70-69-68–207	29000
D Bies	69-71-69–209	21800
J Dent	69-69-71–209	21800

Winner after play-off

Crestar Classic
at Hermitage CC, Manakin-Sabot, Virginia

Name	Score	Prize $
CC Rodriguez	66-69-68–203	52500
R Rhyan	66-68-70–204	27000
J Dent	65-70-69–204	27000
B Charles	66-69-70–205	15750
J Ferree	67-66-72–205	15750
H Henning	69-67-69–205	15750
M Hill	72-67-66–205	15750
A Palmer	70-67-69–206	11000

Digital Senior Classic
at Nashawtuc CC, Concord, Massachusetts

Name	Score	Prize $
B Charles	65-70-65–200	45000
M Hill	65-69-69–203	26000
B Crampton	66-67-71–204	19750
D Douglass	64-69-71–204	19750
M Barber	66-72-67–205	12800
J Ferree	69-71-65–205	12800

Doug Sanders Kingwood Celebrity Classic
at Deerwood Club, Kingwood, Texas

Name	Score	Prize $
H Blancas	73-65-70–208	45000
W Zembriski	70-71-69–210	24750
B Charles	71-71-68–210	24750
G Player	67-70-74–211	16875
C Coody	72-69-70–211	16875

Fairfield Barnett Space Coast Classic
at Suntree CC, Melbourne, Florida

Name	Score	Prize $
B Charles	66-70-67–203	45000
B Baird	67-70-72–209	26000
L Mowry	68-72-70–210	19750
H Henning	69-73-68–210	19750

Name	Score	Prize $
G Player	70-72-69–211	14500
J O'Hern	70-71-71–212	10550
A Geiberger	72-67-73–212	10550

Gatlin Brothers Southwest Classic
at Fairway Oaks G & RC, Abilene, Texas

Name	Score	Prize $
G Archer	69-72-68–209	45000
O Moody	70-70-69–209	23750
J Powell	72-71-66–209	23750
JP Cain	70-70-70–210	12570
B Crampton	71-68-71–210	12570
J Dent	72-68-70–210	12570
M Hill	69-67-74–210	12570
G Player	68-72-70–210	12570
L Ziegler	74-66-71–211	8525
B Baird	68-71-73–212	7450
C Coody	74-68-70–212	7450

General Foods PGA Senior Championship
at PGA National, Palm Beach Gardens, Florida

Name	Score	Prize $
L Mowry	74-69-65-73–281	72000
A Geiberger	69-70-72-71–282	35200
M Barber	72-69-70-71–282	35200
M Hill	67-71-74-75–287	16533
J Jimenez	72-70-72-73–287	16533
D Hill	73-72-70-72–298	16533

The General Tire Classic
at Desert Inn CC, Las Vegas

Name	Score	Prize $
C Coody	67-69-69–205	45000
B Charles	71-67-67–205	24625
CC Rodriguez	70-69-66–205	24625
D Hill	71-68-68–207	18500
A Geiberger	69-68-72–209	15000
G Archer	67-74-69–210	11000
O Moody	70-72-69–211	9669
L Mowry	73-70-68–211	9666
L Elder	69-70-72–211	9666
M Hill	74-70-68–212	8250

Greater Grand Rapids Open
at Elks CC, Grand Rapids, Michigan

Name	Score	Prize $
JP Cain	69-68-66–203	45000
C Sifford	70-69-65–204	23750
D Hill	65-71-68–204	23750
W Zembriski	68-66-71–205	16250
A Geiberger	69-70-66–205	16250

GTE Kaanapali Classic
at Royal Kaanapali, Lahaina, Hawaii

Name	Score	Prize $
D Bies	68-64–132	45000
D Douglass	66-67–133	26000
C Coody	70-65–135	19750
T Shaw	69-66–135	19750
J Jimenez	64-73–137	12800
G Littler	69-68–137	12800
H Henning	72-66–138	9258
M Barber	69-69–138	9258
L Trevino	69-69–138	9258
H Blancas	68-71–139	7800

GTE North Classic
at Broadmoor CC, Indianapolis, Indiana

Name	Score	Prize $
G Player	67-68–135	52500
J Jimenez	68-68–136	24666
A Geiberger	68-68–136	24666
B Casper	67-69–136	24666
M Hill	67-70–137	14333
J Dent	67-70–137	14333
D Douglass	67-70–137	14333
G Brewer	69-69–138	10500
B Crampton	69-69–138	10500

GTE Northwest Classic
at Inglewood CC, Kenmore, Washington

Name	Score	Prize $
A Geiberger	68-68-68–204	52500
F Beard	69-70-68–207	30000
O Moody	70-72-66–208	24000
M Barber	65-74-70–209	15750
H Henning	70-70-69–209	15750

Name	Score	Prize $
M Hill	72-66-71–209	15750
B Crampton	69-71-69–209	15750
D Hill	68-70-72–210	11000

GTE Suncoast Classic
at Tampa Palms G & CC, Tampa, Florida

Name	Score	Prize $
B Charles*	68-70-69–207	45000
J Ferree	72-70-65–207	21833
H Henning	73-67-67–207	21833
D Hill	68-69-70–207	21833
D Sanders	68-70-70–208	14500

GTE West Classic
at Ojai Valley, Ojai, California

Name	Score	Prize $
W Zembriski	64-68-65–197	52500
G Archer	69-64-66–199	27000
J Dent	66-69-64–199	20000
B Charles	66-70-66–202	20000
CC Rodriguez	67-69-67-203	17000
B Baird	71-70-63–204	11750
H Blancas	64-72-68–204	11750
R Botts	69-69-66–204	11750
R Thompson	71-64-69–204	11750
D Bies	71-70-64–205	8366
A Geiberger	69-68-68–205	8366
A Kelley	67-66-72–205	8366

Mazda Champions
at Hyatt Dorado Beach, Puerto Rico

Name	Score	Prize $
P Rizzo & M Hill	65-60-66–191	500000
T Green & D Bies	61-65-66–192	85000
S Turner & C Coody	63-64-65–192	85000
B Daniel & O Moody	63-63-67–193	50000
J Geddes & G Littler	64-62-68–194	35000
P Bradley & D Hill	66-65-63–194	35000
B King & B Charles	68-65-62–195	22000
C Walker & CC Rodriguez	65-67-63–195	22000
C Rarick & M Barber	64-65-66–195	22000
N Lopez & A Geiberger	63-68-65–196	16000

* Winner after play-off

Mazda Senior TPC
at Sawgrass, Ponte Vedra, Florida

Name	Score	Prize $
O Moody	67-69-64-71–271	105000
C Coody	70-70-66-67–273	60000
G Player	68-66-72-68–274	48000
A Palmer	67-69-75-67–278	29600
M Barber	68-68-73-69–278	29600
B Charles	70-69-71-68–278	29600
L Graham	67-72-67-72–278	29600
A Geiberger	69-71-69-69–278	29600

Mony Arizona Classic
at the Pointe GC, Phoenix, Arizona

Name	Score	Prize $
B Crampton	67-64-69–200	45000
B Nichols	62-67-72–201	26000
G Littler	67-65-70–202	18000
R Boldt	70-62-70–202	18000
A Geiberger	65-68-69–202	18000

Mony Syracuse Senior Classic
at Lafayette CC, Jamesville, New York

Name	Score	Prize $
J Dent	69-68-64–201	45000
A Geiberger	73-66-63–202	26000
D Hendrickson	66-66-71–203	21500
G Littler	72-66-67–205	18000
P Rodgers	70-66-71–207	11212
R Beallo	69-70-68–207	11212
T Dill	70-69-68–207	11212
L Graham	69-70-68–207	11212

Murata Seniors Reunion
at Stonebriar CC, Frisco, Texas

Name	Score	Prize $
D Bies	68-67-73–208	45000
H Henning	73-71-70–214	26000
D January	75-69-73–217	21500
M Hill	72-74-74–220	16250
A Geiberger	74-72-74–220	16250

Newport Cup
at Newport CC, Newport, Rhode Island

Name	Score	Prize $
J Dent	67-73-66–206	41500
H Henning	70-65-72–207	25000
T Shaw	71-67-70–208	20500
G Brewer	72-70-68–210	15750
C Evans	70-68-72–210	15750

Northville Long Island Classic
at Meadow Brook CC, Jericho, New York

Name	Score	Prize $
B Baird*	58-62-63–183	52500
F Beard	59-63-61–183	24666
O Moody	59-63-61–183	24666
D Bies	59-62-62–183	24666
L Graham	62-60-63–185	15500
G Lanning	59-61-65–185	15500

Nynex/Golf Digest Commemorative
at Sleepy Hollow CC, Scarborough, New York

Name	Score	Prize $
B Charles	63-65-65–193	45000
D Bies	65-67-66–198	23750
B Crampton	68-64-66–198	23750
C Coody	69-67-65–201	18000
H Henning	69-68-65–202	12800
D Hill	66-67-69–202	12800

Rancho Murieta Senior Gold Rush
at Rancho Murieta CC, Rancho Murieta, California

Name	Score	Prize $
D Hill	69-70-68–207	52500
O Moody	72-68-68–208	30000
D Bies	75-69-65–209	24000

* Winner after play-off

Name	Score	Prize $
K Still	68-71-72–211	15750
P Rodgers	69-73-69–211	15750
Q Gray	71-68-72–211	15750
A Geiberger	70-73-68–211	15750

RJR at the Dominion
at The Dominion CC, San Antonio, Texas

Name	Score	Prize $
L Mowry	66-67-68–201	37500
G Brewer	65-69-68–202	21500
M Barber	66 70 68–204	17800
B Casper	70-69-67–206	14800
H Henning	71-65-71–207	10500
L Graham	66-71-70–207	10500

RJR Bank One Classic
at Mariott's Griffin Gate Resort, Lexington, Kentucky

Name	Score	Prize $
R McBee	68-65-69–202	45000
H Henning	68-66-70–204	26000
L Ziegler	68-70-67–205	21500
O Moody	67-71-68–206	18000
M Hill	69-69-69–207	11866
B Charles	71-67-69–207	11866
J O'Hern	66-71-70–207	11866

RJR Championship
at Tanglewood Park, Clemmons, N Carolina

Name	Score	Prize $
G Player	65-71-71–207	202500
R McBee	68-67-73–208	145000
D Hill	70-70-70–210	107000
M Hill	73-72-66–211	78333
B Charles	73-69-69–211	78333
O Moody	71-71-69–211	78333
Q Gray	67-76-69–212	55000
A Geiberger	73-73-67–213	47500
T Shaw	70-73-70–213	47500
B Crampton	74-68-72–214	37500
L Ziegler	72-69-73–214	37500

The Showdown Classic
at Jeremy Ranch GC, Park City, Utah

Name	Score	Prize $
T Shaw	69-68-70–207	52500
L Mowry	73-66-69–208	30000
H Blancas	69-72-69–210	22000
L Graham	68-72-70–210	22000
G Littler	67-75-69–211	17000

Southwestern Bell Classic
at Quail Creek G & CC, Oklahoma City, Oklahoma

Name	Score	Prize $
B Nicholls*	69-69-71–209	45000
O Moody	69-70-70–209	26000
J Powell	72-68-72–212	19750
A Geiberger	66-71-75–212	19750
B Charles	73-70-70–213	12800
J Dent	69-70-74–213	12800

Sunwest Bank/Charley Pride Senior Golf Classic
at Four Hills CC, Albuquerque, New Mexico

Name	Score	Prize $
B Charles	66-69-68–203	45000
C Coody	66-70-68–204	26000
M Hill	69-72-65–206	21500
G Littler	73-69-65–207	16250
A Geiberger	70-69-68–207	16250
J Dent	67-69-72–208	11100
B Nichols	67-71-71–209	9625
D Hendrickson	71-71-67–209	9625
F Beard	71-72-68–211	8525

The Tradition at Desert Mountain
at Desert Mountain, Scottsdale, Arizona

Name	Score	Prize $
D Bies	71-70-68-66–275	90000
G Player	67-69-72-68–276	52000
H Henning	70-70-70-70–280	45000
B Charles	69-71-73-68–281	34000
C Coody	73-67-72-69–281	34000

Winner after play-off

Transamerica Senior Golf Championship
at Silverado CC, Napa, California

Name	Score	Prize $
B Casper	69-70-68–207	60000
A Geiberger	70-69-71–210	35000
C Coody	67-72-72–211	26600
L Ziegler	71-70-70–211	26600
B Charles	70-70-72–212	19400
D Hill	69-70-74–213	14700
J Dent	70-74-70–214	12533
J Ferree	72-68-74–214	12533

USGA Senior Open
at Laurel Valley CC, Ligonier, Pennsylvania

Name	Score	Prize $
O Moody	72-73-64-70–279	80000
F Beard	70-69-70-72–281	40000
D Douglass	71-70-76-67–284	22267
J Dent	71-73-70-70–284	22267
B Nichols	70-70-74-71–285	13812
C Coody	72-72-71-70–285	13812
A Geiberger	68-72-76-70–286	10955
H Henning	69-74-71-72–286	10955
G Player	72-73-73-69–287	8594
J Powell	74-71-73-69–287	8594
B Charles	73-74-73-67–287	8594
B Crampton	72-72-69-74–287	8594
L Mowry	71-73-73-71–288	7391
M Hill	72-72-73-72–289	7046
B Baird	73-72-69-76–290	6553
D Bies	74-66-77-73–290	6553
T Dill	70-76-72-74–292	6101
CC Rodriguez	75-72-75-72–294	5714
D Hill	70-72-73-79–294	5714
L Graham	77-74-75-69–295	5373
P Thomson	74-74-76-72–296	5028
B Smith	74-74-77-71–296	5028
R McBee	73-71-78-74–296	5028
A Kelley	77-74-72-74–297	4692
D Massengale	74-74-74-77–299	4425
A Chandler	76-76-74-73–299	4425
D Dalziel	73-73-72-81–299	4425

Vintage Chrysler Invitational
at the Vintage Club, Indian Wells, California

Name	Score	Prize $
M Barber	70-70-72-69–281	55500
L Mowry	72-70-71-69–282	25666
D Bies	73-72-68-69–282	25666
B Charles	68-71-73-70–282	25666
JC Goosie	71-68-74-71–284	18000

US Senior Tour Official Statistics, 1989

Scoring Leaders

1	B Charles	69.78
2	A Geiberger	70.32
3	J Dent	70.61
4	D Hill	70.64
5	B Crampton	70.65
6	M Hill	70.72
7	G Littler	70.77
8	D Bies	70.78
9	G Player	70.79
10	L Ziegler	70.85

Greens in Regulation

1	C Coody	.760
2	A Geiberger	.751
3	B Charles	.729
4	J Dent	.719
5	J Ferree	.717
6	D Hill	.709
7	D Bies	.708
8	D Douglass	.694
9	B Crampton	.693
10	L Mowry	.689

Putting Leaders

1	B Charles	1.761
2	H Henning	1.762
3T	D Bies	1.768
	G Brewer	1.768
	G Littler	1.768
6	O Moody	1.769
7	M Barber	1.774
8	A Geiberger	1.778
9	D Hill	1.785
10T	B Crampton	1.788
	M Hill	1.788

Driving Distance

1	J Dent	274.6
2	J Ferree	268.9
3	T Dill	268.0
4	L Ziegler	266.5
5	B Nichols	265.9
6	D Hendrickson	262.3
7	D Bies	259.8
8	B Smith	259.3
9	R Boldt	259.1
10T	A Geiberger	258.7
	B Yancey	258.7

Driving Accuracy

1	C Sifford	.778
2	J Barber	.774
3T	L Elder	.743
	D Simon	.743
5	G Littler	.733
6	W Zembriski	.723
7	G Dickinson	.721
8	R Rhyan	.715
9T	J Fleck	.713
	D Ford	.713

Sand Saves

1	J Barber	.548
2	B Brue	.544
3	R Boldt	.541
4	O Moody	.541
5	D Dalziel	.532
6	R Botts	.529
7	D Douglass	.527
8	B Crampton	.526
9	G Player	.524
10	CC Rodriguez	.516

Safari Tour, 1989

Safari Tour Money List 1989

Pos	Name	Total Prize Money £	Pos	Name	Total Prize Money £
1	V Singh (Fiji)	39344.79	14	D Wood (Wal)	5155.15
2	J Pinsent (Eng)	17212.30	15	S Hamill (N Ire)	4961.07
3	GJ Brand (Eng)	17146.27	16	S McAllister (Scot)	4601.53
4	C Maltman (Scot)	14814.72	17	W Stephens (Eng)	4512.99
5	M Mouland (Wal)	13929.83	18	P Hoad (Eng)	4418.21
6	D Jones (N Ire)	12212.18	19	C Tucker (Eng)	4140.53
7	M Roe (Eng)	9798.26	20	A Cotton (Eng)	4030.53
8	J Morgan (Eng)	8152.54	21	T Stevens (Eng)	3924.20
9	D Llewellyn (Wal)	7053.57	22	J Anderson (Can)	3729.66
10	J Spence (Eng)	7032.43	23	M Miller (Scot)	3720.55
11	I Spencer (Eng)	6197.81	24	R Fish (Eng)	3647.30
12	J Vingoe (Eng)	6055.72	25	C Gray (Eng)	3370.66
13	C Platts (Eng)	5239.00			

Ivory Coast Open
at President GC, Yamoussoukro

Name	Score	Prize £
V Singh	70-65-65-74–274	13808
J Pinsent	69-65-70-71-275	9197
J Morgan	69-69-69-72–279	4664
GJ Brand	68-70-70-71–279	4664
P Hoad	70-70-74-67–281	3204
R Artola	74-64-73-70–281	3204
D Llewellyn	71-66-75-70–282	2485
J Vingoe	75-68-73-69–285	2071

Kenya Open
at Muthaiga, Nairobi

Name	Score	Prize £
D Jones	69-69-65-68–271	11230
M Mouland	67-69-71-67-274	7615
J Spence	70-71-65-69–275	4246
C Tucker	70-66-71-69–276	3092
V Singh	70-68-70-68–276	3092
K Kelsall	71-71-71-64–277	2338
D Wood	71-69-72-67–279	1692
W Stephens	70-71-69-69–279	1692
M Krantz	68-70-68-73–279	1692
C Maltman	67-70-74-68–279	1692

Nigerian Open
at Ikoyi, Lagos

Name	Score	Prize £
V Singh	71-68-72-68–279	10530
GJ Brand	69-71-70-70–280	4711
I Spencer	73-69-71-67–280	4711
J Pinsent	71-70-68-71–280	4711
C Platts	68-68-74-71–281	2680
D Llewellyn	73-67-73-70–283	2212
D Jagger	71-71-71-71–284	1896
J Morgan	71-69-73-72–285	1498
S Richardson	69-76-74-66–285	1498

Zambia Open
at Lusaka Golf Club

Name	Score	Prize £
C Maltman	67-76-72–215	12500
M Roe	76-71-70–217	8320
GJ Brand	76-72-70–218	4690
V Singh	75-73-72–220	3745
A Cotton	75-76-70–221	2897
J Pinsent	72-74-75–221	2897
J Anderson	77-73-72–222	2062
A Hunter	73-78 71–222	2062
J Spence	75-75-73–223	1680
A Edwards	79-74-71–224	1500

Zimbabwe Open
at Royal Harare

Name	Score	Prize £
V Singh	72-67-71-72–282	8168
M Mouland	73-71-67-73–284	5420
D Wood	67-75-75-68–285	3072
GJ Brand	73-69-73-72–287	2077
W Stephens	73-68-72-74–287	2077
J Vingoe	72-70-70-75–287	2077
M Roe	72-73-74-69–288	1478
R Drummond	71-75-72-72–290	1106
S Hamill	71-73-74-72–290	1106
J Spence	73-74-73-70–290	1106

Australia/New Zealand Tour, 1989

Australia/New Zealand Final Order of Merit 1989

Pos	Name	Prize Money $ Aus
1	P Senior	443196
2	G Norman	288600
3	P Fowler	221900
4	R Davis	191311
5	B Ogle	130205
6	R Shearer	129460
7	M Harwood	116797
8	F Nobilo	99804
9	P O'Malley	88831
10	R MacKay	83720
11	J Benepe	83543
12	M Clayton	78412
13	C Parry	77059
14	J Woodland	75177
15	J Clifford	70675
16	T Price	69578
17	T Gale	63561
18	O Moore	62553
19	I Baker-Finch	59745
20	G Waite	56834
21	B Hughes	56588
22	W Smith	54461
23	P McWhinney	52311
24	L Brown	52186
25	D de Long	51543

Asthma Foundation PGA Championship of Victoria
at Keysborough GC

Name	Score	Prize $ Aus
D Ecob	72-69-71-67–279	18000
P Senior	69-69-71-71–280	10000
M Harwood	71-67-71-74–283	6900
J Clifford	71-69-73-71–284	4320
L Brown	71-71-69-73–284	4320
P McWhinney	71-70-70-73–284	4320
M Bradley	68-72-72-73–285	3420
S Owen	70-68-73-75–286	2680
R Gilkey	69-72-72-73–286	2680

Australian Golf Classic
at Melbourne

Name	Score	Prize $ Aus
P Senior	65-72-70-69–276	180000
G Norman	73-71-70-67–281	108000
H Clark	70-72-69-71–282	69000
N Faldo	71-72-71-69–283	43200
B Shearer	72-71-71-69–283	43200
F Nobilo	60-70-72-72–283	43200
P Fowler	72-72-71-69–284	32000
T Gale	70-74-68-72–284	32000
J Cook	72-73-71-69–285	23666
M Clayton	69-69-77-70–285	23666
R Davis	69-73-68-75–285	23666
L Brown	74-73-69-70–286	17200
J Benepe	68-73-70-75–286	17200
C Howell	74-74-69-70–287	13650
M Harwood	70-72-74-71–287	13650
L Stephen	70-71-75-71–287	13650
M Bradley	74-69-71-73–287	13650

Australian Masters
at Huntingdale GC

Name	Score	Prize $ Aus
G Norman	69-69-74-68–280	81000
C Parry	68 67-79-72–286	39825
B Shearer	67-69-74-76–286	39825
G Waite	67-71-76-73–287	22410
P Fowler	67-68-80-73–288	18720
B Franklin	71-70-75-73–289	13752
O Moore	69-72-74-74–289	13752
M Harwood	69-71-78-71–289	13752
M Clayton	72-70-73-74–289	13752
T Yoneyama	71-70-70-78–289	13752

Australian Open
at Kingston Heath GC, Melbourne

Name	Score	Prize $ Aus
P Senior	66-66-69-70–271	90000
P Fowler	68-70-71-69–278	54000
B Ogle	66-71-73-69–279	34500
M Calcavecchia	67-69-69-75–280	24900
N Faldo	68-67-74-72–281	20800
J Woodland	66-69-73-74–282	19100
M Harwood	71-67-71-74–283	16000
G Brand Jr	68-69-71-75–283	16000
H Clark	68-75-72-69–284	11833
F Nobilo	71-72-70-71–284	11833
C Strange	65-71-73-75–284	11833
R Mackay	71-72-75-67–285	8200
S Bann	67-73-72-73–285	8200
I Baker-Finch	71-72-68-74–285	8200
S Bennett	73-70-72-71–286	6800

Australian PGA Championship
at Riverside Oaks, Sydney

Name	Score	Prize $ Aus
P Senior	67-68-68-71–274	90000
J Benepe	72-66-65-72–275	54000
M Harwood	68-69-71-69–277	34500
R Davis	69-70-72-67–278	22850
P Fowler	67-71-72-68–278	22850
W Riley	72-70-68-69–279	19100
F Nobilo	73-69-68-70–280	16000
J Wilson	68-69-72-71–280	16000
C Howell	70-72-69-70–281	13500
I Woosnam	70-70-71-71–282	11000
F Couples	73-69-68-72–282	11000

PGA National Tournament Players Championship
at PGA National, Riverside Oaks

Name	Score	Prize $
G Norman	70-70-69-67–276	90000
R Mackay	67-73-69-69–278	54000
R Davis	72-67-72-69–280	29700
D DeLong	68-70-70-72–280	29700
P Fowler	71-69-71-70–281	19950
C Parry	70-70-70-71–281	19950
F Nobilo	69-74-70-69–282	15166
P Senior	73-70-67-72–282	15166
J Woodland	69-70-67-76–282	15166
B Shearer	70-71-76-66–283	10333
B Hughes	78-68-68-69–283	10333
G Hohnen	70-71-70-72–283	10333

South African Sunshine Circuit

Order of Merit 1988-89

Pos	Name	Official Prize Money–Rand
1	T Johnstone (Zim)	254950
2	J Bland	143448
3	J Hawkes	141677
4	W Westner	103466
5	C Williams	100384
6	I Palmer	91055
7	S Smith	81052
8	F Wadsworth	71167
9	G Levenson	63265
10	B Vaughan (USA)	59952
11	J Daly (USA)	57803
12	J Townsend (USA)	56980
13	JC Anderson (USA)	52063
14	S Van Der Merwe	47202
15	T Lehman (USA)	46360
16	P Harrison (UK)	43608
17	D Feherty (Ire)	41655
18	M Wiltshire	41623
19	H Baiocchi	38766
20	T Webber	33838
21	J Dlamini (Swa)	33350
22	D Durnian (UK)	32710
23	A Pate (USA)	32677
24	D Hayes	32190
25	J Chaffee (USA)	32077

Lexington PGA
at Wanderers

Name	Score	Prize Rand
T Johnstone*	71-65-66-67–269	40000
C Williams	67-68-67-67–269	28750
M Wiltshire	69-63-67-71–270	17500
J Daly	70-69-68-66–273	10666
F Wadsworth	72-67-68-66–273	10666
J Anderson	70-64-68-71–273	10666
D Feherty	70-71-70-63–274	5750
J Bland	68-71-69-66–274	5750
C Moody	70-66-71-67–274	5750
J Hawkes	69-69-68-68–274	6750
B Vaughan	65-69-71-69–274	5750

Winner after play-off

Protea Assurance SA Open Championship
at Glendower

Name	Score	Prize Rand
F Wadsworth	72-68-70-68–278	48000
T Lehman	72-66-68-73–279	34500
J Perenz	75-71-68-67–281	21000
T Johnstone	69-67-74-73–283	15000
J Hawkes	71-69-71-73–284	12600
B Vaughan	73-71-72-69–285	9900
C Bolling	73-67-70-75–285	9900
J Hobday	72-73-69-72–286	7050
G Cesario	72-74-67-73–286	7050
A Cruse	70-65-76-76–287	6000

Trust Bank Tournament of Champions
at Kensington

Name	Score	Prize Rand
J Townsend	67-70-67-71–275	40000
B Vaughan	71-71-70-65–277	28750
I Palmer	73-68-73-65–274	12375
J Bland	70-71-71-67–279	12375
G Levenson	73-69-69-68–279	12375
J Hawkes	69-69-71-70–279	12375
T Robinson	72-71-71-67–281	5750
C Holcombe	72-72-69-68–281	5750
B McDonnell	70-72-68-71–281	5750
J Chaffee	66-72-70-73–281	5750
H Royer	71-74-63-73–281	5750

Sony Ranking 1989

The World Ranking System for Professional Golf

Introduction

In the spring of 1986 the Sony Corporation announced the launch of a world ranking system for professional golf. The Sony Ranking, which is sanctioned by the Championship is a specially developed computerised ranking which provides an authoritative reference source to the relative performance of the world's leading players.

The official events from all the geographical circuits are taken into account and points awarded according to the quality and strength of the players participating in each event. The number of points distributed to each player is dependent upon his finishing position and the scale of bonus points allocated on the basis of the number and ranking of the players in the field. The four Major Championships and the Players Championship have been weighted separately to reflect the higher quality of the events and the strong fields participating.

The Sony Ranking is based on a three year 'rolling' period weighted in favour of the more recent results, and a divisor is used to take account of the number of tournaments played by each ranked player.

The Sony Ranking is issued every Monday at the completion of the week's tournaments from around the world.

Points

50 points are awarded to the winner of a Major Championship with 30 points for second place, 20 for third, 15 for fourth, 12 for fifth down to a single point for a player completing the final round. The Players Championship is awarded 40 points for the winner down to a single point for 50th place.

All other events have a points system 'rated' on the strength of the field which is assessed upon the number and Ranking position of the top 100 Ranked players participating in each event.

Sony Ranking
at 31 December 1989

Pos	(86-88)	Player	Circuit		Points Average	Total Points
1	(2)	Greg Norman	ANZ	1	17.76	1385
2	(4)	Nick Faldo	Eur	1	16.25	1365
3	(1)	Seve Ballesteros	Eur	2	15.03	1097
4	(5)	Curtis Strange	USA	1	13.79	1172
5	(19)	Payne Stewart	USA	2	12.82	1115
6	(13)	Tom Kite	USA	3	12.41	993
7	(15)	J Maria Olazabal	Eur	3	12.00	864
8	(9)	Mark Calcavecchia	USA	4	11.81	1146
9	(6)	Ian Woosnam	Eur	4	11.56	948
10	(8)	Paul Azinger	USA	5	10.95	898
11	(14)	Chip Beck	USA	6	10.49	860
12	(12)	Masashi Ozaki	Jpn	1	10.00	850
13	(11)	David Frost	Afr	1	9.39	836
14	(3)	Sandy Lyle	Eur	5	9.37	862
15	(20)	Fred Couples	USA	7	8.85	814
16	(16)	Bernhard Langer	Eur	6	8.47	720
17	(7)	Ben Crenshaw	USA	8	8.31	673
18	(23)	Mark McCumber	USA	9	8.04	619
19	(24)	Larry Mize	USA	10	7.08	595
20	(17)	Tom Watson	USA	11	6.81	429
21	(57)	Ronan Rafferty	Eur	7	6.73	666
22	(30)	Mike Reid	USA	12	6.57	565
23	(18)	Larry Nelson	USA	13	6.46	465
24	(41)	Scott Hoch	USA	14	6.42	610
25	(10)	Lanny Wadkins	USA	15	6.35	489
26	(47)	Peter Senior	ANZ	2	6.35	641
27	(29)	Mark O'Meara	USA	16	6.20	564
28	(76)	Steve Jones	USA	17	6.09	518
29	(65)	Craig Parry	ANZ	3	6.03	531
30	(32)	Craig Stadler	USA	18	5.90	460
31	(22)	Mark McNulty	Afr	2	5.82	483
32	(35)	Bruce Lietzke	USA	19	5.68	386
33	(21)	Ken Green	USA	20	5.47	509
34	(37)	Isao Aoki	Jpn	2	5.45	518
35	(113)	Tim Simpson	USA	21	5.44	506
36	(25)	Scott Simpson	USA	22	5.33	474
37	(48)	Mark James	Eur	8	5.27	437
38	(33)	Nick Price	Afr	3	4.87	404
39	(34)	Don Pooley	USA	23	4.75	380
40	(43)	Bob Tway	USA	24	4.69	441
41	(38)	Steve Pate	USA	25	4.67	467
42	(85)	Wayne Grady	ANZ	4	4.62	434
43	(31)	Rodger Davis	ANZ	5	4.42	402
44	(28)	Dan Pohl	USA	26	4.36	327
45	(161)	Blaine McCallister	USA	27	4.30	456
46	(62)	Peter Jacobsen	USA	28	4.28	338
47	(39)	Fuzzy Zoeller	USA	29	4.22	274
48	(64)	Naomichi Ozaki	Jpn	3	4.20	395
49	(53)	Jodie Mudd	USA	30	4.17	375
50	(94)	Bill Glasson	USA	31	4.15	349

Men's Amateur

Globe Amateur Order of Merit

Pos	1988 Pos	Name	Club	Points
1	(7)	S Dodd	Brynhill	2896
2	(1)	P McEvoy	Copt Heath	1868
3	(5)	J Milligan	Kilmarnock Barassie	1643
4	(20)	C Cassells	Murcar	1528
5	(2)	G McGimpsey	Bangor	1455
6	(76)	D Clarke	Dungannon	1328
7	(8)	N Anderson	Shandon Park	1121
8	(16)	D Carrick	Douglas Park	1104
9	(11)	E O'Connell	Killarney	1097
10	(6)	R Eggo	L'Ancresse	1061
11	(24)	A Coltart	Thornhill	1033
12	(23)	R Willison	Ealing	1007
13	(21)	A Thomson	Aye Belleisle	965
14	(—)	J Carvill	Warrenpoint	957
15	(—)	J Payne	Sandilands	884
16	(50)	J Cook	Leamington & County	835
17	(10)	C Everett	Cambuslang	825
18	(—)	P McGinley	The Grange	817
19	(4)	S Easingwood	Dunbar	788
20	(12)	J Peters	Southerndown	782
21	(—)	M Smith	Brokenhurst Manor	782
22	(—)	J Metcalfe	Arcot Hall	751
23	(14)	G Wolstenholme	The Leicestershire	713
24	(—)	C Davison	Eaglescliffe	645
25	(65)	L MacNamara	Woodbrook	641
26	(41)	K Hird	Murcar	605
27	(29)	N Goulding	Portmarnock	602
28	(—)	A Elliott	Fereneze	600
29	(51)	K Kearney	Limerick	593
30	(28)	M Macara	Maesdu	585
31	(—)	S Keenan	Gallway	575
32	(52)	A Tait	Irvine	547
33	(39)	R Winchester	Sidmouth	539
34	(—)	G Evans	Worthing	509
35	(26)	M Gannon	County Louth	508
36	(43)	J Lee	Cardiff	470
37	(—)	G Lowson	Auchterarder	464
38	(27)	C Dalgleish	Helensburgh	441
39	(17)	A Nash	Carlyon Bay	433
40	(38)	A Pierse	Tipperary	420
41	(—)	N Williamson	Hunstanton	410
42	(—)	J Fanagan	Milltown	400
43	(—)	C McIntosh	Turnhouse	394
44	(22)	A Rogers	Ealing	390
45	(—)	D Baker	Downpatrick	383
46	(71)	R Roper	Catterick Garrison	382
47	(18)	P Rayfus	Trim	343
48	(18)	E Power	Tramore	321
49	(—)	N Holman	Worlebury	315
50	(40)	G Hay	Hilton Park	300

Walker Cup
at Peachtree, Atlanta

First Day – Foursomes

Great Britain and Ireland	Matches	USA	Matches
R Claydon and D Prosser	0	R Gamez and D Martin (3 and 2)	1
S Dodd and G McGimpsey	½	D Yates and P Mickelson	½
P McEvoy and E O'Connell (6 and 5)	1	G Lesher and J Sigel	0
J Milligan and A Hare (2 and 1)	1	D Eger and K Johnson	0
	2½		1½

Singles

Great Britain and Ireland	Matches	USA	Matches
J Milligan	0	R Gamez (7 and 6)	1
R Claydon (5 and 4)	1	D Martin	0
S Dodd	½	E Meeks	½
E O'Connell (5 and 4)	1	R Howe	0
P McEvoy (2 and 1)	1	D Yates	0
G McGimpsey	0	P Mickelson (4 and 2)	1
C Cassells (1 hole)	1	G Lesher	0
N Roderick	½	J Sigel	½
	5		3

First day's aggregate: Great Britain and Ireland 7½; USA 4½.

Second Day – Foursomes

Great Britain and Ireland	Matches	USA	Matches
P McEvoy and E O'Connell	½	R Gamez and D Martin	½
R Claydon and C Cassells (3 and 2)	1	J Sigel and G Lesher	0
J Milligan and A Hare (2 and 1)	1	D Eger and K Johnson	0
G McGimpsey and S Dodd (2 and 1)	1	P Mickelson and D Yates	0
	3½		½

Singles

Great Britain and Ireland	Matches	USA	Matches
S Dodd	0	R Gamez (1 hole)	1
A Hare	½	D Martin	½
R Claydon	0	G Lesher (3 and 2)	1
P McEvoy	0	D Yates (4 and 3)	1
E O'Connell	½	P Mickelson	½
N Roderick	0	D Eger (4 and 2)	1
C Cassells	0	GK Johnson (4 and 2)	1
J Milligan	½	J Sigel	½
	1½		6½

Second day's aggregate: Great Britain and Ireland 5; USA 7.

Grand match aggregate: Great Britain and Ireland 12½; USA 11½.

The Amateur Championship
at Royal Birkdale

First Round:

J Milligan beat K Fairbairn 2 and 1
S Bouvier beat L Herne 3 and 2
D Bathgate beat G Hickman 4 and 3
J Payne beat R Eggo 2 and 1
C Cassells beat M Wild 5 and 3
N Williamson beat E Els 2 and 1
R Willison beat M Wiggett 4 and 3
J Robson beat C Boardman 5 and 4
G McGimpsey beat B Shields 6 and 5
D Basson beat A Tait 5 and 4
M Hastie beat J Webber 2 holes
B Jackson beat R Claydon at 19th
G Walmsley beat N Graves 1 hole
J Cook beat S Amor 1 hole
G Shaw beat C Everett 3 and 2
C Dalrymple beat S Lovey 5 and 4

P Nyman beat P Robinson 2 and 1
C Davison beat S East 6 and 5
G Vanier beat J Blewett 1 hole
T Foster beat J Lawson 5 and 4
A Hare beat R Henry Jr 5 and 4
G Evans beat S Struver 7 and 6
P McEvoy beat A Elliot at 28th
S Dodd beat D Harding at 20th
K Weeks beat D Horne at 19th
S Wilkinson beat L Peterson 4 and 3
R Bardsley beat D Spriddle 2 and 1
R Karlsson beat U Zilg 3 and 2
M Smith beat G Homewood 1 hole
D Lee beat A Rogers 1 hole
A Coltart beat D Prosser 4 and 3
S McCraw beat W Hewlett 2 and 1

Second Round:

S Bouvier beat J Milligan 3 and 2
J Payne beat D Bathgate 2 and 1
R Willison beat N Williamson 5 and 4
B Jackson beat M Hastie 4 and 3
C Cassells beat D Basson at 19th
G McGimpsey beat J Robson at 22nd
J Cook beat G Walmsley at 19th
P McEvoy beat G Shaw 3 and 1

P Nyman beat C Dalrymple 2 and 1
C Davison beat G Vanier 2 and 1
R Bardsley beat S Wilkinson 4 and 3
S Dodd beat K Weeks 3 and 2
R Karlsson beat T Foster 2 holes
M Smith beat D Lee 2 and 1
A Hare beat A Coltart 4 and 3
S McCraw beat G Evans 3 and 2

Third Round:

J Payne beat S Bouvier 6 and 4
C Cassells beat R Willison 5 and 4
P McEvoy beat J Cook 1 hole
C Davison beat P Nyman 7 and 5

G McGimpsey beat B Jackson 1 hole
S Dodd beat R Bardsley 3 and 1
M Smith beat R Karlsson 2 and 1
S McCraw beat A Hare 4 and 3

Quarter Finals:

C Cassells beat J Payne 1 hole
G McGimpsey beat P McEvoy 2 and 1
S Dodd beat C Davison 3 and 1
S McCraw beat M Smith at 19th

Semi-Finals:

C Cassells beat G McGimpsey 1 hole
S Dodd beat S McCraw 1 hole

Final:

S Dodd beat C Cassells 5 and 3

Berkhamsted Trophy
at Berkhamsted

Name	Score
J Payne	73-69–142
R Claydon	73-70–143
G Walmsley	73-71–144
S Richardson	73-71–144
G Pooley	75-70–145
G Krause	71-74–145
A Rogers	73-73–146
C Bufton	73-73–146

Brabazon Trophy
at Hoylake

Name	Score	Name	Score
RN Roderick	74-69-77-73–293	J Payne	71-76-77-72–296
C Rivett	74-75-69-75–293	J Cook	70-77-74-76–297
AP Hare	71-74-75-74–294	M Wiggett	77-75-74-72–298
J Price	74-74-72-74–294	GS Pooley	68-79-78-73–298
G Hay	74-72-72-76–294	C Cassells	70-80-73-76–299
S Richardson	70-74-76-75–295	P Walton	74-76-72-78–300
G Evans	78-72-75-70–295	MC Reynard	73-76-75-76–300
MJ Smith	74-75-71-75–295	P McEvoy	75-74-75-76–300
R Eggo	78-71-71-75–295	DG Lane	72-77-75-76–300
DM Prosser	74-77-72-73–296	R Claydon	74-76-75-77–302

Cameron Corbett Vase
at Hagg's Castle

Name	Score
A Tait	75-68-70-70–283
S Smith	72-70-70-72–284
S Mackenzie	70-72-70-72–284
G Lowson	69-71-69-75–284

Craigmillar Park Open
at Craigmillar Park

Name	Score
R Roper	71-73-67-67–278
D Prosser	72 66 69 73–280
C Cassells	70-69-70-71–280
G Lowson	70-69-74-70–283

Duncan Putter
at Southerndown

Name	Score
RN Roderick	71-69-68-72–280
P McEvoy	71-71-70-73–285
JP Price	71-73-72-71–287
R Willison	73-71-71-72–287
JL Peters	68-74-74-74–290
S Pardoe	71-74-70-77–292
S Richardson	70-77-72-74–293
MW Calvert	71-71-74-80–296

East of Scotland Open Amateur Stroke-Play
at Lundin Links

Name	Score
K Hird	67-70-72-69–278
G Lowson	68-68-71-72–279
G Macdonald	71-73-72-68–284
S Syme	72-71-71-71–285
D Smith	75-72-71-68–286
C Ronald	69-75-71-71–286

Edward Trophy
at Glasgow Gailes

Name	Score
D Elliot	71-66–137
C Green	72-71–143
B Shields	71-72–143
S Easingwood	71-73–144
A Gourlay	72-73–145

English Amateur Championship
at Royal St George's, Sandwich

Fourth Round:

C Davison beat C Slattery 1 hole
A Dunbar beat P Bembrick 2 holes
R Winchester beat G Boardman 4 and 3
J Cowgill beat T Marsden 3 and 2
R Eggo beat D Hickman 6 and 5
R Claydon beat S Wood 4 and 3
P Hedges beat D Mee 1 hole
D Bathgate beat G Krause 1 hole

G Neilsen beat R Latham at 21st
S Richardson beat G Milne 1 hole
N Holman beat J Hodgson 3 and 2
M Palmer beat R Futerman 1 hole
S Whiffin beat D Gibson 5 and 4
P Robinson beat M Deal 3 and 1
A Sandywell beat J Metcalfe 1 hole
M Wiggett beat R Sadler at 20th

Fifth Round:

C Davison beat M Wiggett 5 and 3
R Eggo beat A Dunbar 2 and 1
R Winchester beat R Claydon at 19th
J Cowgill beat A Sandywell 1 hole

P Hedges beat D Bathgate 4 and 3
S Richardson beat G Neilsen 6 and 5
P Robinson beat S Whiffin 4 and 2
N Holman beat M Palmer 1 hole

Quarter Finals:

R Eggo beat C Davison at 19th
R Winchester beat J Cowgill 2 and 1
S Richardson beat P Hedges 3 and 2
P Robinson beat N Holman at 20th

Semi-Finals:

R Eggo beat R Winchester 2 and 1
S Richardson beat P Robinson 6 and 5

Final:

S Richardson beat R Eggo 2 and 1

English Mid-Amateur Championship
at Moortown

Name	Score
A Mew	76-73-71-70–290
A Carman	74-74-78-81–307
J Docker	71-85-78-75–309
G Clark	76-76-74-84–310

Famous Grouse Scottish Seniors' Championship
at Killermont

Name	Score
S Mayer	72-67–139
G Clark	74-71–145
N McLeod	67-78–145

Name	Score
J Hayes	74-72–146
C Green	72-74–146
A Tune	71-76–147
D Mackie	76-71–147

The Halford Hewitt
at Deal

Third Round:

Shrewsbury 3, Dulwich 2
Repton 3, Bradford 2
Eton 3, Stonyhurst 2
Marlborough 3, St Paul's 2

Tonbridge 4, Merchiston 1
Harrow 3, Charterhouse 2
Oundle 3½, Stowe 1½
Malvern 5, Wreckin 0

Fourth Round:

Malvern 3, Oundle 2
Shrewsbury 4½, Repton ½
Eton 4½, Marlborough ½
Harrow 3½, Tonbridge 1½

Semi-Finals:

Shrewsbury 5, Malvern 0
Eton 3, Harrow 2

Final:

Eton	Matches	Shrewsbury	Matches
NJ Angus and J Merquez	0	MJ Thorpe and JA Skelton (5 and 4)	1
RJG Hurst and JRH Kreetin	0	AL Parsons and JR Campion (3 and 2)	1
B Critchley and AJP Summers (3 and 2)	1	MA Smith and MA Caswell	0
MH Dixon and WGA Clegg (5 and 4)	1	FT Hildrup and JC Mawdsley	0
MJJ Faber and NJ Lindesay-Bethune (1 hole)	1	WI Campion and WR Painter	0
	3		2

Eton 2; Shrewsbury 2

Hampshire Hog
at Blackmoor

Name	Score
P McEvoy	70-73–143
R Claydon	72-72–144
A Rogers	72-72–144
P Dougan	73-72–145
G Krause	74-71–145

Hampshire Salver
at Blackmoor

Name	Score
P Dougan*	286
P McEvoy	286
R Latham	287
A Rogers	288
R Claydon	289

Home Internationals

1989 – at Ganton

England beat Scotland 9 matches to 6
England beat Wales 12 matches to 3
England beat Ireland 8 matches to 7
Scotland beat Ireland 8½ matches to 6½
Scotland beat Wales 8 matches to 7
Ireland beat Wales 11 matches to 4

Winners: England

International Amateur Championship of Greece
at Corfu GC

Nations Cup

Country	Score
Denmark	293
(M Grabow, A Krag, J Svendsen)	
Wales	300
(E Jones, S Jones, S Perdoe)	
Greece	301
(G Nikitaidis, S Vafiadis, M Aronis)	

Individual

Winner	Score
A Krag (Den)	291
S Jones (Wal)	294
M Grabow (Den)	296
G Nikitaidis (Gre)	296
N Boysen (Hol)	303

---

* *Winner after play-off*

Irish Amateur Championship
at Rosses Point

Quarter Finals:

D Clarke beat P O'Looney 7 and 6
N Goulding beat D Baker 5 and 4
P McGinley beat T Cleary 3 and 2
M Morris beat A O'Shea 1 hole

Semi-finals:

N Goulding beat D Clarke 3 and 2
P McGinley beat M Morris 5 and 4

Final:

P McGinley beat N Goulding 3 and 2

Lytham Trophy
at Royal Lytham

Name	Score
N Williamson*	70-71-77-68–286
S Richardson	71-75-69-71–286
D Prosser	68-77-73-73–291
J Payne	74-72-73-72–291
G Evans	68-74-73-76–291
A Hare	69-79-72-72–292
T Foster	72-75-77-68–292
S McCraw	73-76-71-72–292

Midland Open Amateur Championship
at Little Aston

Name	Score
J Cook	70-73-70-70–283
J Payne	72-71-72-70–285
S Robinson	72-73-74-69–288
G Krause	70-76-71-72–289
G Kemble	74-71-74-72–291

Winner after play-off

Oxford *v* Cambridge University Match

for the Grant Thornton Trophy
at Rye GC, Sussex

Cambridge		Oxford	
Foursomes			
	Matches		Matches
J Rumble and R Hall (7 and 6)	1	A Woolnough and K Froggatt	0
J Skelton and M Williams (1 hole)	1	N Burke and J Higgo	0
J Shinton and M Ebert (1 hole)	1	I Henderson and T Tow	0
I Ward and R Haines (6 and 5)	1	D Shaw and J Hampel	0
S Scott and J Borrett	½	A Chilvers and R Youngman	½
	4½		½

Singles			
J Rumble (5 and 4)	1	I Henderson	0
R Hall (7 and 6)	1	N Burke	0
J Skelton (7 and 6)	1	A Woolnough	0
I Ward (6 and 5)	1	A Chilvers	0
J Shinton	0	J Higgo (1 hole)	1
M Ebert	0	T Tew (3 and 2)	1
M Williams	0	K Froggatt (3 and 2)	1
R Haines (6 and 5)	1	R Youngman	0
S Scott (9 and 8)	1	J Hemple	0
J Borrett (6 and 5)	1	D Shaw	0
	7		3

Cambridge 11½; Oxford 3½

President's Putter

at Rye

Fourth Round:

RF Palmer beat RJG Hurst 3 and 2
JJN Caplan beat TR Grew 5 and 4
JMT Warman beat JR Barnett 5 and 4
M Yates beat CLA Edgington 2 and 1

TM Powell beat J Youngman 3 and 2
PM Froggatt beat GD Wuollet 2 and 1
BG Streather beat AJP Summers 3 and 2
JWS Rumble beat TH Theyer at 19th

Fifth Round:

JJN Caplan beat RF Palmer 4 and 3
JMT Warman beat M Yates 1 hole
PM Froggatt beat TM Powell 1 hole
BG Streather beat JWS Rumble 1 hole

Semi-Finals:

JMT Warman beat JJN Caplan 2 and 1
PM Froggatt beat BG Streather 4 and 3

Final:

PM Froggatt beat JMT Warman 3 and 2

Scotland v France
at Rosemount

Scotland		France	
Foursomes			
	Matches		Matches
J Milligan and A Elliott (2 and 1)	1	F Illouz and P Barquez	0
S Easingwood and C Everett	0	C Cevaer and E Giraud (5 and 4)	1
D Carrick and G Hay	0	V Romain and O Edmond (6 and 5)	1
	1		2
Singles			
J Milligan	0	C Cevaer (2 and 1)	1
A Elliott (2 and 1)	1	V Romain	0
S Easingwood (1 hole)	1	E Giraud	0
G Hay	0	O Edmond (4 and 3)	1
D Carrick (3 and 1)	1	F Illouz	0
C Everett (5 and 4)	1	P Barquez	0
	4		2

Scotland 5; France 4

Scottish Amateur Championship
at Moray

Fourth Round:

G Lowson beat R Russell 2 and 1
R Robertson beat B Wann 1 hole
C Dalgleish beat L Campbell 4 and 3
K Hird beat C Watson 1 hole
E Macintosh beat A Mathers 5 and 4
J Grant beat R Ballantyne 4 and 3
A Thomson wo R Blair scr
G Shaw beat G Hay 3 and 1

M McLeman beat R Brechin 3 and 1
A Kidd beat S Bannerman 5 and 4
D Weir beat S Syme 1 hole
F Stewart beat D Kirkpatrick 2 and 1
B Wortley beat J Russell 1 hole
A Tair beat C Mackenzie 2 holes
A Cochrane beat P Macleod at 19th
C Fraser beat S Middleton 1 hole

Fifth Round:

G Lowson beat R Robertson 4 and 3
C Dalgleish beat K Hird 3 and 2
J Grant beat E Macintosh at 19th
A Thomson beat G Shaw 2 and 1

M McLeman beat A Kidd 2 and 1
D Weir beat F Stewart 6 and 5
A Tait beat B Wortley 3 and 2
C Fraser beat A Cochrane 1 hole

Quarter Finals:

C Dalgleish beat G Lowson 2 holes
A Thomson beat J Grant 2 holes
D Weir beat M McLeman 2 holes
A Tait beat C Fraser at 22nd

Semi-Finals:

A Thomson beat C Dalgleish 2 and 1
A Tait beat D Weir 3 and 2

Final:

A Thomson beat A Tait 1 hole

Scottish Open Amateur Stroke-Play Championship
at Rosemount

Name	Score
F Illouz	65-74-69-73–281
C Cassells	72-73-69-69–283
J Milligan	70-72-69-72–283
C Everett	70-71-70-72–283
C Ronald	70-75-69-70–284
S McCraw	67-74-72-71–284
D Carrick	72-73-69-71–285
J Yuille	69-74-71-72–286

Scottish Universities Championship
at Montrose

	P	W	L	D	Pts		
Stirling	7	6	1	0	12	**Individual**	
Edinburgh	7	4	2	1	9	G Moore (Stirling)	154
Aberdeen	7	4	2	1	9	N Hughes (Stirling)	156
St Andrews	7	4	2	1	9	T Gillgrass (Edinburgh	156
Glasgow	7	4	3	0	8	G MacCrossan (Dundee)	157
Strathclyde	7	3	4	0	6	C MacPhail (Edinburgh)	157
Heriot-Watt	7	1	5	1	3		
Dundee	7	0	7	0	0		

Selborne Salver
at Blackmoor

Name	Score
M Stanford	68-72–140
R Willison	73-68–141
P Dougan	71-70–141
R Latham	70-71·141

Sunningdale Foursomes
at Sunningdale

Quarter Finals:

J Wade and V Thomas beat C Cox and V Cox 2 and 1
R Chapman and B Lane beat A Clapp and J Sewell 4 and 3
A Hare and R Claydon beat R Whitehead and L Farmer 2 and 1
B Waites and J Collingham beat C Mason and A Chandler 3 and 1

Semi-Finals:

J Wade and V Thomas beat B Waites and J Collingham 3 and 2
A Hare and R Claydon beat R Chapman and D Lane 3 and 2

Final:

A Hare and R Claydon beat J Wade and V Thomas 4 and 3

TSB Scottish Champion of Champions
at Leven

Name	Score	Name	Score
J Milligan	73-71-78-74–296	C Fraser	71-72-78-80–301
D Carrick	75-72-75-75–297	G Hay	75-73-74-80–302
K Hird	71-75-78-74–298	S Easingwood	74-73-79-76–302
A Thomson	74-75-72-79–300	J Finnigan	70-76-80-77–303
W Bryson	74-77-72-78–301		

US Amateur Championship
at Merion

Quarter Finals:

M Brannan beat T Satterfield 2 holes
C Patton beat K Wentworth 2 and 1
J Courville beat T Himka 2 and 1
D Green beat J Sigel at 19th

Semi-Finals:

C Patton beat M Brannan 3 and 2
D Green beat J Courville 2 holes

Final:

C Patton beat D Green 3 and 1

Welsh Amateur Championship
at Tenby

Quarter Finals:

K Jones beat S Jones 6 and 5
N Roderick beat A Harrhy 6 and 5
J Price beat N Hopwood 1 hole
S Dodd beat J Lee 5 and 4

Semi-Finals:

K Jones beat N Roderick 5 and 4
S Dodd beat J Price at 20th

Final:

S Dodd beat K Jones 2 and 1

WPGET Woolmark Order of Merit, 1989

Place	Name	Official Money £	Place	Name	Official Money £
1	ML de Lorenzi (Fra)	77534	51	L Neumann (Swe)	7710
2	A Nicholas	56529	52	M From (Swe)	7288
3	K Douglas	48534	53	R Bell (Aus)	7173
4	S Strudwick	41966	54	B New	7169
5	D Hutton (Aus)	41541	55	C Nilsmark (Swe)	6367
6	J Connachan	38227	56	N Lowien (Aus)	6340
7	P Conley (USA)	36877	57	J Greco (USA)	6278
8	C Dibnah (Aus)	35622	58	M Jones (USA)	6273
9	L Maritz (SA)	33979	59	J Arnold (NZ)	6214
10	G Stewart	31700	60	WL Li (Tai)	6196
11	F Descampe (Bel)	31003	61	S Nyhus (USA)	6136
12	S Gronberg (Swe)	27230	62	L Mullard (Aus)	6054
13	X Wunsch-Ruiz (Spa)	27190	63	A Sheard (SA)	5850
14	M Garner (Ire)	26923	64	J Rumsey	5410
15	S Moon (USA)	25904	65	E Glass	5020
16	D Dowling	24977	66	J Statham	4978
17	T Abitbol (Spa)	23275	67	K Clark (USA)	4976
18	D Reid	21783	68	K Cornelius (USA)	4821
19	L Davies	21608	69	T Hammond	4789
20	H Alfredsson (Swe)	20356	70	J Furby	4784
21	C Panton	19920	71	L Mills (USA)	4739
22	A Dibos (Peru)	19725	72	T Craik	4321
23	C Soules (Fra)	19500	73	K Hanson (USA)	4217
24	D Barnard	18157	74	M Lunn (Aus)	4124
25	A Oxenstierna (Swe)	18033	75	M Thomson	4117
26	R Hast	17056	76	J Ralls (USA)	4088
27	A Jones (Aus)	15039	77	T Fernando (Sri Lanka)	3984
28	P Gonzalez (Col)	15010	78	J Hennessy (USA)	3900
29	R Lautens (Swi)	15002	79	S Croce (Ita)	3855
30	K Espinasse (Fra)	14343	80	T Yarwood	3818
31	K Lunn (Aus)	13697	81	L Percival	3798
32	C Scholefield (USA)	12963	82	M Navarro Corbachio (Spa)	3643
33	J Soulsby	12854	83	J Brown	3611
34	F Dassu (Ita)	12622	84	L Behan (Ire)	3596
35	S Van Wyk (SA)	12504	85	K Lasken (USA)	3477
36	T Johnson	11681	86	A Munt (Aus)	3404
37	M Walker	11614	87	B Lunsford (USA)	3185
38	D Petrizzi (USA)	11548	88	B Huke	3053
39	C Griffiths	11066	89	K Dallas	2963
40	M McNamara (USA)	10821	90	S Duhig	2668
41	K Davies	10557	91	D Martin	2640
42	S Shapcott	9773	92	M Landehag (Swe)	2530
43	R Comstock (USA)	9577	93	J Forrest	2389
44	D Pavich (Aus)	9576	94	A Rogerson (Can)	2361
45	S Prosser	9010	95	S Andonian-Smith (USA)	2313
46	B Helbig (W Ger)	8843	96	D Baldwin	2310
47	M Burton	8694	97	N Jeanson Decrop (Fr)	2186
48	J Howard (Zim)	8620	98	C Charbonnier (Swi)	2177
49	C Duffy	8503	99	K Spooner (USA)	2157
50	H Andersson (Swe)	7973	100	P Dunlap (USA)	2156

Women's Professional Golf European Tour, 1989

Weetabix Women's British Open
at Ferndown, Dorset

Name	Score	Prize £
J Geddes (USA)	67-67-72-68–274	18000
F Descampe (Bel)	73-66-70-67–276	12340
ML de Lorenzi (Fra)	68-71-67-72–278	8880
P Rizzo (USA)	71-69-68-71–279	6480
M Spencer-Devlin (USA)	72-69-67-71–279	6480
P Conley (GB)	70-67-76-67–280	4860
X Wunsch-Ruiz (Spa)	69-73-72-67–281	4140
K Douglas (GB)	71-70-71-70–282	3540
A Dibos (Peru)	67-75-72-69–283	3060
R Bell (Aus)	71-68-74-72–285	2480
M Figueras-Dotti (Spa)	69-71-72-73–285	2480
H Alfredsson (Swe)	73-70-69-73–285	2480
L Maritz (SA)	67-74-71-74–286	2150
L Davies (GB)	76-71-69-71–287	1924
R Hast (GB)	73-71-73-70–287	1924
A Nicholas (GB)	71-69-71-76–287	1924
M McNamara (USA)	73-70-72-72–287	1924
C Scholefield (USA)	75-72-71-69–287	1924
D Dowling (GB)	69-76-72-71–288	1710
J Furby (GB)	71-72-70-75–288	1710
T Johnson (GB)	72-75-69-73–289	1560
S Strudwick (GB)	70-74-69-75–289	1560
K Davies (GB)	73-70-72-74–289	1560
N Lowien (Aus)	71-70-79-70–290	1440
J Connachan (GB)	72-75-69-75–291	1290
F Dassu (Ita)	74-72-73-72–291	1290
S Moon (USA)	75-71-77-68–291	1290
A Munt (Aus)	73-70-73-75–291	1290
M Jones (Aus)	74-75-70-73–292	1110
L Neumann (Swe)	71-72-75-74–292	1110
C Dibnah (Aus)	69-73-78-73–293	936
K Espinasse (Fra)	73-74-71-75–293	936
J Hill (GB)	73-77-74-69–293	936
J Statham (GB)	72-76-73-72–293	936
D Kortgaard (Can)	72-76-68-77–293	936

AGF Biarritz Ladies Open
at Biarritz, France

Name	Score	Prize £
D Hutton*	68-73-66-67–274	9000
P Conley	70-64-70-70–274	6090
A Nicholas	69-71-70-67–277	3720

Winner after play-off

Name	Score	Prize £
H Alfredsson	64-72-74-67–277	3720
S Mendiburu (Am)	69-70-72-66–277	
C Soules	70-70-70-68–278	2544
D Barnard	71-68-73-67–279	1800
C Griffiths	71-71-68-69–279	1800
S Prosser	71-72-68-68–279	1800
T Johnson	73-73-66-68–280	1272
R Lautens	72-70-68-72–280	1272

Bloor Homes Eastleigh Classic
at Fleming Park, Southampton

Name	Score	Prize £
D Dowling*	69-65-65-62–261	9000
R Hast	67-67-64-63–261	4510
C Panton	66-65-63-67–261	4510
M McNamara	64-66-65-66–261	4510
D Barnard	67-66-67-62–262	1986
P Conley	67-64-68-63–262	1986
A Oxen-Rhodin	66-66-67-63–262	1986
D Pavich	66-65-66-65–262	1986

BMW Ladies' Classic
at Hubbelrath, West Germany

Name	Score	Prize £
ML de Lorenzi	70-72-68-67–277	10500
D Hutton	69-69-70-70–278	7105
C Dibnah	70-70-68-72–280	4900
C Soules	67-69-74-72–282	3780
S Moon	67-72-71-73–283	2968
F Descampe	68-75-67-74–284	2450
M Wennersten From	69-72-71-73–285	2100
S Strudwick	71-73-75-67–286	1750
C Panton	74-72-71-70–287	1568
R Lautens	69-74-74-71–288	1297
A Nicholas	74-75-69-70–288	1297
A Dibos	74-71-69-74–288	1297

Ladies' Danish Open
at Rungsted, Copenhagen

Name	Score	Prize £
T Abitbol*	69-69-73-74–285	9750
ML de Lorenzi	75-70-68-72–285	6600
A Nicholas	74-71-73-69–287	4550
S Strudwick	75-67-77-70–289	3510

Winner after play-off

Name	Score	Prize £
P Conley	69-69-74-80–292	2151
K Douglas	75-73-70-74–292	2151
S Gronberg	75-73-73-71–292	2151
G Stewart	72-72-73-75–292	2151

Expedier Ladies' European Open
at Kingswood, Surrey

Name	Score	Prize £
J Connachan	65-73-70-71–279	10500
G Stewart	75-69-71-67–282	7105
K Lunn	73-76-71-65–285	4340
S van Wyk	70-73-75-67–285	4340
M Garner	69-75-71-71–286	2986
J Howard	75-73-71-68–287	2100
C Soules	72-72-75-68–287	2100

Ford Ladies' Classic
at Woburn

Name	Score	Prize £
ML de Lorenzi	67-74-73-72–286	7500
G Stewart	73-74-76-71–294	5075
S Gronberg	74-79-74-71–298	3100
M Walker	73-75-76-74–298	3100
B Helbig	76-76-76-71–299	1790
K Lunn	73-78-79-69–299	1790
J Soulsby	73-74-75-77–299	1790
A Nicholas	77-74-77-72–300	1185
S Strudwick	78-79-70-73–300	1185
L Davies	74-75-79-75–303	926
R Lautens	77-78-74-74–303	926
A Jones	80-77-73-73–303	926

French Open
at Fourqueux, Paris

Name	Score	Prize £
S Strudwick*	70-69-74-72–285	9000
ML de Lorenzi	78-73-64-70–285	6000
D Petrizzi	72-73-73-72–290	4200
S Nyhus	73-73-74-71–291	3240
R Comstock	73-74-74-71–292	2148
C Duffy	74-72-72-74–292	2148
L Maritz	69-76-75-72–292	2148
C Panton	75-75-72-71–293	1348
D Reid	76-71-71-75–293	1348
MN Corbachio	71-76-71-75–293	1348
C Bourtayre (Am)	77-69-74-73–293	

Winner after play-off

Gisvaled Ladies' Open
at Isaberg, Sweden

Name	Score	Prize £
A Nicholas	73-72-69-74–288	9750
L Neumann	77-68-74-71–290	6600
M Burton	77-75-71-69–292	4030
P Conley	73-73-71-75–292	4030
J Connachan	73-72-74-75–294	2515
D Hutton	77-70-72-75–294	2515
F Dassu	74-72-71-78–295	1505
D Dowling	73-75-73-74–295	1505
M Garner	80-69-73-73–295	1505
X Wunsch-Ruiz	76-72-72-75–295	1505
C Scholefield	76-73-72-74–295	1505

Godiva Ladies' European Masters
at Bercuit, Brussels

Name	Score	Prize £
K Douglas*	69-75-73-70–287	16500
ML de Lorenzi	69-72-76-70–287	11125
H Andersson	72-72-75-70–289	7700
L Maritz	75-72-73-71–291	5302
A Nicholas	73-74-74-70–291	5302
K Espinasse	75-73-74-70–292	3850
J Connachan	76-71-74-73–294	3300

Hennessy Ladies' Cup
at St Germain

Name	Score	Prize £
ML de Lorenzi	68-66-72-73–279	12000
C Dibnah	67-71-70-73–281	6860
J Rosenthal	70-71-70-70–281	6860
L Davies	69-68-70-75–282	4320
L Maritz	71-72-74-70–287	3392
A Dibos	71-72-72-73–288	2800
C Soules	71-71-74-73–289	2064
F Descampe	75-71-71-72–289	2064
L Garbacz	75-72-69-73–289	2064
D Barnard	71-76-71-76–294	1434
J Greco	70-76-73-75–294	1434
A Nicholas	71-75-72-76–294	1434
H Alfredsson	70-72-79-73–294	1434

* Winner after play-off

Ladies' Italian Open
at Carimata, Milan

Name	Score	Prize £
X Wunsch-Ruiz	68-70-72-68—278	12000
J Connachan	67-69-73-71—280	8120
T Johnson	67-71-71-74—283	5600
S Moon	71-67-73-73—284	3856
A Dibbs	70-70-74-70—284	3856
R Lautens	70-70-72-73—285	2600
A Nicholas	71-73-69-72—285	2600
S Strudwick	68-72-73-73—286	2000
L Maritz	73-74-71-70—288	1792
G Stewart	71-71-74-73—289	1536
C Nilsmark	71-74-73-71—289	1536

Laing Charity Ladies' Classic
at Stoke Poges

Name	Score	Prize £
L Davies	72-64-72-68—276	9000
J Connachan	73-68-70-68—279	4018
C Dibnah	71-68-73-67—279	4018
S Moon	67-70-72-70—279	4018
D Reid	69-70-72-68—279	4018
P Conley	70-72-72-66—280	2100
C Scholefield	70-70-70-71—281	1800
F Dassu	73-70-70-69—282	1500
K Lunn	74-70-70-70—284	1272
X Wunsch-Ruiz	68-70-72-74—284	1272

Lufthansa Ladies' German Open
at Worthsee, Munich

Name	Score	Prize £
A Nicholas	67-69-68-65—269	12000
P Gonzales	68-71-66-69—274	8120
S Strudwick	69-68-71-71—279	4960
P Rizzo	67-68-71-73—279	4960
D Barnard	70-70-70-70—280	3096
ML de Lorenzi	70-70-69-71—280	3096
L Maritz	69-72-70-70—281	1948
F Descampe	70-69-71-71—281	1948
M Nause	75-69-68-69—281	1948
H Alfredsson	70-66-74-71—291	1948

Rome Classic
at Olgiata GC, Rome, Italy

Name	Score	Prize £
S Gronberg	70-71-69–210	9750
ML de Lorenzi	71-72-68–211	6600
G Stewart	75-65-72–212	4550
L Maritz	76-69-68–213	3133
F Descampe	71-73-69–213	3133
T Abitbol	72-75-70–217	2112
M Garner	75-72-70–217	2112
K Douglas	71-70-77–218	1460
D Dowling	70-69-79–218	1460
D Reid	72-71-75–218	1460

Qualitair Classic
at La Manga Club, Spain

Name	Score	Prize £
A Nicholas	69-74-70–213	7500
P Conley	69-76-70–215	4287
S Gronberg	70-76-69–215	4287
C Griffiths	74-72-70–216	2410
D Reid	77-69-70–216	2410
R Lautens	74-74-69–217	1500
F Descampe	74-73-70–217	1500
T Yarwood	74-71-72–217	1500

St Moritz Ladies' Classic
at St Moritz

Name	Score	Prize £
K Douglas*	74-71-71-70–286	10500
S Strudwick	74-68-75-69–286	7105
N Lowien	75-72-69-72–288	4900
D Hutton	74-71-75-69–289	2824
L Maritz	73-71-71-74–289	2824
C Panton	71-75-74-69–289	2824
K Hanson	73-71-74-71–289	2824
D Barnard	71-72-75-72–290	1442
ML de Lorenzi	76-72-76-66–290	1442
M Wennersten From	70-75-73-72–290	1422
F Descampe	72-69-73-76–290	1442
M McNamara	72-72-75-71–290	1442

*Winner after play-off

The Players' Championship
at The Tytherington Club, Macclesfield

Name	Score	Prize £
A Oxen-Rhodin	75-74-66-71–286	11250
L Maritz	69-73-73-73–288	7510
M Walker	73-72-74-72–291	5250
J Connachan	73-76-73-70–292	3285
S Gronberg	74-78-70-70–292	3285
S Moon	74-75-74-69–292	3285
P Conley	73-77-75-69–294	1737
C Dibnah	72-73-74-75–294	1737
K Douglas	74-73-75-72–294	1737
M Garner	74-74-73-73–294	1737
S Strudwick	76-70-75-73–294	1737

Variety Club Celebrity Classic
at Calcot Park, Reading

Name	Score	Prize £
C Dibnah	68-70-70-71–279	6500
P Conley	68-71-72-70–281	4400
S Prosser	71-76-71-65–283	3400
J Connachan	70-72-74-70–286	2166
A Nicholas	71-72-73-70–286	2166
S van Wyk	72-71-75-68–286	2166
D Reid	73-71-75-68–287	1350
K Douglas	75-69-74-70–288	1012
D Hutton	72-66-76-74–288	1012
M Garner	70-70-78-71–289	783
R Hast	70-66-74-79–289	783
K Lunn	70-72-72-75–289	783

Woolmark Ladies' Match-play Championship
at Barcelona, Spain

Quarter Finals:

H Alfredsson beat ML de Lorenzi 3 and 2
D Hutton beat T Abitbol 5 and 4
A Jones beat K Douglas 2 and 1
M Garner beat K Espinasse 2 and 1
(Losers each received £2400)

Semi-Finals:

D Hutton beat H Alfredsson at 20th
M Garner beat A Jones 7 and 6
(Losers each received £5000)

Finals:

D Hutton beat M Garner by 2 holes
(D Hutton received £12000 and M Garner received £8000)

USLPGA Money Winners 1989

Place	Name	Official Money $	Place	Name	Official Money $
1	B King	654132	51	T Kerdyk	64644
2	B Daniel	504851	52	C Morse	63422
3	N Lopez	487153	53	C Mackey	61661
4	P Bradley	423714	54	L Adams	61283
5	P Sheehan	253605	55	D Eggeling	56108
6	A Okamoto (Jap)	205745	56	C Keggi	52762
7	C Walker	204666	57	S Haynie	50687
8	T Green	204143	58	L Rittenhouse	50451
9	P Rizzo	198868	59	M Edge	49818
10	S Turner	198353	60	B Mucha	47849
11	C Rarick	196611	61	S Hamlin	47254
12	J Geddes	186485	62	N Foust	45712
13	L Davies (GB)	181574	63	R Walton	45283
14	J Inkster	180848	64	S Steinhauer	44825
15	A Ritzman	177507	65	C Figg-Currier	42894
16	P Hammel	176836	66	L Merten	42832
17	K Postlewait	168192	67	M Mallon	42574
18	A Alcott	168089	68	J Lidback	42418
19	D Coe	143423	69	L Connelly	40492
20	A Finney	143342	70	T Barrett	39776
21	M Nause	138639	71	M Berteotti	38493
22	L Garbacz	138124	72	M Bozarth	37821
23	D Ammaccapane	135109	73	L Rinker	37083
24	H Stacy	134460	74	SA McGetrick	36121
25	S Furlong	133149	75	D White	35814
26	J Rosenthal	132982	76	K Shipman	35193
27	D Mochrie	130830	77	J Crafter (Aus)	35086
28	E Crosby	126899	78	G Hull	34621
29	N Brown	123837	79	J Briles	34277
30	L Neumann (Swe)	119915	80	C Hill	34141
31	S Sanders	112526	81	H Farr	33344
32	R Jones	110671	82	J Wyatt	31794
33	V Fergon	106534	83	S Palmer	31646
34	V Skinner	102089	84	B Thomas	31403
35	A Benz	98129	85	S Quinlan	30944
36	JA Carner	97888	86	K Guadagnino	30110
37	C Johnson	97195	87	S Ertl	29931
38	M Spencer-Devlin	86380	88	L Baugh	29413
39	P Wright (GB)	77951	89	S Redman	28413
40	M Figueras-Dotti (Spa)	77790	90	C Gerring	27649
41	R Hood	74947	91	M Will	26476
42	D Massey	74919	92	MC Cheng (Tai)	25710
43	D McIlaffie	73522	93	H Drew	24670
44	K Albers	72900	94	C Pierce (GB)	24545
45	J Stephenson (Aus)	71550	95	M Floyd	24104
46	M Blackwelder	71250	96	J Dickinson	23460
47	D Richard	70594	97	M Moore	23230
48	M McGeorge	68493	98	K Bauer	23169
49	K Ok-Hee (Kor)	67553	99	J Anderson	22402
50	C Marino	66599	100	L Walters	21979

US Ladies' PGA Tour 1989

US Women's Open
at Indianwood G & CC, Lake Orion, Michigan

Name	Score	Prize $
B King	67-71-72-68–278	80000
N Lopez	73-70-71-68–282	40000
P Hammel	74-73-69-67–283	24250
P Bradley	73-74-68-68–283	24250
D Mochrie	72-70-75-67–284	15043
L Garbacz	71-70-73-70–284	15043
L Davies	73-71-75-66–285	11931
V Fergon	72-74-69-70–285	11931
J Geddes	70-72-72-72–286	9974
C Walker	72-69-71-74–286	9974
A Okamoto	76-72-74-65–287	8304
D Ammaccapane	73-70-74-70–287	8304
M Blackwelder	76-68-71-72–287	8304
ML de Lorenzi	68-74-71-74–287	8304
K Bauer	72-72-73-71–288	7137
M Figueras-Dotti	75-70-70-73–288	7137
G Hull	74-72-72-71–289	6374
J Carner	76-69-71-73–289	6374
P Sheehan	74-67-69-79-289	6374
S Furlong	74-75-73-68–290	5392
B Daniel	73-73-71-73–290	5392
C Keggi	71-73-73-73–290	5391
L Neumann	71-71-75-73–290	5391
K Postlewait	77-70-70-73–290	5392
D Cusano-Wilkins	71-72-71-76–290	5391
S Quinlan	78-71-73-69–291	4680
A Alcott	73-71-73-74–291	4680
K Shipman	74-69-74-74–291	4680
D White	75-73-74-70–292	4172
C Johnson	73-73-75-71–292	4172
N Taylor	74-73-73-72–292	4172
P Rizzo	77-69-73-73–292	4172
D Massey	71-72-75-74–292	4172

A1 Star/Centinela Hospital Classic
at Rancho Park GC, Los Angeles, California

Name	Score	Prize $
P Bradley	72-69-67–208	67500
H Stacy	70-71-68–209	36000
N Lopez	67-73-69–209	36000
B Daniel	71-74-66–211	21375
A Ritzman	69-72-70–211	21375

Atlantic City Classic
at Sands CC, Somers Point, New Jersey

Name	Score	Prize $
N Lopez	67-70-69–206	33750
V Fergon	70-66-71–207	18000
C Johnson	68-68-71-207	17999
J Wyatt	69-70-69–208	11816

Boston Five Classic
at the Sheraton Tara Hotel at Ferncroft Village, Danvers, Massachusetts

Name	Score	Prize $
A Alcott	68-68-68-68–272	52500
C Marino	69-67-71-68–275	32375
M Figueras-Dotti	74-68-66-68–276	23625
B Daniel	69-68-73-67–277	16625
S Furlong	70-66-70-71–277	16625

Cellular One-Ping Golf Championship
at Riverside G & CC, Portland, Oregon

Name	Score	Prize $
M Spencer-Devlin	74-69-71–214	45000
N Lopez	74-72-69–215	19125
T Green	71-74-70–215	19125
S Sanders	71-72-72–215	19125
D Coe	68-71-76–215	19125
B King	72-72-72–216	9675
A Benz	71-73-72–216	9675

Chrysler-Plymouth Classic
at Bamm Hollow CC, Lincroft, New Jersey

Name	Score	Prize $
C Rarick	70-72-72–214	41250
L Davies	70-72-74–216	25437
A Ritzman	72-73-72–217	16500
N Lopez	71-73-73–217	16499

Circle LPGA Tucson Open
at Randolph North GC, Tucson, Arizona

Name	Score	Prize $
L Garbacz	69-68-67-70–274	45000
N Lopez	69-70-72-67–278	27750
K Albers	70-69-72-68–279	14813
J Rosenthal	69-70-70-70–279	14813
J Stephenson	68-69-71-71–279	14812
M Nause	66-69-71-73–279	14812

Crestar Classic
at Greenbrier CC, Chesapeake, Virginia

Name	Score	Prize $
J Inkster	69-72-69–210	45000
B Daniel	75-66-74–215	24000
L Neumann	74-67-74–215	24000

Greater Washington Open
at Bethesda CC, Bethesda, Maryland

Name	Score	Prize $
B Daniel	66-68-71–205	45000
S Turner	73-71-65–209	27750
D Ammaccapane	74-70-66–210	18000
B King	70-72-68–210	18000

Jamaica Classic
at Sandy Bay, Jamaica

Name	Score	Prize $
B King	64-68-70–202	75000
N Lopez	69-70-69–208	46250
L Garbacz	70-71-69-210	30000
M Nause	71-71-68–210	30000
H Stacy	69-71-71–211	17834
B Daniel	76-66-69–211	17833
R Jones	73-71-67–211	17833

Jamie Farr Toledo Classic
at Highland Meadows GC, Sylvania, Ohio

Name	Score	Prize $
P Hammel	69-66-71–206	41250
H Stacy	72-68-68–208	19479
N Lopez	70-70-68–208	19479
L Neumann	68-69-71–208	19478

J C Penney Classic
at Bardmoor CC, Largo, Florida

Name	Score	Prize $
P Bradley/W Glasson*	68-68-65-66–267	100000
P Sheehan/D Waldorf	69-67-64-67–267	60000
T Kerdyk/JD Blake	63-72-64-72–271	35000
S Turner/K Perry	70-64-69-68–271	35000
B Daniel/G Sauers	70-66-63-73–272	24700
L Neumann/G Hallburg	72-66-68-69–275	15750
D Massey/M McCumber	71-67-68-69–275	15750
M Berteotti/R Mediate	71-69-65-70–275	15750
V Skinner/M Hulbert	67-67-70-71–275	15750
D Eggeling/W Lavi	69-69-68-70–276	9500
N Brown/K Knox	69-67-68-72–276	9500

Women's Kemper Open
at Princeville Makai GC, Kauai, Hawaii

Name	Score	Prize $
B King	63-72-67–202	60000
J Geddes	65-69-70–204	37000
B Daniel	67-68-70–205	24000
N Lopez	65-70-70–205	24000
C Morse	66-70-71–207	14267
J Lidback	64-72-71–207	14267
H Stacy	64-72-71–207	14267

Konica San Jose Classic
at Almaden, San Jose, California

Name	Score	Prize $
B Daniel	65-67-73–205	48750
P Bradley	66-69-71–206	30062
V Fergon	71-68-70–209	21937
C Mackey	68-73-69–210	17062
L Connelly	70-71-70–211	12594
L Rittenhouse	69-69-73–211	12593

Winner after play-off

LPGA Corning Classic
at Corning CC, Corning, New York

Name	Score	Prize $
A Okamoto	69-66-67-70–272	48750
B Daniel	70-66-71-71–278	30062
D Coe	67-72-72-70–281	21937
P Sheehan	72-70-69-72–283	17062

du Maurier Ltd Classic
at Beaconsfield GC, Pointe Claire, Canada

Name	Score	Prize $
T Green	68-69-70-72–279	90000
P Bradley	69-75-69-67–280	48000
B King	67-69-74-70–280	48000
P Sheehan	69-74-69-69–281	26000
A Alcott	70-70-72-69–281	26000
P Hammel	71-71-68-71–281	26000

Mazda Japan Classic
at Seta GC, Shiga

Name	Score	Prize $
E Crosby	71-64-70–205	75000
D Coe	69-69-70–208	46250
L Davies	67-73-69–209	33750
A Okamoto	70-67-73–210	26250
C Walker	71-70-70–211	19375
C Rarick	67-73-71–211	19375
P Bradley	71-69-72–212	14750
S Furlong	73-72-68–213	11192
N Brown	72-71-70–213	11192
A Ritzman	71-70-72–213	11192
D Richard	71-70-72–213	11192

Mazda LPGA Championship
at Jack Nicklaus Sports Center, Kings Island, Ohio

Name	Score	Prize $
N Lopez	71-69-68-66–274	75000
A Okamoto	69-68-69-71–277	46250
S Sanders	72-67-71-68–278	33750
A Finney	72-72-66-73–283	23750
P Bradley	67-72-71-73–283	23750
J Geddes	69-73-71-71–284	17500

Mitsubishi Motors Ocean State Open
at Alpine CC, Cranston, Rhode Island

Name	Score	Prize $
T Barrett	67-73-70–210	22500
N Brown	72-69-71–212	13875
M Will	72-73-68–213	8125
M Berteotti	70-73-70–213	8125
J Briles	72-69-72–213	8125
D McHaffie	72-71-71–214	4525
N Rubin	69-73-72–214	4525
D Mochrie	73-67-74–214	4525

Nabisco Dinah Shore
at Mission Hills CC, Rancho Mirage, California

Name	Score	Prize $
J Inkster	66-69-73-71–279	80000
T Green	72-68-75-69–284	34000
J Carner	71-71-71-71–284	34000
B King	73-75-68-71–287	19750
J Rosenthal	69-72-72-74–287	19750

Nestle World Championship
at Stouffer Pine Isle Resort, Budford, Georgia

Name	Score	Prize $
B King	66-71-70-68–275	83500
P Bradley	74-66-68-70–278	34750
P Sheehan	70-66-72-70–278	34750
L Davies	70-72-68-69–279	17500
B Daniel	70-69-71-69–279	17500
R Jones	66-72-74-70–282	10500
J Geddes	71-67-76-69–283	8500

Nippon Travel-MBS Classic
at Los Coyotes CC, Buena Park, California

Name	Score	Prize $
N Lopez	73-69-65-70–277	45000
A Ritzman	70-72-70-67–279	24000
P Wright	70-69-67-73–279	24000
P Bradley	69-69-73-69–280	13000
B Daniel	74-67-69-70–280	13000
C Walker	71-69-69-71–280	13000

Oldsmobile LPGA Classic
at Stonebridge G & CC, Boca Raton, Florida

Name	Score	Prize $
D Mochrie*	69-74-67-69—279	45000
B Daniel	69-68-72-70—279	27750
N Lopez	72-68-69-71—280	20250
S Palmer	73-72-69-69—283	15750

Orix Hawaiian Ladies' Open
at Turtle Bay CC, Oahu, Hawaii

Name	Score	Prize $
S Turner	70-69-66—205	45000
SA McGetrick	69-69-71—209	27750
D Richard	68-74-68—210	18000
C Walker	71-70-69—210	18000
L Neumann	72-70-69-211	10700
J Geddes	69-73-69-211	10700
A Ritzman	69-69-73-211	10700

Rail Charity Classic
at Rail GC, Springfield, Illinois

Name	Score	Prize $
B Daniel	69-70-64—203	41250
B King	71-66-69—206	22000
A Ritzman	69-66-71—206	21999
P Hammel	70-68-69—207	14437
M Spencer-Devlin	73-68-67—208	10656
M Mallon	71-67-70—208	10656

Red Robin Kyocera Inamori Classic
at Stone Ridge CC, San Diego, California

Name	Score	Prize $
P Rizzo	73-67-68-69—277	45000
M Nause	69-68-72-70—279	27750
J Crafter	71-71-68-70—280	18000
J Inkster	71-69-70-70—280	18000
M Edge	72-71-69-69—281	9975
S Turner	69-73-70-69—281	9975
A Alcott	70-69-72-70—281	9975
P Hammel	74-69-67-71—281	9975

* Winner after play-off

Safeco Classic
at Meridian Valley CC, Seattle, Washington

Name	Score	Prize $
B Daniel	69-69-65-70–273	45000
C Rarick	68-69-73-69–279	27750
P Bradley	70-67-70-73–280	20250
B King	71-70-74-66–281	13000
J Geddes	74-70-68-69–281	13000
J Inkster	68-71-70-72–282	13000
L Rittenhouse	70-70-69-73–282	8850

Sara Lee Classic
at Hermitage GC, Nashville, Tennessee

Name	Score	Prize $
K Postlewait	68-66-69–203	63750
V Skinner	68-67-69–204	39312
P Sheehan	66-74-67–207	25500
N Lopez	66-71-70–207	25499

Standard Register Turquoise Classic
at Moon Valley CC, Phoenix, Arizona

Name	Score	Prize $
A Finney	66-69-74-73–282	60000
B Daniel	68-70-70-75–283	37000
J Rosenthal	70-73-72-70–285	27000
R Jones	72-72-69-74–287	19000
P Rizzo	71-68-73-75–287	19000

USX Golf Classic
at Pasadena Yacht & Country Club, St Petersburg, Florida

Name	Score	Prize $
B King*	67-70-72-66–275	37500
L Adams	69-68-68-70–275	23125
L Garbacz	64-73-71-69–277	16875
J Stephenson	70-68-71-70–279	11875
K Postlewait	67-69-73-70–279	11875

Winner after play-off

Women's Amateur

Avia Foursomes
at The Berkshire

Name	Score	Name	Score
J Morley and L Fairclough	224	A Uzieli and E Boatman	237
L Bayman and J Wade	227	V Thomas and S Roberts	242
M McKenna and C Hourihane	228	B Jackson and C Williamson	245
J Collingham and S Robinson	233	K Mitchell and E Secrett	246
H Dobson and A Johns	234	K Tebbet and J Kershaw	248
K Harridge and S Bennett	235	W Wooldridge and C Dunningham	250

(3rd & 4th rounds reduced to 9 holes each due to bad weather)

British Women's Amateur Championship
at Hoylake

First Round:

L Bayman beat S Elliott 1 hole
L Fletcher beat S Lowe 2 and 1
H Dobson beat M McKenna 1 hole
J Hall beat C Marty 3 and 2
J McAvoy beat M Wright 6 and 5
C Lambert beat K Firth 5 and 4
A van der Haegen beat L Kane 2 and 1
J Brown beat C Hourihane 3 and 2

E Farquharson beat L Bolton at 19th
A Johns beat S Bennett 2 holes
K Imrie beat K Mitchell 1 hole
V Thomas beat L Fairclough at 19th
J Forbes beat K Tebbet 2 and 1
L Hackney beat D Lee 2 and 1
C Mourgue d'Algue beat M Koch 3 and 2
A Gardiner beat F Anderson 2 holes

Second Round:

L Fletcher beat L Bayman 2 and 1
H Dobson beat A van der Haegen 3 and 2
J McAvoy beat J Hall 1 hole
C Lambert beat J Brown at 19th

E Farquharson beat A Johns 7 and 6
K Imrie beat V Thomas 3 and 2
L Hackney beat J Forbes 5 and 4
A Gardiner beat C Mourgue d'Algue 2 and 1

Quarter Finals:

H Dobson beat L Fletcher 5 and 4
C Lambert beat J McAvoy at 19th
L Hackney beat A Gardiner 3 and 2
E Farquharson beat K Imrie at 21st

Semi-Finals:

H Dobson beat C Lambert 6 and 5
E Farquharson beat L Hackney 3 and 2

Final:

H Dobson beat E Farquharson 6 and 5

British Women's Stroke-Play Championship
at Southerness

Name	Score	Name	Score
H Dobson	78-77-72-71—298	A McKenna	77-87-73-71—308
N Hall	79-79-73-69—300	A MacDonald	85-77-74-72—308
J Hall	82-81-69-71—303	P Dobson	87-74-73-74—308
A van der Haegen	82-77-71-73—303	V Thomas	79-83-71-76—309
J Forbes	80-81-72-71—304	K Tebbet	81-80-70-78—309
L Fairclough	85-76-73-71—305	S Roberts	80-76-79-74—309
C Lambert	76-83-73-74—306		

Burhill Family Foursomes
at Burhill

Semi-Finals:
Mrs J Lawson and P Lawson beat Miss H Nicholas and A Nicholas 2 holes
Mrs A Wigglesworth and L Wigglesworth beat Mrs J Fox and N Fox 3 and 2

Final:
Mrs J Lawson and P Lawson beat Mrs A Wigglesworth and L Wigglesworth 2 holes

Critchley Salver
at Sunningdale

Name	Score	Name	Score
L Fletcher	72-72—144	L Fairclough	78-75—153
L Bayman	72-73—145	K Fitzgerald	74-81—155
C Caldwell	71-75—146	S Keogh	76-79—155
J Hall	72-76—148	K Mitchell	78-77—155
S Robinson	78-74—152	C Sanders	79-76—155
J Collingham	74-79—153	C Waters	74-81—155

English Women's Stroke-Play Championship
at Hollinwell

Name	Score
S Robinson*	72-74-76-79—302
A Shapcott	75-77-76-74—302
L Hackney	76-74-79-74—303
S Morgan	74-77-77-77—305
K Tebbet	77-76-74-79—306
L Fletcher	74-81-77-75—307
C Breckon	79-80-75-74—308
L Fairclough	79-77-76-77—309
S Keogh	77-77-77-80—311

* Winner after play-off

English Intermediate Championship

Semi-Finals:
L Fairclough beat J Copley 6 and 5
J Hall beat S Morgan 2 and 1

Final:
L Fairclough beat J Hall 4 and 3

European Women's Team Championship
at Pals

France / England
Foursomes Matches — Finals

S Louapre and C Mourgue d'Algue	0	H Dobson and L Bayman (3 and 2)	1
C Bourtayre and D Bourson (6 and 4)	1	J Hall and J Collingham	0
	1		1

Singles

C Mourgue d'Algue (19th hole)	1	H Dobson	0
S Louapre	0	J Hall (2 and 1)	1
C Bourtayre (5 and 4)	1	L Fairclough	0
D Bourson (7 and 6)	1	S Morgan	0
S Mendiburu	0	L Bayman (3 and 2)	1
	3		2

France 4; England 3

Third Place Play-off
Scotland / Italy
Foursomes Matches — Final

E Farquharson and C Lambert (4 and 2)	1	S Cavalleri and S Croce	0
J Forbes and L Anderson	0	C Quintarelli and A Nistri (3 and 2)	1
	1		1

Singles

E Farquharson (3 and 2)	1	C Quintarelli	0
K Imrie	0	I Calogero (5 and 4)	1
C Lambert	0	A Salvi (2 holes)	1
L Anderson	0	S Cavalleri (2 and 1)	1
S Huggan (1 hole)	1	S Croce	0
	2		3

Italy 4; Scotland 2

Welsh Ladies' Close Championship
at Conwy

First Round:

V Thomas beat N Wesley 5 and 4
F Connor beat S Thomas 2 holes
S Turner beat J Foster 1 hole
S Roberts beat D Richards 6 and 5
L Dermott beat D Morgans 1 hole
L Isherwood beat O Davies 6 and 5
K Bradley beat A Prichard at 19th
H Lawson beat A Briggs 4 and 3

Quarter Finals:

V Thomas beat F Connor 2 and 1
S Roberts beat S Turner 2 and 1
L Isherwood beat L Dermott at 19th
H Lawson beat K Bradley 2 holes

Semi-Finals:

V Thomas beat S Roberts 4 and 3
H Lawson beat L Isherwood 2 holes

Final:

H Lawson beat V Thomas 2 and 1

Welsh Women's Open Amateur Championship
at Newport

Name	Score	Name	Score
V Thomas	72-74-74–220	L Hackney	76-77-82–235
S Bennett	70-73-85–228	L Dermott	78-78-80–236
K Tebbet	72-78-78–228	S Elliot	76-80-80–236
J Hall	69-79-81–229	S Palmer	75-83-78–236
J Morley	80-78-76–234	K Mitchell	79-80-79–238
C Lambert	73-78-83–234	L Fetcher	75-78-86–239
C Lesley	76-77-82–235	D Adby	71-81-87–239

Women's Home Internationals
1989 at Westport, Co Mayo

England beat Ireland 5½-3½
England beat Wales 6½-2½
England beat Scotland 8-1
Scotland beat Wales 5-4
Scotland beat Ireland 7-2
Ireland beat Wales 6-3
Result: England 3; Scotland 2, Ireland 1, Wales 0

Juniors and Youths

British Boys' Championship
at Nairn

Quarter Finals:

C Fraser beat S Church 1 hole
N Ludwell beat R Burns 5 and 4
G Williamson beat I Garbutt 5 and 4
C Watts beat D Downie 2 holes

Semi-Finals:

C Fraser beat N Ludwell 4 and 3
C Watts beat G Williamson 2 and 1

Final:

C Watts beat C Fraser 5 and 3

Great Britain and Ireland *v* Continent of Europe
at Nairn

GB and Ireland		Continent of Europe	
Foursomes Matches			
C Fraser and R Robinson (2 and 1)	1	G Hjertserdt and M Persson	0
M Urquhart and R Russell	0	M Florioli and M Gortana (5 and 4)	1
C Watts and I Garbutt (3 and 1)	0	C Beautell and D Borrego	0
P Harrington and R Burns	0	R Berhost and O Rojahn (2 holes)	1
	2		2
Singles			
I Garbutt (3 and 2)	1	M Florioli	0
C Fraser	0	G Hjertserdt (1 hole)	1
R Johnson (3 and 2)	1	M Persson	0
P Harrington (6 and 4)	1	M Gortana	0
R Russell	½	O Rojahn	½
C Watts (4 and 3)	1	C Beautell	0
R Burns	0	R Berhort	1
M Urquhart (7 and 6)	1	D Borrego	0
	5½		2½

Great Britain and Ireland 7½; Continent of Europe 4½

English Girls' Championship
at Edgbaston

Quarter Finals:
H Dobson beat S Tuck 6 and 4
S Germain beat K Stupples 2 and 1
R Bolas beat C Hall 4 and 3
A McDonald beat R Nugent 2 and 1

Semi-Finals:
H Dobson beat S Germain 4 and 3
A McDonald beat R Bolas 3 and 1

Final:
H Dobson beat A McDonald 3 and 1

North of England Open Amateur Youth Championship
at Middlesbrough

Name	Score
SJ Bannerman*	70-67-71-71–279
J Webber	70-67-69-73–279
G Evans	68-72-71-69–280
S Ursell	73-68-72-69–280
A Sandywell	70-67-76-69–282

British Youths' Championship
at Ashburnham

Name	Score	Name	Score
M Smith*	71-74-72-68–285	SM Green	69-72-73-78–292
A Colthart	73-69-69-74–285	D Bathgate	79-71-72-71–293
KG Jones	73-68-73-74–288	A Hill	74-75-71-74–294
E Giraud	73-77-71-68–289	S Bannerman	73-73-72-76–294
C Macphail	73-76-70-70–289	C Watts	72-76-72-74–294
J Webber	71-75-73-71–290	D Arruti	76-72-72-74–294
E McIntosh	74-73-70-73–290		

Winner after play-off

Coca-Cola Schools International Match
at Gullane

Boys
Scotland   England
Foursomes Matches

S Dundas and G Beveridge	0	B Ingleby and P Sherman (4 and 3)	1
R Russell and A Cochrane	0	R Fletcher and A Thomas (1 hole)	1
A Weir and I Weir	0	R Vinall and N Osmond (3 and 2)	1
M Urquhart and D Tait	0	J Barnes and P Oliver (4 and 3)	1
E Mackay and C Gordon	0	M Welch and L Westwood (2 and 1)	1
J Buchan and A Campbell (5 and 4)	1	J Tookey and S Weir	0
	1		5

Singles

S Dundas	0	B Ingleby (3 and 2)	1
R Russell (2 and 1)	1	R Fletcher	0
M Urquhart	0	M Welch (3 and 2)	1
A Weir	½	J Barnes	½
J Buchan	0	P Sherman (2 and 1)	1
G Beveridge	0	A Thomas (1 hole)	1
D Tait	0	J Tookey (2 and 1)	1
I Weir	0	S Weir (1 hole)	1
A Campbell	0	R Vinall (3 and 2)	1
C Gordon (5 and 4)	1	L Westwood	0
A Cochrane	½	N Osmond	½
E Mackay	0	P Oliver (8 and 7)	1
	3		9

Scotland 4; England 14

Girls
Foursomes Matches

M McKinlay and J Moodie (2 and 1)	1	K Smith and N Buxton	0
C Wilson and C Macdonald (2 and 1)	1	E Ratcliffe and F Brown	0
F Mackay and M Mackay (3 and 2)	1	K Whitehead and S Tuck	0
	3		0

Singles

C Macdonald	0	E Ratcliffe (2 and 1)	1
J Moodie (2 and 1)	1	K Smith	0
M McKinlay	0	K Whitehead (1 hole)	1
C Wilson	0	N Buxton (4 and 3)	1
M Mackay	0	S Tuck (2 holes)	1
F Mackay (5 and 4)	1	F Brown	0
	2		4

Scotland 5; England 4

Peter McEvoy Trophy
at Copt Heath

Name	Score
D Bathgate	75-71-77-71–294
R Hurd	75-68-80-73–296
M Garabedian	73-72-76-75–296
C Watts	73-75-74-75–297
P Sherman	73-75-73-77–298
M Smith	71-75-75-77–298
S Pullan	71-73-76-78–298
R Evans	71-75-78-74–298

STV Scottish Boys' Championship
at Dunbar

Quarter Finals:
E Mackay beat H Love at 19th
D Brolls beat C Fraser 5 and 4
N Macrae beat C Farrell 3 and 2
M King beat A Reith at 20th

Semi-Finals:
D Brolls beat E Mackay 1 hole
M King beat N Macrae 2 and 1

Final:
M King beat D Brolls 8 and 7

The Doug Sanders World Boys' Championship
at King's Links, Aberdeen

Name	Score
G Hjerstedt	68-70-71-72–281
G Zorkic	78-70-69-69–286
C Milkhasingh	72-77-67-71–287
H Love	75-69-71-72–287
M Ayers	73-73-70-73–289
T Van Zijl	68-74-71-76–289
C Ste-Marie	77-69-73-80–299
C Walters	79-74-74-73–300

British Girls' Championship
at Carlisle

First Round:

S Eriksson beat L Navarro 5 and 3
E Knuth beat C Hall 2 and 1
J Moodie beat S Lacaze 5 and 3
K Mourgue d'Algue beat D Mendiburu 1 hole
L Ericsson bear M McKay 6 and 5
S Keane beat J Anderson 8 and 6
M McKinlay beat H Helmerson 2 and 1
S Cavalleri beat L Walton at 19th

Quarter Finals:

S Eriksson beat E Knuth 3 and 2
J Moodie beat K Mourgue d'Algue 1 hole
L Ericsson beat S Keane 6 and 4
M McKinlay beat S Cavalleri 2 and 1

Semi-Finals:

S Eriksson beat J Moodie at 20th
M McKinlay beat L Ericsson 3 and 2

Final:

M McKinlay beat S Eriksson at 19th

Scottish Girls' Open Stroke-Play Championship
at Dunblane New

Name	Score	Name	Score
C Lambert	73-71-69–213	K Milne	72-75-76–223
L McCool	67-77-71–215	V Melvin	75-73-78–226
J Moodie	73-68-75–216	C Macdonald	79-74-75–228
M McKinlay	72-74-72–218	L Moretti	76-81-71–228
S Little	77-70-74–221	N Moult	76-76-77–229
J Risby	75-69-78–222		

The Golf Foundation 1989

Chris Plumridge

© Ian Joy, St Andrews

The winning team from Marks Gymnasium, Sweden. From left to right: Niclas Fasth, Jonny Lindström and Pehr Magnebrant. With them are Sandy Sinclair, 1989's R & A captain, and John Panton, Honorary Professional of the R & A.

The main aim of the Golf Foundation has always been to introduce as many young people as possible to the game and thereby sustain the flow of golfers into the adult ranks. The Foundation has never set out to cater for an élite group of youngsters but it is inevitable that, from the thousands of pupils who come under the aegis of the Foundation's Coaching Scheme for Schools and Junior Groups, some of them will make their mark in the upper echelons.

In this respect, 1989 was a particularly gratifying year as Foundation pupils, both past and present, captured more than their fair share of the headlines. Leading the way was Ronan

Rafferty. The former prodigy from Warrenpoint, Northern Ireland, brought his immense talent to fruition with a stunning performance on the Volvo Tour. Consistently challenging for titles throughout the year, Rafferty won three times, including the final event, the Volvo Masters, topped the Order of Merit and was one of the heroes of the Ryder Cup tie at The Belfry when he defeated the Open champion, Mark Calcavecchia, in the singles.

If Rafferty carried the flag in the men's ranks, there was no doubt who the standard-bearer was among the women. Though still a junior in age terms, Helen Dobson had a season that had

© Reg Dutton, Ashley Colour

The champions from each age group: Andrew Cooper, Vicki Hanks, Gary Harris, Keith Harrison, Suzy Boyes, Chris Lane and Nicola Gorman.

everyone scurrying to the record books. Having won the British Girls' title in 1987 and the English Girls' in 1988, the lass from Lincolnshire totally dominated women's amateur golf in 1989. In May she won the English Ladies' Championship and the following month took the British Women's Championship. She retained her English Girls' title in August and then capped a magnificent season by taking the British Stroke Play Championship to become the first player to hold both British titles in the same year.

The two winners of the Golf Foundation Award in 1989 also proved to be wise selections. Ian Garbutt from Yorkshire not only won the English Junior Stroke Play title (Carris Trophy) but also proved to be an exceptional captain of the British Boys' team and a stalwart for his county. The winner of the Award for girls was Lisa Dermott from Clwyd, who also had an outstanding year in capturing the Welsh Girls' title. In addition to these exploits, former Foundation Award winner Matthew Stanford won the Selbourne Salver, one of the premier amateur events in the south of England.

While individual performances such as these were satisfying, there were still many other high spots in the Foundation's year. Chief among these was the staging of the International Final of the Team Championship for Schools at St Andrews. The Final was held over two days with play taking place on the New and Old Courses. From an original entry of 1500 schools throughout the world, 11 gathered at

St Andrews and for all the competitors it was the experience of their young lives. Once again Sweden, represented by the Marks Gymnasium, were the winners but they were chased home by India who were tied for the lead after the first round over the New course. The Swedish team eventually won by ten strokes with their three man team recording five out of the six scores in the 70s. Pehr Magnebrant won the PGA European Tour Trophy for the lowest individual total, 150, but India's Vivek Bhandari broke the Swedish monopoly by taking second place on 153. Sandy Sinclair, then Captain of the Royal and Ancient, presented the R & A Trophy to the winning team after a memorable two days at the Home of Golf.

The third year of the Golf Foundation/NatWest Bank Age Group Championships again attracted an increased entry. Over 2000 boys and girls entered and, following regional qualifying rounds, 51 boys and 27 girls won through to the final at Copt Heath. There was some excellent scoring over the testing Midlands course, with Chris Lane from Kingsthorpe producing the lowest aggregate to win the Boys Under 15s with rounds of 73 and 77. The winner of the Under 16s was Keith Harrison from Cottesmore with rounds of 75 and 76 while Gary Harris from Broome Manor won the Under 14s with a round of 75. The Boys Under 13s was won by Andrew Cooper from Taymouth Castle with the quite outstanding score of 76. In the Girls' section, Suzy Boyes from Wenvoe Castle won the Under 16 title with rounds of 78 and 85, Nicola Gorman from Balmoral won the Under 15s with 78 and 85 and Vicki Hanks from Broome Manor won the Under 14s with an 82. All scores were off scratch with no account taken of handicaps.

In every area of activity the Foundation experienced yet another extremely busy year. The Coaching Scheme catered for an ever increasing number of children and more and more of them went on to embark on the Merit Award Scheme which now has nearly 4000 Award winners in the four categories, with girls dominating the Gold Award list. The year also saw the appointment of 55 Golf Foundation Junior Liaison Officers at 55 clubs throughout the country. Their role will be to co-ordinate junior golf activity within their own club, giving emphasis to the Foundation's various schemes and competitions. At the end of 1990 it is hoped that this idea will be expanded to include more clubs.

As we enter the new decade there are even greater opportunities for the gifted youngster to make his or her way in golf. The Golf Foundation is ready to meet the challenge of the 1990s by continuing to promote and develop the game to youngsters of all ages and all abilities.

Golf Foundation Tournament Winners

Age-group Winners, 1989
at Copt Heath Golf Club, Knowle, West Midlands

Boys
Under 16

Keith Harrison (Cottesmore)	75-76—151
Steven Rees (Carmarthen)	78-76—154
David Hamilton (East Herts)	72-82—154
Richard Craig (Merchants of Edinburgh)	76-81—157

Under 15

Chris Lane (Kingsthorpe)	73–77—150
Anthony Wall (Royal Ascot)	77–76—153
Graham Davidson (Langholm)	76–79—155
Mark Foster (Worksop)	82–76—158

Under 14

Gary Harris (Broome Manor)	75
Danny Payne (Addington Palace)	77
Ben Fillary (Willesley Park)	79
William MacLennan (Inverness)	79
Iain Ferrie (Bedlington)	79

Under 13

Andrew Cooper (Taymouth Castle)	76
Andrew Thomson (Drumpellier)	77
Mark Davis (Durham City)	78
Shaun Webster (Cottesmore)	78
Russell Warner (Shanklin & Sandown)	78

Girls
Under 16

Suzy Boyes (Wenvoe Castle)	78-85—163
Jane Williamson (Hadley Wood)	85-79—164
Lynn Tupholme (Northcliffe)	80-87—167
Tricia Mangan (Ennis)	82-86—168

Under 15

Nicola Gorman (Balmoral)	78-85—163
Louise Nyland (Stoneham)	85-80—165
Charlotte Afford (Drayton Park)	85-84—169
Rebecca Morgan (Monmouth)	90-80—170

Under 14

Vicki Hanks (Broome Manor)	82
Laura McLardy (Duff House Royal)	93
Kerry Robinson (Uttoxeter)	97
Jill Smith (West of Scotland Girls)	99

Team Championship for Schools, 1989

International Final at St Andrews (New and Old Courses)

1st   Sweden
Marks Gymnasium, Skene

Jonny Lindstrom	155
Pehr Magnebrant	150
Niclas Fasth	154
	459

2nd   India
The Modern School, New Delhi

Vivek Bhandari	153
Daniel Chopra	157
Rahul Chawla	159
	469

3rd   Australia
Ballina High School, New South Wales

Scott Hayter	172
Dean Larsson	155
Justin Saxby	163
	490

4th   New Zealand
Gisborne Boys' High School

Waka Donnelly	163
Gavin Cornish	164
Carl Allen	167
	494

5th   Ireland
Summerhill College, Co Sligo

Gerard Sproule	161
Graham Monaghan	169
Noel Quirke	175
	505

6th   Scotland
Madras College, St Andrews, Fife

Philip Lawrie	166
Stephen Simpson	174
Iain Landsburgh	166
	506

7th   England
Trinity School, Croydon, Surrey

Jonathan Good	175
Gary Kirk	165
Ian Golding	169
	509

8th   France
Lycée Maurice Ravel, St Jean de Luz

Thomas Anatole	172
Luc Rakotonjanahary	173
Wilphrid Wayland	170
	515

9th   Iceland
Akranes College, Akranes

Halldor Birgisson	167
Hjalti Nielson	179
Kristin Bjarnason	171
	517

10th   Germany
Pius Gymnasium, Aachen-Seffent

Eric von Lossow	170
Christian von Lossow	177
Philipp Beissel	181
	528

11th   Scotland
Bassaleg Comprehensive, Gwent

Richard Dinsdale	167
Richard Hughes	180
Jonathan Willmore	181
	——
	528

Golf Foundation/Aer Lingus Schools' Team Championship

Year	Winning Team	Country	Venue
1972	Buckhaven High School	Scotland	Ballybunion
1973	Acklam High School	England	Ballybunion
1974	Millfield School	England	Portmarnock
1975	Perth Academy	Scotland	Ballybunion
1976	Brockenhurst College	England	Portmarnock
1977	Millfield School	England	Foxhills
1978	Sundsgardens Folkhogskola	Sweden	Connemara
1979	St Fachtna's	Ireland	Baltray
1980	Hugh Christie School	England	Portmarnock
1981	Tangvallaskolan	Sweden	Portmarnock
1982	Porthcawl Comprehensive	Wales	Carlow
1983	Ysgol John Bright	Wales	Ballybunion
1984	Marr College	Scotland	Lahinch
1985	Marr College	Scotland	Waterville

Golf Foundation Team Championship for Schools
for the R & A Trophy

1986	Tonbridge School	England	Sunningdale
1987	Klippans Gymnasieskola	Sweden	Foxhills
1988	Klippans Gymnasieskola	Sweden	Sunningdale
1989	Marks Gymnasium	Sweden	St Andrews

Golf Foundation Award Winners

1982	Lindsey Anderson	Tain Golf Club
1983	Nigel Osborne-Clarke	Shirehampton Golf Club
1984	Wayne Henry	Redbourn Golf Club
1985	David Grantham	Hull Golf Club
1986	Matthew Stanford	Saltford Golf Club
1987	Jane Marchant	Whittington Barracks Golf Club
1988	*Boys* Ian Garbutt	Wheatley Golf Club
	Girls Lisa Dermott	St Melyd Golf Club

Awards

Golf Writers' Association Trophy

Awarded to the man or woman who, in the opinion of Golf Writers, has done most for golf during the year

1951 Max Faulkner
1952 Miss Elizabeth Price
1953 JB Carr
1954 Mrs Roy Smith (Miss Frances Stephens)
1955 Ladies' Golf Union's Touring Team
1956 JC Beharrell
1957 DJ Rees
1958 Harry Bradshaw
1959 Eric Brown
1960 Sir Stuart Goodwin (sponsor of international golf)
1961 Commdr RCT Roe (ex-hon secretary, PGA)
1962 Mrs Marley Spearman, British Ladies' Champion 1961–1962
1963 MSR Lunt, Amateur Champion, 1963
1964 Great Britain and Ireland Team, winners of Eisenhower Trophy – JB Carr (non-playing Captain), MF Bonallack, MSR Lunt, RDBM Shade, R Foster
1965 Gerald Micklem, golf administrator, President, English Golf Union
1966 RDBM Shade, Scottish Amateur Champion for fourth successive year; Eisenhower Trophy Best individual score, 1966; runner-up Amateur Championship, 1966
1967 John Panton
1968 Michael Bonallack
1969 Tony Jacklin
1970 Tony Jacklin
1971 British Walker Cup Team – MF Bonallack, R Carr, R Foster, CW Green, W Humphreys, JS Macdonald, G McGregor, GC Marks, DM Marsh, HB Stuart
1972 Miss Michelle Walker
1973 PA Oosterhuis
1974 PA Oosterhuis
1975 Golf Foundation
1976 Great Britain and Ireland Team, winners of Eisenhower Trophy – Sandy Saddler (non-playing captain), John Davies, Ian Hutcheon, Mike Kelly, Steve Martin
1977 C O'Connor
1978 Peter McEvoy
1979 S Ballesteros
1980 AWB Lyle
1981 B Langer
1982 G Brand Jr
1983 N Faldo
1984 S Ballesteros
1985 European Ryder Cup Team
1986 Great Britain and Ireland Curtis Cup Team
1987 European Ryder Cup Team
1988 AWB Lyle
1989 British Walker Cup Team – Peter McEvoy, Darren Prosser, Garth McGimpsey, Andrew Hare, Russell Claydon, Craig Cassells, Jim Milligan, Neil Roderick, Stephen Dodd, Eoghan O'Connell

Harry Vardon Trophy

Currently awarded to the PGA member heading the Order of Merit at the end of the season

1937	CA Whitcombe	1966	P Alliss
1938	TH Cotton	1967	ME Gregson
1939	RA Whitcombe	1968	BGC Huggett
1940–45	*In abeyance*	1969	B Gallacher
1946	AD Locke	1970	NC Coles
1947	NG Von Nida	1971	PA Oosterhuis
1948	CH Ward	1972	PA Oosterhuis
1949	CH Ward	1973	PA Oosterhuis
1950	AD Locke	1974	PA Oosterhuis
1951	J Panton	1975	Dale Hayes
1952	H Weetman	1976	S Ballesteros
1953	F van Donck	1977	S Ballesteros
1954	AD Locke	1978	S Ballesteros
1955	DJ Rees	1979	AWB Lyle
1956	H Weetman	1980	AWB Lyle
1957	EC Brown	1981	B Langer
1958	BJ Hunt	1982	G Norman
1959	DJ Rees	1983	N Faldo
1960	BJ Hunt	1984	B Langer
1961	C O'Connor	1985	AWB Lyle
1962	C O'Connor	1986	S Ballesteros
1963	NC Coles	1987	I Woosnam
1964	P Alliss	1988	S Ballesteros
1965	BJ Hunt	1989	R Rafferty

Rookie of the Year

1960	T Goodwin	1976	M James
1961	A Caygill	1977	N Faldo
1962	*No Award*	1978	AWB Lyle
1963	A Jacklin	1979	MJ Miller
1964	*No Award*	1980	P Hoad
1966	R Liddle	1981	J Bennett
1967	*No Award*	1982	G Brand Jr
1968	B Gallacher	1983	G Turner
1969	P Oosterhuis	1984	AP Parkin
1970	S Brown	1985	P Thomas
1971	D Llewellyn	1986	J-M Olazabal
1972	S Torrance	1987	P Baker
1973	P Elson	1988	C Montgomerie
1974	C Mason	1989	P Broadhurst
1975	*No Award*		

Avia Watches' Woman Golfer of the Year

1982	Jane Connachan
1983	Jill Thornhill
1984	Gillian Stewart
	Claire Waite
1985	Belle Robertson
1986	Great Britain and Ireland Curtis Cup Team
1987	Linda Bayman
1988	Great Britain and Ireland Curtis Cup Team
1989	Helen Dobson

Ritz Club-PGA European Tour Golfer of the Year

1987	Ian Woosnam
1988	Severiano Ballesteros
1989	Nick Faldo

The US Vardon Trophy

The award is made to the member of the USPGA who completes 80 rounds or more, with the lowest scoring average over the calendar year.

Year	Winner	Year	Winner
1948	Ben Hogan	1969	Dave Hill
1949	Sam Snead	1970	Lee Trevino
1950	Sam Snead	1971	Lee Trevino
1951	Lloyd Mangrum	1972	Lee Trevino
1952	Jack Burke	1973	Bruce Crampton
1953	Lloyd Mangrum	1974	Lee Trevino
1954	Ed Harrison	1975	Bruce Crampton
1955	Sam Snead	1976	Don January
1956	Cary Middlecoff	1977	Tom Watson
1957	Dow Finsterwald	1978	Tom Watson
1958	Bob Rosburg	1979	Tom Watson
1959	Art Wall	1980	Lee Trevino
1960	Billy Casper	1981	Tom Kite
1961	Arnold Palmer	1982	Tom Kite
1962	Arnold Palmer	1983	Ray Floyd
1963	Billy Casper	1984	Calvin Peete
1964	Arnold Palmer	1985	Don Pooley
1965	Billy Casper	1986	Scott Hoch
1966	Billy Casper	1987	Dan Pohl
1967	Arnold Palmer	1988	Chip Beck
1968	Billy Casper	1989	Greg Norman

Bobby Jones Award

Awarded by USGA for distinguished sportsmanship in golf

Year	Winner	Year	Winner
1955	Francis Ouimet	1974	Byron Nelson
1956	Bill Campbell	1975	Jack Nicklaus
1957	Babe Zaharias	1976	Ben Hogan
1958	Margaret Curtis	1977	Joseph C Dey
1959	Findlay Douglas	1978	Bob Hope and
1960	Charles Evans Jr		Bing Crosby
1961	Joe Carr	1979	Tom Kite
1962	Horton-Smith	1980	Charles Yates
1963	Patty Berg	1981	Mrs JoAnne Carner
1964	Charles Coe	1982	WJ Patton
1965	Mrs Edwin Vare	1983	Mrs Maureen Garrett
1966	Gary Player	1984	J Sigel
1967	Richard Tufts	1985	Fuzzy Zoeller
1968	Robert Dickson	1986	Jess W Sweetser
1969	Gerald Micklem	1987	Tom Watson
1970	Roberto De Vicenzo	1988	Isaac B Grainger
1971	Arnold Palmer	1989	Chi-Chi Rodriquez
1972	Michael Bonallack	1990	Peggy Kirk Bell
1973	Gene Littler		

USPGA Player of the Year Award

Year	Winner	Year	Winner
1948	Ben Hogan	1969	Orville Moody
1949	Sam Snead	1970	Billy Casper
1950	Ben Hogan	1971	Lee Trevino
1951	Ben Hogan	1972	Jack Nicklaus
1952	Julius Boros	1973	Jack Nicklaus
1953	Ben Hogan	1974	Johnny Miller
1954	Ed Furgol	1975	Jack Nicklaus
1955	Doug Ford	1976	Jack Nicklaus
1956	Jack Burke	1977	Tom Watson
1957	Dick Mayer	1978	Tom Watson
1958	Dow Finsterwald	1979	Tom Watson
1959	Art Wall	1980	Tom Watson
1960	Arnold Palmer	1981	Bill Rogers
1961	Jerry Barner	1982	Tom Watson
1962	Arnold Palmer	1983	Hal Sutton
1963	Julius Boros	1984	Tom Watson
1964	Ken Venturi	1985	Lanny Wadkins
1965	Dave Marr	1986	Bob Tway
1966	Billy Casper	1987	Paul Azinger
1967	Jack Nicklaus	1988	Curtis Strange
1968	*Not awarded*	1989	Tom Kite

Arnold Palmer

Awarded to the USPGA leading money-winner

1981	Tom Kite
1982	Craig Stadler
1983	Hal Sutton
1984	Tom Watson
1985	Curtis Strange
1986	Greg Norman
1987	Paul Azinger
1988	Curtis Strange
1989	Tom Kite

Career Money Leaders

1	Tom Kite	$5,600,691
2	Tom Watson	5,160,243
3	Jack Nicklaus	5,102,420
4	Curtis Strange	5,015,720
5	Ben Crenshaw	4,115,074
6	Lanny Wadkins	3,940,949
7	Ray Floyd	3,616,587
8	Payne Stewart	3,606,707
9	Lee Trevino	3,460,416
10	Hale Irwin	3,227,831

Rolex Player of the Year

1980	Beth Daniel
1981	JoAnne Carner
1982	JoAnne Carner
1983	Patty Sheehan
1984	Betsy King
1985	Nancy Lopez
1986	Pat Bradley
1987	Ayako Okamoto
1988	Nancy Lopez
1989	Betsy King

Vare Trophy

		Scoring average
1980	Amy Alcott	71.51
1981	JoAnne Carner	71.75
1982	JoAnne Carner	71.49
1983	JoAnne Carner	71.41
1984	Patty Sheehan	71.40
1985	Nancy Lopez	70.73
1986	Pat Bradley	71.10
1987	Betsy King	71.14
1988	Colleen Walker	71.26
1989	Beth Daniel	70.38

Gatorade Rookie of the Year

1980	Myra Van Hoose
1981	Patty Sheehan
1982	Patti Rizzo
1983	Stephanie Farwig
1984	Juli Inster
1985	Penny Hammel
1986	Jody Rosenthal
1987	Tammie Green
1988	Liselotte Neumann
1989	Pamela Wright

1990 Programme of Events

Column key (diagonal headings, left to right): PGA European Tour · WPG European Tour · UK & Ireland Men's Amateur · UK & Ireland Women's Amateur · USPGA Tour · USLPGA Tour · Others

PGA European Tour	WPG European Tour	UK & Ireland Men's Amateur	UK & Ireland Women's Amateur	USPGA Tour	USLPGA Tour	Others	Date	Event
							January	
				•			4-7	Mony Tournament of Champions, Carlsbad, California
				•			11-14	Northern Telecom Tucson Open, Tucson, Arizona
				•			17-21	Bob Hope Chrysler Classic, La Quinta, California
				•			25-28	Phoenix Open, Scottsdale, Arizona
							February	
				•			1-4	AT&T National Pro-Am, Pebble Beach, California
						•	8-11	Dunhill Cup World Qualifier, Bukit, Singapore
				•			8-11	Hawaiian Open, Honolulu
						•	8-11	Australian Match Play Championship, Melbourne
•							15-18	Atlantic Open, Estela, Oporto
				•			15-18	Shearson Lehman Hutton Open, La Jolla, California
						•	15-18	Australian Masters, Melbourne
						•	15-18	Philippine Open, Manila
•							22-25	Desert Classic, Emirates
				•			22-25	Nissan Los Angeles Open, Pacific Palisades, California
						•	22-25	Chrysler Cup, Sarasota, Florida
						•	22-25	PGA National Tournaments Players Championship, Sydney
						•	22-25	Hong Kong Open, Fanling
							March	
•							1-4	American Express Mediterranean Open, Las Brisas, Spain
						•	1-4	Thailand Open, Bangkok
•							8-11	Renault Open de Baleares, Son Vida, Majorca
				•			8-11	Honda Classic, Coral Springs, Florida
						•	8-11	Indian Open, Calcutta
•							15-18	Catalan Open
				•			15-18	The Players Championship, Ponte Vedra, Florida
						•	15-18	Singapore Open, Bukit
•							22-25	Volvo Open, Ugolino, Florence
				•			22-25	Nestlé Invitational, Orlando, Florida
						•	21-24	Indonesia Open, Jakarta

PGA European Tour	WPG European Tour	UK & Ireland Men's Amateur	UK & Ireland Women's Amateur	USPGA Tour	USLPGA Tour	Others	Date	Event
								March cont'd
•							29-1 Apr	AGF Open, La Grande Motte
				•			29-1 Apr	Independent Insurance Agent Open, The Woodlands, Texas
					•		29-1 Apr	Nabisco Dinah Shore, Rancho Mirage, California
						•	29-1 Apr	Malaysia Open, Ipoh
								April
•							5-8	Jersey Open, La Moye
				•			5-8	**The US Masters, Augusta, Georgia**
				•			5-8	Deposit Guaranty Golf Classic, Hattiesburg, Mississippi
						•	5-8	China Open, Taipei
				•			12-15	MCI Heritage Classic, Hilton Head Island, South Carolina
						•	12-15	PGA Seniors Championship, Palm Beach Gardens, Florida
						•	12-15	Korean Open, Seoul
•							13-16	Crédit Lyonnais Cannes Open, Cannes Mougins
		•					18-19	Peter McEvoy Trophy, Copt Heath
•							19-22	Cepsa Madrid Open, Puerta de Hierro
	•						19-22	Rome Classic, Ogliata
				•			19-22	K Mart Greater Greensboro Open, Greensboro, North Carolina
						•	19-22	Dunlop Open, Ibaraki, Japan
•							26-29	Peugeot Spanish Open, Club de Campo, Madrid
	•						25-28	Ford Ladies Classic, Woburn
				•			26-29	USF&G Classic, New Orleans, Louisiana
								May
				•			3-6	GTE Byron Nelson Classic, Irving, Texas
					•		3-6	Sara Lee Classic, Old Hickory, Tennessee
•							4-7	Benson and Hedges International Open, St Mellion
		•					5-6	Berkshire Trophy, The Berkshire
•							10-13	Volvo Belgian Open, Royal Waterloo
	•						10-13	Hennessy Cup, St Germain-en-Laye, Paris
				•			10-13	Memorial Tournament, Dublin, Ohio
						•	10-13	JPGA Match Play Championship
•							17-20	Lancia Italian Open, Milan
				•			17-20	Southwestern Bell Colonial, Forth Worth, Texas
					•		17-20	Planters Pat Bradley International, High Point, North Carolina
		•					18-20	Brabazon Trophy, Burnham and Berrow
				•			24-27	BellSouth Atlanta Classic, Marietta, Georgia

PGA European Tour	WPG European Tour	UK & Ireland Men's Amateur	UK & Ireland Women's Amateur	USPGA Tour	USLPGA Tour	Others	Date	Event
							May cont'd	
•							25-28	Volvo PGA Championship, Wentworth
		•					25-27	Tillman Trophy, Royal Porthcawl
		•					30-31	Lagonda Trophy, Camberley Heath
		•					30-1 Jun	English Open Seniors Championship, Bridgnorth/Enville
•							31-3 Jun	Dunhill British Masters, Woburn
				•			31-3 Jun	Kemper Open, Potomac, Maryland
							June	
		•					4-9	Amateur Championship, Muirfield/Luffness
•							7-10	Scandinavian Enterprise Open, Drottningholm
	•						7-10	TEC Players' Championship
				•			7-10	Centel Western Open, Oak Brook, Illinois
					•		7-10	McDonald's Championship, Wilmington, Delaware
						•	7-10	Mazda Senior TPC, Dearborn, Michigan
			•				12-16	Ladies British Open Amateur Championship, Dunbar
•							14-17	Wang National Pro-Celebrity, Moor Park
	•						14-17	French Open
		•					14-17	International European Amateur Championship, Aalborg, Denmark
				•			14-17	**US Open, Chicago**
						•	14-17	Trusthouse Forte PGA Seniors Championship, Brough
•							21-24	Carrolls Irish Open, Portmarnock, Dublin
	•						21-24	European Masters, Bercuit, Brussels
				•			21-24	Buick Classic, Rye, New York
		•					22-23	Lytham Trophy, Royal Lytham & St Annes
•							28-1 Jul	Peugeot French Open, Chantilly
	•						28-1 Jul	BMW Classic, Dusseldorf
				•			28-1 Jul	Canon Greater Hartford Open, Cromwell, Connecticut
					•		28-1 Jul	du Maurier Ltd Classic, Kitchener, Ontario
						•	28-1 Jul	USGA Senior Open, Ridgewood, New Jersey
		•					29-30	St Andrews Trophy, El Saler
		•					29-30	Midland Open Amateur Championship, Little Aston/Sutton Coldfield

	PGA European Tour	WPG European Tour	UK & Ireland Men's Amateur	UK & Ireland Women's Amateur	USPGA Tour	USLPGA Tour	Others
July							
4-7 Torras Monte Carlo Open, Mont Agel	•						
5-8 Laing Classic, Stoke Poges		•					
5-8 Anheuser-Busch Golf Classic, Williamsburg, Virginia			•				
11-14 Bell's Scottish Open, Gleneagles	•						
11-15 European Boys Team Championship, Reykjavik				•			
11-15 European Youths Team Championship (Italy)				•			
12-15 Bloor Homes Eastleigh Classic, Fleming Park		•					
12-15 Bank of Boston Classic, Sutton, Massachusetts					•		
12-15 **45th Women's Open, Duluth, Georgia**						•	
19-22 **119th Open Championship, St Andrews**	•	•					
24-26 Carris Trophy, Luffenham Heath				•			
26-29 KLM Dutch Open, Kennemer, Zandvoort	•						
26-29 Volvo Seniors British Open, Turnberry	•						
26-29 Buick Open, Grand Blanc, Michigan					•		
26-29 Mazda LPGA Championship						•	
28-29 Curtis Cup, Somerset Hills, New Jersey				•			
28-29 Ladies British Open, Woburn				•			
30-4 Aug English Amateur Championship, Woodhall Spa			•				
August							
2-5 PLM Open, Bokskogen	•						
2-5 **Weetabix British Open, Woburn**		•					
2-5 Federal Express St Jude Classic, Memphis, Tennessee					•		
2-5 JPGA Championship							•
8-10 British Seniors Championship, The Berkshire	•						
8-10 Girls Internationals, Penrith				•			
8-11 Lufthansa Ladies German Open, Wörthsee, Munich		•					
9-12 Murphy's Cup, Fulford, York	•						
9-12 **PGA Championship, Birmingham, Alabama**					•		
9-10 Boys International, Hunstanton			•				
11 Boys GB & Ireland v Continent of Europe, Hunstanton			•				
13-16 Peugeot Cup: PGA Assistants Championship, Hillside			•				
13-17 Boys Championship, Hunstanton			•				
14-17 Girls British Open Amateur Championship, Penrith			•				
16-19 NM English Open, The Belfry	•						
16-19 Gislaved Ladies Open		•					
16-19 The International, Castle Rock, Colorado					•		

PGA European Tour	WPG European Tour	UK & Ireland Men's Amateur	UK & Ireland Women's Amateur	USPGA Tour	USLPGA Tour	Others	Date	Event
							August cont'd	
			•				22-24	Ladies British Open Amateur Stroke Play Championship, Strathaven
		•					22	Youths Internationals, England v Scotland, Southerness
•							23-26	German Open, Hubbelrath, Dusseldorf
	•						23-26	Swedish Ladies, Stockholm
				•			23-26	NEC World Series Of Golf, Akron, Ohio
					•		23-26	World Championship
		•					23-25	Youths Championship, Southerness
		•					24-26	Mid-Amateur Championship, Wentworth
		•					29-30	Wilson PGA Junior Championship, Selsdon Park
•							30-2 Sept	Ebel European Masters Swiss Open, Crans-sur-Sierre
	•						30-2 Sept	Variety Club Classic, Calcot Park
				•			30-2 Sept	Greater Milwaukee Open, Franklin, Wisconsin
		•					31-1 Sept	Youths International: GB & Ireland v Continent of Europe, Portugal
							September	
		•					3-5	English Boys County Finals, Burford
		•					4-5	Lord Derby's Knowsley Safari Park Tournament, Bury
			•				5-7	Home Internationals, Hunstanton
•							6-9	Panasonic European Open, Sunningdale
				•			6-9	Hardee's Golf Classic, Coal Valley, Illinois
		•					7-8	English Champion Club Tournament, Goring and Streatley
		•					12-14	Home Internationals, Conwy
•							13-16	Lancôme Trophy, St Nom la Breteche, Paris
	•						13-16	Ladies European Open, Kingswood, Surrey
				•			13-16	Canadian Open, Oakville, Ontario
			•				17-23	PGA Cup, Kiawah, South Carolina
•							20-23	Suntory World Match Play, Wentworth
•							20-23	BMW International Open, München Nord-Eichenried
	•						20-23	Paris Open
				•			20-23	BC Open, Endicott, New York
		•					23	English County Champions Tournament, Olton
	•						24-25	Equity & Law Challenge, Royal Mid-Surrey
•							27-30	Epson Grand Prix, St Pierre, Chepstow
				•			27-30	Southern Open, Columbus, Ohio
		•					28-30	English County Finals, Hayling

	PGA European Tour	WPG European Tour	UK & Ireland Men's Amateur	UK & Ireland Women's Amateur	USPGA Tour	USLPGA Tour	Others
October							
2-3 Senior Ladies British Open Amateur Championship, Harrogate				•			
4-7 German Masters, Stuttgart	•						
4-7 Italian Ladies Open		•					
4-7 Central England Open Mixed Foursomes, Woodhall Spa			•	•			
4-7 Nabisco Texas Open, San Antonio					•		
4-7 Centel Classic, Tallahassee, Florida						•	
4-7 Japan Open							•
10-14 Las Vegas Invitational, Las Vegas					•		
11-14 Dunhill Cup, St Andrews	•						
11-14 Austrian Open, Gut Altentann, Salzburg	•						
11-14 AGF Ladies Open		•					
17-19 Golf Plus PGA Fourball Championship, Hillside/Hesketh							•
17-20 Walt Disney World/Oldsmobile Classic, Lake Buena Vista, Florida					•		
18-21 Portuguese Open, Quinta do Lago	•						
18-21 Woolmark Ladies Match Play Championship		•					
18-21 Espirito Santo, Russley, New Zealand				•			
25-28 Volvo Masters, Valderrama, Spain	•						
25-28 Men's World Cup, Russley, New Zealand			•				
25-28 Nabisco Championship, Houston, Texas						•	
November							
1-4 Asahi Glass Four Tours World Championship of Golf, Yomiuri, Tokyo	•				•		
1-4 Mazda Japan Classic, Musashigaoka, Tokyo						•	
7-10 Isuzu Kapalua International, Maui, Hawaii					•		
8-11 Benson and Hedges Trophy (Mixed Team)	•	•					
9-11 USA/Japan Team Matches, Batoh, Japan							•
10-15 Qualifying School, La Grande Motte	•						
16-18 RMCC Invitational, Thousand Oaks, California					•		
23-26 Philip Morris World Cup, Orlando, Florida	•						
27-28 Skins Game, La Quinta, California					•		
29-2 Dec JC Penney Classic, Largo, Florida					•		
29-2 Dec JC Penney Classic, Tarpon Springs, Florida						•	
December							
6-9 Team Championship, Wellington, Florida					•		

Royal & Ancient Venues and Dates For Championships in 1990

THE AMATEUR CHAMPIONSHIP

The Honourable Company of Edinburgh Golfers, Muirfield Luffness New	4-9 June

THE ST ANDREWS TROPHY

El Saler, Spain	29-30 June

THE SENIORS' OPEN AMATEUR CHAMPIONSHIP

The Berkshire	8-10 August

THE BOYS' AMATEUR CHAMPIONSHIP

(a) Internationals

England v Scotland	9 August	
Ireland v Wales	9 August	
Winners of Thursday	10 August	Hunstanton
Losers of Thursday	10 August	
Great Britain & Ireland v Continent of Europe	11 August	
(b) Championship	13-17 August	Hunstanton

THE YOUTHS' OPEN AMATEUR CHAMPIONSHIP

(a) Internationals

Scotland v England	22 August	Southerness
Great Britain & Ireland v Continent of Europe	31 August- 1 September	Portugal
(b) Championship	23-25 August	Southerness

ESPIRITO SANTO TROPHY (WOMEN)

Russley, Christchurch, New Zealand	18-21 October

EISENHOWER TROPHY (MEN)

The Shirley Links, Christchurch, New Zealand	25-28 October

THE OPEN CHAMPIONSHIP

(a) Regional Qualifying Competitions

Blackwell	
Deer Park G&CC	
Hankley Common	
Langley Park	9 July
Ormskirk	
Orsett	
Sherwood Forest	

(b) Final Qualifying Competitions

Ladybank	
Leven Links	
Lundin	15-16 July
Scotscraig	

(c) Championship

Old Course, St Andrews	19-22 July

Part II
Past Tournament Results

The Major Championships

The Open Championship

The Belt

Year	Winner	Score	Venue	Entrants
1860	W Park, Musselburgh	174	Prestwick	8
1861	Tom Morris, sen, Prestwick	163	Prestwick	12
1862	Tom Morris, sen, Prestwick	163	Prestwick	6
1863	W Park, Musselburgh	168	Prestwick	14
1864	Tom Morris, sen, Prestwick	167	Prestwick	6
1865	A Strath, St Andrews	162	Prestwick	10
1866	W Park, Musselburgh	169	Prestwick	12
1867	Tom Morris, sen, St Andrews	170	Prestwick	10
1868	Tom Morris, jun, St Andrews	157	Prestwick	10
1869	Tom Morris, jun, St Andrews	154	Prestwick	8
1870	Tom Morris, jun, St Andrews	149	Prestwick	17

The Belt having been won thrice in succession by young Tom Morris, it became his property, and the Championship remained in abeyance for one year, when the present cup was offered for yearly competition, to be held by the leading club in the district in which the winner resided.

The Cup

Year	Winner	Score	Venue	Entrants
1872	Tom Morris, jun, St Andrews	166	Prestwick	8
1873	Tom Kidd, St Andrews	179	St Andrews	26
1874	Mungo Park, Musselburgh	159	Musselburgh	32
1875	Willie Park, Musselburgh	166	Prestwick	18
1876	Bob Martin, St Andrews	176	St Andrews	34
(David Strath tied but refused to play off)				
1877	Jamie Anderson, St Andrews	160	Musselburgh	24
1878	Jamie Anderson, St Andrews	157	Prestwick	26
1879	Jamie Anderson, St Andrews	169	St Andrews	46
1880	Bob Ferguson, Musselburgh	162	Musselburgh	30
1881	Bob Ferguson, Musselburgh	170	Prestwick	22
1882	Bob Ferguson, Musselburgh	171	St Andrews	40
1883	W. Fernie, Dumfries	159	Musselburgh	41
After a tie with Bob Ferguson, Musselburgh				
1884	Jack Simpson, Carnoustie	160	Prestwick	30
1885	Bob Martin, St Andrews	171	St Andrews	51
1886	D Brown, Musselburgh	157	Musselburgh	46
1887	W. Park, jun, Musselburgh	161	Prestwick	36
1888	Jack Burns, Warwick	171	St Andrews	53
1889	W. Park, jun, Musselburgh	155	Musselburgh	42
After a tie with Andrew Kirkaldy				
1890	John Ball, Royal Liverpool (Am)	164	Prestwick	40
1891	Hugh Kirkaldy, St Andrews	166	St Andrews	82
After 1891 the competition was extended to 72 holes and for the first time entry money was imposed				
1892	HH Hilton, Royal Liverpool (Am)	305	Muirfield	66
1893	W Auchterlonie, St Andrews	322	Prestwick	72
1894	JH Taylor, Winchester	326	Sandwich	94
1895	JH Taylor, Winchester	322	St Andrews	73
1896	H Vardon, Ganton	316	Muirfield	64

After a tie with JH Taylor. Replay scores for 36 holes: H Vardon, 157; Taylor, 161

The Open Championship
continued

Year	Winner	Score	Venue	Entrants
1897	HH Hilton, Royal Liverpool (Am)	314	Hoylake	86
1898	H Vardon, Ganton	307	Prestwick	78
1899	H Vardon, Ganton	310	Sandwich	98
1900	JH Taylor, Mid-Surrey	309	St Andrews	81
1901	James Braid, Romford	309	Muirfield	101
1902	Alex Herd, Huddersfield	307	Hoylake	112
1903	H Vardon, Totteridge	300	Prestwick	127
1904	Jack White, Sunningdale	296	Sandwich	144
1905	James Braid, Walton Heath	318	St Andrews	152
1906	James Braid, Walton Heath	300	Muirfield	183
1907	Arnaud Massy, La Boulie	312	Hoylake	193

Year	Winner	Score	Venue	Qual	Ents
1908	James Braid, Walton Heath	291	Prestwick	180	
1909	JH Taylor, Mid-Surrey	295	Deal	204	
1910	James Braid, Walton Heath	299	St Andrews	210	
1911	Harry Vardon, Totteridge	303	Sandwich	226	

After a tie with Arnaud Massy. The tie was over 36 holes, but Massy picked up at the 35th hole before holing out. He had taken 148 for 34 holes, and when Vardon holed out at the 35th hole his score was 143.

Year	Winner	Score	Venue	Qual	Ents
1912	E Ray, Oxhey	295	Muirfield	215	
1913	JH Taylor, Mid-Surrey	304	Hoylake	269	
1914	Harry Vardon, Totteridge	306	Prestwick	194	
1915-19	No Championship owing to the Great War				
1920	George Duncan, Hanger Hill	303	Deal	81	190
1921	Jock Hutchison, Glenview, Chicago	296	St Andrews	85	158

After a tie with RH Wethered (Am). Royal and Ancient-Replay scores: Jock Hutchison 150; RH Wethered 159.

Year	Winner	Score	Venue	Qual	Ents
1922	Walter Hagen, Detroit, USA	300	Sandwich	80	225
1923	AG Havers, Coombe Hill	295	Troon	88	222
1924	Walter Hagen, Detroit, USA	301	Hoylake	86	277
1925	Jim Barnes, USA	300	Prestwick	83	200
1926	RT Jones, USA (Am)	291	Lytham and St Annes	117	293
1927	RT Jones, USA (Am)	285	St Andrews	108	207
1928	Walter Hagen, USA	292	Sandwich	113	271
1929	Walter Hagen, USA	292	Muirfield	109	242
1930	RT Jones, USA (Am)	291	Hoylake	112	296
1931	TD Armour, USA	296	Carnoustie	109	215
1932	G Sarazen, USA	283	Prince's, Sandwich	110	224
1933	D Shute, USA	292	St Andrews	117	287

After a tie with Craig Wood, USA-Replay scores: D Shute 149; Craig Wood 154.

Year	Winner	Score	Venue	Qual	Ents
1934	TH Cotton, Waterloo, Belgium	283	Sandwich	101	312
1935	A Perry, Leatherhead	283	Muirfield	109	264
1936	AH Padgham, Sundridge Park	287	Hoylake	107	286
1937	TH Cotton, Ashridge	290	Carnoustie	141	258
1938	RA Whitcombe, Parkstone	295	Sandwich	120	268
1939	R Burton, Sale	290	St Andrews	129	254
1940-45	No Championship owing to Second World War				
1946	S Snead, USA	290	St Andrews	100	225
1947	Fred Daly, Balmoral	293	Hoylake	100	263
1948	TH Cotton, Royal Mid-Surrey	284	Muirfield	97	272
1949	AD Locke, South Africa	283	Sandwich	96	224

After a tie with Harry Bradshaw, Kilcroney-Replay Scores: Locke 135; Bradshaw 147.

Year	Winner	Score	Venue	Qual	Ents
1950	AD Locke, South Africa	279	Troon	93	262
1951	M Faulkner, GB	285	Portrush	98	180
1952	AD Locke, South Africa	287	Lytham and St Annes	96	275
1953	Ben Hogan, USA	282	Carnoustie	91	196
1954	PW Thomson, Australia	283	Birkdale	97	349
1955	PW Thomson, Australia	281	St Andrews	94	301
1956	PW Thomson, Australia	286	Hoylake	96	360
1957	AD Locke, South Africa	279	St Andrews	96	282
1958	PW Thomson, Australia	278	Lytham and St Annes	96	362

After a tie with DC Thomas, Sudbury-Replay scores: Thomson 139; Thomas 143.

Year	Winner	Score	Venue	Qual	Ents
1959	GJ Player, South Africa	284	Muirfield	90	285
1960	KDG Nagle, Australia	278	St Andrews	74	410
1961	Arnold Palmer, USA	284	Birkdale	101	364
1962	Arnold Palmer, USA	276	Troon	119	379
1963	RJ Charles, New Zealand	277	Lytham and St Annes	119	261

After a tie with Phil Rodgers, USA-Replay scores: Charles 140; Rodgers 148

Year	Winner	Score	Venue	Qual	Ents
1964	Tony Lema, USA	279	St Andrews	119	327
1965	PW Thomson, Australia	285	Birkdale	130	372
1966	J Nicklaus, USA	282	Muirfield	130	310
1967	R De Vicenzo, Argentina	278	Hoylake	130	326

The Open
Championsh
continued

Year	Winner	Score	Venue	Qual	Ents
1968	GJ Player, South Africa	289	Carnoustie	130	309
1969	A Jacklin, GB	280	Lytham and St Annes	129	424
1970	J Nicklaus USA	283	St Andrews	134	468

After a tie with Doug Sanders, USA-Replay scores: Nicklaus 72; Sanders 73.

Year	Winner	Score	Venue	Qual	Ents
1971	L Trevino, USA	278	Birkdale	150	528
1972	L Trevino, USA	278	Muirfield	150	570
1973	T Weiskopf, USA	276	Troon	150	569
1974	G Player, South Africa	282	Lytham and St Annes	150	679
1975	T Watson, USA	279	Carnoustie	150	629

After a tie with J Newton. Australia-Replay scores: Watson 71; Newton 72.

Year	Winner	Score	Venue	Qual	Ents
1976	J Miller, USA	279	Birkdale	150	719
1977	T Watson, USA	268	Turnberry	150	730
1978	J Nicklaus, USA	281	St Andrews	150	788
1979	S Ballesteros, Spain	283	Lytham and St Annes	150	885
1980	T Watson, USA	271	Muirfield	151	994
1981	B Rogers, USA	276	Sandwich	153	971
1982	T Watson, USA	284	Troon	176	1,121
1983	T Watson, USA	275	Birkdale	151	1,107
1984	S Ballesteros, Spain	276	St Andrews		1,413
1985	A Lyle, GB	282	Sandwich	149	1,361
1986	G Norman, Australia	280	Turnberry	152	1,347
1987	N Faldo, GB	279	Muirfield	153	1,407
1988	S Ballesteros, Spain	273	Lytham and St Annes	153	1,393
1989	M Calcavecchia, USA	275	Royal Troon	156	1,481

1980 at Muirfield

Entries 994. Qualifying aggregates: 144 Luffness New. 146 Gullane No 1. 143 Gullane No 2. Qualified for final 36 holes: 87 competitors (86 Professionals, 1 Amateur) with scores of 149 and below. Qualified for final 18 holes: 65 competitors (64 Professionals, 1 Amateur) with scores of 219 and below.

Name	Score	Prize Money £
T Watson (USA)	68, 70, 64, 69-271	25,000
L Trevino (USA)	68, 67, 71, 69-275	17,500
B Crenshaw (USA)	70, 70, 68, 69-277	13,500
J Nicklaus (USA)	73, 67, 71, 69-280	9,250
C Mason (GB)	72, 69, 70, 69-280	9,250
C Stadler (USA)	72, 70, 69, 71-282	7,250
A Bean (USA)	71, 69, 70, 72-282	7,250
H Green (USA)	77, 69, 64, 72-282	7,250
K Brown (GB)	70, 68, 68, 76-282	7,250
J Newton (Aus)	69, 71, 73, 70-283	5,750
G Morgan (USA)	70, 70, 71, 72-283	5,750
N Faldo (GB)	69, 74, 71, 70-284	4,250
L Nelson (USA)	72, 70, 71, 71-284	4,250
A WB Lyle (GB)	70, 71, 70, 73-284	4,250
I Aoki (Jpn)	74, 74, 63, 73-284	4,250
T Weiskopf (USA)	72, 72, 71, 70-285	2,900
J Bland (SA)	73, 70, 70, 72-285	2,900
J Pate (USA)	71, 67, 74, 73-285	2,900
B Rogers (USA)	76, 73, 68, 69-286	
B Lietzke (USA)	74, 69, 73, 70-286	
N Suzuki (Jpn)	74, 68, 72, 72-286	
S Ballesteros (Spa)	72, 68, 72, 74-286	
P Oosterhuis (GB)	72, 71, 75, 69-287	
M McNulty (SA)	71, 73, 72, 71-287	
W J McColl (GB)	73, 73, 68, 71-287	
GA Cullen (GB)	72, 72, 69, 74-287	
T Kite (USA)	72, 72, 74, 70-288	
N Price (Zim)	72, 71, 71, 74-288	
N Coles (GB)	75, 69, 69, 76-289	
H Baiocchi (SA)	76, 67, 69, 77-289	
D Graham (Aus)	73, 71, 68, 77-289	

Other Totals

M Hayes (USA), T Horton (GB), A Jacklin (GB), J Mahaffey (USA), B Waites (GB), H Clark (GB) 290; J Sigel (USA) (Am), S Torrance (GB), R Davis (Aus), S Ginn (Aus), T Nakamura (Jpn), B Brask Jr (USA), D Hayes (SA) 291; A North (USA), W Armstrong (USA), G Marsh (Aus), M James (GB), E Darcy (Ire), V Fernandez (Arg) 292; A Garrido (Spa), B Gilder (USA), S Hobday (Zim), B Langer (WG), B Shearer (Aus), H Henning (SA), DA Cooper (GB) 293; M Pinero (Spa), B Barnes (GB) 294; R Charles (NZ), D Jagger (GB), M Ozaki (Jpn) 295; P Tupling (GB) 296; S Owen (NZ) 297; D Blies (USA) 298.

1981 at Sandwich

Entries 972. Qualifying aggregates: 146 Littlestone. 146 North Foreland. 148 Princes. 144 Deal. Qualified for final 36 holes: 82 competitors (75 Professionals, 7 Amateurs) with scores of 150 and below. Qualified for final 18 holes: 61 competitors (59 Professionals, 2 Amateurs) with scores of 222 and below.

The Open Championship continued

Name	Score	Prize Money £
B Rogers (USA)	72, 66, 67, 71-276	25,000
B Langer (WG)	73, 67, 70, 70-280	17,500
R Floyd (USA)	74, 70, 69, 70-283	11,750
M James (GB)	72, 70, 68, 73-283	11,750
S Torrance (GB)	72, 69, 73, 70-284	8,500
B Lietzke (USA)	76, 69, 71, 69-285	7,750
M Pinero (Spa)	73, 74, 68, 70-285	7,750
H Clark (GB)	72, 76, 70, 68-286	6,500
B Crenshaw (USA)	72, 67, 76, 71-286	6,500
B Jones (GB)	73, 76, 66, 71-286	6,500
L Trevino (USA)	77, 67, 70, 73-287	5,000
N Faldo (GB)	77, 68, 69, 73-287	5,000
I Aoki (Jpn)	71, 73, 69, 74-287	5,000
E Darcy (Ire)	79, 69, 70, 70-288	3,240
AWB Lyle (GB)	73, 73, 71, 71-288	3,240
D Graham (Aus)	71, 71, 74, 72-288	3,240
B Barnes (GB)	76, 70, 70, 72-288	3,240
N Job (GB)	70, 69, 75, 74-288	3,240
G Marsh (Aus)	75, 71, 72, 71-289	2,013
G Brand (GB)	78, 65, 74, 72-289	2,013
P Townsend (GB)	73, 70, 73, 73-289	2,013
J Pate (USA)	73, 73, 69, 74-289	2,013
M McNulty (SA)	74, 74, 74, 68-290	
N Price (Zim)	77, 68, 76, 69-290	
H Green (USA)	75, 72, 74, 69-290	
J Nicklaus (USA)	83, 66, 71, 70-290	
A Palmer (USA)	72, 74, 73, 71-290	
T Watson (USA)	73, 69, 75, 73-290	
A Jacklin (GB)	71, 71, 73, 75-290	
S Owen (NZ)	71, 74, 70, 75-290	
J Morgan (GB)	77, 72, 73, 69-291	
G Norman (Aus)	72, 75, 72, 72-291	
D Smyth (Ire)	77, 67, 73, 74-291	
T Powell (GB)	75, 68, 73, 75-291	

Other Totals

T Horton (GB), EW Dunk (Aus), B Charles (NZ), M Ozaki (Jpn) 292; S Ballesteros (Spa), F Molina (Arg), N Coles (GB), R Davis (Aus), J Miller (USA) 293; K Brown (GB), R Streck (USA), T Gale (Aus) 294; J Gonzales (Bra), M O'Meara (USA), H Sutton (USA) (Am) 295; D Jones (GB), D Thorpe (GB), B Waites (GB) 296; E Polland (Ire), G Cullen (GB), M Ferguson (GB) 297; N Hunt (GB), W Humphreys (GB) 298; J O'Leary (Ire), D Stewart (GB), G Godwin (GB) (Am) 299; D McLean (USA) 300.

1982 at Troon

Entries 1,121. Qualifying aggregates: 144 Glasgow Gailes. 143 Kilmarnock (Barassie). 140 Prestwick St Nicholas. 145 Western Gailes. Qualified for final 36 holes: 90 competitors (89 Professionals, 1 Amateur) with scores of 152 and below. Qualified for final 18 holes: 60 competitors (59 Professionals, 1 Amateur) with scores of 226 and below.

Name	Score	Prize Money £
T Watson (USA)	69, 71, 74, 70-284	32,000
P Oosterhuis (GB)	74, 67, 74, 70-285	19,300
N Price (SA)	69, 69, 74, 73-285	19,300
T Purtzer (USA)	76, 66, 75, 69-286	11,000
N Faldo (GB)	73, 73, 71, 69-286	11,000
M Kuramoto (Jpn)	71, 73, 71, 71-286	11,000
D Smyth (Ire)	70, 69, 74, 73-286	11,000
F Zoeller (USA)	73, 71, 73, 70-287	8,750
AWB Lyle (GB)	74, 66, 73, 74-287	8,750
J Nicklaus (USA)	77, 70, 72, 69-288	7,350
B Clampett (USA)	67, 66, 78, 77-288	7,350
S Torrance (GB)	73, 72, 73, 71-289	6,300
S Ballesteros (Spa)	71, 75, 73, 71-290	5,400
B Langer (WG)	70, 69, 78, 73-290	5,400
R Floyd (USA)	74, 73, 77, 67-291	3,900
C Strange (USA)	72, 73, 76, 70-291	3,900

Name	Score	Prize Money £
B Crenshaw (USA)	74, 75, 72, 70-291	3,900
D Watson (GB)	75, 69, 73, 74-291	3,900
K Brown (GB)	70, 71, 79, 72-292	2,900
T Nakamura (Jpn)	77, 68, 77, 71-293	2,500
I Aoki (Jpn)	75, 69, 75, 74-293	2,500
J-M Canizares (Spa)	71, 72, 79, 72-294	2,200
J Miller (USA)	71, 76, 75, 72-294	2,200
B Rogers (USA)	73, 70, 76, 75-294	2,200
G Marsh (Aus)	76, 76, 72, 71-295	
B Gallacher (GB)	75, 71, 74, 75-295	
J Haas (USA)	78, 72, 75, 71-296	
G Norman (Aus)	73, 75, 76, 72-296	
A Palmer (USA)	71, 73, 78, 74-296	
L Trevino (USA)	78, 72, 71, 75-296	
D Graham (Aus)	73, 70, 76, 77-296	
L Nelson (USA)	77, 69, 77, 74-297	
M Thomas (GB)	72, 74, 75, 76-297	

The Open
Championship
continued

Other Totals

E Darcy (Ire), J Ferenz (USA), P Way (GB), C Stadler (USA), B Barnes (GB), D Russell (GB) 298; H Henning (SA) 299; B Shearer (NZ), M Lewis (GB) (Am), G Player (SA), T Gale (Aus), N Coles (GB) 300; B Longmuir (GB), T Britz (USA), R Chapman (GB), B Waites (GB) 301; M James (GB), H Sheng-San (Tai), M Pinero (Spa) 302; M McNulty (Zim), P Townsend (GB), M Poxton (GB), K Waters (GB) 303; P Harrison (GB) 304; M King (GB) 305; M Cahill (Aus) 306.

1983 at Birkdale

Entries 1,107. Qualifying aggregates: 143 Hesketh. 145 Southport and Ainsdale. 147 Hillside. 148 West Lancs. Qualified for final 36 holes: 83 competitors (all Professionals) with scores of 146 and below. Qualified for final 18 holes: 63 competitors with scores of 217 and below.

Name	Score	Prize Money £
T Watson (USA)	67, 68, 70, 70-275	40,000
H Irwin (USA)	69, 68, 72, 67-276	23,000
A Bean (USA)	70, 69, 70, 67-276	23,000
G Marsh (Aus)	69, 70, 74, 64-277	15,000
L Trevino (USA)	69, 66, 73, 70-278	13,600
S Ballesteros (Spa)	71, 71, 69, 68-279	12,500
H Henning (SA)	71, 69, 70, 69-279	12,250
D Durnian (GB)	73, 66, 74, 67-280	9,625
C O'Connor, Jr (Ire)	72, 69, 71, 68-280	9,625
B Rogers (USA)	67, 71, 73, 69-280	9,625
N Faldo (GB)	68, 68, 71, 73-280	9,625
P Jacobsen (USA)	72, 69, 70, 70-281	7,250
C Stadler (USA)	64, 70, 72, 75-281	7,250
M Sullivan (USA)	72, 68, 74, 68-282	5,040
G Koch (USA)	75, 71, 66, 70-282	5,040
F Zoeller (USA)	71, 71, 67, 73-282	5,040
R Floyd (USA)	72, 66, 69, 75-282	5,040
D Graham (Aus)	71, 69, 67, 75-282	5,040
G Norman (Aus)	75, 71, 70, 67-283	2,957
H Green (USA)	69, 74, 72, 68-283	2,957
T Britz (SA)	71, 74, 69, 69-283	2,957
B Waites (GB)	70, 70, 73, 70-283	2,957
B Gallacher (GB)	72, 71, 70, 70-283	2,957
S Hobday (SA)	70, 73, 70, 70-283	2,957
J Haas (USA)	73, 72, 68, 70-283	2,957
E Darcy (Ire)	69, 72, 74, 69-284	2,150
H Clark (GB)	71, 72, 69, 72-284	2,150
R Davis (Aus)	70, 71, 70, 73-284	2,150

Other Totals

C-S Lu (Tai), L Wadkins (USA), J Nicklaus (USA), T Kite (USA), M McCullough (USA), H Sutton (USA), M James (GB), T Nakamura (Jpn), C Strange (USA), T Gale (Aus) 285; A Jacklin (GB), K Arai (Jpn), B Gilder (USA), V Fernandez (Arg), C Moody (GB), I Collins (GB) 286; C Tucker (GB), M Muramoto (Jpn), M Pinero (Spa), G Burroughs (GB), T Weiskopf (USA), V Somers (Aus), T Simpson (USA), M McNulty (Zim) 287; B Clampett (USA), L Nelson (USA), S Torrance (GB) 288; B Langer (WG), A Palmer (USA), M Johnson (GB) 289; M Calero (Spa), J O'Leary (Ire) 290; R Rafferty (Ire) 291; M Ingham (GB) 292; Y-S Hseih (Tai) 295.

1984 at St Andrews

Entries 1,413. Regional qualifying courses: Glenbervie, Pleasington, Lindrick, Little Aston, Porters Park, Camberley Heath. Final qualifying courses: Ladybank, Leven, Lundin, Scotscraig. Qualified for final 36 holes: 94 competitors (92 Professionals, 2 Amateurs) with scores of 148 and below. Qualified for final 18 holes: 63 competitors with scores of 219 and below.

Name	Score	Prize Money £
S Ballesteros (Spain)	69, 68, 70, 69-276	55,000
B Langer (W Germany)	71, 68, 68, 71-278	31,900
T Watson (USA)	71, 68, 66, 73-278	31,900
F Couples (USA)	70, 69, 74, 68-281	19,800
L Wadkins (USA)	70, 69, 73, 69-281	19,800
N Faldo (GB)	69, 68, 76, 69-282	16,390
G Norman (Australia)	67, 74, 74, 67-282	16,390
M McCumber (USA)	74, 67, 72, 70-283	14,300
G Marsh (Australia)	70, 74, 73, 67-284	11,264
S Torrance (GB)	74, 74, 66, 70-284	11,264
R Rafferty (Ireland)	74, 72, 67, 71-284	11,264
H Baiocchi (S Africa)	72, 70, 70, 72-284	11,264
I Baker-Finch (Australia)	68, 66, 71, 79-284	11,264
AWB Lyle (GB)	75, 71, 72, 67-285	6,751
K Brown (GB)	74, 71, 72, 68-285	6,751
A Bean (USA)	72, 69, 75, 69-285	6,751
F Zoeller (USA)	71, 72, 71, 71-285	6,751
P Senior (Australia)	74, 70, 70, 71-285	6,751
W Bergin (USA)	75, 73, 66, 71-285	6,751
H Irwin (USA)	75, 68, 70, 72-285	6,751
L Trevino (USA)	70, 67, 75, 73-285	6,751
C Pavin (USA)	71, 74, 72, 69-286	3,850
B Crenshaw (USA)	72, 75, 70, 69-286	3,850
T Kite (USA)	69, 71, 74, 72-286	3,850
P Way (GB)	73, 72, 69, 72-286	3,850
P Jacobsen (USA)	67, 73, 73, 73-286	3,850
G Morgan (USA)	71, 71, 71, 73-286	3,850
T Gale (Australia)	71, 74, 72, 70-287	2,970
J Gonzales (Brazil)	69, 71, 76, 71-287	2,970
C Stadler (USA)	75, 70, 70, 72-287	2,970

Other Totals

P Parkin (GB), R Drummond (GB), B Gallacher (GB), J Miller (USA), J Nicklaus (USA) 288; M Pinero (Spain), J Haas (USA), G Levenson (S Africa), J Heggarty (GB), E Murray (GB), D Dunk (GB), T Nakajima (Japan), JM Canizares (Spain) 289; N Price (S Africa), M Poxon (GB), M James (GB) 290; M Calero (Spain), I Aoki (Japan), D Frost (S Africa), R Charles (New Zealand), R Chapman (GB) 291; H Clark (GB), J Chillas (GB), R Boxall (GB) 292; M Mackenzie (GB), D Russell (GB), W Longmuir (GB), E Rodriguez (Spain) 293; S Fujiki (Japan) 294; J Garner (GB), G Koch (USA), R Hartman (USA), N Ozaki (Japan) 295.

1985 at St Georges

Entries 1,361. Regional qualifying courses: Camberley Heath, Glenbervie, Lindrick, Little Aston, Pleasington, Porters Park, Wildernesse. Final qualifying courses: Royal Cinque Ports Deal, Littlestone, North Foreland. Qualified for final 36 holes: 85 (83 Professionals, 2 Amateurs) with scores of 149 and below. Qualified for final 18 holes: 60 (59 Professionals, 1 Amateur) with scores of 221 and below.

Name	Score	Prize Money £
AWB Lyle (GB)	68, 71, 73, 70-282	65,000
P Stewart (USA)	70, 75, 70, 68-283	40,000
J Rivero (Spain)	74, 72, 70, 68-284	23,600
C O'Connor Jr (Ireland)	64, 76, 72, 72-284	23,600
M O'Meara (USA)	70, 72, 70, 72-284	23,600
D Graham (Australia)	68, 71, 70, 75-284	23,600
B Langer (W Germany)	72, 69, 68, 75-284	23,600
A Forsbrand (Sweden)	70, 70, 69, 70-285	15,566
DA Weibring (USA)	69, 71, 74, 71-285	15,566
T Kite (USA)	73, 73, 67, 72-285	15,566
E Darcy (Ireland)	76, 68, 74, 68-286	11,400
G Koch (USA)	75, 72, 70, 69-286	11,400
J-M Canizares (Spain)	72, 75, 70, 69-286	11,400
F Zoeller (USA)	69, 76, 70, 71-286	11,400
P Jacobsen (USA)	71, 74, 68, 73-286	11,400
S Bishop (GB)	71, 75, 72, 69-287	7,900
S Torrance (GB)	74, 74, 69, 70-287	7,900

Name	Score	Prize Money £
G Norman (Australia)	71, 72, 71, 73-287	7,900
I Woosnam (GB)	70, 71, 71, 75-287	7,900
I Baker-Finch (Australia)	71, 73, 74, 70-288	5,260
J Gonzales (Brazil)	72, 72, 73, 71-288	5,260
L Trevino (USA)	73, 76, 68, 71-288	5,260
G Marsh (Australia)	71, 75, 69, 73-288	5,260
M James (GB)	71, 78, 66, 73-288	5,260
P Parkin (GB)	68, 76, 77, 68-289	3,742
K Moe (USA)	70, 76, 73, 70-289	3,742
J-M Olazabal (Spain) (Am)	72, 76, 71, 70-289	3,742
M Cahill (Australia)	72, 74, 71, 72-289	3,742
D Frost (South Africa)	70, 74, 73, 72-289	3,742
GJ Brand (GB)	73, 72, 72, 72-289	3,742
M Pinero (Spain)	71, 73, 72, 73-289	3,742
R Lee (GB)	68, 73, 74, 74-289	3,742

Other Totals

O Sellberg (Sweden), W Riley (Australia) 290; H Baiocchi (South Africa), B Crenshaw (USA), A Bean (USA), R Shearer (Australia) 291; A Johnstone (Zimbabwe), M Parsson (Sweden), J Pinsent (GB), S Ballesteros (Spain), C Pavin (USA) 292; P Senior (Australia), R Rafferty (N Ireland), D Russell (GB) 293; D Watson (South Africa), M Mouland (GB), G Brand, Jr (GB), B Gallacher (GB), H Clark (GB), T Watson (USA) 294; N Faldo (GB), E Rodriguez (Spain) 295; L Nelson (USA), P Fowler (Australia) 296; D Whelan (GB) 298; D Williams (GB) 300; V Somers (Australia) 301; R Charles (New Zealand) retired.

1986 at Turnberry

Entries 1,347. Regional qualifying courses: Glenbervie, Haggs Castle, Hankley Common, Langley Park, Lindrick, Little Aston, Ormskirk, Porters Park. Final qualifying courses: Glasgow Gailes, Kilmarnock (Barassie), Prestwick St Nicholas, Western Gailes. Qualified for final 36 holes: 77 Professionals. Non-qualifiers after 36 holes: 74 (71 Professionals, 3 Amateurs) with scores of 152 and above.

Name	Score	Prize Money £
G Norman (Australia)	74, 63, 74, 69-280	70,000
GJ Brand (GB)	71, 68, 75, 71-285	50,000
B Langer (W Germany)	72, 70, 76, 68-286	35,000
I Woosnam (GB)	70, 74, 70, 72-286	35,000
N Faldo (GB)	71, 70, 76, 70-287	25,000
S Ballesteros (Spain)	76, 75, 73, 64-288	25,000
G Koch (USA)	73, 72, 72, 71-288	25,000
F Zoeller (USA)	75, 73, 72, 69-289	17,333
B Marchbank (GB)	78, 70, 72, 69-289	17,333
T Nakajima (Japan)	74, 67, 71, 77-289	17,333
C O'Connor Jr (Ireland)	75, 71, 75, 69-290	14,000
D Graham (Australia)	75, 73, 70, 72-290	14,000
J-M Canizares (Spain)	76, 68, 73, 73-290	14,000
C Strange (USA)	79, 69, 74, 69-291	11,500
A Bean (USA)	74, 73, 73, 71-291	11,500
A Forsbrand (Sweden)	71, 73, 77, 71-292	9,000
J-M Olazabal (Spain)	78, 69, 72, 73-292	9,000
R Floyd (USA)	78, 67, 73, 74-292	9,000
R Charles (New Zealand)	76, 72, 73, 72-293	7,250
M Pinero (Spain)	78, 71, 70, 74-293	7,250
R Rafferty (N Ireland)	75, 74, 75, 70-294	5,022
D Cooper (GB)	72, 79, 72, 71-294	5,022
V Somers (Australia)	73, 77, 72, 72-294	5,022
B Crenshaw (USA)	77, 69, 75, 73-294	5,022
R Lee (GB)	71, 75, 75, 73-294	5,022
P Parkin (GB)	78, 70, 72, 74-294	5,022
D Edwards (USA)	77, 73, 70, 74-294	5,022
V Fernandez (Argentina)	78, 70, 71, 75-294	5,022
S Torrance (GB)	78, 69, 71, 76-294	5,022

The Open Championship
continued

Other Totals

I Stanley (Australia), J Mahaffey (USA), M Karamoto (Japan), DA Weibring (USA), A Lyle (Scotland) 295; T Watson (USA), R Chapman (England), A Brooks (Scotland), R Commans (USA), M James (England), P Stewart (USA), G Player (South Africa), G Turner (New Zealand) 296; R Maltbie (USA), M O'Meara (USA), HM Chung (Taiwan) 297; J Nicklaus (USA), M O'Grady (USA), T Charnley (England), F Couples (USA), M Clayton (Australia), L Mize (USA), J Hawkes (South Africa), LS Chuen (Taiwan), R Tway (USA), T Armour III (USA) 298; S Randolph (USA), G Marsh (Australia), C Mason (England) 300; M McNulty (Zimbabwe), M Mackenzie (England), L Trevino (USA), E Darcy (Ireland), T Lamore (USA), F Nobilo (New Zealand) 301; A Chandler (England), J Heggarty (N Ireland), M Gray (Scotland), D Hammond (USA), S Simpson (USA) 302; O Moore (Australia), P Fowler (Australia) 303; D Jones (N Ireland), R Drummond (Scotland) 305; T Horton (Scotland) 306; G Weir (Scotland) 307; K Moe (USA) 314; H Green (USA) retired

The Open Championship
continued

1987 at Muirfield

Entries 1,407. Regional qualifying courses: Glenbervie, Haggs Castle, Hankley Common, Langley Park, Lindrick, Little Aston, Ormskirk, Porters Park. Final qualifying courses: Gullane No 1, Longniddry, Luffness New, North Berwick. Qualified for final 36 holes: 78 (76 Professionals, 2 Amateurs). Non-qualifiers after 36 holes: 75 (65 Professionals, 10 Amateurs) with scores of 147 and above.

Name	Score	Prize Money £
N Faldo (GB)	68, 69, 71, 71-279	75,000
R Davis (Australia)	64, 73, 74, 69-280	49,500
P Azinger (USA)	68, 68, 71, 73-280	49,500
B Crenshaw (USA)	73, 68, 72, 68-281	31,000
P tewart (USA)	71, 66, 72, 72-281	31,000
D Frost (S Africa)	70, 68, 70, 74-282	26,000
T Watson (USA)	69, 69, 71, 74-283	23,000
I Woosnam (GB)	71, 69, 72, 72-284	18,666
N Price (Zimbabwe)	68, 71, 72, 73-284	18,666
C Stadler (USA)	69, 69, 71, 75-284	18,666
M McNulty (Zimbabwe)	71, 69, 75, 70-285	13,500
H Sutton (USA)	71, 70, 73, 71-285	13,500
J-M Olazabal (Spain)	70, 73, 70, 72-285	13,500
M Ozaki (Japan)	69, 72, 71, 73-285	13,500
M Calcavecchia (USA)	69, 70, 72, 74-285	13,500
G Marsh (Australia)	69, 70, 72, 74-285	13,500
W Grady (Australia)	70, 71, 76, 69-286	7,450
AWB Lyle (GB)	76, 69, 71, 70-286	7,450
E Darcy (Ireland)	74, 69, 72, 71-286	7,450
B Langer (W Germany)	69, 69, 76, 72-286	7,450
L Trevino (USA)	67, 74, 73, 72-286	7,450
M Roe (GB)	74, 68, 72, 72-286	7,450
K Brown (GB)	69, 73, 70, 74-286	7,450
R Floyd (USA)	72, 68, 70, 76-286	7,450
G Taylor (Australia)	69, 68, 75, 75-287	5,300
D Feherty (Ireland)	74, 70, 77, 67-288	4,933
G Brand Jr (GB)	73, 70, 75, 70-288	4,933
L Mize (USA)	68, 71, 76, 73-288	4,933

Other Totals

L Wadkins (USA), F Zoeller (USA), K Green (USA), D Edwards (USA), A Forsbrand (Sweden) 289; D Graham (Australia) 290; R Drummond (GB), M Calero (Spain), J Haas (USA), G Norman (Australia), R Tway (USA) 291; D Cooper (GB), F Couples (USA), A Bean (USA), GJ Brand (GB) 292; F Allem (S Africa), B Marshbank (GB), O Moore (Australia), C Mason (GB), L Nelson (USA), J Slaughter (USA) 294; M Lanner (Sweden), S Torrance (GB), S Ballesteros (Spain), P Walton (Ireland) 295; J O'Leary (Ireland), R Chapman (GB), W Andrade (USA) 296; O Sellberg (Sweden), P Mayo (GB) 297; B Jones (Australia), W McColl (GB), T Nakajima (Japan) 298; S Simpson (USA), N Hansen (GB), H Clark (GB), M Martin (Spain) 299; M O'Meara (USA), G Player (S Africa), T Ozaki (Japan), H Baiocchi (S Africa), B Chamblee (USA) 300; W Westner (S Africa) 301; J Nicklaus (USA), T Kite (USA) 302; J Hawkes (S Africa) 303; R Willison (GB) 305; C Moody (GB) 306; D Jones (Ireland) 307; A Stevens (GB) 312.

1988 at Royal Lytham & St. Annes

Entries 1,393. Regional qualifying courses: Beau Desert, Camberley Heath, Glenbervie, Hankley Common, Langley Park, Lindrick, Little Aston, Ormskirk, Porters Park. Final qualifying courses: Blackpool North Shore, Fairhaven, Lytham Green Drive, St Annes Old Links. Qualified for final 36 holes: 71 (70 Professionals, 1 Amateur). Non-qualifiers after 36 holes: 83 (76 Professionals, 7 Amateurs) with scores of 149 and above.

Name	Score	Prize Money £
S Ballesteros (Spa.)	67, 71, 70, 65-273	80,000
N Price (Zim.)	70, 67, 69, 69-275	60,000
N Faldo (Eng.)	71, 69, 68, 71-279	47,000
F Couples (USA)	73, 69, 71, 68-281	33,500
G Koch (USA)	71, 72, 70, 68-281	33,500
P Senior (Aus.)	70, 73, 70, 69-282	27,000
I Aoki (Jap.)	72, 71, 73, 67-283	21,000
P Stewart (USA)	73, 75, 68, 67-283	21,000
D Frost S. Africa)	71, 75, 69, 68-283	21,000
A W B Lyle (Sco.)	73, 69, 67, 74-283	21,000
D Russell (Eng.)	71, 74, 69, 70-284	16,500
B Faxon (USA)	69, 74, 70, 71-284	16,500
C Strange (USA)	79, 69, 69, 68-285	14,000
E Romero (Arg.)	72, 71, 69, 73-285	14,000
L Nelson (USA)	73, 71, 68, 73-285	14,000
J Rivero (Spa.)	75, 69, 70, 72-286	10,500
B Crenshaw (USA)	73, 73, 68, 72-286	10,500
A Bean (USA)	71, 70, 71, 74-286	10,500
D Pooley (USA)	70, 73, 69, 74-286	10,500
T Kite (USA)	75, 71, 73, 68-287	7,000
R Davis (Aus.)	76, 71, 72, 68-287	7,000
G Brand Jr (Sco.)	72, 76, 68, 71-287	7,000
B Tway (USA)	71, 71, 72, 73-287	7,000
R Charles (NZ)	71, 74, 69, 73-287	7,000
J Nicklaus (USA)	75, 70, 75, 68-288	5,500
I Woosnam (Wal.)	76, 71, 72, 69-288	5,500
M O'Meara (USA)	75, 69, 75, 70-289	5,200
H Clark (Eng.)	71, 72, 75, 72-290	4,600
M McNulty (Zim.)	73, 73, 72, 72-290	4,600
T Watson (USA)	74, 72, 72, 72-290	4,600
C Beck (USA)	72, 71, 74, 73-290	4,600
T Armour III (USA)	73, 72, 72, 73-290	4,600
J Benepe III (USA)	75, 72, 70, 73-290	4,600
W Riley (Aus.)	72, 71, 72, 76-291	4,150
L Wadkins (USA)	73, 71, 71, 76-291	4,150
G Brand (Eng.)	73, 74, 72, 73-292	3,950
J Olazabal (Spa.)	73, 71, 73, 75-292	3,950

Other Totals

J Haas (USA), N Ratcliffe (Eng.), B Marchbank (Eng.), R Rafferty (Ire), G March (Aus.), C Pavin (USA), D Russell (Eng.), W Grady (Aus.), K Brown (Eng.) 293; P Kent (Eng.), S Torrance (Sco.), P Azinger (USA), A North (USA), M McCumber (USA) 294; P Fowler (Aus.), F Zoeller (USA), P Walton (Eng.), H Green (USA), J Miller (USA) 295; M Smith (Eng.), C Mason (Eng), P Broadhurst (Am.) (Eng.) 296; C Stadler (USA), G J Player (S. Africa) 297; M James (Eng.), S Bishop (Eng.), A Sherborne (Eng.) 298; M Pinero (Spa.) 299; P Carman 301; G Bruckner, C-H Hsieh 302; B Langer (W. Ger.) 303; G Stafford 305; P Mitchell 308.

United States Open Championship

Year	Winner	Runner-up	Venue	By
1894	W Dunn	W Campbell	St Andrews, NY	2 holes

After 1894 decided by medal play

Year	Winner	Venue	Score
1895	HJ Rawlins	Newport	173
1896	J Foulis	Southampton	152
1897	J Lloyd	Wheaton, Ill	162
1898	F Herd	Shinnecock Hills	328
72 holes played from 1898			
1899	W Smith	Baltimore	315
1900	H Vardon (Eng)	Wheaton, Ill	313
1901	W Anderson	Myopia, Mass	315
1902	L Auchterlonie	Garden City	305
1903	W Anderson	Baltusrol	307
1904	W Anderson	Glenview	304
1905	W Anderson	Myopia, Mass	335
1906	A Smith	Onwentsia	291
1907	A Ross	Chestnut Hill, Pa	302
1908	F McLeod	Myopia, Mass	322
1909	G Sargent	Englewood, NJ	290

Year	Winner	Venue	Score
1910	A Smith	Philadelphia	289
(After a tie with JJ McDermott and Macdonald Smith)			
1911	JJ McDermott	Wheaton, Ill	307
1912	JJ McDermott	Buffalo, NY	294
1913	F Ouimet (Am)	Brookline, Mass	304
(After a tie with H Vardon and E Ray)			
1914	W Hagen	Midlothian	297
1915	JD Travers (Am)	Baltusrol	290
1916	C Evans (Am)	Minneapolis	286
1917-18	No Championship.		
1919	W Hagen	Braeburn	301
1920	E Ray (Eng)	Inverness	295
1921	J Barnes	Washington	289
1922	G Sarazen	Glencoe	288
1923	RT Jones, Jr (Am)	Inwood, LI	295
(After a tie with RA Cruikshank. Play-off: 76; Cruikshank 78)			
1924	C Walker	Oakland Hills	297
1925	W MacFarlane	Worcester	291
1926	RT Jones, Jr (Am)	Scioto	293
1927	TD Armour	Oakmont	301
(After a tie with H Cooper. Play-off: Armour 76; Cooper 79)			
1928	J Farrell	Olympia Fields	294
(After a tie with RT Jones, Jr. Play-off: Farrell 143; Jones 144)			
1929	RT Jones, Jr (Am)	Winged Foot, NY	294
(After a tie with A Espinosa. Play-off: Jones 141; Espinosa 164)			
1930	RT Jones, Jr (Am)	Interlachen	287
1931	B Burke	Inverness	292
(After a tie with G von Elm. Play-off: Burke 149, 148; von Elm 149, 149)			
1932	G Sarazen	Fresh Meadow	286
1933	J Goodman (Am)	North Shore	287
1934	O Dutra	Merion	293
1935	S Parks	Oakmont	299
1936	T Manero	Springfield	282
1937	R Guldahl	Oakland Hills	281
1938	R Guldahl	Cherry Hills	284
1939	Byron Nelson	Philadelphia	284
(After a tie with Craig Wood and D Shute)			
1940	W Lawson Little	Canterbury, Ohio	287
(After a tie with G Sarazen. Tie scores: Little 70; Sarazen 73)			
1941	Craig Wood	Fort Worth, Texas	284
1942-45	No Championship.		
1946	Lloyd Mangrum	Canterbury	284
(After a tie with Byron Nelson and Vic Ghezzie)			
1947	Lew Worsham	St Louis	282
(After a tie with Sam Snead. Replay scores: Worsham 69; Snead 70)			
1948*	Ben Hogan	Los Angeles	276
1949	Dr Cary Middlecoff	Medinah, Ill	286
1950	Ben Hogan	Merion, Pa	287
(After a tie with Lloyd Mangrum and George Fazio. Replay scores: Hogan 69; Mangrum 73; Fazio 75)			
1951	Ben Hogan	Oakland Hills, Mich	287
1952	Julius Boros	Dallas, Texas	281
1953	Ben Hogan	Oakmont	283
1954	Ed Furgol	Baltusrol	284
1955	J Fleck	San Francisco	287
(After a tie with Ben Hogan. Replay scores: Fleck 69; Hogan 72)			
1956	Dr Cary Middlecoff	Rochester	281
1957	Dick Mayer	Inverness	282
(After a tie with Dr Cary Middlecoff. Tie scores: Mayer 72; Middlecoff 79)			
1958	Tommy Bolt	Tulsa, Okla	283
1959	W Casper	Winged Foot, NY	282
1960	Arnold Palmer	Denver, Col	280
1961	Gene Littler	Birmingham, Mich	281
1962	JW Nicklaus	Oakmont	283
(After a tie with Arnold Palmer. Nicklaus 71; Palmer 74)			
1963	Julius Boros	Brookline, Mass	293
(After a tie. Play-off: J Boros, 70; Jack Cupit, 73, Arnold Palmer 76)			
1964	Ken Venturi	Washington	278
1965	Gary Player (SA)	St Louis, Mo	282
(After a tie with KDG Nagle (Aus). Replay scores: Player 71; Nagle 74)			
1966	W Casper	San Francisco	278
(After a tie with Arnold Palmer. Replay scores: Casper 69; Palmer 73)			
1967	JW Nicklaus	Baltusrol	275
1968	Lee Trevino	Rochester	275
1969	Orville Moody	Houston, Texas	281
1970	A Jacklin (Eng)	Chaska, Minn	281
1971	L Trevino	Merion, Pa	280
(After a tie with JW Nicklaus. Play-off: Trevino 68; Nicklaus 71)			
1972	JW Nicklaus	Pebble Beach	290
1973	J Miller	Oakmont, Pa	279
1974	H Irwin	Winged Foot, NY	287
1975	L Graham	Medinah, Ill	287
(After a tie with Mahaffey. Play-off: Graham 71; Mahaffey 73)			

United States Open Championship

continued

Year	Winner	Venue	Score
1976	J Pate	Atlanta, Georgia	277
1977	H Green	Southern Hills, Tulsa	278
1978	A North	Cherry Hills	285
1979	H Irwin	Inverness, Ohio	284
1980	JW Nicklaus	Baltusrol	272
1981	D Graham (Aus)	Merion, Pa	273
1982	T Watson	Pebble Beach	282
1983	L Nelson	Oakmont, Pa	280
1984	F Zoeller	Winged Foot	276

(After tie with G Norman (Aus). Play-off: Zoeller 67; Norman 75)

1985	A North	Oakland Hills, Mich	279
1986	R Floyd	Shinnecock Hills, NY	279
1987	S Simpson	Olympic, San Francisco, Cal	277
1988	C Strange	Brookline, Mass.	278

(After a tie with N Faldo (GB). Play-off Strange 71, Faldo 75)

1989	C Strange	Rochester, NY	278

United States Open Championship

continued

United States Masters' Championship

Venue – Augusta National Golf Course, Augusta, Georgia

Year	Winner	Score	Year	Winner	Score
1934	Horton Smith	284	1965	JW Nicklaus	271
1935	Gene Sarazen	282	1966	JW Nicklaus	288
1936	Horton Smith	285	1967	G Brewer	280
1937	Byron Nelson	283	1968	R Goalby	277
1938	Henry Picard	285	1969	G Archer	281
1939	Ralph Guldahl	279	1970	W Casper	279
1940	Jimmy Demaret	280	1971	C Coody	279
1941	Craig Wood	280	1972	JW Nicklaus	286
1942	Byron Nelson	280	1973	T Aaron	283
1946	Herman Keiser	282	1974	GJ Player (SA)	278
1947	Jimmy Demaret	281	1975	JW Nicklaus	276
1948	Claude Harmon	279	1976	R Floyd	271
1949	Sam Snead	283	1977	T Watson	276
1950	Jimmy Demaret	282	1978	GJ Player (SA)	277
1951	Ben Hogan	280	1979	F Zoeller	280
1952	Sam Snead	286	1980	S Ballesteros (Spa.)	275
1953	Ben Hogan	274	1981	T Watson	280
1954	Sam Snead	289	1982	C Stadler	284
1955	Cary Middlecoff	279	1983	S Ballesteros (Spa.)	280
1956	Jackie Burke	289	1984	B Crenshaw	277
1957	Doug Ford	283	1985	B Langer (WG)	282
1958	Arnold Palmer	284	1986	JW Nicklaus	279
1959	A Wall	284	1987	L Mize	285
1960	Arnold Palmer	282	(After a tie)		
1961	GJ Player (SA)	280	1988	AWB Lyle (GB)	281
1962	Arnold Palmer	280	1989	N Faldo (GB)	283
1963	JW Nicklaus	286	(After a tie)		
1964	Arnold Palmer	276			

United States PGA Championship

Year	Winner	Runner-up	Venue	By
1916	Jim Barnes	Jock Hutchison	Siwanoy	1 hole
1919	Jim Barnes	Fred McLeod	Engineers' Club	6 and 5
1920	Jock Hutchison	Douglas Edgar	Flossmoor	1 hole
1921	Walter Hagen	Jim Barnes	Inwood Club	3 and 2
1922	Gene Sarazen	Emmet French	Oakmont	4 and 3
1923	Gene Sarazen	Walter Hagen	Pelham	38th hole
1924	Walter Hagen	Jim Barnes	French Lick	2 holes
1925	Walter Hagen	WE Mehlhorn	Olympic Fields	6 and 4
1926	Walter Hagen	Leo Diegel	Salisbury	4 and 3
1927	Walter Hagen	Joe Turnesa	Dallas, Texas	1 hole
1928	Leo Diegel	Al Espinosa	Five Farms	6 and 5
1929	Leo Diegel	J Farrell	Hill Crest	6 and 4
1930	TD Armour	G Sarazen	Fresh Meadow	1 hole
1931	T Creavy	D Shute	Wannamoisett	2 and 1
1932	O Dutra	F Walsh	St Paul, Minnesota	4 and 3
1933	G Sarazen	W Goggin	Milwaukee	5 and 4

United States PGA Championship continued

Year	Winner	Runner-up	Venue	By
1934	P Runyan	Craig Wood	Buffalo	38th hole
1935	J Revolta	TD Armour	Oklahoma	5 and 4
1936	D Shute	J Thomson	Pinehurst	3 and 2
1937	D Shute	H McSpaden	Pittsburgh	37th hole
1938	P Runyan	S Snead	Shawnee	8 and 7
1939	H Picard	B Nelson	Pomonok	37th hole
1940	Byron Nelson	Sam Snead	Hershey, Pa	1 hole
1941	Vic Ghezzie	Byron Nelson	Denver, Colo	38th hole
1942	Sam Snead	Jim Turnesa	Atlantic City	2 and 1
1943	*No Championship*			
1944	Bob Hamilton	Byron Nelson	Spokane, Wash	1 hole
1945	Byron Nelson	Sam Byrd	Dayton, Ohio	4 and 3
1946	Ben Hogan	Ed Oliver	Portland	6 and 4
1947	Jim Ferrier	Chick Harbert	Detroit	2 and 1
1948	Ben Hogan	Mike Turnesa	Norwood Hills	7 and 6
1949	Sam Snead	Johnny Palmer	Richmond, Va	3 and 2
1950	Chandler Harper	Henry Williams	Scioto, Ohio	4 and 3
1951	Sam Snead	Walter Burkemo	Oakmont, Pa	7 and 6
1952	Jim Turnesa	Chick Harbert	Big Spring, Louisville	1 hole
1953	Walter Burkemo	Felice Lorza	Birmingham, Michigan	2 and 1
1954	Chick Harbert	Walter Burkemo	St Paul, Minnesota	4 and 3
1955	D Ford	C Middlecoff	Detroit	4 and 3
1956	J Burke	T Kroll	Boston	3 and 2
1957	L Hebert	D Finsterwald	Miami Valley, Dayton	3 and 1

Changed to Stroke Play

Year	Winner	Venue	Score
1958	D Finsterwald	Llanerch, PA	276
1959	Bob Rosburg	Minneapolis, MN	277
1960	Jay Hebert	Firestone, Akron, OH	281
1961	Jerry Barber*	Olympia Fields, IL	277
1962	GJ Player	Aronimink, PA	278
1963	JW Nicklaus	Dallas, TX	279
1964	Bobby Nichols	Columbus, OH	271
1965	D Marr	Laurel Valley, PA	280
1966	Al Geiberger	Firestone, Akron, OH	280
1967	Don January*	Columbine, CO	281
1968	Julius Boros	Pecan Valley, TX	281
1969	Ray Floyd	Dayton, OH	276
1970	Dave Stockton	Southern Hills, OK	279
1971	JW Nicklaus	PGA National, FL	281
1972	GJ Player	Oakland Hills, MI	281
1973	JW Nicklaus	Canterbury, OH	277
1974	L Trevino	Tanglewood, NC	276
1975	JW Nicklaus	Firestone, Akron, OH	276
1976	D Stockton	Congressional, MD	281
1977	L Wadkins*	Pebble Beach, CA	287
1978	J Mahaffey*	Oakmont, PA	276
1979	D Graham*	Oakland Hills, MI	272
1980	JW Nicklaus	Oak Hill, NY	274
1981	L Nelson	Atlanta, GA	273
1982	R Floyd	Southern Hills, OK	272
1983	H Sutton	Pacific Palisades, CA	274
1984	L Trevino	Shoal Creek	273
1985	H Green	Cherry Hills, Denver, CO	278
1986	R Tway	Inverness, Toledo, OH	276
1987	L Nelson*	PGA National, FL	287

*(*After a tie)*

1988	J Sluman	Oaktree, OK	272
1989	P Stewart	Kemper Lakes, IL	276

Ladies' Major Championships

Ladies' British Open Championship
Instituted 1976

Year	Winner	Club/Country	Venue	Score
1976	Miss J Lee Smith	Gosforth Park	Fulford	299
1977	Miss V Saunders	Tyrrells Wood	Lindrick	306
1978	Miss J Melville	Furness	Foxhills	310
1979	Miss A Sheard	South Africa	Southport and Ainsdale	301
1980	Miss D Massey	USA	Wentworth (East)	294
1981	Miss D Massey	USA	Northumberland	295
1982	M Figueras-Dom	Spain	Birkdale	296
1983	*Not played*			
1984	A Okamoto	Japan	Woburn	289
1985	Mrs B King	USA	Moor Park	300
1986	Miss L Davies	GB	Birkdale	283
1987	Miss A Nicholas	GB	St Mellion	296
1988	Miss C Dibnah / Miss S Little	Australia / South Africa } tie	Lindrick	296
(Dibnah won at second play-off hole)				
1989	Miss J Geddes	USA	Ferndown	274

United States Ladies' Open Championship
(American unless stated)

Year	Winner	Venue	By
1946	Miss P Berg	Spokane	5 and 4
Changed to stroke play			

Year	Winner	Venue	Score
1947	Miss B Jamieson	Greensboro	300
1948	Mrs C Zaharias	Atlantic City	300
1949	Miss Louise Suggs	Maryland	291
1950	Mrs G Zaharias	Wichita	291
1951	Miss B Rawls	Atlanta	294
1952	Miss L Suggs	Bala, Philadelphia	284
1953	Miss B Rawls	Rochester, NY	302
(After a tie with Mrs J Pung)			
1954	Mrs G Zaharias	Peabody, Mass	291
1955	Miss F Crocker	Wichita	299
1956	Mrs K Cornelius	Duluth	302
(After a tie with Miss B McIntire)			
1957	Miss B Rawls	Mamaroneck	299
1958	Miss M Wright	Bloomfield Hills, Mich	290
1959	Miss M Wright	Pittsburgh, Pa	287
1960	Miss B Rawls	Worchester, Mass	292
1961	Miss M Wright	Springfield, NJ	293
1962	Mrs M Lindstrom	Myrtle Beach	301
1963	Miss M Mills	Kenwood	289
1964	Miss M Wright	San Diego	290
(After a tie with Miss Ruth Jessen, Seattle)			
1965	Miss C Mann	Northfield, NJ	290
1966	Miss S Spuzich	Hazeltine National GC, Minn	297

Year	Winner	Venue	Score
1967	Miss C Lacoste (Fra.)	Hot Springs, Virginia	294
1968	Mrs SM Berning	Moselem Springs, Pa	289
1969	Miss D Caponi	Scenic-Hills	294
1970	Miss D Caponi	Muskogee, Okla	287
1971	Mrs J Gunderson-Cartner	Erie, Pa	288
1972	Mrs SM Berning	Mamaroneck, NY	299
1973	Mrs SM Berning	Rochester, NY	290
1974	Miss S Haynie	La Grange, Ill	295
1975	Miss S Palmer	Northfield, NJ	295
1976	Mrs J Carner	Springfield, Pa	292
(After a tie with Miss S Palmer)			
1977	Miss H Stacy	Hazeltine, Minn	292
1978	Miss H Stacy	Indianapolis	299
1979	Miss J Britz	Brooklawn, Conn	284
1980	Miss A Alcott	Richland, Tenn	280
1981	Miss P Bradley	La Grange, Illinois	279
1982	Mrs J Alex	Del Paso, Sacramento	283
1983	Miss J Stephenson (Aus.)	Broken Arrow, Oklahoma	290
1984	Miss H Stacy	Salem, Mass	290
1985	Miss K Baker	Baltusrol, NJ	280
1986	Miss J Geddes	NCR	287
1987	Miss L Davies (GB)	Plainfield	285
(After a tie with Mrs J Carner and Miss A Akamoto (Jpn))			
1988	Miss L Neumann (Swe)	Baltimore	277
1989	Miss B King	Indianwood, MI	278

United States Ladies' Open Championship

continued

British and Irish National Championships

Amateur Championship

Year	Winner	Runner-up	Venue	By	Ent
1885	AF MacFie	HG Hutchinson	Hoylake	7 and 6	44
1886	HG Hutchinson	H Lamb	St Andrews	7 and 6	42
1887	HG Hutchinson	J Ball	Hoylake	1 hole	33
1888	J Ball	JE Laidlay	Prestwick	5 and 4	38
1889	JE Laidlay	LMB Melville	St Andrews	2 and 1	40
1890	J Ball	JE Laidlay	Hoylake	4 and 3	44
1891	JE Laidlay	HH Hilton	St Andrews	20th hole	50
1892	J Ball	HH Hilton	Sandwich	3 and 1	45
1893	P Anderson	JE Laidlay	Prestwick	1 hole	44
1894	J Ball	SM Fergusson	Hoylake	1 hole	64
1895	LMB Melville	J Ball	St Andrews	19th hole	68
1896*	FG Tait	HH Hilton	Sandwich	8 and 7	64

*36 holes played on and after this date

Year	Winner	Runner-up	Venue	By	Ent
1897	AJT Allan	J Robb	Muirfield	4 and 2	74
1898	FG Tait	SM Fergusson	Hoylake	7 and 5	77
1899	J Ball	FG Tait	Prestwick	37th hole	101
1900	HH Hilton	J Robb	Sandwich	8 and 7	68
1901	HH Hilton	JL Low	St Andrews	1 hole	116
1902	C Hutchings	SH Fry	Hoylake	1 hole	114
1903	R Maxwell	HG Hutchinson	Muirfield	7 and 5	142
1904	WJ Travis (USA)	E Blackwell	Sandwich	4 and 3	104
1905	AG Barry	Hon O Scott	Prestwick	3 and 2	148
1906	J Robb	CC Lingen	Hoylake	4 and 3	166
1907	J Ball	CA Palmer	St Andrews	6 and 4	200
1908	EA Lassen	HE Taylor	Sandwich	7 and 6	197
1909	R Maxwell	Capt CK Hutchison	Muirfield	1 hole	170
1910	J Ball	C Aylmer	Hoylake	10 and 9	160
1911	HH Hilton	EA Lassen	Prestwick	4 and 3	146
1912	J Ball	A Mitchell	Westward Ho!	38th hole	134
1913	HH Hilton	R Harris	St Andrews	6 and 5	198
1914	JLC Jenkins	CO Hezlet	Sandwich	3 and 2	232
1915-19	No Championship owing to the Great War				
1920	CJH Tolley	RA Gardner (USA)	Muirfield	37th hole	165
1921	WI Hunter	AJ Graham	Hoylake	12 and 11	223
1922	EWE Holderness	J Caven	Prestwick	1 hole	252
1923	RH Wethered	R Harris	Deal	7 and 6	209
1924	EWE Holderness	EF Storey	St Andrews	3 and 2	201
1925	R Harris	KF Fradgley	Westward Ho!	13 and 12	151
1926	J Sweetser (USA)	AF Simpson	Muirfield	6 and 5	216
1927	Dr W Tweddell	DE Landale	Hoylake	7 and 6	197
1928	TP Perkins	RH Wethered	Prestwick	6 and 4	220
1929	CJH Tolley	JN Smith	Sandwich	4 and 3	253
1930	RT Jones (USA)	RH Wethered	St Andrews	7 and 6	271
1931	EM Smith	J De Forest	Westward Ho!	1 hole	171
1932	J De Forest	EW Fiddian	Muirfield	3 and 1	235
1933	Hon M Scott	TA Bourn	Hoylake	4 and 3	269
1934	W Lawson Little (USA)	J Wallace	Prestwick	14 and 13	225
1935	W Lawson Little (USA)	Dr W Tweddell	Lytham St Annes	1 hole	232
1936	H Thomson	J Ferrier (Aus.)	St Andrews	2 holes	283
1937	R Sweeney, Jun (USA)	LO Munn	Sandwich	3 and 2	223
1938	CR Yates (USA)	RC Ewing	Troon	3 and 2	241
1939	AT Kyle	AA Duncan	Hoylake	2 and 1	167
1940-45	Suspended during Second World War				
1946	J Bruen	R Sweeny (USA)	Birkdale	4 and 3	263
1947	WP Turnesa (USA)	RD Chapman (USA)	Carnoustie	3 and 2	200
1948	FR Stranahan (USA)	C Stowe	Sandwich	5 and 4	168
1949	SM McCready	WP Turnesa (USA)	Portmarnock	2 and 1	204
1950	FR Stranahan (USA)	RD Chapman (USA)	St Andrews	8 and 6	324
1951	RD Chapman (USA)	CR Coe (USA)	Porthcawl	5 and 4	192

Amateur
Championship
continued

Year	Winner	Runner-up	Venue	By	Ent
1952	EH Ward (USA)	FR Stranahan (USA)	Prestwick	6 and 5	286
1953	JB Carr	E Harvie Ward (USA)	Hoylake	2 holes	279
1954	DW Bachli (Aus.)	WC Campbell (USA)	Muirfield	2 and 1	286
1955	JW Conrad (USA)	A Slater	Lytham St Annes	3 and 2	240
1956*	JC Beharrell	LG Taylor	Troon	5 and 4	200
1957*	R Reid Jack	HB Ridgley (USA)	Formby	2 and 1	200

*In 1956 and 1957 the Quarter Finals, Semi-Finals and Final were played over 36 holes

Year	Winner	Runner-up	Venue	By	Ent
1958*	JB Carr	A Thirlwell	St Andrews	3 and 2	488

In 1958, Semi-Finals and Final only were played over 36 holes

Year	Winner	Runner-up	Venue	By	Ent
1959	DR Beman (USA)	W Hyndman (USA)	Sandwich	3 and 2	362
1960	JB Carr	R Cochran (USA)	Portrush	8 and 7	183
1961	MF Bonallack	J Walker	Turnberry	6 and 4	250
1962	RD Davies (USA)	J Povall	Hoylake	1 hole	256
1963	MSR Lunt	JG Blackwell	St Andrews	2 and 1	256
1964	GJ Clark	MSR Lunt	Ganton	39th hole	220
1965	MF Bonallack	CA Clark	Porthcawl	2 and 1	176
1966	RE Cole (SA)	RDBM Shade	Carnoustie (18 holes)	3 and 2	206
1967	RB Dickson (USA)	RJ Cerrudo (USA)	Formby	2 and 1	
1968	MF Bonallack	JB Carr	Troon	7 and 6	249
1969	MF Bonallack	W Hyndman (USA)	Hoylake	3 and 2	245
1970	MF Bonallack	W Hyndman (USA)	Newcastle Co Down	8 and 7	256
1971	S Melnyk (USA)	J Simons (USA)	Carnoustie	3 and 2	256
1972	T Homer	A Thirlwell	Sandwich	4 and 3	253
1973	R Siderowf (USA)	PH Moody	Porthcawl	5 and 3	222
1974	T Homer	J Gabrielsen (USA)	Muirfield	2 holes	330
1975	MM Giles (USA)	MH James	Hoylake	8 and 7	206
1976	R Siderowf (USA)	JC Davies	St Andrews	37th hole	289
1977	P McEvoy	HM Campbell	Ganton	5 and 4	235
1978	P McEvoy	PJ McKellar	Troon	4 and 3	353
1979	J Sigel (USA)	S Hoch (USA)	Hillside	3 and 2	285
1980	D Evans	D Suddards (SA)	Porthcawl	4 and 3	265
1981	P Ploujoux (Fr)	J Hirsch (USA)	St Andrews	4 and 2	256
1982	M Thompson	A Stubbs	Deal	4 and 3	245
1983	AP Parkin	J Holtgrieve (USA)	Turnberry	5 and 4	288
1984	J-M Olazabal (Spa)	C Montgomerie	Formby	5 and 4	291
1985	G McGimpsey	G Homewood	Dornoch	8 and 7	457
1986	D Curry	G Birtwell	Lytham St Annes	11 and 9	427
1987	P Mayo	P McEvoy	Prestwick	3 and 1	373
1988	C Hardin (Swe)	B Fouchee (SA)	Porthcawl	1 hole	391
1989	S Dodd	C Cassells	R. Birkdale	5 and 3	378

Senior Open Amateur Championship

Year	Winner	Venue	Score
1969	R Pattinson	Formby	154
1970	K Bamber	Prestwick	150
1971	GH Pickard	Deal	150
1972	TC Hartley	St Andrews	147
1973	JT Jones	Hoylake	142
1974	MA Ivor-Jones	Moortown	149
1975	HJ Roberts	Turnberry	138
1976	WM Crichton	Berkshire	149
1977	Dr TE Donaldson	Panmure	228
1978	RJ White	Formby	225
1979	RJ White	Harlech	226
1980	JM Cannon	Prestwick St Nicholas	218
1981	T Branton	Hoylake	227
1982	RL Glading	Blairgowrie	218
1983	AJ Swann (USA)	Walton Heath	222
1984	JC Owens (USA)	Western Gailes	222
1985	D Morey (USA)	Hesketh	223
1986	AN Sturrock	Panmure	229
1987	B Soyars (USA)	Deal	226
1988	CW Green	Barnton, Edinburgh	221
1989	CW Green	Moortown and Alwoodley	226

Ladies' British Open Amateur Championship

Year	Winner	Runner-up	Venue	By
1893	Lady Margaret Scott	Miss I Pearson	St Annes	7 and 5
1894	Lady Margaret Scott	Miss I Pearson	Littlestone	3 and 2
1895	Lady Margaret Scott	Miss E Lythgoe	Portrush	5 and 4
1896	Miss Pascoe	Miss L Thomson	Hoylake	3 and 2
1897	Miss EC Orr	Miss Orr	Gullane	4 and 2
1898	Miss L Thomson	Miss EC Neville	Yarmouth	7 and 5
1899	Miss M Hezlet	Miss Magill	Newcastle Co Down	2 and 1
1900	Miss Adair	Miss Neville	Westward Ho!	6 and 5
1901	Miss Graham	Miss Adair	Aberdovey	3 and 1
1902	Miss M Hezlet	Miss E Neville	Deal	19th hole
1903	Miss Adair	Miss F Walker-Leigh	Portrush	4 and 3
1904	Miss L Dod	Miss M Hezlet	Troon	1 hole
1905	Miss B Thompson	Miss ME Stuart	Cromer	3 and 2
1906	Mrs Kennon	Miss B Thompson	Burnham	4 and 3
1907	Miss M Hezlet	Miss F Hezlet	Newcastle Co Down	2 and 1
1908	Miss M Titterton	Miss D Campbell	St Andrews	19th hole
1909	Miss D Campbell	Miss F Hezlet	Birkdale	4 and 3
1910	Miss Grant Suttie	Miss L Moore	Westward Ho!	6 and 4
1911	Miss D Campbell	Miss V Hezlet	Portrush	3 and 2
1912	Miss G Ravenscroft	Miss S Temple	Turnberry	3 and 2
(Final played over 36 holes after 1912)				
1913	Miss M Dodd	Miss Chubb	St Annes	8 and 6
1914	Miss C Leitch	Miss G Ravenscroft	Hunstanton	2 and 1
1915-18	*No Championship owing to the Great War*			
1919	*Should have been played at Burnham in October, but abandoned owing to Railway Strike*			
1920	Miss C Leitch	Miss M Griffiths	Newcastle Co Down	7 and 6
1921	Miss C Leitch	Miss J Wethered	Turnberry	4 and 3
1922	Miss J Wethered	Miss C Leitch	Prince's, Sandwich	9 and 7
1923	Miss D Chambers	Miss A Macbeth	Burnham, Somerset	2 holes
1924	Miss J Wethered	Mrs Cautley	Portrush	7 and 6
1925	Miss J Wethered	Miss C Leitch	Troon	37th hole
1926	Miss C Leitch	Mrs Garon	Harlech	8 and 7
1927	Miss Thion de la Chaume (Fra.)	Miss Pearson	Newcastle Co Down	5 and 4
1928	Miss N Le Blan (Fra.)	Miss S Marshall	Hunstanton	3 and 2
1929	Miss J Wethered	Miss G Collett (USA)	St Andrews	3 and 1
1930	Miss D Fishwick	Miss G Collett (USA)	Formby	4 and 3
1931	Miss E Wilson	Miss W Morgan	Portmarnock	7 and 6
1932	Miss E Wilson	Miss CPR Montgomery	Saunton	7 and 6
1933	Miss E Wilson	Miss D Plumpton	Gleneagles	5 and 4
1934	Mrs AM Holm	Miss P Barton	Porthcawl	6 and 5
1935	Miss W Morgan	Miss P Barton	Newcastle Co Down	3 and 2
1936	Miss P Barton	Miss B Newell	Southport and Ainsdale	5 and 3
1937	Miss J Anderson	Miss D Park	Turnberry	6 and 4
1938	Mrs AM Holm	Miss E Corlett	Burnham	4 and 3
1939	Miss P Barton	Mrs T Marks	Portrush	2 and 1
1940-45	*No Championship owing to Second World War*			
1946	Mrs GW Hetherington	Miss P Garvey	Hunstanton	1 hole
1947	Mrs G Zaharias (USA)	Miss J Gordon	Gullane	5 and 4
1948	Miss L Suggs (USA)	Miss J Donald	Lytham St Annes	1 hole
1949	Miss F Stephens	Mrs V Reddan	Harlech	5 and 4
1950	Vicomtesse de Saint Sauveur (Fra.)	Mrs G Valentine	Newcastle Co Down	3 and 2
1951	Mrs PG MacCann	Miss F Stephens	Broadstone	4 and 3
1952	Miss M Paterson	Miss F Stephens	Troon	39th hole
1953	Miss M Stewart (Can)	Miss P Garvey	Porthcawl	7 and 6
1954	Miss F Stephens	Miss E Price	Ganton	4 and 3
1955	Mrs G Valentine	Miss B Romack (USA)	Portrush	7 and 6
1956	Miss M Smith (USA)	Miss MP Janssen (USA)	Sunningdale	8 and 7
1957	Miss P Garvey	Mrs G Valentine	Gleneagles	4 and 3
1958	Mrs G Valentine	Miss E Price	Hunstanton	1 hole
1959	Miss E Price	Miss B McCorkindale	Ascot	37th hole
1960	Miss B McIntyre (USA)	Miss P Garvey	Harlech	4 and 2
1961	Mrs AD Spearman	Miss DJ Robb	Carnoustie	7 and 6
1962	Mrs AD Spearman	Mrs MF Bonallack	Birkdale	1 hole
1963	Miss B Varangot (Fra.)	Miss P Garvey	Newcastle Co Down	3 and 1
1964	Miss C Sorenson (USA)	Miss BAB Jackson	Prince's, Sandwich	37th hole
1965	Miss B Varangot (Fra.)	Mrs IC Robertson	St Andrews	4 and 3
1966	Miss E Chadwick	Miss V Saunders	Ganton	3 and 2
1967	Miss E Chadwick	Miss M Everard	Harlech	1 hole
1968	Miss B Varangot (Fra.)	Mrs C Rubin (Fra.)	Walton Heath	20th hole

Year	Winner	Runner up	Venue	By
1969	Miss C Lacoste (Fra.)	Miss A Irvin	Portrush	1 hole
1970	Miss D Oxley	Mrs IC Robertson	Gullane	1 hole
1971	Miss M Walker	Miss B Huke	Alwoodley	3 and 1
1972	Miss M Walker	Mrs C Rubin (Fra.)	Hunstanton	2 holes
1973	Miss A Irvin	Miss Michelle Walker	Carnoustie	3 and 2
1974	Miss C Semple (USA)	Mrs MF Bonallack	Porthcawl	2 and 1
1975	Mrs N Syms (USA)	Miss S Cadden	St Andrews	3 and 2
1976	Miss C Panton	Miss A Sheard	Silloth	1 hole
1977	Mrs A Uzielli	Miss V Marvin	Hillside	6 and 5
1978	Miss E Kennedy (Aus.)	Miss J Greenhalgh	Notts	1 hole
1979	Miss M Madill	Miss J Lock (Aus.)	Nairn	2 and 1
1980	Mrs A Quast (USA)	Mrs L Wollin (Swe.)	Woodhall Spa	3 and 1
1981	Mrs IC Robertson	Miss W Aitken	Conway	20th hole
1982	Miss K Douglas	Miss G Stewart	Walton Heath	4 and 2
1983	Mrs J Thornhill	Miss R Lautens (Switz.)	Silloth	4 and 2
1984	Miss J Rosenthal (USA)	J Brown	Royal Troon	4 and 3
1985	Miss L Beman (Eire)	C Waite	Ganton	1 hole
1986	Miss McGuire (NZ)	L Briars (Aus.)	West Sussex	2 and 1
1987	Miss J Collingham	Miss S Shapcott	Harlech	19th hole
1988	Miss J Furby	Miss J Wade	Deal	4 and 3
1989	Miss H Dobson	Miss E Farquharson	Hoylake	6 and 5

Ladies' British Open Amateur Championship
continued

Ladies' British Open Amateur Stroke Play Championship

Year	Winner	Club	Venue	Score
1969	Miss A Irvin	Lytham St Annes	Gosforth Park	295
1970	Miss M Everard	Hallamshire	Birkdale	313
1971	Mrs IC Robertson	Dunaverty	Ayr Belleisle	302
1972	Mrs IC Robertson	Dunaverty	Silloth	296
1973	Mrs A Stant	Beau Desert	Purdis Heath	298
1974	Miss J Greenhalgh	Pleasington	Seaton Carew	302
1975	Miss J Greenhalgh	Pleasington	Gosforth Park	298
1976*	Miss J Lee Smith	Gosforth Park	Fulford	299
1977*	Miss M Everard	Hallamshire	Lindrick	306
1978*	Miss J Melville	Furness	Foxhills	310
1979	Miss M McKenna	Donabate	Moseley	305
1980	Miss M Mahill	Portstewart	Brancepeth Castle	304
(After a tie with Miss P Wright)				
1981	Miss J Soulsby	Prudhoe	Norwich	300
1982	Miss J Connachan	Musselburgh	Downfield	294
1983	Miss A Nicholas		Moortown	292
1984	Miss C Waite	Swindon	Caernarvonshire	295
1985	Mrs IC Robertson	Dunaverty	Formby	300
1986	Miss C Hourihane		Blairgowrie	291
(After a tie with Miss P Johnson)				
1987	Mrs L Bayman	Princes	Ipswich	297
1988	Miss K Mitchell	Worthing	Porthcawl	317
1989	Miss H Dobson	Seacroft	Southerness	298

*Played concurrently with Ladies' British Open Championship

Senior Ladies' British Open Amateur Stroke Play Championship
Instituted 1981

Year	Winner	Club	Venue	Score
1981	Mrs BM King	Pleasington	Formby	159
1982	Mrs P Riddiford	Royal Ashdown Forest	Ilkley	161
1983	Mrs M Birtwistle		Troon Portland	167
1984	Mme O Semelaigne	France	Woodbridge	152
1985	Dr G Costello	Formby Ladies	Prestatyn	158
1986	Mrs P Riddiford	Royal Ashdown Forest	Longniddry	154
1987	Mme O Semelaigne	France	Copt Heath	152
1988	Mrs C Bailey	Tandridge	Littlestone	156
1989	Mrs C Bailey	Tandridge	Wrexham	149

English Amateur Championship

Year	Winner	Runner-up	Venue	By
1925	TF Ellison	S Robinson	Hoylake	1 hole
1926	TF Ellison	Sq Ldr CH Hayward	Walton Heath	6 and 4
1927	TP Perkins	JB Beddard	Little Aston	2 and 1
1928	JA Stout	TP Perkins	Lytham St Annes	3 and 2
1929	W Sutton	EB Tipping	Northumberland	3 and 2
1930	TA Bourn	CE Hardman	Burnham	3 and 2
1931	LG Crawley	W Sutton	Hunstanton	1 hole
1932	EW Fiddian	AS Bradshaw	Sandwich	1 hole
1933	J Woollam	TA Bourn	Ganton	4 and 3
1934	S Lunt	LG Crawley	Formby	37th hole
1935	J Woollam	EW Fiddian	Hollinwell	2 and 1
1936	HG Bentley	JDA Langley	Deal	5 and 4
1937	JJ Pennink	LG Crawley	Saunton	6 and 5
1938	JJ Pennink	SE Banks	Moortown	2 and 1
1939	AL Bentley	W Sutton	Birkdale	5 and 4
1946	IR Patey	K Thom	Mid-Surrey	5 and 4
1947	GH Micklem	C Stow	Ganton	1 hole
1948	AGB Helm	HJR Roberts	Little Aston	2 and 1
1949	RJ White	C Stowe	Formby	5 and 4
1950	JDA Langley	IR Patey	Deal	1 hole
1951	GP Roberts	H Bennett	Hunstanton	39th hole
1952	E Millward	TJ Shorrock	Burnham and Berrow	2 holes
1953	GH Micklem	RJ White	Birkdale	2 and 1
1954	A Thirlwell	HG Bentley	Sandwich	2 and 1
1955	A Thirlwell	M Burgess	Ganton	7 and 6
1956	GB Wolstenholme	H Bennett	Lytham St Annes	1 hole
1957	A Walker	G Whitehead	Hoylake	4 and 3
1958	DN Sewell	DA Procter	Walton Heath	8 and 7
1959	GB Wolstenholme	MF Bonallack	Formby	1 hole
1960	DN Sewell	MJ Christmas	Hunstanton	41st hole
1961	I Caldwell	GJ Clark	Wentworth	37th hole
1962	MF Bonallack	MSR Lunt	Moortown	2 and 1
1963	MF Bonallack	A Thirlwell	Burnham and Berrow	4 and 3
1964	Dr D Marsh	R Foster	Hollinwell	1 hole
1965	MF Bonallack	CA Clark	Berkshire	3 and 2
1966	MSR Lunt	DJ Millensted	Lytham St Annes	3 and 2
1967	MF Bonallack	GE Hyde	Woodhall Spa	4 and 2
1968	MF Bonallack	PD Kelley	Ganton	12 and 11
1969	JH Cook	P Dawson	Sandwich	6 and 4
1970	Dr D Marsh	SG Birtwell	Birkdale	6 and 4
1971	W Humphreys	JC Davies	Burnham and Berrow	9 and 8
1972	H Ashby	R Revell	Northumberland	5 and 4
1973	H Ashby	SC Mason	Formby	5 and 4
1974	M James	JA Watts	Woodhall Spa	6 and 5
1975	N Faldo	D Eccleston	Lytham St Annes	6 and 4
1976	P Deeble	JC Davies	Ganton	3 and 1
1977	TR Shingler	J Mayell	Walton Heath	4 and 3
1978	P Downes	P Hoad	Birkdale	1 hole
1979	R Chapman	A Carman	Sandwich	6 and 5
1980	P Deeble	P McEvoy	Moortown	4 and 3
1981	D Blakeman	A Stubbs	Burnham and Berrow	3 and 1
1982	A Oldcorn	I Bradshaw	Hoylake	4 and 3
1983	G Laurence	A Brewer	Wentworth	7 and 6
1984	D Gilford	M Gerrard	Woodhall Spa	4 and 3
1985	R Winchester	P Robinson	Little Aston	1 hole
1986	J Langmead	B White	Hillside	2 and 1
1987	K Weeks	R Eggo	Frilford Heath	37th hole
1988	R Claydon	D Curry	Birkdale	38th hole
1989	S Richardson	R Eggo	Sandwich	2 and 1

English Open Amateur Stroke Play Championship

(formerly Brabazon Trophy)

Year	Winner	Club	Venue	Score
1957	D Sewell	Hook Heath	Moortown	287
1958	AH Perowne	Norwich	Birkdale	289
1959	D Sewell	Hook Heath	Hollinwell	300

Year	Winner	Club	Venue	Score
1960	GB Wolstenholme	Sunningdale	Ganton	286
1961	RDBM Shade	Duddingston	Hoylake	284
1962	A Slater	Wakefield	Woodhall Spa	209
1963	RDBM Shade	Duddingston	Birkdale	306
1964	MF Bonallack	Thorpe Hall	Deal	290
1965	CA Clark / DJ Millensted / MJ Burgess } tie	Ganton / Wentworth / West Sussex	Formby	289
1966	PM Townsend	Porters Park	Hunstanton	282
1967	RDBM Shade	Duddingston	Saunton	299
1968	MF Bonallack	Thorpe Hall	Walton Heath	210
1969	R Foster / MF Bonallack } tie	Bradford / Thorpe Hall	Moortown	290
1970	R Foster	Bradford	Little Aston	287
1971	MF Bonallack	Thorpe Hall	Hillside	294
1972	PH Moody	Notts	Hoylake	296
1973	R Revell	Farnham	Hunstanton	294
1974	N Sundelson	South Africa	Moortown	291
1975	AWB Lyle	Hawkstone Park	Hollinwell	298
1976	P Hedges	Langley Park	Saunton	294
1977	AWB Lyle	Hawkstone Park	Hoylake	293
1978	G Brand, Jr	Knowle	Woodhall Spa	289
1979	D Long	Shandon Park	Little Aston	291
1980	R Rafferty / P McEvoy } tie	Warrenpoint / Copt Heath	Hunstanton	293
1981	P Way	Neville	Hillside	292
1982	P Downes	Coventry	Woburn	299
1983	C Banks	Stanton-on-the-Wolds	Hollinwell	294
1984	M Davis	Thorndon Park	Royal Cinque Ports	286
1985	R Roper / P Baker } tie	Catterick Garrison / Lillieshall Park	Seaton Carew	296
1986	R Kaplan	South Africa	Sunningdale	286
1987	JG Robinson	Woodhall Spa	Ganton	287
1988	R Eggo	L'Ancresse	Saunton	289
1989	C Rivett / RN Roderick } tie		Hoylake	293

English Open Amateur Stroke Play Championship

continued

English Seniors Championship
Inaugurated 1981

Year	Winner	Venue	Score
1981	CR Spalding	Copt Heath	152
1982	JL Whitworth	Lindrick	152
1983	B Cawthray	Ross-on-Wye	154
1984	RL Glading	Thetford	150
1985	JR Marriott	Bristol and Clifton	153
1986	R Hiatt	Northants County	153
1987	I Caldwell	North Hants, Fleet	72
		(curtailed due to storm)	
1988	G Edwards	Bromborough	222
1989	G Clark	West Sussex	212

English Mid-Amateur Championship
Inaugurated 1988

Year	Winner	Club	Venue	Score
1988	P McEvoy	Copt Heath	Little Aston	284
1989	A Mew		Moortown	290

English Club Champions

Year	Winner	Second	Venue	Score
1989	Ealing	Southport and Ainsdale	Southport and Ainsdale	289

English County Championship (Men)

Year	Winner	Year	Winner
1928	Warwickshire	1963	Yorkshire
1929	Lancashire	1964	Northumberland
1930	Lancashire	1965	Northumberland
1931	Yorkshire	1966	Surrey
1932	Surrey	1967	Lancashire
1933	Yorkshire	1968	Surrey
1934	Worcestershire	1969	Berks, Bucks, Oxon
1935	Worcestershire	1970	Gloucestershire
1936	Surrey	1971	Staffordshire
1937	Lancashire	1972	Berks, Bucks, Oxon
1938	Staffordshire	1973	Yorkshire
1939	Worcestershire	1974	Lincolnshire
1947	Staffordshire	1975	Staffordshire
1948	Staffordshire	1976	Warwickshire
1949	Lancashire	1977	Warwickshire
1950	*Not played*	1978	Kent
1951	Lancashire	1979	Gloucestershire
1952	Yorkshire	1980	Surrey
1953	Yorkshire	1981	Surrey
1954	Cheshire	1982	Yorkshire
1955	Yorkshire	1983	Berks, Bucks, Oxon
1956	Staffordshire	1984	Yorkshire
1957	Surrey	1985	Devon
1958	Surrey		Hertfordshire
1959	Yorkshire	1986	Hertfordshire
1960	Northumberland	1987	Yorkshire
1961	Lancashire	1988	Warwickshire
1962	Northumberland	1989	Middlesex

English Ladies' Amateur Championship

Year	Winner	Runner-up	Venue	By
1960	Miss M Nichol	Mrs MF Bonallack	Burnham	3 and 1
1961	Miss R Porter	Mrs P Reece	Littlestone	2 holes
1962	Miss J Roberts	Mrs MF Bonallack	Woodhall Spa	3 and 1
1963	Mrs MF Bonallack	Miss E Chadwick	Liphook	7 and 6
1964	Mrs AD Spearman	Miss M Everard	Lytham St Annes	6 and 5
1965	Miss R Porter	Miss C Cheetham	Whittington Barrcks	6 and 5
1966	Miss J Greenhalgh	Mrs JC Holmes	Hayling Island	3 and 1
1967	Miss A Irwin	Mrs A Pickard	Alwoodley	3 and 2
1968	Mrs S Barber	Miss D Oxley	Hunstanton	5 and 4
1969	Miss B Dixon	Miss M Wenyon	Burnham and Berrow	6 and 4
1970	Miss D Oxley	Mrs S Barber	Rye	3 and 2
1971	Miss D Oxley	Mrs S Barber	Hoylake	5 and 4
1972	Miss M Everard	Mrs MF Bonallack	Woodhall Spa	2 and 1
1973	Miss M Walker	Miss C Le Feuvre	Broadstone	6 and 5
1974	Miss A Irvin	Mrs J Thornhill	Sunningdale	1 hole
1975	Miss B Huke	Miss L Harrold	Birkdale	2 and 1
1976	Miss L Harrold	Mrs A Uzielli	Hollinwell	3 and 2
1977	Miss V Marvin	Miss M Everard	Burnham and Berrow	1 hole
1978	Miss V Marvin	Miss R Porter	West Sussex	2 and 1
1979	Miss J Greenhalgh	Mrs S Hedges	Hoylake	2 and 1
1980	Miss B New	Miss J Walker	Aldeburgh	3 and 2
1981	Miss D Christison	Miss S Cohen	Cotswold Hills	2 holes
1982	Miss J Walter	Miss C Nelson	Brancepeth Castle	4 and 3
1983	Mrs L Bayman	Miss C Mackintosh	Hayling Island	4 and 3
1984	Miss C Waite	Mrs L Bayman	Hunstanton	3 and 2
1985	Miss P Johnson	Mrs L Bayman	Ferndown	1 hole
1986	Mrs J Thornhill	Miss S Shapcott	Princes	3 and 1
1987	Miss J Furby	Miss M King	Alwoodley	4 and 3
1988	Miss J Wade	Miss S Shapcott	Little Aston	19th hole
1989	Miss H Dobson	Miss S Morgan	Burnham and Berrow	4 and 3

English Ladies' Under-23 Championship
Inaugurated 1978

Year	Winner	Venue	Score
1978	Miss S Bamford	Caldy	228
1979	Miss B Cooper	Coxmoor	223
1980	Miss B Cooper	Porters Park	226
1981	Miss J Soulsby	Willesley Park	220
1982	Miss M Gallagher	Highpost	221
1983	Miss P Grice	Hallamshire	219
1984	Miss P Johnson	Moor Park	300
1985	Miss P Johnson	Northants County	301
1986	Miss S Shapcott	Broadstone	301
1987	Miss J Wade	Northumberland	296
1988	Miss J Wade	Wentworth	299
1989	Miss A Shapcott	Notts Ladies	302

English Ladies' Seniors Championship
Inaugurated 1988

Year	Winner	Venue	Score
1988	Mrs A Thompson	Wentworth	158
1989	Mrs C Bailey	Notts Ladies	163

English Ladies' Stroke-Play Championship
Inaugurated 1984

Year	Winner	Venue	Score
1984	Miss P Grice	Moor Park	300
1985	Miss P Johnson	Northants County	301
1986	Miss S Shapcott	Broadstone	301
1987	Miss J Wade	Northumberland	296
1988	Miss S Prosser	Wentworth	297
1989	Miss S Robinson	Notts	302

English Ladies' Intermediate Championship
Inaugurated 1982

Year	Winner	Venue	Score
1982	Miss J Rhodes	Headingley	19th hole
1983	Miss L Davies	Worksop	2 and 1
1984	Miss P Grice	Whittington Barracks	3 and 2
1985	Miss S Lowe	Caldy	2 and 1
1986	Miss S Moorcroft	Hexham	6 and 5
1987	Miss J Wade	Sherringham	2 and 1
1988	Miss S Morgan	Enville, Staffs	20th hole
1989	Miss L Fairclough	Warrington	4 and 3

England and Wales (Ladies') County Championship

Year	Winner	Year	Winner	Year	Winner
1908	Lancashire	1937	Surrey	1968	Surrey
1909	Surrey	1938	Lancashire	1969	Lancashire
1910	Cheshire	1947	Surrey	1970	Yorkshire
1911	Cheshire	1948	Yorkshire	1971	Kent
1912	Cheshire	1949	Surrey	1972	Kent
1913	Surrey	1950	Yorkshire	1973	Northumberland
1920	Middlesex	1951	Lancashire	1974	Surrey
1921	Surrey	1952	Lancashire	1975	Glamorgan
1922	Surrey	1953	Surrey	1976	Staffordshire
1923	Surrey	1954	Warwickshire	1977	Essex
1924	Surrey	1955	Surrey	1978	Glamorgan
1925	Surrey	1956	Kent	1979	Essex
1926	Surrey	1957	Middlesex	1980	Lancashire
1927	Yorkshire	1958	Lancashire	1981	Glamorgan
1928	Cheshire	1959	Middlesex	1982	Surrey
1929	Yorkshire	1960	Lancashire	1983	Surrey
1930	Surrey	1961	Middlesex	1984	Surrey/Yorkshire
1931	Middlesex	1962	Staffordshire	1985	Surrey
1932	Cheshire	1963	Warwickshire	1986	Glamorgan
1933	Yorkshire	1964	Lancashire	1987	Lancashire
1934	Surrey	1965	Staffordshire	1988	Surrey
1935	Essex	1966	Lancashire	1989	Cheshire
1936	Surrey	1967	Lancashire		

Irish National Professional Championship
Instituted 1907

Year	Winner	Club	Venue	Score
1960	C O'Connor	Royal Dublin	Warrenpoint	271
1961	C O'Connor	Royal Dublin	Lahinch	280
1962	C O'Connor	Royal Dublin	Bangor	264
1963	C O'Connor	Royal Dublin	Little Island	271
1964	E Jones	Bangor	Knock	279
1965	C O'Connor	Royal Dublin	Mullingar	283
1966	C O'Connor	Royal Dublin	Warrenpoint	269
1967	H Boyle	Jacobs Golf Centre	Tullamore (3 rounds)	214
1968	C Greene	Mill Town	Knock	282
1969	J Martin	Unattached	Dundalk	268
1970	H Jackson	Knockbracken	Massareene	283
1971	C O'Connor	Royal Dublin	Galway	278
1972	J Kinsella	Castle	Bundoran	289
1973	J Kinsella	Castle	Limerick	284
1974	E Polland	Balmoral	Portstewart	277
1975	C O'Connor	Royal Dublin	Carlow	275
1976	P McGuirk	Co Louth	Waterville	291
From 1977 sponsored by Rank Xerox				
1977	P Skerritt	St Annes	Woodbrook	281
1978	C O'Connor	Royal Dublin	Dollymount	286
1979	D Smyth	Bettystown	Dollymount (54 holes)	215
1980	D Feherty	Balmoral	Dollymount	283
1981	D Jones	Bangor	Woodbrook	283
1982	D Feherty	Balmoral	Woodbrook	287
1983	L Higgins	Waterville	Woodbrook	275
1984	M Sludds		Skerries	277
1985	D J Smyth		Co Louth	204
(Played over 54 holes due to bad weather)				
1986	D J Smyth		Waterville	282
1987	P Walton	Malahide	Co Louth	144
(Played over 36 holes due to bad weather. Walton won play-off)				
1988	E Darcy	Delgany	Castle, Dublin	269
1989	P Walton	Malahide	Castle, Dublin	266

Irish Amateur Championship
Instituted 1893

Year	Winner	Runner-up	Venue	By
1960	M Edwards	N Fogarty	Portstewart	6 and 5
1961	D Sheahan	J Brown	Rosses Point	5 and 4
1962	M Edwards	J Harrington	Baltray	42nd hole
1963	JB Carr	EC O'Brien	Killarney	2 and 1
1964	JB Carr	A McDade	Co Down	6 and 5
1965	JB Carr	T Craddock	Rosses Point	3 and 2
1966	D Sheahan	J Faith	Dollymount	3 and 2
1967	JB Carr	PD Flaherty	Lahinch	1 hole
1968	M O'Brien	F McCarroll	Portrush	2 and 1
1969	V Nevin	J O'Leary	Co Sligo	1 hole
1970	D Sheahan	M Bloom	Grange	2 holes
1971	P Kane	M O'Brien	Ballybunion	3 and 2
1972	K Stevenson	B Hoey	Co Down	2 and 1
1973	RKM Pollin	RM Staunton	Rosses Point	1 hole
1974	R Kane	M Gannon	Portmarnock	5 and 4
1975	MD O'Brien	JA Bryan	Cork	5 and 4
1976	D Brannigan	D O'Sullivan	Portrush	2 holes
1977	M Gannon	A Hayes	Westport	19th hole
1978	M Morris	T Cleary	Carlow	1 hole
1979	J Harrington	MA Gannon	Ballybunion	2 and 1
1980	R Rafferty	MJ Bannon	Co Down	8 and 7
1981	D Brannigan	E McMenamin	Co Sligo	19th hole
1982	P Walton	B Smyth	Woodbrook	7 and 6
1983	T Corridan	E Power	Killarney	2 holes
1984	CB Hoey	L McNamara	Malone	20th hole
1985	D O'Sullivan	D Branigan	Westport	1 hole
1986	J McHenry	P Rayfus	Dublin	4 and 3
1987	E Power	JP Fitzgerald	Tranmore	2 holes
1988	G McGimpsey	D Mulholland	Portrush	2 and 1
1989	P McGinley	N Goulding	Rosses Point	3 and 2

Irish Seniors' Open Amateur Championship

Year	Winner	Venue	Score
1980	GN Fogarty	Galway	144
1981	GN Fogarty	Bundoran	149
1982	J Murray	Douglas	141
1983	F Sharpe	Courtown	153
1984	J Boston	Connemara	147
1985	J Boston	Newcastle	155
1986	J Coey	Waterford	141
1987	J Murray	Castleroy	150
1988	WB Buckley	Westport	154
1989	B McCrea	Royal Belfast	150

Irish Ladies' Amateur Championship
Instituted 1894

Year	Winner	Runner-up	Venue	By
1960	Miss P Garvey	Mrs PG McGann	Cork	5 and 3
1961	Mrs K McCann	Miss A Sweeney	Newcastle	5 and 3
1962	Miss P Garvey	Mrs M Earner	Baltray	7 and 6
1963	Miss P Garvey	Miss E Barnett	Killarney	9 and 7
1964	Mrs Z Fallon	Miss P O'Sullivan	Portrush	37th hole
1965	Miss E Purcell	Miss P O'Sullivan	Mullingar	3 and 2
1966	Miss E Bradshaw	Miss P O'Sullivan	Rosslare	3 and 2
1967	Mrs G Brandom	Miss P O'Sullivan	Castlerock	3 and 2
1968	Miss E Bradshaw	Miss M McKenna	Lahinch	3 and 2
1969	Miss M McKenna	Mrs C Hickey	Ballybunion	3 and 2
1970	Miss P Garvey	Miss M Earner	Portrush	2 and 1
1971	Miss E Bradshaw	Miss M Mooney	Baltray	3 and 1
1972	Miss M McKenna	Mrs I Butler	Killarney	5 and 4
1973	Miss M Mooney	Miss M McKenna	Bundoran	2 and 1

Irish Ladies'
Amateur
Championship
continued

Year	Winner	Runner-up	Venue	By
1974	Miss M McKenna	Miss V Singleton	Lahinch	3 and 2
1975	Miss M Gorry	Miss E Bradshaw	Tramore	1 hole
1976	Miss C Nesbitt	Miss M McKenna	Rosses Point	20th hole
1977	Miss M McKenna	Miss R Hegarty	Ballybunion	2 holes
1978	Miss M Gorry	Mrs I Butler	Grange	4 and 3
1979	Miss M McKenna	Miss C Nesbitt	Donegal	6 and 5
1980	Miss C Nesbitt	Miss C Hourihane	Lahinch	1 hole
1981	Miss M McKenna	Miss M Kenny	Laytown & Bettystown	1 hole
1982	Miss M McKenna	Miss M Madill	Portrush	2 and 1
1983	Miss C Hourihane	Mrs V Hassett	Cork	6 and 4
1984	Miss C Hourihane	Miss M Madill	Rosses Point	19th hole
1985	Miss C Hourihane	Miss M McKenna	Waterville	4 and 3
1986	Mrs T O'Reilly	Miss E Higgins	Castlerock	4 and 3
1987	Miss C Hourihane	Miss C Hickey	Lahinch	5 and 4
1988	Miss L Bolton	Miss E Higgins	Tramore	2 and 1
1989	Miss M McKenna	Miss C Wickham	West Port	19th hole

Scottish Professional Championship
Instituted 1907

Year	Winner	Club	Venue	Score
1960	EC Brown	Buchanan Castle	West Kilbride	278
1961	RT Walker	Downfield, Dundee	Forres	271
1962	EC Brown	Unattached	Dunbar	283
1963	WM Miller	Cardross	Crieff	284
1964	RT Walker	Downfield, Dundee	Machrihanish	277
1965	EC Brown	Cruden Bay	Forfar	271
1966	{ EC Brown / J Panton } tie	Cruden Bay / Glenbervie	Cruden Bay (36 holes)	137
1967	H Bannerman	Aberdeen	Montrose	279
1968	EC Brown	Cruden Bay	Monktonhall	286
1969	G Cunningham	Troon Municipal	Machrihanish	284
1970	RDBM Shade	Duddingston	Montrose	276
1971	NJ Gallacher	Wentworth	Lundin Links	282
1972	H Bannerman	Banchory	Strathaven	268
1973	BJ Gallacher	Wentworth	Kings Links, Aberdeen	276
1974	BJ Gallacher	Wentworth	Drumpellier	276
1975	D Huish	North Berwick	Duddingston	279
1976	J Chillas	Crow Wood	Haggs Castle	286
1977	BJ Gallacher	Wentworth	Barnton	282
1978	S Torrance	Caledonian Hotel	Strathaven	269
1979	AWB Lyle	Hawkstone Park	Glasgow Gailes	274
1980	S Torrance	Caledonian Hotel	East Kilbride	273
1981	B Barnes	Caledonian Hotel	Dalmahoy	275
1982	B Barnes	Caledonian Hotel	Dalmahoy	286
1983	B Gallacher	Wentworth	Dalmahoy	276
(After play-off)				
1984	I Young	Dalmahoy	Dalmahoy	276
1985	S Torrance	Unattached	Dalmahoy	277
1986	R Drummond	Strathclyde Hardware	Glenbervie	270
1987	R Drummond	Strathclyde Hardware	Glenbervie	268
1988	S Stephen	Stephen Architects	Haggs Castle	283
1989	R Drummond	Continental Airlines	Monktonhall	274

Scottish Amateur Championship

Year	Winner	Runner-up	Venue	By
1922	J Wilson	E Blackwell	St Andrews	19th hole
1923	TM Burrell	Dr AR M'Callum	Troon	1 hole
1924	WW Mackenzie	W Tulloch	Aberdeen	3 and 2
1925	JT Dobson	WW Mackenzie	Muirfield	3 and 2
1926	WJ Guild	SO Shepherd	Leven	2 and 1
1927	A Jamieson, Jr	Rev DS Rutherford	Gailes	22nd hole
1928	WW Mackenzie	WE Dodds	Muirfield	5 and 3
1929	JT Bookless	JE Dawson	Aberdeen	5 and 4
1930	K Greig	T Wallace	Carnoustie	9 and 8
1931	J Wilson	A Jamieson, Jr	Prestwick	2 and 1
1932	J McLean	K Greig	Dunbar	5 and 4

Year	Winner	Runner-up	Venue	By
1933	J McLean	KC Forbes	Aberdeen	0 and 4
1934	J McLean	W Campbell	Western Gailes	3 and 1
1935	H Thomson	J McLean	St Andrews	2 and 1
1936	ED Hamilton	R Neill	Carnoustie	1 hole
1937	H McInally	KG Patrick	Barassie	6 and 5
1938	ED Hamilton	R Rutherford	Muirfield	4 and 2
1939	H McInally	H Thomson	Prestwick	6 and 5
1946	EC Brown	R Rutherford	Carnoustie	3 and 2
1947	H McInally	J Pressley	Glasgow Gailes	10 and 8
1948	AS Flockhart	GN Taylor	Balgownie, Aberdeen	7 and 6
1949	R Wright	H McInally	Muirfield	1 hole
1950	WC Gibson	DA Blair	Prestwick	2 and 1
1951	JM Dykes	JC Wilson	St Andrews	4 and 2
1952	FG Dewar	JC Wilson	Carnoustie	4 and 3
1953	DA Blair	JW McKay	Western Gailes	3 and 1
1954	JW Draper	WGH Gray	Nairn	4 and 3
1955	RR Jack	AC Miller	Muirfield	2 and 1
1956	Dr FWG Deighton	A MacGregor	Troon	8 and 7
1957	JS Montgomerie	J Burnside	Balgownie	2 and 1
1958	WD Smith	IR Harris	Prestwick	6 and 5
1959	Dr FWG Deighton	RMK Murray	St Andrews	6 and 5
1960	JR Young	S Saddler	Carnoustie	5 and 3
1961	J Walker	SWT Murray	Western Gailes	4 and 3
1962	SWT Murray	RDBM Shade	Muirfield	2 and 1
1963	RDBM Shade	N Henderson	Troon	4 and 3
1964	RDBM Shade	J McBeath	Nairn	8 and 7
1965	RDBM Shade	GB Cosh	St Andrews	4 and 2
1966	RDBM Shade	CJL Strachan	Western Gailes	9 and 8
1967	RDBM Shade	A Murphy	Carnoustie	5 and 4
1968	GB Cosh	RL Renfrew	Muirfield	4 and 3
1969	JM Cannon	AH Hall	Troon	6 and 4
1970	CW Green	HB Stewart	Balgownie, Aberdeen	1 hole
1971	S Stephen	CW Green	St Andrews	3 and 2
1972	HB Stuart	AK Pirie	Prestwick	3 and 1
1973	IC Hutcheon	A Brodie	Carnoustie	3 and 2
1974	GH Murray	AK Pirie	Western Gailes	2 and 1
1975	D Greig	GH Murray	Montrose	7 and 6
1976	GH Murray	HB Stuart	St Andrews	6 and 5
1977	A Brodie	PJ McKellar	Troon	1 hole
1978	IA Carslaw	J Cuddihy	Downfield	7 and 6
1979	K Macintosh	PJ McKellar	Prestwick	5 and 4
1980	D Jamieson	CW Green	Balgownie, Aberdeen (18 holes)	2 and 1
1981	C Dalgleish	A Thomson	Western Gailes	7 and 6
1982	CW Green	G McGregor	Carnoustie	1 hole
1983	CW Green	J Huggan	Gullane	1 hole
1984	A Moir	K Buchan	Renfrew	3 and 3
1985	D Carrick	D James	Southerness	4 and 2
1986	C Brooks	A Thomson	Monifieth	3 and 2
1987	C Montgomerie	AW Watt	Nairn	9 and 8
1988	J Milligan	A Colthart	Barassie	1 hole
1989	A Thomson	A Tait	Moray	1 hole

Scottish Amateur Championship
continued

Scottish Open Amateur Stroke Play Championship

Year	Winner	Club	Venue	Score
1967	BJ Gallacher	Bathgate	Muirfield and Gullane	291
1968	RDBM Shade	Duddingston	Prestwick and Prestwick St Nicholas	282
1969	JS Macdonald	Dalmahoy	Carnoustie and Monifieth	288
1970	D Hayes	South Africa	Glasgow Gailes and Barassie	275
1971	IC Hutcheon	Monifieth	Leven and Lundin Links	277
1972	BN Nicholas	Nairn	Dalmahoy and Ratho Park	290
1973	DM Robertson / GJ Clark } tie	Dunbar / Whitley Bay	Dunbar and North Berwick	284
1974	IC Hutcheon	Monifieth	Blairgowrie and Alyth	283
1975	CW Green	Dumbarton	Nairn and Nairn Dunbar	295
1976	S Martin	Downfield	Monifieth and Carnoustie	299
1977	PJ McKellar	East Renfrewshire	Muirfield and Gullane	299
1978	AR Taylor	East Kilbride	Keir and Cawder	281
1979	IC Hutcheon	Monifieth	Lansdowne and Rosemount	286

Year	Winner	Club	Venue	Score
1980	G Brand Jr	Knowle	Musselburgh and R Musselburgh (54 holes)	207
1981	F Walton	Malahide	Erskine and Renfrew	287
1982	C Macgregor	Glencourse	Downfield and Camperdown	287
1983	C Murray	Fereneze	Irvine	291
1984	CW Green	Dumbarton	Blairgowrie	287
1985	C Montgomerie	Royal Troon	Dunbar	274
1986	KH Walker	Royal Burgess	Carnoustie	289
1987	D Carrick	Douglas Park	Lundin Links	282
1988	S Easingwood	Dunbar	Cathkin Braes	277
1989	F Illouz	France	Blairgowrie	281

Scottish Open Amateur Stroke Play Championship
continued

Scottish Open Amateur Seniors' Championship
Instituted 1978

Year	Winner	Club	Venue	Score
1978	JM Cannon / GR Carmichael } tie	Irvine / Ladybank	Glasgow Killermont	149
1979	A Sinclair	Drumpellier	Glasgow Killermont	143
1980	JM Cannon	Irvine	Royal Burgess	149
1981	IR Harris / Dr J Hastings } tie / AN Sturrock	Royal Troon / Royal Troon / Royal Troon	Glasgow Killermont	146
1982	JM Cannon / J Niven }	Irvine / Newbury & Crookham	Royal Burgess	143
1983	WD Smith	Prestwick	Glasgow Killermont	145
1984	A Sinclair	Drumpellier	Royal Burgess	148
1985	AN Sturrock	Prestwick	Glasgow Killermont	143
1986	RL Glading	Mitcham	Royal Burgess	153
1987	I Hornsby	Ponteland	Glasgow Killermont	145
1988	J Hayes	Gosforth	Royal Burgess	143
1989	AS Mayer	Torwoodlee	Glasgow Killermont	

Scottish Ladies' Amateur Championship
Instituted 1903

Year	Winner	Runner-up	Venue	By
1960	Miss JS Robertson	Miss DT Sommerville	Turnberry	2 and 1
1961	Mrs I Wright (Miss Robertson)	Miss AM Lurie	St Andrews	1 hole
1962	Miss JB Lawrence	Mrs C Draper	Dornoch	5 and 4
1963	Miss JB Lawrence	Mrs IC Robertson	Troon	2 and 1
1964	Miss JB Lawrence	Mrs SM Reid	Gullane	5 and 3
1965	Mrs IC Robertson	Miss JB Lawrence	Nairn	5 and 4
1966	Mrs IC Robertson	Miss M Fowler	Machrihanish	2 and 1
1967	Miss J Hastings	Miss A Laing	North Berwick	5 and 3
1968	Miss J Smith	Mrs J Rennie	Carnoustie	10 and 9
1969	Mrs JH Anderson	Miss K Lackie	West Kilbride	5 and 4
1970	Miss A Laing	Mrs IC Robertson	Dunbar	1 hole
1971	Mrs IC Robertson	Mrs A Ferguson	Dornoch	3 and 2
1972	Mrs IC Robertson	Miss CJ Lugton	Machrihanish	5 and 3
1973	Mrs I Wright	Dr AJ Wilson	St Andrews	2 holes
1974	Dr AJ Wilson	Miss K Lackie	Nairn	22nd hole
1975	Miss LA Hope	Miss JW Smith	Elie	1 hole
1976	Miss S Needham	Miss T Walker	Machrihanish	3 and 2
1977	Miss CJ Lugton	Miss M Thomson	Dornoch	1 hole
1978	Mrs IC Robertson	Miss JW Smith	Prestwick	2 holes
1979	Miss G Stewart	Miss LA Hope	Gullane	2 and 1
1980	Mrs IC Robertson	Miss F Anderson	Carnoustie	1 hole
1981	Miss A Gemmill	Miss W Aitken	Stranraer	2 and 1
1982	Miss J Connachan	Miss P Wright	Troon	19th hole
1983	Miss G Stewart	Miss F Anderson	North Berwick	3 and 1
1984	Miss G Stewart	Miss A Gemmill	Dornoch	3 and 2
1985	Miss A Gemmill	Miss D Thomson	Barassie	2 and 1
1986	Mrs IC Robertson	Miss L Hope	St Andrews	3 and 2
1987	Miss F Anderson	Miss C Middleton	Nairn	4 and 3
1988	Miss S Lawson	Miss F Anderson	Southerness	3 and 1
1989	Mrs J Huggon	Miss L Anderson	Lossiemouth	5 and 4

Welsh Professional Championship

Instituted 1904

Year	Winner	Club	Venue	Score
1960	RH Kemp, Jr	Unattached	Llandudno	288
1961	S Mouland	Glamorganshire	Southerndown	286
1962	S Mouland	Glamorganshire	Porthcawl	302
1963	H Gould	Southerndown	Wrexham	291
1964	B Bielby	Portmadoc	Tenby	297
1965	S Mouland	Glamorganshire	Penarth	281
1966	S Mouland	Glamorganshire	Conway	281
1967	S Mouland	Glamorganshire	Pyle and Kenfig	
			(54 holes, fog)	219
1968	RJ Davies	South Herts	Southerndown	292
1969	S Mouland	Glamorganshire	Llandudno	277
1970	W Evans	Pennard	Tredegar Park	289
1971	J Buckley	North Wales	St Pierre	291
1972	J Buckley	Rhos-on-Sea	Porthcawl	298
1973	A Griffiths	Wrexham	Newport	289
1974	M Hughes	Aberystwyth	Cardiff	284
1975	C DeFoy	Bryn Meadows	Whitchurch	285
1976	S Cox	Wenvoe Castle	Radyr	284
From 1977 sponsored by Rank Xerox				
1977	C DeFoy	Calcot Park	Glamorganshire	135
1978	BCC Huggett	Cambridgeshire Hotel	Whitchurch	145
1979	*Cancelled*			
1980	A Griffiths	Llanymynech	Cardiff	139
1981	C DeFoy	Coombe Hill	Cardiff	139
1982	C DeFoy	Coombe Hill	Cardiff	137
1983	S Cox	Wenvoe Castle	Cardiff	136
1984	K Jones	Caldy	Cardiff	135
1985	D Llewellyn	Thirsk	Whitchurch	132
1986	P Parkin	Blue Arrow	Whitchurch	142
1987	A Dodman	St Pierre	Cardiff	132
1988	I Woosnam	Wang	Cardiff	137
1989	K Jones	Caldy	Royal Porthcawl	140

Welsh Amateur Championship

Instituted 1895

Year	Winner	Runner-up	Venue	By
1934	SB Roberts	GS Noon	Prestatyn	4 and 3
1935	R Chapman	GS Noon	Tenby	1 hole
1936	RM de Lloyd	G Wallis	Aberdovey	1 hole
1937	DH Lewis	R Glossop	Porthcawl	2 holes
1938	AA Duncan	SB Roberts	Rhyl	2 and 1
1946	JV Moody	A Marshman	Porthcawl	9 and 8
1947	SB Roberts	G Breen Turner	Harlech	8 and 7
1948	AA Duncan	SB Roberts	Porthcawl	2 and 1
1949	AD Evans	MA Jones	Aberdovey	2 and 1
1950	JL Morgan	DJ Bonnell	Southerndown	9 and 7
1951	JL Morgan	WI Tucker	Harlech	3 and 2
1952	AA Duncan	JL Morgan	Ashburnham	4 and 3
1953	SB Roberts	D Pearson	Prestatyn	5 and 3
1954	AA Duncan	K Thomas	Tenby	6 and 5
1955	TJ Davies	P Dunn	Harlech	38th hole
1956	A Lockley	WI Tucker	Southerndown	2 and 1
1957	ES Mills	H Griffiths	Harlech	2 and 1
1958	HC Squirrell	AD Lake	Conway	4 and 3
1959	HC Squirrell	N Rees	Porthcawl	8 and 7
1960	HC Squirrell	P Richards	Aberdovey	2 and 1
1961	AD Evans	J Toye	Ashburnham	3 and 2
1962	J Povall	HC Squirrell	Harlech	3 and 2
1963	WI Tucker	J Povall	Southerndown	4 and 3
1964	HC Squirrell	WI Tucker	Harlech	1 hole
1965	HC Squirrell	G Clay	Porthcawl	6 and 4
1966	WI Tucker	EN Davies	Aberdovey	6 and 5
1967	JK Povall	WI Tucker	Asburnham	3 and 2
1968	J Buckley	J Povall	Conway	8 and 7
1969	JL Toye	EN Davies	Porthcawl	1 hole
1970	EN Davies	J Povall	Harlech	1 hole
1971	CT Brown	HC Squirrell	Southerndown	6 and 5
1972	EN Davies	JL Toye	Prestatyn	40th hole

Year	Winner	Runner-up	Venue	By
1973	D McLean	T Holder	Ashburnham	6 and 4
1974	S Cox	EN Davies	Caernarvonshire	3 and 2
1975	JL Toye	WI Tucker	Porthcawl	5 and 4
1976	MPD Adams	WI Tucker	Harlech	6 and 5
1977	D Stevens	JKD Povall	Southerndown	3 and 2
1978	D McLean	A Ingram	Caernarvonshire	11 and 10
1979	TJ Melia	MS Roper	Ashburnham	5 and 4
1980	DL Stevens	G Clement	Prestatyn	10 and 9
1981	S Jones	C Davies	Porthcawl	5 and 3
1982	D Wood	C Davies	Harlech	8 and 7
1983	JR Jones	AP Parkin	Southerndown	2 holes
1984	JR Jones	A Llyr	Prestatyn	1 hole
1985	ED Jones	MA Macara	Ashburnham	2 and 1
1986	C Rees	B Knight	Conwy	1 hole
1987	PM Mayo	DK Wood	Porthcawl	2 holes
1988	K Jones	RN Roderick	Harlech	40th hole
1989	S Dodd	K Jones	Tenby	2 and 1

Welsh Amateur Championship

continued

Welsh Amateur Stroke Play Championship

Year	Winner	Club	Venue	Score
1967	EN Davies	Llantrisant	Harlech	295
1968	JA Buckley	Rhos-on-Sea	Harlech	294
1969	DL Stevens	Llantrisant	Tenby	288
1970	JK Povall	Whitchurch	Newport	292
1971	{ EN Davies / JL Toye } tie	Llantrisant / Radyr	Harlech	296
1972	JR Jones	Wrexham	Pyle and Kenfig	299
1973	JR Jones	Caernarvonshire	Llandudno (Maesdu)	300
1974	JL Toye	Radyr	Tenby	307
1975	D McLean	Holyhead	Wrexham	288
1976	WI Tucker	Monmouthshire	Newport	282
1977	JA Buckley	Abergele and Pensarn	Prestatyn	302
1978	HJ Evans	Llangland Bay	Pyle and Kenfig	300
1979	D McLean	Holyhead	Holyhead	289
1980	TJ Melia	Cardiff	Tenby	291
1981	D Evans	Leek	Wrexham	270
1982	JR Jones	Langland Bay	Cradoc	287
1983	G Davies	Pontypool	Aberdovey	287
1984	N Roderick	Portardawe	Newport	292
1985	MA Macara	Llandudno	Harlech	291
1986	M Calvert	Aberystwyth	Pyle and Kenfig	299
1987	MA Macara	Llandudno	Llandudno (Maesdu)	290
1988	RN Roderick	Portardawe	Tenby	283
1989	SC Dodd	Brynhill	Conwy (Carnarfonshire)	304

Welsh Seniors' Amateur Championship

Instituted 1975

Year	Winner	Club	Venue	Score
1975	A Marshaman	Brecon	Aberdovey	77 (18 holes)
1976	AD Evans	Ross on Wye	Aberdovey	156
1977	AE Lockley	Swansea Bay	Aberdovey	154
1978	AE Lockley	Swansea Bay	Aberdovey	75 (18 holes)
1979	CR Morgan	Monmouthshire	Aberdovey	158
1980	ES Mills	Llandudno (Maesdu)	Aberdovey	152
1981	T Branton	Newport	Aberdovey	153
1982	WI Tucker	Monmouthshire	Aberdovey	147
1983	WS Gronow	East Berks	Aberdovey	153
1984	WI Tucker	Monmouthshire	Aberdovey	150
1985	NA Lycett	Aberdovey	Aberdovey	149
1986	E Mills	Aberdovey	Aberdovey	154
1987	WS Gronow	East Berks	Aberdovey	146
1988	NA Lycett	Aberdovey	Aberdovey	150
1989	WI Tucker	Monmouthshire	Aberdovey	160

Welsh Ladies' Amateur Championship
Instituted 1905

Year	Winner	Runner-up	Venue	By
1960	Miss M Barron	Mrs E Brown	Tenby	8 and 6
1961	Mrs M Oliver	Miss N Sneddon	Aberdovey	5 and 4
1962	Mrs M Oliver	Miss P Roberts	Radyr	4 and 2
1963	Miss P Roberts	Miss N Sneddon	Harlech	7 and 5
1964	Mrs M Oliver	Mrs M Wright	Southerndown	1 hole
1965	Mrs M Wright	Mrs E Brown	Prestatyn	3 and 2
1966	Miss A Hughes	Miss P Roberts	Ashburnham	5 and 4
1967	Mrs M Wright	Miss C Phipps	Harlech	21st hole
1968	Miss S Hales	Mrs M Wright	Porthcawl	3 and 2
1969	Miss P Roberts	Miss A Hughes	Caernarvonshire	3 and 2
1970	Mrs A Briggs	Miss J Morris	Newport	19th hole
1971	Mrs A Briggs	Mrs EN Davies	Harlech	2 and 1
1972	Miss A Hughes	Miss J Rogers	Tenby	3 and 2
1973	Mrs A Briggs	Mrs J John	Holyhead	3 and 2
1974	Mrs A Briggs	Dr H Lyall	Ashburnham	3 and 2
1975	Mrs A Johnson (*née* Hughes)	Miss K Rawlings	Prestatyn	1 hole
1976	Miss T Perkins	Mrs A Johnson	Porthcawl	4 and 2
1977	Miss T Perkins	Miss P Whitley	Aberdovey	5 and 4
1978	Miss P Light	Mrs A Briggs	Newport	2 and 1
1979	Miss V Rawlings	Mrs A Briggs	Caernarvonshire	2 holes
1980	Miss M Rawlings	Mrs A Briggs	Tenby	2 and 1
1981	Miss M Rawlings	Mrs A Briggs	Harlech	5 and 3
1982	Mrs V Thomas (*née* Rawlings)	Miss M Rawlings	Ashburnham	7 and 6
1983	Mrs V Thomas	Mrs T Thomas (*née* Perkins)	Llandudno	1 hole
1984	Miss S Roberts	K Davies	Newport	5 and 4
1985	Mrs V Thomas	S Jump	Prestatyn	1 hole
1986	Mrs V Thomas	L Isherwood	Porthcawl	7 and 6
1987	Mrs V Thomas	Miss S Roberts	Aberdovey	3 and 1
1988	Miss S Roberts	Miss F Connor	Tenby	4 and 2
1989	Miss H Lawson	Mrs V Thomas	Conwy	2 and 1

Welsh Ladies' Open Amateur Stroke Play Championship
Instituted 1976

Year	Winner	Club	Venue	Score
1980	Mrs T Thomas (*née* Perkins)	Wenvoe Castle	Aberdovey	223
1981	Mrs V Thomas	Pennard	Aberdovey	224
1982	Mrs V Thomas	Pennard	Aberdovey	225
1983	Mrs J Thornhill	Walton Heath	Aberdovey	239
1984	Miss L Davies	West Byfleet	Aberdovey	230
1985	Miss C Swallow		Aberdovey	219
1986	Miss H Wadsworth	Princes	Aberdovey	223
1987	Miss S Shapcott	Knowle	Newport	225
1988	Miss S Shapcott	Knowle	Newport	218
1989	Mrs V Thomas	Pennard	Newport	220

Overseas National Championships
except PGA European Tour Events

Argentine Open Championship
Instituted 1905

Year	Winner	Year	Winner
1980	G Hallberg (USA)	1985	V Fernandez
1981	V Fernandez	1986	V Fernandez
1982	JE Soto	1987	M Fernandez
1983	AD Sowa	1988	M Fernandez
1984	V Fernandez	1989	E Romero

Argentine Amateur Championship
Instituted 1895

Year	Winner	Year	Winner
1980	MA Prado	1985	F Curutchet
1981	JC Devoto	1986	D Ventureira
1982	D Vizzolini	1987	J Rivas
1983	D Vizzolini	1988	J Nougues, Jr
1984	MA Prado	1989	F Alemán

Argentine Ladies' Amateur Championship
Instituted 1904

Year	Winner	Year	Winner
1980	A Felizia	1985	ME Noguerol
1981	S Garmendia	1986	MM Abramoff
1982	S Garmendia	1987	V Podrug
1983	ME Noguerol	1988	ME Noguerol
1984	AM Lagrutta	1989	ME Noguerol

Australian Open Championship

Year	Winner	Score	Year	Winner	Score
1975	JW Nicklaus	279	1983	P Fowler	285
1976	JW Nicklaus	286	1984	T Watson	281
1977	D Graham	284	1985	G Norman	212
1978	JW Nicklaus	284	(54 holes only—rain)		
1979	J Newton	288	1986	R Davies	278
1980	G Norman	284	1987	G Norman	273
1981	B Rogers	282	1988	M Calcavecchia	269
1982	R Shearer	287	1989	P Senior	271

Australian Professional Championship

Year	Winner	Year	Winner
1980	S Torrance	1985	G Norman
1981	S Ballesteros	1986	G Norman
1982	G Marsh	1987	R Mackay
1983	B Shearer	1988	W Grady
1984	G Norman	1989	P Senior

Australian Amateur Championship

Year	Winner	Year	Winner
1980	R Mackay	1985	S Ruangit
1981	O Moore	1986	D Ecob
1982	E Couper	1987	B Johns
1983	W Smith	1988	S Bouvier
1984	B King	1989	S Conran

Australian Ladies' Amateur Championshp
Instituted 1894

Year	Winner	Year	Winner
1980	Mrs C N Coggin	1985	Miss H Greenwood
1981	Miss C Dibnah	1986	Mrs E Kennedy
1982	Miss R Lautens	1987	Miss E Cavill
1983	Mrs S McCaw	1988	Miss C Bourtayre
1984	Mrs S McCaw	1989	Mrs J Higgins

Austrian Amateur Open Championship
Instituted 1909

Year	Winner	Year	Winner
1980	M Lamberg	1985	C-S Hsieh
1981	C Kilian	1986	D Carrick
1982	C-C Yuan	1987	Y-S Chen
1983	C-C Yuan	1988	L Peterson
1984	C-H Yu	1989	U Zilg

Austrian Ladies' Open Championship

Year	Winner	Year	Winner
1980	Miss B-S Huang	1985	Frl P Peter
1981	Miss N Le Roux	1986	Miss W-L Li
1982	Miss J Orley	1987	Miss Y-S Chen
1983	Miss Y-Y Chen	1988	Miss H-F Tseng
1984	Miss M-C Cheng	1989	Miss K Poppmeier

Godiva European Ladies' Masters
(formerly Belgian Ladies' Open Championship)

Year Winner

1985	L Davies
1986	P Grice-Whittaker
1987	ML de Lorenzi
1988	K Lunn
1989	K Douglas

Canadian Open Championship
Instituted 1904

Year	Winner	Year	Winner
1975	T Weiskopf	1983	J Cook
1976	J Pate	1984	G Norman
1977	L Trevino	1985	C Strange
1978	B Lietzke	1986	B Murphy
1979	L Trevino	1987	C Strange
1980	B Gilder	1988	K Green
1981	P Oosterhuis	1989	S Jones
1982	B Lietzke		

Canadian Amateur Championship

Year	Winner	Year	Winner
1980	G Olson	1985	B Franklin
1981	R Zokol	1986	B Franklin
1982	D Roxburgh	1987	B Franklin
1983	D Mijovic	1988	D Roxburgh
1984	W Swartz	1989	P Major

Canadian Ladies' Open Amateur Championship
Instituted 1901

Year	Winner	Year	Winner
1980	Miss E Kennedy	1985	Miss K Williams
1981	Miss J Lock	1986	Miss M O'Connor
1982	Miss C Pleger	1987	Miss T Kerdyk
1983	Miss D Coe	1988	Miss M Hattori
1984	Miss K Williams	1989	Miss C Damphouse

Danish Amateur Stroke Play Championship
Instituted 1981

Year	Winner	Year	Winner
1981	IG Andersen	1986	P Digebjerg
1982	A Sørensen	1987	M Brodersen
1983	T Morsbol	1988	B Tinning
1984	J Rasmussen	1989	R Budde
1985	A Sørensen		

Danish Ladies' Open Championship

Year	Winner
1988	F Descampe
1989	T Abitbol

Danish Ladies' Stroke Play Championship

Instituted 1981

Year	Winner	Year	Winner
1981	A Peitersen	1986	M Meiland
1982	L Eliasen	1987	A Peitersen
1983	M Meiland	1988	J Kragh
1984	M Meiland	1989	M Brandt Anderson
1985	M Meiland		

French Open Amateur Championship

Year	Winner	Year	Winner
1980	A Y Gresham	1985	R Taher
1981	F Illouz	1986	*Not played*
1982	F Illouz	1987	F Lindgren
1983	A Godillot	1988	*Not played*
1984	A Godillot	1989	G Shemano

French Men's Close Amateur Championship

Year	Winner	Year	Winner
1980	A Godillot	1985	J-F Remesy
1981	T Planchin	1986	J van der Velde
1982	A Godillot	1987	G Brizay
1983		1988	P Barquez
1984	Y Houssin	1989	C Cevael

French Ladies' Open Championship

Year	Winner	Score
1987	Miss L Neumann	293
1988	ML de Lorenzi	285
1989	Miss S Strudwick	285

French Ladies' Open Amateur Championship
Instituted 1909

Year	Winner
1984	Miss LA Chen
1985	Miss M Campomanes
1986	*Not played*
1987	Miss S Louapre
1988	*Not played*
1989	Miss E Orley

French Ladies' Close Championship
Instituted 1908

Year	Winner	Year	Winner
1980	E Berthet	1985	Mlle V Pammard
1981	C Soules	1986	ML de Lorenzi
1982	E Berthet	1987	Mlle S Louapre
1983	ML de Lorenzi	1988	Mlle C Marty
1984	Mlle C Soules	1989	Mlle C Bourtayre

International PGA Championship of Germany
(formerly German Close Professional Championship)
Instituted 1927

Year	Winner	Year	Winner
1980	H Heiser	1985	H-P Thül
1981	M Kessler	1986	S Vollrath
1982	H-P Thül	1987	H-P Thül
1983	T Gideon	1988	T Gideon
1984	H-J Kupitz	1989	T Gideon

German Open Amateur Championship
Instituted 1913

Year	Winner	Year	Winner
1980	J Rube	1985	R Thielemann
1981	K Flint	1986	*Not played*
1982	F Schlig	1987	N Sallmann
1983	C Stadler	1988	*Not played*
1984	T Hübner	1989	J Steenkamer

German Close Amateur Championship
Instituted 1938

Year	Winner	Year	Winner
1980	HG Reiter	1985	F Schlig
1981	U Schulte	1986	S Strüver
1982	F Schlig	1987	HG Reiter
1983	C Domin	1988	U Zilg
1984	A Stamm	1989	HG Reiter

German Ladies' Open Championship

Year	Winner
1984	B Huke
1985	J Brown
1986	L Neumann
1987	ML de Lorenzi
1988	L Neumann
1989	A Nicholas

International PGA Championship of Germany (Ladies)
(formerly German Ladies' Close Professional Championship)

Year	Winner
1986	S Eckrodt
1987	S Eckrodt
1988	D Franz
1989	D Franz

German Ladies' Open Amateur Championship
Instituted 1927

Year	Winner	Year	Winner
1980	Miss S Blecher	1985	Mrs M Koch
1981	Miss S Blecher	1986	*Not played*
1982	Miss S Knodler	1987	Miss S Lambert
1983	Miss I Bockelmann	1988	*Not played*
1984	Mrs S Lampert	1989	Miss M Fischer

German Ladies' Close Championship
Instituted 1938

Year	Winner	Year	Winner
1980	Dr B Bohm	1985	Mrs R Ruland
1981	Dr B Bohm	1986	Miss I Bockelmann
1982	Miss E Peter	1987	Mrs P Peter
1983	Miss S Knodler	1988	C Grundherr
1984	Mrs M Koch	1989	M Fischer

Hong Kong Open Championship
Instituted 1959

Year	Winner	Year	Winner
1980	K Chi-Hsiung	1985	M Aebli
1981	CT Ming	1986	S Kanai
1982	K Cox	1987	I Woosnam
1983	G Norman	1988	H Chin-sheng
1984	B Brask	1989	B Claar

Iceland Amateur Championship

Year	Winner	Year	Winner
1980	H Eyvindsson	1985	S Pétursson
1981	R Olafsson	1986	U Jónsson
1982	P Sigurdur	1987	U Jónsson
1983	G Kristinnsson	1988	S Sigurdsson
1984	S Pétursson	1989	U Jónsson

Iceland Ladies' Championship
Instituted 1967

Year	Winner	Year	Winner
1980	S Thorsteinsdóttir	1985	R Sigurdardóttir
1981	S Thorsteinsdóttir	1986	S Saemundsdóttir
1982	S Thorsteinsdóttir	1987	Th. Geirsdóttir
1983	A Sverrisdóttir	1988	S Saemundsdóttir
1984	A Sverrisdóttir	1989	K Saevarsdóttir

India Open Championship

Year	Winner	Year	Winner
1980	K Cox	1985	A Grimes
1981	P Stewart	1986	
1982	HS San	1987	B Tennyson
1983	J Takahashi	1988	L Chien-Soon
(after play-off)		1989	R Bouchard
1984	R Alarcon		

India Men's Amateur Championship

Year	Winner
1984	R Narain
1985	A Sharma
1986	R Mehta
1987	L Singh
1988	KN Perera
1989	

India Ladies' Championship

Year	Winner	Year	Winner
1980	Miss T Fernando	1985	Miss N Lal
1981	Ms M Wallis	1986	Mrs R Grewal
1982	Mrs R Grewal	1987	Mrs E Cavill
1983	Mrs K Kanwar	1988	Miss N Lal
1984	Miss S Saheed	1989	Mrs S Sobti

Italian Professional Championship

Year	Winner	Year	Winner
1980	R Campagnoli	1985	G Cali
1981	M Mannelli	1986	M Mannelli
1982	D Lovato	1987	G Cali
1983	S Locatelli	1988	A Canessa
1984	C Rocca	1989	C Rocca

Italian Open Amateur Championship
Instituted 1906

Year	Winner	Year	Winner
1980	A Canessa	1985	J-M Olazabal
1981	M Durante	1986	A Binaghi
1982	C Francis	1987	P Quirici
1983	J-M Olazabal	1988	E Giraud
1984	M Luzzi	1989	R Victor

Italian Close Amateur Championship
Instituted 1930

Year	Winner	Year	Winner
1980	F Ghirardi	1985	E Nistri
1981	A Canessa	1986	A Binaghi
1982	L Silva	1987	M Grabau
1983	S Grappasonni	1988	M de Rossi
1984	S Prati	1989	G Ferrero

Italian Ladies' Open Championship

Year	Winner	Year	Winner
1980	E Braito	1985	Miss R Lautens
1981	E Berthet	1986	Miss S Moorcroft
1982	M Figueras Dotti	1987	Miss R Lautens
1983	Miss C Maestre	1988	L Davies
1984	Miss R Lautens	1989	X Wunsch-Ruiz

Japan Open Championship

Year	Winner	Year	Winner
1980	S Kikuchi	1985	T Nakajima
1981	Y Hagawa	1986	T Nakajima
1982	A Yabe	1987	I Aoki
1983	B Lane	1988	M Ozaki
1984	K Uehara	1989	M Ozaki

Japan Professional Championship

Year	Winner
1984	T Nakajima
1985	T Ozaki
1986	I Aoki
1987	D Ishii
1988	T Ozaki
1989	M Ozaki

Japan Amateur Championship

Year	Winner
1984	K Nagarta
1985	T Nakagawa
1986	Y Ito
1987	T Suzuki
1988	R Kawagishi
1989	K Oie

Kenya Open Championship

Year	Winner	Year	Winner
1980	B Waites	1985	G Harvey
1981	B Barnes	1986	I Woosnam
1982	E Darcy	1987	C Mason
1983	K Brown	1988	C Platts
1984	J-M Canizares	1989	D Jones

Korea Open Championship

Year	Winner	Year	Winner
1980	Chen Tze Ming	1985	Cho Ho Sang
1981	Chen Tze Ming	1986	Choi Yoon Soo
1982	Choi Yoon Soo	1987	Lee Kang Sun
1983	Choi Sang Ho	1988	Kwak Yu Hyun
1984	Yeom Se Woon	1989	Chul Sang Cho

Malaysian Open Championship

Year	Winner	Year	Winner
1980	M McNulty	1985	T Gale
1981	H-C Lu	1986	S Ginn
1982	D Hepler	1987	T Gale
1983	T Gale	1988	T Tyner
1984	L Chien-Soon	1989	J Maggert

Malaysian Women's Open Championship

Year	Winner
1988	N Neus
1989	T Norimij

New Zealand Open Championship

Year	Winner	Year	Winner
1980	B Allin	1985	DA Weibring
1981	R Shearer	1986	C Pavin
1982	T Gale	1987	R Rafferty
1983	I Baker-Finch	1988	R Rafferty
1984	B Devlin	1989	G Turner

New Zealand Amateur Championship
Instituted 1893

Year	Winner	Year	Winner
1980	PE Hartstone	1985	G Power
1981	T Cochrane	1986	P O'Malley
1982	I Peters	1987	O Kendall
1983	C Taylor	1988	B Hughes
1984	J Wagner	1989	L Peterson

New Zealand Ladies' Open Championship
Instituted 1893

Year	Winner
1984	Mrs D Smith
1985	Miss E Kennedy
1986	Miss A Kita
1987	Miss J Wyatt
1988	Mrs E Cavill
1989	Miss W Sook

Nigerian Open Championship

Year	Winner	Year	Winner
1980	B Longmuir	1985	B Longmuir
1981	P Tupling	1986	GJ Brand
1982	D Jagger	1987	*not played*
1983	GJ Brand	1988	V Singh
1984	E Murray	1989	V Singh

Nordic Men's Open Amateur Championship
(Previously Scandinavian Men's Amateur Open)

Year	Winner
1984	S Tinning
1985	C Härdin
1986	J Ryström
1987	P Hedblom
1988	H Simonsen
1989	P-U Johansson

Nordic Ladies' Open Amateur Championship
(Previously Scandinavian Ladies' Amateur Open)

Year	Winner
1984	T Pors
1985	M Meiland
1986	A. Öquist
1987	H Anderssen
1988	M Binau
1989	K Orum

Pakistan Open Championship

Year	Winner	Year	Winner
1980	A Rashid	1985	G Muhammad
1981		1986	M Ali
1982	G Nabi	1987	T Hassan
1983	G Nabi	1988	G Nabi
1984	G Nabi	1989	F Minosa

Pakistan Men's Amateur Championship

Year	Winner	Year	Winner
1980	T Hassan	1985	T Hassan
1981	T Hassan	1986	T Hassan
1982	I Ahmed	1987	T Hassan
1983	T Hassan	1988	F Qureshi
1984	F Qureshi	1989	M Sajid

Pakistan Ladies' Amateur Championship

Year	Winner	Year	Winner
1980	Miss S Wali	1985	Miss N Shahban
1981	Miss T Butt	1986	Miss N Shahban
1982	*Not Played*	1987	Miss N Shahban
1983	*Not Played*	1988	Mrs Y Mubarik
1984	Mrs Y Mubarik	1989	Miss C Amluwalia

Portuguese Open Amateur Championship

Year	Winner	Year	Winner
1980	IL de Sousa e Melo	1985	M Grabbau
1981	G Brand	1986	R Nissen
1982	M Higgins	1987	S Struven
1983	U Schulte	1988	C Waesberg
1984	A Dantas	1989	S Bjorn

Portuguese Close Amateur Championship

Year	Winner	Year	Winner
1980	NA de Brito e Cunha	1985	C Marta
1981	A Dantas	1986	JS Melo
1982	J Silva Bento	1987	D Silva
1983	A Guerreiro	1988	R Uliveira
1984	J Santos	1989	A Castelo

Portuguese Ladies' Open Amateur Championship

Year	Winner	Year	Winner
1980	Mrs C Caldwell	1985	T Arbitbol
1981	V Dulout	1986	MC Navarizo
1982	Miss S Blecher	1987	MC Navarizo
1983	Miss K Douglas	1988	H Andersson
1984	M Campohanes	1989	S Clauset

Singapore Open Championship

Year	Winner	Year	Winner
1980	K Cox	1985	CT Ming
1981	M Aye	1986	G Turner
1982	HC San	1987	P Fowler
1983	C-S Lu	1988	G Bruckner
(After Play-Off with B Brask)		1989	C-S Lu
1984	T Sieckmann		

Singapore Open Amateur Championship

Year	Winner	Year	Winner
1980	G Suwirjo	1985	D Lim
1981	J Steward	1986	M Sukamdi
1982	Sudjiono	1987	T Wiratchant
1983	P Sachdev	1988	KN Perera
1984	D Ooi	1989	S Gimson

South African Open Championship

Year	Winner	Year	Winner
1980	R Cole	1985	G Levenson
1981	G Player	1986	D Frost
1982	*Not played*	1987	M McNulty
1983	C Bolling	1988	W Westner
1984	A Johnstone	1989	F Wadsworth

South African Masters

Year	Winner	Year	Winner
1980	N Price	1985	M McNulty
1981	M McNulty	1986	M McNulty
1982	M McNulty	1987	D Frost
1983	*Not played*	1988	J Bland
1984	A Johnstone	1989	

South African PGA Championship

Year	Winner	Year	Winner
1980	H Baiocchi	1985	C Williams
1981	*Not played*	1986	B Cole
1982	G Player	1987	F' Allem
1983	C Pavin	1988	D Feherty
1984	G Levenson	1989	A Johnstone

South African Amateur Championship

Year	Winner	Year	Winner
1980	E Groenewald	1985	N Clarke
1981	D Suddards	1986	E Els
1982	N James	1987	B Fouchee
1983	G-C Yuan	1988	N Clarke
1984	M Wiltshire	1989	C Rivett

South African Amateur Stroke Play Championship

Instituted 1969

Year	Winner	Year	Winner
1980	E Groenewald	1985	D van Staden
1981	CC Yuan	1986	C-S Hsieh
1982	WS Li	1987	B Fouchee
1983	P van der Riet	1988	N Clarke
1984	D James	1989	E Els

South African Ladies' Championship

Year	Winner
1984	Miss S Whitfield
1985	Miss W Warrington
1986	Miss G Whitfield
1987	Miss C Low
1988	Miss E Glass
1989	Miss L Maritz

Spanish Open Amateur Championship
Instituted 1911

Year	Winner	Year	Winner
1980	F Illouz	1985	B Quippe de Llano
1981	P Walton	1986	A Haglund
1982	D Williams	1987	M Quirke
1983	J-M Olazabal	1988	
1984	J-M Olazabal	1989	E Giraud

Spanish Amateur Close Championship

Year	Winner
1984	L Garbarda
1985	L Garbarda
1986	BQ de Llano
1987	JM Arruti
1988	TJ Munóz
1989	

Qualitair Ladies' Classic
(formerly Spanish Ladies' Open)

Year	Winner
1986	L Davies
1987	C Dibnah
1988	ML de Lorenzi
1989	A Nicholas

Spanish Ladies' Open Amateur Championship
Instituted 1911

Year	Winner	Year	Winner
1980	ML de Lorenzi	1985	C Espinasse
1981	Marquesa de Artasona	1986	R Lautens
		1987	C Hourihane
1982	C Mourgue D'Algue	1988	I Calogero
1983	ML de Lorenzi	1989	I Calogero
1984	C Navarro		

Spanish Ladies' Amateur Close Championship

Year	Winner
1984	C Maestre
1985	C Navarro
1986	C Navarro
1987	C Navarro
1988	S Navarro
1989	S Navarro

Swedish Professional Championship
Instituted 1976

Year	Winner	Year	Winner
1980	P Lindvall	1985	P Brostedt
1981	G Mueller	1986	M Persson
1982	A Forsbrand	1987	C-M Strömberg
1983	M Lanner	1988	V Singh
1984	P Brostedt	1989	L Hederström

Swedish Open International Stroke Play Championship
Instituted 1964 (before 1984: Amateur)

Year	Winner	Year	Winner
1980	J Rube	1985	Y Nilson
1982	D Carrick	1986	M Lanner
1982	D Carrick	1987	M Pendaries
1983	M Hogberg	1988	P Haugsrud
1984	A Forsbrand	1989	A Gillner

Swedish Close Men's Championship
Instituted 1904 (before 1984: Close Amateur)

Year	Winner	Year	Winner
1980	G Knutsson	1985	Nillso
1981	G Knutsson	1986	M Grankvist
1982	B Svedin	1987	C-M Strömberg
1983	K-G Drotz	1988	M Krantz
1984	M Lanner	1989	M Grankvist

Swedish Ladies' International Open Stroke Play Championship
Instituted 1971 (before 1984: Amateur)

Year	Winner	Year	Winner
1980	MC de Werra	1985	K Espinasse
1981	L Neumann	1986	P Neilsson
1982	L Neumann	1987	M Hattori
1983	A Oxenstierna	1988	H Alfredsson
1984	C Montgomery	1989	S Norberg

Swedish Ladies' Close Championship
Instituted 1911

Year	Winner	Year	Winner
1980	L Wollin	1985	S Gronberg
1981	M Wennersten	1986	H Alfredsson
1982	M Wennersten	1987	H Alfredsson
1983	G Linner ˙	1988	H Alfredsson
1984	L Neumann	1989	P Nilsson

Swiss Open Amateur Championship
Instituted 1007

Year	Winner	Year	Winner
1980	JW Schuchmann	1985	T Hubner
1981	C Staedler	1986	A Binaghi
1982	F Illouz	1987	M Durante
1983	J Lamberg	1988	A Bossert
1984	F Illouz	1989	M Frank

Swiss Close Amateur Championship

Year	Winner	Year	Winner
1980	Y Courturier	1985	M Gottstein
1981	J Storjohann	1986	M Frank
1982	C Rampone	1987	M Frank
1983	P Jaquet	1988	A Bossert
1984	M Buchter	1989	M Frank

Swiss Ladies' Open Amateur Championship
Instituted 1907

Year	Winner	Year	Winner
1980	M Franz	1985	Mrs M Koch
1981	Miss R Lautens	1986	Mrs M Koch
1982	Miss MC de Werra	1987	Miss R Lautens
1983	Miss E Berthet	1988	Mrs M Koch
1984	E Girardi	1989	Miss V Pamard

Swiss Ladies' Close Amateur Championship

Year	Winner	Year	Winner
1980	Miss MC de Werra	1985	Miss E Orley
1981	A Hadorn	1986	Miss E Orley
1982	Miss R Lautens	1987	Miss E Orley
1983	Miss R Lautens	1988	Miss E Orley
1984	Miss R Lautens	1989	Miss C Vannini

United States Amateur Championship

Year	Winner	Runner-up	Venue	By
1946	SE Bishop	S Quick	Baltusrol	37th hole
1947	RH Riegel	J Dawson	Pebble Beach	2 and 1
1948	WP Turnesa	R Billows	Memphis	2 and 1
1949	CR Coe	R King	Rochester	11 and 10
1950	S Urzetta	FR Stranahan	Minneapolis	39th hole
1951	WJ Maxwell	J Cagliardi	Saucon Valley, Pa	4 and 3
1952	J Westland	A Mengert	Seattle	3 and 2
1953	G Littler	D Morey	Oklahoma City	1 hole
1954	A Palmer	R Sweeney	Detroit	1 hole
1955	E Harvie Ward	W Hyndman	Richmond, Va	9 and 8
1956	E Harvie Ward	C Kocsis	Lake Forest, Ill	5 and 4
1957	H Robbins	Dr F Taylor	Brookline	5 and 4

Year	Winner	Runner-up	Venue	By
1958	CR Coe	T Aaron	San Francisco	5 and 4
1959	JW Nicklaus	CR Coe	Broadmoor	1 hole
1960	DR Beman	R Gardner	St Louis, Mo	6 and 4
1961	JW Nicklaus	D Wysong	Pebble Beach	8 and 6
1962	LE Harris, Jr	D Gray	Pinehurst	1 hole
1963	DR Beman	D Sikes	Des Moines	2 and 1
1964	W Campbell	E Tutweiler	Canterbury, Ohio	1 hole
Changed to stroke play				
1965	R Murphy		Tulsa, Okla	291
1966	G Cowan		Ardmore, Penn	285
1967	R Dickson		Colorado	285
1968	B Fleisher		Volumbus	284
1969	S Melnyk		Oakmont	286
1970	L Wadkins		Portland	280
1971	G Cowan		Wilmington	280
1972	M Giles		Charlotte, NC	285
Reverted to match play				
1973	C Stadler	D Strawn	Inverness, Ohio	6 and 5
1974	J Pate	J Grace	Ridgewood, NJ	2 and 1
1975	F Ridley	K Fergus	Richmond, Va	2 holes
1976	B Sander	P Moore	Del Air	8 and 6
1977	J Fought	D Fischesser	Aronimonk, Pa	9 and 8
1978	J Cook	S Hoch	Plainfield, NJ	5 and 4
1979	M O'Meara	J Cook	Canterbury, Ohio	8 and 7
1980	H Sutton	B Lewis	North Carolina	9 and 8
1981	N Crosby	B Lyndley	San Francisco	37th hole
1982	J Sigel	D Tolley	The Country Club,	
			Brookline	8 and 7
1983	J Sigel	C Perry	North Shore, Chicago	8 and 7
1984	S Verplank	S Randolph	Oak Tree, Okla	4 and 3
1985	S Randolph	P Persons	Montclair, NJ	1 hole
1986	S Alexander	C Kite	Shoal Creek	5 and 3
1987	W Mayfair	E Rebmann	Jupiter Hills, Fl	4 and 3
1988	E Meeks	D Yates	Hot Springs, VA	7 and 6
1989	C Patton	D Green	Merion, PA	3 and 1

United States Ladies' Amateur
Championship
Instituted 1895

Year	Winner	Runner-up	Venue	By
1960	Miss J Gunderson	Miss J Ashley	Tulsa, Okla	6 and 5
1961	Mrs A Quast	Miss P Preuss	Tacoma	14 and 13
1962	Miss J Gunderson	Miss A Baker	Rochester, NY	9 and 8
1963	Mrs A Quast	Miss P Conley	Williamstown	2 and 1
1964	Miss B McIntyre	Miss J Gunderson	Prairie Dunes, Kansas	3 and 2
1965	Miss J Ashley	Mrs A Quast	Denver	5 and 4
1966	Mrs D Carner	Mrs JD Streit	Pittsburgh	41st hole
	(Miss Gunderson)			
1967	Miss L Dill	Miss J Ashley	Annandale, Pasadena	5 and 4
1968	Mrs JA Carner	Mrs A Quast	Birmingham, Mich	5 and 4
1969	Miss C Lacoste (Fra)	Miss S Hamlin	Las Colinas, Texas	3 and 2
1970	Miss M Wilkinson	Miss C Hill	Darien, Conn	3 and 2
1971	Miss L Baugh	Miss B Barry	Atlanta	1 hole
1972	Miss M Budke	Miss C Hill	St Louis, Mo	5 and 4
1973	Miss C Semple	Mrs A Quast	Montclair, NJ	1 hole
1974	Miss C Hill	Miss C Semple	Broadmoor, Seattle	5 and 4
1975	Miss B Daniel	Miss D Horton	Brae Burn, Mass	3 and 2
1976	Miss D Horton	Mrs M Bretton	Del Paso, California	2 and 1
1977	Miss B Daniel	Mrs C Sherk	Cincinnati	3 and 1
1978	Mrs C Sherk	Mrs J Oliver	Sunnybrook, Pa	4 and 3
1979	Miss C Hill	Miss P Sheehan	Memphis	7 and 6
1980	Mrs J Inkster	Miss P Rizzo	Prairie Dunes, Kansas	2 holes
1981	Mrs J Inkster	Mrs L Coggan (Aus)	Portland, Oregon	1 hole
1982	Mrs J Inkster	Miss C Hanton	Colorado Springs	4 and 3
1983	Miss J Pacillo	Miss S Quinlan	Canoe Brook, NJ	2 and 1
1984	Miss D Richard	Miss K Williams	Broadmoor, Seattle	37th hole
1985	Miss M Hattori (Jpn.)	Miss C Stacy	Pittsburgh, PA	5 and 4
1986	Miss K Cockerill	Miss K McCarthy	Pasatiempo, California	9 and 7
1987	Miss K Cockerill	Miss T Kerdyk	Barrington, RI	3 and 2
1988	Miss P Sinn	Miss K Noble	Minikahde, MN	6 and 5
1989	Miss V Goetze	Miss B Burton	Pinehurst	4 and 3

Zambian Open Championship
Instituted 1972

Year	Winner	Year	Winner
1980	E Murray	1985	I Woosnam
1981	B Barnes	1986	G Cullen
1982	B Waites	1987	P Carrigill
1983	B Calfee	1988	D Llewellyn
(After Play-Off with E Darcy)		1989	C Maltman
1984	C Mason		

PGA European Tour
and other Men's Professional Tournaments

AGF Open Championship

Year	Winner	Venue	Score
1988	D Llewellyn	Biarritz	258
1989	M James	Montpellier	277

Belgian Open Championship
Instituted 1987

Year	Winner
1987	E Darcy
(three rounds only—rain)	
1988	J-M Olazabal
1989	GJ Brand

Bells' Scottish Open
Formerly Glasgow Classic, 1983-85

Year	Winner	Venue	Score
1983	B Langer	Haggs Castle	274
1984	K Brown	Haggs Castle	266
1985	H Clark	Haggs Castle	274
1986	D Feherty	Haggs Castle	270
1987	I Woosnam	Gleneagles	264
1988	B Lane	Gleneagles	271
1989	M Allen	Gleneagles	272

Benson and Hedges International
at Fulford (1979 – St Mellion)

Year	Winner	Score	Year	Winner	Score
1971	A Jacklin	279	1981	T Weiskopf	272
1972	J Newton	281	1982	G Norman	283
1973	V Baker	276	1983	J Bland	273
1974	P Toussaint	276	1984	S Torrance	270
1975	V Fernandez	266	1985	AWB Lyle	274
1976	G Marsh	272	1986	M James	274
1977	A Garrido	280	1987	N Ratcliffe	275
1978	L Trevino	274	1988	P Baker	271
1979	M Bembridge	272	1989	G Brand, Jr	272
1980	G Marsh	272			

Benson and Hodges Trophy

Year	Winner	Venue	Score
1988	M McNulty/ML de Lorenzi	La Moraleja	276
1989	MA Jimenez/X Wunsch-Ruiz	Aloha	281

Cannes Open Championship
at Cannes Mougins

Year	Winner	Score
1984	D Frost	280
1985	R Lee	280
1986	J Bland	276
1987	S Ballesteros	275
1988	M McNulty	279
1989	P Broadhurst	207*

(*54 holes only)

Carrolls Irish Open
Formerly Carrolls International

Year	Winner	Club/Country	Venue	Score
1971	NC Coles	Coombe Hill	Woodbrook	276
1972	C O'Connor	Royal Dublin	Woodbrook	284
1973	P McGuirk	Co Louth	Woodbrook	277
1974	B Gallacher	Wentworth	Woodbrook	279
1975	C O'Connor, Jr	Carlow	Woodbrook	275
1976	B Crenshaw	USA	Portmarnock	284
1977	H Green	USA	Portmarnock	283
1978	K Brown	GB	Portmarnock	281
1979	M James	Burghley Park	Portmarnock	282
1980	M James	Burghley Park	Portmarnock	284
1981	S Torrance	GB	Portmarnock	276
1982	J O'Leary	Unattached	Portmarnock	287
1983	S Ballesteros	Spain	Dublin	271
1984	B Langer	Germany	Dublin	267
1985	S Ballesteros	Spain	Dublin	278
1986	S Ballesteros	Spain	Portmarnock	285
1987	B Langer	Germany	Portmarnock	269
1988	I Woosnam	Wales	Portmarnock	278
1989	I Woosnam	Wales	Portmarnock	278

Dunhill British Masters'
Formerly sponsored by Dunlop, 1946-62 (1963-83: Silk Cut)

Year	Winner	Club/Country	Venue	Score
1970	BGC Huggett	Betchworth Park	Lytham, St Annes	293
1971	M Bembridge	Little Aston	St Pierre	273
1972	R Charles	New Zealand	Northumberland	277
1973	A Jacklin	Potters Bar	St Pierre	272
1974	B Gallacher	Wentworth	St Pierre	282
1975	B Gallacher	Wentworth	Ganton	289
1976	B Dassu	Italy	St Pierre	271
1977	GL Hunt	Gloucester Hotel	Lindrick	291
1978	TA Horton	Royal Jersey	St Pierre	279
1979	G Marsh	Australia	Woburn (Dukes Course)	283
1980	B Langer	West Germany	St Pierre	270
1981	G Norman	Australia	Woburn	273
1982	G Norman	Australia	St Pierre	267
1983	I Woosnam	Wales	St Pierre	269
1984	Not played			

Year	Winner	Club/Country	Venue	Score
1985	L Trevino	USA	Woburn	278
1986	S Ballesteros	Spain	Woburn	275
1987	M McNulty	Zimbabwe	Woburn	274
1988	AWB Lyle	Scotland	Woburn	273
1989	N Faldo	England	Woburn	267

Dunhill British Masters'
continued

Dutch Open Championship
Instituted 1912

Year	Winner	Year	Winner
1980	S Ballesteros	1985	G Marsh
1981	H Henning	1986	S Ballesteros
1982	P Way	1987	G Brand, Jr
1983	K Brown	1988	M Mouland
1984	B Langer	1989	J-M Olazabal

English Open
Instituted 1988

Year	Winner	Venue	Score
1988	H Clark	Birkdale	279
1989	M James	The Belfry	279

Epson Match-Play
Instituted 1986

Year	Winner	Venue
1986	O Sellberg beat H Clark 3 and 2	St Pierre
1987	M Lanner beat J Hawkes 1 hole	St Pierre
1988	B Langer beat M McNulty 4 and 3	St Pierre
1989	S Ballesteros beat D Durnian 4 and 3	St Pierre

Equity & Law Challenge
Instituted 1987
Venue: Royal Mid-Surrey

Year	Winner	Country	Score
1987	B Lane	England	22 points
1988	R Rafferty	England	21 points
1989	B Ogle	Australia	25 points

French Open Championship

Year	Winner	Score	Year	Winner	Score
1980	G Norman	268	1985	S Ballesteros	263
1981	AWB Lyle	270	1986	S Ballesteros	269
1982	S Ballesteros	278	1987	J Rivero	269
1983	N Faldo	277	1988	N Faldo	274
(After Play-off with J-M Canizares and DJ Russell)			1989	N Faldo	273
1984	B Langer	270			

German Masters
at Stuttgart

Year	Winner	Score
1987	AWB Lyle	278
1988	J-M Olazabal	279
1989	B Langer	276

German Open Championship

Year	Winner	Score	Year	Winner	Score
1980	M McNulty	280	1985	B Langer	183
1981	B Langer	272		*(54 holes only—rain)*	
1982	B Langer	279	1986	B Langer	273
1983	C Pavin	275	1987	M McNulty	259
1984	W Grady	268	1988	S Ballesteros	263
			1989	C Parry	266

Italian Open Championship

Year	Winner	Score	Year	Winner	Score
1980	M Mannelli	276	1986	D Feherty	270
1981	J-M Canizares	280		*(After play-off with R Rafferty)*	
1982	M James	280	1987	S Torrance	271
1983	B Langer	271		*(After play-off with J Rivero)*	
(After Play-Off with K Brown and S Ballesteros)			1988	G Norman	270
1984	AWB Lyle	277	1989	R Rafferty	273
1985	M Pinero	267			

Jersey Open
at La Moye

Formerly British Airways-Avis Tournament and Billy Butlin Open

Year	Winner	Score	Year	Winner	Score
1980	J-M Canizares	281	1985	H Clark	279
1981	A Jacklin	279	1986	J Morgan	275
1982	B Gallacher	273	1987	I Woosnam	279
1983	J Hall	278	1988	D Smyth	273
1984	B Gallacher	274	1989	C O'Connor Jr	281

Lancôme Trophy
at St Nom de la Breteche

Year	Winner	Score	Year	Winner	Score
1970	A Jacklin (54 holes)	206	1981	D Graham	280
1971	A Palmer (54 holes)	202	1982	D Graham	276
1972	T Aaron	279	1983	S Ballesteros	269
1973	J Miller	277	1984	AWB Lyle	278
1974	W Casper	283		*(After tie with S Ballesteros)*	
1975	G Player	278	1985	N Price	275
1976	S Ballesteros	283	1986	S Ballesteros	274
1977	G Marsh	273	1987	I Woosnam	264
1978	L Trevino	272	1988	S Ballesteros	269
1979	J Miller	281	1989	E Romero	266
1980	L Trevino	280			

Madrid Open Championship
at Puerto de Hierro, Madrid

Year	Winner	Score	Year	Winner	Score
1980	S Ballesteros	270	1985	M Pinero	278
1981	M Pinero	279	1986	H Clark	274
1982	S Ballesteros	273	1987	I Woosnam	269
1983	AWB Lyle	285	1988	D Cooper	275
1984	H Clark	274	1989	S Ballesteros	272

Monte Carlo Open Championship
at Mont Agel

Year	Winner	Score
1984	I Mosey	131*
1985	S Torrance	264
1986	S Ballesteros	265
1987	P Senior	260
1988	J Rivero	261
1989	M McNulty	261

*(*36 holes only)*

Panasonic European Open

Year	Winner	Venue	Score
1978	RL Wadkins	Walton Heath	283
1979	AWB Lyle	Turnberry	275
1980	T Kite	Walton Heath	284
1981	G Marsh	Liverpool	275
1982	M Pinero	Sunningdale	266
1983	I Aoki	Sunningdale	274
1984	G Brand, Jr	Sunningdale	270
1985	B Langer	Sunningdale	269
1986	G Norman	Sunningdale	269
1987	P Way	Walton Heath	279
1988	I Woosnam	Sunningdale	260
1989	A Murray	Walton Heath	277

PGA Championship

Year	Sponsor	Winner	Venue	Score
1955		K Bousfield	Pannal	277
1956		CH Ward	Maesdu	282
1957		P Alliss	Maesdu	286
1958		H Bradshaw	Llandudno	287
1959		DJ Rees	Ashburnham	283
1960		AF Stickley	Coventry (63 holes)	247
1961	Schweppes	BJ Bamford	Mid-Surrey	266
1962	Schweppes	P Alliss	Little Aston	287
1963	Schweppes	PJ Butler	Birkdale	306
1964	Schweppes	AG Grubb (Asst)	Western Gailes	287
1965	Schweppes	P Alliss	Prince's	286
1966	Schweppes	GB Wostenholme	Saunton	278
1967	PGA Vice-Presidents	BGC Huggett	Thorndon Park	271
1968	Piccadilly	PM Townsend	Mid-Surrey	275
1969-71	Not played			
1972	Viyella	A Jacklin	Wentworth	279
1973	Viyella	P Oosterhuis	Wentworth	280
1974	Viyella	M Bembridge	Wentworth	278
1975	Penfold	A Palmer	Sandwich	285
1976	Penfold	NC Coles	Sandwich	280
1977	Penfold	M Piner	Sandwich	283
1978	Colgate	N Faldo	Birkdale	278
1979	Colgate	V Fernandez	St Andrews	288
1980	Sun Alliance	N Faldo	Sandwich	283

Year	Sponsor	Winner	Venue	Score
1981	Sun Alliance	N Faldo	Ganton	274
1982	Sun Alliance	A Jacklin	Hillside	284
1983	Sun Alliance	S Ballesteros	Sandwich	278
1984	Whyte & McKay	H Clark	Wentworth	204
(3 rounds only due to weather)				
1985	Whyte & McKay	P Way	Wentworth	282
1986	Whyte & McKay	R Davis	Wentworth	281
1987	Whyte & McKay	B Langer	Wentworth	270
1988	Volvo	I Woosnam	Wentworth	274
1989	Volvo	N Faldo	Wentworth	272

PGA Championship
continued

PLM Open Championship

Year	Winner	Venue	Score
1986	P Senior	Falsterbo	273
1987	H Clark	Ljunghusens	271
1988	F Nobilo	Flommen	270
1989	M Harwood	Bokskogens	271

Portuguese Open Championship

Year	Winner	Year	Winner
1980	Not played	1985	W Humphreys
1981	Not played	1986	M McNulty
1982	S Torrance	1987	R Lee
1983	S Torrance	1988	M Harwood
1984	A Johnstone	1989	C Montgomerie

Renault Open de Baleares
at Santa Ponsa

Year	Winner	Score
1988	S Ballesteros	272
1989	O Sellberg	279

Scandinavian Enterprise Open

Year	Winner	Score	Year	Winner	Score
1973	R Charles	278	1982	B Byman	275
1974	A Jacklin	279	1983	S Torrance	280
1975	G Burns	279	1984	I Woosnam	280
1976	H Baiocchi	271	1985	I Baker-Finch	274
1977	B Byman	275	1986	G Turner	270
1978	S Ballesteros	279	1987	G Brand, Jr	277
1979	A W B Lyle	276	1988	S Ballesteros	270
1980	G Norman	276	1989	R Rafferty	268
1981	S Ballesteros	273			

Spanish Open Championship
Instituted 1912

Year	Winner	Year	Winner
1980	E Polland	1985	S Ballesteros
1981	S Ballesteros	1986	H Clark
1982	S Torrance	1987	N Faldo
1983	A W B Lyle	1988	M James
1984	B Langer	1989	B Langer

Suntory World Match Play Championship
at Wentworth

Sponsored by Piccadilly until 1976 and by Colgate 1977 and 1978
Sponsored by Suntory

Year	Winner	Runner-up	By
1964	A Palmer	NC Coles	2 and 1
1965	G Player	PW Thomson	3 and 2
1966	G Player	JW Nicklaus	6 and 4
1967	A Palmer	PW Thomson	1 hole
1968	G Player	R Charles	1 hole
1969	R Charles	G Littler	37th hole
1970	JW Nicklaus	L Trevino	2 and 1
1971	G Player	JW Nicklaus	5 and 4
1972	T Weiskopf	L Trevino	4 and 3
1973	G Player	G Marsh	40th hole
1974	H Irwin	G Player	3 and 1
1975	H Irwin	A Geiberger	4 and 2
1976	D Graham	H Irwin	38th hole
1977	G Marsh	R Floyd	5 and 3
1978	I Aoki	S Owen	3 and 2
1979	W Rogers	I Aoki	1 hole
1980	G Norman	AWB Lyle	1 hole
1981	S Ballesteros	B Crenshaw	1 hole
1982	S Ballesteros	AWB Lyle	37th hole
1983	G Norman	N Faldo	3 and 2
1984	S Ballesteros	B Langer	2 and 1
1985	S Ballesteros	B Langer	6 and 5
1986	G Norman	AWB Lyle	2 and 1
1987	I Woosnam	AWB Lyle	1 hole
1988	AWB Lyle	N Faldo	2 and 1
1989	N Faldo	I Woosnam	1 hole

Swiss Open Championship

Year	Winner	Year	Winner
1980	N Price	1985	C Stadler
1981	M Pinero *(After Play-Off)*	1986	J-M Olazabal
1982	I Woosnam *(After Play-Off)*	1987	A Forsbrand
1983	N Faldo *(After Play-Off)*	1988	C Moody
1984	J Anderson	1989	S Ballesteros

Volvo Seniors British Open
at Turnberry

Year	Winner	Score
1987	N Coles	279
1988	G Player	272
1989	RJ Charles	269

Wang Four Stars National Pro-Celebrity Tournament
at Moor Park

Year	Winner	Score
1985	K Brown	277
1986	A Garrido	275
1987	M McNulty	273
1988	R Davies	275
1989	C Parry*	273

*(*after a play off)*

Other Men's Professional Tournaments

Club Professionals' Championship

Year	Winner	Club	Venue	Score
1973	DN Sewell	Ferndown	Calcot Park	276
1974	WB Murray	Coombe Wood	Calcot Park	275
1975	DN Sewell	Ferndown	Calcot Park	276
1976	WJ Ferguson	Ilkley	Moortown	283
1977	D Huish	North Berwick	Notts	284
1978	D Jones	Bangor	Pannal	281
1979	D Jones	Bangor	Pannal	278
1980	D Jagger	Selby	Turnberry	286
1981	M Steadman	Cleeve Hill Mun	Woburn	289
1982	D Durnian	Northenden	Hill Valley	285
Sponsored by Wilson				
1983	J Farmer		Heaton Park	270
1984	D Durnian		Bolton Old Links	278
1985	R Mann	Thorpeness	The Belfry	291
1986	D Huish	North Berwick	Birkdale	278
1987	R Weir		Sandiway	273
1988	R Weir		Harlech	269
1989	B Barnes	W Chiltington	Prince's	280

PGA Close Events
Assistants' Championship
Formerly PGA Under-23 Match Play

Year	Winner	Venue	By
1984	G Weir	Coombe Hill	286
1985	G Coles	Coombe Hill	284
Sponsored by Peugeot-Talbot			
1986	J Brennand	Sand Moor	280
1987	J Hawksworth	Coombe Hill	282
1988	J Oates	Coventry	284
1989	C Brooks	Hillside	291

Ryder Scottish Assistants' Championship

Year	Winner	Club	Venue	Score
1980	F Mann	Banchory	Dunbar	294
1981	M Brown	Strathclyde	West Kilbride	290
1982	R Collinson	Windyhill	West Kilbride	294
1983	A Webster	Edzell	Stirling	285
1984	C Elliott	Falkirk Tryst	Stirling	285
1985	C Elliott	Falkirk Tryst	Falkirk Tryst	284
1986	P Helsby	Hilton Park	Erskine	295
1987	C Innes	Turnberry	Hilton Park	284
1988	G Collinson	Windyhill	Turnberry	289
1989	C Brooks	Grangemouth	Windyhill	282

Senior Professional Tournament

From 1957 to 1968 sponsored by Teachers; from 1969 to 1974 sponsored by Pringle; from 1975 sponsored by Ben Sayers and Allied Hotels; from 1977 by Cambridgeshire Hotel; from 1983 by Trust House Forte

Year	Winner	Club/Country	Venue	Score
1970	M Faulkner	Ifield	Longniddry	288
1971	KDG Nagle	Australia	Elie	269
1972	K Bousfield	Coombe Hill	Longniddry	291
1973	KDG Nagle	Australia	Elie	270
1974	E Lester	Astbury	Lundin	282
1975	KDG Nagle	Australia	Longniddry	268
1976	C O'Connor	Royal Dublin	Cambridgeshire Hotel	284
1977	C O'Connor	Royal Dublin	Cambridgeshire Hotel	288
1978	P Skerritt	St Annes, Dublin	Cambridgeshire Hotel	288
1979	C O'Connor	Royal Dublin	Cambridgeshire Hotel	280
1980	P Skerritt	St Annes, Dublin	Gleneagles Hotel	286
1981	C O'Connor	Royal Dublin	North Berwick	287
1982	C O'Connor	Royal Dublin	Longniddry	200
1983	C O'Connor	Royal Dublin	Burnham and Berrow	277
1984	E Jones	Royal Co Down	Stratford-upon-Avon	280
1985	N Coles	Expotel	Pannal, Harrogate	284
1986	N Coles	Expotel	Mere, Cheshire	276
1987	N Coles	Expotel	Turnberry	279
1988	PW Thomson	Australia	North Berwick	287
1989	N Coles	Expotel	West Hill	277

Men's Professional Internationals

Great Britain v USA

Year	Great Britain			USA			Venue
1921 (June 6)	Foursomes Singles	4 6½	10½	Foursomes Singles	1 3½	4½	Gleneagles
1926 (June 4-5)	Foursomes Singles	5 8½	13½	Foursomes Singles	0 1½	1½	Wentworth

The Ryder Cup
Instituted 1927

Year	Great Britain			USA			Venue
1927 (June 3-4)	Foursomes Singles	1 1½	2½	Foursomes Singles	3 6½	9½	Worcester, Mass
1929 (May 26-27)	Foursomes Singles	1½ 5½	7	Foursomes Singles	2½ 2½	5	Moortown
1931 (June 26-27)	Foursomes Singles	1 2	3	Foursomes Singles	3 6	9	Columbus, Ohio
1933 (June 26-27)	Foursomes Singles	2½ 4	6½	Foursomes Singles	1½ 4	5½	Southport and Ainsdale
1935 (Sept 28-29)	Foursomes Singles	1 2	3	Foursomes Singles	3 6	9	Ridgewood, NJ
1937 (June 29-30)	Foursomes Singles	1½ 2½	4	Foursomes Singles	2½ 5½	8	Southport and Ainsdale
1947 (Nov 1-2)	Foursomes Singles	0 1	1	Foursomes Singles	4 7	11	Portland, Oregon
1949 (Sept 16-17)	Foursomes Singles	3 2	5	Foursomes Singles	1 6	7	Ganton
1951 (Nov 2 and 4)	Foursomes Singles	1 1½	2½	Foursomes Singles	3 6½	9½	Pinehurst, N Carolina
1953 (Oct 2-3)	Foursomes Singles	1 4½	5½	Foursomes Singles	3 3½	6½	Wentworth
1955 (Nov 5-6)	Foursomes Singles	1 3	4	Foursomes Singles	3 5	8	
1957 (Oct 4-5)	Foursomes Singles	1 6½	7½	Foursomes Singles	3 1½	4½	Lindrick
1959 (Nov 6-7)	Foursomes Singles	1½ 2	3½	Foursomes Singles	2½ 6	8½	Eldorado, Calif
1961 (Oct 13-14)	Foursomes Singles	2 6	8	Foursomes Singles	6 7	13	Lytham St Annes
1963 (Oct 11-13)	Foursomes Four-ball Singles	1 1 4	6	Foursomes Four-ball Singles	5 5 10	20	Atlanta, Ga.
1965 (Oct 7-9)	Foursomes Four-ball Singles	4 2 5	11	Foursomes Four-ball Singles	4 4 10	18	Birkdale
1967 (Oct 20-22)	Foursomes Four-ball Singles	2 0 4	6	Foursomes Four-ball Singles	5 7 9	21	Houston, Tex.
1969 (Oct 18-20)	Foursomes Four-ball Singles	4 2 4	13	Foursomes Four-ball Singles	3 3 7	13	Birkdale
1971 (Sept 16-18)	Foursomes Four-ball Singles	4 1 6	11	Foursomes Four-ball Singles	3 6 7	16	St Louis, Missouri

Year	Great Britain		USA			Venue
1972	Foursomes	4		Foursomes	3		
(Sept 20-22)	Four-ball	3	10	Four-ball	4	16	Muirfield
	Singles	3		Singles	9		
1975	Foursomes	1		Foursomes	7		
(Sept 19-21)	Four-ball	1	8	Four-ball	4	18	Laurel Valley, Pa.
	Singles	6		Singles	7		
1977	Foursomes	1		Foursomes	3		
(Sept 15-17)	Four-ball	1	7	Four-ball	4	12	Lytham St Annes
	Singles	5		Singles	5		
1979	Foursomes	4		Foursomes	3		
(Sept 14-16)	Four-ball	3	10	Four-ball	5	16	Greenbrier, WVa
	Singles	3		Singles	8		

From 1979 players from Europe became available for selection in addition to those from Great Britain and Ireland

At Walton Heath, 18th, 19th and 20th September, 1981

First Day–Foursomes

GB and Europe

USA

	Matches		Matches
AWB Lyle and M James (2 and 1)	1	W Rogers and B Lietzke	0
B Langer and M Pinero	0	L Trevino and L Nelson (1 hole)	1
B Gallacher and D Smyth (3 and 2)	1	H Irwin and R Floyd	0
P Oosterhuis and N Faldo	0	T Watson and J Nicklaus (4 and 2)	1
	2		2

Four-ball

D Smyth and J-M Canizares (6 and 5)	1	W Rogers and B Leitzke	0
AWB Lyle and M James (3 and 2)	1	B Crenshaw and J Pate	0
S Torrance and H Clark (halved)	0	T Kite and J Miller (halved)	0
B Gallacher and E Darcy	0	H Irwin and R Floyd (2 and 1)	1
	2		1

Second Day–Foursomes

P Oosterhuis and S Torrance	0	L Trevino and J Pate (2 and 1)	1
AWB Lyle and M James	0	W Rogers and R Floyd (3 and 2)	1
B Langer and M Pinero	0	J Nicklaus and T Watson (3 and 2)	1
D Smyth and B Gallacher	0	T Kite and L Nelson (3 and 2)	1
	0		4

Four-Ball

N Faldo and S Torrance	0	L Trevino and J Pate (7 and 5)	1
AWB Lyle and M James	0	L Nelson and T Kite (1 hole)	1
B Langer and M Pinero (2 and 1)	1	R Floyd and H Irwin	0
J-M Canizares and D Smyth	0	J Nicklaus and T Watson (3 and 2)	1
	1		3

Third Day–Singles

S Torrance	0	L Trevino (5 and 3)	1
AWB Lyle	0	T Kite (3 and 2)	1
D Smyth	0	B Crenshaw (6 and 4)	1
B Gallacher (halved)	0	W Rogers (halved)	0
M James	0	L Nelson (2 holes)	1
M Pinero (4 and 2)	1	J Pate	0
B Langer (halved)	0	B Leitzke (haled)	0
N Faldo (2 and 1)	1	J Miller	0
H Clark (4 and 3)	1	T Watson	0
J-M Canizares	0	H Irwin (1 hole)	1
E Darcy	0	J Nicklaus (5 and 3)	1
P Oosterhuis	0	R Floyd (2 holes)	1
	3		7

Match Aggregate: Great Britain and Europe 8; USA 17; 3 halved.

At PGA National, Florida, 14th, 15th and 16th October, 1983

First Day-Foursomes

USA	Matches	GB and Europe	Matches
T Watson and B Crenshaw (4 and 2)	1	B Gallacher and AWB Lyle	0
L Wadkins and C Stadler	0	N Faldo and B Langer (4 and 2)	1
T Kite and C Peete (2 and 1)	1	S Ballesteros and P Way	0
R Floyd and B Gilder	0	J-M Canizares and S Torrance (4 and 3)	1
	2		2

Four-Ball

G Morgan and F Zoeller	0	B Waites and K Brown (2 and 1)	1
T Watson and J Haas (2 and 1)	1	N Faldo and B Langer	0
R Floyd and C Strange	0	S Ballesteros and P Way (1 hole)	1
B Crenshaw and C Peete	0	S Torrance and I Woosnam	0
	1		2

Second Day—Foursomes

R Floyd and T Kite	0	N Faldo and B Langer (3 and 2)	1
J Haas and C Strange (3 and 1)	1	K Brown and B Waites	0
L Wadkins and G Morgan (7 and 5)	1	S Torrance and J-M Canizares	0
B Gilder and T Watson	0	S Ballesteros and P Way (2 and 1)	1
	2		2

Four-Ball

C Stadler and L Wadkins (1 hole)	1	K Brown and B Waites	0
C Peete and B Crenshaw	0	N Faldo and B Langer (2 and 1)	1
G Morgan and J Haas	0	S Ballesteros and P Way	0
T Watson and B Gilder (5 and 4)	1	S Torrance and I Woosnam	0
	2		1

Third Day–Singles

F Zoeller	0	S Ballesteros	0
J Haas	0	N Faldo (2 and 1)	1
G Morgan	0	B Langer (2 holes)	1
B Gilder (2 holes)	1	GJ Brand	0
B Crenshaw (3 and 1)	1	AWB Lyle	0
C Peete (1 hole)	1	B Waites	0
C Strange	0	P Way (2 and 1)	1
C Stadler (3 and 2)	1	I Woosnam	0
T Kite	0	S Torrance	0
L Wadkins	0	J-M Canizares	0
R Floyd	0	K Brown (4 and 3)	1
T Watson (2 and 1)	1	B Gallacher	0
	5		4

Match Aggregate USA 12; Great Britain and Europe 11; 5 halved.
Non-playing Captains: J Nicklaus, USA; A Jacklin, Great Britain and Europe.

At The Belfry, Sutton Coldfield, 13th, 14th and 15th September, 1985

Ryder Cup
continued

First Day-Foursomes

GB and Europe	Matches	USA	Matches
S Ballesteros and M Pinero (2 and 1)	1	C Strange and M O'Meara	0
B Langer and N Faldo	0	C Peete and T Kite (3 and 2)	1
A WB Lyle and K Brown	0	L Wadkins and R Floyd (4 and 3)	1
H Clark and S Torrance	0	C Stadler and H Sutton (3 and 2)	1
	1		3

Four-ball

P Way and I Woosnam (1 hole)	1	F Zoeller and H Green	0
S Ballesteros and M Pinero (2 and 1)	1	A North and P Jacobsen	0
B Langer and J-M Canizares (halved)	0	C Stadler and H Sutton (halved)	0
S Torrance and H Clark	0	R Floyd and L Wadkins (1 hole)	1
	2		1

Second Day—Four-ball

S Torrance and H Clark (2 and 1)	1	T Kite and A North	0
P Way and I Woosnam (4 and 3)	1	H Green and F Zoeller	0
S Ballesteros and M Pinero	0	M O'Meara and L Wadkins (3 and 2)	1
B Langer and A WB Lyle (halved)	0	C Stadler and C Strange (halved)	0
	2		1

Foursomes

J-M Canizares and J Rivero (7 and 5)	1	T Kite and C Peete	0
S Ballesteros and M Pinero (5 and 4)	1	C Stadler and H Sutton	0
P Way and I Woosnam	0	C Strange and P Jacobsen (4 and 2)	1
B Langer and K Brown (3 and 2)	1	R Floyd and L Wadkins	0
	3		1

Third Day–Singles

M Pinero (3 and 1)	1	L Wadkins	0
I Woosnam	0	C Stadler (2 and 1)	1
P Way (2 holes)	1	R Floyd	0
S Ballesteros (halved)	0	T Kite (halved)	0
A WB Lyle (3 and 2)	1	P Jacobsen	0
B Langer (5 and 4)	1	H Sutton	0
S Torrance (1 hole)	1	A North	0
H Clark (1 hole)	1	M O'Meara	0
N Faldo	0	H Green (3 and 1)	1
J Rivero	0	C Peete (1 hole)	1
J-M Canizares (2 holes)	1	F Zoeller	0
K Brown	0	C Strange (4 and 2)	1
	7		4

Match Aggregate: Europe 15; USA 10; 3 halved.
Non-playing Captains: A Jacklin, Europe; L Trevino, USA.

At Muirfield Village, Ohio, 25th, 26th and 27th September, 1987

First Day-Foursomes

USA	Matches	GB and Europe	Matches
C Strange and T Kite (4 and 2)	1	S Torrance and H Clark	0
H Sutton and D Pohl (2 and 1)	1	K Brown and B Langer	0
L Wadkins and L Mize	0	N Faldo and I Woosnam (2 up)	1
L Nelson and P Stewart	0	S Ballesteros and J-M Olazabal (1 up)	1
	2		2

Four-ball

B Crenshaw and S Simpson	0	G Brand Jr and J Rivero (3 and 2)	1
A Bean and M Calcavecchia	0	AWB Lyle and B Langer (1 up)	1
H Sutton and D Pohl	0	N Faldo and I Woosnam (2 and 1)	1
C Strange and T Kite	0	S Ballesteros and J-M Olazabal (2 and 1)	1
	0		4

Second Day—Four-ball

T Kite and C Strange	0	I Woosnam and N Faldo (5 and 4)	1
A Bean and P Stewart (3 and 2)	1	E Darcy and G Brand Jr	0
H Sutton and L Mize (2 and 1)	1	S Ballesteros and J-M Olazabal	0
L Wadkins and L Nelson	0	AWB Lyle and B Langer (1 up)	1
	2		2

Foursomes

C Strange and T Kite (3 and 1)	1	J Rivero and G Brand Jr	0
H Sutton and L Mize (halved)	0	N Faldo and I Woosnam	0
L Wadkins and L Nelson	0	AWB Lyle and B Langer (2 and 1)	1
B Crenshaw and P Stewart	0	S Ballesteros and J-M Olazabal	1
	1		2

Third Day—Singles

A Bean (1 up)	1	I Woosnam	0
D Pohl	0	H Clark (1 up)	1
L Mize (halved)	0	S Torrance	0
M Calcavecchia (1 up)	1	N Faldo	0
P Stewart (2 up)	1	J-M Olazabal	0
S Simpson (2 and 1)	1	J Rivero	0
T Kite (3 and 2)	1	AWB Lyle	0
B Crenshaw	0	E Darcy (1 up)	1
L Nelson (halved)	0	B Langer	0
C Strange	0	S Ballesteros (2 and 1)	1
L Wadkins (3 and 2)	1	K Brown	0
H Sutton (halved)	0	G Brand Jr	0
	6		3

Match Aggregate: USA 11; Europe 13; 4 halved.
Non-playing Captains: J Nicklaus, USA; A Jacklin, Europe.

For 1989 results, see page 39.

Individual Records

(Matches were contested as Great Britain v USA from 1927-71; as Great Britain and Ireland from 1973-7; and as Europe v USA from 1979.)
Bold type indicates captain; in brackets did not play.

Europe

Name	Year	Played	Won	Lost	Halved
Jimmy Adams	*1939-47-49-51-53	7	2	5	0
Percy Alliss	1929-31-33-35-37	6	3	2	1
Peter Alliss	1953-57-59-61-63-65-67-69	30	10	15	5
Laurie Ayton	1949	0	0	0	0
Severiano Ballesteros	1979-83-85-87-89	25	13	8	4
Harry Bannerman	1971	5	2	2	1
Brian Barnes	1969-71-73-75-77-79	26	11	14	1
Maurice Bembridge	1969-71-73-75	16	5	8	3
Aubrey Boomer	1927-29	4	2	2	0
Ken Bousfield	1949-51-55-57-59-61	10	5	5	0
Hugh Boyle	1967	3	0	3	0
Harry Bradshaw	1953-55-57	5	2	2	1
Gordon J Brand	1983	1	0	1	0
Gordon Brand Jr	1987-89	7	2	4	1
Eric Brown	1953-55-57-59-(69)-(71)	8	4	4	0
Ken Brown	1977-79-83-85-87	13	4	9	0
Stewart Burns	1929	0	0	0	0
Dick Burton	1935-37-*39-49	5	2	3	0
Jack Busson	1935	2	0	2	0
Peter Butler	1965-69-71-73	14	3	9	2
Jose-Maria Canizares	1981-83-85-89	11	5	4	2
Alex Caygill	1969	1	0	0	1
Clive Clark	1973	1	0	1	0
Howard Clark	1977-81-85-87-89	13	6	6	1
Neil Coles	1961-63-65-67-69-71-73-77	40	12	21	7
Archie Compston	1927-29-31	6	1	4	1
Henry Cotton	1929-37-*39-**47**-(53)	6	2	4	0
Bill Cox	1935-37	3	0	2	1
Allan Dailey	1933	0	0 0	0	
Fred Daly	1947-49-51-53	8	3	4	1
Eamonn Darcy	1975-77-81-87	11	1	8	2
William Davies	1931-33	4	2	2	0
Peter Dawson	1977	3	1	2	0
Norman Drew	1959	1	0	0	1
George Duncan	1927-29-31	5	2	3	0
Syd Easterbrook	1931-33	3	2	1	0
Nick Faldo	1977-79-81-83-85-87-89	27	16	9	2
John Fallon	1955-**(63)**	1	1	0	0
Max Faulkner	1947-49-51-53-57	8	1	7	0
George Gadd	1927	0	0	0	0
Bernard Gallacher	1969-71-73-75-77-79-81-83	31	13	13	5
John Garner	1971-73	1	0	1	0
Antonio Garrido	1979	5	1	4	0
Eric Green	1947	0	0	0	0
Malcolm Gregson	1967	4	0	4	0
Tom Haliburton	1961-63	6	0	6	0
Jack Hargreaves	1951	0	0	0	0
Arthur Havers	1927-31-33	6	3	3	0
Jimmy Hitchcock	1965	3	0	3	0
Bert Hodson	1931	1	0	1	0
Reg Horne	1947	0	0	0	0
Tommy Horton	1975-77	8	1	6	1
Brian Huggett	1963-67-69-71-73-75-**(77)**	24	8	10	6
Bernard Hunt	1953-57-59-61-63-65-67-69-**(73)**-**(75)**	28	6	16	6
Geoffrey Hunt	1963	3	0	3	0
Guy Hunt	1975	3	0	2	1
Tony Jacklin	1967-69-71-73-75-77-79-**(83)**-**(85)**-**(87)**-**(89)**	35	13	14	8
John Jacobs	1955-**(79)**-**(81)**	2	2	0	0
Mark James	1977-79-81-89	14	5	8	1
Edward Jarman	1935	1	0	1	0
Herbert Jolly	1927	2	0	2	0
Michael King	1979	1	0	1	0
Sam King	1937-*39-47-49	5	1	3	1
Arthur Lacey	1933-37-**(51)**	3	0	3	0
Bernhard Langer	1981-83-85-87-89	22	10	8	4
Arthur Lees	1947-49-51-55	8	4	4	0

Ryder Cup
continued

Name	Year	Played	Won	Lost	Halved
Sandy Lyle	1979-81-83-85-87	10	7	9	2
Jimmy Martin	1965	1	0	1	0
Peter Mills	1957	1	1	0	0
Abe Mitchell	1929-31-33	6	4	2	0
Ralph Moffitt	1961	1	0	1	0
Christy O'Connor, Jr	1975-89	4	1	3	0
Christy O'Connor, Sr	1955-57-59-61-63-65-67-69-71-73	35	11	20	4
Jose-Maria Olazabal	1987-89	10	7	2	1
John O'Leary	1975	4	0	4	0
Peter Oosterhuis	1971-73-75-77-79-81	28	14	11	3
Alf Padgham	1933-35-37-*39	6	0	6	0
John Panton	1951-53-61	5	0	5	0
Alf Perry	1933-35-37	4	0	3	1
Manuel Pinero	1981-85	9	6	3	0
Lionel Platts	1965	5	1	2	2
Eddie Polland	1973	2	0	2	0
Ronan Rafferty	1989	3	1	2	0
Ted Ray	1927	2	0	2	0
Dai Rees	1937-*39-47-49-51-53-**55**-**57**-**59**-**61**-(67)	18	7	10	1
Jose Rivero	1985-87	5	2	3	0
Fred Robson	1927-29-31	6	2	4	0
Syd Scott	1955	2	0	2	0
Des Smyth	1979-81	7	2	5	0
Dave Thomas	1959-63-65-67	18	3	10	5
Sam Torrance	1981-83-85-87-89	18	4	10	4
Peter Townsend	1969-71	11	3	8	0
Brian Waites	1983	4	1	3	0
Charlie Ward	1947-49-51	6	1	5	0
Paul Way	1983-85	9	6	2	1
Harry Weetman	1951-53-55-57-59-61-63-(65)	15	2	11	2
Charles Whitcombe	1927-29-31-33-35-37-*39-(49)	9	3	2	4
Ernest Whitcombe	1929-31-35	6	1	4	1
Reg Whitcombe	1935-*39	1	0	1	0
George Will	1963-65-67	15	2	11	2
Norman Wood	1975	3	1	2	0
Ian Woosnam	1983-85-87-89	17	7	7	3

(Great Britain named eight members of their 1939 side, but the match was not played because of the Second World War.)

United States of America

Name	Year	Played	Won	Lost	Halved
Tommy Aaron	1969-73	6	1	4	1
Skip Alexander	1949-51	2	1	1	0
Paul Azinger	1989	4	3	1	0
Jerry Barber	1955-**61**	5	1	4	0
Miller Barber	1969-71	7	1	4	2
Herman Barron	1947	1	1	0	0
Andy Bean	1979-87	6	4	2	0
Frank Beard	1969-71	8	2	3	3
Chip Beck	1989	4	3	0	1
Homero Blancas	1973	4	2	1	1
Tommy Bolt	1955-57	4	3	1	0
Julius Boros	1959-63-65-67	16	9	3	4
Gay Brewer	1967-73	9	5	3	1
Billy Burke	1931-33	3	3	0	0
Jack Burke	1951-53-55-**57**-59-(73)	8	7	1	0
Walter Burkemo	1953	1	0	1	0
Mark Calcavecchia	1987-89	7	3	4	0
Billy Casper	1961-63-65-67-69-71-73-75-(79)	37	20	10	7
Bill Collins	1961	3	1	2	0
Charles Coody	1971	3	0	2	1
Fred Couples	1989	2	0	2	0
Wilfred Cox	1931	2	2	0	0
Ben Crenshaw	1981-83-87	9	3	5	1
Jimmy Demaret	**1941-47-49-51	6	6	0	0
Gardner Dickinson	1967-71	10	9	1	0
Leo Diegel	1927-29-31-33	6	3	3	0
Dale Douglas	1969	2	0	2	0
Dave Douglas	1953	2	1	0	1
Ed Dudley	1929-33-37	4	3	1	0
Olin Dutra	1933-35	4	1	3	0
Lee Elder	1979	4	1	3	0
Al Espinosa	1927-29-31	4	2	1	1
Johnny Farrell	1927-29-31	6	3	2	1
Dow Finsterwald	1957-59-61-63-(77)	13	9	3	1
Ray Floyd	1969-75-77-81-83-85-(89)	23	7	13	3
Doug Ford	1955-57-59-61	9	4	4	1
Ed Furgol	1957	1	0	1	0

Name	Year	Played	Won	Lost	Halved
Marty Furgol	1955	1	0	1	0
Al Geiberger	1967-75	9	5	1	3
Vic Ghezzi	*1939-**41	0	0	0	0
Bob Gilder	1983	4	2	2	0
Bob Goalby	1963	5	3	1	1
Johnny Golden	1927-29	3	3	0	0
Lou Graham	1973-75-77	9	5	3	1
Hubert Green	1977-79-85	7	4	3	0
Ken Green	1989	4	2	2	0
Ralph Guldahl	1937-*39	2	2	0	0
Fred Haas, Jr	1953	1	0	1	0
Jay Haas	1983	4	2	1	1
Walter Hagen	**1927-29-31-33-35-(37)**	9	7	1	1
Bob Hamilton	1949	2	0	2	0
Chick Harbert	1949-**55**	2	2	0	0
Chandler Harper	1955	1	0	1	0
Dutch (EJ) Harrison	1947-49-51	3	2	1	0
Fred Hawkins	1957	2	1	1	0
Mark Hayes	1979	3	1	2	0
Clayton Heafner	1949-51	4	3	0	1
Jay Hebert	1959-61-**(71)**	4	2	1	1
Lionel Hebert	1957	1	0	1	0
Dave Hill	1969-73-77	9	6	3	0
Jimmy Hines	*1939	0	0	0	0
Ben Hogan	**1941-47-(49)-51-(67)**	3	3	0	0
Hale Irwin	1975-77-79-81	16	11	4	1
Tommy Jacobs	1965	4	3	1	0
Peter Jacobsen	1985	3	1	2	0
Don January	1965-77	7	2	3	2
Herman Keiser	1947	1	0	1	0
Tom Kite	1979-81-83-85-87-89	24	13	7	4
Ted Kroll	1953-55-57	4	3	1	0
Ky Laffoon	1935	1	0	1	0
Tony Lema	1963-65	11	8	1	2
Bruce Lietzke	1981	3	0	2	1
Gene Littler	1961-63-65-67-69-71-75	27	14	5	8
John Mahaffey	1979	3	1	2	0
Mark McCumber	1989	3	2	1	0
Jerry McGee	1977	2	1	1	0
Harold McSpaden	*1939-**41	0	0	0	0
Tony Manero	1937	2	1	1	0
Lloyd Mangrum	**1941-47-49-51-53**	8	6	2	0
Dave Marr	1965-**(81)**	6	4	2	0
Billy Maxwell	1963	4	4	0	0
Dick Mayer	1957	2	1	0	1
Bill Mehlhorn	1927	2	1	1	0
Dick Metz	*1939	0	0	0	0
Cary Middlecoff	1953-55-59	6	2	3	1
Johnny Miller	1975-81	6	2	2	2
Larry Mize	1987	4	1	1	2
Gil Morgan	1979-83	6	1	2	3
Bob Murphy	1975	4	2	1	1
Byron Nelson	1937-*39-**41-47-**(65)**	4	3	1	0
Larry Nelson	1979-81-87	13	9	3	1
Bobby Nichols	1967	5	4	0	1
Jack Nicklaus	1969-71-73-75-77-81-**(83)-(87)**	28	17	8	3
Andy North	1985	3	0	3	0
Ed Oliver	1947-51-53	5	3	2	0
Mark O'Meara	1985-89	5	1	4	0
Arnold Palmer	1961-**63**-65-67-71-73-**(75)**	32	22	8	2
Johnny Palmer	1949	2	0	2	0
Sam Parks	1935	1	0	0	1
Jerry Pate	1981	4	2	2	0
Calvin Peete	1983-85	7	4	2	1
Henry Picard	1935-37-*39	4	3	1	0
Dan Pohl	1987	3	1	2	0
Johnny Pott	1963-65-67	7	5	2	0
Dave Ragan	1963	4	2	1	1
Henry Ransom	1951	1	0	1	0
Johnny Revolta	1935-37	3	2	1	0
Chi Chi Rodriguez	1973	2	0	1	1
Bill Rogers	1981	4	1	2	1
Bob Rosburg	1959	2	2	0	0
Mason Rudolph	1971	3	1	1	1
Paul Runyan	1933-35-*39	4	2	2	0
Doug Sanders	1967	5	2	3	0
Gene Sarazen	1927-29-31-33-35-37-**41	12	7	2	3
Densmore Shute	1931-33-37	6	2	2	2
Dan Sikes	1969	3	2	1	0
Scott Simpson	1987	2	1	1	0
Horton Smith	1929-31-33-35-37-*39-**41	4	3	0	1
JC Snead	1971-73-75	11	9	2	0

Ryder Cup
continued

Name	Year	Played	Won	Lost	Halved
Sam Snead	1937-*39-**41-47-49-51-53-55-59-(69)	13	10	2	1
Ed Sneed	1977	2	1	0	1
Mike Souchak	1959-61	6	5	1	0
Craig Stadler	1983-85	8	4	2	2
Payne Stewart	1987-89	8	5	3	0
Ken Still	1969	3	1	2	0
Dave Stockton	1971-77	5	3	1	1
Curtis Strange	1983-85-87-89	17	6	9	2
Hal Sutton	1985-87	9	3	3	3
Lee Trevino	1969-71-73-75-79-81-(85)	30	17	7	6
Jim Turnesa	1953	1	1	0	0
Joe Turnesa	1927-29	4	1	2	1
Ken Venturi	1965	4	1	3	0
Lanny Wadkins	1977-79-83-85-87-89	25	15	9	1
Art Wall, Jnr	1957-59-61	6	4	2	0
Al Watrous	1927-29	3	2	1	0
Tom Watson	1977-81-83-89	15	10	4	1
Tom Weiskopf	1973-75	10	7	2	1
Craig Wood	1931-33-35-**41	4	1	3	0
Lew Worsham	1947	2	2	0	0
Fuzzy Zoeller	1979-83-85	10	1	8	1

Rydor Cup
continued

(US teams were selected in 1939 (*) and 1941 (**), but the matches were not played because of the Second World War.)

Asahi Glass Four Tours Championship
Formerly Nissan Cup and Kirin Cup

Year	Pos		Year	Pos	
1985	1	US PGA Tour	1988	1	US PGA Tour
	2	PGA European Tour		2	PGA European Tour
	3	PGA Japan Tour		3	Australia/New Zealand Tour
	4	Australia/New Zealand Tour		4	PGA Japan Tour
1986	1	PGA Japan Tour	1989	1	US PGA Tour
	2	PGA European Tour		2	PGA European Tour
	3	Australia/New Zealand Tour		3	PGA Japan Tour
	4	US PGA Tour		4	Australia/New Zealand Tour
1987	1	US PGA Tour			
	2	PGA European Tour			
	3	Australia/New Zealand Tour			
	4	PGA Japan Tour			

Dunhill Cup
Venue: St Andrews
Instituted 1985

Year	Winner	Runner-up
1985	Australia	USA
1986	Australia	Japan
1987	England	Scotland
1988	Ireland	Australia
1989	USA	Japan

PGA Cup
Instituted 1973

Year	Winner	Venue	Result
1973	USA	Pinehurst, USA	13-3
1974	USA	Pinehurst, USA	11½-4½
1975	USA	Hillside	9½-6½
1976	USA	Moortown	9½-6½
1977	Halved	Miss Hills, USA	8½-8½
1978	GB	St Mellion	10½-6½

From 1979 sponsored by Britannia Financial Services

Year	Winner	Venue	Result
1979	GB	Castletown	12½-4½
1980	USA	Oak Tree	15-6
1981	Halved	Turnberry, Isle	10½-10½
1982	USA	Knoxville, Tennessee	13-7
From 1983 sponsored by Bell's Scotch Whisky			
1983	GB&I	Muirfield	14½-6½
1984	GB&I	Turnberry	12½-8½
To be played alternate years			
1986	USA	Knollwood	16-9
1988	USA	The Belfry	15½-10½

PGA Cup
continued

World Cup of Golf
Until 1966, called Canada Cup

Year	Winner	Runners-up	Venue	Score
1953	Argentina (A Cerda and R De Vincenzo)	Canada (S Leonard and B Kerr)	Montreal	287
	(Individual: A Cerda, Argentina, 140)			
1954	Australia (P Thomson and K Nagle)	Argentina (A Cerda and R De Vincenzo)	Laval-Sur-Lac	556
1955	United States (C Harbert and E Furgol)	Australia (P Thomson and K Nagle)	Washington	560
	(Individual: E Furgol, USA, after a play-off with P Thomson and F van Donck, 279)			
1956	United States (B Hogan and S Snead)	South Africa (AD Locke and G Player)	Wentworth	567
	(Individual: B Hogan, USA, 277)			
1957	Japan (T Nakamura and K Ono)	United States (S Snead and J Demaret)	Tokyo	557
	(Individual: T Nakamura, Japan, 274)			
1958	Ireland (H Bradshaw and C O'Connor)	Spain (A Miguel and S Miguel)	Mexico City	579
	(Individual: A Miguel, Spain, after a play-off with P Bradshaw, 286)			
1959	Australia (P Thomson and K Nagle)	United States (S Snead and C Middlecoff)	Melbourne	563
	(Individual: S Leonard, Canada, 275, after a tie with P Thomson, Australia)			
1960	United States (S Snead and A Palmer)	England (H Weetman and BJ Hunt)	Portmarnock	565
	(Individual: F van Donck, Belgium, 279)			
1961	United States (S Snead and J Demaret)	Australia (P Thomson and K Nagle)	Puerto Rico	560
	(Individual: S Snead, USA, 272)			
1962	United States (S Snead and A Palmer)	Argentina (F de Luca and R De Vicenzo)	Buenos Aires	557
	(Individual: R De Vincenzo, Argentina, 276)			
1963	United States (A Palmer and JW Nicklaus)	Spain (S Miguel and R Sota)	St Nom-La-Breteche	482
	(Individual: JW Nicklaus, USA, 237 [63 holes])			
1964	United States (A Palmer and JW Nicklaus)	Argentina (R De Vicenzo and L Ruiz)	Maui, Hawaii	554
	(Individual: JW Nicklaus, USA, 276)			
1965	South Africa (G Player and HR Henning)	Spain (A Miguel and R Sota)	Madrid	571
	(Individual: G Player, South Africa, 281)			
1966	United States (JW Nicklaus and A Palmer)	South Africa (G Player and HR Henning)	Tokyo	548
	(Individual: G Knudson, Canada, and H Sugimoto, Japan, each 272; Knudson won play-off)			
1967	United States (JW Nicklaus and A Palmer)	New Zealand (RJ Charles and W Godfrey)	Mexico City	557
	(Individual: A Palmer, USA, 276)			
1968	Canada (A Balding and G Knudson)	United States (J Boros and L Trevino)	Olgiata, Rome	560
	(Individual: A Balding, Canada, 274)			
1969	United States (O Moody and L Trevino)	Japan (T Kono and H Yasuda)	Singapore	552
	(Individual: L Trevino, USA, 275)			
1970	Australia (B Devlin and D Graham)	Argentina (R De Vicenzo and V Fernandez)	Buenos Aires	545
	(Individual: R De Vicenzo, Argentina, 269)			
1971	United States (JW Nicklaus and L Trevino)	South Africa (H Henning and G Player)	Palm Beach, Florida	555
	(Individual: JW Nicklaus, USA, 271)			

Year	Winner	Runners-up	Venue	Score	World Cup
					continued

1972 Taiwan (H Min-Nan and LL Huan) — Japan (T Kono and T Murakami) — Melbourne — 438
(Individual: H Min-Nan, Taiwan, 217 [3 rounds only])
1973 United States (JW Nicklaus and J Miller) — South Africa (G Player and H Baiocchi) — Marbella, Spain — 558
(Individual: J Miller, USA, 277)
1974 South Africa (R Cole and D Hayes) — Japan (I Aoki and M Ozaki) — Caracas — 554
(Individual: R Cole, South Africa, 271)
1975 United States (J Miller and L Graham) — Taiwan (H Min-Nan and KC Hsiung) — Bangkok — 554
(Individual: J Miller, USA, 275)
1976 Spain (S Ballesteros and M Pinero) — United States (J Pate and D Stockton) — Palm Springs, USA — 574
(Individual: EP Acosta, Mexico, 282)
1977 Spain (S Ballesteros and A Garrido) — Philippines (R Lavares and B Arda) — Manilla, Philippines — 591
(Individual: G Player, South Africa, 289)
1978 United States (J Mahaffey and A North) — Australia (G Norman and W Grady) — Hawaii — 564
(Individual: J Mahaffey, USA, 281)
1979 United States (J Mahaffey and H Irwin) — Scotland (AWB Lyle and K Brown) — Glyfada, Greece — 575
(Individual: H Irwin, USA, 285)
1980 Canada (D Halldorson and J Nelford) — Scotland (AWB Lyle and S Martin) — Bogota — 572
(Individual: AWB Lyle, Scotland, 282)
1981 Not played
1982 Spain (M Pinero and J-M Canizares) — United States (B Gilder and B Clampett) — Acapulco — 563
(Individual: M Pinero, Spain, 281)
1983 United States (R Caldwell and J Cook) — Canada (D Barr and J Anderson) — Pondok Inah, Jakarta — 565
(Individual: D Barr, Canada, 276)
1984 Spain (J-M Canizares and J Rivero) — Scotland (S Torrance and G Brand, Jr) — Olgiata, Rome — 414
(Individual: J-M Canizares, Spain, 205. Played over 54 holes due to storm)
1985 Canada (D Halidorson and D Barr) — England (H Clark and P Way) — La Quinta, Calif. — 559
(Individual: H Clark, England, 272)
1986 Not played
1987 Wales (I Woosnam and D Llewelyn) — Scotland (S Torrance and AWB Lyle) — Kapalua, Hawaii — 574
(Wales won play-off)
(Individual: I Woosnam, Wales, 274)
1988 Unites States (B Crenshaw and M McCumber) — Japan (T Ozaki and M Ozaki) — Royal Melbourne, Australia — 560
1989 Australia (P Fowler and W Grady) — Spain (J-M Olazabal and J-M Canizares) — Las Brisas, Spain
(Individual: P Fowler. Played over 36 holes due to storms.)

Men's Amateur

Berkhamsted Trophy

Year	Winner	Score	Year	Winner	Score
1970	R Hunter	145	1980	R Knott	143
1971	A Millar	144	1981	P Dennett	146
1972	C Cieslewicz	148	1982	DG Lane	148
1973	SC Mason	141	1983	J Hawksworth	146
1974	P Fisher	144	1984	R Willison	139
1975	P Deeble	147	1985	F George	144
1976	J Davies	144	1986	P McEvoy	144
1977	AWB Lyle	144	1987	F George	141
1978	JC Davies	146	1988	J Cowgill	146
1979	JC Davies	147	1989	J Payne	142

Berkshire Trophy

Year	Winner	Score	Year	Winner	Score
1970	MF Bonallack	274	1980	P Downes	280
1971	MF Bonallack / J Davies	277	1981	D Blakeman	280
			1982	S Keppler	278
1972	DP Davidson	280	1983	S Hamer	288
1973	P Hedges	278	1984	JL Plaxton	276
1974	J Downie	280	1985	P McEvoy	279
1975	N Faldo	281	1986	R Muscroft	280
1976	P Hedges	284	1987	J Robinson	275
1977	AWB Lyle	279	1988	R Claydon	276
1978	P Hedges	281	1989	J Metcalfe	
1979	D Williams	274			

Boyd Quaich Tournament

Year	Winner	Year	Winner
1980	ME Lewis	1985	S Elgie
1981	P Gallagher	1986	A Roberts
1982	ME Lewis	1987	M Pask
1983	R Risan	1988	A Mathers
1984	J Huggan	1989	A Mathers

Duncan Putter
Instituted 1959

Year	Winner	Score	Year	Winner	Score
1970	JL Toye	305	1980	P McEvoy	296
1971	W Humphreys	295	1981	R Chapman	294
1972	P Berry (3 rds. fog)	230		PG Way	
1973	JKD Povall	299	1982	D McLean	283
1974	S Cox	302	1983	JG Jermine	297
1975	JG Jermine	295	1984	JP Price	297
1976	W Tucker	286	1985	P McEvoy	299
	H Stott		1986	D Wood	300
1977	H Stott	295	1987	P McEvoy	278
1978	P McEvoy	295	1988	S Dodd	290
1979	HJ Evans	292	1989	N Roderick	280

Edward Trophy
Instituted 1892

Year	Winner	Year	Winner
1980	D Murdoch	1985	GK MacDonald
1981	A Liddle	1986	J Noon
1982	F Dunsmore	1987	S Easingwood
1983	S Morrison	1988	R Blair
1984	K Walker	1989	A Elliott

Frame Trophy
Instituted 1986
Venue: Worplesdon

Year	Winner	Score
1986	DW Frame	220
1987	JRW Walkinshaw	225
1988	DW Frame	229
1989	JRW Walkinshaw	219

Golf Illustrated Gold Vase
Instituted 1909

Year	Winner	Year	Winner
1948	RD Chapman	1970	D Harrison
1949	RJ White	1971	MF Bonallack
1950	AW Whyte	1972	H Ashby
1951	JB Carr	1972	DP Davidson
1952	JDA Langley		R Hunter
1953	JDA Langley	1973	J Davies
1954	H Ridgeley	1974	P Hedges
1955	Major DA Blair	1975	MF Bonallack
1956	Major DA Blair	1976	A Brodie
1957	G Wolstenholme	1977	J Davies
1958	M Lunt	1978	P Thomas
1959	A Bussell	1979	KJ Miller
1960	D Sewell	1980	G Brand, Jr
1961	DJ Harrison	1981	P Garner
	MF Bonallack	1982	I Carslaw
1962	BHG Chapman	1983	S Keppler
1963	RH Mummery	1984	JV Marks
1964	D Moffat	1985	M Davis
1965	C Clark	1986	R Eggo
1966	PM Townsend	1987	D Lane
1967	RA Durrant	1988	M Turner
	MF Bonallack	1989	G Wolstenholme
1968	MF Bonallack		
1969	MF Bonallack		
	J Hayes		

Grafton Morrish Trophy
Public Schools Old Boys' Golf Association

Year	Winner	Year	Winner
1963	Tonbridge	1976	Charterhouse
1964	Tonbridge	1977	Haileybury
1965	Charterhouse	1978	Charterhouse
1966	Charterhouse	1979	Harrow
1967	Charterhouse	1980	Charterhouse
1968	Wellington	1981	Charterhouse
1969	Sedbergh	1982	Marlborough
1970	Sedbergh	1983	Wellington
1971	Dulwich	1984	Sedbergh
1972	Sedbergh	1985	Warwick
1973	Pangbourne	1986	Tonbridge
1974	Millfield	1987	Harrow
1975	Oundle	1988	Robert Gordon's
		1989	Tonbridge

Halford-Hewitt Challenge Cup
Public Schools Old Boys' Tournament
Instituted 1924
Played at Deal

Year	Winner	Year	Winner
1947	Harrow	1968	Eton
1948	Winchester	1969	Eton
1949	Charterhouse	1970	Merchiston
1950	Rugby	1971	Charterhouse
1951	Rugby	1972	Marlborough
1952	Harrow	1973	Rossall
1953	Harrow	1974	Charterhouse
1954	Rugby	1975	Harrow
1955	Eton	1976	Merchiston
1956	Eton	1977	Watsons
1957	Watsons	1978	Harrow
1958	Harrow	1979	Stowe
1959	Wellington	1980	Shrewsbury
1960	Rossall	1981	Watsons
1961	Rossall	1982	Charterhouse
1962	Oundle	1983	Charterhouse
1963	Repton	1984	Charterhouse
1964	Fettes	1985	Harrow
1965	Rugby	1986	Repton
1966	Charterhouse	1987	Merchiston
1967	Eton	1988	Stowe
		1989	Stowe

Hampshire Hog
Played annually at North Hants GC
Instituted 1957

Year	Winner	Year	Winner
1980	RA Durrant	1985	A Clapp
1981	G Brand	1986	R Eggo
1982	A Sherborne	1987	A Rogers
1983	I Gray	1988	S Richardson
1984	J Hawkesworth	1989	P McEvoy

The Lagonda Trophy

Instituted 1975
Venue: Camberley Heath
From 1982 played over 72 holes

Year	Winner	Score	Year	Winner	Score
1980	P McEvoy	139	1985	J Robinson	283
1981	N Mitchell	138	1986	D Gilford	282
1982	A Sherborne	290	1987	DG Lane	290
1983	I Sparkes (3 rounds)	216	1988	R Claydon	275
1984	M Davis	289	1989	T Spence	280

Leven Amateur Championship Gold Medal

Year	Winner	Year	Winner
1980	J Huggan	1985	A Turnball
1981	IC Hutcheon	1986	P-U Johansson
1982	IC Hutcheon	1987	G Macgregor
1983	J Huggan	1988	CE Everett
1984	S Stephen	1989	AJ Coltart

The Lytham Trophy

Venue: Lytham and St Annes

Year	Winner	Score	Year	Winner	Score
1965	MF Bonallack / CA Clark	295	1976	MJ Kelley	292
			1977	P Deeble	296
1966	PM Townsend	290	1978	B Marchbank	288
1967	R Foster	296	1979	P McEvoy	279
1968	R Foster	286	1980	IC Hutcheon	293
1969	T Craddock	290	1981	R Chapman	221
	SG Birtwell		1982	MF Sludds	306
1970	JC Farmer	296	1983	S McAllister	299
	CW Green		1984	J Hawksworth	289
	GC Marks		1985	L Macnamara	144
1971	W Humphreys	292	1986	S McKenna	297
1972	MF Bonallack	281	1987	D Wood	293
1973	MG King / SG Birtwell	292	1988	P Broadhurst	296
			1989	N Williamson	286
1974	CW Green	291			
1975	G Macgregor	299			

Oxford *v* Cambridge

Instituted 1878

Year	Winner	Venue
1946	Cambridge	Lytham and St Annes
1947	Oxford	Rye
1948	Oxford	Sandwich
1949	Cambridge	Hoylake
1950	Oxford	Lytham and St Annes
1951	Cambridge	Rye
1952	Cambridge	Rye
1953	Cambridge	Rye
1954	Cambridge	Rye
1955	Cambridge	Rye
1956	Oxford	Formby
1957	Oxford	Sandwich

Year	Winner	Venue
1958	Cambridge	Rye
1959	Cambridge	Burnham & Berrow
1960	Cambridge	Lytham and St Annes
1961	Oxford	Sandwich
1962	Halved	Hunstanton
1963	Cambridge	Birkdale
1964	Oxford	Rye
1965	Cambridge	Sandwich
1966	Cambridge	Hunstanton
1967	Cambridge	Rye
1968	Cambridge	Porthcawl
1969	Cambridge	Formby
1970	Halved	Sandwich
1971	Oxford	Rye
1972	Cambridge	Formby
1973	Oxford	Saunton
1974	Cambridge	Ganton
1975	Cambridge	Hoylake
1976	Cambridge	Woodhall Spa
1977	Cambridge	Porthcawl
1978	Oxford	Rye
1979	Oxford	Harlech
1980	Oxford	Hoylake
1981	Cambridge	Formby
1982	Cambridge	Hunstanton
1983	Cambridge	Royal St Georges
1984	Cambridge	Sunningdale
1985	Oxford	Rye
1986	Oxford	Ganton
1987	Cambridge	Formby
1988	Cambridge	Royal Porthcawl
1989	Cambridge	Rye

Oxford v Cambridge
continued

Oxford and Cambridge Golfing Society's "President's" Putter
Instituted 1920

Year	Winner	Year	Winner
1947	LG Crawley	1969	P Moody
1948	Major AA Duncan	1970	DMA Steel
1949	PB Lucas	1971	GT Duncan
1950	DHR Martin	1972	P Moody
1951	LG Crawley	1973	AD Swanston
1952	LG Crawley	1974	R Biggs
1953	GH Micklem	1975	CJ Weight
1954	G Huddy	1976	MJ Reece
1955	G Huddy	1977	AWJ Holmes
1956	GT Duncan	1978	MJ Reece
1957	AE Shepperson	1979	*Cancelled due to snow*
1958	Lt-Col AA Duncan	1980	S Melville
1959	ID Wheater	1981	AWJ Holmes
1960	JME Anderson	1982	DMA Steel
1961	ID Wheater	1983	ER Dexter
1962	MF Attenborough	1984	A Edmond
1963	JG Blackwell	1985	ER Dexter
1964	DMA Steel	1986	J Caplan
1965	WI Uzielli	1987	CD Meacher
1966	MF Attenborough	1988	G Woollett
1967	JR Midgley	1989	M Froggatt
1968	AWJ Holmes		

Parliamentary Handicap
Instituted 1891

Year	Winner	Year	Winner
1980	GR Russell	1985	M Morris MP
1981	R Foster	1986	Sir Anthony Grant MP
1982	S Clinton Davis MP	1987	Sir Anthony Grant MP
1983	S Clinton Davis MP	1988	Sir Peter Hordern
1984	S Clinton Davis	1989	Lord Vaux

HRH Prince of Wales Challenge Cup
Instituted 1927
Venue: Deal

Year	Winner	Score	Year	Winner	Score
1980	GM Dunsire and B		1985	RJ Tickner	141
	Nicholson (tied)	149	1986	JM Baldwin	149
1981	JM Baldwin	146	1987	S Finch	148
1982	G Homewood	145	1988	MP Palmer	144
1983	M Davis	141	1989	K Jones	143
1984	DH Niven and				
	F Wood (tied)	146			

Rosebery Challenge Cup
Venue: Ashridge

Year	Winner	Year	Winner
1980	JA Watts	1984	DG Lane
1981	RY Mitchell	1985	P Wharton
	JB Berney	1986	JE Ambridge
	(RY Mitchell won play-off)	1987	HA Wilkerson
1982	DG Lane	1988	N Leconte
1983	N Briggs	1989	C Slattery

St David's Gold Cross
Instituted 1930
Venue: Royal St David's, Harlech

Year	Winner	Year	Winner
1980	CP Hodgkinson	1985	KH Williams
1981	G Broadbent	1986	RN Roderick
1982	MW Calvert	1987	SR Andrew
1983	RD James	1988	MW Calvert
1984	RJ Green	1989	AJ Barnett

St George's Challenge Cup
Instituted 1888
Venue:Royal St George's, Sandwich

Year	Winner	Year	Winner
1980	L Simmance	1984	SJ Wood
1981	MF Bonallack	1985	SJ Wood
1982	{ SJ Wood, G Broadbent, N Taylor (Wood won play-off)	1986	R Claydon
		1987	MR Goodin
		1988	T Ryan
1983	R Willison	1989	S Green

Selborne–Salver
Venue: Blackmoor GC, Hampshire

Year	Winner	Year	Winner
1980	P McEvoy	1985	SM Bottomley
1981	A Sherborne	1986	TE Clarke
1982	I Gray	1987	
1983	D Lane	1988	N Holman
1984	D Curry	1989	M Stanford

Sunningdale Open Foursomes

Year	Winners
1970	R Barrell and Miss A Willard beat R Hunter and Miss M Everard, 2 and 1
1971	A Bird and H Flatman beat J Putt and Miss K Phillips, 3 and 2
1972	JC Davies and MG King beat JK Tullis and AJ Howard, 6 and 5
1973	JA Putt and Miss M Everard beat H Clark and SC Mason, 6 and 5
1974	PJ Butler and C Clark beat HK Clark and DN Brunyard, 1 hole
1975	*Cancelled due to snow*
1976	C Clark and M Hughesdon beat BJ Hunt and IM Stungo, 2 and 1
1977	GN Hunt and D Matthew beat D Huish and G Logan, 3 and 2
1978	GA Caygill and Miss J Greenhalgh beat A Stickley and Mrs C Caldwell, 5 and 4
1979	G Will and R Chapman beat NC Coles and D McClelland, 3 and 2
1980	NC Coles and D McClelland beat SC Mason and J O'Leary, 2 and 1
1981	A Lyddon and G Brand beat MG King and MH Dixon, 1 hole
1982	Miss MA McKenna and Miss M Madill beat Miss C Langford and Miss M Walker, 1 hole
1983	J Davies and M Devetta beat M Hughesdon and Mrs L Bayman, 4 and 3
1984	Miss M McKenna and Miss M Madill beat Miss M Walker and Miss C Langford
1985	J O'Leary and S Torrance beat B Gallacher and P Garner at 25th
1986	R Rafferty and R Chapman beat Mrs M Garner and Miss M McKenna, 1 hole
1987	I Mosey and W Humphries beat Miss G Stewart and D Huish, 3 and 2
1988	C Mason and A Chandler beat Miss M McKenna and Mrs J Garner, 5 and 3
1989	A Hare and R Claydon beat Miss V Thomas and Miss J Wade, 4 and 3

Tennant Cup

This trophy was presented by Sir Charles Tennant to the Glasgow Club in 1880. It is the oldest open amateur stroke play competition in the world

Year	Winner	Year	Winner
1970	CW Green	1980	Allan Brodie
1971	Andrew Brodie	1981	G MacDonald
1972	Allan Brodie	1982	LS Mann
1973	PJ Smith	1983	C Dalgleish
1974	D McCart	1984	E Wilson
1975	CW Green	1985	CJ Brooks
	From 1976, 72 holes	1986	PG Irvan
1976	IC Hutcheon	1987	J Rasmussen
1977	S Martin	1988	C Dalgleish
1978	IA Carslaw	1989	DG Carrick
1979	G Hay		

West of England Open Amateur Championship

Instituted 1912
Venue: Burnham-on-Sea

Year	Winner	Year	Winner
1980	JM Durbin	1985	AC Nash
1981	M Mouland	1986	J Bennett
1982	M Higgins	1987	D Rosier
1983	C Peacock	1988	N Holman
1984	GB Hickman	1989	N Holman

West of England Open Amateur Stroke Play Championship

Instituted 1968

Year	Winner	Year	Winner
1980	P McEvoy	1985	P McEvoy
1981	N Taee	1986	P Baker
1982	MP Higgins	1987	G Wolstenholme
1983	P McEvoy	1988	M Evans
1984	A Sherborne	1989	AD Hare

West of Ireland Open Amateur Championship

Instituted 1923
Venue: Rosses Point

Year	Winner	Year	Winner
1980	A Pierse	1985	J Feeney
1981	D Branigan	1986	P Rayfus
1982	A Pierse	1987	N McGrane
1983	C Glasgow	1988	G McGimpsey
1984	G McGimpsey	1989	P McInerney

West of Scotland Open Amateur Championship

Year	Winner	Year	Winner
1980	DB Howard	1985	JA Thomson
1981	H McMorran	1986	C Brooks
1982	G MacDonald	1987	R Jenkins
1983	C Barrie	1988	S Savage
1984	G Shaw	1989	AJ Elliott

Worplesdon Mixed Foursomes
Instituted 1921

Year	Winners
1980	Mrs L Bayman and I Boyd beat Mrs L Davies and R Hurst, 1 hole
1981	Mrs J Nicholsen and MN Stern beat Mrs S Birley and RL Glading, 2 and 1
1982	Miss B New and K Dobson beat Miss S Cohen and J Tarbuck, 2 and 1
1983	Miss B New and K Dobson beat Miss N McCormack and N Briggs at 19th
1984	Miss L Bayman and MC Hughesdon beat Miss N McCormack and N Briggs, 5 and 4
1985	Mrs H Kaye and D Longmuir beat Mrs J Collingham and GS Melville, 5 and 3
1986	Miss P Johnson and RN Roderick beat Miss C Duffy and L Hawkins, 2 and 1
1987	Mrs J Nicholsen and B White beat Miss T Craik and P Hughes, 4 and 3
1988	Mme A Larrezac and JJ Caplan beat Miss S Bennett and BK Turner, 4 and 3
1989	Miss J Kershaw and M Kershaw beat Mrs H Kaye and D Longmuir, 2 and 1

Amateur International Tournaments and Matches

United States v Great Britain (Walker Cup Matches)

Unofficial

Year	Great Britain		USA		Venue
1921 (May 21)	Foursomes 0 Singles 3	3	Foursomes 4 Singles 5	9	Hoylake

The Walker Cup
Instituted 1922

Year	Great Britain		USA		Venue
1922 (August 29)	Foursomes 1 Singles 3	4	Foursomes 3 Singles 5	8	Long Island, NY
1923 (May 18-19)	Foursomes 3 Singles 2½	5½	Foursomes 1 Singles 5½	6½	St Andrews
1924 (Sept 12-13)	Foursomes 1 Singles 2	3	Foursomes 3 Singles 6	9	Garden City, NY
1926 (June 2-3)	Foursomes 1 Singles 4½	5½	Foursomes 3 Singles 3½	6½	St Andrews
1928 (Aug 30-31)	Foursomes 0 Singles 1	1	Foursomes 4 Singles 7	11	Chicago
1930 (May 15-16)	Foursomes 1 Singles 1	2	Foursomes 3 Singles 7	10	Sandwich
1932 (Sept 1-2)	Foursomes 0 Singles 2½	2½	Foursomes 4 Singles 5½	9½	Brookline, Mass
1934 (May 11-12)	Foursomes 1 Singles 1½	2½	Foursomes 3 Singles 6½	9½	St Andrews
1936 (Sept 2-3)	Foursomes 1 Singles 0½	1½	Foursomes 3 Singles 7½	10½	Pine Valley, NJ
1938 (June 3-4)	Foursomes 2½ Singles 5	7½	Foursomes 1½ Singles 3	4½	St Andrews
1947 (May 16-17)	Foursomes 2 Singles 2	4	Foursomes 2 Singles 6	8	St Andrews
1949 (Aug 19-20)	Foursomes 1 Singles 1	2	Foursomes 3 Singles 7	10	Winged Foot, NY
1951 (May 11-12)	Foursomes 1 Singles 3½	4½	Foursomes 3 Singles 4½	7½	Royal Birkdale
1953 (Sept 4-5)	Foursomes 1 Singles 2	3	Foursomes 3 Singles 6	9	Kittansett, Mass
1955 (May 20-21)	Foursomes 0 Singles 2	2	Foursomes 4 Singles 6	10	St Andrews
1957 (Sept 1-2)	Foursomes 1½ Singles 2	3½	Foursomes 2½ Singles 6	8½	Minikahda
1959 (May 15-16)	Foursomes 0 Singles 3	3	Foursomes 4 Singles 5	9	Muirfield
1961 (Sept 1-2)	Foursomes 0 Singles 1	1	Foursomes 4 Singles 7	11	Seattle, Wash.

From 1963 Foursomes and Singles matches were played on both days, each match over 18 holes.

Year	Great Britain		USA		Venue
1963 (May 24-25)	Foursomes 1 Singles 7	8	Foursomes 6 Singles 6	12	Turnberry
1965 (Sept 3-4)	Foursomes 4 Singles 7	11	Foursomes 3 Singles 8	11	Baltimore, M'land

Year	Great Britain			USA			Venue
1967	Foursomes	3	7	Foursomes	4	13	Sandwich
(May 15-20)	Singles	4		Singles	9		
1969	Foursomes	3	8	Foursomes	3	10	Milwaukee, Wisc.
(Aug 22-23)	Singles	5		Singles	7		
1971	Foursomes	5½	13	Foursomes	2½	11	St Andrews
(May 26-27)	Singles	7½		Singles	8½		
1973	Foursomes	1	10	Foursomes	7	14	Brookline, Mass.
(Aug 24-25)	Singles	9		Singles	7		
1975	Foursomes	3	8½	Foursomes	5	15½	St Andrews
(May 28-29)	Singles	5½		Singles	10½		
1977	Foursomes	3	8	Foursomes	5	16	Shinnecock Hills, NY
(Aug 26-27)	Singles	5		Singles	11		
1979	Foursomes	4	8½	Foursomes	4	15½	Muirfield
(May 30-31)	Singles	4½		Singles	11½		

Walker Cup
continued

At Cypress Point, 28th and 29th August, 1981

First Day—Foursomes

USA	Matches	Great Britain and Ireland	Matches
H Sutton and J Sigel	0	P Walton and R Rafferty (4 and 2)	1
J Holtgrieve and F Fuhrer (1 hole)	1	R Chapman and P McEvoy	0
B Lewis and D von Tacky (2 and 1)	1	P Deeble and T Hutcheon	0
R Commans and C Pavin (5 and 4)	1	D Evans and P Way	0
	3		1

Singles

USA	Matches	Great Britain and Ireland	Matches
H Sutton (3 and 1)	1	R Rafferty	0
J Rassett (1 hole)	1	C Dalgleish	0
R Commans	0	P Walton (1 hole)	1
B Lewis	0	R Chapman (2 and 1)	1
C Pavin (4 and 3)	1	T Hutcheon	0
J Mudd (1 hole)	1	J Godwin	0
D von Tacky	0	P Way (3 and 1)	1
J Sigel (4 and 2)	1	P McEvoy	0
	5		3

First-days' aggregate: USA, 8; Great Britain and Ireland, 4.

Second Day—Foursomes

USA	Matches	Great Britain and Ireland	Matches
H Sutton and J Sigel	0	R Chapman and P Way (1 hole)	1
J Holtgrieve and F Fuhrer	0	P Walton and R Rafferty (6 and 4)	1
B Lewis and D von Tacky	0	D Evans and C Dalgleish (3 and 2)	1
J Rassett and J Mudd (5 and 4)	1	T Hutcheon and J Godwin	0
	1		3

Singles

USA	Matches	Great Britain and Ireland	Matches
H Sutton	0	R Chapman (1 hole)	1
J Holtgrieve (2 and 1)	1	R Rafferty	0
F Fuhrer (4 and 2)	1	P Walton	0
J Sigel (6 and 5)	1	P Way	0
J Mudd (7 and 5)	1	C Dalgleish	0
R Commans (halved)	½	J Godwin (halved)	½
J Rassett (4 and 3)	1	P Deeble	0
C Pavin (halved)	½	D Evans (halved)	½
	6		2

Second-days' aggregate: USA, 7; Great Britain and Ireland, 5.
Grand Match aggregate: USA, 15; Great Britain and Ireland, 9.

At Hoylake, 25th and 26th May, 1983

First Day—Foursomes

Walker Cup
continued

Great Britain and Ireland	USA

	Matches		Matches
M Lewis and M Thompson	0	B Lewis and J Holtgrieve (7 and 6)	1
G Macgregor and P Walton (3 and 1)	1	J Sigel and R Fehr	0
L Mann and A Oldcorn (5 and 4)	1	W Hoffer and D Tentis	0
S Keppler and A Pierse	0	W Wood and B Faxon (3 and 1)	1
	2		2

Singles

Great Britain and Ireland	USA

	Matches		Matches
P Parkin (6 and 4)	1	N Crosby	0
L Mann	0	J Holtgrieve (6 and 5)	1
A Oldcorn (4 and 3)	1	B Tuten	0
P Walton (1 hole)	1	J Sigel	0
S Keppler	0	R Fehr (1 hole)	1
D Carrick	0	B Faxon (3 and 1)	1
G Macgregor (halved)	½	W Wood (halved)	½
A Pierse	0	B Lewis (3 and 1)	1
	3½		4½

First day's aggregate: Great Britain and Ireland, 5½; USA, 6½.

Second Day—Foursomes

Great Britain and Ireland	USA

	Matches		Matches
G Macgregor and P Walton	0	N Crosby and W Hoffer (2 holes)	1
P Parkin and M Thompson (1 hole)	1	B Faxon and W Wood	0
L Mann and A Oldcorn (1 hole)	1	B Lewis and J Holtgrieve	0
S Keppler and A Pierse (halved)	½	J Sigel and R Fehr	½
	2½		1½

Singles

Great Britain and Ireland	USA

	Matches		Matches
P Walton (2 and 1)	1	W Wood	0
P Parkin	0	B Faxon (3 and 2)	1
G Macgregor	0	R Fehr (2 and 1)	1
M Thompson	0	B Tuten (3 and 2)	1
L Mann (halved)	½	D Tentis (halved)	½
S Keppler	0	B Lewis (6 and 5)	1
A Oldcorn (3 and 2)	1	J Holtgrieve	0
D Carrick	0	J Sigel (3 and 1)	1
	2½		5½

Second day's aggregate: Great Britain and Ireland, 5; USA, 7.
Grand Match aggregate: Great Britain and Ireland, 10½; USA 13½.

At Pine Valley, New Jersey, 21st and 22nd August, 1985

First Day—Foursomes

Great Britain and Ireland	Matches	USA	Matches
C Montgomerie and G Macgregor	0	S Verplank and J Sigel (1 hole)	1
J Hawksworth and G McGimpsey (4 and 3)	1	D Waldorf and S Randolph	0
P Baker and P McEvoy (6 and 5)	1	R Sonnier and J Haas	0
C Bloice and S Stephen	½	M Podolak and D Love	½
	2½		1½

Singles

Great Britain and Ireland	Matches	USA	Matches
G McGimpsey	0	S Verplank (2 and 1)	1
P Mayo	0	S Randolph (5 and 4)	1
J Hawksworth	½	R Sonnier	½
C Montgomerie	0	J Sigel (5 and 4)	1
P McEvoy (2 and 1)	1	B Lewis	0
G Macgregor (2 holes)	1	C Burroughs	0
D Gilford	0	D Waldorf (4 and 2)	1
S Stephen (2 and 1)	1	J Haas	0
	3½		4½

First-days' aggregate: Great Britain and Ireland, 6; USA, 6.

Second Day—Foursomes

Great Britain and Ireland	Matches	USA	Matches
P Mayo and C Montgomerie	½	S Verplank and J Sigel	½
J Hawksworth and G McGimpsey	0	S Randolph and J Haas (3 and 2)	1
P Baker and P McEvoy	0	B Lewis and C Burroughs (2 and 1)	1
C Bloice and S Stephen	0	M Podolak and D Love (3 and 2)	1
	½		3½

Singles

Great Britain and Ireland	Matches	USA	Matches
G McGimpsey	½	S Randolph	½
C Montgomerie	0	S Verplank (1 hole)	1
J Hawksworth (4 and 3)	1	J Sigel	0
P McEvoy	0	D Love (5 and 3)	1
P Baker (5 and 4)	1	R Sonnier	0
G Macgregor (3 and 2)	1	C Burroughs	0
C Bloice	0	B Lewis (4 and 3)	1
S Stephen (2 and 1)	1	D Waldorf	0
	4½		3½

Second-days' aggregate: Great Britain and Ireland, 5; USA, 7.
Grand Match aggregate: Great Britain and Ireland, 11; USA, 13.

At Sunningdale, Berkshire, 27th and 28th May 1987

First Day—Foursomes

Great Britain and Ireland	Matches	USA	Matches
C Montgomerie and G Shaw	0	B Alexander and B Mayfair (5 and 4)	1
D Curry and P Mayo	0	C Kite and L Mattice (2 and 1)	1
G Macgregor and J Robinson	0	B Lewis and B Loeffler (2 and 1)	1
J McHenry and P Girvan	0	J Sigel and B. Andrade (3 and 2)	1
	0		4

Singles

Great Britain and Ireland	Matches	USA	Matches
D Curry (2 holes)	1	B Alexander	0
J Robinson	0	B Andrade (7 and 5)	1
C Montgomerie (3 and 2)	1	J Sorenson	0
R Eggo	0	J Sigel (3 and 2)	1
J McHenry	0	B Montgomery (1 hole)	1
P Girvan	0	B Lewis (3 and 2)	1
D Carrick	0	B Mayfair (2 holes)	1
G Shaw (1 hole)	1	C Kite	0
	3		5

First day's aggregate: Great Britain and Ireland, 3, USA, 9.

Second Day—Foursomes

Great Britain and Ireland	Matches	USA	Matches
D Curry and D Carrick	0	B Lewis and B Loeffler (4 and 3)	1
C Montgomerie and G Shaw	0	C Kite and L Mattice (5 and 3)	1
P Mayo and G Macgregor	0	J Sorenson and B Montgomery (4 and 3)	1
J McHenry and J Robinson (4 and 2)	1	J Sigel and B Andrade	0
	1		3

Singles

Great Britain and Ireland	Matches	USA	Matches
D Currey	0	B Alexander (5 and 4)	1
C Montgomerie (4 and 2)	1	B Andrade	0
J McHenry (3 and 2)	1	B Loeffler	0
G Shaw (half)	½	J Sorenson (half)	½
J Robinson (1 hole)	1	L Mattice	0
D Carrick	0	B Lewis (3 and 2)	1
R Eggo	0	B Mayfair (1 hole)	1
P Mayo	0	J Sigel (6 and 5)	1
	3½		4½

Second day's aggregate: Great Britain and Ireland, 4½, USA, 7½.
Grand Match aggregate: Great Britain and Ireland, 7½, USA 16½.

For 1989 see page 102.

Individual Records
Great Britain and Ireland

Walker Cup
continued

Name		Year	Played	Won	Lost	Halved
MF Attenborough	Eng	1967	2	0	2	0
CC Aylmer	Eng	1922	2	1	1	0
P Baker	Eng	1985	3	2	1	0
JB Beck	Eng	1928-(38)-(47)	1	0	1	0
PJ Benka	Eng	1969	4	2	1	1
HG Bentley	Eng	1934-36-38	4	0	2	2
DA Blair	Scot	1955-61	4	1	3	0
C Bloice	Scot	1985	3	0	2	1
MF Bonallack	Eng	(1957)-59-61-63-65-67-69-71-73	25	8	14	3
G Brand	Scot	1979	3	0	3	0
OC Bristowe	Eng	(1923)-24	1	0	1	0
A Brodie	Scot	1977-79	8	5	2	1
A Brooks	Scot	1969	3	2	0	1
Hon WGE Brownlow	Eng	1926	2	0	2	0
J Bruen	Ire	1938-49-51	5	0	4	1
JA Buckley	Wales	1970	1	0	1	0
J Burke	Ire	1932	2	0	1	1
AF Bussell	Scot	1957	2	1	1	0
I Caldwell	Eng	1951-55	4	1	2	1
W Campbell	Scot	1930	2	0	2	0
JB Carr	Ire	1947-49-51-53-55-57-59-61-63-(65)-67	20	5	14	1
RJ Carr	Ire	1971	4	3	0	1
DG Carrick	Scot	1983-87	5	0	5	0
IA Carslaw	Scot	1979	3	1	1	1
C Cassells	Eng	1989	3	2	1	0
JR Cater	Scot	1955	1	0	1	0
J Caven	Scot	1922	2	0	2	0
BHG Chapman	Eng	1961	1	0	1	0
R Chapman	Eng	1981	4	3	1	0
MJ Christmas	Eng	1961-63	3	1	2	0
*CA Clark	Eng	1965	4	2	0	2
GJ Clark	Eng	1965	1	0	1	0
*HK Clark	Eng	1973	3	1	1	1
R Claydon	Eng	1989	4	2	2	0
GB Cosh	Scot	1965	4	3	1	0
T Craddock	Ire	1967-69	6	2	3	1
LG Crawley	Eng	1932-34-38-47	6	3	3	0
B Critchley	Eng	1969	4	1	1	2
D Currey	Eng	1987	4	1	3	0
CR Dalgleish	Scot	1981	3	1	2	0
B Darwin	Eng	1922	2	1	1	0
JC Davies	Eng	1973-75-77-79	13	3	8	2
P Deeble	Eng	1977-81	5	1	4	0
FWG Deighton	Scot	(1951)-57	2	0	2	0
SC Dodd	Wales	1989	4	1	1	2
*NV Drew	Ire	1953	1	0	1	0
AA Duncan	Wales	(1953)	0	0	0	0
JM Dykes	Scot	1936	2	0	1	1
R Eggo	Eng	1987	2	0	2	0
D Evans	Wales	1981	3	1	1	1
RC Ewing	Ire	1936-38-47-49-51-55	10	1	7	2
GRD Eyles	Eng	1975	4	2	2	0
EW Fiddian	Eng	1932-34	4	0	4	0
J de Forest	Eng	1932	1	0	1	0
R Foster	Eng	1965-67-69-71-73-(79)-(81)	17	2	13	2
DW Frame	Eng	1961	1	0	1	0
D Gilford	Eng	1985	1	0	1	0
P Girvan	Scot	1987	3	0	3	0
G Godwin	Eng	1979-81	7	2	4	1
CW Green	Scot	1963-69-71-73-75-(83)-(85)	17	4	10	3
RH Hardman	Eng	1928	1	0	1	0
A Hare	Eng	1989	3	2	0	1
R Harris	Scot	(1922)-23-26	4	1	3	0
RW Hartley	Eng	1930-32	4	0	4	0
WL Hartley	Eng	1932	2	0	2	0
J Hawksworth	Eng	1985	4	2	1	1
P Hedges	Eng	1973-75	5	0	2	3
CO Hezlet	Ire	1924-26-28	6	0	5	1
GA Hill	Eng	1936-(55)	2	0	1	1
Sir EWE Holderness	Eng	1923-26-30	6	2	4	0
TWB Homer	Eng	1973	3	0	3	0
CVL Hooman	Eng	1922-23	3	1**	2	0**
WL Hope	Scot	1923-24-28	5	1	4	0
G Huddy	Eng	1961	1	0	1	0
W Humphreys	Eng	1971	3	2	1	0
IC Hutcheon	Scot	1975-77-79-81	15	5	8	2

Name		Year	Played	Won	Lost	Halved
RR Jack	Scot	1957-59	4	2	2	0
*M James	Eng	1975	4	3	1	0
A Jamieson, jr	Scot	1926	2	1	1	0
MJ Kelley	Eng	1977-79	7	3	3	1
SD Keppler	Eng	1983	4	0	3	1
*MG King	Eng	1969-73	7	1	5	1
AT Kyle	Scot	1938-47-51	5	2	3	0
DH Kyle	Scot	1924	1	0	1	0
JA Lang	Scot	(1930)	0	0	0	0
JDA Langley	Eng	1936-51-53	6	0	5	1
CD Lawrie	Scot	(1961)-(63)	0	0	0	0
ME Lewis	Eng	1983	1	0	1	0
PB Lucas	Eng	(1936)-47-(49)	2	1	1	0
MSR Lunt	Eng	1959-61-63-65	11	2	8	1
*AWB Lyle	Scot	1977	3	0	3	0
AR McCallum	Scot	1928	1	0	1	0
SM McCready	Ire	1949-51	3	0	3	0
JS Macdonald	Scot	1971	3	1	1	1
P McEvoy	Eng	1977-79-81-85-89	18	5	11	2
G McGimpsey	Ire	1985-89	7	2	3	2
G Macgregor	Scot	1971-75-83-85-87	14	5	8	1
RC MacGregor	Scot	1953	2	0	2	0
J McHenry	Ire	1987	4	2	2	0
P McKellar	Scot	1977	1	0	1	0
WW Mackenzie	Scot	1922-23	3	1	2	0
SL McKinlay	Scot	1934	2	0	2	0
J McLean	Scot	1934-36	4	1	3	0
EA McRuvie	Scot	1932-34	4	1	2	1
JFD Madeley	Ire	1963	2	0	1	1
LS Mann	Scot	1983	4	2	1	1
B Marchbank	Scot	1979	4	2	2	0
GC Marks	Eng	1969-71-(87)-(89)	6	2	4	0
DM Marsh	Eng	(1959)-71-(73)-(75)	3	2	1	0
GNC Martin	Ire	1928	1	0	1	0
S Martin	Scot	1977	4	2	2	0
P Mayo	Wales	1985-87	4	0	3	1
GH Micklem	Eng	1947-49-53-55-(57)-(59)	6	1	5	0
DJ Millensted	Eng	1967	2	1	1	0
JW Milligan	Scot	1989	4	2	1	1
EB Millward	Eng	(1949)-55	2	0	2	0
WTG Milne	Scot	1973	4	2	2	0
CS Montgomerie	Scot	1985-87	8	2	5	1
JL Morgan	Wales	1951-53-55	6	2	4	0
P Mulcare	Ire	1975	3	2	1	0
GH Murray	Scot	1977	2	1	1	0
SWT Murray	Scot	1963	4	2	2	0
WA Murray	Scot	1923-24-(26)	4	1	3	0
E O'Connell	Ire	1989	4	2	0	2
A Oldcorn	Eng	1983	4	4	0	0
*PA Oosterhuis	Eng	1967	4	1	2	1
R Oppenheimer	Eng	(1951)	0	0	0	0
P Parkin	Wales	1983	3	2	1	0
JJF Pennink	Eng	1938	2	1	1	0
TP Perkins	Eng	1928	2	0	2	0
AH Perowne	Eng	1949-53-59	4	0	4	0
GB Peters	Scot	1936-38	4	2	1	1
AD Pierse	Ire	1983	3	0	2	1
AK Pirie	Scot	1967	3	0	2	1
MA Poxon	Eng	1975	2	0	2	0
D Prosser	Eng	1989	1	0	1	2
*R Rafferty	Ire	1981	4	2	2	0
J Robinson	Eng	1987	4	2	2	0
RN Roderick	Wales	1989	2	0	1	1
AC Saddler	Scot	1963-65-67-(77)	10	3	5	2
Hon M Scott	Eng	1924-34	4	2	2	0
R Scott, jr	Scot	1924	1	1	0	0
PF Scrutton	Eng	1955-57	3	0	3	0
DN Sewell	Eng	1957-59	4	1	3	0
RDBM Shade	Scot	1961-63-65-67	14	6	6	2
G Shaw	Scot	1987	4	1	2	1
DB Sheahan	Ire	1963	4	2	2	0
AE Shepperson	Eng	1957-59	3	1	1	1
AF Simpson	Scot	(1926)	0	0	0	0
JN Smith	Scot	1930	2	0	2	0
WD Smith	Scot	1959	1	0	1	0
AR Stephen	Scot	1985	4	2	1	1
EF Storey	Eng	1924-26-28	6	1	5	0
JA Stout	Eng	1930-32	4	0	3	1
C Stowe	Eng	1938-47	4	2	2	0
HB Stuart	Scot	1971-73-75	10	4	6	0
A Thirlwell	Eng	1957	1	0	1	0
KG Thom	Eng	1949	2	0	2	0
MS Thompson	Eng	1983	3	1	2	0
H Thomson	Scot	1936-38	4	2	2	0

Name		Year	Played	Won	Lost	Halved
CJH Tolley	Eng	1922-23-**24**-26-30-34	12	4	8	0
TA Torrance	Scot	1924-28-30-**32**-34	9	3	5	1
WB Torrance	Scot	1922	2	0	2	0
*PM Townsend	Eng	1965	4	3	1	0
LP Tupling	Eng	1969	2	1	1	0
W Tweddell	Eng	**1928**-(36)	2	0	2	0
J Walker	Scot	1961	2	0	2	0
P Walton	Ire	1981-83	8	6	2	0
*P Way	Eng	1981	4	2	2	0
RH Wethered	Eng	1922-23-26-**30**-34	9	5	3	1
RJ White	Eng	1947-49-51-53-55	10	6	3	1
J Wilson	Scot	1923	2	2	0	0
JC Wilson	Scot	1947-53	4	0	4	0
GB Wolstenholme	Eng	1957-59	4	1	2	1

Walker Cup
continued

Notes: *Bold Type indicates captain; in brackets, did not play.*
*Players who have also played in the Ryder Cup.
**CVL Hooman and J Sweetser in 1922 were all square after 36 holes; instructions to the
contrary not being readily available,
they played on and Hooman won at the 37th. On all other occasions halved matches have
counted as such.

Individual Records
United States of America

Name	Year	Played	Won	Lost	Halved
*TD Aaron	1959	2	1	1	0
B Alexander	1987	3	2	1	0
DC Allen	1965-67	6	0	4	2
B Andrade	1987	4	2	2	0
ES Andrews	1961	1	1	0	0
D Ballenger	1973	1	1	0	0
R Baxter, jr	1957	2	2	0	0
DR Beman	1959-61-63-65	11	7	2	2
RE Billows	1938-49	4	2	2	0
SE Bishop	1947-49	3	2	1	0
AS Blum	1957	1	0	1	0
J Bohmann	1969	3	1	2	0
M Brannan	1977	3	1	2	0
GF Burns	1975	3	2	1	0
C Burroughs	1985	3	1	2	0
AE Campbell	1936	2	2	0	0
JE Campbell	1957	1	0	1	0
WC Campbell	1951-53-**(55)**-57-65-67-71-75	18	11	4	3
RJ Cerrudo	1967	4	1	1	2
RD Chapman	1947-51-53	5	3	2	0
D Cherry	1953-55-61	5	5	0	0
D Clarke	1979	3	2	0	1
RE Cochran	1961	1	1	0	0
CR Coe	1949-51-53-**(57)**-**59**-61-63	13	7	4	2
R Commans	1981	3	1	1	1
JW Conrad	1955	2	1	1	0
N Crosby	1983	2	1	1	0
BH Cudd	1955	2	2	0	0
RD Davies	1963	2	0	2	0
JW Dawson	1949	2	2	0	0
RB Dickson	1967	3	3	0	0
GT Dunlap, jr	1932-34-36	5	3	1	1
D Edwards	1973	4	4	0	0
HC Egan	1934	1	1	0	0
HC Eger	1989	3	1	2	0
D Eichelberger	1965	3	1	2	0
J Ellis	1973	3	2	1	0
W Emery	1936	2	1	0	1
C Evans, jr	1922-24-28	5	3	2	0
J Farquhar	1971	3	1	2	0
B Faxon	1983	4	3	1	0
R Fehr	1983	4	2	1	1
JW Fischer	1934-36-38-**(65)**	4	3	0	1
D Fischesser	1979	3	1	2	0
MA Fleckman	1967	2	0	2	0
B Fleisher	1969	4	0	2	2
J Fought	1977	4	4	0	0
WC Fownes, jr	**1922**-24	3	1	2	0
F Fuhrer	1981	3	2	1	0
JR Gabrielsen	1977-**(81)**	3	1	2	0
R Gamez	1989	4	3	0	1
RA Gardner	1922-**23**-**24**-**26**	8	6	2	0
RW Gardner	1961-63	5	4	0	1
M Giles	1969-71-73-75	15	8	2	5
HL Givan	1936	1	0	0	1
JG Goodman	1934-36-38	6	4	2	0

Walker Cup
continued

Name	Year	Played	Won	Lost	Halved
M Gove	1979	3	2	1	0
J Grace	1975	3	2	1	0
JA Grant	1967	2	2	0	0
AD Gray, jr	1963-65-67	12	5	6	1
JP Guilford	1922-24-26	6	4	2	0
W Gunn	1926-28	4	4	0	0
*F Haas, jr	1938	2	0	2	0
*J Haas	1975	3	3	0	0
J Haas	1985	3	1	2	0
G Hallberg	1977	3	1	2	0
GS Hamer, jr	(1947)	0	0	0	0
LE Harris, jr	1963	4	3	1	0
V Heafner	1977	3	3	0	0
SD Herron	1923	2	0	2	0
S Hoch	1979	4	4	0	0
W Hoffer	1983	2	1	1	0
J Holtgrieve	1979-81-83	10	6	4	0
JM Hopkins	1965	3	0	2	1
R Howe	1989	1	0	1	0
W Howell	1932	1	1	0	0
W Hyndman	1957-59-61-69-71	9	6	1	2
J Inman	1969	2	2	0	0
JG Jackson	1953-55	3	3	0	0
K Johnson	1989	3	1	2	0
HR Johnston	1923-24-28-30	6	5	1	0
RT Jones, jr	1922-24-26-**28-30**	10	9	1	0
AF Kammer	1947	2	1	1	0
M Killian	1973	3	1	2	0
C Kite	1987	3	2	1	0
*TO Kite	1971	4	2	1	1
RE Knepper	(1922)	0	0	0	0
RW Knowles	1951	1	1	0	0
G Koch	1973-75	7	4	1	2
CR Kocsis	1938-49-57	5	2	2	1
G Lesher	1989	4	1	3	0
B Lewis, jr	1981-83-85-87	14	10	4	0
JW Lewis	1967	4	3	1	0
WL Little, jr	1934	2	2	0	0
*GA Littler	1953	2	2	0	0
B Loeffler	1987	3	2	1	0
D Love	1985	3	2	0	1
MJ McCarthy, jr	(1928)-32	1	1	0	0
BN McCormick	1949	1	1	0	0
JB McHale	1949-51	3	2	0	1
RR Mackenzie	1926-28-30	6	5	1	0
MR Marston	1922-23-24-34	8	5	3	0
D Martin	1989	4	1	1	2
L Mattiace	1987	3	2	1	0
B Mayfair	1987	3	3	0	0
E Meeks	1989	1	0	0	1
SN Melnyk	1969-71	7	3	3	1
P Mickelson	1989	4	1	1	2
AL Miller	1969-71	8	4	3	1
L Miller	1977	4	4	0	0
DK Moe	1930-32	3	3	0	0
B Montgomery	1987	2	2	0	0
G Moody	1979	3	1	2	0
GT Moreland	1932-34	4	4	0	0
D Morey	1955-65	4	1	3	0
J Mudd	1981	3	3	0	0
*RJ Murphy	1967	4	1	2	1
JF Neville	1923	1	0	1	0
*JW Nicklaus	1959-61	4	4	0	0
LW Oehmig	(1977)	0	0	0	0
FD Ouimet	1922-23-24-26-30-**32-34**-(36)-(38)-(47)-(49)	16	9	5	2
HD Paddock, jr	1951	1	0	0	1
*J Pate	1975	4	0	4	0
WJ Patton	1955-57-59-63-65-(69)	14	11	3	0
C Pavin	1981	3	2	0	1
M Peck	1979	3	1	1	1
M Pfeil	1973	4	2	1	1
M Podolak	1985	2	1	0	1
SL Quick	1947	2	1	1	0
S Randolph	1985	4	2	1	1
J Rassett	1981	3	3	0	0
F Ridley	1977-(87)-(89)	3	2	1	0
RH Riegel	1947-49	4	4	0	0
H Robbins, jr	1957	2	0	1	1
*W Rogers	1973	2	1	1	0
GV Rotan	1923	2	1	1	0
*EM Rudolph	1957	2	1	0	1
B Sander	1977	3	0	3	0
CH Seaver	1932	2	2	0	0

Name	Year	Played	Won	Lost	Halved
RL Siderowf	1969-73-75-77-(79)	14	4	8	2
J Sigel	1977-79-81-83-85-87-89	27	14	8	5
RH Sikes	1963	3	1	2	0
JB Simons	1971	2	0	2	0
*S Simpson	1977	3	3	0	0
CB Smith	1961-63	2	0	1	1
R Smith	1936-38	4	2	2	0
R Sonnier	1985	3	0	2	1
J Sorensen	1987	3	1	1	1
*C Stadler	1975	3	3	0	0
FR Stranahan	1947-49-51	6	3	2	1
*C Strange	1975	4	3	0	1
*H Sutton	1979-81	7	2	4	1
JW Sweetser	1922-23-24-26-28-32-(67)-(73)	12	7	4**	1**
FM Taylor	1957-59-61	4	4	0	0
D Tentis	1983	2	0	1	1
RS Tufts	(1963)	0	0	0	0
WP Turnesa	1947-49-51	6	3	3	0
B Tuten	1983	2	1	1	0
EM Tutweiler	1965-67	6	5	1	0
LR Updegraff	1963-65-69-(75)	7	3	3	1
S Urzetta	1951-53	4	4	0	0
K Venturi	1953	2	2	0	0
S Verplank	1985	4	3	0	1
GJ Voigt	1930-32-36	5	2	2	1
G Von Elm	1926-28-30	6	4	1	1
D von Tacky	1981	3	1	2	0
*JL Wadkins	1969-71	7	3	4	0
D Waldorf	1985	3	1	2	0
EH Ward	1953-55-59	6	6	0	0
MH Ward	1938-47	4	2	2	0
M West	1973-79	6	2	3	1
J Westland	1932-34-53-(61)	5	3	0	2
HW Wettlaufer	1959	2	2	0	0
E White	1936	2	2	0	0
OF Willing	1923-24-30	4	4	0	0
JM Winters, Jr	(1971)	0	0	0	0
W Wood	1983	4	1	2	1
FJ Wright	1923	1	1	0	0
CR Yates	1936-38-(53)	4	3	0	1
D Yates	1989	4	1	2	1
RL Yost	1955	2	2	0	0

Notes: Bold type indicates captain: in brackets, did not play.
*Players who have also played in the Ryder Cup.
**CVL Hooman and J Sweetser in 1922 were all square after 36 holes; instructions to the contrary not being readily available, they played on and Hooman won at the 37th. On all other occasions halved matches have counted as such.

Eisenhower Trophy (World Cup)
Instituted 1958

Year	Winners	Runners-up	Venue	Score
1958	Australia	United States	St Andrews	918
(After a tie, Australia won the play-off by two strokes. Australia 222, United States 224)				
1960	United States	Australia	Ardmore, USA	834
1962	United States	Canada	Kawana, Japan	854
1964	Great Britain & Ireland	Canada	Olgiata, Rome	895
1966	Australia	United States	Mexico City	877
1968	United States	Great Britain & Ireland	Melbourne	868
1970	United States	New Zealand	Madrid	857
1972	United States	Australia	Buenos Aires	865
1974	United States	Japan	Dominican Rep.	888
1976	Great Britain	Japan	Penina, Portugal	892
1978	United States	Canada	Fiji	873
1980	United States	South Africa	Pinehurst, USA	848
1982	United States	Sweden	Lausanne	859
1984	Japan	United States	Hong Kong	870
1986	Canada	United States	Caracas, Venezuela	860
1988	Great Britain & Ireland	United States	Ullva, Sweden	882

European Amateur Team Championship

Year	Winner	Second	Venue
1959	Sweden		Brussels, Belgium
1961	Sweden	England	Falsterbo, Sweden
1963	England	Sweden	St George's, England
1965	Ireland	Scotland	Turin, Italy
1967	Ireland	France	Hamburg, W Germany
1969	England	W Germany	Lausanne, Switzerland
1971	England	Scotland	Penina, Portugal
1973	England	Scotland	Killarney, Ireland
1975	Scotland	Italy	The Haagsche, Holland
1977	Scotland	Sweden	Esbjerg, Denmark
1979	England	Wales	St Andrews, Scotland
1981	England	Scotland	Chantilly, France
1983	Ireland	Spain	Halmstad, Sweden
1985	Scotland	Sweden	Murhof, Austria
1987	Ireland	England	Royal Porthcawl
1989	England	Scotland	

Home Internationals

Winners:

1932	Scotland
1933	Scotland
1934	Scotland
1935	Tie: England, Scotland, Ireland
1936	Scotland
1937	Scotland
1938	England
1939–46	No Internationals held
1947	England
1948	England
1949	England
1950	Ireland
1951	Tie: Ireland, Scotland
1952	Scotland
1953	Scotland
1954	England
1955	Ireland
1956	Scotland
1957	England
1958	England
1959	Tie: England, Ireland, Scotland
1960	England
1961	Scotland

Winners:

1962	Tie: England, Ireland, Scotland
1963	Tie: England, Ireland, Scotland
1964	England
1965	England
1966	England
1967	Scotland
1968	England
1969	England
1970	Scotland
1971	Scotland
1972	Tie: Scotland, England
1973	England
1974	England
1975	Scotland
1976	Scotland
1977	England
1978	England
1979	No Internationals held
1980	England
1981	Scotland
1982	Scotland
1983	Ireland
1984	England

1985—At Formby
Winners: England

England beat Wales	11 matches to 4
England beat Scotland	8 matches to 7
England beat Ireland	8½ matches to 6½
Wales beat Scotland	8 matches to 7
Wales beat Ireland	9½ matches to 5½
Ireland beat Scotland	11½ matches to 3½

1986—At Harlech
Winners: Scotland

Scotland beat England	9½ matches to 5½
Scotland beat Ireland	10½ matches to 4½
Scotland beat Wales	10 matches to 5
England beat Wales	9 matches to 6
Ireland beat England	8 matches to 7
Wales halved with Ireland	7½ matches each

1987—At Lahinch
Winners: Ireland

Ireland beat England	6 matches to 4
Ireland beat Scotland	10½ matches to 4½
Ireland beat Wales	8 matches to 7
England beat Scotland	9 matches to 6
England halved with Wales	7 matches each
Scotland beat Wales	6½ matches to 3½

(On the first day the foursomes were abandoned due to bad weather, singles only being played.)

1988—At Muirfield
Winners: England

England beat Wales	11 matches to 4
England beat Scotland	9 matches to 6
England beat Ireland	8 matches to 7
Ireland halved with Wales	7½ matches each
Ireland beat Scotland	10 matches to 5
Wales beat Scotland	8 matches to 7

1989—At Ganton
Winners: England

England beat Ireland	8 matches to 7
England beat Scotland	9 matches to 6
England beat Wales	12 matches to 3
Ireland beat Wales	11 matches to 4
Scotland beat Wales	8 matches to 7
Scotland beat Ireland	8½ matches to 6½

R & A Trophy

This trophy is played between the winners of the England v Scotland and Wales v Ireland International Matches and was introduced in 1985.

Year	Winner	Result	Venue
1985	England / Ireland } tie	7½-7½	Barnton
1986	Ireland	8½-6½	Seaton Carew
1987	Scotland	10½-4½	Barassie
1988	England	14-1	Formby
1989	England	11½-3½	Nairn

St Andrews Trophy (Great Britain v Europe)
Match instituted 1956
Trophy presented 1962

Year	Winner	Venue	Result
1956	Great Britain	Wentworth	12½-2½
1958	Great Britain	St Cloud, France	10-5
1960	Great Britain	Walton Heath	13-5
1962	Great Britain	Halmstead, Sweden	18-12
1964	Great Britain	Muirfield	23-7
1966	Great Britain	Bilbao, Spain	19½-10½
1968	Great Britain	Portmarnock	20-10
1970	Great Britain	La Zoute, Belgium	17½-12½
1972	Great Britain	Berkshire	19½-10½
1974	Europe	Punta Ala, Italy	16-14
1976	Great Britain	St Andrews	18½-11½
1978	Great Britain	Bremen, Germany	20½-9½
1980	Great Britain	St George's	19½-10½

Year	Winner	Venue	Result
1982	Europe	Rosendaelsche, Netherlands	14–10
1984	Great Britain	Taunton, Devon	13-11
1986	Great Britain	Halmstead, Sweden	14½-9½
1988	Great Britain	St Andrews	15½-8½

St Andrews Trophy
continued

Wales v Ireland
Instituted 1972

Year	Winner	Result	Venue
1972	Ireland	5-4	Moortown
1973	Ireland	5½-3½	Blairgowrie
1974	Wales	5-4	Hoylake
1975	Wales	6½-2½	Bruntsfield
1976	Wales	7½-1½	Sunningdale
1977	Ireland	6½-5½	Downfield
1978	Wales	8-4	Seaton Carew
1979	Ireland	9½-2½	Barassie
1980	Wales	6½-5½	Formby
1981	Ireland	8-4	Gullane
1982	Wales	9-3	Burnham & Berrow
1983	Ireland	7-5	Glenbervie
1984	Wales	6½-5½	Porthcawl
1985	Ireland	11½-3½	Barnton
1986	Ireland	8½-6½	Seaton Carew
1987	Wales	10½-4½	Barassie
1988	Wales	8-7	Formby
1989	Wales	10½-4½	Nairn

Ladies' Amateur

Astor Salver
Instituted 1951
Venue: The Berkshire

Year	Winner	Score	Year	Winner	Score
1980	Miss J Lock	141	1985	Miss H Wadsworth	138
1981	Mrs WJ Uzielli	148	1986	Miss C Pierce	144
1982	*Abandoned after one*		1987	Mrs V Thomas	145
	round due to weather		1988	Mrs J Thornhill	136
1983	Mrs L Bayman	148	1989	S Sutton	140
1984	Mrs L Bayman	142			

Hampshire Rose
Instituted 1973
Played annually at North Hants GC

Year	Winner	Year	Winner
1980	Miss B New	1985	Mrs A Uzielli
1981	Mrs J Nicholson	1986	Miss C Hourihane
1982	Mrs J Thornhill	1987	Mrs J Thornhill
1983	Miss J Pool	1988	Mrs J Thornhill
1984	Mrs C Caldwell	1989	Miss A MacDonald

Helen Holm Trophy
Instituted 1973

Year	Winner	Year	Winner
1980	Miss W Aitken	1985	Miss P Wright
1981	Miss G Stewart	1986	Mrs IC Robertson
1982	Miss W Aitken	1987	Miss E Farquharson
1983	Miss J Connachan	1988	Miss E Farquharson
1984	Miss G Stewart	1989	Miss S Robinson

Ladies' Amateur International Tournaments and Matches

British Isles v USA (Ladies) Curtis Cup
Instituted 1932

		British Isles			USA			Venue
1932	Foursomes	0	3½	Foursomes	3	5½		Wentworth
	Singles	3½		Singles	2½			
1934	Foursomes	1½	2½	Foursomes	1½	6½		Chevy Chase
	Singles	1		Singles	5			
1936	Foursomes	1½	4½	Foursomes	1½	4½		Gleneagles
	Singles	3		Singles	3			
1938	Foursomes	2½	3½	Foursomes	½	5½		Essex County Club
	Singles	1		Singles	5			
1948	Foursomes	1	2½	Foursomes	2	6½		Birkdale
	Singles	1½		Singles	4½			
1950	Foursomes	1	1½	Foursomes	2	7½		Buffalo
	Singles	½		Singles	5½			
1952	Foursomes	2	5	Foursomes	1	4		Muirfield
	Singles	3		Singles	3			
1954	Foursomes	0	3	Foursomes	3	6		Merion
	Singles	3		Singles	3			
1956	Foursomes	1	5	Foursomes	2	4		Prince's, Sandwich
	Singles	4		Singles	2			
1958	Foursomes	2	4½	Foursomes	1	4½		Brae Burn GC
	Singles	2½		Singles	3½			
1960	Foursomes	1	2½	Foursomes	2	6½		Lindrick
	Singles	1½		Singles	4½			
1962	Foursomes	0	1	Foursomes	3	8		Colorado Springs
	Singles	1		Singles	5			
1964	Foursomes	3½	7½	Foursomes	2½	10½		Porthcawl
	Singles	4		Singles	8			
1966	Foursomes	1½	5	Foursomes	4½	13		Hot Springs
	Singles	3½		Singles	8½			

		Great Britain & Ireland			USA			Venue
1968	Foursomes	2½	7½	Foursomes	3½	10½		Newcastle, Co Down
	Singles	5		Singles	7			
1970	Foursomes	2½	6½	Foursomes	3½	11½		Brae Burn, USA
	Singles	4		Singles	8			
1972	Foursomes	3½	8	Foursomes	2½	10		Western Gailes
	Singles	4½		Singles	7½			
1974	Foursomes	2½	5	Foursomes	3½	13		San Francisco, Cal.
	Singles	2½		Singles	9½			
1976	Foursomes	2	6½	Foursomes	4	11½		Lytham St Annes
	Singles	4½		Singles	7½			
1978	Foursomes	2½	6	Foursomes	3½	12		Apawamis, NY
	Singles	3½		Singles	8½			

At St Pierre, 6th and 7th June, 1980

First Day–Foursomes

Curtis Cup
continued

Great Britain & Ireland		United States	
Miss M McKenna and Miss C Nesbitt	½	Miss L Smith and Miss T Moody	½
Mrs T Thomas and Miss G Stewart	0	Miss P Sheehan and Miss L Castillo (5 and 3)	1
Miss M Madill and Mrs C Caldwell	½	Mrs J Oliver and Miss C Semple	½
	1		2

Singles

Great Britain & Ireland		United States	
Miss M McKenna	0	Miss P Sheehan (3 and 2)	1
Miss C Nesbitt	½	Miss L Smith	½
Miss J Connachan	0	Miss B Goldsmith (2 holes)	1
Miss M Madill	0	Miss C Semple (4 and 3)	1
Miss L Moore	½	Miss M Hafeman	½
Mrs C Caldwell	0	Mrs J Oliver (1 hole)	1
	1		5

Second Day–Foursomes

Great Britain & Ireland		United States	
Mrs C Caldwell and Miss M Madill	0	Miss P Sheehan and Miss L Castillo (3 and 2)	1
Miss C Nesbitt and Miss M McKenna	0	Miss L Smith and Miss T Moody (6 and 5)	1
Mrs T Thomas and Miss L Moore	0	Mrs J Oliver and Miss C Semple (1 hole)	1
	0		3

Singles

Great Britain & Ireland		United States	
Miss M Madill	0	Miss P Sheehan (5 and 4)	1
Miss M McKenna (5 and 4)	1	Miss L Castillo	0
Miss J Connachan	0	Miss M Hafeman (6 and 5)	1
Miss G Stewart (5 and 4)	1	Miss L Smith	0
Miss L Moore (1 hole)	1	Miss B Goldsmith	0
Mrs T Thomas	0	Miss C Semple (4 and 3)	1
	3		3

Aggregate: United States, 13; Great Britain and Ireland, 5

At Denver, Colorado, USA, on 5th and 6th August, 1982

First Day–Foursomes

Great Britain & Ireland		United States	
Mrs IC Robertson and Miss M McKenna	0	Mrs J Inkster and Miss C Semple (5 and 4)	1
Miss K Douglas and Miss J Soulsby	½	Miss K Baker and Mrs L Smith	½
Miss G Stewart and Miss J Connachan	0	Miss A Benz and Miss C Hanlon (2 and 1)	1
	½		2½

Singles

Great Britain & Ireland		United States	
MIss M McKenna	0	Miss A Benz (2 and 1)	1
Miss J Connachan	0	Miss C Hanlon (5 and 4)	1
Miss W Aitken	0	Mrs M McDougall (2 holes)	1
Mrs IC Robertson	0	Miss K Baker (7 and 6)	1
Miss J Soulsby (2 holes)	1	Mrs J Oliver	0
Miss K Douglas	0	Mrs J Inkster (7 and 6)	1
	1		5

Second Day–Foursomes

Great Britain & Ireland		United States	
Miss J Connachan and Miss W Aitken	0	Mrs J Inkster and Miss C Semple (3 and 2)	1
Miss K Douglas and Miss J Soulsby	0	Miss K Baker and Miss L Smith (1 hole)	1
Miss M McKenna and Mrs IC Robertson (1 hole)	1	Miss A Benz and Miss C Hanlon	0
	1		2

Singles

Great Britain & Ireland		United States	
Miss K Douglas	0	Mrs J Inkster (7 and 6)	1
Miss G Stewart	0	Miss K Baker (4 and 3)	1
Mrs V Thomas	0	Mrs J Oliver (5 and 4)	1
Miss J Soulsby	0	Mrs M McDougall (2 and 1)	1
Miss M McKenna	0	Miss C Semple (1 hole)	1
Mrs IC Robertson (5 and 3)	1	Miss L Smith	0
	1		5

Aggregate: United States, 14½; Great Britain and Ireland, 3½

At Muirfield on 8th and 9th June, 1984

First Day–Foursomes

Great Britain & Ireland		United States	
C Waite and B New (2 holes)	1	J Pacillo and A Sander	0
J Thornhill and P Grice	½	L Smith and J Rosenthal	½
M McKenna and L Davies	0	M Widman and H Farr (1 hole)	1
	1½		1½

Singles

Great Britain & Ireland		United States	
J Thornhill	½	J Pacillo	½
C Waite	0	P Hammel (4 and 2)	1
C Hourihane	0	J Rosenthal (3 and 1)	1
V Thomas (2 and 1)	1	D Howe	0
P Grice (2 holes)	1	A Sander	0
B New	0	M Widman (4 and 3)	1
	2½		3½

Curtis Cup
continued

Second Day–Foursomes

Great Britain & Ireland		United States	
C Waite and B New	0	L Smith and J Rosenthal (3 and 1)	1
J Thornhill and P Grice (2 and 1)	1	M Widman and H Farr	0
V Thomas and C Hourihane	½	D Howe and P Hammel	½
	1½		1½

Singles

Great Britain & Ireland		United States	
J Thornhill	0	J Pacillo (3 and 2)	1
L Davies (1 hole)	1	A Sander	0
C Waite (5 and 4)	1	L Smith	0
P Grice	0	D Howe (2 holes)	1
B New	0	H Farr (6 and 5)	1
C Hourihane (3 and 1)	1	P Hammel	0
	3		3

Aggregate: Great Britain and Ireland 8½; United States 9½

At Prairie Dunes, Kansas, USA on 1st and 2nd August, 1986

Curtis Cup
continued

First Day–Foursomes

Great Britain & Ireland		United States	
L Behan and J Thornhill (7 and 6)	1	K Kessler and C Schreyer	0
P Johnson and K Davies (2 and 1)	1	D Ammaccapane and D Mochrie	0
B Robertson and M McKenna (1 hole)	1	K Gardner and K McCarthy	0
	3		0

Singles

Great Britain & Ireland		United States	
P Johnson (1 hole)	1	L Shannon	0
J Thornhill (4 and 3)	1	K Williams	0
L Behan (4 and 3)	1	D Ammaccapane	0
V Thomas	0	K Kessler (3 and 2)	1
K Davies	½	D Mochrie	½
C Hourihane	0	C Schreyer (2 and 1)	1
	3½		2½

Second Day–Foursomes

Great Britain & Ireland		United States	
P Johnson and K Davies (1 hole)	1	D Ammaccapane and D Mochrie	0
L Behan and J Thornhill (5 and 3)	1	L Shannon and K Williams	0
B Robertson and M McKenna	½	K Gardner and K McCarthy	½
	2½		½

Singles

Great Britain & Ireland		United States	
J Thornhill	½	L Shannon	½
P Johnson (5 and 3)	1	K McCarthy	0
L Behan	0	K Gardner (1 hole)	1
V Thomas (4 and 3)	1	K Williams	0
K Davies	½	K Kessler	½
C Hourihane (5 and 3)	1	C Schreyer	0
	4		2

Aggregate: Great Britain and Ireland 13, United States 5

At Royal St George's, on 10th and 11th June, 1988

Curtis Cup
continued

First Day–Foursomes

Great Britain & Ireland		United States	
L Bayman and J Wade (2 and 1)	1	T Kerdyk and K Scrivner	0
S Shapcott and K Davies (5 and 4)	1	C Scholefield and C Thompson	0
J Thornhill and V Thomas	½	L Shannon and C Keggi	½
	2½		½

Singles

Great Britain & Ireland		United States	
L Bayman	½	T Kerdyk	½
J Wade (2 holes)	1	C Scholefield	0
S Shapcott	0	C Thompson (1 hole)	1
K Davies	0	P Sinn (4 and 3)	1
S Lawson (1 hole)	1	P Cornett	0
J Thornhill (3 and 2)	1	L Shannon	0
	3½		2½

Second Day–Foursomes

Great Britain & Ireland		United States	
L Bayman and J Wade	0	T Kerdyk and K Scrivner (1 hole)	1
S Shapcott and K Davies (2 holes)	1	L Shannon and C Keggi	0
J Thornhill and V Thomas (6 and 5)	1	C Scholefield and C Thompson	0
	2		1

Singles

Great Britain & Ireland		United States	
J Wade	0	T Kerdyk (2 and 1)	1
S Shapcott (3 and 2)	1	C Keggi	0
S Lawson	0	K Scrivner (4 and 3)	1
V Thomas (5 and 3)	1	P Cornett	0
L Bayman (1 hole)	1	P Sinn	0
J Thornhill	0	C Thompson (3 and 2)	1
	3		3

Aggregate: Great Britain and Ireland 11, United States 7

Individual Records

Great Britain and Ireland

Name		Year	Played	Won	Lost	Halved
Jean Anderson (Donald)	Scot	1948	6	3	3	0
Diane Bailey [Frearson] (Robb)	Eng	1962-72-(84)-(86)-(88)	5	2	2	1
Sally Barber (Bonallack)	Eng	1962	1	0	1	0
Pam Barton	Eng	1934-36	4	0	3	1
Linda Bayman	Eng	1988	4	2	1	1
Baba Beck (Pym)	Ire	(1954)	0	0	0	0
Charlotte Beddows [Watson] (Stevenson)	Scot	1932	1	0	1	0
Lilian Behan	Ire	1986	4	3	1	0
Veronica Beharrell (Anstey)	Eng	1956	1	0	1	0
Pam Benka (Tredinnick)	Eng	1966-68	4	0	3	1
Jeanne Bisgood	Eng	1950-52-54-(70)	4	1	3	0
Zara Bolton (Davis)	Eng	1948-(56)-(66)-(68)	2	0	2	0

Name		Year	Played	Won	Lost	Halved
Angela Bonallack						
(Ward)	Eng	1956-58-60-62-64-66	15	6	8	1
Ita Butler (Burke)	Ire	1966	3	2	1	0
Lady Katherine Cairns	Eng	(1952)	0	0	0	0
Carole Caldwell						
(Redford)	Eng	1978-80	5	0	3	2
Doris Chambers	Eng	(1934)-(36)-(48)	0	0	0	0
Carol Comboy (Grott)	Eng	(1978)-(80)	0	0	0	0
Jane Connachan	Scot	1980-82	5	0	5	0
Elsie Corlett	Eng	1932-38-(64)	3	1	2	0
Diana Critchley						
(Fishwick)	Eng	1932-34-(50)	3	1	2	0
Karen Davies	Wales	1986-88	7	4	1	2
Laura Davies	Eng	1984	2	1	1	0
Kitrina Douglas	Eng	1982	4	0	3	1
Marjorie Draper [Peel]						
(Thomas)	Scot	1954	1	0	1	0
Daisy Ferguson	Ire	(1958)	0	0	0	0
Marjory Ferguson						
(Fowler)	Scot	1966	1	0	1	0
Elizabeth Price Fisher						
(Price)	Eng	1950-52-54-56-58-60	12	7	4	1
Maureen Garner (Madill)	Ire	1980	4	0	3	1
Marjorie Ross Garon	Eng	1936	2	1	0	1
Maureen Garrett						
(Ruttle)	Eng	1948-(60)	2	0	2	0
Philomena Garvey	Ire	1948-50-52-54-56-60	11	2	8	1
Carol Gibbs (Le Feuvre)	Eng	1974	3	0	3	0
Jacqueline Gordon	Eng	1948	2	1	1	0
Molly Gourlay	Eng	1932-34	4	0	2	2
Julia Greenhalgh	Eng	1964-70-74-76-78	17	6	7	4
Penny Grice-Whittaker						
(Grice)	Eng	1984	4	2	1	1
Marley Harris						
[Spearman] (Baker)	Eng	1960-62-64	6	2	2	2
Dorothea Hastings						
(Sommerville)	Scot	1958	0	0	0	0
Lady Heathcoat-Amory						
(Joyce Wethered)	Eng	1932	2	1	1	0
Dinah Henson (Oxley)	Eng	1968-70-72-76	11	3	6	2
Helen Holm (Gray)	Scot	1936-38-48	5	3	2	0
Claire Hourihane	Ire	1984-86-88	5	2	2	1
Ann Howard (Phillips)	Eng	1956-68	2	0	2	0
Beverley Huke	Eng	1972	2	0	2	0
Anne Irvin	Eng	1962-68-70-76	12	4	7	1
Bridget Jackson	Eng	1958-64-68	8	1	6	1
Patricia Johnson	Eng	1986	4	4	0	0
Susan Langridge						
(Armitage)	Eng	1964-66	6	0	5	1
Mary Laupheimer						
(Everard)	Eng	1970-72-74-78	15	6	7	2
Joan Lawrence	Scot	1964	2	0	2	0
Shirley Lawson	Scot	1988	2	1	1	0
Wilma Leburn (Aitken)	Scot	1982	2	0	2	0
Jenny Lee Smith	Eng	1974-76	3	0	3	0
Kathryn Lumb (Phillips)	Eng	1970-72	2	1	1	0
Mary McKenna	Ire	1970-72-74-76-78-80-82-84-86	30	10	16	4
Suzanne McMahon						
(Cadden)	Scot	1976	4	0	4	0
Sheila Maher (Vaughan)	Eng	1962-64	4	1	2	1
Vanessa Marvin	Eng	1978	3	1	2	0
Moira Milton (Paterson)	Scot	1952	2	1	1	0
Wanda Morgan	Eng	1932-34-36	6	0	5	1
Beverley New	Eng	1984	4	1	3	0
Maire O'Donnell	Ire	(1982)	0	0	0	0
Margaret Pickard						
(Nichol)	Eng	1968-70	5	2	3	0
Diana Plumpton	Eng	1934	2	1	1	0
Elizabeth Pook						
(Chadwick)	Eng	1966	4	1	3	0
Doris Porter (Park)	Scot	1932	1	0	1	0
Clarrie Reddan (Tiernan)	Ire	1938-48	3	2	1	0
Joan Rennie (Hastings)	Scot	1966	2	0	1	1
Maureen Richmond						
(Walker)	Scot	1974	4	2	2	0
Jean Roberts	Eng	1962	1	0	1	0
Belle Robertson						
(McCorkindale)	Scot	1960-66-68-70-72-(74)-(76)-82-86	24	5	12	7
Claire Robinson						
(Nesbitt)	Ire	1980	3	0	1	2

Curtis Cup

continued

Name		Year	Played	Won	Lost	Halved
Vivien Saunders	Eng	1968	4	1	2	1
Susan Shapcott	Eng	1988	4	3	1	0
Linda Simpson (Moore)	Eng	1980	3	1	1	1
Ruth Slark (Porter)	Eng	1960-62-64	7	3	3	1
Anne Smith [Stant] (Willard)	Eng	1976	1	0	1	0
Frances Smith (Stephens)	Eng	1950-52-54-56-58-60-(62)-(72)	11	7	3	1
Janet Soulsby	Eng	1982	4	1	2	1
Gillian Stewart	Scot	1980-82	4	1	3	0
Tegwen Thomas (Perkins)	Wales	1974-76-78-80	14	4	8	2
Vicki Thomas (Rawlings)	Wales	1982-84-86-88	8	4	2	2
Muriel Thomson	Scot	1978	3	2	1	0
Jill Thornhill	Eng	1984-86-88	12	6	2	4
Angela Uzielli (Carrick)	Eng	1978	1	0	1	0
Jessie Valentine (Anderson)	Scot	1936-38-50-52-54-56-58	13	4	9	0
Julie Wade	Eng	1988	4	2	2	0
Claire Waite	Eng	1984	4	2	2	0
Mickey Walker	Eng	1972	4	3	0	1
Pat Walker	Ire	1934-36-38	6	2	3	1
Verona Wallace-Williamson	Scot	(1938)	0	0	0	0
Nan Wardlaw (Baird)	Scot	1938	1	0	1	0
Enid Wilson	Eng	1932	2	1	1	0
Janette Wright (Robertson)	Scot	1954-56-58-60	8	3	5	0
Phyllis Wylie (Wade)	Eng	1938	1	0	0	1

Bold print: captain; bold print in brackets: non-playing captain
Maiden name in parentheses, former surname in square brackets

Curtis Cup

continued

United States of America

Player	Year	Played	Won	Lost	Halved
Roberta Albers	1968	2	1	0	1
Danielle Ammaccapane	1986	3	0	3	0
Kathy Baker	1982	4	3	0	1
Barbara Barrow	1976	2	1	0	1
Beth Barry	1972-74	5	3	1	1
Larua Baugh	1972	4	2	1	1
Judy Bell	1960-62-(86)-(88)	2	1	1	0
Peggy Kirk Bell (Kirk)	1950	2	1	1	0
Amy Benz	1982	3	2	1	0
Patty Berg	1936-38	4	1	2	1
Barbara Fay Boddie (White)	1964-66	8	7	0	1
Jane Booth (Bastanchury)	1970-72-74	12	9	3	0
Mary Budke	1974	3	2	1	0
JoAnne Carner (Gunderson)	1958-60-62-64	10	6	3	1
Lori Castillo	1980	3	2	1	0
Leona Cheney (Pressler)	1932-34-36	6	5	1	0
Sis Choate	(1974)	0	0	0	0
Peggy Conley	1964-68	6	3	1	2
Mary Ann Cook (Downey)	1956	2	1	1	0
Patricia Cornett	1978-88	4	1	2	1
Jean Crawford (Ashley)	1962-66-68-(72)	8	6	2	0
Clifford Ann Creed	1962	2	2	0	0
Grace Cronin (Lenczyk)	1948-50	3	2	1	0
Carolyn Cudone	1956-(70)	1	1	0	0
Beth Daniel	1976-78	8	7	1	0
Virginia Dennehy	(1958)	0	0	0	0
Mary Lou Dill	1968	3	1	1	1
Alice Dye	1970	2	1	0	1
Heather Farr	1984	3	2	1	0
Jane Fassinger	1970	1	0	1	0
Mary Lena Faulk	1954	2	1	1	0
Carol Sorensen Flenniken (Sorensen)	1964-66	8	6	1	1
Edith Flippin (Quier)	(1954)-(56)	0	0	0	0
Kim Gardner	1986	3	1	1	1
Charlotte Glutting	1934-36-38	5	3	1	1
Brenda Goldsmith	1978-80	4	2	2	0
Aniela Goldthwaite	1934-(52)	1	0	1	0
Joanne Goodwin	1960	2	1	1	0

Player	Year	Played	Won	Lost	Halved
Mary Hafeman	1980	2	1	0	1
Shelley Hamkin	1968-70	8	3	3	2
Penny Hammel	1984	3	1	1	1
Nancy Hammer (Hager)	1970	2	1	1	0
Cathy Hanlon	1982	3	2	1	0
Beverley Hanson	1950	2	2	0	0
Patricia Harbottle					
(Lesser)	1954-56	3	2	1	0
Helen Hawes	(1964)	0	0	0	0
Kathryn Hemphill	1938	1	0	0	1
Helen Hicks	1932	2	1	1	0
Carolyn Hill	1978	2	0	0	2
Cindy Hill	1970-74-76-78	14	5	6	3
Opel Hill	1932-34-36	6	2	3	1
Marion Hollins	(1932)	0	0	0	0
Dana Howe	1984	3	1	1	1
Juli Inkster	1982	4	4	0	0
Ann Casey Johnstone	1958-60-62	4	3	1	0
Mae Murray Jones					
(Murray)	1952	1	0	1	0
Caroline Keggi	1988	3	0	2	1
Tracy Kerdyk	1988	4	2	1	1
Kandi Kessler	1986	3	1	1	1
Dorothy Kielty	1948-50	4	4	0	0
Dorothy Kirby	1948-50-52-54	7	4	3	0
Martha Kirouac					
(Wilkinson)	1970-72	8	5	3	0
Nancy Knight (Lopez)	1976	2	2	0	0
Bonnie Lauer	1974	4	2	2	0
Marjorie Lindsay	1952	2	1	1	0
Patricia Lucey					
(O'Sullivan)	1952	1	0	1	0
Mari McDougall	1982	2	2	0	0
Barbara McIntire	1958-60-62-64-66-72-(76)	16	6	6	4
Lucile Mann (Robinson)	1934	1	0	1	0
Debbie Massey	1974-76	5	5	0	0
Marion Miley	1938	2	1	0	1
Dottie Mochrie (Pepper)	1986	3	0	2	1
Evelyn Monsted	(1968)	0	0	0	0
Terri Moody	1980	2	1	0	1
Judith Oliver	1978-80-82	8	5	1	2
Maureen Orcutt	1932-34-36-38	8	5	3	0
Joanne Pacillo	1984	3	1	1	1
Estelle Page (Lawson)	1938-48	4	3	1	0
Frances Pond (Stebbins)	(1938)	0	0	0	0
Dorothy Germain Porter	1950-(66)	2	1	0	1
Phyllis Preuss	1962-64-66-68-70-(84)	15	10	4	1
Betty Probasco	(1982)	0	0	0	0
Mildred Prunaret	(1960)	0	0	0	0
Anne Quast [Sander]					
[Wetts] [Decker]					
(Quast)	1958-60-62-66-68-74-84	20	9	7	4
Polly Riley	1948-50-52-54-56-58-(62)	10	5	5	0
Barbara Romack	1954-56-58	5	3	2	0
Jody Rosenthal	1984	3	2	0	1
Cindy Scholefield	1988	3	0	3	0
Cindy Schreyer	1986	3	1	2	0
Kathleen McCarthy					
Scrivner (McCarthy)	1986-88	6	2	3	1
Leslie Shannon	1986-88	6	0	4	2
Patty Sheehan	1980	4	4	0	0
Pearl Sinn	1988	2	1	1	0
Grace De Moss Smith					
(De Moss)	1952-54	3	1	2	0
Lancy Smith	1972-78-80-82-84	16	7	5	4
Margaret Smith	1956	2	2	0	0
Hollis Stacy	1972	2	0	1	1
Claire Stancik (Doran)	1952-54	4	4	0	0
Judy Street (Eller)	1960	2	2	0	0
Louise Suggs	1948	2	0	1	1
Nancy Roth Syms (Roth)	1964-66-76-(80)	9	3	5	1
Carol Thompson					
(Semple)	1974-76-80-82	14	7	5	2
Noreen Uihlein	1978	3	1	1	1
Virginia Van Wie	1932-34	4	3	0	1
Glenna Collett Vare					
(Collett)	1932-(34)-36-38-48-(50)	7	4	2	1
Jane Weiss (Nelson)	1956	1	0	1	0
Donna White (Horton)	1976	2	2	0	0
Mary Anne Widman	1984	3	2	1	0
Kimberley Williams	1986	3	0	3	0

Curtis Cup

continued

Player	Year	Played	Won	Lost	Halved
Helen Sigel Wilson (Sigel)	1950-66-(78)	2	0	2	0
Joyce Ziske	1954	1	0	1	0

Bold print: captain; bold print in brackets: non-playing captain.
Maiden name in parenthesis; former surname in square brackets.

Curtis Cup
continued

Commonwealth Tournament (Ladies)

Year	Winner	Venue
1959	Great Britain	St Andrews
1963	Great Britain	Royal Melbourne, Australia
1967	Great Britain	Ancaster, Ontario, Canada
1971	Great Britain	Hamilton, New Zealand
1975	Great Britain	Ganton, England
1979	Canada	Lake Karrinup, Perth, Australia
1983	Australia	Glendale, Edmonton, Canada
1987	Canada	Christchurch, New Zealand
1989		

European Ladies' Amateur Team Championship

Year	Winner	Second	Venue
1967	England	France	Penina, Portugal
1969	France	England	Tylosand, Sweden
1971	England	France	Ganton, England
1973	England	France	Brussels, Belgium
1975	France	Spain	Paris, France
1977	England	Spain	Sotogrande, Spain
1979	Ireland	Germany	Hermitage, Ireland
1981	Sweden	France	Troia, Portugal
1983	Ireland	England	Waterloo, Belgium
1985	England	Italy	Stavanger, Norway
1987	Sweden	Wales	Turnberry, Scotland
1989	France	England	Pals, France

Vagliano Trophy—Great Britain & Ireland v Europe (Ladies)

Played for biennially between teams of women amateur golfers representing the British Isles and Europe. (From 1947 to 1957 was between the British Isles and France.)

Year	Winner	Result	Venue
1959	Great Britain	12-3	Wentworth
1961	Great Britain	8-7	Villa d'Este
1963	Great Britain	20-10	Muirfield
1965	Europe	17-13	Cologne
1967	Europe	15½-14½	Lytham
1969	Europe	16-14	Chantilly
1971	Great Britain	17½-12½	Worplesdon
1973	Great Britain	20-10	Eindhoven
1975	Great Britain	13½-10½	Muirfield
1977	Great Britain	15½-8½	Malmo
1979	Halved	12-12	R Porthcawl
1981	Europe	14-10	P de Hierro
1983	GB & Ireland	14-10	Woodhall Spa
1985	GB & Ireland	14-10	Hamburg
1987	GB & Ireland	15-9	The Berkshire
1989	GB & Ireland	14½-9½	Venice

Women's Home Internationals

Year	Winner	Venue	Year	Winner	Venue
1948	England	Lytham St Annes	1969	England / Scotland	Western Gailes
1949	Scotland	Harlech			
1950	Scotland	Newcastle Co Down	1970	England	Killarney
1951	Scotland	Broadstone	1971	England	Longniddry
1952	Scotland	Troon	1972	England	Lytham St Annes
1953	England	Porthcawl	1973	England	Harlech
1954	England	Ganton	1974	England / Scotland / Ireland	Princes
1955	England / Scotland	Western Gailes			
1956	Scotland	Sunningdale	1975	England	Newport
1957	Scotland	Troon	1976	England	Troon
1958	England	Hunstanton	1977	England	Cork
1959	England	Hoylake	1978	England	Moortown
1960	England	Gullane	1979	Scotland / Ireland	Harlech
1961	Scotland	Portmarnock			
1962	Scotland	Porthcawl	1980	Ireland	Cruden Bay
1963	England	Formby	1981	Scotland	Portmarnock
1964	England	Troon	1982	England	Burnham and Barrow
1965	England	Portrush	1983	Matches abandoned due to weather	
1966	England	Woodhall Spa	1984	England	Gullane
1967	England	Sunningdale	1985	England	Waterville
1968	England	Porthcawl	1986	Ireland	Whittington Barracks

At Ashburnham, Dyfed, 1987

England beat Scotland	5½ matches to 3½
England beat Ireland	5½ matches to 3½
England beat Wales	6 matches to 3
Scotland beat Ireland	6 matches to 3
Scotland beat Wales	7 matches to 2
Ireland beat Wales	8 matches to 1

Result: England 3; Scotland 2; Ireland 1; Wales 0

At Barassie, Ayrshire, 1988

Scotland beat England	5½ matches to 3½
Scotland beat Ireland	5 matches to 4
Scotland beat Wales	7½ matches to 1½
England beat Ireland	6½ matches to 2½
England beat Wales	7 matches to 2
Ireland halved with Wales	4½ matches each

Result: England 2; Scotland 3; Ireland 0; Wales 0

At Westport, Ireland, 1989

Scotland beat Ireland	7 matches to 2
England beat Wales	6½ matches to 2½
Scotland beat Wales	5 matches to 4
England beat Ireland	5½ matches to 3½
England beat Scotland	8 matches to 1
Ireland beat Wales	6 matches to 3

Result: England 3; Scotland 2; Ireland 1; Wales 0

Women's World Amateur Team Championship (Espirito Santo Trophy)

Year	Winners	Runners-up	Venue	Score
1964	France	United States	St Germain	588
1966	United States	Canada	Mexico	580
1968	United States	Australia	Melbourne	616
1970	United States	France	Madrid	598
1972	United States	France	Buenos Aires	583
1974	United States	Great Britain, South Africa	Dominican Republic	620
1976	United States	France	Vilamoura, Portugal	605
1978	Australia	Canada	Fiji	596
1980	United States	Australia	Pinehurst, USA	588
1982	United States	New Zealand	Geneva, Switzerland	579
1984	United States	France	Hong Kong	585
1986	Spain	France	Caracas, Venezuela	580
1988	United States	Sweden	Drottningholm, Sweden	587

Juniors and Youths

Boys' Amateur Championship

Year	Winner	Runner-up	Venue	By
1921	ADD Mathieson	GH Lintott	Ascot	37th hole
1922	HS Mitchell	W Greenfield	Ascot	4 and 2
1923	ADD Mathieson	HS Mitchell	Dunbar	3 and 2
1924	RW Peattie	P Manuevrier	Coombe Hill	2 holes
1925	RW Peattie	A McNair	Barnton	4 and 3
1926	EA McRuvie	CW Timmis	Coombe Hill	1 hole
1927	EW Fiddian	K Forbes	Barnton	4 and 2
1928	S Scheftel	A Dobbie	Formby	6 and 5
1929	J Lindsay	J Scott-Riddell	Barnton	6 and 4
1930	J Lindsay	J Todd	Fulwell	9 and 8
1931	H Thomson	F McGloin	Killermont	5 and 4
1932	IS MacDonald	LA Hardie	Lytham St Annes	2 and 1
1933	PB Lucas	W McLachlan	Carnoustie	3 and 2
1934	RS Burles	FB Allpass	Moortown	12 and 10
1935	JDA Langley	R Norris	Balgownie, Ab'deen	6 and 5
1936	J Bruen	W Innes	Birkdale	11 and 9
1937	IM Roberts	J Stewart	Bruntsfield	8 and 7
1938	W Smeaton	T Snowball	Moor Park	3 and 2
1939	SB Williamson	KG Thom	Carnoustie	4 and 2
1940-45 *Suspended during War*				
1946	AFD MacGregor	DF Dunstan	Bruntsfield	7 and 5
1947	J Armour	I Caldwell	Hoylake	5 and 4
1948	JD Pritchett	DH Reid	Barasssie	37th hole
1949	H MacAnespie	NV Drew	St Andrews	3 and 2
1950	J Glover	I Young	Lytham St Annes	2 and 1
1951	N Dunn	MSR Lunt	Prestwick	6 and 5
1952	M Bonallack	AE Shepperson	Formby	37th hole
1953	AE Shepperson	AT Booth	Dunbar	6 and 4
1954	AF Bussell	K Warren	Hoylake	38th hole
1955	SC Wilson	BJK Aitken	Barassie	39th hole
1956	JF Ferguson	CW Cole	Sunningdale	2 and 1
1957	D Ball	J Wilson	Carnoustie	2 and 1
1958	R Braddon	IM Stungo	Moortown	4 and 3
1959	AR Murphy	EM Shamash	Pollok	3 and 1
1960	P Cros	PO Green	Olton	5 and 3
1961	FS Morris	C Clark	Dalmahoy	3 and 2
1962	PM Townsend	DC Penman	Mid-Surrey	1 hole
1963	AHC Soutar	DI Rigby	Prestwick	2 and 1
1964	PM Townsend	RD Gray	Formby	9 and 8
1965	GR Milne	DK Midgley	Gullane	4 and 2
1966	A Phillips	A Muller	Moortown	12 and 11
1967	LP Tupling	SC Evans	Western Gailes	4 and 2
1968	SC Evans	K Dabson	St Annes Old Links	3 and 2
1969	M Foster	M Gray	Dunbar	37th hole
1970	ID Gradwell	JE Murray	Hillside	1 hole
1971	H Clark	G Harvey	Barassie	6 and 5
1972	G Harvey	R Newsome	Moortown	7 and 5
1973	DM Robertson	S Betti	Blairgowrie	5 and 3
1974	TR Shannon	AWB Lylc	Hoylake	10 and 9
1975	B Marchbank	AWB Lyle	Bruntsfield	1 hole
1976	M Mouland	G Hargreaves	Sunningdale	6 and 5
1977	I Ford	CR Dalgleish	Downfield	1 hole
1978	S Keppler	M Stokes	Seaton Carew	3 and 2
1979	R Rafferty	D Ray	Barassie	6 and 5
1980	D Muscroft	A Llyr	Formby	7 and 6
1981	J Lopez	R Weedon	Gullane	4 and 3
1982	M Grieve	G Hickman	Burnham and Barrow	37th hole
1983	J-M Olazabal	M Pendaries	Glenbervie	6 and 5

Year	Winner	Runner-up	Venue	By
1984	L Vannett	A Mednick	Royal Porthcawl	2 and 1
1985	J Cook	W Henry	Barnton	5 and 4
1986	L Walker	G King	Seaton Carew	5 and 4
1987	C O'Carrol	P Olsson	Barassie	3 and 1
1988	S Pardoe	D Haines	Formby	3 and 2
1989	C Watts	C Fraser	Nairn	5 and 3

English Boys Amateur Open Stroke-Play Championship
(formerly Carris Trophy)

Year	Winner	Score	Year	Winner	Score
1935	R Upex	75	1966	A Black	151
1936	JDA Langley	152	1967	RF Brown	147
1937	RJ White	149	1968	P Dawson	149
1938	IP Garrow	147	1969	ID Gradwell	150
1939	CW Warren	149	1970	MF Foster	146
1946	AH Perowne	158	1971	RJ Evans	146
1947	I Caldwell	159	1972	L Donovan	143
1948	I Caldwell	152	1973	S Hadfield	148
1949	PB Hine	148	1974	KJ Brown	304
1950	J Glover	144	1975	AWB Lyle	270
1951	I Young	154	1976	H Stott	285
1952	N Thygesen	150	1977	R Mugglestone	293
1953	N Johnson	148	1978	J Plaxton	144
1954	K Warren	149	1979	P Hammond	288
1955	ID Wheater	151	1980	MP McLean	290
1956	G Maisey	141	1981	D Gilford	290
1957	G Maisey	145	1982	M Jarvis	298
1958	J Hamilton	149	1983	P Baker	288
1959	RT Walker	152	1984	J Coe	283
1960	PM Baxter	150	1985	P Baker	286
1961	DJ Miller	143	1986	G Evans	292
1962	FS Morris	145	1987	D Bathgate	289
1963	EJ Threlfall	147	1988	P Page	284
1964	PM Townsend	148	1989	I Garbutt	285
1965	G McKay	145			

Peter McEvoy Trophy
Venue: Copt Heath

Year	Winner
1984	W Henry
1985	A Morley
1986	C Mitchell
1987	W Henry
1988	P Sefton
1989	D Bathgate

Queen Elizabeth Coronation Schools' Trophy
Venue: Royal Burgess Golfing Society, Barnton, Edinburgh

Year	Winner	Year	Winner
1980	George Heriots FP	1985	Glasgow High School FP
1981	Ayr Academicals	1986	Watsonians
1982	George Heriots FP	1987	Stewart's-Melville FP
1983	Perth Academy FP	1988	Watsonians
1984	Glasgow High School FP	1989	Kelvinside Academicals

Scottish Boys' Championship

Year	Winner	Runner-up	Venue	By
1960	L Carver	S Wilson	North Berwick	6 and 5
1961	K Thomson	G Wilson	North Berwick	10 and 8
1962	HF Urquhart	S MacDonald	North Berwick	3 and 2
1963	FS Morris	I Clark	North Berwick	9 and 8
1964	WR Lockie	MD Cleghorn	North Berwick	1 hole
1965	RL Penman	J Wood	North Berwick	9 and 8
1966	J McTear	DG Greig	North Berwick	4 and 3
1967	DG Greig	I Cannon	North Berwick	2 and 1
1968	RD Weir	M Grubb	North Berwick	6 and 4
1969	RP Fyfe	IP Doig	North Berwick	4 and 2
1970	S Stephen	M Henry	North Berwick	38th hole
1971	JE Murray	AA Mackay	North Berwick	4 and 3
1972	DM Robertson	G Cairns	North Berwick	9 and 8
1973	R Watson	H Alexander	North Berwick	8 and 7
1974	DM Robertson	J Cuddihy	North Berwick	6 and 5
1975	A Brown	J Cuddihy	North Berwick	6 and 4
1976	B Marchbank	J Cuddihy	Dunbar	2 and 1
1977	JS Taylor	GJ Webster	Dunbar	3 and 2
1978	J Huggan	KW Stables	Dunbar	2 and 1
1979	DR Weir	S Morrison	West Kilbride	5 and 3
1980	R Gregan	AJ Currie	Dunbar	2 and 1
1981	C Stewart	G Mellon	Dunbar	3 and 2
1982	A Smith	J White	Dunbar	39th hole
1983	C Gillies	C Innes	Dunbar	38th hole
1984	K Buchan	L Vannet	Dunbar	2 and 1
1985	AD McQueen	FJ McCulloch	Dunbar	1 hole
1986	AG Tait	EA McIntosh	Dunbar	6 and 5
1987	AJ Coltart	SJ Bannerman	Dunbar	37th hole
1988	CA Fraser	F Clark	Dunbar	9 and 8
1989	M King	D Brolls	Dunbar	8 and 7

Scottish Boys' Open Amateur Stroke Play Championship

Year	Winner	Club	Venue	Score
1970	D Chillas	R Aberdeen	Carnoustie	298
1971	JE Murray	Baberton	Lanark	274
1972	S Martin	Downfield	Montrose	280
1973	S Martin	Carnoustie	Barnton	284
1974	PW Gallacher	Peebles	Lundin Links	290
1975	A Webster	Edzell	Kilmarnock Barassie	286
1976	A Webster	Edzell	Forfar	292
1977	{ J Huggan } tie { L Mann	Winterfield	Renfrew	303
1978	R Fraser	Hilton Park	Arbroath	283
1979	L Mann	Carnoustie	Stirling	289
1980	ASK Glen	Ormesson (France)	Forfar	288
1981	J Gullen	Tillicoultry	Bellshill	296
1982	D Purdie	Turriff	Monifieth	296
1983	L Vannet	Carnoustie	Barassie	286
1984	K Walker	Royal Burgess	Carnoustie	280
1985	G Matthew	Melrose	Baberton	297
1986	G Cassells	Cruden Bay	Edzell	294
1987	C Ronald	Torrance House	Lanark	287
1988	M Urquhart	Inverness	Dumfries and County	280
1989	F Burntside			283

West of Scotland Boys' Championship

Year	Winner	Year	Winner
1980	J Milligan	1985	F O'Callaghan
1981	S Thompson	1986	G King
1982	P Girvan	1987	C Ronald
1983	G Collinson	1988	M King
1984	G Orr	1989	S Dundas

Welsh Boys' Championship

Year	Winner	Runner-up	Venue	By
1960	C Gilford	JL Toye	Llandrindod Wells	5 and 4
1961	AR Porter	JL Toye	Llandrindod Wells	3 and 2
1962	RC Waddilove	W Wadrup	Harlech	20th hole
1963	G Matthews	R Witchell	Penarth	6 and 5
1964	D Lloyd	M Walters	Conway	2 and 1
1965	G Matthews	DG Lloyd	Wenvoe Castle	7 and 6
1966	J Buckley	DP Owen	Holyhead	4 and 2
1967	J Buckley	DL Stevens	Glamorganshire	2 and 1
1968	J Buckley	C Brown	Maesdu	1 hole
1969	K Dabson	P Light	Glamorganshire	5 and 3
1970	P Tadman	A Morgan	Conway	2 and 1
1971	R Jenkins	TJ Melia	Ashburnham	3 and 2
1972	MG Chugg	RM Jones	Wrexham	3 and 2
1973	R Tate	N Duncan	Penarth	2 and 1
1974	D Williams	S Lewis	Llandudno	5 and 4
1975	G Davies	PG Garrett	Glamorganshire	20th hole
1976	JM Morrow	MG Mouland	Caernarvonshire	1 hole
1977	JM Morrow	MG Mouland	Glamorganshire	2 and 1
1978	JM Morrow	A Laking	Harlech	2 and 1
1979	P Mayo	M Hayward	Penarth	24th hole
1980	A Llyr	DK Wood	Llandudno (Maesdu)	2 and 1
1981	M Evans	P Webborn	Pontypool	5 and 4
1982	CM Rees	KH Williams	Prestatyn	2 holes
1983	MA Macara	RN Roderick	Radyr	1 hole
1984	GA Macara	D Bagg	Llandudno	1 hole
1985	B Macfarlane	R Herbert	Cardiff	1 hole
1986	C O'Carroll	GA Macara	Rhuddlan	1 hole
1987	SJ Edwards	A Herbert	Abergavenny	19th hole
1988	C Platt	P Murphy	Holyhead	2 and 1
1989	R Johnson	RL Evans	Southerndown	2 holes

Boys' Internationals
England v Scotland

Year	Winner	Result	Venue
1946	England	8½-3½	Bruntsfield
1947	England	7-5	Hoylake
1948	England	9-3	Barassie
1949	Scotland	8-4	St Andrews
1950	Scotland	8½-3½	Lytham St Annes
1951	England	7-5	Prestwick
1952	England	6½-5½	Formby
1953	Scotland	7-5	Dunbar
1954	England	6½-5½	Hoylake
1955	Scotland	9-3	Barassie
1956	England	7½-4½	Sunningdale
1957	Scotland	7½-4½	Carnoustie
1958	England	7-5	Moortown
1959	England	8½-3½	Pollok
1960	England	10-2	Olton
1961	Scotland	7-5	Dalmahoy

Boys'
Internationals
continued

Year	Winner	Result	Venue
1962	England	6½-5½	Mid-Surrey
1963	Scotland	9-3	Prestwick
1964	England	9-3	Formby
1965	England	10-5	Gullane
1966	England	12-3	Moortown
1967	Scotland	8-7	Western Gailes
1968	England	10-5	St Annes Old Links
1969	England	12-3	Dunbar
1970	England	12-3	Hillside
1971	Halved	7½-7½	Barassie
1972	England	13½-1½	Moortown
1973	England	9-6	Blairgowrie
1974	England	11-4	Liverpool
1975	England	9½-5½	Bruntsfield
1976	Scotland	8-7	Sunningdale
1977	England	8-7	Downfield
1978	Scotland	8½-6½	Seaton Carew
1979	England	11-4	Barassie
1980	England	9-6	Formby
1981	Halved	7½-7½	Gullane
1982	England	8-7	Burnham & Berrow
1983	England	8-7	Glenbervie
1984	England	9½-5½	Porthcawl
1985	England	10-5	Barnton
1986	Scotland	8½-6½	Seaton Carew
1987	Scotland	8-7	Barassie
1988	England	11-4	Formby
1989	England	8-7	Nairn

European Boys' Team Championship

Year	Winner	Second	Venue
1989	England	Spain	Lyckoma, Sweden

Great Britain & Ireland v Continent of Europe, Boys
Instituted 1958

Year	Winner	Result	Venue
1958	Great Britain	11½-½	Moortown
1959	Great Britain	7-2	Pollok
1960	Great Britain	8-7	Olton
1961	Great Britain	11-4	Dalmahoy
1962	Great Britain	11-4	Mid-Surrey
1963	Great Britain	12-3	Prestwick
1964	Great Britain	12-1	Formby
1965	Great Britain	12-1	Gullane
1966	Great Britain	10-2	Moortown
1967-76	*Not played*		
1977	Europe	7-6	Downfield
1978	Europe	7-6	Seaton Carew
1979	Great Britain	9½-2½	Barassie
1980	Great Britain	7-5	Formby
1981	Great Britain	8-4	Gullane
1982	Great Britain	11-1	Burnham & Berrow
1983	Great Britain & Ireland	6½-5½	Glenbervie
1984	Great Britain & Ireland	6½-5½	Porthcawl
1985	Great Britain & Ireland	7½-4½	Barnton
1986	Continent of Europe	8½-3½	Seaton Carew
1987	Great Britain & Ireland	7½-4½	Barassie
1988	Great Britain & Ireland	5½-2½	Formby
1989	Great Britain & Ireland	7½-4½	Nairn

Girls' British Open Amateur Championship

Year	Winner	Runner-up	Venue	By
1960	Miss S Clarke	Miss A L Irvin	Barassie	2 and 1
1961	Miss D Robb	Miss J Roberts	Beaconsfield	3 and 2
1962	Miss S McLaren-Smith	Miss A Murphy	Foxton Hall	2 and 1
1963	Miss D Oxley	Miss B Whitehead	Gullane	2 and 1
1964	Miss P Tredinnick	Miss K Cumming	Camberley Heath	2 and 1
1965	Miss A Willard	Miss A Ward	Formby	3 and 2
1966	Miss J Hutton	Miss D Oxley	Troon Portland	20th hole
1967	Miss P Burrows	Miss J Hutton	Liphook	2 and 1
1968	Miss C Wallace	Miss C Reybroeck	Leven	4 and 3
1969	Miss J de Witt Puyt	Miss C Reybroeck	Ilkley	2 and 1
1970	Miss C Le Feuvre	Miss Michelle Walker	North Wales	2 and 1
1971	Miss J Mark	Miss Maureen Walker	North Berwick	4 and 3
1972	Miss Maureen Walker	Miss S Cadden	Norwich	2 and 1
1973	Miss A M Palli	Miss N Jeanson	Northamptonshire	2 and 1
1974	Miss R Barry	Miss T Perkins	Dunbar	1 hole
1975	Miss S Cadden	Miss L Isherwood	Henbury	4 and 3
1976	Miss G Stewart	Miss S Rowlands	Pyle and Kenfig	5 and 4
1977	Miss W Aitken	Miss S Bamford	Formby Ladies	2 and 1
1978	Miss M L de Lorenzi	Miss D Glenn	Largs	2 and 1
1979	Miss S Lapaire	Miss P Smilie	Edgbaston	19th hole
1980	Miss J Connachan	Miss L Bolton	Wrexham	2 holes
1981	Miss J Connachan	Miss P Grice	Woodbridge	20th hole
1982	Miss C Waite	Miss M Mackie	Edzell	6 and 5
1983	Miss E Orley	Miss A Walters	Leeds	7 and 6
1984	Miss C Swallow	Miss E Farquharson	Maesdu	1 hole
1985	Miss S Shapcott	Miss E Farquharson	Hesketh	3 and 1
1986	Miss S Groce	Miss S Bennett	West Kilbride	5 and 4
1987	Miss H Dobson	Miss S Croce	Barnham Broom	19th hole
1988	Miss A Macdonald	Miss J Posener	Pyle and Kenfig	3 and 2
1989	Miss M McKinlay	Miss S Eriksson	Carlisle	19th hole

English Girls' Championship

Year	Winner	Runner-up	Venue	By
1964	Miss S Ward	Miss P Tredinnick	Wollaton Park	2 and 1
1965	Miss D Oxley	Miss A Payne	Edgbaston	2 holes
1966	Miss B Whitehead	Miss D Oxley	Woodbridge	1 hole
1967	Miss A Willard	Miss G Holloway	Burhill	1 hole
1968	Miss K Phillips	Miss C le Feuvre	Harrogate	6 and 5
1969	Miss C le Feuvre	Miss K Phillips	Hawkstone Park	2 and 1
1970	Miss C le Feuvre	Miss M Walker	High Post	2 and 1
1971	Miss C Eckersley	Miss J Stevens	Liphook	4 and 3
1972	Miss C Barker	Miss R Kelly	Trentham	4 and 3
1973	Miss S Parker	Miss S Thurston	Lincoln	19th hole
1974	Miss C Langford	Miss L Harrold	Knowle	2 and 1
1975	Miss M Burton	Miss R Barry	Formby	6 and 5
1976	Miss H Latham	Miss D Park	Moseley	3 and 2
1977	Miss S Bamford	Miss S Jolly	Chelmsford	21st hole
1978	Miss P Smillie	Miss J Smith	Willesley Park	3 and 2
1979	Miss L Moore	Miss P Barry	Cirencester	1 hole
1980	Miss P Smillie	Miss J Soulsby	Kedleston Park	3 and 2
1981	Miss J Soulsby	Miss C Waite	Worksop	7 and 5
1982	Miss C Waite	Miss P Grice	Wilmslow	3 and 2
1983	Miss P Grice	Miss K Mitchell	West Surrey	2 and 1
1984	Miss C Swallow	Miss S Duhig	Bath	3 and 1
1985	Miss L Fairclough	Miss K Mitchell	Coventry	6 and 5
1986	Miss S Shapcott	Miss N Way	Huddersfield	7 and 6
1987	Miss S Shapcott	Miss S Morgan	Sandy Lodge	1 hole
1988	Miss H Dobson	Miss S Shapcott	Long Ashton	1 hole
1989	Miss H Dobson	Miss A MacDonald	Edgbaston	3 and 1

Irish Girls' Championship

Year	Winner	Runner-up	Venue	By
1961	Miss M Coburn	Miss C McAuley	Portrush	6 and 5
1962	Miss P Boyd	Miss P Atkinson	Elm Park	4 and 3
1963	Miss P Atkinson	Miss C Scarlett	Donaghadee	8 and 7
1964	Miss C Scarlett	Miss A Maher	Milltown	6 and 5
1965	Miss V Singleton	Miss P McKenzie	Ballycastle	7 and 6
1966	Miss M McConnell	Miss D Hulme	Dun Laoghaire	3 and 2
1967	Miss M McConnell	Miss C Wallace	Portrush	6 and 5
1968	Miss C Wallace	Miss A McCoy	Louth	3 and 1
1969	Miss EA McGregor	Miss M Sheenan	Knock	6 and 5
1970	Miss EA McGregor	Miss J Mark	Greystones	3 and 2
1971	Miss J Mark	Miss C Nesbitt	Belfast	3 and 2
1972	Miss P Smyth	Miss M Governey	Elm Park	1 hole
1973	Miss M Governey	Miss R Hegarty	Mullingar	3 and 1
1974	Miss R Hegarty	Miss M Irvine	Castletroy	2 holes
1975	Miss M Irvine	Miss P Wickham	Carlow	2 and 1
1976	Miss P Wickham	Miss R Hegarty	Castle	5 and 3
1977	Miss A Ferguson	Miss R Walsh	Birr	3 and 2
1978	Miss C Wickham	Miss B Gleeson	Killarney	1 hole
1979	Miss L Bolton	Miss B Gleeson	Milltown	3 and 2
1980	Miss B Gleeson	Miss L Bolton	Kilkenny	5 and 3
1981	Miss B Gleeson	Miss E Lynn	Donegal	1 hole
1982	Miss D Langan	Miss S Lynn	Headfort	5 and 4
1983	Miss E McDaid	Miss S Lynn	Ennis	20th hole
1984	Miss S Sheehan	Miss L Tormey	Thurles	6 and 4
1985	Miss S Sheehan	Miss D Hanna	Laytown/Bettystown	5 and 4
1986	Miss D Mahon	Miss T Eakin	Mallow	4 and 3
1987	Miss V Greevy	Miss B Ryan	Galway	8 and 7
1988	Miss L McCool	Miss P Gorman	Courtown	3 and 2
1989	Miss A Rogers	Miss R MacGuigan	Athlone	2 and 1

Scottish Girls' Open Stroke Play Championship

Year	Winner	Venue
1960	Miss J Greenhalgh	Ranfurly Castle
1961	Miss D Robb	Whitecraigs
1962	Miss S Armitage	Dalmahoy
1963	Miss A Irvin	Dumfries
1964	Miss M Nuttall	Dalmahoy
1965	Miss I Wylie	Carnoustie
1966	Miss J Smith	Douglas Park
1967	Miss J Bourassa	Dunbar
1968	Miss K Phillips	Dumfries
1969	Miss K Phillips	Prestonfield
1970	Miss B Huke	Leven
1971	Miss B Huke	Dalmahoy
1972	Miss L Hope	Troon, Portland
1973	Miss G Cadden	Edzell
1974	Miss S Lambie	Stranraer
1975	Miss S Cadden	Lanark
1976	Miss S Cadden	Prestonfield
1977	Miss S Cadden	Edzell
1978	Miss J Connachan	Peebles
1979	Miss A Gemmill	Troon, Portland
1980	Miss J Connachan	Kirkcaldy
1981	Miss K Douglas	Downfield
1982	Miss J Rhodes	Dumfries & Galloway
1983	Miss S Lawson	Largs
1984	Miss S Lawson	Dunbar
1985	Miss K Imrie	Ballater
1986	Miss K Imrie	Dumfries and County
1987	Miss K Imrie	Douglas Park
1988	Miss C Lambert	Baberton
1989	Miss C Lambert	Dunblane New

Scottish Girls' Close Amateur Championship

Year	Winner	Runner-up	Venue	By
1960	Miss J Hastings	Miss A Lurie	Kilmacolm	6 and 4
1961	Miss I Wylie	Miss W Clark	Murrayfield	3 and 1
1962	Miss I Wylie	Miss U Burnet	West Kilbride	3 and 1
1963	Miss M Norval	Miss S MacDonald	Carnoustie	6 and 4
1964	Miss JW Smith	Miss C Workman	West Kilbride	2 and 1
1965	Miss JW Smith	Miss I Walker	Leven	7 and 5
1966	Miss J Hutton	Miss F Jamieson	Arbroath	2 holes
1967	Miss J Hutton	Miss K Lackie	West Kilbride	4 and 2
1968	Miss M Dewar	Miss J Crawford	Dalmahoy	2 holes
1969	Miss C Panton	Miss A Coutts	Edzell	23rd hole
1970	Miss M Walker	Miss L Bennett	Largs	3 and 2
1971	Miss M Walker	Miss S Kennedy	Edzell	1 hole
1972	Miss G Cadden	Miss C Panton	Stirling	3 and 2
1973	Miss M Walker	Miss M Thomson	Cowal, Dunoon	1 hole
1974	Miss S Cadden	Miss D Reid	Arbroath	3 and 1
1975	Miss W Aitken	Miss S Cadden	Leven	1 hole
1976	MIss S Cadden	Miss D Mitchell	Dumfries and County	4 and 2
1977	Miss W Aitken	Miss G Wilson	West Kilbride	2 holes
1978	Miss J Connachan	Miss D Mitchell	Stirling	7 and 5
1979	Miss J Connachan	Miss G Wilson	Dunbar	3 and 1
1980	Miss J Connachan	Miss P Wright	Dumfries and County	21st hole
1981	Miss D Thomson	Miss P Wright	Barassie	2 and 1
1982	Miss S Lawson	Miss D Thomson	Montrose	1 hole
1983	Miss K Imrie	Miss D Martin	Leven	2 and 1
1984	Miss T Craik	Miss D Jackson	Peebles	3 and 2
1985	Miss E Farquharson	Miss E Moffat	West Kilbride	2 holes
1986	Miss C Lambert	Miss F McKay	Nairn	4 and 3
1987	Miss S Little	Miss L Moretti	Stirling	3 and 2
1988	Miss J Jenkins	Miss F McKay	Dumfries and County	4 and 3
1989	Miss J Moodie	Miss V Melvin	Kilmacolm	19th hole

West of Scotland Girls' Championship

Year	Winner	Year	Winner
1980	Miss S Lawson	1985	Miss K Fitzgerald
1981	Miss S Lawson	1986	Miss L Lundie
1982	Miss S Lawson	1987	Miss A Ferguson
1983	Miss A Johnson	1988	Miss A Ferguson
1984	Miss D Jackson	1989	Miss J Risby

Welsh Girls' Amateur Championship

Year	Winner	Runner-up	Venue	By
1960	Miss A Hughes	Miss D Wilson	Llandrindod Wells	6 and 4
1961	Miss J Morris	Miss S Kelly	North Wales	3 and 2
1962	Miss J Morris	Miss P Morgan	Southerndown	4 and 3
1963	Miss A Hughes	Miss A Brown	Conway	8 and 7
1964	Miss A Hughes	Miss M Leigh	Holyhead	5 and 3
1965	Miss A Hughes	Miss A Reardon-Hughes	Swansea Bay	19th hole
1966	Miss S Hales	Miss J Rogers	Prestatyn	1 hole
1967	Miss E Wilkie	Miss L Humphreys	Pyle and Kenfig	1 hole
1968	Miss L Morris	Miss J Rogers	Portmadoc	1 hole
1969	Miss L Morris	Miss L Humphreys	Wenvoe Castle	5 and 3
1970	Miss T Perkins	Miss P Light	Rhuddlan	2 and 1
1971	Miss P Light	Miss P Whitley	Glamorganshire	4 and 3
1972	Miss P Whitley	Miss P Light	Llandudno (Maesdu)	2 and 1
1973	Miss V Rawlings	Miss T Perkins	Whitchurch	19th hole
1974	Miss L Isherwood	Miss S Rowlands	Wrexham	4 and 3
1975	Miss L Isherwood	Miss S Rowlands	Swansea Bay	1 hole

Year	Winner	Runner-up	Venue	By
1976	Miss K Rawlings	Miss C Parry	Rhuddlan	5 and 4
1977	Miss S Rowlands	Miss D Taylor	Clyne	7 and 5
1978	Miss S Rowlands	Miss G Rees	Abergele	3 and 2
1979	Miss M Rawlings	Miss J Richards	St Mellons	19th hole
1980	Miss K Davies	Miss M Rawlings	Vale of Llangollen	19th hole
1981	Miss M Rawlings	Miss F Connor	Radyr	4 and 3
1982	Miss K Davies	Miss K Beckett	Wrexham	6 and 5
1983	Miss N Wesley	Miss J Foster	Whitchurch	4 and 2
1984	Miss J Foster	Miss J Evans	Pwllheli	6 and 5
1985	Miss J Foster	Miss S Caley	Langland Bay	6 and 5
1986	Miss J Foster	Miss L Dermott	Holyhead	3 and 2
1987	Miss J Lloyd	Miss S Bibbs	Cardiff	2 and 1
1988	Miss L Dermot	Miss A Perriam	Builth Wells	2 holes
1989	Miss L Dermot	Miss N Stroud	Carmarthen	4 and 2

Girls' Home Internationals: Stroyan Cup

Year	Winner	Venue
1966	Scotland	Troon (Portland)
1967	England	Liphook
1968	England	Leven
1969	England	Ilkley
1970	England	N Wales
1971	England	N Berwick
1972	Scotland	Royal Norwich
1973	Scotland	Northamptonshire County
1974	England	Dunbar
1975	England	Henbury
1976	Scotland	Pyle and Kenfig
1977	England	Formby Ladies
1978	England	Largs
1979	England	Edgbaston
1980	England	Wrexham
1981	England	Woodbridge
1982	England	Edzell
1983	England	Alwoodley
1984	Scotland	Llandudno (Maesdu)
1985	England	Hesketh GC
1986	England	West Kilbride

1987 at Barnham Broom

England beat Scotland	6½-½
England beat Ireland	7-0
England beat Wales	6-1
Scotland beat Ireland	4-3
Ireland beat Wales	4½-2½
Wales beat Scotland	4-3

Result: England 3; Ireland 1; Scotland 1; Wales 1

1988 at Pyle and Kenfig

England beat Ireland	4-3
England beat Wales	4-3
England halved with Scotland	3½-3½
Ireland beat Wales	4-3
Ireland beat Scotland	5-2
Wales beat Scotland	4-3

Result: England 3; Ireland 2; Scotland 1; Wales 1

1989 at Carlisle

Ireland beat Scotland	4½-2½
England beat Wales	4-3
Ireland beat Wales	4½-2½
England beat Scotland	5-2
Scotland beat Wales	4-3
England beat Ireland	4½-2½

Result: England 3; Ireland 2; Scotland 1; Wales 0

British Youths' Open Amateur Championship

Year	Winner	Club/Country	Venue	Score
1954	JS More	Swanston, Edinburgh	Erskine	287
1955	B Stockdale	Royal Lytham St Annes	Pannal	297
1956	AF Bussell	Coxmoor	Barnton	287
1957	G Will	St Andrews	Pannal	290
1958	RH Kemp	Glamorganshire	Dumfries and County	281
1959	RA Jowle	Moseley	Pannal	286
1960	GA Caygill	Sunningdale	Pannal	279
1961	JS Martin	Kilbirnie Place	Bruntsfield	284
1962	GA Caygill	Sunningdale	Pannal	287
1963	AJ Low	St Andrews University	Pollok	283
1964	BW Barnes	Burnham and Berrow	Pannal	290
1965	PM Townsend	Porters Park	Cosforth Park	281
1966	PA Oosterhuis	Dulwich and Sydenham	Dalmahoy (54 holes)	219
1967	PJ Benka	Addington	Copt Heath	278
1968	PJ Benka	Addington	Ayr Belleisle	281
1969	JH Cook	Calcot Park	Lindrick	289
1970	B Dassu	Italy	Barnton	276
1971	P Elson	Coventry	Northamptonshire	277
1972	AH Chandler	Regent Park	Glasgow Gailes	281
1973	SC Mason	Goring and Streatley	Southport and Ainsdale	284
1974	DM Robertson	Dunbar	Downfield	284
1975	N Faldo	Welwyn Garden City	Pannal	278
1976	ME Lewis	Henbury	Gullane	277
1977	AWB Lyle	Hawkstone Park	Moor Park	285
1978	B Marchbank	Auchterarder	East Renfrewshire	278
1979	G Brand Jr	Knowle	Woodhall Spa	291
1980	G Hay	Hilton Park	Troon	303
1981	T Antevik	Sweden	Gullane	290
1982	AP Parkin	Newtown	St Andrews New	280
1983	P Mayo	Newport	Sunningdale	290
1984	R Morris	Padeswick and Buckley	Blairgowrie	281
1985	J-M Olazabal	Spain	Ganton	281
1986	D Gilford	GB	Carnoustie	283
1987	J Cook / O Nordberg	GB / Sweden } tie	Hollinwell	283
	(Cook won play-off)			
1988	C Cassells / C Cevaer	Murcar / France } tie	Royal Aberdeen	275
	(Cevaer won play-off)			
1989	M Smith	Brokenhurst Manor	Ashburnham	285

Irish Youths' Open Amateur Championship

Year	Winner	Venue	Score
1980	J McHenry	Clandeboye	296
1981	J McHenry	Westport	303
1982	K O'Donnell	Mullingar	286
1983	P Murphy	Cork	287
1984	JC Morris	Bangor	292
1985	J McHenry	Co Sligo	287
1986	JC Morris	Carlow	280
1987	C Everett	Killarney	300
1988	P McGinley	Malone	283
1989	A Mathers	Athlone	280

Scottish Youths' Open Amateur Stroke Play Championship
Instituted 1979

Year	Winner	Club	Venue	Score
1979	A Oldcorn	Ratho Park	Dalmahoy	217
1980	G Brand, Jr	Knowle	Monifieth and Ashludie	281
1981	S Campbell	Cawder	Cawder and Keir	279
1982	LS Mann	Carnoustie	Leven and Scoonie	270
1983	A Moir	McDonald	Mortonhall	284
1984	B Shields	Bathgate	Eastwood, Renfrew	280
1985	H Kemp	Cawder	East Kilbride	282
1986	A Mednick	Sweden	Cawder	282
1987	K Walker	Royal Burgess	Bogside	291
1988	P McGinley	Grange	Ladybank & Glenrothes	281
1989	J Mackenzie	West Linton	Longniddry	281

Ulster Youths' Open Amateur Championship

Year	Winner	Year	Winner
1980	J Jones	1985	J Carvill
1981	M Windebank	1986	DA Mulholland
1982	G Hamill	1987	J Carvill
1983	M Froggatt	1988	G McAllister
1984	G Clarke	1989	G Moore

Great Britain & Ireland *v* Continent of Europe, Youths
Instituted 1967

Year	Winner	Result	Venue
1967	Great Britain	8-7	Copt Heath
1968	Great Britain	11-4	Ayr Belleisle
1969	Great Britain	13½-1½	Lindrick
1970	Great Britain	10½-4½	Barnton
1971	Great Britain	10-5	Northampton County
1972	Great Britain	11½-3½	Glasgow Gailes
1973	Great Britain	10-5	Southport & Ainsdale
1974	Great Britain	10-5	Downfield
1975	Great Britain	9-6	Pannal
1976	Great Britain	17-13	Chantilly
1977	Great Britain	11½-3½	Moor Park
1978	Great Britain	12½-2½	East Renfrewshire
1979	Great Britain	12-3	Woodhall Spa
1980	Europe	13-11	Lunds Akademiska
1981	Great Britain	7½-4½	West Lancs
(Singles curtailed owing to weather)			
1982	Great Britain	7½-4½	St Andrews New
1983	Great Britain	11-13	Punta Ala, Italy
1984	Halved	6-6	Blairgowrie
1985	Great Britain & Ireland	8-4	Ganton
1986	Great Britain & Ireland	13½-10½	Bilbao, Spain
1987	Continent of Europe	7-5	Hollinwell
1988	Great Britain & Ireland	13½-10½	Copenhagen, Denmark
1989	Great Britain & Ireland	8½-3½	Ashburnham

Youths' Internationals
England v Scotland

Year	Winner	Result	Venue
1955	England	13-5	Pannal
1956	Scotland	+17 holes	Burgess
1957	Not played		
1958	England	+4 holes	Dumfries & County
1959	Scotland	12-6	Pannal
1960	Scotland	11½-6½	Pannal
1961	England	11½-6½	Bruntsfield
1962	England	9½-8½	Pannal
1963	Scotland	9-6	Pollok
1964	Scotland	9-6	Pannal
1965	Scotland	10½-3½	Northumberland
1966	England	9½-5½	Dalmahoy
1967	Halved	7½-7½	Copt Heath
1968	Scotland	8½-6½	Ayr Belleisle
1969	England	8½-6½	Lindrick
1970	Scotland	8½-6½	Barnton
1971	England	11-4	Northampton County
1972	England	11-4	Glasgow Gailes
1973	England	10-5	Southport & Ainsdale
1974	England	9-6	Downfield
1975	Scotland	11-4	Pannal
1976	England	8½-6½	Gullane
1977	Scotland	9½-5½	Moor Park
1978	Scotland	8½-6½	East Renfrewshire
1979	Halved	7½-7½	Woodhall Spa
1980	Scotland	9-6	Troon
1981	Scotland	8-7	West Lancs
1982	Halved	7½-7½	St Andrews New
1983	Scotland	8½-6½	Sunningdale
1984	Scotland	9-6	Blairgowrie
1985	Halved	7½-7½	Ganton
1986	Scotland	8-7	Carnoustie
1987	England	9½-5½	Hollinwell
1988	England	10-5	R. Aberdeen
1989	England	9-6	Ashburnham

County and District Championships

Aberdeenshire Ladies' Championship

Year	Winner	Year	Winner
1980	Miss J B Rennie	1985	Miss P Wright
1981	Miss C A Stewart	1986	Miss E Farquharson
1982	Miss P Wright	1987	Miss E Farquharson
1983	Miss E Farquharson	1988	Miss L Urquhart
1984	Miss J Self	1989	Miss J Forbes

Angus Amateur Championship

Year	Winner
1988	D Downie
1989	T Peebles

Angus Ladies' Championship
Instituted pre 1935

Year	Winner	Year	Winner
1980	Miss N Duncan	1985	M Mackie
1981	Miss K Sutherland	1986	Mrs F Farquharson
1982	Miss K Imrie	1987	Mrs F Farquharson
1983	Miss K Imrie	1988	Miss C Hay
1984	Miss K Imrie	1989	Miss C Hope

Argyll and Bute Amateur Championship

Year	Winner	Year	Winner
1980	G Tyre	1985	
1981	M Cannon	1986	
1982	J Ewing	1987	
1983	G Tyre	1988	G Bolton
1984	D MacIntyre	1989	G Tyre

Ayrshire Amateur Championship

Year	Winner	Year	Winner
1980	J Bunting	1985	P Girvan
1981	D Murdoch	1986	G Armstrong
1982	C Evans	1987	B Gemmell
1983	L Crawford	1988	G Blair
1984	J Milligan	1989	D Hawthorn

Ayrshire Ladies' Championship
Instituted 1923

Year	Winner	Year	Winner
1980	Miss A Gemmill	1985	Miss J Leishman
1981	Miss A Gemmill	1986	Miss A Gemmill
1982	Miss A Gemmill	1987	Miss A Gemmill
1983	Miss A Gemmill	1988	Mrs M Wilson
1984	Miss A Gemmill	1989	Miss A Gemmill

Bedfordshire Amateur Championship
Instituted 1923

Year	Winner	Year	Winner
1980	D Ellis	1985	R Harris
1981	C Beard	1986	M Wharton
1982	A Rose	1987	P Wharton
1983	A Rose	1988	P Wharton
1984	MA Stokes	1989	C Staroscik

Bedfordshire Ladies' Championship
Instituted 1926

Year	Winner	Year	Winner
1980	Miss S Kiddle	1985	Mrs S White
1981	Miss S Kiddle	1986	Mrs C Westgate
1982	Miss S Kiddle	1987	Mrs S White
1983	Mrs S White	1988	Miss S Cormack
1984	Mrs S White	1989	Miss T Gale

Berks, Bucks and Oxfordshire Amateur Championship
Instituted 1924

Year	Winner	Year	Winner
1980	DG Lane	1985	M Rapley
1981	M Rapley	1986	DG Lane
1982	DG Lane	1987	F George
1983	M Orris	1988	F George
1984	NG Webber	1989	H Bareham

Berkshire Ladies' Championship
Instituted 1925

Year	Winner	Year	Winner
1980	Mrs A Uzielli	1985	Mrs A Uzielli
1981	Mrs A Uzielli	1986	Mrs A Uzielli
1982	Mrs C Caldwell	1987	Mrs A Uzielli
1983	Mrs A Uzielli	1988	Miss T Smith
1984	Mrs A Uzielli	1989	Miss L Walton

Border Counties Ladies' Championship

Year	Winner	Year	Winner
1980	Miss S Gallacher	1985	Miss S Gallacher
1981	Miss A Hunter	1986	Miss S Gallacher
1982	Mrs S Simpson	1987	Mrs S Simpson
1983	Mrs E White	1988	Miss A Hunter
1984	Miss S Gallacher	1989	Mrs A Fleming

Border Golfers' Association Amateur Championship
Instituted 1893

Year	Winner	Year	Winner
1980	PWJ Gallagher	1985	L Wallace
1981	PWJ Gallagher	1986	L Wallace
1982	DF Campbell	1987	D Ballantyne
1983	B Reid	1988	W Renwick
1984	A Turnbull	1989	A Turnbull

Bucks Ladies' Championship
Instituted 1924

Year	Winner	Year	Winner
1980	Mrs K Copley	1985	Miss E Franklin
1981	Miss J Warren	1986	Miss A Tyreman
1982	Miss J Warren	1987	Mrs C Watson
1983	Miss G Bonallack	1988	Miss C Hourihane
1984	Miss J Warren	1989	Miss C Hourihane

Caernarfonshire and District Amateur Championship
Instituted 1922

Year	Winner	Year	Winner
1980	A Llyr	1985	MA Macara
1981	WG Jones	1986	RI Roberts
1982	D McLean	1987	D McLean
1983	JR Parry / WG Jones	1988	D McLean
1984	S Owen	1989	WE Jones

Caernarfonshire Amateur Championship Cup

Instituted 1989

Year	Winner
1989	M Sheppard

Caernarvonshire and Anglesey Ladies' Championship

Instituted 1924

Year	Winner	Year	Winner
1980	Miss A Thomas	1985	Miss A Lewis
1981	Miss S Jump	1986	Mrs S Turner
1982	Miss F Connor	1987	Miss S Roberts
1983	Miss S Roberts	1988	Mrs S Turner
1984	Miss S Jump	1989	Miss S Roberts

Cambridge Area GU Amateur Championship

Year	Winner	Year	Winner
1980	MT Seaton	1985	DWG Wood
1981	MT Seaton	1986	JGR Miller
1982	RW Guy	1987	R Claydon
1983	JR Gray	1988	R Claydon
1984	NK Hughes	1989	B Jackson

Cambridgeshire and Hunts Ladies' Championship

Year	Winner	Year	Winner
1980	Miss J Richards	1985	Miss J Walter
1981	Miss J Walter	1986	Miss J Walter
1982	Miss J Walter	1987	Mrs R Farrow
1983	Miss J Walter	1988	Miss S Meadows
1984	Miss J Walter	1989	Miss J Hatcher

Channel Islands Ladies' Championship

Year	Winner	Year	Winner
1980	Mrs E Roberts	1985	Miss L Cummins
1981	Miss L Cummins	1986	Miss V Bougourd
1982	Miss V Bougourd	1987	Miss L Cummins
1983	Mrs D Heaton	1988	Miss L Cummins
1984	Mrs E Roberts	1989	Miss L Cummins

Cheshire Amateur Championship
Instituted 1921

Year	Winner	Year	Winner
1980	EI Bradshaw	1985	C Harrison
1981	C Harrison	1986	P Bailey
1982	CR Smethurst	1987	P Jones
1983	CR Smethurst	1988	P Bailey
1984	I Spencer	1989	P Bailey

Cheshire Ladies' Championship
Instituted 1912

Year	Winner	Year	Winner
1980	Mrs A Briggs	1985	Miss L Percival
1981	Mrs A Briggs	1986	Miss J Hill
1982	Miss H Latham	1987	Miss S Robinson
1983	Miss H Latham	1988	Miss J Morley
1984	Miss J Hill	1989	Miss J Morley

Clackmannanshire Amateur Championship

Year	Winner
1988	R Stewart
1989	J Gullen

Cornwall Amateur Championship
Instituted 1896

Year	Winner	Year	Winner
1980	M Boggia	1985	CD Phillips
1981	JR Hirst	1986	RJ Simmons
1982	MC Edmunds	1987	P Clayton
1983	MC Edmunds	1988	P Clayton
1984	RJ Simmons	1989	CD Phillips

Cornwall Ladies' Championship
Instituted 1896

Year	Winner	Year	Winner
1980	Miss L Moore	1985	Miss J Fern
1981	Miss L Moore	1986	Miss J Ryder
1982	Miss S Cann	1987	Miss J Ryder
1983	Miss J Ryder	1988	Mrs S Currie
1984	Miss J Fernleigh	1989	Mrs S Currie

County Champions' Tournament (England)

For President's Bowl

Year	Winner	Year	Winner
1962	GM Edwards, Cheshire A Thirwell, Northumberland	1975	N Faldo, Herts
		1976	RPF Brown, Devon
1963	MJ Burgess, Sussex R Foster, Yorks	1977	M Walls, Cumbria
		1978	IT Simpson, Notts
1964	MF Attenborough, Kent	1979	N Burch, Essex
1965	MG Lees, Lincs	1980	D Lane, Berks, Bucks and Oxon
1966	RP Stephenson, Middx	1981	M Kelly, Yorks
1967	PJ Benka, Surrey	1982	P Deeble, Northumberland
1968	GE Hyde, Sussex	1983	N Chesses, Warwickshire
1969	AW Holmes, Herts	1984	N Briggs, Herts P McEvoy, Warwickshire
1970	MG King, Berks, Bucks and Oxon		
1971	M Lee, Yorks	1985	P Robinson, Herts
1972	P Berry, Glos	1986	A Gelsthorpe, Yorks
1973	AH Chandler, Lancs	1987	F George, Berks, Bucks & Oxon D Fay, Surrey
1974	GE Hyde, Sussex AWB Lyle, Shrops & Hereford		
		1988	R Claydon, Cambridge
		1989	R Willison, Middlesex

Cumbria Amateur Championship

Formerly Cumberland and Westmorland Amateur Championship

Year	Winner	Year	Winner
1980	AR Morrison	1985	J Longcake
1981	J Kirkpatrick	1986	M Ruddick
1982	E Gulliksen	1987	J Longcake
1983	A Drabble	1988	G Waters
1984	M Lowe	1989	G Winter

Cumbria Ladies' Championship

Year	Winner	Year	Winner
1980	Miss D Thomson	1985	Miss J Currie
1981	Miss D Thomson	1986	Mrs H Porter
1982	Miss D Thomson	1987	Miss J McColl
1983	Miss P Brumwell	1988	Miss D Thomson
1984	Miss D Thomson	1989	Miss S Tuck

Denbighshire and Flintshire Ladies' Championship

Year	Winner	Year	Winner
1980	Miss K Davies	1985	Miss E Davies
1981	Mrs E Higgs	1986	Mrs S Thomas
1982	Miss K Davies	1987	Mrs S Thomas
1983	Miss E Davies	1988	Mrs S Thomas
1984	Mrs C Ellis	1989	Mrs S Thomas

Derbyshire Amateur Championship
Instituted 1913

Year	Winner	Year	Winner
1980	JC Thomas	1985	R Davenport
1981	RJ Hall	1986	J Feeney
1982	R Davenport	1987	RP Green
1983	R Davenport	1988	NC Wylde
1984	G Shaw	1989	PM Eastwood

Derbyshire Ladies' Championship
Instituted 1921

Year	Winner	Year	Winner
1980	Miss A Howe	1985	Miss L Holmes
1981	Miss A Howe	1986	Miss E Robinson
1982	Miss V McWilliams	1987	Miss E Clark
1983	Miss J Williams	1988	Miss A Howe
1984	Miss J Williams	1989	Mrs D Andrews

Derbyshire Match-Play Championship
Instituted 1971

Year	Winner	Year	Winner
1980	CRJ Ibbotson	1985	CRJ Ibbotson
1981	N Rowland	1986	J Feeney
1982	MP Higgins	1987	G Shaw
1983	G Shaw	1988	MP Higgins
1984	G Shaw	1989	B Shaw

Derbyshire Open Championship

Year	Winner	Year	Winner
1980	I Gretton (Am)	1985	M McLean
1981	RRW Davenport (Am)	1986	N Furniss (Am)
1982	RRW Davenport (Am)	1987	SA Smith
1983	C Radford (Am)	1988	G Shaw
1984	J Feeney (Am)	1989	DL Clark (Am)

Derbyshire Professional Championship
Instituted 1921

Year	Winner	Year	Winner
1980	P Taylor	1985	J Turnbull
1981	J Lower	1986	J Lower
1982	A Wardle	1987	AR Skingle
1983	PK Seal	1988	M McLean
1984	W Bird	1989	N Hallam

Devon Amateur Championship
Instituted 1912

Year	Winner	Year	Winner
1980	M G Symons	1985	J Langmead
1981	M Jewell	1986	P Newcombe
1982	M G Symons	1987	J Langmead
1983	A Richards	1988	J Langmead
1984		1989	R Barrow

Devon Ladies' Championship
Instituted 1922

Year	Winner	Year	Winner
1980	Mrs J Mason	1985	Miss L Lines
1981	Miss C Stephens	1986	Miss J Hurley
1982	Miss J Hurley	1987	Miss G Jenkinson
1983	Miss J Hurley	1988	Miss J Hurley
1984	Miss J Hurley	1989	Miss S Germain

Devon Open Championship
Instituted 1923

Year	Winner	Year	Winner
1980	M Kemp	1985	A MacDonald
1981	D Sheppard	1986	P Newcombe
1982	M Jewell (Am)	1987	G Milne
1983	T Valentine	1988	D Sheppard
1984	M Symons	1989	D Shappard

Dorset Amateur Championship
Instituted 1924

Year	Winner	Year	Winner
1980	J Nash	1985	J Bloxham
1981	R Hearn	1986	A Lawrence
1982	R Miles	1987	A Lawrence
1983	R Miles	1988	A Lawrence
1984	JD Gordon	1989	A Lawrence

Dorset Ladies' Championship
Instituted 1923

Year	Winner	Year	Winner
1980	Mrs C Stirling	1985	Miss S Lowe
1981	Mrs R Page	1986	Miss H Delew
1982	Mrs B Langley	1987	Mrs J Sugden
1983	Mrs J Sugden	1988	Miss H Delew
1984	Miss S Lowe	1989	Miss T Loveys

Dumfriesshire Ladies' Championship

Year	Winner	Year	Winner
1980	Mrs G Barclay	1985	Mrs R Morrison
1981	Mrs E Hill	1986	Mrs M McKerrow
1982	Mrs B W Hill	1987	Mrs M McKerrow
1983	Miss DM Hill	1988	Miss D Douglas
1984	Miss DM Hill	1989	Miss D Douglas

Dunbartonshire Amateur Championship

Year	Winner	Year	Winner
1980	D G Carrick	1985	S R Millor
1981	J Graham	1986	DG Carrick
1982	DG Carrick	1987	D Shaw
1983	DG Carrick	1988	J Laird
1984	T Eckford	1989	D Shaw

Dunbartonshire Amateur Match Play Championship

Year	Winner	Year	Winner
1980	KW Macintosh	1985	DG Carrick
1981	GF Jack	1986	WG Thom
1982	C White	1987	A Brodie
1983	G Millar	1988	R Blair
1984	RG Fraser	1989	CD Stewart

Dunbartonshire and Argyll Ladies' Championship

Year	Winner	Year	Winner
1980	Mrs MP Grant	1985	Miss V McAlister
1981	Miss V McAlister	1986	Miss J Kinloch
1982	Miss V McAlister	1987	Miss S McDonald
1983	Miss V McAlister	1988	Miss V McAlister
1984	Miss V McAlister	1989	Miss M McKinlay

Durham Amateur Championship
Instituted 1908

Year	Winner	Year	Winner
1980	AJ McLure	1985	A Robertson
1981	D Hawkins	1986	H Ashby
1982	JE Ellwood	1987	P Highmoor
1983	M Ure	1988	JR Ellwood
1984	M Ure	1989	G Bell

Durham Ladies' Championship
Instituted 1923

Year	Winner	Year	Winner
1980	Mrs L Still	1985	Miss M Scullan
1981	Miss C Barker	1986	Miss L Chesterton
1982	Miss P Hunt	1987	Miss B Mansfield
1983	Miss P Hunt	1988	Miss L Chesterton
1984	Miss B Mansfield	1989	Mrs L Still

East Anglian Ladies' Championship

Year	Winner
1986	Miss J Walter
1987	Miss J Walter
1988	Mrs R Farrow
1989	Mrs W Fryer

East Anglian Open Championship

Year	Winner		Year	Winner
1980	S Levermore		1985	C Platts
1981	F Hill		1986	M Stokes
1982	RW Mann		1987	*Not played*
1983	RW Mann		1988	P Kent
1984	M Stokes / K Ashdown	} tie	1989	RY Mitchell

East Lothian Ladies' Championship

Year	Winner	Year	Winner
1980	Miss C Lugton	1985	Miss M Ferguson
1981	Mrs AJR Ferguson	1986	Miss P Lees
1982	*Null and void*	1987	Miss J Ford
1983	Mrs M Thomson	1988	Miss C Lugton
1984	Miss M Ferguson	1989	Miss C Lugton

East of Ireland Open Amateur Championship

Year	Winner	Year	Winner
1980	P Caul	1985	F Ronan
1981	D Branigan	1986	P Hogan
1982	MF Sludds	1987	P Rayfus
1983	AJC Morrow	1988	G McGimpsey
1984	BUM Reddan	1989	D Clarke

Eastern Division Ladies' Championship (Scotland)

Year	Winner	Year	Winner
1980	Mrs J Marshall	1985	Miss L Bennett
1981	Miss E Kimmen	1986	Miss J Harrison
1982	Miss J Bald	1987	Miss A Rose
1983	Mrs J Marshall	1988	Miss J Ford
1984	Miss L Hope	1989	Miss H Rose

East of Scotland Open Amateur Stroke Play

Year	Winner	Year	Winner
1980	D Greig	1985	A McQueen
1981	K Gray	1986	S Knowles
1982	G Macgregor	1987	T Cochrane
1983	S Stephen	1988	C Everett
1984	S Stephen	1989	K Hird

East Region PGA Championship

Year	Winner	
1987	J Pinsent P Kent	} tie
1988	L Farmer	
1989	*Not played*	

Essex Ladies' Championship

Year	Winner	Year	Winner
1980	Mrs E Boatman	1985	Mrs S Barber
1981	Mrs P Jackson	1986	Miss S Moorcroft
1982	Mrs A Bonallack	1987	Miss M King
1983	Mrs E Boatman	1988	Miss W Dicks
1984	Mrs S Barber	1989	Miss A MacDonald

Essex Amateur Championship

Year	Winner	Year	Winner
1980	G Godwin	1985	D Wood
1981	C Davies	1986	M Davis
1982	C Laurence	1987	V Cox
1983	M Davis	1988	R Scott
1984	M Stokes	1989	V Cox

Fife Amateur Championship
Instituted 1935

Year	Winner	Year	Winner
1980	JW Noble	1985	DR Weir
1981	D Ross	1986	D Spriddle
1982	D Weir	1987	SR Meiklejohn
1983	T Cochrane	1988	A Mathers
1984	C Birrell	1989	G Spriddel

Fife County Ladies' Championship

Year	Winner	Year	Winner
1980	Mrs J Louden	1985	Miss L Bennett
1981	Miss J Bald	1986	Miss L Bennett
1982	Miss J Bald	1987	Miss L Bennett
1983	Mrs R Scott	1988	Miss J Lawrence
1984	Miss E Hunter	1989	Mrs J Ford

Galloway Ladies' Championship

Year	Winner	Year	Winner
1980	Miss FM Rennie	1985	Miss M Wright
1981	Miss M Clements	1986	Miss M Wright
1982	Miss M Clements	1987	Miss M Wright
1983	Miss S McDonald	1988	Miss M Wright
1984	Miss S McDonald	1989	Miss F Rennie

Glamorgan Amateur Championship

Year	Winner	Year	Winner
1980	DL Stevens	1985	R Brown
1981	T Melia	1986	LP Price
1982	T Melia	1987	N Roderick
1983	P Bloomfield	1988	I Booth
1984	N Roderick	1989	BR Knight

Glamorgan County Ladies' Championship
Instituted 1927

Year	Winner	Year	Winner
1980	Mrs T Thomas (née Perkins)	1985	Miss P Johnson
		1986	Miss P Johnson
1981	Mrs T Thomas	1987	Mrs V Thomas
1982	Miss M Rawlings	1988	Mrs V Thomas
1983	Mrs T Thomas	1989	Mrs V Thomas
1984	Miss J Foster		

Glasgow Match Play Championship
Instituted 1897

Year	Winner	Year	Winner
1980	D Carrick	1985	S Savage
1981	D Carrick	1986	G Shaw
1982	B Pearson	1987	S Dixon
1983	B Pearson	1988	J Finnigan
1984	I Carslaw	1989	L McLaughlin

Glasgow Stroke Play Championship

Year	Winner
1984	IA Carslaw
1985	IA Carslaw
1986	A Maclaine
1987	S Machin
1988	D Martin
1989	G Shaw

Gloucestershire Amateur Championship
Instituted 1906

Year	Winner	Year	Winner
1980	M Lewis	1985	D Carroll
1981	J Durbin	1986	RJ Broad
1982	D Ray	1987	M Bessell
1983	D Rollo	1988	J Webber
1984	C Robinson	1989	RD Broad

Gloucestershire Ladies' Championship
Instituted 1923

Year	Winner	Year	Winner
1980	Miss K Douglas	1985	Miss C Griffiths
1981	Miss K Douglas	1986	Miss S Shapcott
1982	Miss K Douglas	1987	Mrs R Page
1983	Miss K Douglas	1988	Miss S Elliott
1984	Miss K Douglas	1989	Miss S Elliott

Gwent Amateur Championship
Formerly Monmouthshire Amateur Championship

Year	Winner	Year	Winner
1980	A Disley	1985	M Brimble
1981	A Disley	1986	G Hughes
1982	P Mayo	1987	M Bearcroft
1983	NR Davies	1988	A Williams
1984	P Mayo	1989	P Glyn

Hampshire, Isle of Wight and Channel Islands Open Championship
Instituted 1967

Year	Winner	Year	Winner
1980	R A Doig	1985	I Young
1981	B J Winteridge (Am)	1986	M Desmond
1982	J Hay	1987	T Healey
1983	J Hay	1988	K Bowden
1984	M Desmond	1989	J Coles

Hampshire, Isle of Wight and Channel Islands Amateur Championship
Instituted 1894

Year	Winner	Year	Winner
1980	R W Johnson	1985	R A Alker
1981	B J Winteridge	1986	R Eggo
1982	B J Winteridge	1987	A Mew
1983	K J Weeks	1988	S Richardson
1984	R Eggo	1989	M Smith

Hampshire Ladies' Championship
Instituted 1924

Year	Winner	Year	Winner
1980	Miss C Mackintosh	1985	Mrs C Stirling
1981	Mrs S Pickles	1986	Miss C Hayllar
1982	Miss A Wells	1987	Mrs C Stirling
1983	Miss C Hayllar	1988	Mrs C Stirling
1984	Miss C Mackintosh	1989	Mrs S Pickles

Hampshire Professional Match Play Championship

Year	Winner
1984	J Hay
1985	P Dawson
1986	K Bowden
1987	M Desmond
1988	K Bowden
1989	I Young

Hampshire Professional Stroke Play Championship

Year	Winner
1984	G Stubbington
1985	T Healy
1986	M Desmond
1987	T Healy
1988	G Stubbington
1989	J Coles

Herts Amateur Championship

Year	Winner	Year	Winner
1980	JE Ambridge	1985	PR Robinson
1981	RY Mitchell	1986	PJ Cherry
1982	JE Ambridge	1987	A Clark
1983	C McKay	1988	JE Ambridge
1984	N Briggs	1989	S Hankin

Herts Ladies' Championship
Instituted 1924

Year	Winner	Year	Winner
1980	Mrs H Kaye	1985	Mrs H Kaye
1981	Mrs V Pearson	1986	Miss T Jeary
1982	Miss N McCormack	1987	Mrs H Kaye
1983	Mrs E Provan	1988	Miss T Jeary
1984	Miss K Hurley	1989	Mrs H Kaye

Isle of Wight Ladies' Championship
Instituted 1923

Year	Winner	Year	Winner
1980	Miss G Wright	1985	Miss G Wright
1981	Miss G Wright	1986	Miss M Ankers
1982	Miss G Wright	1987	Miss M Ankers
1983	Miss G Wright	1988	Mrs M Butler
1984	Mrs M Butler	1989	Miss M Ankers

Kent Amateur Championship
Instituted 1925

Year	Winner	Year	Winner
1980	M McLean	1985	J Simmance
1981	M McLean	1986	M Lawrence
1982	S Baldwin	1987	L Batchelor
1983	M Lawrence	1988	W Hodkin
1984	M Lawrence	1989	S Green

Kent Ladies' Championship
Instituted 1920

Year	Winner	Year	Winner
1980	Mrs A Robinson	1985	Mrs L Bayman
1981	Miss J Guntrip	1986	Mrs C Caldwell
1982	Mrs S Hedges	1987	Mrs L Bayman
1983	Miss J Guntrip	1988	Mrs C Caldwell
1984	Mrs S Kitchen	1989	Miss S Sutton

Kent Open Championship

Year	Winner	Year	Winner
1980	I Grant	1985	J Bennett
1981	G Potter	1986	P Mitchell
1982	P Mitchell	1987	M Goodin
1983	G Potter	1988	J Bennett
1984	N Terry	1989	R Cameron

Kent Professional Championship
Instituted 1912

Year	Winner	Year	Winner
1980	R Fidler	1985	G Will
1981	D Russell	1986	J Bennett
1982	R Watkins	1987	S Barr
1983	G Potter	1988	R Cameron
1984	R Cameron	1989	P Lyons

Lanarkshire Amateur Championship

Year	Winner	Year	Winner
1980	H Miller	1985	J Reid
1981	G Banks	1986	WS Bryson
1982	G Jones	1987	S Henderson
1983	R Lynch	1988	WS Bryson
1984	WS Bryson	1989	JS Taylor

Lanarkshire Ladies' County Championship
Instituted 1928

Year	Winner	Year	Winner
1980	Mrs JC Scott	1985	Miss P Hutton
1981	Miss E Dunn	1986	Mrs JC Scott
1982	Mrs W Norris	1987	Mrs A Hendry
1983	Mrs S Roy	1988	Miss F McKay
	(*née* Needham)	1989	Mrs K Dallas
1984	Mrs S Roy		

Lancashire Amateur Championship
Instituted 1910

Year	Winner	Year	Winner
1980	A Squires	1985	RA Bardsley
1981	MJ Wild	1986	MJ Wild
1982	A Squires	1987	T Foster
1983	MPD Wallis	1988	M Kingsley
1984	SG Birtwell	1989	RA Bardsley

Lancashire Ladies' Championship
Instituted 1912

Year	Winner	Year	Winner
1980	Miss A Brown	1986	Mrs J Collingham
1981	Miss A Brown		(née Melville)
1982	Mrs G Costello	1987	Mrs J Collingham
1983	Miss J Melville	1988	Miss L Fairclough
1984	Mrs A Goucher	1989	Miss C Blackshaw
1985	Mrs A Bromilow		

Lancashire Open Championship
Instituted 1973

Year	Winner	Year	Winner
1980	D Clarke	1985	R Green
1981	D Durnian	1986	T Foster (Am)
1982	S Hadfield	1987	S Hamer (Am)
1983	S Hamer (Am)	1988	P Wesselingh
1984	R Longworth	1989	M Jones

Leicestershire and Rutland Amateur Championship
Instituted 1925

Year	Winner	Year	Winner
1980	A Harrison	1985	EW Hammond
1981	EW Hammond	1986	IR Middleton
1982	C Gotla	1987	G Marshall
1983	T Stephens	1988	A Martinez
1984	A Martinez	1989	JD Cayless

Leicestershire and Rutland Open Championship

Year	Winner	Year	Winner
1980	EW Hammond	1985	R Adams
1981	SH Adams (Am)	1986	R Stephenson
1982	I Middleton	1987	*Not played*
1983	EE Feasey (Am)	1988	D Gibson
1984	S Sherratt	1989	R Adams

Leicestershire and Rutland Ladies' Championship

Year	Winner	Year	Winner
1980	Miss J Roberts	1985	Miss A Waters
1981	Mrs R Reed	1986	Mrs V Davis
1982	Miss P Gray	1987	Miss M Page
1983	Mrs R Reed	1988	Miss A Walters
1984	Mrs P Martin	1989	Miss M Page

Lincolnshire Amateur Championship
Instituted 1925

Year	Winner	Year	Winner
1980	A Thain	1985	ACS Robinson
1981	L Brumpton	1986	JA Purdy
1982	S Graves	1987	P Stenton
1983	P Stenton	1988	P Stenton
1984	JA Purdy	1989	J Payne

Lincolnshire Ladies' Championship

Year	Winner	Year	Winner
1980	Mrs E Annison	1985	Miss H Dobson
1981	Miss R Broughton	1986	Miss A Johns
1982	Mrs B Hicks	1987	Miss H Dobson
1983	Mrs B Hicks	1988	Miss H Dobson
1984	Mrs A Burtt	1989	Miss H Dobson

Lincolnshire Open Championship

Year	Winner	Year	Winner
1980	K Daubney (Am)	1985	A Carter
1981	P Davies	1986	GE Stafford
1982	TR Squires	1987	SR Dickinson
1983	S Dickinson (Am)	1988	J Heib
1984	J Taylor	1989	AD Hare

Lothians Amateur Championship

Year	Winner	Year	Winner
1980	ST Knowles	1985	S Easingwood
1981	B Dunlop	1986	S Smith
1982	R Bradley	1987	D Kirkpatrick
1983	A Roy	1988	B Shields
1984	PJ Smith	1989	K Hastings

Manx Amateur Championship
Instituted 1926

Year	Winner	Year	Winner
1980	SJ Boyd	1985	J Sutton
1981	G Kelly	1986	AM Cain
1982	J Sutton	1987	J Sutton
1983	J Sutton	1988	G Kelly
1984	J Sutton	1989	G Ashe

Middlesex Amateur Championship
Instituted 1925

Year	Winner	Year	Winner
1980	NM Curtis	1985	RB Willison
1981	GA Homewood	1986	A Rogers
1982	ML Weir	1987	RB Willison
1983	GA Homewood	1988	A Rogers
1984	RB Willison	1989	RB Willison

Middlesex Ladies' Championship
Instituted 1923

Year	Winner
1984	Miss C Nelson
1985	Miss C Nelson
1986	Mrs A Gems
1987	Mrs A Gems
1988	Miss S Keogh
1989	Miss S Keogh

Middlesex Open Championship

Year	Winner
1983	N Wichelow
1984	L Fickling
1985	P Golding
1986	*Not played*
1987	L Fickling
1988	L Fickling
1989	L Fickling

Midland Ladies' Championship
Instituted 1897

Year	Winner
1984	Miss L Waring
1985	Miss L Waring
1986	Mrs J Collingham
1987	Miss S Roberts
1988	Miss S Roberts
1989	Miss R Bolas

Midland Masters
Instituted 1988

Year	Winner
1988	B Waites
1989	C Haycock

Midland Professional Stroke Play Championship
Instituted 1897

Year	Winner	Year	Winner
1980	DI Vaughan	1985	K Hayward
1981	D Stewart	1986	A Skingle
1982	P Elson	1987	M Mouland
1983	AR Minshall	1988	G Farr
1984	M Mouland	1989	J Higgins

Midland Professional Match Play Championship
Instituted 1899

Year	Winner	Year	Winner
1980	RDS Livingston	1985	D Ridley
1981	P Elson	1986	J Higgins
1982	P Elson	1987	K Hayward
1983	PG Ackerley	1988	J Higgins
1984	P Elson	1989	K Hayward

Midland Counties Amateur Stroke Play Championship

Year	Winner	Year	Winner
1980	P Downes	1985	M Hassall
1981	P Baxter	1986	G Wolstenholme
1982	NJ Chesses	1987	C Suneson
1983	CA Banks	1988	AD Hare
1984	K Valentine	1989	J Cook

Midlothian Ladies' Championship
Instituted 1924

Year	Winner	Year	Winner
1980	Mrs BM Marshall	1985	Mrs F de Vries
1981	Miss MF Allen	1986	Mrs J Marshall
1982	Miss S Little	1987	Miss M Stavert
1983	Mrs J Marshall	1988	Miss M Stavert
1984	Mrs F de Vries	1989	Mrs E Bruce

Mid-Wales Ladies' Championship

Year	Winner
1988	Miss S James
1989	Miss S Wilson

Monmouthshire Ladies' Championship
Instituted 1920

Year	Winner	Year	Winner
1980	Miss M Davis	1985	Miss P Lord
1981	Miss K Beckett	1986	Miss H Buckley
1982	Miss M Davis	1987	Miss H Buckley
1983	Miss K Beckett	1988	Miss H Armstrong
1984	Miss J Lapthorne	1989	Miss B Chambers

Norfolk Amateur Championship
Instituted 1921

Year	Winner	Year	Winner
1980	JG Parkhill	1985	CJ Lamb
1981	MR Few	1986	ID Sperrin
1982	DW Rains	1987	NJ Williamson
1983	MN Sperrin	1988	NJ Williamson
1984	T Hurrell	1989	NJ Williamson

Norfolk Ladies' Championship
Instituted 1912

Year	Winner	Year	Winner
1980	Miss VE Cooper	1985	Mrs M Whybrow
1981	Mrs AM Davies	1986	Mrs N Clarke
1982	Miss VE Cooper	1987	Mrs AM Davies
1983	Mrs M Davies	1988	Mrs L Elliott
1984	Mrs L Elliott	1989	Miss T Keeley

Norfolk Professional Championship
Instituted 1921

Year	Winner	Year	Winner
1980	MT Leeder	1985	M Spooner
1981	SLH Beckham	1986	M Spooner
1982	RJ Page	1987	MJ Elsworthy
1983	RG Foster	1988	M Few
1984	MJ Elsworthy	1989	M Few

Norfolk Professional Match Play Championship

Year	Winner
1986	MT Leeder
1987	RG Foster
1988	M Few
1989	NJ Catchpile

Norfolk Open Championship

Year	Winner	Year	Winner
1980	MT Leeder	1985	T Hurrell
1981	JG Parkhill	1986	M Spooner
1982	RJ Page	1987	MJ Elsworthy
1983	RG Foster	1988	M Few
1984	MJ Elsworthy	1989	M Few

Northamptonshire Amateur Championship
Instituted 1927

Year	Winner	Year	Winner
1980	C Cieslewicz	1985	M McNally
1981	MJ Haddon	1986	M Scott
1982	S McDonald	1987	D Jones
1983	DJJ Warren	1988	D Ellson
1984	M Scott	1989	N Goodman

Northamptonshire Ladies' Championship

Year	Winner	Year	Winner
1980	Mrs M Hutheson	1985	Mrs A Duck
1981	Miss J Dicks	1986	Mrs P Le Vai
1982	Mrs P Coles	1987	Mrs J Kendrick
1983	Miss J Dicks	1988	Mrs A Duck
1984	Mrs A Duck	1989	Mrs C Gibbs

Northern (England) Professional Championship
Instituted 1920

Year	Winner	Year	Winner
1980	G Townhill	1985	A Murray
1981	B Evans	1986	D Stirling
1982	H Muscroft	1987	S Rolley
1983		1988	K Waters
1984		1989	S Bottomley

Northern Counties (Scotland) Ladies' Championship

Year	Winner	Year	Winner
1980	Mrs I McIntosh	1985	Miss A Shannon
1981	Miss S Ross	1986	Miss F McKay
1982	Miss G Stewart	1987	Mrs I McIntosh
1983	Miss L Anderson	1988	Mrs I McIntosh
1984	Miss J Buist	1989	Mrs E Fiskin

North of Ireland Open Amateur Championship

Year	Winner	Year	Winner
1980	MJ Malone	1985	I Elliott
1981	D Long	1986	D Ballantine
1982	D Long	1987	A Pierse
1983	TBC Hoey	1988	N Anderson
1984	G McGimpsey	1989	N Anderson

Northern Scottish Open Championship
Instituted 1931

Year	Winner	Year	Winner
1980	D Huish		
1981	A Thomson	1985	BW Barnes
1982	T Minshall	1986	R Weir
1983	D Cooper	1987	A Hunter
1984	JS Macdonald	1988	D Huish
1984	D Huish	1989	C Brooks

Northern Women's Championship

Year	Winner	Year	Winner
1980	Miss C Barker	1985	Miss C Hall
1981	Miss A Brown	1986	Miss L Fairclough
1982	Miss C Swallow	1987	Miss S Robinson
1983	Miss C Hall	1988	Miss K Tebbet
1984	Miss C Hall	1989	Miss L Fletcher

Northumberland Amateur Championship
Instituted 1907

Year	Winner	Year	Winner
1980	S Smith	1985	D Faulder
1981	D George	1986	D Martin
1982	P Deeble	1987	K Fairbairn
1983	P Deeble	1988	J Metcalfe
1984	J Straker	1989	J Metcalfe

Northumberland Ladies' Championship
Instituted 1921

Year	Winner	Year	Winner
1980	Miss D Glenn	1985	Miss CM Hall
1981	Mrs E Elliot	1986	Miss CM Hall
1982	Mrs M Pickard	1987	Miss C Breckon
1983	Miss J Soulsby	1988	Miss D Glenn
1984	Miss CM Hall	1989	Miss D Glenn

Northern Division Ladies' Championship (Scotland)

Year	Winner	Year	Winner
1980	Miss G Stewart	1986	Miss C Middleton
1981	Miss F McNab	1987	Mrs A Murray
1982	Miss G Stewart		(*née* Shannon)
1983	Miss G Stewart	1988	Miss K Imrie
1984	Miss P Wright	1989	Miss S Wood
1985	Miss A Shannon		

North of Scotland Open Amateur Stroke Play Championship
Instituted 1970

Year	Winner	Year	Winner
1980	BC Milne	1985	JS Macdonald
1981	NS Grant	1986	S Cruickshank
1982	I Hutcheon	1987	S McIntosh
1983	D Kryzanowski	1988	KS Hird
1984	JS Macdonald	1989	GB Hickman

Nottinghamshire Amateur Championship
Instituted 1924

Year	Winner	Year	Winner
1980	T Leigh	1985	M Scothern
1981	CA Banks	1986	G Krause
1982	CA Banks	1987	R Sallis
1983	TM Estrop	1988	CA Banks
1984	G Krause	1989	P Shaw

Nottinghamshire Ladies' Championship
Instituted 1925

Year	Winner	Year	Winner
1980	Miss M Elswood	1985	Miss KM Horberry
1981	Miss KM Horberry	1986	CG Palmer
1982	Miss KM Horberry	1987	Miss M Elswood
1983	Miss M Elswood	1988	Miss A Ferguson
1984	Miss M Elswood	1989	Miss A Peters

Nottinghamshire Open Championship

Year	Winner	Year	Winner
1980	C Banks (Am)	1985	C Jepson
1981	C Banks (Am)	1986	BJ Waites
1982	BJ Waites	1987	CD Hall
1983	C Banks (Am)	1988	C Banks (Am)
1984	CD Hall	1989	P Hinton

One-Armed Championship

Year	Winner	Year	Winner
1980	RP Reid	1985	ASL Robinson
1981	A Robinson	1986	MJ O'Grady
1982	MJ O'Grady	1987	J Cann
1983	ASL Robinson	1988	Q Talbot
1984	ASL Robinson	1989	ASL Robinson

Oxfordshire Ladies' Championship

Year	Winner	Year	Winner
1980	Mrs L Davies	1985	Miss N Sparks
1981	Miss N Sparks	1986	Miss T Craik
1982	Mrs M Glennie	1987	Miss T Craik
1983	Mrs M Glennie	1988	Miss T Craik
1984	Miss T Craik	1989	Miss L King

Perth and Kinross Ladies' Championship

Year	Winner	Year	Winner
1980	Mrs J Aitken	1985	Miss A Guthrie
1981	Mrs J Aitken	1986	Mrs I Shannon
1982	Mrs J Aitken	1987	Miss F Anderson
1983	Miss F Anderson	1988	Miss V Pringle
1984	Miss E Aitken	1989	Miss A Sharp

Perth and Kinross Amateur Stroke Play Championship
Instituted 1930

Year	Winner	Year	Winner
1980	GT Russell	1985	G Lowson
1981	AG Campbell	1986	C Bloice
1982	M Niven	1987	BRM Grieve
1983	ER Lindsay	1988	EJ Lindsay
1984	G Lowson	1989	AG Campbell

Renfrewshire Amateur Championship

Year	Winner	Year	Winner
1980	N Skinner	1985	J McDonald
1981	DB Howard	1986	IG Riddell
1982	A Hunter	1987	DB Howard
1983	G Thomson	1988	ES Grey
1984	DB Howard	1989	RA Clark

Renfrewshire County Ladies' Championship
Instituted 1927

Year	Winner	Year	Winner
1980	Miss W Aitken	1985	Miss S Lawson
1981	Miss W Aitken	1986	Miss S Lawson
1982	Miss W Aitken	1987	Miss S Lawson
1983	Mrs JL Hastings (*née*	1988	Miss S Lawson
	Sommerville)	1989	Miss D Jackson
1984	Dr A Wilson		

Scottish Area Team Championship
Instituted 1977

Year	Winner	Year	Winner
1980	Dunbartonshire	1985	Lothians
1981	Stirlingshire	1986	Ayrshire
1982	Renfrewshire	1987	Lothians
1983	Lothians	1988	Lothians
1984	Glasgow	1989	Lanarkshire

Scottish Champion of Champions
Instituted 1970

Year	Winner	Year	Winner
1970	A Horne	1980	IC Hutcheon
1971	D Black	1981	IC Hutcheon
1972	RS Strachan	1982	G Macgregor
1973	*Not held*	1983	DG Carrick
1974	MM Niven	1984	S Stephen
1975	A Brodie	1985	IR Brotherston
1976	A Brodie	1986	IC Hutcheon
1977	V Reid	1987	G Shaw
1978	DG Greig	1988	IC Hutcheon
1979	B Marchbank	1989	JW Milligan

Scottish Foursome Tournament–*Glasgow Evening Times* Trophy
Instituted 1891

Year	Winner	Year	Winner
1980	Helensburgh	1985	East Renfrewshire
1981	Duddingston	1986	Hamilton
1982	Haggs Castle	1987	Drumpellier
1983	Haggs Castle	1988	Irvine Ravenspark
1984	Royal Musselburgh	1989	Cochrane Leith

Scottish Ladies' County Championship
Instituted 1909

Year	Winner	Year	Winner
1980	Northern Counties	1985	East Lothian
1981	Northern Counties	1986	Aberdeenshire
1982	Renfrewshire	1987	Renfrewshire
1983	Lanarkshire	1988	Lanarkshire
1984	Lanarkshire	1989	Lanarkshire

Scottish Ladies' Foursomes

Year	Winner	Year	Winner
1980	Dumfries and County	1985	*No Championship*
1981	Baberton	1986	Blairgowrie
1982	Aberdour	1987	Baberton
1983	Hamilton	1988	Gullane
1984	Gullane	1989	Gullane

Shropshire and Herefordshire Amateur Championship

Year	Winner	Year	Winner
1980	MA Smith	1985	PA Baker
1981	JA Wilson	1986	C Bufton
1982	NS Kelly	1987	R Dixon
1983	PA Baker	1988	S Thomas
1984	PA Baker	1989	M Welch

Shropshire Ladies' Championship
Instituted 1923

Year	Winner	Year	Winner
1980	Mrs S Pidgeon	1985	Mrs A Johnson
1981	Mrs S Pidgeon	1986	Mrs S Pidgeon
1982	Mrs S Pidgeon	1987	Mrs S Pidgeon
1983	Miss C Gauge	1988	Miss A Jackson
1984	Mrs A Johnson	1989	Miss C Gauge

Somerset Amateur Championship
Instituted 1911

Year	Winner	Year	Winner
1980	LF Millar	1985	PR Hare
1981	J Clifford	1986	CS Edwards
1982	BJ Reeves	1987	G Hickman
1983	DJ Huxtable	1988	CS Edwards
1984	CS Edwards	1989	CS Edwards

Somerset Ladies' Championship
Instituted 1913

Year	Winner	Year	Winner
1980	Miss B New	1985	Miss K Nicholls
1981	Miss B New	1986	Miss K Nicholls
1982	Miss B New	1987	Miss K Nicholls
1983	Miss B New	1988	Mrs C Whiting
1984	Mrs M Perriam	1989	Miss K Nicholls

South-Eastern Ladies' Championship

Year	Winner	Year	Winner
1980	Miss J Rumsey	1985	Mrs J Thornhill
1981	Mrs C Caldwell	1986	Miss S Moorcroft
1982	Mrs J Nicholson	1987	Miss N Way
1983	Miss L Davies	1988	Mrs C Stirling
1984	Miss L Davies	1989	Miss A MacDonald

South Region PGA Championship
Formerly Southern (England) Professional Championship

Year	Winner	Year	Winner
1980	PR Mitchell	1985	C Mason
1981	P Milton	1986	
1982	D McClelland	1987	
1983	M McLean	1988	J Spence
1984	M McLean	1989	W Grant

South of Ireland Open Amateur Championship
Instituted 1895
Venue: Lahinch (Co Clare)

Year	Winner	Year	Winner
1980	M Burns	1985	P O'Rourke
1981	P O'Rourke	1986	J McHenry
1982	M Maurice	1987	B Reddan
1983	AJC Morrow	1988	MA Gannon
1984	N Anderson	1989	S Keenan

South of Scotland Championship
Instituted 1932

Year	Winner	Year	Winner
1980	A Clark	1985	I Brotherston
1981	D James	1986	I Semple
1982	I Brotherston	1987	I Brotherston
1983	I Brotherston	1988	A Coltart
1984	D Ireland	1989	V Reid

Southern Division Ladies' Championship (Scotland)

Year	Winner	Year	Winner
1980	Miss DM Hill	1985	Mrs S Simpson
1981	Miss A Gallagher	1986	Miss M Wright
1982	Miss A Hunter	1987	Miss M Wright
1983	Miss S McDonald	1988	Mrs S Simpson
1984	Miss FM Rennie	1989	Miss F Rennie

South of Scotland Ladies' Championship

Year	Winner	Year	Winner
1980	Miss E Hill	1985	Miss FM Rennie
1981	Mrs A Barclay	1986	Miss FM Rennie
1982	Miss DM Hill	1987	Miss S McDonald
1983	Miss S McDonald	1988	Miss M Wright
1984	Miss M Wright	1989	Miss M Wright

South-Western Ladies' Championship

Year	Winner	Year	Winner
1980	Miss L Isherwood	1985	Miss S Shapcott
1981	Miss L Moore	1986	Miss K Nicholls
1982	Miss L Moore	1987	Miss J Fernley
1983	Miss P Johnson	1988	Mrs V Thomas
1984	Miss P Johnson	1989	Miss C Hall

South-Western Counties Amateur Championship
Instituted 1924

Year	Winner	Year	Winner
1980	CS Mitchell	1985	C Phillips
1981	P Newcombe	1986	C Phillips
1982	D Ray	1987	P Newcombe
1983	C Edwards	1988	J Langmead
1984	M Blaber	1989	K Jones

Staffordshire Amateur Championship
Instituted 1924

Year	Winner	Year	Winner
1980	AR Eden	1985	M Hassall
1981	M Hassall	1986	M Scarrett
1982	A Stubbs	1987	M Hassall
1983	M Hassall	1988	P Sweetsur
1984	M Hassall	1989	CG Poxon

Staffordshire Ladies' Championship
Instituted 1926

Year	Winner	Year	Winner
1980	Mrs A Booth	1985	Miss L Hackney
1981	Miss J Brown	1986	Mrs A Booth
1982	Miss J Brown	1987	Miss D Christison
1983	Miss D Christison	1988	Miss D Boyd
1984	Miss D Boyd	1989	Miss R Bolas

Staffordshire Open Championship

Year	Winner	Year	Winner
1980	P Robinson (Am)	1985	J Annable
1981	J Rhodes	1986	J Higgins
1982	A Stubbs (Am)	1987	J Annable
1983	C Poxon (Am)	1988	J Rhodes
1984	D Gilford	1989	M Passmore

Staffordshire and Shropshire Professional Championship

Year	Winner	Year	Winner
1980	A Sadler	1985	A Stubbs
1981	A Griffiths	1986	J Annable
1982	A Griffiths	1987	J Annable
1983	CM Holmes	1988	J Annable
1984	T Minchell	1989	J Higgins

Staffordshire and Shropshire Stroke Play Championship

Year	Winner
1984	A Minshall
1985	A Stubbs
1986	A Minshall
1987	J Higgins
1988	J Annable
1989	J Higgins

Stirlingshire Amateur Championship

Year	Winner	Year	Winner
1980	DF Wilkie	1985	W Fleming
1981	A Liddle	1986	RA Godfrey
1982	A Liddle	1987	SA Lee
1983	C Gillies	1988	H Anderson
1984	G Barrie	1989	S Russell

Stirling and Clackmannan County Ladies' Championship

Year	Winner	Year	Winner
1980	Miss E Miskimmin	1985	Miss S Michie
1981	Miss E Miskimmin	1986	Miss S Michie
1982	*Null and void*	1987	Miss J Harrison
1983	Miss J Harrison	1988	Miss J Harrison
1984	Mrs W McCallum	1989	Mrs J Abernethy

Suffolk Amateur Championship
Instituted 1924

Year	Winner	Year	Winner
1980	I Whinney	1985	R Barrell
1981	P Buckle	1986	M Clark
1982	CJC Lloyd	1987	CN Coulton
1983	M Turner	1988	J Whitby
1984	S Goodman	1989	M Turner

Suffolk Ladies' Championship
Instituted 1926

Year	Winner	Year	Winner
1980	Miss S Field	1985	Dr J Gibson
1981	Miss D Marriott	1986	J Wade
1982	Miss D Marriott	1987	Miss W Day
1983	Miss D Marriott	1988	Miss S Dawson
1984	Dr J Gibson	1989	Mrs J Hall

Suffolk Open Championship

Year	Winner	Year	Winner
1980	SJ Whymark	1985	KR Preston
1981	P Buckle (Am)	1986	SL Beckham
1982	RW Mann	1987	MR Turner
1983	SJ Whymark	1988	J Maddock
1984	JVT Marks	1989	M Elsworthy

Suffolk Professional Championship
Instituted 1927

Year	Winner	Year	Winner
1980	T Pennock	1985	S Beckham
1981	M Elsworthy	1986	RW Mann
1982	M Elsworthy	1987	S Beckham
1983	RW Mann	1988	S Whymark
1984	RW Mann	1989	S Whymark

Surrey Amateur Championship
Instituted 1924

Year	Winner	Year	Winner
1980	JG Bennet	1985	G Walmsley
1981	SH Keppler	1986	B White
1982	R Boxall	1987	J Paramor
1983	C Lashford	1988	A Carter
1984	PM Talbot	1989	T Lloyd

Surrey Ladies' Championship
Instituted 1921

Year	Winner	Year	Winner
1980	Miss D Dowling	1985	J Nicolson
1981	Mrs J Thornhill	1986	Miss S Prosser
1982	Mrs J Thornhill	1987	Mrs W Wooldridge
1983	Mrs J Thornhill	1988	Mrs C Bailey
1984	Mrs J Thornhill	1989	Mrs J Thornhill

Sussex Amateur Championship
Instituted 1899

Year	Winner	Year	Winner
1980	N Mitchell	1985	MS Jarvis
1981	N Mitchell	1986	A W Schofield
1982	DJ Sewell	1987	D Fay
1983	P Scarles	1988	DW Alderson
1984	JS Spence	1989	P Hurring

Sussex Ladies' Championship
Instituted 1923 (After 1936 Final over 36 holes)

Year	Winner	Year	Winner
1980	Miss C Pierce	1985	Miss N Way
1981	Mrs C Larkin	1986	Miss MJ Cornelius
1982	Mrs C Larkin	1987	Miss K Mitchell
1983	Miss M Gallagher	1988	Miss MJ Cornelius
1984	Miss C Rolph	1989	Miss MJ Cornelius

Sussex Open Championship

Year	Winner	Year	Winner
1980	JC Burrell	1985	JS Spence (Am)
1981	J Pinset (Am)	1986	C Giddins
1982	C Jones	1987	BW Barnes
1983	C Giddins	1988	S Rolley
1984	J Dodds (Am)	1989	M Groombridge (Am)

Ulster Professional Championship
Instituted 1924 (decided by stroke play 1938-39)

Year	Winner	Year	Winner
1980	P Leonard	1985	D Jones
1981	P Leonard	1986	W Todd
1982	P Leonard	1987	W Todd
1983	RB Campbell	1988	J Heggarty
1984	D Carson	1989	D Feherty

Warwickshire Ladies' Championship
Instituted 1923

Year	Winner	Year	Winner
1980	Miss T Hammond	1985	Mrs S Seville
1981	Mrs J Evans	1986	Miss T Hammond
1982	Miss T Hammond	1987	Mrs M Button
1983	Miss T Hammond	1988	Miss S Morgan
1984	Miss M Stevens	1989	Miss S Morgan

Warwickshire Amateur Championship
Instituted 1906

Year	Winner	Year	Winner
1980	P McEvoy	1985	C Suneson
1981	B Wilkes	1986	P Downes
1982	A Roach	1987	W Bladon
1983	NM Chesses	1988	AM Allen
1984	P McEvoy	1989	J Cook

Warwickshire Stroke Play Championship

Year	Winner
1984	A Bownes
1985	P Elson
1986	P Elson
1987	P Elson
1988	C Wicketts
1989	T Rouse

Warwickshire Professional Championship

Year	Winner	Year	Winner
1980	D Steele	1985	
1981	PJ Weaver	1986	P Elson
1982	N Selwyn-Smith	1987	P Elson
1983	PJ Weaver	1988	C Wicketts
1984	A Bownes	1989	T Rouse

Warwickshire Open Championship

Year	Winner	Year	Winner
1980	D Steele		
1981	T Allen (Am)	1985	J Gould
1982	T Allen (Am) / P Downes (Am)	1986	PJ Weaver
		1987	PJ Weaver
1983	PJ Weaver	1988	TM Allen (Am)
1984	P Broadhurst	1989	TM Allen

Welsh Team Championship
Instituted 1895

Year	Winner	Year	Winner
1980	Radyr	1985	Whitchurch
1981	Radyr	1986	Pontnewydd
1982	Newport	1987	Llandudno (Maesdu)
1983	Pontypridd	1988	Ashburnham
1984	Whitchurch	1989	Cardiff

Welsh Ladies' Team Championship
Instituted 1905

Year	Winner	Year	Winner
1980	Monmouthshire	1985	Llandudno (Maesdu)
1981	Porthcawl	1986	Porthcawl
1982	St David's	1987	Whitchurch
1983	Llandudno (Maesdu)	1988	Pennard
1984	Monmouthshire	1989	Llandudno (Maesdu)

West of Scotland Close Amateur Championship
Instituted 1977

Year	Winner	Year	Winner
1980	PJ McKellar	1985	S Savage
1981	DB Howard	1986	S Savage
1982	G Shaw	1987	R Jenkins
1983	D Murdoch	1988	G King
1984	W Erskine	1989	G Lawrie

Western Division Ladies' Championship (Scotland)

Year	Winner	Year	Winner
1980	Miss W Aitken	1985	Mrs IC Robertson
1981	Miss W Aitken	1986	Miss S Lawson
1982	Miss S Lawson	1987	Mrs A Hendry
1983	Miss S Lawson	1988	Miss S Lawson
1984	Dr A Wilson	1989	Mrs K Dallas

West Region PGA Championship
Previously West of England Professional Championship

Year	Winner	Year	Winner
1980	P Ward	1985	D Sheppard
1981	G Brand Jr	1986	S Little
1982	G Smith	1987	A Sherborne
1983	G Marks	1988	M Thomas
1984	M Thomas	1989	G Laing

Wigtownshire Championship
Instituted 1936

Year	Winner	Year	Winner
1980	Dr RNC Douglas	1985	M Gibson
1981	J Young	1986	A Cunningham
1982	Dr RNC Douglas	1987	J Burns
1983	K Hardie	1988	K Hardie
1984	A Burns	1989	D Taylor

Wiltshire Amateur Championship
Instituted 1924

Year	Winner	Year	Winner
1980	RE Searle	1985	S Amor
1981	JN Fleming	1986	G Clough
1982	BF McCallum	1987	RE Searle
1983	D Kingsman	1988	G Clough
1984	NC Garfoot	1989	A Burch

Wiltshire Ladies' Championship

Year	Winner	Year	Winner
1980	Miss C Waite	1985	Miss C Waite
1981	Miss C Waite	1986	Miss S Marks
1982	Miss F Dawson	1987	Mrs J Lawrence
1983	Miss C Waite	1988	Mrs S Sutton
1984	Mrs V Morgan	1989	Mrs J Lawrence

Wiltshire Professional Championship
Instituted 1925
Now known as the "Hills" Wiltshire Pro Champ

Year	Winner	Year	Winner
1980	B Sandry	1985	G Laing
1981	G Smith	1986	B Sandry
1982	R Emery	1987	G Laing
1983	I Bolt	1988	R Emery
1984	G Laing	1989	G Emerson

Worcestershire Amateur Championship
Instituted 1906

Year	Winner	Year	Winner
1980	PR Swinburne	1985	SJ Pimley
1981	MC Reynard	1986	DJ Eddiford
1982	DJ Eddiford	1987	D Prosser
1983	TR Shingler	1988	D Prosser
1984	T Martin	1989	S Braithwaite

Worcestershire Stroke Play Championship

Year	Winner
1984	G Mercer
1985	K Hayward
1986	D Dunk
1987	K Hayward
1988	C Haycock
1989	K Hayward

Worcestershire Ladies' Championship
Instituted 1924

Year	Winner	Year	Winner
1980	Mrs R West	1985	Miss L Waring
1981	Miss J Blaymire	1986	Miss K Cheetham
1982	Miss J Blaymire	1987	Miss L Waring
1983	Miss S Nicklin	1988	Miss J Blaymire
1984	Miss S Nicklin	1989	Miss L Waring

Worcestershire Open Championship

Year	Winner	Year	Winner
1980	RA Jowle (Am)	1985	DJ Eddiford
1981	W Firkins	1986	WR Painter (Am)
1982	MC Reynard (Am)	1987	K Hayward
1983	AJ Hill	1988	D Eddiford
1984	K Hayward	1989	K Hayward

Worcestershire Professional Championship

Year	Winner	Year	Winner
1980	WH Firkins	1985	KA Hayward
1981	R Livingston	1986	D Dunk
1982	WH Firkins	1987	G Mercer
1983	KA Hayward	1988	C Hancock
1984	KA Hayward	1989	KA Hayward

Yorkshire Amateur Championship
Instituted 1894

Year	Winner	Year	Winner
1980	MI Mackenzie	1985	S Field
1981	MJ Kelley	1986	AR Gelsthorpe
1982	S East	1987	RM Roper
1983	JL Plaxton	1988	S Field
1984	J Whiteley	1989	G Harland

Yorkshire Amateur Stroke Play Championship
Instituted 1986

Year	Winner
1986	P Hall
1987	P Hall / RM Roper } tied
1988	CG Rawson
1989	S East

Yorkshire Ladies' Championship
Instituted 1896

Year	Winner	Year	Winner
1980	Miss L Batty	1985	Miss A Farmery
1981	Miss P Grice	1986	Miss P Smillie
1982	Miss P Grice	1987	Miss J Copley
1983	Miss P Grice	1988	Miss J Furby
1984	Miss A Nicholas	1989	Miss K Firth

Yorkshire Professional Championship
Instituted 1921

Year	Winner	Year	Winner
1980	M Ingham	1985	B Jagger
1981	G Townhill	1986	M Ingham
1982	M Mackenzie	1987	D Stirling
1983	P Cowen	1988	M Higginbottom
1984	D Hutchinson	1989	D Stirling

Royal & Ancient Tournaments

Royal & Ancient Club of St Andrews
Captain 1989-90 M Attenborough

Royal Medal
presented by His Majesty King William the Fourth
(First prize at Autumn Meeting)
Instituted 1837

Year		Strokes	Year		Strokes
1930	JN Nock	77	1963	Dr FWG Deighton	72
1931	WL Hartley	75	1964	GA Hill (Captain)	72
1932	Brig Gen AC Critchley	73	1965	RR Jack	71
1933	HE Taylor	73	1966	Dr FWG Deighton	71
1934	CGB Stevens	83	1967	RR Jack	70
1935	Major WHH Aitken	73	1968	TC Schuller	70
1936	LG Crawley	71	1969	HC Maclaine	73
1937	RH Wethered	73	1970	JG Salvesen	73
1938	LG Crawley	72	1971	WD Smith	73
1939-45	*No competition owing*		1972	Dr G Greenhough	71
	to the War		1973	Dr FWG Deighton	69
1946	Dr JC Lawrie	78	1974	HC Maclaine	73
1947	JM Dykes	80	1975	P Davidson	73
1948	Col WHH Aitken	71	1976	BJ Ingham	73
1949	GH Micklem	73	1977	A Sinclair	73
1950	GH Micklem	74	1978	M Lee	73
1951	JG Blackwell	73	1979	P Davidson	73
1952	JM Dykes	74	1980	F Illouz	72
1953	KG Patrick	72	1981	R Foster	72
1954	HJ Ballingall	71	1982	H Campbell	72
1955	Major DA Blair	69	1983	AJ Low	72
1956	Dr FWG Deighton	70	1984	C McLachlan	75
1957	HJ Ballingall	73	1985	GJ Cotla	70
1958	DW Nisbet	74	1986	P Greenhough	70
1959	Dr FWG Deighton	71	1987	HM Campbell	71
1960	R Galloway	73	1988	AM Reid	73
1961	Dr FWG Deighton	69	1989	MJ Reece	70
1962	Major DW Nisbet	71			

Silver Cross
presented by Colonel J Murray Belshes, of Buttergask
(First prize at Spring Meeting)
Instituted 1836

Year		Strokes	Year		Strokes
1928	WA Sievwright	76	1961	JG Salvesen	73
1929	CJH Tolley	73	1962	GW Mackie	73
1930	RK Blair	77	1963	Dr FWG Deighton	74
1931	WB Torrance	74	1964	G Robertson-Durham	75
1932	EM Prain	78	1965	WS McLeod	75
1933	R Harris	77	1966	RR Jack	74
1934	DH Kyle	72	1967	CD Lawrie	71
1935	LG Crawley	77	1968	DA Blair	71
1936	RH Oppenheimer	75	1969	RHJ Mackie	71
1937	CGB Stevens	74	1970	Dr FWG Deighton	72
1938	LG Crawley	73	1971	RHJ Mackie	74
1939	LG Crawley	75	1972	A Sinclair	73
1940-45	No competition owing		1973	Dr FWG Deighton	71
	to the War		1974	DA Blair	74
1946	GW Mackie	75	1975	M Lee	75
1947	D Cameron	74	1976	D Montagu	73
1948	GH Micklem	71	1977	EJ Threlfall	72
1949	RH Oppenheimer	74	1978	DP Davidson	71
1950	TA Torrance	75	1979	PD Kelley	73
1951	D Cameron	72	1980	C McLachlan	75
1952	JC Wilson	72	1981	C McLachlan	66
1953	Dr FWG Deighton	74	1982	P Bucher	73
1954	JC Wilson	68	1983	GM Simmers	74
1955	DA Blair	70	1984	HM Campbell	72
1956	RR Jack	71	1985	Dr DM Lawrie	69
1957	AMM Bucher	70	1986	MJ Reece	73
1958	GH Micklem	70	1987	HM Campbell	71
1959	DA Blair	74	1988	R Foster	73
1960	Dr FWG Deighton	70	1989	Dr DM Lawrie	73

The George Glennie Medal
presented by the Royal Blackheath Golf Club
(lowest aggregate score at Spring and Autumn Meetings)
Instituted 1882

Year		Strokes	Year		Strokes
1930	JH Nock	159	1963	Dr FWG Deighton	159
1931	JG Simpson	154	1964	WR Alexander	150
1932	WB Torrance	160	1965	RR Jack	147
1933	JG Simpson	155	1966	Dr FWG Deighton	148
1934	DH Kyle	150	1967	CD Lawrie	148
1935	LG Crawley	154	1968	CD Lawrie	149
1936	LG Crawley	148	1969	WF Callander, Jr	148
1937	CGB Stevens	149	1970	Dr FWG Deighton	149
1938	LG Crawley	145	1971	WMS Ironside	149
1939-45	No competition owing		1972	M Lee	146
	to the War		1973	Dr FWG Deighton	140
1946	GW Mackie	155	1974	PBM Bucher	155
1947	D Cameron	152	1975	A Sinclair	150
1948	CJH Tolley	148	1976	PBM Bucher	150
1949	CJH Tolley	148	1977	C McLachlan	149
1950	Dr CRD Leeds	155	1978	DP Davidson	145
1951	D Cameron	146	1979	PD Kelley	150
1952	JM Dykes	148	1980	RD Muckart, Jr	152
1953	KG Patrick	150	1981	C McLachlan	139
1954	JC Wilson	140	1982	HM Campbell	147
1955	Major DA Blair	139	1983	AJ Low	147
1956	Dr FWG Deighton	145	1984	HM Campbell	150
1957	DW Nisbet	147	1985	Dr DM Lawrie	148
1958	GH Micklem	144	1986	DW Frame	146
1959	Dr FWG Deighton	149	1987	HM Campbell	142
1960	Dr FWG Deighton	145	1988	HM Campbell	150
1961	JG Salvesen	143	1989	Dr DM Lawrie	148
1962	M Tweddell	150			

Part III
Who's Who in Golf

British Isles Players

Explanations of abbreviations used

Cls	Club membership
PRO	Professional
AM	Amateur
Maj	The Open, US Open, USPGA, US Masters (men) Ladies British Open, US Women's Open, USLPGA (ladies)
Chp	Amateur Championship or Ladies British Open Amateur (or, within text, any championship)
Nat	The player's national championship
Trn	Tournament(s)
Oth	Other national championship or tournament
Reg	Regional tournaments
Int	International team appearances
Eur	European Tour or general European tournament(s)
US	Tournament(s) in United States or Canada
RoW	Tournament(s) in the rest of the world
Sen	Senior
Jun	Junior
Mis	Miscellaneous information
r/u	runner up
s/f	semi-finalist
tied	A lost play-off after first place tie
Eur(L) T Chp	European (Ladies) Amateur Team Championship

Captaincy is indicated by the year printed in **bold** type; years in bold type within brackets indicate non-playing captain.

Aitken, Wilma
See Leburn

Alliss, Peter
Born Berlin on 28th February, 1931. Turned Professional 1946

PRO
Eur   Spanish Open 1956–58. Italian Open, Portuguese Open 1958.
Trn   Daks 1954; Dunlop 1955; PGA Close 1957; Dunlop 1959; Sprite 1960 (shared). PGA Close 1962; Daks 1963 (shared); Swallow–Penfold, Esso Golden 1964; PGA Close, Jeyes 1965; Martini (shared), Rediffusion 1966; Agfa-Gevaert 1967; Piccadilly 1969; Sunningdale Foursomes 1958–61; Wentworth Pro-Am Foursomes 1959
Oth   British Assistants 1952
RoW   Brazilian Open 1961
Reg   West of England Open Professional 1956–58–62–66
Int   Ryder Cup 1953–57–59–61–63–65–67–69; UK v Europe 1954–55–56; England in World Cup 1954–55–57–58–59–61–62–64–66–67; Home International **1967**
Mis   Vardon Trophy 1964–66; PGA Captain 1962–87; Author, TV Commentator

AM
Jun
Int   England Boys 1946

Anderson, Fiona
Born Perth on 24th August, 1954

Cls   Blairgowrie, Gullane Ladies, Craigie Hill
Nat   Scottish Ladies Amateur 1987. r/u 1980–83–88
Reg   North of Scotland Ladies 1977. Scottish Universities Champion 1975
Int   Vagliano Trophy 1987. (Scotland) Home Int 1977–79–80–81–83–84–86–87–88–89; (Eur L T Ch) 1979–83–87

Anderson, Jessie
See Valentine

Anstey, Veronica
See Beharrell

Armitage, Susan
See Langridge

Attenborough, Michael F
Born Britford, nr Salisbury in October, 1939

Cls   Chislehurst, Royal St George's, Royal & Ancient
Oth   Scandinavian Amateur 1965
Trn   Hampshire Hog 1960. President's Putter 1962–66.
      County Champion of Champions 1964. Duncan
      Putter 1966. Prince of Wales Challenge Cup 1969
Reg   Kent Amateur 1963–64–65
Int   Walker Cup 1967. GB v Europe 1966–68. England
      (Home Int) 1964–66–67–68; (Eur T Ch) 1967
Mis   Captain of Royal & Ancient 1989

Bailey, Diane
[Frearson], (*née* Robb)
Born Wolverhampton on 31st August, 1943

Cls   Enville (Hon), Reigate Heath, Betchworth Park
Chp   British Ladies Amateur r/u 1961
Trn   Worplesdon Mixed Foursomes 1971. Avia Foursomes
      1972
Reg   Staffordshire Ladies 1961. Lincolnshire
      Ladies 1966–67. Midland Ladies 1966
Int   Curtis Cup 1962–72–(**84**)–(**86**)–(**88**). Vagliano Trophy
      1961–(**83**)–(**85**). Espirito Santo 1968. England (Home
      Int) 1961–62–71. Commonwealth Team Ch (**1983**).
Mis   Surrey Ladies County Captain 1981–2
Jun   British Girls 1961. Scottish Girls Open Stroke Play
      1959–61
Int   England Girls 1957–61

Baker, Peter
Born 7th October, 1967. Turned Professional 1986

PRO
Eur   Benson & Hedges International 1988
Mis   Rookie of the Year 1987
AM
Nat   English Open Amateur Stroke Play 1985 (shared)
Reg   Shropshire & Herefordshire Amateur 1983–84–85
Int   Walker Cup 1985; GBI v Europe 1986; England
      (Home Int) 1985
Jun   Carris Trophy 1983–85

Bannerman, Harry
Born Aberdeen on 5th March, 1942. Turned Professional 1965

PRO
Oth   Scottish Professional 1967–72. Northern Scottish Open
      1967–69–72. East of Scotland PGA Match Play 1969.
      Scottish Coca Cola 1976
Int   Ryder Cup 1971. Scotland in World Cup 1967–72;
      in Double Diamond 1972–74
Mis   Frank Moran Trophy 1972
AM
Reg   North of Scotland Stroke Play 1962; North-East
      Scotland Stroke Play 1963–64–65
Jun
Int   Scottish Boys 1959

Barber, Sally (*née* Bonallack)
Born Chigwell, Essex on 9th April, 1938. Turned Professional 1979. Reinstated Amateur 1982

AM
Cls   Thorpe Hall, Thorndon Park, Hunstanton (Hon),
      Killarney (Hon)
Nat   English Ladies Amateur 1968; r/u 1970–71
Oth   German Ladies 1958
Trn   Astor Salver 1972; Avia Foursomes 1976

Reg   Essex Ladies 1958–59–60–61–62–63–66–67–70–71;
      London Foursomes 1984
Int   Curtis Cup 1962; Vagliano Trophy 1961–69; England
      (Home Int) 1960–61–62–63–68–70–72–77–(**78**)
      (Eur L T Ch) 1969–71

Barnes, Brian
Born Addington, Surrey on 3rd June, 1945. Turned Professional 1964

PRO
Eur   Agfacolor 1969; Martini International 1972; Dutch
      Open 1974; French Open 1975; Sun Alliance PGA
      Match Play 1976; Spanish Open, Greater Manchester
      Open 1978; Italian Open, Portuguese Open 1979;
      Tournament Players Chp 1981
Oth   Scottish Professional 1981–82; Coca Cola Young
      Professionals 1969; East of Scotland Professional 1975;
      Northern Scottish Open 1978
RoW   Flame Lily (Rhodesia) 1967; Australian Masters 1970;
      Zambian Open 1979–81; Kenya Open 1981
Int   Ryder Cup 1969–71–73–75–77–79; GBI v Europe
      1974–76–78–80; v South Africa 1976; Scotland in
      World Cup 1974–75–76–77; in Double Diamond
      1972–73–74–75–76–77
AM
Reg   Somerset Amateur 1964; South Western Counties
      Amateur 1964
Jun   British Youths 1964
Int   English Youths 1964

Bayman, Linda (*née* Denison-Pender)
Born 10th June, 1948

Nat   English Ladies Amateur 1983; Ladies British
      Amateur Stroke Play 1987
Trn   Avia Foursomes 1969–71–73–79–80; Worplesdon
      Mixed Foursomes 1980–84; Astor Salver 1983–84;
      Critchley Salver 1984
Reg   Kent Ladies 1968–72–73–78
Int   Curtis Cup 1988; Vagliano Trophy 1971–73–85–87;
      Espirito Santo 1988; England (Home Int)
      1971–72–73–83–84–85–87–88; Eur L T Ch 1983–85–87
Jun   Kent Girls 1966
Mis   Avia Woman Golfer of the Year 1987; Doris
      Chambers Trophy 1987–88; Angus Trophy 1987

Beck, Mrs JB (*née* Pim)
Born Cantibeely, Co Dublin on 1st July, 1901

Cls   Royal Portrush, The Berkshire, Prince's
Nat   Irish Ladies 1938, r/u 1949
Oth   Ladies Veteran 1952–55–56–59
Int   Curtis Cup (**1954**); LGU team to South Africa 1951.
      Ireland (Home Int) 1926 to 1950–56
Mis   Irish hockey internationalist 1920

Behan, Lillian
Born Co Kildare on 12th January, 1965. Turned Professional 1986

AM
Chp   Ladies British Open Amateur 1985
Trn   The Curragh Scratch Cup 1986
Int   Curtis Cup 1986; Vagliano Trophy 1985; Ireland
      (Home Int) 1984–85–86; (Eur L T Ch) 1985

Beharrell, John Charles
Born Solihull, Warwickshire on 2nd May, 1938

Cls   Royal & Ancient, Edgbaston, Aldeburgh.
      Hon member of Little Aston, Blackwell, Handsworth
Chp   Amateur Champion 1956
Trn   Antlers Royal Mid-Surrey 1960.

Reg	Central England Mixed Foursomes 1956–57–75
Int	GB v Europe 1956; v Professionals 1956. England (Home Int) 1956
Jun	
Int	English Boy 1955

Beharrell, Veronica (née Anstey)
Born Birmingham on 14th January, 1935

Cls	Edgbaston (Hon), Little Aston
Oth	Australian Ladies, New Zealand Ladies 1955; Victoria Ladies Open 1955
Reg	Warwickshire Ladies 1955–56–57–58–60–71–72–75; Central England Mixed Foursomes 1957–75
Int	Curtis Cup 1956. England (Home Int) 1955–56–58–(61)
Jun	
Int	English Girls 1953

Bembridge, Maurice
Born Worksop on 21st February, 1945. Turned Professional 1960

PRO	
Maj	Leading British player in Open 1968 (5th)
Eur	PGA Match Play, Sumrie 1969; Dunlop Masters 1971; Martini 1973; Piccadilly Medal, Viyella PGA, Double Diamond Individual 1974; German Open 1975; Benson and Hedges International 1979
RoW	Kenya Open 1986–69–70; Caltex (New Zealand) 1970; Lusaka Open 1972
Oth	British Assistants 1967
Int	Ryder Cup 1969–71–73–75; GB v South Africa 1976; England in Double Diamond 1973–74–75; in World Cup 1974–75
Mis	His 63 in the qualifying round for the 1967 Open equals the lowest recorded; second in Order of Merit 1973; scored 64 in last round US Masters 1974 equalling record; his inward half of 30 also equalled the record

Benka, Peter
Born London on 18th September, 1946

Cls	Addington, West Sussex
Nat	Scottish Open Amateur Stroke Play r/u 1969
Oth	Dutch Amateur 1972
Trn	County Champion of Champions 1967; Sunningdale Foursomes 1969; St George's Challenge Cup 1969. Mullingar Trophy 1970; St George's Hill Trophy 1971–75.
Reg	Surrey Amateur 1967–68
Int	Walker Cup 1969; GB v Europe 1970; England (Home Int) 1967–68–69–70; (Eur T Ch) 1969
Jun	British Youths 1967–68.
Int	Boys 1964; Youths 1966–67–68

Bennett, Stephen
Born Cleethorpes on 23rd April, 1959. Turned Professional 1979

PRO	
Eur	Tunisian Open 1985
RoW	Zimbabwe Open 1986
Reg	Lincolnshire Open 1979
AM	
Reg	Lincolnshire Amateur 1977–78

Bentley, Arnold Lewis
Born Southport on 11th June, 1911

Cls	Royal & Ancient, Hesketh (Hon), Royal Birkdale
Nat	English Amateur 1939
Int	England (Home Int) 1936–37; v France 1937–39
Mis	Played for British Seniors 1969

Jun	
Int	Boys 1928

Bentley, Harry Geoffrey
Born Manchester on 13th October, 1907

Cls	Royal & Ancient, Hesketh (Hon), Le Touquet
Nat	English Amateur 1936, r/u 1954; Irish Open Amateur 1934
Oth	French Amateur 1931–32; German Amateur 1933–37–38–39; Italian Amateur 1954
Trn	St George's Challenge Cup 1932; Prince of Wales Cup 1935
Reg	Lancashire Amateur 1931–32–39
Int	Walker Cup 1934–36–38; GB v Professionals 1930–31–32–34–35; England (Home Int) 1931 to 38; 47; v France 1934–36–37–38–39–**54**
Mis	Chairman, Walker Cup selectors 1953; British Seniors Captain 1967; Leading Amateur in French, Belgian, German, Czechoslovakian Opens 1935

Bisgood, Jeanne, CBE
Born Richmond, Surrey on 11th August, 1923

Cls	Parkstone (Hon)
Nat	English Ladies 1951–53–57
Oth	Swedish Ladies 1952; Italian Ladies, German Ladies 1953; Portuguese Ladies 1954; Norwegian Ladies 1955.
Trn	Astor Salver 1951–52–53; Roehampton Gold Cup 1951–52–53. Daily Graphic Cup 1945–51
Reg	South Eastern Ladies 1950–52; Surrey Ladies 1951–53–69
Int	Curtis Cup 1950–52–54–(70); England (Home Int) 1949–50–51–52–53–54–56–58

Bloice, Cecil
Born Aberfeldy on 30th July, 1954

Reg	Perth & Kinross Amateur Stroke Play 1986
Int	Walker Cup 1985; Scotland (Home Int) 1985–86

Bolton, Zara (née Davies)
Born London on 16th March, 1914

Cls	Hon Member of Royal Portrush, Bishop's Stortford, Maccauvlei, County Down, Castlerock, Ballycastle
Nat	English Ladies r/u 1948
Reg	Ulster Scratch Cup 1947–48–49–50–56–60; Herts Ladies 1935; Kent Ladies 1948
Int	Curtis Cup 1948–(56)–(66–(68); GB v France 1948; GB Commonwealth Team (1967); LGU team to South Africa 1951; England (Home Int) 1939–49–50–51–**55**–56

Bonallack, Michael Francis, OBE
Born Chigwell on 31st December, 1934

Cls	Thorpe Hall, Pine Valley, Elie.
Maj	Leading Amateur in Open 1968–71
Chp	Amateur Champion 1961–65–68–69–70; s/f 1958–72–77
Nat	English Amateur 1962–63–65–67–68; r/u 1959; English Open Amateur Stroke Play 1964–68–69 (tied)–71; r/u 1959–66–67
Trn	Berkshire Trophy 1957–61–65–68–70–71 (shared); Hampshire Hog 1957–79; Golf Illustrated Gold Vase 1961 (shared)–67 (shared)–68–69 (shared)–71–75; Scrutton Jug 1961–64–66–68–70–71; Lytham Trophy 1965 (shared)–72; Antlers Royal Mid-Surrey 1964; St George's Challenge Cup 1965–68–81; Prince of Wales Challenge Cup 1967; Sunningdale Foursomes 1959; Worplesdon Mixed Foursomes 1958

Reg Essex Amateur 1954–57–59–60–61–63–64–68–69–70–72; Essex Open 1969; East Anglian Open 1973
Int Walker Cup 1957–59–61–63–65–67–**69**–**71**–73; GB Commonwealth Team 1959–63–**67**–**71**–(**75**); Eisenhower Trophy 1960–62–64–66–**68** (individual winner, shared)–**70**–**72**; v Professionals 1957–58– 59–60; v Europe 1958–60–62–64–66–68–70–72. England (Home Int) 1957 to 72–74 (**1962** to 67); (Eur T Ch) 1959–61– 63–65–67–69–71
Jun British Boys 1952
Mis AGW Trophy 1968; Bobby Jones Award 1972; PGA Chairman 1976; Chairman Golf Foundation 1977; President English Golf Union 1982. Best equal individual score Eisenhower Trophy 1968. Chairman Royal & Ancient Selection Committee 1975 to 1979; Secretary to Royal & Ancient since 1983

Bonallack, Angela (née Ward)
Born Birchington on 7th April, 1937

Cls Prince's, Thorpe Hall, St Rule
Chp Ladies British Open Amateur r/u 1962–74
Nat English Ladies 1958–63, r/u 1960–62–72. British Ladies r/u 1962–74
Oth Swedish Ladies, German Ladies 1955; Scandinavian Ladies 1956; Portuguese Ladies 1957
Trn Astor Salver 1957–58–60–61–66; Worplesdon Mixed Foursomes 1958; Kayser-Bondor Foursomes 1958 (shared); Astor Prince's 1968; Avia Foursomes 1976; Roehampton Gold Cup 1980.
Reg Essex Ladies 1968–69–73–74–76–77–78–82; South East Ladies 1957–65; Kent Ladies' 1955–56–58
Int Curtis Cup 1956–58–60–62–64–66. Vagliano Trophy 1959–61–63. England (Home Int) 1956 to 1964; 1966–72
Jun British Girls 1955
Mis Leading amateur Colgate European Ladies' Open 1975–76

Bousfield, Kenneth
Born Marston Moor on 2nd October, 1919. Turned Professional 1938

Eur German Open 1955–59. Swiss Open, Belgian Open 1958; Portuguese Open 1960–61
Trn News Chronicle 1951; PGA Match Play 1955. PGA Close 1955; Yorkshire Evening News 1956 (shared); Dunlop 1957. Sprite 1959. Irish Hospitals 1960 (shared); Swallow–Penfold 1961
Oth Gleneagles Pro–Am 1964.
Reg Southern England Professional 1951–57–74. Pringle Seniors 1972
Int Ryder Cup 1949–51–55–57–59–61; England in World Cup 1956–57

Bradshaw, Harry
Born Delgany, Co Wicklow on 9th October, 1913. Turned Professional 1934

Maj Open r/u 1949, (tied)
Nat Irish Open 1947–49; Irish Professional 1941–42–43– 44–47–50–51–53–54–57.
Trn Irish Dunlop 1950; Dunlop Masters 1953–55; PGA Close, Penfold–Swallow (tied) 1958
Int Ryder Cup 1953–55–57. Ireland in World Cup 1954–55–56–57–58 (winners)–59
Mis Individual r/u in World Cup 1958

Brand, Gordon J.
Born Cambridge on 6th August, 1955. Turned Professional 1976

PRO
Maj Open r/u 1986
Eur Volvo Belgian Open 1989

RoW Ivory Coast Open 1981; Nigerian Open 1983; Nigerian Open, Ivory Coast Open 1986; Zimbabwe Open 1987; Ivory Coast Open 1988
Int Ryder Cup 1983; Nissan Cup 1986; England in World Cup 1983; Dunhill Cup 1986–87 (winners)
Mis Tooting Bec Cup 1981–86; Braid-Taylor Memorial Medal 1986; Headed Safari Tour Order of Merit 1983, 1986
AM
Int GB v Europe 1976; England (Home Int) 1976

Brand, Gordon Jr
Born Burntisland, Fife on 19th August, 1958. Turned Professional 1981

Cls Hon member of Woodhall Spa, Knowle
PRO
Eur Coral Classic, Bob Hope British Classic 1982; Celtic International, Panasonic European Open 1984; KLM Dutch Open, Scandinavian Enterprise Open 1987; Benson & Hedges International 1989
RoW South Australian Open 1988
Oth PGA Qualifying School winner 1981
Int Ryder Cup 1987–89; Nissan Cup 1985; Kirin Cup 1988; Scotland in World Cup 1984–85–88; in Dunhill Cup 1985–86–87 (r/u)–88–89. GBI v Australia 1988
Mis Rookie of the Year 1982; AGW Trophy 1982
AM
Nat English Open Amateur Stroke Play 1978; Scottish Open Amateur Stroke Play 1980
Oth Swedish Open Amateur Stroke Play 1979; Portuguese Amateur 1981
Trn Golf Illustrated Gold Vase 1980; Sunningdale Foursomes 1981
Reg Gloucestershire Amateur 1977; South-Western Counties Amateur 1977–78
Int Walker Cup 1979; Eisenhower Trophy 1978–80; GB v Europe 1978–80; Scotland (Home Int) 1978–80; v England 1979; v Italy 1979; v France 1980–81; v Belgium 1980; (Eur T Ch) 1979
Jun British Youths 1979; Scottish Youths 1980
Int Youths 1977–78–79

Branigan, Declan
Born Drogheda, Ireland on 22nd July, 1948

Cls Laytown and Bettystown
Nat Irish Amateur 1976–81
Reg West of Ireland Open Amateur 1976–81. East of Ireland Open Amateur 1981
Int Ireland (Home Int) 1975–76–77–80–86; (Eur T Ch) 1977–81; v France, West Germany, Sweden 1976
Jun Irish Youths 1969

Briggs, Audrey (née Brown)
Born Kent on 31st January, 1945

Cls Royal Liverpool
Nat Welsh Ladies 1970–71–73–74, r/u 1978–79–80–81
Reg Sussex Ladies 1969. Cheshire Ladies 1971–73– 76–80–81. North of England Ladies 1976
Int Vagliano Trophy 1971–73. Wales (Home Int) 1969 to 84, (Eur L T Ch) 1969–71–73–75–77–79–81–83; Fiat Trophy 1978–79–80

Broadhurst, Paul
Born Staffordshire on 14th August, 1965. Turned Professional 1988

Maj Leading amateur in Open 1988
PRO
Eur Crédit Lyonnais Cannes Open 1989

AM
Trn Lytham Trophy 1988
Int (GBI) v Europe 1988. England (Home Int) 1986–87.

Brodie, Allan
Born Glasgow on 25th September, 1947

Cls Balmore (Hon), Glasgow
Chp Amateur s/f 1976
Nat Scottish Amateur 1977; r/u 1973. Scottish Open Amateur Stroke Play r/u 1970
Trn Tennant Cup 1972–80; Golf Illustrated Gold Vase 1976
Reg West of Scotland Open Amateur 1974; Dunbartonshire Amateur Stroke Play 1975–76
Int Walker Cup 1977–79; Eisenhower Trophy 1978; GB v Europe 1974–76–78–80; Scotland (Home Int) 1970–72–73–74–75–76–77–78–80; (Eur T Ch) 1973–77–79; v Belgium, Spain 1977; v France 1978; v England, Italy 1979
Jun
Int Youths 1966–67

Brooks, Colin
Born Edinburgh on 14th July, 1965

PRO
Oth Scottish Assistants 1989; British Assistants 1989
AM
Nat Scottish Amateur 1986
Trn Tennant Cup 1985. Gran Primo 1986.
Reg West of Scotland Open Amateur Stroke Play 1986
Int GB v Europe 1986; Scotland (Home Int) 1984–85

Brown, Audrey
See Briggs

Brown, Julie
Born Stoke-on-Trent on 26th December, 1963.

PRO
Eur LBS Ladies German Open 1985
AM
Chp Ladies British Open Amateur r/u 1984
Reg Staffordshire Ladies 1982–83
Int Vilmorin Cup 1984; England (Home Int) 1984

Brown, Kenneth
Born Harpenden, Herts on 9th January, 1957. Turned Professional 1974

Eur Carrolls Irish Open 1978; KLM Dutch Open 1983; Glasgow Classic 1984; Four Stars Pro-Celebrity 1985
US Southern Open 1987
RoW Kenya Open 1983
Oth Hertfordshire Open 1975
Int Ryder Cup 1977–79–83–85–87; Hennessy-Cognac Cup 1978–84; Kirin Cup 1987; Scotland in Double Diamond 1977; Scotland in World Cup 1977–78–79–83
Mis Tooting Bec Cup 1980
Jun Carris Trophy 1974
Int Boys 1974

Buckley, James A
Born Ontario, Canada on 14th September, 1950. Turned Professional 1969. Reinstated Amateur 1976

Cls Abergele, Killarney (Hon)
Nat Welsh Amateur 1968. Welsh Amateur Stroke Play 1968–77, r/u 1978. Welsh Close 1969. Welsh Professional Championship 1971–72

Reg Denbighshire Amateur 1967–68–76–78. North Wales Professional (as Amateur) 1976
Int Walker Cup 1979. Wales (Home Int) 1967–68–69–76–77–78; (Eur T Ch) 1967–69; v Denmark 1976–77
Jun Welsh Boys 1966–67–68

Burke, Ita
See Butler

Bussell, Alan Francis
Born Glasgow on 25th February, 1937

Cls Whitecraigs (Hon), Coxmoor (Hon), Chevin
Chp Amateur s/f 1957
Trn Antlers Royal Mid–Surrey 1956. Golf Illustrated Gold Vase 1959
Reg Nottinghamshire Amateur 1959–60–62–63–64–68–69. Nottinghamshire Open 1960–62. Nottinghamshire Match Play 1960–62. Renfrewshire Amateur 1955
Int Walker Cup 1957. GB v Europe 1956–62; v Professionals 1956–57–59. Scotland (Home Int) 1956–57–58–61; v Scandinavia 1956–60
Jun British Boys 1954. Boy International 1954. British Youths 1956. Youth International 1954–55–56

Butler, Ita *(née Burke)*
Born Nenagh, Co Tipperary

Cls Hon member of Elm Park, Killarney, Woodbrook, Nenagh
Nat Irish Ladies r/u 1972–78
Reg Leinster Ladies three times. Munster and Midland Ladies twice
Int Curtis Cup 1966. World Team Championship 1966. Vagliano Trophy 1965. Ireland (World Cup) 1964; (Home Int) 1962–63–64–65–66–68–71–72–73–76–77–78–79; (Eur T Ch) 1967; Fiat Trophy 1978

Butler, Peter J
Born Birmingham on 25th March, 1932. Turned Professional 1948

Tls French Open 1968. Colombian Open 1975
Trn Swallow–Penfold 1959. Yorkshire Evening News 1962; PGA Close 1963. Bowmaker 1963–67. Cox Moore 1964. PGA Match Play r/u 1964–75. Martini 1965. Piccadilly 1965–67. Penfold, Wills 1968. RTV 1969. Classic International 1971. Sumrie 1974 Evian International 1963. Grand Bahama Invitation Open 1971–72
Reg Midland Open 1956–58–60–65–69. Midland Professional 1961.
Oth Gleneagles Pro-Am 1963. Sunningdale Foursomes 1974
Int Ryder Cup 1965–69–71–73. England in World Cup 1969–70–73. England in Double Diamond 1971–72–76. GB v Europe 1976
Mis Equal lowest round in British events of 61. Second in Order of Merit 1968. PGA Captain 1972

Cadden, Suzanne
See McMahon

Caldwell, Ian
Born Streatham on 17th May, 1930

Cls Royal & Ancient, Sunningdale, Walton Heath
Nat English Amateur 1961
Trn Prince of Wales Challenge Cup 1950–51–52. Boyd Quaich 1954.

Reg Surrey Amateur 1961
Int Walker Cup 1951–55. GB Commonwealth Team 1954.
GB v Europe 1955. England (Home Int) 1950–51–
52–53–54–55–56–57–61
Jun Carris Trophy 1947–48

Caldwell, Carole (née Redford)
Born Kingston, Surrey on 23rd April, 1949

Cls Canterbury (Hon)
Trn Newmark–Avia International 1973. Roehampton Gold
Cup 1973–75–78; Hampshire Rose 1973, 1984; Avia
Foursomes 1974; Critchley Salver 1974; Canadian
Ladies Foursomes 1978; London Foursomes 1984
Oth Portuguese Ladies 1980
Reg South Eastern Ladies 1973–78. Kent Ladies
1970–75–77–86. Berkshire Ladies 1982
Int Curtis Cup 1978–80; Vagliano Trophy 1973; England
(Home Int) 1973–78–79–80
Mis Playing captain of LGU U–23 team to tour Canada
1973. Lost at 27th hole in first round of American
Ladies Amateur 1978

Carr, Joseph B
Born Dublin on 18th February, 1922

Cls Hon member of Sutton
Maj Leading Amateur in Open 1956–58
Chp Amateur Champion 1953–58–60, r/u 1968 s/f 1952–54.
Nat Irish Amateur 1954–57–63–64–65–67, r/u 1951–59.
Irish Open Amateur 1946–50–54–56, r/u 1947–48–51;
US Amateur s/f 1961
Trn Gleneagles Saxone 1955. Golf Illustrated Gold Vase
1951. Berkshire Trophy 1959. Formby Hare 1962.
Mullingar Trophy 1963. Antlers Royal Mid–Surrey
1970
Reg South of Ireland Open Amateur 1948–66–69. East of
Ireland Open Amateur 1941–43–45–46–48–56–57–58–
60–61–64–69. West of Ireland Open Amateur
1946–47–48–51–53–54–56–58–60–61–62–66.
Int Walker Cup 1947–49–51–53–55–57–59–61–**63**–(**65**)–67.
GB v Europe 1954–56–**64**–68. Eisenhower
Trophy 1958–60–(**64**)–(**66**). Ireland (Home Int) 1947
to 1969 (Eur T Ch) 1965–67–69
Mis AGW Trophy 1953. Bobby Jones Award 1961. Walter
Hagen Award 1967

Carr, Roderick J
Born 27th October, 1950. Turned Professional 1971.
Reinstated Amateur 1983

Trn Antlers Royal Mid–Surrey 1970.
Reg East of Ireland Open Amateur 1970. West of Ireland
Open Amateur 1971. Turnberry Pro–Am 1970
Int Walker Cup 1971. Ireland (Home Int) 1970–71; (Eur
T Ch) 1971
Jun Youth International 1970–71
Mis Leading Amateur South African Open 1971

Carrick, David
Born Glasgow on 28th January, 1957

Nat Scottish Amateur 1985. Scottish Open Amateur Stroke
Play 1987
Trn Scottish Champion of Champions 1983. Glasgow
Amateur 1980–81
Reg Dunbartonshire Amateur 1979–80–82–83
Int Walker Cup 1983–87. GB v Europe 1986. Scotland
(Home Int) 1981 to 1989; v Italy 1988; v France 1989;
(Eur T Ch) 1989; v West Germany 1987
Mis Braid Panton Trophy 1989

Carslaw, Iain Alexander
Born Glasgow on 4th October, 1949

Cls Williamwood (Hon), Walton Heath
Chp Amateur s/f 1976
Nat Scottish Amateur 1978
Trn Tennant Cup 1978. Golf Illustrated Gold Vase 1982
Reg Glasgow County Match Play 1977–78–79–80. Glasgow
Amateur 1978
Int Walker Cup 1979. GB v Europe 1978. Scotland
(Home Int) 1976–77–78–80–81; (Eur T Ch) 1977–79;
v Spain 1977; v Belgium 1978; v France 1978–83;
in Fiat Trophy 1978; v Italy 1979; v England 1979;
in Moroccan International 1979
Jun
Int Boys 1967. Youths 1971

Cassells, Craig

Chp Amateur r/u 1989
Reg South–East of Scotland Amateur 1989
Int Walker Cup 1989; England (Home Int) 1989

Cater, John Robert
Born Edinburgh, 1919

Cls Williamwood (Hon), Royal & Ancient, Elie
Chp Amateur s/f 1952
Maj Gleneagles Silver Tassie 1952
Reg West of Scotland Amateur 1951–55. Glasgow County
1957
Int Walker Cup 1955. Scotland (Home Int) 1952–53–54–
55–56; v South Africa 1954; v Scandinavia 1956
Mis Captain of Royal & Ancient 1986

Chadwick, Elizabeth
See Pook

Chapman, Roger
Born in Nakuru, Kenya on 1st May, 1959. Turned
Professional 1981

PRO
RoW Zimbabwe Open 1988
Trn Sunningdale Open Foursomes 1986
AM
Nat English Amateur 1979
Trn Duncan Putter (shared), Lytham Trophy 1981;
Sunningdale Open Foursomes 1979
Int Walker Cup 1981; GB v Europe 1980; England (Home
Int) 1980–81; (Eur T Ch) 1981

Christmas, Martin J
Born 1939

Cls West Sussex, Addington
Chp Amateur s/f 1961–64–65
Nat English Amateur r/u 1960. English Open Amateur
Stroke Play r/u 1960
Trn Gleneagles Pro–Am 1961. Wentworth Pro–Am
Foursomes 1962
Ove Belgian Open Amateur 1976
Reg Sussex Amateur 1962
Int Walker Cup 1961–63. Eisenhower Trophy 1962.
GB v Europe 1960–62–64. England (Home Int)
1960–61–62–63–64

Chugg, Pamela Mary (née Light)
Born Cardiff on 10th May, 1955. Turned Professional
1979. Reinstated Amateur 1986

Cls Whitchurch (Cardiff)
Nat Welsh Ladies 1978. Welsh Ladies Open Stroke Play
1976

Reg   South Western Ladies 1976–78
Int   Wales (Home Int) 1972–73–74–75–76–77–78–86–87–88;
      (Eur L T Ch) 1973–75–77–87
Jun   Welsh Girls 1970. Girl International 1969–70–71–72–73
Mis   Captain of Welsh Juniors 1988

Clark, Clive Anthony
Born Winchester, Hants on 27th June, 1945. Turned Professional 1965

Maj   Open 3rd 1967 (leading British player)
Tls   Danish Open 1966
Chp   Amateur r/u 1965.
Nat   English Amateur r/u 1965. English Open Amateur
      Stroke Play 1965 (tied)
Trn   Lytham Trophy 1965 (tied). Golf Illustrated Gold
      Vase, Scrutton Jug 1965. Bowmaker, Agfa–Gevaert
      1968. John Player Trophy 1970. Sumrie 1974
Oth   Sunningdale Foursomes 1974–76
Int   Walker Cup 1965. GB v Europe 1964. England (Home
      Int) 1964–65. Ryder Cup 1973
Mis   Lost play–off for 1972 French Open. Braid–Taylor
      Memorial Medal; TV commentator.

Clark, Gordon James
Born Newcastle–upon–Tyne on 15th April, 1933. Turned Professional 1974. Reinstated Amateur 1983

Chp   Amateur Champion 1964; s/f 1967
Nat   English Amateur r/u 1961. Scottish Open Amateur
      Stroke Play 1973 (tied)
Oth   Portuguese Amateur 1974
Reg   Northumberland Amateur 1956–71. Northumberland
      Amateur Stroke Play 1967–71
Int   Walker Cup 1965. GB v Europe 1964–66.
      England (Home Int) 1961–64–65–66–67–68–71;
      (Eur T Ch) 1961–65
Jun   English Boy International 1950

Clark, Howard K
Born Leeds on 26th August, 1954. Turned Professional October 1973

PRO
Eur   Portuguese Open, Madrid Open 1978; Cepsa Madrid
      Open, Whyte & Mackay PGA Championship 1984;
      Jersey Open, Glasgow Open 1985; Cepsa Madrid
      Open, Peugeot Spanish Open 1986; Moroccan Open,
      PLM Open 1987; English Open 1988
Oth   U–25 TPD 1976
Int   Ryder Cup 1977–81–85–87–89; Nissan Cup 1985–86;
      Hennessy–Cognac Cup 1978–84; England in World
      Cup 1978–84–85 (individual winner)–87; Dunhill Cup
      1985–86–87 (winners)–89; GBI v Australia 1988
AM
Chp   Amateur s/f 1973
Reg   Yorkshire Amateur 1973
Int   Walker Cup 1973; England (Home Int) 1973
Jun   British Boys 1971
Int   Boys 1969–71; Youths 1971–72–73

Claydon, Russell
Born on 19th November 1965. Turned Professional 1989

Maj   Leading amateur in Open 1989
AM
Nat   English Amateur 1988
RoW   Australian Masters r/u 1989
Trn   St George's Challenge Cup 1986; Berkshire Trophy
      1988; St Andrews Links Trophy 1989; Sunningdale
      Open Foursomes 1989
Reg   Cambridge Amateur 1987–88
Oth   UAP U–25 European Open r/u 1988
Int   Walker Cup 1989; England (Home Int) 1988 (Eur
      T Ch) 1989

Coles, Neil
Born London on 26th September, 1934. Turned Professional 1950

Maj   Open 3rd 1961; r/u 1973; leading British player 1975
      (7th)
Eur   German Open 1971. Spanish Open 1973
Trn   Ballantine 1961. Senior Service 1962. Daks 1963
      (tied)–64–70–71 (tied). Martini 1963 (tied). Bowmaker
      1964–70. PGA Match Play 1964–65–73, r/u 1966–72–78.
      Carrolls 1965–71. Pringle 1966. Dunlop Masters 1966.
      Sumrie 1970–73. Penfold 1971. Sunbeam 1972. Wills
      1974. Penfold PGA 1976. Tournament Players' Cham-
      pionship 1977. Sanyo Open 1983. Engadine Open 1963.
      Shell BP Italy 1970. Walworth Aloyco Italy 1970
Oth   British Assistants 1956. Sunningdale Foursomes
      1962–67–80. Wentworth Pro–Am Foursomes 1963–70.
      Southern England Professionals 1970
Int   Ryder Cup 1961–63–65–67–69–71–73–77. England in
      World Cup 1963–68. England in Double Diamond
      1971–73–75–76–77. GB v Europe 1974–76–78–80
Mis   Harry Vardon Trophy 1963–70. Second in Order
      of Merit 1987
Sen   Seniors British Open 1987

Collingham, Janet (*née* Melville)
Born Barrow–in–Furness on 16th March, 1958

Cls   Notts Ladies
Chp   Ladies British Open Amateur 1987
Nat   Ladies British Open Amateur Stroke Play 1978
Trn   Worplesdon Mixed Foursomes 1979. Northern
      Foursomes 1977–78. Mary McCalley Trophy 1980
Reg   Highland Open 1978. Midland Ladies 1986.
      Lancashire Champion 1983–86
Int   Vagliano Trophy 1979–87. England (Home Int)
      1978–79–81–84–86–87 (Eur L T Ch) 1979. Girls
      International 1976–(**81**)
Mis   Varsity Athlete in golf at Florida International
      University 1980–81; Duncan Salver 1978

Connachan, Jane
Born Haddington, East Lothian on 25th February, 1964. Turned Professional 1984

Cls   Royal Musselburgh (Hon)
PRO
Eur   Jersey Open 1984; British Olivetti, 415/Vantage
      European Match Play 1985; British Olivetti 1987;
      Expedier Ladies European Open 1989
AM
Nat   Scottish Ladies 1982; Ladies British Open Amateur
      Stroke Play 1982, r/u 1981–83
Trn   Helen Holm Trophy 1983
Reg   East Lothian Ladies 1978–79
Int   Curtis Cup 1980–82; Espirito Santo 1980–82; Vagliano
      Trophy 1981–83; Commonwealth Trn 1983; Scotland
      (Home Int) 1979–80–81–82–83; (Eur L T Ch) 1983
Jun   Scottish Girls 1978–79–80; Scottish Girls Open Stroke
      Play 1978–80; British Girls 1980–81; Australian Girls
      1982; Australian Junior Chp 1982
Int   Girls 1976–77–78–79–80; Eur Junior Ladies 1983
Mis   Avia Golfer of the Year 1982; Dinwiddy Trophy 1979;
      Duncan Salver 1982; Angus Trophy 1982; Taunton
      Trophy 1982

Cosh, Gordon B
Born Glasgow on 26th March, 1939

Cls   Troon, Royal Aberdeen, Bruntsfield Links. Hon
      member of Cowglen, Killarney
Nat   Scottish Amateur 1968, r/u 1965. Scottish Open
      Amateur Stroke Play r/u 1968
Trn   Newlands Trophy 1980

Reg	West of Scotland Amateur 1961–64–65–66. Glasgow County Match Play 1965–66. Glasgow Amateur 1969. Glasgow County Stroke Play 1972–74
Int	Walker Cup 1965. Eisenhower Trophy 1966–68. GB Commonwealth Team 1967. GB v Europe 1966–68. Scotland (Home Int) 1964–65–66–67–68–69; (Eur T Ch) 1965-**69**
Jun	
Int	Youths 1959–60

Craddock, Tom
Born Malahide on 16th December, 1931

Cls	Malahide, Donabate, Sutton, The Island Malahide, Malone, Woodbrook, Mullingar, Carlow, Howth, Tara, Killarney
Nat	Irish Amateur 1959, r/u 1965. Irish Open Amateur 1958
Trn	Lytham Trophy 1969
Reg	East of Ireland Open Amateur 1959–65–66
Int	Walker Cup 1967–69. Ireland (Home Int) 1955–56–57–58–59–60–65–66–67–69; (Eur T Ch) 1967–71

Critchley, Bruce
Born 9th December, 1942

Cls	Sunningdale, Killarney (Hon)
Chp	Amateur s/f 1970
Trn	Worplesdon Mixed Foursomes 1961. Sunningdale Foursomes 1964. Hampshire Hog 1969. Antlers Royal Mid–Surrey 1974
Reg	Surrey Amateur 1969
Int	Walker Cup 1969. GB v Europe 1970. England (Home Int) 1962–69–70; (Eur T Ch) 1969
Mis	TV commentator. Co-founder annual match at Deal between former Ryder Cup v Walker Cup Players

Critchley, Diana Lesley (*née* Fishwick)
Born London on 12th April, 1911

Cls	North Foreland, Bramley, Canterbury, Sunningdale, Sunningdale Ladies
Chp	British Ladies 1930.
Nat	English Ladies 1932–49, r/u 1929
Oth	French Ladies 1932. German Ladies 1936–38. Belgian Ladies 1938. Dutch Ladies 1946. Florida (USA) West Coast 1933
Trn	Sunningdale Foursomes 1934
Reg	Kent Ladies 1934. Surrey Ladies 1936–46
Int	Curtis Cup 1932-34–(**50**). GB v France 1931-32-33-34–(**48**); v Canada 1934-50. England (Home Int) 1930-31-32-33-35-36-47
Jun	British Girls 1927–28
Mis	Chairman of ELGA Selection Committee 1967–68–69–70. LGU International Selector 1970–71–72–73. Member LGU Team to tour South Africa 1933

Curry, David H
Born 6th July, 1963

Chp	Amateur Champion 1986
Trn	Selborne Salver 1984
Int	England (Home Int) 1984–86–87. v France 1988. (GB) v Europe 1986–88. Walker Cup 1987

Dalgleish, Colin R
Born Glasgow on 24th September, 1960

Cls	Helensburgh (Hon), Millstone Mills (Hon)
Nat	Scottish Amateur 1981
Trn	Tennant Cup 1983–88
RoW	East of India Amateur 1981. Indian Amateur r/u 1981. Lake Macquarie International Stroke–Play Champion (Australia) 1983

Oth	Scottish Universities Champion 1983
Int	Walker Cup 1981. Scotland (Home Int) 1981–82–83; v France 1982; (Eur T Ch) 1981–83. GB v Europe 1982. Europe v South America 1982
Jun	International Junior Masters 1977. Belgian Junior Championship 1980. British Boys r/u 1977. British Youths r/u 1979–82. Boy International 1976–77–78. Youth International 1979–80–81–82

Daly, Fred
Born Portrush on 11th October, 1911

Maj	Open Champion 1947, r/u 1948, 3rd 1950, 1952
Eur	Irish Open 1946
Trn	PGA Match Play 1947–48–52. Dunlop Southport 1948. Penfold 1948. Lotus 1950. Daks 1952; Irish Dunlop 1946–52
Reg	Ulster Professional 1936–40–41–42–43–46–51–55–56–57–58. Irish Professional 1940–46–52.
Int	Ryder Cup 1947–49–51–53. Ireland 1936–37–38. World Cup 1954–55

Darcy, Eamonn
Born Delgany on 7th August, 1952. Turned Professional 1969

Eur	Spanish Open 1983. Belgian Open 1987
Trn	Sumrie 1976–78. Greater Manchester Open 1977
RoW	Air New Zealand Open 1980. Cock o' the North Open 1981. Kenya Open 1982. Mufulira Open 1984
Oth	Irish Dunlop 1976. Cacharel World Under–25 1976. Irish Match Play 1981
Int	Ryder Cup 1975–77–81–87. Ireland in Double Diamond 1975–76–77. Ireland in World Cup 1976–77–84–85. GB v Europe 1976; v South Africa 1976. Hennessy–Cognac Cup 1976–84. Dunhill Cup 1987–88 (winners)
Mis	Second in Order of Merit 1976

Davies, John C
Born London on 14th February, 1948

Cls	Mid–Surrey, Sunningdale, Royal Cinque Ports, Killarney
Chp	Amateur r/u 1976.
Nat	English Amateur r/u 1971–76. English Open Amateur Stroke Play r/u 1977
Trn	Berkshire Trophy 1969–71 (tied). Royal St George's Challenge Cup 1972–73–74–75–76–77. Sunningdale Foursomes 1968–72. Antlers Royal Mid–Surrey 1969–75–77. Golf Illustrated Gold Vase 1973–77. Prince of Wales Cup 1975. Berkhamsted Trophy 1976–78–79
Oth	Second equal in South African Open Amateur Stroke Play 1974
Reg	Surrey Amateur 1971–72–77
Int	Walker Cup 1973–75–77–79. Eisenhower Trophy 1974–76 (winners). GB v Europe 1972–74–76–78; England (Home Int) 1969–70–71–72–73–74–78; (Eur T Ch) 1973–75–77
Mis	Member of European Team to tour South Africa 1974

Davies, Karen L
Born 19th June, 1965. Turned Professional 1988

Oth	Florida State Tournament 1985. South–Eastern USA Championship 1985
Int	Curtis Cup 1986–88. Wales (Home Int) 1981–82–83 (Eur L U–22) 1981–82–83–84–85–86; (Eur L T Ch) 1987, Commonwealth Team 1987
Jun	Welsh Girls 1980–82

Davies, Laura
Born Coventry on 5th October, 1963. Turned Professional 1985

Maj	Ladies British Open 1986, r/u 1987. US Womens Open 1987
Trn	London Foursomes 1981. Welsh Open Stroke–Play 1984. English Intermediate 1983
Reg	South–Eastern Champion 1983–84
Int	England (Home Int) 1983–84. Vilmorin Cup 1984. Curtis Cup 1984.
Jun	Surrey Girls 1982
Mis	Order of Merit leader 1985–86
Eur	Belgian Ladies Open 1985. McEwan's Lager Classic 1986. Greater Manchester Tournament 1986. Italian Open 1987–88. Ford Ladies Classic, Biarritz Ladies Open 1988. Laing Charity Ladies Classic 1989
US	Tucson Open 1988. Toledo Classic 1988 Lady Keystone Open 1989

Davies, Pamela
See Large

Davies, Zara
See Bolton

Davis, Mark
Born 4th July, 1964. Turned Professional 1986

Nat	English Open Amateur Stroke Play 1984
Trn	Golf Illustrated Gold Vase 1985. Prince of Wales Cup 1983. Lagonda Trophy 1984
Reg	Essex Amateur 1983
Int	England (Home Int) 1984–85

Dawson, Peter
Born Doncaster on 9th May, 1950. Turned Professional 1970

PRO	
Trn	Double Diamond Individual 1975
Int	Ryder Cup 1977. England in World Cup 1977. England in Double Diamond 1977
AM	
Nat	English Amateur r/u 1969
Int	England (Home Int) 1969
Jun	Carris Trophy 1968
Int	Boys 1967; Youths 1969–70
Mis	Plays left-handed

De Bendern, Count John (John de Forest)
Born 1907

Cls	Royal & Ancient, Sunningdale, Addington, Lausanne
Chp	Amateur Champion 1932, r/u 1931
Oth	Austrian Amateur 1937. Czechoslovakian Amateur 1937
Reg	Surrey Amateur 1931–49
Int	Walker Cup 1932. England (Home Int) 1931

Deeble, Peter George
Born Alnwick on 27th February, 1954

Cls	Alnmouth, Alnwick, Ponteland (Hon), Hexham (Hon), Rothbury (Hon), Washington (Hon), Tynedale (Hon)
Nat	English Amateur 1976–80
Trn	Antlers Royal Mid–Surrey 1976. Lytham Trophy 1977. Berkhamsted Trophy 1975. County Champion of Champions 1982
Reg	Northumberland Amateur 1975–82–83. Northumberland Stroke Play 1973–75–77–78–79. Northumberland and Durham Open 1976

Int	Walker Cup 1977–81. GB v Europe 1978. Europe v South America 1980. GB in Colombian International 1978. England (Home Int) 1975–76–77–78–80–81–83; (Eur T Ch) 1979–81; v Scotland 1979; v France 1982. England in Fiat Trophy 1980
Jun	
Int	Boys 1970–71. Youths 1973–75–76

Deighton, Dr FWG
Born Glasgow on 21st May, 1927

Cls	Royal & Ancient, Western Gailes, Elie, Glasgow, Hilton Park (Hon), North Hants
Nat	Scottish Amateur 1956–59
Trn	Edward Trophy 1954. Gleneagles Silver Tassie 1956. Tennant Cup 1958–60–64
Oth	Boyd Quaich 1947 (tied). Royal & Ancient Silver Cross 1953–60–63–70–73. Royal Medal 1956–59–61–63–66–73. Glennie Medal 1956–58–59–60–66–70–73
Reg	West of Scotland Amateur 1959. Dunbartonshire Amateur 1949–50–53–54. Glasgow Amateur 1951–55
Int	Walker Cup 1951–57. GB Commonwealth Team 1954–59. GB v Professionals 1956–57. Scotland (Home Int) 1950–52–53–56–58–59–60; v South Africa 1954; v New Zealand 1954; v Scandinavia 1956
Mis	Member of British Touring Team to South Africa 1952

Dobson, Helen
Cls	Seacroft
Chp	Ladies British Open Amateur 1989
Nat	Ladies British Open Amateur Stroke Play 1989
Int	Vagliano Trophy 1989; England (Home Int) 1987–88–89; (Eur L T Ch) 1989
Jun	British Girls 1987; English Girls 1988
Int	English Girls 1988

Dodd, Stephen
Born Cardiff, on 15th July, 1966

Cls	Brynhill
Chp	Amateur Champion 1989
Nat	Welsh Amateur 1989
Trn	Silver Dragon, WI Tucker Trophy 1987; Duncan Putter, Carad Trophy, Cardiff Feathers, Golden Lamp 1988
Int	Walker Cup 1989; Wales (Home Int) 1985–87–88–89; (Eur T Ch) 1987

Douglas, Kitrina
Born Bristol on 6th September, 1960. Turned Professional 1984

Chp	British Ladies 1982
Oth	Portuguese Champion 1983
Trn	Critchley Salver 1983
Reg	Gloucestershire Champion 1980–81–82–83–84
Int	Curtis Cup 1982. Vagliano Trophy 1983. England (Home Int) 1981–82. Eur L T Ch 1983
Jun	Scottish Girls Stroke–Play 1981
Eur	Ford Classic, Swedish Ladies Open, Rookie of the Year 1984; Mitsubishi Colt Cars, Jersey Open 1986; Hennessy-Cognac Ladies Cup 1987; St Moritz Ladies Classic, Godiva European Masters 1989

Dowling, Deborah
Born Wimbledon on 26th July, 1962. Turned Professional 1981

Reg	Surrey Champion 1980
Int	England (Home Int) 1981 (Eur L T Ch) 1981
Eur	Jersey Open, Woodhall Hills 1983. Portuguese Ladies Open 1985. Eastleigh Classic 1986. Laing Ladies Classic 1986. Blour Homes Eastleigh Classic 1989

Downes, Paul
Born Coventry on 27th September, 1959

Cls	Coventry (Hon)
Nat	English Amateur 1978. English Amateur Stroke Play 1982
Trn	Berkshire Trophy 1980
Oth	Leading Amateur Malaysian Dunlop Masters 1977. Leading Amateur Singapore Open Championship 1978
Reg	Midland Open Amateur Stroke Play 1976–77–80. Warwickshire Match Play 1977–82. Warwickshire Open 1982
Int	England (Home Int) 1976–77–78–80–81–82; (Eur T Ch) 1977–79–81. GB v Europe 1980
Jun	
Int	Boys 1974–75–76–77. Youths 1976–77–78–79–80–81

Drew , Norman Vico
Born Belfast on 25th May, 1932. Turned Professional 1958

PRO	
Trn	Yorkshire Evening News, Irish Dunlop 1959
Oth	Irish Professional 1959; Ulster Professional 1966–72
Int	Ryder Cup 1959; Ireland in World Cup 1960–61
AM	
Nat	Irish Open Amateur 1952–53
Reg	North of Ireland Open Amateur 1950–52; East of Ireland Open Amateur 1952
Int	Walker Cup 1953; Ireland (Home Int) 1952–53

Duncan, Colonel Anthony Arthur, OBE
Born Cardiff on 10th December, 1914

Cls	Royal & Ancient, Southerndown, Hindhead, Royal Porthcawl
Chp	Amateur r/u 1939.
Nat	Welsh Amateur 1938–48–52–54, r/u 1933
Trn	Worplesdon Mixed Foursomes 1946–47. Hampshire Hog 1936. President's Putter 1948–58
Int	Walker Cup **1953**. Wales (Home Int) 1933–34–36–38–47–48–**49**–50–51–52–53–54–55–56–57–**58**–59
Mis	Chairman Walker Cup Selection Committee 1954–55. Won all six matches in 1956 Home Internationals. President Oxford and Cambridge Golfing Society 1979–83

Easingwood, Stephen
Born Edinburgh on 23rd June 1965

Cls	Dunbar, Winterfield
Nat	Scottish Amateur Stroke Play 1988
Trn	Edward Trophy 1987
Reg	Lothians Champion 1985, South-East District Champion 1987–88, Craigmillar Park Open 1986
Int	Scotland (Home Int) 1986–87–88; v France 1987; v Italy 1988
Jun	Scottish Boys v England 1982. Scottish Youths 1983–86
Mis	Braid Panton Trophy 1989

Eggo, Bobby
Born 5th July, 1961

Nat	English Amateur Stroke Play 1988
Trn	Hampshire Hog 1986. Golf Illustrated Gold Vase 1986
Reg	Channel Islands Amateur 1984
Int	Walker Cup 1987. England (Home Int) 1986–87–88; v France 1988. (GBI) v Europe 1988

Evans, Albert David
Born Newton, Brecon, South Wales on 28th August, 1911

Cls	Royal & Ancient, Royal Porthcawl. Hon member of Brecon, Ross-on-Wye, Hereford, Worcestershire, Builth Wells, Pennard, Monmouth, Killarney
Chp	Welsh Amateur 1949–61
Reg	Herefordshire Amateur 1938–46–49–51–53–54–55–59–60–61–62. Breconshire Amateur 1929–31–32–33–34–37
Int	Wales (Home Int) 1931–32–33–34–35–38–39–47–48–49–50–51–52–53–54–55–56,–**60**–**61**–**62**–**63**–**64**–**65**; v Australia 1954
Mis	Walker Cup Selector 1964–75

Evans, Duncan
Born Crewe on 23rd January, 1959

Cls	Leek (Hon), Conway (Hon), Holyhead (Hon), Royal Porthcawl (Hon), Westwood (Hon)
Chp	Amateur 1980.
Nat	Welsh Amateur Stroke Play Championship 1981, r/u 1980
Reg	Staffordshire Amateur 1979. Aberconwy Trophy 1981
Int	GB v Europe. Europe v South America 1980. Wales (Home Int) 1978–80; v Ireland 1979; in Fiat Trophy 1980. Walker Cup 1981; (Eur T Ch) 1981
Jun	
Int	Youths 1980

Evans, Hugh
Born Swansea on 19th May, 1957

Cls	Langland Bay
Nat	Welsh Amateur Stroke Play 1978
Trn	Duncan Putter 1979
Reg	Glamorgan County Champion 1978
Int	Wales (Home Int) 1976–77–78–79–80–81–84–85–87–88; (Eur Team Ch) 1979–81
Mis	Glamorgan County 1974 to 82; **83**–84–**85**–86–87–88

Everard, Mrs D Mary
Born Sheffield on 8th October, 1942

Cls	Hallamshire (Hon), Woodhall Spa (Hon), Kilton Forest (Hon), Lindrick
Maj	Ladies British Open r/u 1977
Chp	Ladies British Open Amateur r/u 1967
Nat	Ladies British Open Amateur Stroke Play 1970–77, r/u 1971–73; English Ladies 1972, r/u 1964–77
Trn	Astor Salver 1967–68–78. Hovis Ladies 1967. Roehampton Gold Cup 1970. Sunningdale Foursomes 1973. Hoylake Mixed Foursomes 1965–67–71–76. Avia Foursomes 1978
Reg	North of England Ladies 1972. Yorkshire Ladies 1964–67–72–73–77
Int	Curtis Cup 1070–72–74 78. Vagliano Trophy 1967–69–71–73. GB Commonwealth Team 1971. World Team Championship 1968–**72**–78, England (Home Int) 1964–67–70–72–73–77–78; (Eur LT Ch) 1967–71–73–77
Mis	Member of British team to tour Australia 1973. Captain English team to tour Kenya 1973

Faldo, Nicholas Alexander, MBE
Born Welwyn Garden City on 18th July, 1957. Turned Professional 1976

PRO	
Maj	Open Champion 1987; 3rd 1988; US Open r/u 1988 (tied); US Masters 1989
Eur	Colgate PGA 1978; Sun Alliance PGA 1980; Sun Alliance 1981; Haig Whisky TPC 1982; French Open, Martini International, Lawrence Batley International, Car Care Plan International, Ebel Swiss Open European Masters 1983; Car Care Plan

International 1984; Peugeot Spanish Open 1987;
Peugeot French Open, Volvo Masters 1988; Volvo
PGA, Dunhill British Masters, Peugeot French
Open, Suntory World Match Play 1989

US Heritage Classic 1984
RoW ICL International 1979
Oth Skol Lager 1977
Int Ryder Cup 1977–79–81–83–85–87–89; Nissan Cup
1986; Kirin Cup 1987–88; GBI v Europe 1978–80–82–84;
England in World Cup 1977; in Double Diamond 1977;
in Dunhill Cup 1985–86–87 (winners)–88
Mis Rookie of the Year 1977; Harry Vardon Trophy
1983; AGW Trophy 1983; Braid-Taylor Memorial
Medal 1983–84–87–88; BBC Sports Personality of the
Year 1989

AM
Nat English Amateur 1975
Trn Berkshire Trophy, Scrutton Jug, County Champion
of Champions 1975
Reg Hertfordshire Amateur 1975
Oth South African GU Special Stroke Chp 1975
Int GB Commonwealth Trn 1975; England (Home Int) 1975
Jun British Youths 1975
Int Boys 1974; Youths 1975

Faulkner, Max
*Born Bexhill, Sussex on 29th July, 1916. Turned
Professional June 1933*

Maj Open Champion 1951
Eur Spanish Open 1952–53–57. Portuguese Open 1968
Trn Dunlop Southport 1946. Dunlop 1949–52. Penfold
Foursomes 1949. Lotus 1949. Dunlop Masters 1951.
PGA Match Play 1953. Irish Hospitals 1959
Reg West of England Open Professional 1947.
Southern England Professional 1964.
Oth Sunningdale Open Foursomes 1964; Pringle
Seniors 1968–70
Int Ryder Cup 1947–49–51–53–57

Feherty, David
*Born in Bangor, NI on 13th August, 1958. Turned
Professional 1976*

Eur Italian Open, Bells Scottish Open 1986;
BMW International Open 1989
RoW ICL International 1984; Lexington PGA 1988
Int Ireland; Dunhill Cup 1986
Mis Braid-Taylor Memorial Medal 1989

Ferguson, Marjory (née Fowler)
Born North Berwick on 15th May, 1937

Cls North Berwick, Gullane, Killarney (Hon)
Nat Scottish Ladies r/u 1966–71
Oth Portuguese Ladies 1960
Reg East of Scotland Ladies 1959–60–62–75. East Lothian
Ladies 1957–58–59–60–61–62–63–64–66–67–69–74–81
Int Curtis Cup 1966. Vagliano Trophy 1965. Scotland
(Home Int) 1959–62–63–64–65–66–67–69–70;
(Eur L T Ch) 1965–67–71

Le Feuvre, Carol
See Gibbs

Fiddian, Eric Westwood
Born Stourbridge on 28th March, 1910

Cls Stourbridge, Handsworth, Lindrick
Chp Amateur r/u 1932.
Nat English Amateur 1932, r/u 1935. Irish Open
Amateur r/u 1933

Reg Worcestershire Amateur 1928–30–50. Midland
Counties 1931
Int Walker Cup 1932–34. England (Home Int) 1929–30–
31–32–33–34–35
Jun Boys 1927.
Int English Boys 1926–27
Mis Had two holes–in–one in the Final of 1933 Irish
Open Amateur

Fishwick, Diana Lesley
See Critchley

Foster, Rodney
Born Shipley, Yorkshire on 13th October, 1941

Cls Royal & Ancient Hon member of Bradford, Halifax,
Leeds, West Bowling, Ilkley, East Bierley
Chp Amateur s/f 1962–65
Nat English Amateur r/u 1964. English Open Amateur
Stroke Play 1969 (tied)–70, r/u 1965
Trn Berkshire Trophy 1964. Lytham Trophy 1967–68.
County Champion of Champions 1963 (tied)
Reg Yorkshire Amateur 1963–64–65–67–70
Int Walker Cup 1965–67–69–71–73 **(79)**. GB v Europe
1964–66–68–70–**(80)**. Eisenhower Trophy 1964–70–
(80). GB Commonwealth Team 1967–71. England
(Home Int) 1963–64–66–67–68–69–70–71–72–**(76)**–**(77)**–
(78); (Eur T Ch) 1963–65–67–69–71–73–**(77)**
Jun
Int Boys 1958. Youths 1959

Fowler, Marjory
See Ferguson

Francis, Craig
Born London on 18th March, 1950

Cls Sunningdale, Lyford Cay, Geneva, Lausanne
Oth Luxembourg Amateur 1972–75–82. Swiss Amateur
1973–74–77. Swiss Amateur Stroke Play 1982. Belgian
Amateur 1975. Italian Amateur 1982, r/u 1972–81. Dutch
Amateur r/u 1976

Frearson, Diane
See Bailey

Furby, Joanne
Born 13th May 1969. Turned Professional 1989

Cls Masham
Chp British Ladies 1988
Nat English Ladies 1987.
Reg Yorkshire Ladies 1988
Int England (Home Int) 1987–88; (Eur L T Ch) 1987

Gallacher, Bernard
*Born Bathgate on 9th February, 1949. Turned Professional
1967*

PRO
Eur Spanish Open 1977; French Open 1979
Trn Schweppes, Wills 1969; Martini International 1971;
Carrolls International, Dunlop Masters 1974; Dunlop
Masters 1975; Tournament Players Chp 1980;
Greater Manchester Open 1981; Martini
International; Jersey Open 1982; Jersey Open 1984
Oth Scottish Professional 1971–73–74–77; Coca-Cola
Young Professionals 1973
RoW Zambia Eagle Open, Zambia Cock o' the North 1969;
Mufulira Open 1970

Int   Ryder Cup 1969–71–73–75–77–79–81–83; Hennessy-Cognac Cup 1974–78–82–84; Scotland in World Cup 1969–71–74–82–83; in Double Diamond 1971–72–73–74–75–76–77; v South Africa 1976

Mis   Rookie of the Year 1968; Harry Vardon Trophy 1969 (then youngest winner); Scottish Sportsman of the Year 1969; Frank Moran Trophy 1973

AM

Nat   Scottish Open Amateur Stroke Play 1967

Int   Scotland (Home Int) 1967

Jun

Int   Boys 1965–66

Gannon, Mark Andrew
Born Drogheda, Ireland on 15th July, 1952

Cls   Co Louth (Hon)

Nat   Irish Amateur 1977, r/u 1974–79

Trn   Mullingar Trophy 1973

Reg   South of Ireland Open Amateur 1973. West of Ireland Open Amateur 1974. East of Ireland Open Amateur 1978

Int   GB v Europe 1974–78. Ireland (Home Int) 1973–74–77–78–80; (Eur T Ch) 1979–81; v France, West Germany and Sweden 1978–80; in Fiat Trophy 1979

Jun   Irish Boys 1968. Irish Youths 1971–72.

Int   Youths 1971

Garner, Maureen (*née* Madill)
Born Coleraine, Co Derry on 1st February, 1958. Turned Professional 1986

Cls   Hon member of Portstewart, Royal Portrush, Milltown, Co Down, Brancepeth Castle, Delamere Forest

Chp Ladies British Amateur 1979

Nat   Ladies British Open Amateur Stroke Play 1980. Irish Foursomes 1980

Maj Avia Foursomes 1980–85.

Reg   North–West Scratch Cup 1978. Ulster Ladies 1980

Int   Curtis Cup 1980. Vagliano Trophy 1979–81–85. GB Commonwealth Team 1979. World Team Championship 1980. Ireland (Home Int) 1978–79–80–81–82–83; (Eur LT Ch) 1979–81–83

Jun

Int   Girls 1972–73–74–75–76

Garrett, Maureen (*née* Ruttle)
Born 22nd August, 1922

Oth   French Ladies 1964

Int   Curtis Cup 1960. England (Home Int) 1960. Vagliano Trophy 1961

Mis   LGU President 1982–85. Bobby Jones Award 1983

Garvey, Philomena K
Born Drogheda, Co Louth on 26th April, 1927. Turned Professional 1964, subsequently reinstated Amateur

Cls   Co Down, Co Louth, Portrush, Milltown

Chp British Ladies 1957, r/u 1946–53–60–63.

Nat   Irish Ladies 1946–47–48–50–51–53–54–55–57–58–59–60–62–63–70

Trn   Worplesdon Mixed Foursomes 1955

Reg   Munster Ladies 1951

Int   Curtis Cup 1948–50–52–54–56–60. GB v France 1949–51–53–55; v Belgium 1951–53. Vagliano Trophy 1959–63. Ireland (Home Int) 1947–48–49–50–51–52–53–54–55–56–59–60–61–62–63–69; v Australia 1950

Mis   Quarter-finalist US Ladies 1950.

Gemmill, Alison
Born 13th September, 1958

Nat   Scottish Ladies 1981–85

Trn   Helen Holm Trophy 1988

Reg   Ayrshire Champion 1980–81–82–83–84–86

Int   Scotland (Home Int) 1981–82–84–85–86–87–88–89; (Eur L T Ch) 1981

Jun   Scottish Girls Stroke–play 1979

Gibbs, Carol (*née* Le Feuvre)
Born Jersey on 18th October, 1951

Cls   Jersey, Lee–on–the–Solent

Nat   English Ladies r/u 1973

Oth   Dutch Ladies 1972

Trn   Avia Foursomes 1974

Reg   Jersey Ladies 1966-67-68. Hampshire Ladies 1970-71-72-73-74-76. South-Eastern Ladies 1974

Int   Curtis Cup 1974. Vagliano Trophy 1973. England (Home Int) 1971–72–73–74; (Eur LT Ch) 1973

Jun   English Girls 1969–70. British Girls 1970.

Int   English Girls 1968–69–70

Mis   Member of LGU Team to tour Australia 1973, and Under–25 team to tour Canada 1973

Gilford, David
Born 14th September, 1965. Turned Professional 1986

PRO

Oth   Silvermere Satellite Trophy 1987

AM

Nat   English Amateur 1984

Trn   Lagonda Trophy 1986

Int   Walker Cup 1985. GB v Europe 1986. England (Home Int) 1983–84–85

Jun   British Youths 1986. Carris Trophy 1981

Girvan, Paul
Born Ayr on 2nd October, 1965. Turned Professional 1988

Reg   Ayrshire Champion 1985

Int   Walker Cup 1987. Scotland (Home Int) 1986

Glover, John
Born Belfast on 3rd March, 1933

Cls   Killarney (Hon), New Club, St Andrews

Trn   Formby Hare 1963

Oth   British Universities 1954–55

Reg   Lancashire Amateur 1970

Int   Ireland (Home Int) 1951–52–53–55–59–60–62–70

Jun   Boy Champion 1950. Carris Trophy 1950

Mis   Secretary Royal & Ancient Rules of Golf Committee

Godwin, Geoffrey Frank
Born Wanstead on 28th July, 1950

Cls   Thorndon Park

Trn   St George's Challenge Cup 1979. Prince of Wales Challenge Cup 1979. Hampshire Hog 1978

Reg   Essex Amateur 1978–80

Int   Walker Cup 1979–81. Europe v South America 1978. England (Home Int) 1976–77–78–80–81; (Eur T Ch) 1979–81; v Scotland 1979; v France 1982

Gorry, Mary Philomena
Born Baltinglass, Co Wicklow on 11th June, 1952

Cls   Baltinglass (Hon), Grange (Hon)

Nat   Irish Ladies 1975–78

Trn   Hermitage Scratch Cup 1978

Reg   South of Ireland Scratch Cup 1975–78–80. Irish
        Midland Ladies 1974–79. Leinster Ladies 1977–79.
        Ulster Ladies 1979. Connaught Ladies 1979
Int   Vagliano Trophy 1977. Ireland (Home Int)1971–72–
        73–74–75–76–77–78–79–80–**88**; (Eur LT Ch) 1971–73–
        75–77–79; in Fiat Trophy 1978
Jun
Int   Girls 1970
Mis   Irish Lady Golfer of the Year 1977–78. Non–play-
        ing captain of Irish team for European Ladies' Junior
        Championship 1983

Gourlay, Miss Mary Perceval (Molly), OBE
Born Kempshott Park, Basingstoke on 14th May, 1898

Cls   Hon member of Camberley Heath, Temple,
        Basingstoke, Dorset, Sunningdale Ladies,
        Beaconsfield, Winchester, Maccauvlei, Bastad
Nat   English Ladies 1926–29, r/u 1931
Trn   Worplesdon Mixed Foursomes 1929–30–34
Eur   French Ladies 1923–28–29. Belgian Ladies 1925–26.
        Swedish Ladies 1932–36–39
Oth   Veteran Ladies 1962
Reg   Surrey Ladies 1923–26–27–31–33–34–38
Int   Curtis Cup 1932–34. GB v Canada 1934; v
        France 1931–32–33–39. England (Home Int)
        1923–24–27–28–29–31–32–33–34
Mis   Member LGU team to tour South Africa 1933. Non–
        playing captain English Ladies 1957. Chairman
        LGU 1957–58–59. President ELGA 1963–65. Retired
        from playing aged 73 when handicap was 4

Green, Charles Wilson
Born Dumbarton on 2nd August, 1932

Cls   Dumbarton, Cardross, Helensburgh
Maj   Leading amateur in Open 1962
Nat   Scottish Amateur 1970–82–83, r/u 1971–80. Scottish
        Open Amateur Stroke Play 1975, 1984, r/u 1967–83.
        British Seniors 1988
Trn   Lytham Trophy 1970 (tied)–74.
        Eden Tournament 1959. Tennant Cup 1968–70–75.
        Edward Trophy 1968–73–74–75
Reg   West of Scotland Amateur 1962–70–79.
        Dunbartonshire Amateur 1960–67–68–73–77.
        Dunbartonshire Match Play 1965–67–69–71–74.
        Glasgow Amateur 1979
Int   Walker Cup 1963–69–71–73–75–(**83**)–(**85**);
        GB v Scandinavia 1962; v Europe 1962–66–68–70–
        72–74–76. Eisenhower Trophy 1970–**72**–84–86. GB
        Commonwealth Team 1971. Scotland (Home Int)
        1961–62–63–64–65–67–68–69–70–71–72–73–74–75–76–
        77–78–(**80**); v Australia 1964; (Eur T Ch) 1965–
        67–69–71–73–75–77–**79**–81–83; v Belgium 1973–
        75–77–78; v Spain 1977; v Italy 1979; v England
        1979
Mis   Frank Moran Trophy 1974. British Selector 1980.
        Scottish Sports Photographer Award 1983

Greenhalgh, Julia
Born Bolton on 6th January, 1941

Cls   Hon member of Pleasington, Killarney, Ganton,
        Hermitage
Chp   Ladies British Open Amateur r/u 1978
Nat   British Ladies Stroke Play 1974–75. Runner–up British
        English Ladies 1966–79. Welsh Ladies Open Amateur
        Stroke Play 1977
Trn   Astor Salver 1969–79. Hermitage Cup 1977.
        Hampshire Rose 1977. Sunningdale Foursomes 1978
Oth   New Zealand Ladies 1963
Reg   Lancashire Ladies 1961–62–66–68–73–75–76–77–78.
        Northern Ladies 1961–62

Int   Curtis Cup 1964–70–74–76–78. Vagliano Trophy
        1961–65–75–77. GB Commonwealth Team 1963–75.
        World Team 1970–**74**–78. England (Home Int)
        1960–61–63–66–69–70–71–76–77–78; (Eur L T Ch)
        1971–75–77–79
Jun   Scottish Girls Open Stroke Play 1960. Girl
        International 1957–58–59
Mis   Leading Amateur (4th) in Australian Wills Ladies
        Open Stroke Play 1974. Daks Woman Golfer of the
        Year 1974. Taunton Trophy 1975–77. Doris Chambers
        Trophy 1977

Gregson, Malcolm Edward
*Born Leicester on 15th August, 1943. Turned Professional
1961*

Trn   Schweppes 1967. RTV 1967. Daks 1967–68.
        Martini 1967 (tied). Sumrie 1972
RoW   Zambia Cock o' the North 1974. Gambian Open 1981
Oth   Pannal Foursomes 1964. British Assistants 1964
Int   Ryder Cup 1967. England in World Cup 1967. England
        1967. GB v France 1966. Sumrie 1972 England in
        Double Diamond 1975
Mis   Harry Vardon Trophy 1967
Am   Boy International 1959–60

Greig, David G
Born Broughty Ferry on 24th January, 1950

Cls   Carnoustie (Hon), Caledonia
Nat   Scottish Amateur 1975
Oth   Boyd Quaich 1972. British Universities Stroke Play
        1969
Reg   Angus Stroke Play 1978. Angus Match Play 1978.
        Scottish Counties Champion of Champions 1978. East
        of Scotland Open Amateur 1980
Int   GB Commonwealth Team 1975. Scotland (Home Int)
        1972–73–75
Jun   Scottish Boys 1967. Boy International 1967. Youth
        International 1969–71

Grice–Whittaker, Penny
*Born Sheffield on 11th September, 1964. Turned
Professional 1985*

Nat   English Intermediate Champion 1984. English
        Stroke–Play 1984
Reg   Yorkshire Champion 1981–82–83. Northern
        Foursomes 1984
Int   Curtis Cup 1984. England (Home Int) 1983–84. (Eur L
        T Ch) 1983. Curtis Cup 1984. Vilmorin Trophy 1984.
        Espirito Santo 1984
Jun   English Girls 1983
Eur   Belgian Open 1986

Hall, Julia (née Wade)

Cls   Felixstowe Ferry
Nat   English Ladies Stroke Play 1987; English Ladies
        1988, r/u British Ladies Amateur Stroke Play 1988
Oth   World Fourball Chp with Helen Wadsworth 1987
Trn   Sunningdale Foursomes with V Thomas
Int   Curtis Cup 1988; England (Home Int) 1987–88–89,
        (Eur L T Ch) 1987–89; GBI Espirito Santo 1988,
        Vagliano Trophy 1989

Hargreaves, Jack
*Born Fleetwood on 12th February, 1914. Turned
Professional 1930*

Maj   Open 3rd 1948
Trn   Spalding 1951. Swallow–Harrogate 1953. Goodwin
        Foursomes 1953
Reg   Midland Professional 1952–60

Int Ryder Cup 1951
Mis Secretary Midland PGA. Captain PGA 1977

Harris, Marley [Spearman] (née Baker)
Born on 11th January, 1928

Cls Sudbury
Chp British Ladies 1961–62.
Nat English Ladies 1964
Trn Sunningdale Foursomes 1965. Kayser–Bondor Foursomes 1958 (tied). Casa Pupo Foursomes 1965. Worplesdon Mixed Foursomes r/u 1956–64. Roehampton Gold Cup 1965. Astor Salver 1964–65. Astor Princes' Trophy 1964–65. Hovis Ladies 1965. Spalding Ladies 1956. London Ladies Foursomes 1960
RoW New Zealand Ladies Stroke Play 1963
Reg Middlesex Ladies 1955–56–57–58–59–61–64–65. South–East Ladies 1956–58–61
Int Curtis Cup 1960–62–64. Vagliano Trophy 1959–61. GB Commonwealth Team 1959–63. England (Home Int) 1955 to 65
Mis AGW Trophy 1962. Non-playing captain English Team European Team Championship 1971

Hastings, Joan
See Rennie

Hastings, Dorothea (née Sommerville)
Born Glasgow on 21st June, 1934

Cls Haggs Castle (Hon), Troon Ladies (Hon), Erskine
Nat Scottish Ladies 1958, r/u 1960
Reg West of Scotland Ladies 1961. Renfrewshire Ladies 1956–57–58–59–61–63–83
Int Curtis Cup 1958. Vagliano Trophy 1963. Scotland (Home Int) 1955 to 63
Jun Junior International 1953. Junior Tour of Australasia 1955

Hawksworth, John
Born 27th March, 1961. Turned Professional 1986

PRO
Trn Peugeot-Talbot Assistants Championship 1987. Broadstone Satellite 1988
AM
Trn Berkhamsted Trophy 1983. Hampshire Hog 1984. Lytham Trophy 1984
Int Walker Cup 1985. England (Home Int) 1984-85

Heathcoat–Amory, Lady
(née Joyce Wethered)
Born 17th November, 1901

Cls Worplesdon
Chp British Ladies 1922–24–25–29, r/u 1921.
Nat English Ladies 1920–21–22–23–24
Trn Worplesdon Mixed Foursomes 1922–23–27–28–31–32–33–36. Sunningdale Foursomes 1935–36
Reg Surrey Ladies 1921–22–24–29–32
Int Curtis Cup 1932. GB v France 1931. England (Home Int) 1921–22–23–24–25–29
Mis Forfeited Amateur status and toured USA in 1935. Reinstated as Amateur after the war

Hedges, Peter J
Born 30th March, 1947

Cls Langley Park (Hon), Royal Cinque Ports, Addington, Wildernesse, Royal & Ancient
Nat English Open Amateur Stroke Play 1976
Trn Royal St George's Challenge Cup 1970. Prince of Wales Challenge Cup 1972–73–74–77. Berkshire Trophy 1973–76–78. Golf Illustrated Gold Vase 1974. Scrutton Jug 1976

Reg Kent Amateur 1968–71–79. Kent Open 1970–74
Int Walker Cup 1973–75. GB v Europe 1974-76 Eisenhower Trophy 1974. England (Home Int) 1970–73–74–75–76–77–78–82; (Eur T Ch) 1973–75–77
Jun Youth International 1968
Mis Member of European Team to tour South Africa 1974

Hedges, Susan Claire (née Whitlock)
Born Beckenham, Kent on 8th May, 1947

Cls Wrotham Heath (Hon), Royal Cinque Ports, Langley Park
Maj Ladies British Open 3rd 1979
Nat Welsh Ladies Open Amateur Stroke Play 1978. English Ladies r/u 1979
Oth Belgian Ladies 1974. Luxembourg Ladies 1976–77. Zaire Ladies 1980
Reg Kent Ladies 1976–79; Central England Mixed Foursomes 1977–81; Hoylake Mixed Foursomes 1982
Int Vagliano Trophy 1979. GB Commonwealth Team 1979. England (Home Int) 1979; (Eur L T Ch) 1979
Mis Smyth Salver 1979

Henson, Dinah (née Oxley)
Born Dorking on 17th October, 1948

Cls West Byfleet (Hon), Killarney (Hon), Fairfield, US (Hon)
Chp British Ladies 1970.
Nat English Ladies 1970-71, r/u 1968. British Ladies Stroke Play r/u 1969
Maj Wills Ladies 1969–70–71. Worplesdon Mixed Foursomes 1968–77. Newmark International 1975 (tied)–77
Reg Surrey Ladies 1967–70–71–76
Int Curtis Cup 1968–70–72–76. Vagliano Trophy 1967–69–71. World Team 1970. GB Commonwealth Team 1967–71. England (Home Int) 1967–68–69–70–75–76–77–78; (Eur L T Ch) 1971–77
Jun British Girls 1963. English Girls 1965. French Girls 1969. Girl International 1964–65–66
Mis Daks Woman Golfer of the Year 1970. Leading Amateur Colgate European Ladies Open 1974

Hetherington, Jean (née McClure)
See Holmes

Hill, George Alec, DSO
Born Northwood, Middlesex in 1908

Cls Royal & Ancient, Royal St George's, Hon Company of Edinburgh Golfers, Sandy Lodge
Int Walker Cup 1936–(55). England (Home Int) 1936–37
Jun Boy International 1926
Mis Chairman R & A Championship Committee 1955. Chairman Rules of Golf Committee 1958–59. Captain Royal & Ancient 1964–65

Hoey, T Brian C

Nat Irish Amateur 1984
Reg North of Ireland Amateur 1979–83
Int Ireland (Home Int) 1970–71–72–73–77–84

Holmes, Jean [Hetherington] (née McClure)
Born Wanstead, Essex on 17th August, 1923

Cls Wanstead, Hunstanton, Thorndon Park
Chp British Ladies 1946, r/u 1958.
Nat English Ladies 1966

Reg Nottinghamshire Ladies 1949-50-51.
Essex Ladies 1956-57
Int England (Home Int) 1957–66–(67)

Homer, Trevor Walter Brian
Born Bloxwich on 8th September, 1943. Turned Professional July 1974. Reinstated as Amateur in 1978

Chp Amateur Champion 1972–74
Trn Leicestershire Fox 1972. Harlech Gold Cross 1970
Int Walker Cup 1973. Eisenhower Trophy 1972. GB v Europe 1972. England (Home Int) 1972–73; (Eur T Ch) 1973

Hope, Miss Lesley Alexandra
Born Gullane, East Lothian on 22nd May, 1955

Cls Gullane Ladies, Catterick
Nat Scottish Ladies Amateur 1975, r/u 1979
Reg East of Scotland Ladies 1977–78
Int Scotland (Home Int) 1975–76–80–84–85–86–87–(88); (Eur LT Ch) 1975–77–79; in Fiat Trophy 1979

Horton, Tommy
Born St Helens, on 16th June, 1941. Turned Professional 1957

Trn RTV 1968. PGA Match Play 1970. Gallaher Ulster 1971. Piccadilly 1972. Penfold 1974. Uniroyal International 1976. Dunlop Masters 1978
RoW South African Open 1970. Nigerian Open 1973. Zambian Open 1977. Tobago Open 1975. Gambian Open 1975
Int Ryder Cup 1975–77. GB v France 1966. England in World Cup 1976. England in Double Diamond 1971–74–75–76–77. GB v Europe 1974–76
Mis Second in Order of Merit 1967. PGA Captain 1978; Braid-Taylor Memorial Medal 1976–77

Hourihane, Claire
Born 18th February, 1958

Cls Woodbrook
Nat Irish Ladies 1983–84–85. British Ladies Stroke Play 1986
Trn Hampshire Rose 1986. South Atlantic (USA) 1983
Reg South Ireland Cup 1977. Leinster Ladies 1980
Int Curtis Cup 1984–86–88. Vagliano Trophy 1981–83– 85–87. Ireland (Home Int) 1979–80–81–82–83–84–85– 86–87–88. (Eur LT Ch) 1981–83–85–87

Howard, Ann (née Phillips)
Born Prestwich on 22nd October, 1934

Cls Whitefield (Hon), Royal Birkdale, Castletown
Oth Danish Ladies 1955
Reg Lancashire Ladies 1957. Manx Ladies 1977–78
Int Curtis Cup 1956–68. GB v France and Belgium 1955–57. England (Home Int) 1953–54–55–56–(79)–(80). Senior European (1981)
Jun British Girls 1952

Huggan, Shirley Margaret (née Lawson)
Born Glasgow on 16th September, 1964

Cls Eastwood, Rock Ridge, USA
Nat Scottish Ladies Amateur 1988–89; Taunton Trophy 1987
Reg West of Scotland Ladies 1986–88; Renfrewshire Ladies 1985–86–87–88
Int Curtis Cup 1988; Scotland (Home Int) 1985–86–87– 88–89; (Eur LT Ch) 1985–87–89; GBI Vagliano Trophy 1989

Jun Scottish Girls 1982; Scottish Girls Stroke Play 1983–84
Int Girls 1980–81–82

Huggett, Brian George Charles, MBE
Born Porthcawl on 18th November, 1936. Turned Professional 1951

Maj Open r/u 1965. 3rd 1962
Eur Dutch Open 1962. German Open 1963. Portuguese Open 1974
Trn Cox–Moore 1963. Smart–Weston 1965. Sumrie 1968–72. PGA Close 1967. Martini 1967 (tied)–68. Shell Winter Tournament 1967–68. PGA Match Play 1968, r/u 1977. Daks 1969–71 (tied). Bowmaker 1969 (tied). Carrolls 1970. Dunlop Masters 1970. British Airways–Avis 1978
RoW Singapore International 1962. Algarve Open 1970
Oth Sunningdale Foursomes 1957. British Assistants 1958. Gleneagles Pro–Am 1961 65. Turnberry Pro–Am 1968. Welsh Professional 1978
Reg East Anglian Open 1962–67
Int Ryder Cup 1963–64–65–68–69–70–71–76–79. Wales in World Cup 1963–64–65–68–69–70–71–76–79. Wales in Double Diamond 1971–72–73–74–75–76–77. GB v Europe 1974–78
Mis Vardon Trophy 1968. European American Express 1972

Hughes, Ann
See Johnson

Huke, Beverly Joan Mary
Born Great Yarmouth on 10th May, 1951. Turned Professional 1978

Cls Cotswold Hills (Hon), Windmill Hill (Hon), Leighton Buzzard, Panmure Barry
Chp British Ladies r/u 1971.
Nat English Ladies 1975
Trn Roehampton Gold Cup 1971. Renfrew Rose Bowl 1976–77–78. Helen Holm Trophy 1977
Reg Gloucestershire Ladies 1972. Angus Ladies 1976
Int Curtis Cup 1972. Vagliano Trophy 1971–75. England (Home Int) 1971–72–75–76–77; (Eur L T Ch) 1975–77
Jun Scottish Girls Open Stroke Play 1970–71. Girl International 1966–67–68
Mis Chairman WPGET 1988
Eur Carlsberg (Ballater) 1979. Carlsberg (Rosemount) 1980. NABS Pro–Am 1st Pro Individual 1981. Brickendon Grange and Stourbridge Pro–Am 1983; Lark Valley Classic 1983 (shared); White Horse Whisky Challenge Trophy 1983. Trusthouse Forte Classic 1985. German Ladies Open 1984. Wester Volkswagen Classic 1986

Humphreys, Warren
Born Kingston, Surrey on 1st April, 1952. Turned Professional 1971

PRO
Eur Portuguese Open 1985
Mis Accles & Pollock Award 1972
AM
Nat English Amateur 1971
Trn Sunningdale Foursomes 1968; Antlers Royal Mid-Surrey 1969; Duncan Putter 1971; Lytham Trophy 1971
Int Walker Cup 1971; GB v Europe 1970; England (Home Int) 1970–71; (Eur T Ch) 1971
Jun
Int Boys 1967–68–69; Youths 1969–70–71

Hunt, Bernard John, MBE
Born Atherstone on 2nd February, 1930. Turned Professional 1946

Maj	Open 3rd 1960; leading British player (4th) 1964
Eur	Belgian Open 1957; German Open 1961; French Open 1967
Trn	Spalding, Goodwin Foursomes, Gleneagles-Saxone 1953; Goodwin Foursomes 1954; Irish Hospitals 1956; Bowmaker 1958 (shared); Martini, Daks 1961; Carrolls, Swallow–Penfold, Smart-Weston, Gevacolour, Dunlop Masters 1963; Rediffusion 1964; Dunlop Masters, Gallaher Ulster 1965; Piccadilly 1966; Gallaher Ulster 1967; Penfold, Sumrie, Agfacolor 1970; Wills 1971; Sumrie 1973
Reg	Southern England Professional 1959–60–62–67; West of England Open Professional 1960–61
Oth	British Assistants 1953; Algarve Open, BP Italy 1969
RoW	Egyptian Open 1956; Brazilian Open 1962
Int	Ryder Cup 1953–57–59–61–63–65–67–69–(73)–(75); England in World Cup 1958–59–60–62–63–64–68; in Double Diamond 1971–72–73
Mis	Harry Vardon Trophy 1958–60–65

Hutcheon, Ian C
Born Monifieth, Angus on 22nd February, 1942

Cls	Monifieth (Hon), Grange and Dundee (Hon)
Nat	Scottish Amateur 1973. Scottish Open Amateur Stroke Play 1971–74–79
Trn	Tennant Cup 1976. Lytham Trophy 1980. Scottish Champion of Champions 1980–81–86–88
Oth	North of Spain Stroke Play 1972
Reg	Scottish Central District Amateur 1972. Angus Match Play 1965–70–72. Angus Stroke Play 1968–71–72–74. North of Scotland District Amateur Stroke Play 1975–76–82
Int	GB v Europe 1974–76. Eisenhower Trophy 1974–76 (winners and joint winning individual)–80. Scotland (Home Int) 1971–72–73–74–75–76–77–78–80; (Eur T Ch) 1973–75–77–79–81; v Spain 1972–77; v Belgium 1973–75–77–78–80; v France 1978–80–81; v Italy 1979; in Fiat Trophy 1979. GB in Dominican International 1973. Walker Cup 1975–77–79–81. GB in Colombian International 1975. GB Commonwealth Team 1975
Mis	Frank Moran Trophy 1976

Imrie, Kathryn
Born Southend on 8th June 1967

Cls	Monifieth
Maj	Leading Amateur in Ladies British Open 1988 (Smyth Salver)
Trn	St Rule Trophy 1985; Riccarton Rosebowl 1985
Reg	Highland Open 1985; North of Scotland Ladies Amateur 1988; Northern Counties Ladies Open Stroke Play 1986–87–88–89; Angus Ladies 1982–83–84–85
Int	Vagliano Trophy 1989; Scotland (Home Int) 1984–88–89; (Eur L T Ch) 1987–89
Mis	Taunton Trophy 1986; winner of two NCAA events whilst at University of Arizona (1985–89)

Irvin, Ann Lesley
Born 11th April, 1943

Cls	Lytham (Hon), Lytham Green Drive (Hon)
Chp	British Ladies 1973, r/u 1969.
Nat	English Ladies 1967–74. British Ladies Stroke Play 1969.
Trn	Roehampton Gold Cup 1967–68–69–72–76. Hovis Ladies 1966–68–70. Avia Foursomes 1968

Reg	Northern Ladies 1963–64. Lancashire Ladies 1965–67–69–71–72–74. Northern Foursomes Championship 1973
Int	Curtis Cup 1962–68–70–76. Vagliano Trophy 1961–63–65–67–69–71–73–75. GB Commonwealth Team 1967–75. England (Home Int) 1962–63–65–67–68–69–70–71–72–73–75; (Eur L T Ch) 1965–67–69–71–73–75
Jun	French Girls 1963.
Int	Girls 1960–61; British Girls 1961
Mis	Daks Woman Golfer of the Year 1968–69. Captain of British Team to tour Australia 1973. Lancashire 1981. County Captain 1979. England Junior Captain. 1981–82. International Selector 1981–82. England Selector 1981–82. County Selector and Junior Organiser

Jack, Robert Reid
Born Cumbernauld on 17th January, 1924

Cls	Hon Company of Edinburgh Golfers, Gullane. Hon member of Buchanan Castle, Dullatur, Bearsden
Maj	Leading Amateur in Open 1959
Chp	Amateur Champion 1957. Scottish Amateur 1955
Nat	Scottish Amateur 1955
Trn	Edward Trophy 1959. Tennant Cup 1961
Oth	Royal & Ancient Royal Medal 1965–67. Silver Cross 1956–66. Glennie Medal 1965
Reg	Glasgow Amateur 1953-54-58. Dunbartonshire Match Play 1949
Int	Walker Cup 1957–59. Eisenhower Trophy 1958. GB Commonwealth Team 1959. GB v Europe 1956. Scotland (Home Int) 1950–51–54–55–56–57–58–59–61; v Scandinavia 1956-58

Jacklin, Tony, CBE
Born Scunthorpe on 7th July, 1944. Turned Professional 1962

PRO	
Maj	Open 1969, 3rd 1971–72; US Open 1970
Eur	Blaxnit 1966; Pringle, Dunlop Masters 1967; Wills, Lancôme Trophy 1970; Benson & Hedges Festival 1971; Viyella PGA Close 1972; Dunlop Masters, Italian Open 1973; Scandinavian Enterprise Open 1874; Kerrygold International Classic 1976; German Open 1979; Jersey Open 1981; Sun Alliance PGA 1982
Oth	British Assistants 1964; English Professional 1977
US	Greater Jacksonville Open 1982
RoW	Kimberley 1966 (shared); Forest Products, New Zealand, New Zealand PGA 1967; Dunlop International Australia 1972; Los Lagartos Open 1973–74; Venezuelan Open 1979
Int	Ryder Cup 1967–69–71–73–75–77–79–(83)–(85)–(87)–(89); Hennessy-Cognac 1976; England in World Cup 1966–70–71–72; in Double Diamond 1972–73–74–76–77
Mis	Rookie of the Year 1963; Hon Life President PGA; first British player since Harry Vardon to hold Open and US Open simultaneously; Braid-Taylor Memorial Medal 1969–70–71–72
AM	
Reg	Lincolnshire Open 1961

Jackson, Barbara Amy Bridget
Born Birmingham on 10th July, 1936

Cls	Royal St David's Edgbaston. Hon member of Handsworth, Hunstanton, Killarney
Chp	British Ladies r/u 1964.
Nat	English Ladies 1956, r/u 1958
Trn	Fairway and Hazard Foursomes 1954. Kayser Bondor Foursomes 1962. Avia Foursomes 1967.

Worplesdon Mixed Foursomes 1960. Astor Prince's 1963
Oth German Ladies 1956. Canadian Ladies 1967
Reg Midland Ladies 1954–56–57–58–59–60–69. Staffordshire Ladies 1954–56–57–58–59–63–64–67–69–76
Int Curtis Cup 1958–64–68. Vagliano Trophy 1959–63–65–67–(**73**)–(**75**). GB Commonwealth Team 1959–67. GB v Belgium 1957; v France 1957. World Team Championship 1964. England (Home Int) 1955–56–57–58–59–63–64–65–66–(**73**)–(**74**); (Eur L T Ch) (**1975**), v France 1964–66
Jun British Girls 1954
Mis LGU International Selector 1983. English and GBI Selector 1983 to 1988. Chairman of English Ladies Association 1970–71

Jacobs, John Robert Maurice
Born Lindrick, Yorkshire on 14th March, 1925. Turned Professional 1947

Eur Dutch Open 1957
RoW South African Match Play 1957
Int Ryder Cup 1955–(**79**)–(**81**). GB v Continent 1954–55–58
Mis Former PGA Tournament Director-General. TV commentator. Coach to many International Teams

James, Mark H
Born Manchester on 28th October, 1953. Turned Professional 1975

PRO
Maj 3rd in Open 1981
Eur Sun Alliance Match Play 1978; Welsh Classic, Carroll's Irish Open 1979; Carroll's Irish Open, Italian Open 1980; Tunisian Open 1983; GSI Open 1985; Benson & Hedges International 1986; Peugeot Spanish Open 1988; Karl Litten Desert Classic, AGF Open, NM English Open 1989
RoW Lusaka Open 1977; Sao Paulo Open 1981; South African TPC 1988
Int Ryder Cup 1977–79–81–89; Hennessy-Cognac 1976–78–80–82 (individual winner)–84; World Cup 1978–79–82–84–87–88; Dunhill Cup 1988–89; Kirin Cup 1988; GBI v Australia 1988
Mis Tooting Bec Cup 1976; Braid-Taylor Memorial Medal 1976–79–81; Rookie of the Year 1976
AM
Chp Amateur r/u 1975
Nat English Amateur 1974
Trn Leicestershire Fox 1974
Int Walker Cup 1975; England (Home Int) 1974–75; (Eur T Ch) 1975
Jun
Int (England) Boys 1971; Youths 1974–75

Johnson, Ann (née Hughes)
Born Llandudno, Gwynedd on 18th October, 1946

Cls Ludlow, Killarney (Hon)
Chp Welsh Ladies 1966–72–75, r/u 1969–76
Reg Caernarvonshire and Anglesey Ladies 1964–68–69–72–78
Int Wales (Home Int) 1964–66·67·68·69·70·71·72·73·74·75·76·78·79; (Eur L T Ch) 1965·67·69·71·75·79
Jun Welsh Girls 1960–63–64–65. Girl International 1965

Johnson, Patricia
Born Bristol on 17th January, 1966. Turned Professional 1987

PRO
Eur McEwan's Wirral Classic, Bloor Homes Eastleigh Classic, Woolmark Match Play 1987

US LPGA Qualifying School 1987
AM
Nat English Ladies 1985. English Ladies Stroke Play 1985
Trn Roehampton Gold Cup 1986
Reg South-Western Ladies 1984
Int Curtis Cup 1986; England (Home Int) 1984–85
Jun Devon Girls 1982

Jones, Emyr O
Born 28th January, 1965

Chp Welsh Amateur 1985
Maj Wales (Home Int) 1983–85–86

Jones, John Roger
Born Old Colwyn, Denbighshire on 14th June, 1944

Cls Langland Bay (Hon)
Nat Welsh Amateur Stroke Play 1972–73–82, r/u 1983. Welsh Amateur Championship 1983
Trn Harlech Gold Cross 1976
Reg Denbighshire Amateur 1969–71. Caernarfonshire and Anglesey Amateur 1970 (tied)–72–74–75. Glamorgan Amateur 1977–79. North Wales Amateur 1976. Carmarthenshire Amateur 1979–80. Landsdowne Trophy (Channel League) Stroke Play 1979–80–83
Int Wales (Home Int) 1970–72–73–77–78–80–81–82–83; (Eur T Ch) 1973–79–81–83; v Denmark 1976–80; v Ireland 1979; v Switzerland 1980; v Spain 1980; in Asian Team Championship 1979

Jones, Keith Glyn
Born Brentwood on 19th July, 1969

Cls Worplesdon, The Berkshire, Lansdown
Nat Welsh Amateur 1988
Reg Bristol Open 1988. Whitchurch Silver Dragon 1988. WI Tucker Trophy 1988
Int Wales (Home Int) 1988
Jun Prince of Wales Trophy 1988

Jones, Stephen P
Born 30th January, 1961

Nat Welsh Amateur 1981
Int Wales (Home Int) 1981–82–83–84–85–86

Kelley, Michael John
Born Scarborough on 6th February, 1945

Cls Ganton, Hon member of Scarborough North Cliff, Bridlington, Bradford
Trn Lytham Trophy 1976. Antlers Royal Mid-Surrey 1972
Reg Yorkshire Amateur 1969–74–81. Yorkshire Open 1969–75. Champion of Champions 1981
Int Walker Cup 1977–79. Eisenhower Trophy 1976 (winners). GB v Europe 1976–78–82; GB in Colombian International 1978. England (Home Int) 1974–75–76–77–78–80–81–82–**88**; (Eur T Ch) 1977–79; v France 1982
Jun
Int Boys 1962. Youths 1965–66

Keppler, Steven D
Born 17th February, 1961

Trn Berkshire Trophy 1982. Golf Illustrated Gold Vase 1983
Reg Surrey Amateur 1981
Int Walker Cup 1983. England (Home Int) 1982–83

King, Michael
Born London on 15th February, 1950. Turned Professional 1974

PRO
Eur   Tournament Players Chp 1979
Int   Ryder Cup 1979; England in World Cup 1979
AM
Trn   St George's Hill Trophy 1970; County Champion of Champions 1970; Sunningdale Foursomes 1972; Lytham Trophy 1973 (shared)
Reg   Berks, Bucks & Oxon Amateur 1968–69–70–73–74; Berks, Bucks & Oxon Open 1968–73
Int   Walker Cup 1969–73; GB Commonwealth Trn 1971; v Europe 1972; England (Home Int) 1971–72–73; (Eur T Ch) 1971–73

King, Samuel Leonard
Born Godden Green, Sevenoaks, Kent on 27th March, 1911

Maj   Open 3rd 1939
Trn   Daily Mail 1937. Yorkshire Evening News 1944–49
Oth   British Assistants 1933. Dunlop–Southern 1936–37. Sunningdale Foursomes 1948. Teachers Senior 1961–62
Int   Ryder Cup 1937–47–49. England 1934–36–37–38

Kyle, Alexander Thomson
Born Hawick on 16th April, 1907

Cls   Royal & Ancient, Easingwold, Sandmoor, Moortown, Harrogate, Knaresborough, Peebles, Fulford (Hon)
Chp   Amateur Champion 1939.
Nat   Irish Open Amateur r/u 1946. English Open Amateur Stroke Play r/u 1952
Trn   Newlands Trophy 1930
Reg   Borders Amateur 1929–30. Yorkshire Amateur 1935–36
Int   Walker Cup 1938–47–51. GB v South Africa 1952. Scotland (Home Int) 1938–47–49–50–51–52–53
Mis   Played for British Seniors 1969–75

Lane, Barry
Born Hayes, Middlesex on 21st June, 1960. Turned Professional 1976

Eur   Equity and Law Challenge 1987. Scottish Open 1988
RoW   Jamaica Open 1983
Int   (England) Dunhill Cup 1988. World Cup 1988

Langley, John DA
Born Northwood, Middlesex on 25th April, 1918

Cls   Sunningdale, Burnham (Hon), Swinley Forest, Fulwell (Hon), Metropolitan (Aus)
Nat   English Amateur 1950, r/u 1936
Trn   Golf Illustrated Gold Vase 1952–53. St George's Hill Trophy 1952
Int   Walker Cup 1936–51–53. England (Home Int) 1950–51–52–53; v France 1950–52
Jun   British Boys 1935. Carris Trophy 1936
Int   Boys 1932–33–34–35
Mis   Chairman Royal & Ancient Selection Committee 1967 to 1969

Langmead, Jonathan
Born 3rd November, 1967

Chp   English Amateur 1986
Int   England (Home Int) 1986
Jun
Int   Youths 1987

Langridge, Susan *(née Armitage)*
Born Huddersfield on 5th April, 1943

Cls   Walsall, Whittington Barracks (Hon)
Reg   Midland Ladies 1961–65
Int   Curtis Cup 1964–66. Vagliano Trophy 1963–65–67. England (Home Int) 1963–64–65–66–67
Jun   Scottish Girls Open Stroke Play 1962

Large, Pamela *(née Davies)*
Born Coventry on 12th April, 1930

Cls   Coventry (Hon)
Nat   English Ladies 1952, r/u 1950
Reg   Midland Ladies 1952. Warwickshire Ladies 1952
Int   England (Home Int) 1950–51–52; v Australia 1950
Jun   British Girls 1949
Mis   Captain English Ladies (Home Int) Team 1981–82

Lawrence, Miss Joan B
Born Kinghorn, Fife on 20th April, 1930

Cls   Hon member Dunfermline, Aberdour, Killarney
Chp   Scottish Ladies 1962–63–64, r/u 1965. Scottish Veteran Ladies Champion 1982
Reg   East of Scotland Ladies 1957–58–59–60–61–62–63–64–65–67–68–69
Int   Curtis Cup 1964. World Team Champion 1964. GB Commonwealth Team 1971. Vagliano Trophy 1963–65. Scotland (Home Int) 1959 to 70–(77); (Eur LT Ch) 1965–67–69–71–(77)
Jun   Girl International 1949
Mis   LGU International Selector 1973–74–75–76–80–81–82–83. Treasurer Scottish Ladies Golfing Association from 1980. Chairman of LGU Executive 1989

Leburn, Wilma *(née Aitken)*
Born 24th January, 1959

Trn   Helen Holm Trophy 1978–80–82. Avia Foursomes 1982
Reg   West of Scotland 1978–80–81. Renfrewshire Champion 1978–79–80–81–82
Int   Curtis Cup 1982. Vagliano Trophy 1981–83. Scotland (Home Int) 1978–79–80–81–82–83. Vilmorin Cup 1979. (Eur L T Ch) 1979–81–83.
Jun   Scottish Girls 1975–77. West of Scotland Girls 1977. British Girls 1977
Int   Scottish Girls 1975–77–78

Lee, Robert
Born in London on 12th October, 1961. Turned Professional 1982

Eur   Cannes Open 1985. Portuguese Open 1987
RoW   Brazilian Open 1985

Lee-Smith, Jenny
Born Newcastle-upon-Tyne on 2nd December, 1948. Turned Professional 1977

Maj   Ladies British Open 1976 (as amateur)
PRO
Eur   Carlsberg 1979; Carlsberg, Robert Windsor Trn, Volvo Swedish International, Manchester Evening News Classic 1980; Sports Space Trn, McEwan's Lager Welsh Classic, Lambert & Butler Match Play 1981; Ford Classic 1982; British Olivetti 1984
AM
Nat   Ladies British Open Amateur Stroke Play 1976
Trn   Wills Match Play 1974; Newmark 1976; Hoylake Mixed Foursomes 1969

Reg   Northumberland Ladies 1972–73–74
Int   Curtis Cup 1974–76; Espirito Santo 1976;
      GB Commonwealth Trn 1975; Colombian International
      1975; England (Home Int) 1973–74–75–76; (Eur L T Ch)
      1975
Mis   Daks Woman Golfer of the Year 1976

Lees, Arthur
Born Sheffield on 21st February, 1908

Eur   Irish Hospitals 1939
Trn   Dunlop Masters 1947. Penfold 1951–53
Oth   Midland Professional 1948–49. Southern England
      Professional 1956. Wentworth Pro–Am Foursomes
      1957. Teachers Seniors 1959
Int   Ryder Cup 1947–49–51–55. England 1938

Lewis, Malcolm Elvet
Born Bristol on 8th January 1959

Cls   Newport, Royal & Ancient, Henbury (Hon)
Maj   Leading amateur in Open, 1982
Oth   Greek Amateur 1979; India Amateur 1981; Dutch
      International Amateur 1982
Trn   British Universities Stroke Play 1978–79–80; British
      Universities Match Play 1980–81; Boyd Quaich 1980–82
Reg   Gloucestershire Amateur 1980; East of India 1982
Int   Walker Cup 1983; England (Home Int) 1980–81–82;
      v France 1982
Jun   British Youths 1976
Int   Boys 1975–76; Youths 1976–77–78–80; Universities
      1978–82

Light, Pamela Mary
See Chugg

Llewellyn, David
*Born Dover on 18th November, 1951. Turned
Professional 1968*

Eur   Biarritz Open 1988.
Oth   Vernons Open 1987; Motorola Classic 1989
RoW   Kenya Open 1972. Ivory Coast Open 1985. Zambian
      Open 1988
Int   Wales in World Cup 1974–85–87 (winners)–88. Dunhill
      Cup 1985–88
Mis   Rookie of the Year 1971

Longmuir, Bill
Born Essex on 10th June, 1953. Turned Professional 1968

RoW   Nigerian Open 1976–80–85. Ivory Coast Open 1983;
      Southlands Classic (NZ) 1976
Mis   Tooting Bec Cup 1979

Lucas, Percy Belgrave, CBE, DSO, DFC
Born Sandwich Bay, Kent on 2nd September, 1915

Cls   Sandy Lodge, Walton Heath, Prince's, Royal West
      Norfolk
Trs   Berkshire Trophy 1947–49. St George's Challenge
      Cup 1947. Prince of Wales Challenge Cup 1947.
      President's Putter 1949
Reg   Herts Amateur 1946–47
Int   Walker Cup 1936–47–(49). GB v Professionals 1935.
      England (Home Int) 1936–48–49; v France 1936–47
Jun   British Boys 1933.
Int   Boys 1930–31–32–33
Mis   President Golf Foundation 1963 to 1966. President
      National Golf Clubs Advisory Association 1963 to 1969.
      President Association of Golf Club Secretaries 1968 to
      1974. Member UK Sports Council 1971 to 1983

Lugton, Constance J, MVO
Born Edinburgh on 17th November, 1936

Cls   Gullane Ladies, Musselburgh
Nat   Scottish Ladies Amateur 1977, r/u 1972
Reg   East of Scotland Ladies 1974, East Lothian Ladies
      1965–68–70–71–72–73–76–77–80
Int   Scotland (Home Int) 1965–68–72–73–(75)–(76)–77–
      78–80 (Eur LT Ch) 1977
Jun   Girl International 1955

Lumb, Kathryn (née Phillips)
Born Bradford on 24th February, 1952

Cls   Hon member of Bradford, West Bowling, Killarney,
      Filton
Reg   Central England Mixed Foursomes 1966–70.
      Yorkshire Ladies 1968–69
Int   Curtis Cup 1970–72. Vagliano Trophy 1969–71.
      England (Home Int) 1968–69–70–71; (Eur L T Ch) 1060
Jun   English Girls 1968. Scottish Girls Open Stroke Play
      1968–69. French Girls 1970.
Int   Girls 1967–68–69

Lunt, Michael Stanley Randle
Born Birmingham on 20th May, 1935

Cls   Royal & Ancient, Walton Heath, St Enodoc, Hon
      member of Blackwell, Royal St David's, Moseley,
      Edgbaston, Stourbridge, Willesley Park, Kibworth,
      Handsworth, King's Norton, Dudley
Chp   Amateur Champion 1963, r/u 1964.
Nat   English Amateur 1966, r/u 1962. English Open
      Amateur Stroke Play r/u 1961
Trn   Golf Illustrated Gold Vase 1958. Harlech Gold Cross
      1959–61–64–65–66–67. Leicestershire Fox 1966
Reg   Midland Counties Amateur 1960–62
Int   Walker Cup 1959–61–62–65. Eisenhower Trophy 1964
      GB Commonwealth Team 1963. England (Home Int)
      1956–57–58–59–60–62–63–64–66–(72)–(73)–(74)–(75).
      (Eur T Ch) (1973)–(75)
Jun   Boy International 1949–50–51–52
Mis   AGW Trophy 1963. President Midland Counties Golf
      Association 1978 to 1980

Lunt, Stanley
Born Moseley, Birmingham on 14th November, 1900

Cls   Royal & Ancient, Hon member of Stourbridge,
      Moseley, Handsworth, Edgbaston, Barnehurst,
      Shifnal, Killarney, Aberdovey, Blackwell
Nat   English Amateur 1934
Trn   Harlech Gold Cross 1953
Reg   Midland Counties Amateur 1934. Worcestershire
      Amateur 1925–36
Int   British Amateurs v Professionals 1932–35.
      England (Home Int) 1932–33–34–35–(52)–(53);
      v France 1934–35–39
Mis   President English Golf Union 1960. Senior Golfers
      Society v USA and Canada 1957–59–61–63–65.
      Captain Senior Golfers' Society 1964

Lyle, Alexander Walter Barr (Sandy), MBE
*Born Shrewsbury on 9th February, 1958. Turned
Professional 1977*

PRO
Maj   Open Champion 1985. US Masters 1988
Eur   Jersey Open, Scandinavian Enterprise Open,
      European Open 1979; Coral Classic 1980;
      French Open, Lawrence Batley International 1981;
      Lawrence Batley International 1982; Madrid Open
      1983; Italian Open, Lancôme Trophy 1984; Benson &
      Hedges International 1985; German Masters 1987;

Dunhill British Masters, Suntory World Match Play 1988
US   Greater Greensboro Open 1986; Tournament Players Championship 1987; Phoenix Open, Greater Greensboro Open 1988
Oth   PGA Qualifying School winner 1977; Scottish Professional Chp 1979
RoW   Nigerian Open 1978; Casio World Open, Kapalua International (Hawaii) 1984
Int   Ryder Cup 1979-81-83-85-87; Nissan Cup 1985-86, Kirin Cup 1987; Hennessy-Cognac Cup 1980-84; Scotland in World Cup 1979-80 (Individual Winner) -87(r/u); Dunhill Cup 1985-86-87(r/u)-88-89; GBI v Australia 1988
Mis   Rookie of the Year 1978; Harry Vardon Trophy 1979-80-85; AGW Trophy 1980-88; Tooting Bec Cup 1982-88; Braid-Taylor Memorial Medal 1985; Frank Moran Trophy 1985; Golfer's Handbook Golfer of the Year 1985
AM
Nat   English Open Amateur Stroke Play 1975-77
Trn   County Champion of Champions 1974; Hampshire Hog, Berkshire Trophy, Scrutton Jug, Berkhamsted Trophy 1977
Reg   Midland Amateur, Shropshire & Herefordshire Amateur 1974; Midland Open 1975; Shropshire & Herefordshire Amateur 1976
Int   Walker Cup 1977; GB Commonwealth Trn 1975; GBI v Europe 1976; England (Home Int) 1975-76-77, (Eur T Ch) 1977
Jun   Carris Trophy 1975; British Youths 1977; r/u British Boys 1974-75
Int   Boys 1972-73-74-75
Mis   In 1975 represented England in Boy, Youth and Full Internationals.

Macara, Michael
Born 31st October, 1965

Nat   Welsh Amateur Stroke Play 1985-87
Int   Wales (Home Int) 1983-84-85-87

McCann, Catherine (née Smye)
Born Clonmel, Co Tipperary in 1922

Cls   Tullamore
Chp   British Ladies 1951.
Nat   Irish Ladies 1949-61, r/u 1947-52-57-60
Reg   Munster Ladies 1958, Irish Midland Ladies 1952-57-58
Int   Curtis Cup 1952. Ireland (Home Int) 1947-48-49-50-51-52-53-54-56-57-58-60-61-62; v New Zealand 1953; v Canada 1953

McClure, Jean
See Holmes

McCorkindale, Isabella
See Robertson

Macdonald, JS
Born St Andrews on 9th July, 1944

Cls   Elgin, Baberton, Killarney (Hon), Frigate Bay (Hon)
Nat   Scottish Amateur Open Stroke Play 1969. English Open Amateur Stroke Play r/u 1970-71.
Oth   Kuwait Open Champion 1977

Trn   Boyd Quaich 1963-65. British Universities 1965
Reg   South East Scotland Amateur 1969-71. North of Scotland Open Amateur Stroke Play 1984-85
Int   Walker Cup 1971. GB v Europe 1970. Scotland (Home Int) 1969-70-71-72; (Eur T Ch) 1971; v Belgium 1973
Jun
Int   Boys 1961. Youths 1962-64-65

McEvoy, Peter
Born London on 22nd March, 1953

Cls   Copt Heath (Hon), Handsworth (Hon), City of Derry (Hon), St Annes (Hon), Chantilly (Hon), L'Ancresse (Hon), Cotswold Hills
Chp   Amateur Champion 1977-78.
Nat   English Open Amateur Stroke Play 1980 (tied), r/u 1978. English Amateur r/u 1980
Trn   Duncan Putter 1978-80-87. Scrutton Jug 1978-80. Lytham Trophy 1979. Selborne Salver 1979-80. Leicestershire Fox 1976. Lagonda Trophy 1980. Berkshire Trophy 1985. County Champion of Champions 1984 (shared). Berkhamsted Trophy 1986. Hampshire Hog 1989
Oth   British Universities Stroke Play 1973
Reg   Warwickshire Match Play 1973-75-81. Warwickshire Amateur 1974-76-77-80. Warwickshire Open 1973-74. West of England Open Amateur Stroke Play 1977-80-83. Midland Open Amateur Stroke Play 1978
Int   Walker Cup 1977-79-81-85-89. Eisenhower Trophy 1978-80-88 (winners). GBI v Europe 1978-80-88. England (Home Int) v Europe 1976-77-78-80-81-83-84-85-86-87-88; (Eur T Ch) 1977-79-81-83; v Scotland 1979; in Fiat Trophy 1980. England v France 1983-88
Jun   Youth International 1974
Mis   Leading amateur Open Championship 1978-79. First British amateur to complete 72 holes in US Masters (1978). AGW Trophy 1978

McGimpsey, Garth M
Born 17th July, 1955

Cls   Bangor, Royal Portrush, Royal Co Down
Chp   Amateur Champion 1985, s/f 1989
Nat   Irish Close Champion 1985; Irish Amateur 1988
Reg   North of Ireland Champion 1978-84, West of Ireland Champion 1984-88, East of Ireland Champion 1988 r/u 1979-80
Int   Walker Cup 1985-89. GBI v Europe 1984-86-88. Eisenhower Trophy 1984-86-88 (winners). Ireland (Home Int) 1978-80-81-82-83-84-85-86-87-88. (Eur T Ch) 1981
Mis   Irish long-driving champion 1977; UK long-driving champion 1979

Macgregor, George
Born Edinburgh on 19th August, 1944

Cls   Glencorse, Killarney (Hon), West Linton (Hon)
Nat   Scottish Open Amateur Stroke Play 1982. r/u 1975-79-80
Trn   Lytham Trophy 1975
Reg   Lothians Amateur 1968. South-East Scotland Amateur 1972-75-79-80-81. East of Scotland Open Amateur 1979-82
Int   Walker Cup 1971-75-83-85-87. GB v Europe 1970-74. GB Commonwealth Team 1971-75. Scotland (Home Int) 1969-70-71-72-73-74-75-76-80-81-82-83-84-85-86-87; (Eur T Ch) 1971-73-75-81-83; v Belgium 1973-75-80; v England 1979; v France 1981-82; Scotland v Sweden 1983

Jun
Int   Youths 1964-65-66
Mis   Leading Amateur Wills PGA Open 1970-71

McHenry, John
Born Cork on 14th March, 1964. Turned Professional 1987

Nat   Irish Amateur 1986
Reg   South of Ireland 1976
Int   Walker Cup 1987. Ireland (Home Int) 1985-86.

Macintosh, Keith William
Born Cardross, Dunbartonshire on 21st June, 1949

Cls   Cardross (Hon), Glasgow
Nat   Scottish Amateur 1979. Scottish Open Amateur Stroke
          Play r/u 1978 (tied)
Oth   Belgian Open Amateur 1980
Trn   Scottish Universities 1969. Cameron Corbett Vase
          1979. Cadzow Cup 1968
Reg   Glasgow District Amateur 1973. Dunbartonshire
          Match Play 1980
Int   GB v Europe 1980. Scotland (Home Int) 1980;
          v England 1979; v France 1980; v Belgium 1980;
          in Fiat Trophy 1980. Moroccan Amateur Team
          Champion 1980. Simon Bolivar Trophy 1979
Jun
Int   Youths 1964

McKellar, Paul James
Born Clarkston, Glasgow on 6th April, 1956

Cls   East Renfrewshire (Hon)
Chp   Amateur r/u 1978, s/f 1977
Nat   Scottish Open Amateur Stroke Play 1977. Scottish
          Amateur r/u 1977-79
Reg   West of Scotland Close 1980
Int   Walker Cup 1977. GB v Europe 1978. Europe v
          South America 1979. Scotland (Home Int) 1976-77-78;
          v Belgium 1978; v France 1978; v England 1979; in
          Caracas International 1979
Jun
Int   Youths 1974-75-76-77-(78)-(79)

McKenna, Mary A
Born Dublin on 29th April, 1949

Cls   Donabate
Nat   British Ladies Open Amateur Stroke Play 1979,
          r/u 1976. Irish Ladies 1969-72-74-77-79-81-82, r/u
          1968-73-76. Irish Women's Close Ch 1981
Trn   Dorothy Grey Stroke Play 1970-71-73. Players No
          6 Cup 1971-72-74. Avia Foursomes 1977-84-86.
          Hermitage Scratch Cup 1975-79
Reg   South of Ireland Scratch Cup 1973-74-76-79
Int   Curtis Cup 1970-72-74-76-78-80-82-84-86. Vagliano
          Trophy 1969-71-73-75-77-79-81-85-87. World Team
          Championship 1970-74-76-86. Ireland
          (Home Int) 1968 to 88 inclusive; (Eur L T Ch)
          1969-71-73-75-77-79-81-83-85-87; in Fiat Trophy
          1979
Mis   Semi-finalist US Women's Western 1972, Broadmoor
          Tournament 1972 and US Women's Amateur 1980.
          Captain of LGU Touring Team to South Africa
          1974. Leading Amateur Colgate European LPGA
          1977 (tied)-79. Daks Woman Golfer of the Year
          1979 Smyth Salver 1984. Taunton Trophy 1976

McLean, David
Born Holyhead on 30th January, 1947

Cls   Holyhead, Baron Hill, Killarney
Nat   Welsh Amateur 1973-78. Welsh Amateur Stroke Play
          1975-79
Trn   Duncan Putter 1982

Reg   North Wales Amateur 1971-75-77-81.
          Caernarfonshire Amateur 1966-68-69-70 (tied)-
          77-79-81-82.
          Anglesey Amateur 1965-67-68-69-70-72-73-74-76-
          78-79-80-81-82
Int   Wales (Home Int) 1968-69-70-71-72-73-74-75-76-
          77-78-80-81-82-83-85-86-88; (Eur T Ch) 1975-
          77-79-81-83; v France 1975-76; v Denmark 1976-
          80-82; v Ireland 1979; v Spain 1980; v Austria 1982;
          v Switzerland 1980-82; in Fiat Trophy 1978-79; in
          Asian Team Championship 1979

McMahon, Suzanne (née Cadden)
Born Old Kilpatrick, Dunbartonshire on 8th October, 1957

Cls   Troon
Chp   British Ladies r/u 1975. British Ladies Stroke Play
          r/u 1975
Nat   Scottish Ladies Foursomes 1972
Reg   Dunbartonshire Ladies 1976-77-79
Int   Curtis Cup 1976. Vagliano Trophy 1975. Scotland
          (Home Int) 1974-75-76-77-79; (Eur L T Ch) 1975
Jun   Scottish Girls 1974-76. Scottish Girls Open Stroke
          Play 1976-77. British Girls 1975. Girl International
          1972-73-74-75-76. World Junior Championship 1973
Mis   Daks Woman Golfer of the Year 1975

Madill, Maureen
See Garner

Maher, Sheila (née Vaughan)
Born Whiston, Liverpool on 9th March, 1942

Cls   Huyton and Prescot
Reg   Lancashire Ladies 1958-63-64
Int   Curtis Cup 1962-64. Vagliano Trophy 1961-65. GB
          Commonwealth Team 1963. England (Home Int)
          1960-61-62-63-64
Jun   British Girls 1959.
Int   England Girls 1956-57-58-59
Mis   In 1963 on tour of Australasia as member of GB
          Commonwealth Team, tied first in Australian Ladies
          Foursomes, won New Zealand Ladies Foursomes and
          won New Zealand Junior Stroke Play

Mann, Lindsay S
Born 28th February, 1962

Trn   Tennant Cup 1982
Int   Walker Cup 1983. Scotland (Home Int) 1982-83

Marchbank, Brian
Born Perth on 20th April, 1958. Turned Professional 1979

Cls   Auchterarder (Hon)
Nat   English Open Amateur Stroke Play r/u 1979
Trn   Lytham Trophy 1978. Scottish Champion of
          Champions 1979
Int   Walker Cup 1979. GB v Europe 1976-78. Eisenhower
          Trophy 1978. Scotland (Home Int) 1978; (Eur T Ch)
          1979; v Italy 1979
Jun   British Boys 1975. Scottish Boys 1976. British
          Youths 1978.
Int   Boys 1973-74-75. Youths 1976-77-78-79

Marks, Geoffrey C
Born Hanley, Stoke-on-Trent, in November, 1938

Cls   Hon member of Trentham, Trentham Park, Greenway
          Hall, Killarney, Walsall, Newcastle, Trevose, Stone.
          Royal & Ancient
Chp   Amateur s/f 1968-75

Nat   English Open Amateur Stroke Play r/u 1973–75
Trn   Scrutton Jug 1967. Prince of Wales Challenge Cup
      1968. Leicestershire Fox 1968. Lytham Trophy 1970
      (tied). Harlech Gold Cup 1974. Homer Salver 1977
Reg   Midland Amateur 1967. Staffordshire
      Amateur1959–60–63–66–67–68–69–73
Int   Walker Cup 1969–71–**87**. Eisenhower Trophy 1970.
      GB v Europe 1968–70. England (Home Int)
      1963–67–68–69–70–71–74–75 (**80**)–(**81**)–(**82**)–(**83**), (Eur
      T Ch) 1967–69–71–75. GB Commonwealth Team 1975.
      GB in Colombian International 1975
Jun
Int   Boys 1955–56. Youths 1957–58–59–60
Mis   England Selector 1980–81–82–83 (chairman)

Marsh, Dr David Max
Born Southport on 29th April, 1934

Cls   Royal & Ancient, Hon member of Southport and
      Ainsdale, Ormskirk, West Lancashire, Worlington
      and Newmarket, Hillside, Clitheroe, Whalley
Nat   English Amateur 1964–70
Trn   Antlers Royal Mid–Surrey 1964–66. Formby Hare
      1968. Boyd Quaich 1957
Int   Walker Cup 1959–71–(**73**)–(**75**); GB v Europe
      1958–(**72**)–(**74**). GB v Professionals 1959. England
      (Home Int) 1956–57–58–59–60–64–65–66–**68**–**69**–**70**–
      71–72; (Eur T Ch) 1971
Jun
Int   Boys 1951
Mis   EGU Selector 1974. British Selector 1975. Chairman
      Royal & Ancient Selection Committee 1979–83.
      President EGU 1987

Martin, Steve W
*Born Dundee on 21st December, 1955. Turned
Professional 1977*

PRO
Int   Scotland in World Cup 1980
AM
Nat   Scottish Open Amateur Stroke Play 1976
Trn   Tennant Cup 1977
Reg   Central District Amateur 1973. Angus Amateur 1973.
      East of Scotland Open Amateur Stroke Play 1976.
Int   Walker Cup 1977. Eisenhower Trophy 1976 (winning
      team). GB v Europe 1976. Scotland (Home Int)
      1975–76–77; (Eur T Ch) 1977; v Belgium 1977;
      v Spain 1977
Jun   Scottish Boys Stroke Play 1972–73.
Int   Boys 1972–73. Youths 1973–75–76–77

Marvin, Vanessa Price
*Born Cosford on 30th December, 1954. Turned
Professional 1978*

Cls   Easingwold (Hon)
PRO
Eur   Carlsberg Trn 1979
AM
Chp   British Ladies Amateur r/u 1977
Nat   English Ladies Amateur 1977–78.
Trn   Hampshire Rose 1975–78 (tied). Roehampton Gold
      Cup 1976. Newmark–Avia 1978
Reg   Yorkshire Ladies 1975–78. North of England Ladies
      1975
Int   Curtis Cup 1978. Vagliano Trophy 1977. England
      (Home Int) 1977–78, (Eur L T Ch) 1977; in Fiat
      Trophy 1978
Mis   Leading amateur Colgate European LPGA 1977.
      Daks Woman Golfer of the Year
      1978.

Mayo, Paul M
*Born Newport, Gwent on 6th January, 1963. Turned
Professional 1988*

Maj   Leading Amateur in Open 1987
Chp   Amateur Champion 1987
Nat   Welsh Amateur 1987
Reg   Gwent Amateur 1982
Int   Walker Cup 1985–87; GB v Europe 1986; Wales
      (Home Int) 1982–87
Jun   British Youths 1983; Welsh Boys 1979

Melia, Terry J
Born Wrexham on 7th July, 1955

Cls   Cardiff
Nat   Welsh Amateur 1979. Welsh Amateur Stroke Play 1980
Reg   Glamorgan County 1981–82
Int   Wales (Home Int) 1976–77–78–80–81–82; (Eur T Ch)
      1977–79; v Denmark 1976–80; v Ireland 1979;
      v Switzerland 1980; v Spain 1980; v S America 1979

Milligan, James W
Born Irvine on 15th June, 1963

Cls   Kilmarnock (Barassie)
Nat   Scottish Amateur 1988
Trn   Scottish Champion of Champions 1989
Int   Walker Cup 1989. Scotland (Home Int) 1986–87–88. v
      West Germany 1987; v Italy 1988. GBI v Europe 1988.
      World Cup (Eisenhower) 1988 (winners)
Jun   Scottish Youths 1984

Milne, William TG
Born Perth on 13th July, 1951. Turned Professional 1973

Trn   Newlands Trophy 1972
Reg   North of Scotland Stroke Play 1971. Perthshire Stroke
      Play 1973
Int   Walker Cup 1973. Scotland (Home Int) 1972–73;
      (Eur T Ch) 1973; v Belgium 1973
Jun   Scotland Youth International 1970–71–72
Mis   Won Lusaka Eagle Open 1974 and Northern
      Scottish Open 1974-75

Milton, Moira (née Paterson)
Born 18th December, 1923

Cls   Turnhouse, Hon Member of Gullane, Lenzie,
      Maccauvlei
Chp   British Ladies 1952.
Nat   Scottish Ladies r/u 1951
Reg   Dunbartonshire Ladies 1949. Midlothian Ladies 1962
Int   Curtis Cup 1952. GB v France 1949–50; v Belgium
      1950. Scotland (Home Int) 1949–50–51–52; v Australia
      1951; v South Africa 1951. (Eur LT Ch) (**1973**)
Mis   Member of LGU Team to South Africa 1951.

Montgomerie, Colin S
*Born Glasgow on 23rd June, 1963. Turned Professional
1987*

PRO
Eur   Portuguese Open 1989
Int   Scotland in Dunhill Cup 1988; in World Cup 1988
Mis   Rookie of the Year 1988
AM
Nat   Scottish Open Amateur Stroke Play 1985; Scottish
      Amateur 1987
Int   Walker Cup 1985–87; Eisenhower Trophy 1984–86;
      GB v Europe 1986; Scotland (Home Int) 1984–85–86
      (Eur T Ch) 1985; v Sweden 1984–86; v France 1985

Montgomerie, John Speir
Born Cambuslang on 7th August, 1913

Cls	Royal & Ancient, Cambuslang, Kilmarnock (Barassie), Pollok
Nat	Scottish Amateur 1957
Reg	Lanarkshire Amateur 1951–54
Int	Scotland (Home Int) 1957–(62)–(63); v Scandinavia 1958
Mis	Non-playing captain Scottish Team (Eur T Ch) 1965. Walker Cup Selector 1957 to 1965. President Scottish Golf Union 1965–66

Moore, Linda
See Simpson

Morgan, John
Born Oxford on 3rd September, 1943. Turned Professional 1968

Eur	Jersey Open 1986
RoW	Nigerian Open 1979. Lusaka Open 1979. Ivory Coast 1982

Morgan, John Llewellyn
Born Llandrindod Wells on 23rd June, 1918

Cls	Llandrindod Wells, Sutton Coldfield, Builth Wells, Little Aston, Aberystwyth, Killarney, St Deiniol, Ashburnham
Nat	Welsh Amateur 1950–51, r/u 1952
Trn	Berkshire Trophy 1953. Duncan Putter 1968. Harlech Gold Cross 1951–55
Sen	Welsh Seniors 1974
Reg	Midlands Amateur 1949–50–52. Midlands Open 1950. Warwickshire Amateur 1951
Int	Walker Cup 1951–53–55. Wales (Home Int) 1948–49–50–51–52–53–54–56–57–58–59–60–61–62–63–64–66–67. (Eur T Ch) 1965
Mis	Professional for 4 years subsequently reinstated as Amateur

Morgan, Wanda
Born Lymm, Cheshire on 22nd March, 1910

Cls	Canterbury, Westgate, St Enodoc, Herne Bay, Belmont, Chestfield, Rochester and Cobham Park, Cooden Beach, Littlestone, Prince's, Seasalter, Barnehurst, Hon Life member of ALL clubs listed
Chp	British Ladies 1935, r/u 1931.
Nat	English Ladies 1931-36-37
Trn	Sunningdale Foursomes 1948. Worplesdon Mixed Foursomes 1948. Fairway and Hazard Foursomes 1956. Daily Graphic 1941–42
Reg	Kent Ladies 1930–31–33–35–36–37–53
Int	Curtis Cup 1932–34–36. GB v France 1932–33–34–35–36–37; v Canada 1934. England (Home Int) 1931–32–33–34–35–36–37–53

Mosey, Ian
Born Keighley on 29th August, 1951. Turned Professional 1972

Maj	Monte Carlo Open 1984
Oth	Merseyside International 1980.
RoW	Kalahari Classic 1980. Holiday Inns, SA 1981

Mouland, Mark
Born Wales on 23rd April, 1961. Turned Professional 1981

PRO	
Eur	Car Care Plan International 1986. KLM Open 1988
Reg	Midland Professional Stroke Play 1984
Int	Wales: in Dunhill Cup 1986–87–88–89; World Cup 1988; Kirin Cup 1988

AM	
Jun	British Boys 1976

Mulcare, Pat
Born Ballybunion, 1945

Cls	Woodbrook (Hon), Dublin (Hon)
Maj	East of Ireland Open Amateur 1971–72–73. South of Ireland Open Amateur 1971
Int	Walker Cup 1975. Ireland (Home Int) 1968–69–70–71–72–73–74–78–80; (Eur T Ch) 1975–79; v France, West Germany and Sweden 1978–80

Murray, Gordon H
Born Paisley on 19th December, 1936

Cls	Fereneze (Hon)
Nat	Scottish Amateur 1974–76, r/u 1975; Scottish Stroke Play 1983
Reg	West of Scotland Amateur 1971–73–76–78
Int	Walker Cup 1977. GB v Europe 1978. Scotland (Home Int) 1973–74–75–76–77–78–83 (Eur T Ch) 1975–77; v Spain 1974–77; v Belgium 1975–77

Murray, Stuart WT
Born Paisley on 10th November, 1933. Turned Professional 1963

Nat	Scottish Amateur 1962, r/u 1961
Trn	Tennant Cup 1963. Edward Trophy 1960–61
Reg	West of Scotland Amateur 1958. Renfrewshire Amateur 1958–59. Glasgow Amateur 1960. Hampshire Amateur 1963. Midland Professional 1964-67-68. Middlesex Open 1973
Int	Walker Cup 1963. GB Commonwealth Team 1963 GB v Europe. 1958–62. Scotland (Home Int) 1959–60–61–62–63, v Scandinavia 1960

Needham, Sandra Claire
See Roy

Nesbitt, Claire
See Robinson

New, Beverley Jayne
Born Bristol on 30th July, 1960. Turned Professional 1984

PRO	
Eur	Broadway Group Wirral Classic 1988
RoW	Thailand Ladies Open 1987; Malaysian Ladies Open 1988
AM	
Nat	English Ladies 1980; Welsh Ladies Stroke Play r/u 1979
Trn	Hampshire Rose 1980; WPGA United Friendly Insurance Trn, Worplesdon Mixed Foursomes 1982; Roehampton Gold Cup, Worplesdon Mixed Foursomes, Martin Bowl 1983
Reg	Somerset Ladies 1979–80–81–82–83; Bristol & District Open 1983
Int	Curtis Cup 1984; Vagliano Trophy 1983; England (Home Int) 1980–81–82–83; (Eur L T Ch) 1981–83; Fiat Trophy 1980
Mis	Doris Chambers Trophy 1983

Nichol, Margaret
See Pickard

Nicholas, Alison
Born Gibraltar on 6th March, 1962. Turned Professional 1984

PRO	
Maj	Ladies British Open 1987, 3rd 1988

Eur   Laing Charity Classic 1987; Variety Club Classic,
      British Olivetti, Guernsey Open 1988; Lufthansa
      German Open, Gislaved Open 1989
AM
Nat   Ladies British Open Amateur Stroke Play 1983
Reg   Yorkshire Ladies 1984; Northern Foursomes 1983
Jun   North of England Girls 1982–83
Mis   Taunton Trophy 1983; Duncan Salver 1983

O'Connell, Eoghan

Int   Walker Cup 1989; Eisenhower Trophy 1988 (winners);
      GB v Europe 1988; Ireland (Home Int) 1985; (Eur T Ch)
      1989

O'Connor, Christy
Born Galway on 21st December, 1924

Maj   Open Championship r/u 1965, 3rd 1961.
Trn   Swallow–Penfold 1955. Dunlop Masters 1956–59.
      Spalding 1956 (tied). PGA Match Play 1957. Daks
      1959. Ballantine 1960. Irish Hospitals 1960–62.
      Carling–Caledonian 1961. Martini 1963 (tied)–64.
      Jeyes 1964. Carrolls 1964–66–67–72. Senior Service
      1965; Gallaher Ulster 1966–68–69. Alcan International
      1968 (tied). Bowmaker 1970. John Player Classic 1970.
Oth   Ulster Professional 1953–54. Irish Professional 1958–
      60–61–62–63–65–66–71–75–77. Irish Dunlop 1962–
      65–66–67. Gleneagles Pro–Am 1962. Southern Ireland
      Professional 1969–76. Sean Connery Pro–Am 1970.
Sen   PGA Seniors 1976–77–81–82. World Seniors
      1976–77
Int   Ryder Cup 1955–57–59–61–63–65–67–69–71–73. GB
      v Commonwealth 1956. Ireland in World Cup
      1956–57–58 (winners) –59–60–61–62–63–64–66–67–68–
      69–71–75. Ireland in Double Diamond
      1971–72–73–74–75–76–77
Mis   Harry Vardon Trophy 1961–62. Second in order of
      Merit 1964 (equal)–65–66–69–70. AGW Trophy 1977

O'Connor, Christy, Jr
Born Galway on 19th August, 1948. Turned Professional
1965

Maj   Open 3rd 1985
Eur   Martini 1975 (tied). Carrolls Irish Open 1975. Sumrie
      1976–78
Oth   Irish Dunlop 1974. Carrolls Irish Match Play 1975–77
RoW   Zambian Open 1974
Int   Ryder Cup 1975–89. Ireland in Double Diamond
      1974–75–76–77. Ireland in World Cup 1974–75–78–85.
      Hennessy-Cognac 1974–84. GB v South Africa 1976.
      Dunhill Cup 1985–89

Oldcorn, Andrew
Born Bolton on 31st March, 1960. Turned Professional 1983

Nat   English Amateur 1982
Int   Walker Cup 1983. England (Home Int) 1982–83
Jun   Scottish Youths Stroke Play 1979

O'Leary, John E
Born Dublin on 19th August, 1949. Turned Professional
1970

PRO
Trn   Sumrie 1975. Greater Manchester Open 1976.
      Carrolls Irish Open 1982; Irish Dunlop 1972
RoW   Holiday Inns (Swaziland) 1975
Int   Ryder Cup 1975. Ireland in World Cup 1972–80–82.
      Ireland in Double Diamond 1972–73–74–75–76–77. GB
      v Europe 1976–78–82

AM
Reg   South of Ireland Amateur 1970.
Int   Ireland (Home Int) 1969–70; (Eur T Ch) 1969
Jun
Int   Youths 1970

Oosterhuis, Peter A
Born London on 3rd May, 1948. Turned Professional
November 1968

PRO
Maj   Open r/u 1974–82; leading British player 1975 (7th),
      1978 (6th) US Masters 3rd 1973
Eur   Agfacolor, Sunbeam Pro-Am, Piccadilly 1971; Penfold
      1972; French Open, Piccadilly, Viyella PGA 1973;
      French Open, Italian Open 1974
US   Canadian Open 1981
RoW   General Motors South Africa 1970; Transvaal Open,
      Schoeman Park, Rhodesian Dunlop Masters 1971;
      Glen Anil Classic 1972; Rothman's Match Play South
      Africa, Maracaibo Open 1973; El Paraiso Open 1974
Oth   Sunningdale Foursomes 1969; Coca-Cola Young
      Professionals 1970–72
Reg   Southern England Professional 1971
Int   Ryder Cup 1971–73–75–77–79–81; Hennessy-Cognac
      1974; England in World Cup 1971–73, in Double
      Diamond 1973–74
Mis   Rookie of the Year 1969; Harry Vardon Trophy
      1971–72–73–74; AGW Trophy 1973–74
AM
Trn   Berkshire Trophy 1966
Int   Walker Cup 1967; Eisenhower Trophy 1968; England
      (Home Int) 1966–67–68
Jun   British Youths 1966
Int   Boys 1964–65; Youths 1966–67–68

O'Reilly, Therese (*née* Moran)
Born 29th January, 1954

Cls   Grange
Nat   Irish Ladies' Amateur 1986
Reg   Leinster Ladies 1975–78. Irish Midland Ladies 1974
Int   Ireland (Home Int) 1977–78–86–88; (Eur L T Ch)
      1988

O'Sullivan, Denis

Nat   Irish Amateur 1985
Int   Ireland (Home Int) 1985-86–87

O'Sullivan, Dr William M
Born Killarney on 13th March, 1911

Cls   Killarney (Hon), Dooks (Hon), Tralee (Hon),
      Muskerry (Hon), Cork (Hon), Ballybunion (Hon),
      Waterville
Chp   Irish Open Amateur 1949, r/u 1936–53.
      Irish Amateur r/u 1940
Int   Ireland (Home Int) 1934–35–36–37–38–47–48–
      49–50–51–53–54. President Golfing Union of Ireland
      1959–60

Oxley, Dinah
See Henson

Panton, Catherine Rita
Born Bridge of Allan, Stirlingshire on 14th June, 1955.
Turned Professional 1978

Cls   Glenbervie (Hon), Pitlochry (Hon), Silloth (Hon),
      South Herts
PRO
Eur   Carlsberg Tournament 1979. State Express Ladies

Championship 1979 and headed WPGA Order of Merit. In 1980 won Elizabeth Ann Classic. European Ladies Champion 1981, also won two WPGA events. Moben Kitchens Classic 1982. Qualified for USLPGA Tour, January 1983. Won Smirnoff Irish Classic 1983. UBM Northern Classic 1983, Dunham Forest Pro-Am 1983. McEwans Wirral Caldy Classic 1985. Delsjö Open 1985. Portuguese Open 1986–87. Scottish Open 1988

AM	
Chp	Ladies British Open Amateur 1976
Reg	East of Scotland Ladies 1976
Int	World Team Championship 1976. Vagliano Trophy 1977. Scotland (Home Int) 1972–73–76–77–78; (Eur L T Ch) 1973–77
Jun	Scottish Girls 1969. Girl Int 1969-70-71-72-73
Mis	Scottish Sportswoman of the Year 1976. Member of LGU under–25 team to tour Canada 1973

Panton, John MBE
Born Pitlochry, Perthshire on 9th October, 1916. Turned Professional 1935

Maj	Leading British player in 1956 Open (5th)
Trn	Silver King 1950. Daks 1951. North–British–Harrogate 1952. Goodwin Foursomes 1952. Yorkshire Evening News 1954. PGA Match Play 1956, r/u 1968
Eur	Woodlawn Invitation Open (Germany) 1958–59–60
Oth	West of Scotland Professional 1947–48–52–54– 55–61–63. Scottish Professional 1948–49–50–51–54–55– 59–66 (tied). Northern Open 1948–51–52–56–59–60–62. West of Scotland PGA Match Play 1954–55–56–64. Goodwin Foursomes 1952. Gleneagles–Saxone 1956.
Sen	Pringle Seniors 1967–69. World Seniors 1967
Int	Ryder Cup 1951–53–61. Scotland in World Cup 1955–56–57–58–59–60–62–63–64–65–66–68
Mis	Harry Vardon Trophy 1951. AGW Trophy 1967. Hon Professional to Royal & Ancient from 1988

Parkin, Philip
Born Doncaster on 12th December, 1961. Turned Professional 1984

PRO	
Int	Wales in World Cup 1984; Dunhill Cup 1985–86–87–89; Hennessy-Cognac Cup 1984
Mis	Rookie of the Year 1984
AM	
Chp	Amateur Champion 1983
Int	Walker Cup 1983. Wales (Home Int) 1980–81–82.
Jun	British Youths 1982

Paterson, Moira
See Milton

Peel, Marjorie
See Draper

Perkins, Tegwen
See Thomas

Perowne, Arthur Herbert
Born Norwich on 21st February, 1930

Cls	Royal Norwich, Hunstanton, West Norfolk
Chp	English Open Amateur Stroke Play 1958
Oth	Swedish Amateur 1974
Trn	Berkshire Trophy 1958 (tied)
Reg	East Anglia Open 1952. Norfolk Amateur 1948–51–52– 53–54–55–56–57–58–60–61. Norfolk Open 1964

Int	Walker Cup 1949–53–59. Eisenhower Trophy 1958. GB v Denmark 1955; v Professionals 1956–58. England (Home Int) 1947–48–49–50–51–53–54–55–57; v France 1950–54–56–59; v Sweden 1947; v Denmark 1947
Jun	Carris Trophy 1946
Int	Boys 1946

Phillips, Ann
See Howard

Phillips, Kathryn
See Lumb

Pickard, Margaret (*née* Nichol)
Born on 25th April, 1938

Cls	Alnmouth (Hon)
Nat	English Ladies 1960, r/u 1957–67
Reg	Northern Ladies 1957–58. Northumberland Ladies 1956–57–58–61–62–64–65–66–67–69–70–71–76–77–82
Int	Curtis Cup 1968–70. Vagliano Trophy 1959–61–67. England (Home Int) 1957–58–59–60–61–67–69–(83). (Eur L T Ch) (1983)

Pierse, Arthur D'Arcy
Born Dublin on 30th April 1952

Reg	West of Ireland Open Amateur 1980–82. North of Ireland Amateur 1987. East of Ireland 1979
Int	Walker Cup 1983, GB v Europe 1980–82. Ireland (Home Int) 1976–77–78–80–81–82–83–84–85–87–88 (Eur T Ch) 1981. Eisenhower Trophy 1982

Pirie, Alex Kemp
Born Aberdeen on 21st June, 1942

Cls	Hazelhead (Hon), Cruden Bay
Nat	Scottish Amateur r/u 1972–74
Trn	Eden Tournament 1963.
Reg	Northern Scottish Open 1970. West of Scotland Open Amateur 1972. East of Scotland Open Amateur Stroke Play 1975. North East Scotland Match Play 1964–66–67–68–71–73. Aberdeenshire Stroke Play 1966–68
Int	Walker Cup 1967. GB v Europe 1970. Scotland (Home Int) 1966–67–68–69–70–71–72– 73–74–75; (Eur T Ch) 1967–69; v Belgium 1973–75; v Spain 1974

Polland, Eddie
Born Newcastle, Co Down on 10th June, 1947. Turned Professional 1967

Eur	Spanish Open 1976–80
Trn	Penfold 1973. Sun Alliance PGA Match Play 1975. Irish Dunlop 1973–75. Irish Professional 1974. Carrolls Irish Match Play 1974. Ulster Professional 1976
Int	Ryder Cup 1973. Ireland in World Cup 1973–74–76–77– 78–79. Ireland in Double Diamond 1972–73–74–75–76– 77. GB v Europe 1974–76–78–80; v South Africa 1976

Pook, Elizabeth (*née* Chadwick)
Born Inverness on 4th April, 1943

Cls	Mendip
Chp	British Ladies 1966–67.
Nat	English Ladies r/u 1963
Reg	Central England Mixed Foursomes 1962–63–64 North of England Ladies 1965–66–67. Cheshire Ladies 1963–64–65–66–67
Int	Curtis Cup 1966. England (Home Int) 1963–65–66–67; (Eur L T Ch) 1967; v France 1965
Jun	Girl International 1961

Porter, Ruth
See Slark

Power, Eddie
Born Waterford on 17th January, 1965

Cls	Tramore (Hon) Enniscorthy (Hon)
Nat	Irish Amateur 1987, r/u 1983
Int	Ireland (Home Int) 1987–88
Jun	Boy International 1982. Youth International 1984–86. European Boys 1982. Junior World Cup 1982

Price Fisher, Elizabeth
Born London on 17th January, 1923. Turned Professional 1968, reinstated as Amateur 1971

Cls	Hankley Common, Farnham, Berkshire
Chp	British Ladies 1959, r/u 1954–58.
Nat	English Ladies r/u 1947–54–55
Oth	Danish Ladies 1952. Portuguese Ladies 1964
Trn	Spalding Ladies 1955–59. Astor Salver 1955–56–59. Fairway and Hazard Foursomes 1954–60. Kayser Bondor Foursomes 1958 (tied). Roehampton Gold Cup 1960. Central England Mixed Foursomes 1971–76–82
Reg	South Eastern Ladies 1955–59–60–69. Surrey Ladies 1954–55–56–57–58–59–60
Int	Curtis Cup 1950–52–54–56–58–60. Vagliano Trophy 1959. GB v Canada 1950–54–58; v France 1953–55–57; v Belgium 1953–55–57. GB Commonwealth Team 1955–59. England (Home Int) 1948–51–52–53–54–55–56–57–58–59–60
Mis	AGW Trophy 1952.

Rafferty, Ronan
Born Newry on 13th January, 1964. Turned Professional 1981

PRO	
Eur	Equity & Law Challenge 1988; Lancia Italian Open, Scandinavian Enterprise Open, Volvo Masters 1989
RoW	Venezuelan Open 1982; South Australian Open, New Zealand Open 1987; Australian Match Play 1988
Int	Ryder Cup 1989; Kirin Cup 1988; GBI v Australia 1988; Hennessy-Cognac 1984; Ireland in World Cup 1983–84–87–88; Dunhill Cup 1986–87–88(winners)–89
Mis	Harry Vardon Trophy 1989
AM	
Nat	Irish Amateur 1980; English Amateur Open Stroke Play 1980(tied)
Int	Walker Cup 1981; Eisenhower Trophy 1980; GB v Europe 1980; Ireland (Home Int) 1980; v Wales 1979; v France, Germany, Sweden 1980; Fiat Trophy 1980; (Eur T Ch) 1981
Jun	British Boys 1979; Irish Youths 1979; Ulster Youths 1979
Int	Boys 1978–79; Youths 1979–80

Rawlings, Mandy
Born Bargoed, Glamorganshire on 15th June, 1964

Cls	Bargoed, Whitchurch, Radyr (Hon)
Nat	Welsh Ladies 1980–81
Int	Wales (Home Int) 1978–79–80; in Fiat Trophy 1980. Girls International 1981. Senior International 1981–83–84. Vagliano Trophy 1981
Jun	Welsh Girls 1979–81. Girl International 1976–77–78–79–80. De Beers Ch 1980

Rawlings, Vicki
See Thomas

Reddan, Clarrie (née Tiernan)
Born Drogheda on 3rd July, 1916

Cls	Co Louth
Chp	British Ladies r/u 1949
Nat	Irish Ladies 1936, r/u 1946–48.
US	New Jersey State Ladies 1937. Canadian Ladies r/u 1938
Int	Curtis Cup 1938–48. GB v Canada 1938. Ireland (Home Int) 1935–36–37–38–39–47–48–49

Redford, Carole
See Caldwell

Rees, Christopher

Nat	Welsh Amateur 1986
Int	Wales (Home Int) 1986–88
Jun	Welsh Boys 1982

Reid, Dale
Born Ladybank, Fife on 20th March, 1959. Turned Professional 1979

PRO	
Eur	Carlsberg (Coventry) 1980. Carlsberg (Gleneagles), Moben Kitchens 1981. Guernsey Open 1982. United Friendly, International Classic 1983. Caldy Classic 1983. UBM Classic, JS Bloor Classic 1984. Ulster Volkswagen Classic, Brend Hotels International 1985. British Olivetti 1986. Volmac Open, European Open, Bowring Scottish Ladies Open, Volkswagen Classic 1987. European Open, Toshiba Players Ch 1988.
Mis	Order of Merit leader 1984
AM	
Int	Scotland (Home Int) 1978
Jun	Fife Girls 1973–75. Scottish Girls International 1974–75–76–77

Rennie, Joan Kerr (née Hastings)
Born Troon on 29th May, 1941

Cls	Aberdeen Ladies, Hon member of Troon Bentinck, Kilmarnock (Barassie), Troon Municipal
Nat	Scottish Ladies 1967, r/u 1968
Reg	Ayrshire Ladies 1960–61–63–64–66–67. Aberdeenshire Ladies 1980
Int	Curtis Cup 1966. Vagliano Trophy 1961–67. Scotland (Home Int) 1961–65–66–67–71–72; (Eur L T Ch) 1973
Jun	Scottish Girls 1980.
Int	Girls 1957–58–59

Richmond, Maureen (née Walker)
Born Kilmacolm on 22nd April, 1955

Cls	Kilmacolm (Hon), Troon, Shiskine (Hon)
Int	Curtis Cup 1974. Vagliano Trophy 1975. Scotland (Home Int) 1972–73–74–75–77–78; (Eur L T Ch) 1973–75
Jun	British Girls 1972. Scottish Girls 1970–71–73.
Int	Girls International 1969–70–71–72–73
Mis	Member of LGU Under-25 Team to tour Canada 1973.

Robb, Diane
See Bailey

Roberts, Sharon
Born Penmaenmawr on 8th June, 1964

Cls	Llandudno (Maesdu)
Nat	Welsh Ladies Amateur 1984–88 r/u 1987
Trn	Keighley Open 1987. Birkdale Open 1988
Reg	Midlands Match Play 1987–88
Int	Wales (Home Int) 1983–84–85–86–87–88; (Eur L T Ch) 1983–87

Robertson, Isabella (Belle), MBE
Born Southend, Argyll, on 11th April, 1936

Cls	Dunaverty (Hon)
Maj	Ladies British Open: leading amateur (Smyth Salver); r/u 1980–81
Chp	Ladies British Open Amateur 1981; r/u 1959–65–70
Nat	Ladies British Open Amateur Stroke Play 1971–72–85; Scottish Ladies 1965–66–71–72–78–80; r/u 1959–63–70
Oth	New Zealand Ladies Match Play 1971
Trn	Sunningdale Foursomes 1960; Avia Foursomes 1972–81–84–86; Helen Holm Trophy 1973–79–86; Players No 6 Cup 1973–76; Roehampton Gold Cup 1978 (tied)–79–81–82
Reg	West of Scotland Ladies 1957–64–66–69; Dunbartonshire Ladies 1958 to 1963, 1965–66–68–69–78
Int	Curtis Cup 1960–66–68–70–72–(74)–(76)–82–86; Vagliano Trophy 1959–63–65–69–71–81; Espirito Santo 1964–66–**68**–72–80–82; GB Commonwealth Team 1071–(**75**), Scotland (Home Int) 1958 to 1966, 69–72–73–78–80–81–82 (Eur L T Ch) 1965–**67**–69–71–73–81–83; Fiat Trophy 1978–80
Mis	Daks Woman Golfer of the Year 1971–81; Frank Moran Trophy 1971; leading qualifier in US Ladies Amateur 1978; Scottish Sportswoman of the Year 1968–71–78–81; Avia Golfer of the Year 1985

Robertson, Janette
See Wright

Robinson, Jeremy
Born 21st January, 1966. Turned Professional 1987

Nat	English Amateur Stroke Play (Brabazon Trophy) 1987
Trn	Lagonda Trophy 1985
Int	Walker Cup 1987. England (Home Int) 1986

Robinson, Claire (née Nesbitt)
Born 7th March, 1953

Nat	Irish Ladies Amateur 1976–80
Reg	Ulster Ladies 1976–78
Int	Curtis Cup 1980. Vagliano Trophy 1979. Ireland (Home Int) 1974 to 81. (Eur L T Ch) 1975–77–79

Roderick, R Neil
Born Swansea on 8th March, 1966

Cls	Pontardawe
Nat	Welsh Amateur Stroke Play 1984–88. English Open Amateur Stroke Play 1989
Trn	Tenby Eagle 1988. Harlech Gold Cross 1986. Southerndown Silver Ram 1984–85–86. Worplesdon Mixed Foursomes 1986. Duncan Putter 1989
Int	Walker Cup 1989. Wales (Home Int) 1983–84–85–86–87–88. GBI v Europe 1988
Jun	Welsh Boys 1982–83

Roper, Roger
Born 15th April, 1962

Nat	English Open Amateur Stroke Play 1985 (shared)
Int	England (Home Int) 1984–85–86–87

Roy, Sandra Clair (née Needham)
Born Bishopton, Renfrewshire on 8th March, 1946

Cls	Cawder (Hon), Machrihanish (Hon), Troon
Nat	Scottish Ladies 1976
Trn	Helen Holm Trophy 1974
Reg	West of Scotland Ladies 1967–71–72–73–75. Lanarkshire Ladies 1969–72–73–77–83–84

Int	Vagliano Trophy 1973–75, Scotland (Home Int) 1969–71–72–73–74–75–76–83; (Eur L T Ch) 1969–75–77
Mis	Member of LGU team to tour South Africa 1974

Russell, David J
Born Birmingham on 2nd May, 1954. Turned Professional 1973

Eur	Car Care Plan International 1985

Saddler, AC
Born Forfar, Angus on 11th August, 1935

Cls	Forfar, Carnoustie
Nat	Scottish Amateur r/u 1960
Trn	Berkshire Trophy 1962
Int	Walker Cup 1963–65–67–(**77**) Eisenhower Trophy 1962–(**76**) (winners)–78. GB Commonwealth Team 1959–63–67; v Europe 1960–62–66–(**76**)–(**78**); v Professionals 1959–61. Scotland (Home Int) 1959–60–61–62–63–65–(**74**)–(**75**)–(**76**)–(**77**); (Eur T Ch) (**1975**)–(**77**)

Saunders, Vivien Inez
Born Sutton on 24th November, 1946. Turned Professional 1969

PRO	
Maj	Ladies British Open 1977
Trn	Avia Foursomes 1978; Keighley Trophy 1981; British Car Auctions 1980
US	1969 First European to qualify for LPGA tour
RoW	Schweppes-Tarax Open (Australia), Chrysler Open (Australia) 1973
Mis	Founder WPGA & Chairman 1978–79
AM	
Chp	Ladies British Open Amateur r/u 1966
Trn	Avia Foursomes 1967
Int	Curtis Cup 1968; Vagliano Trophy 1967; GB Commonwealth Team 1967; England (Home Int) 1967–68 (Eur L T Ch) 1967; v France 1966–67
Jun	
Int	Girls 1964–65–66–67

Sewell, Douglas
Born Woking on 19th November, 1929. Turned Professional 1960

PRO	
Trn	Martini International 1970 (shared); Wentworth Pro-Am Foursomes 1968
Reg	West of England Open Professional 1968–70
AM	
Nat	English Amateur 1958–60; English Open Amateur Stroke-Play 1957–59
Trn	Scrutton Jug 1959; Golf Illustrated Gold Vase 1960; Sunningdale Foursomes 1959
Reg	Surrey Amateur 1954–56–58
Int	Walker Cup 1957–59; Eisenhower Trophy 1960; GB Commonwealth Team 1959; England (Home Int) 1956–57–58–59–60

Shapcott, Susan
Born 2nd November, 1969

Cls	Knowle
Chp	Ladies British Open Amateur r/u 1987
Nat	English Women's Stroke Play 1986. Welsh Open Amateur Stroke Play 1987–88. English Ladies Close r/u 1986
Reg	Gloucestershire Ladies 1986
Int	Curtis Cup 1988. England (Home Int) 1986–88
Mis	Dinwiddy Trophy 1985–87
Jun	British Girls 1985. English Girls 1986–87

Shaw, Graeme
Born Glasgow on 6th June, 1960

Reg   Glasgow Amateur 1986. Scottish Champion of Champions 1987
Int   Walker Cup 1987. (Scotland) Home Int 1984–86–87–88; v West Germany 1987

Sheahan, Dr David B
Born Southsea, England on 25th February, 1940

Cls   Grange
Nat   Irish Amateur 1961–66–70
Trn   Jeyes Professional 1962 (as an Amateur)
Oth   Boyd Quaich 1962
Int   Walker Cup 1963. GB v Europe 1962–64. Ireland (Home Int) 1961–62–63–64–65–66–67–70; (Eur T Ch) 1965–67 (winners on both occasions)

Shepperson, AE
Born Sutton–in–Ashfield on 8th April, 1936

Cls   Coxmoor (Hon), Notts
Nat   English Open Amateur Stroke Play r/u 1958–62
Trn   President's Putter 1957
Reg   Nottinghamshire Amateur 1955–58–61–65. Nottinghamshire Open 1955–58
Int   Walker Cup 1957–59. England (Home Int) 1956–57–58–59–60–62
Jun   British Boys 1953

Simpson, Linda (*née* Moore)
Born 7th October, 1961

Reg   Cornwall Ladies 1979–80–81. South–West Ladies 1981
Int   Curtis Cup 1980. England (Home Int) 1979–80. (Eur L T Ch) 1981

Sinclair, Alexander
Born West Kilbride, Ayrshire on 6th July, 1920

Cls   Royal & Ancient, West Kilbride (Hon), Drumpellier (Hon), Bothwell Castle (Hon), Royal Troon (Hon)
Trn   Newlands Trophy 1950
Oth   Royal & Ancient Silver Cross 1972. Royal Medal 1977. Scottish Open Amateur Seniors 1979
Reg   West of Scotland Amateur 1950. Lanarkshire Amateur 1952–59–61. Glasgow Amateur 1961
Int   Scotland (Home Int) 1950–(**66**)–(**67**). (Eur T Ch) (**1967**)
Mis   Chairman R & A Selection Committee from 1969 to 1975. Leading Amateur (joint second) in Northern Open 1948. President Scottish Golf Union 1976–78. Frank Moran Trophy 1978. Chairman R & A Amateur Status Committee 1979–81. President European Golf Association 1981–82–83. Captain of Royal & Ancient 1988

Slark, Ruth (*née* Porter)
Born Chesterfield on 6th May, 1939

Cls   Long Ashton (Hon), Bath, Burnham and Berrow, Reigate Heath, Walton Heath
Nat   English Ladies 1959–61–65, r/u 1978
Oth   Australian Ladies r/u 1963
Trn   Astor Prince's 1961. Fairway and Hazard Foursomes 1958. Roehampton Gold Cup 1963. Astor Salver 1962–63. Hovis Ladies 1966 (tied). Avia Foursomes 1968
Reg   South Western Ladies 1956–57–60–61–62–64–65–66–67–69–72–77–79. Gloucestershire Ladies 1957–59–61–62–63–64–66–67–69–73–74–75–76–77
Int   Curtis Cup 1960–62–64. Vagliano Trophy 1959–61–65.

Smith, Anne [Stant], (*née* Willard)
Born Calcutta, India on 23rd May, 1950

Cls   Walsall, Hon member of Gorleston, Purdis Heath (Ipswich), Ganton, Beau Desert
Nat   British Ladies Stroke Play 1973
Trn   Sunningdale Foursomes 1970. Central England Mixed Foursomes 1968. Hoylake Mixed Foursomes 1978
Reg   Suffolk Ladies 1967–69–70–71. Midland Ladies 1973–75. Staffordshire Ladies 1975–78–79, r/u 1977
Int   Curtis Cup 1976. Vagliano Trophy 1975. GB Commonwealth Team 1975. England (Home Int) 1974–75–76; (Eur L T Ch) 1975
Jun   British Girls 1965. English Girls 1967. Girl International 1965–66–67–68
Mis   Member of LGU Touring Team to South Africa 1974

Smith, William Dickson
Born Glasgow on 2nd February, 1918

Cls   Prestwick (Hon), Royal & Ancient, Royal Troon, Selkirk (Hon), Southerness, Gullane
Maj   Leading amateur (5th) in Open 1957
Nat   Scottish Amateur 1958. Scottish Senior Open Amateur 1983
Oth   Indian Open Amateur 1945. Portuguese Open Amateur 1967–70.
Trn   Worplesdon Mixed Foursomes 1957. Royal & Ancient Royal Medal 1971
Reg   Border Amateur 1949–51–57–63. Dumfriesshire Amateur 1956
Int   Walker Cup 1959. GB v Europe 1958. Scotland (Home Int) 1957–58–59–60–63–(**83**); v Scandinavia 1958–60

Smye, Catherine
See McCann

Smyth, Des
Born Drogheda on 12th February, 1953. Turned Professional 1973

PRO
Trn   PGA Match Play 1979. Newcastle Brown 900, Greater Manchester Open 1980. Coral Classic 1981. Sanyo Open 1983. Jersey Open 1988
Oth   Irish Professional 1979. Carrolls Irish Match Play, Irish Dunlop 1980
Int   Ryder Cup 1979–81. Ireland in World Cup 1979–80–82–83. Hennessy–Cognac Cup 1980–82–84. Dunhill Cup 1985–86–87–88 (winners)
AM
Int   Ireland (Home Int) 1972–73; (Eur T Ch) 1973

Sommerville, Dorothea
See Hastings

Soulsby, Janet
Born Corbridge on 25th December, 1964. Turned Professional 1985

Nat   Ladies British Open Amateur Stroke Play 1981
Reg   Northumberland Ladies 1983
Int   Curtis Cup 1982
Mis   Taunton Trophy, Duncan Salver, Dinwiddy Trophy 1981

Spearman, Marley
See Harris

Squirrell, Hew Crawford
Born Cardiff on 15th August, 1932

Cls   Hon member of Cardiff, Moseley, Killarney
Nat   Welsh Amateur 1958–59–60–64–65, r/u 1962–71
Trn   Antlers Royal Mid-Surrey 1959–61. Hampshire Hog
      1961. Berkhamsted Trophy 1960–63. Boyd Quaich 1955
Reg   Glamorgan Amateur 1959–65. Herts Amateur 1963–73
Int   Wales (Home Int) 1955–56–57–58–59–60–61–62–63–
      64–65–66–67–68–**69–70–71**–73–74–75; (Eur T Ch)
      1965–67–69–71–75; v France 1975
Mis   Deputy-Director Golf Foundation

Stant, Anne
See Smith

Stephen, Alexander R (Sandy)
Born St Andrews on 8th January, 1954. Turned
Professional 1985

Cls   Lundin (Hon), Muckhart (Hon), Broomieknowe
PRO
Trn   Scottish Professional Chp 1988
AM
Nat   Scottish Amateur 1971
Trn   Scottish Champion of Champions 1984
Reg   North of Scotland Open Amateur 1972–77. Fife
      Amateur 1973. Lothians Amateur 1978; East of Scotland
      Open Amateur 1974–77–83–84. West of Scotland Open
      Amateur 1975.
Int   Walker Cup 1985. GB v Europe 1972. Scotland (Home
      Int) 1971–72–73–74–75–76–77–84–85; (Eur T Ch) 1975;
      v Spain 1974; v Belgium 1975–77–78.
Jun   Scottish Boys 1970.
Int   Boys 1970–71. Youths 1972–73–74–75
Mis   Finished third in World Boys International Trophy
      (USA) 1970

Stevens, David Llewellyn
Born Church Village, Glamorgan on 14th April, 1950

Cls   Llantrisant and Pontyclun, Southerndown, Killarney
      (Hon)
Nat   Welsh Amateur Stroke Play 1969. Welsh Amateur
      1977–80
Reg   Glamorgan Amateur 1974–76–80
Int   Wales (Home Int) 1968–69–70–74–75–76–78–80–82;
      (Eur T Ch) 1969–77; v France 1976; v Denmark
      1977; in Fiat Trophy 1980

Stewart, Gillian
Born Inverness on 21st October, 1958. Turned
Professional 1985

Cls   Inverness (Hon), Nairn
PRO
Eur   IBM European Open 1984 (as amateur). Ford Ladies
      Classic 1985–87
AM
Nat   Scottish Ladies 1979–83–84. Ladies British Open
      Amateur r/u 1982
Trn   Helen Holm Trophy 1981–84
Reg   Northern Counties Ladies 1976–78–82. North of
      Scotland Ladies 1975–78–80-82-83.
Int   Curtis Cup 1980–82. GB Commonwealth Team
      1979–83. Vagliano Trophy 1979–81–83. World Cup
      1982–84. Scotland (Home Int) 1979–80–81–82–83–84;
      (Eur L T Ch) 1979–81–83.
Jun   British Girls 1976. Scottish U–19 Stroke Play Champion
      1975

Int   Girls 1975–76–77
Mis   Member of Scottish team which won the 1980
      European Junior Team Championship. Avia Golfer
      of the Year 1984.

Storey, Eustace Francis
Born Lancaster on 30th August, 1901

Cls   Swinley Forest
Maj   Leading Amateur in Open Championship 1938
Chp   Amateur Championship r/u 1924
Trn   Worplesdon Mixed Foursomes 1938–48. President's
      Putter 1926 (tied)
Int   Walker Cup 1924–26–28. England (Home Int)1924–
      25–26–27–28–30–36; v France 1936

Stowe, Charles
Born Sandyfields, Sedgley on 11th January, 1909

Cls   Penn, Brocton Hall, Beau Desert, Shifnal
Chp   Amateur Championship r/u 1948.
Nat   English Open Amateur Stroke Play 1948–53. English
      Amateur r/u 1947–49
Trn   Prince of Wales Challenge Cup 1937–49
Reg   Midland Counties Amateur 1935–48–59–63.
      Staffordshire Amateur 1934–39–46–48–53–54–57–64.
      Staffordshire Open 1948
Int   Walker Cup 1938–47. England (Home Int) 1935–36–
      37–38–46–49; v France 1938–39
Mis   Played for British Seniors 1967

Stuart, Hugh Bannerman
Born Forres on 27th June, 1942

Cls   Forres (Hon), Murcar (Hon)
Chp   Amateur s/f 1974
Nat   Scottish Amateur 1972, r/u 1970–76
Reg   North of Scotland Amateur 1967–74. Moray
      Amateur 1960. Nairnshire Amateur 1966
Int   Walker Cup 1971–73–75. GB Commonwealth Team
      1971. Eisenhower Trophy 1972. GB v Europe
      1968–
      72–74. Scotland (Home Int) 1967–68–70–71–72–73–
      74–76; (Eur T Ch) 1969–71–73–75; v Belgium 1973–75
Jun   Scottish Boys 1959.
Int   Boys 1959
Mis   Won all his matches in 1971 Walker Cup. Member
      of European Team to tour South Africa 1974

Swallow, Carole
Born 9th August, 1967. Turned Professional 1985

Nat   Welsh Ladies Open Amateur Stroke Play 1985
Int   England (Eur L T Ch) 1985; (Home Int) 1985
Jun   British Girls 1984. English Girls 1984
Mis   Dinwiddy Trophy 1984

Thirlwell, Alan
Born 8th August, 1928

Cls   Gosforth, Formby
Chp   Amateur r/u 1958–72.
Nat   English Amateur 1954–55, r/u 1963. English Open
      Amateur Stroke Play r/u 1964
Trn   County Champion of Champions 1962. Wentworth
      Pro-Am Foursomes 1960–61–68
Reg   Northumberland Amateur 1952–55–62–64.
      Northumberland and Durham Open 1960
Int   Walker Cup 1957. GB Commonwealth Team 1954–63.
      GB v Europe 1956–58; v Denmark 1955;
      v Professionals 1963. England (Home Int) 1951–52–54–
      55–56–57–58–59–63–64; v France 1954–56-59

Mic   Canadian Amateur s/f 1957, EGU Selector 1974 to
      1977. Secretary CONGU

Thom, Kenneth Gordon
Born 1st March, 1922

Cls	Hendon
Nat	English Amateur r/u 1946
Reg	Middlesex Amateur 1947-48
Int	Walker Cup 1949. England (Home Int) 1947–48–49–53
Jun	Boy International 1939

Thomas, David C
Born Newcastle–upon–Tyne on 16th August, 1934. Turned Professional 1949

Maj	Open r/u 1958 (lost play-off for title), r/u 1966
Eur	Belgian Open 1955. Dutch Open 1958. French Open 1959
Trn	Esso Golden 1961 (tied)–62–66. PGA Match Play, Olgiata Trophy (Rome) 1963. Silentnight 1965 (tied). Penfold–Swallow, Jeyes 1966. Penfold 1968 (tied). Graham Textiles 1969. Pains–Wessex 1969
RoW	Caltex (NZ) 1958–59.
Oth	British Assistants 1955. Wentworth Pro–Am Foursomes 1960–61
Int	Ryder Cup 1959–63–65–67. Wales in World Cup 1957–58–59–60–61–62–63–66–67–69–70. Wales in Double Diamond 1972–73
Mis	Won qualifying competition for US Open 1964

Thomas, Tegwen (née Perkins)
Born Cardiff on 2nd October, 1955

Cls	Wenvoe Castle, Porthcawl, Pennard
Nat	Welsh Ladies Amateur 1976–77. Welsh Ladies Open Amateur Stroke Play 1980. British Ladies Amateur Stroke Play r/u 1974
Trn	Wills Match Play 1973. Avia Foursomes 1977. Worplesdon Mixed Foursomes 1973–78
Reg	South–Western Ladies 1973–74–76. Glamorganshire Ladies 1972–74–75–77–78–80–81–83
Int	Curtis Cup 1974–76–78–80. World Team Championship 1974. GB Commonwealth Team 1975–79. GB in Colombian International 1977–79. Wales (Home Int) 1972 to 84; (Eur L T Ch) 1975–77–79–81-83; in Fiat Trophy 1978.
Jun	Welsh Girls 1970.
Int	Girls 1970–71–72–73
Mis	Member of LGU Team to tour South Africa 1974. First Welsh player in Curtis Cup Team. In 1976 became first Welsh Woman player to win all matches in Home Internationals. Daks Woman Golfer of the Year 1976 (joint). Taunton Trophy 1974. Duncan Salver 1974–76. Dinwiddy Trophy 1973–74

Thomas, Vicki (née Rawlings)
Born Northampton on 27th October, 1954

Cls	Pennard
Nat	Welsh Ladies Amateur 1979–82–83–85–86–87. British Ladies Amateur Stroke Play r/u 1979. Welsh Ladies Open Stroke Play 1981–82–89, r/u 1980
Trn	Roehampton Gold Cup 1983–85. Cotswold Gold Vase 1983. Keithley Trophy 1983. Sunningdale Foursomes 1989
Reg	Glamorganshire Ladies 1970–71–79
Int	Curtis Cup 1982–83–86–88. GB Commonwealth Team 1979–83–87. Vagliano Trophy 1979–83–85–87–89. Wales (Home Int) 1971 to 89; (Eur L T Ch) 1973–75–77–79–81–83–87.
Jun	Welsh Girls 1973.
Int	Girls 1969–70–71–72–73
Mis	Taunton Trophy 1979, Smyth Salver 1986

Thompson, Martyn S
Born 27th January, 1964

Chp	Amateur Champion 1982
Int	Walker Cup 1983. England (Home Int) 1982

Thomson, James Allan
Born Prestwick on 2nd May 1958

Cls	Ayr Belleisle
Nat	Scottish Amateur 1989; r/u 1981–86; s/f 1983–88
Reg	West of Scotland Amateur 1985
Int	Scotland (Home Int) 1981–82–83–84–85–86–87–88–89; v West Germany 1987; v Italy 1988

Thomson, Muriel
Born Aberdeen on 12th December, 1954. Turned Professional 1979

PRO	
Eur	Carlsberg, Viscount Double Glazing, Barnham Broom 1980; Elizabeth Ann Classic 1981; Guernsey Open, Sands International 1984; Laing Ladies Classic 1985; Irish Open, Ford Ladies Classic 1986
Mis	Order of Merit winner 1980–83; Frank Moran Trophy 1981
AM	
Nat	Scottish Ladies r/u 1977
Trn	Helen Holm Trophy 1975–76; Canadian Ladies Foursomes 1978
Reg	North of Scotland Ladies 1973–74; Aberdeenshire Ladies 1977
Int	Curtis Cup 1978; Vagliano Trophy 1977; Espirito Santo 1978; GB in Colombian International 1979; Scotland (Home Int) 1974–75–76–77–78; (Eur L T Ch) 1975–77

Thornhill, Jill
Born 18th August, 1942

Cls	Walton Heath, Silloth-on-Solway
Chp	Ladies British Open Amateur 1983
Nat	English Ladies 1986, r/u 1974. Ladies British Open Amateur Stroke Play r/u 1987
Trn	Avia Foursomes 1970–83. Astor Salver 1972–75. Newmark International 1974. Worplesdon Mixed Foursomes 1975. Hampshire Rose 1982–87
Eur	Belgian Ladies 1967
Reg	South Eastern Ladies 1964–64–85. Surrey Ladies 1962–64–65–73–74–77–78–81–82–83–84
Int	Curtis Cup 1984–86–88. Vagliano Trophy 1965–83–85-87. England (Home Int) 1964–65–74–82–83–84–85–86 –87–88. Commonwealth Team Ch 1983; (Eur L T Ch) 1983. Avia Golfer of the Year 1983
Mis	Doris Chambers Trophy 1986

Tiernan, Clarrie
See Reddan

Torrance, Sam
Born Largs, Ayrshire on 24th August, 1953. Turned Professional 1970

PRO	
Eur	Piccadilly Medal, Martini International 1976; Carrolls Irish Open 1981; Spanish Open, Portuguese Open 1982; Scandinavian Enterprise Open, Portuguese Open 1983; Tunisian Open, Benson & Hedges International, Sanyo Open 1984; Monte Carlo Open 1985; Lancia Italian Open 1987
Oth	U-25 Match Play 1972; Scottish Uniroyal 1975; Scottish Professional 1978–80
RoW	Zambian Open 1975; Colombian Open 1979

Int   Ryder Cup 1981–83–85–87–89; Hennessy-Cognac Cup
      1976–80–82–84; Nissan Cup 1985; Scotland in World
      Cup 1976–78–82–84–85; Double Diamond 1973–76–77;
      Dunhill Cup 1985–86–87–89
Mis   Rookie of the Year 1972; Tooting Bec Cup 1984
AM
Jun
Int   Scottish Boys 1970

Townsend, Peter Michael Paul
*Born Cambridge on 16th September, 1946. Turned
Professional 1966*

PRO
Eur   Dutch Open 1967; Swiss Open, Carrolls Irish Match
      Play 1971; Carrolls Irish Match Play 1976; Irish Dunlop
      1977
Oth   PGA Close, Coca-Cola Young Professionals 1968
US   Chesterfield 1968
RoW   Western Australia Open 1968; Caracas Open 1969;
      Walworth Aloyco 1971; Los Lagaratos Open 1972;
      ICL International (South Africa) 1975; Moroccan Grand
      Prix, Los Lagaratos Open, Caribbean Open, Zambian
      Open 1978; Laurent Perrier 1981
Int   Ryder Cup 1969–71; Hennessy-Cognac 1974; England
      in World Cup 1969–74; in Double Diamond 1971–72–74
AM
Nat   English Open Amateur Stroke Play 1966
Trn   Duncan Putter 1965; Mullingar Trophy 1965–66;
      Lytham Trophy 1966; Golf Illustrated Golf Vase
      1966; Prince of Wales Challenge Cup 1966; St
      George's Challenge Cup 1966; Berkhamsted Trophy
      1966
Reg   Herts Amateur 1964
Int   Walker Cup 1965; Eisenhower Trophy 1966; GB v
      Europe 1966; England (Home Int) 1965–66
Jun   British Boys 1962–64; British Youths 1965
Int   Boys 1961–62–63–64; Youths 1965
Mis   Captain PGA 1984

Tucker, William Iestyn
Born Nantyglo, Monmouth on 9th December, 1926

Cls   Monmouthshire, Brecon, Killarney, Morlais Castle,
      Tredegar and Rhymney, Pontynewydd, Llantrisant,
      Radyr, Whitehall
Nat   Welsh Amateur 1933–36, r/u 1951–56–64–67–75–76.
      Welsh Amateur Stroke Play 1976
Trn   Duncan Putter 1960–61 (tied)–63–69–76
Reg   Monmouthshire Amateur 1949, 1952 to 63, 1967–69–74.
      Gwent Amateur 1976
Int   Wales (Home Int) 1949 to 72, 1974–75; (Eur T Ch)
      1965-67-69-75; v Australia 1953; v France 1975. Captain
      Welsh Team 1966-67-68

Uzielli, Angela (née Carrick)
Born Swanton Morley, Norfolk on 1st February, 1940

Cls   Berkshire (Hon),
Chp   British Ladies Open Amateur 1977.
Nat   English Ladies Amateur r/u 1976
Trn   Astor Salver 1971–73 (tied)–77–81. Roehampton Gold
      Cup 1977. Avia Foursomes 1982. Hampshire Rose 1985
Reg   Berkshire Ladies 1976–77–78–79–80–81
Int   Curtis Cup 1978. Vagliano Trophy 1977. England
      (Home Int) 1976–77–78; (Eur L T Ch) 1977
Mis   Daks Woman Golfer of the Year 1977

Valentine, Jessie, MBE (née Anderson)
Born Perth on 18th March, 1915. Turned Professional 1960

Cls   Hon member of Craigie Hill, St Rule, Hunstanton,
      Blairgowrie, Murrayshall
Chp   British Ladies 1937–55–58, r/u 1950–57.

Nat   Scottish Ladies 1938–39–51–53–55–56, r/u 1934–54
Oth   New Zealand Ladies 1935. French Ladies 1936
Trn   Spalding Ladies 1957. Kayser Bondor Foursomes
      1959–61. Worplesdon Mixed Foursomes 1963–64–65
Reg   East of Scotland Ladies
Int   Curtis Cup 1936–38–50–52–54–56–58. GB v France
      1935–36–38–39–47–49–51–55; v Belgium 1949–51–
      54–55; v Canada 1938–50. GB Commonwealth
      Team 1953–55–(59). Scotland (Home Int) 1934–35–
      36–37–38–39–47–49–50–51–52–53–54–55–56–57–58
Jun   British Girls 1933
Mis   Canadian Ladies s/f 1938. Member of LGU Team
      to Australia and New Zealand 1935. Frank Moran
      Trophy 1967

Vaughan, Sheila
See Maher

Wade, Julie
See Hall

Wadsworth, Helen
Born on the Gower, Swansea on 7th April, 1964

Cls   Royal Cinque Ports
Nat   Welsh Ladies Open Amateur Stroke Play 1986
Oth   World Fourball Chp with Julie Wade 1987
Trn   Astor Salver 1985.
Int   Wales (Home Int) 1987–88–89; (Eur L T Ch) 1985–87
Jun   South–East Girls 1981

Waite, Claire
*Born Marlborough on 4th November, 1964. Turned
Professional 1985*

Nat   English Ladies 1984. British Ladies Stroke Play 1984
Oth   Australian Stroke Play Team 1982. South Atlantic
      (USA) 1984. Trans National (USA) 1984
Reg   Wiltshire Ladies 1980–81–83
Int   Curtis Cup 1984. Vagliano Trophy 1983.
      Commonwealth Trn 1983. Espirito Santo 1984.
      England (Home Int) 1981–82–83. (Eur L T Ch)
      1983.
Jun   British Girls 1982.
Int   English Girls 1982
Mis   Avia Golfer of the Year 1984

Waites, Brian J
Born Bolton on 1st March, 1940. Turned Professional 1957

Eur   Tournament Players' Championship 1978. Car Care
      Plan International 1982
RoW   Kenya Open 1980. Mufulira Open (Zambia) 1980–82.
      Cock o' the North (Zambia) Open 1985
Reg   Midland Open 1971–76–81. Midland Professional
      Stroke Play 1972–77–78–79. Midland Professional
      Match Play 1972–73–74.
Int   GB v Europe 1980. Hennessy–Cognac Cup 1984.
      England in World Cup 1980–82–83

Walker, Carole Michelle (Mickey)
*Born Alwoodley, nr Leeds on 17th December, 1952.
Turned Professional 1973*

PRO
Maj   Ladies British Open r/u 1979
Eur   Carlsberg 1979; Lambert & Butler Match Play
      1980; Carlsberg 1981; Sands International 1983;
      Baume-Mercier Classic, Lorne Stewart Match Play
      1984
Oth   Sunningdale Foursomes 1982
AM
Chp   Ladies British Open Amateur 1971–72; r/u 1973

Nat   Ladies British Open Amateur Stroke Play r/u 1972;
      English Ladies 1973
Oth   Portuguese Ladies Amateur, US Trans-Mississippi
      1972; Spanish Ladies Amateur 1973
Trn   Hovis Ladies 1972
Int   Curtis Cup 1972; GB Commonwealth Team 1971;
      Espirito Santo 1972; Vagliano Trophy 1971; England
      (Home Int) 1970–72 (Eur L T Ch) 1971–73
Jun   French Girls U–22 Open 1971
Int   English Girls 1969–70–71
Mis   AGW Trophy 1972; Daks Women Golfer of the Year
      1972; Duncan Salver 1972

Walker, Mrs JB, MBE
Born Ireland on 21st June, 1896

Cls   Gosforth, Hon member of Troon, Island, Malahide,
      Alnmouth, Foxton Hall
Nat   Irish Ladies 1930, r/u 1934
Oth   Australian Ladies 1935. New Zealand Ladies r/u 1935
Reg   Ayrshire Ladies 1934–37–38
Int   Curtis Cup 1934–36–38. GB v France 1935–38–39;
      v Canada 1938. Ireland (Home Int) 1928 to 38–48
Mis   Two holes-in-one in the same week

Walker, James
Born Bartonholme, by Irvine, on 11th February, 1921

Cls   Irvine Bogside
Chp   Amateur Championship r/u 1961
Nat   Scottish Amateur 1961
Reg   West of Scotland Amateur 1954. Ayrshire Amateur
      1956 (tied)
Int   Walker Cup 1961. GB v Europe 1958–60;
      v Professionals 1958–60. Scotland (Home Int)
      1954–55–57–58–60–61–62–63

Walker, Kenneth
Born Edinburgh on 1st December, 1966

Nat   Scottish Open Amateur Stroke Play 1986
Trn   Edward Trophy 1984
Oth   Scottish Universities Individual 1985
Int   Scotland (Home Int) 1986

Walker, Maureen
See Richmond

Walton, Philip
Born Dublin on 28th March, 1962. Turned Professional 1983

PRO
Trn   Irish Professional 1989
Int   Dunhill Cup 1989
AM
Nat   Scottish Open Amateur Stroke Play 1981. Irish
      Amateur 1982
Int   Walker Cup 1981–83. Ireland (Home Int) 1980–81;
      (Eur T Ch) 1981

Ward, Angela
See Bonallack

Ward, Charles Harold
Born Birmingham on 16th September, 1911

Maj   Open 3rd 1948–51, leading British player (4th) 1946
Trn   Daily Mail Victory 1945. Silver King (tied),
      Yorkshire Evening News 1948. Spalding, North
      British–Harrogate, Dunlop Masters 1949. Daily Mail
      1950. Dunlop, Lotus 1951. PGA Close 1956

Oth   West of England Open Professional 1937. Daily
      Telegraph Pro–Am 1947–48. Midland Professional
      1933–34–50–53–55–63. Midland Open 1949–51–52–
      54–57
Int   Ryder Cup 1947–49–51
Mis   Vardon Trophy 1948–49

Way, Paul
Born Kingsbury, Middx on 12th March, 1963. Turned Professional 1981

PRO
Eur   KLM Dutch Open 1982. Whyte & McKay PGA 1985.
      European Open 1987
RoW   South African Charity Classic 1985
Int   Ryder Cup 1983–85. England in World Cup 1985.
      Dunhill Cup 1985
AM
Nat   English Open Amateur Stroke Play 1981
Int   Walker Cup 1981

Weeks, Kevin
Nat   English Amateur 1987
Int   England (Home Int) 1987–88; v France 1988

Wethered, Joyce
See Lady Heathcoat–Amory

White, Ronald James
Born Wallasey on 9th April, 1921

Cls   Hon member of Royal Birkdale, Woolton, Buxton
      and High Peak, Killarney
Nat   English Amateur 1949 r/u, 1953. English Open
      Amateur Stroke Play 1950–51
Trn   Golf Illustrated Gold Vase 1949. Daily Telegraph
      Pro–Am 1947–49
Sen   British Seniors Open Amateur 1978–79
Reg   Lancashire Amateur 1948
Int   Walker Cup 1947–49–51–53–55. England (Home Int)
      1947–48–49–53; France 1947–48
Jun   Carris Trophy 1937
Int   Boys 1936–37–38

Whitlock, Susan
See Hedges

Willard, Anne
See Smith

Wilson, Miss Enid
Born Stonebroom, nr Alfreton, Derbyshire on 15th March, 1910

Cls   Hon member of Notts, Sherwood Forest, Chesterfield,
      Bramley, Sandy Lodge, Knole Park, North Hants,
      Crowborough
Chp   British Ladies 1931–32–33.
Nat   English Ladies 1928–30, r/u 1927; US Ladies Amateur
      s/f 1931–33
Trn   Roehampton Gold Cup 1930
Reg   Midland Ladies 1926–28–29–30. Derbyshire Ladies
      1925–26. Cheshire Ladies 1933
Int   Curtis Cup 1932. England (Home Int) 1928–29–30
Jun   British Girls 1925

Winchester, Roger
Born 28th March, 1967

Chp   English Amateur 1985
Int   England (Home Int) 1985–87–89. Youth (GBI) v Europe
      1987

Wood, David K
Born 27th March, 1963

Nat	Welsh Amateur 1982
Trn	Lytham Trophy 1987
Int	Wales (Home Int) 1982–83–84–85–86–87

Woosnam, Ian
Born Oswestry 2nd March, 1958. Turned Professional 1976

PRO	
Maj	Open 3rd 1986; US Open r/u 1989
Eur	Swiss Open 1982; Silk Cut Masters 1983; Scandinavian Enterprise Open 1984; Lawrence Batley TPC 1986; Jersey Open, Cepsa Madrid Open, Bell's Scottish Open, Lancôme Trophy, Suntory World Match Play 1987; Volvo PGA, Carrolls Irish Open, Panasonic European Open 1988; Carrolls Irish Open 1989
Oth	News of the World U–23 Match Play 1979; Cacharel U–25 Chp 1982
RoW	Zambian Open 1985, Kenya Open 1986; Hong Kong Open 1987
Int	Ryder Cup 1983–85–87–89; Nissan Cup 1985–86; Kirin Cup 1987; GBI v Australia 1988; Hennessy-Cognac Cup 1982–84; Wales in World Cup 1980–82–83–84–85–87 (winners; also individual winner); in Dunhill Cup 1985–86–87–88–89
Mis	Harry Vardon Trophy 1987
AM	
Reg	Shropshire & Herefordshire Amateur 1975

Wright, Janette (*née* Robertson)
Born Glasgow on 7th January, 1935

Cls	Hon member of Lenzie, Troon, Cruden Bay, Aboyne, St Rule
Nat	Scottish Ladies 1959–60–61–73, r/u 1958
Trn	Kayser Bondor Foursomes 1958 (tied)–61. Worplesdon Mixed Foursomes 1959
Reg	North of Scotland Ladies 1970. Lanarkshire Ladies 1954–55–56–57–58–59. West of Scotland Ladies 1956–58–59
Int	Curtis Cup 1954–56–58–60. Vagliano Trophy 1959–61. GB v France 1957; v Belgium 1957; v Canada 1954. GB Commonwealth Team 1959. Scotland (Home Int) 1952–53–54–55–56–57–58–59–60–61–63–65–66–67–73–(78)–(79)–(80). (Eur L T Ch) 1965–73–(79)
Jun	British Girls 1950.
Int	Girls 1950–51–52–53

Overseas Players

Aaron, Tommy
Born Gainesville, Georgia, USA on 22nd February, 1937.
Turned Professional 1961

PRO
Maj   US Masters 1973; USPGA r/u 1972
Eur   Lancôme Trophy 1972
US   Canadian Open 1969; Georgia-Pacific Atlanta Golf
      Classic 1970
Int   Ryder Cup 1969–73
AM
Nat   US Amateur r/u 1958
Int   Walker Cup 1959

Alcott, Amy
Born Kansas City, Missouri, USA on 22nd February,
1956. Turned Professional 1975

PRO
Maj   US Women's Open 1980
US   27 LPGA wins to end of 1988; Boston Five Classic 1989
Mis   Gatorade Rookie of the Year 1975; Vare Trophy,
      Golf Magazine Player of the Year 1980; Founders
      Cup 1986
AM
Jun   USGA Girls 1973

Aoki, Isao
Born Abiko, Chiba, Japan on 31st August, 1942. Turned
Professional 1964

Eur   World Match Play Chp 1978. European Open 1983
RoW   Japan PGA 1973–81–86; Japan Open 1983–87. Hawaiian
      Open 1983, Dunlop Jap International 1987
Int   Japan v US 1982–83–84. Dunhill Cup 1985. Nissan
      Cup 1985. Kirin Cup 1987

Azinger, Paul William
Born Holyoke Massachusetts, USA on 6th January, 1960.
Turned Professional 1981

Maj   Open r/u 1987; USPGA r/u 1988
US   1987–three; 1988–one; 1989–one (Great Hartford
      Open)
Int   Ryder Cup 1989
Mis   USPGA Player of the Year 1987

Baiocchi, Hugh
Born Johannesburg, South Africa on 17th August, 1946.
Turned Professional 1971

PRO
Eur   Swiss Open 1973; Dutch Open 1975; Scandinavian
      Enterprise Open 1976; PGA Match Play 1977; Swiss
      Open 1979; State Express Classic 1983
RoW   South African Open 1978; South African PGA 1980;

Western Province Open, SA International Classic
1973; Transvaal Open 1974–76; Rhodesian Dunlop
Masters, Swaziland Holiday Inns, Transvaal Open
1976; Zimbabwe Open, Vaal Reefs Open 1980
Int   South Africa in World Cup 1973–77–79;
      Hennessy-Cognac Cup 1982
Mis   Captain SA PGA 1978–79
AM
Nat   South African Amateur 1970
Oth   Brazilian Amateur 1968

Baker, Kathy
Born Albany, New York, USA on 20th March, 1961.
Turned Professional 1983.

PRO
Maj   US Women's Open 1985
AM
Int   Curtis Cup 1982; Espirito Santo 1982 (winners)

Baker–Finch, Ian
Born Nambour, Queensland, Australia on 24th October,
1960. Turned Professional 1979

Eur   Scandinavian Open 1985
US   Colonial National Invitation 1989
RoW   Australian Match Play 1987; Australian Masters 1988;
      Western Australian Open, NSW Open, Queensland
      PGA 1984; Victoria Open 1985; Golf Digest 1987;
      Pocari Sweat Open 1988
Int   Nissan Cup 1986; Kirin Cup 1987–88

Ballesteros, Severiano
Born Pedrena, Spain on 9th April, 1957. Turned
Professional 1974

Maj   Open 1979–84–88; r/u 1976. US Open 3rd 1987. US
      Masters 1980–83 r/u 1985–87; 3rd 1982
Eur   Dutch Open, Lancôme Trophy 1976; French
      Open, Uniroyal International, Swiss Open 1977;
      Martini International, German Open, Scandinavian
      Enterprise Open, Swiss Open 1978; English Classic
      1979; Madrid Open, Martini International, Dutch Open
      1980; Scandinavian Enterprise Open, Spanish Open,
      Suntory World Match Play 1981; French Open,
      French Open, Suntory World Match Play 1982;
      Sun Alliance PGA, Irish Open, Lancôme Trophy
      1983. Suntory World Match Play 1984; Irish Open,
      French Open, Sanyo Open, Spanish Open, Suntory
      World Match Play 1985; British Masters, Irish Open,
      Monte Carlo Open, French Open, Dutch Open,
      Lancôme Trophy (tied) 1986; Suze Open 1987; Open
      de Baleares, Scandinavian Enterprise Open, German
      Open, Lancôme Trophy 1988. Cepsa Madrid Open;
      Epson Grand Prix; Ebel European Masters-Swiss
      Open 1989
US   Greater Greensboro Open 1978; Westchester Classic
      1983; USF&G Classic 1985; Westchester Classic 1988

RoW Japanese Open, Dunlop Phoenix , Otago Classic 1977;
Japanese Open, Kenya Open 1978; Dunlop Phoenix,
Australian PGA 1981; Visa Taiheiyo Masters 1988
Int   Ryder Cup 1979–83–85–87–89; Hennessy-Cognac
Cup 1976–78; Spain in World Cup
1975–76(winners)–77(winners); Dunhill Cup
1985–86–88
Mis Harry Vardon Trophy 1976–77–78–86–88; AGW
Trophy 1979; Ritz Club Golfer of the Year 1988

Barber, Miller
Born Shreveport, Louisiana, USA on 31st March, 1931.
Turned Professional 1958

US   11 wins 1964–78
Sen US Seniors PGA 1981. US Seniors Open 1982.
Int   Ryder Cup 1969–71

Bean, Andy
Born Lafayette, Georgia on 13th March, 1953. Turned
Professional 1975

Maj Open r/u 1983, USPGA r/u 1980–89, 3rd 1985
US   11 wins 1977–86
Int   Ryder Cup 1979–87

Beck, Chip
Born Fayetteville, North Carolina, USA on 12th
September, 1956. Turned Professional 1978

Maj US Open r/u 1986–89
US   Los Angeles Open, USF & G Classic 1988
Int   Ryder Cup 1989, Dunhill Cup 1988

Beman, Dean R
Born Washington, DC, USA on 22nd April, 1938. Turned
Professional 1987

Maj US Open r/u 1969, leading amateur 1962
PRO
US   Texas Open 1969; Greater Milwaukee Open; Quad
Cities Open 1972; Shrine-Robinson Classic 1973
Mis Commissioner of USPGA since 1974; Herb Graffis
Award 1987
AM
Chp Amateur 1959
Nat US Amateur 1960–63, r/u 1966
Reg Eastern Amateur 1960–61–63–64
Int   Walker Cup 1959–61–63–65; Eisenhower Trophy
1960(winners)–62(winners)–64–66(r/u)

Berg, Patty
Born Minneapolis, USA on 13th February, 1918. Turned
Professional 1940 (Founder member of LPGA)

PRO
Maj US Women's Open 1946, r/u 1957
US   57 LPGA wins 1941–62 (incl Western
Open 1941–48–51–55–57–58; Titleholders Chp
1948–53–55–57)
Mis Leading money winner 1954–55–57; Bobby Jones
Award 1963; Ben Hogan Award 1975; first President
of USLPGA; LPGA Hall of Fame 1951; World Golf Hall
of Fame 1974; Old Tom Morris Award 1986
AM
Nat US Ladies Amateur 1938
Reg Western Amateur 1938
Trn 29 amateur wins 1934–40
Int   Curtis Cup 1936–38

Bevione, Isa
See Goldschmid

Bland, John
Born Johannesburg, South Africa on 22nd September,
1945. Turned Professional 1970

Eur Benson & Hedges International 1983; Suze Cannes
Open 1986
RoW South African PGA 1977; 13 trn wins in Southern
Africa 1970–88; Tournament of Champions 1988.
Int   South Africa in World Cup 1975; Hennessy-Cognac
Cup 1982

Boros, Julius
Born Fairfield, Connecticut on 3rd March, 1920. Turned
Professional 1950

Maj US Open 1952–63, r/u 1956, 3rd 1958–60; USPGA
1968; US Masters 3rd 1963
US   15 wins 1952–1968
Sen USPGA Seniors 1971–77; Legends of Golf 1979
Int   Ryder Cup 1959–63–65–67; USA in World Cup
1963–68(r/u)
Mis US leading money winner 1952–55; USPGA Player
of the Year 1952–63

Bradley, Pat
Born Westford, Massachusetts, USA on 24th March, 1951.
Turned Professional 1974

Maj US Women's Open 1981, 3rd 1989; USLPGA 1986
US   22 LPGA wins 1976–87; Centinela Hospital Classic
1989
RoW Colgate Far East Open 1975
Mis Rolex Player of the Year 1986; Vare Trophy 1986;
Mazda–LPGA Series 1983–86; Golf Magazine Player
of the Year 1986

Burke, Jack, Jr
Born Fort Worth, Texas, USA in January, 1923. Turned
Professional 1940

Maj USPGA 1956; US Masters 1956, r/u 1952
US   15 wins 1950–63
Int   Ryder Cup 1951–53–55–**57**–59–(**73**)
Mis USPGA Player of the Year 1956

Calcavecchia, Mark
Born Laurel, Nebraska, USA on 12th June 1960. Turned
Professional 1981

Maj Open 1989; US Masters r/u 1988
US   WSW Golf Classic 1986 Honda Classic 1987, Bank
of Boston Classic 1988; Phoenix Open, Nissan Los
Angeles Open 1989
Int   Ryder Cup 1987–89; Kirin Cup 1987

Campbell, William Cammack
Born West Virginia, USA on 5th May, 1923

Chp Amateur r/u 1954
Nat US Amateur 1964
Oth Canadian Amateur r/u 1952–54–65; Mexican Amateur
1956
Reg North & South Amateur 1950–53–57–67. Tam O'Shanter
World Amateur 1948–49. Ontario Amateur 1967
Sen USGA Seniors 1979–80
Int   Walker Cup 1951–53–**55**–57–65–67–71–75. Eisenhower
Trophy 1964–(**68**)
Mis Bobby Jones Award 1956. President USGA 1983.
Captain Royal & Ancient 1987

Canizares, José–Maria
Born Madrid on 18th February, 1947. Turned Professional
1967

Eur Avis Jersey Open; Bob Hope British Classic 1980;
Italian Open 1981; Bob Hope British Classic 1983
Oth Lancia D'Oro 1972

RoW Kenya Open 1984
Int Ryder Cup 1981–83–85–87; Hennessy-Cognac Cup
1974–76–78–80–82–84; Spain in World Cup
1974–80–82(winners)–83–84(winners; individual
winner)–85–87; Dunhill Cup 1985–87–89

Caponi, Donna
*Born Detroit, Michigan, USA on 29th January, 1945.
Turned Professional 1965*

Maj US Women's Open 1969–70. USLPGA 1979–81
Eur Colgate European Open 1975
US 24 LPGA wins 1969–81
Mis LA Times Woman Golfer of the Year 1970

Carner, JoAnne (*née* Gunderson)
*Born Kirkland, Washington, USA on 4th April, 1939.
Turned Professional 1970*

PRO
Maj US Women's Open 1971–76, r/u 1975–78–82–83–87;
USLPGA r/u 1974–82
US 42 LPGA wins 1970–85
RoW Australian Ladies Open 1975
Mis Rolex Player of the Year 1974–81–82; Vare Trophy
1974–75–81–82–83; Gatorade Rookie of the Year 1970;
Golf Magazine Player of the Year 1974–81–82; LPGA
Hall of Fame 1982; World Golf Hall of Fame 1985;
Bobby Jones Award 1981

AM
Nat US Ladies Amateur 1957–60–62–66–68, r/u 1956–64
Trn LPGA Burdine's Invitational 1969 (as amateur)
Reg Western Ladies Open Amateur 1959
Int Curtis Cup 1958–60–62–64
Jun US Girls 1956

Casper, Billy
*Born in San Diego, California, USA on 24th June, 1931.
Turned Professional 1954*

Maj US Open 1959–66; USPGA r/u 1958–65–71; US Masters
1970, r/u 1969
Eur Lancôme Trophy 1974; Italian Open 1975
Oth Lancia D'Oro 1974
US 51 wins 1956–75; Canadian Open 1967
RoW Moroccan Grand Prix 1973–75; Mexican Open
1977
Sen Arizona Classic 1987
Int Ryder Cup 1961–63–65–67–69–71–73–75–(79)
Mis Vardon Trophy 1960–63–65–66–68; leading money
winner 1966–68. USPGA Player of the Year 1966–70;
Byron Nelson Award 1966–68–70. World Golf Hall of
Fame 1978; USPGA Hall of Fame 1982

Charles, Robert J (Bob)
*Born Carterton, New Zealand on 14th March, 1936.
Turned Profesional 1960*

PRO
Maj Open 1963, r/u 1968–69; US Open 3rd 1964–70;
USPGA r/u 1968
Eur Bowmaker 1961; Engadine Open, Swiss Open,
Daks 1962; Piccadilly World Match Play 1969,
r/u 1968; John Player Classic, Dunlop Masters
1972; Scandinavian Enterprise Open 1973; Swiss
Open 1974
US 4 wins 1963–74; Canadian Open 1968
RoW New Zealand Open 1954 (as amateur)–66–70–73, r/u
1974; New Zealand Professional 1961–79–80; 17 other
trn wins in New Zealand 1961–78; South African Open
1973
Sen Volvo Seniors British Open 1989
Int New Zealand in World Cup 1962 to 1968, 1971–72;
Dunhill Cup 1985–86

Mis First New Zealander and first left-handed player
to win the Open
AM
Int Eisenhower Trophy 1960

Coe, Charles R
Born Oklahoma City, USA on 26th October, 1923

Maj US Masters r/u 1961
Chp Amateur r/u 1951
Nat US Amateur 1949–58; r/u 1959
Reg Western Amateur 1950
Int Walker Cup 1949–51–53–(57)–59–61–63. Eisenhower
Trophy 1960
Mis Bobby Jones Award 1964

Cole, Robert
*Born Springs, South Africa on 11th May, 1948. Turned
Professional 1966*

PRO
Maj Open 3rd 1975
US Buick Open 1977
RoW South African Open 1974–80; Dunlop Masters (SA)
1969; Natal Open 1969–70–72; Cape Classic 1970;
Transvaal Open 1972; Rhodesian Masters 1972;
Vavasseur (SA) 1974
Int South Africa in World Cup 1969–74 (winners;
individual winner)–76
AM
Chp Amateur 1966
Nat English Open Amateur Stroke Play r/u 1966
Int Eisenhower Trophy 1966

Collett, Glenna
See *Vare*

Couples, Fred
*Born Seattle, Washington, USA on 3rd October, 1959.
Turned Professional 1980*

Maj US Open leading amateur 1978; USPGA 3rd 1982
US Kemper Open 1983; Tournament Players Chp 1984;
Byron Nelson Classic 1987
Int Ryder Cup 1989

Crenshaw, Ben
*Born Austin, Texas, USA on 11th January, 1952. Turned
Professional 1973*

PRO
Maj Open r/u 1978–79, 3rd 1980; US Open leading amateur
1970, 3rd 1975; USPGA r/u 1979; US Masters 1984, r/u
1976–83, 3rd 1989
Eur Carrolls Irish Open 1976
US 13 wins 1973–87
RoW Australian Open r/u 1978; Mexican Open 1982
Int Ryder Cup 1981–83–87; US in World Cup
1972–87–88(winners; individual winner); Kirin Cup
1988
Mis Rookie of the Year 1974; Byron Nelson Award
1976
AM
Trn NCAA Chp 1971–72(shared)–73
Int Eisenhower Trophy 1972(winners)

Crosby, Nathaniel
*Born Los Angeles, California, USA on 29th October,
1961. Turned Professional 1984*

Nat US Amateur 1981
Int Walker Cup 1983. Eisenhower Trophy 1982
(winners)

Daniel, Beth
Born Charleston, South Carolina, USA on 14th October, 1956. Turned Professional October, 1978

PRO
US   18 LPGA wins 1979–89
RoW World Ladies Championship (Japan) 1979
Mis USLPGA Rookie of the Year 1979. USLPGA leading money winner 1980. USLPGA Player of the Year 1980
AM
Nat US Women's Amateur 1975–77
Int Curtis Cup 1976–78

Davies, Richard
Born USA on 29th October, 1930

Maj Leading amateur US Open 1963
Chp Amateur 1962
Int Walker Cup 1963

Davis, Rodger
Born Sydney, New South Wales, Australia on 18th May, 1951. Turned Professional 1974

Maj Open r/u 1987
Eur State Express Classic 1981. Whyte & Mackay PGA 1986. Wang Four Stars 1988
RoW Australian Open 1986. South Australia Open 1978. Victoria Open 1979
Int World Cup 1985–87. Dunhill Cup 1986 (winners)–87–88. Nissan Cup 1986. Kirin Cup 1987–88, Test Match v GBI 1988

Decker, Anne
See Sander

Dibnah, Corinne
Born Brisbane, Australia on 29th July, 1962. Turned Professional 1984

Maj Ladies British Open 1988
PRO
Trn Trusthouse Forte Ladies Classic, Kristianstad Open 1986; Guernsey Open, Spanish Open 1987; Eastleigh Classic 1988
AM
Nat Australian Ladies 1981. New Zealand Champion 1983
Int Commonwealth Tournament 1983 (winners)

Dickson, Robert B
Born McAlester, Oklahoma, USA on 25th January, 1944. Turned Professional 1968

PRO
US   2 wins 1968–73
AM
Chp Amateur 1967
Nat US Amateur 1967
Int Walker Cup 1967
Mis One of only four to win British and US Amateur titles in the same year. Bobby Jones Award 1968.

Fernandez, Vicente
Born Corrientes, Argentina on 5th April, 1946. Turned Professional 1964

Eur Dutch Open 1970; Benson & Hedges 1975; Colgate PGA 1979
RoW Argentine Open 1968–69–81; Maracaibo Open 1972; Brazil Open 1977–83–84

Int World Cup 1970–72–78–84–85. Dunhill Cup 1986–88–89. Hennessy-Cognac 1982

Finsterwald, Dow
Born Athens, Ohio, USA on 6th September, 1929. Turned Professional 1951

Maj US Open 3rd 1960; USPGA 1958; r/u 1957; US Masters r/u 1962 (tied), 3rd, 1960
US   11 wins 1955–63; Canadian Open 1956
Int Ryder Cup 1957–59–61–63–(**77**)
Mis Vardon Trophy 1957; USPGA Player of the Year 1958

Floyd, Ray
Born Fort Bragg, North Carolina, USA on 4th September, 1942. Turned Professional 1961

Maj Open r/u 1978; 3rd 1981; US Open 1986; US Masters 1970, r/u 1985, USPGA 1969–82, r/u 1976
US   19 wins 1963–86
RoW Brazilian Open 1978
Int Ryder Cup 1969–75–77–83–(**89**). Dunhill Cup 1985–86. Nissan Cup 1985
Mis Rookie of the Year 1963

Ford, Doug
Born West Haven, Connecticut, USA on 6th August, 1922. Turned Professional 1949

Maj US Masters 1957; r/u 1958. USPGA 1955
US   15 wins 1955–62; Canadian Open 1959–63
Sen 1987-one
Int Ryder Cup 1955–57–59–61
Mis USPGA Player of the Year 1955

Frost, David
Born South Africa

Eur Cannes Open 1984
RoW South African Open 1986
US   1988-one; 1989-one (NEC World Series)

Garrido, Antonio
Born Madrid on 2nd February, 1944. Turned Professional 1961

Eur Benson & Hedges International 1977. Standard Four Stars National 1986. Madrid Open 1977. Spanish Open 1972. Tunisian Open 1982
Int Ryder Cup 1979. Spain in World Cup 1977(winners)–78–79. Hennessy-Cognac Cup 1976–78–80– 82–84

Geddes, Jane
Born Huntingdon, New York, USA on 5th February, 1960. Turned Professional 1983

Maj Ladies British Open 1989; US Women's Open 1986; USLPGA 1987
US   Boston Five Classic 1986; Women's Kemper Open, GNA Glendale Federal Classic, LPGA Championship, Toledo Classic, Boston Five Classic 1987

Giles, Marvin
Maj Leading amateur US Open 1973
Chp Amateur Champion 1975
Nat US Amateur Champion 1972, r/u 1967–68–69
Int Walker Cup 1969–71–73–75. Eisenhower Trophy (winners) 1968–70–72

Goldschmid, Isa (née Bevione)
Born Italy

Nat   Italian Ladies' Close 1947-51-53-54-55-56-57-
58-59-60-61-62-63-64-65-66-67-69-71-73-74. Italian
Ladies' Open 1952-57-58-60-61-63-64-67-68-69
Oth   Spanish Ladies 1952. French Ladies 1975
Trn   Kayser Bondor 1963
Int   Vagliano Trophy 1959-61-63-65-67-69-71-73-(77)
Eur v United States 1968. Italy in Espirito Santo
1964-66-68-70-72

Grady, Wayne
Born Brisbane, Queensland, Australia on 26th July 1957.
Turned Professional 1978

Maj   Open r/u 1989
Eur   German Open 1984
US   Westchester Classic
RoW   West Lakes Classic (Aust)
Int   Australia in World Cup 1978-83; Nissan Cup 1985;
Dunhill Cup 1989

Graham, David
Born Windsor, Tasmania on 23rd May, 1946. Turned
Professional 1962

Maj   Open 3rd 1985; US Open 1981; USPGA 1979
Eur   French Open 1970; Piccadilly World Match Play
1976; Lancôme Trophy 1982
US   5 wins 1972-83
RoW   Australian Open 1977, r/u 1972; Australian Wills
Masters 1975; Thailand Open, Victoria Open,
Tasmanian Open, Yomiuri Open 1970; Caracas Open,
Japanese Airlines 1971; Chunichi Crowns (Japan) 1976;
West Lakes Classic (Aust), New Zealand Open 1979;
Queensland Open 1987

Graham, Lou
Born Nashville, Tennessee, USA on 7th January, 1938.
Turned Professional 1962

Maj   US Open 1975; r/u 1977
US   1967-one. 1972-one. 1979-three.
Int   Ryder Cup 1973-75-77. World Cup 1975 (winners)

Green, Hubert
Born Birmingham, Alabama, USA on 18th December,
1946. Turned Professional 1970

Maj   US Open 1977. US Masters r/u 1978. USPGA 1985
Eur   Carrolls Irish Open 1977
US   16 wins 1971-84
RoW   Dunlop Phoenix (Japan) 1975
Int   Ryder Cup 1977-79-85. USA in World Cup 1977
Mis   Rookie of the Year 1971

Green, Ken
Born Danbury, Connecticut, USA on 23rd July 1958.
Turned Professional 1979

US   Buick Open 1985; The International 1986; Canadian
Open, Greater Milwaukee Open 1988; Greater
Greensboro Open 1989
Int   Ryder Cup 1989

Gunderson, JoAnne
See Carner

Härdin Christian
Born Sweden

Chp   Amateur Champion 1988
Int   (Eur) v GBI 1988

Harper, Chandler
Born Portsmouth, Virginia, USA on 10th March, 1914.
Turned Professional 1934

Maj   USPGA 1950
US   Won over 20 tournaments. Ten times Virginia Open
Champion.
Sen   National Seniors 1965 World Senior Professional,
USPGA Seniors 1968.
Int   Ryder Cup 1955
Mis   Elected to USPGA Hall of Fame 1969. Holder of
USPGA 54- and 36-hole records (see *Record*
Scoring). In 1941 scored round of 58 (29-29) on
6100 yards, Portsmouth, Virginia

Hayes, Dale
Born Pretoria, South Africa on 1st July, 1952. Turned
Professional 1970

PRO
Eur   Spanish Open 1971; Swiss Open 1975; Italian Open,
French Open 1978; Spanish Open 1979
Oth   Coca-Cola Young Professionals 1974; PGA U-25 1975
RoW   South African Open 1976, leading amateur 1969; South
African PGA 1974-75-76; 12 wins in Southern Africa
1970-76; Brazilian Open 1970; Bogota Open 1979
Int   South Africa in World Cup 1974(winners)-76
Mis   Accles & Pollock Award 1973; Harry Vardon Trophy
1975
AM
Nat   South African Amateur Stroke Play 1969-70
Oth   English Open Amateur Stroke Play r/u 1969; German
Amateur 1969; Scottish Open Amateur Stroke Play
1970
Int   Eisenhower Trophy 1970(r/u individual)
Jun   World Junior Chp 1969

Haynie, Sandra
Born Fort Worth, Texas, USA on 4th June 1943. Turned
Professional 1961

Maj   US Open 1965-74, r/u 1963-70-82; USLPGA 1974,
r/u 1975-83
US   42 LPGA wins 1962-82
Mis   Rolex Player of the Year 1970; LPGA Hall of Fame 1977

Henning, Harold
Born Johannesburg, South Africa on 3rd October, 1934.
Turned Professional 1953

Maj   Open 3rd 1960-70.
Trn   Daks 1958 (tied). Yorkshire Evening News 1958
(tied). Spalding 1959 (tied). Sprite 1960. Pringle 1964
Nat   South African Open 1957-62. South African PGA
1965-66-67-72
Eur   Italian Open 1957. Swiss Open 1960-64. Danish Open
1960-64-65. German Open 1965.
RoW   Malaysian Open 1966
US   2 wins 1966-70
Oth   Transvaal Open 1957. Natal Open 1957. Western
Province Open 1957-59. Cock o' the North 1959.
Engadine Open 1966. South African International
Classic 1972. ICL International (SA) 1980
Int   South Africa in World Cup 1957-58-59-61-65
(winners)-66-67-69-70-71

Hogan, Ben W
Born Dublin, Texas, USA on 13th August, 1912. Turned
Professional 1929

Maj   Open 1953; US Open 1948-50-51-53; r/u 1955-56.
USPGA 1946-48. US Masters 1951-53; r/u
1942-46-54-55
US   57 wins 1938-59

Int   Ryder Cup 1947–49–51–(67). World Cup 1956 (winners and individual winner)–58
Mis   USPGA Player of the Year 1948–50–51–53. US leading money winner 1940–41–42–46–48. Sportsman of the Decade Award 1946–56. Had a serious car crash in 1949 which seemed likely to prevent him playing golf again but returned to win more major victories. In 1965 was named the greatest professional of all time by US golf writers. Bobby Jones Award 1976

Hyndman, William III
Born 25th December, 1915

Chp   Amateur r/u 1959–69–70
Nat   US Amateur r/u 1955
Sen   US Seniors 1973
Int   Walker Cup 1957–59–61–71. Eisenhower Trophy 1958–60

Inkster, Juli
Born Santa Cruz, California, USA on 24th June, 1960. Turned Professional 1983

PRO
US   13 wins 1983–89
AM
Nat   US Ladies Amateur 1980–81–82
Int   Curtis Cup 1982; World Cup 1980–82

Irwin, Hale
Born Joplin, Montana, USA on 3rd June, 1945. Turned Professional 1968

Maj   Open r/u 1983; US Open 1974–79, 3rd 1975
Eur   Piccadilly World Match Play 1974–75
US   16 wins 1971–86
RoW   Australian PGA 1978. South African PGA 1978. Bridgestone 1981
Int   Ryder Cup 1975–77–79–81. USA in World Cup 1974–79 (winners and individual winner)

January, Don
Born Plainview, Texas, USA on 20th November, 1929. Turned Professional 1955

Maj   USPGA 1967; r/u 1961–76
US   11 wins 1956–76
Sen   1987–one
Int   Ryder Cup 1965–67

Kennedy, Edwina
Born 10th June, 1959

Nat   Ladies Amateur 1978.
Oth   Canadian Ladies Amateur 1980
Int   World Cup 1978 (winners) 80–84–86. Commonwealth Tournament 1979–83

King, Betsy
Born Reading, Pennsylvania, USA on 13th August, 1955. Turned Professional 1977

Maj   Ladies British Open 1986; US Woman's Open 1989; USLPGA r/u 1987
US   19 wins 1984–89

Kite, Tom
Born Austin, Texas, USA on 9th December, 1949. Turned Professional 1972

PRO
Maj   Open r/u 1978; US Masters r/u 1983–86, 3rd 1977
US   13 wins 1976–89
RoW   Auckland Classic (NZ) 1974

Int   Ryder Cup 1979–81–83–85–87–89; Kirin Cup 1987(individual winner); Dunhill Cup 1989(winners); World Cup 1984–85
Mis   Rookie of the Year 1973; Vardon Trophy 1981–82; Palmer Award 1981; Bobby Jones Award 1979; Golf Writers Player of the Year 1981
AM
Chp   Amateur s/f 1971
Nat   US Amateur r/u 1970
Trn   NCAA Chp 1972(shared)
Int   Walker Cup 1971; Eisenhower Trophy 1970(winners)

Knight, Nancy
See Lopez

Kuramoto, Masahiro
Born Hiroshima City, Hiroshima, Japan on 9th September, 1955. Turned Professional 1981

RoW   Japan Amateur 1975–77–00. Japan PGA 1982
Eur   14 wins 1983–88
Int   Dunhill Cup 1985

Lacoste, Catherine
See Prado

Langer, Bernhard
Born Anhausen, West Germany on 27th August, 1957. Turned Professional 1972

Maj   Open r/u 1981–84, 3rd 1985–86; US Masters 1985
Eur   Dunlop Masters 1980; German Open, Bob Hope Classic 1981; German Open 1982; Italian Open, Glasgow Golf Classic, St Mellion TPC 1983; French Open, Dutch Open, Irish Open, Spanish Open 1984; German Open, European Open 1985; Lancôme Trophy(shared), German Open 1986; Whyte & Mackay PGA, Irish Open 1987; Epson Grand Prix 1988; Peugeot Spanish Open, German Masters 1989
Oth   German Close Professional, Cacherel U–25 Chp 1979; Belgian Classic 1987
US   Sea Pines Heritage Classic 1985
RoW   Colombian Open 1980; Johnnie Walker Tournament, Casio World Open 1983; Australian Masters, Sun City Challenge 1985
Int   Ryder Cup 1981–83–85–87–89; Hennessy-Cognac Cup 1976–78–80–82; Germany in World Cup 1976–77–78–79–80; Nissan Cup 1985–86, Kirin Cup 1987
Mis   Harry Vardon Trophy 1981–84

Lewis, Bob

Nat   US Amateur r/u 1980
Int   Walker Cup 1981–83–85–87. Eisenhower Trophy (winners) 1982

Littler, Gene
Born San Diego, California, USA on 21st July, 1930. Turned Professional 1954

PRO
Maj   US Open 1961, r/u 1954; USPGA r/u 1977; US Masters r/u 1970(tied)
US   26 wins 1955–1977; Canadian Open 1965
RoW   Taiheiyo Pacific Masters 1974–75; Australian Masters 1980; Yellow Pages (SA) 1977
Sen   1987–two
Int   Ryder Cup 1961–63–65–67–69–71–75
Mis   Byron Nelson Award 1959; Bobby Jones Award, Ben Hogan Award 1973
AM
Nat   US Amateur 1953
Int   Walker Cup 1953

Lopez, Nancy
Born Torrance, California, USA on 6th January, 1957.
Turned Professional July, 1977

Maj	US Women's Open r/u 1975(leading amateur)–77–89; USLPGA 1978–85–89
PRO	
Eur	Colgate European 1978–79
US	39 LPGA wins 1978–88; Atlantic City Classic, Nippon Travel–MBS Classic 1989
RoW	Colgate Far East 1978
Mis	Rolex Player of the Year 1978–79–85–88; Vare Trophy 1978–79–85; Mazda-LPGA Series 1985; Gatorade Rookie of the Year 1978; Powell Award 1987; Golf Magazine Player of the Year 1978–79–85; LPGA Hall of Fame 1987
AM	
Oth	Mexican Ladies Amateur 1975
Int	Curtis Cup 1976; Espirito Santo 1976(winners)
Jun	US Girls 1972–74

de Lorenzi, Marie-Laure
Born Biarritz, France on 21st January 1961. Turned Professional 1986

PRO	
Maj	Ladies British Open 3rd 1989
Eur	BMW Ladies German Open, Belgian Ladies Godiva Open 1987; French Open, Volmac Open, Hennessy Ladies Cup, Gothenburg Ladies Open, Laing Charity Classic, Woolmark Match Play Chp, Qualitair Ladies Spanish Open, Benson & Hedges Trophy (with M McNulty) 1988; Ford Ladies Classic, Hennessy Ladies Cup, BMW Ladies Classic 1989
Mis	Woolmark Order of Merit winner 1988
AM	
Nat	French Close Chp 1983
Oth	Spanish Ladies 1978–80–83
Int	France (Eur L T Ch) 1977–83; Vagliano Trophy 1983
Jun	French Girls 1976; British Girls 1978
Mis	Doris Chambers Trophy 1982–85; Angus Trophy 1980

McCumber, Mark
Born Jacksonville, Florida, USA on 7th September, 1951.
Turned Professional 1974

Maj	US Open r/u 1989
US	Doral-Eastern Open 1979; Western Open 1983; Pensacola Open 1983; Doral-Eastern Open 1985; Anheuser-Busch Classic 1987; Tournament Players Championship 1988. Beatrice Western Open 1989
Int	Ryder Cup 1989. Dunhill Cup 1988

McGuire, Marnie
Born New Zealand

Nat	Ladies British Amateur 1986

McIntire, Barbara

Maj	US Women's Open r/u 1956
Chp	Ladies British Amateur 1960
Nat	US Ladies Amateur 1959–64
Int	Curtis Cup 1958–60–62–64–66–72

McNulty, Mark
Born Zimbabwe on 25th October, 1953. Turned Professional 1977

Eur	Greater Manchester Open 1979; German Open 1980; Portuguese Open 1986; German Open, 4 Stars Pro-Celebrity, Dunhill Masters 1987; Cannes Open 1988; Torres Monte Carlo Open 1989
RoW	SAF Open 1987, SAF Masters 1982–86; 19 wins 1980–89; Malay Open 1980

Mahaffey, John Drayton
Born Kerrville, Texas, USA on 9th May, 1948. Turned Professional 1971

PRO	
Maj	US Open leading Amateur 1970, r/u 1975;
US	8 wins 1973–86; St Jude Classic 1989; USPGA 1978
Int	Ryder Cup 1979, US in World Cup 1978 (winners; individual winner) 1979 (winners)
AM	
Trn	NCAA Champion 1970

Marsh, Graham, MBE
Born Kalgoorlie, Western Australia on 14th January, 1944. Turned Professional 1968

Eur	Swiss Open 1970; German Open 1972; Sunbeam Electric 1973; Benson & Hedges International 1976; Colgate World Match Play, Lancôme Trophy 1977; Dutch Open, Dunlop Masters 1979; Benson & Hedges International 1980; European Open 1981; Dutch Open 1985
US	1977–one
RoW	Watties Open (NZ) 1970; Indian Open, Spalding Masters (NZ) 1971; Indian Open, Thailand Open 1973; Malaysian Open 1974; Malaysian Open 1975; Western Australian Open 1976; 17 wins in Japan 1972–81; Sapporo–Tokyu Open (Jap) 1989
Int	Dunhill Cup 1985(winners); Nissan Cup 1986; Kirin Cup 1987
Mis	USPGA Rookie of the Year 1977; Australian Sportsman of the Year 1977

Massey, Debbie
Born Grosse Pointe, Michigan, USA on 5th November 1950. Turned Professional 1977.

Maj	Ladies British Open 1980–81; US Women's Open leading amateur 1974; USLPGA 3rd 1983
PRO	
US	Mizuno Japan Classic 1977; Wheeling Classic 1979
Mis	Gatorade Rookie of the Year 1977
AM	
Oth	Canadian Ladies Amateur 1974–75–76
Reg	Western Amateur 1972–75; Eastern Amateur 1975
Int	Curtis Cup 1974–76; Espirito Santo 1976
Mis	Doris Chambers Trophy 1976; Angus Trophy 1976

Melynk, Steven Nicholas
Born Brunswick, Georgia, USA on 26th February, 1947. Turned Professional 1971

AM	
Maj	Open leading amateur 1970; US Masters leading amateur 1970
Chp	Amateur 1971
Nat	US Amateur 1969
Reg	Western Amateur 1969. Eastern Amateur 1970
Int	Walker Cup 1969–71
Mis	US Amateur Golfer of the Year 1969

Middlecoff, Cary
Born Halls, Tennessee, USA on 6th January, 1921. Turned Professional 1947

Maj	US Open 1949–56, r/u 1957; USPGA r/u 1955; US Masters 1955, r/u 1948
US	37 wins 1947–61
Int	Ryder Cup 1953–55–59; World Cup 1959
Mis	Byron Nelson Award 1955; Vardon Trophy 1956; USPGA Hall of Fame 1974; World Golf Hall of Fame 1986

Miller, Johnny Lawrence
Born San Francisco, USA on 29th April, 1947. Turned Professional 1969

Maj　Open 1976, r/u 1973, 3rd 1975; US Open 1973, leading amateur 1966; US Masters r/u 1971–75
Eur　Lancôme Trophy 1973–79
US　21 wins 1971–87
RoW　Dunlop Phoenix International (Japan) 1974. Otago Classic (NZ) 1972
Int　Ryder Cup 1975–81; World Cup 1973 (winners; individual winner)–75 (winners; individual winner)–80; v Japan 1983
Mis　USPGA Player of the Year 1974. US leading money winner 1974

Mize, Larry Hogan
Born Augusta, Georgia, USA on 23rd September, 1958. Turned Professional 1980

Maj　US Masters 1987
US　Memphis Classic 1983
RoW　Casio World Open (Jap) 1988
Int　Ryder Cup 1987

Nagle, Kelvin DG
Born North Sydney, Australia on 21st December, 1920. Turned Professional 1946

Maj　Open 1960, r/u 1962; US Open r/u 1965 (tied)
Eur　Irish Hospitals, Dunlop, French Open 1961. Bowmaker 1962–65. Esso Golden 1963–67
US　Canadian Open 1964
RoW　Australian Open 1959. Australian Professional 1949–54–58–59–65–68. New Zealand Professional 1957–58–60–70–73–74–75. New Zealand Open 1957–58–62–64–67–68–69. In New Zealand BP 1968; Caltex 1969, Garden City, 1969, Otago Charity Classic 1970–76. Stars Travel 1970. In Australia: West End Open 1969, NBN Newcastle 1970, New South Wales Professional 1971, South Coast Open 1975, Western Australia PGA 1977
Sen　World Seniors 1971–75; British Seniors 1971–73–75 (winners)
Int　Australia in World Cup 1954 (winners) 55–58–59–(winners)–60–61–62–65–66
Mis　Honorary Member of Royal & Ancient.

Nakajima, Tsuneyuki
Born Kiryu City, Gumma, Japan on 20th October, 1954. Turned Professional 1975

Maj　USPGA 3rd 1988
RoW　Japan Amateur 1973. Japan Open 1985–86. Japan PGA 1983–84–86; 12 wins 1984–87
Int　Dunhill Cup 1986. Nissan Cup 1986(individual winner). Kirin Cup 1987

Nelson, Byron
Born Fort Worth, Texas, USA on 4th February, 1912. Turned Professional 1932

Maj　US Open 1939; r/u 1946; USPGA 1940–45, r/u 1939–41–44; US Masters 1937–42, r/u 1941–47
Eur　French Open 1955
US　54 wins 1935–one 1936–one 1937–two 1938–two 1939–three 1940–two 1941–three 1942–three 1944–six 1945–fifteen 1946–five
Int　Ryder Cup 1937–47

Mis　Vardon Trophy 1939; leading money winner 1944–45; USPGA Hall of Fame 1953; World Golf Hall of Fame 1974; Bobby Jones Award 1974; 11 consecutive tour wins March-August 1945, and 18 for the year.

Nelson, Larry Gene
Born Fort Payne, Alabama, USA on 10th September, 1947. Turned Professional 1971

Maj　US Open 1983. USPGA 1981–87.
US　4 wins 1979-88
Int　Ryder Cup 1979–81–87

Neumann, Liselotte
Born Finspang, Sweden on 20th May, 1966. Turned Professional 1985

PRO
Maj　US Women's Open 1988
Eur　5 wins 1985–88
RoW　Singapore Open 1987
AM
Nat　Swedish Champion 1982–83; Swedish Match Play Champion 1983
Int　Sweden (Eur L T Ch) 1984. Espirito Santo 1982–84

Newton, Jack
Born Sydney, Australia on 30th January, 1950. Turned Professional 1969

Maj　Open r/u 1975 (tied); US Masters r/u 1980
Nat　Australian Open 1979
Eur　Benson & Hedges Festival 1972. Benson & Hedges PGA Match Play 1974. Sumrie 1975. Dutch Open 1972
US　1978–one
RoW　City of Auckland Classic (NZ) 1972. Amoco Forbes (Aust) 1972. Nigerian Open 1974. Cock o' the North (Zambia) 1976. Mufulira Open 1976. New South Wales Open 1976–79
Mis　Seriously injured on tarmac by aeroplane propeller accident 1983

Nicklaus, Jack William
Born Columbus, Ohio, USA on 21st January, 1940. Turned Professional 1961

Maj　Open 1966–70–78, r/u 1964–67–72–76–79, 3rd 1963–74–75; US Open 1962–67–72–80, r/u 1960 (leading amateur)–68–71(tied)–82, leading amateur (4th) 1961; USPGA 1963–71–73–75–80, r/u 1964–65–74–83, 3rd 1967–77; US Masters 1963–65–66–72–75–86, r/u 1964–71–77–81, 3rd 1973–76
PRO
Eur　Piccadilly World Match Play 1970, r/u 1966–71
US　71 wins 1962–84; World Series 1962–63–67–70–76
RoW　Australian Open 1964–68–71–75–76–78; Dunlop International (Aust) 1971
Int　Ryder Cup 1969–71–73–75–77–81–(83)–(87); World Cup 1963(winners; individual winner) –64(winners; individual winner) –65–66(winners) –67(winners) –71(winners; individual winner) –73(winners)
Mis　Rookie of the Year 1962; USPGA Player of the Year 1967–72–73–75–76; leading money winner 1964–65–67–71–72–73–75–76; Byron Nelson Award 1964–65–67–72–73; Bobby Jones Award 1975; Walter Hagen Award 1980; World Golf Hall of Fame 1974; US Sportsman of the Year 1978; Card Walker Award 1983
AM
Nat　US Amateur 1959–61
Trn　NCAA Chp 1961
Int　Walker Cup 1959–61; Eisenhower Trophy 1960(winners; individual winner)

Norman, Greg
Born Mt Isa, Queensland, Australia on 10th February, 1955. Turned Professional 1976

Maj   Open 1986, r/u 1989(tied); US Open r/u 1984(tied); USPGA r/u 1986; US Masters r/u 1986–1987(tied), 3rd 1989

Eur   Martini 1977; Martini 1979; Scandinavian Enterprise Open, French Open, Suntory World Match Play 1980; Martini, Dunlop Masters 1981; Dunlop Masters, Benson & Hedges International, State Express Classic 1982; Suntory World Match Play 1983; European Open, Suntory World Match Play 1986; Italian Open 1988

US   Kemper Open, Canadian Open 1984; Panasonic-Las Vegas Invitational, Kemper Open 1986; MCI Heritage Classic 1988; The International, Greater Milwaukee Open 1989

RoW   Australian Open 1980–85; Australian Masters 1984–87; Australian PGA 1984–85; Australian Open 1976; South Seas Classic (Fiji), NSW Open 1978; Hong Kong Open 1979; NSW Open, Hong Kong Open 1983; Victoria Open 1984; NSW Open, Queensland Open, South Australian Open, Western Australian Open 1986; ESP Open, Palm Meadows Cup 1988

Int   Australia in World Cup 1976–78; Dunhill Cup 1985(winners)–1986(winners)–87–88–89; Nissan Cup 1985–86; Kirin Cup 1987; test match v GBI 1988

Mis   Harry Vardon Trophy 1982; Arnold Palmer Award 1986

North, Andy
Born Thorp, Wisconsin, USA on 9th March, 1950. Turned Professional 1972

Maj   US Open 1978–85
US   2 wins 1977–78
Int   US in World Cup 1978

Okamoto, Ayako
Born Hiroshima, Japan on 2nd April, 1951. Turned Professional 1976

Maj   Ladies British Open 1984; US Women's Open r/u 1987(tied); USLPGA r/u 1989
US   15 wins 1982–89
Mis   Rolex Player of the Year 1987; Mazda-LPGA Series 1984–87

Olazabal, José-Maria
Born Fuenterrabia, Spain on 5th February, 1966. Turned Professional 1985

PRO
Eur   Ebel European Masters – Swiss Open, Sanyo Open 1986; Volvo Belgian Open, German Masters 1988; Tenerife Open, KLM Dutch Open 1989
Int   Ryder Cup 1987–89; Kirin Cup 1987; Spain in Dunhill Cup 1986–87–88–89

AM
Chp   Amateur 1984
Nat   Spanish Open Amateur 1983
Oth   Italian Open Amateur 1983
Jun   British Boys 1983; Belgian International Youths Chp 1984; British Youths 1985

O'Meara, Mark
Born Goldsboro, North Carolina, USA on 13th January, 1957. Turned Professional 1980

PRO
Maj   Open 3rd 1985; US Open 3rd 1988
Eur   Lawrence Batley International 1987

US   Greater Milwaukee Open 1984; Bing Crosby Pro-Am, Hawaiian Open 1985; AT&T Pebble Beach National Pro-Am 1989
RoW   Kapalua International, Fuji Sankei Classic (Jap) 1985; Australian Masters 1986
Int   Ryder Cup 1985–89; Nissan Cup 1985; Dunhill Cup 1985–86–87; US v Japan 1984
Mis   Rookie of the Year 1981
AM
Nat   US Amateur 1979
Oth   Mexican Amateur 1979

Ozaki, Masashi
Born Kaiman Town, Tokushima, Japan on 24th January, 1947. Turned Professional 1980

RoW   Japan Open 1974–88–89; Japan PGA 1971–74–89; Japan tour 20 wins 1984–89
Int   Nissan Cup 1986; Kirin Cup 1987

Palmer, Arnold
Born Latrobe, Pennsylvania, USA on 10th September, 1929. Turned Professional 1954

PRO
Maj   Open 1961–62, r/u 1960; US Open 1960, r/u 1962–63(tied)–66(tied)–67, 3rd 1972; USPGA r/u 1964–68–70; US Masters 1958–60–62–64, r/u 1961–65, 3rd 1959

Eur   Piccadilly World Match Play 1964–67; Lancôme Trophy 1971; Penfold PGA, Spanish Open 1975
US   61 wins 1956–four 1957–four 1958–two 1959–three 1960–six 1961–five 1962–six 1963–seven 1964–one 1965–one 1966–four 1967–four 1968–two 1969–two 1970–one 1971–four 1973–one. Canadian Open 1955; Canadian PGA 1980
RoW   Australian Open 1966
Int   Ryder Cup 1961–63–65–67–71–73–(**75**); World Cup 1960–62–63–64–66–67 (winners each year; individual winner 1967)
Mis   USPGA Player of the Year 1960–62; Vardon Trophy 1961–62–64–67; leading money winner 1958–60–62–63; Byron Nelson Award 1950–61–62–63; World Golf Hall of Fame 1974; USPGA Hall of Fame 1980; Bobby Jones Award 1971; William Richardson Award 1970; Walter Hagen Award 1981; Old Tom Morris Award 1983
AM
Nat   US Amateur 1954

Parry, Craig
Born Sunshine, Victoria, Australia on 12th January, 1966. Turned Professional 1985

Eur   Wang Four Stars National Pro-Celebrity, German Open 1989
US   Canadian TPC 1987
RoW   NSW Open, South Australian PGA 1987
Int   Kirin Cup 1988; test match vGBI 1988

Pate, Jerry
Born Macon, Georgia, USA on 16th September, 1953. Turned Professional 1975

PRO
Maj   US Open 1976; r/u 1979; USPGA 1978; US Masters 3rd 1982
US   4 wins 1977–82; Canadian Open 1976
RoW   Taiheiyo Pacific Masters 1976; Brazilian Open 1980
Int   USA in World Cup 1976
Mis   Rookie of the Year 1976
AM
Nat   US Amateur 1974
Int   Walker Cup 1975

Pavin, Corey
Born Oxnard, California, USA on 16th November, 1959.
Turned Professional 1981

PRO
Eur German Open 1983.
US 7 wins 1984–88
RoW SA PGA 1983
Int Nissan Cup 1985
AM
Int Walker Cup 1981

Peete, Calvin
Born Detroit, USA on 18th July, 1943. Turned Professional
1971

Maj USPGA 3rd 1982
US 12 wins 1979–86
Oth Vardon Trophy 1984
Int Ryder Cup 1983–85. Nissan Cup 1985–86
Mis Ben Hogan Award 1984

Pinero, Manuel
Born Badajoz, Spain on 1st September, 1952. Turned
Professional 1968

Eur Madrid Open 1974; Swiss Open 1976; Penfold PGA
1977; English Classic 1980; Madrid Open, Swiss Open
1981; European Open 1982; Cepsa Madrid Open,
Italian Open 1985
Oth Spanish Professional 1972–73
Int Ryder Cup 1981–85; Hennessy-Cognac Cup
1974–76–78– 80–82; Spain in World Cup
1974–76(winners)– 78–79–80–82(winners; individual
winner)–83–85–88; Dunhill Cup 1985

Player, Gary
Born Johannesburg, South Africa on 1st November, 1935.
Turned Professional 1953

Maj Open 1959–68–74, 3rd 1967; US Open 1965, r/u 1958–79;
USPGA 1962–72, r/u 1969; US Masters 1961–74–78, r/u
1962(tied)–65, 3rd 1970
Eur Dunlop 1956; Piccadilly World Match Play
1965–66–68–71–73; Ibergolf European Chp 1974;
Lancôme Trophy 1975
US 21 wins 1958–78; World Series 1965–68–72
RoW South African Open 1956–60–65–66–67–
68–69–72–75–76–77–79–81; South African
PGA 1968–79–81; South African Masters
1959–60–64–67–71–72–73–74–76–76(2)–79; Australian
Open 1958–62–63–65–69–70–74; Australian PGA 1957;
Brazilian Open 1972–74; Chile Open 1980; Ivory
Coast Open 1980; Transvaal Open 1959–60–62–66;
Natal Open 1958–60–66–68; Western Province Open
1968–71–72; General Motors (SA) 1971–75–76;
Rothmans Match Play (SA) 1973; International Classic
(SA) 1974; ICL International (SA) 1977; Johannesburg
International, Sun City Classic 1979; Wills Masters
(Aust) 1968; Dunlop International (Aust) 1970; Japan
Airlines Open 1972
Sen USGA Senior Open 1987–88; Senior TPC 1987; Volvo
Seniors British Open 1988
Int South Africa in World Cup 1956–57–58–59–
60–62–63–64–65(winners; individual winner)
–66–67–68–71–72–73–77(individual winner)
Mis US leading money winner 1961; Bobby Jones
Award 1966; World Golf Hall of Fame 1974;
William Richardson Award 1976; SA PGA captain
1977, president 1978

Ploujoux, Philippe
Born La Bouille, Seine Maritime, France on 20th February,
1955

Chp Amateur 1981
Nat French Amateur Close Match Play 1977
Oth International Moroccan Stroke Play 1977
Int Continental Team (St Andrews Trophy) five times
(including winners 1982) Continental Youth Team four
times. Represented France more than fifty times
Jun French Youths Match Play 1972–73–74–75–76. French
Boys 1969–70

Pohl, Dan
Born Mt Pleasant, Michigan, USA on 1st April, 1955.
Turned Professional 1977

PRO
Maj US Open 3rd 1982; US Masters r/u 1982
US 2 wins 1986
Int Ryder Cup 1987
AM
Reg Michigan State Champion 1975–77

Prado, Catherine (née Lacoste)
Born Paris on 27th June, 1945

Maj US Women's Open 1967
Chp Ladies British Open Amateur 1969
Nat French Ladies Open Amateur 1967–69–70–72. French
Ladies Close Amateur 1968–69
Oth US ladies' Amateur 1969; Spanish Ladies Amateur
1969–72–76
Reg Western Ladies Amateur 1968
Trn Astor Princes' 1966; Worplesdon Foursomes 1967;
Hovis 1969
Int Espirito Santo 1964 (winners; individual winner)–68
(individual winner)
Mis Doris Chambers Trophy 1967–69; First amateur, first
non-American and youngest player at that time to win
the US Women's Open

Price, Nick
Born Durban, South Africa on 28th January, 1957. Turned
Professional 1977

Maj Open r/u 1982–1988
Eur Swiss Open 1980; Lancôme Trophy 1985
US World Series 1983
RoW South African Masters 1980; Vaal Reefs Open (SAF)
1982; ICL International (SAF) 1985

Quast, Anne
See Sander

Randolph, Sam
Born Santa Barbara, California, USA on 13th May 1964.
Turned Professional 1987

PRO
US 1987–one (Bank of Boston Classic)
AM
Nat US Amateur 1985
Int Walker Cup 1985

Rawls, Betsy
Born Spartanburg, South Carolina, USA on 4th May 1928.
Turned Professional 1951

Maj US Women's Open 1951–53–57–60, r/u 50(as
amateur)–61; USLPGA 1959–69
US 55 LPGA wins 1951–72 (incl Western Open 1952–59)
Mis Vare Trophy 1959; LPGA Hall of Fame 1960; World
Golf Hall of Fame 1987; Patty Berg Award 1980

Reid, Mike
Born Bainbridge, Maryland, USA on 1st July 1954. Turned Professional 1976

Maj	US Open leading amateur 1976; USPGA r/u 1989
US	Seiko Tucson Open 1987; NEC World Series 1988
Int	World Cup 1980

Rivero, José
Born Spain on 20th September, 1955. Turned Professional 1973

Eur	Lawrence Batley International 1984. French Open 1987. Monte Carlo Open 1988
Int	Ryder Cup 1985–87. World Cup 1984 (winners)–87–88. Dunhill Cup 1986–87–88. Kirin Cup 1988

Rogers, William Charles (Bill)
Born Waco, Texas, USA on 10th September, 1951. Turned Professional 1974

PRO
Maj	Open 1981; US Open r/u 1981, 3rd 1982
Eur	Suntory World Match Play 1979
US	1978–one, 1981–three, 1983–one
Oth	Pacific Masters 1977
RoW	Suntory Open (Jap) 1980; NSW Open, Australian Open, Suntory Open (Jap) 1981
Int	Ryder Cup 1981
Mis	USPGA Player of the Year 1981

AM
Int	Walker Cup 1973

Rosenthal, Jody
Born Minneapolis, Minnesota, USA on 18th October, 1962. Turned Professional 1985

PRO
US	United Virginia Bank Classic, du Maurier Classic 1987
Mis	Gatorade Rookie of the Year 1986

AM
Chp	Ladies British Open Amateur 1984
Int	Curtis Cup 1984; Espirito Santo 1984(winners)

St Sauveur, Vicomtesse de
See Segard

Sander, Anne [Welts] [Decker] (née Quast)
Chp	Ladies British Open Amateur 1980.
Nat	US Ladies Amateur 1958–61–63, r/u 1965–68–73
Int	Curtis Cup 1958–60–62–66–68–74–84; Espirito Santo 1966(winners)–68(winners)
Mis	Doris Chambers Trophy 1973–74; Angus Trophy 1974

Sarazen, Gene
Born Harrison, New York, USA on 27th February, 1902. Turned Professional 1920

Maj	Open 1932, r/u 1928, 3rd 1931–33; US Open 1922–32, r/u 1934–40; USPGA 1922–23–33, r/u 1930; US Masters 1935
Eur	North of England Professional 1923
US	1922–one 1925–one 1927–two 1928–two 1930–two 1935–one 1936–one 1937–two 1938–one 1939–one 1941–one; USPGA Seniors 1954–58
RoW	Australian Open 1936
Int	Ryder Cup 1927–29–31–33–35–37
Mis	PGA Hall of Fame 1940; World Golf Hall of Fame 1974; William Richardson Award 1966; Old Tom Morris Award 1988; one of the few to win the Open and the US Open in the same year; Honorary Member of the Royal & Ancient Golf Club

Segard, Mme Patrick [Vcmtsse De St Sauveur] (née Lally Vagliano)
Chp	British Ladies 1950.
Trn	Worplesdon Foursomes 1962. Avia Foursomes 1966. Kayser–Bondor Foursomes 1960
Nat	French Ladies' Open 1948–50–51–52. French Ladies' Close 1939–46–49–50–51–54
Oth	Swiss Ladies 1949–65. Luxembourg Ladies 1949. Italian Ladies 1949–51. Spanish Ladies 1951
Int	France 1937–38–39–47–48–49–50–51–52–53–54–55–56–57–58–59–60–61–62–63–64–65–70. Vagliano Trophy 1959–61–63–65–(75)
Jun	British Girls 1937
Mis	Chairman of The Women's Committee of World Amateur Golf Council 1964 to 1972

Semple, Carol (Thompson)
Chp	British Ladies 1974.
Nat	US Ladies' Amateur 1973
Trn	Newmark International 1975 (tied), r/u 1974
Int	Curtis Cup 1974–77–80–82. World Team Championship 1974(winners)–80 (winners)

Senior, Peter
Born Singapore on 31st July, 1959. Turned Professional 1978

Eur	PLM Open 1986. Monte Carlo Open 1987
RoW	Queensland Open, New South Wales PGA 1984; New South Wales PGA, Rich River Classic, (South Australian Open 1979). Queensland PGA 1987
Int	Australia in Dunhill Cup 1987. Kirin Cup 1987; World Cup 1988; test match v GBI 1988

Sheehan, Patty
Born Middlebury, Vermont, USA on 27th October, 1956. Turned Professional 1980

PRO
Maj	US Women's Open r/u 1983–88; USLPGA 1983–84, r/u 1986
US	17 LPGA wins 1981–86; Sarasota Classic, Mazda Japan Classic 1988; Rochester International 1989

AM
Int	Curtis Cup 1980

Siderowf, R
Maj	US Open leading amateur 1968
Chp	Amateur 1973–76
Oth	Canadian Amateur 1971
Int	Walker Cup 1969–73–75–77–(79). Eisenhower Trophy 1968–76

Sigel, Jay
Chp	Amateur 1979
Nat	US Amateur 1982–83
Int	Walker Cup 1977–79–81–83–85–87–89
Mis	Most wins (14) in Walker Cup matches

Simpson, Scott William
Born San Diego, California, USA on 17th September 1955. Turned Professional 1977

PRO
Maj	US Open 1987
US	1980–one. 1984–one. 1987–one (Greater Greensboro Open). Bell South Atlanta Classic 1989
RoW	1984–two (Chunichi Crowns, Dunlop Phoenix)

Int Ryder Cup 1987. Kirin Cup 1987
AM
Trn NCAA Chp 1976–77

Sluman, Jeff
Born Rochester, New York, USA on 11th September, 1957. Turned Professional 1980

Maj USPGA 1988

Snead, Samuel Jackson
Born Hot Springs, Virginia, USA on 27th May, 1912. Turned Professional 1934

Maj Open 1946; US Open r/u 1937–47–49–53; USPGA
     1942–49–51, r/u 1938–40, 3rd 1974; US Masters
     1949–52–54, r/u 1939–57
US   84 wins 1936–65; Canadian Open 1938–40–41
Sen USPGA Seniors 1964–65–67–70–72–73 World Senior
     Professional 1964–65–70–72–73
Int Ryder Cup 1937–47–49–**51**–53–55–59–(**69**); USA in
     World Cup 1954–56–57–58–59–60–61–62; (winners
     56–60–61–62; individual winner 1961)
Mis US leading money winner 1938–49–50. USPGA
     Player of the Year 1949. Oldest professional
     to win a major tournament 1965. Unofficially
     credited with 164 victories (including 84 official
     USPGA tournaments) in his long career of which
     full details are not available. Finished 2nd equal
     in a 1974 USPGA tournament aged 61 and 3rd
     equal in 1974 USPGA Championship aged 62. 24
     holes–in–one

Somerville, Charles Ross
Born London, Ontario, Canada on 4th May, 1903

Nat Canadian Amateur 1926–28–30–31–35–37; r/u
     1924–25–34–38
Oth US Amateur 1932
Reg Ontario Amateur 1927–28–29–37. Manitoba Amateur
     1926. Canadian Seniors 1960–61 (tied)–65–66 (tied)
Mis President Royal Canadian Golf Association 1957

Stacy, Hollis
Born Savannah, Georgia, USA on 16th March, 1954. Turned Professional 1974

PRO
Maj US Women's Open 1977–78–84; r/u 1980
US   14 wins 1977–85
AM
Int Curtis Cup 1972
Jun US Girls 1969–70–71

Stadler, Craig
Born San Diego, California, USA on 2nd June, 1953. Turned Professional 1975

PRO
Maj US Masters 1982, 3rd 1988
US   1980–two. 1981–one. 1982–three. 1984–one
Int Ryder Cup 1983–85
Mis Arnold Palmer Award 1982
AM
Nat US Amateur 1973
Int Walker Cup 1975

Stephenson, Jan
Born Sydney, NSW, Australia on 22nd December 1951. Turned Professional 1973

Chp US Women's Open 1983. LPGA 1982
Nat Australian Ladies Open 1973–77
US   13 wins 1976–86; 1987–two

Stewart, Payne
Born Springfield, Missouri, USA on 30th January, 1957. Turned Professional 1979

Maj Open r/u 1985; USPGA 1989
US   1982–two 1983–one 1987–one 1989–one (MCI Heritage
     Classic)
RoW Indian Open, Indonesian Open 1981; Tweed
     Head Classic (Aust) 1982; Jun Classic (Jap)
     1985
Int Ryder Cup 1987–89; Nissan Cup 1986; Kirin Cup
     1988

Stockton, Dave
Born San Bernardino, California, USA on 2nd November, 1941. Turned Professional 1964

Maj US Open r/u 1978. USPGA 1970–76. US Masters r/u
     1974.
US   1967–two. 1968–two. 1971–one. 1973–one. 1974–three
     9 wins 1967–74
Int Ryder Cup 1971–77. World Cup 1970–76

Stranahan, Frank R
Born Toledo, Ohio, USA on 5th August, 1922. Turned Professional 1954

Maj Open r/u 1947–53, leading amateur 1947–49–50–51–53
PRO
US   1955–one 1958–one
AM
Chp Amateur 1948–50, r/u 1952
Nat US Amateur r/u 1950
Oth Mexican Amateur 1946–48–51; Canadian Amateur
     1947–48
Reg North & South Amateur 1946–49–52; Western Amateur
     1946–49–51–53; Tam o' Shanter All-American Amateur
     1948–49–50–51–52–53; Tam o' Shanter World Amateur
     1950–51–52–53–54
Int Walker Cup 1947–49–51

Strange, Curtis
Born Norfolk, Virginia, USA on 20th January, 1955. Turned Professional 1976

PRO
Maj US Open 1988–89, 3rd 1984; USPGA r/u 1989; US
     Masters r/u 1985
Oth Canadian Open 1985–87
US   14 wins 1979–88
Int Ryder Cup 1983–85–87–89. Dunhill Cup
     1985–87–88–89(winners). Nissan Cup 1985. Kirin
     Cup 1987–88
Mis Arnold Palmer Award 1985–87
AM
Int Walker Cup 1975; Eisenhower Trophy 1974

Streit, Marlene Stewart
Born Cereal, Alberta, Canada on 9th March, 1934

Chp Ladies British Amateur 1953
Nat Canadian Ladies' Open 1951–54–55–56–58–
     59–63–68–72–73. Canadian Ladies' Close 1951 to 1957,
     1963–68
Oth US Ladies Amateur 1956; r/u 1966. Australian Ladies
     1963
Reg Ontario Provincial 1951–56–57–58. US North and South
     Ladies 1956
Int Canadian Commonwealth Team 1959–63–**79**
Mis Canadian Athlete of the Year 1951–53–56. Canadian
     Woman Athlete of the Year 1951–53–56–60–63

Suggs, Louise

Born Atlanta, Georgia, USA on 7th September, 1923.
Turned Professional 1948 (Founder Member of LPGA)

PRO
Maj US Women's Open 1949–52, r/u 1951–55–58–59–63;
     USLPGA 1957, r/u 1955–60–61–63
US   50 LPGA wins 1949–62 (incl Titleholders Chp 1946(as
     amateur)–54–56–59; Western Open 1946–47(both as
     amateur)–49–53)
Mis Leading money winner 1953–60; Vare Trophy 1957;
     LPGA Hall of Fame 1951; World Golf Hall of Fame 1979
AM
Chp British Ladies 1948
Nat US Ladies Amateur 1947
Int Curtis Cup 1948

Sutton, Hal

Born Shreveport, Louisiana, USA on 28th April, 1958.
Turned Professional 1981

Maj USPGA 1983
US   1982–one 1983–one 1985–two 1986–two
Int Ryder Cup 1985–87; Nissan Cup 1986; v Japan 1983
Mis Arnold Palmer Award 1983; Golf Writers Player of
     the Year 1983; USPGA Player of the Year 1983
AM
Nat US Amateur 1980
Int Walker Cup 1979–81

Thompson, Carol

See Semple

Thomson, Peter W CBE

Born Melbourne, Australia on 23rd August, 1929. Turned
Professional 1949

Maj Open 1954–55–56–58–65, r/u 1952–53–57. 3rd 1969
Eur PGA Match Play 1954; Yorkshire Evening News 1957;
     Dunlop, Daks(shared) 1958; Italian Open, Spanish
     Open 1959; German Open, Yorkshire Evening News,
     Bowmaker, Daks 1960; PGA Match Play, Yorkshire
     Evening News, Esso Golden(shared), Dunlop Masters
     1961; Martini International, Piccadilly 1962; Daks 1965;
     PGA Match Play 1966; Alcan International, PGA Match
     Play, Esso Golden(tied) 1967; Dunlop Masters 1968;
     Martini International 1970(shared); Wills 1972
US   1956–one 1957–one
RoW Australian Open 1951–67–72, r/u 1950, leading amateur
     1948; Australian Professional 1967; New Zealand
     Open 1950–51–53–55–59–60–61–65–71; New Zealand
     Professional 1953; Hong Kong Open 1960–65–67; India
     Open 1964–76; Philippines Open 1964; New Zealand
     Caltex 1967; Victorian Open 1973
Int Australia in World Cup 1953–54(winners)–55–56–67–
     59(winners)–60–61–62–65–69
Mis Honorary Member of Royal & Ancient Golf Club

Trevino, Lee

Born Dallas, Texas, USA on 1st December, 1939. Turned
Professional 1961

Maj Open 1971–72, r/u 1980, 3rd 1970; US Open 1968–71;
     USPGA 1974–84, r/u 1985
Eur Benson & Hedges International, Lancôme Trophy
     1978; Lancôme Trophy 1980; Dunhill British Masters
     1985

US   27 wins 1968–one 1969–one 1970–two 1971–three
     1972–three 1973–two 1974–one 1975–one 1976–one
     1978–one 1980–three 1981–one; World Series 1974;
     Canadian Open 1971–77–79; Canadian PGA 1979–83
RoW Chrysler Classic (Aust) 1973; Mexican Open 1975;
     Moroccan Grand Prix 1977
Int Ryder Cup 1969–71–73–75–79–81–(85); World Cup
     1968–69(winners; individual winner) –70–71(winners)
     –74
Mis Rookie of the Year 1967; leading money winner
     1970; USPGA Player of the Year 1971; Vardon Trophy
     1970–71–72–74–80; Byron Nelson Award 1971; Ben
     Hogan Award 1981; World Golf Hall of Fame 1981;
     William Richardson Award 1985

Tway, Bob

Born Oklahoma City, USA on 4th May, 1959. Turned
Professional 1981

Maj USPGA 1986
US   1986–three 1989–one (Memorial Trn)
Int Nissan Cup 1986
Mis USPGA Player of the Year 1986

Vagliano, Lally

See Segard

Van Donck, Flory

Born Tervueren, Brussels, Belgium on 23rd June, 1912.
Turned Professional 1934

Maj Open r/u 1956–59
Trn PGA Match Play r/u 1947–52; Silver King 1951–53;
     North British Harrogate 1951; South of England
     Professional 1952; Yorkshire Evening News 1953
Nat Belgian Open 1939–46–47–53–56, r/u 1935–51;
     Belgian Professional 1935–38–39–52–53–54–55–56–
     57–59–60–63–64–65–66–68
Eur Dutch Open 1936–37–46–51–53; Italian Open
     1938–47–53–58; Swiss Open 1953–55; French Open
     1954–57–58; German Open 1953–56; Portuguese Open
     1955; Danish Open 1959
RoW Uruguay Open 1954; Venezuelan Open 1957
Int Belgium in World Cup 1954 to 1970, 1972–79(individual
     winner 1960); Europe v GB 1954–55–56–58
Mis Harry Vardon Trophy 1953

Varangot, Brigitte

Born Biarritz, France on 1st May, 1940

Chp Ladies British Open Amateur 1963–65–68
Nat French Ladies Open Amateur 1961–62–64–65–66–73,
     r/u 1960–63–67–70; French Ladies Close Amateur
     1959–61–63–70
Oth Italian Ladies 1970
Trn Kayser-Bondor Foursomes; Casa Pupo Foursomes
     1965; Avia Foursomes 1966–73
Int France in Vagliano Trophy 1959–61–63–65–69–71;
     Espirito Santo 1964(winners)–66–68–70–72–74

Vare, Glenna (née Collett)

Born New Haven, Connecticut, USA on 20th June 1903

Chp British Ladies Amateur r/u 1929–30
Nat US Ladies' Amateur 1922–25–28–29–30–35; r/u 1931–32
Oth Canadian Ladies 1923–24
Reg North and South Ladies six times; Eastern Ladies
     seven times
Int Curtis Cup 1932–36–38–**48**–(**50**)
Mis Bobby Jones Award 1965; World Golf Hall of Fame
     1975

Verplank, Scott
Born Dallas, Texas, USA on 9th July, 1964. Turned Professional 1986

PRO
US   Buick Open 1988
AM
Nat   US Amateur 1984
US   Western Open (USPGA circuit) 1985
Trn   NCAA Chp 1986
Reg   Western Amateur 1984
Int   Walker Cup 1985

De Vicenzo, Roberto
Born Buenos Aires, Argentina on 14th April, 1923. Turned Professional 1938

Maj   Open 1967, r/u 1950, 3rd 1948–49–56–60–64–69; US Masters r/u 1968
Eur   Belgian Open, Dutch Open, French Open 1950; French Open 1960; French Open, German Open 1964; Spanish Open 1966
US   1951–two 1953–one 1957–two 1966–one
RoW   Argentine Open 1944–49–51–52–58–65–67–70–74; Argentine Professional 1944–45–47–48–49–51–52; Chile Open 1946; Colombia Open 1947; Uruguay Open 1949; Mexican Open 1951; Panama Open 1952; Mexican Open 1953; Jamaican Open 1956; Brazilian Open, Jamaican Open 1957; Brazilian Open 1960–63–64; Bogota Open 1969; Panama Open, Brazilian Open, Caracas Open 1973; Panama Open 1974
Sen   USPGA Seniors 1974; World Senior Professional 1974; Legends of Golf 1979; US Senior Open 1980
Int   Argentina in World Cup 1953(winners) –54–55–62(individual winner) –63–64–65–66–68–69–70 (individual winner) –71–72–73–74; Mexico in World Cup 1956–59–60–61
Mis   Bobby Jones Award 1970; William Richardson Award 1971; Honorary Member of the Royal & Ancient Golf Club 1976; Walter Hagen Award 1979

Wadkins, Lanny
Born Richmond, Virginia, USA on 5th December, 1949. Turned Professional 1971

PRO
Maj   US Open r/u 1986; USPGA 1977, r/u 1982–84–87, 3rd 1973
US   1972–one 1973–two 1979–two 1982–two 1983–two 1985–three 1987–one 1988–two World Series 1977
RoW   Victoria PGA (Aust) 1978
Int   Ryder Cup 1977–79–83–85–87–89; World Cup 1977–84–85; v Japan 1982–83; Nissan Cup 1985; Kirin Cup 1987
Mis   USPGA Player of the Year 1985; Rookie of the Year 1972
AM
Nat   US Amateur 1970
Reg   Western Amateur 1970; Southern Amateur 1968 70; Eastern Amateur 1969
Int   Walker Cup 1969–71; Eisenhower Trophy 1970(winners)

Ward, Harvie
Born Tarboro, North Carolina, USA in 1926. Turned Professional 1973

Chp   Amateur 1952; r/u 1953
Nat   US Amateur 1955–56

Oth   Canadian Amateur 1964
Trn   NCAA Chp 1949
Reg   North and South Amateur 1948
Int   Walker Cup 1953–55–59

Watson, Tom
Born Kansas City, Missouri, USA on 4th September, 1949. Turned Professional 1971

Maj   Open 1975–77–80–82–83, r/u 1984; US Open 1982, r/u 1983–87, 3rd 1980; USPGA r/u 1978; US Masters 1977–81, r/u 1978–79–84
US   32 wins 1974–one 1975–one 1977–three 1978–five 1979–five 1980–five 1981–four 1982–two 1984–three 1987–one; World Series 1975–80
RoW   Phoenix Open (Jap) 1980
Int   Ryder Cup 1977–81–83–89; v Japan 1982–84
Mis   Vardon Trophy 1977–78–79; leading money winner 1977–78–79–80–84; USPGA Player of the Year 1977–78–79–80–84; Bobby Jones Award 1986

Weiskopf, Tom
Born Massillon, Ohio, USA on 9th November, 1942. Turned Professional 1964

Maj   Open 1973; US Open r/u 1976; 3rd 1973–77; USPGA 3rd 1975; US Masters r/u 1969–72–74–75
Eur   Piccadilly World Match Play 1972
US   1968–two 1971–two 1972–one 1973–three 1975–one 1977–one 1978–one 1982–one World Series 1973; Canadian Open 1973–75
RoW   South African PGA 1973; Argentine Open 1979
Int   Ryder Cup 1973–75; USA in World Cup 1972

Welts, Anne
See Sander

Whitworth, Kathy
Born Monahans, Texas, USA on 27th September, 1939. Turned Professional 1959

Maj   US Open r/u 1971; USLPGA 1967–71–75, r/u 1968–70
US   88 LPGA wins 1962–85 (incl Titleholder's Chp 1965–66; Western Open 1967)
Mis   Rolex Player of the Year 1966–67–68–69–71–72–73. Vare Trophy 1965–66–67–69–70–71–72. William Richardson Award 1986; Woman Athlete of the Year 1965–66; LPGA Hall of Fame; World Golf Hall of Fame 1982; Powell Award 1986; Patty Berg Award 1987

Wright, Mary Kathryn (Mickey)
Born San Diego, California, USA on 14th February, 1935. Turned Professional 1954

Maj   US Open 1958–59–61–64, r/u 1968, leading amateur 1954; USLPGA 1958–60–61–63, r/u 1964–66
PRO
US   82 LPGA wins 1956–73 (incl Titleholders Chp 1961–62; Western Open 1962–63–66; 13 wins in 1963)
Mis   Leading money winner 1961–62–63–64; Vare Trophy 1960–61–62–63–64; LPGA Hall of Fame 1964; World Golf Hall of Fame 1976; Woman Athlete of the Year 1963–64

Yates, Charles Richard
Born Atlanta, Georgia, USA on 9th September, 1913

Maj   US Masters leading amateur 1934–39–40
Chp   Amateur 1938
Reg   Western Amateur 1935.
Int   Walker Cup 1936–38–(**53**)

Zoeller, Frank Urban (Fuzzy)

Born New Albany, Indiana, USA on 11th November, 1951. Turned Professional 1973

Maj US Open 1984; USPGA r/u 1981; US Masters 1979
US   1979–two 1983–two 1985–one 1986–three
Int Ryder Cup 1979–83–85
Mis Ben Hogan Award 1986

British Isles International Players, Professional Men

Adams, J
(Scotland): v England 1932-33-34-35-36-37-38; v Wales 1937-38; v Ireland 1937-38. (GB): v America 1947-49-51-53

Ainslie, T
(Scotland): v Ireland 1936

Alliss, Percy
(England): v Scotland 1932-33-34-35-36-37; v Ireland 1932-38; v Wales 1938. (GB): v France 1929; v America 1929-31-33-35-37

Alliss, Peter
(England): in Canada Cup 1954-55-57-58-59-61-62-64-66; in World Cup 1967. (GB): v America 1953-57-59-61-63-65-67-69

Anderson, Joe
(Scotland): v Ireland 1932

Anderson, W
(Scotland): v Ireland 1936; v England 1937; v Wales 1937

Ayton, LB
(Scotland): v England 1910-12-13-33-34

Ayton, JB, jr
(Scotland): v England 1937. (GB): v America 1949

Ballantine, J
(Scotland): v England 1932-36

Ballingall, J
(Scotland): v England 1938; Ireland 1938; v Wales 1938

Bamford, BJ
(England): in Canada Cup 1961

Bannerman, H
(Scotland): in World Cup 1967-72. (GB): v America 1971

Barber, T
(England): v Ireland 1932-33

Barnes, BW
(Scotland): in World Cup 1974-75-76-77. (GB): v America 1969-71-73-75-77-79; v Europe 1974-76-78-80; v South Africa 1976

Batley, JB
(England): v Scotland 1912

Beck, AG
(England): v Wales 1938; v Ireland 1938

Bembridge, M
(England): in World Cup 1974-75. (GB): v America 1969-71-73-75; v South Africa 1976

Boomer, A
(England): (GB): v America 1926-27-29

Bousfield, K
(England): in Canada Cup 1956-57. (GB): v America 1949-51-55-57-59-61

Boyle, HF
(Ireland): in World Cup 1967. (GB): v America 1967

Bradshaw, H
(Ireland): in Canada Cup 1954-55-56-57-58-59; v Scotland 1937-38; v Wales 1937; v England 1938. (GB): v America 1953-55-57

Braid, J
(Scotland): v England 1903-04-05-06-07-09-10-12. (GB): v America 1921

Branch, WJ
(England): v Scotland 1936

Brand, G, jr
(Scotland): in World Cup 1984-85; in Dunhill Cup 1985-86-87-88-89; (Eur): in Nissan Cup 1985; Kirin Cup 1988; (GB): v America 1987-89; v Australia 1988

Brand,GJ
(England): in World Cup 1983; in Dunhill Cup 1986-87 (winners). (GB): v America 1983; (Eur) Nissan Cup 1986

Brown, EC
(Scotland): in Canada Cup 1954-55-56-57-58-59-60-61-62-65-66; in World Cup 1987-68. (GB): v America 1953-55-57-59

Brown, K
(Scotland): in World Cup 1977-78-79-83. (GB): v America 1977-79-83-85-87; v Europe 1978; (Eur) Kirin Cup 1987

Burns, S
(Scotland): v England 1932. (GB): v America 1929

Burton, J
(England): v Ireland 1933

Burton, R
(England): v Scotland 1935-36-37-38; v Ireland 1938; v Wales 1938. (GB): v America 1935-37-49

Busson, JH
(England): v Scotland 1938

Busson, JJ
(England): v Scotland 1934-35-36-37. (GB): v America 1935

Butler, PJ
(England): in World Cup 1969-70-73. (GB): v America 1965-69-71-73; v Europe 1976

Callum, WS
(Scotland): v Ireland 1935

Campbell, J
(Scotland): v Ireland 1936

Carrol, LJ
(Ireland): v Scotland 1937-38; v Wales 1937; v England 1938

Cassidy, J
(Ireland): v England 1933; v Scotland 1934-35

Cassidy, D
(Ireland): v Scotland 1936-37; v Wales 1937

Cawsey, GH
(England): v Scotland 1906-07

Caygill, GA
(England): (GB): v America 1969

Clark, C
(England): (GB): v America 1973

Clark, HK
(England): in World Cup 1978-84-85-87; in Dunhill Cup 1985-86-87 (winners)-89. (GB): v America 1977-81-85-87-89; v Australia 1988; v Europe 1978-84. (Eur): in Nissan Cup 1985

Coles, NC
(England): in Canada Cup 1963; in World Cup 1968.
(GB): v America 1961-63-65-67-69-71-73-77;
v Europe 1974-76-78-80

Collinge, T
(England): v Scotland 1937

Collins, JF
(England): v Scotland 1903-04

Coltart, F
(Scotland): v England 1909

Compston, A
(England): v Scotland 1932-35; v Ireland 1932.
(GB): v America 1926-27-29-31; v France 1929

Cotton, TH
(England): (GB): v America 1929-37-47; v France 1929

Cox, S
(Wales): in World Cup 1975

Cox, WJ
(England): v Scotland 1935-36-37. (GB): v America 1935-37

Curtis, D
(England): v Scotland 1934-38; v Ireland 1938; v Wales 1938

Dabson, K
(Wales): in World Cup 1972

Dailey, A
(Scotland): v England 1932-33-34-35-36-38; v Ireland
1938; v Wales 1938. (GB): v America 1933

Daly, F
(Ireland): v Scotland 1936-37-38; v England 1938;
v Wales 1937; in Canada Cup 1954-55.
(GB): v America 1947-49-51-53

Darcy, E
(Ireland): in World Cup 1976-77-83-84-85-87;
Dunhill Cup 1987-88 (winners). (GB): v America 1975-77-
81-87; v Europe 1976-84; v South Africa 1976

Davies, R
(Wales): in World Cup 1968

Davies, WH
(England): v Scotland 1932-33; v Ireland 1932-33.
(GB): v America 1931-33

Davis, W
(Scotland): v Ireland 1933-34-35-36-37-38;
v England 1937-38; v Wales 1937-38

Dawson, P
(England): in World Cup 1977. (GB): v America 1977

De Foy, CB
(Wales): in World Cup 1971-73-74-75-76-77-78

Denny, CS
(England): v Scotland 1936

Dobson, T
(Scotland): v England 1932-33-34-35-36-37; v Ireland
1932-33-34-35-36-37-38; v Wales 1937-38

Don, W
(Scotland): v Ireland 1935-36

Donaldson, J
(Scotland): v England 1932-35-38; v Ireland 1937;
v Wales 1937

Dornan, R
(Scotland): v Ireland 1932

Drew, NV
(Ireland): in Canada Cup 1960-61. (GB): v America 1959

Duncan, G
(Scotland): v England 1906-07-09-10-12-13-32-34-35-36-
37. (GB): v America 1921-26-27-29-31

Durnian, D
(England): in Dunhill Cup 1989

Durward, JG
(Scotland): v Ireland 1934; v England 1937

Easterbrook, S
(England): v Scotland 1932-33-34-35-38; v Ireland 1933.
(GB): v America 1931-33

Edgar, J
(Ireland): v Scotland 1938

Fairweather, S
(Ireland): v England 1932; v Scotland 1933. (Scotland):
v England 1933-35-36; v Ireland 1938; v Wales 1938

Faldo, NA
(England): in World Cup 1977; in Dunhill Cup 1985-86-
87 (winners) -88. (GB): v America 1977-79-81-83-85-87-89;
v Europe 1978-80-82-84; v Rest of World 1982.
(Eur) Nissan Cup 1986. Kirin Cup 1987

Fallon, J
(Scotland): v England 1936-37-38; v Ireland 1937-38;
v Wales 1937-38. (GB): v America 1955

Faulkner, M
(England): (GB): v America 1947-49-51-53-57

Feherty, D
(Ireland): in Dunhill Cup 1985-86

Fenton, WB
(Scotland): v England 1932; v Ireland 1932-33

Fernie, TR
(Scotland): v England 1910-12-13-33

Foster, M
(England): in World Cup 1976. (GB): v Europe 1976

Gadd, B
(England): v Scotland 1933-35-38; v Ireland 1933-38;
v Wales 1938

Gadd, G
(England): (GB): v America 1926-27

Gallacher, BJ
(Scotland): in World Cup 1969-71-74-82-83. (GB): v
America 1969-71-73-75-77-79-81-83; v Europe 1974-78-
82-84; v South Africa 1976; v Rest of World 1982

Garner, JR
(England): (GB): v America 1971-73

Gaudin, PJ
(England): v Scotland 1905-06-07-09-12-13

Good, G
(Scotland): v England 1934-36

Gould, H
(Wales): in Canada Cup 1954-55

Gow, A
(Scotland): v England 1912

Grabham, C
(Wales): v England 1938; v Scotland 1938

Grant, T
(Scotland): v England 1913

Gray, E
(England): v Scotland 1904-05-07

Green, E
(England): (GB): v America 1947

Green, T
(England): v Scotland 1935. (Wales): v Scotland 1937-38;
v Ireland 1937; v England 1938

Greene, C
(Ireland): in Canada Cup 1965

Gregson, M
(England): in World Cup 1967. (GB): v America 1967

Haliburton, TB
(Scotland): v Ireland 1935-36-38; v England 1938; v Wales 1938; in Canada Cup 1954. (GB): v America 1961-63

Hamill, J
(Ireland): v Scotland 1933-34-35; v England 1932-33

Hargreaves, J
(England): (GB): v America 1951

Hastings, W
(Scotland): England 1937-38; v Wales 1937-38; v Ireland 1937-38

Havers: AG
(England): v Scotland 1932-33-34; v Ireland 1932-33. (GB): v America 1921-26-27-31-33; v France 1929

Healing, SF
(Wales): v Scotland 1938

Hepburn, J
(Scotland): v England 1903-05-06-07-09-10-12-13

Herd, A
(Scotland): v England 1903-04-05-06-09-10-12-13-32

Hill, EF
(Wales): v Scotland 1937-38; v Ireland 1937; v England 1938

Hitchcock, J
(England): (GB): v America 1965

Hodson, B
(England): v Ireland 1933. (Wales): v Scotland 1937-38; v Ireland 1937; v England 1938. (GB): v America 1931

Holley, W
(Ireland): v Scotland 1933-34-35-36-38; v England 1932-33-38

Horne, R
(England): (GB): v America 1947

Horton, T
(England): in World Cup 1976. (GB): v Europe 1974-76; v America 1975-77

Houston, D
(Scotland): v Ireland 1934

Huggett, BGC
(Wales): in Canada Cup 1963-64-65; in World Cup 1968-69-70-71-76-79. (GB): v America 1963-67-69-71-73-75; v Europe 1974-78

Huish, D
(Scotland): in World Cup 1973

Hunt, BJ
(England): in Canada Cup 1958-59-60-62-63-64; in World Cup 1968. (GB): v America 1953-57-59-61-63-65-67-69

Hunt, GL
(England): in World Cup 1972-75. (GB): v Europe 1974; v America 1975

Hunt, Geoffrey M
(England): (GB): v America 1963

Hunter, W
(Scotland): v England 1906-07-09-10

Hutton, GC
(Scotland): v Ireland 1936-37; v England 1937-38; v Wales 1937

Ingram, D
(Scotland): in World Cup 1973

Jacklin, A
(England): in Canada Cup 1966; in World Cup 1970-71-72. (GB): v America 1967-69-71-73-75-77-79-83 (captain) -85(captain) -87(captain) -89(captain); v Europe 1976-82; v Rest of World 1982

Jackson, H
(Ireland): in World Cup 1970-71

Jacobs, JRM
(England): (GB): v America 1955

Jagger, D
(England): (GB): v Europe 1976

James, G
(Wales): v Scotland 1937; v Ireland 1937

James, MH
(England): in World Cup 1978-79-82-84-87; in Dunhill Cup 1988-89. (GB): v America 1977-79-81-89; v Europe 1978-80-82; v Rest of World 1982; v Australia 1988; (Eur): Kirin Cup 1988

Jarman, EW
(England): v Scotland 1935. (GB): v America 1935

Job, N
(England): (GB): v Europe 1980

Jolly, HC
(England): (GB): v America 1926-27; v France 1929

Jones, DC
(Wales): v Scotland 1937-38; v Ireland 1937; v England 1938

Jones, E
(Ireland): in Canada Cup 1965

Jones, R
(England): v Scotland 1903-04-05-06-07-09-10-12-13

Jones, T
(Wales): v Scotland 1936; v Ireland 1937; v England 1938

Kenyon, EWH
(England): v Scotland 1932; v Ireland 392

King, M
(England): in World Cup 1979. (GB): v America 1979

King, SL
(England): v Scotland 1934-36-37-38; v Wales 1938; v Ireland 1938. (GB): v America 1937-47-49

Kinsella, J
(Ireland): in World Cup 1968-69-72-73

Kinsella, W
(Ireland): v Scotland 1937-38; v England 1938

Knight, G
(Scotland): v England 1937

Lacey, AJ
(England): v Scotland 1932-33-34-36-37-38; v Ireland 1932-33-38; v Wales 1938. (GB): v America 1933-37

Laidlaw, W
(Scotland): v England 1935-36-38; v Ireland 1937; v Wales 1937

Lane, B
(England): in Dunhill Cup 1988

Lees, A
(England): v Scotland 1938; v Wales 1938; v Ireland 1938. (GB): v America 1947-49-51-55

Llewellyn, D
(Wales): in World Cup 1974-85-87 (winners); in Dunhill Cup 1985-88. (GB): v Europe 1984

Lloyd, F
(Wales): v Scotland 1937-38; v Ireland 1937; v England 1938

Lockhart, G
(Scotland): v Ireland 1934-35

Lyle, AWB
(Scotland): in World Cup 1979-80-87; in Dunhill Cup 1985-86-87-88-89. (GB): v America 1979-81-83-85-87; v Europe 1980-82-84; v Rest of World 1982; v Australia 1988. (Eur): in Nissan Cup 1985-86; Kirin Cup 1987.

McCartney, J
(Ireland): v Scotland 1932-33-34-35-36-37-38;
v England 1932-33-38; v Wales 1937

McCulloch, D
(Scotland): v England 1932-33-34-35-36-37;
v Ireland 1932-33-34-35

McDermott, M
(Ireland): v England 1932; v Scotland 1932

McDowall, J
(Scotland): v England 1932-33-34-35-36;
v Ireland 1933-34-35-36

McEwan, P
(Scotland): v England 1907

McIntosh, G
(Scotland): v England 1938; v Ireland 1938;
v Wales 1938

McKenna, J
(Ireland): v Scotland 1936-37-38; v Wales 1937-38;
v England 1938

McKenna, R
(Ireland): v Scotland 1933-35; v England 1933

McMillan, J
(Scotland): v England 1933-34-35; v Ireland 1933-34

McMinn, W
(Scotland): v England 1932-33-34

McNeill, H
(Ireland): v England 1932

Mahon, PJ
(Ireland): v Scotland 1932-33-34-35-36-37-38;
v Wales 1937-38; v England 1932-33-38

Martin, J
(Ireland): in Canada Cup 1962-63-64-66;
in World Cup 1970. (GB): v America 1965

Martin, S
(Scotland): in World Cup 1980

Mason, SC
(England): in World Cup 1980. (GB): v Europe 1980

Mayo, CH
(England): v Scotland 1907-09-10-12-13

Mills, RP
(England): (GB): v America 1957

Mitchell, A
(England): v Scotland 1932-33-34. (GB): v America
1921-26-29-31-33

Moffitt, R
(England): (GB): v America 1961

Montgomerie, C
(Scotland): in Dunhill Cup 1988

Mouland, M
(Wales): in Dunhill Cup 1986-87-88-89. (Eur): Kirin
Cup 1988.

Mouland, S
(Wales): in Canada Cup 1965-66; in World Cup 1967

O'Brien, W
(Ireland): v Scotland 1934-36-37; v Wales 1937

Ockenden, J
(England): (GB): v America 1921

O'Connor, C
(Ireland): in Canada Cup 1956-57-58-59-60-61-62-63-64-66;
in World Cup 1967-68-69-71-73. (GB): v America 1955-57-
59-61-63-65-67-69-71-73

O'Connor, C, jr
(Ireland): in World Cup 1974-75-78-85; in Dunhill
Cup 1985-89. (GB): v Europe 1974-84; v America
1975-89; v South Africa 1976

O'Connor, P
(Ireland): v Scotland 1932-33-34-35-36; v England 1932-33

Oke, WG
(England): v Scotland 1932

O'Leary, JE
(Ireland): in World Cup 1972-80-82. (GB): v America 1975;
v Europe 1976-78-82; v Rest of World 1982

O'Neill, J
(Ireland): v England 1933

O'Neill, M
(Ireland): v Scotland 1933-34; v England 1933

Oosterhuis, PA
(England): in World Cup 1971. (GB): v America 1971-
73-75-77-79-81; v Europe 1974

Padgham, AH
(England): v Scotland 1932-33-34-35-36-37-38; v Ireland
1932-33-38; v Wales 1938. (GB): v America 1933-35-37

Panton, J
(Scotland): in Canada Cup 1955-56-57-58-59-60-61-62-63-64-
65-66; in World Cup 1968. (GB): v America 1951-53-61

Park, J
(Scotland): v England 1909

Parkin, P
(Wales): in World Cup 1984; in Dunhill Cup 1985-86-87-
89. (GB): v Europe 1984

Patterson, E
(Ireland): v Scotland 1933-34-35-36; v England 1933;
v Wales 1937

Perry, A
(England); v Ireland 1932; v Scotland 1933-36-38.
(GB): v America 1933-35-37

Pickett, C
(Wales): v Scotland 1937-38; v Ireland 1937; v England 1938

Platts, L
(Wales): (GB): v America 1965

Polland, E
(Ireland): in World Cup 1973-74-76-77-78-79.
(GB): v America 1973; v Europe 1974-76-78-80;
v South America 1976

Pope, CW
(Ireland): v England 1932; v Scotland 1932

Rafferty, R
(Ireland): in World Cup 1983-84-87; in Dunhill Cup 1986-
87-88 (winners)-89 (GB): v Europe 1984; v Australia 1988.
(Eur): v America 1989; Kirin Cup 1988

Rainford, P
(England): v Scotland 1903-07

Ray, E
(England): v Scotland 1903-04-05-06-07-09-10-12-13.
(GB): v America 1921-26-27

Rees, DJ
(Wales): v Scotland 1937-38; v Ireland 1937; England 1938;
in Canada Cup 1954-56-57-58-59-60-61-62-64.
(GB): v America 1937-47-49-51-53-55-57-59-61

Reid, W
(England): v Scotland 1906-07

Renouf, TG
(England): v Scotland 1903-04-05-10-13

Ritchie, WL
(Scotland): v England 1913

Robertson, F
(Scotland): v Ireland 1933; v England 1938

Robertson, P
(Scotland): v England 1932; v Ireland 1932-34

Robson, F
(England): v Scotland 1909-10. (GB): v America
1926-27-29-31
Rowe, AJ
(England): v Scotland 1903-06-07

Sayers, B, jr
(Scotland): v England 1906-07-09
Scott, SS
(England): (GB): v America 1955
Seymour, M
(England): v Scotland 1932-33; v Ireland 1932-33.
(Scotland): v Ireland 1932
Shade, RDBM
(Scotland): in World Cup 1970-71-72
Sherlock, JG
(England): v Scotland 1903-04-05-06-07-09-10-12-13.
(GB): v America 1921
Simpson, A
(Scotland): v England 1904
Smalldon, D
(Wales): in Canada Cup 1955-56
Smith, CR
(Scotland): v England 1903-04-07-09-13
Smith, GE
(Scotland): v Ireland 1932
Smyth, D
(Ireland): in World Cup 1979-80-82-83; in Dunhill Cup
1985-86-87-88 (winners). (GB): v America 1979-81; v Europe
1980-82-84; v Rest of World 1982
Snell, D
(England): in Canada Cup 1965
Spark, W
(Scotland): v Ireland 1933-35-37; v England 1935;
v Wales 1937
Stevenson, P
(Ireland): v Scotland 1933-34-35-36-38;
v England 1933-38
Sutton, M
(England): in Canada Cup 1955

Taylor, JH
(England): v Scotland 1903-04-05-06-07-09-10-12-13
(GB): v America 1921
Taylor, JJ
(England): v Scotland 1937
Taylor, Josh
(England): v Scotland 1913. (GB): v America 1921
Thomas, DC
(Wales): in Canada Cup 1957-58-59-60-61-62-63-66; in
World Cup 1967-69-70. (GB): v America 1959-63-65-67
Thompson, R
(Scotland): v England 1903-04-05-06-07-09-10-12
Tingey, A
(England): v Scotland 1903-05
Torrance, S
(Scotland): in World Cup 1976-78-82-84-85-87; in Dunhill
Cup 1985-86-87-89. (GB): v Europe 1976-78-80-82-84;
v America 1981-83-85-87-89; v Rest of World 1982.
(Eur): in Nissan Cup 1985
Townsend, P
(England): in World Cup 1969-74. (GB): v
America
1969-71; v Europe 1974
Twine, WT
(England): v Ireland 1932

Vardon, H
(England): (GB): v America 1921
Vaughan, DI
(Wales): in World Cup 1972-73-77-78-79-80

Waites, BJ
(England): in World Cup 1980-82-83. (GB): v Europe
1980-82-84; v Rest of World 1982; v America 1983
Walker, RT
(Scotland): in Canada Cup 1964
Wallace, L
(Ireland): v England 1932; v Scotland 1932
Walton P
(Ireland): in Dunhill Cup 1989
Ward, CH
(England): v Ireland 1932. (GB): v America 1947-49-51
Watt, T
(Scotland): v England 1907
Watt, W
(Scotland): v England 1912-13
Way, P
(England): in Dunhill Cup 1985; in World Cup 1985.
(GB): v America 1983-85
Weetman, H
(England): in Canada Cup 1954-56-60. (GB): v America
1951-53-55-57-59-61-63
Whitcombe, CA
(England): v Scotland 1932-33-34-35-36-37-38;
v Ireland 1933. (GB): v America 1927-29-31-33-35-37;
v France 1929
Whitcombe, EE
(England): v Scotland 1938; v Wales 1938; v Ireland 1938
Whitcombe, ER
(England): v Scotland 1932; v Ireland 1933.
(GB): v America 1926-29-31-35; v France 1929
Whitcombe, RA
(England): v Scotland 1933-34-35-36-37-38.
(GB): v America 1935
White, J
(Scotland): v England 1903-04-05-06-07-09-12-13
Wilcock, P
(England): in World Cup 1973
Will, G
(Scotland): in Canada Cup 1963; in World Cup 1969-70.
(GB): v America 1963-65-67
Williams, K
(Wales): v Scotland 1937-38; v Ireland 1937;
v England 1938
Williamson, T
(England): v Scotland 1904-05-06-07-09-10-12-13
Wilson, RG
(England): v Scotland 1913
Wilson, T
(Scotland): v England 1933-34; v Ireland 1932-33-34
Wolstenholme, GB
(England): in Canada Cup 1965
Wood, N
(Scotland): in World Cup 1975. (GB): v America 1975
Woosnam, I
(Wales): in World Cup 1980-82-83-84-85-87 (winners).
Dunhill Cup 1985-86-87-88-89. (GB): v Europe 1982-84; v
Rest of World 1982; v America 1983-85-87-89; v Australia
1988. (Eur): in Nissan Cup 1985-86. Kirin Cup 1987

British Isles International Players, Amateur Men

Abbreviations:
(GB)   played for Great Britain or Great Britain and Ireland;
Com Tnmt   Commonwealth Tournament;
Eur T Ch   played in European Team Championship for home country;
Home Int   played in Home International matches

Adams, MPD
(Wales): Home Int 1969-70-71-72-75-76-77; Eur T Ch 1971

Aitken, AR
(Scotland): v England 1906-07-08

Alexander, DW
(Scotland): Home Int 1958; v Scandinavia 1958

Allison, A
(Ireland): v England 1928; v Scotland 1929

Anderson, N
(Ireland): Home Int 1985-86-87-88-89. Eur T Ch 1989. (GB): v Europe 1988

Anderson, RB
(Scotland): v Scandinavia 1960-62; Home Int 1962-63

Andrew, R
(Scotland): v England 1905-06-07-08-09-10

Armour, A
(Scotland): v England 1922

Armour, TD
(GB): v America 1921

Ashby, H
(England): Home Int 1972-73-74. (GB): in Dominican Int 1973. (GB): v Europe 1974

Atkinson, HN
(Wales): v Ireland 1913

Attenborough, M
(England): Home Int 1964-66-67-68; Eur T Ch 1967. (GB): v Europe 1966-68; v American 1967

Aylmer, CC
(England): v Scotland 1911-22-23-24. (GB): v America 1921-22

Babington, A
(Ireland): v Wales 1913

Baker, P
(England): Home Int 1985. (GB): v America 1985; v Europe 1986

Baker, RN
(Ireland): Home Int 1975

Ball, J
(England): v Scotland 1902-03-04-05-06-07-08-09-10-11-12

Bamford, JL
(Ireland): Home Int 1954-56

Banks, C
(England): Home Int 1983

Banks, SE
(England): Home Int 1934-38

Bannerman, S
(Scotland): Home Int 1988

Bardsley, R
(England): Home Int 1987; v France 1988

Barker, HH
(England): v Scotland 1907

Barnett, A
(Wales): Home Int 1989

Barrie, GC
(Scotland): Home Int 1981-83

Barry, AG
(England): v Scotland 1906-07

Bayliss, RP
(England): v Ireland 1929; Home Int 1933-34

Bayne, PWGA
(Wales): Home Int 1949

Beamish, CH
(Ireland): Home Int 1950-51-53-56

Beck, JB
(England): v Scotland 1926-30; Home Int 1933. (GB): v America 1928-38 (Captain) -47 (Captain)

Beddard, JB
(England): v Wales/Ireland 1925; v Ireland 1929; v Scotland 1927-28-29

Beharrell, JC
(England): Home Int 1956

Bell, HE
(Ireland): v Wales 1930; Home Int 1932

Bell, RK
(England): Home Int 1947

Benka, PJ
(England): Home Int 1967-68-69-70; Eur T Ch 1969. (GB): v America 1969; v Europe 1970

Bennett, H
(England): Home Int 1948-49-51

Bennett, S
(England): v Scotland 1979

Bentley, AL
(England): Home Int 1936-37; v France 1937-39

Bentley, HG
(England): v Ireland 1931; v Scotland 1931. Home Int 1932-33-34-35-36-37-38-47; v France 1934-35-36-37-39-54. (GB): v America 1934-36-38

Berry, P
(England): Home Int 1972. (GB): v Europe 1972

Bevan, RJ
(Wales): Home Int 1964-65-66-67-73-74

Beveridge, HW
(Scotland): v England 1908

Birtwell, SG
(England): Home Int 1968-70-73

Black, D
(Scotland): Home Int 1966-67

Black, FC
(Scotland): Home Int 1962-64-65-66-68; v Scandinavia 1962; Eur T Ch 1965-67. (GB): v Europe 1966

Black, GT
(Scotland): Home Int 1952-53; v South Africa 1954

Black, JL
(Wales): Home Int 1932-33-34-35-36

Black, WC
(Scotland): Home Int 1964-65

Blackwell, EBH
(Scotland): v England 1902-04-05-06-07-09-10-12-23-24-25

Blair, DA
(Scotland): Home Int 1948-49-51-52-53-55-56-57; v Scandinavia 1956-58-62. (GB): v America 1955-61; in Com Tnmt 1954

Blakeman, D
(England): Home Int 1981; v France 1982

Bloice, C
(Scotland): Home Int 1985-86. (GB): v America 1985

Bloxham, JA
(England): Home Int 1966

Blyth, AD
(Scotland): v England 1904

Bonallack,MF
(England): Home Int 1957-58-59-60-61-62-63-64-65-66-67-68-69-70-71-72-73-74; Eur T Ch 1969-71. (GB): v America 1957-59-61-63-65-67-69 (Captain) -71 (Captain) -73; v Europe 1958-62-64-66-68-70-72; in Com Tnmt 1959-63-67-71; in World Team Ch 1960-62-64-66-68-70-72

Bonnell, DJ
(Wales): Home Int 1949-50-51

Bookless, JT
(Scotland): v England 1930-31; v Ireland 1930; v Wales 1931

Bottomley, S
(England): Home Int 1986

Bourn, TA
(England): v Ireland 1928; v Scotland 1930; Home Int 1933-34; v France 1934. (GB): v Australia 1934

Bowen, J
(Ireland): Home Int 1961

Bowman, TH
(England): Home Int 1932

Boxall, R
(England): Home Int 1980-81-82; v France 1982

Boyd, HA
(Ireland): v Wales 1913-23

Bradshaw, AS
(England): Home Int 1932

Bradshaw, EI
(England): v Scotland 1979; Eur T Ch 1979

Braid, H
(Scotland): v England 1922-23

Bramston, JAT
(England): v Scotland 1902

Brand, GJ
(England): Home Int 1976. (GB) v Europe 1976

Brand, G
(Scotland): Home Int 1978-80; v England 1979; Eur T Ch 1979; v Italy 1979; v Belgium 1980; v France 1980. (GB); v Europe 1978-80; in World Team Ch 1978-80; v America 1979; v France 1981

Branigan, D
(Ireland): Home Int 1975-76-77-80-81-82-86; Eur T Ch 1977-81; v West Germany, France, Sweden 1976

Bretherton, CF
(England): v Scotland 1922-23-24-25; v Wales/Ireland 1925

Briscoe, A
(Ireland): v England 1928-29-30-31; v Scotland 1929-30-31; v Wales 1929-30-31; Home Int 1932-33-38

Bristowe, OC
(GB): v America 1923-24

Broad, RD
(Wales): v Ireland 1979; Home Int 1980-81-82-84; Eur T Ch 1981

Broadhurst, P
(England): Home Int 1986-87; v France 1988. (GB) v Europe 1988

Brock, J
(Scotland) v Ireland 1929; Home Int 1932

Brodie, Allan
(Scotland): Home Int 1970-72-73-74-75-76-77-78-80; Eur T Ch 1973-77-79; v England 1979; v Italy 1979; v Belgium 1977; v Spain 1977; v France 1978. (GB): v America 1977-79; v Europe 1974-76-78-80;in World Team Ch 1978

Brodie, Andrew
(Scotland): Home Int 1968-69; v Spain 1974

Bromley-Davenport, E
(England): Home Int 1938-51

Brooks, A
(Scotland): Home Int 1968-69; Eur T Ch 1969. (GB): v America 1969

Brooks, CJ
(Scotland): Home Int 1984-85. (GB): v Europe 1986

Brotherton, IR
(Scotland): Home Int 1984-85

Brough, S
(England): Home Int 1952-55-59-60; v France 1952-60. (GB): v Europe 1960

Brown, CT
(Wales): Home Int 1970-71-72-73-74-75-77-78-80-88 (captain); Eur T Ch 1973; v Denmark 1977-80; v Ireland 1979; v Switzerland, Spain 1980

Brown, D
(Wales): v Ireland 1923-30-31; v England 1925; v Scotland 1931

Brown, JC
(Ireland): Home Int 1933-34-35-36-37-38-48-52-53

Brownlow, Hon WGE
(GB): v America 1926

Bruen, J
(Ireland): Home Int 1937-38-49-50. (GB): v America 1938-49-51

Bucher, AM
(Scotland): Home Int 1954-55-56; v Scandinavia 1956

Buckley, JA
(Wales): Home Int 1967-68-69-76-77-78; Eur T Ch 1967-69; v Denmark 1976-77. (GB): v America 1979

Burch, N
(England): Home Int 1974

Burgess, MJ
(England): Home Int 1963-64-67; Eur T Ch 1967

Burke, J
(Ireland): v England 1929-30-31; v Wales 1929-30-31; v Scotland 1930-31; Home Int 1932-33-34-35-36-37-38-47-48-49. (GB): v America 1932

Burns, M
(Ireland): Home Int 1973-75-83

Burnside, J
(Scotland): Home Int 1956-57

Burrell, TM
(Scotland): v England 1924

Bussell, AF
(Scotland): Home Int 1956-57-58-61; v Scandinavia 1956-60. (GB): v America 1957; v Europe 1956-62

Butterworth, JR
(England): v France 1954

Cairnes, HM
(Ireland): v Wales 1913-25; v England 1904; v Scotland 1904-27

Caldwell, I
(England): Home Int 1950-51-52-53-54-55-56-57-58-59-61; v France 1950. (GB): v America 1951-55

Calvert, M
(Wales): Home Int 1983-84-86-87-89

Cameron, D
(Scotland): Home Int 1938-51

Campbell, Bart, Sir Guy C
(Scotland): v England 1909-10-11

Campbell, HM
(Scotland): Home Int 1962-64-68; v Scandinavia 1962; v Australia 1964; Eur T Ch 1965.(GB): v Europe 1964

Campbell, JGS
(Scotland): Home Int 1947-48

Campbell, W
(Scotland): v Ireland 1927-28-29-30-31; v England 1928-29-30-31; v Wales 1931; Home Int 1933-34-35-36. (GB): v America 1930

Cannon, JHS
(England): v Ireland/Wales 1925

Cannon, JM
(Scotland): Home Int 1969; v Spain 1974

Carman, A
(England): v Scotland 1979; Home Int 1980

Carr, FC
(England): v Scotland 1911

Carr, JB
(Ireland): Home Int 1947-48-49-50-51-52-53-54-55-56-57-58-59-60-61-62-63-64-65-66-67-68-69; Eur T Ch 1965-67-69. (GB): v America 1947-49-51-53-55-57-59-61-63-65 (Captain) -67 (Captain); v Europe 1954-56-64-66-68; in World Team Ch 1958-60

Carr, JJ
(Ireland): Home Int 1981-82-83

Carr, JP
(Wales): v Ireland 1913

Carr JR
(Ireland): v Wales 1930-31; v England 1931; Home Int 1933

Carr, R
(Ireland): Home Int 1970-71; Eur T Ch 1971. (GB): v America 1971

Carrgill, PM
(England): Home Int 1978

Carrick, DG
(Scotland): Home Int 1981-82-83-84-85-86-87-88-89; v West Germany 1987; v Italy 1988; v France 1989; Eur T Ch 1989. (GB): v America 1983-87; v Europe 1986

Carroll, CA
(Ireland): v Wales 1924

Carroll, JP
(Ireland): Home Int 1948-49-50-51-62

Carroll, W
(Ireland): v Wales 1913-23-24-25; v England 1925; v Scotland 1929; Home Int 1932

Carslaw, LA
(Scotland): Home Int 1976-77-78-80-81; Eur T Ch 1977-79; v England 1979; v Italy 1979; v Spain 1977; v Belgium 1978; v France 1978. (GB): v Europe 1978; v America 1979

Carvill, J
(Ireland): Home Int 1989; Eur T Ch 1989

Cashell, BG
(Ireland): Home Int 1978; v France, West Germany, Sweden 1978

Cassells, C
(England): Home Int 1989

Castle, H
(England): v Scotland 1903-04

Cater, JR
(Scotland): Home Int 1952-53-54-55-56. (GB): v America 1955

Caul, P
(Ireland): Home Int 1968-69-71-72-73-74-75

Caven, J
(Scotland): v England 1926. (GB): v America 1922

Chapman, BHG
(England): Home Int 1961-62. (GB): v America 1961; v Europe 1962

Chapman, JA
(Wales): v Ireland 1923-29-30-31; v Scotland 1931; v England 1925

Chapman, R
(Wales): v Ireland 1929; Home Int 1932-34-35-36

Chapman, R
(England): v Scotland 1979; Home Int 1980-81; Eur T Ch 1981. (GB): v Europe 1980; v America 1981

Charles, WB
(Wales): v Ireland 1924

Chillas, D
(Scotland): Home Int 1971

Christmas, MJ
(England): Home Int 1960-61-62-63-64. (GB): v America 1961-63; v Europe 1962-64; in World Team Ch 1962

Clark, CA
(England): Home Int 1964. (GB): v Europe 1964; v America 1965

Clark, D
(Ireland): Home Int 1987-89

Clark, GJ
(England): Home Int 1961-64-66-67-68-71. (GB): v Europe 1964-66; v America 1965.

Clark, HK
(England): Home Int 1973. (GB): v America 1973

Clark, MD
(Wales): v Ireland 1947

Clay, G
(Wales): Home Int 1962

Claydon, R
(England): Home Int 1988; Eur T Ch 1989. (GBI): v America 1989

Cleary, T
(Ireland): Home Int 1976-77-78-82-83-84-85-86; v Wales 1979; v France, West Germany, Sweden 1976

Clement, G
(Wales): v Ireland 1979

Cochran, JS
(Scotland): Home Int 1966

Colt, HS
(England): v Scotland 1908

Coltart, A
(Scotland): Home Int 1988-89; Eur T Ch 1989

Cook, J
(England): Home Int 1989

Cook, JH
(England): Home Int 1969

Corridan, T
(Ireland): Home Int 1983-84

Corcoran, DK
(Ireland): Home Int 1972-73; Eur T Ch 1973

Cosh, GB
(Scotland): Home Int 1964-65-66-67-68-69; Eur T Ch 1965-69.
(GB): v America 1965; v Europe 1966-68; in Com Tnmt
1967; in World Team Ch 1966-68

Coulter, JG
(Wales): Home Int 1951-52

Coutts, FJ
(Scotland): Home Int 1980-81-82; Eur T Ch 1981;
v France 1981-82

Cox, S
(Wales): Home Int 1970-71-72-73-74; Eur T Ch 1971-73

Crabbe, JL
(Ireland): v Wales 1925; v Scotland 1927-28

Craddock, T
(Ireland): Home Int 1955-56-57-58-59-60-67-68-69-70;
Eur T Ch 1971. (GB): v America 1967-69

Craigan, RM
(Ireland): Home Int 1963-64

Crawley, LG
(England): v Ireland 1931; v Scotland 1931; Home Int 1932-
33-34-36-37-38-47-48-49-54-55; v France 1936-37-38-49.
(GB): v America 1932-34-38-47

Critchley, B
(England): Home Int 1962-69-70; Eur T Ch 1969.
(GB): v America 1969; v Europe 1970

Crosbie, GF
(Ireland): Home Int 1953-55-56-57-88 (captain)

Crowley, M
(Ireland): v England 1928-29-30-31; v Wales 1929-31;
v Scotland 1929-30-31; Home Int 1932

Cuddihy, J
(Scotland): Home Int 1977

Curry, DH
(England): Home Int 1984-86-87; v France 1988. (GB): v
Europe 1986–88 v America 1987

Dalgleish, CR
(Scotland): Home Int 1981-82-83-89; v France 1982;
Eur T Ch 1981; Nixdorf Nations Cup 1989. (GB): v America
1981

Darwin, B
(England): v Scotland 1902-04-05-08-09 10 23 24.
(GB): v America 1922

Davies, EN
(Wales): Home Int 1959-60-61-62-63-64-65-66-67-68-69-
70-71-72-73-74; Eur T Ch 1969-71-73

Davies, JC
(England) Home Int 1969-71-72-73-74-78; Eur T Ch 1973-
75-77. (GB): v Europe 1972-74-76-78; v America 1973-75-
77-79; in World Team Ch 1974-76

Davies, FE
(Ireland): v Wales 1923

Davies, G
(Wales): v Denmark 1977; Home Int 1981-82-83

Davies, HE
(Wales): Home Int 1933-34-36

Davies, M
(England): Home Int 1984-85

Davies, TJ
(Wales): Home Int 1954-55-56-57-58-58-60

Davison, C
(England): Home Int 1989

Dawson, JE
(Scotland): v Ireland 1927-29-30-31; v England 1930-31;
v Wales 1931; Home Int 1932-33-34-37

Dawson, M
(Scotland): Home Int 1963-65-66

Dawson, P
(England): Home Int 1969

Doboys, A
(Scotland): Home Int 1956-59-60; v Scandinavia 1960

Deeble, P
(England): Home Int 1975-76-77-78-80-81-83-84;
v Scotland 1979; Eur T Ch 1979-81. (GB): v America 1977-81;
v Europe 1978; v France 1982; in Colombian Int 1978

Deighton, FWG
(Scotland): Home Int 1950-52-53-56-57-58-59-60.
(GB): v America 1951-57; v South Africa 1952;
in Com Tnmt 1954-59

Denholm, RB
(Scotland): v Ireland 1929-31; v Wales 1931; v England
1931; Home Int 1932-33-34-35

Dewar, FG
(Scotland): Home Int 1952-53-55

Dick, CE
(Scotland): v England 1902-03-04-05-09-12

Dickson, HM
(Scotland): v Ireland 1929-31

Dickson, JR
(Ireland): Eur T Ch 1977; Home Int 1980

Disley, A
(Wales): Home Int 1976-77-78; v Denmark 1977;
v Ireland 1979

Dodd, SC
(Wales):Home Int 1985-87-88-89. (GBI): v America 1989

Donellan, B
(Ireland): Home Int 1952

Dowie, A
(Scotland): Home Int 1949

Downes, P
(England): Home Int 1976-77-78-80-81-82;
Eur T Ch 1977-79-81. (GB): v Europe 1980

Downie, JJ
(England): Home Int 1974

Draper, JW
(Scotland): Home Int 1954

Drew, NV
(Ireland): Home Int 1952-53. (GB): v America 1953

Duffy, I
(Wales): Home Int 1975

Duncan, AA
(Wales): Home Int 1933-34-36-38-47-48-49-50-51-52-53-
54-55-56-57-58-59. (GB): v America (Captain) 1953

Duncan, GT
(Wales): Home Int 1952-53-54-55-56-57-58

Duncan, J, jr
(Wales): v Ireland 1913

Duncan, J
(Ireland): Home Int 1959-60-61

Dunn, NW
(England): v Ireland 1928
Dunn, P
(Wales): Home Int 1957-58-59-60-61-62-63-65-66
Dunne, E
(Ireland): Home Int 1973-74-76-77; v Wales 1979;
Eur T Ch 1975
Durrant, RA
(England): Home Int 1967; Eur T Ch 1967
Dykes, JM
(Scotland): Home Int 1934-35-36-48-49-51.
(GB): v America 1936

Easingwood, SR
(Scotland): Home Int 1986-87-88; v Italy 1988; v France
1989; Eur T Ch 1989
Eaves, CH
(Wales): Home Int 1935-36-38-47-48-49
Edwards, B
(Ireland): Home Int 1961-62-64-65-66-67-68-69-73
Edwards, M
(Ireland): Home Int 1956-57-58-60-61-62
Edwards, TH
(Wales): Home Int 1947
Egan, TW
(Ireland): Home Int 1952-53-59-60-62-67-68;
Eur T Ch 1967-69
Eggo, R
(England): Home Int 1986-87-88-89; v France 1988. (GB):
v America 1987; v Europe 1988
Elliot, A
(Scotland): Home Int 1989; v France 1989; Eur T Ch 1989
Elliot, C
(Scotland): Home Int 1982
Elliot, IA
(Ireland): Home Int 1975-77-78; Eur T Ch 1975,
v France, West Germany, Sweden 1978
Ellis, HC
(England): v Scotland 1902-12
Ellison, TF
(England): v Scotland 1922-25-26-27
Emerson, T
(Wales): Home Int 1932
Emery, G
(Wales): v Ireland 1925; Home Int 1933-36-38
Evans, AD
(Wales): v Scotland 1931-35; v Ireland 1931; Home Int 1932-
33-34-35-38-47-49-50-51-52-53-54-55-56-61
Evans, Duncan
(Wales): Home Int 1978-80-81; v Ireland 1979;
Eur T Ch 1981. (GB) v Europe 1980; v America 1981
Evans, G
(England): Home Int 1961
Evans, HJ
(Wales): Home Int 1976-77-78-80-81-84-85-87-88;
v France 1976; v Denmark 1977-80; v Ireland 1979;
Eur T Ch 1979-81; v Switzerland, Spain 1980
Evans, M Gear
(Wales): v Ireland 1930-31; v Scotland 1931
Everett, C
(Scotland): Home Int 1988-89; v Italy 1988; v France 1989;
Eur T Ch 1989; Nixdorf Nations Cup 1989
Ewing, RC
(Ireland): Home Int 1934-35-36-37-38-47-48-49-50-51-53-
54-55-56-57-58. (GB): v America 1936-38-47-49-51-55

Eyles, GR
(England): Home Int 1974-75; Eur T Ch 1975. (GB): v
America 1975; v Europe 1974; in World Team Ch 1974
Fairbairn, KA
(England): Home Int 1988
Fairchild, CEL
(Wales): v Ireland 1923; v England 1925
Fairchild, LJ
(Wales): v Ireland 1924
Fairlie, WE
(Scotland): v England 1912
Faldo, N
(England): Home Int 1975. (GB): in Com Tnmt 1975
Fanagan, J
(Ireland): Home Int 1989
Farmer, JC
(Scotland): Home Int 1970
Ferguson, M
(Ireland): Home Int 1952
Ferguson, WJ
(Ireland): Home Int 1952-54-55-58-59-61
Fergusson, S Mure
(Scotland): v England 1902-03-04
Ffrench, WF
(Ireland): v Scotland 1929; Home Int 1932
Fiddian, EW
(England): v Scotland 1929-30-31; v Ireland 1929-30-31;
Home Int 1932-33-34-35; v France 1934. (GB): v America
1932-34
Fitzgibbon, JF
(Ireland): Home Int 1955-56-57
Fitzsimmons, J
(Ireland): Home Int 1938-47-48
Flaherty, JA
(Ireland): Home Int 1934-35-36-37
Flaherty, PD
(Ireland): Home Int 1967; Eur T Ch 1967-69
Fleming, J
(Scotland): Home Int 1987
Fleury, RA
(Ireland): Home Int 1974
Flockhart, AS
(Scotland): Home Int 1948-49
Fogarty, GN
(Ireland): Home Int 1956-58-63-64-67
Fogg, HN
(England): Home Int 1933
Forest, J de (now Count J de Bendern)
(England): v Ireland 1931; v Scotland 1931.
(GB): v America 1932
Foster, MF
(England): Home Int 1973
Foster, R
(England): Home Int 1963-64-66-67-68-69-70-71-72;
Eur T Ch 1967-69-71-73. (GB): v Europe 1964-66-68-70;
v America 1965-67-69-71-73-79 (Captain) -81 (Captain);
in Com Tnmt 1967-71; in World Team Ch 1964-70
Fowler, WH
(England): v Scotland 1903-04-05
Fox, SJ
(England): Home Int 1956-57-58
Frame, DW
(England): Home Int 1958-59-60-61-62-63.
(GB): v America 1961
Francis, F
(England): Home Int 1936; v France 1935-36

Frazier, K
(England): Home Int 1938
Froggatt, P
(Ireland): Home Int 1957
Fry, SH
(England): v Scotland 1902-03-04-05-06-07-09

Gairdner, JR
(Scotland): v England 1902
Gallacher, BJ
(Scotland): Home Int 1967
Galloway, RF
(Scotland): Home Int 1957-58-59;
v Scandinavia 1958
Gannon, MA
(Ireland): Home Int 1973-74-77-78-80-81-83-84-87-88-89;
v France, West Germany, Sweden 1978-80;
Eur T Ch 1979-81-89. (GB) v Europe 1974-78
Garner, PF
(England): Home Int 1977-78-80; v Scotland 1979
Garnet, LG
(England): v France 1934. (GB): v Australia 1934
Garson, R
(Scotland): v Ireland 1928-29
Gent, J
(England): v Ireland 1930; Home Int 1938
Gibb, C
(Scotland): v England 1927; v Ireland 1928
Gibson, WC
(Scotland): Home Int 1950-51
Gilford, CF
(Wales): Home Int 1963-64-65-66-67
Gilford, D
(England): Home Int 1983-84-85. (GB): v America 1985;
v Europe 1986
Gill, WJ
(Ireland): v Wales 1931; Home Int 1932-33-34-35-36-37
Gillies, HD
(England): v Scotland 1908-25-26-27
Girvan, P
(Scotland): Home Int 1986; West Germany 1987.
(GB): v America 1987
Glossop, R
(Wales): Home Int 1935-37-38-47
Glover, J
(Ireland): Home Int 1951-52-53-55-59-60-70
Godwin, G
(England): Home Int 1976-77-78-80-81; v Scotland 1979;
v France 1982; Eur T Ch 1979-81. (GB): v America 1979-81
Goulding, N
(Ireland): Home Int 1988-89
Graham, AJ
(Scotland): v England 1925
Graham, J
(Scotland): v England 1902-03-04-05-06-07-08-09-10-11
Graham, JSS
(Ireland): Home Int 1938-50-51
Gray, CD
(England): Home Int 1932
Green, CW
(Scotland): Home Int 1961-62-63-64-65-66-67-68-69-70-71-72-
73-74-75-76-77-78; Eur T Ch 1965-67-69-71-73-75-77-79;
v Scandinavia 1962; v Belgium 1973-75-77-78; v Spain 1977; v
Italy 1979; v England 1979. (GB): v Europe 1962-66-68-70-72-
74-76; v America 1963-69-71-73-75-83 (Captain) -85 (Captain)
in Com Tnmt 1971; in World Team Ch 1970-72

Green, HB
(England): v Scotland 1979
Green, PO
(England): Home Int 1961-62-63. (GB): in Com Tnmt 1963
Greene, R
(Ireland): Home Int 1933
Greig, DG
(Scotland): Home Int 1972-73-75. (GB): in Com Tnmt 1975
Greig, K
(Scotland): Home Int 1933
Griffiths, HGB
(Wales): v Ireland 1923-24-25
Griffiths, HS
(Wales): v England 1958
Griffiths, JA
(Wales): Home Int 1933
Guild, WJ
(Scotland): v England 1925-27-28; v Ireland 1927-28

Hales, JP
(Wales): v Scotland 1963
Hall, AH
(Scotland): Home Int 1962-66-69
Hall, D
(Wales): Home Int 1932-37
Hall, K
(Wales): Home Int 1955-59
Hambro, AV
(England): v Scotland 1905-08-09-10-22
Hamilton, CJ
(Wales): v Ireland 1913
Hamilton, ED
(Scotland): Home Int 1936-37-38
Hamer, S
(England): Home Int 1983-84
Hanway, M
(Ireland): Home Int 1971-74
Hardman, RH
(England): v Scotland 1927-28. (GB): v America 1928
Hare, A
(England): Home Int 1988; Eur T Ch 1989. (GBI) v America
1989
Hare, WCD
(Scotland): Home Int 1953
Harrhy, A
(Wales): Home Int 1988-89
Harrington, J
(Ireland): Home Int 1960-61-74-75-76; Eur T Ch 1975;
v Wales 1979
Harris, IR
(Scotland): Home Int 1955-56-58-59
Harris, R
(Scotland): v England 1905-08-10-11-12-22-23-24-25-26-27-28
(GB): v America 1922 (Captain) -23 (Captain) -26 (Captain)
Harrison, JW
(Wales): Home Int 1937-50
Hartley, RW
(England): v Scotland 1926-27-28-29-30-31; v Ireland 1928-
29-30-31; Home Int 1933-34-35. (GB): v America 1930-32
Hartley, WL
(England): v Ireland/Wales 1925; v Scotland 1927-31;
v Ireland 1928-31; Home Int 1932-33; v France 1935.
(GB): v America 1932
Hassall, JE
(England): v Scotland 1923; v Ireland/Wales 1925

Hastings, JL
(Scotland): Home Int 1957-58; v Scandinavia 1958
Hawksworth, J
(England): Home Int 1984-85. (GB): v America 1985
Hay, G
(Scotland): v England 1979; Home Int 1980–88; v Belgium 1980; v France 1980-89; v Italy 1988. (GB): v Europe 1986
Hay, J
(Scotland): Home Int 1972
Hayes, JA
(Ireland): Home Int 1977
Hayward, CH
(England): v Scotland 1925; v Ireland 1928
Healy, TM
(Ireland): v Scotland 1931; v England 1931
Heather, D
(Ireland): Home Int 1976; v France, West Germany, Sweden 1976
Hedges, PJ
(England): Home Int 1970-73-74-75-76-77-78-82-83; Eur T Ch 1973-75-77. (GB): v America 1973-75; v Europe 1974-76; in World Team Ch 1974
Hegarty, J
(Ireland): Home Int 1975
Hegarty, TD
(Ireland): Home Int 1957
Helm, AGB
(England): Home Int 1948
Henderson, J
(Ireland): v Wales 1923
Henderson, N
(Scotland): Home Int 1963-64
Henriques, GLQ
(England): v Ireland 1930
Henry, W
(England): Home Int 1987; v France 1988
Herlihy, B
(Ireland): Home Int 1950
Herne, KTC
(Wales): v Ireland 1913
Heverin, AJ
(Ireland): Home Int 1978; v France, West Germany, Sweden 1978
Hezlet, CO
(Ireland): v Wales 1923-25-27-29-31; v Scotland 1927-28-29-30-31; v England 1929-30-31. (GB): v America 1924-26-28; v South Africa 1927
Higgins, L
(Ireland): Home Int 1968-70-71
Hill, GA
(England): Home Int 1936-37. (GB): v America 1936-55 (Captain)
Hilton, HH
(England): v Scotland 1902-03-04-05-06-07-09-10-11-12
Hird, K
(Scotland): Home Int 1987-88-89; Nixdorf Nations Cup 1989
Hoad, PGJ
(England): Home Int 1978; v Scotland 1979
Hodgson, C
(England): v Scotland 1924
Hoey, TBC
(Ireland): Home Int 1970-71-72-73-77-84; Eur T Ch 1971-77
Hogan, P
(Ireland): Home Int 1985-86-87-88
Holderess, Sir EWE
(England): v Scotland 1922-23-24-25-26-28. (GB): v America 1921-23-26-30

Holmes, AW
(England): Home Int 1962
Homer, TWB
(England): Home Int 1972-73; Eur T Ch 1973. (GB): v America 1973; v Europe 1972; in World Team Ch 1972
Homewood, G
(England): Home Int 1985
Hooman, CVL
(England): v Scotland 1910-22. (GB): v America 1922-23
Hope, WL
(Scotland): v England 1923-25-26-27-28-29. (GB): v America 1923-24-28
Horne, A
(Scotland): Home Int 1971
Hosie, JR
(Scotland): Home Int 1936
Howard, DB
(Scotland): v England 1979; Home Int 1980-81-82-83; v Belgium 1980; v France 1980-81; Eur T Ch 1981. (GB): v Europe 1980.
Howell, HR
(Wales): v Ireland 1923-24-25-29-30-31; v England 1925; v Scotland 1931; Home Int 1932-34-35-36-37-38-47
Howell, H Logan
(Wales): v Ireland 1925
Huddy, G
(England): Home Int 1960-61-62. (GB): v America 1961
Huggan, J
(Scotland): Home Int 1981-82-83-84; v France 1982; Eur T Ch 1981
Hughes, I
(Wales): Home Int 1954-55-56
Hulme, WJ
(Ireland): Home Int 1955-56-57
Humphrey, JG
(Wales): v Ireland 1925
Humphreys, AR
(Ireland): v England 1957
Humphreys, DI
(Wales): Home Int 1972
Humphreys, W
(England): Home Int 1970-71; Eur T Ch 1971. (GB): v Europe 1970; America 1971
Hunter, NM
(Scotland): v England 1903-12
Hunter, WI
(Scotland): v England 1922
Hutcheon, I
(Scotland): Home Int 1971-72-73-74-75-76-77-78-80; v Belgium 1973-77-78-80; v Spain 1977; v France 1978-80-81; v Italy 1979; Eur T Ch 1973-75-77-79-81. (GB): v Europe 1974-76; v America 1975-77-79-81; in World Team Ch 1974-76-80; in Com Tnmt 1975; in Dominican Int 1973; in Colombian Int 1975
Hutchings, C
(England): v Scotland 1902
Hutchinson, HG
(England): v Scotland 1902-03-04-06-07-09
Hutchison, CK
(Scotland): v England 1904-05-06-07-08-09-10-11-12
Hyde, GE
(England): Home Int 1967-68

Illingworth, G
(England): v Scotland 1929; v France 1937

Inglis, MJ
(England): Home Int 1977
Isitt, GH
(Wales): v Ireland 1923

Jack, RR
(Scotland): Home Int 1950-51-54-55-56-57-58-59-61;
v Scandinavia 1958. (GB): v America 1957-59; v
Europe 1956; in World Team Ch 1958; in Com Tnmt
1959
Jack, WS
(Scotland): Home Int 1955
Jacob, NE
(Wales): Home Int 1932-33-34-35-36
James, D
(Scotland): Home Int 1985
James, M
(England). Home Int 1974-75; Eur T Ch 1975
(GB): v America 1975
James, RD
(England): Home Int 1974-75
Jameson, JF
(Ireland): v Wales 1913-24
Jamieson, A, jr
(Scotland): v England 1927-28-31; v Ireland 1928-31;
v Wales 1931; Home Int 1932-33-36-37.
(GB): v America 1926
Jamieson, D
(Scotland): Home Int 1980
Jenkins, JLC
(Scotland): v England 1908-12-22-24-26-28;
v Ireland 1928. (GB): v America 1921
Jermine, JG
(Wales): Home Int 1972-73-74-75-76-82; Eur T Ch
1975-77; v France 1975
Jobson, RH
(England): v Ireland 1928
Johnson, TWG
(Ireland): v England 1929
Johnston, JW
(Scotland): Home Int 1970-71
Jones, A
(Wales): Home Int 1989
Jones, DK
(Wales): Home Int 1973
Jones, EO
(Wales): Home Int 1983-85-86
Jones, JG Parry
(Wales): Home Int 1959-60
Jones, JL
(Wales): Home Int 1933-34-36
Jones, JR
(Wales): Home Int 1970-72-73-77-78-80-81-82-83-84-85;
Eur T Ch 1973-79-81; v Denmark 1976-80; v Ireland
1979; v Switzerland, Spain 1980; v Ireland 1979
Jones, JW
(England): Home Int 1948-49-50-51-52-54-55
Jones, KG
(Wales): Home Int 1988
Jones, MA
(Wales): Home Int 1947-48-49-50-51-53-54-57
Jones, Malcolm F
(Wales): Home Int 1933
Jones, SP
(Wales): Home Int 1981-82-83-84-85-86-88-89

Kane, RM
(Ireland): Home Int 1967-68-71-72-74-78; Eur T Ch
1971-79; v Wales 1979. (GB): v Europe 1974
Kearney, K
(Ireland): Home Int 1988-89
Keenan, S
(Ireland): Home Int 1989
Kelleher, WA
(Ireland): Home Int 1962
Kelley, MJ
(England): Home Int 1974-75-76-77-78-80-81-82-88 (Captain);
v France 1982; Eur T Ch 1977-79. (GB): v America
1977-79; v Europe 1976-78; in World Team Ch 1976;
in Colombian Int 1978
Kelley, PD
(England): Home Int 1965-66-68
Kelly, NS
(Ireland): Home Int 1966
Keppler, SD
(England): Home Int 1982-83; v France 1982.
(GB): v America 1983
Kilduff, AJ
(Ireland): v Scotland 1928
Killey, GC
(Scotland): v Ireland 1928
King, M
(England): Home Int 1969-70-71-72-73; Eur T Ch 1971-73 (GB):
v America 1969-73; v Europe 1970-72; in Com Tnmt 1971
Kissock, B
(Ireland): Home Int 1961-62-74-76; v France, West
Germany, Sweden 1978
Kitchin, JE
(England): v France 1949
Knight, B
(Wales): Home Int 1986
Knipe, RG
(Wales): Home Int 1953-54-55-56
Knowles, WR
(Wales): v England 1948
Kyle, AT
(Scotland): Home Int 1938-47-49-50-51-52-53.
(GB): v America 1938-47-51; v South Africa 1952
Kyle, D
(Scotland): v England 1924-30. (GB): v America 1924
Kyle, EP
(Scotland): v England 1925

Laidlay, JE
(Scotland): v England 1902-03-04-05-06-07-08-09-10-11
Lake, AD
(Wales): Home Int 1958
Lang, JA
(Scotland): v England 1929-31; v Ireland 1929-30-31;
v Wales 1931. (GB): v America 1930
Langley, JDA
(England): Home Int 1950-51-52-53; v France 1950.
(GB): v America 1936-51-53
Langmead, J
(England): Home Int 1986
Lassen, EA
(England): v Scotland 1909-10-11-12
Last, CN
(Wales): Home Int 1975
Laurence, C
(England): Home Int 1983-84-85

Lawrie, CD
(Scotland): Home Int 1949-50-55-56-57-58; v Scandinavia
1958. (GB): v South Africa 1952; v America 1961
(Captain) -63 (Captain)

Layton, EN
(England): v Scotland 1922-23-26; v Ireland/Wales 1925

Lee, IGF
(Scotland): Home Int 1958-59-60-61-62; v Scandinavia
1960

Lee, JN
(Wales): Home Int 1988-89

Lee, M
(England): Home Int 1950

Lee, MG
(England): Home Int 1965

Lehane, N
(Ireland): Home Int 1976; v France, West Germany,
Sweden 1976

Lewis, DH
(Wales): Home Int 1935-36-37-38

Lewis, DR
(Wales): v Ireland 1925-29-30-31; v Scotland 1931;
Home Int 1932-34

Lewis, ME
(England): Home Int 1980-81-82; v France 1982.
(GB): v America 1983

Lewis, R Cofe
(Wales): v Ireland 1925

Leyden, PJ
(Ireland): Home Int 1953-55-56-57-59

Lincoln, AC
(England): v Scotland 1907

Lindsay, J
(Scotland): Home Int 1933-34-35-36

Lloyd, HM
(Wales): v Ireland 1913

Lloyd, RM de
(Wales): v Scotland 1931; v Ireland 1931; Home Int
1932-33-34-35-36-37-38-47-48

Llyr, A
(Wales): Home Int 1984-85

Lockhart, G
(Scotland): v England 1911-12

Lockley, AE
(Wales): Home Int 1956-57-58-62

Logan, GW
(England): Home Int 1973

Long, D
(Ireland): Home Int 1973-74-80-81-82-83-84;
v Wales 1979; Eur T Ch 1979

Low, AJ
(Scotland): Home Int 1964-65; Eur T Ch 1965

Low, JL
(Scotland): v England 1904

Lowe, A
(Ireland): v Wales 1924; v England 1925-28; v Scotland
1927-28

Lowson, G
(Scotland): Home Int 1989

Lucas, PB
(England): Home Int 1936-48-49; v France 1936.
(GB): v America 1936-47-49 (Captain)

Lunt, MSR
(England): Home Int 1956-57-58-59-60-62-63-64-66.
(GB): v America 1959-61-63-65; v Europe 1964;
in Com Tnmt 1963; in World Team Ch 1964

Lunt, S
(England): Home Int 1932-33-34-38, v France 1001 00 00

Lygate, M
(Scotland): Home Int 1970-75-88 (Captain); Eur T Ch 1971

Lyle, AWB
(England): Home Int 1975-76-77; Eur T Ch 1977.
(GB): v America 1977; in Com Tnmt 1975; v Europe 1976

Lyon, JS
(England): Home Int 1937-38

Lyons, P
(Ireland): Home Int 1986

McAllister, SD
(Scotland): Home Int 1983

Macara, MA
(Wales): Home Int 1983-84-85-87-89

McArthur, W
(Scotland): Home Int 1952-54

McBeath, J
(Scotland): Home Int 1964

McBride, D
(Scotland): Home Int 1932

McCallum, AR
(Scotland): v England 1929. (GB): v America 1928

McCarrol, F
(Ireland): Home Int 1968-69

McCart, DM
(Scotland): Home Int 1977; v Belgium 1978

McCarthy, L
(Ireland): Home Int 1953-54-55-56

McConnell, FP
(Ireland): v Wales 1929-30-31; v England 1929-30-31;
v Scotland 1930-31; Home Int 1934

McConnell, RM
(Ireland): v Wales 1924-25-29-30-31; v England 1925-28-
29-30-31; v Scotland 1927-28-29-31; Home Int 1934-35-36-37

McConnell, WG
(Ireland): v England 1925

McCormack, JD
(Ireland): v Wales 1913-24; v England 1928, Home Int
1932-33-34-35-36-37

McCrea, WE
(Ireland): Home Int 1965-66-67; Eur T Ch 1965

McCready, SM
(Ireland): Home Int 1947-49-50-52-54. (GB): v America
1949-51

McDaid, B
(Ireland): v Wales 1979

MacDonald, GK
(Scotland): Home Int 1978-81-82; v England 1979; v France
1981-82

McDonald, H
(Scotland): Home Int 1970

Macdonald, JS
(Scotland): Home Int 1969-70-71-72; v Belgium 1973;
Eur T Ch 1971. (GB): v Europe 1970; v America 1971

McEvoy, P
(England): Home Int 1976-77-78-80-81-83-84-85-86-87-88-89;
v Scotland 1979; v France 1982–88; Eur T Ch 1977-79-81-89;
(GB): v America 1977-79-81-85-89; v Europe 1978-80-86-88;
in World Cup 1978-80-88 (winners)

Macfarlane, CB
(Scotland): v England 1912

McGimpsey, G
(Ireland): Home Int 1978-80-81-82-83-84-85-86-87-88-89;

v Wales 1979; Eur T Ch 1981-89. (GB): v America 1985-89;
v Europe 1986-88; World Cup 1988 (winners)

McGinley, P
(Ireland): Home Int 1989

Macgregor, A
(Scotland): v Scandinavia 1956

Macgregor, G
(Scotland): Home Int 1969-70-71-72-73-74-75-76-80-81-82-83-
84-85-86-87; v Belgium 1973-75-80; v England 1979; Eur T Ch
1971-73-75-81. (GB): v Europe 1970-74; v America 1971-75-83-
85-87; in Com Tnmt 1971-75; v France 1981-82

MacGregor, RC
(Scotland): Home Int 1951-52-53-54. (GB): v America 1953

McHenry, J
(Ireland): Home Int 1985-86. (GB): v America 1987

McInally, H
(Scotland): Home Int 1937-47-48

McInally, RH
(Ireland): Home Int 1949-51

McIntosh, E
(Scotland): Home Int 1989

Macintosh, KW
(Scotland): v England 1979; Home Int 1980; v France 1980;
v Belgium 1980. (GB): v Europe 1980

McKay, G
(Scotland): Home Int 1969

McKay, JR
(Scotland): Home Int 1950-51-52-54

McKellar, PJ
(Scotland): Home Int 1976-77-78; v Belgium 1978;
v France 1978; v England 1979. (GB): v America 1977;
v Europe 1978

Mackenzie, F
(Scotland): v England 1902-03

Mackenzie, WW
(Scotland): v England 1923-26-27-29; v Ireland 1930.
(GB): v America 1922-23

Mackeown, HN
(Ireland): Home Int 1973; Eur T Ch 1973

Mackie, GW
(Scotland): Home Int 1948-50

McKinna, RA
(Scotland): Home Int 1938

McKinlay, SL
(Scotland): v England 1929-30-31; v Ireland 1930; v Wales
1931; Home Int 1932-33-35-37-47. (GB): v America 1934

McKinnon, A
(Scotland): Home Int 1947-52

McLean, D
(Wales): Home Int 1968-69-70-71-72-73-74-75-76-77-78-
80-81-82-83-85-86-88; Eur T Ch 1975-77-79-81;
v France 1975-76; v Denmark 1976-80; v Ireland 1979;
v Switzerland, Spain 1980

McLean, J
(Scotland): Home Int 1932-33-34-35-36. (GB): v America
1934-36; v Australia 1934

McLeod, AE
(Scotland): Home Int 1937-38

McLeod, WS
(Scotland): Home Int 1935-37-38-47-48-49-50-51

McMenamin, E
(Ireland): Home Int 1981

McMullan, C
(Ireland): Home Int 1933-34-35

McNair, AA
(Scotland): v Ireland 1929

MacNamara, L
(Ireland): Home Int 1977-83-84-85-86-87-88-89; Eur T Ch 1977

McRuvie, EA
(Scotland): v England 1929-30-31; v Ireland 1930-31;
v Wales 1931; Home Int 1932-33-34-35-36.
(GB): v America 1932-34

McTear, J
(Scotland): Home Int 1971

Madeley, JFD
(Ireland): Home Int 1959-60-61-62-63-64. (GB): v Europe
1962; v America 1963

Mahon, RJ
(Ireland): Home Int 1938-52-54-55

Maliphant, FR
(Wales): Home Int 1932

Malone, B
(Ireland): Home Int 1959-64-69-71-75; Eur T Ch 1971-75

Manford, GC
(Scotland): v England 1922-23

Manley, N
(Ireland): v Wales 1924; v England 1928; v Scotland 1927-28

Mann, LS
(Scotland): Home Int 1982-83. (GB): v America 1983

Marchbank, B
(Scotland): Home Int 1978; v Italy 1979; Eur T Ch 1979.
(GB): v Europe 1976-78; in World Team Ch 1978;
v America 1979

Marks, GC
(England): Home Int 1963-67-68-69-70-71-74-75-82; Eur
T Ch 1967-69-71-75. (GB): v Europe 1968-70; v America
1969-71-87 (Captain)-89 (Captain); in World Team Ch 1970;
in Com Tnmt 1975; in Colombian Int 1975. Non playing
captain v France 1982

Marren, JM
(Ireland): v Wales 1925

Marsh, DM
(England): Home Int 1956-57-58-59-60-64-66-68-69-70-
71-72; Eur T Ch 1971. (GB): v Europe 1958; v America
1959-71-73 (Captain) -75 (Captain)

Marshman, A
(Wales): Home Int 1952

Marston, CC
(Wales): v Ireland 1929-30-31; v Scotland 1931

Martin, DHR
(England): Home Int 1938; v France 1934-49

Martin, GNC
(Ireland): v Wales 1923-29; v Scotland 1928-29-30;
v England 1929-30. (GB): v America 1928

Martin, S
(Scotland): Home Int 1975-76-77; Eur T Ch 1977; v Belgium
1977; v Spain 1977. (GB): v America 1977; v Europe 1976;
in World Team Ch 1976

Mason, SC
(England): Home Int 1973

Mathias-Thomas, FEL
(Wales): v Ireland 1924-25

Matthews, RL
(Wales): Home Int 1935-37

Maxwell, R
(Scotland): v England 1902-03-04-05-06-07-09-10

Mayo, PM
(Wales): Home Int 1982-87. (GB): v America 1985-87

Meharg, W
(Ireland): Home Int 1957

Melia, TJ
(Wales): Home Int 1976-77-78-80-81-82; v Ireland 1979;

Eur T Ch 1977-79; v Denmark 1976-80; v Switzerland, Spain 1080

Mellin, GL
(England): v Scotland 1922

Melville, LM Balfour
(Scotland): v England 1902-03

Melville, TE
(Scotland): Home Int 1974

Menzies, A
(Scotland): v England 1925

Metcalfe, J
(England): Home Int 1989

Micklem, GH
(England): Home Int 1947-48-49-50-51-52-53-54-55. (GB): v America 1947-49-53-55-57 (Captain) -59 (Captain); in World Team 1958

Mill, JW
(Scotland): Home Int 1953-54

Millensted, DJ
(England): Home Int 1966; Eur T Ch 1967. (GB): v America 1967; in Com Tnmt 1967

Miller, AC
(Scotland): Home Int 1954-55

Miller, MJ
(Scotland): Home Int 1974-75-77-78; v Belgium 1978; v France 1978

Milligan, JW
(Scotland): Home Int 1986-87-88-89; v West Germany 1987; v Italy 1988; v France 1989; Eur T Ch 1989; Nixdorf Nations Cup 1989. (GB): v Europe 1988; World Cup 1988 (winners). (GBI): v America 1989

Mills, ES
(Wales): Home Int 1957

Millward, EB
(England): Home Int 1950-52-53-54-55. (GB): v America 1949-55

Milne, WTG
(Scotland): Home Int 1972-73; Eur T Ch 1973; v Belgium 1973. (GB): v America 1973

Mitchell, A
(England): v Scotland 1910-11-12

Mitchell, CS
(England): Home Int 1975-76-78

Mitchell, FH
(England): v Scotland 1906-07-08

Mitchell, JWH
(Wales): Home Int 1964-65-66

Moffat, DM
(England): Home Int 1961-63-67; v France 1959-60

Moir, A
(Scotland): Home Int 1983-84

Montgomerie, CS
(Scotland): Home Int 1984-85-86; v West Germany 1987. (GB): v America 1985-87; v Europe 1986

Montgomerie, JS
(Scotland): Home Int 1957; v Scandinavia 1958

Montgomerie, RH de
(England): v Scotland 1908; v Wales/Ireland 1925; v South Africa 1927. (GB): v America 1921

Moody, JV
(West): Home Int 1947-48-49-51-56-58-59-60-61

Moody, PH
(England): Home Int 1971-72. (GB): v Europe 1972

Moore, GJ
(Ireland): v England 1928; v Wales 1929

Morgan, JL
(Wales): 1948-49-50-51-52-53-54-55-56-57-58-59-60-61-62-64-68 (GB): v America 1951-53-55

Morris, FS
(Scotland): Home Int 1963

Morris, MF
(Ireland): Home Int 1978-80-82-83-84; v Wales 1979; Eur T Ch 1979; v France, West Germany, Sweden 1980

Morris, R
(Wales): Home Int 1983-86-87

Morris, TS
(Wales): v Ireland 1924-29-30

Morrison, JH
(Scotland): v Scandinavia 1960

Morrison, JSF
(England): v Ireland 1930

Morrow, AJC
(Ireland): Home Int 1975-83

Morrow, JM
(Wales): v Ireland 1979; Home Int 1980-81; Eur T Ch 1979-81; v Denmark, Switzerland, Spain 1980

Mosey, IJ
(England): Home Int 1971

Moss, AV
(Wales): Home Int 1965-66-68

Mouland, MG
(Wales): Home Int 1978-81; v Ireland 1979; Eur T Ch 1979

Moxon, GA
(Wales): v Ireland 1929-30

Mulcare, P
(Ireland): Home Int 1968-69-70-71-72-74-78-80; v France, West Germany, Sweden 1978-80; Eur T Ch 1975-79. (GB): v Europe 1972; v America 1975

Mulholland, D
(Ireland): Home Int 1988

Munn, E
(Ireland): v Wales 1913-23-24; v Scotland 1927

Munn, L
(Ireland): v Wales 1913-23-24; Home Int 1936-37

Munro, RAG
(Scotland): Home Int 1960

Murdoch, D
(Scotland): Home Int 1964

Murphy, AR
(Scotland): Home Int 1961-65-67

Murphy, P
(Ireland): Home Int 1985-86

Murray, GH
(Scotland): Home Int 1973-74-75-76-77-78-83; v Spain 1974-77; v Belgium 1975-77; Eur T Ch 1975-77. (GB): v America 1977; v Europe 1978

Murray, SWT
(Scotland): Home Int 1959-60-61-62-63; v Scandinavia 1960. (GB): v Europe 1958-62; v America 1963

Murray, WA
(Scotland): v England 1923-24-25-26-27. (GB): v America 1923-24

Murray, WB
(Scotland): Home Int 1967-68-69; Eur T Ch 1969

Muscroft, R
(England): Home Int 1986

Nash A
(England): Home Int 1988-89

Neech, DG
(England): Home Int 1961

Neill, JH
(Ireland): Home Int 1938-47-48-49
Neill, R
(Scotland): Home Int 1936
Nestor, JM
(Ireland): Home Int 1962-63-64
Nevin, V
(Ireland): Home Int 1960-63-65-67-69-72; Eur T Ch 1967-69-73
Newey, AS
(England): Home Int 1932
Newman, JE
(Wales): Home Int 1932
Newton, H
(Wales): v Ireland 1929
Nicholson, J
(Ireland): Home Int 1932
Noon, GS
(Wales): Home Int 1935-36-37
Noon, J
(Scotland): Home Int 1987

O'Boyle, P
(Ireland): Eur T Ch 1977
O'Brien, MD
(Ireland): Home Int 1968-69-70-71-72-75-76-77; Eur T Ch 1971; v France, West Germany, Sweden 1976
O'Carroll, C
(Wales): Home Int 1989
O'Connell, A
(Ireland): Home Int 1967-70-71-71
O'Connell, E
(Ireland): Home Int 1985; Eur T Ch 1989. (GB): v Europe 1988; World Cup 1988 (winners). (GBI): v America 1989
O'Leary, JE
(Ireland): Home Int 1969-70; Eur T Ch 1969
O'Neill, JJ
(Ireland): Home Int 1968
Oldcorn, A
(England): Home Int 1982-83. (GB): v America 1983
Oosterhuis, PA
(England): Home Int 1966-67-68. (GB): v America 1967; v Europe 1968; in World Team Ch 1968
Oppenheimer, RH
(England): v Ireland 1928-29-30; v Scotland 1930. (GB): v America 1957 (Captain)
O'Rourke, P
(Ireland): Home Int 1980-81-82-84-85
O'Sullivan, D
(Ireland): Home Int 1985-86-87
O'Sullivan, DF
(Ireland): Home Int 1976; Eur T Ch 1977
O'Sullivan, WM
(Ireland): Home Int 1934-35-36-37-38-47-48-49-50-51-53-54
Osgood, TH
(Scotland): v England 1925
Owen, JB
(Wales): Home Int 1971
Owens, GF
(Wales): Home Int 1960-61
Ownes, GH
(Ireland): Home Int 1935-37-38-47

Palferman, H
(Wales): Home Int 1950-53
Palmer, DJ
(England): Home Int 1962-63

Parfitt, RWM
(Wales): v Ireland 1924
Parkin, AP
(Wales): Home Int 1980-81-82. (GB): v America 1983
Parry, JR
(Wales): Home Int 1966-75-76-77; v France 1976
Patey, IR
(England): Home Int 1952; v France 1948-49-50
Patrick, KG
(Scotland): Home Int 1937
Patterson, AH
(Ireland): v Wales 1913
Pattinson, R
(England): Home Int 1949
Payne, J
(England): Home Int 1950-51
Payne J
(England): Home Int 1989
Pearson, AG
(GB): v South Africa 1927
Pearson, MJ
(England): Home Int 1951-52
Pease, JWB (later Lord Wardington)
(England): v Scotland 1903-04-05-06
Pennink, JJF
(England): Home Int 1937-38-47; v France 1937-38-39. (GB): v America 1938
Perkins, TP
(England): v Scotland 1927-28-29. (GB): v America 1928
Perowne, AH
(England): Home Int 1947-48-49-50-51-53-54-55-57. (GB): v America 1949-53-59; in World Team Ch 1958
Peters, GB
(Scotland): Home Int 1934-35-36-37-38. (GB): v America 1936-38
Peters, JL
(Wales): Home Int 1987-88-89
Phillips, LA
(Wales): v Ireland 1913
Pierse, AD
(Ireland): Home Int 1976-77-78-80-81-82-83-84-85-87-88; v Wales 1979; v France, West Germany, Sweden 1980; Eur T Ch 1981. (GB): v Europe 1980; v America 1983
Pinch, AG
(Wales): Home Int 1969
Pirie, AK
(Scotland): Home Int 1966-67-68-69-70-71-72-73-74-75; Eur T Ch 1967-69; v Belgium 1973-75; v Spain 1974. (GB): v America 1967; v Europe 1970
Plaxton, J
(England): Home Int 1983-84
Pollin, RKM
(Ireland): Home Int 1971; Eur T Ch 1973
Pollock, VA
(England): v Scotland 1908
Povall, J
(Wales): Home Int 1960-61-62-63-65-66-67-68-69-70-71-72-73-74-75-76-77; Eur T Ch 1967-69-71-73-75-77; v France 1975-76; v Denmark 1976. (GB): v Europe 1962
Powell, WA
(England): v Scotland 1923-24; v Wales/Ireland 1925
Power, E
(Ireland): Home Int 1987-88
Power, M
(Ireland): Home Int 1947-48-49-50-51-52-54

Poxon, MA
(England): Home Int 1076 76; Eur T Ch 1975
(GB): v America 1975
Pressdee, RNG
(Wales): Home Int 1958-59-60-61-62
Pressley, J
(Scotland): Home Int 1947-48-49
Price, JP
(Wales): Home Int 1986-87-88
Prosser, D
(England): Eur T Ch 1989
Pugh, RS
(Wales): v Ireland 1923-24-29
Purcell, J
(Ireland): Home Int 1973

Raeside, A
(Scotland): v Ireland 1929
Rafferty, R
(Ireland): v Wales 1979; Home Int 1980-81; v France, West
Germany, Sweden 1980; Eur T Ch 1981. (GB): v Europe
1980; in World Team Ch 1980; v America 1981
Rainey, WHE
(Ireland): Home Int 1962
Rawlinson, D
(England): Home Int 1949-50-52-53
Ray, D
(England): Home Int 1982; v France 1982
Rayfus, P
(Ireland): Home Int 1986-87–88
Reade, HE
(Ireland): v Wales 1913
Reddan, B
(Ireland): Home Int 1987
Rees, CN
(Wales): Home Int 1986-88-89
Rees, DA
(Wales): Home Int 1961-62-63-64
Renfrew, RL
(Scotland): Home Int 1964
Renwick, G, jr
(Wales): v Ireland 1923
Revell, RP
(England): Home Int 1972-73; Eur T Ch 1973
Ricardo, W
(Wales): v Ireland 1930-31; v Scotland 1931
Rice, JH
(Ireland): Home Int 1947-52
Rice-Jones, L
(Wales): v Ireland 1924
Richards, PM
(Wales): Home Int 1960-61-62-63-71
Richardson, S
(England): Home Int 1986-87-88
Risdon, PWL
(England): Home Int 1935-36
Robb, J, jr
(Scotland): v England 1902-03-05-06-07
Robb, WM
(Scotland): Home Int 1935
Roberts, AT
(Scotland): v Ireland 1931
Roberts, G
(Scotland): Home Int 1937-38

Roberts, GP
(England): Home Int 1951-53; v France 1949
Roberts, HJ
(England): Home Int 1947-48-53
Roberts, J
(Wales): Home Int 1937
Roberts, SB
(Wales): Home Int 1932-33-34-35-37-38-47-48-49-50-51-
52-53-54
Roberts, WJ
(Wales): Home Int 1948-49-50-51-52-53-54
Robertson, A
(England): Home Int 1986-87; v France 1988
Robertson, CW
(Ireland): v Wales 1930; v Scotland 1930
Robertson, DM
(Scotland): Home Int 1973-74; v Spain 1974
Robertson-Durham, JA
(Scotland): v England 1911
Robinson, J
(England): v Ireland 1928
Robinson, J
(England): Home Int 1986. (GB): v America 1987
Robinson, S
(England): v Scotland 1925; v Ireland 1928-29-30
Roderick, RN
(Wales): Home Int 1983-84-85-86-87-88. (GB) v Europe 1988.
(GBI): v America 1989
Rolfe, B
(Wales): Home Int 1963-65
Roobottom, EL
(Wales): Home Int 1967
Roper, HS
(England): v Ireland 1931; v Scotland 1931
Roper, MS
(Wales): v Ireland 1979
Roper, R
(England): Home Int 1984-85-86-87
Rothwell, J
(England): Home Int 1947-48
Rutherford, DS
(Scotland): v Ireland 1929
Rutherford, R
(Scotland): Home Int 1938-47

Saddler, AC
(Scotland): Home Int 1959-60-61-62-63-64-66; Eur T Ch
1965-67. (GB): v Europe 1960-62-64--66; v America 1963-
65-67-77 (Captain); in Com Tnmt 1959-63-67; in World
Team Ch 1962
Scannel, BJ
(Ireland): Home Int 1947-48-49-50-51-53-54
Scott, KB
(England): Home Int 1937-38; v France 1938
Scott, Hon M
(England): v Scotland 1911-12-23-24-25-26.
(GB): v America 1924-34 (Captain); v Australia 1934
Scott, Hon O
(England): v Scotland 1902-05-06
Scott, R, jr
(Scotland): v England 1924-28. (GB): v America 1924
Scratton, EWHB
(England): v Scotland 1912
Scroggie: FH
(Scotland): v England 1910

Scrutton, PF
(England): Home Int 1950-55. (GB): v America 1955-57

Sewell, D
(England): Home Int 1956-57-58-59-60. (GB): v America 1957-59; in Com Tnmt 1959; in World Team Ch 1960

Shade, RDBM
(Scotland): Home Int 1957-60-61-62-63-64-65-66-67-68; v Scandinavia 1960-62; Eur T Ch 1965-67. (GB): v America 1961-63-65-67; v Europe 1962-64-66-68; in World Team Ch 1962-64-66-68; in Com Tnmt 1963-67

Shaw, G
(Scotland): Home Int 1984-86-87-88; v West Germany 1987. (GB): v America 1987

Sheals, HS
(Ireland): v Wales 1929; v England 1929-30-31; v Scotland 1930; Home Int 1932-33

Sheahan, D
(Ireland): Home Int 1961-62-63-64-65-66-67-70. (GB): v Europe 1962 64 67; v America 1963

Sheilds, B
(Scotland):Home Int 1986

Shepperson, AE
(England): Home Int 1956-57-58-59-60-62. (GB): v America 1957-59

Sherborne, A
(England): Home Int 1982-83-84

Shingler, TR
(England): Home Int 1977

Shorrock, TJ
(England): v France 1952

Simcox, R
(Ireland): v Wales 1930-31; v Scotland 1930-31; v England 1931; Home Int 1932-33-34-35-36-38

Simpson, AF
(Scotland): v Ireland 1928; v England 1927

Simpson, JG
(Scotland): v England 1906-07-08-09-11-12-22-24-26. (GB): v America 1921

Sinclair, A
(Scotland): Home Int 1950

Slark, WA
(England): Home Int 1957

Slater, A
(England): Home Int 1955-62

Slattery, B
(Ireland): Home Int 1947-48

Sludds, MF
(Ireland): Home Int 1982

Smith, Eric M
(England): v Ireland 1931; v Scotland 1931

Smith, Everard
(England): v Scotland 1908-09-10-12

Smith, GF
(England): v Scotland 1902-03

Smith, JN
(Scotland): v Ireland 1928-30-31; v England 1929-30-31; v Wales 1931; Home Int 1932-33-34. (GB): v America 1930

Smith, JR
(England): Home Int 1932

Smith, LOM
(England): Home Int 1963

Smith, VH
(Wales): v Ireland 1924-25

Smith, W
(England): Home Int 1972. (GB): v Europe 1972

Smith, WD
(Scotland): Home Int 1957-58-59-60-63; v Scandinavia 1958-60. (GB): v Europe 1958; v America 1959

Smyth, D
(Ireland): Home Int 1972-73; Eur T Ch 1973

Smyth, DW
(Ireland): v Wales 1923-30; v England 1930; v Scotland 1931; Home Int 1933

Smyth, HB
(Ireland): Home Int 1974-75-76-78; Eur T Ch 1975-79; v France, West Germany, Sweden 1976. (GB): v Europe 1976

Smyth, V
(Ireland): Home Int 1981-82

Snowdon, J
(England): Home Int 1934

Soulby, DEB
(Ireland): v Wales 1929-30; v England 1929-30; v Scotland 1929-30

Spiller, EF
(Ireland): v Wales 1924; v England 1928; v Scotland 1928-29

Squirrell, HC
(Wales): Home Int 1955-56-57-58-59-60-61-62-63-64-65-66-67-68-69-70-71-73-74-75; Eur T Ch 1967-69-71-75; v France 1975

Staunton, R
(Ireland): Home Int 1964-65-72; Eur T Ch 1973

Steel, DMA
(England): Home Int 1970

Stephen, AR
(Scotland): Home Int 1971-72-73-74-75-76-77-84-85; Eur T Ch 1975; v Spain 1974; v Belgium 1975-77-78. (GB): v Europe 1972; v America 1985

Stevens, DI
(Wales): Home Int 1968-69-70-74-75-76-77-78-80-82; Eur T Ch 1969-77; v France 1976; v Denmark 1977

Stevens, LB
(England): v Scotland 1912

Stevenson, A
(Scotland): Home Int 1949

Stevenson, JB
(Scotland): v Ireland 1931; Home Int 1932-38-47-49-50-51

Stevenson, JF
(Ireland): v Wales 1923-24; v England 1925

Stevenson, K
(Ireland): Home Int 1972

Stockdale, B
(England): Home Int 1964-65

Stoker, K
(Wales): v Ireland 1923-24

Stokoe, GC
(Wales): v England 1925; v Ireland 1929-30

Storey, EF
(England): v Scotland 1924-25-26-27-28-30; Home Int 1936; v France 1936. (GB): v America 1924-26-28

Stott, HAN
(England): Home Int 1976-77

Stout, JA
(England): v Scotland 1928-29-30-31; v Ireland 1929-31. (GB): v America 1930-32

Stowe, C
(England): Home Int 1935-36-37-38-47-49-54; v France 1938-39-49. (GB): v America 1938-47

Strachan, CJL
(Scotland): Home Int 1965-66-67; Eur T Ch 1967

Straker, R
(England): Home Int 1932

Stuart, HB
(Scotland): Home Int 1967-68-70-71-72-73-74-76; Eur T
Ch 1969-71-73-75; v Belgium 1973-75. (GB): v Europe
1968-72-74; v America 1971-73-75; in Com Tnmt 1971; in
World Team Ch 1972

Stuart, JE
(Scotland): Home Int 1959

Stubbs, AK
(England): Home Int 1982

Suneson, C
(England): Home Int 1988; Eur T Ch 1989

Sutherland, DMG
(England): Home Int 1947

Sutton, W
(England): v Scotland 1929-31; v Ireland 1929-30-31

Symonds, A
(Wales): v Ireland 1925

Taggart, J
(Ireland): Home Int 1953

Tait, AG
(Scotland): Home Int 1987-88-89; Nixdorf Nations Cup 1989

Tate, JK
(England): Home Int 1954-55-56

Taylor, GN
(Scotland): Home Int 1948

Taylor, HE
(England): v Scotland 1911

Taylor, JS
(Scotland): v England 1979; Home Int 1980; v Belgium 1980;
v France 1980

Taylor, LG
(Scotland): Home Int 1955-56

Taylor, TPD
(Wales): Home Int 1963

Thirlwell, A
(England): Home Int 1951-52-54-55-56-57-58-63-64. (GB): v
Europe 1956-58-64; v America 1957; in Com Tnmt 1953-64

Thirsk, TJ
(England): v Ireland 1929; Home Int 1933-34-35-36-37-38;
v France 1935-36-37-38-39

Thom, KG
(England): Home Int 1947-48-49-53. (GB): v America 1949

Thomas, I
(England): Home Int 1933

Thomas, KR
(Wales): Home Int 1951-52

Thompson, ASG
(England): Home Int 1935-37

Thompson, MS
(England): Home Int 1982. (GB): v America 1983

Thomson, AP
(Scotland): Home Int 1970; Eur T Ch 1971

Thomson, H
(Scotland): Home Int 1934-35-36-37-38. (GB): v America
1936-38

Thomson, JA
(Scotland): Home Int 1981-82-83-84-85-86-87-88-89;
v West Germany 1987; v Italy 1988

Thorburn, K
(Scotland): v England 1928; v Ireland 1927

Timbey, JC
(Ireland): v Scotland 1928-31; v Wales 1931

Timmis, CW
(England): v Ireland 1930; Home Int. 1936-
37

Tipping, EB
(England): v Ireland 1930

Tipple, ER
(England): v Ireland 1928-29; Home Int 1932

Tolley, CJH
(England): v Scotland 1922-23-24-25-26-27-28-29-30;
Home Int 1936-37-38; v Ireland/Wales 1925; v France 1938.
(GB): v America 1921-22-23-24 (Captain) -26-30-34;
v South Africa 1927

Tooth, EA
(Wales): v Ireland 1913

Torrance, TA
(Scotland): v England 1922-23-25-26-28-29--30; Home Int
1933. (GB): v America 1924-28-30-32 (Captain) -34

Torrance, WB
(Scotland): v England 1922-23-24-26-27-28-30; v Ireland
1928-29-30. (GB): v America 1922

Townsend, PM
(England): Home Int 1965-66. (GB): v America 1965;
v Europe 1966; in World Team Ch 1966

Toye, JL
(Wales): Home Int 1963-64-65-66-67-69-70-71-72-73-74-
76-78; Eur T Ch 1971-73-75-77; v France 1975

Tredinnick, SV
(England): Home Int 1950

Tucker, WI
(Wales): Home Int 1949-50-51-52-53-54-55-56-57-58-59-
60-61-62-63-64-65-66-67-68-69-70-71-72-74-75; Eur
T Ch 1967-69-75; v France 1975

Tulloch, W
(Scotland): v England 1929-30-31; v Ireland 1930-31;
v Wales 1931; Home Int 1932

Tupling, LP
(England): Home Int 1969; Eur T Ch 1969.
(GB): v America 1969

Turnbull, CH
(Wales): v Ireland 1913-25

Turner, A
(England): Home Int 1952

Turner, GB
(Wales): Home Int 1947-48-49-50-51-52-55-56

Tweddell, W
(England): v Scotland 1928-29-30; Home Int 1935.
(GB): v America 1928 (Captain) -36 (Captain)

Vannet, L
(Scotland): Home Int 1984

Waddell, G
(Ireland): v Wales 1925

Walker, J
(Scotland): Home Int 1954-55-57-58-60-61-62-63; v
Scandinavia 1958-62. (GB): v Europe 1958-60; v America
1961

Walker, KH
(Scotland): Home Int 1985-86

Walker, MS
(England): v Ireland/Wales 1925

Walker, RS
(Scotland): Home Int 1935-36

Wallis, G
(Wales): Home Int 1934-36-37-38

Walls, MPD
(England): Home Int 1980-81-85

Walters, EM
(Wales): Home Int 1967-68-69; Eur T Ch
1969

Walton, AR
(England): Home Int 1934-35

Walton, P
(Ireland): v Wales 1979: Home Int 1980-81; v France, Germany, Sweden 1980; Eur T Ch 1981. (GB): v America 1981-83

Warren, KT
(England): Home Int 1962

Watt, A
(Scotland): Home Int 1987

Way, P
(England): Home Int 1981; Eur T Ch 1981, (GB): v America 1981.

Webster, A
(Scotland): Home Int 1978

Webster, F
(Ireland): Home Int 1949

Weeks, K
(England): Home Int 1987-88; v France 1988

Welch, L
(Ireland): Home Int 1936

Wemyss, DS
(Scotland): Home Int 1937

Werner, LE
(Ireland): v Wales 1925

West, CH
(Ireland): v England 1928; Home Int 1932

Wethered, RH
(England): v Scotland 1922-23-24-25-26-27-28-29-30. (GB): v America 1921-22-23-26-30 (Captain) -34

White, RJ
(England): Home Int 1947-48-49-53-54. (GB): v America 1947-49-51-53-55

Whyte, AW
(Scotland): Home Int 1934

Wilkie, D
(Scotland): Home Int 1962-63-65-67-68

Wilkie, G
(Scotland): v England 1911

Wilkie, GT
(Wales): Home Int 1938

Willcox, FS
(Wales): v Scotland 1931; v Ireland 1931

Williams, DF
(England): v Scotland 1979

Williams KH
(Wales): Home Int 1983-84-85-86-87

Williams, PG
(Wales): v Ireland 1925

Williamson, SB
(Scotland): Home Int 1947-48-49-51-52

Willison, R
(England): Home Int 1988-89; Eur T Ch 1989

Wilson, F
(Scotland): Home Int 1985

Wilson, J
(Scotland): v England 1922-23-24-26. (GB): v America 1923

Wilson, JC
(Scotland): Home Int 1947-48-49-51-52-53. (GB): v America 1947-53; v South Africa 1952; in Com Tnmt 1954

Wilson, P
(Scotland): Home Int 1976; Belgium 1977

Winchester, R
(England): Home Int 1985-87-89

Winfield, HB
(Wales): v Ireland 1913

Wise, WS
(England): Home Int 1947

Wolstenholme, G
(England): Home Int 1953-55-56-57-58-59-60 (GB): v America 1957-59; in World Team Ch 1958-60; in Com Tnmt 1959

Wolstenholme, G
(England): Home Int 1988-89; v France 1988

Wood, DK
(Wales): Home Int 1982-83-84-85-86-87

Woollam, J
(England): Home Int 1933-34-35; v France 1935

Woolley, FA
(England): v Scotland 1910-11-12

Woosnam, I
(Wales): v France 1976

Worthington, JS
(England): v Scotland 1905

Wright, I
(Scotland): Home Int 1958-59-60-61; v Scandinavia 1960

Yeo, J
(England): Home 1971

Young, D
(Ireland): Home Int 1969-70-77

Young, ID
(Scotland): Home Int 1981-82; v France 1982

Young, JR
(Scotland): Home Int 1960-61-65; v Scandinavia 1960. (GB): v Europe 1960

Zacharias, JP
(England): Home Int 1935

Zoete, HW de
(England): v Scotland 1903-04-06-07

British Isles International Players, Amateur Ladies

Abbreviations:
(GB) played for Great Britain or Great Britain and Ireland; Eur L T Ch played in European Ladies Amateur Team Championship; Home Int played in Home International matches; CW played in Commonwealth International. Previous surnames are shown in brackets.

Aitken, E (Young)
(Scotland): Home Int 1954

Alexander, M
(Ireland): Home Int 1920-21-22-30

Allen, F
(England): Home Int 1952

Allington Hughes, Miss
(Wales): Home Int 1908-09-10-12-14-22-25

Anderson, E
(Scotland): Home Int 1910-11-12-21-25

Anderson, F
(Scotland): Home Int 1977-79-80-81-83-84-86-87-88-89; Eur L T Ch 1987. (GB): in Vagliano Trophy 1987

Anderson, H
(Scotland): Home Int 1964-65-68-69-70-71; Eur L T Ch 1969. (GB): in Vagliano Trophy 1969

Anderson, J (Donald)
(Scotland): Home Int 1947-48-49-50-51-52-53. (GB): in Curtis Cup in 1948-50-52

Anderson, L.
(Scotland): Home Int 1986-87-88-89; Eur L T Ch 1987-89

Anderson, VH
(Scotland): Home Int 1907

Arbuthnot, M
(Ireland): Home Int 1921

Archer, A (Rampton)
(England): Home Int 1968 (Captain)

Armstrong, M
(Ireland): Home Int 1906

Ashcombe, Lady [Bromley-Davenport] (Isabella Rieben)
(Wales): Home Int 1932-33-34-35-36-48-50-51-52-53-54-55

Aubertin, Mrs
(Wales): Home Int 1908-09-10

Bailey, D [Frearson] (Robb)
(England): Home Int 1961-62-71; Eur L T Ch 1968. (GB): in Curtis Cup 1962–72-84 (Captain)–86(Captain)-88(Captain); in Vagliano Trophy 1961-83(Captain)-85(Captain); CW 1983

Bald, J
(Scotland): Home Int 1968-69-71; Eur L T Ch 1969

Barber, S (Bonallack)
(England): Home Int 1960-61-62-68-70-72-77-78 (Captain); Eur L T Ch 1969-71. (GB): in Curtis Cup 1962; in Vagliano Trophy 1961-63-69

Barclay, C (Brisbane)
(Scotland): Home Int 1953-61-68

Bargh Etherington, B (Whitehead)
(England): Home Int 1974

Barlow, Mrs
(Ireland): Home Int 1921

Barron, M
(Wales): Home Int 1929-30-31-34-35-36-37-38-39-47-48-49-50-51-52-53-54-55-56-57-58-60-61-62-63

Barry, L
(England): Home Int 1911-12-13-14

Barry, P
(England): Home Int 1982

Barton, P
(England): Home Int 1935-36-37-38-39. (GB): in Curtis Cup 1934-36

Bastin, G
(England): Home Int 1920-21-22-23-24-25

Bayliss, Mrs
(Wales): Home Int 1921

Bayman, L (Denison Pender)
(England): Home Int 1971-72-73-83-84-85-87-88; Eur L T Ch 1985-87-89. (GB): in Curtis Cup 1988; in Vagliano Trophy 1971-85-87; in Espirito Santo 1988

Baynes, Mrs CE
(Scotland): Home Int 1921-22

Beck, B (Pim)
(Ireland): Home Int 1930-31-32-33-34-36-37-47-48-49-50-51-52-53-54-55-56-58-59-61

Beckett, J
(Ireland): Home Int 1962-66-67-68; Eur L T Ch 1967

Beddows, C [Watson] (Stevenson)
(Scotland): Home Int 1913-14-21-22-23-27-29-30-31-32-33-34-35-36-37-39-47-48-49-50-51. (GB): in Curtis Cup 1932

Behan, L
(Ireland): Home Int 1984-85-86. (GB): in Curtis Cup 1986; in Vagliano Trophy 1985

Beharrell, V (Anstey)
(England): Home Int 1955-56-57-61(Captain). (GB): in Curtis Cup 1956

Benka, P (Tredinnick)
(England): Home Int 1967. (GB): in Curtis Cup 1966-68; in Vagliano Trophy 1967

Bennett, L
(Scotland): Home Int 1977-80-81

Benton, MH
(Scotland): Home Int 1914
Birmingham, M
(Ireland): Home Int 1967(Captain)
Bisgood, J
(England) Home Int 1949-50-51-52-53-54-56-58. (GB): in
Curtis Cup 1950-52-54-70(Captain)
Blair, N (Menzies)
(Scotland): Home Int 1955
Blake, Miss
(Ireland): Home Int 1931-32-34-35-36
Blaymire, J
(England): Home Int 1971-88-89(Captain)
Bloodworth, D (Lewis)
(Wales): Home Int 1954-55-56-57-60
Bolton, L
(Ireland): Home Int 1981-82-88-89
Bolton, Z (Bonner Davis)
(England): Home Int 1939-48-49-50-51-55-(Captain)-56. (GB):
in Curtis Cup 1948-56(Captain)-66(Captain)-68(Captain);
CW 1967
Bonallack, A (Ward)
(England): Home Int 1956-57-58-59-60-61-62-63-64-65
(Captain)-66-72. (GB): in Curtis Cup 1956-58-60-62-64-66;
in Vagliano Trophy 1959-61-63
Bostock, M
(England): Home Int 1954(Captain)
Bourn, Mrs
(England): Home Int 1909-12
Bowhill, M (Robertson-Durham)
(Scotland): Home Int 1936-37-38
Boyd, J
(Ireland): Home Int 1912-13-14
Bradley, K (Rawlings)
(Wales): Home Int 1975-76-77-78-79-82-83
Bradshaw, E
(Ireland): Home Int 1964-66-67-68-69-70-71-74-75-80
Captain)-81(Captain); Eur L T Ch 1969-71-75. (GB): in
Vagliano Trophy 1969-71
Brandom, G
(Ireland): Home Int 1965-66-67-68; Eur L T Ch 1967. (GB)
in Vagliano Trophy 1967
Brearley, M
(Wales): Home Int 1937-38
Brennan, R (Hegarty)
(Ireland): Home Int 1974-75-76-77-78-79-81
Bridges, Mrs
(Wales): Home Int 1933-38-39
Briggs, A (Brown)
(Wales): Home Int 1969-70-71-72-73-74-75-76-77-78-79-80-
81(Captain)-82(Captain)-83(Captain)-84; Eur L T Ch 1971-
75. (GB): in Vagliano Trophy 1971-75
Brinton, Mrs
(Ireland): Home Int 1922
Brook, D
(Wales): Home Int 1913
Brooks, E
(Ireland): Home Int 1953-54-56
Broun, JG
(Scotland): Home Int 1905-06-07-21
Brown, B
(Ireland): Home Int 1960
Brown, E (Jones)
(Wales): Home Int 1947-48-49-50-52-53-57-58-59-60-61-62-
63-64-65-66-68-69-70

Brown, Mrs FW (Gilroy)
(Scotland): Home Int 1905-06-07-08-09-10-11-13-21
Brown, J
(Wales): Home Int 1960-61-62-64-65; Eur L T Ch
1965-69
Brown, J
(England): Home Int 1984
Brown, TWL
(Scotland): Home Int 1924-25
Brown, Mrs
(Wales): Home Int 1924-25-27
Brownlow, Miss
(Ireland): Home Int 1923
Bryan-Smith, S
(Wales): Home Int 1947-48-49-50-51-52-56
Burke, Mrs
(Ireland): Home Int 1948
Burrell, Mrs
(Wales): Home Int 1939
Burton, H (Mitchell)
(Scotland): Home Int 1931-55-56-59(Captain). (GB): in
Vagliano Trophy 1961
Burton, M
(England): Home Int 1975-7
Butler, I (Burke)
(Ireland): Home Int 1962-63-64-65-66-68-70-71-72-73-76-77-
78-79-86(Captain)-87(Captain); Eur L T Ch 1967. (GB): in
Curtis Cup 1966; in Vagliano Trophy 1965; in Espirito Santo
1964-66
Byrne, A (Sweeney)
(Ireland): Home Int 1959-60-61-62-63

Cadden, G
(Scotland): Home Int 1974-75
Cairns, Lady Katherine
(England): Home Int 1947-48-50-51-52-53-54. (GB): in Curtis
Cup 1952(Captain)
Caldwell, C (Redford)
(England): Home Int 1973-78-79-80. (GB): in Curtis Cup
1978-80; in Vagliano Trophy 1973
Campbell, J (Burnett)
(Scotland): Home Int 1960
Cann, M (Nuttall)
(England): Home Int 1966
Carrick, P (Bullard)
(England): Home Int 1939-47
Caryl, M
(Wales): Home Int 1929
Casement, M (Harrison)
(Ireland): Home Int 1909-10-11-12-13-14
Cautley, B (Hawtrey)
(England): Home Int 1912-13-14-22-23-24-25-27
Chambers, D
(England): Home Int 1906-07-09-10-11-12-20 24 25. (GB): in
Curtis Cup 1934(Captain)-36(Captain)-38(Captain)
Christison, D
(England): Home Int 1981
Chugg, P (Light)
(Wales): Home Int 1973-74-75-76-77-78-86-87-78; Eur L T
Ch 1975-87
Clark, G (Atkinson)
(England): Home Int 1955
Clarke, Mrs ML
(England): Home Int 1933-35

Clarke, P
(England): Home Int 1081

Clarke, Mrs
(Ireland): Home Int 1922

Clarkson, H (Reynolds)
(Wales): Home Int 1935-38-39

Clay, E
(Wales): Home Int 1912

Clement, V
(England): Home Int 1932-34-35

Close, M (Wenyon)
(England): Home Int 1968-69; Eur L T Ch 1969. (GB) in Vagliano Trophy 1969

Coats, Mrs G
(Scotland): Home Int 1931-32-33-34

Cochrane, K
(Scotland): Home Int 1924-25-28-29-30

Collett, P
(England): Home Int 1910

Collingham, J (Melville)
(England): Home Int 1978-79-81-84-86-87; Eur L T Ch 1989. (GB): in Vagliano Trophy 1979-87; CW 1987

Colquhoun, H
(Ireland): Home Int 1959-60-61-63

Comboy, C (Grott)
(England): Home Int 1975(Captain)-76(Captain). (GB): in Curtis Cup 1978(Captain)-80(Captain); in Vagliano Trophy 1977(Captain)-1979(Captain); in Espirito Santo 1978(Captain); CW 1979

Connachan, J
(Scotland): Home Int 1979-80-81-82-83. (GB): in Curtis Cup 1980-82; in Vagliano Trophy 1981-83; in Espirito Santo 1980-82; CW 1983

Coote, Miss
(Ireland): Home Int 1925-28-29

Copley, K (Lackie)
(Scotland): Home Int 1974-75

Corlett, E
(England): Home Int 1927-29-30-31-32-33-35-36-37-38-39. (GB): in Curtis Cup 1932-38-64(Captain)

Costello, G
(Ireland): Home Int 1973-84(Captain)-85(Captain)

Cotton, S (German)
(England): Home Int 1967-68; Eur L T Ch 1967. (GB): in Vagliano Trophy 1967

Couper, M
(Scotland): Home Int 1929-34-35-36-37-39-56

Cowley, Lady
(Wales): Home Int 1907-09

Cox, Margaret
(Wales): Home Int 1924-25

Cox, Nell
(Wales): Home Int 1954

Craik, T
(Scotland): Home Int 1988

Cramsie, F (Hezlet)
(Ireland): Home Int 1905-06-07-08-09-10-13-20-24

Crawford, I (Wylie)
(Scotland): Home Int 1970-71-72

Cresswell, K (Stuart)
(Scotland): Home Int 1909-10-11-12-14

Critchley, D (Fishwick)
(England): Home Int 1930-31-32-33-35-36-47. (GB): in Curtis Cup 1932-34-50(Captain)

Croft, A
(England): Home Int 1927

Cross, M
(Wales): Home Int 1922

Cruickshank, DM (Jenkins)
(Scotland): Home Int 1910-11-12

Crummack, Miss
(England): Home Int 1909

Cuming, Mrs
(Ireland): Home Int 1910

Cunninghame, S
(Wales): Home Int 1922-25-29-31

Cuthell, R (Adair)
(Ireland): Home Int 1908

Dampney, S
(Wales): Home Int 1924-25-27-28-29-30

David, Mrs
(Wales): Home Int 1908

Davidson, B (Inglis)
(Scotland): Home Int 1928

Davies, K
(Wales): Home Int 1981-82-83; Eur L T Ch 1987. (GB): in Curtis Cup 1986-88; in Vagliano Trophy 1987; CW 87

Davies, L
(England): Home Int 1983-84. (GB): in Curtis Cup 1984; CW 1987

Davies, P (Griffiths)
(Wales): Home Int 1965-66-67-68-70-71-73; Eur L T Ch 1971

Deacon, Mrs
(Wales): Home Int 1912-14

Denny, A (Barrett)
(England): Home Int 1951

Dering, Mrs
(Ireland): Home Int 1923

Dermott, Lisa
(Wales): Home Int 1987-88-89

Dickson, M
(Ireland): Home Int 1909

Dobson, H
(England): Home Int 1987-88-89; Eur L T Ch 1989. (GBI): in Vagliano Trophy 1989

Dod, L
(England): Home Int 1905

Douglas, K
(England): Home Int 1981-82-83. (GB): in Curtis Cup 1982; in Vagliano Trophy 1983

Dowling, D
(England): Home Int 1979

Draper, M [Peel] (Thomas)
(Scotland): Home Int 1929-34-38-49-50-51-52-53-54(Captain)-55(Captain)-56-57-58-61(Captain)-62. (GB): in Curtis Cup 1954; in Vagliano Trophy 1963(Captain)

Duncan, B
(Wales): Home Int 1907-08-09-10-12

Duncan, M
(Wales): Home Int 1922-23-28-34

Duncan, MJ (Wood)
(Scotland): Home Int 1925-27-28-39

Durlacher, Mrs
(Ireland): Home Int 1905-06-07-08-09-10-14

Durrant, B [Green] (Lowe)
(England): Home Int 1954

Dwyer, Mrs
(Ireland): 1928

Eakin, P (James)
(Ireland): 1967
Earner, M
(Ireland): Home Int 1960-61-62-63-70
Edwards, E
(Wales): Home Int 1949-50
Edwards, J
(Wales): Home Int 1932-33-34-36-37
Edwards, J (Morris)
(Wales): Home Int 1962-63-66-67-68-69-70-77(Captain)-78 (Captain)-79(Captain); Eur L T Ch 1967-69
Ellis, E
(Ireland): Home Int 1932-35-37-38
Ellis Griffiths (Mrs)
(Wales): Home Int 1907-08-09-12-13
Emery, MJ
(Wales): Home Int 1928-29-30-31-32-33-34-35-36-37-38-47
Evans, H
(England): Home Int 1908
Evans, N
(Wales): Home Int 1908-09-10-13
Everard, M
(England): Home Int 1964-67-69-70-72-73-77-78; Eur L T Ch 1967-71-77. (GB): in Curtis Cup 1970-72-74-78; in Vagliano Trophy 1967-69-71-73; in Espirito Santo 1968-72-78; CW 1971

Fairclough, L
(England): Home Int 1988-89; Eur L T Ch 1989. (GBI): Vagliano Trophy 1989
Falconer, V (Lamb)
(Scotland): Home Int 1932-36-37-47-48-49-50-51-52-53-54-55-56
Farie-Anderson, J
(Scotland): Home Int 1924
Farquharson, E
(Scotland): Home Int 1987-88-89; Eur L T Ch 1989. (GBI): in Vagliano Trophy 1989
Ferguson, A
(Ireland): Home Int 1989
Ferguson, D
(Ireland): Home Int 1927-28-29-30-31-32-34-35-36-37-38-61 (Captain). (GB): in Curtis Cup 1958(Captain)
Ferguson, M (Fowler)
(Scotland): Home Int 1959-62-63-64-65-66-67-69-70-85; Eur L T Ch 1965-67-71. (GB): in Curtis Cup 1966; in Vagliano Trophy 1965
Ferguson R (Ogden)
(England): Home Int 1957
Fitzgibbon, M
(Ireland): Home Int 1920-21-29-30-31-32-33
FitzPatrick, O (Heskin)
(Ireland): Home Int 1967
Fletcher, L
(England): Home Int 1989
Fletcher, P (Sherlock)
(Ireland): Home Int 1932-34-35-36-38-39-54-55-66(Captain)
Forbes, J
(Scotland): Home Int 1985-86-87-88-89; Eur L T Ch 1987-89
Foster, C
(England): Home Int 1905-06-09
Foster, J
(Wales): Home Int 1984-85-86-87; Eur L T Ch 1987
Fowler, J
(England): Home Int 1928
Franklin Thomas, E
(Wales): Home Int 1909

Freeguard, C
(Wales): Home Int 1927
Furby, J
(England): Home Int 1987-88; Eur L T Ch 1987
Fyshe, M
(England): Home Int 1938

Gallagher, S
(Scotland): Home Int 1983-84
Gardiner, A
(Ireland): Home Int 1927-29
Garfield Evans, PR (Whittaker)
(Wales): Home Int 1948-49-50-51-52-53-54-55(Captain)-56 (Captain)-57 (Captain)-58(Captain)
Garner, M (Madill)
(Ireland): Home Int 1978-79-80-81-82-83-84-85. (GB): in Curtis Cup 1980; in Vagliano Trophy 1979 81 85; in Espirito Santo 1980; CW 1979
Garon, MR
(England): Home Int 1927-28-32-33-34-36-37-38. (GB): in Curtis Cup 1936
Garrett, M (Ruttle)
(England): Home Int 1947-48-50-53-59(Captain)-60(Captain)-63(Captain). (GB): in Curtis Cup 1948-60(Captain); in Vagliano Trophy 1959
Garvey, P
(Ireland): Home Int 1947-48-49-50-51-52-53-54(Captain)-56-57(Captain) -58(Captain)-59(Captain)-60(Captain)-61-62-63-68-69. (GB): in Curtis Cup 1948-50-52-54-56-60; in Vagliano Trophy 1959-63
Gaynor Fallon, Z
(Ireland): Home Int 1952-53-54-55-56-57-58-59-60-61-62-63-64-65-66-68-69-70-72 (Captain). (GB): in Espirito Santo 1964
Gear Evans, A
(Wales): Home Int 1932-33-34
Gee, Hon. J (Hives)
(England): Home Int 1950-51-52
Gemmill, A
(Scotland): Home Int 1981-82-84-85-86-87-88-89
Gethin Griffith, S
(Wales): Home Int 1914-22-23-24-28-29-30-31-35
Gibb, M (Titterton)
(England): Home Int 1906-07-08-10-12
Gibbs, C (Le Feuvre)
(England): Home Int 1971-72-73-74. (GB): in Curtis Cup 1974; in Vagliano Trophy 1973
Gibbs, S
(Wales): Home Int 1933-34-39
Gildea, Miss
(Ireland): Home Int 1936-37-38-39
Glendinning, D
(Ireland): Home Int 1937-54
Glennie, H
(Scotland): Home Int 1959
Glover, A
(Scotland): Home Int 1905-06-08-09-12
Gold, N
(England): Home Int 1929-31-32
Gordon, J
(England): Home Int 1947-48-49-52-53. (GB): in Curtis Cup 1948
Gorman, S
(Ireland): Home Int 1976-79-80-81-82
Gorry, Mary
(Ireland): Home Int 1971-72-73-74-75-76-77-78-79-80-88-89;(Captain) Eur L T Ch 1971-75. (GB): in Vagliano Trophy 1977

Gotto, Mrs C
(Ireland): Home Int 1923
Gotto, Mrs L
(Ireland): Home Int 1920
Gourlay, M
(England): Home Int 1923-24-27-28-29-30-32-33-34-38-57
(Captain). (GB): in Curtis Cup 1932-34
Gow, J
(Scotland): Home Int 1923-24-27-28
Graham, MA
(Scotland): Home Int 1905-06
Graham, N
(Ireland): Home Int 1908-09-10-12
Granger Harrison, Mrs
(Scotland): Home Int 1922
Grant-Suttie, E
(Scotland): Home Int 1908-10-11-14-22-23
Grant-Suttie, R
(Scotland): Home Int 1914
Green, B (Pockett)
(England): Home Int 1939
Grice-Whittaker, P (Grice)
(England): Home Int 1983-84. (GB): in Curtis Cup 1984;
in Espirito Santo 1984
Griffith, W
(Wales): Home Int 1981
Griffiths, M
(England): Home Int 1920-21
Greenlees, E
(Scotland): Home Int 1924
Greenlees, Y
(Scotland): Home Int 1928-30-31-33-34-35-38
Guadella, E (Leitch)
(England): Home Int 1908-10-20-21-22-27-28-29-30-33
Gubbins, Miss
(Ireland): Home Int 1905

Haig, J (Mathias Thomas)
(Wales): Home Int 1938-39
Hall, CM
(England): Home Int 1985
Hall, J (Wade)
(England): Home Int 1987-88-89; Eur L T Ch 1987-89. (GBI):
in Curtis Cup 1988; in Espirito Santo 1988; in Vagliano Tro-
phy 1989
Hall, Mrs
(Ireland): Home Int 1927-30
Hamilton, S (McKinven)
(Scotland): Home Int 1965
Hambro, W (Martin Smith)
(England): Home Int 1914
Hamilton, J
(England): Home Int 1937-38-39
Hammond, T
(England): Home Int 1985
Hampson, M
(England): Home Int 1954
Hanna, D
(Ireland): Home Int 1987-88
Harrington, D
(Ireland): Home Int 1923
Harris, M [Spearman] (Baker)
(England): Home Int 1955-56-57-58-59-60-61-62-63-64-65; Eur
L T Ch 1965-71. (GB): in Curtis Cup 1960-62-64; in Vagliano
Trophy 1959-61-65; in Espirito Santo 1964

Harrold, L
(England): Home Int 1974-75-76
Hartill, D
(England): Home Int 1923
Hartley, E
(England): Home Int 1964(Captain)
Hartley, R
(Wales): Home Int 1958-59-62
Hastings, D (Sommerville)
(Scotland): Home Int 1955-56-57-58-59-60-61-62-63. (GB): in
Curtis Cup 1958; in Vagliano Trophy 1963
Hay, J (Pelham Burn)
(Scotland): Home Int 1959
Hayter, J (Yuille)
(England): Home Int 1956
Hazlett, VP
(Ireland): Home Int 1956(Captain)
Head, EA [Boatman] (Collis)
(England): Home Int 1974-80-84(Captain)-85(Captain); Eur
L T Ch 1985(Captain)-87(Captain)
Healy, B (Gleeson)
(Ireland): Home Int 1980-82
Heathcoat-Amory, Lady (Joyce Wethered)
(England): Home Int 1921-22-23-24-25-29. (GB): in Curtis
Cup 1932(Captain)
Hedges, S (Whitlock)
(England): Home Int 1979. (GB): in Vagliano Trophy 1979;
CW 1979
Hedley Hill, Miss
(Wales): Home Int 1922
Hegarty, G
(Ireland): Home Int 1955-56-64(Captain)
Helme, E
(England): Home Int 1911-12-13-20
Heming Johnson, G
(England): Home Int 1909-11-13
Henson, D (Oxley)
(England): Home Int 1967-68-69-70-75-76-77-78; Eur L T
Ch 1971-77. (GB): in Curtis Cup 1968-70-72-76; in Vagliano
Trophy 1967-69-71; in Espirito Santo 1970; CW 1967-71
Heskin, A
(Ireland): Home Int 1968-69-70-72-75-77-82(Captain)-83
(Captain)
Hetherington, Mrs (Gittens)
(England): Home Int 1909
Hewett, G
(Ireland): Home Int 1923-24
Hezlet, Mrs
(Ireland): Home Int 1910
Hickey, C
(Ireland): Home Int 1969-75(Captain)-76(Captain)
Higgins, E
(Ireland): Home Int 1981-82-83-84-85-86-87-88; Eur L T Ch
1987
Hill, J
(England): Home Int 1986
Hill, Mrs
(Wales): Home Int 1924
Hodgson, M
(England): Home Int 1939
Holland, I (Hurst)
(Ireland): Home Int 1958
Holm, H (Gray)
(Scotland): Home Int 1932-33-34-35-36-37-38-47-48-50-51-55-
57. (GB): in Curtis Cup 1936-38-48

Holmes, A
(England): Home Int 1931
Holmes, J [Hetherington] (McClure)
(England): Home Int 1957-66-67(Captain)
Hooman, EM [Gavin]
(England): Home Int 1910-11
Hope, LA
(Scotland): Home Int 1975-76-80-84-85-86-87-88(Captain)
Hort, K
(Wales): Home Int 1929
Hourihane, C
(Ireland): Home Int 1979-80-81-82-83-84-85-86-87-88-89; Eur
L T Ch 1987. (GB): in Curtis Cup 1984-86-88; in Vagliano
Trophy 1981-83-85-87-89; in Espirito Santo 1986
Howard, A (Phillips)
(England): Home Int 1953-54-55-56-57-58-79(Captain)-80
(Captain). (GB): in Curtis Cup 1956-58
Huggan, S (Lawson)
(Scotland): Home Int 1985-86-87-88-89; Eur L T Ch 1985-
87-89. (GBI): in Curtis Cup 1988, in Vagliano Trophy 1989
Hughes, J
(Wales): Home Int 1967-71-88-89(Captain); Eur L T Ch 1971
Hughes, Miss
(Wales): Home Int 1907
Huke, B
(England): Home Int 1971-72-75-76-77. (GB): in Curtis Cup
1972; in Vagliano Trophy 1975
Hulton, V (Hezlet)
(Ireland): Home Int 1905-07-09-10-11-12-20-21
Humphreys, A (Coulman)
(Wales): Home Int 1969-70-71
Humphreys, D (Forster)
(Ireland): Home Int 1951-52-53-55-57
Hunter, D (Tucker)
(England): Home Int 1905
Hurd, D [Howe] (Campbell)
(Scotland): Home Int 1905-06-08-09-11-28-30
Hurst, Mrs
(Wales): Home Int 1921-22-23-25-27-28
Hyland, B
(Ireland): Home Int 1964-65-66

Imrie, K
(Scotland): Home Int 1984-85-89. Eur L T Ch 1987–89 (GBI):
in Vagliano Trophy 1989;
Inghram, E (Lever)
(Wales): Home Int 1947-48-49-50-51-52-53-54-55-56-57-58-
64-65
Irvin, A
(England): Home Int 1962-63-65-67-68-69-70-71-72-73-75; Eur
L T Ch 1965-67-69-71. (GB): in Curtis Cup 1962-68-70-76; in
Vagliano Trophy 1961-63-65-67-69-71-73-75; in Espirito Santo
1982(Captain); CW 1967-75
Irvine, Miss
(Wales): Home Int 1930
Isaac, Mrs
(Wales): Home Int 1924
Isherwood, L
(Wales): Home Int 1972-76-77-78-80-86-88-89

Jack, E (Philip)
(Scotland): Home Int 1962-63-64-81(Captain)-82(Captain)
Jackson, B
(Ireland): Home Int 1937-38-39-50

Jackson, B
(England): Home Int 1955-56-57-58-59-63-64-65-66-73
(Captain)-74(Captain). (GB): in Curtis Cup 1958-64-68; in
Vagliano Trophy 1959-63-65-67-73(Captain)-75(Captain);
Espirito Santo 1964; CW in 1959-67
Jackson, Mrs H
(Ireland): Home Int 1921
Jackson, J
(Ireland): Home Int 1912-13-14-20-21-22-23-24-25-27-28-29-30
Jackson, Mrs L
(Ireland): Home Int 1910-12-14-20-22-25
Jameson, S (Tobin)
(Ireland): Home Int 1913-14-20-24-25-27
Jenkin, B
(Wales): Home Int 1959
Jenkins, J (Owen)
(Wales): Home Int 1953-56
John, J
(Wales): Home Int 1974
Johns, A
(England): Home Int 1987-88-89
Johnson, A (Hughes)
(Wales): Home Int 1964-66-67-68-69-70-71-72-73-74-75-76-
78-79-85; Eur L T Ch 1965-67-69-71
Johnson, J (Roberts)
(Wales): Home Int 1955
Johnson, M
(England): Home Int 1934-35
Johnson, R
(Wales): Home Int 1955
Johnson, T
(England): Home Int 1984-85-86; Eur L T Ch 1985. (GB):
in Curtis Cup 1986; in Vagliano Trophy 1985; in Espirito
Santo 1986
Jones, A (Gwyther)
(Wales): Home Int 1959
Jones, K
(Wales): Home Int 1959(Captain)-1960(Captain)-61(Captain)
Jones, M (De Lloyd)
(Wales): Home Int 1951
Jones, Mrs
(Wales): Home Int 1932-35
Justice, M
(Wales): Home Int 1931-32

Kaye, H (Williamson)
(England): Home Int 1986(Captain)-87(Captain)
Keenan, D
(Ireland): Home Int 1989
Keiller, G [Style]
(England): Home Int 1948-49-52
Kelway Bamber, Mrs
(Scotland): Home Int 1923-27-33
Kennedy, D (Fowler)
(England): Home Int 1923-24-25-27-28-29
Kennion, Mrs (Kenyon Stow)
(England) Home Int 1910
Kerr, J
(Scotland): Home Int 1947-48-49-54
Kidd, Mrs
(Ireland): Home Int 1934-37
King Mrs
(Ireland): Home Int 1923-25-27-29
Kinloch, Miss
(Scotland): Home Int 1913-14

Kirkwood, Mrs
(Ireland): Home Int 1955
Knight, Mrs
(Scotland): Home Int 1922
Kyle, B [Rhodes] (Norris)
(England): Home Int 1937-38-39-48-49
Kyle, E
(Scotland): Home Int 1909-10

Laing, A
(Scotland): Home Int 1966-67-70-71-73(Captain)-74(Captain);
Eur L T Ch 1967. (GB): in Vagliano Trophy 1967
Lambert, C
(Scotland): Home Int 1989; Eur L T Ch 1989
Lambert, S (Cohen)
(England): Home Int 1979-80. (GB): in Vagliano Trophy 1979
Lambie, S
(Scotland): Home Int 1976
Laming Evans, Mrs
(Wales): Home Int 1922-23
Langford, Mrs
(Wales): Home Int 1937
Langridge, S (Armitage)
(England): Home Int 1963-64-65-66; Eur L T Ch 1965. (GB):
in Curtis Cup 1964-66; in Vagliano Trophy 1963-65
Large, P (Davies)
(England): Home Int 1951-52-81(Captain)-82(Captain)
Larkin, C (McAuley)
(Ireland): Home Int 1966-67-68-69-70-71-72; Eur L T Ch 1971
Latchford, B
(Ireland): Home Int 1931-33
Latham Hall, E (Chubb)
(England): Home Int 1928
Lauder, G
(Ireland): Home Int 1911
Lauder, R
(Ireland): Home Int 1911
Lawrence, JB
(Scotland): Home Int 1959-60-61-62-63-64-65-66-67-68-69-70-
77(Captain); Eur L T Ch 1965-67-69-71. (GB): in Curtis Cup
1964; in Vagliano Trophy 1963-65; in Espirito Santo 1964;
CW 1971
Lawson, H
(Wales): Home Int 1989
Lebrun, W (Aitken)
(Scotland): Home Int 1978-79-80-81-82-83-85. (GB): in Curtis
Cup 1982; in Vagliano Trophy 1981-83
Leaver, B
(Wales): Home Int 1912-14-21
Lee Smith, J
(England): Home Int 1973-74-75-76. (GB): in Curtis Cup
1974-76; in Espirito Santo 1976; CW 1975
Leete, Mrs IG
(Scotland): Home Int 1933
Leitch, C
(England): Home Int 1910-11-12-13-14-20-21-22-24-25-27-28
Leitch, M
(England): Home Int 1912-14
Llewellyn, Miss
(Wales): Home Int 1912-13-14-21-22-23
Lloyd, J
(Wales): Home Int 1988
Lloyd, P
(Wales): Home Int 1935-36
Lloyd Davies, VH
(Wales): Home Int 1913

Lloyd Roberts, V
(Wales): Home Int 1907-08-10
Lloyd Williams, Miss
(Wales): Home Int 1909-10-12-14
Lobbett, P
(England): Home Int 1922-24-27-29-30
Lowry, Mrs
(Ireland): Home Int 1947
Luckin, B (Cooper)
(England): Home Int 1980
Lugton, C
(Scotland): Home Int 1968-72-73-75(Captain)-76(Captain)-
77-78-80
Lumb, K (Phillips)
(England): Home Int 1968-69-70-71; Eur L T Ch 1969. (GB):
Curtis Cup 1972; in Vagliano Trophy 1969-71
Lyons, T (Ross Steen)
(England): Home Int 1959. (GB): in Vagliano Trophy 1959

MacAndrew, F
(Scotland): Home Int 1913-14
Macbeth, M (Dodd)
(England): Home Int 1913-14-20-21-22-23-24-25
MacCann, K
(Ireland): Home Int 1984-85-86
MacCann, K (Smye)
(Ireland): Home Int 1947-48-49-50-51-52-53-54-56-57-58-60-
61-62-64-65(Captain)
McCarthy, A
(Ireland): Home Int 1951-52
McCarthy, D
(Ireland): Home Int 1988
McCulloch, J
(Scotland): Home Int 1921-22-23-24-27-29-30-31-32-33-35-
60(Captain)
McDaid, E (O'Grady)
(Ireland): Home Int 1959
McDaid, ER
(Ireland): Home Int 1987-88-89; Eur L T Ch 1987
Macdonald, K
(Scotland): Home Int 1928-29
MacGeach, C
(Ireland): Home Int 1938-39-48-49-50
McGreevy, V
(Ireland): Home Int 1987
McIntosh, B (Dixon)
(England): Home Int 1969-70; Eur L T Ch 1969. (GB):
in Vagliano Trophy 1969
McIntyre, J
(England): Home Int 1949-54
MacKean, Mrs
(Wales): Home Int 1938-39-47
McKenna, M
(Ireland): Home Int 1968-69-70-71-72-73-74-75-76-77-78-79-
80-81-82-83-84 -85-86-87-88-89; Eur L T Ch 1969-71-75-87.
(GB): in Curtis Cup 1970-72-74-76-78-80-82-84-86; in Vagliano
Trophy 1969-71-73-75-77-79-81-85-87; in Espirito Santo 1970-
74-76-86(Captain)
Mackenzie, A
(Scotland): Home Int 1921
McLarty, E
(Scotland): Home Int 1966(Captain)-67(Captain)-68(Captain)
McMahon, S (Cadden)
(Scotland): Home Int 1974-75-76-77-79. (GB): in Curtis Cup
1976; in Vagliano Trophy 1975

McNair, W
(England): Home Int 1921
McNeil, K
(Scotland): Home Int 1969(Captain)-70(Captain)
McNeile, CL
(Ireland): Home Int 1906
McQuillan, Y
(Ireland): Home Int 1985-86
MacTier, Mrs
(Wales): Home Int 1927
Madeley, M (Coburn)
(Ireland): Home Int 1964-69; Eur L T Ch 1969
Madill, Mrs
(Ireland): Home Int 1920-24-25-27-28-29-33
Magill, J
(Ireland): Home Int 1907-11-13
Maher, S (Vaughan)
(England): Home Int 1960-61-62-63-64. (GB): in Curtis Cup 1962-64; in Vagliano Trophy 1961; CW 1963
Mahon, D
(Ireland): Home Int 1989
Main, M (Farquhar)
(Scotland): Home Int 1950-51
Maitland, M
(Scotland): Home Int 1905-06-08-12-13
Mallam, Mrs S
(Ireland): Home Int 1922-23
Marks, Mrs T
(Ireland): Home Int 1950
Marks, Mrs
(Ireland): Home Int 1930-31-33-35
Marley, MV (Marley)
(Wales): Home Int 1921-22-23-30-37
Marr, H (Cameron)
(Scotland): Home Int 1927-28-29-30-31
Martin, P [Whitworth Jones] (Low)
(Wales): Home Int 1948-50-56-59-60-61
Marvin, V
(England): Home Int 1977-78; Eur L T Ch 1977. (GB): in Curtis Cup 1978; in Vagliano Trophy 1977
Mason, Mrs
(Wales): Home Int 1923
Mather, H
(Scotland): Home Int 1905-09-12-13-14
Mellis, Mrs
(Scotland): Home Int 1924-27
Menton, D
(Ireland): Home Int 1949
Menzies, M
(Scotland): Home Int 1962(Captain)
Merrill, J (Greenhalgh)
(England): Home Int 1960-61-63-66-69-70-71-75-76-77-78; Eur L T Ch 1971-77. (GB): in Curtis Cup 1964-70-74-76-78; in Vagliano Trophy 1961-65-75-77; in Espirito Santo 1970-74(Captain)-78; CW 1963
Millar, D
(Ireland): Home Int 1928
Milligan, J (Mark)
(Ireland): Home Int 1971-72-73
Mills, I
(Wales): Home Int 1935-36-37-39-47-48
Milton, M (Paterson)
(Scotland): Home Int 1948-49-50-51-52. (GB): in Curtis Cup 1952

Mitchell, J
(Ireland): Home Int 1930
Mooney, M
(Ireland): Home Int 1972-73; Eur L T Ch 1971. (GB): in Vagliano Trophy 1973
Moorcroft, S
(England): Home Int 1985-86; Eur L T Ch 1985-87
Moore, S
(Ireland): Home Int 1937-38-39-47-48-49-68(Captain)
Moran, V (Singleton)
(Ireland): Home Int 1970-71-73-74-75; Eur L T Ch 1971-75
Morant, E
(England): Home Int 1906-10
Morgan, S
(England): Home Int 1989; Eur L T Ch 1989
Morgan, W
(England): Home Int 1931-32-33-34-35-36-37. (GB): in Curtis Cup 32-34-36
Morgan, Miss
(Wales): Home Int 1912-13-14
Moriarty, M (Irvine)
(Ireland): Home Int 1979
Morris, L (Moore)
(England): Home Int 1912-13
Morris, Mrs de B
(Ireland): Home Int 1933
Morrison, G (Cheetham)
(England): Home Int 1965-69(Captain). (GB): in Vagliano Trophy 1965
Morrison, G (Cradock-Hartopp)
(England): Home Int 1936
Mountford, S
(Wales): Home Int 1989
Murray, Rachel
(Ireland): Home Int 1952
Murray, S (Jolly)
(England): Home Int 1976
Musgrove, Mrs
(Wales): Home Int 1923-24
Myles, M
(Scotland): Home Int 1955-57-59-60-67

Neill-Fraser, M
(Scotland): Home Int 1905-06-07-08-09-10-11-12-13-14
Nes, K (Garnham)
(England): Home Int 1931-32-33-36-37-38-39
Nevile, E
(England): Home Int 1905-06-08-10
New, B
(England): Home Int 1980-81-82-83. (GB): in Curtis Cup 1984; in Vagliano Trophy 1983
Newell, B
(England): Home Int 1936
Newman, L
(Wales): Home Int 1927-31
Newton, B (Brown)
(England): Home Int 1930-33-34-35-36-37
Nicholls, M
(Wales): Home Int 1962(Captain)
Nicholson, J (Hutton)
(Scotland): Home Int 1969-70; Eur L T Ch 1971; CW 1971
Nicholson, Mrs WH
(Scotland): Home Int 1910-13
Nimmo, H
(Scotland): Home Int 1936-38-39

Norris, J (Smith)
(Scotland): Home Int 1966-67-68-69-70-71-72-75-76-77-78-79-83(Captain)-84(Captain)-84(Captain); Eur L T Ch 1971. (CB): in Vagliano Trophy 1977

Norwell, I (Watt)
(Scotland): Home Int 1954

Nutting, P (Jameson)
(Ireland): Home Int 1927-28

O'Brien, A
(Ireland): Home Int 1969

O'Brien Kenney, S
(Ireland): Home Int 1977-78-83-84-85-86

O'Donnell, M
(Ireland): Home Int 1974-77(Captain)-78(Captain)-79 (Captain); Eur L T Ch 1980(Captain). (GB): in Curtis Cup 1982; in Vagliano Trophy 1981(Captain)

O'Donohoe, A
(Ireland): Home Int 1948-49-50-51-53-73(Captain)-74 (Captain)

O'Hare, S
(Ireland): Home Int 1921-22

O'Reilly, T (Moran)
(Ireland): Home Int 1977-78-86-88; Eur L T Ch 1987

O'Sullivan, A
(Ireland): Home Int 1982-83-84

O'Sullivan, P
(Ireland): Home Int 1950-51-52-53-54-55-56-57-58-59-60-63-64-65-66-67-69 (Captain)-70(Captain)-71(Captain); Eur L T Ch 1971(Captain)

Oliver, M (Jones)
(Wales): Home Int 1955-60-61-62-63-64-65-66. (GB): in Espirito Santo 1964

Ormsby, Miss
(Ireland): Home Int 1909-10-11

Orr, P (Boyd)
(Ireland): Home Int 1971

Orr, Mrs
(Wales): Home Int 1924

Owen, E
(Wales): Home Int 1947

Panton, C
(Scotland): Home Int 1972-73-76-77-78. (GB): in Vagliano Trophy 1977; in Espirito Santo 1976

Park, Mrs
(Scotland): Home Int 1952

Parker, S
(England): Home Int 1973

Patey, Mrs
(Scotland): Home Int 1922-23

Pearson, D
(England): Home Int 1928-29-30-31-32-34

Percy, G (Mitchell)
(Scotland): Home Int 1927-28-30-31

Perriam, A
(Wales): Home Int 1988

Phelips, M
(Wales): Home Int 1913-14-21

Phillips, ME
(England): Home Int 1905

Phillips, Mrs
(Wales): Home Int 1921

Pickard, M (Nichol)
(England): Home Int 1958-59-60-61-67-69-83(Captain). (GB): in Curtis Cup 1968-70; in Vagliano Trophy 1959-61-67

Pim, Mrs
(Ireland): Home Int 1908

Pook, E (Chadwick)
(England): Home Int 1963-65-66-67; Eur L T Ch 1967. (GB): in Curtis Cup 1966; in Vagliano Trophy 1963-67; CW 1967

Porter, D (Park)
(Scotland): Home Int 1922-25-27-29-30-31-32-33-34-35-37-38-47-48. (GB): in Curtis Cup 1932

Porter, M (Lazenby)
(England): Home Int 1931-32

Powell, M
(Wales): Home Int 1908-09-10-12

Price, M (Greaves)
(England): Home Int 1956(Captain)

Price Fisher, E (Price)
(England): Home Int 1948-51-52-53-54-55-56-57-58-59-60. (GB): in Curtis Cup 1950-52-54-56-58-60; in Vagliano Trophy 1959; CW 1959

Proctor, Mrs
(Wales): Home Int 1907

Provis, I (Kyle)
(Scotland): Home Int 1910-11

Purcell, E
(Ireland): Home Int 1965-66-67-72-73

Purvis-Russell-Montgomery, C
(Scotland): Home Int 1921-22-23-25-28-29-23-31-32-33-34-35-36-37-38-39-47-48-49-50-52

Pyman, B
(Wales): Home Int 1925-28-29-30-32-33-34-35-36-37-38

Rabbidge, R
(England): Home Int 1931

Rawlings, M
(Wales): Home Int 1979-80-81-83-84-85-86-87. (GB): in Vagliano Trophy 1981

Rawlinson, T (Walker)
(Scotland): Home Int 1970-71-73-76. (GB): in Vagliano Trophy 1973

Read, P
(England): Home Int 1922

Reddan, C (Tiernan)
(Ireland): Home Int 1935-36-38-39-47-48-49. (GB): in Curtis Cup 1938-48

Reddan, MV
(Ireland): Home Int 1955

Reece, P (Millington)
(England): Home Int 1966(Captain)

Rees, G
(Wales): Home Int 1981

Rees, MB
(Wales): Home Int 1927-31

Reid, A (Lurie)
(Scotland) Home Int 1960-61-62-63-64-66. (GB): in Vagliano Trophy 1961

Reid, A (Kyle)
(Scotland): Home Int 1923-24-25

Reid, D
(Scotland): Home Int 1978-79

Remer, H
(England): Home Int 1909

Rennie, J (Hastings)
(Scotland): Home Int 1961-65-66-67-71-72; Eur L T Ch 1967. (GB): in Curtis Cup 1966; in Vagliano Trophy 1961-67

Rhys, J
(Wales): Home Int 1979

Rice, J
(Ireland): Home Int 1924-27-29

Richards, J
(Wales): Home Int 1980-82-83-85

Richards, S
(Wales): Home Int 1967

Richardson, Mrs
(England): Home Int 1907-09

Richmond, M (Walker)
(Scotland): Home Int 1972-73-74-75-77-78. (GB): in Curtis Cup 1974; in Vagliano Trophy 1975

Rieben, Mrs
(Wales): Home Int 1927-28-29-30-31-32-33

Rigby, F (Macbeth)
(Scotland): Home Int 1912-13

Ritchie, C (Park)
(Scotland): Home Int 1939-47-48-51-52-53-64(Captain)

Roberts, B
(Wales): Home Int 1984(Captain)-85(Captain)-86(Captain)

Roberts, E (Pentony)
(Ireland): Home Int 1932-33-34-35-36-39

Roberts, E (Barnett)
(Ireland): Home Int 1961-62-63-64-65; Eur L T Ch 1964

Roberts, G
(Wales): Home Int 1949-52-53-54

Roberts, M (Brown)
(Scotland): Home Int 1965(Captain). (GB): in Espirito Santo 1964

Roberts, P
(Wales): Home Int 1950-51-53-55-56-57-58-59-60-61-62-63-64(Captain)-65 (Captain)-66(Captain)-67(Captain)-68-69-70; Eur L T Ch 1965-67-69. (GB) in Espirito Santo 1964

Roberts, S
(Wales): Home Int 1983-84-85-86-87-88-89; Eur L T Ch 1987

Robertson, B (McCorkindale)
(Scotland): Home Int 1958-59-60-61-62-63-64-65-66-69-72-73-78-80-81-82-84 -85-86; Eur L T Ch 1965-67(Captain)-69-71(Captain). (GB): in Curtis Cup 1960-66-68-70-72-74 (Captain)-76(Captain)-82-86; in Vagliano Trophy 1959-63-69-71-81-85; in Espirito Santo 1959-63-69-71-81-85; CW 1971-75(Captain)

Robertson, D
(Scotland): Home Int 1907

Robertson, E
(Scotland): Home Int 1924

Robertson, G
(Scotland): Home Int 1907-08-09

Robinson, C (Nesbitt)
(Ireland): Home Int 1974-75-76-77-78-79-80-81. (GB): in Curtis Cup 1980; in Vagliano Trophy 1979

Robinson, R (Bayly)
(Ireland): Home Int 1947-56-57

Robinson, S
(England): Home Int 1989

Roche, Mrs
(Ireland): Home Int 1922

Rogers, J
(Wales): Home Int 1972

Roskrow, M
(England): Home Int 1948-50

Ross, M (Hezlet)
(Ireland): Home Int 1905-06-07-08-11-12

Roy, S (Needham)
(Scotland): Home Int 1969-71-72-73-74-75-76-83. (GB): in Vagliano Trophy 1973-75

Rudgard, G
(England): Home Int 1931-32-50-51-52

Rusack, J
(Scotland): Home Int 1908

Sabine, D (Plumpton)
(England): Home Int 1934-35. (GB): in Curtis Cup 1934

Saunders, V
(England): Home Int 1967-68; Eur L T Ch 1967. (GB): in Curtis Cup 1968; in Vagliano Trophy 1967; CW 1967

Scott Chard, Mrs
(Wales) Home Int 1928-30

Seddon, N
(Wales): Home Int 1962-63-74(Captain)-75(Captain)-76 (Captain)

Selkirk, H
(Wales): Home Int 1925-28

Shapcott, A
(England): Home Int 1989

Shapcott, S
(England): Home Int 1986-88; Eur L T Ch 1987. (GB): in Curtis Cup 1988; in Vagliano Trophy 1987; CW 1987; in Espirito Santo 1988

Shaw, P
(Wales): Home Int 1913

Sheldon, A
(Wales): Home Int 1981

Sheppard, E (Pears)
(England): Home Int 1947

Simpson, L (Moore)
(England): Home Int 1979-80

Singleton, B (Henderson)
(Scotland): Home Int 1939-52-53-54-55-56-57-58-60-61-62-63-64-65

Slade, Lady
(Ireland): Home Int 1906

Slark, R (Porter)
(England): Home Int 1959-60-61-62-64-65-66-68-78; Eur L T Ch 1965. (GB): in Curtis Cup 1960-62-64; in Vagliano Trophy 1959-61-65; in Espirito Santo 1964-66(Captain); CW 1963

Slocombe, E (Davies)
(Wales): Home Int 1974-75

Smalley, Mrs A
(Wales): Home Int 1924-25-31-32-33-34

Smillie, P
(England): Home Int 1985-86

Smith, A [Stant] (Willard)
(England): Home Int 1974-75-76. (GB): in Curtis Cup 1976; in Vagliano Trophy 1975; CW 1959-63

Smith, F (Stephens)
(England): Home Int 1947-48-49-50-51-52-53-54-55-59-62 (Captain)-71(Captain) -72(Captain). (GB): in Curtis Cup 1950-52-54-56-58-60-62(non-playing Captain)-72 (non-playing Captain); in Vagliano Trophy 1959-71; CW 1959-63

Smith, Mrs L
(Ireland): Home Int 1913-14-21-22-23-25

Smythe, M
(Ireland): Home Int 1947-48-49-50-51-52-53-54-55-56-58-59-62(Captain)

Sowter, Mrs
(Wales): Home Int 1923

Speir, M
(Scotland): Home Int 1957-64-68-71(Captain)-72(Captain)

Starrett, L (Malone)
(Ireland): Home Int 1975-76-77-78-80

Stavert, M
(Scotland): Home Int 1979

Steel, Mrs DC
(Scotland): Home Int 1925

Steel, E
(England): Home Int 1905-06-07-08-11

Stewart, G
(Scotland): Home Int 1979-80-81-82-83-84; Eur L T Ch 1982-84. (GB): in Curtis Cup 1980-82; in Vagliano Trophy 1979-81-83; CW 1979-83

Stewart, L (Scraggie)
(Scotland): Home Int 1921-22-23

Stocker, J
(England): Home Int 1922-23

Stockton, Mrs
(Wales): Home Int 1949

Storry, Mrs
(Wales): Home Int 1910-14

Stroud, N
(Wales): Home Int 1989

Stuart, M
(Ireland): Home Int 1905-07-08

Stuart-French, Miss
(Ireland): Home Int 1922

Sugden, J (Machin)
(England): Home Int 1953-54-55

Summers, M (Mackie)
(Scotland): Home Int 1986

Sumpter, Mrs
(England): Home Int 1907-08-12-14-24

Sutherland Pilch, R (Barton)
(England): Home Int 1947-49-50-58(Captain)

Swallow, C
(England): Home Int 1985; Eur L T Ch 1985

Tamworth, Mrs
(England): Home Int 1908

Taylor, I
(Ireland): Home Int 1930

Teacher, F
(Scotland): Home Int 1908-09-11-12-13

Temple, S
(England): Home Int 1913-14

Temple Dobell, G (Ravenscroft)
(England): Home Int 1911-12-13-14-20-21-25-30

Thomas, C (Phipps)
(Wales): Home Int 1959-63-64-65-66-67-68-69-70-71-72-73-76-77-80

Thomas, I
(Wales): Home Int 1910

Thomas, O
(Wales): Home Int 1921

Thomas, S (Rowlands)
(Wales): Home Int 1977-82-84-85

Thomas, T (Perkins)
(Wales): Home Int 1972-73-74-75-76-77-78-79-80-81-82-83-84; Eur L T Ch 1975. (GB): in Curtis Cup 1974-76-78-80; in Vagliano Trophy 1973-75-77-79; in Espirito Santo 1979; CW 1975-79

Thomas, V (Rawlings)
(Wales): Home Int 1971-72-73-74-75-76-77-78-79-80-81-82-83-84-85-86-87-88-89; Eur L T Ch 1975-87. (GB): in Curtis Cup 1982-84-86-88; in Vagliano Trophy 1979-83 -85-87-89; CW 1979-83-87.

Thompson, M
(Wales): Home Int 1937-38-39

Thompson, M (Wallis)
(England): Home Int 1948-49

Thompson, M
(Scotland): Home Int 1949

Thomson, D
(Scotland): Home Int 1982-83-85-87

Thomson, M
(Scotland): Home Int 1907

Thomson, M
(Scotland): Home Int 1974-75-76-77-78; Eur L T Ch 1978. (GB): in Curtis Cup 1978; in Vagliano Trophy 1977

Thornhill, J (Woodside)
(England): Home Int 1965-74-82-83-84-85-86-87-88; Eur L T Ch 1965-85-87. (GB): in Curtis Cup 1984-86-88; in Vagliano Trophy 1965-83-85-87-89(Captain); CW 1983-87

Thornhill, Miss
(Ireland): Home Int 1924-25

Thornton, Mrs
(Ireland): Home Int 1924

Todd, Mrs
(Ireland): Home Int 1931-32-34-35-36

Thomlinson, J [Evans] (Roberts)
(England): Home Int 1962-64. (GB): in Curtis Cup 1962; in Vagliano Trophy 1963

Treharne, A [Mills]
(Wales): Home Int 1952-61

Turner, B
(England): Home Int 1908

Turner, S (Jump)
(Wales): Home Int 1982-84-85-86

Tynte, V
(Ireland): Home Int 1905-06-08-09-11-12-13-14

Uzielli, A (Carrick)
(England): Home Int 1976-77-78; Eur L T Ch 1977. (GB): in Curtis Cup 1978; in Vagliano Trophy 1977

Valentine, J (Anderson)
(Scotland): Home Int 1934-35-36-37-38-39-47-49-50-51-52-53-54-55-56 (Captain)-57-58. (GB): in Curtis Cup 1938-48-50-52-54-56-58; CW 1959

Valentine, P (Whitley)
(Wales): Home Int 1973-74-75-77-78-79-80

Veitch, F
(Scotland): Home Int 1912

Wadsworth, H
(Wales): Home Int 1987-88-89; Eur L T Ch 1987

Waite, C
(England): Home Int 1981-82-83-84, Eur L T Ch 1985. (GB): in Curtis Cup 1984; in Vagliano Trophy 1983; in Espirito Santo 1984; CW 1983

Wakelin, H
(Wales): Home Int 1955

Walker, B (Thompson)
(England): Home Int 1905-06-07-08-09-11

Walker, M
(England): Home Int 1970-72; Eur L T Ch 1971. (GB): in Curtis Cup 1972; in Vagliano Trophy 1971; CW 1971

Walker, P
(Ireland): Home Int 1928-29-30-31-32-33-34-35-36-37-38-39-48. (GB): in Curtis Cup 1934-36-38

Walker-Leigh, F
(Ireland): Home Int 1907-08-09-11-12-13-14

Wallace-Williamson, V
(Scotland): Home Int 1932. (GB): in Curtis Cup 1938 (Captain)

Walsh, R
(Ireland): Home Int 1987

Walter, J
(England): Home Int 1974-79-80-82-86

Wardlaw, N (Baird)
(Scotland): Home Int 1932-35-36-37-38-39-47-48. (GB): in
Curtis Cup 1938

Watson, C (Nelson)
(England): Home Int 1982

Webster, S (Hales)
(Wales): Home Int 1968-69-72

Wesley, N
(Wales): Home Int 1986

Westall, S (Maudsley)
(England): Home Int 1973

Weston, R
(Wales): Home Int 1927

Whieldon, Miss
(Wales): Home Int 1908

Wickham, C
(Ireland): Home Int 1983 80

Wickham, P
(Ireland): Home Int 1976-83-87; Eur L T Ch 1987

Williams, M
(Wales): Home Int 1936

Wliamson, C (Barker)
(England): Home Int 1979-80-81

Willock-Pollen, G
(England): Home Int 1907

Wilson, A
(Scotland): Home Int 1973-74-85 (Captain)

Wilson, E
(England): Home Int 1928-29-30. (GB): in Curtis Cup 1932

Wilson, Mrs
(Ireland): Home Int 1931

Wilson Jones, D
(Wales): Home Int 1952

Winn, J
(England): Home Int 1920-21-23-25

Wooldridge, W (Shaw)
(Scotland): Home Int 1982

Wragg, M
(England): Home Int 1929

Wright, J (Robertson)
(Scotland): Home Int 1952-53-54-55-56-57-58-59-60-61-63-65-
67-73-78 (Captain-79(Captain)-80(Captain)-86(Captain); Eur
L T Ch 1965. (GB): in Curtis Cup 1954-56-58-60; in Vagliano
Trophy 1959-61-63; CW 1959

Wright, N (Cook)
(Wales): Home Int 1938-47-48-49-51-52-53-54-57-58-59-60-
62-63-64-66-67-68-71 (Captain)-72(Captain)-73(Captain); Eur
L T Ch 1965-71 (Captain). (GB): in Espirito Santo 1964

Wright, P
(Scotland): Home Int 1981-82-83-84; Eur L T Ch 1987. (GB):
in Vagliano Trophy 1981

Wylie, P (Wade)
(England): Home Int 1934-35-36-37-38-47. (GB): in Curtis
Cup 1938

*Note: As will be seen, there is a good
deal still missing in these lists. Records,
particularly of the early days, are not easily
found. The Editor will be pleased to receive
any additions or corrections from players or
their relatives.*

Association of Golf Writers

Adams, Jack
Daily Record, Glasgow

Andrew, Harry H

(L) Baker, John E

Ballantine, John

Bisher, Firman
Atlanta-Journal Constitution,

Blackstock, Dixon
Sunday Mail, Glasgow

Blighton, Bill
Today

Blomquist, Jan
Golf Digest Sverige

Bolze, Gerd A

Booth, Alan

Bowden, Ken

Britten, Mike

(H) Butler, Frank

Caird, Douglas

Callander, Colin
Golf Monthly

Campbell, John G
The Daily Telegraph

Campbell, Malcolm
Golf Monthly

Chapman, Jeremy
The Sporting Life

Clark, Bill
Sunday Mirror, Belfast

Clough, Frank
The Sun

Coffman, Ron
Golf World

Creighton, Brian
Reuters

Dabell, Norman

Davies, Bob
Shropshire Star

Davies, David
The Guardian

Davies, Patricia

Dobereiner, Peter

Dodd, Richard
The Yorkshire Post

Donald, Peter

Ebbinge, Jan B
Dutch Golf Wegener Tijl

(L) Edwards, Leslie

Elliott, Bill
The Daily Star

Ellison, Stanley
Turf Management

Elsey, Neil
Golf Illustrated Weekly

Farquharson, Colin
Press and Journal, Aberdeen

(H) Fenton, John
BBC Radio

Ferrie, Kevin
Dundee Courier and Advertiser

Ferrier, Bob
Elite World of Sport Ltd

Figar, Jose
Adesport, Madrid

Fraser, Alan
Scotland on Sunday

Frederick, Adrian

Garrod, Mark
Press Association

Gilleece, Dermot
The Irish Times

Glover, Tim
The Independent

Goodner, Ross
Golf Digest, USA

Green, Bob
The Associated Press, New York

Green, Robert
Golf World

Grimsley, Will

Hamilton, David
Golf Illustrated Weekly

Hamilton, Eddie

Hardy, Martin
Daily Express

Haslam, Peter
Golf World

(L) Hart, Maurice

Hedley, Alan
The Journal, Newcastle-upon-Tyne

Hennessy, John
The Times

Herron, Allan

Higgs, Peter
Mail on Sunday

Hopkins, John
The Sunday Times

(L) Huggins, Percy

Ingham, John

Jacobs, Raymond
Glasgow Herald

Jenkins, Bob
Sunday Post, Glasgow

Jenkins, Dan
Golf Digest, USA

Johnson, Bill
Bolton Evening News

Kahn, Elizabeth

Lafaurie, André-Jean
Golf European, Paris

Laidlaw, Renton
Evening Standard

Lawrenson, Derek
Birmingham Post and Mail

(L) Lincoln, Stanley

MacCallum, Scott
Golf Monthly

McDonnell, Michael
Daily Mail

(H) McKinlay, S L

Macniven, Ian
Edinburgh Evening News

MacVicar, Jock
Scottish Daily Express

Mackie, Keith

Magowan, Jack
Belfast Telegraph

Mair, Norman
The Scotsman

Mair, Lewine

Maitland, Bobby
Scottish Daily Express

Mancinelli, Piero

Mearing, Paddy

Miró, Miguel
Diario Deportivo, Madrid

Moody, John

Morgan, John
Home Counties Golfer

Moseley, Ron
Press Association

Mossop, James
Sunday Express

Mulqueen, Charles
Cork Examiner

(H) Neale, Bert
Action Photos

Nicol, Alister
Daily Record, Edinburgh

Oakley, John

Ortega, Jesús Ruiz
Golf, Madrid

Ostermann, Ted
Golf Vertrieb, Hamburg
Pargeter, John

Pastor, Nuria
La Vanguardia, Barcelona

Pinner, John
Golf World Wales

(H) Place, Tom
US Tour, Ponte Vedra Beach, Florida

Platts, Mitchell
The Times

Plumridge, Chris
The Illustrated London News

Price, Charles

Price-Fisher, Elizabeth
The Daily Telegraph

Ramsoy, Tom
News Limited, North Sydney

Redmond, John
Irish Press

Reece, John K

Riach, Ian
Scottish Sunday Express

Richardson, Gordon

Roberts, Steve

Robertson, Bill
Today's Golfer

Robertson, Jack
Evening Times, Glasgow

Rodrigo, Robert (Bob Rodney)

Ross, John M
The Met Golfer, USA

Ruddy, Pat
Golfers Companion

Ryde, Peter

St John, Lauren
Today's Golfer

(L) Scatchard, Charles

Seitz, Nick
Golf Digest/Tennis, USA

Severino, Dick
Golf Features Service, San Diego

Simpson, Gordon
Press Association, Glasgow

Skelton, Ronald
Dundee Courier and Advertiser

Smart, Chris
Mid-Glamorgan Press Agency

Smith, Colm
Independent Newspapers, Dublin

Sommers, Robert
US Golf Association

Spander, Art
San Francisco Examiner

Steel, Donald
The Sunday Telegraph

Stobbs, John

Taylor, Dick
Golf World, USA

(H) Thornberry, Henry W

(H) Ullyett, Roy
Daily Express

Van Esbeck, Edmund
The Irish Times

Ward, Barry E
Golfing Life

Whitbread, John S
Surrey Herald Newspapers

White, Gordon S
New York Times

Wills, Ron
Daily Mirror

Williams, Michael
The Daily Telegraph

(L) Wilson, Enid

Wilson, Mark
PGA European Tour, Wentworth

Wind, Herbert Warren
The New Yorker

Wright, Ben

Zachrisson, Goran

(L) = Life member
(H) = Honorary member

British Association of Golf Course Architects

Members

Full

J Hamilton Stutt

Hamilton Stutt & Co, Bergen, 12 Bingham Ave, Poole, Dorset BW14 8NE *Tel* (0202) 708406

Donald Harradine, Peter Harradine

CH 6987, Caslano, Switzerland *Tel* (091) 711561

Fred Hawtree, Martin Hawtree, Simon Gidman

Hawtree & Son, 5 Oxford Street, Woodstock, Oxford OX7 1TQ *Tel* (0993) 811976

Donald Steel

Donald Steel & Co Ltd, The Forum, Stirling Road, Chichester, West Sussex, PO19 2EN *Tel* (0243) 531901

Tom McAuley

38 Moira Drive, Bangor, Co Down, N Ireland BT20 4RW *Tel* (0247) 465953

Provisional

Peter Bellchambers, Steven Macfarlane

Hawtree & Son, 5 Oxford Street, Woodstock, Oxford OX7 1TQ *Tel* (0993) 811976

Alistair Rae

26 Tannoch Road, Uplawmoor, Glasgow G78 4AD *Tel* (050 585) 371

Stephan Quenouille

c/o Tom McAuley, 38 Moira Drive, Bangor, Co Down, N Ireland BT20 4RW *Tel* (0247) 465953

Cameron Sinclair

21 Lauds Road, Crick, Northamptonshire NN6 7TJ

Jeremy Pern

13 Lotissement des Chênes, Aussonne 31700, Blagnac (Toulouse), France *Tel* 61 85 09 02

Overseas (Full)

Eddie Hackett

28 Ailesbury Drive, Dublin 4, Eire *Tel* (0001) 691592

Joan Dudok Van Heel

Beukenlaan 4, B-1640, St Genesius-Rode, nr Brussels, Belgium *Tel* (02) 3583387

Pier Mancinelli

21 Via Achille Papa 00195, Rome, Italy *Tel* (06) 36036-35

Jan Sederholm

K Kristoffersweg 3A, S 253 34 Helsingborg, Sweden *Tel* (042) 371 84

Overseas (Provisional)

Kurt Rossknecht

Dennenmoos 5a, 8990 Lindau-Bad, Schachen, W Germany *Tel* 08382 230 05

R Berthet

Château du Tremblay, s/Mauldre, 78490 Montfort L'Amaury, France *Tel* (1)34879200

Tjasa Gregoric   Kobilarna Lipica, 66 210 Sezatia, Yugoslavia

Gerard Jol   Landschapsarchitekt bnt, Middenduinerweg 15, 2082 LC
                             Santpoort, Netherlands *Tel* (023) 376449

Honorary Member

G S Cornish   Fiddlers Green, Amherst, Mass 01002, USA

The most exciting new museum in Scotland tees off Summer 1990!

it's British

The British Golf Museum tells the story of golf from its misty origins to the present day.

it's more than just golf

It combines highly visual presentations with the most advanced forms of visitor-participation displays

and it's more than just a museum

Located opposite the world-famous Royal & Ancient Golf Club House, the musuem is an exciting experience for the whole family.

Contact:
The British Golf Museum,
Golf Place, St Andrews,
Fife KY16 9JD.
Tel: 0334 73423.

The British Golf Museum gratefully acknowledges the support given by the Scottish Tourist Board and Philips Interactive Media Systems.

Golfing Hotel Compendium

This year the Golfing Hotel Compendium *has again increased in size and continues to be a primary source of information for golfers wishing to find the most comfortable place to stay at or close to some of the finest golf courses in the country. This section has been compiled from the premier hotels of the British Isles which include golf among their many attractions.*

If readers wish to especially recommend an establishment which is not listed in this edition of the Royal & Ancient Golfer's Handbook *the editors will be happy to be advised.*

Please note that from 6th May 1990 telephone codes for London will change. If you require help call Freefone 0800 800 873

England: South West

The Anchorage Hotel
The Quay, Instow, Bideford, N Devon.
Tel (0271) 860655
Golf parties catered for, any number from two to thirty-two. We arrange every aspect of your holiday. Concessionary green fees at Saunton and Royal North Devon – starting times guaranteed. Come and be pampered at Devon's No.1 golf hotel. (See advertisement page 403 for further details.)

Bel Alp House Country Hotel
Haytor, Near Bovey Tracey, South Devon.
Tel (03646) 217
Small elegant country house in a most spectacular setting providing a remarkable standard of food, comfort and hospitality. Close to many excellent South Devon golf courses plus perfect peace and quiet.

Boskerris Hotel
Carbis Bay, St Ives, Cornwall TR26 2NQ.
Tel (0736) 795295
Boskerris Hotel does not have its own golf course, but by a unique arrangement with 10 of Cornwall's clubs, is able to offer free golf within the price of accommodation. (See advertisement page 401 for further details.)

Budock Vean Golf and Country House Hotel
Mawnan Smith, Falmouth, Cornwall TR11 5LG.
Tel (0326) 250288
Challenging 9 hole (18 tee) private golf course set in sub-tropical grounds, free to guests. Excellent amenities, luxurious surroundings, top quality service and cuisine. (See advertisement page 399 for further details.)

Burnham & Berrow Golf Club
St Christopher's Way, Burnham-on-Sea, Somerset TA8 2PE.
Tel (0278) 785760
18 hole championship links golf course and 9 hole course. (See advertisement page 401 for further details.)

The Coombe Bank Hotel
Landscore Road, Teignmouth, Devon
TQ14 9JL.
Tel (0626) 772369
Devon golfing holidays. Four different courses.
Societies welcome. From only £125 inclusive.

The Crown Hotel
West Street, Blandford, Dorset DT11 7AJ.
Tel (0258) 456626
A superb Georgian building ideally situated
for the many fine golf courses in the area.

The Dormy Hotel and Leisure Club
New Road, Ferndown, Dorset BH22 8ES.
Tel (0202) 872121
De Vere 4 Star hotel adjacent to Ferndown golf
course, offering sporting and leisure activities
combined with a high standard of accommodation and cuisine. (See advertisement page 399
for further details.)

Fairlight Hotel
1 Golf Links Road, Broadstone, Dorset
BH18 8BE.
Tel (0202) 694316
16 courses within 20 miles radius as well as
beaches, coast and countryside, Bournemouth
and Poole, theatres and shops etc. Broadstone
Club few hundred yards. Ideal base for golfing
or mixed holidays. Doubles from £26. Full
English breakfast, excellent 4 course dinner
at this private licensed hotel. Friendly welcome
assured.

Gleneagles Hotel *** RAC
Asheldon Road, Wellswood, Torquay
TQ1 2QS.
Tel (0803) 293637
42 bedrooms all en-suite with sun balconies,
colour television, telephone and room service.
Heated pool, jacuzzi, solarium, superb cocktail
lounge and poolside restaurant. Four golf
courses close by. (See advertisement page
399 for further details.)

Graftonbury Hotel
Grafton Lane, Hereford HR2 8BN.
Tel (0432) 356411
Garden hotel close to city centre. House
and garden rooms. Conference facilities.
Gym, sauna, jacuzzi, sun bed, heated covered
swimming pool (May-September). Wedding
receptions. Fully licensed. Two miles from
Belmont golf course.

The Grosvenor Hotel
10 Summerleaze Crescent, Bude, Cornwall
EX23 8HH.
Tel (0288) 352062
Golfing family hotel with views of beach, canal,
river and "A good 3 wood from the golf course,"
or choice of three other golf courses to play. B/B
dinner and green fees, VAT included. £36.75
daily. (See advertisement page 401 for further
details.)

Hotel Collingwood
11 Priory Road, Bournemouth BH2 5DF.
Tel (0202) 27575
Situated in central Bournemouth with 9 golf
courses within 6 miles. Tee times arranged.
Parking, indoor pool, leisure centre, snooker,
nightly entertainment. Early breakfast, late
evening meal available from £28.00 DBB

Kittiwell House Hotel & Restaurant
Croyde, North Devon EX33 1PG.
Tel (0271) 890247
Special concessions with Saunton and Royal
North Devon golf clubs. 16th century thatched
Devon long house. 12 bedrooms all en-suite.
High standard cuisine and well stocked bar.
Walking distance from sea.

Langstone Cliff Hotel
Dawlish, Devon EX7 0NA.
Tel (0626) 865155
64 bedroom hotel overlooking the sea. Set in
19 acre grounds. Indoor and outdoor heated
swimming pool, snooker, table tennis, hard
court tennis. Six 18 hole golf courses within
12 miles.

Lansdown Grove Hotel
Lansdown, Bath BA1 5EH.
Tel (0225) 315891
An attractive hotel overlooking historic Bath.
45 en-suite bedrooms with TV, telephone,
mini-bar and tea/coffee making facilities.
Excellent restaurant. Five local golf courses.
A Best Western Hotel. AA/RAC 3 Star.

Manor Crest Hotel
Hendford, Yeovil, Somerset BA20 1TG.
Tel (0935) 23116 *Tx* 46580 *Fax* (0935) 706607
Centrally located off the A30 this 1735 manor
house has been converted into a 41 bedroom
3 Star hotel. Personal service is our key to
success. Only 7 minutes from Yeovil golf club.

RAC ***   **TORQUAY DEVON TQ1 2QS**   RAC ***

This modern 42 bedroom hotel overlooking one of the most beautiful locations in south Devon - Anstey's Cove and Redgate beach, access to both through the hotel grounds. All bedrooms en-suite with sun balcony, television, telephone etc.

For your enjoyment, poolside restaurant, cocktail lounge, jacuzzi, solarium, plus much more.

Why chance where you stay for that well deserved golfing holiday/break. Gleneagles is a family run hotel which has a renowned reputation as one of the leading hotels in the West Country.

SPECIAL 10% DISCOUNT OFFERED TO ALL GOLFING GUESTS BOOKING VIA THIS GUIDE.

Reservations: (0803) 293637/297011

LUXURY CORNISH GOLFING HOTEL

Set in 65 acres of sub-tropical grounds, with beautifully laid out private golf course, championship all-weather tennis courts and fabulous indoor pool – this hotel offers superb facilities free to all guests.

Idyllically situated on the banks of the romantic Helford River, with private foreshore for boating, both the hotel and golf course enjoy delightful views.

All guest rooms offer style and comfort, and excellent standards of service combined with top class cuisine prepared and presented with care and originality make us confident of satisfying the most discerning guest.

We invite you to visit the hotel and enjoy the luxury of a peaceful, healthy holiday, in elegant surroundings.

BUDOCK VEAN
GOLF AND COUNTRY HOUSE HOTEL

MAWNAN SMITH FALMOUTH CORNWALL TR11 5LG TEL. (0326) 250288

'OU CONCENTRATE ON YOUR ROUND. WE'LL TAKE CARE OF THE REST.

With Ferndown's championship course right on your doorstep – and 14 other courses within easy reach – there's nowhere better for golfers to stay than the Dormy Hotel.
Reduced green fees on Ferndown's new course, luxury en-suite accommodation, special weekend rates and free use of our superb Leisure Club, with swimming pool, tennis and squash courts, gym, sauna, solarium, steam baths and snooker room. *Phone or write for further details.*

THE DORMY HOTEL
& LEISURE CLUB

DE VERE HOTELS   NEW ROAD, FERNDOWN, NR. BOURNEMOUTH DORSET BH22 8ES   TEL. (0202) 872121   AA ★ ★ ★ ★ RAC

The Manor House Hotel
Moretonhampstead, Devon TQ13 8RE.
Tel (0647) 40355
18 hole championship golf course with its
own Jacobean style country house hotel on
the edge of Dartmoor National Park. Par 3
course, under-cover driving bay. Professional
tuition available. Golf fully inclusive in room
rate. (See advertisement page 403 for further
details.)

Marstan Hotel
Meadfoot Sea Road, Torquay TQ1 2LQ.
Tel (0803) 292837
An elegant detached Victorian hotel, 4 Crown
ETB standard, near beach and conveniently
situated for golf courses. Bedrooms all en-suite,
direct dial telephones, coloured TV, outdoor
heated swimming pool, licensed bar. Special
rates for golfers.

Oxford Arms Hotel
Duke Street, Kington, Herefordshire.
Tel (0544) 230322
16th century coaching inn located one mile
from Kington golf course – highest course
in England and Wales. Challenging 18 hole
course. Ten other courses within a half hour
drive.

Pines Hotel
Burlington Road, Swanage, Dorset.
Tel (0929) 425211
50 bedroom family run three star hotel. All
bedrooms have private bathroom, telephone
and colour TV. One and a half miles from Isle
of Purbeck golf club. Within easy reach of all
Dorset courses.

St Brannocks House Hotel
St Brannocks Road, Ilfracombe EX34 8EQ.
Tel (0271) 63873
Friendly family run hotel. En-suite rooms.
Licensed bar. Large car park. TV/Tea making
in all rooms. Pets welcome. Open all year. From
£150 DB & B including 5 days golf. Reductions
for non-golfers, parties and societies.

St Mellion Hotel
St Mellion Golf & Country Club, St Mellion,
Saltash, Cornwall PL12 6SD.
Tel (0579) 50101
Modern hotel situated next to the St Mellion
complex. 24 rooms. AA and RAC***. Two golf
courses (the Nicklaus and the Old), indoor pool,
tennis, squash and badminton courts.

Trevose Golf and Country Club
Constantine Bay, Padstow, Cornwall PL28 8JB.
Tel (0841) 520208 *Fax* (0841) 521057
Located on the north coast of Cornwall Trevose
offers an idyllic golfing paradise. 18 and 9
hole courses. 3 tennis courts, swimming pool.
Self catering accommodation and restaurant.
Brochure on request.

White Hart Hotel
Broad Street, Launceston, Cornwall PL15 8AA.
Tel (0566) 2013
A very popular hotel amongst the golfing
fraternity, with the local course at Launceston
being one of the finest in the South West.
Golf packages, bargain breaks and conference
facilities.

England: South East

Ashdown Forest Hotel
Chapel Lane, Forest Row, East Sussex.
Tel (0342) 82 4866
Family owned and run hotel offering
comfortable accommodation and good food
and wines. Royal Ashdown Forest new course
operated by hotel exclusively for residents and
visitors.

Briggens House Hotel
Stanstead Road, Stanstead Abbotts, Ware,
Hertfordshire SG12 8LD.
Tel (027979) 2416
18th century stately house set in 45 acres
of Hertfordshire countryside. 54 superbly
appointed bedrooms are complemented by an
excellent restaurant. The golf course employs a
full time professional for tuition and coaching all
year round.

The Clarendon Hotel
Beach Street, Deal CT14 6HY.
Tel (0304) 374748
Family run seafront hotel offering traditional
English cooking and real ales. Entertainment
throughout year. Fishing and golfing outings
arranged. Bedrooms: 3 single, 4 double and
8 twin. Bed and breakfast £15.20 single, £30
double. (See advertisement page 403 for
further details.)

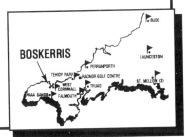

Cooden Resort Hotel
Cooden Beach, Bexhill-on-Sea, East Sussex TN39 4TT.
Tel (0424) 32281
Situated on the beach just 200 yards from mainline station and adjacent to golf club. Indoor health club, Sovereign bar, candlelit dinners in grill room. All rooms with bath/shower, TV, direct dial telephone. Ideal for conferences.

The Copthorne Effingham Park
Copthorne, West Sussex RH10 3EU.
Tel (0342) 714994
A newly built hotel set in 40 acres of parkland. Superb 4 Star facilities. Convenient location (M23 - 5 minutes). Parking. 122 rooms. Various restaurants and bars. Comprehensive sports and leisure centre. 9 hole golf course. Pro-shop.

The Cottage – Royal Eastbourne Golf Club
Paradise Drive, Eastbourne BN20 8BP
Tel (0323) 29738
The cottage is situated near the 1st tee of the long course. The accommodation consists of two twin-bedded rooms, lounge, kitchen and bathroom. Parking on the premises. From £300 per week including golf. (See advertisement page 403 for further information.)

Friendly Lodge Hotel
Monks Way, Two Mile Ash, Milton Keynes MK8 8LY.
Tel (0908) 561666
A 50 bedroom 3 Star hotel and restaurant overlooking Abbey Hill golf course, and just a short drive from Woburn. Excellent value weekend rates available on request.

Guildford House Hotel
49 Beach Street, Deal, Kent CT14 6HY.
Tel (0304) 375015
16th century privately run hotel situated on the promenade opposite pier. All rooms have showers, colour TV etc. Own private bar. Three championship golf courses close by. Group rates and green fee bookings.

Hendon Hall Hotel
Ashley Lane (off Parsons Street), Hendon, London NW4 1HF.
Tel 01-203 3341
Discover the comfort, warmth and hospitality of David Garrick's Country House! Whether it's a board meeting or a business lunch, a leisurely dinner in our pavilion restaurant or a stay in one of our fully equipped bedrooms.

Lansdowne Hotel
King Edward's Parade, Eastbourne, East Sussex BN21 4EE.
Tel (0323) 25174 *Fax* (0323) 39721
Play 36 holes a day on choice of six courses; we book your tee-off time. Two nights with green fees, light lunch at club and use of our drying room. 14 January to 31 March £97; 1 April to 31 May £100; 1 June to 31 August £105; 1 October to 29 December £105. Extra days pro rata. (See advertisement page 407 for further details.)

Lythe Hill Hotel
Petworth Road, Haslemere, Surrey GU27 3BQ.
Tel (0428) 51251
A luxurious, privately owned country hotel with two superb restaurants and beautifully appointed bedrooms and suites situated in 14 acres of parkland gardens in the Surrey hills. Tennis, sauna and croquet in the grounds and four excellent golf courses within 10 miles: Old Thorns, Hindhead, Liphook and Cowdray Park. Special weekend bargain breaks available.

Old Thorns Golf Course, Hotel and Restaurants
Old Thorns, Longmoor Road, Liphook, Hampshire GU30 7PE.
Tel (0428) 724555
Old Thorns is a rare combination of an 18 hole championship golf course. European and Japanese resturants, hotel and leisure centre set in 400 acres of magnificent Hampshire countryside.

Quinns Hotel
48 Sheen Road, Richmond, Surrey TW9 1AW.
Tel 01-940 5444
Very quiet and centrally located hotel close to many sporting venues. Standard and en-suite rooms available all with radio, intercom, colour television. Car parking in own grounds. Unbeatable rates available.

Selsdon Park Hotel
Sanderstead, Croydon, Surrey CR2 8YA.
Tel 01-657 8811 *Tx* 945003 *Fax* 01-651 6171
Traditional country house set in 200 acres of parkland with an 18 hole championship course. Green fee players welcome. Residents' exclusive tropical leisure complex. (See advertisement page 405 for further details.)

Channel Islands

Les Arches Hotel
Archirondel, Gorey, St Martin, Jersey.
Tel (0534) 53839 *Fax* (0534) 56660
Overlooking France. Private access to beach.
All rooms en-suite with TV. One and a half
miles from Royal Jersey golf club. Swimming
pool, garden, tennis court, putting green, golf
net, nightclub, sauna, mini-gym and bars.

England: East (East Anglia)

Abbotsley Golf & Squash Club
Eynesbury Hardwicke, St Neots,
Cambridgeshire.
Tel (0480) 215153
Cosy moated country house amidst picturesque
golf course. Beamed dining room with delightful
inglenook fireplace. All bedrooms en-suite.
Internationally renowned golf schools with
Vivien Saunders. Squash and golf range.
(See advertisement page 407 for further
details.)

Anglia Court Hotel
5 Runton Road, Cromer, Norfolk NR27 9AR.
Tel (0263) 512443
Golf at Royal Cromer and Sheringham courses.
Friendly 1 star hotel. En-suite rooms, excellent
cuisine. 2 – 5 day breaks arranged for golfers
by golfers. Special rates for party bookings.
Write or telephone NOW for details.

Barnham Broom Hotel
Golf & Leisure Centre, Honingham Road,
Barnham Broom, Norwich, Norfolk NR9 4DD.
Tel (060 545) 393 *Fax* (060 545) 8224
East Anglia's top Conference and Leisure
Centre lies in 250 acres of countryside. 52
fully equipped bedrooms include family rooms,
served by Flints Restaurant and sports snack
bar. 4 squash courts, snooker, heated indoor
swimming pool with spa jets, tennis and 36 hole
golf. Golfing Getaway £124. (See advertisement
page 409 for further details.)

The Blakeney Hotel
Blakeney, Nr Holt, Norfolk NR25 7NE.
Tel (0263) 740797
Situated near the coastal golf courses at
Sheringham, Brancaster and Hunstanton.
Overlooking National Trust harbour, traditional
privately owned friendly hotel with 50 en-suite
bedrooms. Enjoy good fresh food and the
heated indoor pool. Midweek and Weekend
breaks. (See advertisement page 411 for further
details.)

Burlington Hotel
The Esplanade, Sheringham, Norfolk NR26 8LJ
Tel (0263) 822224
The hotel that really overlooks the sea.
Sheringham golf course 4 minutes away.
Cromer golf club 4 miles away. Our friendly
staff and elegant surroundings will help you to
relax during your stay with us. For the more
discerning, real ales are served in our bar.

Hintlesham Hall
Hintlesham, Ipswich, Suffolk IP8 3NS.
Tel (047 387) 671
Luxurious 16th century country hotel set in its
own park. Offering superb hospitality, food and
accommodation. 18 hole championship length
golf course, designed by Hawtree & Son,
opening Autumn 1990. AA 3 Red Stars, RAC
Blue Ribbon. (See advertisement page 411 for
further details.)

The Imperial Hotel
North Drive, Great Yarmouth, Norfolk
NR30 1EQ.
Tel (0493) 851113 *Fax* (0493) 852229
Comfortable surroundings, friendly service and
superb food is "Par for the Course" at the
Imperial. A family run hotel of the highest
standard. Golf inclusive holidays are played
at the Great Yarmouth and Caistor course.

King's Head Hotel
Norwich Street, Dereham, Norfolk NR19 1AB.
Tel (0362) 693342 *Fax* (0362) 693776
A modernised 17th century hotel within easy
reach of Norwich. The restaurant offers a full
a la carte and table d'hote menu. Amenities
available include grass tennis court and an
outdoor bowling green.

Le Strange Arms Hotel
Golf Course Road, Old Hunstanton, Norfolk PE36 6JJ.
Tel (04853) 34411
Three star country house hotel with lawns sweeping down to the beach. 28 bedrooms with private facilities. Snooker room and themed pub. An ideal base for Hunstanton, Royal West Norfolk and King's Lynn golf courses.

The Links Country Park Hotel & Golf Club
West Runton, Cromer, Norfolk NR27 9QH.
Tel (0263) 75691 *Fax* (0263) 758264
The hotel is privately owned and run; situated in 35 acres of its own grounds. Superb 9 hole golf course, with tight hilly fairways and tricky greens. Other leisure facilities are a large heated indoor swimming pool, tennis court, sauna and solarium. (All leisure facilities FREE to residents.) The renowned golf courses of Sheringham, Cromer and Hunstanton are nearby, making the 'Links' an ideal base. (See advertisement page 407 for further details.)

Thorpeness Golf Club Hotel
Thorpeness, Near Leiston, Suffolk IP16 4NH.
Tel (0728) 452176
Modern luxury hotel adjoining the clubhouse on one of East Anglia's finest 18 hole courses. Situated on the lovely, unspoiled Suffolk coast. Ideal too for non-golfers. (See advertisement page 411 for further details.)

White Horse Hotel
Station Road, Leiston, Suffolk IP16 4HD.
Tel (0728) 830694 *Fax* (0728) 833105
Close to three excellent courses, in the heart of Suffolk heritage coast. Friendly bars, excellent food, 12 rooms (6 en-suite) all with TV and telephone. Bargain weekend breaks all year.

England: Midlands

Broomhill Hotel
Holdenby Road, Spratton, Northampton NN6 8LD.
Tel (0604) 84595
A privately owned 3 star country house hotel offering high standard cuisine and 13 superb en-suite bedrooms. Five miles from Northampton, 3 miles from Northamptonshire County golf course. Fully licensed.

Castle Hotel
Ladybank, Tamworth, Staffordshire B79 7NB.
Tel (0827) 57181
Lying in the shadows of historic Tamworth Castle in the centre of this ancient town. Located in the Midlands with easy access to A5, M42 and access to M6 and M5. 5 miles from Belfry Golf Centre.

The Dower House Hotel
The Manor Estate, Woodhall Spa, Lincs LN10 6PY.
Tel (0526) 52588
Situated in its own grounds. Adjacent to Woodhall Spa golf course and town centre. Ideal for individual golfers and small societies.

George Hotel
Bird Street, Lichfield, Staffs WS13 6PR.
Tel (0543) 414822
38 en-suite bedrooms with colour TV, radio, telephone, tea and coffee making facilities. Old coaching inn set in Dr Johnson's historic city. Less than 15 minutes from the Belfry championship course.

The Grange and Links Hotel
Sea Lane, Sandilands, Sutton-on-Sea, Lincolnshire.
Tel (0521) 41334
Grade A 30 bedroom hotel with own 18 hole links course. Two tennis courts, snooker room, ballroom. Renowned for good food, friendliness, comfort and service. Within easy reach are Seacroft and Woodhall Spa golf clubs.

The Greenway
Shurdington, Cheltenham, Gloucestershire GL51 5UG.
Tel (0242) 862352 *Tx* 437216 *Fax* (0242) 862780
16th century country house hotel set in formal gardens and surrounded by hundreds of acres of parkland. Convenient for Lilley Brook, Cotswold Hills, Cirencester and Broadway golf clubs.

Hawkstone Park
Weston-Under-Redcastle, Shrewsbury, Shropshire SY4 5UY.
Tel (093924) 611 *Fax* (093924) 311
Where Sandy Lyle learned his game. Two 18 hole parkland golf courses. Hawkstone 6465 yds surrounded by hills and antiquities, and Weston 5368 yds. Busy 3 Star hotel with 59 rooms all en-suite. Located 14 miles north of Shrewsbury on A49. It is advisable to book tee times in advance. Open all year to non-residents.

Courses to choose from!

Hollies Hotel
Chester Road, Whitchurch, Shropshire
SY13 1LZ.
Tel (0948) 2184
Play Hill Valley, Hawkstone Park, Market
Drayton. All tee times in advance. All rooms
en-suite, tea/coffee making and colour TV. Bed,
breakfast, dinner – Golf, from £40.

The Limes Country House Hotel
Gainsborough Road, Market Rasen,
Lincolnshire LN8 3JW.
Tel (0673) 842357 *Fax* (0673) 844540
This Victorian country house, set in three acres
of pleasant tree-lined gardens on the edge of
the Wolds, offers 17 en-suite fully equipped
bedrooms. As well as the Limes Restaurant and
two bars overlooking the gardens, the hotel also
incorporates a squash club.

The Olde School and Manor Hotel
Church Street, Bloxham, Nr Banbury, Oxon
OX15 4ET.
Tel (0295) 720369
Old style country hotel near museum,
thatched cottages, open countryside. 40
bedrooms with facilities, ironing boards,
hairdryers. Six conference rooms, games
room, art studio for art weekend, open
fires.

Sutton Court Hotel
60-66 Lichfield Road, Sutton Coldfield,
West Midlands B74 2NA.
Tel (021) 355 6071
Privately owned 3 Star hotel, 64 individually
designed bedrooms and Courtyard Restaurant
enjoying a fine reputation for international
cuisine. 8 golf courses within 15 minutes drive,
including Belfry Ryder Cup course.

Telford Hotel Golf and Country Club
Great Hay, Sutton Hill,
Telford, Shropshire TF7 4DT.
Tel (0952) 585642
Overlooking the Ironbridge Gorge and
encompassed by its own 9 and 18 hole
golf courses, this hotel offers comfort and
style in addition to extensive leisure facilities
featuring swimming, snooker and squash. (See
advertisement page 413 for further details.)

Terrick Hall Country Hotel
Hill Valley, Whitchurch, Shropshire
SY13 4JZ.
Tel (0948) 3031/3020
Surrounded by the Hill Valley golf courses.
Prime tee times each day for residents. First
class accommodation, all 22 rooms en-suite,
excellent restaurant and bar. Tennis, snooker
and squash.

Tewkesbury Park Hotel Golf and Country Club
Lincoln Green Lane, Tewkesbury,
Gloucestershire GL20 7DN.
Tel (0684) 295405
This 82 bedroom hotel with modern facilities
is surrounded by its own 18 hole course. It
also offers heated indoor pool, sauna, whirlpool,
steam room, multi-gym, snooker, squash and
all-weather tennis courts.

Welcombe Hotel and Golf Course
Warwick Road, Stratford-upon-Avon,
Warwickshire CV37 0NR.
Tel (0789) 295252
A 4 Star Jacobean-style mansion set within its
own 6,202 yards private golf course. A newly
created clubhouse and pro's shop within the
hotel's 157 acres enhances the parkland course.

England: North

Alma Lodge
149 Buxton Road, Stockport, Greater
Manchester.
Tel (061) 483 4431
Located on the southern edge of Stockport,
within easy access to M63, M56, M6 and M62.
58 bedrooms with 1 suite, all rooms have radio,
colour TV, direct dial telephone, hairdryer, tea
and coffee making facilities, etc. Extensive car
park. 7 miles from Manchester Airport.

Appleby Manor Country House Hotel
Roman Road, Appleby-in-Westmorland,
Cumbria CA16 6JD.
Tel (07683) 51571
Swim, Bubble and Golf! Enjoy your par 68 on
Appleby's 18 moorland holes (5895 yds), then
return to your favourite country house hotel for
a refreshing swim and a relaxing jacuzzi in
the indoor leisure club. Mouth-watering meals,
too! (See advertisement page 415 for further
details.)

BARNHAM BROOM
▪ HOTEL ▪ GOLF ▪ LEISURE ▪

Discover the world of recreation offered to you by Barnham Broom Hotel, amid 250 acres of delightful Norfolk countryside in our river valley setting. Spend time with us and take your pleasure in luxurious surroundings.

The hotel and leisure facilities were purpose designed with you in mind and appeal equally to holiday makers and the business community alike.

The beautifully appointed hotel looks out over two magnificent 18 hole golf courses with a par 72. This valley setting is maintained in top condition by experienced staff who liaise with golfing professionals to create a challenging course; and for beginners, special practice holes and putting green areas are available.

The jewel in the crown of the Leisure Centre is the splendid new swimming pool with its sparkling jet stream and spa pool. Swimmers can test their technique while friends relax in the shallow spa or nearby sauna.

Guests can try the steam room or in the same complex a fully equipped gymnasium is run by well trained professionals. Other purpose designed on-site amenities include squash and tennis courts with top class coaches giving regular lessons.

Barnham Broom Hotel,
Conference and Leisure Centre
Barnham Broom, Norwich NR9 4DD

Telephone: (060 545) 393/6
Telex: 975711 Fax: (060 545) 8224

Peter Ballingall
Golf Schools. 1990

The early season Schools fill really quickly........ BOOK EARLY to avoid disappointment

Each year he runs more schools. Each year they are fully subscribed. At least 30 % of each year's places are taken up by clients returning a second or more times to attend one of his special schools for Former Pupils.

Why? Because being one of the premier teachers in the game, he has the rare ability to bring out the best in his pupils, to remove their confusions and give them a much clearer understanding of what is required.

His sound knowledge, infinite patience and total commitment will ensure that you will also leave with a healthier self image and a firm belief that you can, and will, play BETTER GOLF, NATURALLY.

Classes are restricted to a maximum of 12 per school (3, 4 or 5 Day) so it matters not whether you have a Single Figure Handicap or are an absolute novice.

You will enjoy his "Golf School Experience" and leave with happy memories of a time well spent in the company of others of like mind and outlook.....as hundreds of others have done.

Peter Ballingall is on the Teaching Panel of Golf Monthly.

Please send me your 1990 Peter Ballingall Golf School Brochure

Name _____

Address _____

_____

Peter Ballingall Golf Schools
Barnham Broom Hotel & Country Club
Norwich, Norfolk NR9 4DD
or Telephone No. (STD 060545 741 - 24 hour service)

The Bold Hotel
Lord Street, Southport PR9 0BE.
Tel (0704) 32578/38497
Situated centrally on one of the most beautiful
boulevards in Britain. Surrounded by some of
the best golfing courses in Britain. There
are also superb shops, parks and historical
monuments.

Brabyns Hotel
Shaftesbury Avenue, Blackpool, Lancs
FY2 9QQ.
Tel (0253) 54263
Two star hotel – open all year. Appointed
to high standard. Restaurant offers excellent
and varied menus – vegetarian dishes. Choice
of golf courses including Royal Lytham. Easy
access from M55 – car park. Near Blackpool
North Shore.

Dane Lodge Hotel
92/94 Northenden Road, Sale, Cheshire
M33 3HB.
Tel (061) 973 6666 *Tx* 635091 DANLO
Fax (061) 905 2446
A family run hotel giving a warm, friendly
atmosphere. All bedrooms are en-suite having
colour TV, telephone and coffee/tea making
facilities. All sports are well catered for in the
area with golf at the fore. Manchester Airport
is 10 minutes away.

Devonport Hotel
Middleton-One-Row, Darlington, Co Durham.
Tel (0325) 332255
A friendly family run hotel with sixteen
comfortable bedrooms, all with private facilities,
and good food. Four 18 hole courses within
five minutes with a further 12 inland and links
courses within thirty minutes' drive.

The Dormy, Lancaster Golf & Country Club Ltd
Ashton Hall, Ashton-with-Stodday, Lancaster
LA2 0AJ.
Tel (0524) 751247
Ideal for small parties of up to 18 persons.
For terms and reservations please apply to
the secretary. (See advertisement page 399
for further details.)

The Dormy House
Royal Lytham & St Anne's Golf Club, Links
Gate, Lytham St Anne's, Lancashire FY8 3LQ.
Tel (0253) 724206
Ideal for small parties wishing to play
the championship course. Accommodation
for men only. Apply to the secretary.
(See advertisement page 413 for further
details.)

Downe Arms
Wykeham, Scarborough, North Yorkshire
YO13 9QB.
Tel (0723) 862471
Situated on A170, 6 miles from Ganton and
Scarborough. Rooms en-suite, colour TV and
tea making facilities. Bars and restaurant. Ring
Philip Mort for reservations.

Esplanade Hotel
Belmont Road, Scarborough YO11 2AA.
Tel (0723) 360382
Superbly appointed in a warmly welcoming
period style in keeping with its origins, the
Esplanade Hotel is situated in a commanding
position on Scarborough's south cliff, convenient
for several golf clubs including Ganton
championship course. (See advertisement page
413 for further details.)

The Grand Crest Hotel
South Promenade, St Annes on Sea, Lancashire
FY8 1NB.
Tel (0253) 721288 *Tx* 67481
Fax (0253) 714459
A beautiful Edwardian hotel overlooking the sea
front, with 40 individual comfortable bedrooms
including 4 suites, 2 Spa bathrooms and sea
view rooms. Elegant restaurant and cocktail bar
and informal grand lounge. Within a stroke from
Royal Lytham Golf Links. (See advertisement
page 413 for further details.)

Harewood Arms Hotel
Harrogate Road, Harewood, Nr Leeds,
West Yorkshire LS17 9LH.
Tel (0532) 886566 *Fax* (0532) 886064
Ideally located for businessmen and tourists.
Seven miles from the commercial centre of
Leeds and seven miles from the Spa town of
Harrogate. The hotel is conveniently situated
for discovering the charm of the Yorkshire Dales,
with an abundance of things to see and do. (See
advertisement page 417 for further details.)

Leasowe Castle Hotel
Moreton, Wirral.
Tel (051) 606 9191
All bedrooms have bath/shower, colour television, trouser press, hairdryer. There are 12 golf courses in the area. Special golf break tariff. Sea fishing. (See advertisement page 415 for further details.)

Metropole Hotel
3 Portland Street, Southport, Merseyside PR8 1LL.
Tel (0704) 36836
RAC/AA** hotel situated within 5 minutes of Royal Birkdale. Fully licensed, full size snooker table, private facilities, special golf terms. Golfing proprietors can assist with golf bookings. Colour brochure on request.

Motel Leeming
Bedale, North Yorkshire DL9 1DT.
Tel (0677) 23611
Modern family run hotel in the middle of North Yorkshire. Four courses within 20 minutes. Special packages at sensible prices. Clean rooms, good cooking and laundry service.

Prince of Wales
Lord Street, Southport PR8 1JS.
Tel (0704) 36688
Less than an hour's drive from twelve top class golf courses. 98 bedrooms, 6 suites, 2 restaurants and famous clubhouse bar. The hotel offers an ideal venue for golfing parties from 2 to 100 or more. (See advertisement page 429 for further details.)

Shaw Hill Hotel Golf and Country Club
Preston Road, Whittle-Le-Woods, Chorley, Lancashire PR6 7PP.
Tel (02572) 69221
RAC and AA 3 Star hotel golf and country club. A la carte restaurant. 22 bedrooms, all en-suite, overlooking an 18 hole golf course. Special mini break rates available. (See advertisement page 415 for further details.)

Shrigley Hall Hotel Golf & Country Club
Shrigley Park, Pott Shrigley, Nr Macclesfield, Cheshire SK10 5SB.
Tel (0625) 575757
Four Star country house on the edge of the Peak District, with magnificent views over the 18 hole course to the Cheshire plain below. Adjoining leisure club has swimming pool, squash, snooker, tennis, steam, sauna and solaria.

The Sunningdale Private Hotel
21/22 Lucker Road, Bamburgh, Northumberland NE69 7AX.
Tel (06684) 334
A friendly family run hotel close to all local amenities. 19 bedrooms, some en-suite. All rooms have central heating and tea and coffee making facilities. Resident cocktail lounge adjoining snooker/games room and two comfortable lounges. Open all year.

Washington Moat House Hotel
Stone Cellar Road, Washington, Tyne and Wear NE37 1PH.
Tel (091) 417 2626
Everything for the golfer, championship 18 hole course, 9 hole par 3, floodlit driving range and well stocked pro shop. Hotel accommodation offers superbly appointed bedrooms, restaurant and bars. Snooker, squash and leisure centre with pool.

The Wensleydale Heifer
West Witton, Wensleydale, North Yorkshire DL8 4LS.
Tel (0969) 22322
A 17th century Dales inn with 19 en suite bedrooms, restaurant and bistro. Ideally placed for Catterick, Richmond and Bedale courses. Golfing breaks a speciality. A Consort Hotel. AA/RAC 2 Star. (See advertisement page 415 for further details.)

Isle of Man

Castletown Golf Links Hotel
Derbyhaven, Castletown, Isle of Man.
Tel (0624) 822201
Situated on our own peninsula, our championship golf course of 6,700 yards, with all holes having sea views, is a real test of links golf. The hotel facilities are of a luxurious 3 star standard.

Wales: North

The Beach Hotel
Trearddur Bay, Isle of Anglesey, Gwynedd, North Wales.
Tel (0407) 860332
Play golf on Britain's Treasure Island, three superb golf courses. Championship and links. Most comprehensive prestige hotel and leisure complex in North Wales. Facilities include: sauna, swim spa, jacuzzi, sun beds, fitness room, squash and snooker. (See advertisement page 417 for further details.)

Bryn Morfydd Hotel
Llanrhaeadr, Nr Denbigh, Clwyd LL16 4NP.
Tel (074578) 280
Country house hotel nestling on the hillside overlooking the Vale of Clwyd and the Clwydian range beyond. Residents enjoy free use of our 9 hole course. There are three 18 hole courses within a ten mile radius. (See advertisement page 417 for further details.)

Hotel 70°
Penmaenhead, Old Colwyn, Colwyn Bay, Clwyd.
Tel (0492) 516555
Luxury modern hotel situated on the cliff tops with breathtaking views. Each of the 44 bedrooms has every modern facility. Superb award winning restaurant. (See advertisement page 417 for further details.)

Linksway Hotel
Morfa Nefyn, Gwynedd, North Wales LL53 6BG.
Tel (0758) 720258
Adjacent to the golf course and the beach, this very popular hotel has 26 bedrooms all en-suite with radio and colour TV. Welcoming bar, friendly staff and good food. We can offer all year round golf. (See advertisement page 419 for further details.)

The Marine Hotel
The Promenade, Llandudno, Gwynedd LL30 1AN.
Tel (0492) 77521
Imposing 82 bedroom hotel on seafront of delightful Victorian resort. The three competition 18 hole courses in close proximity to the hotel are Maesdu, North Wales and Conwy, all offering excellent standards for the discerning golfer.

The Royal Sportsman
High Street, Porthmadoc, Gwynedd.
Tel (0766) 512015
Situated near the picturesque Llyn Peninsula. The hotel offers 20 bedrooms of very high standard throughout. Porthmadoc, Nefyn, Criccieth and Pwllheli 18 hole competition courses of excellent standard are in close proximity.

St George's Hotel
The Promenade, Llandudno, Gwynedd LL30 2LG.
Tel (0492) 77544
87 bedrooms with satellite TV systems. The hotel facilities include a la carte restaurant, coffee shop, residents bar, sports bar and Shape health and beauty salon. Local attractions: Dry ski slope, Snowdonia National Park and historic castles.

Trearddur Bay Hotel
Trearddur Bay, Holyhead, Anglesey.
Tel (0407) 860 301
Excellent facilities at this prestigious three star establishment including an indoor heated swimming pool. Four golf courses within 20 miles radius. Holyhead course one mile away. Ideally situated for watersports and country pursuits. Open all year.

Trefeddian Hotel
Aberdovey, Gwynedd, Wales LL35 0SB.
Tel (065 472) 213
Three Star hotel with 46 rooms all with bath or shower en-suite, central heating, telephone and colour TV. Indoor pool, putting green, tennis court, games room. Overlooks the golf links and sea. Golfers' tariff and brochure sent on request.

The Westminster Hotel
East Parade, Rhyl, Clwyd.
Tel (0745) 342241
Health and leisure club. Excellent reputable night club. Located on the seafront. 57 bedrooms. In close proximity to Rhyl, Rhuddlan, Prestatyn and Abergele 18 hole golf courses and Kinmel Bay driving range.

Wales: Central

Belle Vue Royal Hotel
The Promenade, Aberystwyth, Dyfed.
Tel (0970) 617558
Situated on the seafront overlooking Cardigan
Bay. Free golf at Aberystwyth golf club
(Monday to Friday) available to residents,
half green fees at weekends. Getaway breaks
available for individuals or parties.

Bodfor Hotel
Sea Front, Aberdovey, Gwynedd, Wales.
Tel (0654 72) 475 *Fax* (0654 72) 679
Most rooms en-suite with sea view overlooking
Dovey Estuary. All rooms have television,
telephone, tea making facilities. Residential
and restaurant licence. Excellent restaurant
offering table d'hote and a la carte menus. Car
park and beach opposite. Golf parties welcome
(concessionary green fees). (See advertisement
page 419 for further details.)

Wales: South

The Cawdor Arms Hotel
Llandeilo, Dyfed, S W Wales SA19 6EN.
Tel (0558) 823500
Original 18th century coaching inn set
in beautiful Vale of Towy. Individually
furnished bedrooms all en-suite, excellent and
imaginative food. Ashburnham championship
golf course within short distance, Glenhir
close by. Fishing and shooting available.
AA*** RAC***

Fairways Hotel
Seafront, Porthcawl CF36 3LS.
Tel (0656) 2085
A recently renovated, privately owned hotel,
overlooking the Bristol Channel. Situated five
minutes from the M4. 28 bedrooms, many with
bathroom and shower en-suite. Three 18 hole
golf courses, the Royal Porthcawl, Pyle and
Kenfig and Southerndown all within a few
minutes' drive. Table d'hote and full a la carte
menu. (See advertisement page 419 for further
information.)

Heronston Hotel
Ewenny, Bridgend, Mid-Glamorgan CF35 5AW.
Tel (0656) 68811
4 miles off M4. Three championship courses
within 3 miles of hotel. Indoor and outdoor
heated swimming pools with sauna, steam room,
solarium and jacuzzi. Transport can be arranged
to various activities. Special terms for weekend
breaks. (See advertisement page 419 for further
details.)

Hotel Marinera
Mariners Square, Haverfordwest,
Pembrokeshire SA61 2DU
Tel (0437) 763353
17th century hotel situated in quiet town
centre. All rooms have colour television and
are en-suite. Fully licensed with bar lunches
and dinner. 2 miles to golf course. Own car
park. Special weekend rates.

St Pierre Hotel Golf & Country Club
Chepstow, Gwent NP6 6YA
Tel (0291) 625261
14th century mansion house, comprising 148
bedrooms, en-suite facilities and leisure club
including swimming pool, squash, badminton,
tennis, snooker, spa bath, sauna, steam room,
gymnasium, health and beauty salon, and crown
green bowling with restaurants and bars.

Scotland: West

Abbotsford Hotel
Corsehill Road, Ayr.
Tel (0292) 261506
"Open golf country": Royal Troon, Old Prestwick,
Turnberry. Adjacent to Belleisle and Seafield
golf courses, all rooms en-suite, colour TV and
tea makers. We will undertake all golf bookings
and arrange a package that will suit all grades
of golfer. Dinner, bed and breakfast from £33.
Society Rates. Contact Allan Hunter.

Ardlochan Hotel
Maidens Culzean, Near Maybole, Ayrshire
KA19 8LA.
Tel (06556) 254
The hotel and caravan site is situated next to
the beach. It has 4 double rooms with toilet and
shower en-suite. There are also self catering,
furnished chalets and touring pitches available.
5 minutes to Culzean country park, 2 miles from
Turnberry golf course.

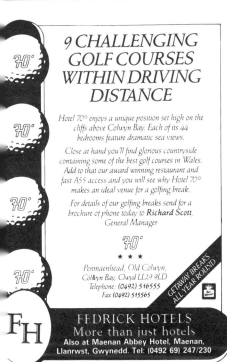

The Ardshiel Hotel
Kilkerran Road, Campbeltown, Argyll.
Tel (0586) 52133
A comfortable small hotel within easy reach
of golf course and airport. Golfing packages
available.

Beechwood Country House Hotel
Harthope Place, Moffat, Dumfriesshire
DG10 9RS.
Tel (0683) 20210
Situated in a delightful garden overlooking
Moffat and the Upper Annan Valley which
is renowned for fishing and walking. Golf,
tennis and riding available nearby. Excellent
restaurant and wine list.

Buccleuch and Queensberry Hotel
Drumlanrig Street, Thornhill, Dumfriesshire
DG3 5LU.
Tel (0848) 30215
A warm and friendly hotel. Thornhill golf
course close by - SSS 70 6124 yds. Other
courses within driving distance. Salmon and
trout fishing also available. 12 rooms, 9 en-suite.
Car parking. Highly recommended. AA/RAC
listed. (See advertisement page 421 for further
details.)

Buchanan Highland Hotel
Main Street, Drymen by Lochlomond,
Stirlingshire G63 0BQ.
Tel (0360) 60588
Hotel situated short drive from Glasgow and
Stirling in country village. Facilities include
leisure centre, bowling green. Golf at Buchanan
Castle, Strathendrick, Hiltonpark and Aberfoyle,
along with clay pigeon shooting and salmon
fishing which can be arranged.

Clonyard House Hotel
Colvend, Dalbeattie, Kirkshire DG5 4QW.
Tel (055) 663 372
Family run country hotel in quiet grounds.
Excellent restaurant, also informal meals in
our lively bar. Ground floor rooms with
facilities including direct dial telephones. Four
golf courses within a 10 mile radius.

The Fernhill Golf Hotel
Heugh Road, Portpatrick, Nr Stranraer
DG9 8TD.
Tel (077 681) 220
Golf package holidays available throughout
the year in this 3 Star AA and RAC hotel.
Golf at the scenic Portpatrick club and
championship Stranraer. Send for illustrated
coloured brochure.

Hospitality Inn
46 Annick Road, Irvine, Ayrshire KA11 4LD.
Tel (0294) 74272
Built around a temperature-controlled Hawaiian
lagoon. this modern hotel offers excellent
cuisine in surroundings resembling Tangiers
in the 30's. Our own 9 hole golf course, putting
green and driving range are currently under
construction.

Kinloch Hotel
Blackwaterfoot, Isle of Arran.
Tel (077086) 444
Beside the world's only 12 hole golf course.
Breathtaking test of links skill. Six other courses
nearby. Swimming pool, tennis, sauna, squash
court, solarium. Full en-suite facilities. Special
golfers' rates.

Kirkton Jean's Hotel
47 Main Street, Kirkoswald, Ayrshire.
Tel (06556) 220
Play golf at the famous Turnberry golf
course, or any of twenty superb golf courses
including Royal Troon, Prestwick and five Open
qualifying courses all within 35 minutes. Or visit
Culzean Castle and National Park which is
nearby. This 18th century coaching inn situated
in the heart of the Burns country, offers 9 twin
rooms with en-suite showers, colour TV and tea
and coffee making facilities.

Kirroughtree Hotel
Newton Stewart, Galloway, SW Scotland
DG8 6AN.
Tel (0671) 2141
Unlimited free golf at 2 courses including a
championship course. Luxurious country house
hotel with finest French cuisine provided by
our top continental trained chefs. Please send
for details. AA 4 Star RAC. (See advertisement
page 421 for further details.)

Malin Court
Turnberry, Ayrshire KA26 9PB.
Tel (0655) 31457
Malin Court has recently undergone extensive
refurbishment. You may dine in our beautiful
restaurant with its breathtaking views of the
mystical Isle of Arran. All our bedrooms have
private en-suite bathrooms and exquisite sea
views. (See advertisement page 423 for further
details.)

LINKSWAY

A.A. ** **HOTEL** R.A.C. **

Two minutes from Morfa Nefyn beach the Linkway is a modern spacious 26 bedroom hotel. The restaurant offers varied and interesting menus served by friendly experienced staff. Week and Mini Golf breaks on our 18 hole course is available and tuition can be arranged with our Golf pro, John Pilkington. Five other challenging courses within a short drive.

*Morfa Nefyn,
Gwynedd, North Wales*

*Tel: Reception: Nefyn 0758 720-258
Visitors: Nefyn 0758 720-392*

RAC ACCLAIMED

Wales Tourist Board

SEA FRONT ABERDOVEY GWYNEDD LL35 0EA

Tel: (065472) 475 & 314 • Fax: (065472) 679

Most rooms en-suite with sea view over looking Dovey Estuary. *All rooms have television, telephone, Tea making facilities. *Residential & Restaurant Licence. *Excellent Restaurant offering Table D'Hote and A la Carte menus. *Car park and Beach opposite. *Golf parties welcome (Concessionary Green Fees).

Fairways

FAIRWAYS HOTEL

Seafront · Porthcawl · Mid Glamorgan
Telephone: (0656) 2085/3544

A recently renovated, privately owned Hotel, overlooking the Bristol Channel. Situated just five minutes off the M4, Junction 27. 28 bedrooms, many with bathroom or shower en-suite. Three 18 hole Golf Courses, the Royal Porthcawl, Pyle & Kenfig, and Southerndown are all within a few minutes' drive. Table d'hote and full a la carte Menu always available.

Please write or telephone for more information.

The Heronston Hotel
Bridgend Mid-Glamorgan

Luxury Hotel with 76 Superb Suites
Situated 4 miles off the M4

Three Golf Championship Courses within 3 miles of hotel

Indoor and Outdoor Heated Swimming Pool with Sauna, Steam Room, Solarium and Jacuzzi

Transportation can be arranged to various activities

Special Terms for Weekend Breaks

The Hotel with the Personal Touch

The HERONSTON HOTEL
Ewenny, Bridgend, Mid-Glamorgan.
Tel 0656 68811 Telex 498232 Fax 0656 767391

The Marine Highland Hotel
Troon, Ayrshire KA10 6HE.
Tel (0292) 314444
Magnificent 4 Star hotel overlooking 18th
fairway of Royal Troon championship course. It
comprises 72 bedrooms and suites, leisure and
sports club, conference and banqueting centre,
two restaurants and three bars.

North West Castle Hotel
Seafront, Stranraer, South West Scotland
DG9 8EH.
Tel (0776) 4413
This 4 Star hotel offers free golf midweek
at Stranraer golf club. Facilities include indoor
swimming pool and well equipped games room.
Weekly terms from £210 DBB. Taste of Scotland
Town Hotel of the Year 1989.

Portpatrick Hotel
Portpatrick, Nr Stranraer, Wigtownshire,
Scotland DG9 8TA.
Tel (077 681) 333
This majestic hotel commands one of the
most spectacular sea views in Britain. Three
excellent golf courses including Portpatrick
where special golf package offers free
week-day golf. Dinner B & B from £85
(except July and August).

Turnberry Hotel and Golf Courses
Turnberry, Ayrshire KA26 9LT.
Tel (0655) 31000 *Tx* 777779 *Fax* (0655)
31706
Situated overlooking Scotland's South West
Ayrshire coast. Within its 360 acres are a luxury
hotel, golf and leisure resort with few equals in
the world.

Scotland: East

Alton Burn Hotel
Alton Burn Road, Nairn IV12 5ND.
Tel (0667) 52051
Superb family run hotel overlooking Nairn golf
course, with many courses a short drive away.
All 27 bedrooms – private facilities, teamakers,
TV's. Special rates for golfing parties. We can
arrange tee times etc. for you.

Angus Thistle Hotel
101 Marketgait, Dundee DD1 1QU.
Tel (0382) 26874
The Angus Thistle is a modern four star hotel in
the centre of Dundee and is particularly handy
for the superb golf courses at Carnoustie and St
Andrews. It has 58 bedrooms including three
luxury suites with jacuzzi. All rooms have colour
TV, trouser press, hairdryer, tea and coffee
making facilities, etc.

Balcraig House Hotel
By Scone, Perth PH2 7PG.
Tel (0738) 51123 *Fax* (0738) 33449
Country house hotel with luxury accommo-
dation, in parkland setting. We are in close
proximity to all major courses in the area,
including Gleneagles, Carnoustie, St Andrews,
Blairgowrie and others. Special group rates
on request. Assistance with itinerary. Contact
Derek MacKintosh.

Balgeddie House Hotel
Balgeddie Way, Glenrothes KY6 3ET.
Tel (0592) 742511 *Fax* (0592) 621702
Beautifully situated in immaculate gardens
with panoramic view over Glenrothes. All
bedrooms have private bathrooms, satellite
TV, radio, telephone, tea making facilities.
Elegant cocktail bar/restaurant – table d'hote/a
la carte menus. Golf packages arranged. AA***
RAC*** STB 4 Crowns.

The Bein Inn Hotel
Glenfarg, Perthshire PH2 9PY.
Tel (057) 73216
Excellent facilities in beautiful surroundings.
8 miles from Perth and within 30 minutes of
Carnoustie, Gleneagles, St Andrews, Downfield
and Ladybank. (See advertisement page 425
for further details.)

Clarendon Hotel
18-24 Grosvenor Street, Edinburgh EH12 5EG.
Tel (031) 337 7033
The Clarendon Hotel is situated at the west end
of Edinburgh within easy access to the Forth
Bridge and St Andrews to the east, and M9
motorway to Gleneagles in the central region.

The Buccleuch & Queensberry Hotel Thornhill, Dumfriesshire. DG3 5LU (0848) 30215
* Thornhill golf course close by, SSS 70 6124 yds.
* Other courses within driving distance, Dumfries, Powfoot, Southern Ness
* Salmon and Trout fishing also available
* 12 rooms, 9 en-suite
* Car parking
* Highly recommended
* AA/RAC listed

A warm and friendly hotel

Come Golfing in Scotland
Play Gullane Muirfield and North Berwick

and stay at the

MARINE HOTEL
Cromwell Road, North Berwick,
East Lothian EH39 4LZ Telephone (0620) 2406

***Awarded:* 1985 International Trophy to Tourist and Hotel Industry as the most outstanding hotel**

KIRROUGHTREE HOTEL
Newton Stewart, Galloway SW Scotland
Tel. 0671-2141
AA ★ ★ ★ ★ RAC Ashley Courtney
Egon Ronay Grade 1   Good Food Guide
Scottish Tourist Board ⠶⠶⠶⠶
Commended

LUXURY AND FINEST CUISINE—PLUS FREE GOLF AT 2 COURSES

Recognised as one of Britain's most delightful and peaceful Country House Hotels, bedrooms are exquisitely furnished in every detail. Coloured bathroom suites, colour TV etc., 4 honeymoon/wedding anniversary suites. Two beautiful dining rooms – one for non-smokers – and elegant public rooms with period furnishings.

Finest French Cuisine by continent trained chefs.

An excellent centre for trout and salmon fishing, shooting and deer stalking.

For garden lovers 8 acres of landscaped gardens with beautiful views, putting, croquet and tennis. One of the mildest climates in Britain because of the gulf-stream. You will be accorded attentive service in a very friendly and relaxing atmosphere.

Please send for full details.

Clifton House

Nairn, Scotland IV12 4HW.
Tel (0667) 53119 *Fax* (0667) 52836
Having been 'home' to the owner for fifty nine
years, Clifton has a high standard to maintain
and welcomes all those who appreciate good
food and wines. It is small, elegant, charming
and very personal. (See advertisement page
429 for further details.)

Craigard Country House Hotel

Kinchurdy Road, Boat of Garten,
Inverness-shire.
Tel (047 983) 206
Situated overlooking Boat of Garten golf course.
Elegant country house hotel ideally placed for
golfing holiday. Within easy reach of six local
courses. Excellent cuisine served by friendly
local staff. Golf packages and parties arranged.
(See advertisement on page 052052 for further
details.)

Darroch Learg Hotel

Braemar Road, Ballater, Grampian AB3 5UX.
Tel (03397) 55443
The Darroch Learg sits in a high position
overlooking the River Dee and Grampian
mountains. It is a few minutes from the course
at Ballater and convenient for others in the north
east of Scotland.

Eight Acres Hotel

Sheriff Mill, Elgin, Moray.
Tel (0343) 543077
Modern 3 Star hotel set in landscaped grounds.
All rooms with private facilities. Full leisure
complex offering swimming pool, squash,
gymnasium, sauna, sunbeds, table tennis,
snooker etc. 10 golf courses available locally.
Special golfing breaks available.

Fernie Castle Hotel

Letham, By Cupar, Fife KY7 7RU.
Tel (033 781) 381
Steeped in 13th century history in delightful
scenic surroundings our small luxury hotel offers
comfort, good food and friendly service. For
golfers the world famous St Andrews is only
a short distance with a choice of seven further
courses close by. (See advertisement page 423
for further details.)

Forest Hills Hotel

The Square, Auchtermuchty, Fife, Scotland.
Tel (0337) 28318
This old inn is situated in the village square,
surrounded by rich farming country and forests.
Only 25 minutes from St Andrews and close to
many golf courses, make this hotel ideal for your
golfing holiday. STB 2 Crowns.

Glencoe Hotel

8 Links Parade, Carnoustie, Angus DD7 7JF.
Tel (0241) 53273
Directly opposite the 1st tee of the
championship course. 11 bedrooms, the
majority with private bathrooms. All with colour
television and direct dial telephones. 2 Star AA
and RAC.

Golf Hotel

34 Dirleton Avenue, North Berwick, East Lothian
EH39 4BH.
Tel (0620) 2202
Family run hotel ideal for golfers wishing to
play any of East Lothian's 16 courses. Starting
times arranged. Lounge bar, TV lounge, rooms
with private bathroom and colour TV.

Greenlawns

13 Seafield Street, Nairn IV12 4HG.
Tel (0667) 52738
Greenlawns is situated close to golf courses,
beaches, bowling greens, tennis/squash courts,
swimming pool, riding stables and fishing.
Within easy reach of Loch Ness, Cawdor
and Brodie Castles, Culloden Battlefield. An
ideal centre for touring northern Scotland.

Greywalls

Muirfield, Gullane, East Lothian EH31 2EG.
Tel (0620) 842144
Set in the heart of Golf Country, 10 courses
within 5 miles and located overlooking
Muirfield. For those who enjoy the best of
golf, we provide the best food, comfort and
service.

Houstoun House Hotel and Restaurant

Uphall, West Lothian EH52 6JS.
Tel (0506) 853831
Thirty magnificent bedrooms – many with four
poster - in this 16th century house. Excellent
dining facilities with only fresh produce used.
A central base for your golf holiday. Over 100
courses within one hour's drive. Edinburgh
Airport nearby.

The Kenmore Hotel
Kenmore, Perthshire PH15 2NU.
Tel (08873) 205 *Fax* (08873) 262
Scotland's oldest inn is uniquely situated on
the banks of the river and Loch Tay. We offer
modern, comfortable rooms, exciting menus,
a fine cellar and our own 18 hole, par 69
Taymouth Castle golf course.

Kings of Kinloch Hotel
Meigle, Perthshire PH12 8QX.
Tel (08284) 273
A luxury country house hotel with modest prices
and a warm welcome (family managed) within
easy reach of 30 golf courses. We have en-suite
bedrooms and self catering chalets. Special 2/3
day breaks available.

Letham Grange
Colliston, by Arbroath DD11 4RL.
Tel (024) 189 373 *Fax* (024) 189 414
20 bedroom Victorian mansion, with 18 hole
championship standard golf course, first
class facilities set in the heartland of
golf. Company/Society golf outings/breaks
welcome. (See advertisement page 423 for
further details.)

Marine Hotel
Cromwell Road, North Berwick, East Lothian
EH39 4LZ.
Tel (0620) 2406
Golfers in North Berwick have a choice of
14 splendid courses and the superb Marine
Hotel overlooks the famous West Links. (See
advertisement page 421 for further details.)

Nivingston House Hotel
Cleish, Kinross-shire KY13 7LS.
Tel (05775) 216
Nivingston House Hotel, run by Allan Deeson –
a golfing enthusiast – is superbly and centrally
located for golfers. Driving net and Putting
available. Ask for details of many other
activities, including fishing, shooting and
motor-racing. (See advertisement page 427
for further details.)

The Park Hotel
John Street, Montrose, Angus DD10 8RJ.
Tel (0674) 73415 *Tx* 76367 *Fax* (0674) 77091
A short distance from Montrose Medal Course.
Privately owned hotel, 59 bedrooms all with
colour TV and most with private bathrooms.
(See advertisement page 425 for further
details.)

Parkway Hotel
Abbotshall Road, Kirkcaldy, Fife KY2 5PQ.
Tel (0592) 262143
3 Star hotel geared to golfers' needs within
30 minutes' drive of 35 courses including
Gleneagles and St Andrews. Superb restaurant
serving many specialities and well stocked bar.
Two night breaks from £55 pp DBB.

Queens Hotel
160 Nethergate, Dundee.
Tel (0382) 22515
The Queens Hotel is a prestigious city centre
hotel. Built in 1878, this privately owned hotel
has all the charm and elegance of a 19th
century Victorian retreat combined with the
quality and efficiency of a modern hotel. (See
advertisement page 427 for further details.)

The Queens Hotel
Church Street, Inverkeithing, Fife KY11 1LJ.
Tel (0383) 413075 *Fax* (0383) 416761
Compact family run hotel. Ideally situated for
all the major golf courses in Edinburgh and the
East of Scotland. Only one mile from the Forth
Road Bridge and ten miles from Edinburgh. Golf
trips organised. (See advertisement page 425
for further details.)

Rescobie Hotel and Restaurant
Valley Drive, Leslie, Glenrothes, Fife KY6 3BQ.
Tel (0592) 742143
A comfortable country house hotel with 8
well equipped bedrooms and an established
reputation locally for excellent food. Positioned
centrally between Carnoustie, Dalmahoy,
Gleneagles and St Andrews. There are
100 golf courses within easy driving range.

Rosemount Golf Hotel
Golf Course Road, Blairgowrie, Perthshire
PH10 6LJ.
Tel (0250) 2604
Rosemount (and Lansdowne) close by. St
Andrews, Gleneagles, Carnoustie and 75
others all within easy reach. We have 12
en-suite rooms, 2 self-catering cottages in
lovely gardens. AA**RAC. STB 3 Crowns
commended.

The Scores Hotel

The Scores, St Andrews, Fife, Scotland.
Tel (0334) 72451
Overlooking St Andrews Bay and the Royal
and Ancient Clubhouse, this famous 3 Star
hotel is only yards from the first tee of
the Old Course. Facilities include 30 en-suite
bedrooms, restaurant, coffee shop and bars.
Golfing packages available.

Seafield Lodge Hotel

Woodside Avenue, Grantown-on-Spey
PH26 3JN.
Tel (0479) 2152 *Fax* (0479) 2340
STB four Crowns commended. A 2 Star hotel
run by the resident proprietors, Nancy and
Peter Austen. Too small for coaches, yet large
enough to provide a good restaurant and
comfortable lounge bar, where a cosmopolitan
group of sportsmen congregate. The subject of
a major refurbishment, all rooms now boast
private bathrooms, colour TV, tea making
equipment and direct dial telephones. Two
luxury suites, with sitting rooms and jacuzzis!

Skean Dhu Hotel

Farburn Terrace, Dyce, Aberdeen AB2 0DW.
Tel (0224) 723101
Approximately 5 miles from Aberdeen with
219 bedrooms containing full private facilities.
Restaurant, coffee shop, catering/conference
for 300 and own leisure complex. Nearby
are several high standard golf courses.

St Andrews Golf Hotel

St Andrews, Fife KY16 9AS.
Tel (0334) 72611 *Fax* (0334) 72188
Most comfortable, traditional Scottish hotel (all
bedrooms en-suite). Fine restaurant. Extensive
cellar. On the seafront 200 yards from the 'Old
Course'. Let us arrange your golf in Scotland.

Stakis Earl Grey Hotel

Earl Grey Place, Dundee DD1 4DE.
Tel (0382) 29271
Luxury hotel located within 45 minutes of
50 major golf courses with St Andrews and
Carnoustie on the doorstep. Car park and
leisure facilities available. Special golfing
holidays available.

Station Hotel

Station Road, Carnoustie, Angus DD76.
Tel (0241) 52447
Close to Carnoustie championship course,
Burnside and Buddon, this hotel is ideal
for golfers. Family run, meals temptingly
served with ample portions, rooms with
shower en-suite, colour TV. Public and lounge
bars. Friendly atmosphere.

Stirling Arms Hotel

Stirling Road, Dunblane, Perthshire FK15 9EP.
Tel (0786) 822156
17th century coaching inn on the banks of
the Allan Water, conveniently situated for
main road/rail access, perfect location for
businessmen, tourists, golfers (Gleneagles 10
minutes) and anglers. Excellent restaurant.

Scotland: North

Burghfield House Hotel

Dornoch, Sutherland IV25 3HN.
Tel (0862) 810212
42 bedroom country house hotel a few minutes
from the golf course. Superb restaurant. Golf
packages on Royal Dornoch and nearby
courses.

Dornoch Castle

Dornoch, Sutherland IV25 3SD.
Tel (0862) 810216
Formerly a Bishop's palace, the hotel has
19 bedrooms. The panelled cocktail bar,
elegant lounge and Bishop's Room restaurant
overlook historic Dornoch Cathedral. An
INTER hotel AA RAC STB commended 3
Crowns. (See advertisement page 427 for
further details.)

Sutherland Arms Hotel

Lairg, Sutherland IV27 4AT.
Tel Lairg (0549) 2291
The location of the Sutherland Arms Hotel is
ideal for the golfer – Dornoch's championship
course; also the challenging links courses at
Golspie and Brora, all within 35 minutes' drive
from the hotel.

Scotland: Central

Burnside Apartments

19 West Moulin Road, Pitlochry, Perthshire PH16 5EA.
Tel (0796) 2203
EXCITING, NEW holiday concept providing the style and luxury of hotel living, with the comfort and independence golfers require. Quality suites or apartments, with daily housekeeping service – ideal for Perthshire and East Coast courses.

Gleneagles Hotel

Auchterader, Perthshire PH3 1NF.
Tel (07646) 2231
In addition to four championship golf courses Gleneagles boasts an indoor sports and leisure complex, tennis courts, the Jackie Stewart Shooting School and, of course, the luxury of Scotland's first and foremost five star hotel. (See advertisement page 15 for further details.)

Keppoch House Hotel

Perth Road, Crieff, Perthshire PH7 3EQ.
Tel (0764) 4341
The Hotel offers excellent en-suite accommodation, fine food and is fully licensed. Only two minute walk from Crieff golf club with 18 and 9 hole courses. Also the choice of 20 courses within a 20 mile radius.

Murray Park Hotel

Crieff, Perthshire PH7 3DJ.
Tel (0764) 3731 *Fax* (0764) 5311
A charming pink stoned Victorian house, set in its own grounds, it has been tastefully altered over the years to keep in touch with today's standards. Murray Park is an important golf hotel which specialises in good food and good cheer. Special golf packages arranged. 4 Crowns commended. AA 2 Stars and Taste of Scotland. (See advertisement page 429 for further details.)

Buyer's Guide to Good Golfing and Golf Course Maintenance

This compact but informative guide to manufacturers and organisations offering services to Golf Clubs and individual golfers has once again been expanded to include a greater number of categories. The editors do not necessarily endorse the information supplied.

Please note that from May 6th 1990 telephone codes for London will change. If you require help call Freefone 0800 800 873

Club Management and Training Courses

Club Management Services
50 Town Street, Duffield, Derby DE6 4GG.
Tel (0332) 840075
Provision of training courses in Golf Club Management. Existing correspondence courses for Secretary/Managers and Stewards. Management consultancy and staff recruitment for Golf Clubs in Great Britain and in Europe.

Clubhouse Fixtures & Fittings

Prospec International Ltd
PO Box 48, Canklow Meadows Estate, West Bawtry Road, Rotherham, South Yorkshire S60 2XP.
Tel (0709) 377147
Prospec offers ranges of hardwood and laminate lockers and a selection of benches ideally suited to golf clubs. Many British clubs are already enjoying the benefits. Local representation and layout service. Contact Prospec (0709) 377147.

Summit Carpet Industries
75/77 Margaret Street, London W1N 7HB.
Tel 01-631 0307
Manufacturers of contract carpet and carpet tiles. Spike-proof carpet from Karastan. (PGA endorsed). Heavy contract rating for locker-rooms; spike bars and pro shops.

Driving Range Equipment

J Knez AB (Range Servant)
Skallebackavagen 11, S-302 41 Halmstad Sweden.
Tel (035-10) 92 40
Manufacturers of high quality driving range equipment including ball dispensers, ball washers and motorized ball pickers. The labour saving combination including motorized elevator connecting the washer to the dispenser is a unique Swedish concept. (See advertisement page 439 for further details.)

Universal Materials Co Ltd
5-7 High Street, Dorchester-on-Thames, Oxfordshire OX9 8HH.
Tel (0865) 341580 *Fax* (0865) 341575
Probably the widest choice of mats for driving ranges, winter tees and practice grounds, including the ever-popular "AstroTurf", together with other range equipment and accessories and the par T Golf simulator. A consultancy service is also available.

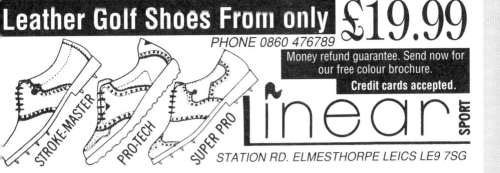
HAWTREE AND SON

GOLF COURSE ARCHITECTS

Since 1912

5 Oxford Street, Woodstock,
Oxford, OX7 1TQ.
Woodstock (0993) 811976.

Telex: 837853 MIMO G
Fax: (0993) 812448

Founder Members: British Association of Golf Course Architects.

SPORTS GROUND IRRIGATION CO.

6 Stuart Road, Market Harborough, LE16 9PQ.
Tel: Market Harborough 63153   Fax: 0858 410085
Official Buckner Pop-up Sprinkler Installation Engineers

Ask About Our Annual Maintenance Contract

Any Spares — Any System   Free Survey — No Obligation

Driving Ranges & Leisure Complexes

Gosforth Park Golfing Complex Ltd
High Gosforth Park, Newcastle-upon-Tyne.
Tel (091) 236 8840
The Complex has an 18 hole golf course, 30 bay floodlit driving range, 9 hole Pitch and Putt course and putting green: Also pro shop; bar and restaurant. Open to non members.

Silvermere Golf & Leisure Ltd
Redhill Road, Cobham, Surrey KT11 1EF.
Tel (0932) 66007
Silvermere is a championship golf course situated half a mile from junction 10 on the M25 with A3. 34 bay floodlit driving range – full catering facilities. Society Days from £39.50 per person. Telephone (0932) 66007 for a full information pack.

Event Organisers

3D Golf Promotion plc
62 Carcluie Crescent, Ayrshire KA7 4SZ.
Tel (0292) 42206/43989 *Tx* 776483
Fax (0292) 4261
UK'S NO 1 GOLF SPECIALIST PGA approved organisers of overseas Pro-Am series golf tuition week and golf school series with the UK's top teachers, home and abroad. FULL COLOUR BROCHURE AVAILABLE.

Footwear

Daniels
Unit 41, Oleander Crescent, Northampton NN3 4QP.
Tel (0604) 412706
Manufacturers of most types of specialist golf shoes. Models include Goodyear welted brogues, waterproof leather styles, lightweight brogues, trainer styles, and shoes for beginners. Available with spiked or gripper soles. Men's and ladies' ranges. All made in UK. (See advertisement page 435 for further details.)

Linear Sport Shoes
Station Road, Elmesthorpe, Leics LE9 7SG.
Tel (0860) 476789
Linear Sport are sole suppliers of the superb range of Linear Golf Shoes. They are only available on a mail order basis, which makes prices extremely competitive. All products are made in UK. Styles include both welted and conventional constructions. (See advertisement page 431 for further details.)

Man o' Leisure
Manor House, Mill Lane, Pirbright, Surrey GU24 0BN.
Tel (048 67) 88587
Distributer for Okespor 100% waterproof golf shoe available in 5 different colours plus a golf wellington boot again 100% waterproof. Available in two colours.

Golf Accessory Suppliers

Cypress Point International
Golf House, Ivinghoe, Nr Leighton Buzzard, Beds.
Tel (0296) 668696
Manufacturing the Cypress Point range of clubs, bags and other accessories for supply to the golf profession.

Dunlop Golf Division
P O Box 8, Normanton, West Yorkshire WF6 1YX.
Tel (0924) 896868
Manufacturers of golf balls (Maxfli DDH 500 Tour Ltd MD, Maxfli 65 and Powermax) and golf clubs under the Maxfli brand. A wide range of bags, gloves, holdalls, umbrellas and accessories is also available.

Lawradale Ltd
PO Box 184, Purley, Surrey CR2 1JA.
Tel 01-660 0822 *Fax* 01-681 2440
Manufacturers. Bespoke bag tags, "Pitch Forks For Your Sales Pitch" hand knitted 100% lambswool golf scene pullovers, with your club name. Agents for St. Andrews fine bone china. His and hers 8 inch pewter golfing models. (See advertisement page 435 for further details.)

Slazenger Golf Division
P O Box 8, Normanton, West Yorkshire WF6 1YX.
Tel (0924) 896868
Slazenger manufacture a range of stylish equipment. Balls include 480 Interlok balata, surlyn and two piece. Clubs include Silver Panther, Seve Ballesteros forged irons; Slazenger Persimmon, Black Panther and XTC. Stylish bags, luggage and accessories to complement the range.

Tanaka of Japan
Unit 4, Hambridge Lane Industrial Estate,
Newbury, Berks.
Tel (0635) 31374
High technology wood heads of various
materials eg. persimmon, graphite, laminates,
ceramic or 17.4 metals, which can be fitted
with various types of shafts and grips, to match
forged or investment cast irons. Putters, golf
bags and accessories are also available.

Golf Ball Manufacturers

Dunlop Golf Division
P O Box 8, Normanton, West Yorkshire
WF6 1YX.
Tel (0924) 896868
Manufacturers of golf balls (Maxfli DDH 500
Tour Ltd MD, Maxfli 65 and Powermax) and
golf clubs under the Maxfli brand. A wide
range of bags, gloves, holdalls, umbrellas and
accessories is also available.

Kestrel Products Ltd
Unit 34, Cwmdu Estate, Skewen, Neath, West
Glamorgan SA10 6RP.
Tel (0792) 817884 *Fax* (0792) 812913
One piece golf balls and rubber tees for
ranges and golf mats. Includes low bounce
for crazy golf, mid-compression for ranges
and practice and high compression for higher
handicap golfers and up-market ranges.

Slazenger Golf Division
P O Box 8, Normanton, West Yorkshire
WF6 1YX.
Tel (0924) 896868
Slazenger manufacture a range of stylish
equipment. Balls include 480 Interlok balata,
surlyn and two piece. Clubs include Silver
Panther, Seve Ballesteros forged irons;
Slazenger Persimmon, Black Panther and
XTC. Stylish bags, luggage and accessories
to complement the range.

Golf Carts, Trolleys & Buggies

Kingkaddy Ltd
Ninelands Lane, Garforth, Leeds LS25 1NT.
Tel (0532) 320151 *Fax* (0532) 860739
Kingkaddy powered golf caddies have been
tested by professionals over the most arduous
courses. The Kingkaddy Mark 2 and the
Kingkaddy Pacer are designed for reliable
service at a realistic price. Available from your

pro-shop. Sole UK concessionaires for Yamaha
golf cars. Details from the above address.

Mitsui Machinery Sales (UK) Ltd
Oakcroft Road, Chessington, Surrey KT9 1SA.
Tel 01-397 5111
Suppliers of top selling Yamaha golf car.
Available through a national network of
distributors. Various schemes include lease
purchase or seasonal hire contracts to
Clubs.

Quillgold Marketing
Quillgold House, Kingswood Road, Hampton
Lovett, Droitwich, Worcestershire WR9 0QH.
Tel (0905) 795963 *Fax* (0905) 795958
Telex 334831 VAX APP G
The Pardrive Electric Golf Trolley is the only
electric golf trolley to be officially approved
by the PGA It is sold only through PGA
Members and there are 250 Service Centres
nationwide. (See advertisement page 4 for
further details.)

Golf Clothing & Rainwear

Maddocks & Dick Ltd
231 Canongate, Royal Mile, Edinburgh, Scotland.
Tel (031) 556 6012
Manufacturers and suppliers of golf club and
company ties, badges, neckwear etc. Produced
in pure silk, silk mixtures and polyesters. Also
ladies' scarves all exclusively designed and
produced in the Royal Mile Scotland. (See
advertisement page 433 for further details.)

Matchplay
PO Box 2, Nottingham Road, Somercotes,
Derbyshire DE55 4SB.
Tel (0773) 607321
Matchplay leisurewear is a competitively
priced, colour coordinated collection of
knitted and woven shirts, trousers and
knitwear designed for both on and off the golf
course.

SR Leisure
26 Stirling Close, Pattison South Industrial
Estate, District 8, Washington, Tyne & Wear
NE38 8QD.
Tel (091) 415 3344
That – specialist ladies outer clothing, jackets,
gilets, skirts, trousers plus 2's, cullottes, in
polycottons, trevira, poly-viscose and corduroy.
Also showerproof oversuits in the comfortable
micro-fibre finesse fabric, 100% waterproof suits
with the cyclone membrane, Tactel Outers.

435

Sunderland Sportswear Ltd
P O Box 14, Glasgow G2 1ER.
Tel (041) 552 3261 *Fax* (041) 552 8518
Sunderland Sportswear manufacture high-
quality golf rainwear in Scotland, all rainsuits
are tour tested and guaranteed waterproof, a
variety of fabrics including Gore-tex and Vent-x
being used. Official supplier to PGA.

Golf Club & Equipment Manufacturers

Ben Hogan (UK) Ltd
21 Cratfield Road, Bury St Edmunds, Suffolk
IP32 7DF.
Tel (0284) 752152 *Fax* (0284) 753114
UK subsidiary of Ben Hogan Company, Texas,
USA. Supplies all the golf professionals and
network of European distributors. Complete
Hogan product range of clubs, balls, bags,
accessories and golf shirts.

Browning Sports Ltd
37d Milton Trading Estate, Milton, Abingdon,
Oxon OX14 4RT.
Tel (0235) 833939
Browning are established manufacturers of
quality clubs, bags and accessories. Club
ranges to suit all standards of play include
Ceramic Plus, Tour Class, Mirage, Lady Mirage,
DP900, Eclipse and Premier.

Confidence Golf Ltd
Brook Farm, Linstead Parva, Nr. Halesworth,
Suffolk IP19 0LA.
Tel (098 685) 332 *Fax* (098 685) 485
Golf club manufacturers offering a range of
models across the price and design range
from forging to starter set and including
two game improvement models. Play with
'Confidence'- you can't win without it!

Criterion Sports (NI) Ltd
17b Springtown Industrial Estate, Londonderry
Northern Ireland BT48 0LY.
Tel (0504) 371624 *Fax* (0504) 371640
Manufacturer and distributor of Criterion range
of golf equipment including clubs, bags, trolleys
and accessories. Manufacturing base: Criterion
Sports Limited, Millbrae, Buncrana, Co.
Donegal, Republic of Ireland.
Tel (077) 61856.

J B Halley & Co Ltd
2/3 Charterhouse Square, London EC1M 6ES.
Tel 01-253 5581 *Fax* 01-250 1528
Manufacturers of golf clubs and accessories for
over 100 years. Over 90% of our equipment is

British made and we supply 76 countries around
the world.

Pro Drive UK
Pro Drive House, 5 Epsom Downs Metro
Centre, Waterfield, Tadworth, Surrey
KT20 5LR.
Tel (0737) 373949
Manufacturers and distributors of the Pro Drive
range of golf clubs, bags, shirts and accessories
throughout the UK and Europe. Clubs include
Monaco, Powersole and Tempest as well as
the new Ultimate flow weight system, Dynamo
320 and Enforcer ranges. Steel, Graphite and
Boron shafts. Men's and Ladies', right and left
hand available. (See advertisement page 433
for further details.)

Slazenger Golf Division
P O Box 8, Normanton, West Yorkshire
WF6 1YX.
Tel (0924) 896868
Slazenger manufacture a range of stylish
equipment. Balls include 480 Interlok balata,
surlyn and two piece. Clubs include Silver
Panther, Seve Ballesteros forged irons;
Slazenger Persimmon, Black Panther and
XTC. Stylish bags, luggage and accessories
to complement the range.

Slotline Golf Europe Ltd
Largo Road, St Andrews, Fife.
Tel (0334) 77017 *Fax* (0334) 75950 Call Free
0800 83 33 77
Manufacturers of INERTIAL PUTTERS, E-MAX
IRONS and WOODS and the new LADY
RAMPANT COPPER/GRAPHITE IRONS and
WOODS. Free advice and customisation
service always available from professional
staff.

Taylor Made (Great Britain) Ltd
Annecy House, Gastons Wood, Reading Road,
Basingstoke, Hants RG24 0TW.
Tel (0256) 479797 *Fax* (0256) 479357
Taylor Made metalwoods continue to be the
number one choice of touring professionals.
The comprehensive range of metalwoods and
TPF irons have a choice of steel, titanium and
graphite shafts. New putters and bags are also
available.

Yamaha UK (IMS Ltd)
545-549 Wallisdown Road, Poole, Dorset
BH12 5AD.
Tel (0202) 538877
UK distributors for Yamaha golf equipment
featuring an extensive range of mens' and
ladies' graphite clubs, left handed clubs, bags
and headcovers.

Golf Course Architects

British Association of Golf Course Architects
Hon Secretary, 5 Oxford Street, Woodstock, Oxford OX7 1TQ.
Tel (0993) 811976
Professional Association of qualified golf course architects officially recognised by the R & A and English Golf Union.

Golf Development International NV
(Joan F Dudok Van Heel) 4 Beukenlaan, 1640 St Genesius-Rode, Belgium.
Tel (02) 358 3387
Architecture, design and construction – supervision of golf courses. Consultancy on golf course and club management. Feasibility studies - promoting and developing the game of golf.

Hamilton Stutt & Co
12 Bingham Avenue, Poole, Dorset BH14 8NE.
Tel (0202) 708406
Founder member of the British Association of Golf Course Architects. One of Europe's most experienced golf architects. Personal attention to each new project – only a limited number accepted each year.

Hawtree & Son
5 Oxford Street, Woodstock, Oxford OX7 1TQ.
Tel (0993) 811976
Hawtree & Son celebrates 77 years of golf architectural service throughout the world. (See advertisement page 431 for further details.)

John Jacobs Golf Associates Ltd
68A High Street, Walkern, Stevenage, Herts SG2 7PG.
Tel (0438) 86 438 *Fax* (0438) 86 788
Golf architects/consultants offering a complete service, through feasibility, design and contract management. Leaders in the golf centre design and development field. Architects of the new South Course at Wentworth. (See advertisement page 32 for further details.)

Golf Course Maintenance

Ransomes Sims & Jefferies Ltd
Ransomes Way, Ipswich IP3 9QG.
Tel (0473) 270000
Ransomes offer the most comprehensive range of golf course maintenance equipment available today, from the mowing of tees and fairways to the superb grooming of golf greens and

surrounds. (See advertisement page 18 for further details.)

Watermation Ltd
Monument Way E, Woking, Surrey GU21 5LY.
Tel (0483) 770303
Manufacturers and installers of top quality golf course irrigation equipment, including computer controllers (TW1 and TW2) and pop-up sprinklers (GN range) made from brass and bronze with rubber covers.

Golf Course Project Management

I R H (Development Services) Ltd
5 Coates Crescent, Edinburgh EH3 7AL.
Tel (031) 220 1707 *Fax* (031) 220 1626
Co-ordination and management of all project elements including concept, planning approvals, golf course design and construction, related infrastructure and landscaping. Projects range from course alterations to substantial integrated developments as at Collingtree Park, Northampton. (See advertisement page 433 for further details.)

International Golfers Club Ltd
Albert Building, 49 Queen Victoria Street, London EC4N 4SA.
Tel 01-248 4435
International Golfers Club provides the complete golf management solution to clubs across Europe. Its totally integrated system with hardware and software installed free of charge provides a start-time system, membership and handicap package and nominal ledger. Member clubs can obtain start times at other clubs within the network. IGC is offering highly competitive financing, advice on increasing club profitability and consultancy on course improvement and maintenance. (See advertisement on page 28 for further details.)

Golf Financial Services

Golf Plus – Golf Financial Services Ltd
308-314 Kings Road, Reading, Berkshire RG1 4PA.
Tel (0734) 61022 *Tx* 848511 *Fax* (0734) 662237
Golf Plus, the credit card designed exclusively for golfers. Approved by the PGA, Golf Plus offers members a comprehensive range of golfing services and benefits through the Golf Plus Club.

Golf Holidays

Meridian Holidays
12-16 Dering Street, London W1R 9AE.
Tel 01-493 2777
Choose Meridian for over 10 years experience
in arranging golf holiday packages in Europe.
Self-catering or hotel holidays in France,
Spain or Portugal with value and style.
ABTA/IATA/ATOL.

Golf Practice Equipment

Evergreen Products Ltd
Curtis Road, Dorking, Surrey RH4 1XD.
Tel (0306) 881546
Manufacturers of the finest range of golf mats
for driving ranges, golf courses and practise
use. Artificial surfaces such as putting greens,
fairways and safety surfaces also undertaken.
Please contact us for our brochure.

Universal Materials Co Ltd
5-7 High Street, Dorchester-on-Thames,
Oxfordshire OX9 8HH.
Tel (0865) 341580 *Fax* (0865) 341575
Probably the widest choice of mats for driving
ranges, winter tees and practice grounds,
including the ever-popular "AstroTurf", together
with other range equipment and accessories
and the par T Golf simulator. A consultancy
service is also available.

Golfing Gifts & Novelties

Another Gift Idea Co
Virginia Mills, Higher Hillgate, Stockport,
Cheshire SK1 3JG.
Tel (061) 480 8991
Supply of golfing gifts to golf professionals and
retailers. Portfolio includes exclusive lines from
US, Japan and Far East. Products include the
Sipper, all sports air fresheners, Its-a-Lock, and
English bone china figurines.

Central Sales and Marketing Ltd
13 Grosvenor Gardens, London
SW1W 0BD.
Tel: 01-828 2469
Distributors of Walt Disney golfing goods –
club covers, golf balls and towels. Novelty
gifts for the golfer such as 3-dimensional
golf ice cubes, ice buckets and glasses.
Exploding, floating and trick golf
balls.

Golfing Tuition

Peter Ballingall Golf School
Barnham Broom Hotel Golf and Country Club
Norwich, Norfolk.
Tel (060 545) 393
Residential golf schools where clients,
regardless of experience, can improve their
golf on a 3, 4 or 5 day course with Peter
Ballingall, one of the premier teachers of the
game. (See advertisement page 409 for further
details.)

Headwear & Embroidery

David Allan & Co Ltd
(Dept.GH) Unit 8, 2 North Avenue, Clydebank
Business Park, Glasgow, Scotland G81 2DR.
Tel (041) 941 3133 *Fax* (041) 951 1827
We are the European distributor of Kangol
headwear and offer a complete embroidery
service onto this comprehensive range of ladies'
and gents' hats. The Company also manufacture
casual jackets and sweatshirts.

Prostitch
Pin Hi, Wentworth Close, Gravesend, Kent
DA11 7NL.
Tel (0474) 333397
Full computerised embroidery service on
all golf and sportswear. Sweaters, shirts,
sweatshirts, caps, visors, etc supplied. Any
logo/badge designed for societies, clubs,
companies – large or small. Please contact
for further details.

Irrigation Equipment & Installation

Sportsground Irrigation Co
6 Stuart Road, Market Harborough LE16 9PQ.
Tel (0858) 63153 *Fax* (0858) 410085
Irrigation engineers, specialising in golf
course equipment and installations. Annual
service contracts offered on any system.
(See advertisement page 431 for further
details.)

Watermation Ltd
Monument Way E, Woking, Surrey GU21 5LY.
Tel (0483) 770303
Manufacturers and installers of top quality
golf course irrigation equipment, including
computer controllers (TW1 and TW2) and
pop-up sprinklers (GN range) made from brass
and bronze with rubber covers.

Professional Bodies

British Association of Golf Course Architects
Hon Secretary, 5 Oxford Street, Woodstock, Oxford OX7 1TQ.
Tel (0993) 811976
Professional Association of qualified golf course architects officially recognised by the R & A and English Golf Union.

Institute of Groundsmanship
19-23 Church Street, The Agora, Wolverton, Milton Keynes, Bucks MK12 5LG.
Tel (0908) 312511
Educational and training programmes; turf advisory service; annual conference; monthly journal; 10G sports and leisure world trade exhibitions; Groundsman of the Year awards. The professional body for groundsmen and greenkeepers.

Suppliers of Golf Awards & Prizes

Derek Burridge Trophies
5-11 Hanbury Road, Acton, London W3 8RF.
Tel 01-992 5948/7313 *Fax* 01-993 4814
The country's leading suppliers of golf prizes. We offer a vast range of silverplate, crystal, china, clocks, leather goods and sporting trophies, all at trade prices. Glass and silver plate in-house engraving service. (See advertisement page 437 for further details.)

Trade Suppliers

Golf Equip (GB) Ltd
Gladonian Road, Littlehampton, West Sussex BN17 6JW.
Tel (0903) 724500
Manufacturers of golf course and range equipment. Specialist in heavy duty machinery and mats. All requirements and advice for golf ranges and practice centres. Trade sales only. (See advertisement page 435 for further details.)

Index of Advertisers

Abbotsley Golf & Squash Club Ltd	407	Hotel 70°	417
Appleby Manor Hotel	415	International Golfers Club	28
Avon Industrial Polymers	437	IRH (Development Services) Ltd	433
Barnham Broom Hotel	409	J Knez AB	439
The Beach Hotel	417	John Jacobs Golf Associates	32
Bein Inn	425	Kirroughtree Hotel	421
Blakeney Hotel	411	Lancaster Golf & Country Club	411
Bodfor Hotel	419	Lansdowne Hotel	407
Boskerris Hotel	401	Lawradale Ltd	435
Bryn Morfydd Hotel	417	Leasowe Castle Hotel	415
Buccleuch & Queensberry Hotel	421	Letham Grange	423
Budock Vean Hotel	399	Linear Sports Shoes	431
Burnham & Berrow Golf Club	401	Links Country Park Hotel	407
Clarendon Hotel	403	Linksway Hotel	419
Clifton House	429	Maddocks & Dick	433
Craigard Country House Hotel	427	Malin Court Hotel	423
Daniels Sportslines	435	Manor House Hotel	403
Deneavon Hotel Group	429	Marine Hotel	421
Derek Burridge Trophies	437	Murray Park Hotel	429
Dormy Hotel & Leisure Club	399	Nivingston House Hotel	427
The Dormy House – Royal Lytham &		Park Hotel	425
St Anne's	413	Peter Ballingall Golf School	409
Dornoch Castle	427	Prince of Wales	429
Esplanade Hotel	413	Pro Drive UK Ltd	433
Fairways Hotel	419	Queen's Hotel – Dundee	427
Fernie Castle	423	Queens Hotel – Fife	425
Ford Motor Company	8	Quillgold Marketing Ltd	4
Gleneagles Hotel – Torquay	399	Ransomes Sims & Jefferies	18
Gleneagles Hotel – Auchterader	15	Royal Eastbourne Golf Club	403
Golf Equipment (GB Ltd)	435	Selsdon Park Hotel	415
Grand Crest Hotel	413	Shaw Hill Hotel	405
Grosvenor Hotel	401	Sports Ground Irrigation	431
Harewood Arms Hotel	417	Telford Hotel Golf & Country Club	413
Hawtree & Son	431	Thorpeness Golf Club Hotel	411
Heronston Hotel	419	Wensleydale Heifer	415
Hintlesham Hall	411		

Part IV
Clubs and Courses in the UK and Europe

1990 Centenary Clubs

England

Alresford

The Club was started as a tentative venture by a few people. Its first recorded activity was in the report of a competition held on 15th November 1890 on an 80 acre expanse of Tichborne Down, already in use by a sheep farmer, a racehorse trainer and two cricket clubs.

By 1911 the Club had acquired the tenancy and leased extra land for an extension from 9 to 18 holes, but the new land reverted to agricultural use in 1914.

The Club remained fairly prosperous until 1946 when various post-war difficulties arose, but it was saved by the formation of a Company and stability was further assured when rented accommodation adjoining a public house was abandoned and a railway coach adapted as a Clubhouse on the course.

Membership increased rapidly as golf became popular in the 1960s. In 1964 the members agreed to purchase the assets of the Company which had served its invaluable purpose. The freehold of the course was bought in 1968 and the present Clubhouse built in 1969.

Three holes were lost in the construction of the Alresford bypass, but the Club has worked hard to incorporate the compensating land into a redesigned 9 hole course, as attractive as the old one. It is always hoping that the course will one day be extended to 18 holes.

Captain 1990: Stephen H Robinson
Secretary: Peter Kingston
Professional: Malcolm R Scott

Banstead Downs

Banstead Downs Golf Club started life in 1890 as the Sutton Ladies Golf Club but the Club historians of 1895 recorded, 'After a few months husbands, brothers and friends grew envious and their desire to share the privileges and responsibilities of the new Club were well received.'

The course, which has changed over the years, is laid out on the 'bright and breezy Banstead Downs' and measures some 6200 yards. With its mostly tight fairways it can be a testing SSS 69, especially as the cutting of the rough in the spring has to be restricted until the majority of the chalkland flora has seeded because the course was, in 1985, declared by the National Conservancy Council to be a Site of Special Scientific Interest.

Golf is played under licence on common land which is divided by the Brighton Road, with 6 holes to the east of the road and 12 to the west. These 12 holes were the whole of the course until 1904. The course is undoubtedly unusual inasmuch as it has five short holes all running from north to south.

There are around 600 members who enjoy playing their golf some 500 feet above sea level on Banstead Downs which, according to Daniel Defoe in the eighteenth century, 'needs no description other than it is perfectly agreeable, the ground soft, level and dry; they conspire to make the most delightful spot in all this part of England.'

Captain 1990: D Knill-Jones
Secretary: R S Barrett
Professional: I Marr

Belton Park

Belton Park Golf Club is one of the oldest golf clubs in Lincolnshire. It was founded in 1890, but the first captain (HJ Hildyard) and management committee was not elected until 1892.

During the First World War Belton Park was used as a vast army camp; thousands of troops were stationed in the area, many in huts on the course. The course was closed from 1914 until 1922 when it was redesigned by Tom Williamson and reopened by the Club President, Lord Brownlow.

During the 1930s there were minor alterations to the course and Clubhouse. The Club
managed to survive through 1935–45, despite
lack of staff and petrol; it became a haven of
golf for the American forces stationed in the
area. After the war VG Richards, the professional, supervised reconstruction with the help
of members.

In 1975 a long lease of the course was
successfully negotiated with the Belton Trust
Estate. The whole course was fenced in, and
with the extra land available the Club was able
to construct a further 9 holes, making 27 holes
in all, each 9 holes having starting tees and last
greens adjacent to the Clubhouse.

The ground makes full use of the beautiful
parkland trees and the natural lakes, providing
an undulating course of 6420 yards which is a
very good test of golf. The new inner 9 holes
have recently been extended and can now also
be used for competitions.

Several Open competitions are organised
throughout the year as well as a PGA-organised
Pro-Am competition, in which many of the leading Midlands professionals compete.

Captain 1990: Trevor Ireland
Manager: Terry Measure
Professional: Brian McKee

Berkhamsted

Berkhamsted Golf Club lies amid the natural
beauty of Berkhamsted Common and is one of
the original four clubs founded in Hertfordshire
in 1890.

A group of masters from Berkhamsted School
met on 12th December 1890 to form the Club.
Permission to play golf on the Common was obtained from Lord Brownlow, who later became
President of the Club. Within a year, there were
40 members, subscriptions being one guinea for
gentlemen and a half guinea for ladies.

The original Clubhouse was a wooden hut
set in the valley by Berkhamsted Castle, and a
9 hole course ran up to the Common and back
down into the valley. In 1901, a new Clubhouse
was erected on the Common where the 9 hole
course lay. Gradual extensions to the course
were made in the early years of the century.

After Lord Brownlow's death in 1921, the estate was broken up, the land bought by Edwin
Williams and a Trustee Company formed to hold
the land for the benefit of the Golf Club. At this
stage, James Braid was called in to advise on the
further lengthening of the course and a new 18
hole layout was opened in November 1927.

Early in the golfing year, Berkhamsted plays
host to the country's best amateur golfers with
the Berkhamsted Trophy, started in 1960 to
commemorate the golfing achievements of
Harold Rance, a Berkhamsted member and
County golfer. The Trophy attracts a very strong
entry, and is one of the premier 36 hole scratch
competitions in the country.

The course is narrow, on good common land
turf. Gorse, heather and grass bunkers are the
main hazards. It is 6605 yards long, SS 72, plays
well all the year and continues to provide all
golfers with a considerable challenge.

Captains 1990: CD Bennett, ME Hearon
Secretary: JF Robinson
Professional: BJ Proudfoot

Berwick-upon-Tweed (Goswick)

The Club was formed at a meeting of golf
enthusiasts held in the Kings Arms Hotel,
Berwick-upon-Tweed, on 21st October 1889.
Six months later, on 19th April 1890, the first
ball was struck by Lady Crossman at the opening of a 9 hole course which had been made on
the seaside links at Goswick, five miles south
of Berwick, through the courtesy of Sir William
Crossman, the land owner. The course was extended to 18 holes in 1893 and gradually moved
northwards on to links land of Windmill Hill and
Cheswick Farms. These seaside links were described by Bernard Darwin as 'one of the most
naturally magnificent pieces of golfing ground
that ever swam into the ken of the golfing explorer.'

Willie Park (1903), James Braid (1930) and
JFF Pennink (1964) have all had a hand in
making Goswick into the most delightful and
testing of golf courses. The Clubhouse has recently been extended to provide facilities for
the ever increasing numbers of visitors who
are learning of this little golfing paradise on
the lovely unspoilt north Northumbrian coast.

Captain 1990: JH Fleming
Secretary: RC Oliver
Professional: M Leighton

Bournemouth

In 1885 a few residents of Bournemouth arranged
to play golf on wasteland at Brokenhurst. They
were joined by regular visitors from London who
came by train, as did those from Bournemouth,
on specially reduced fares for golfers. They
formed the Bournemouth Golf Club in 1890 and
played at Brokenhurst until 1894. That year the
Bournemouth Corporation was given 118 acres of
land on which to lay out a golf course. Tom Dunn
designed it at Meyrick Park which became the

first Municipal course in England. Years ahead of all the others, it had piped water to every green, probably the first course in the country to have it.

A Clubhouse was built in 1895, another in 1905 and a third soon afterwards at Queen's Park, where another Municipal course was laid out in 1906. Bournemouth Club members could play on both courses until 1946 when it confined its activities to Meyrick Park. In 1988 Bournemouth and Meyrick Park Clubs merged and a new Clubhouse is to be built.

From 1925-61 Ernest Whitcombe, the eldest of the three Dorset brothers from Came Down, was professional at Meyrick Park; he played in three early Ryder Cup matches and twice finished close to the winner of the Open.

Captain 1990: I Cole
Secretary: RL Pike
Professional: J Sharkey

Boxmoor

Boxmoor Golf Club, founded in 1890, has played on the same ground ever since. It has 9 holes and the layout of the course has hardly changed since the early days. A hand-drawn map, dated 1914, in the Clubhouse shows that some holes have been lengthened by moving tees but few other changes.

The old minute book records that the first committee meeting was held in a first-class carriage of a train heading for Euston from Hemel Hempstead. Half-a-dozen golfers living in the Boxmoor area came together, formed their Club and wrote to the Boxmoor Trust to obtain permission to use Sheephanger Common for 'the purpose of golf'. The Boxmoor Trust minutes record that permission was granted on 13th August 1890.

The Club has always had a small membership; one of the most illustrious early members from 1895 to 1907 was the Hon Lionel Walter Rothschild, MP for Aylesbury,who succeeded to the title of the second Baron in 1915. In 1987 Lord Rothschild's grandniece, The Hon Mrs ML Lane, presented the Club with a photograph of Lord Rothschild which now hangs in the Clubhouse.

Being a members' Club, many a financial crisis and two World Wars, have affected it over the years and the membership has fluctuated from 40 or so, to today's 200.

The course is difficult, on hilly terrain and it can be very unforgiving. Once known, its challenge is appreciated and accuracy improves.

Captain 1990: Colin G Witney
Hon Secretary: E Duell

Bridgnorth

The Editor regrets his failure to include Bridgnorth in the 1989 edition and is pleased to make good his error this year.

The Club was started in 1887, but the centenary was celebrated in 1989. The original 9 holes of 2308 yards (average 258 yards!) at Hook Farm, Tasley, followed the course of the Cantreyn Brook. In 1906 the Club moved to its present site in Stanley Lane, nearer to the River Severn, but it was not until the 1930s that the Club really moved out of the Edwardian age. Development began with a new Clubhouse, the gift of the landlord and President, Major AW Foster, which added rooms to the old changing shed. Further extensions were made in 1950 and 1970, which provided more amenities for members. A new Clubhouse was built in 1975–76 financed by members' loans and further developments were completed in its centenary year.

It was not until 1930 that a professional, Bert Gadd, a winner of the French Open Championship, also to be greenkeeper and bar steward, was appointed. Since then the Club has continued to be well served by its staff, with each of Gadd's three jobs now being undertaken by a separate individual.

Bridgnorth has in recent years been a prominent Club in the Shropshire and Herefordshire Union. With its improved Clubhouse facilities, it will no doubt continue to be a leader in the two counties.

The Ladies section has played a prominent part in the Club since the 1930s and has produced county players and officials. Equally several men members have figured in County and National affairs without yet producing a national champion.

Captain 1989: Michael Cooksey
Secretary: EH Thomas
Professional: Paul Hinton

Burghley Park, Stamford

At a meeting held at the George Hotel on 29th October 1890, it was resolved to establish the Burghley Park Golf Club, with Mr Hubert Eaton as Secretary. Lord Exeter had kindly given leave for the links to be in the High Park. The subscription was settled to be 10s 6d per member.

The following were present at the original meeting and became members: F Coventry, J Scott, H Eaton, VG Stapleton, N Cayley, CP Phillips, C Handson, J Phillips, DJ Evans, MS Young, HO Edmonds, E Phillips, CE Hare, CJ Godfrey, JE Parble and C Thorpe; the Committee to consist of Messers Cayley, CP Phillips and Scott. The Marquis of Exeter was appointed President of the Club.

Following on from the minutes of that first meeting it has been possible to trace the progress through what, at times, must have seemed insurmountable difficulties to reach the richness of the present day's well established and strongly supported Club. From the mere handful of members, who at times had to keep the Club going by their own efforts in maintaining the course and by dipping into their pockets to overcome losses, Burghley Park Golf Club today has 920 members.

The popularity of golf is at a premium and the many who enjoy the well manicured, delightful surroundings of our course in 1990 must spare a thought for those who first cut the hay to form a course in 1890.

Captain 1990: Ian Yarham
Secretary: P Howard Mulligan
Professional: Glenn Davies

Burnham & Berrow

The Burnham Golf Club (it became Burnham & Berrow Golf Club in 1910) was formed at a meeting convened at the Royal Clarence Hotel, Bridgwater on 3rd September 1890 with 11 gentlemen present.

Originally there were 9 holes, laid out in the autumn of 1891 by Charles Gibson, the professional at Westward Ho!. They were on what was known as the 'Berrow Warren', let to the Club by JH Palmer, the agent for the Lords of the Manor, at a rate of £10 per annum for seven years. These 9 holes were altered and extended by Gibson in 1897 and four long holes, of over 400 yards length, were made. Over the years many changes and improvements have been made to the 18 hole course and in 1977 a new 9 hole course, situated between the sea marshlands and main links, was opened.

The Burnham Ladies Golf Club was instituted on 2nd May 1892, when the entrance fee was half a guinea and the annual subscription 11 shillings.

Burnham is one of the natural Championship Links courses and through the years has gained an honoured place in golf. Situated close to the M5, it has panoramic views of the Somerset hills and the Devon coastline sweeping across famed reed beds and the Bristol Channel, with the islands of Steepholm and Flatholm standing out against the Welsh coastline. The course is a protected area, due to the abundance of wild flowers and in particular varieties of orchids.

Captain 1990: RW Wyatt
Secretary: Elizabeth Sloman
Professional: Nigel Blake

Bury

Bury Golf Club, with Sir Henry James, the local MP as first President, was formed in 1890. The course was on farmland at Redvales, an area south of the town. Its first professional was Harry Vardon who was appointed greenkeeper/professional in 1891 after a spell at Studley Royal Golf Club, Ripon. By 1896, when he won the first of his Open Championships he had left Bury for Ganton but the Bury Members gave him a clock in recognition of his success. His handwritten letter of thanks is one of the Club's treasured possessions.

During the First World War the land was needed for agricultural purposes and golf at Redvales virtually came to an end. In 1920 however a new site was acquired at Unsworth on 'the turnpike road' to Manchester. Unsworth Hall had been the residence of the first Mayor of Bury and 9 holes were opened in 1921 with a further 9 in 1922. The professional at that time was Tom Cooke who later moved to Saltburn and whose son, Bernard, is a well-known and respected professional in Essex. In 1935, Tom Jarman, one of five golfing brothers, was appointed professional and served the Club until he retired in 1973.

The course is of 18 holes (5961 yards, SS69) over undulating land which provides an interesting test of golf. The Clubhouse has been recently refurbished and new locker rooms provided.

The Club's Patron is the Rt Hon Earl of Derby MC.

Captain 1990: M Fleming
Secretary: JP Meikle
Professional: M Peel

Charnwood Forest

Often described as one of the most attractive 9 hole courses in the country, this, the oldest club in Leicestershire, is situated some three miles from Loughborough, overlooking the village of Woodhouse Eaves. The course is played around the ancient pre-Cambrian rocks of Charnwood, known as the Hanging Stone Rocks, with splendid views of the surrounding countryside.

It was founded in 1890 by the local Vicar of Quorn, the Rev RC Faithfull, who secured the approval of the owner of the historic Beaumanor Estate, for part of it to be used as a golf course. The Club started with some 40 members. In 1915 the estate passed to Colonel the Hon Curzon Herrick, who in 1897 had been elected the Club's first President. From 1919 to 1926 the course was rented by him at a rate of £25 per annum. The annual subscription at that time was 3 guineas for gentlemen and 2 guineas for ladies and the President then proposed that he would raise his subscription to £25 to cover the cost of the rental. This happy arrangement was terminated in 1946 when the Beaumanor Estate was sold and the Club was able to establish its independence by purchasing the course.

In 1890 members enjoyed the use of the lodgekeeper's house and after 1900 clubhouse facilities were provided at two successive neighbouring farmhouses. A purpose-built Clubhouse was opened in 1957 but destroyed by fire in 1977. An enlarged building has since been erected on the same site which happily serves the needs of the present membership of 250 men and women members.

Captain 1990: GG Smith
Honorary Secretary: AG Stanley

Chipping Norton

Instituted on 11th March 1890 with 40 members and an annual subscription of 10 shillings, 'the green' was situated on Chipping Norton Common, quite close to the railway station. The first President was Dr G Wright Hutchinson and many family names among members of the first committee were stalwarts of the Club in future years.

While all records prior to 1932 have been lost, research suggests that the Club moved to its present site, some 700 feet above sea level and the highest point in Oxfordshire, in 1908. The loss of records is due to the Club almost folding in 1932. It survived due to the efforts of Councillor George Hannis, the Mayor, who called a special meeting of those thought to be interested in the continuation of the Club. About 40 supported the proposal; the following year the farm, of which the course formed a part, was offered for sale. £600 was raised to purchase 58½ acres and although 40 acres came under the plough in 1942 to support the war effort, this land now forms the back 9 of the present course. There were problems again in the mid-1950s which almost resulted in closure, but fortunately negotiations to sell the course failed.

Since then the Club has not looked back. The little wooden hut was replaced by a new Clubhouse in 1968 which has been extended twice since and the big step forward was the purchase of a further 52 acres of adjoining land in 1985 to add another 9 holes. With much help from members, the full 18 holes of 6280 yards was opened in April 1988, the par three third over the lake being particularly interesting. It still remains a members' club enabling subscriptions to be kept at a modest level.

Captain 1990: Michael White
Secretary: John Norman
Professional: Bob Gould

Chorleywood

It was the idea of a group of Harrow schoolmasters that the Club was founded in 1890 to play golf on Chorleywood Common. Most of the early members were from London, including many men from both Houses of Parliament, among them AJ Balfour, later Prime Minister. For 30 years and more, playing golf on the Common was opposed by many local residents who objected to *their* Common being so used, mostly by men who lived elsewhere. It was not until 1926 that, after years of opposition from the Council and Commoners, that Sunday play was allowed.

Sometime after the First World War the Club, somewhat grudgingly, invited locals to join. Concurrently the course was reduced from 18 to 9 holes at which it remains. The original course was laid out by the ubiquitous Tom Dunn.

The first Clubroom, little more than a tin shed, with refreshment to be had from the house adjoining, was in use until recently when, with the sale of a plot of land, a new Clubhouse was built on the same site. The membership is now mostly local and the Club thrives.

The Ladies, who had a poor deal until the middle 1920s, now have an active section. Max MacCready, the 1949 Amateur Champion, was a welcome member who often played at the weekends.

Captain 1990: TJ Fox
Secretary: LW Turner

Churston

The Club was born in November 1890 when eight golfing enthusiasts from Kingswear and Paignton met to discuss the feasibility of playing golf at the nearby Galmpton Warborough Common. Within a matter of weeks a primitive 9 hole course was laid out, the only hazards being patches of gorse, copses and roads and footpaths criss-crossing the uncut fairways.

The Club was fortunate in having Lord Churston, grandfather of the present holder of the title as one of its founder members for, besides being an enthusiastic golfer, he brought his considerable influence to bear on the Club's development. He became the first President and in 1896 the course was extended to 18 holes, the cost of £200 being borne entirely by him.

By 1920, the committee became painfully aware that playing on the common was becoming extremely hazardous, not only to golfers, but more so to the increasing numbers using that open space for walking, cricket, football and other sporting activities. In 1922 Mr HS Colt and Mr Hawtree of Bromley advised on a new layout.

The land to be used was part of the Churston Estate and Colt, who laid out the course, reported 'From much of the ground, there are magnificent views of Torbay and the situation and surroundings are admirable in every way. I consider £5000 outlay would be amply justified by the increased value of surrounding land for building purposes.'

The new course was opened in 1924, and, apart from minor adjustments for safety and improved golf equipment, this is the course we enjoy today.

Ted Ray, British and American Open Champion was professional at Churston between 1899 and 1903.

Captain 1990: Brian Harris
Secretary: Andrew Chaundy
Professional: R Penfold

Datchet

The Club was formed in 1890 on land leased from the Commissioners of Woods and Forest and was previously used by King Charles I for steeplechasing and King Charles II for angling at Black Potts. The formation was led by RAH Mitchell, an Eton College master, together with a number of local residents who were keen cricketers. Thus Datchet Golf Club became one of the first 400 in the United Kingdom and the third in Berkshire.

The Club's association with the Royal Family started with the renting of the course from the Crown Commissioners, but on a more personal basis, two of Queen Victoria's grandsons, namely Prince Albert of Schleswig-Holstein and Prince Leopold of Battenberg, were members of the Club. Prince Albert played in Club matches as well as presiding at the AGM. King Edward VII played the course on numerous occasions when he was Prince of Wales.

Captain 1990: P Francis
Secretary: GS East
Professional: Max Taylor

Eltham Warren

Eltham Warren Golf Club is situated on the eastern outskirts of Eltham, in south-east London, with access from Bexley Road.

It was founded on 7th May 1890 when a group of eight friends met to form a small private club. They rented a field, 'The Warren Field,' from a Mr Edwards at a cost of £10 per annum and laid out a 6 hole course. At first the name was Eltham Golf Club, but it was soon changed to The Warren and then to the present Eltham Warren. After a few years the original playing area was lost for building development but the Club was able to lease from the Crown Agents a large tract of land extending towards Falconwood which is more or less the site of the present 9 hole course.

At first one or more rooms were rented for essential accommodation until, in 1912, membership and funds justified building a pleasant Clubhouse on the course. This was destroyed by fire in 1957 and replaced with the present larger building on the same site.

Eltham Warren has always been a supporter of competitive golf and the Club takes part in all local inter-club competitions. It was also a founder member of the Society of London Golf Captains, the Society of London Lady Golf Captains and the Society of Kent Golf Captains and has over the years provided Captains of all three.

Captain 1990: J Coleman
Secretary: DJ Clare
Professional: Ian Coleman

Ilkley

Ilkley Golf Club was founded in June 1890 and is the third oldest golf club in Yorkshire. The first Ilkley course was a 9 hole links on Rombald's Moor where stone walls, streams, ravines, bracken and boulders all came into play. Although the greens were good, the bogey score of 40 for a fairly short 9 hole course gives some idea of the difficulty. Tom Vardon was one of the Club's early professionals and his more famous brother, Harry, actually won his first prize as a professional golfer on this course in 1893. This was £5 for a 36 hole score of 162.

The desire for an 18 hole course made the Committee look elsewhere and they finally settled on the Club's present site by the beautiful River Wharfe. Work commenced on the new course in February 1898 and the Club actually played its first medal competition in June of that year.

The course is set in beautiful country with each hole giving delightful and fresh views of the river, the surrounding moors or attractive woodland and farmland. Although the planting of trees on the course around 1970 has had a major effect on both the scenic and golfing aspects of the course, it is the river that dominates the opening holes. Sacrificing length for straightness can often be a sensible policy. However, Ilkley is not a severe test of golf, more a most enjoyable challenge on a first class course in delightful surroundings.

Captain 1990: Ricky Cockcroft
Secretary: G Hirst
Professional: John L Hammond

Lamberhurst

The golf course at Lamberhust is dominated by Court Lodge, a Jacobean house which has been the Morland family home since 1734. In 1890 the Squire's younger son, Major (later Lt Col) Henry Courtenay Morland, commissioned estate labour to construct a 9 hole golf course on the 'two Denes' north of the River Teise. Henry's maxim was 'everything in a straight line' and his original course was true to this.

The course was enjoyed by the Morland family and their guests, one of whom was the First World War poet Siegfried Sassoon who wrote fondly of playing 'to the cries of the school children and the smell of the brewery'. After the First World War the family felt unable to maintain the course privately. In 1920 a members' club was formed 'on the undertaking of about a dozen local men, that they would, individually or in pairs, be responsible for maintaining a green apiece.'

The Army commandeered the course during the Second World War and caused extensive damage. In 1946 restoration work began and in 1965 the course was extended to 5304 yards. In 1968 a new Clubhouse was opened and 1976 saw a full 18 hole course. Many trees were lost in 1987 to the hurricane but sufficient remain to provide an enjoyable but stern test of golf.

Captain 1990: A Tisdall
Secretary: P Gleeson
Professional: M Travers

Leicestershire

The Club was formed in June 1890, and permission was obtained in December 1890 to use part of the Leicester Racecourse as a golf course. It was instituted in February 1891 as the Leicester Golf Club and moved to a new site north of Stoughton Lane, Oadby, in 1892, where a 9 hole course was laid out over grazing land. The main hazards were hedgerows, spinneys, ditches and the Evington Brook. It was officially opened in October 1894 with an exhibition match between Sandy Herd and George

Smith, the resident professional, who probably designed this course and the extended 18 hole course which was opened in 1899.

'Leicestershire' was substituted for 'Leicester' in the Club's title in 1894 to substantiate its claim to represent the County in matches against other County Clubs, such as Nottinghamshire, until the Leicestershire and Rutland Golf Union was established in 1910.

Improvements were made to the course on the advice of James Braid in 1910, and of HS Colt in 1921, and it was redesigned and extended by Major Charles Mackenzie in 1935. It was again redesigned by CK Cotton in 1965 and the new Clubhouse was built on Evington Lane, when the old Clubhouse and part of the course was lost under the Ring Road. Further improvements have recently been undertaken on the advice of Donald Steel. The present course measures 6312 yards off the back tees.

Captain 1990: WM Harvison
Secretary: JL Adams
Professional: JR Turnbull

North Wilts

North Wilts Golf Club is situated high on the Wiltshire Downs between the towns of Calne and Devizes and enjoys panoramic views over much of the county. The Golfing Annual of 1890-91 reveals that it was instituted on 1st September 1890 with 30 members who paid an entrance fee and annual subscription of 5 shillings each. We learn also that, in 1982, a Clubroom had been erected and stabling for six horses was in course of construction – progress indeed!

In the early years, the land was rented from a farmer whose sheep kept the grass down, a common practice in those days. In the 1930s the land was leased from the Crown Estates, who remain the landlords, and was fenced in.

Sadly, very few records exist prior to 1926. However, it is known that JH Taylor inspected the course and advised on alterations. Further advice was sought from HS Colt, the designer of many famous courses. The present Clubhouse was constructed in 1937 and has since been extended.

In 1966 further land was acquired for the Club to grow from 9 to 18 holes. The new holes were designed by CK Cotton and were opened for play in 1972. Since then, automatic watering has been installed.

Shortly after winning the Open Championship in 1936, AH Padgham played an exhibition match and during their time in the armed services the Club could boast that Cecil Beamish, Gordon Huddy and Guy Wolstenholme were members.

This is essentially a 'Members' Club' that has provided pleasure for many over the years. Who knows what the next century may bring – FORE!

Captain 1990: JW Taylor
Secretary: JBW McKelvie
Professional: GJ Laing

Penrith

On 13th May 1890 a group of members of the Inglewood Club met to consider the formation of a golf club on the local racecourse and such was the enthusiasm that within 14 days the Inglewood Golf Club was established and equipped with a lawnmower, a grasscutter and a spade. Nine holes were laid out around the local racetrack and members had to contend with thick undergrowth of gorse and hoof-marks made by horses in training.

In 1913 racing had ceased and the course was extended to 18 holes by renting adjacent land, the occasion being marked by an exhibition match in which Ted Ray and Harry Vardon played the home professional and the Club champion. In 1935 the racecourse land was purchased from the Trustees, and the ownership of the complete 18 holes finally secured in 1948 when the land on the Beacon side was purchased from the Lowther Estate.

Over the years what was originally the Racecourse Grandstand has been converted into a fine Clubhouse with appropriate facilities. The course, having benefitted from advice given by W Fernie of Troon in 1911 and Dr Mackenzie in 1920, now presents a fine test of golf and has earned a growing reputation for its unrivalled situation and the immaculate condition in which it is maintained.

Captain 1990: D Noble
Secretary: J Carruthers
Professional: CB Thomson

Royal Guernsey

It would appear that golf had been played on the links in Guernsey for some years before the formation of the Guernsey Golf Club in 1890 by some 37 members. The original Clubhouse, a cottage, still exists. Royal status was granted in 1891 and a new course designed by old Tom Morris in 1894 on a large expanse of common land at L'Ancresse. The course is bordered by two large sandy bays which, from the raised tees at the northern end, produce some fine vistas. The plan of the new course was adjusted to fit in with the building of a new Clubhouse some distance from the original one.

The newly-built enlarged Clubhouse was but a shell after the German Occupation 1940–45 and the redesigned course had disappeared. A new course, designed by Mackenzie Ross, with the Clubhouse rebuilt, was opened in 1948; it was further extended and changes to the course made by Messers Hawtree in 1968.

Club membership is 1465, the standard scratch score is 70 and the length 6206 yards.

Well-known golfers associated with the Club have been Ted Ray, who was the Club professional at the turn of the century, Henry Cotton, who lived as a boy near the links and learnt to play there and the brothers Jolly, the best known being Berty (HC Jolly of Foxgrove) who played in the Ryder Cup in 1927.

Captain 1990: WJ Gaudion
Secretary: GJ Nicolle
Professional: N Wood

St Enodoc

Deep into Cornwall, St Enodoc is a haven for golfers who are prepared to travel to play the game on a splendid seaside course with no pretentions to grandeur, but where the welcome is cordial. The many devotees of St Enodoc, be they local members, summer visitors who return annually for their holiday golf, or the occasional golfer who enjoys links golf, all regard a round here as a memorable experience. Few visit the course without a burning desire to return.

Bernard Darwin, that most perceptive of writers, did not come to St Enodoc until late in his career. Yet his enthusiasm for the course as 'eminently natural, amusing and dramatic in a country of glorious and terrific sandhills' remains its reputation today. He emphasises how much enjoyment can be had from a course of modest length but where the terrain insists that each shot be carefully considered before it is played.

The early days of St Enodoc are not well chronicled, its origins being misty. Golf was played there in 1888 and a few holes were laid out in 1889, but the St Enodoc Club was not formed until 'about the year 1890'. As with most courses new ground near the original layout was rented and later acquired. Although many holes have been altered over the years, the course is essentially now where it began. Between 1967 and 1982 a new 18 hole short course of 4165 yards was constructed which has proved popular with members and visitors alike.

A new Clubhouse was opened in time for the English Ladies Championship in 1937, but due to the long trek to reach St Enodoc, it has been generally off the beat for national events.

Not perhaps that the members mind that too much.

Captain 1990: H Watts
Secretary: Col L Guy
Professional: N Williams

St Neots

Formed in October 1890 by 33 gentlemen of St Neots, the Club played originally over 9 holes laid out on St Neots Common. Because the land was used in summer for grazing cattle, play was permitted from August to March only, and even then parts were flooded in winter to provide skating for the public. Par for the course was originally 48, made up holo by hole as 0, 6, 4, 4, 7, 7, 5, 5, 4. In 1892, 21 Ladies joined the Club and the Ladies Section was the 12th to be formed in the country. The par for their course was 40, hole by hole being 5, 5, 3, 4, 5, 3, 6, 3, 6.

In 1909, the Club moved to a new course some two miles away, and in 1912 to its present location, with 9 holes laid out by Harry Vardon. Another 9 holes were added in 1966.

For some years, the Club rented a room in the nearby Cannon Inn for use as a 'headquarters'. In 1905 a 'pavilion' was erected on the Common close to the 1st tee, the site now being occupied by a Second World War pillbox. This pavilion was moved to the new course in 1909, and again to the present course in 1912. It has been replaced twice, the present structure being prestigious, with dining accommodation for over 100 people at a time.

The SSS of the present course is 69 and is a good test of amateur and professional, SSS having been equalled or bettered by only three of the latter.

The Club is fortunate to own all the ground over which the course is played and so is secure from rising rents. Its close proximity to the A1 makes it a very popular venue for visitors and with a membership of over 600 is well known for its welcome and hospitality.

Captain 1990: Barry Stearns
Secretary: Roger Marsden
Professional: Graham Bithrey

West Herts

The Club was founded in March 1890 to play on 19 acres of 'uncut and unrolled land' in the grounds of Bushey Hall, a health establishment. Hugh Kirkaldy, Open Champion in 1891, became our first professional following the addition of an extra 9 holes in 1891. Membership soon grew to over 300, mainly drawn from the professional classes of North London.

In 1897 the opportunity was taken to move to the beautiful grounds of Cassiobury Park. The soil formation of gravel over chalk ensured fine turf and excellent drainage. Old Tom Morris laid out the course and the bunkers were sited by JH Taylor. Under the influence of Lord Essex, the Club's landlord, Lord Clarendon, Lord Ridley and AJ Balfour the membership grew both in numbers and prestige. In 1903 West Herts was included in the Golfer's Handbook list of the 31 largest golf clubs in the world. The Club's Annual Dinners, held at the Hotel Cecil or Café Monico, became nationally famous, mainly owing to the witty after-dinner playlets written by Richard André, the Club poet.

When the land west of the Gade was sold in 1911 the Club lost its Clubhouse and four holes. After advice from HS Colt and Harry Vardon, five new holes were constructed. The present Clubhouse, designed by Sir Guy Dawber, was erected on the site of the old 3rd green.

In 1922 the course was lengthened and improved by one of the finest of all golf architects, Alistair Mackenzie.

Watford Borough Council, who acquired the land in 1932, announced in 1987 its intention to municipalise the course. In the High Court in May 1989 the Club succeeded in its application for Judicial Review. It now awaits an approach from the Council which it is hoped will lead to a solution acceptable to both parties.

Captain 1990: Jim Denton
Secretary: RAS Gordon
Professional: Charles Gough

Whitley Bay

From 1890 to 1900 golf was only played in the winter at Whitley Bay, the 9 hole course on the shore being released to holidaymakers in the summer. After 10 years land was also found for a 9 hole summer course nearby and for another six years summer and winter play took place on the two separate courses. 1906 saw a new 9 holes, to be 18 by 1910, at South Hartley Farm and Briar Dene. The Dene, a deep gulley with a stream running to the sea, provided a difficult hazard to cross for tee shots at four holes.

In 1949 Briar Dene was requisitioned for open-cast coal mining. Carters, the Raynes Park Seed Merchants, designed a new 9, cleverly arranged to provide good golf without interfering with the open-cast workings. This involved moving many thousands of tons of soil, clay and rock. As a result this part of the course has many interesting features with splendid sea views, only a mile from the town centre.

Captain 1990: CP Armatage
Secretary: B Dockar
Professional: WJ Light

Wildernesse

The name suggests a Club hard to locate. Situated in quiet parkland at Seal near Sevenoaks, it has always been a members' Club of distinction. Its foundation was inspired by Lord Hillingdon of the Glynn Mills banking family, who with his descendants, were Patrons and Presidents of the Club until after the First World War. The 18 hole course has undergone many changes but the most recent, in 1956, is the layout now much appreciated by all who are fortunate to play here.

In 1924 a group of members defected to found the nearby Knole Park Club; however the relationship between the two Clubs has always been friendly. Before the Second World War when many amateur golf tournaments were regarded as interesting and as important as much of the professional circuit today, the Bishop's Bowl Trophy attracted a formidable entry of Walker Cup, International and Oxford and Cambridge Blues almost as good as for the Amateur Championship.

The two best known golfers connected with the Club are the late Gerald Micklem and Sam King. Both learnt their golf at Wildernesse. Sam King was a Ryder Cup player of note and Gerald Micklem was one of the last Corinthians as player, Royal and Ancient Captain and administrator.

A new Clubhouse was built in 1956; previously a fine mansion of the Hillingdon family had been used.

Captain 1990: D Stirling
Secretary: M Blanford
Professional: W Dawson

Wilpshire

Wilpshire, the oldest golf club in East Lancashire, was established by a Mr James Birtwistle and nine other gentlemen who paid 10 shillings each to raise the annual rent required by a local farmer for land adjacent to the A666 between Blackburn and Clitheroe. Not surprisingly the first Clubroom was situated in the Wilpshire Hotel, until a move was made into a new Clubhouse in 1910.

The new 18 hole course was played for the first time in October 1909; alterations and improvements continued until the 1930s since when developments on the course have been more of a cosmetic than an intrinsic nature.

The most prestigious golfing event in the Club's calendar is the Wilpshire Trophy which, since its inception in 1931, has always been played on the first Saturday in July. The splendid silver trophy is based on the historic Warwick Vase and the Trophy was one of the first 36 hole amateur events to be held in Lancashire. In its early days it always attracted a field of county and international golfers.

The Club now has a thriving membership of over 700 of which 350 are men and 110 ladies.

Captain 1990: John Davidson
Hon Secretary: Brian Grimshaw
Professional: Walter Slaven

Woodford

Following the opening of Epping Forest to the public in 1882, a group of Woodford businessmen obtained permission in 1890 from the Corporation of London to play golf over that part of the Forest adjoining Sunset Avenue.

Work commenced immediately on the course, which was to be of 9 holes to a design by Tom Dunn, under greenkeeper and professional Lambert of Musselburgh. Fifty members were obtained in the first month and the first competition was held at Easter 1891, with the winner's score being 137. The scratch score was 83 although the length (for 18 holes) was approximately 5500 yards.

In 1894 a lease was taken on a cottage and adjoining land in Sunset Avenue, next to the 1st tee. The cottage housed the greenkeeper and one room was used by the few lady members. In the same year, a Clubroom for men only was erected on the adjoining land, where it still stands albeit with replacement parts. The Ladies Section elected its first captain in 1902 and obtained its first pavilion in 1922, built by the side of the Clubroom.

During the Second World War the course had very restricted use as anti-landing trenches were dug in the fairways. These were not filled in and the ground restored until 1950. The Clubroom was extended to incorporate the ladies in 1969 and further extended in 1984 as the first act in the run-up to the centenary.

Captain 1990: John Peters
Secretary: GJ Cousins
Professional: Ashley Johns

York

The Club was founded in September 1890, and for the next 14 years played on one of the city commons, Knavemire, the site of

York Racecourse. The original 9 hole course was penal in character, making full use of the available hazards: a gravel pit, pond, whins, ditches, and the racecourse rails themselves. Other major difficulties were the frequent intrusions from the general public (particularly those exercising horses) allied with lack of proper clubhouse facilities.

These problems were solved in 1904 by the move to the present 18 hole course at Strensall, six miles north of York. The course was designed by JH Taylor on open farmland which had latterly been used by the army for training purposes. Although Taylor's layout is largely unchanged, many bunkers have been filled in as the course has gradually reverted to its fundamental birch heathland character.

The Club has always had strong links with the military garrison in York, its most notable early member being Lt Freddie Tait, whose brief association with it (as the current amateur champion), was inspirational during a difficult period of its existence.

Despite other major difficulties during both World Wars, and after a disastrous Clubhouse fire in 1969, the Club has prospered at Strensall.

Captain 1990: CT Bailey
Secretary: F Appleyard
Professional: Tony Mason

Ireland

Ballycastle

Ballycastle Golf Club was founded in 1890 by Commander Alfred Causton who had retired from the Royal Navy to become Chief Inspector of the Coastguard in Ballycastle. Following a visit to Royal Portrush, he apparently recognised the suitability of the 'Warren' as a links course. The first competition was played in 1891 and earlier the same year Ballycastle became one of the founder members of the Irish Golf Union. The original 9 hole course on the Warren area of dunes was expanded early in the century to include some land to the east of the links. The major change occurred when more land was bought in the 1920s and the 18 hole course was opened by the Duke of Abercorn in 1926. It has remained essentially unchanged since that time.

The first five holes skirt Bon-a-Margy Abbey, a Franciscan friary in the grounds of which are buried sailors from *HMS Drake* which was torpedoed in Rathlin Sound during the First World War. Six holes remain in the Warren links and seven others cover an area of upland heath.

The panoramic views of Fair Head, the Mull of Kintyre, Rathlin Island, the North Antrim Coast and the Glens of Antrim make this one of the most scenic courses in Ireland. The course, though not long by golfing standards at 5882 yards, requires accurate wood and iron play and provides an excellent foil to the remaining North Coast courses for those players who, over the last 25 years, have taken part in the prestigious Causeway Coast Tournament, played each June.

Captain 1990: Hugh Sayers
Hon Secretaries: Tim Sheehan, Michael Page
Professional: Trevor Stewart

Bushfoot

Bushfoot is one mile from County Antrim's Giant's Causeway, not far from Royal Portrush, whose centenary was in 1988, and Ballycastle, also celebrating this year. Bushfoot is 9 holes, par 70 (SS 67) and particularly suits the holiday golfer with a family. Many eminent Irish names were members in the Club's early days when the annual subscription was 10 shillings and family membership £1.

The Club became affiliated to the Irish Golf Union in 1906 and the Ladies section to the Irish Ladies' Golf Union in 1933. That year Sir Malcolm MacNaughton was granted Life Membership of the Club in appreciation of his generosity towards building a new Clubhouse, completed in 1934 at a cost of £450. Fifty-five years on the Club has a beautiful new building for the centenary, which cost rather more than the earlier one!

A well-known member of the Club was J Fitzsimmons who won the Irish Amateur in 1934 and the North of Ireland Amateur in 1947 and 1948. He was elected an Honorary member of the Club.

Captain 1990: J Torrens
Hon Secretary: P Ritchie

Dungannon

The Club was instituted on 22nd November 1890 and golf was played over land generously provided by the Earl of Ranfurley, who became President of the Club and of the Irish Golf Union in 1891. At first play was restricted to winter months as in the summer the land was taken over for farming. This resulted in acrimonious relations with the farmer who had little regard for the game. From 1897–1904 the Earl was absent abroad as Governor-General of New Zealand and without his presence members found the situation vis-à-vis the farmer increasingly intolerable.

Later, during the First World War, new ground on which to play had to be found. Eventually a new 9 hole course was established at the Oaks road site. The Club moved again in 1957 to its present ground, first with 9 holes and in 1960 18, with a par of 71 (SSS 68).

The Clubhouse has suffered from bomb damage on several occasions, yet, despite these unwanted interruptions, golf has continued to be played all the time.

Captain 1990: Alan J Shiells
Hon Secretary: Joseph McCausland

Sutton, Dublin

This 9 hole course at Cush Point was once the home of the Dublin Golf Club before it moved to Phoenix Park and then Dolllymount in 1890, when the Sutton Club was founded. A rent of one shilling per month was paid to Lord Howth for the land.

The Sutton course, over which the leasehold has been the subject of many negotiations, has suffered from soil erosion. In 1964 a new lease on nearby land, which had been a corporation dump, was secured and a few new holes made and merged with some of the old. It involved major renovation, including £10,000 of top-soil and an artificial lake.

A new Clubhouse was completed in 1965, replacing the corrugated iron shed which had served for 75 years. It was opened by Mr Charles Haughey, now the Prime Minister.

Sutton will always be associated with its most famous son, Joe Carr, the best Amateur golfer in the British Isles from 1946 to 1970. Three times British Amateur Champion, 11 Walker Cup appearances, 22 consecutive Home Internationals for Ireland and winner of countless Irish titles, his record is quite unique. Other well-known players from Sutton have been Roddy Carr, JP Carroll, W Gill and Mrs Madill.

Captain 1990: Joe Carr
Secretary: JJ Geary
Professional: Nick Lynch

Scotland

Aberfoyle

Aberfoyle Golf Club was founded on 26th December 1890 with a membership of 30 and an annual subscription of 10 shillings. The course, which originally consisted of 9 holes with 'excellent hazards', was extended to 18 holes in the early 1980s and has scenic views of both the Campsie Fells and the glens at the foot of Ben Lomond.

Early in the Club's existence a small Clubroom was built for the comfort of the members. As the membership and the popularity of the Club grew, the original clubroom was unable to meet the needs of the players and a new Clubhouse was built in 1970.

The first recorded competition, held during August 1891 for the Lee Challenge Medal, was won by Mr A Blair with rounds of 52 and 53. Unfortunately Club records prior to the early 1960s have been lost and details of other competitive events are very scant.

The current membership stands at close to 400 and plans are at hand for an extension to be made to the existing Clubhouse.

Captain 1990: John Stokoe
Secretary: Alan McDonald

Anstruther

At a meeting in West Anstruther Town Hall on 3rd November 1890 it was decided to form a golf club to play over the land west of the town and that the name of the club would be 'Anstruther Golf Club'. The course at the Billowness was officially opened by playing for the Robertson Medal on Wednesday 8th April 1891, the first AGM taking place in October the same year.

The original course consisted of 7 holes until 1923 when more ground was leased to extend it to 9 holes. During the 1920s many unsuccessful attempts were made to purchase land to extend the course further to 18 holes. The first Clubhouses were small buildings, which are still integral parts of the course. In 1923 two rooms of a large private house named Marsfield were leased. This arrangement continued until 1945 when the rooms were gifted to the Club.

In 1957 the Club received a gift of an 18 hole putting green near the 1st tee and at the same time watering facilities were provided at all greens on the course. In 1979 a licence to sell liquor was obtained and a small bar was made in the existing building. This was later extended to the spacious lounge which overlooks Anstruther Harbour. The first Anstruther Open Competition took place in May 1983 and is now established on the calendar of many golfers in the area.

Captain 1990: Tom Reid
Secretary: Marjory Yuill

Callander

In September 1889 a group of local professional and businessmen decided to form a golf club. After looking at several sites Mr Baillie-Hamilton was approached to allow play on part of the Moor of Gart on Cambusmore estate. Tom Morris was invited to lay out a course and Callander Golf Club's 6 holes were opened in June 1890. The annual subscription was 10 shillings. Even at that time ladies were allowed to play in men's competitions and Miss Baillie-Hamilton was Club Champion three times.

The Club expanded quickly. In 1892 9 holes were constructed on Lord Ancaster's land behind the railway station. Later the Town Council purchased Lord Ancaster's site with additional ground for 9 more holes, now the present 18 hole course.

For many years visitors and Societies have supplemented the Club's income. The Club flourishes with 540 members and a new Clubhouse was built in 1980. Important Club competitions are the Club Championship, the Ancaster Cup and the James Johnston and Henry Hill Medals. Since 1909 the Ladies have had their own Captain and this section is very active and continues to expand.

The Club has always encouraged youth with both Durham Burt and Gordon MacDonald helping young golfers until a professional was appointed. For a small Club, Callander has done well to produce two members, Gordon and Sandy Barrie, who have played for Scotland in recent years.

Captain 1990: FC Leatherby
Secretary: J McClements
Professional: W Kelly

Dollar

At the end of the last century, nestling in the foothills of the Ochils, Dollar's life revolved round the Academy which attracted many from abroad to settle for a time to educate their families; an early rule still in existence is that members living out of Scotland until the 15th May are only required to pay half the annual subscription.

The club started out with a flat 9 hole course which was abandoned to the Ladies Club in 1896 in favour of a more challenging one at the appropriately named Gloomhill on the slopes of the Ochils. The layout of the present course, opened in 1906, was started by Dickson who left for Portmarnock and completed by Ben Sayers who realised that the contours of the small raised greens made bunkers unnecessary.

As the only 18 hole course in the area at the time, the Club was host to County and District Championships and Inter County Matches, much

to the chagrin of the Fife players from their links courses.

In 1908 the caddies organised a strike for an increase in their fee from 6d to 9d, but this was quashed before Sandy Herd and George Duncan played a four-ball against John Ball and Ted Ray which was halved. Ray returned in 1921 to win a match against Harry Vardon, holing the course in a record 67 to Vardon's 76.

Due to the development of more and larger courses in the area, the prominence of Dollar declined and the Club returned to the comparative tranquillity of its early years. For the enjoyment of the course's challenge, its splendid views and the return to the 19th in Brewlands House, we owe a debt of gratitude to our founders.

Captain 1990: H Galloway
Secretary: MB Shea

Glencorse

Milton Bridge was not the original home of Glencorse Golf Club. It was along the road at Rosslynlee where golf was played in the fields at an annual rent of £15, with members being charged 5 shillings. In 1894 at the Fishers Tryst in Milton Bridge 20 members met and proposed a move to a more extended course between Milton Bridge and Auchendinny, belonging to Mr Alexander Inglis, who gave the ground free for a few years after the Club moved there in 1895. Entry fee was one guinea and the annual subscription 7s 6d.

In 1900 Glencorse was described as one of the finest inland courses in Scotland. The higher holes commanded a fine view of the Pentland Hills, while in Auchendinny Glen the scenery and sporting character of the holes could not be excelled.

From the start Glencorse had 18 holes laid out by Willie Park Jr. Leslie Balfour-Melville, the 1895 Amateur Champion, was one of the Club's first members. George Macgregor, the Centenary Captain, represented Britain and Ireland in five Walker Cup matches between 1971 and 1987 and made 160 appearances for Scotland. Robin Wight and Colin Brooks, now a professional, were both amateur Scottish champions. The late Ronnie Shade learnt his golf at Glencorse where his father had been Head Greenkeeper.

In 1965 the purchase of the course for £20,500 brought lasting benefits to members. In 1987 the disused 16-arch railway viaduct spanning the course was declared dangerous and blown up.

Captain 1990: George Macgregor
Secretary: Dan McNiven
Professional: Cliffe Jones

Grantown-on-Spey

The Club was founded in 1890 by local gentlemen who felt a golf course was essential to improve amenities in an expanding Highland holiday area. The land for the original course was leased from the Countess of Seafield and designed by AC Brown. The 1911 18 hole lay-out was by Willie Park Jr, with further alterations later by James Braid. The course divides itself into three sections of six holes: the first in parkland has destroyed many a round before crossing the road to the next six set in typical Highland woodland, with the 9th providing one of the many beautiful views in Scottish golf. The remaining holes revert to parkland with out-of-bounds demanding tee-shot accuracy.

The Clubhouse, rebuilt after a fire in 1933, was extended in the 1980s to provide a comfortable 19th hole with magnificent views over the Crondall Hills and the Cairngorms.

The Club's most famous golfing son was Bobby Cruikshank, whose successful US golf career included tying with Bobby Jones for the US Open in 1923, but losing the play-off. A trophy at the Club, presented by his grand-daughter, reminds today's members of the 'great wee Scot', as he was affectionately known.

Captain 1990: WP Lawson
Secretary: D Shepherd
Professional: W Mitchell

Greenock

In 1873 the Rev John Ireland and the Rev WW Tulloch arrived in Greenock from St Andrews to be inducted in local churches, bringing their golf clubs with them. Sparking off local interest, they took a lease of Bow Farm and laid out 6 holes. Soon a dispute with the local farmer meant the closure of the course and the Club's disbandment. In 1890 the Greenock Club was founded on flat ground at Battery Park and J Campbell Park was elected Captain of 50 members.

In 1892 the Club moved to new ground above Battery Park; 9 holes were laid out and a Clubhouse built. The course was extended over the years and in 1924 James Braid was invited to advise on reconstruction; the leased farmlands were purchased and an 18 and a 9 hole course built. During the Second World War much of the course was taken over by the military. In 1946 the ground was recovered to form the present courses which have a delightful setting and fine views to Glasgow and south-west to the Firth of Clyde and Arran.

The Club has hosted several championships on the SSS 68 part parkland and part moorland course. Open Champions JH Taylor and Willie Fernie in 1893 and Harry Vardon with Sandy Herd in 1905 played exhibition matches, while more recently Roberto De Vicenzo, Fred Daly, Dai Rees, John Panton, Ronnie Shade, Jack Newton and Sam Torrance have demonstrated their skills to members. Panton's Professional record of 66 in 1956 still stands.

Captain 1990: Rodger Clark
Secretary: Eric Black
Professional: Graham Ross

Stornoway

Stornoway Golf Club, instituted in 1890, was originally laid out as 9 holes on the Melrost links, three miles from the town. Neither the designer nor the date it was extended to 18 holes is known, due to the absence of minute books before 1933.

From the mid-1930s part of the course, being flat, was used as a civil landing ground and from 1940 the whole of it was used as an RAF station, which is now Stornoway airport. Thus the Club's activities were suspended until 1947 when a new 18 hole course in Lews Castle Park was constructed with Air Ministry compensation. For some years it was reduced to 12 holes, due to drainage difficulties, but between 1970 and 1977 six additional holes were laid out, whilst preserving the 'Dardanelles' hole, said to be the most difficult par 5 in Europe.

The small membership of 200 greatly enjoys the course, which is conveniently situated close to the town and has superb views of seas and moorland. Visitors are welcome; no starting times are necessary.

Captain 1990: CS Kelso
Secretary: P Dickie

Stromness

The Club was officially formed in 1890 at Wharbeth, one and a half miles from the town centre, although it is known that golf was played earlier in the district. It was a 9 hole course until 1924 when 18 holes were laid out at Ness, the farm there having been sold. Golfers raised £1600 to purchase the land and more to lay out the fairways and greens. This was supervised by George Smith of Lossiemouth and opened in 1924 by Dr McNish.

Until 1963 the barn of the farm was the Clubhouse. It was then extended to include a bar run by the Social Club, which was formed to organise and raise funds for a modern Club-house. This was built in the late 1960s and has recently been enlarged and improved.

A unique feature of the course is two large, concrete bunkers with their deep ravine-like access. They are remnants of old munition stores and gun emplacements from the war. Woe betide anyone who lands in these! A further feature was the sheep which still grazed on the course, but this ceased in December 1988.

Situated on the shore overlooking Hoy Sound with views to the north of Scotland and Scapa Flow, Stromness must rank among the most picturesque courses in the Kingdom. Every year the Club, with a membership increasing annually, plays golf at midnight on 21st June, the longest day.

Captain 1990: K Anderson
Secretary: FJ Groundwater

Tain

Situated on the southern shore of the Dornoch Firth between the heather and the sea lies Tain Golf Course.

Celebrating its centenary this year, the Club was founded by Alexander MacBean, a gentleman retired from banking service in India when he had enjoyed golf. He and a number of Tain businessmen summoned the great Tom Morris to design the course and, to this day, it bears the stamp of his authority. A feature of the course is the Tain River which winds its way through the early and late holes, making it a strict SSS 70. From the Box Tees, a very pleasurable SSS 68 can be played.

In August, the Tain Tournament is held when Open One-Day, 4-Day, Mixed Foursomes and Ladies' Tournaments are held – a real family occasion.

Captain 1990: Anthony Watson
Secretary: WW Russell

West Linton

On 7th June 1890 a meeting was convened by Robert Miller, schoolmaster, in the Public School at West Linton, Peeblesshire for the purpose of initiating a golf club. The course was laid out by Robert Miller who was largely responsible for the growth of the Club during its early years. The course, which was originally 9 holes, is on heathland almost 1000 feet above sea level amid peace and tranquillity and affords magnificent views of the Pentlands and the Lyne Valley to the Moorfoot Hills.

For many years the course was popular with seasonal visitors from Edinburgh who spent their summers in West Linton. The Club's serious expansion began in the 1960s with the erection of a new Clubhouse, followed closely in the early 1970s with the extension of the course to 18 holes. Thereafter the Club was able to purchase the land on which the course is situated from the local landowner, Colonel Sutherland, and numerous improvements have since been made rendering the course an opponent which is not easily conquered.

The Club has an enthusiastic playing membership of 500 and is extremely popular with visitors. Although there have been many changes to the course and the facilities over the years, the superb scenery and beauty of the surroundings remain unaltered, making it an extremely agreeable place to relax and play golf.

Captain 1990: RS Buchan
Secretary: G Scott
Professional: DI Stewart

Wales

Conwy (Caernavonshire)

Golf has been played near the sea at Conwy from 1869. Hoylake members improved the course in 1876, but the Caernarvonshire Club was not founded until 1890, when 50 members secured a five-year lease to play golf on Conwy Morfa Links. They also acquired a military mess-hut of the Volunteers as a Clubhouse. The course record of 71 was held by Alex Herd until George Duncan, winner of the Open Championship in 1920 and the Club's professional, went round in 65 in 1910, a really remarkable score at the time. Soon afterwards he was dismissed for playing football on Saturday afternoons when he was about to sign forms for Liverpool FC.

The Club and course suffered in both wars through military incursion, but the committee managed to ensure golf continued to be played resulting in a steadily increased membership in the following years. In 1933 the Clubhouse, along with many valuable records, was completely destroyed by fire. One early register of members which survives shows that out of 129 members only 15 men and four ladies had Conwy addresses. The absentee members included famous amateur, Harold Hilton who won the Open twice, in 1892 and 1897. The Club was a founder member of the Welsh Golfing Union.

Captain 1990: Don Dent
Secretary: Cyril Roberts
Professional: Peter Lees

Glamorganshire

Founded in October 1890, Glamorganshire was the first parkland course in Wales. Most of the early members came from Penarth. With 9 holes laid out nearby on rising ground and views over five counties and the Bristol Channel, membership grew fast. The course was soon extended to 18 holes and the Welsh Amateur Championship was played there as soon as 1897.

Members who were early Welsh Champions included TM Barlow, the Club's first Captain, and James Hunter. The Club won the Welsh Team Championship 11 times in 30 years from 1899.

Another leading amateur of the Club was Henry Howell, eight times Welsh Champion, who played for Wales for 29 years in the Home Internationals. On one occasion he beat the Champions of England, Scotland and Ireland on three consecutive days and was still not selected for the Walker Cup side. He later became Secretary of the Club which now has close on 1000 members and continues to flourish.

Captain 1990: CJ Harrison
Secretary: GC Crimp
Professional: A Kerr Smith

Rhyl

The original course opened in 1890, comprised 9 holes, with a further 9 holes being added in 1908, supervised by James Braid. Situated between the sea and the Rhyl–Prestatyn main road, with panoramic views of the Clwydian Hills, the course is an excellent test of golf, especially against the prevailing winds from the sea.

Many Welsh Amateur Championships have been held here and Rhyl members have won a number of these events. In 1909 the Welsh Professional Championship held here saw A Matthew of Rhyl emerge as the winner. During the period 1895 to 1955, Rhyl won the Welsh Team Championship eight times, and between 1895 and 1920 provided three Chairmen of the WGU of which it is a founder member.

About 1949, following a heavy storm, huge quantities of sand were deposited on the Prestatyn end of the course, with the subsequent closure of 9 holes, which is how the course remains to date. However, the Club Course Committee has recently acquired the land which was lost in the storm from the Borough Council and is negotiating with various interested parties to restore the course to something near its former glory, a decision which has yet to be put before the members.

Captain 1990: Malcolm Herrington
Secretary: GK Watkin

Clubs also celebrating their centenary in 1990: Newquay (Cornwall), Tavistock (Devon), Ffestiniog (Gwynedd) and The Island (Dublin).

The Editors regret that limitations on space have meant that illustrations of the Centenary Clubs could not be included.

Golf Clubs and Courses in the UK and Europe

How to use this section

1. Geographical divisions

Clubs are listed in alphabetical order within counties, which are themselves listed alphabetically. All clubs are now listed under their geographical county and not the county of affiliation. In Scotland, counties are grouped under the recognised Scottish administrative regions.

European clubs are in alphabetical order by country, grouped under useful regional headings as a further guide. In addition, all clubs and courses are listed in the index at the back of the book.

2. Explanation of details given

a After the name of the club is the date of foundation (where available).

b Courses are private unless otherwise stated. Many public courses have members' clubs which play over them; information on these clubs can be obtained from the course concerned.

c The address is the postal address of each club or course. If the postal county is different from the one under which the club or course is listed, it will be shown in the address.

d The membership figure denotes the total number of members. The number of lady members (L), the number of juniors (J) and of five day members (5) are sometimes shown separately.

e Telephone numbers for secretaries and professionals are shown if different from the club telephone number.

f Fees: green fees are only quoted for visitors if they are permitted to play unaccompanied by a

member. The basic cost per round is shown first, then in brackets, the cost of a weekend and/or Bank Holiday round where this is available to unaccompanied visitors. Green fees for visitors playing with a member are not given. Weekly (W), monthly (M) and fortnightly (F) terms are shown where available. *Green fees quoted are the most up to date supplied by each club.*

3. Abbreviations

V'trs this shows what restrictions (if any) are in force for visitors.
WD Weekdays
WE Weekends
BH Bank Holidays
  (If no days stated, the particular restrictions apply at all times)
U Unrestricted, ie casual visitors may play without restriction on the days stated.
M with a member, ie casual visitors are not allowed. Only visitors playing with a member are permitted on the days stated.
H Handicap certificate required
I Introduction, ie visitors are permitted on the days stated if they have a letter of introduction from their own club, their own club's membership card, or a handicap certificate.
XL No ladies allowed on the days stated
NA No visitors allowed
SOC Recognised Golfing Societies welcome if previous arrangements made with secretary

Information given us is up to date as possible at the time of going to press. Great reliance on the accuracy of this information is placed on details received from club secretaries, for whose assistance we are indebted, but we would be grateful to be notified of any inaccuracies.

County Index

England

Avon (Map 3) 492
Bedfordshire (Map 4) 493
Berkshire (Map 2) 494
Buckinghamshire (Map 2) 496
Cambridgeshire (Map 4) 497
Channel Islands 498
Cheshire (Map 8) 499
Cleveland (Map 9) 501
Cornwall (Map 3) 502
Cumbria (Map 9) 503
Derbyshire (Map 6) 505
Devon (Map 3) 506
Dorset (Map 3) 508
Durham (Map 9) 510
Essex (Map 4) 511
Gloucestershire (Map 3) 514
Greater Manchester (Map 8) 536
Hampshire (Map 2) 515
Hereford & Worcester (Map 6) 519
Hertfordshire (Map 4) 520
Humberside (Map 7) 523
Isle of Man (Map 8) 524
Isle of Wight (Map 2) 525
Kent (Map 1) 525
Lancashire (Map 8) 530
Leicestershire (Map 5) 533
Lincolnshire (Map 5) 535
Merseyside (Map 8) 541
Middlesex (Map 1) 544
Norfolk (Map 4) 546
Northants (Map 5) 548
Northumberland (Map 9) 549
Nottinghamshire (Map 5) 550
Oxfordshire (Map 2) 552
Shropshire (Map 6) 552
Somerset (Map 3) 553
Staffordshire (Map 6) 554
Suffolk (Map 4) 556
Surrey (Map 1) 568
Sussex, East (Map 1) 563
Sussex, West (Map 1) 565
Tyne & Wear (Map 9) 567

Warwickshire (Map 6) 568
West Midlands (Map 6) 569
Wiltshire (Map 3) 573
Yorkshire, North (Map 7) 574
Yorkshire, South (Map 7) 576
Yorkshire, West (Map 7) 578

Ireland (Map 10)

Connacht
Co Galway 591
Co Leitrim 593
Co Mayo, 594
Co Roscommon 596
Co Sligo 596

Leinster
Co Carlow 585
Dublin City 589
Co Dublin 590
Co Kildare 592
Co Kilkenny 593
Co Laois 593
Co Longford 594
Co Louth 594
Co Meath 595
Co Offaly 596
Co Westmeath 598
Co Wexford 598
Co Wicklow 598

Munster
Co Clare 585
Co Cork 586
Co Kerry 592
Co Limerick 593
Co Tipperary 596
Co Waterford 597

Ulster
Co Antrim 583
Co Armagh 584
Belfast 584
Co Cavan 585
Co Donegal 587

Co Down 588
Co Fermanagh 591
Co Londonderry 594
Co Monaghan 595
Co Tyrone 597

Scotland

Borders (Map 11)
Berwickshire 599
Peebleshire 599
Roxburghshire 599
Selkirkshire 599

Central (Map 13)
Clackmannanshire 600
Perthshire (part) 600
Stirlingshire (part) 600

Dumfries & Galloway (Map 12)
Dumfriesshire 601
Kirkcudbrightshire 602
Wigtownshire 602

Fife (Map 13) 603

Grampian (Map 14)
Aberdeenshire 605
Banffshire 607
Kincardineshire 608
Morayshire 608

Highland (Map 14)
Caithness 608
Inverness 609
Nairnshire 609
Ross & Cromarty 609
Sutherland 610

Lothian (Map 11)
East Lothian 610
Midlothian 612
West Lothian 614

Orkney & Shetland (Map 14) 614

Strathclyde (Map 12)
Argyll 615
Ayrshire 615
Bute 617

Dunbartonshire 618
Lanarkshire 619
Renfrewshire 622
Stirlingshire (part) 624

Tayside (Map 13)
Angus 624
Kinross-shire 625
Perthshire (part) 626

Western Isles (Map 14) 627

Wales (Map 15)

Clwyd 628
Dyfed 629
Gwent 630
Gwynedd 631
Isle of Anglesey 632
Mid Glamorgan 632
Powys 633
South Glamorgan 634
West Glamorgan 635

England: South-East

Kent
1 Aquarius
2 Ashford
3 Barnehurst
4 Bearsted
5 Beckenham Place Park
6 Bexley Heath
34 Bromley
7 Broome Park
8 Canterbury
9 Cherry Lodge
10 Chestfield (Whitstable)
11 Chislehurst
12 Cobtree Manor Park
13 Corinthian
14 Cranbrook
15 Cray Valley
16 Darenth Valley
17 Dartford
18 Deangate Ridge
19 Edenbridge G&CC
20 Eltham Warren
21 Faversham
22 Gillingham
23 Hawkhurst
24 Herne Bay
25 High Elms
26 Holtye
27 Hythe Imperial
28 Knole Park
29 Lamberhurst
30 Langley Park
31 Leeds Castle
32 Littlestone
33 Lullingstone Park
35 Mid Kent
36 Nevill
37 North Foreland
38 Poult Wood
39 Prince's
40 Rochester & Cobham Park
41 Royal Blackheath
42 Royal Cinque Ports
43 Royal St George's
44 Ruxley
45 St Augustines
46 Sene Valley Folkestone & Hythe
47 Sheerness
48 Shooter's Hill
49 Shortlands
50 Sidcup
51 Sittingbourne & Milton Regis
52 Sundridge Park
53 Tenterden
54 Tunbridge Wells
55 Walmer & Kingsdown
56 West Kent
57 West Malling
58 Westgate & Birchington
59 Whitstable & Seasalter
60 Wildernesse
61 Woodlands Manor
62 Wrotham Heath
New for 1990
63 Tudor Park

Middlesex
1 Airlinks
2 Ashford Manor
3 Brent Valley
4 Bush Hill Park
5 Crews Hill
6 Ealing
7 Enfield
8 Finchley
9 Fulwell
10 Grim's Dyke
11 Hampstead
12 Harefield Place
13 Harrow School
14 Haste Hill
15 Hendon
16 Highgate
17 Hillingdon
18 Holiday Inn
19 Horsenden Hill
20 Hounslow Heath
21 Lime Trees Park
22 Mill Hill
23 Muswell Hill
24 North Middlesex
25 Northwood
26 Perivale Park
27 Picketts Lock
28 Pinner Hill
29 Ruislip
30 Stanmore
31 Strawberry Hill
32 Sudbury
33 Trent Park
34 Twickenham
35 West Middlesex
36 Whitewebbs
37 Wyke Green

Surrey
1 The Addington
2 Addington Court
3 Addington Palace
4 Banstead Downs
5 Barrow Hills
6 Betchworth Park
7 Bramley
8 Burhill
9 Camberley Heath
10 Chessington Golf Centre
11 Chipstead
12 Coombe Hill
13 Coombe Wood
14 Coulsdon Court
15 Croham Hurst
16 Crondall
17 Cuddington
18 Dorking
19 Drift
20 Dulwich & Sydenham Hill
21 Effingham
22 Epsom
23 Farnham
24 Farnham Park
25 Fernfell G&CC
26 Foxhills
27 Gatton Manor Park
28 Goal Farm
29 Guildford
30 Hankley Common
31 Hindhead
32 Hoebridge Golf Centre
33 Home Park
34 Kingswood
35 Laleham
36 Leatherhead
37 Limpsfield Chart
38 Malden
39 Mitcham
40 Moore Place
41 New Zealand
42 North Downs
43 Oaks Sports Centre
44 Purley Downs
45 Puttenham
46 RAC Country Club
47 Redhill & Reigate
48 Reigate Heath
49 Richmond
50 Richmond Park
51 Roehampton
52 Royal Mid Surrey
53 Royal Wimbledon
54 St George's Hill
55 Sandown Park
56 Selsdon Park Hotel
57 Shillinglee Park
58 Shirley Park
59 Silvermere (Sunningdale: see Berkshire, Map 2)
60 Surbiton
61 Tandridge
62 Thames Ditton & Esher
63 Tyrrells Wood
64 Walton Heath
65 Wentworth
66 West Byfleet
67 West Hill
68 West Surrey
69 Wimbledon Common
70 Wimbledon Park
71 Windlemere
72 Woking
73 Woodcote Park
74 Worplesdon
New for 1990
75 Lingfield Park

Sussex (East)
1 Ashdown Forest Hotel
2 Brighton & Hove
3 Cooden Beach
4 Crowborough Beacon
5 Dale Hill
6 The Dyke
7 East Brighton
8 Eastbourne Downs
9 Hastings
10 Highwoods (Bexhill)
11 Hollingbury Park (Brighton)
12 Horam Park
13 Lewes
14 Peacehaven
15 Piltdown
16 Royal Ashdown Forest
17 Royal Eastbourne
18 Rye
19 Seaford
20 Seaford Head
21 Waterhall
22 West Hove
23 Willingdon
New for 1990
24 East Sussex National

Sussex (West)
1 Bognor Regis
2 Copthorne
3 Cottesmore
4 Cowdray Park
5 Effingham Park
6 Gatwick Manor
7 Goodwood
8 Ham Manor
9 Haywards Heath
10 Hill Barn
11 Ifield
12 Littlehampton
13 Mannings Heath
14 Pyecombe
15 Selsey
16 Tilgate
17 West Chiltington
18 West Sussex
19 Worthing
New for 1990
20 Pease Pottage

Public courses are set in bold

Map 1   463

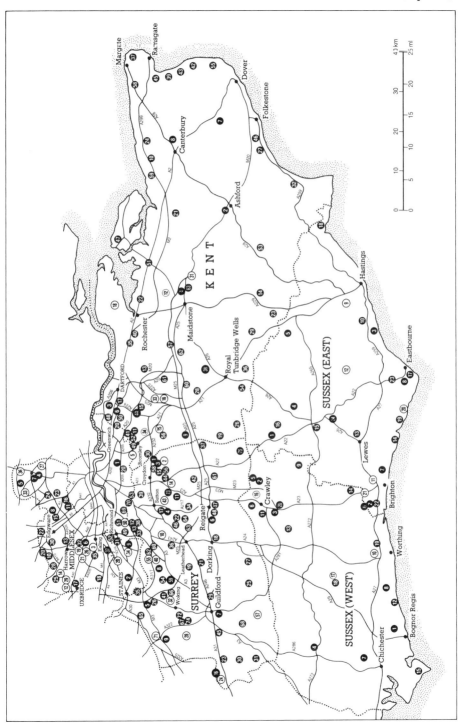

England: South

Berkshire
1 Bearwood
2 Berkshire
3 Calcot Park
4 Datchet
5 Downshire
6 East Berkshire
7 Eton College
8 Goring & Streatley
9 Hawthorn Hill
10 Hurst
**11 Lavender Park Golf
Centre**
12 Maidenhead
13 Newbury &
   Crookham
14 Reading
15 Royal Ascot
16 The Royal Household
17 Sonning
18 Sunningdale
19 Sunningdale Ladies
   (Sunningdale clubs
   listed under Surrey)
20 Swinley Forest
21 Temple
22 West Berkshire
23 Winter Hill
New for 1990
24 Donnington Valley
25 Mill Ride

Buckinghamshire
1 Abbey Hill
2 Beaconsfield
3 Buckingham
4 Burnham Beeches
5 Chesham & Ley Hill
6 Chiltern Forest
7 Denham
8 Ellesborough
9 Farnham Park
10 Flackwell Heath
11 Gerrards Cross
12 Harewood Downs
13 Hazlemere G&CC
14 Iver
15 Ivinghoe
16 Little Chalfont
17 Stroke Poges
18 Stowe
19 Weston Turville
20 Wexton Park
21 Whiteleaf
22 Windmill Hill
23 Woburn
New for 1990
24 Chartridge Park

Hampshire
1 Alresford
2 Alton
3 Ampfield Par Three
4 Andover
5 Army Golf Club
6 Barton-on-Sea
7 Basingstoke
8 Basingstoke Hospitals
9 Bishopswood
10 Blackmoor
11 Bramshaw
12 Brokenhurst Manor
13 Burley
14 Corhampton
15 Dibden
16 Dunwood Manor
17 Fleetlands
18 Fleming Park
19 Gosport & Stokes Bay
20 Great Salterns
21 Hartley Wintney
22 Hayling
23 Hockley
24 Leckford & Longstock
25 Lee-on-the-Solent
26 Liphook
27 Meon Valley Hotel
28 New Forest
29 North Hants
30 Old Thorns Hotel CC
31 Ordnance Survey
32 Petersfield
33 Portsmouth
34 Romsey
35 Rowlands Castle
36 Royal Winchester
37 Southampton
38 Southwick Park
39 Southwood
40 Stoneham
41 Tidworth Garrison
42 Tylney Park
43 Waterlooville
New for 1990
44 Sandford Springs

Isle of Wight
1 Cowes
2 Freshwater
3 Newport IW
4 Osborne
5 Ryde
6 Shanklin & Sandown
7 Ventnor

Oxfordshire
1 Badgemore Park
2 Burford
3 Cherwell Edge
4 Chesterton
5 Chipping Norton
6 Frilford Heath
7 Henley
8 Huntercombe
9 North Oxford
10 RAF Benson
11 Southfield
12 Tadmarton Heath

*Public courses are set
in bold*

Map 2   465

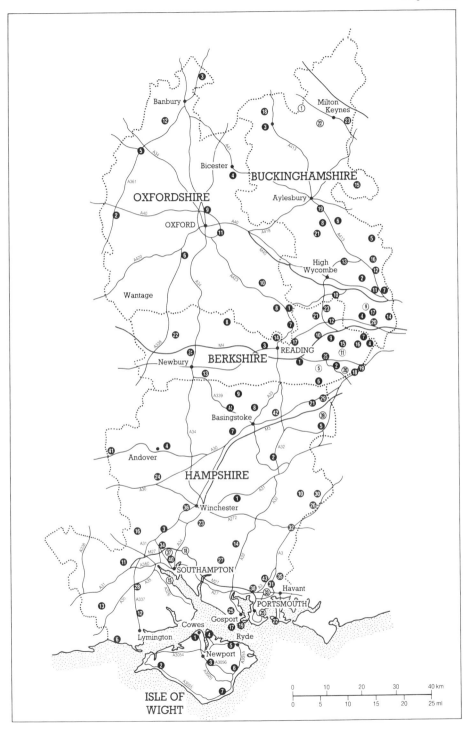

Banbury

Milton
Keynes

Bicester

BUCKINGHAMSHIRE

OXFORDSHIRE

Aylesbury

OXFORD

High
Wycombe

Wantage

READING

Newbury

BERKSHIRE

Basingstoke

Andover

HAMPSHIRE

Winchester

SOUTHAMPTON

Havant

PORTSMOUTH

Cowes

Gosport

Ryde

Lymington

Newport

ISLE OF
WIGHT

| 0 | 10 | 20 | 30 | 40 km |

| 0 | 5 | 10 | 15 | 20 | 25 ml |

England: South-West

Avon
1 Bath
2 Bristol & Clifton
3 Chipping Sodbury
4 Clevedon
5 **Entry Hill**
6 Filton
7 Fosseway CC
8 Henbury
9 Knowle
10 Lansdown
11 Long Ashton
12 Mangotsfield
13 Saltford
14 Shirehampton Park
15 Tracy Park
16 Weston-super-Mare
17 Worlebury

Cornwall
1 Bude & North
  Cornwall
2 Budock Vean Hotel
3 Carlyon Bay
4 Culdrose
5 Falmouth
6 Isles of Scilly
7 Launceston
8 Looe Bindown G&CC
9 Mullion
10 Newquay
11 Perranporth
12 Praa Sands
13 St Austell
14 St Enodoc
15 St Mellion
16 Tehidy Park
17 Tregenna Castle
  Hotel
18 Trevose
19 Truro
20 West Cornwall
21 Whitsand Bay Hotel

Devon
1 Axe Cliff
2 Bigbury
3 Chulmleigh
4 Churston
5 Downes Crediton
6 East Devon
7 Elfordleigh Hotel
  G&CC
8 Exeter G&CC
9 Holsworthy
10 Honiton
11 Ilfracombe
12 Manor House Hotel
13 Newton Abbot
  (Stover)
14 Okehampton
15 Royal North Devon
16 Saunton

17 Sidmouth
18 Staddon Heights
19 Tavistock
20 Teignmouth
21 Thurlestone
22 Tiverton
23 Torquay
24 Torrington
25 Warren
26 Wrangaton (South
  Devon)
27 Yelverton

Dorset
1 Ashley Wood
2 Bridport & West
  Dorset
3 Broadstone
4 Came Down
5 **Christchurch**
6 Ferndown
7 Highcliffe Castle
8 Isle of Purbeck
9 Knighton Heath
10 East Dorset (Lakey
  Hill)
11 Lyme Regis
12 **Meyrick Park**
13 Parkstone
14 **Queen's Park**
15 Sherborne
16 Wareham
17 Weymouth
New for 1990
18 Canford School
19 Halstock

Gloucestershire
1 Broadway
2 Cirencester
4 **Cleeve Hill**
5 Cotswold Edge
6 Cotswold Hills
7 Forest of Dean
8 Gloucestershire Hotel
9 Lilley Brook
10 Lydney
11 Minchinhampton
12 Painswick
13 Stinchcombe Hill
14 Tewkesbury Park
  Hotel
15 Westonbirt

Somerset
1 Brean
2 Burnham & Berrow
3 Enmore Park
4 Kingweston
5 Mendip
6 Minehead & West
  Somerset

7 Taunton & Pickeridge
8 **Vivary Park**
9 Wells
10 Windwhistle G&CC
11 Yeovil

Wiltshire
1 Bremhill Park
2 Brinkworth
3 **Broome Manor**
4 Chippenham
5 High Post
6 Kingsdown
7 Marlborough
8 North Wilts
9 RAF Upavon
10 RMCS Shrivenham
11 Salisbury & South
  Wilts
12 Swindon
13 West Wilts

*Public courses are set
in bold*

Map 3   467

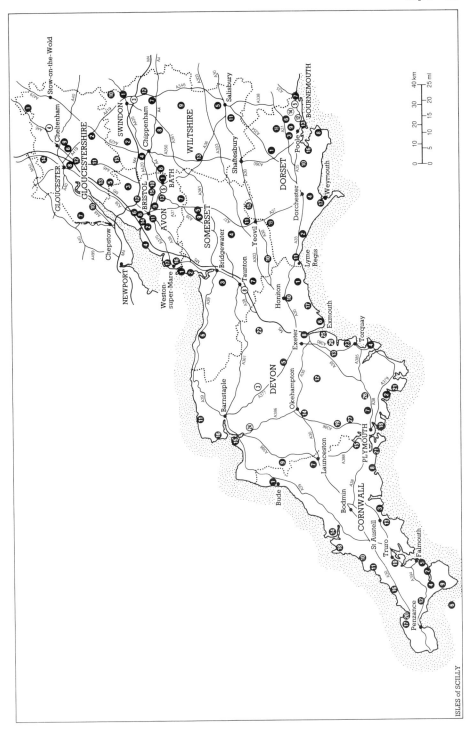

England: East Anglia

Bedfordshire
1 Aspley Guise &
  Woburn Sands
2 Beadlow Manor Hotel
  G&CC
3 Bedford & County
4 Bedfordshire
5 Colworth
6 Dunstable Downs
7 Griffin
8 John O'Gaunt
9 Leighton Buzzard
10 Millbrook
11 **Mowsbury**
12 South Beds
13 **Stockwood Park**
14 **Tilsworth**
15 **Wyboston Lakes**
New for 1990
16 RAF Henlow

Cambridgeshire
1 Abbotsley
2 Cambridgeshire Moat
  House Hotel
3 Ely City
4 Girton
5 Gog Magog
6 March
7 **Orton Meadows**
8 Peterborough Milton
9 Ramsey
10 St Ives (Hunts)
11 St Neot's
12 **Thorpe Wood**

Essex
1 Abridge G&CC
2 Ballards Gore
3 **Basildon**
4 **Belfairs**
5 **Belhus Park Municipal**
6 Bentley G&CC
7 Birch Grove
8 Boyce Hill
9 Braintree
10 **Bunsay Downs**
11 Burnham-on-Crouch
12 Canons Brook
13 Channels
14 Chelmsford
15 Chigwell
16 **Chingford**
17 Clacton
18 Colchester
19 **Fairlop Waters**
20 Forrester Park
21 Frinton
22 **Hainault Forest**
23 **Hartswood**
24 Harwich & Dovercourt
25 **Havering**
26 Ilford

27 Maldon
28 Maylands
29 Orsett
30 Pipps Hill CC
31 Quietwaters
32 Rochford Hundred
33 Romford
34 **Royal Epping Forest**
35 Saffron Walden
36 Skips
38 Stoke by Nayland
39 Theydon Bois
40 Thorndon Park
41 Thorpe Hill
42 Three Rivers
43 Towerlands
44 Upminster
45 Wanstead
46 Warley Park
47 Warren
48 West Essex
49 Woodford
New for 1990
50 Castle Point

Hertfordshire
1 Aldenham G&CC
2 Arkley
3 Ashridge
4 **Batchwood Hall**
5 Berkhamsted
6 Bishops Stortford
7 Boxmoor
8 Brickendon Grange
9 Brookmans Park
10 Bushey G&CC
11 Bushey Hall
12 Chadwell Springs
13 **Cheshunt Park**
14 Chorleywood
15 Dyrham Park CC
16 East Herts
17 Elstree
18 Hadley Wood
19 Harpenden
20 Harpenden Common
21 Hartsbourne CC
22 Hatfield London
23 Knebworth
24 Letchworth
25 **Little Hay**
26 Mid Herts
27 Moor Park
28 Old Ford Manor
29 **Panshanger**
30 Porters Park
31 Potters Bar
32 Redbourn
33 **Rickmansworth**
34 Royston
35 Sandy Lodge
36 South Herts
37 **Stevenage**
38 Verulam

39 Welwyn Garden City
40 West Herts
41 Whipsnade Park

Norfolk
1 Barnham Broom Hotel
2 Bawburgh
3 Costessey Park
4 Dereham
5 Eaton
6 Fakenham
7 Feltwell
8 Gorleston
9 Great Yarmouth &
  Caister
10 Hunstanton
11 King's Lynn
12 Links Country Park
  Hotel
13 Mundesley
14 RAF Marham
15 Royal Cromer
16 Royal Norwich
17 Royal West Norfolk
18 Ryston Park
19 Sheringham
20 Sprowston Park
21 Swaffham
22 Thetford

Suffolk
1 Aldeburgh
2 Beccles
3 Bungay & Waveney
  Valley
4 Bury St Edmunds
5 **Cretingham**
6 Diss
7 Felixstowe Ferry
8 Flempton
9 Fornham Park
10 Haverhill
11 Ipswich (Purdis
  Heath)
12 Links (Newmarket)
13 Newton Green
14 Rookery Park
15 Royal Worlington &
  Newmarket
16 Rushmere
17 Southwold
18 Stowmarket
19 Thorpeness Hotel
20 Waldringfield Heath
21 Warren Heath
22 Woodbridge

*Public courses are set
in bold*

Map 4   469

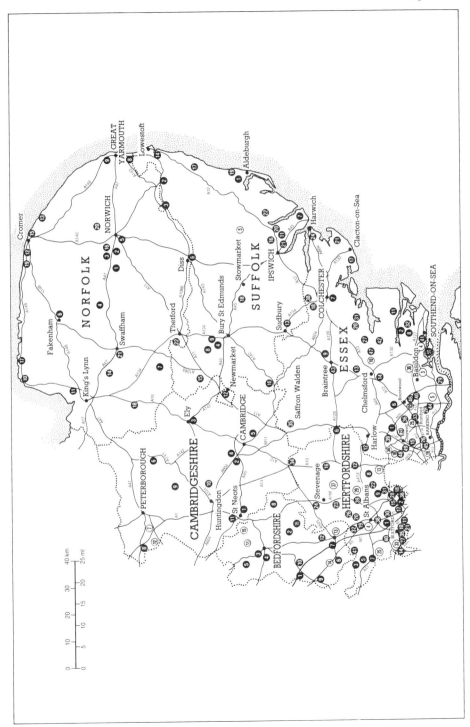

England: East Midlands

Leicestershire
1 Birstall
2 Charnwood Forest
3 Cosby
4 Enderby
5 Glen Gorse
6 Hinckley
7 Humberston Heights
8 Kibworth
9 Kirby Muxloe
10 Leicestershire
11 Lingdale
12 Longcliffe
13 Luffenham Heath
14 Lutterworth
15 Market Harborough
16 Melton Mowbray
17 Oadby
18 RAF North Luffenham
19 Rothley Park
20 Scraptoft
22 Western Park
23 Whetstone
24 Willesley Park

Lincolnshire
1 Belton Park
2 Blankney
3 Boston
4 Burghley Park
5 Canwick Park
6 Carholme
7 Elsham
8 Gainsborough
9 Lincoln
10 Louth
11 Market Rasen
       & District
12 Millfield
13 North Shore
14 RAF Waddington
15 Sandilands
16 Seacroft
17 Sleaford
18 Spalding
19 Stoke Rochford
20 Sutton Bridge
21 Woodhall Spa
New for 1990
22 Woodthorpe Hall

Northamptonshire
1 Cold Ashby
2 Daventry & District
3 Delapre
4 Kettering
5 Kingsthorpe
6 Northampton
7 Northamptonshire
       County
8 Oundle
9 Priors Hall
10 Rushden
11 Staverton Park
12 Wellingborough
13 Woodlands Vale

Nottinghamshire
1 Beeston Fields
2 Bulwell Forest
3 Chilwell Manor
4 Coxmoor
5 Edwalton
6 Kilton Forest
**20 Mansfield
       Woodhouse**
7 Mapperley
8 Newark
9 Nottingham City
10 Notts
11 Oxton
12 Radcliffe on Trent
13 Retford
14 Ruddington Grange
15 Rushcliffe
16 Serlby Park
17 Sherwood Forest
18 Stanton-on-the-Wolds
19 Wollaton Park
21 Worksop

*Public courses are set
in bold*

Map 5 471

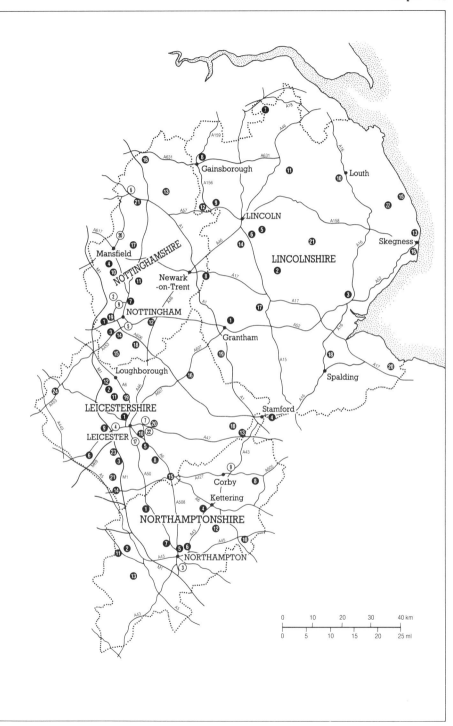

England: West Midlands

Derbyshire
1 Alfreton
2 **Allestree Park**
3 Ashbourne
4 Bakewell
5 Blue Circle
6 Breadsall Priory
7 Buxton & High Peak
8 Cavendish
9 Chapel-en-le-Frith
10 Chesterfield
11 **Chesterfield Municipal**
12 Chevin
13 **Derby**
14 Erewash Valley
15 Glossop & District
16 Hallowes
17 **Ilkeston**
18 Kedleston Park
19 Matlock
20 Mickleover
21 Ormonde Fields
22 Pastures
23 Shirland
24 Sickleholme
25 Stanedge

Hereford & Worcester
1 Belmont House
2 Blackwell
3 Churchill and Blakedown
4 Droitwich
5 Evesham
6 Habberley
7 Herefordshire
8 Kidderminster
9 King's Norton
10 Kington
11 Leominster
12 Little Lakes
13 **Pitcheroak**
14 Redditch
15 Ross-on-Wye
16 Tolladine
17 Worcester G&CC
18 Worcestershire
New for 1990
19 Abbey Park

Shropshire
1 Bridgnorth
2 Church Stretton
3 Hawkstone Park
4 Hill Valley G&CC
5 Lilleshall Hall
6 Llanymynech
7 Ludlow
8 Market Drayton
9 **Meole Brace**
10 Oswestry
11 Shifnal
12 Shrewsbury
13 Telford Hotel G&CC
14 Wrekin

Staffordshire
1 Alsager G&CC
2 Barlaston
3 Beau Desert
4 Branston
5 Brocton Hall
6 Burslem
7 Burton-on-Trent
8 **Craythorne Golf Centre**
9 Drayton Park
10 **Goldenhill**
11 Greenway Hall
12 Ingestre Park
13 Lakeside (Rugeley)
14 Leek
15 **Newcastle Municipal**
16 Newcastle-under-Lyme
17 Onneley
18 Stafford Castle
19 Stone
20 **Tamworth**
21 Trentham
22 Trentham Park
23 Uttoxeter
24 Westwood
25 Whittington Barracks
26 Wolstanton
New for 1990
27 **Park Hall**

Warwickshire
1 Atherstone
2 **City of Coventry (Brandon Wood)**
3 Kenilworth
4 Ladbrook Park
5 Leamington & County
6 Maxstoke Park
7 **Newbold Comyn**
8 Nuneaton
9 Purley Chase
10 Rugby
11 Stratford-on-Avon
12 **Warwick**
13 Welcombe Hotel

West Midlands
1 **The Belfry**
2 Bloxwich
3 **Boldmere**
4 **Brand Hall**
5 Calderfields
6 **Cocks Moor Woods**
7 Copt Heath
8 Coventry
9 Coventry Hearsall
10 Dartmouth
11 Druids Heath
12 Dudley
13 Edgbaston
14 Enville
15 Forest of Arden G&CC
16 Fulford Heath
17 Gay Hill
18 Grange
19 Great Barr
20 Hagley
21 Halesowen
22 Handsworth
23 Harborne
24 Harborne Church Farm
25 Hatchford Brook
26 Hilltop
27 **Himley Hall**
28 **Lickey Hills**
29 Little Aston
30 Moor Hall
31 Moseley
32 North Warwickshire
33 North Worcestershire
34 Olton
35 Oxley Park
36 Patshull Park
37 Penn
38 **Pype Hayes**
39 Robin Hood
40 Sandwell Park
41 Shirley
42 South Staffordshire
43 Sphinx
44 Stourbridge
45 Sutton Coldfield
46 Swindon
47 Walmley (Wylde Green)
48 Walsall
49 **Warley**

Public courses are set in bold

Map 6   473

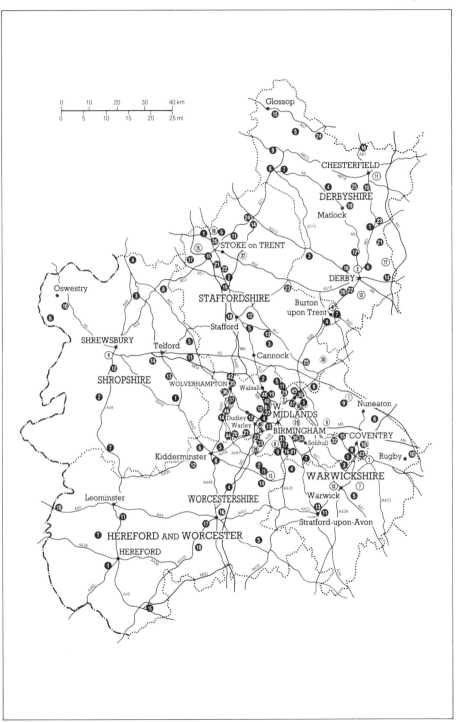

England: Yorkshire & Humberside

Humberside
1 Beverley & East Riding
2 Boothferry (Spaldington)
3 Bridlington
4 Brough
5 Cleethorpes
6 Driffield
7 Flamborough Head
8 Ganstead Park
9 Grimsby
10 Hainsworth Park
11 Hessle
12 Holme Hall
13 Hornsea
14 Hull
15 Immingham
16 Kingsway
17 Normanby Hall
18 Scunthorpe
19 Springhead Park
20 Sutton Park
21 Withernsea
22 Cave Castle Hotel

Yorkshire (North)
1 Aldwark Manor
2 Ampleforth College
3 Bedale
4 Bentham
5 Catterick Garrison
6 Crimple Valley
7 Easingwold
8 Filey
9 Fulford (York)
10 Ganton
11 Ghyll
12 Harrogate
13 Heworth
14 Kirkbymoorside
15 Knaresborough
16 Malton & Norton
17 Masham
18 Oakdale
19 Pannal
20 Pike Hills
21 Richmond
22 Ripon City
23 Scarborough North Cliff
24 Scarborough South Cliff
25 Selby
26 Settle
27 Skipton
28 Thirsk & Northallerton
29 Whitby
30 York
New for 1990
31 Loftus Hill

Yorkshire (South)
1 Abbeydale
2 Austerfield Park
3 Barnsley
4 Beauchief Municipal
5 Birley Wood
6 Concord Park
7 Crookhill Park
8 Doncaster
9 Doncaster Town Moor
10 Dore & Totley
11 Grange Park
12 Hallamshire
13 Hickleton
14 Hillsborough
15 Lees Hall
16 Lindrick
17 Phoenix
18 Renishaw Park
19 Rotherham
20 Roundwood
21 Sheffield Transport Dept
22 Silkstone
23 Sitwell Park
24 Stocksbridge & District
25 Tankersley Park
26 Thorne
27 Tinsley Park
28 Wath-upon-Dearne
29 Wheatley
New for 1990
30 Wombwell Hillies

Yorkshire (West)
1 Alwoodley
2 Baildon
3 Ben Rhydding
4 Bingley (St Ives)
5 Bradford
6 Bradford Moor
7 Bradley Park
8 Branshaw
9 Calverley
10 Castle Fields
11 City of Wakefield
12 Clayton
13 Cleckheaton & District
14 Crosland Heath
15 Dewsbury District
16 East Bierley
17 Elland
18 Ferrybridge 'C'
19 Fulneck
20 Garforth
21 Gotts Park
22 Halifax
23 Halifax Bradley Hall
24 Halifax West End
25 Hanging Heaton
26 Headingley
27 Headley

28 Horsforth
29 Howley Hall
30 Huddersfield
31 Ilkley
32 Keighley
33 Leeds
34 Lightcliffe
35 Longley Park
36 Low Laithes
37 Marsden
38 Meltham
39 Middleton Park
40 Moor Allerton
41 Moortown
42 Mount Skip
43 Normanton
44 Northcliffe
45 Otley
46 Outlane
47 Painthorpe House
48 Phoenix Park
49 Pontefract & District
50 Pontefract Park
51 Queensbury
52 Rawdon
53 Riddlesden
54 Roundhay
55 Ryburn
56 Sand Moor
57 Scarcroft
58 Shipley
59 Silsden
60 South Bradford
61 South Leeds
62 Temple Newsam
63 Todmorden
64 Wakefield
65 West Bowling
66 West Bradford
67 Wetherby
68 Whitwood
69 Woodhall Hills
70 Woodsome Hall
71 Wortley

Public courses are set in bold

Map 7   475

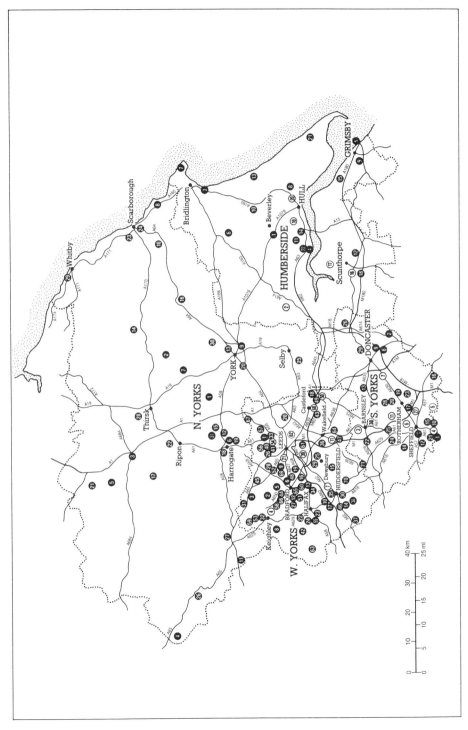

England: North-West

Cheshire
1 Alderley Edge
2 Astbury
3 Avro
4 Birchwood
5 Bramhall
6 Chester
7 Congleton
8 Crewe
9 Delamere Forest
10 Eaton
11 **Ellesmere Port**
12 Helsby
13 **Knights Grange**
14 Knutsford
15 Lymm
16 Macclesfield
17 **Malkins Bank**
18 Mere G&CC
19 New Mills
20 Poulton Park
21 Prestbury
22 **Queen's Park**
23 Romiley
24 Runcorn
26 Sandbach
27 Sandiway
28 Stockport
29 The Tytherington
30 Upton-by-Chester
31 Vicars Cross
32 **Walton Hall**
33 Warrington
34 Widnes
35 **Widnes Municipal**
36 **Wilmslow**

Isle of Man
1 Castletown
2 **Douglas Municipal**
3 Howstrake
4 Peel
5 **Port St Mary**
6 **Ramsey**
7 Rowany

Lancashire
1 Accrington & District
2 **Alt**
3 Ashton & Lea
4 Bacup
5 Baxenden & District
6 Blackburn
7 Blackpool North Shore
8 **Blackpool Park**
9 Burnley
10 Chorley
11 Clitheroe
12 Colne
13 Darwen
14 Dean Park
15 **Duxbury Park**

16 Fairhaven
17 Fishwick Hall
18 Fleetwood
19 Great Harwood
20 Green Haworth
21 Heysham
22 Hindley Hall
23 Ingol Golf & Squash Club
24 Knott End
25 Lancaster G&CC
26 Lansil
27 Leyland
28 Lobden
29 Longridge
30 Lytham (Green Drive)
31 **Marsden Park**
32 Morecambe
33 Nelson
34 Ormskirk
35 Penwortham
36 Pleasington
37 Poulton-le-Fylde
38 Preston
39 Rishton
40 Rossendale
41 Royal Lytham & St Annes
42 St Annes Old Links
43 Shaw Hill G&CC
44 Silverdale
45 **Towneley**
46 Turton
47 Whalley
48 Wilpshire

Manchester (Greater)
1 **Altrincham Municipal**
2 Ashton-on-Mersey
3 Ashton-under-Lyne
4 **Beacon Park**
5 Blackley
6 Bolton
7 **Bolton Municipal**
8 Bolton Old Links
9 **Brackley Municipal**
10 Bramall Park
11 Breightmet
12 Brookdale
13 Bury
14 Castle Hawk
15 Cheadle
16 Chorlton-cum-Hardy
17 Crompton & Royton
18 Davenport
19 Davyhulme Park
20 Deane
21 Denton
22 Didsbury
23 Disley
24 Dukinfield
25 Dunham Forest G&CC
26 Dunscar
27 Ellesmere

28 Fairfield Golf Sailing Club
29 Flixton
30 Gathurst
31 Gatley
32 Great Lever & Farnworth
33 Greenmount
34 **Haigh Hall**
35 Hale
36 Harwood
37 Hazel Grove
38 Heaton Moor
39 **Heaton Park**
40 Horwich
41 Houldsworth (Levenshulme)
42 Leigh
43 Lowes Park
44 Manchester GC Ltd
45 Marple
46 Mellor & Townscliffe
47 North Manchester
48 Northenden
49 Oldham
50 Pike Fold
51 Prestwich
52 Reddish Vale
53 Ringway
54 Rochdale
55 Saddleworth
56 Sale
57 **Springfield Park**
58 Stamford
59 Stand
60 Swinton Park
61 Tunshill
62 Walmersley
63 Werneth
64 Werneth Low
65 Westhoughton
66 Whitefield
67 Whittaker
68 Wigan
69 **William Wroe**
70 Withington
71 Worsley

Merseyside
1 **Allerton Park**
2 **Arrowe Park**
3 Ashton-in-Makerfield
4 Bidston
5 Bootle
6 **Bowring**
7 Bromborough
8 Caldy
9 Childwall
10 Eastham Lodge
11 Formby
12 Formby Ladies'
13 Grange Park
14 Haydock Park
15 Hesketh

16 Heswall
17 Hillside
18 **Hoylake Municipal**
19 Huyton & Prescot
20 Leasowe
21 Lee Park
22 **Liverpool Municipal**
23 Prenton
24 Royal Birkdale
25 Royal Liverpool
26 **St Helens**
27 Southport & Ainsdale
28 **Southport Municipal**
29 Southport Old Links
30 Wallasey
31 **Warren**
32 West Derby
33 West Lancashire
34 Wirral Ladies
35 Woolton
New for 1990
37 **Brackenwood**

Public courses are set in bold

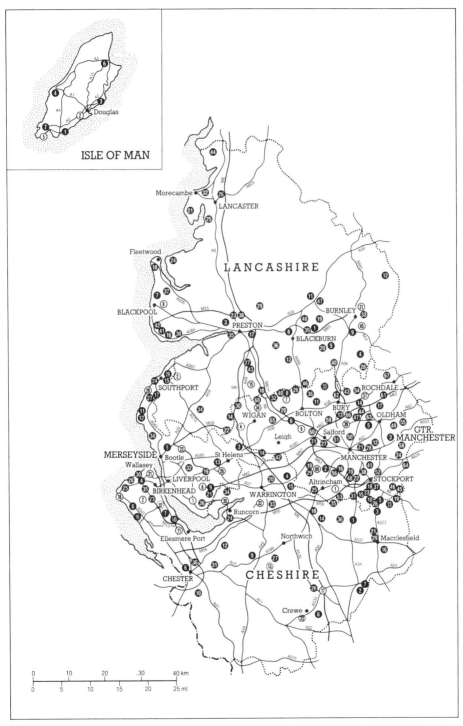

Map 8   477

ISLE OF MAN

Douglas

Morecambe   LANCASTER

Fleetwood

LANCASHIRE

BLACKPOOL

BURNLEY

PRESTON

BLACKBURN

ROCHDALE

SOUTHPORT

WIGAN   BOLTON   BURY   OLDHAM

Salford

Leigh   GTR.
MANCHESTER

MERSEYSIDE   St Helens

Wallasey   Bootle

LIVERPOOL   MANCHESTER

BIRKENHEAD   Altrincham   STOCKPORT

WARRINGTON

Runcorn

Northwich   Macclesfield

Ellesmere Port

CHESHIRE

CHESTER

Crewe

0   10   20   30   40 km

0   5   10   15   20   25 ml

England: North

Cleveland
1 Billingham
2 Castle Eden &
   Peterlee
3 Cleveland
4 Eaglescliffe
5 Hartlepool
6 Middlesbrough
**7 Middlesbrough
   Municipal**
8 Saltburn
9 Seaton Carew
10 Tees-side
11 Wilton

Cumbria
1 Alston Moor
2 Appleby
3 Barrow
4 Brampton (Talkin
   Tarn)
5 Carlisle
6 Cockermouth
7 The Dunnerholme
8 Furness
9 Grange Fell
10 Grange-over-Sands
11 Kendall
12 Keswick
13 Kirkby Lonsdale
14 Maryport
15 Penrith
16 St Bees
17 Seascale
18 Sedbergh
19 Silecroft
20 Silloth-on-Solway
21 Stoneyholme
22 Ulverston
23 Windermere
24 Workington

Durham
1 Aycliffe
2 Barnard Castle
3 Beamish Park
4 Bishop Auckland
5 Blackwell Grange
6 Brancepeth Castle
7 Chester-Le-Street
8 Consett & District
9 Crook
10 Darlington
11 Dinsdale Spa
12 Durham City
13 Hobson Municipal
14 Mount Oswald
15 Roseberry Grange
16 Seaham
17 South Moor
18 Stressholme
19 Woodham G&CC

Northumberland
1 Allendale
2 Alnmouth
3 Alnmouth Village
4 Alnwick
5 Arcot Hall
6 Bamburgh Castle
7 Bedlingtonshire
8 Bellingham
9 Berwick-upon-Tweed
10 Blyth
11 Dunstanburgh Castle
12 Hexham
13 Magdalene Fields
14 Morpeth
15 Newbiggin-by-
   the-Sea
16 Ponteland
17 Prudhoe
18 Rothbury
19 Seahouses
20 Stocksfield
21 Tynedale
22 Warkworth
23 Wooler
New for 1990
24 Haltwhistle
25 Slaley Hall

Tyne & Wear
1 Backworth
2 Birtley (Portobello)
3 Boldon
4 City of Newcastle
5 Close House
6 Garesfield
8 Gosforth
9 Gosforth Park
10 Heworth
11 Houghton-le-Spring
12 Newcastle United
13 Northumberland
14 Ravensworth
15 Ryton
16 South Shields
17 Tynemouth
18 Tyneside
19 Wallsend
20 Washington
21 Wearside
22 Westerhope
23 Whickham
24 Whitburn
25 Whitley Bay

*Public courses are set
in bold*

Map 9   479

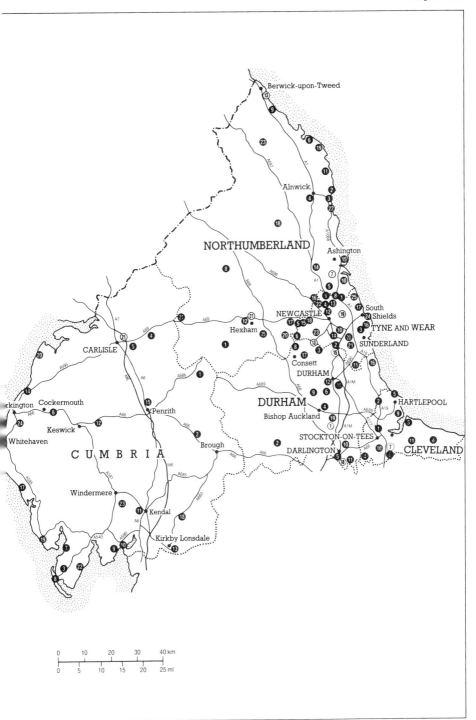

Ireland

Connacht

Co Galway
1 Athenry
2 Ballinasloe
3 Connemara
4 Galway
5 Gort
6 Loughrea
7 Mount Bellew
8 Oughterard
9 Portumna
10 Tuam

Co Leitrim
11 Ballinamore
12 Carrick-on-Shannon

Co Mayo
13 Achill Island
14 Ballina
15 **Ballinrobe**
16 Ballyhaunis
17 Belmullet
18 Castlebar
19 Claremorris
20 **Mulrany**
21 Swinford
22 Westport

Co Roscommon
23 Athlone
24 Ballaghaderreen
25 Boyle
26 Castlerea
27 Roscommon

Co Sligo
28 Ballymote
29 County Sligo
30 Enniscrone
31 Strandhill

Leinster

Co Carlow
1 Borris
2 Carlow

Co Dublin
3 Balbriggan
4 Ballinascorney
5 Beaverstown
6 Beech Park
7 **Corballis**
8 **Deer Park**
9 Donabate
10 Dun Laoghaire
11 Forrest Little
12 Hermitage
13 The Island
14 Killiney
15 **Kilternan Hotel**
16 Lucan
17 Malahide
18 Newlands
19 Portmarnock

20 Rush
21 Skerries
22 Slade Valley
23 Woodbrook

Dublin City
24 Carrickmines
25 Castle
26 Clontarf
27 Edmondstown
28 Elm Park G&SC
29 Foxrock
30 Grange
31 Howth
32 Milltown
33 Rathfarnham
34 Royal Dublin
35 St Anne's
36 Stackstown
37 Sutton

Co Kildare
38 Athy
39 Bodenstown
40 Cill Dara
41 Clongowes
42 Curragh
43 Knockanally
44 Naas

Co Kilkenny
45 Callan
46 Castlecomer
47 Kilkenny

Co Laois
48 Abbey Leix
49 Heath (Portlaoise)
50 Mountrath
51 Portarlington
52 Rathdowney

Co Longford
53 Co Longford

Co Louth
54 Ardee
55 County Louth
56 Dundalk
57 Greenore

Co Meath
58 Gormanston College
59 Headfort
60 Laytown and
   Bettystown
61 Royal Tara
62 Trim
New for 1990
82 Blackbush

Co Offaly
63 Birr
64 Edenderry
65 Tullamore

Co Wexford
66 Courtown
67 Enniscorthy
68 New Ross

69 Rosslare
70 Wexford

Co Westmeath
71 Moate
72 Mullingar

Co Wicklow
73 Arklow
74 Baltinglass
75 Blainrow
76 Bray
77 Coollattin
78 Delgany
79 Greystones
80 Wicklow
81 Woodenbridge
New for 1990
83 Old Conna

Munster

Co Clare
1 **Drumoland Castle**
2 Ennis
3 Kilkee
4 **Kilrush**
5 Lahinch
6 Shannon
7 Spanish Point

Co Cork
8 Bandon
9 Bantry
10 Charleville
11 Cobh
12 Cork
13 Doneraile
14 Douglas
15 Dunmore
16 East Cork
17 Fermoy
18 Glangarriff
19 Kanturk
20 Kinsale
21 Macroom
22 Mallow
23 Mitchelstown
24 Monkstown
25 Muskerry
26 Skibbereen
27 Youghal

Co Kerry
28 Ballybunion
29 Ceann Sibeal
30 Dooks
31 Kenmare
32 Killarney
33 Parknasilla
34 Tralee
35 Waterville

Co Limerick
36 Adare Manor
37 Castletroy
38 Limerick
39 Newcastle West

Co Tipperary
40 Cahir Park
41 Carrick-on-Suir
42 Clonmel
43 Nenagh
44 Rockwell College
45 Roscrea
46 Templemore
47 Thurles
48 Tipperary

Co Waterford
49 Dungarvan
50 Lismore
51 Tramore
52 Waterford

Ulster

Co Antrim
1 Ballycastle
2 Ballyclare
3 Ballymena
4 Bushfoot
5 Cairndhu
6 Carrickfergus
7 Cushendall
8 Dunmurry
9 Greenisland
10 Larne
11 Lisburn
12 Massereene
13 Royal Portrush
14 Whitehead

Co Armagh
15 County Armagh
16 **Craigavon**
17 Lurgan
18 Portadown
19 Tandragee

Belfast
20 **Ballyearl Golf Centre**
21 Balmoral
22 Belvoir Park
23 Cliftonville
24 Fortwilliam
25 **Gilnahirk**
26 The Knock
27 Knockbracken
28 Malone
29 Ormeau
30 Shandon Park

Co Cavan
31 Belturbet
32 Blacklion
33 Cabra Castle
34 County Cavan
35 Virginia

List continued on p. 482

Map 10   481

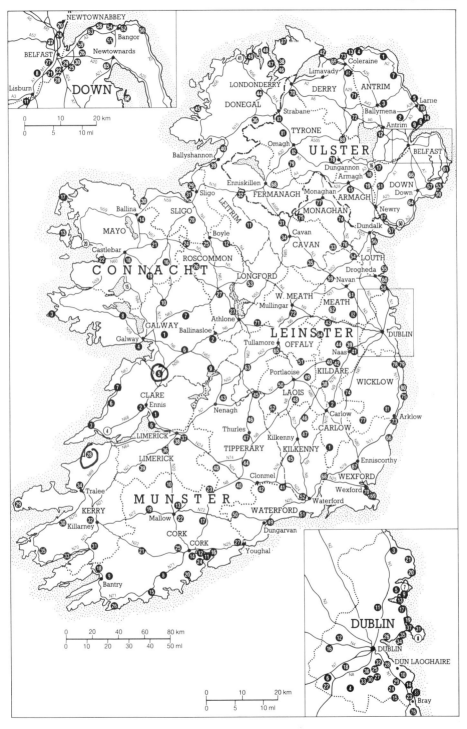

Ireland continued

Scotland

Co Donegal
36 Ballbofey & Stranorlar
37 Ballyliffin
38 Buncrana
39 Bundoran
40 Donegal
41 Dunfanaghy
42 Greencastle
43 Gweedore
44 Letterkenny
45 Narin & Portnoo
46 North West
47 Otway
48 Portsalon
49 Rosapenna

Co Down
50 Ardglass
51 Banbridge
52 Bangor
53 Bright Castle
54 Carnalea
55 Clandeboye
56 Donaghadee
57 Downpatrick
58 Helen's Bay
59 Holywood
60 Kilkeel
61 Kirkistown Castle
62 Mahee Island
63 Royal Belfast
64 Royal County Down
65 Scrabo
66 The Spa
67 Warrenpoint

Co Fermanagh
68 Eniskillen

Co Londonderry
New for 1990
84 Brown Trout
69 Castlerock
70 City of Derry
71 Kilrea
72 Moyola Park
73 Portstewart

Co Monaghan
74 Castleblayney
75 Clones
76 Nurenmore
77 Rossmore

Co Tyrone
78 Dungannon
79 Fintona
80 Killymoon
81 Newtownstewart
82 Omagh
83 Strabane

*Public courses are set
in bold*

Border Region

Berwickshire
1 Duns
2 Eyemouth
3 The Hirsel
4 Lauder

Peebleshire
5 Innerleithen
6 Peebles
7 West Linton

Roxburghshire
8 Hawick
9 Jedburgh
10 Kelso
11 Melrose
12 Minto
13 St Boswells

Selkirkshire
14 Galashiels
15 Selkirk
16 Torwoodlee

Lothian

East Lothian
17 Burgh Links
18 Dunbar
19 Gifford
20 Gullane
21 Haddington
22 The Honourable
    Company of
    Edinburgh Golfers
23 Kilspindie
24 Longniddry
25 Luffness New
26 Musselburgh
27 Musselburgh Old
    Course
28 North Berwick
29 Royal Musselburgh
30 Winterfield

Midlothian
31 Baberton
32 Braidhills No 1
33 Braidhills No 2
34 Broomieknowe
35 Bruntsfield Links
36 Carrick Knowe
37 Craigentinny
38 Craigmillar park
39 Dalmahoy
40 Duddington
41 Glencorse
42 Kingsknowe
43 Liberton
44 Lothianburn
45 Merchants of
    Edinburgh
46 Mortonhall
47 Murrayfield
48 Newbattle
49 Portobello
50 Prestonfield
51 Ratho Park
52 Ravelston
53 Royal Burgess Golfing
    Society of
    Edinburgh
54 Silverknowes
55 Swanston
56 Torphin Hill
57 Turnhouse

West Lothian
58 Bathgate
59 Deer Park
60 Dundas park
61 Greenburn
62 Harburn
63 Linlithgow
64 Niddry Castle
65 Polkemmet
66 Pumpherston
67 Uphall
68 West Lothian

*Public courses are set
in bold*

Map 11 483

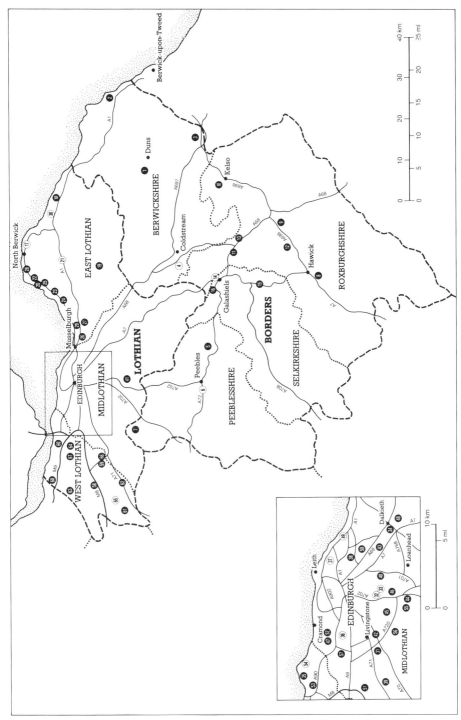

Dumfries & Galloway

Dumfriesshire
1 Crichton Royal
2 Dumfries & County
3 Dumfries & Galloway
4 Langholm
5 Lochmaben
6 Lockerbie
7 Moffat
8 Powfoot
9 Sanquhar
10 Southerness
11 Thornhill

Kirkudbrightshire
12 Castle Douglas
13 Colvend
14 Dalbeattie
15 Gatehouse
16 Kirkcudbright
17 New Galloway

Wigtownshire
18 Newton Stewart
19 Portpatrick Dunskey
20 St Medan
21 Stranraer
22 Wigtown & Bladnoch
23 Wigtownshire County

Strathclyde

Argyll
24 Blairmore & Strone
25 Carradale
26 Colonsay
27 Cowal
28 Craignure
29 Dunaverty
30 Glencruitten
31 Innellan
32 Kyles of Bute
33 Lochilphead
34 Machrie Hotel
35 Machrihanish
36 Tarbert
37 Tobermory
38 Vaul

Ayrshire
39 Annanhill
40 Ardeer
41 Auchenharvie
42 Ballochmyle
43 Beith
44 Belleisle
45 Caprington
46 Dalmilling
47 Girvan
48 Glasgow Gailes
49 Irvine
50 Irvine Ravenspark
51 Kilbirnie Place
52 Kilmarnock
   (Barassie)
53 Largs
54 Loudoun Gowf Club
55 Maybole
56 New Cumnock
57 Prestwick
58 Prestwick St
   Cuthbert
59 Prestwick St
   Nicholas
60 Routenburn
61 Royal Troon
62 Seafield
63 Skelmorlie

64 Troon Municipal
65 Turnberry Hotel
66 West Kilbride
67 Western Gailes

Bute
68 Brodick
69 Bute
70 Corrie
71 Lamlash
72 Lochranza
73 Machrie Bay
74 Millport
75 Port Bannatyne
76 Rothesay
77 Shiskine
78 Whiting Bay

Dunbartonshire
79 Bearsden
80 Cardross
81 Clober
82 Clydebank & District
**83 Clydebank
   Municipal**
84 Cumbernauld
85 Dougalston
86 Douglas Park
87 Dullatur
88 Dumbarton
89 Glasgow
90 Hayston
91 Helensburgh
92 Hilton Park
93 Kirkintilloch
94 Milngavie
95 Vale of Leven
96 Windyhill

Lanarkshire
97 Airdrie
98 Alexandra Park
99 Bellshill
100 Biggar
101 Bishopbriggs

102 Blairbeth
103 Bothwell Castle
104 Calderbraes
105 Cambuslang
106 Carluke
107 Carnwath
108 Cathkin Braes
109 Cawder
110 Coatbridge
111 Colville Park
112 Cowglen
113 Crow Wood
114 Deaconsbank
115 Douglas Water
116 Drumpellier
117 East Kilbride
118 Easter Moffat
119 Haggs Castle
120 Hamilton
121 Hollandbush
122 King's Park
123 Kirkhill
124 Knightswood
125 Lanark
126 Larkhall
127 Leadhills
128 Lenzie
129 Lethamhill
130 Linn Park
131 Littlehill
132 Mount Ellen
133 Pollok
134 Ruchill
135 Sandyhills
136 Shotts
137 Strathaven
138 Strathclyde Park
139 Torrance House
140 Wishaw

Renfrewshire
141 Barshaw
142 Bonnyton
143 Caldwell
144 Cathcart Castle
145 Cochrane Castle
146 East Renfrewshire

147 Eastwood
148 Elderslie
149 Erskine
150 Fereneze
151 Gleddoch
152 Gourock
153 Greenock
154 Kilmacolm
155 Lochwinnoch
156 Old Ranfurly
157 Paisley
158 Port Glasgow
159 Ralston
160 Ranfurly Castle
161 Renfrew
162 Whinhill
163 Whitecraigs
164 Williamwood

Stirlingshire
165 Aberfoyle
166 Kilsyth Lennox

*Public courses are set
in bold*

Map 12   485

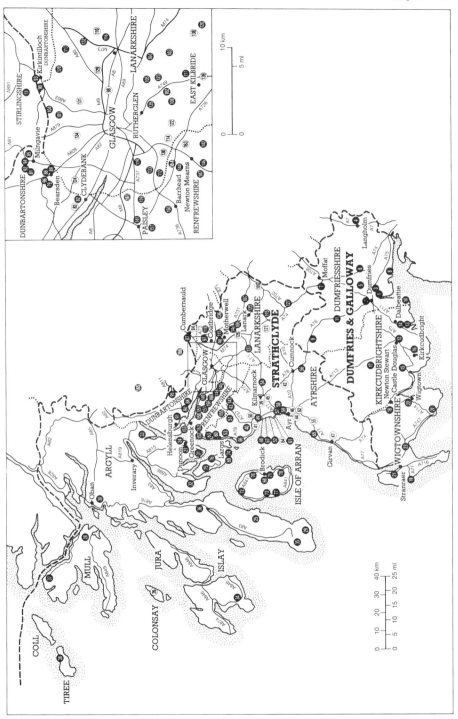

Central Region

Clackmannanshire
1 Alloa
2 Alva
3 Braehead
4 Dollar
5 Muckhart
6 Tillicoultry
7 Tulliallan

Perthshire
8 Callander
9 Dunblane New
10 Killin

Stirlingshire
11 Balmore
12 Bonnybridge
13 Bridge of Allan
14 Buchanan Castle
15 Campsie
16 Falkirk
17 Falkirk Tryst
18 Glenbervie
19 **Grangemouth**
20 Polmont
21 Stirling
22 Strathendrick

Fife

Fife
23 Aberdour
24 Anstruther
25 Auchterderran
26 Balbirnie Park
27 **Ballingry**
28 Burntisland Golf
    House Club
29 Canmore
30 Crail Golfing Society
31 Cupar
32 Dunfermline
33 **Dunnikier Park**
34 **Falkland**
35 **Glenrothes**
36 Golf House Club
37 **Kinghorn**
38 Kirkcaldy
39 Ladybank
40 Leslie (Fife)
41 Leven Links
42 **Leven Municipal**
43 Lochgelly
44 Lundin
45 Lundin Ladies
46 Pitreavie
47 St Andrews
48 St Michaels
49 Saline
50 Scotscraig
51 Thornton

Tayside Region

Angus
52 **Arbroath**
53 Brechin Golf & Squash
54 **Buddon Links**
55 **Burnside**
56 **Caird Park**
57 **Caird Park**
58 **Camperdown**
59 **Carnoustie**
    Championship
60 Downfield
61 Edzell
62 Forfar
63 Kirriemuir
64 Letham Grange
65 Monifieth Golf Links
66 **Montrose**
67 Panmure

Kinross-shire
68 Bishopshire
69 Green Hotel
70 Milnathort

Perthshire
71 Aberfeldy
72 Alyth
73 Auchterarder
74 Blair Atholl
75 Blairgowrie
76 Comrie
77 Craigie Hill
78 Crieff
79 **Dalminzie**
80 Dunkeld & Birnam
81 Dunning
82 Glenalmond
83 Gleneagles Hotel
84 King James VI
85 Murrayshall
86 Muthill
87 **North Inch**
88 Pitlochry
89 Royal Perth Golfing
    Society
90 St Fillans
91 Strathtay
92 Taymouth Castle

Public course are set in bold

Map 13   487

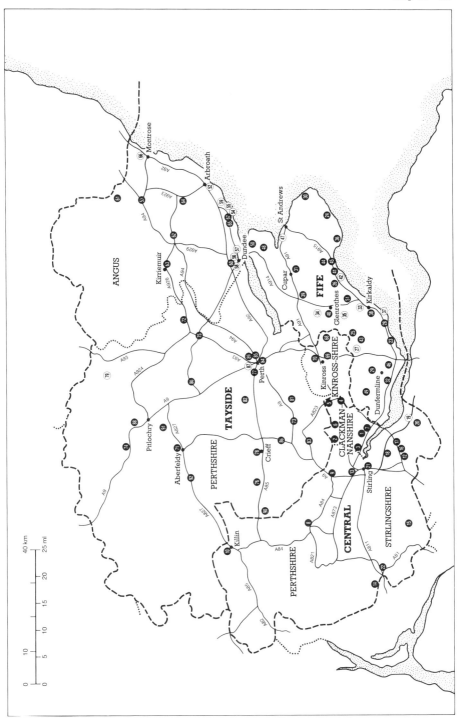

Grampian

Aberdeenshire
1 Aboyne
2 **Auchmill**
3 Ballater
4 **Balnagask**
5 Braemar
6 Cruden Bay
7 Deeside
8 Dunecht House
9 Fraserburgh
10 **Hazlehead**
11 Huntly
12 Insch
13 **Inverallochy**
14 Inverurie
15 Kemnay
16 **King's Links**
17 Kintore
18 McDonald
19 Murcar
20 Newburgh-on-Ythan
21 Oldmeldrum
22 Peterhead
23 Royal Aberdeen
24 Tarland
25 Torphins
26 Turriff
27 Westhill

Banffshire
28 Buckpool
29 Cullen
30 Duff House Royal
31 Dufftown
32 Keith
33 Royal Tarlair
34 Strathlene

Kincardineshire
35 **Auchenblae**
36 Banchory
37 Stonehaven

Morayshire
38 Elgin
39 Forres
40 Garmouth and
    Kingston
41 Grantown
42 Hopeman
43 Moray
44 Spey Bay

Orkney & Shetland Region

Orkney & Shetland
78 Orkney
79 Shetland
80 Stromness
81 Westray

Western Isles Region

Western Isles
82 Askernish
83 Stornoway

*Public courses are set
in bold*

Highland Region

Caithness
45 Lybster
46 Reay
47 **Thurso**
48 Wick

Inverness-shire
49 Abernethy
50 Boat-of-Garten
51 Carrbridge
52 Fort Augustus
53 Fort William
54 Inverness
55 Kingussie
56 Newtonmore
57 Sconser
58 **Skeabost**
59 **Torvean**
60 Traigh

Nairnshire
61 Nairn
62 Nairn Dunbar

Ross & Cromarty
63 Alness
64 Fortrose &
    Rosemarkie
65 Gairloch
66 Invergordon
67 Lochcarron
68 Muir of Ord
69 Strathpeffer Spa
70 Tain
71 Tarbat

Sutherland
72 Bonar-Bridge
    & Ardgay
73 Brora
74 **Durness**
75 Golspie
76 Helmsdale
77 Royal Dornoch

Map 14   489

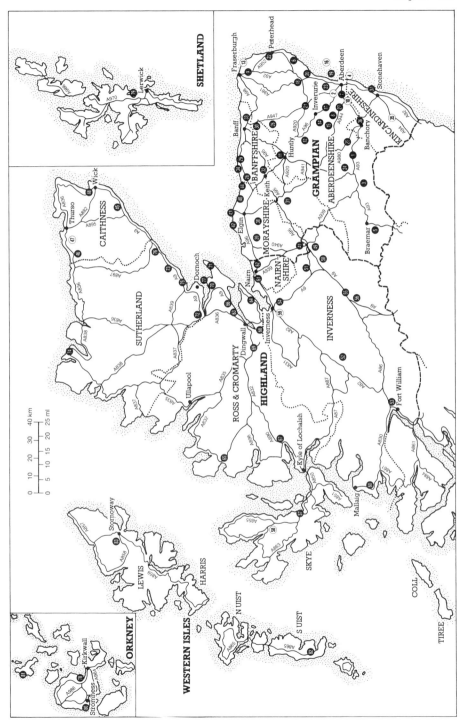

Wales

Clwyd
1 Abergele & Pensarn
2 Bryn Morfydd
3 Denbigh
4 Flint
5 Hawarden
6 Holywell
7 Mold
8 Old Colwyn
9 Old Padeswood
10 Padeswood & Buckley
11 Prestatyn
12 Rhuddlan
13 Rhyl
14 Ruthin-Pwllglas
15 St Melyd
16 Vale of Llangollen
17 Wrexham

Dyfed
1 Aberystwyth
2 Ashburnham
3 Borth & Ynyslas
4 Cardigan
5 Carmarthen
6 Cilgwyn
7 Glynhir
8 Haverfordwest
9 Milford Haven
10 Newport (Pembs)
11 St Davids City
12 South Pembrokeshire
13 Tenby

Gwent
1 Blackwood
2 Caerleon
3 Greenmeadow
4 Llanwern
5 Monmouth
6 Monmouthshire
7 Newport
8 Pontnewydd
9 Pontypool
10 Rolls of Monmouth
11 St Mellons
12 St Pierre
13 Tredegar & Rhymney
14 Tredegar Park
15 West Monmouthshire

Gwynedd
1 Aberdovey
2 Abersoch
3 Bala
4 Betws-y-Coed
5 Caernarfon
6 Conwy
   (Caernarvonshire)
7 Criccieth
8 Dolgellau
9 Ffestiniog

10 Llandudno (Maesdu)
11 Llandudno
   (North Wales)
12 Llanfairfechan
13 Nefyn & District
14 Penmaenmawr
15 Portmadoc
16 Pwllheli
17 Rhos-on-Sea
   Residential
18 Royal St David's
19 St Deiniol
   New for 1990
20 Bala Lake

Isle of Anglesey
1 Anglesey
2 Baron Hill
3 Bull Bay
4 Holyhead
5 Llangefni

Mid Glamorgan
1 Aberdare
2 Bargoed
3 Bryn Meadows G&CC
4 Caerphilly
5 Castell Heights
6 Creigiau
7 Llantrisant &
   Pontyclun
8 Maesteg
9 Merthyr Tydfil
10 Morlais Castle
11 Mountain Ash
12 Mountain Lakes
13 Pontypridd
14 Pyle & Kenfig
15 Rhondda
16 Royal Porthcawl
17 Southerndown
18 Whitehall

Powys
1 Brecon
2 Builth Wells
3 Cradoc
4 Knighton
5 Llandrindod
6 Machynlleth
7 Old Rectory
   Hotel
8 St Giles GC Newtown
9 Llanidloes (St Idloes)
10 Welshpool

South Glamorgan
1 Brynhill
2 Cardiff
3 Dinas Powis
4 Glamorganshire

5 Llanishen
6 Radyr
7 RAF St Athan
8 Wenvoe Castle
9 Whitchurch (Cardiff)

West Glamorgan
1 Clyne
2 Fairwood Park
3 Glynneath
4 Inco
5 Langland Bay
6 Morriston
7 Neath
8 Palleg
9 Pennard
10 Pontardawe
11 Swansea Bay

*Public courses are set
in bold*

Map 15   491

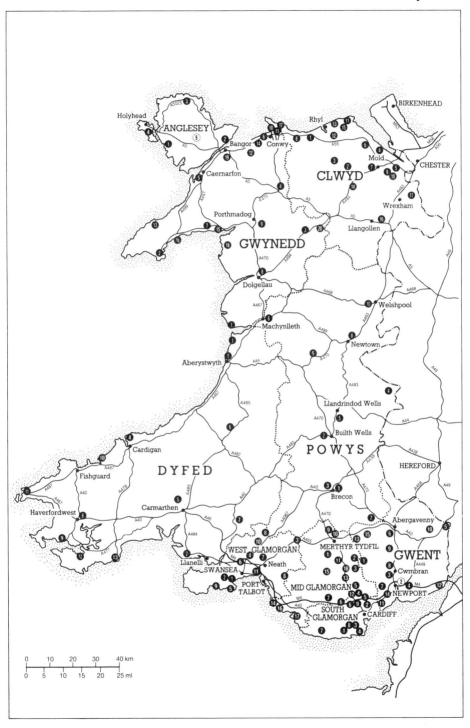

Golf Courses of the UK and Europe

England

Avon

Bath (1880)
Sham Castle, North Road, Bath
BA2 6JG
Tel   (0225) 425182
Mem 650
Sec   PB Edwards (0225) 463834
Pro   P Hancox (0225) 466953
Holes 18 L 6369 yds SSS 70
Recs Am-65 CS Edwards
      Pro-68 G Brand
V'trs H SOC
Fees £12 (£15) 1989 prices
Loc   1¹/₂ miles SE of Bath off
      A36

Bristol & Clifton (1891)
Beggar Bush Lane, Failand, nr Clifton,
Bristol BS8 3TH
Tel   (0272) 393117/393474
Mem 800
Sec   Cdr PA Woollings RN
      (0272) 393474
Pro   P Mawson (0272) 393031
Holes 18 L 6294 yds SSS 70
Recs Am-65 P Godsland
      Pro-64 P Oosterhuis
V'trs WD-UH WE/BH-MH
Fees On request
Loc   2 miles W of suspension
      bridge. 4 miles S of M5
      Junction 19

Chipping Sodbury (1954)
The Common, Chipping Sodbury,
Bristol BS17 6PU
Tel   (0454) 312024 (Members)
Mem 750
Sec   KG Starr (0454) 319042
Pro   SC Harris (0454) 314087
Holes New 18 L 6912 yds SSS 73
      Old 9 L 6194 yds SSS 69
Recs New Am-66 D Wood (1988)
      Pro-68 J Nicholas (1988)
V'trs WD-U SOC WE/BH-pm only
      M Sat/Sun am-XL
Fees New £8 D-£12 (£10 D-£16)
      Old £2.50
Loc   M4 Junction 18, 5 miles.
      M5 Junction 14, 9 miles.
      12 miles NE of Bristol
Mis   (0454) 315822 (Steward)

Clevedon (1908)
Castle Road, Clevedon BS21 7AA
Tel   (0272) 873140
Mem 700
Sec   Capt (Rctd) M Sullivan
      (0272) 874057
Pro   Miss C Langford (0272) 874704
Holes 18 L 5887 yds SSS 69
Recs Am-65 S Wyllie
      Pro-67 G Ryall (1987)
V'trs WD-U H exc Wed am-NA
      WE/BH-H I NA before 11am
      SOC-Mon only
Fees £12 (£15)
Loc   Holly Lane, Walton, Clevedon.
      M5 Junction 19 or 20

Entry Hill (1985)
Public
Entry Hill, Bath BA2 5NA
Tel   (0225) 834248
Pro   T Tapley
Holes 9 L 4206 yds SSS 61
Recs Am-65 R Blannin
V'trs WD-U WE-booking only
Fees 18 holes-£5.20 9 holes-£3.30
Loc   1 mile S of Bath off A367
Mis   Entry Hill GC plays here

Filton (1909)
Golf Course Lane, Bristol BS12 7QS
Tel   (0272) 692021
Mem 700
Sec   DF O'Leary (0272) 694169
Pro   JCN Lumb (0272) 694158
Holes 18 L 6277 yds SSS 69
Recs Am-66 S Hurley
V'trs WD-U WE/BH-M
Fees £14
Loc   4 miles N of Bristol

Fosseway CC (1970)
Charlton Lane, Midsomer Norton,
Bath BA3 4BD
Tel   (0761) 412214
Mem 280
Sec   RF Jones (Mgr)
Holes 9 L 4148 yds SSS 61
Recs Am-55 M Chedgy (1985)
V'trs U exc Wed-M after 5pm
      Sun-NA before 1.30pm
Fees £8 (£9)
Loc   10 miles SW of Bath on
      A367

Henbury (1891)
Westbury-on-Trym, Bristol BS10 7QB
Tel   (0272) 500660
Mem 330 85(L) 48(J) 157(5)
Sec   JW Estill (0272) 500044
Pro   P Stow (0272) 502121
Holes 18 L 6039 yds SSS 70
Recs Am-63 R Tugwell
      Pro-67 B Sandry
V'trs WD-H WE-M SOC-Tues & Fri
Fees £15
Loc   3 miles N of Bristol.
      M5 Junction 17

Knowle (1905)
Fairway, Knowle, Brislington, Bristol
BS4 5DF
Tel   (0272) 776341
Mem 700
Sec   Mrs JD King (0272) 770660
Pro   GM Brand (0272) 779193
Holes 18 L 6016 yds SSS 69
Recs Am-64 SD Hurley, D Hares
      Pro-64 S Brown
V'trs WD-H or I exc Thurs
      WE/BH-H or I SOC-Thurs
Fees £12 (£15)
Loc   3 miles S of Bristol, Brislington
      Hill off A4

Lansdown (1894)
Lansdown, Bath BA1 9BT
Tel   (0225) 425007
Mem 725
Sec   (0225) 422138
Pro   T Mercer (0225) 420242
Holes 18 L 6267 yds SSS 70
Recs Am-65 C Edwards, A Lyddon
      (1984)
      Pro-65 D Ray (1987)
V'trs WD-U WE-H SOC
Fees £14
Loc   2 miles NW of Bath, by
      racecourse. M4 Junction 18
      6 miles

Long Ashton (1893)
Long Ashton, Bristol BS18 9DW
Tel   (0272) 392229
Mem 700
Sec   RE Burniston (0272) 392316
Pro   DP Scanlan (0272) 392265
Holes 18 L 6051 yds SSS 70
Recs Am-64 A Rogers, J Bickerton
      Pro-65 D Snell

V'trs WD–U H WE/BH–I H
SOC–Wed
Fees £15 (£18)
Loc 3 miles S of Bristol on B3128

Mangotsfield (1975)

Carsons Road, Mangotsfield, Bristol
BS17 3LW
Tel (0272) 565501
Mem 600
Sec J Hill
Pro C Trewin
Holes 18 L 5297 yds SSS 66
V'trs U
Fees £7 (£10)
Loc Bristol 3 miles

Saltford (1904)

Golf Club Lane, Saltford
Tel (0225) 873220
Mem 650
Sec V Radnedge (0225) 873513
Pro D Millensted (0225) 872043
Recs Am–68 S Godfrey
Pro–P Evans
V'trs U
Fees £14 (£16)
Loc Bath 6 miles. Bristol 7 miles

Shirehampton Park (1907)

Park Hill, Shirehampton, Bristol
BS11 0UL
Tel (0272) 823059
Mem 600
Sec BJG Manning (0272) 822083
Pro (0272) 822488
Holes 18 L 5493 yds SSS 67
Recs Am–63 R Abbott
Pro–63 K Spurgeon
V'trs WD–U WE–M
Fees £13
Loc M5 Junction 18, 1¹/₂ miles

Tracy Park (1976)

Tracy Park, Bath Road, Wick,
nr Bristol BS15 5RN
Tel (027 582) 2251
Mem 1000
Sec Capt J Seymour–Williams
Pro G Aitken (027 582) 3521
Holes 27–Avon L 6834 yds SSS 73;
Bristol L 6861 yds SSS 73;
Cotswold L 6203 yds SSS 70
Recs Am–66 M Stephens
Pro–72 M Dennis
V'trs WD/WE(phone first)
SOC–WD/WE
Fees £12 (£15)
Loc 8 miles E of Bristol off A420
Bristol–Chippenham road.
5 miles N of Bath, M4
Junction 18

Weston-super-Mare (1892)

Uphill Road, Weston-super-Mare
Tel (0934) 621360
Mem 700
Sec A Hickox (0934) 626968
Pro T Murray (0934) 633360

Holes 18 L 6308 yds SSS 70
Recs Am–69 GT Irlam
Pro–69 A Lees, WJ Branch
V'trs U SOC
Fees £14 (£18) W–£45
Loc Weston-super-Mare

Worlebury (1908)

Monks Hill, Weston-super-Mare
BS22 9SX
Tel (0934) 623214
Mem 640
Sec RT Bagg (0934) 625789
Pro G Marks (0934) 418473
Holes 18 L 5921 yds SSS 69
Recs Am–67 P Simmonds
V'trs U SOC–WD
Fees £11 (£17)
Loc 2 miles NE of Weston

Bedfordshire

Aspley Guise & Woburn Sands (1914)

West Hill, Aspley Guise, Milton
Keynes MK17 8DX
Tel (0908) 582264
Mem 530
Sec TE Simpson (0908) 583596
Pro G McCarthy (0908) 582974
Holes 18 L 6248 yds SSS 70
Recs Am–67 M Wharton
Pro–68 P Webster
V'trs WD–UH WE/BH–MH
SOC–Wed & Fri
Fees £13 D–£16
Loc 2 miles W of M1 Junction 13

Beadlow Manor Hotel G & CC

Beadlow, Shefford SG17 5PH
Tel (0525) 60800
Mem 700
Pro (0525) 61292
Holes 18 L 6238 yds SSS 71
9 L 6042 yds SSS 70
Recs Am–71 C Skinner
Pro–68 KF Robson
V'trs U H SOC
Fees On application
Loc 2 miles W of Shefford on
A507

Bedford & County (1912)

Green Lane, Clapham, Bedford
MK41 6ET
Tel (0234) 52617
Mem 600
Sec E Bullock
Pro E Bullock (0234) 59189
Holes 18 L 6347 yds SSS 70
Recs Am–66 C Allen (1980)
Pro–66 M King (1978)
V'trs WD–U WE–M SOC

Fees WD–£15
Loc 2 miles NW of Bedford on
A6

Bedfordshire (1891)

Bromham Rd, Biddenham, Bedford
MK40 4AF
Tel (0234) 53241
Mem 600
Sec TA Nutt (0234) 61669
Pro G Buckle (0234) 53653
Holes 18 L 6185 yds SSS 69
Recs Am–64 CM Beard
Pro–65 K Warren
V'trs WD–U (phone first) WE–M
before noon SOC–WD
Fees On application
Loc 1¹/₂ miles NW of Bedford
boundary (A428)

Colworth (1985)

Unilever Research, Sharnbrook,
Bedford MK44 1LQ
Tel (0234) 222654
Mem 350
Sec SG Pound
Holes 9 L 2500 yds
Recs Am–57 J Barrett (1988)
V'trs NA
Loc 10 miles N of Bedford off A6

Dunstable Downs (1907)

Whipsnade Road, Dunstable LU6 2NB
Tel (0582) 604472
Mem 696
Sec PJ Nightingale
Pro M Weldon (0582) 662806
Holes 18 L 6184 yds SSS 70
Recs Am–65 RA Durrant
Pro–67 J Macdonald, SL King
V'trs WD–H WE–M SOC–Tues &
Thurs
Fees On application
Loc 2 miles SW of Dunstable on
B4541. M1 Junction 11

Griffin (1985)

c/o 3 Hillcrest Avenue, Luton LU2 7AB
Tel (0582) 415573
Mem 350
Sec Mrs L Weedon (0582) 579511
Holes 9 L 5354 yds SSS 66
Recs Am–73 A Halliday (1987)
V'trs WD–U WE/BH–M (exc Sun
am–NA) SOC
Fees £3 (£5)
Loc 3 miles W of Luton on
A505 between Dunstable and
Caddington. M1 Junction 11

John O'Gaunt (1948)

Sutton Park, Sandy, Biggleswade
SG19 2LY
Tel (0767) 260360
Mem 1250
Sec DJ Wallace
Pro R Round (0767) 260094

Holes John O'Gaunt 18 L 6513 yds
SSS 71; Carthagena 18 L 5869
yds SSS 68
Recs Am–64 N Wharton
Pro–67 SC Evans
V'trs WD–U WE–H
Fees £25 (£40)
Loc 3 miles NE Biggleswade on
B1040
Mis Advisable phone before visit

Leighton Buzzard (1925)

Plantation Road, Leighton Buzzard
Tel (0525) 373811/2
Mem 600
Sec FJ Clements (0525) 373811
Pro LJ Muncey (0525) 372143
Holes 18 L 5366 yds SSS 68
Recs Am–65 D Horne
V'trs WD exc Tues–U WE/BH–MH
Fees £15 D–£20
Loc 1 mile N of L Buzzard

Millbrook

Millbrook, Ampthill
Tel (0525) 404683
Mem 250
Sec CF Grimwood (0525) 712001
Pro T Devine (0525) 402269
Holes 18 L 6473 yds SSS 72
V'trs WD–U exc Thurs WE–NA
before 9.30am
Fees £10 (£15)
Loc Millbrook

Mowsbury (1975)

Public
Kimbolton Road, Bedford MK41 8DQ
Tel (0234) 771042
Sec E Thompson (Mgr)
Pro P Ashwell
Holes 18 L 6514 yds SSS 71
Recs Pro–66
Fees £4 (£6)
Loc 3 miles N of Bedford on B660
Mis Driving range

RAF Henlow (1985)

RAF Henlow, Henlow SG16 6DN
Mem 200
Sec Sgt R Chaytor (0462) 815016
(Ext 2267)
Holes 9 L 5616 yds SSS 67
Recs Am–75 JWG Morgan (1988)
V'trs M
Fees D–£2
Loc 3 miles SW of Shefford on
A600

South Beds (1892)

Warden Hill, Luton
Tel (0582) 575201
Mem 750
Sec AJ Messing (0582) 591500
Pro E Cogle (0582) 591209
Holes 18 L 6342 yds SSS 70
9 L 4954 yds SSS 64

V'trs WD–U WE/BH–H exc comp
days–NA SOC Ladies Day–
Tues
Fees 18 hole:£14 D–£21 (£18 D–£25)
9 hole: £7 (£10)
Loc 3 miles N of Luton on E side
of A6

Stockwood Park (1973)

Public
London Rd, Stockwood Park, Luton
LU7 4LX
Tel (0582) 413704
Pro D Hunt
Holes 18 L 5567 yds SSS 69
Recs Am–73 RM Harris
Pro–66 T Minshall
Fees £3.40 (£5.10)
Loc 1 mile S of Luton on A6

Tilsworth

Public
Dunstable Rd, Tilsworth, Dunstable
Tel (0525) 210721/210722
Pro N Webb
Holes 9 L 2773 yds SSS 35
V'trs U
Fees £3 (£4)
Loc 2 miles N of Dunstable (A5)

Wyboston Lakes (1978)

Public
Wyboston Lakes, Wyboston
MK44 3AL
Tel (0480) 219200
Sec B Chinn (Mgr)
Pro P Ashwell (0480) 212501
Holes 18 L 5721 yds SSS 69
V'trs WD–U SOC WE–booking
Fees £7 (£10)
Loc S of St Neots off A1 and
St Neots by-pass

Berkshire

Bearwood (1986)

Mole Road, Sindlesham RG11 5DB
Tel (0734) 761330
Mem 570
Sec C Dyer OBE (0734) 760060
Pro B Tustin (Mgr) (0734) 760643
Holes 9 L 2814 yds SSS 67
Recs Am–72 J Twamley (1989)
V'trs WD–H before 4pm –M after
4pm WE/BH–M
Fees 18 holes–£12. 9 holes–£7
Loc B3030, 1½ miles N of
Arborfield Cross. M4 Junction
10
Mis 9 hole pitch and putt

Berkshire (1928)

Swinley Road, Ascot SL5 8AY
Tel (0990) 21495
Mem 935
Sec Maj PD Clarke (0990) 21496
Pro KA Macdonald (0990) 22351

Holes Red 18 L 6356 yds SSS 70
Blue 18 L 6258 yds SSS 70
V'trs WD–I WE/BH–M
Fees On application
Loc 3 miles from Ascot on A332

Calcot Park (1930)

Calcot, nr Reading
Tel (0734) 427124
Mem 700
Sec SD Chisholm
Pro A Mackenzie (0734) 427797
Holes 18 L 6283 yds SSS 70
Recs Am–66 SA Scott
Pro–63 C Defoy
V'trs WD–U WE/BH–M
Fees £18
Loc 3 miles W of Reading on A4

Datchet (1890)

Buccleuch Road, Datchet
Tel (0753) 43887
Mem 200 50(L) 25(J) 110(5)
Sec GS East
Pro M Taylor (0753) 42755
Holes 9 L 5978 yds SSS 69
Recs Am–66 R Blyfield
Pro–63 N Wood
V'trs WD–U before 3pm
M–after 3pm WE–M
Fees £12 D–£18
Loc Slough, Windsor 2 miles

Donnington Valley

Oxford Road, Donnington, Newbury
RG16 9AG
Tel (0635) 32488
Mem 250
Sec C Cox
Pro D Cox
Holes 18 L 4033 yds SSS 60
V'trs U
Loc N of Newbury

Downshire (1973)

Public
Easthampstead Park, Wokingham
Tel (0344) 424066
Pro G Legouix
Holes 18 L 6382 yds SSS 70
Recs Am–67 T Smith
Pro–66 M King
V'trs U SOC
Fees Summer–£6.50 Winter–£4.50
Loc Off Nine Mile Ride
Mis Easthampstead GC and
Downshire GC play here

East Berkshire (1904)

Ravenswood Ave, Crowthorne
Tel (0344) 772041
Mem 700
Sec WH Short
Pro A Roe (0344) 774112
Holes 18 L 6315 yds SSS 70
Recs Am–65 J Davies
Pro–65 N Coles
V'trs I WE/BH–M SOC H
Fees £24
Loc Nr Crowthorne Station

Eton College (1973)

Eton College, Windsor
Tel   (0753) 866461
Mem   500
Sec   PTC Croker (0753) 855299
Holes   9 L 3560 yds SSS 58
Recs   Am–55 DL Morkill
V'trs   NA

Goring & Streatley (1893)

Rectory Road, Streatley-on-Thames
RG8 9QA
Tel   (0491) 872688
Mem   740 110(L) 80(J) 120(5)
Sec   J Menzies (0491) 873229
Pro   R Mason (0491) 873715
Holes   18 L 6266 yds SSS 70
Recs   Am–65 DG Lane
        Pro–65 C DeFoy
V'trs   WD–U WE/BH–M SOC–WD
Fees   £18
Loc   10 miles NW of Reading on
        A417

Hawthorn Hill (1985)

Public

Drift Road, Hawthorn Hill, Maidenhead
SL6 3ST
Tel   (0628) 771030/75588
Sec   CD Smith
Pro   G Edmonds
Holes   18 L 6212 yds SSS 70
Fees   £7.20 (£8.70)
Loc   4 miles S of Maidenhead
        on A330
Mis   Floodlit driving range

Hurst (1979)

Public

Sandford Lane, Hurst, Wokingham
Tel   (0734) 345143
Pro   G Legouix
Holes   9 L 3015 yds SSS
Fees   Summer–£2.50 Winter–£1.65
Loc   Reading 5 miles.
        Wokingham 3 miles

Lavender Park

Public

Swinley Road, Ascot SO5 1BD
Tel   (0344) 884074
Pro   G Casy
Holes   9 L 1104 yds SSS 27
V'trs   U
Fees   £3.10
Loc   W of Ascot on B3017
Mis   Driving range

Maidenhead (1898)

Shoppenhangers Road, Maidenhead
SL6 2PZ
Tel   (0628) 24693
Mem   730
Sec   PW Clash
Pro   L Elstone (0628) 24067
Holes   18 L 6360 yds SSS 70

Recs   Am–66 M Briggs (1985),
        L Hawkins (1986)
        Pro–04 AN Walker,
        G Wolstenholme
V'trs   WD–by appointment Fri–M
        after 12 noon WE–M
Fees   £15 R/D
Loc   Maidenhead Station ½ mile

Mill Ride

Mill Ride, North Ascot SL5 8LT
Tel   (0344) 885444
Sec   J Deeming
Pro   R Newman (0344) 890433
Holes   9 L 6601 yds SSS 72
V'trs   M
Loc   2 miles W of Ascot

Newbury & Crookham (1873)

Bury's Bank Road, Greenham
Common, Newbury RG15 8BZ
Tel   (0635) 40035
Mem   626
Pro   DW Harris (0635) 31201
Holes   18 L 5880 yds SSS 68
Recs   Am–63 D Rosier (1984)
        Pro–61 M Howell (1986)
V'trs   WD–U WE–M (recognised
        club members) H
Fees   £15
Loc   2 miles SE of Newbury

Reading (1910)

Kidmore End Road, Emmer Green,
Reading RG4 8SG
Tel   (0734) 472169
Mem   700
Sec   ANH Weekes (0734) 472909
Pro   TP Morrison (0734) 476115
Holes   18 L 6204 yds SSS 70
Recs   Am–65 MG King
        Pro–64 AP Morley
V'trs   Mon–Thurs–U Fri/WE/BH–M
Fees   £19
Loc   2 miles N of Reading off
        Peppard Road (B481)

Royal Ascot (1887)

Winkfield Road, Ascot SL5 7LJ
Tel   (0990) 25175
Mem   600
Sec   J Young
Pro   C Dell (0990) 24656
Holes   18 L 5709 yds SSS 68
Recs   Am–66 K Rixon
V'trs   WD–U before 5pm
        M after 5pm SOC
Fees   £12
Loc   Bracknell 3 miles.
        Windsor 4 miles
Mis   Within boundaries of
        racecourse

The Royal Household

Buckingham Palace, London SW1
Tel   (071) 930 4832
Mem   200
Sec   A Jarred

Holes   9 L 4560 yds SSS 62
V'trs   Strictly by invitation
Loc   Home Park, Windsor Castle

Sonning (1914)

Sonning-on-Thames
Tel   (0734) 693332
Mem   500
Sec   PF Williams
Pro   RT McDougall (0734) 692910
Holes   18 L 6345 yds SSS 70
Recs   Am–66 MT Rapley
        Pro–65 B Lane
V'trs   WD–U WE–M
Fees   On application
Loc   S of A4, nr Sonning

Swinley Forest (1909)

Coronation Road, Ascot SL9 5LE
Tel   (0990) 20197
Mem   335
Sec   IL Pearce
Pro   RC Parker
Holes   18 L 6001 yds
Recs   Am–64 EF Storey, ER Sermon
        Pro–64 P Alliss
V'trs   M
Loc   S of Ascot

Temple (1909)

Henley Road, Hurley, Maidenhead
SL6 5LH
Tel   (062 882) 4248
Mem   500
Sec   DW Kirkland (062 882) 4795
Pro   A Dobbins (062 882) 4254
Holes   18 L 6206 yds SSS 70
Recs   Am–66 AR Millar
V'trs   WD–I WE/BH–M SOC
Fees   £25
Loc   Between Maidenhead and
        Henley on A423. M4 Junction
        8/9. M40 Junction 3

West Berkshire (1975)

Chaddleworth, Newbury RG16 0HS
Tel   (04882) 574
Mem   700
Sec   W Richardson
Pro   D Sheppard (04882) 8851
Holes   18 L 7053 yds SSS 74
Recs   Am–74 J Pocock, D Murphy,
        B Claringbold
        Pro–69 M Howell, B Laing
V'trs   U SOC
Fees   £15 (£20)
Loc   On A338 to Wantage. M4
        Junction 14

Winter Hill (1976)

Grange Lane, Cookham SL6 9RP
Tel   (062 85) 27613
Mem   800
Sec   GB Charters–Rowe
Pro   P Hedges (062 85) 27610

For explanation of abbreviations, see page 460.

Holes   18 L 6408 yds SSS 71
Recs   Am–70 K Boulter (1988)
V'trs   WD–U WE–M SOC
Fees   £15
Loc   Maidenhead 3 miles

Buckinghamshire

Abbey Hill (1975)

Public
Monks Way, Two Mile Ash, Milton
Keynes MK8 8AA
Tel   (0908) 563845
Pro   S Harlock
Holes   18 L 6193 yds SSS 69
Recs   Am–67 T Mernagh
        Pro–67 H Stott
Fees   On application
Loc   2 miles S of Stony Stratford.
        N of Milton Keynes

Beaconsfield (1914)

Beaconsfield HP9 2UR
Tel   (0494) 676545
Mem   862
Sec   PI Anderson
Pro   M Brothers (0494) 676616
Holes   18 L 6469 yds SSS 71
Recs   Am–66 D Haines
        Pro–63 E Murray
V'trs   WD–H WE–N/A
Fees   £20
Loc   8 miles N of Slough.
        2 miles E of Beaconsfield

Buckingham (1914)

Tingewick Road, Buckingham
MK18 4AE
Tel   (0280) 813282
Mem   680
Sec   D Rolph (0280) 815566
Pro   T Gates (0280) 815210
Holes   18 L 6082 yds SSS 69
Recs   Am–71 RJ Gillam
        Pro–67 S Watson
V'trs   WD–U WE–M SOC
Fees   £18
Loc   1½ miles on Oxford road
        (A421)

Burnham Beeches (1891)

Burnham, Slough SL1 8EG
Tel   (0628) 661150
Mem   670
Sec   AJ Buckner (Mgr) (0628)
        661448
Pro   T Buckner (0628) 661661
Holes   18 L 6415 yds SSS 71
Recs   Am–67 M Orris
        Pro–64 H Flatman
V'trs   WD–I WE/BH–M
Fees   £18 D–£27
Loc   4 miles W of Slough

Chartridge Park (1989)

Marand Grange, Chartridge, Chesham
HP5 2TF
Tel   (0494) 775919
Mem   300
Sec   Mrs A Gibbins
Pro   P Gibbins
Holes   9 L 3550 yds SSS 74
V'trs   WD–U SOC WE–NA
Fees   £10
Loc   Chartridge, 2 miles NW of
        Chesham

Chesham & Ley Hill (1919)

Ley Hill, Chesham HP5 1UZ
Tel   (0494) 784541
Mem   384
Sec   K Brown (Mgr)
Holes   9 L 5240 yds SSS 66
Recs   Am–64 GA Knowes
        Pro–65 M Lovegrove
V'trs   Mon & Thurs–U Wed–U after
        12 noon Fri–U before 1pm –M
        after 1pm Tues–M after 3pm
        WE/BH–M SOC–Thurs only
Fees   £12
Loc   Chesham 2 miles
Mis   Course closed Sun after 2pm
        from 1st Apr–30th Sept

Chiltern Forest (1921)

Aston Hill, Halton, Aylesbury
HP22 5NQ
Tel   (0296) 630899
Mem   570
Sec   LEA Clark (0296) 631267
Pro   C Skeet
Holes   9 L 6038 yds SSS 70
Recs   Am–67 D Ball (1989)
V'trs   WD–U WE–M SOC
Fees   £10
Loc   5 miles SE of Aylesbury

Denham (1910)

Tilehouse Lane, Denham UB9 5DE
Tel   (0895) 832022
Mem   550
Sec   Wg Cdr D Graham
Pro   J Sheridan (0895) 832801
Holes   18 L 6439 yds SSS 71
Recs   Am–66 DMA Steel
        Pro–68 J Sheridan
V'trs   Mon–Thurs–I H Fri–Sun/BH–M
Fees   £14 D–£23
Loc   3 miles NW of Uxbridge

Ellesborough (1906)

Butlers Cross, nr Aylesbury
HP17 0TZ
Tel   (0296) 622375
Mem   780
Sec   KM Flint (0296) 622114
Pro   S Watkins (0296) 623126
Holes   18 L 6310 yds SSS 70
Recs   Am–66 N Lucas, NM Allen,
        P Stevens
        Pro–68 G Will

V'trs   WE/BH–M WD–I or H
        SOC–Wed & Thurs only
Fees   On application
Loc   1 mile W of Wendover

Farnham Park (1974)

Public
Park Road, Stoke Poges, Slough
SL2 4PJ
Tel   (028 14) 3332
Sec   Mrs M Brooker (Hon)
Pro   S Cannon
Holes   18 L 5847 yds SSS 68
Recs   Am–69 N Harrison, D Ivall
        Pro–68 T Bowers
Fees   £4.80 (£7)
Loc   2 miles N of Slough

Flackwell Heath (1920)

High Wycombe HP10 9PE
Tel   (062 85) 20027
Mem   750
Sec   JJR Barton (062 85) 20929
Pro   B Plucknett (062 85) 23017
Holes   18 L 6150 yds SSS 69
Recs   Am–65 P Dougan
        Pro–65 J Hoskison, E Murray
V'trs   WD–H WE–M SOC–Wed &
        Thurs
Fees   £19
Loc   Between High Wycombe &
        Beaconsfield off the A40. M40
        Junction 3 from London

Gerrards Cross (1934)

Chalfont Park, Gerrards Cross
SL9 0QA
Tel   (0753) 883263
Mem   780
Sec   PH Fisher
Pro   AP Barr (0753) 885300
Holes   18 L 6295 yds SSS 70
Recs   Am–65 JB Berney
        Pro–63 AP Barr
V'trs   WD–H WE/BH–M
Fees   £23, £17 after 3pm
Loc   1 mile from station off A413

Harewood Downs (1908)

Cokes Lane, Chalfont St Giles
HP8 4TA
Tel   (0494) 762308
Mem   350
Sec   RM Lennard (0494) 762184
Pro   GC Morris (0494) 764102
Holes   18 L 5958 yds SSS 69
Recs   Am–65 AL Parsons
        Pro–65 JM Hume
V'trs   WD–H WE/BH–M SOC
Loc   Off A413 to Amersham

Hazlemere G & CC (1982)

Penn Road, Hazlemere, High
Wycombe HP15 7LR
Tel   (0494) 714722
Mem   560
Sec   DE Hudson

Pro   SR Morvell (0494) 718298
Holes 18 L 6039 yds SSS 69
Recs   Pro–65 J Bennett, R Green
       (1987)
V'trs WD–U WE–booking req
       SOC–WD
Fees   £14 (£18)
Loc   3 miles NE of High Wycombe
       on B474
Mis   Buggies available for hire

Iver (1983)

Hollow Hill Lane, Iver SL0 0JJ
Tel   (0753) 655615
Mem   500
Sec   T Notley
Pro   T Notley
Holes 9 L 3107 yds SSS
V'trs U SOC
Fees   18 holes–£5.60 (£8)
       9 holes–£3.60 (£4.60)
Loc   ½ mile from Langley station,
       off Langley Park Road

Ivinghoe (1967)

Wellcroft, Ivinghoe, nr Leighton
Buzzard LU7 9EF
Tel   (0296) 668696
Mem   250
Sec   Mrs SE Garrad (0296) 662478
Pro   PW Garrad
Holes 9 L 4508 yds SSS 62
Recs   Am–61 J Dillon (1984)
       Pro–60 R Garrad (1967)
V'trs WD–U WE–U after 8am
Fees   18 holes–£4.50 (£6)
       36 holes–£5.50 (£7)
Loc   Tring 3 miles. Dunstable 4
       miles. M1 Junction 11, 5 miles

Little Chalfont (1981)

Lodge Lane, Little Chalfont,
nr Amersham
Tel   (024 04) 4877
Mem   450
Sec   JM Dunne
Pro   W Lowe (024 04) 2942
Holes 9 L 5852 yds SSS 68
Recs   Am–76 D Brown
       Pro–65 S Parker
V'trs WD–U WE–M
Fees   £7 (£9)
Loc   Station 1½ miles

Stoke Poges (1908)

Park Road, Stoke Poges
SL2 4PG
Tel   (0753) 26385
Mem   700
Sec   RC Pickering
Pro   K Thomas (0753) 23609
Holes 18 L 6654 yds SSS 71
Recs   Am–65 BA Price
       Pro–65 J Hudson
V'trs WD–I or H WE/BH–M
Fees   £8 (£14)
Loc   2 miles N of Slough

Stowe (1974)

Stowe, Buckingham MK18 5EH
Tel   (0280) 813650
Mem   300
Sec   Mrs SA Cross (0280) 813684
Holes 9 L 4573 yds SSS 63
V'trs WD/WE dawn–1pm & after
       7pm–M; School holidays–M
       SOC
Fees   £5
Loc   M1 Junction 16–A5–A43–A413.
       4 miles from Buckingham
       on A413 to Brackley.

Weston Turville (1974)

New Road, Weston Turville,
nr Aylesbury HP22 5QT
Tel   (0296) 24084
Mem   460
Sec   AK Holden
Pro   G George (0296) 25949
Holes 18 L 6100 yds SSS 69
Recs   Am–73 B Duff
V'trs U (exc Sun am) Sat–booking
Fees   £8 (£10)
Loc   2½ miles SE of Aylesbury

Wexham Park (1979)

Wexham Street, Wexham, nr Slough
SL3 6NB
Tel   (028 16) 663271
Mem   650
Sec   JWE Mulley
Pro   D Morgan (028 16) 663425
Holes Wexham 18 L 5836 yds SSS 68;
       Old Grange 9 L 2383 yds SSS 32
V'trs U SOC–WD
Fees   18 hole: £5.60 (£8)
       9 hole: £3.60 (£4.60)
Loc   2 miles N of Slough
Mis   Further 9 holes opening 1990

Whiteleaf (1904)

Whiteleaf, Aylesbury
Tel   (084 44) 3097
Mem   300
Sec   DG Bullard
Pro   KS Ward (084 44) 5472
Holes 9 L 2756 yds SSS 66
Recs   Am–64 M Copping
       Pro–63 MM Caines
V'trs WD–U WE–M
Fees   18 holes–£15 36–holes £20
Loc   Princes Risborough 2 miles

Windmill Hill (1972)

Public
Tattenhoe Lane, Bletchley,
Milton Keynes MK3 7RB
Tel   (0908) 648149 (Fax) 0908 271478
Pro   C Clingan
Holes 18 L 6773 yds SSS 72
Recs   Am–69 RJ Long
       Pro–66 C Defoy
V'trs U SOC
Fees   £3.75 (£5.30)
Loc   4 miles M1 Junction 14 on A421
Mis   Floodlit driving range

Woburn (1976)

Bow Brickhill, Milton Keynes
Tel   (0908) 370756
Pro   A Hay (0908) 647987
Holes Duke's 18 L 6940 yds SSS 74;
       Duchess 18 L 6641 yds SSS 72
Recs   Duke's Am–68
       Pro–64 P Mitchell
V'trs WD–H (by arrangement)
       WE–M
Fees   By arrangement
Loc   4 miles W of M1 Junction 13

Cambridgeshire

Abbotsley (1986)

Eynesbury Hardwicke, St Neots
PE19 4XN
Tel   (0480) 215153
Mem   700
Sec   J Wisson (0480) 74000
Pro   V Saunders
Holes 18 L 6150 yds SSS 71
Recs   Am–72 J Morrow (1987)
       Pro–69 S Whymark (1984)
V'trs WD–U SOC WE–M before
       10am –U after 10am BH–U
Fees   £8 (£13)
Loc   2 miles SE of St Neots
       on B1046. 12 miles W of
       Cambridge. M11 Junction 13,
       on to A45
Mis   Floodlit driving range.

Cambridgeshire Moat House Hotel (1974)

Bar Hill, Cambridge CB3 8EU
Tel   (0954) 780555
Mem   450
Sec   GW Huggett
Pro   GW Huggett (0954) 780098
Holes 18 L 6734 yds SSS 72
Recs   Am–68 P Way
       Pro–68 P Townsend
V'trs I
Fees   £18 (£25)
Loc   5 miles NW of Cambridge
       on A604
Mis   Buggies for hire

Ely City (1961)

Cambridge Road, Ely CB7 4HX
Tel   (0353) 2751
Mem   750
Sec   GA Briggs
Pro   F Rowden (0353) 3317
       (Touring Pro H Baiocchi)
Holes 18 L 6686 yds SSS 72
Recs   Am–68 N Evans
       Pro–66 L Trevino
V'trs WD–H WE–H SOC–Tues–Fri
Fees   £14 (£20)
Loc   12 miles N of Cambridge

For explanation of abbreviations, see page 460.

Girton (1936)

Dodford Lane, Cambridge
Tel   (0223) 276169
Mem   700
Sec   Mrs MA Cornwell
Pro   J Sharkey
Holes   18 L 6085 yds SSS 69
V'trs   WD–U WE/BH–M SOC
Fees   WD–£14
Loc   3 miles N of Cambridge
        (A604)

Gog Magog (1901)

Shelford Bottom, Cambridge
CB2 4AB
Tel   (0223) 247626
Mem   1050
Sec   JE Riches
Pro   I Bamborough (0223) 246058
Holes   Old 18 L 6386 yds SSS 70
        New 9 L 5833 yds SSS 68
Recs   Am–64 RW Guy, MT Seaton,
        DWG Woods, R Claydon
        Pro–64 G Wolstenholme,
        PJ Butler
V'trs   WD–I WE/BH–M SOC–Tues
        & Thurs
Fees   Old–£20 New–£10
Loc   2 miles S of Cambridge on
        A1307

March (1922)

Frogs Abbey, Grange Rd, Knights
End, March
Tel   (0354) 52364
Mem   300
Sec   RA Philpott (0354) 54604
Pro   F Kiddie
Holes   9 L 6278 yds SSS 70
Recs   Am–68 JW Kisby
V'trs   H WE–M
Fees   £7
Loc   18 miles E of Peterborough

Orton Meadows (1987)

Public
Ham Lane, Peterborough PE2 0UU
Tel   (0733) 237478
Pro   N Grant
Holes   18 L 5800 yds SSS 68
Recs   Am–74 N Cornell (1989)
        Pro–67 R Mann (1987)
V'trs   U (always phone Pro)
Fees   £4.20 (£6.50)
Loc   2 miles SW of Peterborough
        on A605
Mis   12 hole pitch and putt

Peterborough Milton (1937)

Milton Ferry, Peterborough
PE6 7AG
Tel   (0733) 380204
Mem   800
Sec   PJ Bishop (0733) 380489

Pro   NS Bundy (0733) 380793
Holes   18 L 6431 yds SSS 71
Recs   Am–67 J Mitchell (1988)
        Pro–68 J Hawkesworth, A Jolly,
        R Larratt
V'trs   WD–U WE–M SOC
Fees   £18
Loc   4 miles W of Peterborough
        on A47

Ramsey (1964)

4 Abbey Terrace, Ramsey,
Huntingdon PE17 1DD
Tel   (0487) 813573
Mem   750
Sec   R Muirhead (0487) 812600
Pro   BJ Puttick (0487) 813022
Holes   18 L 6145 yds SSS 70
Recs   Am–66 DP Smith (1987)
        Pro–67 F Kiddie (1989)
V'trs   WD–H WE/BH–M SOC
Fees   £15
Loc   12 miles SE of Peterborough

St Ives (Hunts) (1923)

St Ives, Huntingdon PE17 4RS
Tel   (0480) 64459
Mem   320
Sec   R Hill IPFA (0480) 68392
Pro   A Headley (0480) 66067
Holes   9 L 6100 yds SSS 69
Recs   Am–67 Fl–Lt CJB Murdoch
        Pro–61 P Alliss
V'trs   WD–U WE–NA
Fees   £10 (£15)
Loc   5 miles E of Huntingdon

St Neot's (1890)

Crosshall Road, St Neot's PE19 4AE
Tel   (0480) 74311
Mem   600
Sec   RJ Marsden (0480) 72363
Pro   G Bithrey (0480) 76513
Holes   18 L 6027 yds SSS 69
Recs   Am–67 JR Gray
        Pro–65 M Gallagher, H Flatman
V'trs   H WE–M
Fees   WD–£15 D–£20
Loc   1 mile W of St Neot's on
        A45
Mis   Buggy £12 D–£20

Thorpe Wood (1975)

Public
Nene Parkway, Peterborough
PE3 6SE
Tel   (0733) 267701
Pro   D Fitton, R Fitton
Holes   18 L 7086 yds SSS 74
Recs   Am–74 N Brownlie, JN Dodd,
        J Brady
        Pro–71 R Fitton
V'trs   U
Fees   £4.20 (£6.50)
Loc   3 miles W of Peterborough,
        on A47

Channel Islands

Alderney (1969)

Route des Carrières, Alderney
Tel   (048 182) 2835
Mem   520
Sec   A Eggleston
Holes   9 L 2528 yds SSS 33
Recs   Am–29 M Hugman
        Pro–28 PL Cunningham
V'trs   U
Fees   £8 (£10)
Loc   1 mile E of St Anne

L'Ancresse

L'Ancresse, Guernsey
Tel   (0481) 47408
Mem   315
Sec   M Russell (0481) 55805
Holes   Share L'Ancresse course
        with Royal Guernsey

La Moye (1902)

La Moye, St Brelade
Tel   (0534) 42701
Mem   1250
Sec   D Lowton (0534) 43401
Pro   D Melville (0534) 43130
Holes   18 L 6741 yds SSS 72
Recs   Am–69 BJ McCarthy (1987)
        Pro–62 G Brand Jr
V'trs   IH SOC–after 9.30am
Fees   £22 (£25) W–£100
Loc   6 miles W of St Helier

Royal Guernsey (1890)

L'Ancresse, Guernsey
Tel   (0481) 47022
Mem   1520
Sec   GJ Nicolle (0481) 46523
Pro   N Wood (0481) 45070
Holes   18 L 6206 yds SSS 70
Recs   Am–64 R Eggo (1986)
        Pro–64 P Cunningham
V'trs   WD–H WE–NA
Fees   £10.50 D–£12.50 W–£40 F–£60
Loc   5 miles N of St Peter Port

Royal Jersey (1878)

Grouville, Jersey
Tel   (0534) 54416
Mem   1300
Sec   RC Leader
Pro   T Horton (0534) 52234
Holes   18 L 6023 yds SSS 69
Recs   Am–64 R Harrop (1989)
        Pro–64 P Le Chevalier (1988)
V'trs   WD–H after 10am WE/BH–H
        after 2.30pm (Winter 12.30pm)
Fees   £22 (£30)
Loc   4 miles E of St Helier

St Clements (1925)

Public
St Clements, Jersey
Tel   (0534) 21938
Pro   R Marks
Holes   9 L 3972 yds SSS 61

Recs   Am–61 T Gray, B McCarthy
V'trs   H Sun am–NA
Fees   £8
Loc   1 mile E of St Helier
Mis   Book by telephone

Western Golf Range

Public
The Mount, Val de la Mare,
St Quens, Jersey
Tel   (0534) 81947/82787
Sec   J Le Brun (Mgr) (0534) 82629
Pro   C Wackeb (0534) 82787
Holes   12 holes Par 3 SSS 36
V'trs   U
Fees   12 holes £3 (£3.25)
Loc   Five Mile Road, St Quens Bay
Mis   Driving range

Cheshire

Alderley Edge (1907)

Brook Lane, Alderley Edge SK9 7RU
Tel   (0625) 585583
Mem   212 80(L) 40(J) 40(5)
Sec   AJ Hayes (0625) 523213
Pro   M Stewart (0625) 584493
Holes   9 L 5836 yds SSS 68
Recs   Am–65 FA Hardy, DJ Austin
Pro–65 BR Boughey
V'trs   M or H
Fees   £10 (£13)
Loc   12 miles S of Manchester

Astbury (1922)

Peel Lane, Astbury, nr Congleton
CW12 4RE
Tel   (0260) 272772
Mem   600
Sec   T Williams
Pro   SR Bassil
Holes   18 L 6269 yds SSS 70
Recs   Am–65 AJA Hurst (1983)
Pro–69 I Mosey (1979)
V'trs   WD–H or M WE–M
SOC–Thurs only
Fees   £12
Loc   1 mile S of Congleton off A34,
via Astbury

Avro (1980)

British Aerospace, Woodford
Tel   (061) 439 5050
Mem   400
Sec   AP Johnson (0625) 874402
Holes   9 L 5735 yds SSS 68
Recs   Am–72 R Wheeler (1989)
V'trs   M
Fees   £4 (£6)

Birchwood (1979)

Kelvin Close, Birchwood, Warrington
Tel   (0925) 818819
Mem   1009
Sec   A Jackson
Pro   D Cooper
Holes   18 L 6808 yds SSS 73

Recs   Am–64 MJ Conroy
Pro–65 P Affleck
V'trs   U SOC–Mon & Thurs
Fees   £11 (£15)
Loc   M62 Junction 11, 2 miles

Bramhall (1905)

Ladythorn Road, Bramhall,
Stockport SK7 2EY
Tel   (061) 439 4057
Mem   300 160(L) 85(J) 100(5)
Sec   F Chadfield (061) 439 4393
Pro   B Nield (061) 439 1171
Holes   18 L 6300 yds SSS 70
Recs   Am–64 AE Hill (1987)
Pro–66 I Higby (1987)
V'trs   U exc Thurs SOC
Fees   £15 (£20)
Loc   Stockport

Chester (1900)

Curzon Park, Chester CH4 8AR
Tel   (0244) 675130
Mem   840
Sec   PM Pritchard (0244) 677760
Pro   G Parton (0244) 671185
Holes   18 L 6487 yds SSS 71
Recs   Am–68 M Weetman
Pro–66 D Screeton
V'trs   U H SOC
Fees   £15 (£20)
Loc   Chester 1 mile

Congleton (1897)

Biddulph Road, Congleton CW12 3LZ
Tel   (0260) 273540
Mem   425
Sec   FT Pegg
Pro   JA Colclough (0260) 271083
Holes   9 L 5704 yds SSS 65
Recs   Am–60 M Griffiths (1989)
Pro–59 N Coles (1968)
V'trs   U
Fees   On application
Loc   1½ miles from Congleton
on A527

Crewe (1911)

Fields Road, Haslington, Crewe
CW1 1TB
Tel   (0270) 584227 (Steward)
Mem   601
Sec   DG Elias B.Sc (0270) 584099
Pro   R Rimmer (0270) 585032
Holes   18 L 6181 yds SSS 69
Recs   Am–66 VG McCandless
Pro–68 A Thompson
V'trs   WD–U WE/BH–M SOC
Fees   £13 1989 prices
Loc   2 miles NE of Crewe Station,
off A534. 5 miles W of M6
Junction 16

Delamere Forest (1910)

Station Road, Delamere, Northwich
CW8 2JE
Tel   (0606) 882807
Mem   400
Sec   L Parkin

Pro   EB Jones (0606) 883307
Holes   18 L 6305 yds SSS 70
Recs   Am 66 B Stockdale
Pro–63 M Bembridge
V'trs   WD–U WE–2 ball only SOC
Fees   £15 (£20)
Loc   10 miles E of Chester

Eaton (1965)

Eaton Park, Eccleston, Chester
CH4 9JF
Tel   (0244) 671420
Sec   RT Robinson (0244) 680474
Pro   A Mitchell (0244) 680170
Holes   18 L 6446 yds SSS 71
V'trs   I SOC–WD
Loc   3 miles S of Chester

Ellesmere Port (1971)

Public
Chester Road, Hooton, South Wirral
L66 1QH
Tel   (051) 339 7502
Pro   D Yeats
Holes   18 L 6432 yds SSS 71
Recs   Am–69 A Waterhouse
Pro–67 B Evans, A Caygill
V'trs   SOC–WD WE–Arrange with
Pro
Fees   £2.90 (£3.60)
Loc   9 miles N of Chester on A41

Helsby (1902)

Tower's Lane, Helsby, Warrington
WA6 0JB
Tel   (09282) 2021
Mem   600
Sec   N Littler
Pro   I Wright (09282) 5457
Holes   18 L 6204 yds SSS 70
Recs   Am–69 F Wood, JJ Spruce
Pro–68 I Wright
V'trs   WE–NA SOC
Fees   £10
Loc   Off A56 into Primrose Lane,
first right Towers Lane

Knights Grange (1983)

Public
Grange Lane, Winsford CW7 2PT
Tel   (06065) 52780
Pro   G Moore
Holes   9 L 6240 yds SSS 70
V'trs   U SOC
Fees   18 holes–£2.10 (£2.80)
9 holes–£1.60 (£2.10)
Loc   Signposted to Knights Grange
Sports Complex

Knutsford (1891)

Mereheath Lane, Knutsford
Tel   (0565) 3355
Mem   135
Sec   D Francis
Pro   A Wilson
Holes   9 L 6288 yds SSS 70
Recs   Am–65 B Stockdale
Pro–65 D Cooper

For explanation of abbreviations, see page 460.

V'trs I exc Wed pm–NA SOC
Fees £10 (£15)
Loc Knutsford ¹/₄ mile

Lymm (1907)

Whitbarrow Road, Lymm WA13 9AN
Tel (092 575) 2177
Mem 400 100(L) 75(J) 50(5)
Sec JM Pearson (092 575) 5020
Pro GJ Williams (092 575) 5054
Holes 18 L 6304 yds SSS 70
Recs Am–68 CN Brown (1987)
      Pro–69 S Lyle (1987)
V'trs H
Fees £11 (£13) 1989 prices
Loc 5 miles SE of Warrington

Macclesfield (1889)

The Hollins, Macclesfield 3K11 7EA
Tel (0625) 23227
Mem 600
Sec W Eastwood (0625) 615845
Pro T Taylor (0625) 616952
Holes 12 L 6184 yds SSS 69
Recs Am–69 RA Johnson,
      B Hodkinson
      Pro–67 M Gregson
V'trs WD/BH–I WE–M
Fees £10
Loc 1 mile SE of Macclesfield

Malkins Bank

Public
Malkins Bank, Sandbach
Tel (0270) 765931
Pro D Wheeler
Holes 18 L 6071 yds SSS 69
Recs Am–71 JR Dabecki (1989)
V'trs U SOC
Fees £3.40 (£4.10)
Loc 2 miles S of Sandbach via
      A534/A533. M6 Junction 17

Mere G & CC (1934)

Mere, Knutsford WA16 6LJ
Tel (0565) 830155
Mem 375 175(L) 100(J)
Sec AB Turner
Pro EP Goodwin (0565) 830219
Holes 18 L 6849 yds SSS 73
Recs Am–68 CR Smethurst
      Pro–69 N Faldo
V'trs WE/BH–NA Wed & Fri–NA
      Mon/Tues/Thurs–H SOC
Fees £30
Loc 1 mile E of M6 Junction 19
Mis Driving range. Buggies

New Mills (1907)

Shaw Marsh, New Mills
Tel (0663) 43485
Mem 250
Sec W Hyde (0663) 43816
Pro I Scott (0663) 46161
Holes 9 L 5924 yds SSS 68
Recs Am–72 R Palmer, S Hewson
      Pro–67 A Ellis, A Murray
V'trs WD–U WE–M SOC
Fees D–£6

Poulton Park (1980)

Dig Lane, Cinnamon Brow
Tel (0925) 812034
Mem 360
Sec B Carr
Pro S McCarthy (0925) 825220
Holes 9 L 4918 metres SSS 66
Recs Am–66 S Bennett
V'trs WD–NA 5–6pm
      WE–NA noon to 2pm
Fees £8 (£10)
Loc Off Crab Lane, Fearnhead

Prestbury (1920)

Macclesfield Road, Prestbury,
Macclesfield SK10 4BJ
Tel (0625) 829388
Mem 725
Sec JL Carter (0625) 828241
Pro TW Rastall (0625) 828242
Holes 18 L 6359 yds SSS 71
Recs Am–66 R Foster, JE Allen
      Pro–68 M Faulkener
V'trs WD–I WE–M SOC–Thurs
Fees £20
Loc 2¹/₂ miles NW of Macclesfield

Queen's Park (1985)

Public
Queen's Park Gardens, Crewe
CW2 7SB
Tel (0270) 666724
Pro M Williams
Holes 9 L 5370 yds Par 68
V'trs WD–U WE–U after 8.30am SOC
Fees £2.50 (£3)
Loc 1¹/₄ miles from Crewe, off
      Victoria Avenue

Romiley (1897)

Goosehouse Green, Romiley,
Stockport SK6 4LJ
Tel (061) 430 2392
Mem 750
Sec F Beard (061) 430 7257
Pro G Butler (061) 430 7122
Holes 18 L 6335 yds SSS 70
Recs Am–64 N Ryan
      Pro–67 D Roberts
V'trs U SOC
Fees £11 (£16)
Loc Station ³/₄ mile

Runcorn (1909)

Clifton Road, Runcorn
Tel (0928) 572093 (members)
Mem 375 80(L) 80(J)
Sec GE Povey OBE JP
      (0928) 574214
Pro G Berry (0928) 564791
Holes 18 L 6035 yds SSS 69
Recs Am–67 I Rockliffe
V'trs WD–U exc comp days H SOC
Fees £10 (£12)
Loc Runcorn (A557). M56 Junction
      12

St Michael Jubilee

Public
Dundalk Road, Widnes
Tel (051) 424 0989
Mem 300
Sec W Hughes
Holes Play over Widnes Municipal

Sandbach (1923)

Middlewich Road, Sandbach
CW11 9EA
Tel (0270) 762117
Mem 215 110(L) 50(J)
Sec AF Pearson
Holes 9 L 5614 yds SSS 67
Recs Am–64 K Brooks
V'trs WD–U WE/BH–M
Fees £10
Loc Sandbach 1 mile

Sandiway (1921)

Sandiway CW8 2DJ
Tel (0606) 882606
Mem 750
Sec VFC Wood (0606) 883247
Pro I Clark (0606) 883180
Holes 18 L 6435 yds SSS 72
Recs Am–67 AE Hill
      Pro–65 D Huish
V'trs I H
Fees £20 (£25)
Loc Chester 15 miles on A556

Stockport (1906)

Offerton Road, Offerton, Stockport
SK2 5HL
Tel (061) 427 2001
Mem 495
Sec HE Bagshaw (061) 427 4425
Pro R Tattersall (061) 427 2421
Holes 18 L 6319 yds SSS 71
Recs Am–65 KR Gorton
      Pro–66 E Lester
V'trs U SOC
Fees £15 (£20)
Loc 1 mile along A627 from
      Hazel Grove to Marple

The Tytherington (1986)

Macclesfield SK10 2JP
Tel (0625) 617622
      (Fax) 0625 611076
Mem 200
Sec Ms R Dawson
Pro S Wilson
Holes 18 L 6737 yds SSS 72
V'trs U
Fees £16 D–£22 (£20 D–£30)
Loc Nr Macclesfield on
      Manchester road

Upton-by-Chester (1934)

Upton Lane, Chester CH2 1EE
Tel (0244) 381183
Mem 750
Sec JB Durban
Pro PA Gardner
Holes 18 L 5875 yds SSS 68

Recs   Am–63 JD Norbury
       Pro–66 A Perry
V'trs U SOC–WD
Fees   £13 (£15)
Loc   Off Liverpool Road,
       near 'Frog' PH

Vicars Cross (1939)

Vicars Cross, Chester
Tel   (0244) 335174
Mem   650
Sec   DC Chilton
Pro   JA Forsythe
Holes 18 L 5857 yds SSS 68
Recs   Am–63 MK Jones
V'trs U exc Fri–M
Fees   £15 D–£18
Loc   2 miles E of Chester on A51

Walton Hall

Public
Warrington Road, Higher Walton,
Warrington WA4 5LU
Tel   (0925) 66775
Sec   D Judson (0925) 571028
Pro   MJ Slater (0925) 63061
Holes 18 L 6843 yds SSS 73
Recs   Am–70 R Davies (1988)
V'trs U
Fees   £3.65 (£4.50)
Loc   2 miles S of Warrington

Warrington (1903)

Hill Warren, Appleton
Tel   (0925) 61620
Mem   875
Sec   RO Francis (0925) 61775
Pro   AW Fryer (0925) 65431
Holes 18 L 6305 yds SSS 70
Recs   Am–66 JR Bennett
       Pro–65 EG Lester
V'trs U SOC–Wed & Thurs
Fees   £9.50 (£14)
Loc   3 miles S of Warrington

Widnes (1924)

Highfield Road, Widnes WA8 7DT
Tel   (051) 424 2440
Mem   800
Sec   MM Cresswell
       (051) 424 2995
Pro   F Robinson (051) 424 2995
Holes 18 L 5719 yds SSS 68
Recs   Am–65 F Whitfield (1985),
       WK George (1986),
       T Skold (1989)
       Pro–64 A Murray
V'trs WD–U WE–NA on comp days
       SOC–WD
Fees   £10 (£12)
Loc   Station ¹⁄₂ mile

Widnes Municipal (1977)

Public
Dundalk Road, Widnes WA8 8BS
Tel   (051) 424 6230
Pro   R Bilton (0295) 65241
Holes 18 L 5612 yds SSS 67
Recs   Am–67 I O'Connor (1989)

V'trs U
Fees   £2.70 (£3.35)
Mis   St Michael Jubilee Club
       plays here

Wilmslow (1889)

Great Warford, Mobberley, Knutsford
WA16 7AY
Tel   (056 587) 2579
Mem   670
Sec   CA Skelton (056 587) 2148
Pro   J Nowicki (056 587) 3620
Holes 18 L 6500 yds SSS 71
Recs   Am–68 A O'Connor, TB Taylor
       Pro–64 J O'Leary
V'trs U exc Wed–NA before 2pm
Fees   On application
Loc   3¹⁄₂ miles W of Alderley Edge

Cleveland

Billingham (1967)

Sandy Lane, Billingham TS22 5NA
Tel   (0642) 554494/533816
Mem   800
Sec   DJ Bruce OBE (0642) 533816
Pro   P Bradley (0642) 557060
Holes 18 L 6430 yds SSS 71
Recs   AM–66 M Ure (1988)
       Pro–65 P Harrison (1988)
V'trs WD–H after 9am WE/BH–M
       SOC
Fees   D–£12 (NA)
Loc   W boundary of Billingham by
       A19, E of bypass

Castle Eden & Peterlee (1927)

Castle Eden, Hartlepool
Tel   (0429) 836220
Mem   650
Sec   P Robinson
Pro   T Jenkins (0429) 836689
Holes 18 L 6297 yds SSS 70
Recs   Am–66 G Border (1987)
V'trs U
Fees   £10 (£16)
Loc   2 miles S of Peterlee

Cleveland (1887)

Queen Street, Redcar TS10 1BT
Tel   (0642) 483693
Mem   674
Sec   LR Manley (0642) 471798
Pro   D Masey (0642) 483462
Holes 18 L 6707 yds SSS 72
Recs   Am–68 M Watson (1978)
       Pro–70 B Hardcastle (1976)
V'trs WD–U after 9.30am SOC
       Sun/BH–no parties
Fees   £10 (£15)
Loc   S bank of River Tees

Eaglescliffe (1914)

Yarm Road, Eaglescliffe,
Stockton-on-Tees
Tel   (0642) 780098
Mem   470
Sec   AH Painter (0642) 780238

Pro   J Munro (0642) 780588
Holes 18 L 6275 yds SSS 70
Recs   Am–67 B Skipper
       Pro–67 J Munro
V'trs H
Fees   £11 (£15)
Loc   3 miles S of Stockton-on-Tees

Hartlepool (1906)

Hart Warren, Hartlepool
Tel   (0429) 274398
Mem   600
Sec   WE Storrow (0429) 870282
Pro   ME Cole (0429) 267473
Holes 18 L 6215 yds SSS 70
Recs   Am–65 G Bell (1989)
       Pro–66 G Brown (1987)
V'trs WD–U SOC
Fees   £12 (£20)
Loc   N boundary of Hartlepool

Middlesbrough (1908)

Brass Castle Lane, Middlesbrough
TS8 9EE
Tel   (0642) 316430
Mem   900
Sec   JM Jackson (0642) 311515
Pro   DJ Jones (0642) 311766
Holes 18 L 5582 metres SSS 69
Recs   Am–61 R Boxall
       Pro–66 D Jagger
V'trs U
Fees   D–£12.50 (£15)
Loc   3 miles S of Middlesborough

Middlesbrough Municipal (1977)

Public
Ladgate Lane, Middlesbrough
TS5 7YZ
Tel   (0642) 315533
Sec   J Dilworth (Hon)
Pro   M Nutter (0642) 315361
Holes 18 L 6314 yds SSS 70
Recs   Am–69 NBJ Fick
       Pro–67 B Gallagher
V'trs U
Fees   £3.75 (£5)
Loc   3 miles S of Middlesborough,
       on A174
Mis   Floodlit driving range

Saltburn (1894)

Hob Hill, Saltburn-by-the-Sea
Tel   (0287) 22812
Mem   800
Sec   I Mackay (0287) 32768
Pro   R Broadbent (0287) 24653
Holes 18 L 5846 yds SSS 68
V'trs U
Fees   £8 (£10)

Seaton Carew (1874)

Tees Road, Hartlepool TS25 1DE
Tel   (0429) 266249
Mem   650
Sec   T Waite (0429) 267645
Pro   W Hector

For explanation of abbreviations, see page 460.

Holes	Old L 6604 yds SSS 72
	Brabazon L 6802 yds SSS 73
Recs	Am–66 M Kelley
	Pro–67 JW Johnson
V'trs	U SOC
Fees	£16 (£20)
Loc	Hartlepool 2 miles

Tees-side (1901)

	Acklam Road, Thornaby TS17 7JS
Tel	(0642) 676249
Mem	600
Sec	W Allen (0642) 616516
Pro	K Hall (0642) 673822
Holes	18 L 6472 yds SSS 71
V'trs	WD–before 4.30pm WE–after
	11am BH–M before 11am SOC
Fees	£8 (£12)
Loc	2 miles S of Stockton on A1130.
	1/2 mile from A19 on A1130

Wilton (1949)

	Wilton, Redcar TS10 4QY
Tel	(0642) 465265
Mem	700
Sec	DW Lewis (0642) 477570
Pro	AL Maskell
Holes	18 L 6104 yds SSS 69
Recs	Am–64 N Crapper
	Pro–68 S Hunt
V'trs	WD–U Sat–NA Sun/BH–U SOC
Fees	£10
Loc	3 miles W of Redcar on A174

Cornwall

Bude & North Cornwall (1891)

	Burn View, Bude EX23 8BY
Tel	(0288) 352006
Mem	320 135(L) 60(J)
Sec	BWA Watson
Pro	P Sanders
Holes	18 L 6202 yds SSS 70
Recs	Am–67 D Cann
	Pro–70 C Pennington
V'trs	U SOC
Fees	£9 W–£30 F–£45
Loc	In Bude

Budock Vean Hotel (1922)

	Falmouth
Tel	(0326) 250288
Mem	250
Sec	FG Benney (0326) 250060
Holes	9 L 5007 yds SSS 65
Recs	Am–61 RJ Sadler
	Pro–64 D Short
V'trs	H
Fees	£7 (£9)
Loc	Falmouth 5 miles

Carlyon Bay (1926)

	Carlyon Bay, St Austell
Tel	(072 681) 4250
Mem	600
Sec	CH Farmer

Pro	NJ Sears (072 681) 4228
Holes	18 L 6510 yds SSS 71
Recs	Am–69 M Boggia
	Pro–65 N Coles
V'trs	U
Fees	£8.50 (£10) W–£40
Loc	2 miles E of St Austell
Mis	Buggies for hire

Culdrose

	Royal Naval Air Station, Culdrose
Tel	(0326) 574121 (Ext 7113)
Mem	130
Sec	DG Guy (Ext 2388)
Holes	9 L 6412 yds SSS 71
V'trs	M

Falmouth (1928)

	Swanpool Road, Falmouth
Tel	(0326) 311262
Mem	600
Sec	DJ de C Sizer (Mgr)
	(0326) 40525
Pro	D Short (0326) 316229
Holes	18 L 5581 yds SSS 67
Recs	Am–60 JL Gresson (1988)
	Pro–65 G Brand Jr (1981)
V'trs	U SOC
Fees	£10 (£10) W–£42
Loc	1/2 mile W of Swanpool Beach

Isles of Scilly (1904)

	St Mary's, Isles of Scilly TR21 0NF
Tel	(0720) 22692
Mem	380
Holes	9 L 5974 yds SSS 69
Recs	Am–69 M Twynham
V'trs	U Sun–M
Fees	£7 W–£15.50
Loc	Hughtown 11/2 miles

Launceston (1928)

	St Stephen, Launceston
Tel	(0566) 3442
Mem	750
Sec	BJ Grant
Pro	J Tozer
Holes	18 L 6374 yds SSS 70
Recs	Am–67 H Reid
	Pro–67 G Smith
V'trs	U SOC
Fees	£10 (£12)
Loc	1 mile N of Launceston, off
	Bude road

Looe (1933)

	Bin Down, nr Looe PL13 1PX
Tel	(05034) 239
Mem	450
Sec	G Bond (Gen Mgr)
Holes	18 L 5940 yds SSS 68
V'trs	U SOC
Fees	£10 (£12)
Loc	3 miles E of Looe

Mullion (1895)

	Cury Helston TR12 7BP
Tel	(0326) 240276
Mem	800
Sec	D Watts (0326) 240685
Pro	M Singleton (0326) 241176
Holes	18 L 5610 yds SSS 67
Recs	Am–66 PA Gilbert
	Pro–68 BJ Hunt, P Alliss
V'trs	H (restricted comp days and
	open days) SOC–WD
Fees	£12 W–£40 F–£60
Loc	6 miles S of Helston

Newquay (1890)

	Tower Road, Newquay TR7 1LT
Tel	(0637) 872091
Mem	500
Sec	G Binney (0637) 874354
Pro	P Muscroft (0637) 874830
Holes	18 L 6140 yds SSS 69
Recs	Am–63 P Clayton (1989)
	Pro–69 PJ Yeo
V'trs	WD/Sat–H Sun–H
Fees	£12 (£15) W–£48
Loc	1/2 mile from Newquay

Perranporth (1927)

	Budnick Hill, Perranporth
	TR6 0AB
Tel	(0872) 572454
Mem	550
Sec	VG Hill
Pro	DC Mitchell (0872) 572317
Holes	18 L 6208 yds SSS 70
Recs	Am–65
	Pro–68
V'trs	H SOC
Loc	1/2 mile NW of Perranporth

Praa Sands (1971)

	Praa Sands, Germoe Cross Roads,
	Penzance TR20 9TQ
Tel	(0736) 763445
Mem	350
Sec	D & K Phillips (Props)
Pro	RA Hamilton
Holes	9 L 4036 yds SSS 60
Recs	Am–59 P Lorys
V'trs	U exc Sunday am
Fees	£6 W–£28
Loc	7 miles from Penzance on
	A394 Penzance–Helston road,
	at Praa Sands

St Austell (1912)

	Tregongeeves, St Austell
Tel	(0726) 74756
Mem	780
Sec	SH Davey
Pro	M Rowe (0726) 68621
Holes	18 L 5981 yds SSS 69
Recs	Am–67 AC Nash
V'trs	SOC exc comp days
Fees	£9 (£12)
Loc	11/2 miles W of St Austell

St Enodoc (1890)

Rock, Wadebridge PL27 6LB
Tel   (020 886) 3216
Mem   1050
Sec   Col L Guy OBE
Pro   NJ Williams (020 886) 2402
Holes   Church 18 L 6207 yds SSS 70
        Holywell 18 L 4165 yds SSS 61
Recs   Am–65 K Jones
        Pro–67 Dai Rees
V'trs   Main course–H SOC
        Short course–U
Fees   Church £15 W–£54
        Holywell £9 W–£36
Loc   Wadebridge 6 miles
Mis   Max handicap 24

St Mellion (1976)

St Mellion, nr Saltash PL12 6SD
Tel   (0579) 50101
Mem   700
Sec   DM Webb (Mgr)
Pro   T Moore (0579) 50724
Holes   Old 18 L 5927 yds SSS 68
        Jack Nicklaus Course 18 L
        6626 yds SSS 72
V'trs   H SOC
Loc   Tamar Bridge
Mis   Buggies. Driving range

Tehidy Park (1922)

Camborne TR14 0HH
Tel   (0209) 842208
Mem   1000
Sec   RD Parry
Pro   J Dumbreck (0209) 842914
Holes   18 L 6241 yds SSS 70
Recs   Am–67 N Rogers
        Pro–70 M Grieve
V'trs   H
Fees   £12 (£16)
Loc   3 miles N of Camborne

Tregenna Castle Hotel (1982)

St Ives TR26 2DE
Tel   (0736) 795254 (Ext 121)
Mem   184
Sec   J Goodman
Holes   18 L 3645 yds SSS 57
Recs   Am–62 G Thomas (1989)
        Pro–54 L Knapp (1986)
V'trs   U SOC
Fees   £8 (£9)
Loc   St Ives 1 mile

Trevose (1924)

Constantine Bay, Padstow PL28 8JB
Tel   (0841) 520208
Mem   625
Sec   P Gammon (Prop)
        GL Grindley (Sec/Mgr)
Pro   G Alliss (0841) 520261

Holes   18 L 6608 yds SSS 72
        9 L 1367 yds SSS 29
Recs   Am–67 C Phillips
        Pro–66 N Burch
V'trs   H SOC
Fees   On application
Loc   4 miles W of Padstow
Mis   3 & 4 ball starting times
        restricted all year–phone Club

Truro (1937)

Treliske, Truro TR1 3LG
Tel   (0872) 72640
Mem   900
Sec   BE Heggie (0872) 78684
Pro   NK Bicknell (0872) 76595
Holes   18 L 5347 yds SSS 66
Recs   Am–61 AJ Ring
        Pro–63 M Hoyle
V'trs   U SOC
Fees   £12 (£15) W–£48 M–£100
Loc   2 miles W of Truro on A390

West Cornwall (1889)

Lelant, St Ives TR26 3DZ
Tel   (0736) 753319
Mem   825
Sec   WS Richards (0736) 753401
Pro   P Atherton (0736) 753177
Holes   18 L 5854 yds SSS 68
Recs   Am–65 MC Edmunds,
        P Darlington
        Pro–64 G Emerson
V'trs   H
Fees   £10 (£14) W–£30
Loc   2 miles E of St Ives

Whitsand Bay Hotel (1909)

Portwrinkle, Torpoint
Tel   (0503) 30470/30276 (Hotel)
Mem   400
Sec   GG Dyer (0503) 30418
Pro   S Poole (0503) 30778
Holes   18 L 5512 yds SSS 67
Recs   Am–62 GG Dyer (1981)
        Pro–63 M Faulkner (1948)
V'trs   H SOC
Fees   £10 (£12)
Loc   Plymouth 6 miles

Cumbria

Alston Moor (1906)

The Hermitage, Alston CA9 3DB
Tel   (0498) 81675
Mem   150
Sec   A Dodd (0498) 81953
Holes   9 L 5880 yds SSS 64
Recs   Am–67 A Rutherford
V'trs   U SOC
Fees   £4 (£5)
Loc   Alston 2 miles on B6277

Appleby (1903)

Appleby
Tel   (076 83) 51432
Mem   600
Sec   BW Rimmer
Holes   18 L 5914 yds SSS 68
Recs   Am–63 K Bush
        Pro–69 SS Scott
V'trs   U
Fees   £8 (£10)
Loc   2 miles SE of Appleby. 1/2 mile
        N of A66

Barrow (1921)

Rakesmoor Lane, Hawcoat,
Barrow-in-Furness
Tel   (0229) 25444
Mem   385 109(L) 80(J)
Sec   I Booth (0229) 35213
Pro   M Booth (0229) 23121
Holes   18 L 6209 yds SSS 70
Recs   Am–66 NL Brooks
V'trs   U
Fees   £8 (£8) W–£25
Loc   Hawcoat

Brampton (Talkin Tarn) (1907)

Brampton
Tel   (069 77) 2255
Mem   750
Sec   IJ Meldrum (0228) 23155
Pro   S Harrison (069 77) 2000
Holes   18 L 6420 yds SSS 71
Recs   Am–70 N Johnstone (1988)
V'trs   U
Fees   £7 (£9) W–£24
Loc   B6413, 1 mile SE of Brampton

Carlisle (1908)

Aglionby, Carlisle
Tel   (0228) 513303
Mem   870
Sec   C Baker, JA Griffiths
Pro   JS More (0228) 513241
Holes   18 L 6278 yds SSS 70
Recs   Am–65 M Ruddick (1989)
        Pro–65 D Pearce (1988)
V'trs   WD–U after 9.30am & 1.30pm
        Tues pm/comp days–NA
        Sat–U after 10am & 2.30pm
        Sun–M SOC–Mon/Wed/Fri
Fees   £15 (£20)
Loc   1/2 mile E of M6 Junction 43,
        on A69

Cockermouth (1896)

Embleton, Cockermouth
Tel   (059 681) 223
Mem   497
Sec   RD Pollard (0900) 822650
Holes   18 L 5496 yds SSS 67
Recs   Am–65 S Gabb
V'trs   WD–U before 5pm exc Wed
        Sun–NA before 11am and
        2–2.30pm SOC
Fees   £6 (£8)
Loc   4 miles E of Cockermouth

For explanation of abbreviations, see page 460.

The Dunnerholme (1905)

Askam-in-Furness
Tel   (0229) 62675
Mem   400
Sec   JH Mutton (0229) 62979
Holes   10 L 6101 yds SSS 69 (18 tees)
Recs   Am–68 H Bayliff
          Pro–70 JB Ball
V'trs   U
Fees   £6 (£8)
Loc   6 miles N of Barrow on A595
          Whitehaven–Workington road

Furness (1872)

Walney Island, Barrow-in-Furness
Tel   (0229) 41232
Mem   700
Sec   WT French
Pro   K Bosward
Holes   18 L 6363 yds SSS 71
Recs   Am–67 A Miles (1986)
          Pro–65 A Chandler,
          GJ Brand (1984)
V'trs   U
Fees   £10 (£10)
Loc   Walney Island

Grange Fell (1952)

Cartmel Road, Grange-over-Sands
LA11 6HB
Tel   (05395) 32536
Mem   260
Sec   JB Asplin (05395) 32021
Holes   9 L 4826 metres SSS 66
Recs   Am–68 GB Wolstenholme
          AI Bremner, N Bremner,
          D Airey, G Park
          Pro–66 F Robinson
V'trs   U
Fees   £8 (£10)

Grange-over-Sands (1919)

Meathop Road, Grange-over-Sands
LA11 6QX
Tel   (05395) 33180
Mem   255 95(L) 25(J)
Sec   JR Green (05395) 32717
Holes   18 L 5660 yds SSS 68
Recs   Am–64 S McMillan
          Pro–67 G Cuthbert
V'trs   U
Fees   £9 (£12)
Loc   Grange station ¹/₂ mile

Kendal (1891)

The Heights, Kendal
Tel   (0539) 724079
Mem   460
Sec   EF Millar (0539) 720840
Pro   D Turner (0539) 723499
Holes   18 L 5550 yds SSS 67
Recs   Am–63 J Brennand
          Pro–63 P Tupling, GC Norton
V'trs   U H SOC
Fees   £9 (£12.50)

Keswick (1978)

Threlkeld Hall, nr Keswick CA12 4HH
Tel   (07687) 83324
Mem   470
Sec   DS Cowen (07687) 72147
Holes   18 L 6175 yds SSS 72
Recs   Am–71 BD Airey (1987)
          Pro–69 I Clark (1984)
V'trs   U SOC
Fees   £10 (£12)
Loc   4 miles E of Keswick A66

Kirkby Lonsdale

Casterton Road, Kirkby Lonsdale
Mem   130 30(L) 20(J)
Sec   P Jackson (0468) 72085
Holes   9 L 4058 yds SSS 60
V'trs   U
Fees   £3
Loc   1 mile on Sedbergh road

Maryport (1905)

Bankend, Maryport CA15 6PA
Tel   (0900) 812605
Mem   275
Sec   F Wilkinson
Holes   18 L 6272 yds SSS 71
Recs   Am–70 JA Scott
V'trs   U
Fees   D–£6 (£8) Mon–Fri–£20
Loc   1 mile N of Maryport off B5300

Penrith (1890)

Salkeld Road, Penrith CA11 8SG
Tel   (0768) 62217/65429
Mem   850
Sec   J Carruthers (0768) 62217
Pro   CB Thomson (0768) 62217
Holes   18 L 6026 yds SSS 69
Recs   Am–64 JM Nutter
          Pro–65 K Bousefield
V'trs   H WE/BH–10.06–11.30am &
          after 3pm
Fees   £10 (£12)
Loc   ¹/₂ mile E of Penrith

St Bees (1931)

Rhoda Grove, Rheda, Frizington
CA26 3TE
Tel   (0946) 812105
Mem   325
Sec   JB Campbell
Holes   9 L 5082 yds SSS 65
Recs   Am–66 E Gulliksen
V'trs   U
Fees   £5 (£6)
Loc   4 miles S of Whitehaven

Seascale (1893)

The Banks, Seascale CA20 1QL
Tel   (094 67) 28202/28800
Mem   550
Sec   C Taylor (094 67) 28662
Holes   18 L 6416 yds SSS 71
Recs   Am–67 D Weston, ID Stavert,
          G Shuttleworth (1987)
          Pro–68 EC Anderson

V'trs   U SOC
Fees   £10 (£12)
Loc   15 miles S of Whitehaven

Sedbergh (1896)

The Riggs, Sedbergh
Mem   70
Sec   AD Lord (0587) 20993
Holes   9 L 2067 yds SSS 61
Recs   Am–64 S Gardner
V'trs   U
Fees   £2
Loc   1 mile S of Sedbergh at
          Millthorp

Silecroft (1903)

Silecroft, Millom LA18 4AG
Tel   (0229) 774250
Mem   370
Sec   M O'N Wilson JP (0229)
          774160
Holes   9 L 5712 yds SSS 68
Recs   Am–68 D Temple
V'trs   WD–U WE/BH–often restricted
          until 5.30pm SOC
Fees   £5 R/D
Loc   3 miles N of Millom towards
          shore

Silloth-on-Solway (1892)

Silloth, nr Carlisle CA5 4AD
Tel   (0965) 31179
Mem   600
Sec   GS Hartley, G Lowther
Holes   18 L 6343 yds SSS 70
Recs   Am–66 C Wallace, DL
          Watson
V'trs   U H SOC
Fees   D–£11 (D–£16) 5D–£40
Loc   Silloth, 22 miles W of
          Carlisle

Stoneyholme (1974)

Public
St Aidan's Road, Carlisle CA7 1LS
Tel   (0228) 34856
Pro   S Ling
Holes   18 hole course
Recs   Am–69
V'trs   U
Fees   £3.90
Loc   1 mile E of Carlisle

Ulverston (1894)

Bardsea Park, Ulverston
Tel   (0229) 52824
Mem   700
Sec   D Weston (0229) 52963
Pro   MR Smith (0229) 52806
Holes   18 L 6122 yds SSS 69
Recs   Am–66 AJ Edwards (1989)
          Pro–71 JA Raisbeck
V'trs   U
Fees   £14 (£18) 3D–£36
Loc   1¹/₂ miles SW of Ulverston on
          A5087

Windermere (1892)

Cleabarrow, Windermere
LA23 3NB
Tel   (096 62) 3123
Mem   870
Sec   KR Moffat
Pro   WSM Rooke (096 62) 3550
Holes   18 L 5006 yds SSS 65
Recs   Am–58 P Chapman (1988)
        Pro–59 G Brand (1989)
V'trs   H SOC
Fees   £15 (£20)
Loc   1¹/₂ miles E of Bowness

Workington (1922)

Branthwaite Road, Workington
Tel   (0900) 603460
Mem   475 125(L) 100(J)
Sec   JK Walker (0900) 605420
Pro   N Summerfield
Holes   18 L 6252 yds SSS 70
Recs   Am–65 A Drabble
V'trs   H SOC
Fees   £10 (£15)
Loc   2 miles E of Workington

Derbyshire

Alfreton (1893)

Oakerthorpe, Alfreton
Tel   (0773) 832070
Mem   260
Sec   D Tomlinson (0246) 862661
Holes   9 L 5074 yds SSS 65
Recs   Am–64 N Cluskey
        Pro–65 J Smith
V'trs   WD exc Mon–U before 4.30pm
        –M after 4.30pm WE/Mon–M
        SOC
Fees   £6.50 (£8)
Loc   Alfreton

Allestree Park (1949)

Public
Allestree Hall, Allestree, Derby
Tel   (0332) 550616
Pro   RG Brown
Holes   18 L 5749 yds SSS 68
Recs   Am–66 J McCann
V'trs   U WE–booking req SOC
Fees   £3.50 (£4.60)
Loc   2 miles N of Derby on
        A6

Ashbourne (1910)

Clifton, Ashbourne
Tel   (0335) 42078
Mem   350
Sec   NPA James (0335) 42077
Holes   9 L 5388 yds SSS 66
V'trs   U SOC
Fees   £6 (£8)
Loc   2 miles W of Ashbourne on
        A515 Litchfield road

Bakewell (1899)

Station Road, Bakewell DE1 1CB
Tel   (0629) 812307
Mem   205 67(L) 40(J) 21(5)
Sec   PS Newell
Pro   TE Jones
Holes   9 L 5240 yds SSS 66
Recs   Am–64 MH Piggott
V'trs   U SOC
Fees   £6 (£10)
Loc   ¹/₂ mile NE of Bakewell and A6

Blue Circle (1985)

Cement Works, Hope S30 2RP
Tel   (0433) 20317
Mem   116
Sec   DS Smith
Holes   9 L 5252 yds SSS 66
Recs   Am–69 B Harper
V'trs   NA
Loc   Hope Valley

Breadsall Priory Hotel G & CC (1976)

Moor Road, Morley, Derby DE7 6DL
Tel   (0332) 832235
Mem   550
Sec   A Busman (Gen Mgr)
Pro   A Smith (0332) 834425
Holes   18 L 6402 yds SSS 71
Recs   Am–66 A Thomas
        Pro–66 M Glynn
V'trs   WD–U SOC–WD only
Fees   £18 (£20)
Loc   A61 Breadsall, left into Croft
        Lane, left into Rectory Lane,
        right on to Moor Road

Buxton & High Peak (1887)

Townend, Buxton SK17 7JB
Tel   (0298) 23453
Mem   450
Sec   B Webb
Pro   A Wardle (0298) 23112
Holes   18 L 5954 yds SSS 69
Recs   Am–63 N Hallam
        Pro–66 P Anderson, P Norton
V'trs   U
Fees   £10 (£12)
Loc   NE boundary of Buxton (A6)

Cavendish (1925)

Gadley Lane, Buxton SK17 6XD
Tel   (0298) 23494
Mem   650
Sec   DN Doyle–Davidson
        (0298) 23256
Pro   J Nolan (0298) 25052
Holes   18 L 5833 yds SSS 68
Recs   Am–65 J Slack (1983)
        Pro–63 I Buckley (1988)
V'trs   U SOC–by prior arrangement
        with Pro
Fees   £14 (£16)
Loc   ³/₄ mile W of Buxton Station

Chapel-en-le-Frith (1905)

The Cockyard, Manchester Road,
Chapel-en-le-Frith, Stockport
SK12 6UH
Tel   (0298) 812118
Mem   617
Sec   JW Dranfield (0298) 813943
Pro   DJ Cullen
Holes   18 L 6089 yds SSS 69
V'trs   U
Fees   £10 (£15)
Loc   Stockport 13 miles on A6
        (B5470)

Chesterfield (1897)

Walton, Chesterfield S42 7LA
Tel   (0246) 279256
Mem   551
Sec   CD Yates (0246) 566032
Pro   M McLean (0246) 276297
Holes   18 L 6326 yds SSS 70
Recs   Am–65 I Wyatt
        Pro–66 K Nagle, B Hutchison
V'trs   WD–U WE–M SOC
Fees   £15
Loc   2 miles SW of Chesterfield on
        A263

Chesterfield Municipal (1934)

Public
Murray House, Crow Lane,
Chesterfield S41 0EQ
Tel   (0246) 273887
Pro   J Delany
Holes   18 L 6013 yds SSS 69
V'trs   U
Fees   £3.50 (£4.50)
Loc   ¹/₄ mile past Chesterfield
        station
Mis   Tapton Park play here

Chevin (1894)

Duffield, Derby
Tel   (0332) 841864
Mem   500 66(L) 61(J) 8(5)
Sec   CP Elliott
Pro   W Bird (0332) 841112
Holes   18 L 6057 yds SSS 69
Recs   Am–65 C Radford (1987)
        Pro–65 DJ Russell (1985)
V'trs   WD–U WE–M SOC exc Sat
Fees   £15
Loc   5 miles N of Derby on
        A6

Derby (1923)

Public
Shakespeare Street, Sinfin, Derby
DE2 9HD
Tel   (0332) 766323
Pro   RG Brown (0332) 766462
Holes   18 L 6144 yds SSS 69
Recs   Am–66
V'trs   U
Fees   £3.50 (£4.50)

For explanation of abbreviations, see page 460.

Erewash Valley (1905)

Stanton-by-Dale, nr Ilkeston
Tel   (0602) 323258
Mem   450
Sec   D Knowles (0602) 322984
Pro   MJ Ronan (0602) 324667
Holes   18 L 6487 yds SSS 71
Recs   Am–67 R Claydon
        Pro–68 MJ Ronan
V'trs   WE/BH–NA before noon
        SOC–WD
Fees   £12 (£16)
Loc   Between Nottingham and
        Derby. M1 Junction 25

Glossop & District (1894)

Sheffield Road, Glossop
Tel   (045 74) 3117
Mem   250
Sec   J Dickson (045 74) 62713
Pro   C Wadsworth
Holes   11 L 5716 yds SSS 68
Recs   Am–66 DM Pike
        Pro–68 S Sewgolum
V'trs   U SOC
Fees   £6 (£7)
Loc   1 mile E of Glossop off A57

Hallowes (1892)

Dronfield, Sheffield S18 6UA
Tel   (0246) 413149
Mem   600
Sec   EE Vessey (0246) 413734
Pro   P Seal (0246) 411196
Holes   18 L 6342 yds SSS 71
Recs   Am–67 JW Benson
        Pro–67 R Ellis
V'trs   WD–U WE/BH–M (phone first)
Fees   £7 D–£10
Loc   6 miles S of Sheffield on A61
        (not by–pass)

Ilkeston (1929)

Public
Peewit West End Drive, Ilkeston
Tel   (0602) 304550
Holes   9 L 4116 yds SSS 60
V'trs   U
Fees   £4
Loc   ½ mile E of Ilkeston

Kedleston Park (1947)

Kedleston, Derby DE6 4JD
Tel   (0332) 840035
Mem   853
Sec   K Wilson
Pro   J Hetherington (0332) 841685
Holes   18 L 6643 yds SSS 72
Recs   Am–65 M Betteridge
        Pro–66 J Lower
V'trs   U
Fees   £20 (£25)
Loc   4 miles N of Derby. NT signs
        to Kedleston Hall

Matlock (1907)

Chesterfield Road, Matlock DE4 5LF
Tel   (0629) 582191
Mem   375 50(L) 65(J) 95(5)
Sec   AJ Box
Pro   M Deeley (0629) 584934
Holes   18 L 5989 yds SSS 69
V'trs   WD–U WE–M SOC–WD
Fees   D–£15 W–£60 M–£120
Loc   1½ miles NE of Matlock (A632)

Mickleover (1923)

Uttoxeter Road, Mickleover
Tel   (0332) 513339 (clubhouse)
Mem   650
Sec   D Rodgers
Pro   S Hadfield (0332) 518662
Holes   18 L 5708 yds SSS 68
Recs   Am–64 CRJ Ibbotson
        Pro–63 A Skingle
V'trs   U SOC–Tues & Thurs
Fees   £12 (£14)
Loc   3 miles W of Derby on
        A516/B5020

Ormonde Fields

Nottingham Road, Codnor, Ripley
Tel   (0773) 42987
Mem   460
Sec   RN Walters (0773) 47301
Pro   S Illingworth
Holes   18 L 5812 yds SSS 68
Recs   Am–67 S Clarke, S Butt
        Pro–67 C Jepson
V'trs   U SOC
Fees   £5 (£7)
Loc   A610 Ripley to Nottingham
        road. M1 Junction 26 5 miles

Pastures (1969)

Pastures Hospital, Mickleover
Tel   (0332) 513921 (Ext 348)
Mem   320
Sec   S McWilliams
Holes   9 L 5005 yds SSS 64
Recs   Am–62 C Whyatt (1989)
V'trs   M SOC–WD
Loc   4 miles W of Derby

Shirland (1977)

Lower Delves, Shirland DE5 6AU
Tel   (0773) 832515
Mem   360
Sec   RT Yorke (0773) 604764
Pro   NB Hallam (0773) 834935
Holes   18 L 5948 yds SSS 69
Recs   Pro–71 NB Hallam
V'trs   U SOC
Fees   £8 (£12)
Loc   1 mile N of Alfreton, off A61
        by Shirland Church

Sickleholme (1898)

Bamford, Sheffield S30 2BH
Tel   (0433) 51306
Mem   250 100(L) 72(J) 80(5)
Sec   WT Scott
Pro   PH Taylor

Holes   18 L 6064 yds SSS 69
Recs   Am–63 IL Fletcher
        Pro–65 AP Highfield
V'trs   U exc Wed am
Fees   £15 (£20) 1989 prices
Loc   W of Sheffield, between
        Hathersage and Hope (A625)

Stanedge (1934)

Walton Hay Farm, nr Chesterfield
Tel   (0246) 566156
Mem   300
Sec   W Tyzack (0246) 276568
Holes   9 L 4867 yds SSS 64
Recs   Am–64 W Steel Jr (1982)
        Pro–65 A Skingle (1987)
V'trs   WD–U before 2pm –M after
        2pm Sat–M Sun–NA before
        4pm M after 4pm
Fees   £7
Loc   5 miles SW of Chesterfield
        off B5057

Tapton Park (1934)

Public
Murray House, Crow Lane,
Chesterfield S41 0EQ
Mem   450
Sec   D Griffiths (0246) 475260
Holes   Play over Chesterfield
        Municipal

Devon

Axe Cliff (1896)

Squires Lane, Axmouth, Seaton
EX12 2BJ
Tel   (0297) 20499
Mem   400
Sec   YG Keep
Holes   18 L 5111 yds SSS 65
Recs   Am–65 P Cricard
V'trs   U H SOC
Fees   £10
Loc   Axmouth ¾ mile, nr Yacht
        Club at Axmouth Bridge

Bigbury (1923)

Bigbury, Kingsbridge TQ7 4BB
Tel   (0548) 810207
Mem   850
Sec   BJ Perry (0548) 810557
Pro   S Lloyd (0548) 810412
Holes   18 L 6076 yds SSS 69
Recs   Am–65 CS Yeoman
        Pro–67 S Lloyd
V'trs   I H SOC
Fees   £12
Loc   Plymouth 15 miles

Chulmleigh (1976)

Leigh Road, Chulmleigh EX18 7BL
Tel   (0769) 80519
Mem   150
Sec   PN Callow
Holes   18 L 1440 yds Par 3
Recs   Am–52 H Gillibrand
        Pro–54 D Sheppard

Holsworthy (1937)

Kilatree, Holsworthy
Tel (0409) 253177
Mem 350
Sec B Megson
Holes 18 L 6012 yds SSS 69
Recs Am–66 A Ramsey
Pro–67 G Ryall, R Troake
V'trs WD–U Sun–U after 12 noon
Fees £7 W–£28
Loc 1 mile W of Holsworthy

Honiton (1896)

Middlehills, Honiton EX14 8TR
Tel (0404) 3633
Mem 820
Sec D Holloway (0404) 44422
Pro (0404) 2943
Holes 18 L 5931 yds SSS 68
Recs Am–70 R Bumpstead
Pro–65 I Read
V'trs U (recognised club member)
BH–NA SOC
Fees £14 (£17)
Loc 1 mile S of Honiton.
M5 Junction 25

Ilfracombe (1892)

Hele Bay, Ilfracombe EX34 9RT
Tel (0271) 62176
Mem 593
Sec RC Beer
Pro D Hoare (0271) 63328
Holes 18 L 5857 yds SSS 68
Recs Am–67 RC Beer
V'trs H SOC WD–NA 12–2pm
WE/BH–U after 10am
–NA 12–2pm
Fees £10 5D–£35
Loc Between Ilfracombe and
Combe Martin

Manor House Hotel (1929)

Moretonhampstead
Tel (0647) 40355
Mem 250
Sec R Lewis
Pro R Lewis
Holes 18 L 6016 yds SSS 69
Recs Pro–65 R Emerson
V'trs U SOC
Fees £12 (£15)
Loc 15 miles SW of Exeter

Newton Abbot (Stover) (1930)

Newton Abbot TQ12 6QQ
Tel (0626) 52460
Mem 861
Sec R Smith
Pro M Craig (0626) 62078
Holes 18 L 5852 yds SSS 68
Recs Am–63 M Pym (1989)
Pro–67 B Barnes (1977)
V'trs H SOC–Thurs
Fees £15 R/D
Loc 3 miles N of Newton Abbot
on A382

Churston (1890)

Churston, Brixham
Tel (0803) 842218
Mem 640
Sec AM Chaundy (0803) 842751
Pro R Penfold (0803) 842894
Holes 18 L 6201 yds SSS 70
Recs Am–64 RHP Knott
Pro–67 JM Green
V'trs U (recognised club members)
Tues am–NA
Fees £16 (£20)
Loc Torquay 5 1/4 miles

Downes Crediton (1976)

Hookway, Crediton EX17 3PT
Tel (036 32) 3991
Mem 700
Sec WJ Brooks (036 32) 3025
Pro H Finch (036 32) 4464
Holes 18 L 5868 yds SSS 68
V'trs U
Fees £12 (£15)
Loc Off A377 on Exeter side of
Crediton

East Devon (1902)

North View Road, Budleigh Salterton
EX9 6DQ
Tel (039 54) 2018
Mem 850
Sec RSB Luckman (039 54) 3370
Pro T Underwood (039 54) 5195
Holes 18 L 6214 yds SSS 70
Recs Am–65 R Winchester
Pro–67 S Little
V'trs H SOC
Fees £20 (£25)
Loc 12 miles SE of Exeter

Elfordleigh Hotel G & CC (1932)

Elfordleigh, Plympton, Plymouth
Tel (0752) 336428
Mem 400
Sec A Dunstan (0752) 703824
Pro I Marshall (0752) 345071
Holes 9 L 5759 yds SSS 68
V'trs WD–U WE–phone first
Fees £12 (£12)
Loc 4 miles E of Plymouth

Exeter G & CC (1895)

Countess Wear, Exeter EX2 7AE
Tel (039 287) 4139
Mem 896
Sec C Greetham
Pro M Rowett (039 287) 5028
Holes 18 L 6061 yds SSS 69
Recs Am–63 G Milne (1988)
Pro–64 G Laing
V'trs WD–U WE–I SOC–Thurs only
Fees £15

Okehampton (1913)

Okehampton EX20 1EF
Tel (0837) 52113
Mem 500
Sec S Chave
Pro P Blundell (0837) 53541
Holes 18 L 5300 yds SSS 67
Recs Am–67 MS Moore
Pro–H Finch
V'trs U SOC
Fees On application
Loc S boundary of Okehampton,
signposted from traffic lights

Royal North Devon (1864)

Golf Links Road, Westward Ho!
EX39 1HD
Tel (023 72) 473824
Mem 900
Sec EJ Davies (023 72) 473817
Pro G Johnston (023 72) 477598
Holes 18 L 6644 yds SSS 72
Recs Am–66 D Boughey
Pro–66 P Dawson, KDG Nagle,
MF Foster
V'trs On request
Fees £14 (£18)
Loc Bideford 2 miles

Saunton (1897)

Saunton, nr Braunton
Tel (0271) 812436
Mem 1080
Sec WE Geddes
Pro JA McGhee (0271) 812013
Holes East 18 L 6703 yds SSS 73
West 18 L 6322 yds SSS 71
Recs East Am–67 T Nash
Pro–69 B Huggett
West Am–67 ME Jewell
Pro–69 P Berry
V'trs U H
Fees £17 (£19) W–£85
Loc 9 miles W of Barnstaple

Sidmouth (1889)

Cotmaton Road, Sidmouth
EX10 8SX
Tel (0395) 513023
Mem 700
Sec DE Matthews (0395) 513451
Pro M Kemp (0395) 516407
Holes 18 L 5188 yds SSS 65
Recs Am–59 N Winchester
Pro–64 E Murray
V'trs U SOC
Fees D–£10 (£12) W–£40
Loc 1/2 mile W of Sidmouth.
12 miles SE of M5 Junction 30

Staddon Heights (1895)

Plymstock, Plymouth PL9 9SP
Tel (0752) 402475
Mem 620
Sec MG Holliday
Pro M Grieve (0752) 492630

V'trs U
Fees £3 D–£6
Loc 1 mile N of A377 Barnstaple–
Exeter road

For explanation of abbreviations, see page 460.

Holes 18 L 5861 yds SSS 68
Recs Am–64 R Clark, D Roberts
Pro–62 GC Smale
V'trs WE–H SOC–WD
Fees £9 D–£11 (£12 D–£14)
5D–£30 Summer £25 Winter
Loc SE Plymouth

Tavistock (1890)

Down Road, Tavistock PL19 9AQ
Tel (0822) 612049
Mem 650
Sec BG Steer (0822) 612344
Pro R Hall (0822) 612316
Holes 18 L 6250 yds SSS 70
Recs Am–66 MG Symons
Pro–69 S Chadwick, N Bicknell
V'trs H SOC–WD
Fees £12 (£15)
Loc Whitchurch Down

Teignmouth (1924)

Teignmouth TQ14 9NY
Tel (062 67) 73614
Mem 900
Sec D Hankins (062 67) 74194
Pro P Ward (062 67) 72894
Holes 18 L 6142 yds SSS 69
Recs Am–65 JH Laidler (1980)
Pro–66 P Millhouse (1987)
V'trs H (recognised club member)
SOC–WD WE–M before 4pm
Fees £15 (£20)
Loc 2 miles N of Teignmouth on
B3192

Thurlestone (1897)

Thurlestone, nr Kingsbridge
Tel (0548) 560405/560221
Mem 700
Sec R Marston (0548) 560405
Pro N Whitley (0548) 560715
Holes 18 L 6337 yds SSS 70
Recs Am–66 RP Knott
Pro–67 PJ Yeo
V'trs I or H
Fees £15 W–£65 1989 prices
Loc Kingsbridge 5 miles

Tiverton (1932)

Post Hill, Tiverton EX16 4NE
Tel (0884) 252114 (clubhouse)
Mem 475 130(L) 45(J) 250(5)
Sec Maj DLJ Hicks (0884) 252187
Pro RE Freeman (0884) 254836
Holes 18 L 6263 yds SSS 71
Recs Am–65 SC Waddington
Pro–70 A Moore
V'trs I H
Fees On application
Loc 5 miles W of M5 Junction 27.
1 1/2 miles E of Tiverton on
B3391

Torquay (1910)

Petitor Road, St Marychurch,
Torquay TQ1 4QF
Tel (0803) 314591
Mem 800
Sec BG Long
Pro M Ruth (0803) 329113
Holes 18 L 6192 yds SSS 69
Recs Am–62 AR Copping
Pro–66 D Short
V'trs H SOC
Fees £15 (£17)
Loc Torquay

Torrington (1932)

Weare Trees, Torrington EX38 7EZ
Tel (0805) 22229
Mem 405
Sec GSC Green (Hon)
Holes 9 L 4418 yds SSS 62
Recs Am–65 P Wheeler
V'trs U Sun am–NA SOC
Fees £8 (£10)
Loc Torrington 1 mile on Weare
Gifford road

Warren (1892)

Dawlish
Tel (0626) 862255
Mem 550
Sec TE Allen
Pro G Wicks (0626) 864002
Holes 18 L 5968 yds SSS 69
Recs Am–65 J Langmead (1987)
V'trs U
Fees £10 (£12) W–£45
Loc 1 1/2 miles E of Dawlish

Wrangaton (South Devon) (1895)

Wrangaton, South Brent TQ10 9HJ
Tel (0364) 73229
Mem 350
Sec RR Hine
Holes 9 L 5790 yds SSS 68
Recs Am–66 SR Bryant
Pro–67 FG Robins
V'trs U exc Wed pm and Sun
(Mar–Oct)
Fees £10 (£15)
Loc Dartmoor, 10 miles SW of
Ashburton
Mis Further 9 holes opening 1990

Yelverton (1904)

Golf Links Road, Yelverton PL20 6BN
Tel (0822) 853618
Mem 700
Sec Maj (Retd) DR Bettany
(0822) 852824
Pro A MacDonald (0822) 853593
Holes 18 L 6288 yds SSS 70
Recs Am–67 P Newcombe (1987)
V'trs H SOC
Fees £10 (£12) W–£25
Loc 6 miles N of Plymouth on A386

Dorset

Ashley Wood (1896)

Tarrant Rawston, Blandford Forum
DT11 9HN
Tel (0258) 452253
Mem 500
Sec P Fry
Pro S Taylor
Holes 9 L 6227 yds SSS 70
Recs Am–68 D Thorn, S Ricketts,
N Rodgers
Pro–67 S Taylor (1988)
V'trs WD–U WE–NA before noon
SOC
Fees £10 (£12)
Loc 1 1/2 miles SW of Blandford

Boscombe (1938)

Public
Queen's Park, Bournemouth
Mem 337
Sec JHH Burdett (0202) 483017
Holes Play over Queen's Park

Boscombe Ladies (1953)

Queen's Park Pavilion, Queen's Park,
West Drive, Bournemouth BH8 9BY
Tel (0202) 36198
Mem 90
Sec Mrs S Dean (0202) 426042
Holes Play over Queen's Park
Loc

Bournemouth & Meyrick Park (1890)

Meyrick Park, Bournemouth
BH2 6LH
Tel (0202) 290307
Mem 600
Sec RL Pike
Holes Play over Meyrick Park

Bridport & West Dorset (1891)

East Cliff, West Bay, Bridport
DT6 4EP
Tel (0308) 22597
Mem 700
Sec PJ Ridler (0308) 421095
Pro JE Parish (0308) 421491
Holes 18 L 5246 yds SSS 66
Recs Am–63 M Rees, M Berrett
(1984)
Pro–66 S Bishop (1980),
R Crockford (1983)
V'trs U
Fees £10 (£15)
Loc 1 1/2 miles S of Bridport at West
Bay

Broadstone (1898)

Wentworth Drive, Station Approach,
Broadstone BH18 8DQ
Tel (0202) 693363
Mem 750
Sec JM Cowan (0202) 692595

Pro N Tokely (0202) 603936
Holes 18 L 6183 yds SSS 70
Recs Am–65 JH Nash (1988)
Pro–64 S Hamill (1988)
V'trs WD–H after 9.30am
WE/BH–NA SOC–WD
Fees £18 D–£22
Loc 4 miles N of Poole

Came Down (1905)

Came Down, Dorchester DT2 8NR
Tel (030 581) 2531
Mem 700
Sec D Matthews (Mgr)
(030 581) 3494
Pro R Preston (030 581) 2670
Holes 18 L 6224 yds SSS 71
Recs Am–69
V'trs H Sun am–NA SOC
Fees £12.50 (£16) W–£45
Loc 2 miles S of Dorchester

Canford School

Canford School, Wimborne BH21 3AD
Tel (0202) 841254
Mem 200
Sec HA Jarvis
Holes 9 L 5918 yds SSS 68
V'trs M SOC
Fees £5
Loc 2 miles SE of Wimborne, off A341

Christchurch (1977)

Public
Iford Bridge, Barrack Road, Christchurch
Tel (0202) 473817
Pro P Troth
Holes 9 L 4824 yds SSS 64
Recs Am–65 D Pearcey
V'trs U
Fees £3.40 (£3.90)
Loc Boundary of Bournemouth on Christchurch Road
Mis Driving range

East Dorset (Lakey Hill) (1978)

Hyde, Wareham BH20 7NT
Tel (0929) 471776/471941
Mem 900
Sec JI Mullins
Pro G Packer (0929) 471574
Holes 18 L 6146 yds SSS 69
V'trs WD–U WE–M SOC–WD
Fees £10 (£12)
Loc Worgret, 4 miles from Worgret Heath
Mis Driving range

Ferndown (1923)

119 Golf Links Road, Ferndown BH22 8BU
Tel (0202) 872022
Mem 700
Sec R White (0202) 874602

Pro DN Sewell (0202) 873825
Holes 18 L 6442 yds SSS 71
9 L 5604 yds SSS 68
Recs Old Am–66 JHA Leggett
Pro–68 DN Sewell
New Am–67 G Howell
Pro–68 DN Sewell
V'trs WD–I H after 9.30am SOC–WD
Fees Old £25 New £15
Loc 6 miles N of Bournemouth

Halstock

Common Lane, Halstock
Tel (0935) 89689
Mem 200
Sec R Clifton
Pro RF & RG Clifton
Holes 9 L 2083 yds SSS
Recs Am–33 G Ashwood
Pro–32 RG Clifton
V'trs U SOC
Fees 9 holes–£4.50
Loc 6 miles S of Yeovil, off A37
Mis Driving range

Highcliffe Castle (1913)

107 Lymington Road, Highcliffe-on-Sea, Christchurch BH23 4LA
Tel (042 52) 72953
Mem 350 100(L) 50(J)
Sec DW Blakeman (042 52) 72210
Pro R Crockford (042 52) 6640
Holes 18 L 4655 yds SSS 63
Recs Am–58 S Jenkins
Pro–60 D Sewell
V'trs I H SOC
Fees £11 (£15)
Loc Bournemouth 8 miles

Isle of Purbeck (1892)

Studland BH19 3AB
Tel (092 944) 361
Mem 600
Sec J Robinson
Pro P Sowerby (092 944) 354
Holes 18 L 6283 yds SSS 71
9 L 2022 yds SSS 30
Recs Am–67 N Holman
Pro–72 K Sparkes
V'trs U H SOC
Fees Purbeck £16 (£18)
Dene £8
Loc Swanage 2 miles

Knighton Heath (1976)

Francis Avenue, West Howe, Bournemouth BH11 8NX
Tel (0202) 572633
Mem 700
Sec R Bestwick
Pro M Torrens (0202) 578275
Holes 18 L 6206 yds SSS 70
Recs Am–65 P Holbert (1988)
Pro–65 M Thomas (1988)

V'trs WD–H after 9.30am WE–H after 10.30am
Fees On request
Loc 3 miles N of Poole nr junction of A348/A3049

Lyme Regis (1894)

Timber Hill, Lyme Regis
Tel (029 74) 2963
(029 74) 2043 (Steward)
Mem 650
Sec RG Fry
Pro A Black (029 74) 3822
Holes 18 L 6262 yds SSS 70
Recs Am–68 J Thompson (1988)
Pro–66 MD Dack (1987)
V'trs H WD–U after 9.30am
(1pm Thurs) Sun–U after 12 noon SOC
Fees £15 (£18)
Loc Between Lyme Regis and Charmouth off A3502/A35

Meyrick Park (1894)

Public
Bournemouth BH2 6LH
Tel (0202) 290871
Pro J Sharkey
Holes 18 L 5878 yds SSS 69
Recs Am–66 GG Burton
V'trs U
Fees £6.50 (£7.50)
Mis Closed Sun pm. Bournemouth Club plays here

Parkstone (1910)

Links Road, Parkstone, Poole BH14 9JU
Tel (0202) 708025
Mem 500 160(L) 50(J)
Sec AS Kinnear (0202) 707138
Pro N Blenkarne (0202) 708092
Holes 18 L 6250 yds SSS 70
Recs Am–65 RA Latham, T Spence
Pro–63 P Alliss
V'trs H WD–NA before 9.30am and 12.30–2.10pm WE–NA before 9.45am and 12.30–2.30pm
Fees £20 D–£25 (£25 D–£30)
Loc 3 miles W of Bournemouth, off A35

Queen's Park (1905)

Public
Queen's Park, South Drive, Bournemouth
Tel (0202) 36198
Sec JG Sharkey (0202) 36817
Holes 18 L 6505 yds SSS 72
Recs Am–69 M Butcher
Pro–66 A Caygill, H Boyle
V'trs U SOC
Fees Oct–Apr £6 May–Sept £7
Loc 2 miles NE of Bournemouth
Mis Closed Sun pm. Boscombe club plays here

For explanation of abbreviations, see page 460.

Sherborne (1895)

Clatcombe, Sherborne DT9 4RN
Tel   (0935) 812475
Sec   A Mouncer (0935) 814431
Pro   A Pakes (0935) 812274
Holes 18 L 5949 yds SSS 68
Recs   Am–66 S Edgeley (1987)
       Pro–63 M Thomas
V'trs H
Fees   £12 (£15)
Loc   1 mile N of Sherborne

Wareham (1922)

Sandford Road, Wareham
BH20 4DH
Tel   (0929) 554147
Mem   550
Sec   EPM Dorrington
Pro   A Frampton
Holes 18 L 5332 yds SSS 66
Recs   Am–67 K Knott (1989)
V'trs WD–U WE–M SOC
Fees   £10
Loc   1 mile NE of Wareham,
       on A351

Weymouth (1909)

Weymouth DT4 0PF
Tel   (0305) 784994
Mem   650
Sec   E Dickinson (0305) 773981
Pro   D Lochrie (0305) 773997
Holes 18 L 5980 metres SSS 69
Recs   Am–68 L Peters
       Pro–65 D Bennett
V'trs WD/WE–H SOC
Fees   £10 (£13)
Loc   A354, off Manor roundabout

Durham

Aycliffe (1977)

Public
School Lane, Newton Aycliffe
Tel   (0325) 300700
Pro   R Lister (0325) 310820
Holes 9 L 6054 yds SSS 69
V'trs U
Fees   £2.20 (£3.30)
Loc   Sports complex on A6072
       from A68. 1¹/₂ miles from
       Aycliffe
Mis   Floodlit driving range

Barnard Castle (1898)

Harmire Road, Barnard Castle
Tel   (0833) 37237
Mem   600
Sec   AW Lavender (0833) 38355
Pro   J Harrison (0833) 31980
Holes 18 L 5838 yds SSS 68
Recs   Am–65 M Porter (1984)
       Pro–64 C Hamilton (1983),
       J Harrison (1989)

V'trs U SOC
Fees   £10 (£15) 5D–£20
Loc   N boundary of Barnard Castle

Beamish Park (1950)

Beamish, Stanley DH9 0RH
Tel   (091) 370 1133
Mem   520
Sec   AD Stewart (091) 370 1382
Pro   C Cole (091) 370 1984
Holes 18 L 6205 yds SSS 70
Recs   Am–67 A Stewart
V'trs WD/Sat–U before 4pm
       Sun–NA SOC
Fees   £11
Loc   Beamish, nr Stanley

Bishop Auckland (1893)

High Plains, Bishop Auckland
Tel   (0388) 602198
Mem   680
Sec   J Carr (0388) 663648
Pro   W Laird (0388) 661618
Holes 18 L 6420 yds SSS 71
Recs   Am–67 RL Aisbitt
       Pro–65 BL Hunt
V'trs H (closed Good Friday and
       Christmas Day)
Fees   £12 (£15)
Loc   ¹/₂ mile NE of Bishop
       Auckland

Blackwell Grange (1930)

Briar Close, Blackwell, Darlington
DL3 8QX
Tel   (0325) 464464
Mem   650
Sec   F Hewitson (Hon)
       (0325) 465265
Pro   R Givens (0325) 462088
Holes 18 L 5621 yds SSS 67
Recs   Am–64 HP Jolly, S Santon,
       MW Rogers
       Pro–63 M Gregson
V'trs U exc Wed 11am–2.30pm–NA
       Sat–booking only. Sun–comps
       in progress SOC
Fees   £10 (£12)
Loc   1 mile S of Darlington on
       A66

Brancepeth Castle (1924)

Brancepeth Village, Durham
DH7 8EA
Tel   (091) 378 0075
Mem   768 118(L) 74(J) 114(5)
Sec   DC Carver
Pro   D Howdon (091) 378 0183
Holes 18 L 6415 yds SSS 71
Recs   Am–67 D Curry, P Page
V'trs SOC–WD WE–NA
Fees   £16 (£20)
Loc   4¹/₂ miles W of Durham on
       A690

Chester-Le-Street (1909)

Lumley Park, Chester-Le-Street
DH3 4NS
Tel   (091) 388 3218
Mem   400 130(L) 90(J)
Sec   WB Dodds
Pro   MA Strong (091) 389 0157
Holes 18 L 6054 yds SSS 69
Recs   Am–67 SJ Watson
V'trs WD–H WE–NA before 10.30am
       or 12–2pm or by arrangement
Fees   £10 (£15)
Loc   ¹/₄ mile E of Chester–Le–Street

Consett & District (1911)

Elmfield Road, Consett DH8 5NN
Tel   (0207) 502186
Mem   650
Sec   J Horrill (0207) 562261
Pro   S Corbally (0207) 580210
Holes 18 L 6001 yds SSS 69
Recs   Am–65 H Ashby
V'trs WD–U SOC–exc Sat
Fees   £8 (£12)
Loc   12 miles NW of Durham on
       A691. Gateshead 12 miles on
       A692

Crook (1919)

Low Job's Hill, Crook
Tel   (0388) 762429
Mem   450
Sec   R King
Holes 18 L 6075 yds SSS 69
Recs   Am–66 N Tweddle
V'trs U SOC
Fees   £6 (£7)
Loc   ¹/₂ mile E of Crook (A690)

Darlington (1908)

Haughton Grange, Darlington
DL1 3JD
Tel   (0325) 463936
Mem   410 87(L) 110(J) 70(5)
Sec   J Welsh (0325) 355324
Pro   I Todd (0325) 462955
Holes 18 L 6272 yds SSS 70
Recs   Am–64 H Teschner
       Pro–67 M Gallacher
V'trs U 9.30–12 & 1.30–5pm SOC
Fees   £10 (£12)
Loc   Off Salters Lane, NE of
       Darlington

Dinsdale Spa (1910)

Middleton St George, Darlington
DL2 1DW
Tel   (0325) 332222
Mem   826
Sec   PJ Wright (0325) 332297
Pro   D Dodds (0325) 332515
Holes 18 L 6078 yds SSS 69
Recs   Am–64 PF Ward (1984)
       Pro–69 DM Edwards (1980)
V'trs WD–U WE–M BH–M SOC
Fees   £10 D–£12.50
Loc   5 miles SE of Darlington

Durham City (1887)

Littleburn, Langley Moor DH7 8HL
Tel   (091) 378 0069
Mem   750
Sec   JT Ross
Pro   S Corbally (091) 378 0029
Holes 18 L 6211 yds SSS 69
Recs Am–66 A Ramshaw,
      K Cheseldine
V'trs WD–U WE–NA SOC
Fees £8 (£12)
Loc   1½ miles W of Durham

Hobson Municipal (1978)

Public
Hobson, nr Burnopfield,
Newcastle–upon–Tyne
Tel   (0207) 70941
Pro   J Ord (0207) 71605
Holes 18 L 6502 yds SSS 71
Recs Am–69 D Dunn (1987)
V'trs U SOC
Fees £4.50 (£6)
Loc   Between Gateshead and
      Consett on A692

Mount Oswald

South Road, Durham City DH1 3TQ
Tel   (091) 386 7527
Mem   106
Sec   SE Reeve
Holes 18 L 6009 yds SSS 69
Recs Am–64 J Mee (1986)
      Pro–66 J Mathews (1984)
V'trs U SOC
Fees £5.50 D–£8 (£6.50 D–£10)
Loc   SW of Durham on A1050

Roseberry Grange

Public
Grange Villa, Chester-Le-Street
DH2 3NF
Tel   (091) 370 0670
Pro   A Hartley (091) 370 0660
Holes 18 L 5628 yds SSS 68
Recs Am–66 D Brolls (1989)
      Pro–65 B Rumney (1988)
V'trs U SOC
Fees £4 (£5)
Loc   3 miles W of Chester-Le-Street
      on A693

Seaham (1911)

Dawdon, Seaham SR7 7RD
Tel   (091) 581 2354
Mem   550
Sec   V Smith (091) 581 5413
Holes 18 L 5972 yds SSS 69
Recs Am–64 J Sanderson Jr (1984)
V'trs U SOC
Fees £6 (£12)
Loc   Dawdon, 2 miles NE of
      A19

South Moor (1925)

The Middles, Craghead, Stanley
DH9 6AG
Tel   (0207) 232848
Mem   530
Sec   R Harrison (091) 370 0515
Holes 18 L 6445 yds SSS 71
Recs Am–67 JE Handy
      Pro–65 A Webster
V'trs U
Fees On application
Loc   8 miles NW of Durham

Stressholme (1976)

Public
Snipe Lane, Darlington
Tel   (0325) 353073
Pro   FC Thorpe (0325) 461002
Holes 18 L 6511 yds SSS 71
Recs Am–69 S Aitken
      Pro–64 N Coles
V'trs U
Fees £5 (£6)
Loc   2 miles S of Darlington
      on A167

Woodham G & CC (1983)

Burnhill Way, Newton Aycliffe
DH5 4PM
Tel   (0325) 320574
Mem   400
Sec   GE Golightly
Pro   J Graham
Holes 18 L 6727 yds SSS 72
Recs Am–74 S Raby
      Pro–71 D Stirling
V'trs U SOC WE–booking
Fees £7 (£10)
Loc   1 mile N of Newton Aycliffe

Essex

Abridge G & CC (1964)

Epping Lane, Stapleford Tawney
RM4 1ST
Tel   (04028) 388
Mem   560
Sec   PG Pelling (04028) 396/7
Pro   B Cooke (04028) 333
Holes 18 L 6703 yds SSS 72
Recs Am–68 NK Burch
      Pro–68 D Feherty
V'trs WD–H WE/BH–NA
Fees £17
Loc   Theydon Bois/Epping Stations
      3 miles

Ballards Gore (1980)

Gore Road, Canewdon, Rochford
Tel   (0702) 258917
Mem   600
Sec   NG Patient
Pro   M Pierce (0702) 258924
Holes 18 L 7062 yds SSS 74
V'trs WD–U WE–M after 12.30pm
      (summer) 11.30am (winter)
      SOC
Fees WD–£14
Loc   1½ miles NE of Rochford

Basildon (1967)

Public
Clayhill Lane, Sparrow's Hearn,
Kingswood, Basildon
Tel   (0268) 533297
Pro   W Paterson (0268) 533532
Holes 18 L 6120 yds SSS 69
Recs Am–67 R Reeve
      Pro–63 W Longmuir
V'trs U SOC
Fees £5.25 (£10)
Loc   1 mile S of Basildon off A176
      at Kingswood roundabout

Belfairs (1926)

Public
Eastwood Road North, Leigh-on-Sea
SS9 4LR
Tel   (0702) 526911
Pro   R Foreman (0702) 520202
Holes 18 L 5871 yds SSS 68
V'trs WD–U exc Thurs am
      WE/BH–booking
Fees £6 (£9)
Mis   Southend GC and Belfairs GC
      play here

Belhus Park Municipal (1972)

Public
Belhus Park, South Ockendon
RM15 4QR
Tel   (0708) 854260
Sec   L Bourne (Mgr) (0708) 852248
Pro   S Wimbleton
Holes 18 L 5450 yds SSS 66
Recs Am–67 M Jennings, J Bearman
      Pro–63 R Joyce
V'trs U
Fees £3.95 (£6)
Loc   1 mile N of A13/M25 Dartford
      Tunnel
Mis   Floodlit driving range

Bentley G & CC (1972)

Ongar Road, Brentwood CM15 9SS
Tel   (0277) 73179
Mem   525
Sec   JA Vivers
Pro   K Bridges (0277) 72933
Holes 18 L 6709 yds SSS 72
Recs Am–71 J Moody (1987)
      Pro–69 S Cipa (1988),
      B Smith (1988)
V'trs WD–UH WE–M after noon
      BH–after 11am SOC–WD
Fees £15 D–£20
Loc   18 miles E of London. M25
      Junction 28 3 miles

Birch Grove (1970)

Layer Road, Colchester CO2 0HS
Tel   (0206) 34276
Mem   250
Sec   Mrs M Marston
Holes 9 L 4108 yds SSS 60
Recs Am–63 A Green (1988)
      Pro–62

For explanation of abbreviations, see page 460.

V'trs   WD/BH–U WE–Sun after 1pm
        SOC
Fees   £6 (£8)
Loc   3 miles S of Colchester on
        B1026

Boyce Hill (1921)

Vicarage Hill, Benfleet SS7 1PD
Tel   (0268) 793625
Mem   600
Sec   JE Atkins
Pro   G Burroughs (0268) 752565
Holes   18 L 5882 yds SSS 68
Recs   Am–65 RCD Gilbert
        Pro–61 G Burroughs
V'trs   WD–UH WE/BH–MH
        SOC–Thurs only
Fees   £15 R/D
Loc   4 miles W of Southend

Braintree (1891)

Kings Lane, Stisted, Braintree
CM7 8DA
Tel   (0376) 24117
Mem   600
Sec   HW Hardy (0376) 46079
Pro   T Parcell (0376) 43465
Holes   18 L 6026 yds SSS 69
Recs   Am–65 M Hawes, M Davis
        Pro–65 P Golding
V'trs   WD–U WE/BH–H SOC
Fees   £14 (£17.50)
Loc   1 mile W of Braintree, off A120
        towards Stisted

Bunsay Downs (1982)

Public
Little Baddow Road, Woodham
Walter, nr Maldon CM9 6RW
Tel   (024 541) 2648/2369
Holes   9 L 2913 yds SSS 68
V'trs   WD–U WE/BH–tee booking up
        to 1 week in advance
Fees   18 holes £6.50 (£7)
        9 holes £5 (£5.50)
Loc   7 miles E of Chelmsford off
        A414
Mis   Indoor driving range

Burnham-on-Crouch (1923)

Creeksea, Burnham-on-Crouch
Tel   (0621) 782282
Mem   450
Sec   TG Barnes
Holes   9 L 5866 yds SSS 68
Recs   Am–66 D Clarke
        Pro–64 FJ Winser
V'trs   WD–H WE/BH M
Fees   WD–£12
Loc   1½ miles W of Burnham

Canons Brook (1962)

Elizabeth Way, Harlow CM19 5BE
Tel   (0279) 21482
Mem   650
Sec   GE Chambers
Pro   R Yates (0279) 418357

Holes   18 L 6745 yds SSS 73
Recs   Am–68 H Cornick
        Pro–65 G Burroughs
V'trs   WD–U WE/BH–NA
Fees   £15 R/D
Loc   25 miles N of London

Castle Point (1989)

Canvey Island SS8 8HQ
Tel   (0268) 510830
Sec   VW Russell
Pro   J Hudson
Holes   18 L 5627 yds SSS 69
V'trs   U
Loc   Waterside Farm, Canvey
        Island

Channels (1983)

Belsteads Farm Lane, Little Waltham,
Chelmsford
Tel   (0245) 440005
Mem   650
Sec   SM Everitt
Pro   IB Sinclair (0245) 441056
Holes   18 L 6033 yds SSS 69
V'trs   WD SOC–WD
Fees   £8.75
Loc   3 miles N of Chelmsford
Mis   Pitch and putt course

Chelmsford (1893)

Widford, Chelmsford
Tel   (0245) 250555
Mem   650
Sec   Wg Cdr BA Templeman–
        Rooke (0245) 256483
Pro   GD Bailey (0245) 257079
Holes   18 L 5912 yds SSS 68
Recs   Am–67 G Turner
        Pro–65 C Platts
V'trs   WD–I WE/BH–M
Fees   On application
Loc   Off A1016 at Widford
        roundabout

Chigwell (1925)

High Road, Chigwell IG7 5BH
Tel   (081) 500 2059
Mem   650
Sec   G Kitson
Pro   R Beard (081) 500 2384
Holes   18 L 6279 yds SSS 70
Recs   Am–66 AM Ronald
        Pro–66 H Flatman
V'trs   WD–I WE/BH–M
Fees   £20 R/D 1989 prices
Loc   13½ miles NE of London
        (A113)

Chingford (1923)

Public
158 Station Road, Chingford,
London E4
Tel   (081) 529 2107
Pro   LH and R Gowers (081) 529
        5708
Holes   18 L 6136 yds SS 70

Recs   Am–65 P Barnes
        Pro–65 R Gowers
V'trs   U
Fees   £7
Mis   Red coats must be worn

Clacton (1892)

West Road, Clacton-on-Sea CO15 1AJ
Tel   (0255) 424331
Mem   475
Sec   IM Simpson (0255) 421919
Pro   SJ Levermore (0255) 426304
Holes   18 L 6243 yds SSS 70
Recs   Am–67 A Hull
        Pro–65 S Bryan
V'trs   WE/BH–1st tee after 11am
        10th tee after 12.30pm SOC
Fees   £12 (£18)
Loc   On sea front

Colchester (1909)

Braiswick, Colchester CO4 5AU
Tel   (0206) 852946
Mem   330 90(L) 70(J) 160(5)
Sec   Mrs J Boorman (0206) 853396
Pro   P Hodgson (0206) 853920
Holes   18 L 6319 yds SS 70
Recs   Am–63 B Booth
        Pro–68 A Parcell
V'trs   WD–H WE/BH–NA SOC
Fees   £12 D–£16
Loc   ¾ mile NW of Colchester
        North Station, towards West
        Bergholt

Fairlop Waters (1987)

Public
Forest Road, Barkingside, Ilford
IG6 3JA
Tel   (081) 500 9911
Pro   A Bowers (081) 501 1881
Holes   18 L 6288 yds SSS 72
V'trs   U
Fees   £3.75 (£6)
Loc   2 miles from S end of M11, by
        Fairlop underground station
Mis   Driving range. 9 hole Par 3

Forrester Park (1975)

Beckingham Road, Great Totham,
Maldon
Tel   (0621) 891406
Mem   550
Sec   T Forrester–Muir
Holes   18 L 6073 yds SSS 69
V'trs   WD–U WE–NA before 2pm
        SOC–WD
Fees   £10 (£14)
Loc   3 miles NE of Maldon on
        Tiptree Road (B1022)

Frinton (1896)

1 The Esplanade, Frinton-on-Sea
CO13 9EP
Tel   (0255) 764618
Mem   800
Sec   PB Stokes

Pro P Taggart (0255) 671618
Holes 18 L 6259 yds SS 70
9 L 2508 yds SSS 33
Recs Am–67 IA Quick
Pro–66 CS Denny
V'trs H WE/BH–NA before 11.30am
SOC
Fees £18 R/D 9 holes–£6
Loc 18 miles E of Colchester

Hainault Forest (1912)

Public
Chigwell Row, Hainault Forest
Tel (081) 500 2097
Sec HG Richards (Sec/Mgr)
(04023) 44435
Pro AE Frost (081) 500 2131
Holes No 1 18 L 5754 yds SSS 67
No 2 18 L 6600 yds SSS 71
Recs No 1 Am–65 TG Patmore
Pro–65 A Frost
No 2 Am–68 S Middleton
Pro–68 AE Frost Jr
V'trs U
Fees £5 (£7)
Loc Hog Hill, Redbridge

Hartswood (1967)

Public
King George's Playing Fields,
Brentwood CM14 5AE
Tel (0277) 218714
Sec J Turner (0277) 218850
Pro J Stanion
Holes 18 L 6238 yds SSS 70
Recs Am–70 A Cornell
Pro–70 W Longmuir
V'trs U SOC
Fees £5 (£7.50)
Loc E of Brentwood on Ingrave
road (A128)
Mis Hartswood Club plays here

Harwich & Dovercourt (1906)

Parkeston Road, Harwich
Tel (0255) 3616
Mem 350
Sec BQ Dunham
Holes 9 L 2931 yds SSS 68
V'trs WD–U SOC
Fees On application
Loc A120 to roundabout to
Parkeston Quay, course
entrance 20 yds on left

Havering

Public
Risebridge Chase, Lower Bedfords
Road, Romford
Tel (0708) 41429
Sec P Jennings
Pro P Jennings
Holes 18 L 6252 yds SSS 70
9 hole Par 3
V'trs WD–U WE–at certain times
Fees £2.95 (£4.50)
Loc 2 miles from Brentwood
Junction of M25, off A12
Mis Risebridge Club plays here

Ilford (1907)

Wanstead Park Road, Ilford
Tel (081) 554 5174
Mem 597
Sec PGB Smyth–Pigott
(081) 554 2930
Pro K Ashdown (081) 554 0094
Holes 18 L 5702 yds SSS 68
Recs Am–63 M Pinner
Pro–64 B Huggett, A Campbell
V'trs U WE–telephone Pro
Fees £8 (£10)

Maldon (1891)

Beeleigh Langford, Maldon CM9 7SS
Tel (0621) 53212
Mem 460
Sec JC Rigby
Holes 9 L 6197 yds SSS 69
Recs Am–71 R Byford
Pro–67 S Levermore
V'trs WD–U WE–M SOC
Fees £7 D–£9 (£8 D–£10)
Loc 3 miles NW of Maldon on
B1019

Maylands (1936)

Harold Park, Romford
Tel (040 23) 42055
Mem 600
Sec (040 23) 73080
Pro JS Hopkin (040 23) 46466
Holes 18 L 6351 yds SSS 70
Recs Am–67 G Johnson
Pro–67 H Flatman
V'trs WD–I WE/BH–M SOC
Fees £16 (£25)
Loc 2 miles E of Romford
on A12. 1 mile from M25
Junction 28
Mis Buggies available for hire

Orsett (1898)

Brentwood Road, Orsett RM16 3DS
Tel (0375) 891352
Mem 900
Sec RA Bond
Pro R Newberry (0375) 891797
Holes 18 L 6614 yds SSS 72
Recs Am–68 A Pollock, I Quick
Pro–69 H Flatman, G Burroughs
V'trs WD–H SOC–Mon–Wed only
Fees £20
Loc 4 miles NE of Grays on A128.
M25 Junction 30/31

Pipps Hill CC

Aquatels Recreation Centre,
Cranes Farm Road, Basildon
Tel (0268) 23456
Holes 9 L 2829 yds SSS 67
V'trs U SOC
Fees On application
Loc Adjacent A127 London–
Southend road

Quietwaters (1974)

Colchester Road, Tolleshunt D'Arcy,
nr Maldon CM9 8HX
Tel (0621) 860410
Mem 585
Sec PD Keeble (Mgr)
Pro D Pugh (0621) 860576
Holes 18 L 6204 yds SSS 70
Recs Am–71 M Keeble (1988)
Pro–68 K Ashdown (1988)
V'trs U BH–U after 1pm SOC
Fees On application
Loc 8 miles S of Colchester
off B1026

Rochford Hundred (1893)

Rochford
Tel (0702) 544302
Mem 340 150(L) 60(J) 210(S)
Sec D Gardner
Pro GN Shipley
Holes 18 L 6256 yds SSS 70
Recs Am–65 DK Wood
Pro–65 C Tucker
V'trs WD–U WE–M
Fees On application
Loc 4 miles N of Southend-on-Sea

Romford (1894)

Heath Drive, Gidea Park, Romford
RM2 5QB
Tel (0708) 40007 (Members)
Mem 690
Sec BE Fox (0708) 40986
Pro H Flatman (0708) 49393
Holes 18 L 6377 yds SSS 70
Recs Am–68 D Girdlestone
V'trs WD–I WE–NA SOC
Fees £13 D–£20
Loc 1 mile E of Romford. 3 miles
W of M25 Junction 29

Royal Epping Forest (1888)

Public
Forest Approach, Station Road,
Chingford, London E4 7AZ
Tel (081) 529 6407
Mem 278 43(L) 25(J)
Sec JH Shaw (081) 529 2195
Pro R Gowers (081) 529 2708
Holes 18 L 6220 yds SSS 70
Recs Am–68 A Johns
Pro–65 R Gowers
V'trs WE–booked times
Fees £4.50 (£6.50)
Loc Bury Road, London E4.
250 yds E of Chingford Stn
Mis Red coats or trousers
compulsory

Saffron Walden (1919)

Windmill Hill, Saffron Walden
CB10 1BX
Tel (0799) 22689 (Members)
Mem 900
Sec KW Reddall (Mgr) (0799) 22786
Pro P Davis (0799) 27728
Holes 18 L 6608 yds SSS 72

For explanation of abbreviations, see page 460.

Recs   Am–67 AD Emery (1988)
       Pro–68 S Jackson (1983)
V'trs WD–UH WE/BH–M SOC
Fees   £20
Loc   On B184 at entry to town.

Skips (1973)

Horsemanside, Tysea Hill,
Stapleford Abbots RM4 1JU
Tel   (040 23) 48234
Sec   D Brautigan
Holes 18 L 6146 yds SSS 71
V'trs NA–Season tickets only
Loc   Romford 3 miles off B175

Stoke by Nayland (1972)

Keepers Lane, Leavenheath,
Colchester CO6 4PZ
Tel   (0206) 262836
Mem   1250
Sec   J Loshak
Pro   K Lovelock (0206) 262769
Holes Gainsborough 18 L 6516 yds
       SSS 71; Constable 18 L 6544
       yds SSS 71
Recs   Gainsborough Am–66
       RW Mann
       Pro–69 PL Cowan
V'trs WD–U WE/BH–H after 10am
       SOC
Fees   £15 (£18)
Loc   Off A134 Colchester–Sudbury
       road on to B1036

Theydon Bois (1897)

Theydon Bois, Epping CM16 4EH
Tel   (037 881) 2279
Mem   600
Sec   I McDonald (037 881) 3054
Pro   R Joyce (037 881) 2460
Holes 18 L 5472 yds SSS 68
Recs   Am–66 S Allen (1986),
       T Moncur (1988)
V'trs Thurs am–restricted WE–M
Fees   £16 (£24)
Loc   1 mile S of Epping

Thorndon Park (1920)

Ingrave, Brentwood CM13 3RH
Tel   (0277) 811666
Mem   300 140(L) 60(J) 130(5)
Sec   JE Leggitt (0277) 810345
Pro   BV White (0277) 810736
Holes 18 L 6455 yds SSS 71
Recs   Am–66 MES Davis
       Pro–65 BJ Hunt, B Waites
V'trs WD–I WE/BH–M
Fees   £20 D–£30
Loc   2 miles SE of Brentwood on
       A128

Thorpe Hall (1907)

Thorpe Hall Avenue, Thorpe Bay
SS1 3AT
Tel   (0702) 582205
Mem   750
Sec   RCP Hunter
Pro   G Harvey (0702) 588195
Holes 18 L 6286 yds SSS 71

Recs   Am–68 B Hillsden
       Pro–67 L Platts
V'trs WD–H WE/BH–M
Fees   On application
Loc   E of Southend-on-Sea

Three Rivers (1973)

Stow Road, Purleigh, nr Chelmsford
CM3 6RR
Tel   (0621) 828631
Mem   600
Sec   G Stafford
Pro   L Platts
Holes 18 L 6609 yds SSS 72
       9 L 1071 yds Par 3 course
V'trs WD–U WE/BH–M SOC–Tues
       & Thurs
Fees   £12 R/D WE–NA
Loc   5 miles S of Maldon

Towerlands (1985)

Panfield Road, Braintree CM7 5BJ
Tel   (0376) 26802
Mem   325
Sec   DJ Collar
Holes 9 L 2703 yds SSS 66
V'trs WD–U WE–U after 2pm
       SOC–WD
Fees   18 holes–£6.50 (£9)
       9 holes–£5
Loc   1 mile NW of Braintree
Mis   Driving range

Upminster (1928)

114 Hall Lane, Upminster
Tel   (040 22) 20249
Mem   900
Sec   Mrs J Wylie (040 22) 22788
Pro   N Carr (040 22) 20000
Holes 18 L 5951 yds SSS 68
Recs   Am–64 AT Bird
V'trs WD–U WE/BH–NA
Fees   £16
Loc   Station 3/4 mile

Wanstead (1893)

Wanstead, London E11 2LW
Tel   (081) 989 0604
Mem   650
Sec   K Jones (081) 989 3938
Pro   G Jacom (081) 989 9876
Holes 18 L 6262 yds SSS 69
Recs   Am–64 BJ Hilsdon
       Pro–64 N Coles, P Brown
V'trs WD–I WE/BH–M
Fees   £17.50
Loc   Epping Forest boundary

Warley Park (1975)

Magpie Lane, Little Warley,
Brentwood
Tel   (0277) 231352
Mem   600
Sec   SP Greene (0277) 224891
Pro   P O'Conner (0277) 212552
Holes 18 L 6261 yds SSS 70
       9 L 3166 yds SSS 35

Recs   Am–69 B Preston
V'trs WD–U WE–M
Fees   £15
Loc   2 miles S of Brentwood

Warren (1932)

Woodham Walter, Maldon CM9 6RW
Tel   (024 541) 3258/3198
Mem   800
Pro   M Walker (024 541) 4662
Holes 18 L 6211 yds SSS 69
Recs   Am–66 C Laurence
       Pro–66 H Flatman
V'trs WD–I H WE–M
Fees   £14 D–£17
Loc   7 miles E of Chelmsford off
       A414

West Essex (1900)

Bury Road, Stewardstonebury,
Chingford, London E4 7QL
Tel   (081) 529 0928
Mem   645
Sec   PH Galley MBE (081) 529 7558
Pro   C Cox (081) 529 4367
Holes 18 L 6317 yds SSS 70
Recs   Am–66 KG Budd
       Pro–EE Whitcombe
V'trs WD–UH WE/BH–MH
       SOC–Mon/Wed/Fri
Fees   £15 D–£18
Loc   3/4 mile N of Chingford Station.
       M25 Junction 26

Woodford (1890)

2, Sunset Avenue, Woodford Green
Tel   (081) 504 0553/4254
Mem   400 64(L) 52(J) 80(5)
Sec   GJ Cousins (081) 504 3330
Pro   A Johns (081) 504 4254
Holes 9 L 5806 yds SSS 68
Recs   Am–64 M Everitt
V'trs WD–U before 3pm exc Tues
       & Thurs am–NA WE–M SOC
Fees   £9
Loc   11 miles NE of London

Gloucestershire

Broadway (1896)

Willersey Hill, Broadway, Worcs
WR12 7LG
Tel   (0386) 858997
Mem   400 120(L) 70(J) 140(5)
Sec   KS Lawrance (0386) 853683
Pro   J Freeman (0386) 853275
Holes 18 L 6211 yds SSS 70
Recs   Am–66 DM Fletcher
       Pro–66 D Steele, R Adams
V'trs H Sat–M
Fees   £16 (£19)
Loc   1 1/2 miles E of Broadway (A44)

Cirencester (1893)

Cheltenham Road, Cirencester
GL7 7BH
Tel (0285) 653939
Mem 700
Sec ND Jones (0285) 652465
Pro M Thomas (0285) 656124
Holes 18 L 6021 yds SSS 69
Recs Am-64 D Rollo
Pro-67 DJ Rees
V'trs BH-H SOC-WD
Fees £18 (£25)
Loc 1½ miles N of Cirencester
on A435

Cleeve Hill (1976)

Public
Cleeve Hill, nr Cheltenham
Tel (024 267) 2025
Pro D Finch (024 267) 2592
Holes 18 L 6444 yds SSS 71
V'trs U exc Sun am-NA SOC
Fees £5 (£6)
Loc 3 miles N of Cheltenham on
A46 to Winchcombe

Cotswold Edge (1980)

Upper Rushmire, Wotton-under-Edge
GL12 7PT
Tel (0453) 844167
Mem 800
Sec NJ Newman
Pro I Watts (0453) 844398
Holes 18 L 6170 yds SSS 69
Recs Am-N Barlow (1986)
Pro-K Spurgeon (1985)
V'trs WD-U WE-M SOC
Fees £10 (£10)
Loc 2 miles NE of Wotton-under-
Edge on B4058 Tetbury road

Cotswold Hills (1902)

Ullenwood, nr Cheltenham GL53 9QT
Tel (0242) 522421
Mem 750
Sec Lt Col PG Roberson
(0242) 515264
Pro N Boland (0242) 515263
Holes 18 L 6716 yds SSS 72
Recs Am-68 R Day
Pro-68 SD Brown (1987)
V'trs I (recognised club members)
Fees £17 (£22)
Loc 3 miles S of Cheltenham

Forest of Dean (1974)

Lords Hill, Coleford GL16 8BD
Tel (0594) 32583
Mem 450
Sec R Sanzen-Baker
Pro J Nicol (0594) 33689
Holes 18 L 5519 yds SSS 67
V'trs U SOC
Fees £10 (£15)
Loc ½ mile from Coleford on
Parkend Road

Gloucestershire Hotel (1976)

Matson Lane, Gloucester
Tel (0452) 25653
Mem 500
Sec R Jewell
Pro R Jewell, P Darnell
(0452) 411331
Holes 18 L 6127 yds SSS 69
9 L 1980 yds SSS 27
Recs Am-69 J Northam
Pro-65 P Darnell
V'trs U
Fees £14 (£18)
Loc 2 miles S of Gloucester, off
Painswick road

Lilley Brook (1922)

Cirencester Road, Charlton Kings,
Cheltenham GL53 8EG
Tel (0242) 526785
Mem 700
Sec K Skeen
Pro F Hadden (0242) 525201
Holes 18 L 6226 yds SSS 70
Recs Am-64 B Mitten (1987)
Pro-66 G Ryall, G Laing (1989)
V'trs H or I (recognised club
members) SOC-WD
Fees D-£16 (£20)
Loc 3 miles SE of Cheltenham
on A435

Lydney (1909)

Lydney
Tel (0594) 842614
Mem 300
Sec DA Barnard (0594) 843940
Holes 9 L 5382 yds SSS 66
Recs Am-63 MA Barnard (1988)
Pro-68 F Goulding
V'trs WD-U WE-M SOC
Fees £8 W-£25
Loc Off Lakeside Avenue

Minchinhampton (1889)

Minchinhampton, Stroud GL6 8BE
Tel (045 383) 2642 (Old course)
(045 383) 3866 (New course)
Mem 1721
Sec DR Vickers (045 383) 3866
Pro C Steele (045 383) 3860
Holes Old 18 L 6295 yds SSS 70
New 18 L 6675 yds SSS 72
Recs Old Am-67 PH Fisher, L Scott
Old-67 RA Brown
New Am-68 RD Broad (1988)
Pro-67 GH Marks, G Ryall
V'trs U-subject to availability of
starting times SOC
Fees Old course £8 (£10)
New course £15 (£20)
Loc Old-3 miles E of Stroud.
New-5 miles E of Stroud

Painswick (1891)

Painswick, nr Stroud
Tel (0452) 812180
Mem 300

Sec RJ May
Holes 18 L 4780 yds SSS 64
Roou Am 61 J Woolley
V'trs WD/Sat-U Sun-M SOC
Fees £6 (£8)
Loc Painswick
Mis Sun-course closes at 2pm
Apr-Oct

Stinchcombe Hill (1889)

Stinchcombe Hill, Dursley GL11 6AQ
Tel (0453) 542015
Mem 500
Pro A Valentine (0453) 543878
Holes 18 L 5723 yds SSS 68
Recs Am-64 PC French (1979)
Pro-64 I Bolt (1984)
V'trs WD-U WE/BH-NA before
10.30am SOC
Fees £12 (£14) W-£30 F-£50 M-£80
Loc Dursley 1 mile

Tewkesbury Park Hotel (1976)

Lincoln Green Lane, Tewkesbury
GL20 7DN
Tel (0684) 295405
Mem 560
Sec Maj. JD McCarthy
Pro P Cane (0684) 294892
Holes 18 L 6533 yds SSS 72
Recs Am-68 RN Roper
Pro-68 N Job
V'trs WD-U H SOC-WD
WE-residential SOC only
Fees £18 (£22)
Loc ½ mile S of town on A38.
2 miles M5 Junction 9
Mis 6 hole Par 3-£2. 4 bay practice
range

Westonbirt (1971)

Westonbirt, Tetbury GL8 8QG
Tel (066 88) 242
Mem 200
Sec Bursar, Westonbirt School
Pro C Steele (045 383) 3860
Holes 9 L 4504 yds SSS 61
Recs Am-62 S Dunlop
V'trs U SOC-WD
Fees D-£5 (£5)
Loc 3 miles S of Tetbury off A433

Hampshire

Alresford (1890)

Cheriton Road, Alresford SO24 0PN
Mem 490
Sec P Kingston (0962) 733746
Pro M Scott (0962) 733998
Holes 12 L 6038 yds SSS 69
Recs Pro-67 J Hay
V'trs U H WE-after 12 noon SOC
Fees £10.50 D-£15 (£20)
Loc 1 mile S of Alresford

For explanation of abbreviations, see page 460.

Alton (1908)

Old Odiham Road, Alton GU34 4BU
Tel   (0420) 82042
Mem   340
Sec   JHJ Powers (0252) 613061
Pro   M Smith (0420) 86518
Holes 9 L 5744 yds SSS 68
Recs   Am–65 I McInally (1987)
       Pro–65 A Stevens (1988)
V'trs U (exc comp days) SOC–WD
Fees   £8 (£12)
Loc   2 miles N of Alton. 6 miles
       S of Odiham off A32

Ampfield Par Three (1963)

Winchester Road, Ampfield,
nr Romsey SO51 9BQ
Tel   (0794) 68480
Mem   500
Sec   Mrs S Baker
Pro   R Benfield (0794) 68750
Holes 18 L 2478 yds SSS 53
Recs   Am–49 R Bailey
       Pro–49 A Timms
V'trs WD–U WE/BH–H (phone first)
       SOC
Fees   £5 (£10)
Loc   On A31 Winchester to Romsey

Andover (1907)

51 Winchester Road, Andover
SP10 2EF
Tel   (0264) 23980
Mem   415 60(L) 40(J)
Sec   Maj BF Gerhard MBE
       (0264) 58040
Pro   A Timms (0264) 24151
Holes 9 L 5933 yds SSS 68
Recs   Am–69 D Critcher (1988)
       Pro–67 A Timms (1985)
V'trs WD–U WE/BH–NA before
       noon SOC
Fees   £10 (£20)
Loc   1/2 mile S of Andover on A3057

Army Golf Club (1883)

Laffan's Road, Aldershot GU11 2HF
Tel   (0252) 541104
Mem   800
Sec   RT Crabb(Sec/Mgr) (0252)
       540638
Pro   P Thompson (0252) 547232
Holes 18 L 6579 yds SSS 71
Recs   Am–69 G Young
       Pro–69 I Young
V'trs WD–I WE–M
Fees   £16 (special rates for Forces)
Loc   Between Aldershot and
       Farnborough

Barton-on-Sea (1897)

Marine Drive, Barton-on-Sea
BH25 7DY
Tel   (0425) 615308
Mem   392 117(L) 30(J)
Sec   CJ Wingfield

Pro   P Coombs (0425) 611210
Holes 18 L 5565 yds SSS 67
Recs   Am–63 RM Tuddenham
       Pro–66 P Alliss
V'trs H WD–U WE/BH–NA before
       11.15am SOC–Wed & Fri
Fees   £18 (£21) R/D
Loc   New Milton, 1 1/2 miles M27
       Junction 1

Basingstoke (1928)

Kempshott Park, Basingstoke
RG23 7LL
Tel   (0256) 465990
Mem   725
Sec   PA Gill
Pro   I Hayes (0256) 51332
Holes 18 L 6309 yds SSS 70
Recs   Am–67 C Tuck (1989)
       Pro–65 G Stubbington (1989)
V'trs WD–H WE–M SOC–Wed &
       Thurs
Fees   £14
Loc   3 miles W of Basingstoke
       on A30. M3 Junction 7
Mis   Buggy hire £10 per round

Basingstoke Hospitals

Aldermaston Road, Basingstoke
Tel   (0256) 20347
Mem   275
Sec   EEL Rowlands
Holes 9 L 5480 yds SSS 67
V'trs WD–U WE–contact Mgr SOC
Fees   £6.50 (£9)
Loc   1 1/2 miles N of Basingstoke

Bishopswood (1978)

Bishopswood Lane, Tadley,
Basingstoke RG26 6AT
Tel   (0734) 815213
Mem   400
Sec   MW Phillips (Mgr)
       (0734) 812200
Pro   K Pickett
Holes 9 L 6474 yds SSS 71
Recs   Am–69 C Wilkins (1987)
       Pro–68 R Boxall (1983)
V'trs Tues/Thurs/Fri–U Mon &
       Wed–M WE–M
Fees   WD–£8
Loc   6 miles N of Basingstoke
       off A340
Mis   Floodlit driving range

Blackmoor (1913)

Whitehill Bordon GU35 9EH
Tel   (04203) 2775
Mem   680 85(L) 60(J)
Sec   Maj HRG Spiller
Pro   A Hall (04203) 2345
Holes 18 L 6213 yds SSS 70
V'trs H WE–NA
Fees   £15 D–£23 WE–NA
Loc   1/2 mile W of Whitehill on A325

Bohunt Manor (1923)

Liphook
Mem   60
Sec   IR Baker, 29 Headley Road,
       Liphook
Holes Play over Liphook

Bramshaw (1880)

Brook, Lyndhurst SO43 7HE
Tel   (0703) 813433
Mem   900 116(L) 39(J) 195(5)
Sec   FS Prince
Pro   W Wiltshire (0703) 813434
Holes Forest 18 L 5753 yds SSS 68
       Manor 18 L 6257 yds SSS 70
Recs   Forest Am–67 G Hill
       Pro–66 W Wiltshire
       Manor Am–67 G Lovelady
       Pro–67 D Allen
V'trs WD–U WE–M
Fees   On application
Loc   Southampton 10 miles

Brokenhurst Manor (1919)

Sway Road, Brockenhurst
Tel   (0590) 23332
Mem   800
Sec   CF Mackintosh
Pro   C Bonner (0590) 23092
Holes 18 L 6222 yds SSS 70
Recs   Am–64 K Weeks
       Pro–66 D Haslam
V'trs WD–after 9.30am H SOC
       NA–Tues–Ladies' Day
Fees   £20 (£30)
Loc   Brockenhurst 1 mile on B3055
       to Sway

Burley (1905)

Burley, Ringwood BH24 4BB
Tel   (04253) 2431
Mem   470
Sec   GR Kendall
Holes 9 L 3126 yds SSS 69
Recs   Am–70 N Carpenter, W Medd
V'trs U
Fees   £10 (£10) W–£40
Loc   4 miles SE of Ringwood

Corhampton (1885)

Sheeps Pond Lane, Droxford,
Southampton SO3 1QZ
Tel   (0489) 877279
Mem   600
Sec   P Taylor
Pro   J Harris (0489) 877638
Holes 18 L 6088 yds SSS 69
Recs   Am–66 R Edwards (1988)
       Pro–65 P Dawson (1987)
V'trs WD–UH WE/BH–M
       SOC–Mons & Thurs
Fees   £11 D–£16.50
Loc   9 miles S of Winchester
Mis   Buggies for hire £10 per round

Dibden (1974)

Public
Main Road, Dibden, Southampton
SO4 5TB
Tel (0703) 845596
Pro A Bridge
Holes 18 L 6206 yds SSS 70
Recs Pro–63 I Young (1988)
V'trs U
Fees £4.30 (£6.30)
Loc 10 miles W of Southampton.
 1/2 mile from Dibden
 roundabout on A326 Fawley
 road

Dunwood Manor (1969)

Shootash Hill, Romsey SO5 10GF
Tel (0794) 40549
Mem 700
Sec Mrs H Johnson, K Heathcote
 (Gen Mgr)
Pro G Stubbington (0794) 40663
Holes 18 L 6004 yds SSS 69
Recs Am–71 A Devlin
 Pro–61 G Stubbington
V'trs WE/BH–restricted SOC–WD
Fees £10 (£15)
Loc Romsey 4 miles off A27

Fleetlands (1961)

Fareham Road, Gosport PO13 0AW
Tel (0705) 822351
Mem 120
Sec A Eade (Ext 44384)
Holes 9 L 4775 yds SSS 63
Recs Am–65 M Squibb
V'trs M at all times
Loc 2 miles S of Fareham on A32
 Gosport road. M27 Junction 12

Fleming Park (1973)

Public
Fleming Park, Eastleigh
Tel (0703) 612797
Pro D Miller
Holes 18 L 4436 yds SSS 62
Recs Am–61 B Rose (1987)
 Pro–I Young
V'trs U
Fees £3.85 (£5.95)
Loc 6 miles N of Southampton

Gosport & Stokes Bay (1885)

Military Road, Fort Road, Haslar,
Gosport PO12 2AT
Tel (0705) 581625
Mem 170
Sec T Jopling (0705) 527941
Holes 9 L 5668 yds SSS 69
Recs Am–68 M Cousins (1989)
 Pro–65 P Dawson (1985)
V'trs U Sun–NA before noon
Fees D–£8 (May–Oct)
 D–£6 (Nov–Apr)
Loc S boundary of Gosport

Great Salterns (1914)

Public
Portsmouth Golf Centre, Eastern Road,
Portsmouth PO3 6QB
Tel (0705) 664549
Pro T Healey
Holes 18 L 5970 yds SSS 68
V'trs U
Fees £5
Loc 1 mile off M27 on A2030
Mis Southsea Club plays here.
 Driving range

Hartley Wintney (1891)

London Road, Hartley Wintney,
nr Basingstoke
Tel (025 126) 2214
Mem 410
Sec BD Powell (025 126) 4211
Pro T Barter (025 126) 3779
Holes 9 L 6096 yds SSS 69
Recs Am–70 M Wild
 Pro–63 R Lewington
V'trs Wed–Ladies' Day SOC–Tues
 & Thurs WE/BH–restricted
Fees £10 (£18)
Loc A30 between Camberley and
 Basingstoke

Hayling (1883)

Ferry Road, Hayling Island PO11 0BX
Tel (0705) 463712/463777
Mem 900
Sec RCW Stokes (0705) 464446
Pro R Gadd (0705) 464491
Holes 18 L 6489 yds SSS 71
Recs Pro–66 F Gilbride
 Am–66 D Harrison, K Weeks
V'trs H WE/BH–after 11.30am SOC
Loc 5 miles S of Havant on
 A3023

Hockley (1915)

Twyford, nr Winchester SO21 1PL
Tel (0962) 713165
Mem 750
Pro T Lane (0962) 713678
Holes 18 L 6279 yds SSS 70
Recs Am–67 PE Anthony, CJ Hyde,
 GP Cole
 Pro–65 T Underwood
V'trs WD–U WE/BH–M
Fees £17 (£21)
Loc Winchester Station 2 miles on
 A3335

Leckford & Longstock (1929)

Leckford, Stockbridge SO20 6SG
Tel (0264) 810710
Mem 200
Sec LG Lucas
Pro LG Lucas
Holes 9 L 3251 yds SSS 71
V'trs M
Loc 5 miles W of Andover

Lee-on-the-Solent (1905)

Brune Lane, Lee-on-the-Solent
Tel (0705) 550207
Mem 700
Sec (0705) 551170
Pro John Richardson (0705) 551181
Holes 18 L 5991 yds SSS 69
Recs Am–65 S Richardson
 Pro–66 M Faulkner
V'trs WD–UH WE–MH
 SOC–Thurs
Fees D–£14
Loc 3 miles S of Fareham

Liphook (1922)

Liphook GU30 7EH
Tel (0428) 723271
Mem 800
Sec Maj JB Morgan MBE
 (0428) 723785
Pro I Large
Holes 18 L 6207 yds SSS 70
Recs Am–70 R Tuddenham,
 M Wiggett
 Pro–66 TR Pinner
V'trs IH (max 24) Sun–NA before
 1pm
Fees £15 D–£25 (£25 D–£30)
Loc 18 miles SW of Guildford
 on A3
Mis Bohunt Manor Club plays
 here

Meon Valley Hotel G & CC (1977)

Sandy Lane, Shedfield, Southampton
SO3 2HQ
Tel (0329) 833455
Mem 550
Sec T Hussey (Gen Mgr)
 CM Terry (Sec)
Pro J Stirling
Holes 18 L 6519 yds SSS 71
Recs Am–69 CW A'Court (1986)
 Pro–67 J Garner (1987)
V'trs H SOC
Fees £18 (£22)
Loc 2 miles NW of Wickham.
 N off A334

New Forest (1888)

Southampton Road, Lyndhurst
SO43 7BU
Tel (042 128) 2450/2752
Mem 850
Sec Mrs W Swann
Pro K Gilhespy
Holes 18 L 5748 yds SS 68
Recs Am–65 C White
 Pro–67 S Clay, R Brown
V'trs U exc Sun am
Fees £10 (£12)
Loc On A35 Bournemouth to
 Southampton road

For explanation of abbreviations, see page 460.

North Hants (1904)

Minley Road, Fleet GU13 8RE
Tel (0252) 616443
Mem 700
Sec IR Goodliffe
Pro S Porter (0252) 616655
Holes 18 L 6257 yds SSS 70
Recs Am–66 MC Hughesdon (1976)
JS Cheetham, J Dodds (1988)
Pro–67 B Hunt
V'trs WD–UH WE/BH–MH
SOC–Tues & Wed
Fees £15 D–£20
Loc 3 miles W of Farnborough on B3013. M3 Junction 4

Old Thorns Hotel (1982)

London Kosaido Company Ltd,
Longmoor Road, Liphook GU30 7PE
Tel (0428) 724555
Sec GM Jones
Pro Philip Loxley
Holes 18 L 6447 yds SSS 71
Recs Pro–69 I Aoki (1982)
V'trs U SOC
Fees £18 (£28) SOC–£45
Loc 1 mile off A3 from Liphook
Mis 34 buggies for hire

Ordnance Survey (1934)

Southampton Municipal, Bassett,
Southampton
Tel (0703) 768407
Mem 90
Sec MB Swan, 68A Wolsley Road,
Freemantle, Southampton
(0703) 788393
Holes Play over Southampton
Municipal

Petersfield (1900)

Heath Road, Petersfield GU31 4EJ
Tel (0730) 63725
Mem 470(M) 87(L) 77(J)
Sec P Heraud (0730) 62386
Pro S Clay (0730) 67732
Holes 18 L 5720 yds SSS 68
Recs Am–70 P Tupper
Pro–66 J Hay
V'trs U WE–NA before 10.30am
Fees £12 D–£18 (£18 D–£24)
Loc 1/2 mile E of Petersfield

Portsmouth (1926)

Public
Crookhorn Lane, Widley, Portsmouth
PO7 5QL
Tel (0705) 372210
Pro R Brown
Holes 18 L 6259 yds SSS 70
V'trs U SOC (arrange with Pro)
Fees £6.40
Loc 1 mile N of Portsmouth, on B2177

Romsey (1925)

Nursling, Southampton SO1 9XW
Tel (0703) 732218
Mem 825

Sec RJ Priestley (0703) 734637
Pro M Desmond (0703) 736673
Holes 18 L 5752 yds SSS 68
Recs Am–66 NP Woodward (1981)
Pro–64 J Slade (1985)
V'trs WD–U WE/BH–M H
Fees £12
Loc 2 miles SE of Romsey on
Southampton road (A3057).
Nr M27/M271 Junction 3

Rowlands Castle (1902)

Links Lane, Rowlands Castle
PO9 6AE
Tel (0705) 412216
Mem 500 150(L) 60(J)
Sec Capt. AW Aird (0705) 412784
Pro P Klepacz (0705) 412785
Holes 18 L 6627 yds SSS 72
Recs Am–70 N Cole, C Anderson
Pro–66 M Gregson
V'trs WD–UH WE–phone first Sat–M
SOC–Tues/Thurs/Fri
Fees £16 R/D (£20) 1989 prices
Loc 9 miles S of Petersfield off
A3(M). 3 miles N of Havant

Royal Winchester (1888)

Sarum Road, Winchester SO22 5QE
Tel (0962) 52462
(0962) 65048 (Members)
Mem 700
Sec RD Tingey
Pro DP Williams (0962) 62473
Holes 18 L 6218 yds SSS 70
Recs Am–67 J Curren
Pro–67 B Lane, D Feherty
V'trs WD–UH WE/BH–M SOC–WD
Fees £20
Loc W of Winchester off A31

Sandford Springs (1989)

Wolverton, Basingstoke RG26 5RT
Tel (0635) 297881
Mem 400
Sec K Brake (Dir)
Pro K Brake, A Dillon
(0635) 297883
Holes 18 L 6064 yds SSS 70
V'trs WD–prior booking WE–M
SOC
Fees £15 D–£24
Loc Between Basingstoke and
Newbury on A339

Southampton (1935)

Public
Golf Course Road, Bassett,
Southampton
Tel (0703) 768407
Pro J Cave
Holes 18 L 6218 yds SSS 70
9 L 2391 yds SSS 33
Recs Am–64 P Dedman
Pro–62 SW Murray
V'trs U
Fees 18 holes £4.20 (£6)
9 holes £2.10 (£3)
Loc 2 miles N of Southampton

Southsea (1972)

The Mansion, Eastern Road,
Portsmouth
Tel (0705) 664549
Mem 650
Sec KP Parker (0705) 812435
Holes Play over Great Salterns

Southwick Park (1977)

Pinsley Drive, Southwick PO17 6EL
Tel (0705) 380131
Mem 600 60(L)
Sec NW Price
Pro J Green (0705) 380442
Holes 18 L 5855 yds SSS 68
Recs Am–67 R Edwards, R Berry
Pro–64 G Hughes
V'trs WD–U before 11am only
SOC–Tues
Fees On application. Servicemen
reduced rate
Loc Southwick village 1/2 mile

Southwood (1977)

Public
Ively Road, Farnborough
GU14 0LJ
Tel (0252) 548700
Sec RE Smith (Hon)
Pro R Hammond
Holes 18 L 5553 yds SSS 67
Recs Am–69 (1988)
Pro–64 M Fagan (1988)
V'trs U
Fees £8
Loc 1 mile W of Farnborough
off A325

Stoneham (1908)

Bassett, Southampton SO2 3NE
Tel (0703) 768151
Mem 800
Sec Mrs AM Wilkinson
(0703) 769272
Pro I Young (0703) 768397
Holes 18 L 6310 yds SSS 70
Recs Am–65 R Park
Pro–63 J Martin
V'trs WD–U WE–NA
SOC–Mon/Thurs/Fri
Fees £18
Loc 2 miles N of Southampton

Tidworth Garrison (1908)

Tidworth
Tel (0980) 42321 (Steward)
Mem 600
Sec Lt Col DFT Tucker
(0980) 42301
Pro T Godsen (0980) 42393
Holes 18 L 5990 yds SSS 69
Recs Am–65 JN Flemming, A Litton
Pro–65 I Young
V'trs SOC–Tues/Thurs/Fri
WE/BH–NA before 3pm
Fees £15 (£18)
Loc Tidworth 1 mile on Bulford
road

Tylney Park (1973)

Rotherwick, Basingstoke
Tel (0256) 762079
Mem 700
Sec AD Bewley
Pro C de Bruin (Mgr)
Holes 18 L 6108 yds SSS 69
Recs Am–70 D Curd
Pro–68 S Watson (1988)
V'trs WD–U WE–M or H SOC
Fees £13 (£20)
Loc 2 miles NW of Hook.
M3 Junction 5

Waterlooville (1907)

Cherry Tree Ave, Cowplain,
Portsmouth PO8 8AP
Mem 800
Sec C Chamberlain
(0705) 263388
Pro J Hay (0705) 256911
Holes 18 L 6647 yds SSS 72
Recs Am–66 D Hickman (1987)
Pro–66 H Stott (1988)
V'trs WD/WE–MH (Sun am–XL)
SOC
Fees £14 D–£17
Loc 10 miles N of Portsmouth on A3

Hereford & Worcester

Abbey Park G & CC

Bordesley Lodge Farm, Dagnell End
Road, Redditch, Worcs
Tel (0527) 63918
Mem 1200
Sec ME Bradley
Pro RK Cameron
Holes 18 L 6398 yds SSS 71
V'trs WD–U
Fees £4.50 (£5.50)
Loc B4101, off A441 Redditch–
Birmingham road
Mis Driving range

Belmont House (1983)

Belmont, Hereford HR2 9SA
Tel (0432) 277445
Mem 370
Sec MJ Francis
Pro M Welsh
Holes 18 L 6448 yds SSS 71
V'trs U SOC
Fees On application
Loc 1½ miles S of Hereford
on A465

Blackwell (1893)

Blackwell, nr Bromsgrove B60 1PY
Tel (021) 445 1781
Mem 300 100(L) 30(J)
Sec S Allen (021) 445 1994
Pro H MacDonald (021) 445 3113
Holes 18 L 6202 yds SSS 71
Recs Am–68 AJ Thomson
Pro–64 M Bembridge

V'trs WD–U WE/BH–M
Fees £18
Loc 3 miles E of Bromsgrove

Churchill & Blakedown (1926)

Churchill Lane, Blakedown,
nr Kidderminster
Tel (0562) 700200
Mem 350
Sec JH Lidstone (0384) 73161
Holes 9 L 5399 yds SSS 67
Recs Am–64 CMM Lea
Pro–61 R Livingston
V'trs WD–U WE–M
Fees D–£7.50
Loc 3 miles N of Kidderminster
on A453

Droitwich (1897)

Ford Lane, Droitwich WR9 0BQ
Tel (0905) 770129
Mem 728
Sec MJ Taylor (0905) 774344
Pro CS Thompson (0905) 770207
Holes 18 L 6040 yds SSS 69
Recs Am–63 J Bickerton
V'trs WD–U WE/BH–M SOC–Wed
& Fri
Fees £16.50
Loc 1 mile N of Droitwich off A38.
M5 Junction 5

Evesham (1894)

Craycombe Links, Fladbury, Pershore,
Worcs WR10 2QS
Tel (0386) 860395
Mem 340
Sec FG Vincent (0386) 552373
Pro JR Gray
Holes 9 L 6415 yds SSS 71
V'trs WD–M H NA on comp/match
days SOC
Fees £10
Loc Fladbury, 4 miles W of
Evesham (B4084)

Habberley (1924)

Trimpley Road, Kidderminster
DY11 5RG
Tel (0562) 745756
Mem 400
Sec DB Lloyd (0562) 823509
Holes 9 L 5440 yds SSS 67
Recs Am–62 D Kwei
V'trs WD–U WE–M SOC
Fees £7
Loc 3 miles NW of Kidderminster

Herefordshire (1909)

Raven's Causeway, Wormsley,
nr Hereford HR4 8LY
Tel (0432) 71219
Mem 600 75(L) 85(J) 55(5)
Sec C Jones (0432) 760662
Pro D Hemming (0432) 71465
Holes 18 L 6069 yds SSS 69

Recs Am–66 J Wilson
Pro–61 B Barnes
V'tro U
Fees £8 (£10) W–£35
Loc 6 miles NW of Hereford
Mis Buggy for hire

Kidderminster (1909)

Russell Road, Kidderminster
Tel (0562) 822303
Mem 800
Sec W Wiltshire (Mgr)
Pro NP Underwood (0562) 740090
Holes 18 L 6223 yds SSS 70
V'trs WD only
Fees £18
Loc Kidderminster Station 1 mile

King's Norton (1892)

Brockhill Lane, Weatheroak
Tel (0564) 826789
Mem 950
Sec LNW Prince (Sec/Mgr)
Pro C Haycock (0564) 822822
Holes 18 L 6754 yds SSS 72
9 L 3290 yds SSS 36
Recs Am–67 PR Swinburne
Pro–65 G Farr
V'trs WD–U WE–NA SOC
Fees £20, £16 after 3pm
Loc 8 miles S of Birmingham.
M42 Junction 3, 2 miles

Kington (1926)

Bradnor Hill, Kington
Mem 420
Sec GE Long (0497) 820542
GR Wictome (05448) 270
Pro R Bott
Holes 18 L 5840 yds SSS 68
Recs Am–65 K Alexander
V'trs SOC WE–NA before 10.15am
–restricted 1.30–2.45pm
Fees £10 (£14)
Loc 1 mile N of Kington

Leominster (1967)

Ford Bridge, Leominster,
Herefordshire HR6 0LE
Tel (0568) 2863
Mem 460
Sec JA Ashcroft (043 272) 493
Pro R Price
Holes 9 L 2657 yds SSS 66
Recs Am–65 G Price
Pro–66
V'trs I or H
Fees £10 (£13)
Loc 3 miles S of Leominster on
A49 (Leominster By–pass)

Little Lakes (1975)

Lye Head, Bewdley DY12 2UZ
Tel (0299) 266385
Mem 400 50(L)
Sec T Norris
Pro M Laing
Holes 9 L 6247 yds SSS 72

Recs Am–75 R Dean (1987)
Pro–70 R Lane (1986)
V'trs WD–U WE–NA SOC
Fees WD–£10
Loc 2¹/₂ miles W of Bewdley off
A456

Pitcheroak (1973)

Public
Plymouth Road, Redditch B97 4PB
Tel (0527) 41054
Pro D Stewart
Holes 9 L 4584 yds SSS 62
V'trs U
Fees £2.80 (£3.50)
Loc Plymouth Road, Redditch
Mis Redditch Kingfisher plays here

Redditch (1913)

Lower Grinsty, Green Lane,
Callow Hill, Redditch B97 5PJ
Tel (0527) 43309
Mem 756
Sec C Holman
Pro F Powell (0527) 46372
Holes 18 L 6671 yds SSS 72
V'trs WD–U SOC
Fees £15
Loc 3 miles SW of Redditch.
Heathfield Road off A441

Ross-on-Wye (1903)

Two Park, Gorsley, Ross-on-Wye
HR9 7UT
Tel (098 982) 267
Mem 740
Sec GH Cason
Pro A Clifford (098 982) 439
Holes 18 L 6500 yds SSS 73
Recs Am–69 J Stordy
Pro–71 G Brand Jr
V'trs U SOC Wed–Fri (2 per week
for 16+ players)
Fees £16 (£20)
Loc 5 miles N of Ross-on-Wye.
M50 Junction 3

Tolladine (1895)

The Fairway, Tolladine Road,
Worcester WR4 9BA
Tel (0905) 21074
Mem 350
Sec AJ Wardle (0905) 54841
Holes 9 L 5174 yds SSS 67
V'trs WD–U before 4pm –M after
4pm WE/BH–M SOC
Fees £10
Loc M5 Junction 6 Warndon 1 mile

Worcester G & CC (1898)

Boughton Park, Worcester
Tel (0905) 422555
Mem 1100
Sec JM Kennedy
Pro C Colenso (0905) 422044
Holes 18 L 5946 yds SSS 68
Recs Am–67 M Jeffs
V'trs WD–U WE–M SOC
Fees £18
Loc 1 mile W of Worcester

Worcestershire (1879)

Wood Farm, Malvern Wells
WR14 4PP
Tel (0684) 573905
Mem 770
Sec GR Scott (0684) 575992
Pro GM Harris (0684) 564428
Holes 18 L 6449 yds SSS 71
Recs Am–67 PM Guest,
MC Reynard, S Braithwaite
Pro–66 R Larratt
V'trs WD–H WE–H after 10am
Fees £12 (£15) W–£45 1989 prices
Loc 2 miles S of Gt Malvern
off A449/B4209

Hertfordshire

Aldenham G & CC (1975)

Radlett Road, Aldenham, nr Watford
Tel (0923) 85 3929
Mem 520
Sec DW Phillips
Pro A McKay (0923) 85 7889
Holes 18 L 6500 yds SSS 71
Recs Am–67 P Wharton (1987)
Pro–69 B Charles (1982)
V'trs U
Fees £8 D–£12 (£15)
Loc M1 Junction 5–A41–B462

Arkley (1909)

Rowley Green Road, Barnet EN5 3HL
Tel (081) 449 0394
Mem 350
Sec GD Taylor
Pro M Squire (081) 440 8473
Holes 9 L 6045 yds SSS 69
Recs Am–67 SN McWilliams
Pro–63 LV Baker
V'trs WD–U WE–M SOC–Wed–Fri
Fees £12 D–£15
Loc NW of Barnet, off A1(M)

Ashridge (1932)

Little Gaddesden, Berkhamsted
HP4 1LY
Tel (044 284) 2244
Mem 750
Sec Mrs MA West
Pro G Pook (Golf Mgr)
(044 284) 2307
Holes 18 L 6508 yds SSS 71
Recs Am–64 C Slattery
Pro–66 JRM Jacobs
V'trs Ring Sec for bookings
Fees On application
Loc 5 miles NW of Berkhamsted
on B4506

Batchwood Hall (1935)

Public
Batchwood Hall, St Albans
Tel (0727) 33349
Sec BR Mercer (Hon)
Pro J Thomson
Holes 18 L 6465 yds SSS 71

Recs Am–67 M Cassidy
Pro–62 PP Wynne
V'trs U
Fees £5 (£6)
Loc NW of St Albans on A5081.
5 miles S of M1 Junction 9

Berkhamsted (1890)

The Common, Berkhamsted HP4 2QB
Tel (0442) 863730
Mem 280 113(L) 119(J) 150(5)
Sec JF Robinson (0442) 865832
Pro BJ Proudfoot (0442) 865851
Holes 18 L 6605 yds SSS 72
Recs Am–69 J Payne (1989)
Pro–69 S Proudfoot (1987)
V'trs U H WE–M before 11.30am
SOC–Wed & Fri
Fees On application
Loc 1 mile NE of Berkhamsted

Bishop's Stortford (1910)

Dunmow Road, Bishop's Stortford
CM23 5HP
Tel (0279) 654027 (Clubhouse)
Mem 700
Sec Maj C Rolls (0279) 654715
Pro V Duncan (0279) 651324
Holes 18 L 6440 yds SSS 71
Recs Am–69 M Whitlock
Pro–66 J Bennett
V'trs WD–U WE–M SOC
Fees £15
Loc E of B Stortford on A120. M11
Junction 8
Mis Buggies for hire

Boxmoor (1890)

18 Box Lane, Hemel Hempstead
Tel (0442) 42434
Mem 225
Sec E Duell (0442) 62427
Holes 9 L 4854 yds SSS 64
Recs Am–57 D Boyd, A Reeves
V'trs U Sun–NA
Fees £5 Sat–£6
Loc 1 mile W of Hemel on B4505
to Chesham

Brickendon Grange (1964)

Brickendon, nr Hertford
Tel (099 286) 228
Mem 650
Sec N Martin (099 286) 258
Pro J Hamilton (099 286) 218
Holes 18 L 6325 yds SSS 70
Recs Am–70 J Paterson,
M Passingham
Pro–67 S James, K Robson
V'trs WD–U WE/BH–M SOC
Fees On application
Loc Bayford, 3 miles S of Hertford

Brookmans Park (1930)

Brookmans Park, Hatfield AL9 7AT
Tel (0707) 52487
Sec To be appointed
Pro MMR Plumbridge (0707) 52468
Holes 18 L 6454 yds SSS 71

Recs Am–67 P Embleton
Pro–66 GR Burroughs
V'trs WD–UH WE/BH–M SOC
Fees D–£15
Loc 3 miles S of Hatfield, off A1000

Bushey G & CC (1980)

High Street, Bushey WD2 1BJ
Tel (081) 950 2283
Mem 600
Sec Mr and Mrs Paterson
Pro G Atkinson (081) 950 2215
Holes 9 L 3000 yds SSS 69
V'trs WD–before 6pm WE/BH–after
2pm Wed–closed
Fees 18 holes–£9 (£12)
9 holes–£5 (£7)
Loc 2 miles S of Watford on A4008
Mis Driving range

Bushey Hall (1896)

Bushey Hall Drive, Bushey WD2 2EP
Tel (0923) 225802
Mem 550
Sec CA Brown
Pro D Fitzsimmons (0923) 222253
Holes 18 L 6099 yds SSS 69
Recs Am–65 G Kemble
V'trs WD–H WE/BH–M
Loc 1 mile SE of Watford

Chadwell Springs (1974)

Hertford Road, Ware SG12 9LE
Tel (0920) 463647
Mem 350
Sec K Horner (0920) 461447
Pro AN Shearn (0920) 462075
Holes 9 L 3021 yds SSS 69
V'trs WD–U WE–M
Fees WD–£12
Loc Between Ware and Hertford
on A119

Cheshunt Park (1976)

Public
Park Lane, Cheshunt EN7 6QD
Tel (0992) 24009
Pro AC Newton (0992) 24009
Holes 18 L 6608 yds SSS 71
V'trs U
Fees £4.50 (£6)
Loc A10 London–Cambridge; turn
off at College Road junction.
Proceed along Churchgate

Chorleywood (1890)

Common Road, Chorleywood
WD3 5LN
Tel (092 78) 2009
Mem 200 55(L) 40(J)
Sec LW Turner
Holes 9 L 2838 yds SSS 67
Recs Am–65 SM McCready
Pro–64 H Bradshaw
V'trs WD–U exc Tues & Thurs am
WE–Sat pm only
Fees £8 (£10)
Loc 3 miles W of Rickmansworth
off A404. M25 Junction 18

Dyrham Park CC (1963)

Galley Lane, Barnet
Tel (081) 440 3361
Mem 300
Sec DU Prentice
Pro W Large (081) 440 3904
Holes 18 L 6369 yds SSS 70
V'trs WD–M SOC–Wed
Loc 10 miles N of London, W off A1
Mis Guests must be accompanied
by a member

East Herts (1898)

Hamels Park, Buntingford
SG9 9NA
Tel (0920) 821923
Mem 700
Sec JA Harper (0920) 821978
Pro James Hamilton
(0920) 821922
Holes 18 L 6449 yds SSS 71
Recs Am–68 JA Watts
Pro–64 R Joyce
V'trs WD–H WE–M
Fees On application
Loc 1/4 mile N of Puckeridge
on A10

Elstree (1984)

Watling Street, Elstree WD6 3AA
Tel (081) 953 6115
Mem 550
Sec G Stoneman
Pro G Stoneman (081) 207 5680
Holes 18 L 6100 yds SSS 69
Recs Am–68 C Woodcock (1987)
V'trs U SOC
Fees On application
Loc A5183, 1 mile N of Elstree.
8 miles N of London.
M1 Junction 4, 2 miles
Mis Private covered floodlit golf
range

Hadley Wood (1922)

Beech Hill, Hadley Wood, Barnet
EN4 0JJ
Tel (081) 449 4486
Mem 600
Sec JE Linaker (Sec/Mgr)
(081) 449 4328
Pro A McGinn (081) 449 3285
Holes 18 L 6473 yds SSS 71
Recs Am–67 CC Holton (1983),
N Leconte (1989)
Pro–67 PP Elson (1980)
V'trs WD–H or I WE/BH–M
Fees On application
Loc 10 miles N of London off
A111 between Potters Bar
and Cockfosters. 2 miles
S of M25 Junction 24

Harpenden (1894)

Hammonds End, Harpenden
Tel (0582) 712580
Mem 800
Sec H Pitcock
Pro DH Smith (0582) 767124

Holes 18 L 6363 yds SSS 70
Recs Am–67 B Bulmer (1987)
V'trs WD–U WE/BH–M SOC–WD
exc Thurs (Ladies Day)
Fees £15 D–£22
Loc 6 miles N of St Albans on B487

Harpenden Common (1931)

East Common, Harpenden AL5 1BL
Tel (0582) 712856
Mem 700
Sec HN Hobbs (0582) 715959
Pro N Lawrence (0582) 460655
Holes 18 L 5651 yds SSS 67
Recs Pro–63 N Brown, M Squires
(1989)
V'trs WD–U WE–M SOC H
Fees £11
Loc 5 miles N of St Albans, on A1081

Hartsbourne CC (1946)

Hartsbourne Avenue, Bushey Heath
WD2 1JW
Tel (081) 950 1113
Mem 400
Sec RJH Jourdan
Pro G Hunt (081) 950 2836
Holes 18 L 6305 yds SSS 70
9 L 5432 yds SSS 70
Recs Am–67 E Silver
Pro–62 P Oosterhuis
V'trs NA
Loc 5 miles SE of Watford, off A4008

Hatfield London (1976)

Bedwell Park, Essendon, Hatfield
AL9 6JA
Tel (0707) 42624
Mem 100
Sec T Takizawa
Holes 18 L 6878 yds SSS 73
V'trs U
Fees £9 (£18)
Loc B158

Knebworth (1908)

Deards End Lane, Knebworth
SG3 6NL
Tel (0438) 814681 (Clubhouse)
Mem 900
Sec JC Wright (0438) 812752
Pro MW Blainey (0438) 812757
Holes 18 L 6428 yds SSS 71
Recs Am–68 PR Robinson
Pro–65 W Henry
V'trs WD–U H WE–M SOC–WD
Fees On application
Loc 1 mile S of Stevenage on B197

Letchworth (1905)

Letchworth SG6 3NQ
Tel (0462) 683203
Mem 900
Sec BM Barber
Pro SJ Mutimer (0462) 682713
Holes 18 L 6057 yds SSS 69

For explanation of abbreviations, see page 460.

Recs   Am–67 RF Croft
        Pro–66 NC Coles
V'trs   WD–U WE–M SOC–Wed–Fri
Fees   £16
Loc   Letchworth, S off A505

Little Hay Golf Complex (1977)

Public
Box Lane, Bovingdon,
Hemel Hempstead
Tel   (0442) 833798
Pro   D Johnson (Golf Dir)
Holes   18 L 6610 yds SSS 72
Recs   Pro–69
V'trs   U
Fees   £4.40 (£6.40)
Loc   2 miles W of Hemel on B4505
        to Chesham

Mid Herts (1893)

Gustard Wood, Wheathampstead
AL4 8RS
Tel   (058 283) 2242
Mem   500(M) 125(L)
Sec   CJ Bowen
Pro   NG Brown (058 283) 2788
Holes   18 L 6060 yds SSS 69
Recs   Am–68 P Mayles (1987)
        Pro–66 H Baiocchi, R Morris,
        J Pinsent (1987)
V'trs   WD–UH exc Tues & Wed pm
        WE/BH–M SOC
Fees   On application
Loc   6 miles N of St Albans on B651

Moor Park (1923)

Rickmansworth
Tel   (0923) 773146
Mem   1950
Sec   JA Davies
Pro   ER Whitehead
Holes   High 18 L 6903 yds SSS 73
        West 18 L 5823 yds SSS 68
Recs   High Am–69 RY Mitchell
        Pro–67 M King
        West Am- 63 AJ Eisner
        Pro–63 AD Locke, A Lees,
        EE Whitcombe
V'trs   WD–I WE/BH–M
Fees   On request
Loc   1 mile SE of Rickmansworth,
        off Batchworth roundabout
        (A4145). M25 Junction 18, 1
        mile

Old Fold Manor (1910)

Hadley Green, Barnet EN5 4QN
Tel   (081) 440 9185
Mem   520
Sec   DV Dalingwater
Pro   P Jones (081) 440 7488
Holes   18 L 6473 yds SSS 71
Recs   Am–66 A Clark
        Pro–68 SL King
V'trs   WD–I/H WE–M
Fees   £18 D–£28
Loc   1 mile N of Barnet on A1000

Panshanger (1976)

Public
Old Herns Lane, Welwyn Garden City
Tel   (0707) 339507
Mem   352
Pro   B Lewis, M Corlass
Holes   18 L 6626 metres SSS 72
Recs   Am–71 S Walton (1987)
        Pro–70 R Green
V'trs   U
Fees   £5.50 (£6)
Loc   2 miles off A1, via B1000
        to Hertford

Porters Park (1899)

Shenley Hill, Radlett WD7 7AZ
Tel   (0923) 854127
Mem   550
Sec   JH Roberts (Mgr)
Pro   D Gleeson (0923) 854366
Holes   18 L 6313 yds SSS 70
Recs   Am–65 J Putt
        Pro–64 P Townsend
V'trs   WD–H (phone first) WE/BH–M
        SOC–Wed&Thurs
Fees   £22–£30
Loc   ½ mile E of Radlett on Shenley
        road

Potters Bar (1923)

Darkes Lane, Potters Bar EN6 1DE
Tel   (0707) 52020
Mem   550
Sec   A Williams (Mgr)
Pro   K Hughes (0707) 52987
Holes   18 L 6273 yds SSS 70
Recs   Am–66 RR Davis
        Pro–65 D McClelland
V'trs   WD–H WE–M SOC–Mon & Fri
Loc   1 mile N of M25 Junction 24,
        off A1000

Redbourn (1970)

Kinsbourne Green Lane, Redbourn,
nr St Albans
Tel   (0582) 793493
Sec   WM Dunn (0582) 792150
Pro   S Baldwin
Holes   18 L 6407 yds SSS 71
        9 L 1361 yds SSS 27
V'trs   18 hole: WD–U exc 4.30–6.15pm
        WE/BH–NA before 3pm SOC. 9
        hole: WD/WE–U
Fees   18 hole £7.50 (£9)
        9 hole £3 (£4.50)
Loc   4 miles N of St Albans.
        4 miles S of Luton.
        1 mile S of M1 Junction 9
Mis   Driving range

Rickmansworth (1937)

Public
Moor Lane, Rickmansworth
WO3 1QL
Tel   (0923) 773163
Pro   I Duncan (0923) 775278
Holes   18 L 4412 yds SSS 62
Recs   Am–62 L Silver

Panshanger — V'trs

V'trs   U
Fees   £4.40 (£6.30)
Loc   ½ mile SE of Rickmansworth
        off Batchworth roundabout
        (A4145). M25 Junction 18, 1
        mile
Mis   9 hole pitch & putt

Royston (1892)

Baldock Road, Royston
Tel   (0763) 242177 (Members)
Mem   700
Sec   Mrs S Morris (0763) 242696
Pro   M Hatcher (0763) 243476
Holes   18 L 6032 yds SSS 69
Recs   Am–65 T Moss
        Pro–63 B Waites
V'trs   WD–U WE/BH–M SOC
Fees   £15
Loc   SW of Royston on A505

Sandy Lodge (1910)

Northwood, Middx
Tel   (092 74) 25429
Mem   700
Sec   JN Blair
Pro   A Fox (092 74) 25321
Holes   18 L 6340 yds SSS 70
Recs   Am–67 JM Brew, IC Goode
        Pro–64 A Jacklin
V'trs   WD/WE/BH–M H
Fees   £18
Loc   Adjacent Moor Park Station,
        Rickmansworth

South Herts (1899)

Totteridge Lane, London N20 8QU
Tel   (081) 445 0117
Mem   800
Sec   AA Dogan (081) 445 2035
Pro   RS Livingston (081) 445 4633
Holes   18 L 6470 yds SSS 71
        9 L 1581 yds
Recs   Am–67 R Neil (1964)
        Pro–66 D Thomas (1966)
V'trs   WD–IH WE/BH–M
Fees   On application
Loc   10 miles N of London on A5109

Stevenage (1980)

Public
Aston Lane, Stevenage SG2 7EL
Tel   (043 888) 424
Pro   K Bond
Holes   18 L 6451 yds SSS 71
Recs   Am–70 A Archer (1988)
        Pro–65 R Green (1989)
V'trs   U
Fees   £4.50 (£6)
Loc   Off A602 to Hertford.
        A1(M) Junction 7
Mis   Driving range. 9 hole Par 3

Verulam (1905)

London Road, St Albans AL1 1JG
Tel   (0727) 53327
Mem   600
Sec   GD Eastwood
Pro   P Anderson (0727) 61401
Holes   18 L 6432 yds SSS 71

Recs Am–70
Pro–65 R Mitchell
V'trs WD–U WE/BH–NA
Fees £14 (reduced Mon–£10)
Loc 1 miles SE of St Albans on A1081

Welwyn Garden City (1922)

Mannicotts, High Oaks Road,
Welwyn Garden City AL8 7BP
Tel (0707) 322722
Mem 700
Sec JL Carragher (0707) 325243
Pro H Arnott (0707) 325525
Holes 18 L 6100 yds SSS 69
Recs Am–65 J Bickerton (1989)
Pro–63 N Faldo (1988)
V'trs UH Sun–M after noon
Fees £16 (£25)
Loc 3/4 mile N of Hatfield.
A1(M)–B197 to Valley Road

West Herts (1890)

Cassiobury Park, Watford WD1 7SL
Tel (0923) 224264
Mem 650
Sec RAS Gordon (0923) 36484
Pro CS Gough (0923) 220352
Holes 18 L 6488 yds SSS 71
Recs Am–68 SA Masson
Pro–67 R Whitehead
V'trs WD–I WE/BH–M SOC–Wed & Fri
Fees £12.50
Loc Off A412 between Watford and Rickmansworth

Whipsnade Park (1974)

Studham Lane, Dagnall HP4 1RH
Tel (044284) 2330
Mem 400
Sec D Whalley
Pro M Lewendon
Holes 18 L 6812 yds SSS 72
Recs Am–71 A Calder
V'trs WD–U WE–M SOC–WD
Fees £15 D–£20
Loc 10 miles N of Hemel
Hempstead off A4146, between Dagnall and Studham

Humberside

Beverley & East Riding (1889)

The Westwood, Beverley HU17 8RG
Tel (0482) 867190
Mem 460
Sec A Walker (0482) 868757
Pro I Mackie (0482) 869519
Holes 18 L 6164 yds SSS 69
Recs Am–66 N Burnley
V'trs U SOC–WD
Fees £6.50 (£9)
Loc Beverley–Walkington road

Boothferry (1981)

Public
Spaldington Lane, Spaldington,
Howden, Goole
Tel (0430) 430364
Pro S Wilkinson
Holes 18 L 6593 yds SSS 72
Recs Am–70 R Giles (1988)
Pro–70 M Ingham (1984)
S Rolley (1987)
Fees £4 (£7)
Loc 3 miles N of Howden on B1288.
M62 Junction 37

Bridlington (1905)

Belvedere Road, Bridlington
YO15 3NA
Tel (0262) 672092
Mem 663
Sec C Wilson (0262) 674679
Pro D Rands (0262) 674721
Holes 18 L 6330 yds SSS 70
V'trs U Sun–after 11.15am
Fees £10 (£15)
Loc Bridlington Station 1 1/2 miles

Brough (1891)

Brough HU15 1HB
Tel (0482) 667374
Mem 650
Sec HJ Oldroyd (0482) 667291
Pro G Townhill (0482) 667483
Holes 18 L 6183 yds SSS 69
Recs Am–64 PWJ Greenhough,
MJ Kelley
Pro–63 A Thompson
V'trs WD–U exc Wed–NA before 2pm
Fees £15
Loc 10 miles W of Hull on A63

Cave Castle Hotel (1989)

South Cave, N Humberside
HU15 2EU
Tel (0403) 422245
Sec JR Brodigan
Holes 18 L 6851 yds SSS 73
V'trs U
Loc South Cave, 10 miles W of Hull

Cleethorpes (1894)

Kings Road, Cleethorpes DN35 0PN
Tel (0472) 814060
Mem 750
Sec GB Standaloft
Pro E Sharp
Holes 18 L 6015 yds SSS 69
Recs Am–64 A Hare
Pro–64 D Ramsey
V'trs Wed pm–NA Sat pm/Sun am–XL
Fees £10 (£13)
Loc Cleethorpes 1 mile

Driffield (1938)

Sunderlandwick, Driffield
Tel (0377) 43116
Mem 384
Sec K Pickles (0377) 44069
Holes 9 L 6227 yds SSS 70
V'trs U
Fees £6 (£10)
Loc 10 miles S of Bridlington

Flamborough Head (1932)

Lighthouse Road, Flamborough,
Bridlington YO15 1AR
Tel (0262) 850333
Mem 400
Sec WR Scarle (0262) 676494
Holes 18 L 5438 yds SSS 66
Recs Am–63 GR Allen
Pro–63 P Dawson
V'trs U
Fees £7 (£9) W–£28
Loc 5 miles NE of Bridlington

Ganstead Park (1976)

Longdales Lane, Coniston, Hull
HU11 4LB
Tel (0482) 811280
Mem 350
Sec RB Barker
Pro M Smee (0482) 811121
Holes 18 L 6534 yds SSS
Recs Am–67 M Smee (1987)
Pro–67 H Clark
V'trs U H WE–NA before noon SOC
Fees £6 (£9)
Loc 2 miles E of Hull on A165

Grimsby (1923)

Littlecoates Road, Grimsby DN34 4LU
Tel (0472) 342823
Mem 550 150(L) 70(J)
Sec AD Houlihan (0472) 342630
Pro S Houltby (0472) 356981
Holes 18 L 6068 yds SSS 69
Recs Am–66 M James
Pro–66 BJ Hunt
V'trs WD–U Sat pm/Sun am–XL
Fees £12.50 (£15) W–£45
Loc 1 mile W of Grimsby

Hainsworth Park (1983)

Brandesburton, Driffield YO25
Tel (0964) 542362
Mem 400
Sec BW Atkin (Prop)
Holes 9 L 5360 yds SSS 66
V'trs WD–U WE–U after 4pm
SOC–WD
Fees £5 (£7.50)
Loc 8 miles N of Beverley (A165).
Bridlington 15 miles

For explanation of abbreviations, see page 460.

Hessle (1906)

Westfield Road, Cottingham
Tel (0482) 650171
Mem 600
Sec RL Dorsey
Pro G Fieldsend (0482) 650190
Holes 18 L 6638 yds SSS 72
Recs Am–68 A Wright (1984)
Pro–69 B Thompson (1980)
V'trs WD–U exc Tues 9.15am–1pm
WE–M
Fees £13 (£20)
Loc 3 miles SW of Cottingham

Holme Hall (1908)

Holme Lane, Bottesford, Scunthorpe
DN16 3RF
Tel (0724) 849185 (Steward)
Mem 490 110(L) 75(J) 3(5)
Sec AHF Holtby (0724) 862078
Pro M Haines (0724) 851816
Holes 18 L 6475 yds SSS 71
Recs Am–67 S Steele, A Thain,
K Blow, FW Wood
Pro–66 B Thompson
V'trs WD–U WE–M H SOC–WD
Fees £8 D–£12
Loc 4 miles SE of Scunthorpe.
M180 Junction 4

Hornsea (1908)

Rolston Road, Hornsea HU18 1XG
Tel (0964) 532020
Mem 550
Sec BW Kirton
Pro B Thompson (0964) 534989
Holes 18 L 6461 yds SSS 71
Recs Am–65 P Binnington (1986)
Pro–67 B Thompson (1985)
V'trs WD–U WE–Restricted SOC
Fees £13 (£18)
Loc 300 yds past Hornsea Pottery

Hull (1921)

The Hall, 27 Packman Lane,
Kirk Ella, Hull HU10 7JT
Tel (0482) 653026
Mem 756
Sec R Toothill (Gen Mgr)
(0482) 658919
Pro D Jagger (0482) 653074
Holes 18 L 6242 yds SSS 70
Recs Am–64 JD Dockar, R Roper
Pro–66 D Dunk, N Hunt,
S Smith, D Jagger
V'trs U WE–NA
Fees £15 R/D
Loc 5 miles W of Hull

Immingham (1975)

Church Lane, Immingham, Grimsby
DN40 2EO
Tel (0469) 75298
Mem 600
Sec E Cowton
Pro J Moffat (0469) 75493
Holes 18 L 5809 yds SSS 68

V'trs WE–M Sun–NA before noon
Fees £8 D–£12 (£12)
Loc Civic Centre, 1/2 mile behind
St Andrew's Church

Kingsway

Public
Kingsway, Scunthorpe DN15 7ER
Tel (0724) 840945
Sec C Mann
Pro C Mann
Holes 9 L 1915 yds SSS 59
V'trs U
Fees £1.40 (£1.80)
Loc 3/4 mile W of Scunthorpe

Normanby Hall (1978)

Public
Normanby Park, Scunthorpe
Tel (0724) 720226
Pro C Mann
Holes 18 L 6548 yds SSS 71
Recs Am–68
Pro–68 N Bundy
V'trs U SOC–WD
Fees £5.50 (£7)
Loc 5 miles N of Scunthorpe

Scunthorpe (1936)

Ashby Decoy, Burringham Road,
Scunthorpe DN17 2AB
Tel (0724) 842913/866561
Mem 450 105(L) 50(J)
Sec EA Willsmore
Pro G Bailey (0724) 868972
Holes 18 L 6281 yds SSS 71
Recs Am–67 J Payne
Pro–67 K Waters
V'trs U SOC–WD
Fees £12 (Sat–£12 Sun–NA)
Loc 2 miles SW of Scunthorpe

Springhead Park (1903)

Public
Willerby Road, Hull HU5 5JE
Tel (0482) 656309
Sec F Coggrave (Hon)
Pro B Herrington
Holes 18 L 6439 yds SSS 71
Recs Am–69 AD Hill, A Wright
Pro–65 S Rolley
V'trs U
Fees £2.85 (£4)
Loc 4 miles W of Hull on Willerby
road

Sutton Park (1935)

Public
Salthouse Road, Hull
Tel (0482) 74242
Sec CD Smith (Hon)
Pro P Rushworth (0482) 711450
Holes 18 L 6251 yds SSS 70
Recs Am–67 A Wright
Pro–64 L Herrington
V'trs U
Fees £2.85 (£4)
Loc 3 miles E of Hull

Withernsea (1909)

Chestnut Avenue, Withernsea
HU19 2PG
Tel (0964) 612258
Mem 329 55(L) 40(J) 236(5)
Sec F Buckley (0964) 612214
Holes 9 L 5112 yds SSS 64
Recs Am–62 SH Kellet
Pro–63 G Townhill
V'trs WD–U WE–NA Sun am SOC
Fees £5 (£5) 5D–£25 W–£30
Loc 17 miles E of Hull on B1033.
S side of Withernsea

Isle of Man

Castletown (1092)

104 Ballycriy Park, Colby
Tel (0624) 834422
Mem 300
Sec TH Dore
Pro MC Crowe (0624) 822125
Holes 18 L 6716 yds SSS 72
Recs Am–68 WR Ennett
V'trs U SOC (arrange with Pro)
Fees £7 (£8)
Loc 1 1/4 miles E of Castletown

Douglas Municipal (1927)

Public
Pulrose Park, Douglas
Tel (0624) 75952
Pro K Parry
Holes 18 L 6080 yds SSS 69
Recs Am–63
V'trs U
Fees £5 W–£20
Loc Douglas Pier 1 mile
Mis Douglas Club plays here

Howstrake (1914)

Groudle Road, Onchan
Tel (0624) 20430
Mem 400
Sec JC Davies
Holes 18 L 5367 yds SSS 66
Recs Am–62 TP Kniveton
Pro–69
V'trs U SOC
Fees £5 (£7)
Loc 1 mile N of Douglas

Peel (1896)

Rheast Lane, Peel
Tel (062 484) 2227
Mem 500
Sec DR Forth (062 484) 3456
(mornings)
Holes 18 L 5914 yds SSS 68
Recs Am–64 J Sutton
V'trs WD–U WE/BH–NA before
10.30am SOC
Fees £8 (£10)
Loc 10 miles W of Douglas

Port St Mary

Public
Kallow Road, Port St Mary
Tel   (0624) 834932
Holes   9 L 2711 yds SSS 66
Recs   Am–66 A Horne (1989)
V'trs   U
Fees   WD/WE–£3
Loc   Port St Mary, nr sea shore

Ramsey

Tel   (0624) 813365/812244
Mem   870
Sec   SA Lockwood (0624) 812397
Holes   18 L 6019 yds SSS 69
Recs   Am–65 S Boyd
        Pro–65 S Lyle
V'trs   U H for comps SOC
Fees   £8 (£10)
Loc   W boundary of Ramsey

Rowany (1895)

Port Erin
Tel   (0624) 834108
Mem   520
Sec   RJS Mawson (Mgr)
        (0624) 834988
Holes   18 L 5840 yds SSS 69
Recs   Am–68 A Cain
V'trs   U H for open comps SOC
Fees   £8 (£9)
Loc   6 miles W of Castletown

Isle of Wight

Cowes (1908)

Crossfield Avenue, Cowes
PO31 8HN
Tel   (0983) 292303
Mem   250
Sec   RE Wootton (0983) 295802
Holes   9 L 5880 yds SSS 68
Recs   Am–69 I Graham
V'trs   H Thurs–NA before 4pm
        (Ladies Day) Fri–NA after
        5pm Sun am–NA
Fees   £10 W–£37.50
Loc   Crossfield Avenue (private
        road), nr Cowes High School

Freshwater Bay

Afton Down, Freshwater
Tel   (0983) 752955
Mem   500
Sec   HGV Gordon
Holes   18 L 5662 yds SSS 68
Recs   Am–67 K Garrett,
        S McArthur (1989)
        Pro–66 T Underwood (1981)
V'trs   U SOC
Fees   £12 (£14) W–£60 2W–£80
Loc   400 yds off Military Road

Newport IW (1896)

St George's Down, nr Shide, Newport
PO30 3BA
Tel   (0983) 525076
Mem   350
Sec   J Ambrose
Holes   9 L 5704 yds SSS 68
Recs   Am–65 J Burton (1987)
V'trs   WD–U Sat–NA before 3.30pm
        Sun–NA before noon
Fees   £10
Loc   1 mile SE of Newport

Osborne (1903)

Club House, East Cowes
Tel   (0983) 295421
Mem   260 90(L)
Sec   Mrs M Butler
Pro   I Taylor (0983) 295649
Holes   9 L 6286 yds SSS 70
V'trs   WD–U exc Ladies' Day
        11am–2.30pm–NA Sun–NA
        after 11.30am SOC
Fees   £12 5D–£36
Loc   S of East Cowes in grounds
        of Osborne House

Ryde (1921)

Ryde House Park, Ryde
Tel   (0983) 614809
Mem   450
Sec   F Cockayne (0983) 64388
Pro   S Ward (0983) 62088
Holes   9 L 5220 yds SSS 66
Recs   Am–64 M Groves, D Chalon
        Pro–64 T Underwood,
        D Allen
V'trs   U
Fees   £10 (£12.50)
Loc   On main Ryde/Newport road

Shanklin & Sandown (1900)

Fairway Lake, Sandown PO36 9PR
Tel   (0983) 403217
Mem   700
Sec   GA Wormald
Pro   P Warner (0983) 404424
Holes   18 L 6000 yds SSS 69
Recs   Am–65 D McToldridge
        Pro–65 R Wynn
V'trs   WD–U SOC–WD WE–NA
        before 4pm(summer) 12 noon
        (winter)
Fees   £16 (£18) 5D–£65
Loc   Sandown

Ventnor (1892)

Steephill Down Road, Ventnor
Tel   (0983) 853326
Mem   180
Sec   R Hose (0983) 853198
Holes   9 L 5772 yds SSS 68
Recs   Am–73 IH Guy
V'trs   U
Fees   £6 (£7)
Loc   NW boundary of Ventnor

Kent

Aquarius (1913)

Marmora Rd, Honor Oak, London SE22
Tel   (081) 693 1626
Mem   400
Sec   PA Mutton
Pro   F Private
Holes   9 L 5034 yds SSS 65
Recs   Am–62 R Hare
        Pro–63 F Private
V'trs   M
Loc   SE London

Ashford (1904)

Sandyhurst Lane, Ashford TN25 4NT
Tel   (0233) 620180
Mem   650
Sec   AH Story (0223) 622655
Pro   H Sherman (0233) 629644
Holes   18 L 6246 yds SSS 70
Recs   Am–67 KC Elvin, SM Green
        Pro–63 RS Fidler
V'trs   WD–H SOC WE/BH–H
Fees   D–£16 (D–£20)
Loc   Ashford 1½ miles (A20)

Barnehurst (1903)

Mayplace Road, East Barnehurst
DA7 6JU
Tel   (0322) 523746
Mem   250
Sec   GE Audsley (0322) 54612
Pro   S Barr (0322) 51205
Holes   9 L 5320 yds SSS 66
Recs   Am–64
        Pro–64
V'trs   Mon/Wed/Fri–U Other days
        restricted
Fees   £3.60 (£5.70)
Loc   Between Crayford and
        Bexley Heath

Bearsted (1898)

Ware Street, Bearsted, nr Maidstone
Tel   (0622) 38389
Mem   648
Sec   (0622) 38198
Pro   T Simpson (0622) 38024
Holes   18 L 6253 yds SSS 70
Recs   Am–68 D Jenner (1987)
        Pro–69 G Norton (1982)
V'trs   WD–I H WE–H M Recognised
        GC members only SOC
Fees   £14 D–£20
Loc   Maidstone 2½ miles

Beckenham Place Park (1907)

Public
Beckenham Hill Road,
Beckenham SE6
Tel   (081) 650 2292
Pro   B Woodman (081) 658 5374
Holes   18 L 5722 yds SSS 68

For explanation of abbreviations, see page 460.

Recs   Am–62 S Champion
        Pro–65 T Cotton
V'trs   WD–U WE–U after 2pm
Fees   £5.90 (£8.40) WE booking fee
Loc   2 miles S of Catford SE6
Mis   Braeside GC and Foxgrove
        GC play here

Bexley Heath (1907)

Mount Road, Bexley Heath BR8 7RJ
Tel   (081) 303 6951
Mem   350
Sec   SE Squires
Holes   9 L 5239 yds SSS 66
Recs   Am–65 D Fillary
V'trs   WD–H before 4pm
Fees   £8
Loc   Station 1 mile

Braeside (1947)

Public
The Mansion, Beckenham Place Park,
Beckenham
Tel   (081) 650 2292
Mem   150
Sec   R Oliver
Holes   Play over Beckenham Place
        Park

Bromley (1948)

Public
Magpie Hall Lane, Bromley
Tel   (081) 462 7014
Pro   A Hodgson
Holes   9 L 5538 yds SSS 66
Recs   Am–66 HE Harding,
        KW Miles
V'trs   U
Fees   £1.70 (£2.40)
Loc   Off Bromley Common (A21)

Broome Park (1981)

Barham, nr Canterbury CT4 6QX
Tel   (0227) 831701
Sec   D Lees (Hon)
Pro   T Britz (Ext 264)
Holes   18 L 6610 yds SSS 72
Recs   Am–64 A Roberts
        Pro–66 B Impett (1984)
V'trs   H WE–NA before noon SOC
Fees   £15 (£17)
Loc   M2/A2–A260 Folkestone road,
        1¹⁄₂ miles on RH side

Canterbury (1927)

Scotland Hills, Canterbury CT1 1TW
Tel   (0227) 463586
Mem   720
Sec   G Good (0227) 453532
Pro   P Everard (0227) 462865
Holes   18 L 6245 yds SSS 70
Recs   Am–66 RJ Davies
        Pro–64 K Redford
V'trs   WD–UH Sat–NA before 10am
        Sun am–NA SOC–Tues &
        Thurs
Fees   £16 D–£20 (£22)
Loc   1 mile E of Canterbury on
        A257

Cherry Lodge (1969)

Jail Lane, Biggin Hill, nr Westerham
TN16 3AX
Tel   (0959) 72250
Mem   840
Sec   IR Westwater (Mgr)
Pro   N Child (0959) 72989
Holes   18 L 6908 yds SSS 74
Recs   Am–70 N Lancaster (1984)
        Pro–69 B Cameron (1986)
V'trs   WD–U WE–M
Fees   £18 D–£25
Loc   15 miles SE of London
Mis   Buggies available

Chestfield (Whitstable)
(1925)

103 Chestfield Road, Whitstable
CT5 3LU
Tel   (022 779) 4411
Sec   RW Leaver
Pro   J Brotherton (022 779) 3563
Holes   18 L 6126 yds SSS 69
Recs   Am–66 S Wood
        Pro–64 B Cameron
V'trs   WD–H WE–Sat after 11am
        Sun after 3pm
Fees   On application
Loc   1 mile S of A229 and Chestfield
        Station

Chislehurst (1894)

Camden Place, Chislehurst BR7 5HJ
Tel   (081) 467 3055
Mem   740
Sec   NE Pearson (081) 467 2782
Pro   AS Costorphine (081) 467
        6798
Holes   18 L 5128 yds SSS 65
Recs   Am–62 DC Theobald (1987)
        Pro–61 J Bennett
V'trs   WD–H WE–M
Fees   D–£20
Loc   M25 Junction 3–A20–A222

Cobtree Manor Park

Public
Chatham Road, Boxley, Maidstone
Tel   (0622) 53276
Pro   M Drew
Holes   18 L 5716 yds SSS 68
V'trs   WD–U WE/BH–(book 1 wk in
        advance) SOC–WD
Fees   £5 (£7.50)
Loc   Maidstone 3 miles on A229
        to Chatham

Corinthian (1987)

Gay Dawn Farm, Fawkham,
nr Dartford, DA3 8LZ
Tel   (04747) 7559
Mem   350
Sec   SJ Billings
Holes   9 L 3118 yds SSS 35
V'trs   WD–UH WE/BH–M SOC
Fees   £7.50

Loc   4 miles S of Dartford Tunnel.
        E of Brands Hatch along
        Fawkham Valley road
Mis   Artificial greens

Cranbrook (1969)

Benenden Road, Cranbrook
TN17 4AL
Tel   (0580) 712833/712934
Mem   700
Sec   HM Borissow (0580) 712833
Pro   G Potter (0580) 712934
Holes   18 L 6128 yds SSS 70
Recs   Am–67 S Coulter
        Pro–70 S Barr
V'trs   WD–U WE/BH–U exc comp
        days SOC
Fees   £8 (£11)
Loc   15 miles S of Maidstone.
        Sissinghurst 1¹⁄₄ miles
Mis   Buggies for hire Apr–Oct

Cray Valley (1972)

Sandy Lane, St Paul's Cray, Orpington
Tel   (0689) 31927
Mem   700
Sec   R Hill (0689) 39677
Pro   T Morgan (0689) 37909
Holes   18 L 5624 yds SSS 67
        9 L 2100 yds SSS 60
V'trs   WD–U WE–H SOC
Fees   £6 (£10)
Loc   15 miles SW of London

Darenth Valley (1973)

Public
Station Road, Shoreham, nr Sevenoaks
TN14 7SA
Tel   (09592) 2944 (Clubhouse)
Pro   P Edwards (09592) 2922
Holes   18 L 6356 yds SSS 71
Recs   Am–69 W Leo
        Pro–68 B Owens, P Edwards
V'trs   WD–U SOC
Fees   £6.50 (£9)
Loc   3 miles N of Sevenoaks off
        A225

Dartford (1897)

Dartford Heath, Dartford
Tel   (0322) 23616
Mem   600
Sec   PJH Smith (0322) 26455
Pro   A Blackburn (0322) 26409
Holes   18 L 5914 yds SSS 68
Recs   Am–66 G Wright
        Pro–66 C Tucker
V'trs   WD–I WE–M H
Fees   £20
Loc   Dartford 2 miles

Deangate Ridge (1972)

Public
Hoo, Rochester ME3 8RZ
Tel   (0634) 251180
Pro   B Aram
Holes   18 L 6300 yds SSS 70
Recs   Am–67 AJ Rossiter (1985)
        Pro–66 AJ Russell (1986),
        W Grant (1989)

V'trs U
Fees £3.30 (£4.65)
Loc Nr Isle of Grain

Edenbridge G & CC (1973)
Crouch House Road, Edenbridge
TN8 5LQ
Tel (0732) 865097
Mem 800
Sec Mrs S Mitchell
Pro (0732) 865202
Holes 18 L 6604 yds SSS 72
     9 hole course
Recs Am-72 I Martyr
V'trs WE-booking necessary
Fees £10 (£12)
Loc M25 Junction 6. Gatwick
    Airport 20 mins
Mis 16 bay floodlit driving range

Eltham Warren (1890)
Clubhouse, Bexley Road, Eltham,
London SE9 2PE
Tel (081) 850 1166
Mem 400
Sec DJ Clare (081) 850 4477
Pro IA Coleman
Holes 9 L 5840 yds SSS 68
Recs Am-66 G Janes
V'trs WD-I WE/BH-M SOC
Fees £14
Loc Eltham

Faversham (1910)
Belmont Park, Faversham
Tel (079 589) 251
Mem 700
Sec DB Christie (079 589) 561
Pro GG Nixon (079 589) 275
Holes 18 L 6021 yds SSS 69
Recs Am-65 R Chapman
     Pro-67 P Clark
V'trs WD-I or H WE-M SOC
Fees £16
Loc Faversham and M2, 2 miles

Gillingham (1908)
Woodlands Road, Gillingham
Tel (0634) 50999
Mem 450 100(L) 50(J) 120(5)
Sec LP O'Grady (0634) 53017
Pro S Barrow (0634) 55862
Holes 18 L 5911 yds SSS 68
Recs Am-65 T Williamson
     Pro-64 P Clark
V'trs WD-I H WE/BH-M
Fees £11 D-£16.50
Loc A2/M2, 2 miles

Hawkhurst (1968)
High Street, Hawkhurst TN18 4JS
Tel (0580) 752396
Mem 450
Sec AW Shipley
Pro T Collins (0580) 753600
Holes 9 L 5769 yds SSS 68
Recs Am-70 B Betts
     Pro-68 R Cameron

V'trs WD-U
Fees £10 (£14)
Loc 14 miles S of Tunbridge Wells
    on A268

Herne Bay (1902)
Eddington, Herne Bay CT6 7PG
Tel (0227) 374097
Mem 480
Sec B Warren (0227) 373964
Pro D Lambert (0227) 374727
Holes 18 L 5466 yds SSS 67
Recs Am-60 SJ Wood
     Pro-65 C Clark
V'trs WD-U WE/BH-H after 11am
     SOC-WD
Fees £12 D-£16.50 (£16.50)
Loc Herne Bay/Canterbury road

High Elms (1969)
Public
High Elms Road, Downe, Orpington
Tel (0689) 58175
Sec C Poulter (Hon)
Pro A Hodgson
Holes 18 L 6210 yds SSS 70
Recs Am-68 I Farman
     Pro-A Hodgson
V'trs U
Fees £4.50 (£6.80)
Loc Off A21 via Shire Lane

Holtye (1893)
Holtye, Cowden TN8 7ED
Tel (034 286) 635
Mem 480
Sec JP Holmes (034 286) 576
Pro M Scarles
Holes 9 L 5259 yds SSS 66
Recs Am-65 PD Scarles, JA Couling
     Pro-64 S Frost
V'trs WD-U WE-NA before noon
     SOC-Tues only
Fees On application
Loc 4 miles E of E Grinstead on
    A264. 6 miles W of Tunbridge
    Wells

Hythe Imperial (1950)
Prince's Parade, Hythe CT21 5RN
Tel (0303) 67441
Mem 300
Sec PI Kaye (0303) 67554
Pro G Ritchie
Holes 9 L 5533 yds SSS 67
Recs Am-63 PI Kaye
     Pro-64 SH Sherman
V'trs U H SOC
Fees £10 (£15)
Loc On coast, 4 miles W of
    Folkestone

Knole Park (1924)
Seal Hollow Road, Sevenoaks
TN15 0HJ
Tel (0732) 452709
Mem 700
Sec DJL Hoppe (0732) 452150
Pro PE Gill (0732) 451740

Holes 18 L 6249 yds SSS 70
Recs Am-64 RW Seamer
V'trs WD-restricted WE/BH-M H
     SOC
Fees £16 D-£26
Loc Seal Hollow Road
Mis Sevenoaks Town GC plays
    here

Lamberhurst (1890)
Church Road, Lamberhurst TN3 8DT
Tel (0892) 890241
Mem 700
Sec P Gleeson (0892) 890591
Pro M Travers (0892) 890552
Holes 18 L 6257 yds SSS 70
Recs Am-71 MJ Collett
     Pro-69 H Stott
V'trs WD-UH WE-M
Fees £20 (£25)
Loc 5 miles SE of Tunbridge
    Wells

Langley Park (1910)
Barnfield Wood Road, Beckenham
BR3 2SZ
Tel (081) 650 2090
Mem 650
Sec JL Smart (081) 658 6849
Pro GT Ritchie (081) 650 1663
Holes 18 L 6488 yds SSS 71
Recs Am-66 T Trodd
     Pro-65 P Mitchell (1987)
V'trs WD-I WE-M SOC-WD
Fees £20
Loc Bromley South Station 1 mile

Leeds Castle (1928)
Public
Leeds Castle, nr Maidstone ME17 1PL
Tel (0622) 880467
Pro C Miller
Holes 9 L 2910 yds Par 34
Recs Pro-66
V'trs U SOC-WD
Fees £6.95 (9 holes)
Loc A20, 1 mile from M20 at Park
    Gate Inn entrance
Mis 6-day advance booking
    system for 9 holes

Littlestone (1888)
Littlestone, New Romney TN28 8RB
Tel (0679) 62310
Mem 450
Sec JD Lewis (0679) 63355
Pro Glynne Williams
     (0679) 62231
Holes 18 L 6417 yds SSS 71
     9 L 3996 yds Par 64
Recs Am-67 G Godmon (1984),
     S Wood (1988)
     Pro-67 T Gale (1985)
V'trs WD-H WE-by arrangement
Fees On application
Loc 2 miles E of New Romney.
    15 miles SE of Ashford

Lullingstone Park (1967)

Public
Parkgate Road, Chelsfield,
nr Orpington
Tel   (0959) 34542
Pro   G Lloyd
Holes   18 and 9 hole courses
Fees   18 holes-£7.50. 9 holes-£4.25
Loc   Off Orpington by-pass A224

Mid Kent (1909)

Singlewell Road, Gravesend DA11 7RB
Tel   (0474) 568035
Mem   1050
Sec   AF Reid
Pro   R Lee (0474) 332810
Holes   18 L 6206 yds SSS 70
V'trs   WD-H WE-M
Fees   On application
Loc   25 miles SE of London

Nevill (1914)

Benhall Mill Road, Tunbridge Wells
TN2 5JW
Tel   (0892) 27820
Mem   400 200(L) 120(J) 150(5)
Sec   RA White (0892) 25818
Pro   P Huggett (0892) 32941
Holes   18 L 6336 yds SSS 70
Recs   Am-66 A Sykes (1975)
         Pro-66 M Warner (1988)
V'trs   WD-H WE/BH-M
Fees   WD-£18
Loc   Tunbridge Wells 1 mile

North Foreland (1903)

Kingsgate, Broadstairs, Thanet
Tel   (0843) 62140
Mem   800
Sec   BJ Preston
Pro   M Lee (0843) 69628
Holes   18 L 6374 yds SSS 70
         18 hole Approach and Putt
Recs   Am-66 P Walton
         Pro-66 M Lawrence
V'trs   WD-H WE-NA am -H pm
Fees   Summer £13 (£17) Winter £11
         (£16) Approach & Putt £5
Loc   Broadstairs Station 1¹/₂ miles

Poult Wood (1974)

Poult Wood, Higham Lane, Tonbridge
Tel   (0732) 364039
Mem   500
Sec   A Hope (Prop) (0732) 366180
         S Taylor (Hon)
Pro   K Adwick
Holes   18 L 5569 yds SSS 67
V'trs   U SOC-WD
Fees   £4.75 (£7)
Loc   2 miles N of Tonbridge off A227

Prince's (1904)

Sandwich Bay, Sandwich
Tel   (0304) 611118
Mem   550
Sec   G Rowlands (0304) 612000
Pro   P Sparks (0304) 613797

Holes   27 hole course (3x
         9 holes):
         Dunes/Himalayas/Shore.
         Length 6238-6947 yds.
         Par 71-72 SSS 70-73
Recs   Himalayas/Shore
         Am-67 M Goodin
         Pro-69 M Mannelli
         Dunes/Himalayas
         Am-69 S Wood
V'trs   U SOC-WD/WE (book with
         G Ramm)
Fees   £25 D-£27 (£32 D-£34)
Loc   Sandwich Bay

Rochester & Cobham Park (1891)

Park Pale, by Rochester ME2 3UU,
Tel   (047 482) 3411
Mem   720
Sec   Maj JW Irvine (Mgr)
Pro   M Henderson (047 482) 3658
Holes   18 L 6467 yds SSS 71
Recs   Am-67 JW Baldwin
         Pro-67 M Henderson
V'trs   WD-UH WE-M before 5pm
         SOC-Tues & Thurs
Fees   £18 WD/WE
Loc   3 miles E of Gravesend turn
         on A2

Royal Blackheath (1608)

Court Road, Eltham, London SE9 5AF
Tel   (081) 850 1795
Mem   700
Sec   Wg Cdr R Barriball RAF (Rtd)
Pro   I McGregor (081) 850 1763
Holes   18 L 6209 yds SSS 70
Recs   Am-66 DM Woolmer
         Pro-66 WC Thomas
V'trs   WD-I WE/BH-M SOC
Fees   £25
Loc   Between Eltham and
         Mottingham, N of A20

Royal Cinque Ports (1892)

Golf Road, Deal
Tel   (0304) 374328
Mem   1015
Sec   NS Phillips (0304) 374007
Pro   A Reynolds (0304) 374170
Holes   18 L 6744 yds SSS 72
Recs   Am-65 MF Bonallack
         Pro-63 GD Manson
V'trs   I
Fees   On application
Loc   Deal

Royal St George's (1887)

Sandwich CT13 9PB
Tel   (0304) 617308
Mem   700
Sec   Capt. RJ Hitchen RN
         (0304) 613090
Pro   N Cameron (0304) 615236
Holes   18 L 6534 yds SSS 72
Recs   Am-67 H Berwick
         Pro-64 C O'Connor Jr

V'trs   WD-IH SOC-WD WE-M
Fees   £25 D-£35 1989 prices
Loc   Sandwich 1 mile

Ruxley (1975)

Sandy Lane, St Paul's Cray, Orpington
Tel   (0689) 71490
Mem   250
Sec   D Simpson (Prop)
Pro   R Cornwell
Holes   18 L 5017 yds SSS 65
Recs   Am-63 D Curtis
         Pro-63 L Turner
V'trs   WD-U WE/BH-before 11.30am
Fees   £7 (£9)
Loc   Off A20 Ruxley roundabout at
         Sidcup

St Augustines (1907)

Cottington Road, Cliffsend, Ramsgate
Tel   (0843) 590333
Mem   300 80(L) 55(J) 120(5)
Sec   R James
Pro   DB Scott (0843) 590222
Holes   18 L 5138 yds SSS 65
Recs   Am-59 Dr S Hutton
         Pro-61 P Mitchell
V'trs   H SOC-WE
Fees   £15 (£17) W-£47 M-£112
Loc   2 miles S of Ramsgate. Follow
         signs to St Augustines Cross

Sene Valley Folkestone & Hythe (1888)

Sene, Folkestone CT18 8BL
Mem   650
Sec   GL Hills (0303) 68513
Pro   T Dungate (0303) 68514
Holes   18 L 6287 yds SSS 70
Recs   Am-65 J Hamilton
         Pro-69 G Will
V'trs   WD-H or I SOC
Fees   £16 (£20)
Loc   2 miles N of Hythe on B2065

Sheerness (1906)

Power Station Road, Sheerness
ME12 3AE
Tel   (0795) 662585
Mem   550
Sec   JW Gavins
Holes   18 L 6500 yds SSS 71
Recs   Am-68 JD Simmance
V'trs   WD-U WE-M SOC
Fees   £10 (£12)
Loc   Sittingbourne 9 miles.
         M20, M2 or A2 to A249

Shooter's Hill (1903)

Lowood, Eaglesfield Road, London
SE18 3DA
Tel   (081) 854 1216
Mem   310 60(L) 31(J) 265(5)
Sec   BR Adams (081) 854 6368
Pro   M Ridge (081) 854 0073
Holes   18 L 5736 yds SSS 68
Recs   Am-63 M Holland
         Pro-64 N Coles, G Will, S Scott

V'trs   WD–I WE/BH–M SOC–Tues &
        Thurs only
Fees   £18 WD only
Loc   Blackheath 4 miles

Shortlands (1897)

Meadow Road, Shortlands, Bromley
BR2 0PB
Tel   (081) 460 2471
Mem   525
Sec   Mrs L Burrows
Pro   J Bates
Holes   9 L 5261 yds SSS 66
Recs   Am–64 B Kent
        Pro–61 D Pratt
V'trs   M
Loc   Bromley, Kent

Sidcup (1891)

Hurst Road, Sidcup DA15 9AE
Tel   (081) 300 2864
Mem   350
Sec   C Baker
Pro   R Taylor
Holes   9 L 5692 yds SSS 67
Recs   Am–65 R Harris
        Pro–64 D Webb
V'trs   WD–H WE/BH–M
Fees   £10
Loc   On A222. A2/A20, 2 miles

Sittingbourne & Milton Regis (1929)

Wormdale, Newington, Sittingbourne
ME9 7PX
Tel   (0795) 842261
Mem   325 100(L) 72(J) 175(5)
Sec   HDG Wylie
Pro   JR Hearn (0795) 842775
Holes   18 L 6121 yds SSS 69
Recs   Am–66
        Pro–62
V'trs   WD–H Sat–NA Sun–M
        SOC–Tues & Thurs
Fees   £13
Loc   1 mile N of M2 Junction 5
        on A249

Sundridge Park (1902)

Garden Lane, Bromley BR1 3NE
Tel   (081) 460 1822
Mem   1167 99(L) 51(J) 189(5)
Sec   (081) 460 0278
Pro   B Cameron (081) 460 5540
Holes   East 18 L 6410 yds SSS 71
        West 18 L 6027 yds SSS 69
Recs   East Am–65 W Hodkin (1988)
        Pro–64 R Cameron
        West Am–67 P Lyons (1987)
        Pro–65 R Fidler
V'trs   H SOC–WD
Fees   £25
Loc   1 mile N of Bromley off
        Plaistow Lane, opposite
        Sundridge Park Station.
        M25 Junction 3 Southbound.
        M25 Junction 4 Northbound

Tenterden (1905)

Woodchurch Road, Tenterden
Tel   (058 06) 3987
Mem   450
Sec   DF Hunt (058 06) 4612
Pro   G Pottern
Holes   9 L 5141 yds SSS 65
V'trs   WD–U WE/BH–M Sun–NA
        before noon
Fees   On application
Loc   Tenterden 1 mile

Tudor Park (1989)

Ashford Road, Bearsted, Maidstone
ME14 4NQ
Tel   (0622) 34334
Sec   P Dawson
Holes   18 L 6000yds Par 70
V'trs   H SOC–Tues–Thurs

Tunbridge Wells (1889)

Langton Road, Tunbridge Wells
TN4 8XH
Tel   (0892) 23034
Mem   325 80(L) 48(J)
Sec   EM Goulden (0892) 36918
Pro   K Smithson (0892) 41386
Holes   9 L 4684 yds SSS 62
Recs   Am–59 EC Chapman
        Pro–59 J Humphrey
V'trs   WD–U WE/BH–M
Fees   £15 D–£20
Loc   Tunbridge Wells, by Spa Hotel

Walmer & Kingsdown (1909)

The Leas, Kingsdown, Deal CT14 8EP
Tel   (0304) 373256
Mem   620
Sec   BW Cockerill
Pro   T Hunt (0304) 363017
Holes   18 L 6451 yds SSS 71
Recs   Am–69 A Randall
        Pro–70 M Lee
V'trs   WD–U WE–after 12 noon SOC
Fees   D–£15 (£17) W–£67 F–£102
Loc   2¹⁄₂ miles S of Deal on clifftop

West Kent (1916)

West Hill, Downe, Orpington BR6 7JJ
Tel   (0689) 53737
Mem   385 100(L) 140(5)
Sec   AM Watt (0689) 51323
Pro   RS Fidler (0689) 56863
Holes   18 L 6369 yds SSS 70
Recs   Am–62 DC Smith
        Pro–65 H Baiocchi
V'trs   WD–HI WE/BH–M
Fees   £17.50
Loc   Orpington 5 miles

West Malling (1974)

Addington, nr Maidstone
Tel   (0732) 844785
Mem   550
Sec   MR Ellis

Pro   P Foston
Holes   Spitfire 18 L 6142 yds Par 70
        Hurricane 18 L 6240 yds Par 70
Recs   Am–70 R Parkhouse
        Pro–71 P Way
V'trs   WD–U WE–UH after 11.30am
Fees   £14 (£16)
Loc   A20 London Road

Westgate & Birchington (1893)

176, Canterbury Road, Westgate-on-
Sea CT8 8LT
Tel   (0843) 31115
Mem   325
Sec   JM Wood
Pro   R Game
Holes   18 L 4926 yds SSS 64
Recs   Am–60 Miss W Morgan
        Pro–60 J Hickman
V'trs   H or I WD–NA before 10am
        WE–NA before 12 noon
Fees   £10 (£12)
Loc   Westgate Station ¹⁄₄ mile

Whitstable & Seasalter (1910)

Collingwood Road, Whitstable
CT5 1EB
Tel   (0227) 272020
Mem   250
Sec   D Spratt (0227) 273589
Holes   18 L 5284 yds SSS 63
V'trs   WD–U WE–M
Fees   £10
Loc   Whitstable Station 1 mile

Wildernesse (1890)

Seal, Sevenoaks
Tel   (0732) 61526
Mem   750
Sec   M Blanford (0732) 61199
Pro   W Dawson (0732) 61527
Holes   18 L 6478 yds SSS 72
Recs   Am–66 P Benka, M Pinner
        Pro–65 I Grant
V'trs   WD–I H
Fees   £18.50 D–£27.50
Loc   2 miles E of Sevenoaks (A25)

Woodlands Manor (1928)

Woodlands, Sevenoaks TN15 6AB
Tel   (095 92) 3805
Mem   650
Sec   EF Newman, J Mills (095 92)
        3806
Pro   N Allen (095 92) 4161
Holes   18 L 5858 yds SSS 68
Recs   Pro–65 N Coles
V'trs   WD–U WE–H NA before noon
        SOC–WD
Fees   £9 (£15)
Loc   4 miles S of M25 Junction 3.
        Off A20 between W Kingsdown
        and Otford

For explanation of abbreviations, see page 460.

Wrotham Heath (1906)

Seven Mile Lane Comp, Sevenoaks
TN15 8QZ
Tel   (0732) 884800
Mem   200 70(L) 55(J) 50(5)
Sec   JD Majendie (0732) 883099
Pro   H Dearden (0732) 883854
Holes 9 L 5823 yds SSS 68
Recs   Am–66 R Sloman (1983)
V'trs   WD–H WE/BH–M SOC–Fri
Fees   £12 D–£15
Loc   8 miles W of Maidstone on
         B2106. M26/A20 Junction 1
         mile

Lancashire

Accrington & District (1893)

West End, Oswaldtwistle, Accrington
Tel   (0254) 32734
Mem   350
Sec   JE Pilkington (0254) 35070
Pro   W Harling (0254) 31091
Holes 18 L 5954 yds SSS 69
Recs   Am–64 J Rothwell
V'trs   WD/WE–U SOC
Fees   £8.50 (£11)

Alt (1975)

Public
Park Road, West Southport
Tel   (0704) 30435
Pro   W Fletcher (0704) 35268
Holes 18 L 5939 yds SSS 69
V'trs   U (Phone to book)
Fees   £2.40 (£3)
Loc   N of Marine Lake

Ashton & Lea (1913)

Tudor Ave, off Blackpool Rd,
Lea, nr Preston PR4 0XA
Tel   (0772) 726480
Mem   900
Sec   MG Gibbs (0772) 735282
Pro   P Laugher (0772) 720374
Holes 18 L 6289 yds SSS 70
Recs   Am–65 K Wallbank (1989)
         Pro–66 J Hawkesworth (1988)
V'trs   U SOC
Fees   £12.50 (£17)
Loc   3 miles W of Preston off A583

Bacup (1912)

Maden Road, Bacup OL13 8HY
Tel   (0706) 873170
Mem   395
Sec   J Garvey (0706) 874485
Holes 9 L 5656 yds SSS 67
Recs   Am–65 M Butcher
         Pro–67 H Higgins
V'trs   U
Fees   £6 (£7)
Loc   Bankside Lane

Baxenden & District (1913)

Top o' th'Meadow, Baxenden,
nr Accrington
Tel   (0254) 34555
Mem   250
Sec   L Howard (0706) 213394
Holes 9 L 5740 yds SSS 68
Recs   Am–67 JJ Walsh
         Pro–66 C Tobin
V'trs   U
Fees   £4 (£5)
Loc   2 miles SE of Accrington

Blackburn (1894)

Beardwood Brow, Blackburn BB2 7AX
Tel   (0254) 51122
Mem   420 110(L) 120(J)
Sec   PD Haydock
Pro   (0254) 66042
Holes 18 L 6100 yds SSS 70
Recs   Am–64 GH Readett
         Pro–66 M Foster
V'trs   U SOC–WD WE/BH–restricted
Fees   £12 (£15)
Loc   Blackburn

Blackpool North Shore (1904)

Devonshire Road, Blackpool FY2 0RD
Tel   (0253) 51017
Mem   820
Sec   DS Walker (0253) 52054
Pro   B Ward (0253) 54640
Holes 18 L 6443 yds SSS 71
Recs   Am–67 T Foster (1988)
         Pro–63 C O'Connor
V'trs   U SOC WE–restricted
Fees   £14 (£16)
Loc   ½ mile behind North prom

Blackpool Park (1925)

Public
North Park Drive, Blackpool FY3 8LS
Tel   (0253) 33960
Pro   B Purdie (0253) 31004
Holes 18 L 6192 yds SSS 69
Recs   Am–65 AV Moss
         Pro–68 D Lewis
V'trs   U
Fees   £4 (£5)
Loc   1½ miles E of centre,
         adjacent to Stanley Park

Burnley (1905)

Glen View, Burnley BB11 3RW
Tel   (0282) 21045
Mem   600
Sec   G Dean (0282) 24328
Pro   RM Cade (0282) 55266
Holes 18 L 5891 yds SSS 69
Recs   Am–65 ID Gradwell,
         L Samuels, DA Brown,
         GD Haworth
         Pro–66 JS Steer
V'trs   U SOC
Fees   £11 (£12)
Loc   From centre via Manchester
         Road to Glenview Road

Chorley (1898)

Hall o' th' Hill Heath, Charnock,
nr Chorley PR6 9HX
Tel   (0257) 480263
Mem   400
Sec   GA Birtill (025 72) 63024
Pro   P Wesselingh (0257) 481245
Holes 18 L 6277 yds SSS 70
Recs   Am–65 WG Bromilow
         Pro–66 M Hughes
V'trs   WD–I WE–by arrangement
         SOC
Fees   On application
Loc   1 mile S of Chorley

Clitheroe (1891)

Whalley Road, Clitheroe BB7 1PP
Tel   (0200) 22618
Mem   750 122(L) 68(J)
Sec   JB Kay (0200) 22292
Pro   P Geddes (0200) 24242
Holes 18 L 6045 yds SSS 71
Recs   Am–68 P Marlow, M Gray
V'trs   U
Fees   £15 (£18)
Loc   2 miles S of Clitheroe

Colne (1901)

Law Farm, Skipton Old Road, Colne
Tel   (0282) 863391
Mem   290
Holes 9 L 5961 yds SSS 69
Recs   Am–69 J Gallagher
V'trs   U exc comp days SOC
Fees   £8 (£10)
Loc   1½ miles N of Colne. From
         end of M65, signs to Keighley
         and Lothersdale

Darwen (1893)

Winter Hill, Darwen
Tel   (0254) 701287
Mem   360 70(L) 100(J) 40(5)
Sec   J Kenyon (0254) 581983
Pro   W Lennon (0254) 776370
Holes 18 L 5752 yds SSS 68
Recs   Am–66
         Pro–65
V'trs   U
Fees   £10 (£15)
Loc   Darwen 1½ miles

Dean Wood (1922)

Laford Lane, Up Holland,
Skelmersdale WN8 0QZ
Tel   (0695) 622980
Mem   850
Sec   J Walls (0695) 622219
Pro   AB Coop
Holes 18 L 6129 yds SSS 70
Recs   Am–66 D Dawber,
         JB Dickinson, D Parkin
         Pro–66 RA Morris
V'trs   WD–U WE/BH–M SOC
Fees   £13.50 (£17.50)
Loc   4 miles W of Wigan (A577)

Duxbury Park (1975)

Public
Duxbury Hall Road, Duxbury Park,
Chorley PR7 4AS
Tel   (025 72) 41634 (Clubhouse)
Pro   D Clarke (025 72) 65380
Holes   18 L 6270 yds SSS 70
Recs   Am–74 A Jones
            Pro–66 J Anglada
V'trs   U
Fees   £3 (£4)
Loc   1 1/2 miles S of Chorley off
            Wigan Lane

Fairhaven (1895)

Lytham Hall Park, Ansdell,
Lytham St Annes FY8 4JU
Mem   900
Sec   B Hartley (0253) 736741
Pro   (0253) 736976
Holes   18 L 6883 yds SSS 73
Recs   Am–65 SG Birtwell
            Pro–65 R Commans
V'trs   U SOC–WD WE–NA before
            9.30am
Fees   £15 (£20)
Loc   Lytham 2 miles. St Annes
            2 miles. M55 Junction 4

Fishwick Hall (1912)

Glenluce Drive, Farringdon Park,
Preston PR1 5TB
Tel   (0772) 798300
Mem   500
Sec   RR Gearing (0772) 796866
Pro   H Smith (0772) 795870
Holes   18 L 6028 yds SSS 69
Recs   Am–66 C Cross
V'trs   Apply to Sec SOC
Fees   £12 (£18)
Loc   1 mile E of Preston, nr junction
            of A59 and M6 Junction 31

Fleetwood (1932)

Golf House, Princes Way, Fleetwood
FY7 8AF
Tel   (039 17) 3114
Mem   548
Sec   K Volter (039 17) 3661
Pro   CT Burgess (039 17) 3661
Holes   L 18 L 6723 yds SSS 72
Recs   Am–69 JC Roberts
            Pro–70 S Bennett
V'trs   U SOC
Fees   £14 (£16)
Loc   1 mile W of Fleetwood

Great Harwood (1895)

Harwood Bar, Great Harwood
Tel   (0254) 884391
Mem   162 60(L) 30(J)
Sec   A Garraway (0254) 886802
Pro   K Caven (0254) 886728
Holes   9 L 6413 yds SSS 71
Recs   Am–68 J Aspinall
            Pro–64 AH Padgham

Vtrs   U
Fees   £7 (£8)
Loc   Nr Blackburn

Green Haworth (1914)

Green Haworth, Accrington
BB5 3SL
Tel   (0254) 37580
Mem   200
Sec   K Lynch
Holes   9 L 5470 yds SSS 67
Recs   Am–66 R Peters
V'trs   WD–U WE/BH–M SOC
            Ladies only after 5pm Wed
Fees   £5 (£6)
Loc   Willows Lane

Heysham (1910)

Trumacar Park, Middleton Road,
Heysham, Morecambe LA3 3JH
Tel   (0524) 51011
Mem   900
Sec   A Hesketh
Pro   R Williamson (0524) 52000
Holes   18 L 6224 yds SSS 70
Recs   Am–66 PW Coyle (1984),
            B Bielby, S Swinton (1988)
            Pro–64 H Clark (1978)
V'trs   U
Fees   £10 D–£13 (Sat £12 D–£16
            Sun £18)
Loc   Morecambe 2 miles. 5 miles
            from M6

Hindley Hall (1905)

Hall Lane, Hindley, Wigan
WN2 2SQ
Tel   (0942) 55131
Mem   430
Sec   R Bell (0942) 58356
Pro   S Yates (0942) 55991
Holes   18 L 5840 yds SSS 68
Recs   Am–63 JB Dickinson
            Pro–65
V'trs   I SOC
Fees   £13 (£18)
Loc   2 1/2 miles S of Wigan.
            M61 Junction 6

Ingol Golf & Squash Club (1983)

Tanterton Hall Road, Ingol, Preston
PR2 7BY
Tel   (0772) 734556
Mem   500
Sec   H Parker
Holes   18 L 6345 SSS 70
V'trs   U SOC
Fees   £8 (£10)
Loc   A6 1 1/2 miles NW of Preston.
            M6 Junction 32

Knott End (1911)

Wyreside, Knott End on Sea,
Blackpool FY6 0AA
Tel   (0253) 810254
Mem   660
Sec   C Desmond (0253) 810576

Pro   K Short (0253) 811365
Holes   18 L 5351 metres SSS 68
Recs   Am–66 DJ Martel
V'trs   WD–U WE/BH–by
            arrangement SOC–WD
Fees   £13 (£15)
Loc   Over Wyre, Knott End on Sea

Lancaster G & CC (1932)

Ashton Hall, Ashton–with–Stodday,
nr Lancaster LA2 0AJ
Tel   (0524) 752090
Mem   525 165(L) 125(J) 50(5)
Sec   Mrs J Hayhurst (0524) 751247
Pro   R Head (0524) 751802
Holes   18 L 6465 yds SSS 71
Recs   Am–66 M Brooks
V'trs   H (arrange with Sec or Pro)
Fees   £18
Loc   2 1/2 miles S of Lancaster
            on A588

Lansil (1947)

Caton Road, Lancaster LA1 3PD
Tel   (0524) 39269
Mem   310
Sec   FM Parker (0524) 67143
Holes   9 L 5608 yds SSS 67
Recs   Am–68 DC Whiteway
V'trs   WD–U WE–U after 1pm
Fees   £4 (£6)
Loc   A683, 2 miles E of
            Lancaster

Leyland (1924)

Wigan Road, Leyland
Tel   (0772) 421359
Mem   400
Sec   GD Copeman (0772) 436457
Pro   C Burgess (0772) 423425
Holes   18 L 6123 yds SSS 69
Recs   Am–66 G Norris
            Pro–66 D Screeton
V'trs   WD–U WE–M
Fees   £13
Loc   M6 Junction 28, 1 mile

Lobden (1888)

Whitworth, nr Rochdale
Tel   (0706) 343228
Mem   220
Sec   A Taylor (0706) 49000
Holes   9 L 5770 yds SSS 68
Recs   Am–67 C Turner
V'trs   U
Fees   £5 (£6.50)
Loc   4 miles N of Rochdale

Longridge (1877)

Fell Barn, Jeffrey Hill, Longridge,
nr Preston
Tel   (0772) 783291
Mem   400
Sec   J Greenwood (0772) 782765

Pro NS James (0772) 783291
Holes 18 L 5726 yds SSS 68
Recs Am–68 RP Wood
V'trs U
Fees £10 (£12)
Loc 8 miles NE of Preston
off B6243

Lytham (Green Drive) (1922)

Ballam Road, Lytham FY8 4LE
Tel (0253) 734782
Mem 700
Sec R Kershaw (0253) 737390
Pro I Howieson (0253) 737379
Holes 18 L 6159 yds SSS 69
Recs Am–64 C Rymer (1988)
Pro–64 E Romero (1988)
V'trs U H WE–NA SOC–WD
Fees £16.50 (£20)
Loc Lytham St Annes

Marsden Park (1969)

Public
Townhouse Road, Nelson BB9 8DG
Tel (0282) 67525
Pro N Brown
Holes 18 L 5806 yds SSS 68
Recs Am–66 MN Davies
Pro–74 T Gillett
V'trs U
Fees D–£3.85 (D–£4.95)
Loc Signposted Walton Lane,
Nelson

Morecambe (1904)

Bare, Morecambe LA4 6AJ
Tel (0524) 418050
Mem 1200
Sec Maj. BC Hodgson
(0524) 412841
Pro D Helmn (0524) 415596
Holes 18 L 5766 yds SSS 68
Recs Am–64 J Swallow, DP Carney
Pro–63 B Gallacher,
P Oosterhuis
V'trs U H SOC
Fees £10 (£14)
Loc On sea front

Nelson (1902)

Kings Causeway, Brierfield, Nelson
BB9 0EU
Tel (0282) 64583
Mem 500
Sec RW Baldwin
Pro R Geddes (0282) 67000
Holes 18 L 5967 yds SSS 69
Recs Am–65 S Duerden (1987),
N Uttley (1989)
Pro–68 H Shoesmith
V'trs WD–U exc Thurs pm SOC
WE–U exc Sat before 4pm
Fees £10 (£12)
Loc 2 miles N of Burnley

Ormskirk (1899)

Cranes Lane, Lathom, Ormskirk
L40 5UJ
Tel (0695) 572112
Mem 300
Sec PD Dromgoole (0695) 572227
Pro J Hammond (0695) 572074
Holes 18 L 6350 yds SSS 70
Recs Am–63 DJ Eccleston
Pro–67 MJ Slater
V'trs I Sat–NA SOC
Fees £20 (£25) Wed–£25
Loc 2 miles E of Ormskirk

Penwortham (1908)

Blundell Lane, Penwortham, Preston
PR1 0AX
Tel (0772) 743207
Mem 700
Sec J Parkinson (0772) 744630
Pro J Wright (0772) 742345
Holes 18 L 5915 yds SSS 68
Recs Am–62 A Gillespie
Pro–66 W Fletcher
V'trs WD–U WE–no parties
Fees £15 (£18)
Loc 1½ miles W of Preston

Pleasington (1890)

Nr Blackburn BB2 5JF
Tel (0254) 201028
Mem 442
Sec L Ingham (0254) 202177
Pro GJ Furey (0254) 201630
Holes 18 L 6445 yds SSS 71
Recs Am–64 SG Birtwell (1983)
Pro–66 S Holden (1988)
V'trs H
Fees £15 (£20)
Loc 3 miles W of Blackburn

Poulton-le-Fylde (1982)

Myrtle Farm, Breck Road, Poulton,
nr Blackpool
Tel (0253) 892444
Mem 250
Sec (0253) 893150
Holes 9 L 2979 yds SSS 69
Recs Am–74 D Barker (1986)
Pro–70 J Wraith (1985)
V'trs U
Fees £2.50 (£3.50)
Loc 3 miles E of Blackpool

Preston (1892)

Fulwood Hall Lane, Fulwood, Preston
PR2 4DD
Tel (0772) 794234 (Clubhouse)
(0772) 700436 (Steward)
Mem 800
Sec JB Dickinson (0772) 700011
Pro PA Wells (0772) 700022
Holes 18 L 6249 yds SSS 70
Recs Am–65 MA Holmes, J Wright
Pro–66 JM Hulme

Ormskirk continued

V'trs U H SOC–WD
Fees £15 D–£18 (£20)
Loc 1½ miles W of M6 Junction
32

Rishton (1925)

Eachill Links, Hawthorn Drive, Rishton
BB1 4HG
Tel (0254) 884442
Mem 250
Sec G Haworth (0254) 60226
(after 6pm)
Holes 9 L 6199 yds SSS 69
Recs Am–66 G Walmsley
Pro–70 G Furey
V'trs WD–U WE–M
Fees £6
Loc 3 miles E of Blackburn

Rossendale (1903)

Ewood Lane, Head Haslingden,
Rossendale BB4 6LH
Tel (0706) 213056
Mem 600
Sec WP Whittaker
(0706) 831339/216234
Pro SJ Nicholls (0706) 213616
Holes 18 L 6262 yds SSS 70
Recs Am–67 A Siddle
Pro–68 S Holden
V'trs WD/Sun–U Sat–M
Fees £11 (£14)
Loc 7 miles N of Bury near end
of M66 (Haslingden exit)

Royal Lytham & St Annes (1886)

Links Gate, Lytham St Annes
FY8 3LQ
Tel (0253) 724206
Mem 600
Sec Maj AS Craven (Retd)
Pro E Birchenough (0253) 720094
Holes 18 L 6673 yds SSS 73
Recs Am–66 R Foster, T Craddock
Pro–65 C O'Connor,
BGC Huggett, W Longmuir,
S Ballesteros
V'trs WD–I H
Fees £30 D–£40
Loc St Annes 1 mile

St Annes Old Links (1901)

Highbury Road, Lytham St Annes
FY8 2LD
Tel (0253) 723597
Mem 975
Sec DJM Hemsted
Pro GG Hardiman (0253) 722432
Holes 18 L 6647 yds SSS 72
Recs Am–66 RD Squire, AC Nash
Pro–66 AD Sowa, T Webber,
GL Parslow
V'trs WD–NA before 9.15am and
12–2pm WE/BH–arrange with
Sec SOC
Fees £20 (£23)
Loc Midway between St Annes
and Blackpool off A584

Shaw Hill G & CC

Whittle-le-Woods, Chorley
Tel   (025 72) 69221
Mem   500
Sec   F Wharton
Pro   I Evans (025 72) 79222
Holes   18 L 6467 yds SSS 71
Recs   Am–68 A Squires
        Pro–69 I Evans
V'trs   WD–U
Fees   £17 R/D
Loc   A6, 1 1/2 miles N of Chorley.
        M61 Junction 8. M6 Junction
        28

Silverdale (1906)

Red Bridge Lane, Silverdale, Carnforth
LA5 0SP
Tel   (0524) 701300
Mem   513
Sec   EF Wright (05395) 63782
Pro
Holes   9 L 5288 yds SSS 67
Recs   Am–66
V'trs   U exc Sun (Summer)–M
Fees   £6 (£10)
Loc   3 miles NW of Carnforth, by
        Silverdale station

Towneley (1932)

Public
Towneley Park, Todmorden Road,
Burnley
Tel   (0282) 51636
Pro   D Whittaker (0282) 38473
Holes   18 L 5840 yds SSS 68
        9 hole course
V'trs   U
Fees   £2.95 (£3.40)
Loc   1 1/2 miles E of Burnley

Turton (1907)

Woodend Farm, Bromley Cross,
nr Bolton
Tel   (0204) 852235
Mem   200 47(L) 31(J) 25(5)
Sec   D Jackson (0204) 594171
Holes   9 L 5805 yds SSS 68
Recs   Am–67 TD Bullough
V'trs   U Comp days–NA Sun–M
        before 10am
Fees   £6
Loc   3 1/2 miles N of Bolton

Whalley (1912)

Long Leese Barn, Clerkhill, Whalley,
nr Blackburn
Tel   (025 482) 2236
Mem   475
Sec   PC Burt (025 482) 2367
Pro   K Caven
Holes   9 L 5953 yds SSS 69
Recs   Am–67 G Richards
V'trs   WD/WE/BH–U exc Sat
        (Apr–Oct) SOC–WD
Fees   £5 (£8)
Loc   7 miles E of Blackburn

Wilpshire (1890)

72 Whalley Road, Wilpshire,
Blackburn BB1 9LF
Tel   (0254) 248260/249691
Mem   650
Pro   W Slaven (0254) 249558
Holes   18 L 5911 yds SSS 68
Recs   Am–64 H Green, MJ Savage
        Pro–61 J Hawkesworth
V'trs   WD–U WE/BH–on request
Fees   £13 (£17)
Loc   3 miles NE of Blackburn
        off A666

Leicestershire

Birstall (1901)

Station Road, Birstall, Leicester
Tel   (0533) 674450
Mem   350 86(L) 57(J)
Sec   Ms S Wells (0533) 674322
Pro   R Ball (0533) 675245
Holes   18 L 6203 yds SSS 70
Recs   Am–68 K Wells, NH Abel,
        D Hunter Walker
        Pro–67 L Platts
V'trs   Mon/Wed/Fri–I Other days–M
Fees   £15
Loc   3 miles N of Leicester

Charnwood Forest (1890)

Breakback Road, Woodhouse Eaves,
Loughborough LE12 8TA
Tel   (0509) 890259
Mem   300
Sec   AG Stanley (0509) 890588
Holes   9 L 5960 yds SSS 69
Recs   Am–65 G Wolstenholme (1987)
V'trs   H SOC
Fees   £12 (£15)
Loc   M1 Junction 23, 3 miles

Cosby (1895)

Chapel Lane, off Broughton Road,
Cosby, nr Leicester
Tel   (0533) 864759
Mem   650
Sec   MD Riddle (0533) 775597
Pro   D Bowring (0533) 848275
Holes   18 L 6277 yds SSS 70
V'trs   WD–U before 4pm WE/BH–M
        SOC–WD–H
Fees   £15
Loc   7 miles S of Leicester.
        1/4 mile S of Cosby

Enderby (1986)

Public
Mill Lane, Enderby, Leicester
Tel   (0533) 849388
Sec   LJ Speake (0533) 841133
Pro   C D'Araujo
Holes   9 L 4356 yds SSS 61
V'trs   U
Fees   18 holes–£2.25 (£2.75)
Loc   Enderby 2 miles. M2 Junction
        21/M69 Junction 1

Glen Gorse (1933)

Glen Road, Oadby, Leicester
LE2 4RF
Tel   (0533) 712226/714159
Mem   358 96(L) 65(J)
Sec   K McKay (0533) 714159
Pro   R Larratt (0533) 713748
Holes   18 L 6641 yds SSS 72
Recs   Am–68 IR Middleton, P Toon
        Pro–66 DT Steele
V'trs   WD–U WE/BH–M SOC–WD
Fees   £14
Loc   3 miles S of Leicester on A6

Hinckley (1983)

Leicester Road, Hinckley LE10 3DR
Tel   (0455) 615124
Mem   500
Sec   J Toon
Pro   R Jones (0455) 615014
Holes   18 L 6462 yds SSS 71
Recs   Pro–67 K Dickens (1987)
V'trs   WD–U WE–NA Sun after noon
        SOC
Fees   £15
Loc   NE of Hinckley on A47

Humberstone Heights (1978)

Public
Gipsy Lane, Leicester
Tel   (0533) 761905
Sec   S Day (0533) 674835
Pro   P Highfield (0533) 764674
Holes   18 L 6444 yds SSS 71
Recs   Am–69 D Butler (1987)
        Pro–67 R Adams (1985)
V'trs   U
Fees   £3.50 (£4.50)
Loc   3 miles E of Leicester off A47

Kibworth (1905)

Weir Road, Kibworth Beachamp,
Leicester LE8 0LP
Tel   (053 753) 792304
Mem   550
Sec   Mrs W Potter
Pro   A Strange (053 753) 792283
Holes   18 L 6282 yds SSS 70
Recs   Am–67 EE Feasey
        Pro–67 J Briars
V'trs   WD–U WE–M SOC
Fees   £12
Loc   9 miles SE of Leicester on A6

Kirby Muxloe (1910)

Station Road, Kirby Muxloe,
nr Leicester LE9 9EN
Tel   (0533) 393107
Mem   425
Sec   SF Aldwinckle (0533) 393457
Pro   RT Stephenson
        (0533) 392813
Holes   18 L 6303 yds SSS 70
Recs   Am–69 M Reay
        Pro–65 P Thomson

For explanation of abbreviations, see page 460.

V'trs	WD–U before 3.45pm exc
	Tues–NA SOC–H
Fees	£12.50 D–£15 (£12.50 with
	Captain's permission only)
Loc	3 miles W of Leicester

Leicestershire (1890)

Evington Lane, Leicester
LE5 6DJ

Tel	(0533) 736035
Mem	750
Sec	JL Adams (0533) 738825
Pro	JR Turnbull (0533) 736730
Holes	18 L 6330 yds SSS 70
Recs	Am–65 A Martinez,
	G Wolstenholme
	Pro–63 H Henning, I Mosey,
	S Sherratt
V'trs	U H SOC
Fees	£17 (£20)
Loc	2 miles E of Leicester

Lingdale (1967)

Joe Moores Lane, Woodhouse Eaves,
Loughborough

Tel	(0509) 890035
Mem	450
Sec	D Wardle
Pro	P Sellears (0509) 890684
Holes	9 L 6114 yds SSS 72
Recs	Am–71 DS Cameron
V'trs	U SOC
Fees	D–£9 (£12)
Loc	Loughborough 6 miles.
	4 miles from M1 Junction 23

Longcliffe (1905)

Nanpantan, Loughborough

Tel	(0509) 216321
Mem	550
Sec	G Harle (0509) 239129
Pro	I Bailey (0509) 231450
Holes	18 L 6551 yds SSS 71
Recs	Am–69 M Wilson
	Pro–68 M Reay
V'trs	WD–U WE–M
Fees	£17
Loc	Loughborough 2¹/₂ miles.
	M1 Junction 23

Luffenham Heath (1911)

Ketton, Stamford, Lincs PE9 3UU

Tel	(0780) 720205
Mem	555
Sec	IF Davenport
Pro	JA Lawrence (0780) 720298
Holes	18 L 6254 yds SSS 70
Recs	Am–66 RD Christian, E Lloyd
	Pro–67 PJ Butler, RL Moffitt
V'trs	U SOC–WD
Fees	£22 (£28)
Loc	5 miles W of Stamford on A6121

Lutterworth (1904)

Lutterworth, Leicester

Tel	(045 55) 2532
Mem	500
Sec	JC Bonfield
Pro	N Melvin

Holes	18 L 5570 yds SSS 67
Recs	Am–67 M Moore
	Pro–71 M Faulkner
V'trs	WD–U WE–M SOC
Fees	£10
Loc	¹/₄ mile M1. 4 miles M6

Market Harborough (1898)

Oxendon Road, Market Harborough

Tel	(0858) 63684
Mem	360
Sec	JNT Lord (0536) 771771
Pro	N Gilks
Holes	9 L 6080 yds SSS 69
Recs	Am–68 RC Gadd, W Sneath
	Pro–69 P Highfield, R Adams
V'trs	WD–U SOC
Fees	£18
Loc	1 mile S of M Harborough

Melton Mowbray (1925)

Waltham Rd, Thorpe Arnold,
Melton Mowbray

Tel	(0664) 62118
Mem	380
Sec	Mrs TD Hudson (0664) 78312
Holes	9 L 6200 yds SSS 70
Recs	Am–65 N Street (1985)
	Pro–66 W Hill
V'trs	U before 3pm –M after 3pm
Fees	£9 (£12)
Loc	2 miles NE of Melton Mowbray

Oadby (1974)

Public
Leicester Road Racecourse, Oadby,
Leicester LE2 4AB

Tel	(0533) 700326/700215
Pro	S Ward (0533) 709052
Holes	18 L 6228 yds SSS 69
Recs	Am–65 S Davis (1988)
	Pro–73 C O'Connor Jr
V'trs	U SOC–WD
Fees	£3 (£4)
Loc	2 miles S of Leicester

RAF North Luffenham (1975)

RAF North Luffenham, Oakham
LE15 8RL

Tel	(0780) 720041 (Ext 273/240)
Mem	229 62(L) 25(J)
Sec	CJ Sheffield (Ext 273)
Holes	9 L 6006 yds SSS 69
Recs	Am–72 KP Hickman
V'trs	M
Fees	£4.50 (£5.50)
Loc	RAF N Luffenham, ¹/₂ mile
	from S shore of Rutland
	Water

Rothley Park (1911)

Westfield Lane, Rothley, Leicester
LE7 7LH

Tel	(0533) 302019
Sec	BS Durham (0533) 302809
Pro	PJ Dolan (0533) 303023

Holes	18 L 6487 yds SSS 71
Recs	Am–67 EE Feasey
	Pro–68 PJ Dolan
V'trs	U
Fees	£20 (£25)
Loc	6 miles N of Leicester, W of A6

Scraptoft (1928)

Beeby Road, Scraptoft, Leicester
LE7 9SJ

Tel	(0533) 419000
Mem	500
Sec	T White (0533) 418863
Pro	S Sherratt (0533) 419138
Holes	18 L 6166 yds SSS 70
Recs	Am–66 D Gibson, CM Harries
	Pro–A Bownes
V'trs	WD–U WE–M SOC–WD
Fees	£12 (£16)
Loc	3 miles E of Leicester

Ullesthorpe Court (1976)

Frolesworth Road, Ullesthorpe,
Lutterworth

Tel	(0455) 209023
Mem	600
Sec	PE Woolley
Pro	N Warburton (0455) 209150
Holes	18 L 6540 yds SSS
Recs	Am–69 M Manship (1989)
	Pro–68
V'trs	U SOC–WD
Fees	£11.50
Loc	3 miles NW of Lutterworth

Western Park (1920)

Public
Scudamore Road, Leicester
LE3 1UQ

Tel	(0533) 872339/876158
Pro	BN Whipham (0533) 872339
Holes	18 L 6532 yds SSS 71
V'trs	U
Fees	£3.50 (£4.50)
Loc	4 miles W of Leicester

Whetstone (1965)

Cambridge Road, Cosby, Leicester
LE9 5SH

Tel	(0533) 861424
Mem	500
Sec	B Bywater
Pro	N Leatherland
Holes	18 L 5700 yds SSS 69
V'trs	U
Fees	£6 (£7.50)
Loc	S boundary of Leicester

Willesley Park (1921)

Measham Road, Ashby-de-la-Zouch
LE6 5PF

Tel	(0530) 411532
Mem	600 99(L) 38(J)
Sec	NH Jones (0530) 414596
Pro	C Hancock (0530) 414820
Holes	18 L 6310 yds SSS 70
Recs	Am–66 G Wolstenholme
	Pro–65 L Jones

V'trs WD–H WE/BH–H after 9.30am
       SOC
Fees   £20 (£25)
Loc   2 miles S of Ashby on B5006.
       M1 Junctions 22/23/24.
       A42(M) Junction 10

Lincolnshire

Belton Park (1890)

Belton Lane, Londonthorpe Road,
Grantham NG31 9SH
Tel   (0476) 63355
Mem   950
Sec   T Measures (Mgr)
       (0476) 67399
Pro   B McKee (0476) 63911
Holes 27 Brownlow L 6412 yds
       SSS 71; Ancaster L 6109 yds
       SSS 69; Belmont L 5857 yds
       SSS 68
Recs   Am–69 DF Price
       Pro–65 S Bennett
V'trs U SOC–WD 9.30am–12.30pm
       and 2–5pm
Fees   18 holes £13 (£16)
       27/36 holes £18 (£20)
Loc   Grantham 2 miles

Blankney (1903)

Blankney, Lincoln
Tel   (0526) 20263
Mem   400 100(L) 60(J) 100(5)
Sec   BH Clipsham
Pro   G Bradley (0526) 20202
Holes 18 L 6402 yds SSS 71
Recs   Am–68
       Pro–69
V'trs WD–U WE–M SOC
Fees   £12 D–£16 (£20)
Loc   10 miles SE of Lincoln on
       B1188

Boston (1962)

Cowbridge, Horncastle Road, Boston
PE22 7EL
Tel   (0205) 62306
Mem   650 112(L) 43(J)
Sec   DE Smith (0205) 350589
Pro   TR Squires
Holes 18 L 5825 yds SSS 68
Recs   Am–67 SG Wood
       Pro–64 S Edwards (1989)
V'trs U
Fees   £10 (£15)
Loc   2 miles N of Boston on B1183

Burghley Park (1890)

St Martin's, Stamford PE9 3JX
Tel   (0780) 53789
Mem   500 80(L) 80(J) 200(5)
Sec   PH Mulligan
Pro   G Davies (0780) 62100
Holes 18 L 6133 yds SSS 69
Recs   Am–65 PG Barker
       Pro–70 B Thomson
V'trs WD–I or H WE/BH–M SOC

Fees   £15
Loc   1 mile S of Stamford, off A1
       at roundabout

Canwick Park (1893)

Canwick Park, Washingborough
Road, Lincoln
Tel   (0522) 22166
Mem   500
Sec   M Hodgkinson (0526) 398978
Pro   S Williamson (0522) 536870
Holes 18 L 6257 yds SSS 70
Recs   Am–66 J Shelton
V'trs WD–U WE–M
Fees   £8 (£12)
Loc   1 mile S of Lincoln

Carholme (1906)

Lincoln
Tel   (0522) 36811
Mem   550
Sec   BW Robinson (0522) 751580
Pro   G Leslie (0522) 33263
Holes 18 L 6086 yds SSS 69
Recs   Am–69 R Taylor
V'trs U (exc Sun)
Fees   On application
Loc   Lincoln 1 mile

Elsham (1900)

Barton Road, Elsham, nr Brigg
DN20 0LS
Tel   (0652) 688382
Mem   600
Sec   HG Markham (0652) 680291
Pro   R McKiernan (0652) 680432
Holes 18 L 6411 yds SSS 71
Recs   Am–72 A Shepherd
       Pro–69 MT Hoyle
V'trs WE–M SOC–WD
Fees   £15
Loc   Off M180 nr Brigg

Gainsborough (1900)

Thonock, Gainsborough DN21 1PZ
Tel   (0427) 613088
Mem   470
Sec   DJ Garrison (Mgr)
Pro   G Stafford
Holes 18 L 6527 yds SSS 71
Recs   Am–66
V'trs U H WE/BH–M SOC–WD
Fees   £12 D–£14
Loc   Gainsborough
Mis   Floodlit driving range

Lincoln (1891)

Lincoln
Tel   (042 771) 210
Mem   600
Sec   D Boag (042 771) 721
Pro   A Carter (042 771) 273
Holes 18 L 6400 yds SSS 70
Recs   Am–66 A Thain, P Taylor
       Pro–65 M James
V'trs H WE–by appointment
Fees   £14 D–£18 (£14 D–£18)
Loc   12 miles W of Lincoln

Louth (1965)

Crowtree Lane, Louth LN11 9LJ
Tel   (0507) 603664
Mem   900
Sec   Maj E Coombes (0507) 603681
Pro   AJ Blundell (0507) 604648
Holes 18 L 6477 yds SSS 71
Recs   Am–70 A Murray (1985),
       L Johnson (1986)
       Pro–69 C Hall (1989)
V'trs U SOC–WD
Fees   £10 D–£12 (£12 D–£14)
Loc   Louth 1/2 mile

Market Rasen (1922)

Legsby Road, Market Rasen
LN8 3DZ
Tel   (0673) 842416
Mem   550
Sec   E Hill (0673) 842319
Pro   AM Chester
Holes 18 L 6043 yds SSS 69
Recs   Am–66 C Osbourne (1985)
       Pro–65 S Bennett (1989)
V'trs WD–I WE/BH–M SOC
Fees   £10 D–£15
Loc   1 mile E of Market Rasen

Millfield (1985)

Laughterton, Lincoln
Tel   (042 771) 255
Sec   A Hunter
Pro   P Lester
Holes 18 L 5583 yds SSS 67
Fees   £3 R/D
Loc   12 miles W of Lincoln
Mis   Inland links course

North Shore (1910)

North Shore Road, Skegness
PE25 1DN
Tel   (0754) 3298
Mem   525
Sec   RC Sykes (0754) 67280
Pro   J Cornelius (0754) 4822
Holes 18 L 6134 yds SSS 69
Recs   Am–71 G Hunter (1989)
V'trs H SOC–WD
Fees   £17 (£22)
Loc   1 mile N of Skegness

RAF Waddington

Waddington, Lincoln LN5 9NB
Tel   (0522) 720271
Mem   45
Sec   Cpl JDT Richardson (Ext 244)
Holes 18 L 5223 yds SSS 66
Recs   Am–68 T Graham (1987)
V'trs By prior arrangement
Fees   £2
Loc   A607 Lincoln–Grantham

Sandilands (1900)

Sandilands, Sutton-on-Sea LN12 2RJ
Tel   (0521) 41432
Mem   400
Sec   D Mumby (0521) 41617
Pro   D Vernon (0521) 41600

For explanation of abbreviations, see page 460.

Holes	18 L 5995 yds SSS 69
Recs	Am–66 JR Payne
	Pro–63 FG Allott
V'trs	U SOC
Fees	£8 D–£10 (£10 D–£12)
Loc	1 mile S of Sutton-on-Sea off A52

Seacroft (1895)

	Seacroft, Skegness PE25 3AU
Tel	(0754) 3020
Mem	340 190(L) 90(J)
Sec	HK Brader
Pro	R Lawie (0754) 69624
Holes	18 L 6478 yds SSS 71
Recs	Am–64 TH Bowman
	Pro–67 J Heib (1988)
V'trs	WD–U WE–XL before 11am
Fees	£15 (£20)
Loc	S boundary of Skegness

Sleaford (1905)

	South Rauceby, Sleaford NG34 8PL
Tel	(052 98) 273
Mem	650
Sec	DBR Harris (0529) 303535
Pro	SD Harrison (052 98) 644
Holes	18 L 6443 yds SSS 71
Recs	Am–65 A Hare (1988)
	Pro–
V'trs	U H SOC–WD
Fees	£12 (£20)
Loc	1 mile W of Sleaford on A153

Spalding (1922)

	Surfleet, Spalding PE11 4DG
Tel	(077 585) 234
Sec	WE Codling (077 585) 386
Pro	J Spencer (077 585) 474
Holes	18 L 5807 yds SSS 68
Recs	Am–65 G Palmer
	Pro–65 J Spencer
V'trs	U H SOC–Thurs
Fees	On application
Loc	4 miles N of Spalding off A16

Stoke Rochford (1924)

	Great North Rd, nr Grantham
Tel	(047 683) 275
Mem	515
Sec	JM Butler
Pro	A Dow (047 683) 218
Holes	18 L 6204 yds SSS 70
Recs	Am–64 A Hare, J Payne, M Wilson
	Pro–65 A Dow
V'trs	WE–U after 10.30am
Fees	On application
Loc	6 miles S of Grantham, at service station on A1

Sutton Bridge (1914)

	New Road, Sutton Bridge
Tel	(0406) 350323
Mem	340
Sec	KC Buckle (0945) 870455
Pro	To be appointed

Holes	9 L 5804 yds SSS 68
Recs	Pro–62 CJ Norton
V'trs	WD–H WE–NA
Fees	£12
Loc	Wisbech 8 miles

Woodhall Spa (1905)

	Woodhall Spa LN10 6PU
Tel	(0526) 52511
Mem	450
Sec	SR Sharp
Pro	P Fixter
Holes	18 L 6866 yds SSS 73
Recs	Am–68 FW Wood
	Pro–68 EB Williamson
V'trs	U–booking essential SOC
Fees	£12 (£14.50)
Loc	19 miles SE of Lincoln

Woodthorpe Hall (1986)

	Woodthorpe, Alford LN13 0DD
Tel	(0507) 450294
Mem	210
Sec	PC Bell (Hon)
Holes	9 L 1990 yds SSS 59
V'trs	U
Fees	D–£4.50
Loc	3½ miles from Alford off B1371

Manchester (Greater)

Altrincham Municipal

	Public
	Stockport Road, Timperley, Altrincham
Tel	(061) 928 0761
Pro	R West
Holes	18 L 6204 yds SSS 69
Recs	Am–67
	Pro–67
V'trs	U
Fees	£3 (£4.50)
Loc	9 miles SW of Manchester

Ashton-on-Mersey (1898)

	Church Lane, Sale, Cheshire M33 5QQ
Tel	(061) 973 3220
Mem	180 70(L) 40(J) 60(5)
Sec	AH Marsland
Pro	MJ Williams (061) 962 3727
Holes	9 L 3073 yds SSS 69
Recs	Am–68 B Armitage, M Gleave
	Pro–67 R Williamson, D Cooper
V'trs	WD–U (exc Tues after 5pm & Wed before 5pm) WE–M
Fees	£8
Loc	5 miles W of Manchester

Ashton-under-Lyne (1913)

	Gorsey Way, Hurst, Ashton-under-Lyne
Tel	(061) 330 1537
Mem	450

Sec	G Musgrave (061) 339 8655
Pro	C Boyle (061) 308 2095
Holes	18 L 6209 yds SSS 70
V'trs	WD–U WE/BH–M SOC
Fees	£11
Loc	8 miles E of Manchester

Beacon Park (1982)

	Public
	Beacon Lane, Dalton, Up Holland, Wigan WN8 7RU
Tel	(0695) 622700
Sec	JC McIlroy (Hon)
Pro	R Peters
Holes	18 L 5927 yds SSS 69
Recs	Am–68 D Parkin, I Donaldson
V'trs	U
Fees	£2.95 (£3.95)
Loc	Nr Ashurst Beacon and M58/M6
Mis	Beacon Club plays here

Blackley (1907)

	Victoria Avenue, East Manchester M9 2HW
Tel	(061) 643 2980
Mem	500
Sec	CB Leggott (061) 643 4116
Pro	M Barton (061) 643 3912
Holes	18 L 6235 yds SSS 70
Recs	Am–65 D Royle
	Pro–66 J Nixon
V'trs	WD–U WE–M
Fees	£8
Loc	N Manchester area

Bolton (1912)

	Lostock Park, Bolton BL6 4AJ
Tel	(0204) 43278
Mem	600
Sec	H Cook (0204) 43067
Pro	R Longworth (0204) 43073
Holes	18 L 6215 yds SSS 70
Recs	Am–66 JB Hope, DE Roocroft
	Pro–67 WSM Rooke
V'trs	U SOC
Fees	Mon/Tues & Thurs/Fri–£15 Wed/WE/BH–£20
Loc	3½ miles W of Bolton. M61 Horwich exit 1½ miles

Bolton Municipal (1931)

	Public
	Links Road, Chorley New Road, Bolton BL6 4AF
Tel	(0204) 42336
Pro	AK Holland
Holes	18 L 6012 yds SSS 69
Recs	Am–67 PK Abbott
	Pro–68 L Alamby
V'trs	U SOC–WD
Fees	£3 (£4)
Loc	A673, 3 miles W of Bolton. M61 Junction 6
Mis	Regent Park Club plays here

Bolton Old Links (1898)

Chorley Old Road, Montserrat, Bolton
BL1 5SU
Tel   (0204) 40050
Mem   650
Sec   E Monaghan (0204) 42307
Pro   P Horridge (0204) 43089
Holes 18 L 6406 yds SSS 72
Recs   Am–66 L Mooney (1981)
       Pro–65 I Spencer (1989)
V'trs   U H exc comp Sats SOC
Fees   £15 (£20)
Loc   3 miles NW of Bolton on
       B6226

Brackley Municipal (1977)

Public
Bullows Road, Little Hulton
Tel   (061) 790 6076
Pro   K Bates
Holes 9 L 3003 yds SSS 69
V'trs   U
Fees   £2.30 (£3) 9 holes
Loc   Walkden 2 miles off A6

Bramall Park (1894)

20 Manor Road, Bramhall, Stockport
SK7 6NW
Tel   (061) 485 3119
Mem   715
Sec   JC O'Shea
Pro   RL Johnson (061) 485 2205
Holes 18 L 6214 yds SSS 70
Recs   Am–68 B Steele
V'trs   I
Fees   £15 (£20)
Loc   8 miles S of Manchester.
       A6 to Bramhall Lane A5102.
       Turn right at Carrwood
       Road

Breightmet (1911)

Red Bridge, Ainsworth, nr Bolton
Tel   (0204) 27381
Mem   200
Sec   R Weir
Holes 9 L 6416 yds SSS 71
Recs   Am–69 G Stanley (1982)
       Pro–68 P Alliss (1971)
V'trs   WE–NA SOC–WD
Fees   £8 (£10)
Loc   3 miles on Bury side

Brookdale (1905)

Woodhouses, Failsworth
Tel   (061) 681 4534
Mem   650
Sec   G Glass (061) 681 8996
Pro   P Devalle (061) 681 2655
Holes 18 L 6040 yds SSS 68
Recs   Am–65 G Lever
V'trs   U SOC–WD
Fees   £8 (£12)
Loc   5 miles N of Manchester

Bury (1890)

Unsworth Hall, Blackford Bridge,
Bury BL9 9TJ
Tel   (061) 766 2213
Mem   410
Sec   JP Meikle
Pro   M Peel
Holes 18 L 5961 yds SSS 69
Recs   Am–66 PD Hilton
       Pro–PWT Evans
V'trs   U SOC
Fees   £12 (£15)
Loc   A56, 5 miles N of Manchester.
       3 miles N of M62 Junction 17

Castle Hawk (1975)

Heywood Road, Castleton, Rochdale
Tel   (0706) 40841
Mem   200
Sec   A Kershaw
Pro   K Caven
Holes 27 L 3160 yds SSS 55
Recs   Am–57 R Baker
       Pro–56 G Bond
V'trs   U SOC
Fees   £3 (£4)
Loc   Castleton Station 1 mile

Cheadle (1885)

Shiers Drive, Cheadle SK8 1HW
Tel   (061) 428 2160
Mem   350
Sec   PP Webster (061) 485 4540
Pro   NR Harding (061) 428 9878
Holes 9 L 5006 yds SSS 65
Recs   Am–62 RP Bullock, PR Shortt
       Pro–63 F Memmott
V'trs   H I M NA–Tues & Sat SOC
Fees   D–£8 (£10)
Loc   1 mile S of Cheadle

Chorlton-cum-Hardy (1903)

Barlow Hall, Manchester M21 2JJ
Tel   (061) 881 3139
Mem   350
Sec   FE Collis (061) 881 5830
Pro   D Screeton (061) 881 9911
Holes 18 L 6003 metres SSS 69
Recs   Am–63 JR Berry
       Pro–65 FS Boobyer
V'trs   U SOC
Fees   £12 (£15)
Loc   4 miles S of Manchester
       A5103/A5145

Crompton & Royton (1913)

High Barn, Royton, Oldham OL2 6RW
Tel   (061) 624 2154
Mem   620
Sec   T Donovan (061) 624 0986
Pro   DA Melling
Holes 18 L 6212 yds SSS 70
Recs   Am–65 JA Osbaldeston
       Pro–65 D Durnian
V'trs   U SOC–WD
Fees   £9 (£12)
Loc   Oldham 3 miles

Davenport (1913)

Middlewood Road, Poynton, Stockport
Tel   (0636) 877321
Mem   600
Sec   TD Swindells (0625) 876951
Pro   W Harris (0625) 877319
Holes 18 L 6066 yds SSS 69
Recs   Am–68 C Banfield
       Pro–67 B Evans
V'trs   U (exc Sat–NA)
Fees   £12 (£18)
Loc   5 miles S of Stockport

Davyhulme Park (1910)

Gleneagles Road, Davyhulme,
Manchester M31 2SA
Tel   (061) 748 2856
Mem   600
Sec   EW Travis (061) 748 2260
Pro   H Lewis (061) 748 3931
Holes 18 L 6237 yds SSS 70
Recs   Am–67 TF Sharp, B Connor
       Pro–68 KG Geddes, D Rees
V'trs   U Comp days–M after 3pm
       SOC
Fees   £9.50 (£11.50)
Loc   7 miles SW of Manchester

Deane (1906)

Off Junction Road, Deane, Bolton
BL3 4NB
Tel   (0204) 61944
Mem   300
Sec   P Flaxman (0204) 651808
Pro   D Martindale
Holes 18 L 5583 yds SSS 67
Recs   Am–62 N Hazzleton
V'trs   WD–U WE–Restricted
Fees   £10
Loc   2 miles W of Bolton

Denton (1909)

Manchester Road, Denton M34 2NU
Tel   (061) 336 3218
Mem   520
Sec   R Wickham
Pro   R Vere (061) 336 2070
Holes 18 L 6290 yds SSS 70
Recs   Pro–68 D Cooper, S Scanlon,
       D Durnian
V'trs   WD–U WE/BH–M SOC
Fees   £7
Loc   5 miles SE of Manchester

Didsbury (1891)

Ford Lane, Northenden, Manchester
M22 4NQ
Tel   (061) 998 9278
Mem   776
Sec   B Hughes (Sec/Mgr)
Pro   P Barber (061) 998 2811
Holes 18 L 6273 yds SSS 70
Recs   Am–65 RI Walker
V'trs   WD–UH after 10am WE–M
Fees   £10 (£12)
Loc   6 miles S of Manchester

For explanation of abbreviations, see page 460.

Disley (1889)

Stanley Hall Lane, Disley, Stockport
Tel   (0663) 62071
Mem 600
Sec   JA Lomas (Hon)
Pro   AG Esplin (0663) 62884
Holes 18 L 6015 yds SSS 69
Recs Am–68 A Peck
      Pro–63 B Charles
V'trs Wed–Fri/BH–NA
Fees £10 (£12)
Loc   6 miles S of Stockport

Dukinfield (1913)

Yew Tree Lane, Dukinfield
Tel   (061) 338 2340
Mem 199 46(L) 27(J)
Sec   KP Parker (061) 338 2669
Holes 16 L 5544 yds SSS 67
Recs Am–69 S Woolley
V'trs WD–U exc Wed WE–M
Fees £6
Loc   6 miles E of Manchester

Dunham Forest G & CC (1961)

Oldfield Lane, Altrincham
WA14 4TY
Tel   (061) 928 2605
Mem 600
Sec   Mrs S Klaus
Pro   I Wrigley (061) 928 2727
Holes 18 L 6636 yds SSS 72
V'trs WD–U WE/BH–M SOC exc
      12.45–1.45pm
Fees £16 (£20)
Loc   1 mile SW of Altrincham

Dunscar (1908)

Longworth Lane, Bromley Cross,
Bolton BL7 9QY
Tel   (0204) 53321
Mem 420
Sec   TM Yates (0204) 51090
Pro   G Treadgold (0204) 592992
Holes 18 L 5968 yds SSS 69
Recs Am–64 JW Smethurst
      Pro–66 W Slater
V'trs U WE–Restricted
Fees £12.50 (£15)
Loc   3 miles N of Bolton off
      A666

Ellesmere (1913)

Old Clough Lane, Worsley,
nr Manchester M28 5HZ
Tel   (061) 790 2122
Mem 330 80(L) 75(J) 50(5)
Sec   AC Kay (061) 790 7108
Pro   J Pennington (061) 790 8591
Holes 18 L 5957 yds SSS 69
Recs Am–67 JA Pugh
      Pro–66 G Weir
V'trs U exc comp days (recognised
      club members, check first with
      Pro) SOC–WD

Fees £9 (£12)
Loc   6 miles W of Manchester, nr
      junction of M62/A580

Fairfield Golf & Sailing Club (1892)

Booth Road, Audenshaw, Manchester
M34 5GA
Tel   (061) 370 1641
Mem 550
Sec   J Humphries (061) 336 3950
Pro   DM Butler (061) 370 2292
Holes 18 L 5664 yds SSS 68
Recs Am–65 PW Wrigley,
      ARS Pownell
V'trs U SOC–WD
Fees £9 (£10)
Loc   East boundary A635

Flixton (1893)

Church Road, Flixton, Manchester
Tel   (061) 748 2116
Mem 400
Sec   JG Frankland (061) 747 0296
Pro   N Rothe
Holes 9 L 6410 yds SSS 71
Recs Am–63 MJ Wallwork (1988)
      Pro–65 P Reeves (1985)
V'trs U WE/BH–M
Fees £10
Loc   6 miles SW of Manchester on
      B5213

Gathurst (1913)

Miles Lane, Shevington, nr Wigan
WN6 8EW
Tel   (025 75) 2861
Mem 300
Sec   J Clarke (025 75) 2432
Pro   D Clarke (025 75) 4909
Holes 9 L 6308 yds SSS 70
Recs Am–67 S Ainscough
      Pro–66 D Clarke
V'trs WD–U before 5pm
      WE/BH/Wed–M SOC–WD
Fees £10
Loc   4 miles W of Wigan.
      1 mile S of M6 Junction 27

Gatley (1911)

Waterfall Farm, Styal Road,
Heald Green, Cheadle SK8 3TW
Tel   (061) 437 2091
Mem 400
Sec   WW Tibbitts (061) 485 2943
Pro   M Proffitt (061) 436 2830
Holes 9 L 5934 yds SSS 68
Recs Am–62 M Hoyland
      Pro–63 C Timperley
V'trs WE/Tues–NA Other days–by
      prior arrangement with Sec
Fees £10
Loc   7 miles S of Manchester.
      Manchester Airport 2 miles

Great Lever & Farnworth

Lever Edge Lane, Bolton
Tel   (0204) 62582
Mem 470
Sec   PJ Holt (0204) 72550
Holes 18 L 5859 yds SSS 69
Recs Am–67 D Barr
      Pro–65 SC Evans
V'trs U
Fees £9 (£12.50)
Loc   Bolton 1½ miles

Greenmount (1920)

Greenmount, nr Bury
Tel   (020 488) 3712
Mem 180
Sec   HI Billingham (020 488)
      3401
Holes 9 L 4920 yds SSS 64
Recs Am–62 G Dalziel
V'trs WD–U exc Tues WE–M
Fees £6
Loc   3 miles N of Bury

Haigh Hall (1972)

Public
Haigh Hall Country Park, Haigh, Wigan
WN2 1PE
Tel   (0942) 833337 (Clubhouse)
Pro   I Lee (0942) 831107
Holes 18 L 6423 yds SSS 71
Recs Am–67 J Silcock (1987)
      Pro–66 K Waters (1988)
V'trs U
Fees £3 (£5)
Loc   3 miles NW of Wigan

Hale (1903)

Rappax Road, Hale WA15 0NU
Tel   (061) 980 4225
Mem 300
Sec   RV Nichols
Holes 9 L 5780 yds SSS 68
Recs Pro–65 D Durnian
V'trs WD–U exc Thurs–NA before
      5pm SOC WE/BH–M
Fees £10
Loc   2 miles SE of Altrincham

Harwood (1926)

"Springfield", Roading Brook Road,
Bolton BL2 5HT
Tel   (0204) 22878
Mem 360
Sec   D Bamber (0204) 22878
Pro   MW Evans (0204) 398472
Holes 9 L 5960 yds SSS 69
Recs Am–67 PM Lay, N Stirling
V'trs WD–U WE–M SOC
Fees £10
Loc   Harwood, 4 miles NE of
      Bolton

Hazel Grove (1912)

Club House, Hazel Grove,
nr Stockport SK7 6LU
Tel   (061) 483 3217
Mem   550
Sec   HAG Carlisle (061) 483 3978
Pro   ME Hill (061) 483 7272
Holes   18 L 6300 yds SSS 70
Recs   Am–67 A Hill
        Pro–67 M Slater
V'trs   U
Fees   £15 (£20)
Loc   3 miles S of Stockport

Heaton Moor (1892)

Heaton Mersey, Stockport
Tel   (061) 432 2134
Mem   350
Sec   AA Gibbon (061) 432 6458
Pro   CR Loydall (061) 432 0846
Holes   18 L 5876 yds SSS 68
Recs   Am–66 D Howorth
        Pro–66 D Cooper
V'trs   U
Fees   £10 (£14)
Loc   Greater Manchester

Heaton Park (1912)

Public
Heaton Park, Prestwich, Manchester
M25 5SW
Tel   (061) 798 0295
Pro   J Pennington
Holes   18 L 5849 yds SSS 68
Recs   Am–66 J Griffiths (1986),
        S Pilling (1988)
        Pro–65 AP Thomson, B Evans,
        I Collins, M Gray
V'trs   U
Fees   £4 (£6)
Loc   N Manchester via M62 and
        M66 to Middleton Road

Horwich (1895)

Victoria Road, Horwich BL6 5PH
Tel   (0204) 696980
Mem   180
Sec   GR Sharp (0204) 696298
Holes   9 L 5404 yds SSS 67
Recs   Am–65 M Derbyshire
V'trs   M SOC–WD
Loc   5 miles W of Bolton

Houldsworth (Levenshulme) (1910)

Wingate House, Higher Levenshulme,
Manchester M19 3JW
Tel   (061) 224 5055
Mem   300
Sec   JB Hogg (061) 336 5044
Pro   David Naylor (061) 224 4571
Holes   18 L 6078 yds SSS 69
Recs   Am–67 R Arnold
        Pro–63 D Vaughan
V'trs   U SOC
Fees   £6 (£8)
Loc   4 miles S of Manchester

Leigh (1906)

Kenyon Hall, Culcheth, Warrington
WA3 4BG
Tel   (092 576) 3130
Mem   700
Sec   GD Riley (092 576) 2943
Pro   A Baguley (092 576) 2013
Holes   18 L 5853 yds SSS 68
Recs   Am–64 J Critchely
        Pro–67 D Coles
V'trs   U H SOC
Fees   £11 (£16)
Loc   At Culcheth

Lowes Park (1914)

Hill Top, Walmersley, Bury BL9 6SU
Tel   (061) 764 1231
Mem   250
Sec   E Brierley (0706) 67331
Holes   9 L 6043 yds SSS 69
Recs   Am–69 MJ Bailey (1984)
V'trs   WD–U exc Wed–NA Sat comp
        days–NA Sun–by appointment
        only
Fees   WD–£7 Sun–£8
Loc   2 miles NE of Bury off
        A56

Manchester GC Ltd (1882)

Hopwood Cottage, Rochdale Road,
Middleton, Manchester M24 2QP
Tel   (061) 643 2718
Mem   600
Sec   KG Flett (061) 643 3202
Pro   B Conner (061) 643 2638
Holes   18 L 6450 yds SSS 72
Recs   Am–66 RE Tattersall,
        M Russell
        Pro–65 I Mosey, D Cooper
V'trs   WD–H WE–NA
Fees   £13
Loc   7 miles N of Manchester.
        M62 Junction 20

Marple (1892)

Hawk Green, Marple, Stockport
Tel   (061) 427 2311
Mem   300 70(L) 60(J) 30(5)
Sec   M Gilbert (061) 427 6364
Pro   I Scott (061) 449 0690
Holes   18 L 5506 yds SSS 67
Recs   Am–66 T Christie (1984)
V'trs   WD–U exc Thurs–NA
        WE/BH–M SOC
Fees   £7.50
Loc   2 miles from High Lane North
        off A6

Mellor & Townscliffe (1894)

Tarden, Gibb Lane, Mellor,
nr Stockport SK6 5NA
Tel   (061) 427 2208
Mem   470
Sec   K Bounds
Pro   MJ Williams (061) 427 5759
Holes   18 L 5939 yds SSS 69

Recs   Am–67 CW Axon, MG Senior,
        GD Williams
        Pro–64 MJ Slater
V'trs   WD–U WE–M 3OC
Fees   £10 (£15)
Loc   7 miles SE of Stockport

North Manchester (1894)

Rhodes House, Manchester Old Road,
Middleton, Manchester M24 4PE
Tel   (061) 643 2941
Mem   300 60(L) 38(J) 80(5)
Sec   J Fallon (061) 643 9033
Pro   M Vipond (061) 643 7094
Holes   18 L 6542 yds SSS 72
Recs   Am–66 J Cheetham
        Pro–66 G Furey
V'trs   U
Fees   £14 (£15)
Loc   5 miles N of Manchester.
        M62 Junction 18

Northenden (1913)

Palatine Road, Manchester M22 4FR
Tel   (061) 998 4738
Mem   600
Sec   JM Fleet (Mgr)
        RH Newall (Hon Sec)
Pro   WJ McColl (061) 945 3386
Holes   18 L 6435 yds SSS 71
Recs   Am–67 JEB Waddell
        Pro–64 D Durnian
V'trs   U SOC
Fees   £13.50 (£17)
Loc   5 miles S of Manchester

Old Manchester (1818)

Tel   (061) 766 4157
Mem   60
Sec   PT Goodall
Holes   Club without a course

Oldham (1892)

Lees New Road, Oldham
Tel   (061) 624 4986
Mem   300 45(L) 35(J)
Sec   BC Heginbotham
        (0457) 876326
Pro   A Laverty (061) 626 8346
Holes   18 L 5045 yds SSS 65
Recs   Am–66 D Maloney (1987)
        Pro–65 E Smith
V'trs   U SOC–WD
Fees   £8 (£10)
Loc   Off Oldham–Stalybridge road

Pike Fold (1909)

Cooper Lane, Victoria Avenue,
Blackley, Manchester M9 2QQ
Tel   (061) 740 1136
Mem   200
Sec   GVW Kendell (061) 766 6788
Holes   9 L 5789 yds SSS 68

For explanation of abbreviations, see page 460.

Recs Am–66 P Bradley (1989)
Pro–66 JE Wiggett
V'trs WD–U WE/BH–M SOC
Fees £5 R/D (WE–M)
Loc 5 miles N of Manchester.
M62 Junction 18, 2 miles

Prestwich (1908)

Hilton Lane, Prestwich
Tel (061) 773 2544
Mem 470
Sec WV Trees (061) 773 4578
Pro GP Coope
Holes 18 L 4522 yds SSS 63
Recs Am–60 J Lunosz
V'trs WD–H WE–NA before 3pm
SOC
Fees £10 (£12)
Loc 2½ miles N of Manchester

Reddish Vale (1912)

Southcliffe, Reddish, Stockport
SK5 7EE
Tel (061) 480 2359
Mem 500
Sec JL Blakey (061) 432 6544
Pro RA Brown (061) 480 3824
Holes 18 L 6086 yds SSS 69
Recs Am–64 KR Gorton, D Young
Pro–67 R Williamson
V'trs WD–U WE–M SOC
Fees £12
Loc 1 mile NNE of Stockport

Ringway (1909)

Hale Mount, Hale Barns, Altrincham
WA15 8SW
Tel (061) 904 9609
Mem 345 165(L) 41(J) 25(5)
Sec D Wright (061) 980 2630
Pro N Ryan (061) 980 8432
Holes 18 L 6494 yds SSS 71
Recs Am–67 RE Preston
V'trs Fri/Tues before 2pm & Sun
before 11am–M
Fees £18 (£22)
Loc 8 miles S of Manchester off
M56 Junction 6 (A538)

Rochdale (1888)

Edenfield Road, Bagslate, Rochdale
OL11 5YR
Tel (0706) 46024 (Clubhouse)
Mem 625
Sec (0706) 43818
Pro FW Accleton (0706) 522104
Holes 18 L 6002 yds SSS 69
Recs Am–66 J Hawkard, R Kershaw,
B Crabtree
Pro–65 G Hammond
V'trs U
Fees £11 (£14)
Loc M62 Junction 20, 3 miles on
A680

Saddleworth (1904)

Uppermill, nr Oldham, Lancs
Tel (04577) 3653
Mem 620
Sec IG Bennett
Pro ET Shard
Holes 18 L 5976 yds SSS 69
Recs Am–67 P Smethurst
Pro–69 M Melling, A Gillies
V'trs U
Fees £8 (£10.50)
Loc 5 miles E of Oldham
Mis Buggy for hire

Sale (1913)

Sale Lodge, Golf Road, Sale
M33 2LU
Tel (061) 973 3404
Mem 580
Sec J Blair (061) 973 1638
Pro M Lake (061) 973 1730
Holes 18 L 6351 yds SSS 70
Recs Am–67 JR Barlow
V'trs U SOC–WD
Fees £12 (£18)
Loc North boundary of Sale

Springfield Park (1928)

Public
Marland, Rochdale
Tel (0706) 49801
Pro D Wills
Holes 18 L 5209 yds SSS 66
Recs Am–68 B Walsh
Pro–67 ME Hill
V'trs U
Fees £3.20 (£3.20) 1989 prices
Loc W boundary of Rochdale

Stamford (1900)

Oakfield House, Huddersfield Road,
Stalybridge SK15 3PY
Tel (04575) 2126
Mem 500
Sec FE Rowles
Pro B Badger (04575) 4829
Holes 18 L 5524 yds SSS 67
Recs Am–66 H Fletcher
V'trs WD–U WE comp days–after
2.30pm SOC–WD (min 12
members)
Fees £8 (£12.50)
Loc NE boundary of Stalybridge
on B6175

Stand (1904)

The Dales, Ashbourne Grove,
Whitefield, Manchester M25 7NL
Tel (061) 766 2388
Mem 700
Sec TE Thacker (061) 766 3197
Pro M Dance (061) 766 2214
Holes 18 L 6411 yds SSS 71
Recs Am–68 JE Cooke
Pro–67 PM Eales

Saddleworth — V'trs continued

V'trs U SOC–WD
Fees £10 (£14)
Loc 5 miles N of Manchester.
M62 Junction 17

Swinton Park (1926)

East Lancashire Road, Swinton,
Manchester M27 1LX
Tel (061) 794 1785
Mem 425 100(L) 50(J)
Sec F Slater (061) 794 0861
Pro J Wilson (061) 793 8077
Holes 18 L 6675 yds SSS 72
Recs Am–66 J Thornley (1984)
V'trs WD–U WE–M SOC–Tues
Fees £12D–£16
Loc On A580, 5 miles NW of
Manchester

Tunshill (1901)

Club House, Kiln Lane, Milnrow,
nr Rochdale
Tel (0706) 342095
Mem 180
Sec D Kennedy
Pro P Lunt (0706) 861982
Holes 9 L 5812 yds SSS 68
Recs Am–66 D Williams (1981), KM
Hardy (1984), R Hopley (1989)
V'trs WD–U WE–NA Mar–Oct SOC
Fees £6 (£6.50) 1989 prices
Loc 2 miles E of Rochdale.
M62 Junction 21

Walmersley (1906)

Garrett's Close, Walmersley, Bury
Tel (061) 764 1429
Mem 350
Sec C Stock (061) 764 5057
Holes 9 L 5588 metres SSS 70
Recs Am–67 I Bamborough
V'trs U exc Tues–(Ladies Day)
Sat–(Mens Comp day) Sun–M
SOC–Wed–Fri
Fees £6
Loc 2 miles N of Bury (A56).
M66 Junction 1

Werneth (1909)

Green Lane Garden Suburb, Oldham
OL8 3AZ
Tel (061) 624 1190
Mem 350
Sec JH Barlow
Pro T Morley
Holes 18 L 5363 yds SSS 66
Recs Am–62 LA Lawton
Pro–63 S Holden
V'trs WD–U WE–M SOC
Fees WD–£10
Loc 2 miles S of Oldham

Werneth Low (1912)

Gee Cross, Hyde, Tameside
Tel (061) 368 2503
Mem 245 50(L) 60(J)

Sec R Watson (061) 368 7388
Pro A Bacchus (061) 336 6908
Holes 9 L 5734 yds SSS 68
Recs Am–67 ST Madden
Pro–57 D Cooper
V'trs U Sun–NA BH–M
Fees £8.50 (Sat £13.50)
Loc On Werneth Low–2 miles from centre

Westhoughton (1929)

Long Island, Westhoughton, Bolton BL5 2BR
Tel (0942) 811085
Mem 200
Sec DJ Kinsella
Pro S Brian
Holes 9 L 5834 yds SSS 68
Recs Am–64 T Woodward
V'trs WD–U WE/BH–M
Fees £8
Loc 4 miles SW of Bolton

Whitefield (1932)

Higher Lane, Whitefield, Manchester M25 7EZ
Tel (061) 766 2728
Mem 500
Sec Mrs RL Vidler (061) 766 2904
Pro P Reeves (061) 766 3096
Holes 18 L 6041 yds SSS 69
18 L 5714 yds SSS 68
V'trs U SOC–WD
Fees £11.50 (£17)
Loc 4 miles N of Manchester. M62 Junction 17

Whittaker (1906)

Littleborough OL15 0LH
Tel (0706) 78310
Mem 120
Sec GA Smith (0484) 428546
Holes 9 L 5576 yds SSS 67
Recs Am–61 D Kernick
Pro–65 MT Hoyle
V'trs WD/Sat–U Sun–NA
Fees £6 (£8)
Loc 1¹/₂ miles N of Littleborough off A58

Wigan (1898)

Arley Hall, Haigh, Wigan WN1 2UH
Tel (0257) 421360
Mem 250
Sec J Crompton (0257) 41051
Holes 9 L 6058 yds SSS 69
Recs Am–68 RM Hodson
V'trs WD–U
Fees £10 (£12)
Loc 4 miles N of Wigan off A5106/B5239. M6 Junction 27

William Wroe (1973)

Public
Pennybridge Lane, Flixton, Manchester
Tel (061) 748 8680
Pro R West

Holes 18 L 4395 yds SSS 60
Recs Am–60 C Meadows, D Dunwoodie
V'trs U (24–hour booking req)
Fees £3 (£4.50)
Loc 6 miles SW of Manchester, by M63
Mis Acre Gate Club plays here

Withington (1892)

243 Palatine Road, West Didsbury, Manchester M20 8UD
Tel (061) 445 3912
Mem 340 97(L) 38(J) 30(5)
Sec A Larsen (061) 445 9544
Pro RJ Ling (061) 445 4861
Holes 18 L 6410 yds SSS 71
Recs Am–69 C Webb (1989)
V'trs WD–U before 4pm WE–U after 2.30pm SOC
Fees £12 (£15)
Loc 6 miles S of Manchester

Worsley (1894)

Stableford Avenue, Monton Green, Eccles, Manchester
Tel (061) 789 4202
Mem 625
Sec B Dean
Pro C Cousins
Holes 18 L 6217 yds SSS 70
Recs Am–66 B Dean
Pro–68 FS Boobyer
V'trs I NA–9–9.45am and 12.15–1.30pm
Fees £12
Loc 5 miles W of Manchester

Merseyside

Allerton Park (1934)

Public
Allerton Road, Liverpool
Tel (051) 428 1046
Pro B Large
Holes 18 L 5084 yds SSS 64
V'trs U
Fees £2.70
Loc 5 miles S of Liverpool

Arrowe Park (1931)

Public
Arrowe Park, Woodchurch, Birkenhead, Wirral
Tel (051) 677 1527
Pro C Scanlon
Holes 18 L 6377 yds SSS 70
V'trs U
Fees £3.25
Loc 3 miles from Birkenhead on A552. M53 Junction 3, 1 mile

Ashton-in-Makerfield (1902)

Garswood Park, Liverpool Road, Ashton-in-Makerfield
Tel (0942) 727267
Mem 500
Sec H Howard Elce (0942) 727745
Pro P Allan (0942) 724229
Holes 18 L 6120 yds SSS 69
Recs Am–67 GS Lacy
V'trs WD–restricted Wed WE/BH–M SOC
Fees £7
Loc Ashton 1 mile

Bidston (1913)

Scoresby Road, Leasowe, Moreton L46 1QQ
Tel (051) 638 3412
Mem 500
Sec LA Kendrick (051) 638 8685
Pro JR Law (051) 630 6650
Holes 18 L 6207 yds SSS 70
Recs Am–67 P Whitehouse
Pro–68 JM Hume
V'trs WD–U WE–M SOC
Fees £7.50 (£12)
Loc Off Leasowe Road

Bootle (1934)

Dunnings Bridge Road, Litherland L30 2PP
Tel (051) 928 6196
Mem 300
Sec J Morgan (Hon)
Pro G Brown (051) 928 1371
Holes 18 L 6362 yds SSS 70
Recs Am–64 S Ashcroft
Pro–69 R Boobyer
V'trs U SOC
Fees £2.55 (£3.75)
Loc 5 miles N of Liverpool
Mis Book by phone

Bowring (1913)

Public
Bowring Park, Roby Road, Huyton
Tel (051) 489 1901
Pro D Weston
Holes 9 L 5592 yds SSS 66
Recs Am–67 G Spurrier
V'trs U
Fees £2.70
Loc M62 motorway

Brackenwood

Public
Brackenwood Park, Bebington, Wirral L63 2LY
Tel (051) 608 3093
Pro C Disbury
Holes 18 L 6131 yds SSS 69
Recs Am–67 D Charlton
Pro–64 C Disbury
V'trs U
Fees £3.20
Loc Nr M53 Junction 4

For explanation of abbreviations, see page 460.

Bromborough (1904)

Raby Hall Road, Bromborough
Tel (051) 334 2155
Mem 600
Sec LB Silvester (051) 334 2978
Pro P Andrew (051) 334 4499
Holes 18 L 6650 yds SSS 73
Recs Am–68 DP Jones
V'trs U (Arrange with Pro in advance)
Fees £12 (£15)
Loc Mid Wirral, M53 Junction 4

Caldy (1908)

Links Hey Road, Caldy, Wirral L48 1NB
Tel (051) 625 5660
Mem 800
Sec JK Mayberry
Pro K Jones (051) 625 1818
Holes 18 L 6675 yds SSS 73
Recs Am–69 PT Bailey
V'trs WD–M until 9.30am –U from 9.30am–1pm –M from1–2pm –U after 2pm. Advance booking req.
Fees D–£20 After 2pm–£15
Loc 1$^1/_2$ miles S of West Kirby
Mis Buggies for hire

Childwall (1913)

Naylor's Road, Gateacre, Liverpool L27 2YB
Tel (051) 487 0654
Mem 650
Sec L Upton
Pro N Parr (051) 487 9871
Holes 18 L 6425 yds SSS 71
Recs Am–66 M Gamble
V'trs WE/BH/Tues–restricted
Fees £10.50 (£16)
Loc 7 miles E of Liverpool. M62, 2 miles

Eastham Lodge (1973)

Ferry Road, Eastham, Wirral L62 0AP
Tel (051) 327 1483
Mem 520
Sec CS Camden (051) 327 3003
Pro I Jones (051) 327 3008
Holes 15 L 5826 yds SSS 68
Recs Am–64 EI Bradshaw Pro–66 I Jones
V'trs WD–U WE/BH–M SOC–Tues
Fees £11
Loc 6 miles S of Birkenhead on A41. M53 Junction 5. Signs to Eastham village

Formby (1884)

Golf Road, Formby, Liverpool L37 1LQ
Tel (070 48) 74273
Mem 600
Sec A Thirlwell (070 84) 72164
Pro C Harrison (070 48) 73090
Holes 18 L 6871 yds SSS 73

Recs Am–67 DJ Eccleston Pro–65 NC Coles
V'trs I
Fees £30 (£35)
Loc By Freshfield Station

Formby Ladies' (1896)

Formby, Liverpool L37 1YL
Tel (070 48) 74127
Sec Mrs V Bailey (070 48) 73493
Pro C Harrison (070 48) 73090
Holes 18 L 5426 yds SSS 71
Recs Am–60 CD Lee
V'trs U
Fees £19 (£22)
Loc Near Southport

Grange Park (1891)

Toll Bar, Prescot Road, St Helens WA10 3AD
Tel (0744) 22980 (Members)
Mem 700
Sec DA Wood (0744) 26318
Pro PG Evans (0744) 28785
Holes 18 L 6480 yds SSS 71
Recs Am–68 GS Lacy (1988) Pro–66 R Ellis (1986)
V'trs I
Fees £15 (£21.50)
Loc 1$^1/_2$ miles W of St Helens on A58

Haydock Park (1877)

Golborne Park, Rob Lane, Newton-le-Willows WA12 0HX
Tel (0925) 224389
Mem 390 120(L)
Sec G Tait (0925) 228525
Pro PE Kenwright (0925) 226944
Holes 18 L 6014 yds SSS 69
Recs Am–65 D Pilkington, P Boydell, K Sargent
V'trs H or I SOC–WD exc Tues
Fees £15
Loc M6 Junction 23

Hesketh (1885)

Cockle Dick's Lane, Cambridge Road, Southport PR9 9QQ
Tel (0704) 30226
Mem 580
Sec PB Seal (0704) 36897
Pro J Donoghue (0704) 30050
Holes 18 L 6478 yds SSS 72
Recs Am–68 G Brand Pro–64 D Hayes
V'trs WD–U WE/BH–limited SOC
Fees £15 D–£20 (£20 D–£25)
Loc 1 mile N of Southport

Heswall (1901)

Cottage Lane, Gayton Heswall, Wirral L60 8PB
Tel (051) 342 2193
Mem 902
Sec CPR Calvert (051) 342 1237
Pro AE Thompson (051) 342 7431

Holes 18 L 6472 yds SSS 72
Recs Am–67 J Butterworth (1986) Pro–64 K Jones (1986)
V'trs U BH–NA SOC–Wed & Fri
Fees D–£16 (D–£20) SOC–£16 (Min 24)
Loc 8 miles NW of Chester

Hillside (1909)

Hastings Road, Southport
Tel (0704) 69902
Mem 800
Sec PW Ray (0704) 67169
Pro B Seddon (0704) 68360
Holes 18 L 6850 yds SSS 74
Recs Am–67 S Struurr Pro–66 M O'Grady, R Craig
V'trs By arrangement with Sec
Fees D–£25 (£30)
Loc Southport

Hoylake Municipal

Public
Carr Lane, Hoylake, Wirral L47 4BQ
Tel (051) 632 2956
Pro R Boobyer
Holes 18 L 6330 yds SSS 70
Recs Am–67 S Roberts (1983) Pro–64 T Bennett (1982)
V'trs U SOC WE–phone booking 1 week in advance
Fees £3.20
Loc Liverpool 10 miles
Mis West Hoyle Club plays here

Huyton & Prescot (1905)

Hurst Park, Huyton
Tel (051) 489 1138
Mem 700
Sec Mrs E Holmes (051) 489 3948
Pro R Pottage (051) 489 2022
Holes 18 L 5738 yds SSS 68
Recs Am–67
V'trs WD–U WE–M
Fees £12 (£15)
Loc 7 miles E of Liverpool. 1 mile from A57 Prescot

Leasowe (1891)

Leasowe Road, Moreton, Wirral L46 3RD
Tel (051) 677 5852
Mem 450
Sec R Kerr
Pro I Higby (051) 678 5460
Holes 18 L 6204 yds SSS 70
Recs Am–63 J Maddocks
V'trs U Sun–M
Fees £10 (£12)

Lee Park (1954)

Childwall Valley Road, Gateacre, Liverpool L27 3YA
Tel (051) 487 9861 (clubhouse)
Mem 450
Sec Mrs D Barr (051) 487 3882

Holes 18 L 6024 yds SSS 69
Recs Am–69 RA Knight
Pro–67 I Bramall
V'trs U
Fees On application
Loc Liverpool 7 miles

Liverpool Municipal (1967)

Public
Ingoe Lane, Kirkby, nr Liverpool
L32 4SS
Tel (051) 546 5435
Pro D Weston
Holes 18 L 6571 yds SSS 71
Recs Am–70 J Paton (1986)
Pro–70
V'trs U WE–booking required
Fees £2.20 (£2.20)
Loc M57 exit to B5192
Mis Kirkby Club plays here

Prenton (1905)

Golf Links Road, Prenton, Birkenhead
Tel (051) 608 1461
Mem 360 100(L) 69(J) 70(5)
Sec PE Manley (051) 608 1053
Pro R Thompson (051) 608 1636
Holes 18 L 6411 yds SSS 71
Recs Am–68 CJ Farey, AJ Rainford,
WJ Beattie
V'trs U SOC–Mon/Wed/Fri
Fees £15 (£18)
Loc Outskirts of Birkenhead.
M53 Junction 3

RLGC Village Play (1895)

Hoylake, Wirral
Mem 40
Sec J Chapman (051) 625 7013
Holes Play over Royal Liverpool

Royal Birkdale (1889)

Waterloo Road, Birkdale, Southport
PR8 2LX
Tel (0704) 69903
Sec NT Crewe (0704) 67920
Pro R Bradbeer (0704) 68857
Holes 18 L 6703 yds SSS 73
Recs Am–68 C Cassells
Pro–64 M O'Meara
V'trs I H SOC
Fees £30 D–£45 (£45)
Loc 1½ miles S of Southport

Royal Liverpool (1869)

Meols Drive, Hoylake L47 4AL
Tel (051) 632 3101/2
Mem 650
Sec JR Davidson
Pro J Heggarty (051) 632 5868

Holes 18 L 6804 yds SSS 74
Recs Am–69 R Hayes
Pro–64 B Waites
V'trs I SOC
Fees £25 (£30)
Loc 10 miles W of Liverpool

St Helens (1985)

Public
St Helens, Lancs
Tel (0744) 813149
Sec MH Devenish (0744) 31955
Pro PR Parkinson
Holes 18 L 5941 yds SSS 69
Recs Am–74 D Tierney, M Venney
V'trs U
Fees £2.10
Loc Sherdley Park, 2 miles E of
town on A570
Mis Sherdley Park Club plays here

Southport & Ainsdale (1907)

Bradshaws Lane, Ainsdale, Southport
PR8 3LG
Tel (0704) 78092
Mem 340 100(L) 60(J) 130(5)
Sec DA Wood (0704) 78000
Pro M Houghton (0704) 77316
Holes 18 L 6612 yds SSS 73
Recs Am–67 JB Dickinson (1982),
JL Plaxton (1983)
Pro–67 DJ Russell, DI Vaughan
(1983)
Pro (L)–69 B New, M Walker,
K Ehrnlund (1984)
V'trs WD–I before 4pm –M after
4pm WE/BH–M SOC
Fees £17 (NA)
Loc 3 miles S of Southport on A565

Southport Municipal

Public
Park Road, Southport
Tel (0704) 35286
Pro W Fletcher
Holes 18 L 6253 yds SSS 69
Recs Pro–67 W Fletcher (1986)
V'trs U
Fees £2.50 (£3.50)
Loc N end of Southport promenade
Mis Park Club plays here

Southport Old Links (1926)

Moss Lane, Southport
Tel (0704) 24294/28207
Mem 390
Sec WAD Sims
Holes 9 L 6486 yds SSS 71
Recs Am–68 J Robinson
V'trs U exc WE comp days BH–NA
SOC–WD
Fees £10 (£15) SOC–£9.50
Loc Churchtown, 3 miles NE of
Southport

Wallasey (1891)

Bayswater Road, Wallasey L45 8LA
Tel (051) 639 3630
Mem 350 90(L) 50(J) 45(5)
Sec DF Haslehurst (051) 691 1024
Pro M Adams (051) 638 3888
Holes 18 L 6607 yds SSS 73
Recs Am–68 P Morgan
Pro–66 P Barber
V'trs U
Fees £18 (£22)
Loc M53–signs to New Brighton

Warren (1911)

Public
Grove Road, Wallasey, Wirral
Tel (051) 639 8223 (Clubhouse)
Pro K Lamb (051) 639 5730
Holes 9 L 5914 yds SSS 68
Recs Am–66 J Hayes
Pro–66 JA MacLachlan
V'trs U
Fees £3
Loc Wallasey

West Derby (1896)

Yew Tree Lane, Liverpool L12 9HQ
Tel (051) 228 1540
Mem 575
Sec S Young (051) 254 1034
Pro N Brace (051) 220 5478
Holes 18 L 6322 yds SSS 70
Recs Am–66 M Gamble
Pro–67 AC Coop
V'trs U
Fees £12 (£16)
Loc 2 miles E of Liverpool off
A580–West Derby Junction

West Lancashire (1873)

Blundellsands, Crosby, Liverpool
L23 8SZ
Tel (051) 924 4115
Mem 700
Sec DE Bell (051) 924 1076
Pro D Lloyd (051) 924 5662
Holes 18 L 6756 yds SSS 73
Recs Am–69 G Boardman
Pro–66 C Mason
V'trs U SOC
Fees £14 (£17) £8 after 4pm
Loc Midway between Liverpool
and Southport off A565
Mis Traditional links

Wirral Ladies (1894)

93 Bidston Road, Birkenhead, Wirral
L43 6TS
Tel (051) 652 5797
Mem 550
Sec Mrs DP Cranston–Miller
(051) 652 1255
Pro M Jones (051) 652 2468
Holes 18 L 4966 yds SSS 70 (Ladies)
18 L 5170 yds SSS 66 (Men)

Recs Am–71 Miss H Lyall
V'trs U
Fees £12
Loc Birkenhead $^1/_2$ mile.
    M53 2 miles

Woolton (1901)

Doe Park, Speke Road, Woolton,
Liverpool L25 7TZ
Tel (051) 486 1601
Mem 750
Sec KG Jennions (051) 486 2298
Holes 18 L 5706 yds SSS 68
Recs Am–63 J Edwards
    Pro–66 DJ Rees
V'trs U exc comp days
Fees £13 (£19)
Loc South Liverpool
Mis Buggy hire

Middlesex

Airlinks (1984)

Public
Southall Lane, Hounslow TW5 9PE
Tel (081) 561 1418
Sec J Shortland (Mgr)
Pro S Smith
Holes 18 L 5883 yds SSS 69
Recs Am–60 K Dempster
V'trs WD–U Sat am–NA
Fees £5.50 (£7.50)
Loc Just off M4

Ashford Manor (1898)

Fordbridge Road, Ashford TW15 3RT
Tel (0784) 252049
Mem 800
Sec BJ Duffy (0784) 257687
Pro M Finney (0784) 255940
Holes 18 L 6372 yds SSS 70
Recs Am–65 GA Homewood (1989)
    Pro–64 D Talbot
V'trs H
Fees £20 (£25)
Loc Ashford, off A308

Brent Valley (1938)

Public
Church Road, Hanwell, London
W7
Tel (081) 567 1287 (bookings)
Sec P Bryant
Pro P Bryant
Holes 18 L 5426 yds SSS 66
Recs Am–65 S Harper (1985)
    Pro–61 R Green (1988)
V'trs U SOC
Fees £4 D £6 (£6.50)
Loc Off Greenford Avenue,
    Hanwell

Bush Hill Park (1895)

Bush Hill, Winchmore Hill, London
N21 2BU
Tel (081) 360 5738
Mem 665
Sec DJ Clark

Pro GW Low (081) 360 4103
Holes 18 L 5809 yds SSS 68
Recs Am–63 T Sheaff
    Pro–64 L Farmer
V'trs WD–U WE–M SOC
Fees £14
Loc 9 miles N of London

Crews Hill (1920)

Cattlegate Road, Crews Hill,
Enfield EN2 8AZ
Tel (081) 363 0787
Mem 600
Sec EJ Hunt (081) 363 6674
Pro J Reynolds (081) 366 7422
Holes 18 L 6208 yds SSS 70
Recs Am–68 S Bishop
    Pro–66 P Hunt
V'trs WD–U H WE/BH–M SOC
Fees On application
Loc $2^1/_2$ miles N of Enfield.
    M25 Junction 24

Ealing (1923)

Perivale Lane, Greenford UB6 8SS
Tel (081) 997 2595
Mem 600
Sec CFS Ryder (081) 997 0937
Pro A Stickley (081) 997 3959
Holes 18 L 6216 yds SSS 70
Recs Am–65 A Rogers
    Pro–64 R Verwey
V'trs WD–U WE–M
Fees On application
Loc Marble Arch 6 miles on A40

Enfield (1893)

Old Park Road South, Enfield
EN2 7DA
Tel (081) 363 0083/3921
Mem 625
Sec AJ Hollis (081) 363 3970
Pro I Martin (081) 366 4492
Holes 18 L 6137 yds SSS 70
Recs Am–66 A Rogers
    Pro–66 L Fickling
V'trs WD–H WE/BH–M SOC–WD
Fees £16 D–£20
Loc 1 mile NE of Enfield

Finchley (1929)

Nether Court, Frith Lane, London
NW7 1PU
Tel (081) 346 2436
Mem 500
Sec JR Pearce
Pro D Brown (081) 346 5086
Holes 18 L 6411 yds SSS 71
Recs Am–65 D Chatterton
    Pro–67 T Moore
V'trs WD–U WE–pm only SOC
Fees £20 (£25)
Loc 8 miles NW of Charing Cross

Fulwell (1904)

Hampton Hill TW12 1JY
Tel (081) 977 3188
Mem 600
Sec MCN Reding (081) 977 2733
Pro D Haslam (081) 977 3844

Holes 18 L 6490 yds SSS 71
Recs Am–68 KD Corcoran, SR Warin
    Pro–63 P Buchan
V'trs WD–I WE–M
Fees £15 (£20)
Loc Opposite Fulwell Station

Grim's Dyke (1910)

Oxhey Lane, Hatch End, Pinner
HA5 4AL
Tel (081) 428 4093
Mem 575
Sec PH Payne (081) 428 4539
Pro C Williams (081) 428 7484
Holes 18 L 5600 yds SSS 67
Recs Am–65 J Thornton (1988)
    Pro–64 BJ Hunt (1978)
V'trs U Sun–M H SOC
Fees D–£25 Sat–£30
Loc 2 miles W of Harrow (A4008)

Hampstead (1894)

Winnington Road, London N2 0TU
Tel (081) 455 0203
Mem 533
Sec KF Young
Pro PJ Brown (081) 455 7089
Holes 9 L 5812 yds SSS 68
Recs Am–66 RDA Smith
    Pro–65 D Stevenson
V'trs WD–H WE–H
Fees £15 D–£20 (£20)
Loc N of Hampstead Heath off
    Hampstead Lane

Harefield Place (1947)

Public
The Drive, Harefield Place, Uxbridge
UB10 8PA
Tel (0895) 31169
Pro P Howard (0895) 37287
Holes 18 L 5711 yds SSS 68
Recs Am–65 S Mylward
    Pro–64 A Barr G Cullen
V'trs U
Fees £4.50 (£7)
Loc 2 miles N of Uxbridge

Harrow School (1978)

Harrow-on-the-Hill
Mem 250 100(L) 40(J)
Sec DA Fothergill (081) 869 1214
Holes 9 L 1775 yds SSS 30
V'trs M
Loc Harrow School

Haste Hill (1933)

Public
The Drive, Northwood
Tel (092 74) 22877
Sec T Le Brocq (Mgr)
Pro T Le Brocq
Holes 18 L 5794 yds SSS 68
Recs Am–68 J Joyce
V'trs U
Fees £3.50 (£5.50)

Hendon (1900)

off Sanders Lane, Devonshire Road,
London NW7 1DG
Tel   (081) 346 6023
Mem   525
Sec   DE Cooper
Pro   S Murray (081) 346 8990
Holes 18 L 6241 yds SSS 70
Recs   Am–68 AL MacLeod
        Pro–66 SWT Murray
V'trs   WD–U WE/BH–bookings SOC
Fees   £18 D–£25 (£30)
Loc   10 miles N of London.
        M1 Junction 2

Highgate (1904)

Denewood Road, Highgate, London
N6 4AH
Tel   (081) 340 1906
Mem   593
Sec   J Zuill (081) 340 3745
Pro   R Turner (081) 340 5467
Holes 18 L 5964 yds SSS 69
Recs   Am–66 D Kingsman, P Bax
        Pro–66 I Martin (1987)
V'trs   WD–U exc Wed–NA
        WE/BH–M SOC
Fees   £16
Loc   London 5 miles off A1

Hillingdon (1892)

18 Dorset Way, Hillingdon,
Uxbridge UB10 0JR
Tel   (0895) 39810
Mem   375
Sec   LAN Holland (0895) 33956
Pro   DJ McFadden (0895) 51980
Holes 9 L 5459 yds SSS 67
Recs   Am–67 M Weir
        Pro–69 P Cheyney
V'trs   WD–U exc Thurs 12–4pm WE
        pm–M H SOC–Mon/Tues/Fri
Fees   18 holes D–£15
Loc   1 mile E of Uxbridge, by RAF
        Station, Uxbridge

Holiday Inn (1975)

Stockley Road, West Drayton
Mem   80
Sec   J O'Loughlin (0895) 444232
Pro   NC Coles
Holes 9 L 3800 yds SSS 62
V'trs   U SOC
Fees   18 holes–£3 (£3.50)
Loc   In grounds of Holiday Inn

Horsenden Hill (1935)

Public
Woodland Rise, Greenford
Tel   (081) 902 4555
Pro   T Martin
Holes 9 L 3264 yds SSS 56
V'trs   U
Fees   £2.30 (£3.50)
Loc   Greenford

Hounslow Heath (1979)

Public
Staines Road, Hounslow TW4 5DS
Tel   (081) 570 5271
Pro   P Cheyney
Holes 18 L 5820 yds SSS 68
V'trs   WD–U WE–booking essential
Fees   £4 (£5)
Loc   Opposite Green Lane,
        Staines Road, Hounslow

Lime Trees Park (1984)

Public
Ruislip Road, Northolt UB5 6QZ
Tel   (081) 845 3180
Pro   B Mylward
Holes 9 L 5789 yds SSS 69
V'trs   U SOC
Loc   Turn off Western Avenue (A40)
        at Polish war memorial towards
        Yeading
Mis   Course renovation 1990

Mill Hill (1925)

100 Barnet Way, Mill Hill,
London NW7 3AL
Tel   (081) 959 2282
Mem   450
Sec   FH Scott (081) 959 2339
Pro   A Daniel (081) 959 7261
Holes 18 L 6309 yds SSS 70
Recs   Am–65 H Aarons
        Pro–67 J Hudson
V'trs   WD–UH WE/BH–UH after
        11.30am SOC
Fees   £16 (£25)
Loc   1 mile from Mill Hill
        Broadway, off A1. Approach
        via Marsh Lane and Hankins
        Lane

Muswell Hill (1893)

Rhodes Avenue, Wood Green,
London N22 4UT
Tel   (081) 888 2044
Mem   500
Sec   JAB Connors (081) 888 1764
Pro   IB Roberts (081) 888 8046
Holes 18 L 6474 yds SSS 71
Recs   Am–67 PJ Montague
        Pro–65 H Weetman
V'trs   U SOC
Fees   £23 (£30–book with Pro)
Loc   Bounds Green station 1 mile

North Middlesex (1928)

The Manor House, Friern Barnet Lane,
London N20 0NL
Tel   (081) 445 1732
Mem   560
Sec   MC Reding (Mgr)
        (081) 445 1604
Pro   ASR Roberts (081) 445 3060
Holes 18 L 5611 yds SSS 67
Recs   Am–65 M Cohen
        Pro–64 S Levermore

V'trs   WD–I WE/BH–restricted at
        certain times
Fees   £15 (£22)
Loc   Between Barnet and Finchley

Northwood (1891)

Rickmansworth Road, Northwood
HA6 2QW
Tel   (092 74) 25329
Mem   420 240 (L)50(J) 111(5)
Sec   IM Kirkwood (092 74) 21384
Pro   CJ Holdsworth (092 74)
        20112
Holes 18 L 6493 yds SSS 71
Recs   Am–68 BE Marsden(1987)
        Pro–67 J Bland (1977)
V'trs   WD–H WE/BH–NA SOC
Fees   £20 1989 price
Loc   3 miles E of Rickmansworth

Perivale Park (1932)

Public
Ruislip Road, Greenford
Tel   (081) 575 8655
Pro   J Hamlyn
Holes 9 L 5296 yds SSS 65
Recs   Am–64
V'trs   U
Fees   £3.50 (£4.50)
Loc   1 mile E of Greenford

Picketts Lock (1973)

Public
Picketts Lock Lane, Edmonton,
London N9 0AS
Tel   (081) 803 3611
Pro   RG Gerken
Holes 9 L 2496 yds SSS 64
Recs   Am–31 M Yates
        Pro–30 JTB Rayner
V'trs   WD–U WE–booking advisable
Fees   £2.50 (£3)

Pinner Hill (1927)

Pinner Hill HA5 3YA
Tel   (081) 866 0963
Mem   750
Sec   M Crouch
Pro   J Rule (081) 866 2109
Holes 18 L 6293 yds SSS 70
Recs   Am–63 SR Warrin
        Pro–67 TH Cotton, G Player,
        T Wilkes, G Low, J Warren
V'trs   WD–H Sun/BH–M
Fees   On request
Loc   West Pinner Green 1 mile

Ruislip (1936)

Public
Ickenham Road, Ruislip
Tel   (0895) 632004/638081
Pro   D Nash (0895) 638835
Holes 18 L 5235 yds SSS 67
Recs   Am–64 W Bennet
        Pro–64 H Flatmann
V'trs   U
Fees   £4.50 (£7)
Loc   W Ruislip BR/LTE Station

For explanation of abbreviations, see page 460.

Stanmore (1893)

Gordon Avenue, Stanmore HA7 2RL
Tel   (081) 954 4661
Mem 500
Sec   PF Wise (081) 954 2599
Pro   VR Law (081) 954 2646
Holes 18 L 5881 yds SSS 68
Recs Am–66 H Preston
      Pro–66 G Low
V'trs WD–H WE/BH–M SOC
Fees WD–£15 (£6 public days)
Loc   E boundary of Harrow

Strawberry Hill (1900)

Wellesley Road, Twickenham
Tel   (081) 894 1246
Mem 350
Sec   RC Meer (081) 894 0165
Pro   P Buchan (081) 892 2082
Holes 9 L 2381 yds SSS 62
Recs Am–61 RE Heryet
      Pro–59 H Fullicks,
      K Bousfield, R Gerken
V'trs WD–U WE–M(XL)
Fees £8
Loc   Strawberry Hill Station

Sudbury (1920)

Bridgewater Road, Wembley
HA0 1AL
Tel   (081) 902 0218
Mem 640
Sec   JA Smith (081) 902 3713
Pro   N Jordan (081) 902 7910
Holes 18 L 6282 yds SSS 70
Recs Am–63 T Greenwood
      Pro–65 J Gill
V'trs WD–H Sun–M
Fees £20 (£30)
Loc   Junction of A4005/A4090

Trent Park (1973)

Public
Bramley Road, Southgate, London N14
Tel   (081) 366 7432
Pro   C Easton
Holes 18 L 6008 yds SSS 69
Recs Am–65 M Skinner (1989)
      Pro–64 V Law (1979)
V'trs WD–U SOC WE–NA before
      11am
Fees £4.50 (£6)
Loc   Opp Oakwood Tube,
      Piccadilly Line

Twickenham (1977)

Public
Staines Road, Twickenham
Tel   (081) 979 6946
Pro   T Morgan (081) 783 1698
Holes 9 L 6014 yds SSS 69
V'trs U
Fees £3 (£4)
Loc   2 miles NW of Hampton Court,
      nr Rugby Ground

West Middlesex (1891)

Greenford Road, Southall
Tel   (081) 574 3450
Mem 700
Sec   PJ Furness
Pro   L Farmer (081) 574 1800
Holes 18 L 6242 yds SSS 70
Recs Am–65 J Walsh
      Pro–64 L Farmer
V'trs WD–U WE–after 3pm
Fees Tues/Thurs/Fri–£9.50 (£16)
      Mon & Wed–£6.50
Loc   Junction of Uxbridge Road
      and Greenford Road

Whitewebbs (1932)

Public
Beggars Hollow, Clay Hill, Enfield
EN2 9JN
Tel   (081) 363 2951
Pro   D Lewis (081) 363 4454
Holes 18 L 5755 yds SSS 68
Recs Am–61 C Smith
      Pro–68 D Lewis
V'trs U
Fees £3.80 (£5.10)
Loc   1 mile N of Enfield Town

Wyke Green (1928)

Syon Lane, Isleworth
Tel   (081) 560 8777
Mem 618
Sec   Maj. WE Lyndon Moore
Pro   A Fisher (081) 847 0685
Holes 18 L 6242 yds SSS 70
Recs Am–65 MR Johnson
      Pro–64 C DeFoy
V'trs U
Fees £12 (£17)
Loc   1/2 mile from Gillettes Corner
      (A4)

Norfolk

Barnham Broom Hotel (1977)

Barnham Broom, Norwich NR9 4DD
Tel   (060 545) 393
Mem 560
Sec   A Long (Man Dir)
      P Ballingall (Golf Dir)
Pro   S Beckham
Holes Valley 18 L 6470 yds SSS 71;
      Hill 18 L 6628 yds SSS 72
V'trs I or H WE/BH–NA (exc hotel
      residents) SOC
Fees £20 (NA) £17.50–residents
Loc   8 miles SW of Norwich off A47.
      4 miles NW of Wymondham
      off A11

Bawburgh

Long Lane, Bawburgh
Tel   (0603) 746390
Mem 400
Sec   RJ Mapes
Pro   R Waugh
Holes 9 L 5278 yds SSS 66
Recs Am–67 S Manser
      Pro–69 R Waugh
V'trs Sun–Restricted before 11am
      SOC–WD by arrangement
Fees 18 holes £10 (£12.50)
      9 holes £6
Loc   S of A47, 1 mile from Norwich
      ring road. Turn left at Round
      Well PH. Rear of Royal Norfolk
      Showground

Costessey Park (1983)

Costessey Park, Costessey, Norwich
NR8 5AL
Tel   (0603) 746333
Mem 500
Sec   BA Howson
Pro   D Johnson (0603) 747085
Holes 18 L 5853 yds SSS 68
V'trs U SOC–WD
Fees £10 (£12)
Loc   3 miles W of Norwich, turn
      off A47 at Round Well PH

Dereham (1934)

Quebec Road, Dereham NR19 2DS
Tel   (0362) 693122
Mem 520
Sec   N Dodds (0362) 695900
Pro   S Fox (0362) 695631
Holes 9 L 6225 yds SSS 70
Recs Am–63 L Varney
      Pro–65 M Elsworthy
V'trs H WE–M
Fees £12.50
Loc   Dereham 1/2 mile

Eaton (1910)

Newmarket Road, Norwich NR4 6SF
Tel   (0603) 52881
Mem 425 130(L) 70(J) 205(5)
Sec   J Drinkwater (0603) 51686
Pro   F Hill (0603) 52478
Holes 18 L 6135 yds SSS 69
Recs Am–65 SW Abel (1987)
      Pro–65 M Spooner (1988)
V'trs I WE–NA before noon
Fees £14 (£18)
Loc   S Norwich

Fakenham (1973)

Fakenham
Tel   (0328) 2867
Mem 450
Sec   G Cocker (0328) 55665
Pro   J Westwood (0328) 3534
Holes 9 hole course
Recs Am–70 D Hood
      Pro–70 M Leeder

V'trs WD–U WE–starting times
alternate Sun am SOC
Fees £8 (£11)
Loc Racecourse

Feltwell (1976)

Thor Ave, off Wilton Road, Feltwell
Mem 340
Sec Mrs C Sharp (0366) 728035
Holes 9 L 6260 yds SSS 70
V'trs U
Fees £7 (£10)
Loc 1 mile S of Feltwell Village
on B1112
Mis Course laid out on former
Feltwell aerodrome.

Gorleston (1906)

Warren Road, Gorleston, Gt Yarmouth
NR31 6JT
Tel (0493) 661802
Mem 800
Sec PG Rudd (0493) 661911
Pro RL Moffit (0493) 662103
Holes 18 L 6400 yds SSS 71
Recs Am–68 J Maddock (1981)
V'trs U H SOC
Fees £12 (£14) W–£35
Loc S of Gorleston off A12

Granary Hotel G & CC

Little Dunham, King's Lynn PE32 2DF
Tel (0328) 701310
Sec J Harris (Prop)
Pro C Denny (0362) 694383
Holes 9 L 2023 yds SSS 60
V'trs U
Loc 4 miles NE of Swaffham

Great Yarmouth & Caister (1882)

Beach House, Caister-on-Sea,
Gt Yarmouth
Tel (0493) 720421
Mem 700
Sec AA Hunton (0493) 728699
Pro N Catchpole
Holes 18 L 6284 yds SSS 70
Recs Am–67 M Sperrin
Pro–66 E Murray
V'trs WE–NA before noon SOC
Fees £8 (£10)
Loc Caister-on-Sea

Hunstanton (1891)

Hunstanton
Tel (048 53) 2811
Mem 650 250(L) 60(J)
Sec RH Cotton
Pro J Carter (048 53) 2751
Holes 18 L 6670 yds SSS 72
Recs Am–65 S Robertson (1989)
Pro–65 ME Gregson (1967)
V'trs WD–U after 9.30am WE/BH–U
after 10.30am SOC
Fees £20 (£25) W–£93
Loc ½ mile NE of Hunstanton

King's Lynn (1923)

Castle Rising, King's Lynn PE31 6BD
Tel (055 387) 656
Mem 980
Sec GJ Higgins (055 387) 654
Pro C Hanlon (055 387) 655
Holes 18 L 6646 yds SSS 72
Recs Am–74 S Webster (1988)
Pro–68 M Davis (1988)
V'trs WD–UH WE/BH–NA SOC
Fees £14 (£20)
Loc 4 miles NE of King's Lynn

Links Country Park Hotel (1979)

West Runton, Cromer
Tel (026 375) 691
Mem 300
Sec SG Mansfield
Pro M Jubb
Holes 9 L 4814 yds Par 66 SSS 64
Recs Am–64 CJ Lamb (1988)
Pro–65 R Mann, GR Harvey
(1987)
V'trs U
Fees D–£12 (D–£14)
Loc Midway between Cromer and
Sheringham

Mundesley (1903)

Links Road, Mundesley NR11 8ES
Tel (0263) 720279
Mem 400
Sec BD Baxter (0263) 720095
Pro TG Symmons
Holes 9 L 5410 yds SSS 66
V'trs U exc Wed 12–3pm Sun–NA
before 11.30am
Fees £10 (£16)
Loc 7 miles S of Cromer

RAF Marham (1974)

RAF Marham, Kings Lynn PE33 9NP
Mem 200
Sec Flt Lt M Gilligan
(0760) 337261 (Ext 604)
Holes 9 L 5244 yds SSS 66
Recs Am–71
V'trs By prior arrangement–course
situated on MOD land; U exc
Sun am
Fees £3 (£7)
Loc Near Narborough, 11 miles
SE of Kings Lynn
Mis Course may be closed
without prior notice

Royal Cromer (1888)

Overstrand Road, Cromer NR27 0JH
Tel (0263) 512884
Mem 675
Sec Flt Lt E Robertson
Pro RJ Page (0263) 512267
Holes 18 L 6508 yds SSS 71
Recs Am–68 M Williamson (1989)
Pro–70 M Few (1988)
V'trs H SOC–WD
Fees £18 (£22)
Loc 1 mile E of Cromer

Royal Norwich (1893)

Drayton High Road, Hellesdon,
Norwich
Tel (0603) 45712
Mem 780
Sec DF Cottier (0603) 429928
Pro B Lockwood (0603) 408459
Holes 18 L 6603 yds SSS 72
Recs Am–67 A Barker
Pro–66 HJ Boyle
V'trs WE/BH–Restricted SOC
Fees £15 R/D
Loc ½ mile W of Norwich ring
road, on Fakenham road

Royal West Norfolk (1892)

Brancaster, King's Lynn PE31 8AX
Tel (0485) 210223
Mem 760
Sec Maj. N Carrington Smith
Pro RE Kimber (0485) 210616
Holes 18 L 6428 yds SSS 71
Recs Am–67 AH Perowne
Pro–66 M Elsworthy
V'trs WD–by prior arrangement
WE–M BH–NA SOC–max 12
Fees £20 (£25)
Loc 7 miles E of Hunstanton on A419

Ryston Park (1932)

Ely Road, Denver, Downham Market
PE38 0HH
Tel (0366) 382133
Mem 320
Sec AJ Wilson (0366) 383834
Holes 9 L 6292 yds SSS 70
Recs Am–66 JP Alflatt (1975)
V'trs WE–M
Fees £15
Loc 1 mile S of Downham
Market on A10

Sheringham (1891)

Sheringham
Tel (0263) 822038
Mem 750
Sec MJ Garrett (0263) 823488
Pro MT Leeder (0263) 822980
Holes 18 L 6464 yds SSS 71
Recs Am–69 SD Miller
Pro–69 M Few
V'trs WD–U after 9.15am H SOC
Fees £20 (£25)
Loc ½ mile W of Sheringham

Sprowston Park (1980)

Wroxham Road, Sprowston, Norwich
NR7 8RP
Tel (0603) 410657
Mem 650
Sec TA Mower
Pro C Potter (0603) 415557
Holes 18 L 5985 yds SSS 69
Recs Am–69 S Terrington
Pro–65 N Catchpole
V'trs WD–U H before 5pm WE–NA
Loc 2 miles NE of Norwich
Mis Floodlit driving range

For explanation of abbreviations, see page 460.

Swaffham (1922)

Cley Road, Swaffham
Tel   (0760) 721611
Mem   450
Sec   R Joslin (0760) 22487
Pro   CJ Norton (036 621) 284
Holes 9 L 6252 yds SSS 70
Recs   Am–68 G Head
       Pro–64 CJ Norton
V'trs WD–U WE–M Sun am–NA
Fees   £12
Loc   Swaffham 1¹/₂ miles

Thetford (1912)

Brandon Road, Thetford IP24 3NE
Tel   (0842) 752258
Mem   650
Sec   RJ Ferguson (0842) 752169
Pro   N Arthur (0842) 752662
Holes 18 L 6879 yds SSS 73
Recs   Am–69 RE Clarke
       Pro–69 B White
V'trs H SOC
Fees   £15 (D–£20)
Loc   Brandon Road (B1107) off A11

Northamptonshire

Cold Ashby (1974)

Cold Ashby, nr Northampton
NN6 7EP
Tel   (0604) 740548
Mem   600 40(L) 40(J)
Sec   D Croxton
Pro   T Skingle (0604) 740099
Holes 18 L 5957 yds SSS 69
Recs   Am–68 S Crowson (1989)
       Pro–61 D Dunk (1985)
V'trs WD–U WE–U after 2pm
       (if booked) SOC
Fees   £10 (£12)
Loc   5 miles E of M1 Junction
       18, between Leicester and
       Northampton

Daventry & District (1922)

Norton Road, Daventry
Tel   (0327) 702829
Mem   300
Sec   F Higham (0327) 703204
Pro   M Higgins
Holes 9 L 2871 yds SSS 67
V'trs WD–U Sun–NA before 11am
       SOC
Fees   £4.50 (£5.50)
Loc   Norton Road

Delapre (1976)

Public
Eagle Drive, Nene Valley Way,
Northampton
Tel   (0604) 64036/63957
Pro   J Corby (0604) 64036
Holes 18 L 6293 yds SSS 70
       2 x 9 hole Par 3 courses

Recs   Am–66 M McNally
V'trs U SOC
Fees   £3.75 (WE/BH £4.75)
Loc   M1 Junction 15, 3 miles (A508)
Mis   Pitch and putt. Driving range

Kettering (1891)

Headlands, Kettering
Tel   (0536) 512074
Mem   380 100(L) 45(J) 65(5)
Sec   T Cave (0536) 511104
Pro   K Theobald (0536) 81014
Holes 18 L 6035 yds SSS 69
Recs   Am–67 J Campbell
       Pro–67 J Gallagher
V'trs WD–U WE/BH–M SOC
Fees   £12
Loc   S boundary of Kettering

Kingsthorpe (1908)

Kingsley Road, Northampton NN2 7BU
Tel   (0604) 711173
Mem   450
Sec   NC Liddington (0604) 710610
Pro   P Smith (0604) 719602
Holes 18 L 6006 yds SSS 69
Recs   Am–63 S McDonald
       Pro–64 B Larratt
V'trs WD–U WE/BH–MH SOC–WD
Fees   £16 R/D
Loc   Northampton

Northampton (1893)

Kettering Road, Northampton
NN3 1AA
Tel   (0604) 711054
Mem   500 100(L) 70(J)
Sec   TCA Knight (0604) 719453
Pro   M Chamberlain (0604) 714897
Holes 18 L 6002 yds SSS 69
Recs   Am–66 C Cieslewicz (1972)
       Pro–64 M Gallagher (1983)
V'trs WD–U H WE–M
Fees   £18
Loc   2 miles E of Northampton,
       on A43

Northamptonshire County (1909)

Church Brampton, Northampton
Tel   (0604) 842170
Mem   600
Sec   GG Morley (0604) 843025
Pro   SD Brown (0604) 842226
Holes 18 L 6503 yds SSS 71
Recs   Am–67 C Poxon (1986)
       Pro–65 M Ingham (1987)
V'trs WD–H WE–I H XL before
       3.30pm Sat and 11.15am Sun
Fees   £13 (£15)
Loc   5 miles NW of Northampton
       off A50

Oundle (1894)

Oundle
Tel   (0832) 273267
Mem   600
Sec   R Davis
Holes 18 L 5507 yds SSS 67

Recs   Am–68
       Pro–67
V'trs WD–U WE–M before 10.30am
       –U after 10.30am
Fees   £12 (£15)

Priors Hall (1965)

Public
Tel   (0536) 60756
Pro   M Summers
Holes 18 L 6677 yds SSS 72
Recs   Am–75 R Beekie, M Scott,
       WF Kearney
       Pro–70 RH Kemp
V'trs U
Fees   £2.80 (£4.30)
Loc   A43

Rushden (1919)

Kimbolton Road, Chelveston,
Wellingborough
Tel   (0933) 312581
Mem   350
Sec   R Tomlin (0933) 312197
Holes 9 L 6381 yds SSS 70
Recs   Am–67
V'trs WD–U exc Wed pm WE–M
       Sat pm/Sun am–XL BH–U SOC
Fees   £12
Loc   On A45, 2 miles E of Higham
       Ferrers

Staverton Park (1977)

Staverton, nr Daventry NN11 6JJ
Mem   (0327) 705911
Sec   AL McLundie
Pro   B Mudge (0327) 705506
Holes 18 L 6634 yds SSS 72
Recs   Am–67
       Pro–64
V'trs H SOC
Fees   £12.50 (£19.50)
Loc   1 mile S of Daventry off A425.
       M1 Junctions 16/18, 15 mins

Wellingborough (1893)

Harrowden Hall, Great Harrowden,
Wellingborough NN9 5AD
Tel   (0933) 677234/673022
Mem   850
Sec   Maj. AS Furnival (0933) 677234
Pro   D Clifford (0933) 678752
Holes 18 L 6620 yds SSS 72
Recs   Am–69 AI Marshall
       Pro–69 D Clifford
V'trs W–U exc Tues pm I WE–M
       SOC–Wed & Thurs
Fees   £20 D–£25
Loc   2 miles N of Wellingborough
       on A509 to Kettering

Woodlands Vale (1974)

Farthingstone, nr Towcester
Tel   (032 736) 291
Mem   650
Sec   DC Donaldson (Prop)
Pro   M Gallagher
Holes 18 L 6330 yds SSS 71

Recs   Am–69 A Deakin (1984)
       Pro–66 D Thorp (1985)
       M Gallagher (1986)
V'trs U SOC
Fees   £9 (£12)
Loc   6 miles W of M1 Junction 16.
       3 miles W of A5 at Weedon,
       on Farthingstone road
Mis   Buggies for hire

Northumberland

Allendale (1923)

Thornley Gate, Allendale, Hexham
NE47 9LG
Mem   90 20(L) 9(J)
Sec   JC Hall (091) 267 5875
Holes 9 L 4410 yds SSS 63
V'trs U SOC
Fees   £3 (£4) W–£16.50
Loc   10 miles SW of Hexham

Alnmouth (1869)

Foxton Hall, Alnmouth
Tel   (0665) 830231
Mem   600
Sec   FK Marshall (0665) 830368
Holes 18 L 6414 yds SSS 71
Recs   Am–65 P Deeble
V'trs U SOC–Mon–Thurs
Fees   £11 (£14) 1989 prices
Loc   5 miles SE of Alnwick
Mis   Dormy House accommodation

Alnmouth Village (1869)

Marine Road, Alnmouth
Tel   (0665) 830370
Mem   340
Sec   W Maclean (0665) 602096
Holes 9 L 6020 yds SSS 70
Recs   Am–63 D Weddell
V'trs U SOC
Fees   £6 (£10) W–£25
Loc   Alnmouth

Alnwick (1907)

Swansfield Park, Alnwick
Tel   (0665) 602632
Mem   400
Sec   LE Stewart (0665) 602499
Holes 9 L 5387 yds SSS 66
Recs   Am–62 P Deeble
V'trs U
Fees   £6 R/D
Loc   Alnwick

Arcot Hall (1909)

Dudley, Cramlington NE23 7QP
Mem   540
Sec   AG Bell (091) 236 2794
Pro   GM Cant (091) 236 2147
Holes 18 L 6389 yds SSS 70

Recs   Am–67 N McDonald (1986),
       J Metcalfe (1987), N Ferriman
       (1989)
       Pro–67 S Harrison, P Harrison
V'trs WD–U SOC
Fees   £14 (£18)
Loc   7 miles N of Newcastle off A1

Bamburgh Castle (1904)

Bamburgh NE69 7DE
Tel   (066 84) 378
Mem   650
Sec   TC Osborne (066 84) 321
Holes 18 L 5465 yds SSS 67
Recs   Am–63 RS Rutter (1984)
V'trs U BH–NA SOC
Fees   £12 R/D (£12 D–£16) W–£45
Loc   Bamburgh, 7 miles E of A1
       via B1341 or B1342
Mis   Buggy for hire (summer)

Bedlingtonshire (1972)

Public
Acorn Bank, Bedlington
Tel   (0670) 822457
Sec   R Partis (Hon)
Pro   M Webb (0670) 822087
Holes 18 L 6224 metres SSS 73
Recs   Am–68 D Gray
       Pro–65 K Waters
V'trs U
Fees   £4.50 D–£6 (£6 D–£8)
Loc   12 miles N of Newcastle

Bellingham (1893)

Bellingham NE48 2DT
Tel   (0434) 220530
Mem   250
Sec   TH Thompson (0434) 220281
Holes 9 L 5226 yds SSS 66
Recs   Am–63 I Wilson
V'trs U exc comp days SOC
Fees   £6 (£7.50)
Loc   15 miles N of Hexham

Berwick-upon-Tweed (1890)

Goswick Beal, Berwick-upon-Tweed
TD15 2RW
Tel   (0289) 87256
Mem   450
Sec   RC Oliver
Pro   M Leighton (0289) 87380
Holes 18 L 6425 yds SSS 71
Recs   Am–64 J Cotton
V'trs WD–U WE–U 10am–2.30pm
       (1st tee) SOC
Fees   £9 D–£12 (£12 D–£18) W–£30
Loc   5 miles S of Berwick off A1

Blyth (1905)

New Delaval, Blyth
Tel   (0670) 367728
Mem   580 120(L) 120(J)
Sec   WJF Lightley
Pro   K Phillips (0670) 356514

Holes 18 L 6498 yds SSS 71
Recs   Am–66 P Simpson (1989)
V'trs WD–U WE–M BH–NA
       SOC–WD
Fees   £8 D–£10 WE–M
Loc   W end of Plessey Road, Blyth

Dunstanburgh Castle (1907)

Embleton NE66 3XQ
Tel   (066 576) 562
Mem   256
Sec   PFC Gilbert
Holes 18 L 6357 yds SSS 70
Recs   Am–69
V'trs U
Fees   £8 (£11)
Loc   7 miles NE of Alnwick on B1339

Haltwhistle

Greenhead, Nr Haltwhistle
Tel   (069) 72367
Mem   250
Sec   WE Barnes (Hon)
Pro   J Metcalf
Holes 12 5968 yds SSS 69
V'trs U SOC
Fees   £5 (£5)
Loc   Greenhead, 3 miles W of
       Haltwhistle

Hexham (1906)

Spital Park, Hexham NE46 3RZ
Tel   (0434) 602057
Mem   700
Sec   JC Oates (0434) 603072
Pro   I Waugh (0434) 604904
Holes 18 L 6272 yds SSS 70
Recs   Am–66 A Hinds
       Pro–67 I Waugh
V'trs U
Fees   £8 (£11) W–£32 M–£70
Loc   21 miles W of Newcastle

Magdalene Fields (1903)

Public
Magdalene Fields, Berwick-upon-
Tweed
Tel   (0289) 306384
Sec   R Patterson (0289) 305758
Holes 18 L 6551 yds SSS 71
Recs   Am–70 J Patterson
V'trs U
Fees   £6.25 (1989)
Loc   Berwick centre 5 mins

Morpeth (1907)

The Common, Morpeth
Tel   (0670) 519980
Mem   500
Sec   T Weddell (0670) 55828
Pro   MR Jackson (0670) 512065
Holes 18 L 5671 metres SSS 70
V'trs H
Fees   £6.50 (£8)
Loc   1 mile S of Morpeth on A197

For explanation of abbreviations, see page 460.

Newbiggin-by-the-Sea (1884)

Newbiggin-by-the-Sea
Tel   (0670) 817344
Mem   500
Sec   D Lyall (0670) 815062
Pro   D Fletcher (0670) 817833
Holes   18 L 6450 yds SSS 71
Recs   Am–67 B Bennett
        Pro–68 K Saint
V'trs   U after 10am SOC
Fees   £5.50 (£7.50) W–£25
Loc   Newbiggin, near Church Point

Ponteland (1927)

53 Bell Villas, Ponteland,
Newcastle–upon–Tyne NE20 9BD
Tel   (0661) 72844/71872
Mem   460 150(L) 80(J) 30(5)
Sec   G Weetman (0661) 22689
Pro   A Crosby (0661) 22689
Holes   18 L 6512 yds SSS 71
Recs   Am–66 J Hayes, WMM Jenkins,
        DG Potter (1987)
        Pro–66 G Burrows
V'trs   WD–U WE/BH–M
Fees   £10 D–£12
Loc   6 miles NW of Newcastle on
        A696, nr Airport

Prudhoe (1930)

Eastwood Park, Prudhoe-on-Tyne
NE42 5DX
Tel   (0661) 32466
Mem   400
Sec   GB Garratt (0661) 34134
Pro   J Crawford (0661) 36188
Holes   18 L 5812 yds SSS 68
Recs   Am–65 DH Curry
        Pro–65 A Crosby
V'trs   WD–U WE–M SOC
Fees   £7 (£8)
Loc   15 miles W of Newcastle

Rothbury (1891)

Old Race Course, Rothbury, Morpeth
Tel   (0669) 21271 (Clubhouse)
Mem   300
Sec   WT Bathgate (0669) 20718
Holes   9 L 5560 yds SSS 67
Recs   Am–64 S Twynholm
V'trs   WD–U WE–U before noon
        NA–after noon
Fees   £3.50 (£6)
Loc   15 miles N of Morpeth on A1.
        W side of Rothbury

Seahouses (1913)

Beadnell Road, Seahouses NE68 7XT
Tel   (0665) 720794
Mem   350
Sec   G Hogg (0665) 720091
Holes   18 L 5374 yds SSS 66

Recs   Am–65 RS Rutter (1989)
V'trs   U SOC
Fees   £8 (£10.50)
Loc   14 miles N of Alnwick.
        9 miles off A1

Slaley Hall G & CC (1988)

Slaley, Hexham
Tel   (0434) 673691
Mem   200
Sec   BW Patterson
Pro   B Patterson
Holes   18 L 6995 yds SSS 74
V'trs   U H SOC
Fees   £22.50 D–£35
Loc   16 miles W of Newcastle.
        7 miles S of Corbridge off A68

Stocksfield (1913)

New Ridley NE43 7RE
Tel   (0661) 843041
Mem   341 79(L) 70(J)
Sec   DB Moon
Pro   K Driver
Holes   18 L 5594 yds SSS 68
Recs   Am–61 GED Bradley
        Pro–66 P Harrison
V'trs   U SOC
Fees   £10 (£15)
Loc   3 miles E of A68.
        1 mile S of A686

Tynedale (1908)

Public
Tyne Green, Hexham
Holes   9 L 5706 yds SSS 68
Recs   Am–64 A Varty
V'trs   U exc Sun–booking req
Fees   £3 (£5) 1989 prices
Loc   S side of Hexham

Warkworth (1891)

The Links, Warkworth, Morpeth
Tel   (0665) 711596
Mem   400
Sec   JW Anderson (0665) 75608
Holes   9 L 5817 yds SSS 68
Recs   Am–67 AB Barrett
V'trs   U
Fees   £6 (£10)
Loc   15 miles NE of Morpeth

Wooler (1975)

Doddington, Wooler
Mem   200
Sec   JH Curry (0668) 81956
Holes   9 L 6353 yds SSS 70
Recs   Am–72 N Graham
V'trs   U SOC
Fees   D–£4 (D–£5) W–£18
Loc   3 miles N of Wooler on B6525

Nottinghamshire

Beeston Fields (1923)

Beeston, Nottingham
Tel   (0602) 257062
Mem   400 150(L) 52(J)
Sec   DW Newbold
Pro   M Pashley (0602) 257503
Holes   18 L 6404 yds SSS 71
Recs   Am–66 P Benson
V'trs   U SOC
Fees   £15 (£17)
Loc   4 miles W of Nottingham.
        M1 Junction 25

Bulwell Forest (1902)

Public
Hucknall Road, Bulwell,Nottingham
NG6 9LQ
Tel   (0602) 770576
Sec   D Stubbs (Hon)
Pro   CD Hall (0602) 763172/278008
Holes   18 L 5746 yds SSS 68
Recs   Am–62 DN Smedley,
        D Newham, JP Smith
        Pro–62 CD Hall
V'trs   U
Fees   £3.20
Loc   4 miles N of Nottingham.
        M1 Junction 26

Chilwell Manor (1906)

Meadow Lane, Chilwell, Nottingham
NG9 5AE
Tel   (0602) 257050
Mem   620
Sec   GA Spindley (0602) 258958
Pro   E McCausland (0602) 258993
Holes   18 L 6379 yds SSS 69
        18 L 5438 yds SSS 67
Recs   Am–67 C Gray
        Pro–66 B Waites
V'trs   WD–U WE–NA SOC
Fees   £9 D–£12
Loc   4 miles W of Nottingham

Coxmoor (1913)

Coxmoor Road, Sutton-in-Ashfield
NG17 5LF
Tel   (0623) 557359
Mem   650
Sec   J Tyler
Pro   DJ Ridley (0623) 559906
Holes   18 L 6501 yds SSS 72
Recs   Am–67 M Nunn
        Pro–65 B Waites
V'trs   H SOC (Ladies Day–Tues)
Fees   £16 (£20)
Loc   1½ miles S of Mansfield.
        3 miles from M1 Junction 27

Edwalton (1982)

Public
Edwalton, Nottingham
Tel   (0602) 234775
Sec   JF Shepperson (Hon)
Pro   J Staples

Holes	9 L 3336 yds SSS 36
	9 hole Par 3 course
V'trs	U
Fees	£2.30 (£2.80)
Loc	2 miles S of Nottingham

Kilton Forest (1978)

Public

Blyth Road, Worksop S81 0TL

Tel	(0909) 472488
Sec	EL James (Hon)
Pro	PW Foster (0909) 486563
Holes	18 L 6569 yds SSS 72
Recs	Am–69 SJ Thorpe (1988)
	Pro–72 DJ Ridley (1988)
V'trs	U
Fees	£4.50 (£5.50)
Loc	1 mile NE of Worksop
	on B6045

Mansfield Woodhouse (1973)

Public

Mansfield Woodhouse NG19 9EU

Tel	(0623) 23521
Holes	9 L 2411 yds SSS 65
Recs	Am–67 S Fisher
	Pro–L Highfield Jr
V'trs	U
Fees	£2
Loc	2 miles N of Mansfield

Mapperley (1913)

Central Avenue, Plains Road,
Mapperley, Nottingham NG3 5RH

Tel	(0602) 265611
Mem	600
Sec	SJD Kinghan
Pro	R Daibell (0602) 202227
Holes	18 L 6224 yds SSS 70
Recs	Am–68 B Tones (1986)
	Pro–68 R Daibell (1986)
V'trs	U SOC
Fees	£9 (£11)
Loc	3 miles NE of Mapperley

Newark (1901)

Kelwick, Coddington, Newark

Tel	(0636 84) 241
Mem	575
Sec	JN Simpson (0636 84) 282
Pro	A Bennett (0636 84) 492
Holes	18 L 6486 yds SSS 71
Recs	Am–70 C Bentley
	Pro–69 CW Gray, DJ Britten
V'trs	I H
Fees	£10 (£15)
Loc	4 miles E of Newark on A17

Nottingham City (1910)

Public

Lawton Drive, Bulwell, Nottingham
NG6 8BL

Tel	(0602) 278021
Sec	DA Griffiths (Hon)
Pro	CR Jepson (0602) 272767

Holes	18 L 6218 yds SSS 70
Recs	Am–66 T Payne (1987)
	Pro–66 T Smart
V'trs	WD–U WE–NA before noon
	SOC
Fees	£3.75 (£4)
Loc	M1 Junction 28, 3 miles

Notts (1887)

Hollinwell, Kirby-in-Ashfield
NG17 7QR

Tel	(0623) 752042/753225
Mem	500
Sec	JR Walker (0623) 753225
Pro	BJ Waites (0623) 753087
Holes	18 L 7020 yds SSS 74
Recs	Am–67 IT Simpson,
	I MacKenzie
	Pro–64 J Bland
V'trs	WD–H WE/BH–M
Fees	On application
Loc	4 miles S of Mansfield.
	M1 Junction 27

Oxton (1974)

Oaks Lane, Oxton

Tel	(0602) 653545
Mem	550
Sec	GC Norton
Pro	GC Norton
Holes	18 L 6600 yds SSS 72
	9 L 3300 yds SSS 37
Recs	Am–70 J Vaughan
	Pro–68 D Dunk, B Waites,
	D Snell, D Ridley
V'trs	WD–U WE/BH–arrange times
	with Mgr SOC
Fees	£7.50 (£9)
Loc	9 miles N of Nottingham on
	A614 to Doncaster
Mis	Floodlit driving range

Radcliffe-on-Trent (1909)

Dewberry Lane, Cropwell Road,
Radcliffe-on-Trent NG12 2JH

Tel	(0602) 333000
Mem	650
Sec	PJ Newton
Pro	P Hinton (0602) 332396
Holes	18 L 6423 yds SSS 71
V'trs	U H SOC
Fees	£14 (£18)
Loc	6 miles E of Nottingham
	off A52

Retford (1921)

Brecks Road, Ordsall, Retford
DN22 7UA

Tel	(0777) 703733
Mem	360
Sec	A Harrison (0777) 703389
Holes	9 L 6230 yds SSS 70
Recs	Am–68 MD Walker (1987)
V'trs	WD–U WE–M SOC–WD
Fees	£4 (£6)
Loc	2 miles SW of Retford off
	A638 or A620. 16 miles E
	of M1 Junction 30

Ruddington Grange

Wilford Road, Ruddington,
Nottingham NG11 6NB

Tel	(0602) 846141
Mem	600
Sec	J Aston
Pro	RJ Ellis (0602) 211951
Holes	18 L 6467 yds SSS 71
Recs	Am–71 DJT Johnson (1988)
	Pro–71 C Hall (1989)
V'trs	UH BH–U exc comp days SOC
Fees	£15 D–£20 (£18 D–£24)
Loc	3 miles S of Nottingham

Rushcliffe (1910)

East Leake, nr Nottingham

Tel	(050 982) 2209
Mem	500
Sec	MG Booth (050 982) 2959
Pro	T Smart (050 982) 2701
Holes	18 L 6090 yds SSS 69
V'trs	NA
Loc	9 miles S of Nottingham

Serlby Park (1905)

Serlby, Doncaster, S Yorks
DN10 6BA

Tel	(0777) 818268
Mem	250
Sec	M Hunter (0302) 851349
Holes	9 L 5370 yds SSS 66
Recs	Am–63 A Pugsley (1988)
	Pro–65 M Bembridge (1965)
V'trs	M
Loc	12 miles S of Doncaster
	between A614 and A638

Sherwood Forest (1904)

Eakring Road, Mansfield
NG18 3EW

Tel	(0623) 23327
Mem	600
Sec	K Hall (0623) 26689
Pro	K Hall (0623) 27403
Holes	18 L 6710 yds SSS 73
Recs	Am–65 PM Baxter
	Pro–68 C Gray, G Stafford
V'trs	U H SOC
Fees	£15 D–£20 (£20)
Loc	2 miles E of Mansfield

Stanton-on-the-Wolds (1906)

Stanton Lane, Keyworth

Tel	(060 77) 2044
Mem	500 167(L) 100(J)
Sec	HG Gray (0602) 787291
Pro	N Hernon ((060 77) 2390
Holes	18 L 6437 yds SSS 71
Recs	Am–67 CA Banks
	Pro–69 C Jepson
V'trs	U exc Sat comp days–NA XL
	SOC
Fees	£13 (£15)
Loc	9 miles S of Nottingham

For explanation of abbreviations, see page 460.

Wollaton Park (1927)

Nottingham NG8 1BT
Tel (0602) 787574
Mem 600
Sec B Morris BSc PhD
Pro R Hastings (0602) 784834
Holes 18 L 6494 yds SSS 71
Recs Am–66 C Banks, L White
V'trs U SOC
Fees £11 (£17)
Loc Nottingham 2 miles

Worksop (1914)

Windmill Lane, Worksop S80 2SQ
Tel (0909) 472696
Mem 500
Sec PG Jordan (0909) 477731
Pro JR King (0909) 477732
Holes 18 L 6651 yds SSS 72
Recs Am–70 D Bagshaw
 Pro–69 A Carter
V'trs WD–U H (phone first)
 WE/BH–M SOC
Fees £13 R/D (£16)
Loc 1 mile SE of Worksop, off
 A6009 via by–pass

Oxfordshire

Badgemore Park (1972)

Henley-on-Thames
Tel (0491) 573667 (Clubhouse)
Mem 750
Sec LA Booker (0491) 572206
Pro M Howell (0491) 574175
Holes 18 L 6112 yds SSS 69
Recs Am–67 SJ Mann
 Pro–65 M Howell
V'trs WD–U WE–M SOC–WD
Fees £18 SOC–£19
Loc 3/4 mile W of Henley on B290

Burford (1936)

Burford OX8 4JG
Tel (099 382) 2149
Mem 680
Sec R Cane (099 382) 2583
Pro N Allen (099 382) 2344
Holes 18 L 6405 yds SSS 71
Recs Am–67 DE Giles
 Pro–67 H Weetman
V'trs WD–H SOC
Loc 19 miles W of Oxford on A40

Cherwell Edge (1980)

Public
Chacombe, Banbury OX17 2EN
Tel (0295) 711591
Sec R Davies
Pro R Davies
Holes 18 L 5925 yds SSS 69
Recs Am–71
V'trs U SOC–WD
Fees £3.80 D–£6.50 (£4.90)
Loc 3 miles E of Banbury on
 B4525 (A422)

Chesterton (1973)

Chesterton, nr Bicester OX6 8TE
Tel (0869) 241204
Mem 650
Sec BT Carter
Pro JW Wilkshire (0869) 242023
Holes 18 L 6224 yds SSS 70
Recs Am–68
 Pro–68
V'trs WD–U WE/BH–H SOC–WD
Fees £10 (£15)
Loc 2 miles SW of Bicester

Chipping Norton (1890)

Southcombe, Chipping Norton
OX7 5QH
Tel (0608) 2383
Mem 825
Sec AJB Norman
Pro R Gould (0608) 3356
Holes 18 L 6280 yds SSS 70
Recs Am–67 A Perrie, J Morewood
V'trs WD–U WE–M
Fees £14
Loc 1 mile E of Chipping Norton

Frilford Heath (1908)

Frilford Heath, Abingdon OX13 5NW
Tel (0865) 390864
Mem 750
Sec JW Kleynhans
Pro DC Craik (0865) 390887
Holes Red 18 L 6768 yds SSS 73
 Green 18 L 6006 yds SSS 69
Recs Red Am–68 S Walker
 Green Am–65 G Wolstenholme
V'trs WD–U H WE/BH–M H SOC
Fees £22 (£30)
Loc 3 miles W of Abingdon on
 A338 Oxford/Wantage road

Henley (1908)

Harpsden, Henley-on-Thames
RG9 4HG
Tel (0491) 573304
Mem 750
Sec J Hex (0491) 575742
Pro J Cook (0491) 575710
Holes 18 L 6329 yds SSS 70
Recs Am–65 D Griffin (1989)
 Pro–64 P Harrison (1989)
V'trs WD–H WE–M
Fees £18 R/D 1989 price
Loc Henley Station 1 mile

Huntercombe (1901)

Nuffield, Henley-on-Thames RG9 5SL
Tel (0491) 641207
Mem 700
Sec Lt Col TJ Hutchison
Pro JB Draycott (0491) 641241
Holes 18 L 6261 yds SSS 70
Recs Am–65 A Jackson
 Pro–63 J Morris
V'trs WD–H after 10am WE/BH–NA
 SOC
Fees £23
Loc 6 miles W of Henley on A423
Mis Foursomes and singles only

North Oxford (1908)

Banbury Road, Oxford OX2 8EZ
Tel (0865) 54415
Mem 701
Sec W Forster (0865) 54924
Pro R Harris (0865) 53977
Holes 18 L 5805 yds SSS 67
Recs Am–64 S Donaghey
 Pro–M Faulkner
V'trs U SOC
Fees £18 (£25)
Loc Between Oxford and
 Kidlington

RAF Benson (1975)

Royal Air Force, Benson
Tel (0491) 37766
Mem 175
Sec Sqn Ldr WB Sowerby MVO
 RAF (Ret'd) (0235) 848472
Holes 9 L 4395 yds SSS 61
V'trs M
Loc 3$^{1}/_{2}$ miles NE of Wallingford

Southfield (1875)

Hill Top Road, Oxford OX4 1PF
Tel (0865) 242158
Mem 500
Sec AG Hopcraft
Pro A Rees (0865) 244258
Holes 18 L 6230 yds SSS 70
Recs Am–66 CM Barrett, GL Morley
 Pro–61 A Rees
V'trs WD–U WE/BH–MH SOC
Fees £16
Loc 2 miles E of Oxford

Tadmarton Heath (1922)

Wigginton, Banbury OX15 5HL
Tel (0608) 737649
Mem 600
Sec RE Wackrill (0608) 737278
Pro Les Bond (0608) 730047
Holes 18 L 5917 yds SSS 69
Recs Am–66 R Welsh
 Pro–63 G Smith
V'trs WD–U H WE–M SOC
Fees £18
Loc 5 miles W of Banbury off B4035

Shropshire

Bridgnorth (1889)

Stanley Lane, Bridgnorth
WV16 4SF
Tel (0746) 3315
Mem 435
Sec EH Thomas (07462) 2400
Pro P Hinton (07462) 2045
Holes 18 L 6638 yds SSS 72
Recs Am–67 C Banks (1985)
 Pro–66 P Hinton (1989)
V'trs U SOC
Fees £12.50 (£18)
Loc 1 mile N of Bridgnorth

Church Stretton (1898)

Trevor Hill, Church Stretton
Tel   (0694) 722281
Mem   470
Sec   R Broughton (0694) 722633
Holes   18 L 5008 yds SSS 66
Recs   Am–63 J Griffiths (1987)
V'trs   H SOC WE–NA before 10.30am
Fees   £7 (£11)
Loc   1/2 mile W of Church Stretton,
        off A49

Hawkstone Park (1921)

Weston-under-Redcastle,
nr Shrewsbury SY4 5UY
Tel   (093924) 611
Mem   400
Sec   KL Brazier Mgr)
        AWB Lyle (Golf Dir)
Pro   K Williams (093924) 209
Holes   Hawkstone 18 L 6465 yds
        SSS 71; Weston 18 L 5368 yds
        SSS 66
Recs   Am–67 AWB Lyle, MA Smith
        Pro–65 A Jacklin
V'trs   U after 10.35am SOC
Fees   Hawkestone £13 (£16)
        Weston £8.50 (£9.50)
Loc   7 miles S of Whitchurch.
        14 miles N of Shrewbury
        on A49
Mis   Buggies for hire. Golf hotel

Hill Valley G & CC (1975)

Terrick Road, Whitchurch
Tel   (0948) 3584
Mem   500
Sec   RB Walker
Pro   AR Minshall (0948) 3032
Holes   18 L 6050 yds SSS 69
        9 L 5106 yds SSS 65
        9 hole Par 3 course
Recs   Am–69 K Valentine
        Pro–64 W Milne
V'trs   U
Fees   £11 (£15) 9 holes–£7
        Par 3 course–£3
Loc   1 mile N of Whitchurch, off
        A41/A49
Mis   John Garner golf school

Lilleshall Hall (1937)

Abbey Road, Lilleshall, nr Newport
TF10 9AS
Tel   (0952) 603840
Mem   600
Sec   AP Thwaite (0952) 604776
Pro   NW Bramall (0952) 604104
Holes   18 L 5861 yds SSS 68
Recs   Am–65 P Baker
        Pro–70 J Anderson
V'trs   WD–U WE–M
Fees   £12.50 (BH+ day after–£18)

Llanymynech (1933)

Pant, nr Oswestry SY10 8LB
Tel   (0691) 830542
Mem   760
Sec   NE Clews (0691) 830983

Pro   A Griffiths (0691) 830879
Holes   18 L 6114 yds SSS 69
Recs   Am–66 M Evans
        Pro–65 I Woosnam
V'trs   U before 4.30pm –M after
        4.30pm SOC
Fees   £10 (£15)
Loc   5 miles S of Oswestry on A483

Ludlow (1889)

Bromfield, nr Ludlow
Tel   (058 477) 285
Mem   500
Sec   RPJ Jones (058 477) 334
Pro   G Farr (058 477) 366
Holes   18 L 6240 yds SSS 70
Recs   Am–67 T Clare
        Pro–65 PA Brookes
V'trs   U
Fees   £8 (£10)
Loc   A49, 2 miles N of Ludlow

Market Drayton (1925)

Sutton, Market Drayton
Tel   (0630) 2266
Mem   450
Sec   JJ Moseley (0630) 3661 (day)
Pro   R Clewes
Holes   18 L 6225 yds SSS 70
V'trs   WD–U WE–NA
Fees   £10
Loc   1 mile S of Market Drayton

Meole Brace (1976)

Public
Meole Brace, Shrewsbury SY2 6QQ
Tel   (0743) 64050
Pro   I Doran
Holes   9 L 2915 yds SSS 68
Recs   Am–68 J Mansell
        Pro–68 R Cockcroft
V'trs   U
Fees   £2.55 (£3.20) 18 holes
Loc   Junction A5/A49 Meole Brace

Oswestry (1930)

Aston Park, Oswestry
Tel   (069 188) 221
Mem   700
Sec   Mrs PM Lindner (069 188) 535
Pro   D Skelton (069 188) 448
Holes   18 L 6038 yds SSS 69
Recs   Am–62 AL Strange
        Pro–68 JW Walker
V'trs   M or H SOC–WD
Fees   £10 (£14)
Loc   3 1/4 miles E of Oswestry on A5

Shifnal (1929)

Decker Hill, Shifnal
Tel   (0952) 460467/460330
Mem   500
Sec   J Bell (0952) 460330
Pro   J Flanaghan (0952) 460457
Holes   18 L 6422 yds SSS 71

Recs   Am–66 R Howells
        Pro–67 IN Doran
V'trs   WD–phone first WE/BH–M
Loc   M54 Junction 4, 2 miles.
        1 mile NE of Shifnal

Shrewsbury (1891)

Condover, Shrewsbury
Tel   (074 372) 2976
Mem   450 160(L) 75(J)
Sec   JA Morrison (074 372) 2977
Pro   P Seal (074 372) 3751
Holes   18 L 6212 yds SSS 70
Recs   Am–60 JR Burn
V'trs   H SOC
Fees   £12 (£18)
Loc   4 miles SW of Shrewsbury

Telford Hotel G & CC (1981)

Great Hay, Sutton Hill, Telford
TF7 4DT
Tel   (0952) 585642
Mem   400
Sec   Cdr JG Brigham (Ext 274)
Pro   S Marr (0952) 586052
Holes   18 L 6766 yds SSS 72
Recs   Am–66 C Bufton (1986)
        Pro–62 D Thorpe
V'trs   H SOC
Fees   £16 (£20)
Loc   1 mile SE of Telford,
        off A442

Wrekin (1905)

Wellington, Telford
Tel   (0952) 244032
Mem   500 85(L) 90(J) 30(5)
Sec   S Leys
Pro   K Housden
Holes   18 L 5657 yds SSS 67
Recs   Am–65 GC Clayton,R Jones,
        P Baker, F Tart
        Pro–67 C Holmes
V'trs   WD–U before 5pm
        M after 5pm SOC
Fees   £10 (£12)
Loc   Wellington, off B5061

Somerset

Brean (1973)

Coast Road, Brean TA28 2RF
Tel   (027 875) 570
Mem   400
Sec   WS Martin (027 875) 409
Holes   18 L 5711 yds SSS 68
Recs   Am–67 C Clarke (1987)
V'trs   WD/Sat–U Sun–M after 11am
        –U after noon SOC
Fees   £6.50 (£10.50)
Loc   3 miles N of Burnham-on-Sea

For explanation of abbreviations, see page 460.

Burnham & Berrow (1890)

St Christopher's Way,
Burnham-on-Sea TA8 2PE
Tel (0278) 783137
Mem 800
Sec Mrs EL Sloman (0278) 785760
Pro NP Blake (0278) 784545
Holes 18 L 6547 yds SSS 73
9 L 6550 yds SSS 72
Recs Medal Am–68 G Thomas
C'ship Am–66 P Baker
V'trs I SOC
Fees £18 (£25) W–£100 9 hole–£6
Loc 1 mile N of Burnham-on-Sea

Enmore Park (1932)

Enmore, Bridgwater
Tel (027 867) 244
Mem 730
Sec DH Smith (027 867) 481
Pro N Wixon (027 867) 519
Holes 18 L 6443 yds SSS 71
Recs Am–67 CS Edwards
Pro–65 G Carter
V'trs U SOC–WD
Fees £14 (£17)
Loc 3 miles W of Bridgwater, off
Durleigh road. M5 Junction
23

Kingweston (1983)

Somerton
Tel (0458) 43921
Mem 200
Sec JG Willetts
Holes 9 L 4516 yds SSS 62
V'trs M Wed & Sat 2–5pm–NA
Fees NA

Mendip (1908)

Gurney Slade, Bath BA3 4UT
Tel (0749) 840570
Mem 594 95(L) 85(J)
Sec MJ Lee
Pro RF Lee (0749) 840793
Holes 18 L 5982 yds SSS 69
Recs Am–65 RH Flower
Pro–64 N Blenkarne
V'trs WD–U WE–M H SOC–WD
Fees £12 (£20)
Loc 3 miles N of Shepton Mallet
(A37)

Minehead & West Somerset (1882)

Warren Road, Minehead
Tel (0643) 2057
Mem 473
Sec RA Lawrence
Pro I Read (0643) 4378
Holes 18 L 6130 yds SSS 70
Recs Am–68 GE Vaulter
Pro–66 BJ Hunt
V'trs U after 9.15am SOC
Fees £12 (£15) W–£45
Loc E end of sea front

Taunton & Pickeridge (1892)

Corfe, Taunton TA3 7BY
Tel (082 342) 240
Mem 600
Sec GW Sayers (082 342) 537
Pro G Glew (082 342) 790
Holes 18 L 5927 yds SSS 68
Recs Am–66 CS Edwards (1989)
Pro–65 G Emerson (1984)
V'trs H SOC
Fees On application
Loc 5 miles S of Taunton on
B3170

Vivary Park

Public
Taunton
Tel (0823) 289274 (Clubhouse)
Pro J Wright (0823) 333875
Holes 18 L 4620 yds SSS 63
V'trs U exc Wed evenings–M
Booking necessary through
Pro
Fees £5.25
Loc Taunton
Mis Vivary Club plays here

Wells (1900)

East Horrington Road, Wells
Tel (0749) 72868
Mem 670
Sec MW Davis (0749) 75005
Pro A England
Holes 18 L 5354 yds SSS 67
Recs Am–64 RW Davis (1985)
Pro–65 R Clifton (1986)
V'trs WD–U WE–H SOC–WD
Fees £8 (£10) Mon–Fri £27.50
Loc Town centre 1½ miles, off
Radstock Road

Windwhistle G & CC (1932)

Cricket St Thomas, Chard
Tel (046 030) 231
Mem 300
Sec I Dodd
Pro N Morris
Holes 12 L 6055 yds SSS 69
Recs Am–71 P Knight
Pro–70 D Colgan
V'trs U WE–phone first
Fees On application
Loc On A30, opposite Cricket St
Thomas Wildlife Park

Yeovil (1919)

Sherborne Road, Yeovil BA21 5BW
Tel (0935) 75949
Mem 695 150(L) 70(J)
Sec J Riley (0935) 22965
Pro G Kite (0935) 73763
Holes 18 L 6144 yds SSS 69
Recs Am–66 J Pounder (1986)
Pro–65 G Laing (1987),
R Troake (1989)

V'trs WD–U WE–H (phone Pro for
starting time) BH–H SOC
Fees £12 (£14)
Loc 1 mile from Yeovil on A30
to Sherborne

Staffordshire

Alsager G & CC (1977)

Audley Road, Alsager, Stoke-on-Trent
Tel (0270) 875700
Mem 640
Sec Mrs EE Wynne
Pro D Clare (0270) 877432
Holes 18 L 6192 yds SSS 70
V'trs WD–U before 5pm –M after
5pm WE/BH–M SOC
Fees £10
Loc 2 miles E of M6 Junction
16. Crewe 5 miles. Stoke 7
miles

Barlaston

Meaford Road, Barlaston, Stone
Tel (078 139) 2795
Mem 450
Sec M Degg
Holes 18 L 5800 yds SSS 68
Recs Am–69 S Ashcroft (1983)
V'trs U
Fees £9 (£12)
Loc ¼ mile S of Barlaston.
¾ mile N of Stone

Beau Desert (1921)

Hazel Slade, Cannock
WS12 5PJ
Tel (054 38) 2773
Mem 500
Sec IE Williams (054 38) 2626
Pro B Stevens (054 38) 2492
Holes 18 L 6279 yds SSS 71
Recs Am–68 WR Probert
Pro–64 T Minshall
V'trs WD–U SOC BH–NA
WE–phone in advance
Fees £20
Loc 4 miles NE of Cannock

Branston (1975)

Burton Road, Branston, Burton-on-
Trent
Tel (0283) 43207
Mem 420 50(L) 60(J)
Sec KL George
Pro S Warner
Holes 18 L 6480 yds SSS 71
Recs Am–69 T Bailey (1987)
Pro–67 P Kent
V'trs WD–U WE–M before noon
SOC
Fees £10 (£12)
Loc ½ mile towards Burton from
A38/A5121 junction

Brocton Hall (1923)

Brocton, Stafford ST17 0TH
Tel   (0785) 662627
Mem   500
Sec   WR Lanyon (0785) 661901
Pro   R Johnson (0785) 661485
Holes 18 L 6095 yds SSS 69
Recs   Am–67 WB Taylor
V'trs   I H SOC
Fees   £15 (£17)
Loc   4 miles SE of Stafford off
       A34

Burslem (1907)

Wood Farm, High Lane, Stoke-on-
Trent ST6 7JT
Tel   (0782) 837006
Mem   250
Sec   RJ Sutton (0782) 837704
Holes 11 L 5527 yds SSS 67
Recs   Am–64 M Keeling (1988)
       Pro–66 T Williamson
V'trs   M Sun–NA
Fees   £7
Loc   Burslem 2 miles

Burton-on-Trent (1893)

43 Ashby Road, East Burton-on-Trent
DE15 0PS
Tel   (0283) 68708
Mem   600
Sec   A Maddock (0283) 44551
Pro   JM Lower (0283) 62240
Holes 18 L 6555 yds SSS 71
Recs   Am–69 JE Roberts
       Pro–67 DA Stewart
V'trs   I or M
Fees   £9 (£13)
Loc   Burton 3 miles

Craythorne Golf Centre (1972)

Public
Craythorne Road, Stretton, Burton-on-
Trent DE13 0AZ
Tel   (0283) 64329
Sec   J Bissell (Gen Mgr)
Pro   (0283) 33745
Holes 18 L 5230 yds SSS 66
       9 hole course
Recs   Am–62 PCR Smith (1987)
V'trs   WD–U SOC
Fees   £7 (£9)
Loc   1½ miles N Burton-on-Trent
       (A38). Junction A5121, signpost
       Stretton
Mis   Driving range

Drayton Park (1897)

Drayton Park, Tamworth B78 3TN
Tel   (0827) 251139
Mem   450
Sec   AO Rammell JP
Pro   MW Passmore (0827) 251478
Holes 18 L 6414 yds SSS 71
Recs   Am–66 M Biddle (1984)
       Pro–65 DJ Russell (1987)

V'trs   WD–H WE/BH–NA SOC–Tues
       & Thurs
Fees   £18 R/D
Loc   2 miles S of Tamworth (A4091)

Goldenhill (1983)

Public
Mobberley Road, Goldenhill,
Stoke-on-Trent ST6 5SS
Pro   A Clingan (0782) 784715
Holes 18 L 5957 yds SSS 68
V'trs   U WE/BH–book with Pro
Fees   £3.60 (£4.20)
Loc   Between Tunstall and
       Kidsgrove off A50

Greenway Hall (1908)

Stockton Brook, Stoke-on-Trent
Tel   (0782) 503158
Mem   390
Sec   EH Jones (Mgr) (0782) 503095
Holes 18 L 5676 yds SSS 67
Recs   Am–65 A Bailey, A Dathan
V'trs   Mon/Wed/Fri–H Tues &
       Thurs–U WE–U Sun pm SOC
Fees   On application
Loc   5 miles N of Stoke

Ingestre Park (1977)

nr Stafford
Tel   (0889) 270061
Mem   600
Sec   DD Humphries (Mgr)
       (0889) 270845
Pro   D Scullion (0889) 270304
Holes 18 L 6334 yds SSS 70
Recs   Am–69 S Smith, N Jackson
       Pro–68 D Scullion
V'trs   WD–U WE/BH–M
Fees   £15
Loc   6 miles E of Stafford

Lakeside (Rugeley) (1969)

Rugeley Power Station, Rugeley
WS15 1PR
Tel   (08894) 3181
Mem   250
Sec   TA Yates
Holes 9 L 4768 yds SSS 63
V'trs   M
Loc   Rugeley Power Station.
       2 miles SE of Rugeley on A513

Leek (1892)

Big Birchall, Leek ST13 5RE
Tel   (0538) 385889
Mem   400 90(L) 45(J) 100(5)
Sec   F Cutts (0538) 384779
Pro   P Stubbs (0538) 384767
Holes 18 L 6240 yds SSS 70
Recs   Am–63 D Evans
       Pro–66 CH Ward
V'trs   U H before 3pm –M after 3pm
       SOC–Wed only
Fees   £18 (£24)
Loc   ½ mile from Leek on Stone
       road (A520)

Newcastle Municipal (1973)

Public
Keele Road, Newcastle-under-Lyme
Tel   (0782) 627596
Pro   C Smith
Holes 18 L 5822 metres SSS 70
Recs   Am–70 P Rowe
       Pro–68 P Rowe
V'trs   U
Fees   £2.75 (£3.15)
Loc   2 miles NW on A525 opposite
       Keele University

Newcastle-under-Lyme (1908)

Whitmore Road, Newcastle-under-
Lyme
Tel   (0782) 616583
Mem   575
Sec   RB Irving
Pro   P Symonds (0782) 618526
Holes 18 L 6450 yds SSS 71
Recs   Am–67 MC Hassall
       Pro–66 AR Sadler
V'trs   WD–U WE/BH–M
Fees   £10
Loc   Newcastle

Onneley (1968)

Onneley, nr Crewe, Cheshire
Tel   (0782) 750577
Mem   324
Sec   WJ Paterson (0270) 624818
Holes 9 L 5584 yds SSS 67
Recs   Am–68 D Gilford
V'trs   WD–U Sat/BH–M Sun–NA
Fees   £10
Loc   Nr Woore, 1 mile off A51
       to Newcastle

Park Hall (1989)

Public
Hulme Road, Weston Coyney,
Stoke-on-Trent ST3 5BH
Pro   A Clingan (0782) 599584
Holes 18 L 2335 yds Par 54
V'trs   WD–U WE/BH–book with Pro
Fees   £2.70. (£3.20)
Loc   1 mile from Longton

Stafford Castle (1907)

Newport Road, Stafford
ST16 1BP
Tel   (0785) 223821
Mem   400
Sec   MH Fisher
Holes 9 L 6462 yds SSS 71
Recs   Am–70 S Sturgess
V'trs   WD–U WE–after 1pm
Fees   £7 (£10)
Loc   ½ mile W of Stafford

For explanation of abbreviations, see page 460.

Stone (1892)

Filleybrooks, Stone ST15 0NB
Tel   (0785) 813103
Mem   168 52(L) 22(J) 30(5)
Sec   MG Pharaoh (088 97) 224
Holes 9 L 6299 yds SSS 70
Recs   Am–69 A Hurst (1988)
V'trs WD–U WE/BH–M SOC–WD
Fees   £10
Loc   1/2 mile W of Stone on A34

Tamworth (1978)

Public
Eagle Drive, Amington, Tamworth
B77 4EG
Tel   (0827) 53850
Sec   BN Jones (0827)53858
Pro   BN Jones
Holes 18 L 6695 yds SSS 72
Recs   Am–67 CJ Christison
       Pro–65 BN Jones
V'trs U SOC–WD
Fees   £3.35
Loc   21/2 miles E of Tamworth
       on B5000. M42 3 miles.

Trentham (1895)

14 Barlaston Old Road, Trentham,
Stoke-on-Trent ST4 8HB
Tel   (0782) 642347
Mem   680
Sec   Lt Cdr JR Smith RN(Retd)
       (0782) 658109
Pro   D MacDonald (0782) 657309
Holes 18 L 6644 yds SSS 72
Recs   Am–66 DJ Boughey (1987)
V'trs WD–U H WE/BH–M (or
       enquire Sec) SOC–WD
Fees   £15 (£18) 1989 prices
Loc   3 miles S of Newcastle off
       A34. M6 Junction 15

Trentham Park (1936)

Trentham Park, Stoke-on-Trent
ST4 8AE
Tel   (0782) 642245
Mem   300 70(L) 70(J) 100(5)
Sec   CH Lindop (0782) 658800
Pro   R Clarke (0782) 642125
Holes 18 L 6403 yds SSS 71
Recs   Am–67 PG Nuthall
V'trs U SOC–Wed & Fri
Fees   £15 (£17)
Loc   4 miles S of Newcastle on
       A34. M6 Junction 15, 1 mile

Uttoxeter (1975)

Wood Lane, Uttoxeter
Tel   (0889) 564884
Mem   450
Sec   Mrs G Davies
Holes 18 L 5695 yds SSS 69
Recs   Am–69
V'trs WD–U WE–by arrangement
       SOC
Fees   £10 (£15)
Loc   Uttoxeter racecourse 1/2 mile

Westwood (1923)

Newcastle Road, Walbridge, Leek
Tel   (0538) 383060
Mem   300
Sec   AJ Lawton (0782) 503780
Holes 13 L 4766 yds SSS 68
Recs   Am–68 SD Spooner
V'trs WD–U Sat–M BH–H SOC
Fees   WD–£8
Loc   W boundary of Leek on A53

Whittington Barracks (1886)

Tamworth Road, Lichfield WS14 9PW
Tel   (0543) 432212
Mem   670
Sec   M Scargill (0543) 432317
Pro   AR Sadler (0543) 432261
Holes 18 L 6457 yds SSS 71
Recs   Am–65 CG Marks, CG Poxon
       Pro–67 AR Sadler
V'trs WD–H I WE/BH + day after–M
       SOC–Wed & Thurs
Fees   £18 R/D
Loc   21/2 miles from Lichfield on
       Tamworth road

Wolstanton (1904)

Dimsdale Old Hall, Newcastle
ST5 9DR
Tel   (0782) 616995
Mem   550
Sec   KI Colderick (0782) 622413
Pro   J Darling (0782) 622718
Holes 18 L 5807 yds SSS 68
Recs   Am–65 P Sweetsur, M Hassall,
       R Maxfield
       Pro–66 CH Ward
V'trs WD–I WE–M
Fees   £8
Loc   11/2 miles NW of Newcastle

Suffolk

Aldeburgh (1884)

Aldeburgh IP15 5PE
Tel   (0728) 452408
Mem   750
Sec   RC Van de Velde
       (0728) 452890
Pro   K Preston (0728) 453309
Holes 18 L 6330 yds SSS 71
       9 L 2114 yds SSS 64
Recs   Am–65 J Lloyd
       Pro–67 JM Johnson
V'trs I
Fees   On application
Loc   6 miles E of A12, midway
       between Ipswich and
       Lowestoft

Beccles (1899)

The Common, Beccles
Tel   (0502) 712244
Mem   200
Sec   Mrs LW Allen (0402) 712479
Pro   K Allen

Holes 9 L 2696 yds SSS 67
Recs   Pro–64 K Allen
V'trs WD–U Sun–M SOC
Fees   £6 (£7)
Loc   Lowestoft 10 miles.
       Norwich 18 miles

Bungay & Waveney Valley (1889)

Bungay
Tel   (0986) 2337
Mem   600
Sec   WJ Mann
Pro   N Whyte
Holes 18 L 5944 yds SSS 68
Recs   Am–67 R Kidd
       Pro–64 T Spurgeon
V'trs WD–U WE–M SOC
Fees   £12 R/D
Loc   Bungay 1/2 mile

Bury St Edmunds (1922)

Tut Hill, Bury St Edmunds
Tel   (0284) 755979
Mem   830 130 (L) 34(J) 100(5)
Sec   CD Preece
Pro   M Jillings (0284) 755978
Holes 18 L 6615 yds SSS 72
Recs   Am–69 S Goodman, A Currie
       Pro–67 K Golding
V'trs WD–U WE–H NA before 10am
       BH–U SOC
Fees   £12.50 (£16)
Loc   2 miles W of Bury St Edmunds
       on B1106

Cretingham (1983)

Public
Grove Farm, Cretingham,
Woodbridge IP13 7BA
Tel   (072882) 275
Sec   J Austin (Prop)
Holes 9 L 1955 yds Par 30
Recs   Am–28 R Watts (1986)
V'trs U
Fees   £5 (£6) 18 holes
Loc   2 miles SE of Earl Soham

Diss (1903)

Stuston Common, Diss
Tel   (0379) 642847
Mem   500
Sec   J Bell (0379) 642679
Pro   N Taylor (0379) 644399
Holes 9 L 5900 yds SSS 68
Recs   Am–68 JE Doe
       Pro–T Pennock
V'trs WD–NA after 4pm WE–NA
Fees   £10
Loc   Diss 1/2 mile

Felixstowe Ferry (1880)

Ferry Road, Felixstowe IP4 9RY
Tel   (0394) 286834
Mem   750
Sec   IH Kimber

Pro   I Macpherson (0394) 283975
Holes 18 L 6308 yds SSS 70
Recs Am–68 I Whinney
      Pro–65 I Richardson
V'trs UH WE–M before 10.30am
      SOC
Fees £15 (£18)
Loc 2 miles NE of Felixstowe,
      towards Felixstowe Ferry

Flempton (1895)

Bury St Edmunds
Tel (028 484) 291
Mem 250
Sec PH Nunn (0638) 750100
Pro M Jillings
Holes 9 L 6704 yds SSS 69
Recs Am–67 Lt J Reynolds
      Pro–69 J Arbon
V'trs WD–H WE/BH–M H
Fees £15 D–£20
Loc 5 miles NW of Bury St Edmunds
      on A1101

Fornham Park (1974)

Fornham St Martin, Bury St Edmunds
IP28 6UG
Tel (0284) 63426
Mem 500
Sec Mrs J Matthews
Pro S Wright
Holes 18 L 6212 yds SSS 70
Recs Am–68 S Blanshard (1987)
      Pro–65 S Wright (1986)
V'trs U SOC
Fees £8.50 (£12.50)
Loc From Cambridge, 1st exit on
      A45; from Ipswich, 3rd exit on
      A45

Haverhill (1974)

Coupals Road, Haverhill CB9 7UW
Tel (0440) 61951
Mem 350
Sec Mrs J Webster
Pro S Mayfield (0440) 712628
Holes 9 L 5707 yds SSS 68
Recs Am–65 T Barton
      Pro–66 C Cook
V'trs U SOC
Fees £10 (£15)
Loc Haverhill, 1 mile off A604.
      Signs to Calford Green

Ipswich (Purdis Heath) (1895)

Purdis Heath, Ipswich
Tel (0473) 728941
      (0473) 727474 (Steward)
Mem 800
Sec AE Howell
Pro SJ Whymark (0473) 724017
Holes 18 L 6405 yds SSS 70
      9 L 1950 yds Par 31
Recs Am–64 JVT Marks
      Pro–67 RA Knight

V'trs 18 hole–H or I 9 hole–U SOC
Fees 18 hole:£14 (£16)
      9 hole:£7 (£8)
Loc 3 miles E of Ipswich

Links (Newmarket) (1902)

Cambridge Road, Newmarket
CB8 0TG
Tel (0638) 662708
Mem 685
Sec Mrs T MacGregor
      (0638) 663000
Pro DP Thomson (0638) 662395
Holes 18 L 6402 yds SSS 71
Recs Am–69 B Jackson
      Pro–70 S Barlow
V'trs WD–H WE/BH–H Sun–MH
      before 11.30am SOC
Fees £15 (£20)
Loc 1 mile S of Newmarket

Newton Green (1907)

Newton Green, Sudbury
Tel (0787) 77501/77216
Mem 400
Sec G Bright (0787) 71119
Pro K Lovelock
Holes 9 L 5488 yds SSS 67
Recs Am–60 R Rowland
      Pro–29 A Davey (9 holes)
V'trs WD–U WE–M
Fees £10
Loc 4 miles E of Sudbury

Rookery Park (1975)

Carlton Colville, Lowestoft
NR33 8HJ
Tel (0502) 560380
Mem 750
Sec J Almond
Pro M Elsworthy (0502) 515103
Holes 18 L 6649 yds SSS 72
      Par 3 course
Recs Am–71 G Long (1985)
      Pro–69 P Kent (1985)
V'trs WD–U SOC Sat/BH–after 11am
      Sun–NA
Fees £12 (£14)
Loc West Lowestoft (A146)

Royal Worlington & Newmarket (1895)

Worlington, Bury St Edmunds
IP28 8SD
Tel (0638) 712216
Mem 328
Sec WN White MC MA
Pro M Hawkins (0638) 715224
Holes 9 L 6218 yds SSS 70
Recs Am–67 DJ Millensted
      Pro–66 EE Beverley
V'trs U–phone first WE–NA
Fees £18.50
Loc Mildenhall 2 miles

Rushmere (1895)

Rushmere Heath, Ipswich
Tel (0473) 727109
Mem 750
Sec RW Whiting (0473) 725648
Pro NTJ McNeill (0473) 728076
Holes 18 L 6287 yds SSS 70
Recs Am–66 F Knights (1989)
      Pro–67 NTJ McNeil (1984),
      S Beckham (1985)
V'trs WD–U WE/BH–after 2.30pm
Fees On application
Loc Ipswich, off Woodbridge road
      (A12)

Southwold (1884)

The Common, Southwold
Tel (0502) 723234
Mem 450
Sec IG Guy (0502) 723248
Pro B Allen (0502) 723790
Holes 9 L 6001 yds SSS 69
Recs Am–67 S Fitzgerald
      Pro–65 R Mann
V'trs U (subject to fixtures)
Fees On application
Loc 35 miles N of Ipswich

Stowmarket (1962)

Lower Road, Onehouse, Stowmarket
IP14 3DA
Tel (044 93) 392
Mem 600
Sec PW Rumball (044 93) 473
Pro C Aldred
Holes 18 L 6119 yds SSS 69
Recs Am–67 I Oakes
      Pro–66 H Flatman
V'trs WD/WE–H SOC–Thurs & Fri
Fees £10 (£16.50)
Loc 2¹/₂ miles SW of Stowmarket

Thorpeness Hotel

Thorpeness
Tel (0728) 452176
Mem 400
Sec NW Griffin
Pro T Pennock (0728) 452524
Holes 18 L 6208 yds SSS 71
Recs Am–66 J Marks
      Pro–67 K McDonald
V'trs U
Fees £15 (£25)
Loc 2 miles N of Aldeburgh
Mis Hotel adjacent to course

Waldringfield Heath (1983)

Newbourne Road, Waldringfield,
Woodbridge IP12 4PT
Tel (0473) 36768
Mem 450
Sec LJ McWade (0473) 36791
Holes 18 L 5837 yds SSS 68
V'trs WD–U WE/BH–M before noon
      SOC–WD
Loc 3 miles N of Ipswich off A12

For explanation of abbreviations, see page 460.

Warren Heath

Bucklesham Road, Ipswich IP3 8TZ
Tel   (0473) 726821
Mem   150
Sec   BP Johnson
Pro   JW Johnson
Holes   9 L 3162 yds SSS 34
Recs   Pro–64 JW Johnson
V'trs   U SOC
Fees   £2.50
Loc   Between Bucklesham road and Old Felixstowe road

Woodbridge (1893)

Bromeswell Heath, nr Woodbridge
Tel   (039 43) 2038
Mem   930
Sec   Capt LA Harpum RN
Pro   LA Jones (039 43) 3213
Holes   18 L 6314 yds SSS 70
        9 L 2243 yds SSS 31
Recs   Am–64 JVT Marks (1983)
        Pro–65 F Sunderland (1970)
V'trs   H WE/BH–M SOC
Fees   £15 D–£20 1989 prices
Loc   2 miles E of Woodbridge.
        Turn off A12 Woodbridge
        by–pass towards Orford B1084

Surrey

The Addington (1913)

Shirley Church Road, Croydon
CR50 5AB
Tel   (081) 777 1055
Sec   Miss E Kennedy (081) 777 6057
Pro   E Campbell (081) 777 1701
Holes   18 L 6242 yds SSS 71
Recs   Am–66 P Benka
        Pro–68 F Robson
V'trs   H SOC–WD
Fees   On application
Loc   E Croydon 2¹/₂ miles

Addington Court (1931)

Public
Featherbed Lane, Addington,
Croydon CR0 9AA
Tel   (081) 657 028¹/₂/3
Sec   G Cotton
Pro   G Cotton
Holes   Old 18 L 5577 yds SSS 67
        New 18 L 5513 yds SSS 66
        Lower 9 L 1812 yds SSS 62
        18 hole Pitch and Putt course
Recs   Pro–63 C Phillips
V'trs   U
Fees   Winter: Old £5 New £4.10
        9 hole £3. Summer: Old £6
        New £5.25 9 hole £3.50
Loc   3 miles E of Croydon

Addington Palace (1923)

Gravel Hill, Addington, Croydon
CR0 5BB
Tel   (081) 654 3061
Mem   700
Sec   J Robinson
Pro   M Pilkington (081) 654 1786
Holes   18 L 6410 yds SSS 71
Recs   Am–63 R Glading
        Pro–65 AD Locke
V'trs   WD–M or I WE/BH–M
Fees   £22
Loc   2 miles E of Croydon Station

Banstead Downs (1890)

Burdon Lane, Belmont, Sutton
SM2 7DD
Tel   (081) 642 2284
Mem   650
Sec   RS Barrett
Pro   I Marr (081) 642 6884
Holes   18 L 6169 yds SSS 69
Recs   Pro–MLA Perry
V'trs   WD–I WE/BH–M
Fees   £20
Loc   1 mile S of Sutton

Barrow Hills (1970)

Longcross, Chertsey KT16 0DS
Mem   250
Sec   RW Routley (0932) 848117
Holes   18 L 3090 yds SSS 53
Recs   Am–58 EJ Sewell
V'trs   M
Loc   4 miles W of Chertsey

Betchworth Park (1913)

Reigate Road, Dorking RH4 1NZ
Tel   (0306) 882052
Mem   725
Sec   DAS Bradney
Pro   A King (0306) 884334
Holes   18 L 6266 yds SSS 70
Recs   Am–68 CJ Copus
        Pro–65 NC Coles
V'trs   WD–by arrangement exc Tues
        & Wed am–NA WE–NA exc
        Sun pm
Fees   £20 (£27)
Loc   1 mile E of Dorking on A25

Bramley (1913)

Bramley, nr Guildford GU5 0AL
Tel   (0483) 893042
Mem   700
Sec   Mrs M Lambert (0483) 892696
Pro   G Peddie (0483) 893685
Holes   18 L 5966 yds SSS 68
Recs   Am–66 MI Farmer
        Pro–63 PR Gill
V'trs   WD–U WE–M SOC–WD

Burhill (1907)

Walton-on-Thames KT12 4BL
Tel   (0932) 227345
Mem   1100
Sec   AJ Acres
Pro   L Johnson (0932) 221729
Holes   18 L 6224 yds SSS 70
Recs   Am–66 RJ Pollitt (1987)
        Pro–65 G Orr (1988)
V'trs   WD–H WE/BH–M
Fees   On application
Loc   Between Walton-on-Thames
        and Cobham, off Burwood
        Road

Fees   £15 D–£20
Loc   3 miles S of Guildford on A281
Mis   Buggies for hire

Camberley Heath (1913)

Golf Drive, Camberley GU15 1JG
Tel   (0276) 23258
        (Fax) 0276 692505
Mem   725
Pro   Gary Smith (0276) 27905
Holes   18 L 6402 yds SSS 71
Recs   Am–66 C Laurence
        Pro–67 A Perry
V'trs   WD–I WE–M SOC H
Fees   £17 D–£25
Loc   1¹/₄ miles S of Camberley on
        Old Portsmouth Road (A325)

Chessington Golf Centre (1983)

Public
Garrison Lane, Chessington KT9 2LW
Tel   (081) 391 0948
Sec   A Maxted (Mgr) (081) 974 1705
Pro   B Cuff, J Fitzpatrick, J Rodger
Holes   9 L 1400 yds SSS 54
Recs   Am–60 N Murphy
        Pro–54 R Hunter
V'trs   WD–U WE–NA before noon
Fees   9 holes–£2.50 (£3)
Loc   Off A243, opposite Chessington
        South Station. M25 Junction 9

Chipstead (1906)

How Lane, Chipstead, Coulsdon
CR3 3PR
Tel   (0737) 551053
Mem   600
Sec   SLD Spencer–Skeen
        (0737) 555781
Pro   (0737) 554939
Holes   18 L 5450 yds SSS 67
Recs   Am–63 A Davey (1986)
        Pro–63 N Child (1980)
V'trs   WD–U WE/BH–M
Fees   £20; after 2pm–£15
Loc   Chipstead Station 200 yds

Coombe Hill (1911)

Kingston Hill
Tel (081) 942 2284
Mem 437
Sec AL Foster
Pro C De Foy (081) 949 3713
Holes 18 L 6286 yds SSS 71
Recs Am–67 L Freedman,
   RL Glading
   Pro–64 BJ Hunt
V'trs I or H SOC
Fees By arrangement
Loc Off Coombe Lane West.
   1 mile from New Malden.
   ¹/₂ mile off A3 on A238

Coombe Wood (1904)

George Road, Kingston Hill,
Kingston–upon–Thames
KT2 7NS
Tel (081) 942 3828 (Steward)
Mem 620
Sec T Duncan (081) 942 0388
Pro D Butler (081) 942 6764
Holes 18 L 5210 yds SSS 66
Recs Am–62 FJ Cocker
   Pro–60 D Butler (1987)
V'trs WD–UH after 9am WE/BH–M
   SOC–WD
Fees £20
Loc 1 mile N of Kingston–upon–
   Thames, off A3 at Robin Hood
   roundabout

Coulsdon Court (1937)

Public
Coulsdon Road CR3 2LL
Tel (081) 660 0468
Pro C Staff (081) 660 6083
Holes 18 L 6030 yds SSS 70
Recs Pro–66 G Ralph
V'trs U
Fees £5 (£7.25)
Loc 5 miles S of Croydon on
   B2030
Mis Public course, now privately
   operated

Croham Hurst (1911)

Croham Road, South Croydon
CR2 7HJ
Tel (081) 657 2075
Mem 284 110(L) 80(J) 175(5)
Sec R Stallard (Mgr)
Pro E Stillwell (081) 657 7705
Holes 18 L 6274 yds SSS 70
Recs Am–64 SF Robson
   Pro–66 B Firkins
V'trs WD–I WE/BH–M
Fees £21
Loc 1 mile from S Croydon.
   M25 Junction 6–A22–B270–B269

Crondall (1984)

Oak Park, Heath Lane, Crondall,
nr Farnham GU10 5PB
Tel (0252) 850880
Mem 400

Sec Mrs R Smythe (Prop)
Pro P Rees (0252) 850066
Holes 18 L 6278 yds SSS 70
V'trs U SOC
Fees £12 (£17)
Loc Off A287 Farnham to Odiham
   road
Mis Covered driving range

Cuddington (1929)

Banstead Road, Banstead SM7 1RD
Tel (081) 393 0952
Mem 850
Sec DM Scott
Pro R Gardner (081) 393 5850
Holes 18 L 6352 yds SSS 70
Recs Am–69 PJ Gibbons
   Pro–63 W Grant
V'trs WD–I WE–M (by appointment)
Fees £24
Loc Banstead Station 200 yds

Dorking (1897)

Chart Park, Dorking
Tel (0306) 889786
Mem 380
Sec RM Payne (0306) 886917
Pro P Napier
Holes 9 L 5106 yds SSS 65
Recs Am–65 J Houston
   Pro–62 A King
V'trs WD–U WE/BH–M
   SOC–WD
Fees £10
Loc 1 mile S of Dorking on A24

Drift (1976)

The Drift, East Horsley KT24 5HD
Tel (048 65) 4641
Mem 700
Sec C Rose
Pro J Hagen (048 65) 4772
Holes 18 L 6414 yds SSS 71
Recs Am–72 J Scarfe
   Pro–72 TM Powell
V'trs WD–U SOC
Fees £20 before 1pm
   £13 after 1pm
Loc 2 miles off A3. London 20
   miles. 2 miles off M25

Dulwich & Sydenham Hill (1893)

Grange Lane, College Road, London
SE21 7LH
Tel (081) 693 3961
Mem 850
Sec B Harmer
Pro D Baillie (081) 693 8491
Holes 18 L 6051 yds SSS 69
Recs Am–62 T Bridle
   Pro–63 LF Rowe
V'trs WD–I WE/BH–M SOC
Fees £16
Loc Charing Cross 5 miles

Effingham (1927)

Effingham Crossroads, Effingham
KT24 5PZ
Tel (0372) 52203/4
Mem 1200
Sec Miss SD Cousins
Pro S Hoatson (Mgr) (0372) 52606
Holes 18 L 6488 yds SSS 71
Recs Am–67 I Hawson (1986)
   Pro–63 AD Locke
V'trs WD–H WE/BH–M
Fees WD–£25 before 2pm
   £20 after 2pm
Loc 8 miles N of Guildford

Epsom (1889)

Longdown Lane, South Epsom
KT17 4JR
Tel (037 27) 23363
Mem 600
Sec KH Watson (037 27) 21666
Pro R Wynn (037 27) 41867
Holes 18 L 5607 yds SSS 67
Recs Am–68 R Goudie
   Pro–68 R Wynn
V'trs WD–U WE/BH–U after 12 noon
   SOC–Wed & Fri
Fees £10 (£12.50)
Loc S Epsom Downs Rail Station

Farnham (1896)

The Sands, Farnham GU10 1PX
Tel (025 18) 3163
Mem 700
Sec (025 18) 2109
Pro G Cowlishaw (025 18) 2198
Holes 18 L 6313 yds SSS 70
Recs Am–67 G Walmsley
V'trs WD–H WE–M SOC–Wed &
   Thurs
Fees £18 D–£21
Loc Signposted off A31, about
   1 mile E of Farnham

Farnham Park (1966)

Public
Farnham Park, Farnham GU9 0AU
Tel (0252) 715216
Sec P Chapman
Pro P Chapman
Holes 9 L 1163 yds Par 54
Recs Am–61 JA Pike
   Pro–56 G Wheeler
V'trs U
Fees £1.80 (£2.10)
Loc By Farnham Castle

Fernfell G & CC (1985)

Barhatch Lane, Cranleigh GU6 7NG
Tel (0483) 276626
Mem 1000
Sec Miss GL Petersen (Mgr)
Pro (0483) 277188
Holes 18 L 5258 yds SSS 66
Recs Am–59 RJ Martin (1988)
V'trs WD–U WE/BH–NA am
   SOC–WD

For explanation of abbreviations, see page 460.

Fees £12 (£15)
Loc 1 mile from Cranleigh,
off A281. A3, 8 miles.
M25, 11 miles

Foxhills (1975)

Stonehill Road, Ottershaw KT16 0EL
Tel (093 287) 2050
Mem 647
Sec A Dupuy
Pro B Hunt (093 287) 3961
Holes 18 L 6880 yds SSS 73
18 L 6747 yds SSS 72
Recs Pro–65 P Dawson
V'trs U SOC
Fees £22 D–£30
Loc London 20 miles.
Heathrow 10 miles
Mis Buggies for hire

Gatton Manor Hotel (1969)

Ockley, nr Dorking RH5 5PQ
Tel (030 679) 555
Mem 250
Sec DG Heath
Pro R Sargent (030 679) 557
Holes 18 L 6903 yds SSS 72
Recs Am–72 J McLaren (1985)
Pro–73 R Sargent (1985)
V'trs U exc Sun before noon–M
SOC–WD
Fees £9 (£11)
Loc 1½ miles SW of Ockley off
A29. M25 Junction 9, S on A24
Mis Buggies–£20 per day

Goal Farm (1977)

Public
Goal Road, Pirbright GU24 0P2
Tel (048 67) 3183/3205
Holes 9 hole 1273 yds Par 3
course
Recs Am–27
V'trs Sat–reserved for club comps
SOC–WD
Fees 18 holes £3.80 (£4.20)
9 holes £2 (£2.20)

Guildford (1886)

High Path Road, Merrow, Guildford
GU1 2HL
Tel (0483) 575243
Mem 600
Sec HJ Warburton (0483) 63941
Pro PG Hollington (0483) 66765
Holes 18 L 6080 yds SSS 70
Recs Am–64 DG Lintott (1989)
Pro–67 PG Hollington (1987)
V'trs WD–U WE–M SOC–WD
Fees £20
Loc 2 miles E of Guildford

Hankley Common (1895)

Tilford, Farnham GU10 2DD
Tel (025 125) 2493
Mem 700
Sec JKA O'Brien
Pro W Brogden (025 125) 3761

Holes 18 L 6418 yds SSS 71
Recs Am–66 J Lee (1987)
Pro–62 H Stott (1988)
V'trs WD–I WE–At discretion of
Sec
Fees £20 D–£27.50
Loc 3 miles SE of Farnham on
Tilford road

Hindhead (1904)

Churt Road, Hindhead GU26 6HX
Tel (042 873) 4614
Mem 300 50(L) 100(J) 100(5)
Sec ML Brown
Pro N Ogilvy (042 873) 4458
Holes 18 L 6357 yds SSS 70
Recs Am–65 W Rowland
Pro–65 DJ Rees
V'trs WD–UH WE/BH–NA before
noon SOC–Wed & Thurs
Fees £22 (£27)
Loc 1½ miles N of Hindhead on
A287

Hoebridge Golf Centre (1982)

Public
The Club House, Old Woking Road,
Old Woking GU22 8JH
Tel (0483) 722611
Sec TD Powell
Pro TD Powell
Holes 18 L 6587 yds SSS 71
Intermediate 9 L 2294 yds
Par 3 18 L 2298 yds
V'trs U
Fees 18 hole–£8.50 Inter–£5
Par 3–£4.50
Loc Between Old Woking and
West Byfleet. 2 miles off A3
on A247
Mis 25 bay floodlit driving range

Home Park (1895)

Hampton Wick, Kingston–upon–
Thames KT1 4AD
Tel (081) 977 6645
Mem 500
Sec CHH Gray (081) 977 2423
Pro L Roberts (081) 977 2658
Holes 18 L 6519 yds SSS 71
V'trs U
Fees £10.50 (£18)
Loc 1 mile W of Kingston

Kingswood (1928)

Sandy Lane, Kingswood, Tadworth
KT20 6NE
Tel (0737) 832188
Mem 640
Sec M Fletcher (Admin)
Pro R Blackie (0737) 832334
Holes 18 L 6855 yds SSS 73
Recs Am–70 P Stanford
Pro–67 R Blackie
V'trs H SOC
Fees £25 (£30)
Loc 5 miles S of Sutton on A217.
M25 Junction 8, 2 miles

Laleham (1907)

Laleham Reach, Chertsey KT16 8RP
Tel (093 28) 564211
Mem 600
Sec MA Ford
Pro T Whitton (093 28) 62877
Holes 18 L 6203 yds SSS 70
Recs Am–68 C Poulton
Pro–66 R Mandeville,
J Hitchcock
V'trs WD–U before 4.30pm WE–M
SOC–Mon–Wed
Fees £17
Loc 2 miles S of Staines

Leatherhead (1904)

Kingston Road, Leatherhead
KT22 0DP
Mem 500
Sec W Betts (037 284) 3966
Holes 18 L 6060 yds SSS 69
Recs Am–68 PW Wynn
Pro–65 R Wynn
V'trs U SOC
Fees £27.50 (£32.50)
Loc ½ mile from Leatherhead
junction of M25, on A243
to Chessington

Limpsfield Chart (1889)

Limpsfield RH8 0SL
Tel (0883) 723405
Mem 395
Sec WG Bannochie (0883) 713097
Holes 9 L 5718 yds SSS 68
Recs Am–67 N Simmons
Pro–64 B Huggett
V'trs WD–Tues/Fri/Wed pm
Apr–Oct Sun–NA after 1pm
Fees On application
Loc 2 miles E of Oxted

Lingfield Park (1987)

Racecourse Road, Lingfield
RH7 6PQ
Tel (0342) 834602
Mem 600
Sec C Manktelow
Pro T Collingwood (0342) 832659
Holes 18 L 6500 yds SSS 72
Recs Pro–67 B Stillwell (1987)
V'trs WD–U WE/BH–M SOC
Fees £15 (£20)
Loc Next to Lingfield racecourse
M25 Junction 6
Mis Driving range

London Scottish (1865)

Windmill Enclosure, Wimbledon
Common, London SW19 5NQ
Tel (081) 788 0135
Mem 250
Sec J Johnson (081) 789 7517
Pro M Barr (081) 789 1207
Holes 18 L 5486 yds SSS 67
Recs Am–64 A Glickberg
Pro–63 D Butler, A King

V'trs WD–U WE–M BH–NA
       SOC–WD
Fees   £6 D–£10
Loc   Wimbledon Station 2 miles
Mis   Club has joint use with
       Wimbledon Common GC

Malden (1926)

Traps Lane, New Malden KT3 4RS
Tel   (081) 942 0654
Mem   680
Sec   Mrs C Penhale
Pro   G Howard (081) 942 6009
Holes 18 L 6201 yds SSS 70
Recs   Am–65 G Lashford
       Pro–67 A Waters
V'trs WD–U WE–restricted (apply
       Sec) SOC–Wed–Fri
Fees   £19.50 (£25)
Loc   Close to A3 between
       Wimbledon and Kingston

Mitcham (1897)

Carshalton Road, Mitcham Junction
CR4 4HN
Tel   (081) 648 1508
Mem   450
Sec   CA McGahan (Hon)
Pro   JA Godfrey (081) 640 4280
Holes 18 L 5931 yds SSS 68
Recs   Am–D Wilde
V'trs U WE–NA 8am–2pm SOC
Fees   £8 (£8)
Loc   Mitcham Junction Station

Mitcham Village (1907)

Tel   (081) 648 1508
Mem   240 10(J)
Sec   RL Scriven (081) 764 1861
Holes Play over Mitcham Course

Moore Place

Public
Portsmouth Road, Esher KT10 9LN
Tel   (0372) 63533
Sec   J Darby (Hon)
Pro   D Allen
Holes 9 L 3512 yds SSS 58
Recs   Am–29 W Cavanagh
       Pro–25 P Loxley
V'trs U
Fees   £3.50 (£4.50)
Loc   Centre of Esher on Portsmouth
       road

New Zealand (1895)

Woodham Lane, Woodham,
Weybridge KT15 3QD
Tel   (093 23) 45049
Mem   300
Sec   MJ Wood (093 23) 42891
Pro   VR Elvidge (093 23) 49619
Holes 18 L 6012 yds SSS 69
Recs   Am–66 P Cannings
       Pro–72 Alex Herd
V'trs WD–H WE/BH–NA
Fees   On application
Loc   Woking 3 miles. West Byfleet
       1 mile. Weybridge 5 miles

North Downs (1899)

Northdown Road, Woldingham
Tel   (0883) 653298
Mem   650
Sec   JAL Smith (Mgr)
       (0883) 652057
Pro   P Ellis (0883) 653004
Holes 18 L 5787 yds SSS 68
Recs   Am–66 M Smallcorn (1989)
       Pro–65 W Humphreys (1987)
V'trs WD–U WE–M
       SOC–Tues/Wed/Fri
Fees   £16 1989 price
Loc   3 miles E of Caterham

Oaks Sports Centre (1973)

Public
Woodmansterne Road, Carshalton
Tel   (081) 643 8363
Pro   G Horley
Holes 18 L 5975 yds SSS 69
       9 L 1590 yds SSS 29
Recs   18–hole Pro–66 G Horley
       9–hole Pro–27 J Woodroffe
V'trs U
Fees   18–hole £5.20 (£7)
       9–hole £2.50 (£3)
Loc   Sutton 2 miles
Mis   Floodlit driving range

Purley Downs (1894)

106 Purley Downs Road, Purley
CR2 0RB
Tel   (081) 657 8347
Mem   600
Sec   Miss KNR Pudner
Pro   G Wilson (081) 651 0819
Holes 18 L 6243 yds SSS 70
Recs   Am–66 M Hayes
       Pro–69 M Gregson
V'trs WD–I WE–M
Fees   On application
Loc   3 miles S of Croydon

Puttenham (1894)

Puttenham, nr Guildford
Tel   (0483) 810498
Mem   500
Sec   G Simmons
Pro   G Simmons (0483) 810277
Holes 18 L 5300 yds SSS 66
Recs   Am–65 P Bivona
       Pro–59 R Donald
V'trs WD–H WE/BH–M SOC–Wed
       & Thurs
Fees   On application
Loc   Midway between Guildford
       and Farnham on Hog's Back

RAC Country Club (1913)

Woodcote Park, Epsom KT18 7EW
Tel   (0372) 276311
Sec   K Symons
Pro   P Butler
Holes 18 L 6672 yds SSS 72
       18 L 5520 yds SSS 67
V'trs M SOC
Loc   Epsom Station 1³/₄ miles

Redhill & Reigate (1887)

Clarence Lodge, Pendleton Road,
Redhill RH1 6LB
Tel   (0737) 244626/244433
Mem   500
Sec   FR Cole (0737) 240777
Pro   B Davies (0737) 244433
Holes 18 L 5238 yds SSS 66
V'trs WD–U WE–NA before 11am
       Sun–NA June–Sept
Fees   £10 (£12)
Loc   Redhill 1 mile on A23

Reigate Heath (1895)

Reigate Heath RH2 8QR
Tel   (0737) 242610
Mem   250 90(L) 50(J)
Sec   Mrs DM Howard (0737) 245530
Pro   WH Carter
Holes 9 L 5554 yds SSS 67
Recs   Am–65 D Mahaney
       Pro–65 P Loxley
V'trs WD–U Sun/BH–M SOC–Wed
       & Thurs
Fees   On application
Loc   W boundary

Richmond (1891)

Sudbrook Park, Richmond TW10 7AS
Tel   (081) 940 1463
Mem   500
Sec   JF Stocker (081) 940 4351
Pro   N Job (081) 940 7792
Holes 18 L 5965 yds SSS 69
Recs   Am–63 J Lawson
       Pro–61 J Bennett
V'trs WD–U
Fees   £25
Loc   Between Richmond and
       Kingston–upon–Thames

Richmond Park (1923)

Public
Roehampton Gate, Richmond Park,
London SW15 5JR
Tel   (081) 876 3205/1795
Pro   J Slinger
Holes Dukes 18 L 5940 yds SSS 68
       Princes 18 L 5969 yds SSS 68
V'trs U SOC
Fees   £5.50 (£8)
Loc   3 miles SW of Putney along
       Priory Lane
Mis   Centurion GC plays here

Roehampton (1901)

Roehampton Lane, London SW15 5LR
Tel   (081) 876 5505
Mem   900
Sec   RW Varley
Pro   AL Scott (081) 876 3858
Holes 18 L 6057 yds SSS 69
Recs   Am–65 AK Scott
       Pro–62 H Stott
V'trs WD–Introduced by member
       WE–M
Loc   Nr Barnes

Royal Mid–Surrey (1892)

Old Deer Park, Richmond TW9 2SB
Tel   (081) 940 1894
Mem   1200
Sec   MSR Lunt
Pro   D Talbot (081) 940 0459
Holes   Outer 18 L 6337 yds SSS 70
        Inner 18 L 5446 yds SSS 71
Recs   Outer Am–66 GH Micklem,
        JC Davies, D Gilford
        Pro–64 R Charles,
        B Gallacher
V'trs   WD–H or M WE/BH–M SOC
Fees   £30
Loc   Nr Richmond roundabout, off
        A316

Royal Wimbledon (1865)

29 Camp Road, Wimbledon, London
SW19 4UW
Tel   (081) 946 2125
Mem   800
Sec   Maj. GE Jones
Pro   H Boyle (081) 946 4606
Holes   18 L 6300 yds SSS 70
Recs   Am–66 JFM Connolly
        Pro–71 R Burton
V'trs   WD–I or M WE–M
Fees   £27
Loc   S of Wimbledon Common

St George's Hill (1912)

Weybridge KT13 0NL
Tel   (0932) 842406
Mem   600
Sec   MR Tapsell (0932) 847758
Pro   AC Rattue (0932) 843523
Holes   18 L 6492 yds SSS 71
        9 L 2360 yds SSS 35
Recs   Am–65 D Swanston
        Pro–65 M Faulkner
V'trs   WD–IH WE/BH–NA 9 hole–U
Fees   D–£35 –£24 after 1.45pm
        9 hole £8 –£7 after 1.45pm
        £6 after 4pm
Loc   ¹/₂ mile N of M25/A3 Junction
        on A245 to Woking

Sandown Park (1970)

Public
More Lane, Esher KT10 8AN
Tel   (0372) 63340
Sec   P Barriball (Mgr)
Pro   N Bedward
Holes   9 L 5658 yds SSS 67
        9 hole Par 3
Recs   Am–69 P O'Halloran
V'trs   U (Closed on race day until
        30 mins after last race)
Fees   £2.80 (£3.75)
Loc   Sandown Park Racecourse
Mis   Floodlit driving range.
        Sandown Park Club plays
        here

Selsdon Park Hotel (1929)

Addington Road, Sanderstead,
S Croydon CR2 8YA
Tel   (081) 657 8811
        (Fax) 081 651 6171

Pro   T O'Keefe, I Naylor
        (081) 657 4129
Holes   18 L 6402 yds SSS 71
Recs   Am–68 M Welch
V'trs   U SOC (min 12 golfers)
Fees   £20 Sat–£25 Sun/BH–£30
Loc   3 miles S of Croydon on
        A2022 Purley–Addington road
Mis   Unsuitable for novice golfers

Shillinglee Park (1980)

Public
Chiddingfold, Godalming GU8 4TA
Tel   (0428) 53237
Sec   R Mace
Pro   R Mace
Holes   9 L 2400 yds Par 32
V'trs   U SOC
Fees   £11.50 D–£13.50 (£13.50
        D–£15.50) 9 holes–£6.50
        (£7)
Loc   2¹/₂ miles SE of Chiddingfold

Shirley Park (1914)

Addiscombe Road, Croydon CR0 7LB
Tel   (081) 654 1143
Mem   900
Sec   A Baird
Pro   H Stott (081) 654 8767
Holes   18 L 6210 yds SSS 70
Recs   Am–66 J Good
        Pro–65 J Bennett
V'trs   WD–U WE/BH–M SOC
Fees   £17.50
Loc   On A232, 1 mile E of Croydon
        Station

Silvermere (1976)

Redhill Road, Cobham KT11 1EF
Tel   (0932) 67275
Mem   600
Sec   Mrs P Devereux (Hon)
Pro   D McClelland
Holes   18 L 6333 yds SSS 71
Recs   Pro–65 S Rolley (1986)
V'trs   WD–U WE–NA before 1pm
        SOC
Fees   £10 (£14)
Loc   Between Cobham and Byfleet.
        ¹/₂ mile from M25 Junction 10
        on B366 to Byfleet
Mis   Floodlit driving range

Sunningdale (1901)

Sunningdale SL5 9RW
Tel   (0990) 21681
Mem   800
Sec   K Almond
Pro   K Maxwell (0990) 20128
Holes   Old 18 L 6586 yds SSS 71
        New 18 L 6676 yds SSS 71
Recs   Old Am–66 MC Hughesdon
        Pro–62 N Faldo
        New Am–65 M Lunt
        Pro–64 GJ Player
V'trs   WD–I WE–M
Fees   £47
Loc   Sunningdale Station ¹/₄ mile on
        A30

Sunningdale Ladies (1902)

Cross Road, Sunningdale
Tel   (0990) 20507
Mem   400
Sec   BWJ Ford
Holes   18 L 3622 yds SSS 60
Recs   Am –
V'trs   WD/WE–by appointment.
        No 3 or 4 balls before 11am
Fees   D–Ladies £11 (£13)
        Men £14 (£16)
Loc   Sunningdale Station ¹/₄ mile

Surbiton (1895)

Woodstock Lane, Chessington
Tel   (081) 398 3101
Mem   750
Sec   GA Keith MBE
Pro   P Milton (081) 398 6619
Holes   18 L 6211 yds SSS 70
Recs   Am–66 N Pimm
        Pro–66 P Milton
V'trs   WD–H WE/BH–M
Fees   £20 D–£30
Loc   2 miles E of Esher

Tandridge (1925)

Oxted
Tel   (0883) 712273/4
Mem   650
Sec   ID Wheater
Pro   A Farquhar (0883) 713701
Holes   18 L 6250 yds SSS 70
Recs   Am–68 JC Robson
        Pro–69 BGC Huggett
V'trs   Mon/Wed/Thurs only–I
        SOC–Mon/Wed/Thurs BH–M
Fees   £21
Loc   5 miles E of Redhill off A25.
        M25 Junction 6

Thames Ditton & Esher (1892)

Portsmouth Road, Esher KT10 9AL
Tel   (081) 398 1551
Mem   300
Sec   BAJ Chandler
Pro   R Hutton
Holes   9 L 5415 yds SSS 65
Recs   Am–61 T Petitt
        Pro–61 D Regan
V'trs   WD–U WE–by arrangement
Fees   £6 (£8)

Tyrrells Wood (1924)

Leatherhead KT22 8QP
Tel   (0372) 376025 (2 lines)
Mem   744
Sec   GD Lawson
Pro   P Taylor (0372) 375200
Holes   18 L 6219 yds SSS 70
Recs   Am–67 P Earl (1988)
        Pro–65 P Hoad (1988)

V'trs   WD–I SOC BH/Sat–NA
        Sun–NA before noon
Fees   £22 (£30)
Loc   2 miles from Leatherhead
       off A24 nr Headley.
       M25 Junction 9, 1 mile

Walto.· Heath (1904)
Tadworth KT20 7TP
Tel   (0737) 812060
Mem   900
Sec   (0737) 812380
Pro   K Macpherson (0737) 812152
Holes Old 18 L 6813 yds SSS 73
       New 18 L 6659 yds SSS 72
Recs   Old Am–68 R Revell
       Pro–65 P Townsend
       New Am–67 JK Tate
       Pro–64 C Clark
V'trs WD–IH WE/BH–M SOC
Fees   £30
Loc   3 miles S of Epsom.
       M25 Junction 8, 2 miles

Wentworth (1924)
Virginia Water GU25 4LS
Tel   (099 04) 2201
Mem   2335
Sec   JAR Doyle–Davidson
Pro   B Gallacher (099 04) 3353
Holes West 18 L 6945 yds SSS 74
       East 18 L 6176 yds SSS 70
       South 18 L 6979 yds SSS 73
       Executive 9 L 1902 yds Par 54
Recs   West Am–72 P McEvoy
       Pro–64 H Clarke
       East Am–65 GB Wolstenholme
       Pro–62 DN Sewell, G Will
V'trs WD–H by prior arrangement
       WE–M SOC–Tues–Thurs
Fees   On application
Loc   21 miles SW of London at
       A30/A39 junction
Mis   South course opening July 1990

West Byfleet (1922)
Sheerwater Road, West Byfleet
KT14 6AA
Tel   (093 23) 45230
Mem   550
Sec   DG Smith (093 23) 43433
Pro   D Regan (093 23) 46584
Holes 18 L 6211 yds SSS 70
Recs   Am–66 W Calderwood
       Pro–67 P Thomson
V'trs WD–I WE/BH–NA
Fees   £20
Loc   West Byfleet ½ mile on A245
       M25 Junction 10

West Hill (1909)
Brookwood, nr Woking
Tel   (048 67) 4365/2110
Mem   550
Sec   WD Leighton MBE
Pro   JA Clements (048 67) 3172
Holes 18 L 6368 yds SSS 70

Recs   Am–66 WA Murray
       Pro–66 N Coles
V'trs WD–H WE–M SOC
Fees   £24
Loc   5 miles W of Woking on A322

West Surrey (1909)
Enton Green, nr Godalming GU8 5AF
Tel   (048 68) 21275
Mem   750
Sec   RS Fanshawe
Pro   J Hoskison (048 68) 7278
Holes 18 L 6247 yds SSS 70
Recs   Am–66 SD Cook
       Pro–67 B Lane
V'trs H SOC–WD
Fees   £16 (£30)
Loc   ½ mile SE of Milford Station

White Lodge (1923)
Public
Priory Lane, Richmond Park,
London SW15
Tel   (081) 876 3205
Mem   126
Sec   FE Carpenter
Holes Play over Richmond Park
       municipal courses

Wimbledon Common (1908)
19 Camp Road, Wimbledon Common,
London SW19 4UW
Tel   (081) 946 0294
Mem   250
Sec   BK Cox (081) 946 7571
Pro   JE Jukes
Holes 18 L 5438 yds SSS 66
Recs   Am–65 T Mahon, MC Ball
       Pro–64 JS Jukes
V'trs WD–U WE–M Sun pm BH–NA
Fees   £10
Mis   Pillarbox red outer garment
       must be worn. London Scottish
       play here

Wimbledon Park (1898)
Home Park Road, London SW19
Tel   (081) 946 1002
Mem   580
Sec   MK Hale (081) 946 1250
Pro   D Wingrove (081) 946 4053
Holes 18 L 5465 yds SSS 67
Recs   Am–61 SJ Bennett, B King
       Pro–60 M Gerrard
V'trs WD–H I WE/BH–after 3pm
       SOC
Fees   D–£20
Loc   Central London 8 miles

Windlemere (1978)
Public
Windlesham Road, West End, Woking
GU24 9QL
Tel   (0276) 858727
Sec   CD Smith

Pro   D Thomas
Holes 9 L 5346 yds SSS 66
V'trs U
Fees   £4 (£4.80)
Loc   A319 at Lightwater
Mis   Floodlit driving range

Woking (1893)
Pond Road, Hook Heath, Woking
GU22 0JZ
Tel   (0483) 760053
Mem   500
Sec   AW Riley
Pro   J Thorne (0483) 769582
Holes 18 L 6322 yds SSS 70
Recs   Am–65 PJ Benka
V'trs WD–I WE–M
Fees   £20
Loc   2½ miles W of Woking off
       Hollybank Road

Woodcote Park (1912)
Bridle Way, Meadow Hill, Coulsdon
CR3 2QQ
Tel   (081) 660 0176 (Clubhouse)
Mem   750
Sec   (081) 668 2788
Pro   I Martin (081) 668 1843
Holes 18 L 6624 yds SSS 71
Recs   Am–66 S Keppler
       Pro–66 C Bonner
V'trs WD–U WE–M
Fees   £20
Loc   Purley 2 miles

Worplesdon (1908)
Heath House Road, Woking GU22 0RA
Tel   (04867) 89876 (Steward)
Mem   560
Sec   Maj REE Jones (04867) 2277
Pro   J Christine (04867) 3287
Holes 18 L 6422 yds SSS 71
Recs   Am–64 KG Jones (1988)
       Pro–62
V'trs WD–H WE–M
Fees   On application
Loc   E of Woking off A322.
       5 miles S of M3 Junction 3

Sussex (East)

Ashdown Forest Hotel
Chapel Lane, Forest Row RH18 5BB
Tel   (0342 82) 4866
Mem   150
Sec   AJ Riddick, RL Pratt
Pro   H Padgham (0342 82) 2247
Holes 18 L 5510 yds SSS 67
V'trs U SOC
Fees   £10 (£12.50)
Loc   4 miles S of E Grinstead off
       A22. 12 miles W of Tunbridge
       Wells
Mis   Hotel specialises in golf breaks

Beauport Park

Battle Road, St Leonards-on-Sea
TN38 0TA
Tel   (0424) 52977
Mem   300
Sec   DC Funnell
Holes Play over Hastings Public
       Course

Brighton & Hove (1887)

Dyke Road, Brighton BN1 8YJ
Tel   (0273) 556482
Mem   270
Sec   SC Cawkwell
Holes 9 L 5722 yds SSS 68
Recs   Am–67
V'trs U SOC Sun–NA before noon
Fees   £12 (£18) 9 holes–£6
Loc   15 mins N of Brighton

Cooden Beach (1912)

Cooden Beach, nr Bexhill-on-Sea
Tel   (042 43) 2040
Mem   450
Sec   RA Wilkins
Pro   K Robson (042 43) 3938
Holes 18 L 6450 yds SSS 71
Recs   Am–67 G Burton, CM Skinner,
       Sir H Birkmyre
       Pro–65 AG Harrison
V'trs U
Fees   £17 (£20)
Loc   W boundary of Bexhill

Crowborough Beacon (1895)

Beacon Road, Crowborough TN6 1UJ
Tel   (0892) 661511
Mem   700
Sec   M Swatton (0892) 661511
Pro   D Newnham (0892) 653877
Holes 18 L 6279 yds SSS 70
Recs   Am–67 GCD Carter, SF Robson
       Pro–67 K Ashdown,
       K MacDonald
V'trs I H WE/BH–NA before 3pm
Fees   £20 (£20)
Loc   7 miles S of Tunbridge Wells
       on A26

Dale Hill (1973)

Ticehurst, nr Wadhurst TN5 7DQ
Tel   (0580) 200112
Mem   600
Sec   AG Smith
Pro   A Malcolm (0580) 201090
Holes 18 L 6055 yds SSS 69
Recs   Pro–68 K MacDonald
V'trs WD–U WE/BH–H after 10.30am
       SOC
Fees   £12.50 (£16.50)
Loc   B2087, off A21 at Flimwell

The Dyke (1908)

Dyke Road, Brighton BN1 8YJ
Tel   (079 156) 296
Mem   750
Sec   B Gazzard

Pro   P Longmore (079 156) 260
Holes 18 L 6577 yds SSS 71
Recs   Am–68 N O'Byrne
       Pro–65 C Jones
V'trs U exc Sun–NA
Fees   £14 D–£16 (£20)
Loc   4 miles N of Brighton

East Brighton (1893)

Roedean, Brighton BN2 5RA
Tel   (0273) 604838
Mem   700
Sec   KR Head
Pro   WH Street
Holes 18 L 6337 yds SSS 70
Recs   Am–68 A Turner
       Pro–63 S King
V'trs WD–U WE–NA before 11am
       SOC
Fees   £15 (£20)
Loc   N from Marina, Black Rock

East Sussex National (1989)

Little Horsted, Uckfield TN22 5TS
Tel   (0825) 75577
Mem   1000
Sec   J McLaughlin (Golf Dir)
Pro   P Dellanzo
Holes East 18 L 7112 yds SSS
       West 18 L 7072 yds SSS
Fees   D–£100 Hotel guests–£57.50
Loc   2 miles S of Uckfield off A22
Mis   Driving range. Golf academy

Eastbourne Downs (1907)

East Dean Road, Eastbourne
BN20 8ES
Tel   (0323) 20827
Mem   700
Sec   DJ Eldrett
Pro   T Marshall (0323) 32264
Holes 18 L 6635 yds SSS 72
Recs   Am–67 J Collison (1988)
       Pro–70 B Gallacher
V'trs U Sun–after 1pm
Fees   £10 (£12)
Loc   1 mile W of Eastbourne on
       A259

Hastings (1973)

Public
Beauport Park, Battle Road,
St Leonards-on-Sea TN38 0TA
Tel   (0424) 52977
Sec   M Barton (0424) 52981
Pro   M Barton (0424) 52981
Holes 18 L 6248 yds SSS 71
Recs   Am–69 V Massarella (1981)
       Pro–72 S Hall (1987)
V'trs U–booking necessary SOC
Fees   £6.50 (£8)
Loc   3 miles N of Hastings off A2100
       Battle to St Leonards road
Mis   Beauport Park Club plays
       here.

Highwoods (Bexhill) (1925)

Ellerslie Lane, Bexhill-on-Sea
TN39 4LJ
Tel   (0424) 212625
Mem   800
Sec   P Robins
Pro   MJ Andrews (0424) 212770
Holes 18 L 6218 yds SSS 70
Recs   Am–66 JAL Smith (1987)
       Pro–68 C Clark (1976)
V'trs WD/Sat–H Sun am–M
       Sun pm–H
Fees   £18 (£22)
Loc   2 miles N of Bexhill

Hollingbury Park (1911)

Public
Ditching Road, Brighton BN1 7HS
Tel   (0273) 552010
Pro   P Brown (0273) 500086
Holes 18 L 6415 yds SSS 71
Recs   Am–68 G Derkson (1988)
       Pro–66 B Norton (1988)
V'trs U SOC
Fees   £8 D–£12 (£10)
Loc   1 mile NE of Brighton

Horam Park (1985)

Public
Chiddingly Road, Horam TN21 0JJ
Tel   (04353) 3477
Pro   R Foster
Holes 9 L 5688 yds SSS 66
Recs   Pro–64 J Pinsent (1988)
V'trs U SOC Sat–M before 4pm
Fees   £12.50 D–£18 (£14 D–£19)
       9 holes £6.50 (£7)
Loc   1/2 mile S of Horam towards
       Chiddingley. 12 miles N of
       Eastbourne on A267
Mis   Floodlit driving range

Lewes (1896)

Chapel Hill, Lewes
Tel   (0273) 473245
Mem   545
Sec   GJ Cull (0273) 473074
Pro   E Goldring
Holes 18 L 5951 yds SSS 69
Recs   Am–70 D Cosham
       Pro–67 CA Burgess
V'trs U SOC
Fees   £10 (£12)
Loc   1/2 mile from Lewes at
       E end of Cliffe High Street

Peacehaven (1896)

Brighton Road, Newhaven BN9 9UH
Tel   (0273) 514049
Mem   290
Sec   DT Jenkins (0273) 512571
Pro   G Williams (0273) 512602
Holes 9 L 5235 yds SSS 66
Recs   Am–67 A Browning (1985)
V'trs WD–U WE/BH–after 11am SOC
Fees   On application
Loc   8 miles E of Brighton on A259

Piltdown (1904)

Uckfield TN22 3XB
Tel (082 872) 0000
Mem 350
Sec REH King (Hon)
Pro J Amos (082 572) 2389
Holes 18 L 6059 yds SSS 69
Recs Am–67 A Smith (1988)
Pro–69 S Frost, P Lovesey
V'trs I or H exc Tues am/
Thurs am/Sun am
Fees £25 (£25)
Loc 1 mile W of Maresfield off
A272, towards Isfield

Royal Ashdown Forest (1888)

Chapel Lane, Forest Row,
E Grinstead RH18 5LR
Tel (034 282) 2018/3014
(034 282) 4866 (New Course)
Mem 450
Sec KPA Mathews
Pro M Landsborough
Holes Old 18 L 6477 yds SSS 71
New 18 L 5549 yds SSS 69
Recs Am–67 RA Darlington
Pro–62 HA Padgham
V'trs On application (phone first)
Fees £20 (£25) 1989 prices
Loc 4 miles S of E Grinstead
on B2100 Hartfield road.
M25 Junction 6

Royal Eastbourne (1887)

Paradise Drive, Eastbourne BN20 8BP
Tel (0323) 30412
Mem 900
Sec R Passingham (0323) 29738
Pro R Wooller (0323) 36986
Holes 18 L 6109 yds SSS 69
9 L 2147 yds SSS 32
Recs Am–65 J Beland (1980)
Pro–62 J Pinsent (1987)
V'trs U H SOC
Fees 18 hole £17.50 (£25)
9 hole £10 (£12)
Loc 1/2 mile from Town Hall

Rye (1894)

Camber, Rye TN31 7QS
Tel (0797) 225241
Mem 800 105(L) 40(J)
Sec JM Bradley
Pro P Marsh (0797) 225218
Holes 18 L 6301 yds SSS 71
9 L 6625 yds SSS 72
Recs Am–64 P Hurring (1988)
Pro–67 C Ledger (1988)
V'trs M
Loc 3 miles E of Rye

Seaford (1887)

East Blatchington, Seaford
BN25 2JD
Tel (0323) 892597
Mem 420 110(L) 37(J) 88(5)
Sec MB Hichisson (0323) 892442
Pro P Stevens (0323) 894160
Holes 18 L 6241 yds SSS 70
Recs Am–66 EA Snow, A Flygt
Pro–67 H Weetman
V'trs WD–U WE–M
Fees £20, £15 after 12 noon
£10 after 3pm
Loc 1 mile N of Seaford
Mis Dormy House accommodation

Seaford Head (1907)

Public
Southdown Road, Seaford BN25 4JS
Tel (0323) 890139
Pro AJ Lowles
Holes 18 L 5812 yds SSS 68
Recs Am–66 J Crawford
Pro–66 M Andrews
V'trs U
Fees £6 D–£8.50 (£7.50 D–£9)
Loc 8 miles W of Eastbourne.
3/4 mile S of A259

Waterhall (1921)

Public
Devils Dyke Road, Brighton BN1 8YN
Tel (0273) 508658
Sec D Birch (Hon)
Pro P Charman
Holes 18 L 5775 yds SSS 68
Recs Am–68 S Maplesden
V'trs U
Fees £8 (£10)
Loc 3 miles N of Brighton between
A23 and A27. 1 mile N of A2308

West Hove (1910)

369 Old Shoreham Road, Hove
BN3 7GD
Tel (0273) 413411
Sec R Charman (0273) 419738
Pro C White (0273) 413494
Holes 18 L 6038 yds SSS 69
Recs Am–66 N O'Byrne
Pro–62 C Moody
V'trs WD–U WE–M
Fees £7 (£9)
Loc 300 yds N of Postslade &
West Hove Station on A27

Willingdon (1898)

Southdown Road, Eastbourne
BN20 9AA
Tel (0323) 410983
Mem 500
Sec B Kirby (0323) 410981
Pro DJ Ashton (0323) 410984
Holes 18 L 6049 yds SSS 69

Recs Am–64 DM Sewell (1986)
Pro–63 P Mitchell (1987)
V'trs WD–U WE–MH SOC–H
Fees £17 (£20) R/D
Loc 1/2 mile N of Eastbourne, off
A22 to London

Sussex (West)

Bognor Regis (1892)

Downview Road, Felpham,
Bognor Regis PO22 8JD
Tel (0243) 865867
Mem 570 173(L)
Sec BD Poston (0243) 821929
Pro R Day (0243) 865209
Holes 18 L 6238 yds SSS 70
Recs Am–65 G Evans
Pro–66 R Wynn
V'trs H WE (Apr–Sept)–M
Fees £16 (£20)
Loc 2 miles E of Bognor

Copthorne (1892)

Borers Arm Road, Copthorne
RH10 3LL
Tel (0342) 712508
Mem 565
Sec J Appleton
Pro J Burrell (0342) 712405
Holes 18 L 6505 yds SSS 71
Recs Am–68 D Arnold, M Logan
Pro–68 C Mason, R Boxall
V'trs WD–U WE/BH–after 1pm SOC
Fees £17 (£30)
Loc E Grinstead 1 mile on A264.
M23 Junction 10

Cottesmore (1974)

Buchan Hill, Crawley RH11 9AT
Tel (0293) 28256
Mem 1600
Sec MF Rogerson
Pro P Webster (0293) 35399
Holes 18 L 6097 yds SSS 70
18 L 5321 yds SSS 68
Recs Old Am–69 I Geddes
Pro–70 D Russell
V'trs U
Fees £14 (£18)
Loc 4 miles S of Crawley

Cowdray Park (1949)

Midhurst GU29 0BB
Tel (0730) 812088
Mem 700
Sec Mrs JD Huggett (0730) 813599
Pro S Hall (0730) 812091
Holes 18 L 6212 yds SSS 70
Recs Am–69 D Fay
Pro–68 G Ralph

V'trs I or H WD–NA before
9am Sat–NA before 11am
Sun/BH–NA before 3pm SOC
Fees £10–£14 (£20)
Loc 1 mile E of Midhurst on A272

Effingham Park (1980)

nr Copthorne
Tel (0342) 716528
Mem 400
Pro I Dryden
Holes 9 L 1749 yds Par 30
Recs Am–29
Pro–26
V'trs WD–U WE–M before 12 noon
–U after 12 noon
Fees £6 D–£8.50 (£7 D–£10)
Loc B2028/B2039

Gatwick Manor (1975)

Crawley
Tel (0293) 24470
Sec C Hemsley
Pro BC Hemsley
Holes 9 L 1109 yds SSS 27
V'trs U
Loc A23 to Crawley, 1 mile past
Gatwick Airport

Goodwood (1892)

Goodwood, nr Chichester PO18 0PN
Tel (0243) 785012 (Members)
Mem 900
Sec M Hughes–Narborough
(0243) 774968
Pro K MacDonald (0243) 774994
Holes 18 L 6383 yds SSS 70
Recs Am–68 SB Ursell (1989)
Pro–66 K MacDonald (1988)
V'trs WD–U H after 9.30pm
WE–H after 10am SOC
Fees £16 (£25)
Loc 3 miles NE of Chichester, on
road to racecourse

Ham Manor (1936)

West Drive, Angmering,
nr Littlehampton BN16 4JE
Tel (0903) 783288
Mem 860
Sec PH Saubergue
Pro S Buckley (0903) 783732
Holes 18 L 6216 yds SSS 70
Recs Am–64 F Wieland (1987)
Pro–62 TA Horton
V'trs WD/WE–H
Fees On application
Loc Between Worthing and
Littlehampton

Haywards Heath (1922)

High Beech Lane, Haywards Heath
RH16 1SL
Tel (0444) 414310
Mem 625
Sec J Duncan (0444) 414457

Pro M Henning (0444) 414866
Holes 18 L 6202 yds SSS 70
Recs Am–69 G Batt–Rawden,
R Arnold
V'trs WD/WE–H–restricted
SOC–Wed & Thurs
Fees £15 (£25)
Loc 2 miles N of Haywards Heath

Hill Barn (1935)

Public
Hill Barn Lane, Worthing
Tel (0903) 37301
Pro P Higgins
Holes 18 L 6224 yds SSS 70
Recs Am–66 H Francis, B Roberts
Pro–63 J Kinsella
V'trs U
Fees £7 (£8)
Loc NE of A27 at Warren Road
roundabout

Ifield (1927)

Rusper Road, Ifield, Crawley
RH11 0LN
Tel (0293) 20222
Mem 800
Sec DT Howe
Pro C Strathearn (0293) 23088
Holes 18 L 6314 yds SSS 70
Recs Am–67 M Groombridge
Pro–65 P Mitchell,
G Cowlishaw
V'trs WD–H WE–M
Fees £15 D–£20
Loc Nr Crawley

Littlehampton (1889)

170 Rope Walk, Littlehampton
BN17 5DL
Tel (0903) 717170
Mem 650
Sec KR Palmer (Sec/Mgr)
Pro CA Burgess (0903) 716369
Holes 18 L 6244 yds SSS 70
Recs Am–68 S Graham
Pro–66 C Giddings
V'trs WD–U after 9.30am
WE/BH–NA before noon SOC
Fees £18 (£25)
Loc W bank of River Arun,
Littlehampton

Mannings Heath (1908)

Mannings Heath, Horsham
Tel (0403) 210168
Mem 800
Sec JD Coutts (0403) 210228
Pro M Denny (0403) 210332
Holes 18 L 6402 yds SSS 71
Recs Am–66 PG Way
Pro–64 G Ralph
V'trs WD–H–M after 5pm WE–NA
SOC
Fees £15
Loc 3 miles SE of Horsham (A281)

Pease Pottage (1986)

Horsham Road, Pease Pottage,
Crawley
Tel (0293) 21706
Mem 40
Sec M Cooper (0403) 50301
Pro C Morley, N Lee
Holes 9 L 3511 yds SSS 57
Recs Am–64 M Roberts (1988)
V'trs U
Fees £5 (£7)
Loc S of Crawley off A23
Mis Floodlit driving range

Pyecombe (1894)

Pyecombe, Brighton BN4 7FF
Tel (079 18) 4176
Mem 550
Sec WM Wise MA (079 18) 5372
Pro CR White (079 18) 5398
Holes 18 L 6234 yds SSS 70
Recs Am–67 C Morris
Pro–67 J Debenham
V'trs WD–U exc Tues after 9.45am
Sat–U after 2pm Sun–U after
3pm SOC–WD exc Tues
Fees £16 (£25)
Loc 6 miles N of Brighton on A272

Selsey (1906)

Golf Links Lane, Selsey PO20 9DR
Tel (0243) 602203
Mem 400
Sec EC Rackstraw (0243) 602029
Pro P Grindley
Holes 9 L 5932 yds SSS 68
Recs Am–66 A Kelly
V'trs U
Fees £9 (£12)
Loc 7 miles S of Chichester

Tilgate (1982)

Public
Titmus Drive, Tilgate, Crawley
Tel (0293) 30103
Pro H Spencer, D McClelland
(0293) 545411
Holes 18 L 6359 yds SSS 70
Recs Am–74 M Hearn (1988)
Pro–68 J Hodgkinson (1986)
V'trs U SOC–Mon–Thurs
Fees £6.50 D–£12.50 (£9.50)
Loc 1¹⁄₂ miles SE of Crawley,
off M23 Junction 11

West Chiltington (1988)

Public
Broadford Bridge Road, W.Chiltington
RH20 2YA
Tel (07983) 3574
Sec SE Coulson (Man Dir)
Pro BW Barnes (07983) 2115
Holes 18 L 5969 yds SSS 69
V'trs U SOC
Fees £8.50 (£12)
Loc 2 miles E of Pulborough
Mis Driving range

West Sussex (1930)

Hurston Lane, Pulborough RH20 2EN
Tel   (079 82) 2563
Mem   800
Sec   GR Martindale
Pro   T Packham (079 82) 2426
Holes 18 L 6156 yds SSS 70
Recs   Am–63 DJ Harrison
V'trs WD–I H after 9.30am exc
       Tues–M SOC–Wed & Thurs
Fees   On application
Loc   1 1/2 miles E of Pulborough on
       A283

Worthing (1905)

Links Road, Worthing BN14 9QZ
Tel   (0903) 60801
Mem   1150
Sec   Maj RB Carroll
Pro   S Rolley (0903) 60718
Holes Lower 18 L 6477 yds SSS 72
       Upper 18 L 5243 yds
       SSS 66
Recs   Lower Am–67 G Evans
       (1988)
       Pro–66 J Bennett (1989)
V'trs WD–U WE–confirm in
       advance with Sec
Fees   £22 (£26)
Loc   Central Station 1 1/2 miles
       (A27)
       1/4 mile from A24 Junction

Tyne & Wear

Backworth (1937)

The Hall, Backworth, Shiremoor,
Newcastle-upon-Tyne ME27 0AH
Tel   (091) 268 1048
Mem   400
Holes 9 L 5930 yds SSS 69
Recs   Am–66
V'trs Mon & Fri–U Tues–Thurs–M
       after 5pm WE–after 12.30pm
       exc comp Sats–after 6pm
Fees   £5 (£6.25)
Loc   Off Tyne Tunnel link road,
       Holystone roundabout

Birtley (Portobello) (1922)

Portobello Road, Birtley DH3 2LR
Tel   (091) 410 2207
Mem   220
Sec   GK Blain (091) 410 0710
Holes 9 L 5660 yds SSS 67
Recs   Am–64 G Hammond
V'trs WD–U exc Fri–NA after 3pm
       WE/BH–M SOC
Fees   £6 W–£20
Loc   Birtley service area
       3 miles on A1(M)

Boldon (1912)

Dipe Lane, East Boldon
Tel   (091) 536 4182
Mem   600
Sec   RE Jobes (091) 536 5360
Pro   Phipps Golf (091) 536 5835
Holes 18 L 6348 yds SSS 70
Recs   Am–67 GR Simpson (1987)
       Pro–66 P Tupling (1980)
V'trs U
Fees   £7 (£9)
Loc   East Boldon

City of Newcastle (1892)

Three Mile Bridge, Great North
Road, Gosforth, Newcastle-upon-
Tyne NE3 2DR
Tel   (091) 285 1775
Mem   400 110(L) 60(J)
Sec   AJ Matthew
Pro   AJ Matthew (091) 285 5481
Holes 18 L 6508 yds SSS 71
Recs   Am–67 M Blackburn (1989)
       Pro–67 W Tyrie (1988)
V'trs U
Fees   £9 (£13)
Loc   A1, 3 miles N of Newcastle

Close House (1968)

Close House, Heddon on the wall,
Newcastle-upon-Tyne NE15 0HT
Tel   (0661) 852953
Mem   850
Sec   Mrs L Steel (0661) 852303
Holes 18 L 5511 yds SSS 67
Recs   Am–66 W Parker (1984),
       R Ingham (1986)
V'trs M SOC–WD
Loc   9 miles W of Newcastle on
       A69

Garesfield (1922)

Chopwell NE17 7AP
Tel   (0207) 561278/561309
Mem   440
Sec   JE Ward (091) 414 3838
Pro   (0207) 561309
Holes 18 L 6196 yds SSS 70
Recs   Am–69 A McClure
       Pro–70 D Dunk
V'trs U SOC
Fees   £4.50 (£6)
Loc   7 miles SW of Newcastle
       between High Spen and
       Chopwell

Gosforth (1906)

Broadway East, Gosforth,
Newcastle-upon-Tyne NE3 5ER
Tel   (091) 285 6710
Mem   370 90(L) 40(J) 40(5)
Sec   HV Smith (091) 285 3495
Pro   D Race (091) 285 0553
Holes 18 L 6030 yds SSS 69
Recs   Am–67 J Hattrick (1987)
V'trs U SOC
Fees   £10 (£15)
Loc   3 miles N of Newcastle
       off A6125

Gosforth Park Golfing Complex (1971)

High Gosforth Park, Newcastle 3
Tel   (091) 236 4480/4867
Mem   450
Sec   A Mair (Dir)
Pro   G Garland
Holes 18 L 5807 yds SSS 68
Recs   Am–68 M Simpkin
       Pro–65 B Rumney
V'trs U
Fees   £7.50
Loc   5 miles N of Newcastle
Mis   9 hole pitch & putt course

Heworth (1912)

Gingling Gate, Heworth, Gateshead
Tel   (091) 469 2137
Mem   600
Sec   G Holbrow (091) 469 9832
Holes 18 L 6462 yds SSS 71
Recs   Am–65 D Moralee
       Pro–69 P Highmoor
V'trs WD–U WE–after noon
Fees   £5 (£7.50)
Loc   SE boundary of Gateshead

Houghton-le-Spring (1912)

Copt Hill Links, Houghton-le-Spring
Tel   (091) 584 1198
Mem   500
Sec   N Wales
Pro   (0783) 584 7421
Holes 18 L 6416 yds SSS 71
Recs   Am–69 J Hogg
V'trs U SOC
Fees   £8 (£12)
Loc   6 miles SW of Sunderland

Newcastle United (1892)

60 Ponteland Road, Newcastle-upon-
Tyne NE5 3JW
Tel   (091) 286 4693 (Clubhouse)
Mem   500
Sec   J Simpson
Pro   (091) 286 9998
Holes 18 L 6484 yds SSS 71
Recs   Am–64 N Graham
V'trs WD–U WE–M SOC
Fees   £6 (£8)
Loc   Nuns Moor, Cowgate

Northumberland (1898)

High Gosforth Park,
Newcastle-upon-Tyne NE3 5HT
Tel   (091) 236 2009
Mem   500
Sec   D Lamb (091) 236 2498
Holes 18 L 6629 yds SSS 72
Recs   Am–68 DP Davidson,
       PWS Bent, DM Moffat
       Pro–65 A Jacklin, T Horton
V'trs WD–I WE/BH–M
Fees   WD–£17.50
Loc   4 miles N of Newcastle

For explanation of abbreviations, see page 460.

Ravensworth (1906)

Mossheaps, Wrekenton, Gateshead
NE9 7UU
Tel	(091) 487 6014/2843
Mem	480
Sec	JN Davison (091) 469 3782
Holes	18 L 5872 yds SSS 68
Recs	Am–63 K Kelly
	Pro–64 T Horton
V'trs	U
Fees	£8 (£12)
Loc	3 miles S of Newcastle on B1296

Ryton (1891)

nr Stanners, Clara Vale NE40 3TD
Tel	(091) 413 3737
Mem	460
Sec	RW Charlton (091) 413 3048
Holes	18 L 6300 yds SSS 69
Recs	Am–69 PR Brougham
V'trs	WD–U WE–U exc 8–9.30am and 12–1.30pm SOC
Fees	£8 (£10)
Loc	7 miles W of Newcastle, off A69

South Shields (1893)

Cleadon Hills, South Shields
NE34 8EG
Tel	(091) 456 0475
Mem	700
Sec	WH Loades (091) 456 8942
Pro	G Parsons (091) 456 0110
Holes	18 L 6264 yds SSS 70
Recs	Am–65 J Ellwood (1988)
	Pro–64 M Gregson
V'trs	U SOC–WD
Fees	£10 (£15)
Loc	Cleadon Hills, South Shields

Tynemouth (1913)

Spital Dene, Tynemouth, North Shields
NE30 2ER
Tel	(091) 257 4578
Mem	813
Sec	W Storey (091) 257 3381
Pro	J McKenna (091) 258 0728
Holes	18 L 6403 yds SSS 70
Recs	Am–64 CR Hinson
	Pro–64 J Ord
V'trs	WD–U SOC Sat/Sun am–NA
Fees	£10 (£12)
Loc	E of Newcastle-upon-Tyne

Tyneside (1879)

Westfield Lane, Ryton NE40 3QE
Tel	(091) 413 2177
Mem	660
Sec	JR Watkin (091) 413 2742
Pro	M Gunn
Holes	18 L 6055 yds SSS 69
Recs	Am–66 J Surtees, M Dunn, PS Highmoor
	Pro–65 JR Harrison
V'trs	WD–U (exc 11.30–1.30pm) WE–NA before 3pm SOC
Fees	£10 (£16)
Loc	7 miles W of Newcastle. S of river, off A695

Wallsend (1973)

Public
Bigges Main, Wallsend NE28 8XF
Tel	(091) 262 1973
Pro	P Eaton (091) 262 2431
Holes	18 L 6608 yds SSS 72
V'trs	U
Fees	£6.50 (£8)
Loc	Between Newcastle and Wallsend on coast road

Washington

Stone Cellar Road, Washington
Mem	450
Sec	DV Duffy (Hon)
Pro	D Howden (091) 417 8346
Holes	18 L 6604 yds SSS 72
Recs	Am–71 D Armstrong (1984)
	Pro–66 N Briggs (1987)
V'trs	U
Fees	£4.35 (£6)
Loc	By A1(M)–North turning to Washington
Mis	Hotel. Driving range. 9 hole pitch & putt

Wearside (1892)

Coxgreen, Sunderland SR4 9JT
Tel	(091) 534 2518
Mem	650
Sec	KD Wheldon (091) 534 1193
Pro	S Wynn (091) 534 4269
Holes	18 L 6315 yds SSS 70
Recs	Am–67 L Naisby, D Curry, D Wood
	Pro–68 A Bickerdike
V'trs	WD–H WE–MH SOC
Fees	£7 D–£9 (£10)
Loc	2 miles W of Sunderland, off A183. ¼ mile W of A19

Westerhope

Whorlton Grange, Westerhope,
Newcastle-upon-Tyne NE5 1PP
Tel	(091) 286 9125
Mem	700
Sec	GS Bazley (091) 286 7636
Pro	N Brown (091) 286 0594
Holes	18 L 6407 yds SSS 71
Recs	Am–66 A Morrison, R Roper
	Pro–67 D Russell
V'trs	U
Fees	£9
Loc	5 miles W of Newcastle

Whickham (1911)

Hollinside Park, Whickham,
Newcastle-upon-Tyne NE16 5BA
Tel	(091) 488 7309
Mem	500
Sec	N Weightman (091) 488 1576
Pro	GN Towne (091) 488 8591
Holes	18 L 6129 yds SSS 69
Recs	Am–68
V'trs	U
Fees	£10 D–£12 (D–£15)
Loc	5 miles SW of Newcastle

Whitburn (1931)

Lizard Lane, South Shields NE34 7AF
Tel	(091) 529 2144
Mem	380 73(L) 61(J) 79(5)
Sec	W Anderson (091) 456 0388
Pro	D Stephenson (091) 529 4210
Holes	18 L 6046 yds SSS 69
Recs	Am–65 KW Fleming (1988)
	Pro–70 M Gunn
V'trs	U SOC
Fees	£7.50 (£12)
Loc	2 miles N of Sunderland on coast

Whitley Bay (1890)

Claremount Road, Whitley Bay
NE26 3UF
Tel	(091) 252 0180
Mem	700
Sec	B Dockar
Pro	WJ Light (091) 252 5688
Holes	18 L 6614 yds SSS 72
Recs	Am–68 GJ Clark
	Pro–66 J Fourie
V'trs	WD–U WE–M
Fees	£10
Loc	10 miles E of Newcastle

Warwickshire

Atherstone (1894)

The Outwoods, Atherstone
Tel	(0827) 713110
Mem	265 40(L) 40(J)
Sec	AG Sarson (0827) 714579
Holes	18 L 6239 SSS 70
Recs	Am–66 M Reay
	Pro–65
V'trs	H WE/Tues–M SOC–WD
Fees	D–£10
Loc	½ mile from Atherstone (Coleshill road)
Mis	

City of Coventry (Brandon Wood) (1977)

Public
Brandon Lane, Coventry CV8 3GQ
Tel	(0203) 543141
Pro	C Gledhill
Holes	18 L 6530 yds SSS 71
Recs	Pro–68 AR Sadler
V'trs	U SOC
Fees	£5 (£6.50)
Loc	6 miles SE of Coventry, off A45 (southbound)
Mis	Floodlit driving range

Kenilworth (1889)

Crew Lane, Kenilworth
Tel	(0926) 54296
Mem	830
Sec	BV Edwards (0926) 58517
Pro	S Mouland (0926) 512732
Holes	18 L 6408 yds SSS 71
Recs	Am–69 P Broadbent

V'trs U
Fees £11 (£15)
Loc 5 miles S of Coventry

Ladbrook Park (1908)

Poolhead Lane, Tamworth-in-Arden,
Solihull B94 5ED
Tel (05644) 2220 (Members)
Mem 740
Sec Mrs GP Taylor (05644) 2264
Pro GR Taylor (05644) 2581
Holes 18 L 6407 yds SSS 71
Recs Am–67 PJ Sant
Pro–65 RDS Livingston
V'trs WD–U H WE/BH–M H
Fees On application
Loc 12 miles S of Birmingham.
M42 Redditch/Evesham
Junction

Leamington & County (1908)

Golf Lane, Whitnash, Leamington Spa
CV31 2QA
Tel (0926) 420298
Mem 600
Sec SM Cooknell (0926) 425961
Pro I Grant (0926) 428014
Holes 18 L 6430 yds SSS 71
Recs Am–65 RG Hiatt
Pro–66 D Thomas
V'trs U SOC
Fees £12 D–£15 (£18)
Loc 1$\frac{1}{2}$ miles S of Leamington Spa

Maxstoke Park (1896)

Castle Lane, Coleshill, Birmingham
B46 2RD
Tel (0675) 621518
Mem 450
Sec JC Evans (Hon)
Pro RA Young (0675) 64915
Holes 18 L 6460 yds SSS 71
Recs Am–66 AM Allen
Pro–71 PJ Butler
V'trs WD–U WE–M
Fees £14
Loc 3 miles S of Coleshill

Newbold Comyn (1973)

Public
Newbold Terrace East, Leamington
Spa
Tel (0926) 421157
Pro D Knight
Holes 18 L 6221 yds SSS 70
Recs Am–70 G Knight
Pro–S Hutchinson (1987)
V'trs WD–U WE–booking 1 week
in advance
Fees £3.40 (£4.40)
Loc Off Willes Road (B4099)

Nuneaton (1906)

Golf Drive, Whitestone, Nuneaton
Tel (0203) 347810
(0203) 344268 (Steward)
Mem 650
Sec T Rosser

Pro PF Kowalik (0203) 340201
Holes 18 L 6412 yds SSS 71
Recs Am–67 P Broadhurst
Pro–67 C Holmes
V'trs WD–U H WE–M SOC
Fees £12
Loc 2 miles S of Nuneaton

Purley Chase (1980)

Pipers Lane, Ridge Lane,
nr Nuneaton CV10 0RB
Tel (0203) 393118
Mem 600
Sec RG Place
Pro D Llewelyn (0203) 395348
Holes 18 L 6604 yds SSS 72
Recs Am–72 P Broadhurst
Pro–64 P Elson
V'trs WD/BH–U WE–U after 2.30pm
SOC
Fees £10 D–£12 (£15 D–£16)
Loc 4 miles WNW of Nuneaton
on
B4114 (A47). 1$\frac{1}{2}$ miles SW of
A5 Mancetter Island
Mis 13 bay driving range

Rugby (1891)

Clifton Road, Rugby CV21 3RD
Tel (0788) 542306
Mem 550
Sec B Poxon (0788) 810066
Pro D Sutherland (0788) 75134
Holes 18 L 5457 yds SSS 67
Recs Am–65 R Clynick
Pro–68 D Sutherland
V'trs WD–U WE/BH–M SOC
Fees £12 R/D
Loc 1 mile N of Rugby on B5414

Stratford-on-Avon (1894)

Tiddington Road, Stratford-on-Avon
Tel (0789) 414546
Mem 770
Sec JH Standbridge (0789) 205749
Pro ND Powell (0789) 205677
Holes 18 L 6309 yds SSS 70
Recs Am–67 PB Rodgers,
NCF Dainton
Pro–65 J Whitehead
V'trs U
Fees On application
Loc $\frac{1}{2}$ mile E of Stratford on B4086

Warwick (1971)

Public
Warwick Racecourse, Warwick
CV34 6HW
Tel (0926) 494316
Sec Mrs R Dunkley
Pro P Sharp (0926) 491284
Holes 9 L 2682 yds SSS 66
Recs Am–67 R Buckingham
Pro–70 P Sharp
V'trs U exc while racing in progress
Fees £2 (£2.50)
Loc Centre of racecourse
Mis Driving range

Welcombe Hotel

Warwick Road, Stratford-on-Avon
CV37 0NR
Tel (0789) 299012 (Clubhouse)
Sec PJ Day (Golf Mgr)
BAK Miller (Hotel Mgr)
(0789) 295252
Holes 18 L 6202 yds SSS 70
Recs Am–67 R Fletcher
V'trs WD–U H WE/BH–UH after
noon
Fees £20 (£25)
Loc Stratford 1$\frac{1}{2}$ miles on A439
towards Warwick

West Midlands

The Belfry (1977)

Public
Wishaw B76 9PR
Tel (0675) 70301
Sec SD Butler (Ext 280)
Pro P McGovern (Ext 267)
Holes Brabazon 18 L 6975 yds SSS 73
Derby 18 L 6127 yds SSS 70
Recs Brabazon Pro–63 E Darcy
Derby Pro–69 J Brown
V'trs U
Fees Brabazon £20 (£22)
Derby £9 (£11)
Loc 4 miles N of M6 Junction 4

Bloxwich (1924)

Stafford Road, Bloxwich WS3 3PQ
Tel (0922) 405724
Mem 500
Sec AD Perry (0922) 476593
Pro B Janes (0922) 476889
Holes 18 L 6277 yds SSS 70
Recs Am–67 JPG Windsor
Pro–65 J Rhodes
V'trs WD–U WE–M SOC
Fees D–£14
Loc On A34 N of Walsall

Boldmere

Public
Monmouth Drive, Birmingham, Sutton
Coldfield CJ3 6JR
Tel (021) 354 3379
Sec D Dufty
Pro T Short
Holes 18 L 4463 yds SSS 62
Recs Am–57 G Marston (1987)
Pro–57 P Weaver (1987)
V'trs U
Fees £3.90 (£4.60)
Loc By Sutton Park, 1 mile from
Sutton Coldfield

Brand Hall (1946)

Public
Heron Road, Oldbury, Warley
Tel (021) 552 7475
Pro (021) 552 2195
Holes 18 L 5813 yds SSS 68
Recs Am–64 B Burlison

Calderfields

V'trs   U exc first 2 hrs Sat/Sun
Fees   £3
Loc   6 miles NW of Birmingham.
        M5 Junction 2, 1¹/₂ miles

Calderfields

Aldridge Road, Walsall WS4 2JS
Tel   (0922) 640540 (Clubhouse)
Mem   550
Sec   M Quinn
Pro   R Griffin (0922) 32243
Holes   18 L 6636 yds SSS 69
V'trs   U
Fees   £8 D–£15 (£10)
Loc   1 mile N of Walsall

Cocks Moor Woods (1926)

Public
Alcester Road, South King's
Heath, Birmingham BK1 6ER
Tel   (021) 444 3584
Pro   S Ellis
Holes   18 L 5742 yds SSS 67
Recs   Am–65 V Pailing
        Pro–71 B Jones, K Dodsworth
V'trs   U
Fees   £3.90 (£4.60)
Loc   6¹/₂ miles S of Birmingham

Copt Heath (1910)

1220 Warwick Road, Knowle, Solihull
B93 9LN
Tel   (0564) 772650
Mem   700
Sec   W Lenton
Pro   BJ Barton
Holes   18 L 6504 yds SSS 71
Recs   Am–66 P McEvoy
        Pro–65 BJ Barton
V'trs   WD–H SOC WE/BH–M
Fees   £20
Loc   2 miles S of Solihull on A41

Coventry (1887)

Finham Park, Coventry CV3 6PJ
Tel   (0203) 411123
Mem   750
Sec   JE Jarman (0203) 414152
Pro   P Weaver (0203) 411298
Holes   18 L 6613 yds SSS 72
Recs   Am–66 P Downes
        Pro–66 P Weaver
V'trs   WD–H
Fees   £17.50
Loc   2 miles S of Coventry on A444

Coventry Hearsall (1896)

Beechwood Avenue, Coventry
CV5 6DF
Tel   (0203) 713470
Mem   450
Sec   WG Doughty
Pro   T Rouse (0203) 713156
Holesz
        18 L 5963 yds SSS 69
Recs   Am–70 J Marley (1987)
        Pro–66 B Morris (1987)
V'trs   WD–U WE–M
Fees   D–£14
Loc   1¹/₂ miles S of Coventry

Dartmouth (1910)

Vale Street, West Bromwich B71 4DW
Tel   (021) 588 2131
Mem   250
Sec   RH Smith
Holes   18 L 6060 yds SSS 69
Recs   Am–68 P Griffiths
        Pro–70 P Lester
V'trs   WD–U WE–restricted
Fees   £9
Loc   1 mile from W Bromwich,
        behind Churchfields High
        School. Nr Junction M5/M6

Druids Heath (1974)

Stonnall Road, Aldridge WS9 8JZ
Tel   (0922) 55595
Mem   500 40(L) 35(J)
Sec   To be appointed
Pro   M Daubney (0922) 59523
Holes   18 L 6914 yds SSS 73
Recs   Am–69 M Pearce
V'trs   WD–U WE–M
Fees   £12 (£17)
Loc   6 miles NW of Sutton Coldfield

Dudley (1894)

Turners Hill, Rowley Regis, Warley
Tel   (0384) 53719
Mem   300
Sec   RP Fortune (0384) 233877
Pro   D Down (0384) 54020
Holes   18 L 5715 yds SSS 67
Recs   Am–66 AA Davies
        Pro–63 R Livingstone
V'trs   WD–U WE–M
Fees   £12
Loc   2 miles S of Dudley

Edgbaston (1896)

Church Road, Birmingham B15 3TB
Tel   (021) 454 1736
Mem   830
Sec   Maj DB Sullivan
Pro   A Bownes (021) 454 3226
Holes   18 L 6118 yds SSS 69
Recs   Am–67 T Allen
        Pro–65 J Rhodes
V'trs   U
Fees   £20 (£25)
Loc   S of Birmingham

Enville (1935)

Highgate Common, Enville,
nr Stourbridge DY7 5BN
Tel   (0384) 872551
Mem   900
Sec   RJ Bannister (Sec/Mgr)
        (0384) 872074
Pro   S Power (0384) 872585
Holes   Highgate 18 L 6451 yds SSS 72
        Lodge 18 L 6207 yds SSS 70
Recs   Highgate Am–68 A Stubbs
        Pro–66 PH Hinton
        Lodge Am–65 C Elston (1989)

Dartmouth (continued)

V'trs   WD–U WE/BH–M H SOC
Fees   £15 D–£20
Loc   6 miles W of Stourbridge
Mis   Buggies for hire

Forest of Arden G & CC

Maxstoke Lane, Meriden, Coventry
CV7 7HR
Tel   (0676) 22118
Mem   600
Sec   KJ Shaw (Mgr)
Pro   M Tarn
Holes   18 L 6900 yds Par 72
V'trs   U SOC
Fees   £12 (£15)
Loc   Off A45 Birmingham–Coventry
        road. M42 Junction 6. M6
        Junction 4. NEC 3 miles

Fulford Heath (1934)

Tanners Green Lane, Wythall,
Birmingham B47 6BH
Tel   (0564) 822806 (Clubhouse)
        (0564) 824758 (Office)
Mem   675
Sec   RG Bowen (021) 705 5480
Pro   KA Hayward (0564) 822930
Holes   18 L 6256 yds SSS 70
Recs   Am–66 KJ Miller
        Pro–67 M James
V'trs   WD–H WE/BH–M SOC
Fees   £12 D–£15
Loc   8 miles S of Birmingham

Gay Hill (1913)

Hollywood Lane, Birmingham B47 5PP
Tel   (021) 430 6523/7077
Mem   700
Sec   Mrs EK Devitt (021) 430 8544
Pro   A Hill (021) 474 6001
Holes   18 L 6532 yds SSS 71
Recs   Am–67 P Adams
        Pro–66 R Livingston
V'trs   WD–U WE–M SOC
Fees   £18
Loc   7 miles S of Birmingham on
        A435. M42 Junction 3, 3 miles

Grange (1924)

Copsewood, Coventry CV3 1HS
Tel   (0203) 451465
Mem   350
Sec   E Soutar (0203) 446324
Holes   9 L 6002 yds SSS 69
V'trs   WD–U before 2.30pm Sat–NA
        Sun–NA before noon
Fees   £7 D–£10 Sun–£10
Loc   East Coventry

Great Barr (1961)

Chapel Lane, Birmingham B43 7BA
Tel   (021) 357 1232
Mem   600
Sec   K Pembridge (021) 358 4376
Pro   SM Doe (021) 357 5270

Holes	18 L 6545 yds SSS 72
Recs	Am–67 CM Lambert
	Pro–71 J Higgins
V'trs	WD–U WE–I (h'cap max 18)
Fees	£12 (£15)
Loc	6 miles NW of Birmingham.
	M6 Junction 7

Hagley (1980)

Wassell Grove, Hagley, nr Stourbridge
Tel	(0562) 883701
Mem	600
Sec	VC Lewis
Holes	18 L 6353 SSS 72
Recs	Am–73 S Hull (1989)
V'trs	WD–U exc Wed before 1.30pm
	WE–M after 1pm SOC–WD
Fees	£12 D–£14

Halesowen (1909)

The Leasowes, Halesowen B62 8QF
Tel	(021) 550 1041
Mem	600
Sec	Mrs M Bateman (021) 501 3606
Pro	M Smith (021) 503 0593
Holes	18 L 5754 yds SSS 68
Recs	Am–65 D Henn
	Pro–66
V'trs	WD–U WE–M SOC–WD exc
	Wed
Fees	£10 D–£12
Loc	M5 Junction 3, 2 miles

Handsworth (1895)

Sunningdale Close, Handsworth Wood, Birmingham B20 1NP
Tel	(021) 554 0599
Mem	850
Sec	RL Neale (Hon)
Pro	M Hicks (021) 523 3594
Holes	18 L 6297 yds SSS 70
Recs	Am–65 DJ Russell
	Pro–71 HF Boyce
V'trs	WD–U WE/BH–M SOC
Fees	£20 (£20)
Loc	3 miles NW of Birmingham.
	M5 Junction 1. M6 Junction 7

Harborne (1893)

40 Tennal Road, Harborne, Birmingham B32 2JE
Tel	(021) 427 1728
Mem	500
Sec	RA Eddy (021) 427 3058 (am)
Pro	A Quarterman (021) 427 3512
Holes	18 L 6240 yds SSS 70
Recs	Am–65 JA Fisher, R Ellis
	Pro–65 E Cogle
V'trs	WD–U WE/BH–M SOC
Fees	£15 R/D
Loc	3 miles SW of Birmingham.
	M5 Junction 3

Harborne Church Farm

Public
Vicarage Road, Harborne, Birmingham B17 0SN
Tel	(021) 427 1204
Pro	M Hampton

Holes	9 L 4514 yds SSS 62
Recs	Am–63 J Sankey
	Pro–60 PR Rudge
V'trs	U
Fees	£3.20 (£4) 18 holes
	£1.70 (£2.10) 9 holes
Loc	5 miles SW of Birmingham

Hatchford Brook (1969)

Public
Coventry Road, Sheldon, Birmingham B26 3PY
Tel	(021) 743 9821
Pro	P Smith
Holes	18 L 6164 yds SSS 69
Recs	Am–69 A Allen (1987)
	Pro–68 P Smith (1988)
V'trs	U SOC–WD
Fees	£3.90 (£4.60)
Loc	City boundary close to airport.
	A45/M42 Junction

Hilltop (1979)

Public
Park Lane, Handsworth, Birmingham B21 8LJ
Tel	(021) 551 3229 (Clubhouse)
Pro	K Highfield (021) 554 4463
Holes	18 L 6114 yds SSS 69
Recs	Am–66 H Ali
	Pro–65 BN Jones
V'trs	U
Fees	£3.90 (£4.60)
Loc	M5 West Brom, opposite
	Hawthorns Football Ground

Himley Hall (1980)

Public
Himley Hall Park, Dudley
Tel	(0902) 895207
Holes	9 L 3090 yds SSS 35
V'trs	WD–U WE/BH–restricted
Fees	18 holes £3.50 (£4)
	9 holes £2.20 (£2.70)
Loc	Grounds of Himley Hall Park,
	nr Dudley

Lickey Hills

Public
Rednal, Birmingham
Tel	(021) 453 3159
Pro	MS March
Holes	18 L 6010 yds SSS 69
Recs	Am–74 MSR Lunt
	Pro–72 R Livingston
V'trs	U
Fees	£2 (£2)
Loc	10 miles SW of Birmingham
Mis	Rose Hill Club plays here

Little Aston (1908)

Streetly, Sutton Coldfield B74 3AN
Tel	(021) 353 2066
Mem	250
Sec	NH Russell (021) 353 2942
Pro	J Anderson (021) 353 2942

Holes	18 L 6724 yds SSS 73
Recs	Am–66
	Pro–68
V'trs	By prior arrangement WE–XL
Fees	On application
Loc	4 miles NW of Sutton Coldfield

Moor Hall (1932)

Four Oaks, Sutton Coldfield
Tel	(021) 308 6130
Mem	525
Sec	WC Brodie
Pro	A Partridge (021) 308 5106
Holes	18 L 6219 yds SSS 70
Recs	Am–65 J Cook
	Pro–67 NR McDonald
V'trs	WD–U exc Thurs–U after
	12.30pm WE/BH–M
Fees	£17 D–£23
Loc	1 mile E of Sutton

Moseley (1892)

Springfield Road, King's Heath, Birmingham B14 7DX
Tel	(021) 444 2115
Mem	600
Sec	PT Muddiman (021) 444 4957
	(10am–1pm)
Pro	G Edge (021) 444 2063
Holes	18 L 6227 yds SSS 70
Recs	Am–64 A Forrester
	Pro–64 FE Miller
V'trs	M or I
Fees	£25
Loc	S Birmingham

North Warwickshire (1894)

Hampton Lane, Meriden, Coventry CV7 7LL
Tel	(0676) 22259
Mem	400
Sec	EG Barnes (Hon)
Pro	D Bradley
Holes	9 L 6362 yds SSS 70
Recs	Am–67 P Broadhurst, M Biddle
V'trs	WD–U WE/BH–M SOC
Fees	£10 (£14)
Loc	Coventry 6 miles.
	Birmingham 13 miles

North Worcestershire (1907)

Frankley Beeches Road, Northfield, Birmingham B31 5LP
Tel	(021) 475 1047
Mem	550
Sec	KS Reading
Pro	K Jones (021) 475 5721
Holes	18 L 5907 yds SSS 69
Recs	Am–64 DJ Russell
	Pro–63 K Dickens (1988)
V'trs	WD–U WE/BH–NA
Fees	£10
Loc	7 miles SW of Birmingham

For explanation of abbreviations, see page 460.

Olton (1893)

Mirfield Road, Solihull B91 1JH
Tel   (021) 705 1083
Mem   600
Sec   MA Perry (0564) 777953
Pro   D Playdon (021) 705 7296
Holes 18 L 6229 yds SSS 71
Recs Am–65 T Allen
      Pro–66 D Llewellyn
V'trs WD–U exc Wed am WE–M
Fees £16
Loc   7 miles S of Birmingham

Oxley Park (1914)

Stafford Road, Bushbury,
Wolverhampton WV10 6DE
Tel   (0902) 20506
Mem   400
Sec   Mrs K Mann (0902) 20892
      (mornings)
Pro   LA Burlison (0902) 25445
Holes 18 L 6168 yds SSS 69
Recs Am–64 CS White
      Pro–65 D Thorp, P Weaver
V'trs U SOC
Fees £14 (£16)
Loc   1 1/2 miles N of Wolverhampton

Patshull Park (1980)

Pattingham, Wolverhampton
WV6 7HR
Tel   (0902) 700342 (Golf Admin)
Mem   375
Sec   T Gray
Pro   DJ McDowall (Golf Dir)
      I Woosnam (Golf Dir)
Holes 18 L 6412 yds SSS 71
Recs Pro–66 P Elson
V'trs U SOC
Fees £17 D–£25 (£20 D–£30)
Loc   7 miles W of Wolverhampton.
      M54 Junction 3, 5 miles

Penn (1908)

Penn Common, Wolverhampton
Tel   (0902) 341142
Mem   500
Sec   PW Thorrington
Pro   A Briscoe (0902) 330472
Holes 18 L 6465 yds SSS 71
Recs Am–68 RJ Green
      Pro–70 J Rhodes, R Cameron
V'trs WD–U WE–M SOC
Fees £12
Loc   2 miles SW of Wolverhampton

Pype Hayes (1932)

Public
Eachelhurst Road, Walmley,
Sutton Coldfield B76 8EP
Tel   (021) 351 1014
Pro   JF Bayliss
Holes 18 L 5811 yds SSS 68
Recs Am–62 L Jacks (1985)
      Pro–59 J Cawsey (1954)

V'trs U
Fees £4
Loc   5 miles NE of Birmingham

Robin Hood (1893)

St Bernards Road, Solihull
B92 7DJ
Tel   (021) 706 0159
Mem   650
Sec   (021) 706 0061
Pro   FE Miller (021) 706 0806
Holes 18 L 6609 yds SSS 72
Recs Am–68 J Draper (1988)
      Pro–68 A Miller
V'trs WD–U WE/BH–M SOC–WD
Fees £16 D–£20
Loc   7 miles S of Birmingham

Sandwell Park (1896)

Birmingham Road, West Bromwich
B71 4JJ
Tel   (021) 553 0260
Mem   650
Sec   HB Medley (Mgr)
      (021) 553 4637
Pro   AW Mutton (021) 553 4384
Holes 18 L 6470 yds SSS 72
Recs Am–67 B Charlton (1983)
      Pro–67 J Rhodes
V'trs WD–U WE–MH SOC–WD
Fees £14 D–£20
Loc   West Bromwich/Birmingham
      boundary. By M5 Junction 1

Shirley (1956)

Stratford Road, Monkspath, Shirley,
Solihull B90 4EW
Tel   (021) 744 6001
Mem   450
Sec   AJ Phillips
Pro   C Wicketts (021) 745 4979
Holes 18 L 6510 yds SSS 71
Recs Am–68 M Payne
      Pro–68
V'trs WD–U WE–M
Fees £15 D–£25
Loc   8 miles S of B'ham. 400 yds
      city side of M42 Junction 4

South Staffordshire (1892)

Danescourt Road, Tettenhall,
Wolverhampton WV6 9BQ
Tel   (0902) 751065
Mem   600
Sec   H Williams
Pro   J Rhodes (0902) 754816
Holes 18 L 6621 yds SSS 72
Recs Am–67 D Gifford
      Pro–66 A Sadler
V'trs WD–U WE/BH–M SOC
Fees £14 D–£18 1989 prices
Loc   3 miles W of Wolverhampton
      off A41

Sphinx (1948)

Siddeley Avenue, Stoke, Coventry
CV3 1FZ
Tel   (0203) 451361
Mem   400
Sec   GE Brownbridge
      (0203) 597731
Holes 9 L 4104 yds SSS 60
Recs Am–62 PR Thorpe
V'trs U exc Sun am
Fees £3.50
Loc   Nr Birley Road, Coventry

Stourbridge (1892)

Worcester Lane, Pedmore,
Stourbridge
Tel   (0384) 393062
Mem   720
Sec   FR McLachlan (0384) 395566
Pro   WH Firkins (0384) 393129
Holes 18 L 6178 yds SSS 69
Recs Am–65 J Fisher
      Pro–63 WH Firkins
V'trs WD–U exc Wed before
      4pm–M WE/BH–M
Fees £15

Sutton Coldfield (1889)

Thornhill Road, Sutton Coldfield
B74 3ER
Tel   (021) 353 2014
Mem   517
Sec   AJ Bishop, M McClean
      (021) 353 9633
Pro   JK Hayes (021) 353 9633
Holes 18 L 6541 yds SSS 71
Recs Am–65 L Jacks (1986)
      Pro–64 PA Elson (1978)
V'trs U H SOC
Fees £18 (£20)
Loc   9 miles N of Birmingham

Swindon (1986)

Bridgnorth Road, Swindon, Dudley
DY3 4PU
Tel   (0902) 897031
Mem   500
Sec   E Greenway (Mgr)
Pro   P Lester (0902) 896191
Holes 18 L 6042 yds SSS 69
      9 hole Par 3 1135 yds
Recs Am–68 B Cotterill
      Pro–68 K Bayliss
V'trs U SOC–WD
Fees £12 (£18)
Loc   5 miles from Wolverhampton,
      Dudley and Stourbridge on
      B4176
Mis   Driving range

Walmley (Wylde Green) (1902)

Brooks Road, Wylde Green,
Sutton Coldfield B72 1HR
Tel   (021) 373 0029
Mem   700
Sec   JPG Windsor
Pro   MJ Skerritt (021) 373 7103

Holes	18 L 6537 yds SSS 72
Recs	Am–71 R Soen
	Pro–72 B Waites
V'trs	WD–U WE–M
Fees	£18 D–£25
Loc	N boundary of Birmingham

Walsall (1907)

Broadway, Walsall
Tel	(0922) 22710
Mem	700
Sec	E Murray (0922) 613512
Pro	R Lambert (0922) 26766
Holes	18 L 6232 yds SSS 70
Recs	Am–66 RG Hiatt, D Blakeman
	Pro–66 N Brunyard
V'trs	WD–U WE–M SOC
Fees	£12.50 (£18)
Loc	1 mile S of Walsall

Warley (1921)

Public
Lightwoods Hill, Warley B67 5EO
Tel	(021) 429 2440
Pro	D Owen
Holes	9 L 2606 yds SSS 64
Recs	Am–62 M Daw
	Pro–58 B Fereday
V'trs	U
Fees	£3.20 (£4)
Loc	5 miles W of Birmingham

Wiltshire

Bremhill Park (1967)

Shrivenham, Swindon
Tel	(0793) 782946
Sec	R Bentley (0793) 783846
Pro	P Borham
Holes	18 L 5889 yds SSS 70
Recs	Am–68
	Pro–66 M Howell (1988)
V'trs	U
Fees	£8 (£10)
Loc	4 miles E of Swindon

Brinkworth (1984)

Longmans Farm, Brinkworth,
Chippenham SN15 5DG
Tel	(066 641) 277
Mem	250
Sec	R Sheppard
Holes	9 L 6086 yds SSS 69
V'trs	U SOC
Fees	£3 (£3.50) 1988 prices
Loc	Brinkworth 2 miles on Wootton Bassett–Malmesbury road

Broome Manor (1976)

Public
Pipers Way, Swindon SN3 1RG
Tel	(0793) 532403
Sec	T Watt (Mgr)(0793) 495761
Pro	B Sandry (0793) 532403
Holes	18 L 6359 yds SSS 70
	9 L 2745 yds SSS 67

Recs	Am–69 A Norman–Thorpe, S Robertson
	Pro–66 M Bevan
V'trs	U
Fees	18 hole:£4.75 (£5.25) 9 hole:£2.85 (£3.15)
Loc	Swindon 2 miles
Mis	25 bay floodlit driving range

Chippenham (1896)

Malmesbury Road, Chippenham
Tel	(0249) 652040
Mem	650
Sec	V J Carlisle
Pro	W Creamer (0249) 655519
Holes	18 L 5540 yds SSS 67
Recs	Am–62 M Darbyshire
	Pro–64 B Sandry
V'trs	H WE–M SOC
Fees	£15 (£18)
Loc	Chippenham 1 mile. M4 Junction 17

High Post (1922)

Great Durnford, Salisbury SP4 6AT
Tel	(0722) 73231
Mem	600
Sec	WWR Goodwin (0722) 73356
Pro	AJ Harman (0722) 73219
Holes	18 L 6267 yds SSS 70
Recs	Am–64 K Weeks, RJ Searle
	Pro–65 P Alliss, N Sutton
V'trs	WD–U WE/BH–H SOC
Fees	£14 D–£17 (£20) SOC–£23
Loc	4 miles N of Salisbury on A345

Kingsdown (1880)

Kingsdown, Corsham SN14 9BS
Tel	(0225) 742530
Mem	475 100(L) 45(J)
Sec	SH Phipps (0225) 743472
Pro	R Emery (0225) 742634
Holes	18 L 6445 yds SSS 71
Recs	Am–67 R Vinall (1989)
	Pro–68 G Clough (1989)
V'trs	WD–U Comp days–M
Fees	£15 (NA)
Loc	5 miles E of Bath

Marlborough (1888)

The Common, Marlborough SN8 1DU
Tel	(0672) 52147
Mem	710
Sec	L Ross (Mgr), S Lynch (Admin)
Pro	W McAdams (0672) 52493
Holes	18 L 6440 yds SSS 71
Recs	Am–65 J Tomlinson
	Pro–67 J Cook
V'trs	WD/WE–H SOC
Fees	£15 D–£18 (£20)
Loc	1 mile N of Marlborough (A345)

North Wilts (1890)

Bishops' Cannings, Devizes SN10 2LP
Tel	(038 086) 257
Mem	600 95(L) 53(J)
Sec	Lt Cdr JBW McKelvie (038 086) 627

Pro	GJ Laing (038 086) 330
Holes	18 L 5898 metres SSS 71
Recs	Am–66 EAJ Pulleyblank
	Pro–67 GJ Laing
V'trs	U
Fees	£10 (£16)
Loc	1 mile from A4 at Calne

RAF Upavon (1918)

York Road, Upavon, Pewsey
SN9 6BE
Tel	(0980) 630787
Mem	300
Sec	Sqn Ldr IF Davidson (0980) 630351 (Ext 654)
Holes	9 L 5597 yds SSS 67
Recs	Am–66 Wg Cdr RB Duckett
V'trs	WD–U Sat am/Sun am–M SOC
Fees	£8 (£8)
Loc	Upavon 3 miles on A342 to Andover

RMCS Shrivenham (1953)

RMCS Shrivenham, Swindon
SN6 8LA
Tel	(0793) 782551 (Ext 2355)
Mem	350
Sec	GM Moss
Holes	9 L 5206 yds SSS 66
V'trs	M SOC
Loc	In grounds of Royal Military College of Science, Shrivenham. Entry must be arranged with Sec

Salisbury & South Wilts (1888)

Netherhampton, Salisbury
Tel	(0722) 742131
Mem	810
Sec	Wg Cdr AW Pawson (0722) 742645
Pro	G Emerson (0722) 742929
Holes	18 L 6130 yds SSS 70
Recs	Am–61 RS Blake
	Pro–62 N Blenkarne
V'trs	WD–U WE–H SOC
Fees	D–£13 (D–£20)
Loc	Wilton 2 miles on A3094. Salisbury 2 miles

Swindon (1907)

Ogbourne St George, Marlborough,
nr Swindon
SN8 1TB
Tel	(067 284) 217
Mem	600
Sec	A Grant (067 284) 327
Pro	C Harraway (067 284) 287
Holes	18 L 6226 yds SSS 70
Recs	Am–66 RJ Binsted, S Robertson
	Pro–65 I Bolt
V'trs	U SOC–WD
Fees	On application
Loc	5 miles S of M4 Junction 15 on A345

For explanation of abbreviations, see page 460.

West Wilts (1891)

Elm Hill, Warminster BA12 0AU
Tel   (0985) 212702
Mem 420 70(L) 55(J) 40(5)
Sec   Maj LR Weaver (0985) 213133
Pro   A Harvey (0985) 212110
Holes 18 L 5701 yds SSS 68
Recs Am–62 CG Burton (1989)
      Pro–64 R Emery (1985)
V'trs WD–U H WE–U H after noon
      –NA before noon
Fees £15 (£23)
Loc   Off A350 on Westbury road
      from Warminster

Yorkshire (North)

Aldwark Manor (1977)

Aldwark Manor, Aldwark Alne, York
YO6 2NF
Tel   (03473) 353
Sec   GF Platt
Holes 9 L 2569 yds SSS 66
Recs Pro–67 S Deller (1988),
      B Hessay (1989)
V'trs SOC
Fees £8 (£14) Hotel Residents free
Loc   5 miles SE of Boroughbridge
      off A1. 13 miles NW of York
      off A19

Ampleforth College (1962)

56 High Street, Helmsley, York
YO6 5AE
Mem 130
Sec   JE Atkinson (0439) 70678
Holes 10 L 4018 yds SSS 63
V'trs U exc WD 2–4pm SOC–WD
Fees £4 (£6)
Loc   Driveway to Gilling Castle
      in centre of Gilling East.
      18 miles N of York (B1363)
Mis   Green fees payable at
      Fairfax Arms, Gilling East

Bedale (1896)

Leyburn Road, Bedale DL8 1EZ
Tel   (0677) 22568
Mem 450 100(L) 60(J)
Sec   GA Shepherdson
      (0677) 22451
Pro   AD Johnson (0677) 22443
Holes 18 L 5737 yds SSS 68
Recs Am–66 J Swain
      Pro–64 J Hughes
V'trs U SOC
Fees £10 (£15)
Loc   N boundary of Bedale

Bentham (1922)

Robin Lane, Bentham, Lancaster
Tel   (05242) 61018
Mem 370
Sec   JM Philipson (05242) 62455
Holes 9 L 5752 yds SSS 69
Recs Am–69 J Carter (1989)
V'trs U
Fees £7 (£9) W–£15

Loc   NE of Lancaster on B6480
      towards Settle. 13 miles E
      of M6 Junction 34

Catterick Garrison (1930)

Leyburn Road, Catterick Garrison
DL9 3QE
Tel   (0748) 833268
Mem 670
Sec   Maj. L Layton (Rtd)
Pro   S Bradley (0748) 833671
Holes 18 L 6336 yds SSS 70
Recs Am–65 CS Carveth
      Pro–69 D Edwards
V'trs U
Fees £10 (£15)
Loc   6 miles SW of Scotch Corner,
      off A1 towards Catterick
      Garrison

Crimple Valley (1976)

Hookstone Wood Road, Harrogate
Tel   (0423) 883485
Mem 200
Sec   J Lumb
Pro   J Lumb
Holes 9 L 2500 yds SSS 33
V'trs U
Fees £3
Loc   Next to Yorkshire Fairground,
      Harrogate

Easingwold (1930)

Stillington Road, Easingwold, York
YO6 3ET
Tel   (0347) 21486
Mem 575
Sec   KC Hudson
Pro   J Hughes (0347) 21964
Holes 18 L 6262 yds SSS 70
Recs Am–67 GW Mutch
      Pro–65 G Brown
V'trs U
Fees D–£14 (£18)
Loc   12 miles N of York on A19.
      S end of Easingwold

Filey (1897)

West Ave, Filey YO14 9BQ
Tel   (0723) 513293
Mem 937
Sec   TM Thompson
Pro   DW Currey (0723) 513134
Holes 18 L 6030 yds SSS 69
Recs Am–67 AS Roberts
      Pro–64 AS Murray
V'trs U H SOC
Fees £11 (£14) 1989 prices

Fulford (York) (1909)

Heslington Lane, York YO1 5DY
Tel   (0904) 413579
Mem 580
Sec   JCA Gledhill
      (Requests for visits)
Pro   B Hessay (0904) 412882
Holes 18 L 6779 yds SSS 72

Recs Am–66 G Harland (1989)
      Pro–62 I Woosnam
V'trs By arrangement
Fees £20 (£23)
Loc   2 miles S of York

Ganton (1891)

Station Road, Ganton, Scarborough
YO12 4PA
Tel   (0944) 70329
Mem 600
Sec   Air Vice Marshal RG Price
Pro   G Brown (0944) 70260
Holes 18 L 6693 yds SSS 73
Recs Am–67 G Boardman
      Pro–65 N Coles
V'trs By prior arrangement
Fees On application
Loc   Scarborough 11 miles on
      A64

Ghyll (1907)

Ghyll Brow, Barnoldswick, Colne
BB8 6JQ
Tel   (0282) 842466
Mem 310
Sec   JL Gill (0282) 813205
Holes 9 L 5708 yds SSS 68
Recs Am–64 M Boardman (1989)
V'trs U Sun–NA
Fees £6 (£8)
Loc   Barnoldswick 1 mile

Harrogate (1892)

Forest Lane Head, Harrogate
HG2 7TF
Tel   (0423) 863158
Mem 620
Sec   J McDougall (0423) 862999
Pro   P Johnson (0423) 862547
Holes 18 L 6241 yds SSS 70
Recs Am–65 P Hall
      Pro–64 D Durnian
V'trs WD–U WE/BH–enquire first
      SOC–Tues & Fri
Fees £18 (£25)
Loc   Harrogate 2 miles on
      Knaresborough Road (A59)

Heworth (1912)

Muncaster House, Muncastergate,
York YO3 9JX
Tel   (0904) 424618
Mem 245 80(L) 50(J) 70(5)
Sec   JR Richards
Pro   SI Robinson (0904) 422389
Holes 11 L 6141 yds SSS 69
V'trs U
Fees £10 (£12)
Loc   NE boundary of York (A1036)

Kirkbymoorside (1951)

Manor Vale, Kirkbymoorside, York
YO6 6EG
Tel   (0904) 31525
Mem 500
Sec   DG Saunders
Holes 18 L 6027 yds SSS 69
Recs Am–S Dunn, C Fletcher (1989)

V'trs U
Fees £10 (£15)
Loc A170 between Helmsley and Pickering

Knaresborough (1919)

Boroughbridge Road, Knaresborough HG5 0QQ
Tel (0423) 863219
Mem 757
Sec Gp Capt JI Barrow (0423) 862690
Pro K Johnstone (0423) 864865
Holes 18 L 6281 yds SSS 70
Recs Am–68 D Walker Pro–65 J King
V'trs U
Fees £10 (£16)
Loc 1½ miles N of Knaresborough

Loftus Hill (1989)

Boroughbridge Road, Ferrensby, Knaresbrough HG5 9JT
Tel (0423) 340731
Sec J Townsend
Holes 9 L 5106 yds SSS 65
V'trs WD–U WE–pm only
Fees £8 D–£10 (£10 D–£12)
Loc 3 miles N of Knaresbrough

Malton & Norton (1923)

Welham Park, Norton, Malton YO17 9QE
Tel (0653) 692959
Mem 700
Sec WG Wade (0653) 697912
Pro ML Henderson (0653) 693882
Holes 18 L 6401 yds SSS 71
V'trs WD–U WE–restricted on match days H
Fees £11.50 (£15.50) W–£50
Loc Between York and Scarborough, off Welham Road, Norton

Masham (1900)

Burnholme, Swinton Road, Masham, Ripon HG4 4DX
Tel (0765) 89379
Mem 280
Sec Mrs MA Willis (0765) 89491
Holes 9 L 5244 yds SSS 66
Recs Am–69 G Furby (1987)
V'trs WD–U before 5pm WE–M BH–NA
Fees £10
Loc 10 miles N of Ripon

Oakdale (1914)

Oakdale, Harrogate HG1 2LN
Tel (0423) 567162
Mem 775
Sec FR Hindmarsh
Pro N Summer (0423) 560510
Holes 18 L 6456 yds SSS 71
Recs Am–66 G Cuthbert (1989) Pro–66 P Hall (1989)
V'trs WD–U 9.30–12.30 and after 2pm SOC

Fees £15 (£20)
Loc ½ mile NE of Royal Hall, Harrogate

Pannal (1906)

Follifoot Road, Pannal, Harrogate HG3 1ES
Tel (0423) 871641
Mem 815
Sec WK Davies (0423) 872628
Pro M Burgess (0423) 872620
Holes 18 L 6659 yds SSS 72
Recs Am–66 J Whitehead (1988) Pro–66 J Beattie, M James, D Jones
V'trs WD–H 9.30am–12 and after 1.30pm WE–after 10am and after 2.30pm
Fees £17 D–£22 (£22)
Loc 2½ miles S of Harrogate

Pike Hills (1920)

Tadcaster Road, Copmanthorpe, York YO2 3UW
Tel (0904) 706566
Mem 800
Sec G Wood
Pro I Gradwell (0904) 708756
Holes 18 L 6048 yds SSS 69
V'trs WD–UH before 4.30pm M–after 4.30pm WE/BH–M SOC
Fees Summer £14 Winter £10
Loc 3 miles W of York on Leeds road

Richmond (1892)

Bend Hagg, Richmond
Tel (0748) 2457
Mem 454
Sec BD Aston (0748) 4775
Pro P Jackson
Holes 18 L 5704 yds SSS 68
Recs Am–64 G Catt Pro–64 P Tupling
V'trs U
Fees £8 (£12)
Loc 3 miles S of Scotch Corner

Ripon City (1905)

Palace Road, Ripon HG4 3HH
Tel (0765) 3640
Mem 280 50(L) 30(J) 70(5)
Sec E Bentley (0765) 3991
Pro T Davis (0765) 700411
Holes 9 L 5752 yds SSS 68
Recs Am–65 M Grant Pro–66 B Hutchinson
V'trs U
Fees £5 (£7)
Loc 1 mile N of Ripon, on A6108

Scarborough North Cliff (1927)

North Cliff Avenue, Burniston Road, Scarborough YO12 6PP
Tel (0723) 360786
Mem 800
Sec JR Freeman

Pro SN Deller (0723) 365920
Holes 18 L 6425 yds SSS 71
Recs Am–66 MJ Kelly, R Newton
V'trs U exc Sun before 10am and comp days H SOC
Fees £12 (£16)
Loc 2 miles N of Scarborough on coast road

Scarborough South Cliff (1903)

Deepdale Avenue, off Filey Road, Scarborough YO11 2WE
Tel (0723) 360522
Mem 500
Sec JA Sword (0723) 374737
Pro DM Edwards (0723) 365150
Holes 18 L 6085 yds SSS 69
Recs Am–68 SJ Thorpe (1987) Pro–66 MJ Slater (1987)
V'trs U H
Fees £11.50 (£15)
Loc 1 mile S of Scarborough

Selby (1907)

Mill Lane, Brayton, Selby YO8 9LD
Tel (075 782) 622
Mem 691
Sec BLC Moore
Pro A Smith (075 782) 785
Holes 18 L 6246 yds SSS 70
Recs Am–65 L Walker Pro–64 D Matthew
V'trs H SOC–Wed/Thurs/Fri WE–NA
Fees £13 D–£16
Loc 3 miles SW of Selby off A19

Settle (1896)

Giggleswick, Settle
Tel (072 92) 3912
Mem 250
Sec L Whitaker
Holes 9 L 2276 yds SSS 31
Recs Am–62 P Robinson
V'trs U SOC
Fees £4 (£5)
Loc 1 mile N of Settle on A65

Skipton (1905)

Off NW Bypass, Skipton BD23 1LL
Tel (0756) 3922
Mem 605
Sec JC Varley (Mgr) (0756) 2128
Pro J Hammond (0756) 3257
Holes 18 L 6087 yds SSS 70
Recs Am–69 RR Taylor (1989)
V'trs U
Fees £10 (£15)
Loc Skipton 1 mile off NW Bypass

Thirsk & Northallerton (1914)

Thornton-le-Street, Thirsk YO7 4AB
Tel (0845) 22170
Mem 300
Sec HD Swarbrick (0845) 587350

For explanation of abbreviations, see page 460.

Pro A Marshall, D Llewellyn
(Touring Pro)
Holes 9 L 6257 yds SSS 70
Recs Am–69 R Cable
Pro–69 P Blaze
V'trs WD–U Sun–M SOC
Fees £10 D–£15 Sat/BH–£15 Sun–M
Loc 2 miles N of Thirsk nr A19
and A168 roundabout

Whitby (1892)

Low Straggleton, Whitby
YO21 3SR
Tel (0947) 602768
Mem 800
Sec A Dyson (0947) 600660
Pro A Brook (0947) 602719
Holes 18 L 5710 yds SSS 67
Recs Am–67
Pro–68
V'trs U SOC
Fees £10 (£15) W–£45

York (1890)

Lords Moor Lane, Strensall, York
YO3 5XF
Tel (0904) 491840
Mem 340 110(L) 120(J)
Sec F Appleyard
Pro A Mason (0904) 490304
Holes 18 L 6285 yds SSS 70
Recs Am–64 S East
Pro–66 P Fowler
V'trs U (phone Pro) SOC–WD &
Sun
Fees £17 (£21)
Loc 3 miles N of York ringroad
(A1237)

Yorkshire (South)

Abbeydale (1895)

Twentywell Lane, Dore, nr Sheffield
S17 4QA
Tel (0742) 360763
Mem 700
Sec Mrs KM Johnston
Pro SJ Cooper (0742) 365633
Holes 18 L 6419 yds SSS 71
V'trs U SOC–Tues & Fri
Fees £15 (£20)
Loc 5 miles S of Sheffield

Austerfield Park (1974)

Cross Lane, Austerfield, nr Bawtry
Doncaster DN10 6RF
Tel (0302) 710841
Mem 425 45(L) 40(J) 80(5)
Sec A Bradley (0709) 540928
Pro A Stothard (0302) 719461
Holes 18 L 6824 yds SSS 73
Recs Am–72 R Taylor (1989)
Pro–67 J Brennand (1988)
V'trs U
Fees £10 (£12)
Loc 2 miles NE of Bawtry off A614
Mis 10 bay driving range

Barnsley (1925)

Public
Wakefield Road, Staincross, Barnsley
S75 6JZ
Tel (0226) 382856
Pro M Melling (0226) 382954
Holes 18 L 6048 yds SSS 69
Recs Am–64 RI Shaw (1988)
Pro–62 M Melling
V'trs U
Fees £3.25 (£4.40)
Loc 4 miles N of Barnsley on A61

Beauchief Municipal (1925)

Public
Abbey Lane, Sheffield S8 0DB
Tel (0742) 367274/620040
Pro B English
Holes 18 L 5428 yds SSS 66
Recs Am–65 PW Hickinson
Pro–63 P Tupling
V'trs U
Fees £4.50 (£4.50)
Loc A621 Sheffield

Birley Wood (1974)

Public
Birley Lane, Sheffield S12 3BP
Tel (0742) 390099
Pro S Sherratt
Holes 18 L 6275 yds SSS 70
V'trs U
Fees £3.50 (£5)
Loc 4 miles S of Sheffield on
A616 to M1

Concord Park (1952)

Public
Shiregreen Lane, Sheffield S5 6AE
Tel (0742) 570274/570053
Holes 18 L 4321 yds SSS 62
V'trs U
Fees £4.50
Loc M1 Junction 34, 1 mile

Crookhill Park (1973)

Public
Conisborough, nr Doncaster
DN12 2AH
Tel (0709) 862979
Pro R Swaine
Holes 18 L 5846 yds SSS 68
Recs Am–67 R Jones
Pro–70
V'trs U
Fees £4
Loc 3 miles W of Doncaster (A630)

Doncaster (1895)

Bawtry Road, Bessacarr, nr Doncaster
DN4 7PD
Tel (0302) 868316
Mem 375
Sec F Colley (0302) 537815
Pro S Fox (0302) 868404
Holes 18 L 6230 yds SSS 70
Recs Am–66 H Green
Pro–66 H Clark

V'trs UH WE/BH–after 11.30am
SOC–WD
Fees £14 (£17.50)
Loc 4½ miles S of Doncaster

Doncaster Town Moor (1900)

c/o The Belle Vue Club, Bellevue,
Doncaster DN4 5HV
Tel (0302) 535286
Mem 400
Sec JC Padley (0302) 535458
Pro G Bailey
Holes 18 L 6314 yds SSS 69
Recs Am–64 AJ Miller (1989)
Pro–69 D Snell
V'trs U exc Sun before 11.30am SOC
Fees £9 (£11)
Loc Inside Racecourse

Dore & Totley (1913)

Bradway Road, Bradway, nr Sheffield
S17 4QR
Tel (0742) 360492
Mem 600
Sec Mrs C Milner (0742) 369872
Pro M Pearson (0742) 366844
Holes 18 L 6301 yds SSS 70
Recs Am–S Field
Pro–P Cowen
V'trs WD–U WE/BH–M
Fees £13
Loc 5 miles SW of Sheffield

Grange Park (1972)

Public
Upper Wortley Road, Kimberworth,
Rotherham S61 2SJ
Tel (0709) 558884
Pro E Clark (0709) 559497
Holes 18 L 6461 yds SSS 71
Recs Am–68 J Beckitt
Pro–68 G Tickell
V'trs U
Fees £2.75 (£3.60)
Loc 2 miles W of Rotherham on
A629

Hallamshire (1897)

Sandygate, Sheffield S10 4LA
Tel (0742) 302153
Mem 600
Sec R Burns
Pro G Tickell (0742) 305222
Holes 18 L 6396 yds SSS 71
Recs Am–66 W Bremner
Pro–63 JW Wilkinson
V'trs I
Fees £17 (£25)
Loc W boundary of Sheffield

Hickleton (1909)

Hickleton, nr Doncaster
Tel (0709) 892496
Mem 485
Sec R Jowett (0709) 893506
Pro P Shepherd (0709) 895170
Holes 18 L 6403 yds SSS 71

Recs Am–69 P Goodwin (1988)
V'trs WD/Sat am/Sun pm–U SOC
Fees £10 (£15)
Loc 6 miles W of Doncaster, on A635 between Doncaster and Barnsley

Hillsborough (1920)

Worrall Road, Sheffield S6 4BE
Tel (0742) 343608
Mem 710
Sec AW Platts (0742) 349151
Pro G Walker (0742) 332666
Holes 18 L 5672 metres SSS 70
V'trs U
Fees £14 (£20)
Loc Wadsley, Sheffield

Lees Hall (1907)

Hemsworth Road, Norton, Sheffield S8 8LL
Tel (0742) 554402
Mem 700
Sec NE Westworth (0742) 552900
Pro JR Wilkinson
Holes 18 L 6137 yds SSS 69
Recs Am–65 AR Gellsthorpe
     Pro–63 B Hutchinson
V'trs U SOC
Fees £11.50 (£17.25)
Loc ¹/₂ miles S of Sheffield. E of A61

Lindrick (1891)

Lindrick Common, nr Worksop, Notts S81 8BH
Tel (0909) 485802
Mem 500
Sec G Bywater (0909) 475282
Pro (0909) 475820
Holes 18 L 6615 yds SSS 72
Recs Am–65 DF Livingston
     Pro–65 G Bond, J Morgan
V'trs U with prior arrangement
     Tues am–NA SOC–WD
Fees £25 (£30) Winter £18
Loc 4 miles W of Worksop on A57. M1 Junction 31–4¹/₂ miles towards Worksop

Phoenix (1932)

Brinsworth, Rotherham
Tel (0709) 382624
Mem 700
Sec J Burrows (0709) 370759
Pro A Limb
Holes 18 L 6170 yds SSS 69
V'trs U
Fees £10 (£14)
Loc Rotherham 2 miles. Bawtry road off M1 Tinsley roundabout

Renishaw Park (1911)

Golf House, Renishaw, Sheffield S31 9UZ
Tel (0246) 432044
Mem 400
Sec DG Rossington (0246) 811646

Pro S Elliott (0246) 435484
Holes 18 L 6253 yds SSS 70
Recs Am–65 AR Gelsthorpe
     Pro–66 D Dunk, R Emory, J Rhodes
V'trs U
Fees £14 (£16)
Loc 7 miles from Sheffield. 2 miles from M1 Junction 30

Rotherham (1903)

Thrybergh Park, Rotherham S65 4NU
Tel (0709) 850466
Mem 400
Sec F Green (0709) 850812
Pro B Ellis (0709) 850480
Holes 18 L 6324 yds SSS 70
Recs Am–66 MJ Kelly
     Pro–66 B Hutchison
V'trs U
Fees £17 (£20)
Loc 4 miles E of Rotherham on A630

Roundwood (1976)

Green Lane, Rawmarsh, Rotherham S62 6LA
Tel (0709) 523471
Mem 400
Sec T Barnfield (0709) 541792
Holes 9 L 5646 yds SSS 67
V'trs WE–not before 2.30pm on comp days
Fees £5 (£7)
Loc 2 miles N of Rotherham on A633

Sheffield Transport Dept (1923)

Meadow Head, Sheffield
Tel (0742) 373216
Mem 100
Sec AE Mason
Holes 18 L 3966 yds SSS 62
Recs Am–62 VR Hutton
V'trs M
Fees 50p
Loc S of Sheffield on A61

Silkstone (1905)

Field Head, Silkstone, nr Barnsley
Tel (0226) 790328
Mem 450
Sec G Speight (0226) 244796
Pro K Guy (0226) 790128
Holes 18 L 6045 yds SSS 70
Recs Am–66 TG Garner,
     JG Clapham
V'trs WD–U WE–M SOC–WD
Fees £10
Loc 1 mile from M1

Sitwell Park (1913)

Shrogs Wood Road, Rotherham
Tel (0709) 541046
Mem 500
Sec J Straffen (0709) 365830
Pro N Taylor

Holes 18 L 6250 yds SSS 70
Recs Am–67 RN Portas
V'trs U
Fees £10 (£11)
Loc 2¹/₂ miles E of Rotherham

Stocksbridge & District (1925)

30 Royd Lane, Townend, Deepcar, nr Sheffield S30 5RZ
Tel (0742) 882003
Mem 200
Sec S Lee (0742) 882408
Holes 15 L 5055 yds SSS 65
Recs Am–61 CR Dale (1977)
     Pro–61 TJ Brookes (1986)
V'trs U SOC
Fees £6 (£7)
Loc 7 miles W of Sheffield

Tankersley Park (1907)

High Green, Sheffield S30 4LG
Tel (0742) 468247
Mem 574
Sec S Jessop
Pro I Kirk (0742) 455583
Holes 18 L 6241 yds SSS 70
Recs Am–66 N Grice
     Pro–69 W Atkinson
V'trs WD–U WE–M SOC–WD
Fees £10 D–£12 (£12)
Loc Chapeltown, 7 miles N of Sheffield. M1 Junction 35A (northbound)

Thorne (1980)

Kirton Lane, Thorne, Doncaster DN8 5RJ
Tel (0405) 812054
Sec P Kittridge (0302) 813827
Pro RD Highfield
Holes 18 L 5146 yds SSS 65
V'trs U
Fees £4 (£5)
Loc M18 Junction 5/6

Tinsley Park (1920)

Public
Darnall, Sheffield
Tel (0742) 560237
Sec S Conroy (Hon)
Pro AP Highfield
Holes 18 L 6045 yds SSS 69
Recs Am–70 D Robbins
     Pro–66 D Snell
V'trs U
Fees £4.50
Loc M1 Junction 32, 1 mile

Wath–upon–Dearne (1904)

Abdy Rawmarsh, Rotherham
Tel (0709) 872149
Mem 400
Sec B Lawrence (0709) 526727
Pro SC Poole (0709) 878677

For explanation of abbreviations, see page 460.

Holes	18 L 5776 yds SSS 68
V'trs	WD–U WE/BH–M SOC
Fees	£10
Loc	Abdy Farm, 1½ miles S of Wath–upon–Dearne

Wheatley (1913)

Armthorpe Road, Doncaster
DN2 5QB

Tel	(0302) 831655
Mem	385 100(L) 50(J) 5(5)
Sec	KW Percival
Pro	T Parkinson (0302) 834085
Holes	18 L 6345 yds SSS 70
Recs	Am–65 B Bremner
	Pro–63 G Walker
V'trs	U SOC
Fees	£12 (£16)
Loc	3 miles E of Doncaster

Wombwell Hillies (1989)

Public
Wentworth View, Wombwell,
Barnsley S73 0LA

Tel	(0226) 754433
Sec	R Burkinshaw (Mgr)
Holes	9 L 2019 yds SSS 60
V'trs	U
Fees	18 holes–£2.20 (£3.15)
	9 holes–£1.55 (£2.10)
Loc	4 miles SE of Barnsley

Yorkshire (West)

Alwoodley (1908)

Wigton Lane, Alwoodley, Leeds
LS17 8SA

Tel	(0532) 681680
Mem	450
Sec	TG Turnbull
Pro	J Foss
Holes	18 L 6686 yds SSS 72
Recs	Am–68 F Haughton
	Pro–68 D Fitton
V'trs	WD–U SOC–WD
Fees	£25 (£30)
Loc	5 miles N of Leeds on A61

Baildon (1898)

Moorgate, Baildon, Shipley BD17 5PP

Tel	(0274) 584266
Mem	700
Sec	D Farnsworth (0274) 584684
Pro	R Masters (0274) 595162
Holes	18 L 6085 yds SSS 70
Recs	Am–66 D Farnsworth
	Pro–64 G Brand, D Durnian
V'trs	WD–U before 5pm (limited Tues) Sat–U after 3.30pm Sun–U after 9.30am
Fees	£9 (£12)
Loc	5 miles NW of Bradford

Ben Rhydding (1948)

High Wood, Ben Rhydding, Ilkley

Tel	(0943) 608759
Mem	185 60(L) 36(J)
Sec	JDB Watts
Holes	9 L 4711 yds SSS 64

Recs	Am–64 H Barker
	Pro–64 GJ Brand
V'trs	WD–U WE–M
Fees	£5
Loc	Ilkley

Bingley (St Ives) (1931)

Public
St Ives Estate, Bingley BD16 1AT

Tel	(0274) 562506
Sec	J Crolla (Hon)
Pro	R Firth
Holes	18 L 6466 yds SSS 71
Recs	Am–70 WM Hopkinson
	Pro–62 N Faldo
V'trs	WD–U before 4.30pm
Fees	£5 D–£7 (£8.50 D–£14)
Loc	6 miles W of Bradford

Bradford (1891)

Hawksworth Lane, Guiseley, Leeds
LS20 8NP

Tel	(0943) 75570
Mem	500
Sec	P Atkinson
Pro	S Weldon (0943) 73719
Holes	18 L 6259 yds SSS 70
Recs	Am–67 R Foster, N Ludwell
V'trs	WD–U WE–after noon SOC–WD
Loc	8 miles N of Bradford

Bradford Moor (1907)

Scarr Hall, Pollard Lane, Bradford

Tel	(0274) 638313
Mem	375
Sec	D Armitage
Pro	R Hughes (0274) 631163
Holes	9 L 5854 yds SSS 68
Recs	Am–68 I Helliwell
	Pro–69 H Waller
V'trs	U
Fees	£7.50 (£8)

Bradley Park (1978)

Public
Bradley Road, Huddersfield HD2 1PZ

Tel	(0484) 539988
Pro	PE Reilly
Holes	18 L 6202 yds SSS 70
	9 hole Par 3
Recs	Am–69 R Hall
	Pro–64 P Carman
V'trs	U SOC
Fees	£4.25 (£5.50)
Loc	M62 Junction 25, 1½ miles
Mis	Floodlit driving range

Branshaw (1912)

Branshaw Moor, Oakworth,
nr Keighley BD22 7ES

Tel	(0535) 43235
Mem	445
Sec	DA Town (0535) 605003

Holes	18 L 5858 yds SSS 69
Recs	Am–68 I Houldsworth
V'trs	WD–U SOC
Fees	£8 (£10)
Loc	2 miles SW of Keighley on B6143

Calverley (1984)

Woodhall Lane, Pudsey LS28 5JX

Tel	(0532) 569244
Mem	425
Sec	WW Gardner
Holes	18 L 5348 yds SSS 66
	9 hole course
Recs	Am–66 M Woodhall
V'trs	WD–U WE–pm only
Fees	£10, 9 holes–£4
Loc	4 miles NE of Bradford
Mis	Driving range

Castle Fields (1900)

Rastrick Common, Brighouse

Mem	140
Sec	P Bentley (0484) 712108
Holes	6 L 2406 yds SSS 50
V'trs	M
Fees	£1.50
Loc	1 mile S of Brighouse

City of Wakefield (1936)

Public
Lupset Park, Horbury Road, Wakefield
WF2 8QS

Tel	(0924) 374316
Pro	R Holland (0924) 360282
Holes	18 L 6405 yds SSS 71
Recs	Am–66 PE Monaghan, DA Ware
	Pro–67 P Cowen
V'trs	WD–U WE/BH–NA SOC–WD
Fees	£3.60 (£5.80)
Loc	A642, 2 miles W of Wakefield. 2 miles E of M1 Junction 39/40

Clayton (1906)

Thornton View Road, Clayton,
Bradford

Tel	(0274) 880047
Mem	180 35(L) 35(J) 40(5)
Sec	FV Wood (0274) 574203
Holes	9 L 5515 yds SSS 67
Recs	Am–65 ND Hawkins
V'trs	WD–U Sat–U Sun–after 4pm
Fees	£5 (£8)
Loc	2 miles W of Bradford

Cleckheaton & District (1900)

483 Bradford Road, Cleckheaton
BD19 6BU

Tel	(0274) 874118
Mem	550
Sec	H Thornton (0274) 851266

Pro   M Ingham (0274) 851267
Holes   18 L 5994 yds SSS 69
Recs   Am–62 CA Bloice
         Pro–63 GA Caygill
V'trs   U SOC
Fees   £11 (£17.50)
Loc   Nr M62 Junction 26–A638

Crosland Heath (1914)

Crosland Heath, Huddersfield
Tel   (0484) 653216
Mem   320
Sec   D Walker (0484) 653262
Pro   R Jessop (0484) 653877
Holes   18 L 5961 yds SSS 70
Recs   Am–66 S Ellis
         Pro–65 SW Dellar
V'trs   U SOC
Fees   On application
Loc   3 miles W of Huddersfield

Dewsbury District (1891)

The Pinnacle, Mirfield
Tel   (0924) 492399
Mem   500
Pro   N Hirst (0924) 496030
Holes   18 L 6256 yds SSS 71
Recs   Am–68 M Colcombe
         Pro–68 R Masters
V'trs   U SOC
Fees   £9
Loc   W boundary of Dewsbury

East Bierley (1928)

South View Road, Bradford
Tel   (0274) 681023
Mem   156 47(L) 30(J)
Sec   Mrs M Welch
Holes   9 L 4692 yds SSS 63
Recs   Am–59 R Watts
         Pro–62 B Hill
V'trs   U exc Mon–NA after 4pm
         Sun–NA
Fees   £6 (£8)
Loc   4 miles SE of Bradford

Elland (1910)

Hullen Edge, Elland
Tel   (0422) 372505
Mem   350
Sec   WH Pearson (0442) 373276
Pro   J Tindall (0442) 374886
Holes   9 L 2763 yds SSS 66
Recs   Am–64 C Hartland
V'trs   U
Fees   £6 (£10)
Loc   Elland ¹/₂ mile.
         M62 Junction 24 (Blackley)

Ferrybridge 'C' (1976)

PO Box 39, Stranglands Lane,
Knottingley
WF11 8SQ
Tel   (0977) 84188 (Ext 256)
Mem   274
Sec   NE Pugh (0977) 793884

Holes   9 L 5138 yds SSS 65
Recs   Am–67 R MacDonald (1989)
V'trs   M
Loc   Ferrybridge 'C' Power Station.
         ¹/₂ mile off A1 on B6136

Fulneck (1892)

Pudsey
Tel   (0532) 565191
Mem   230
Sec   J Allan (0532) 663349
Holes   9 L 5564 yds SSS 67
Recs   Am–64 I Holdsworth
V'trs   WD–U WE/BH–M SOC
Fees   £6
Loc   5 miles W of Leeds

Garforth (1913)

Long Lane, Garforth, Leeds LS25 2DS
Tel   (0532) 862021
Mem   550
Sec   FA Readman (0532) 863308
Pro   K Findlater (0532) 862063
Holes   18 L 6327 yds SSS 70
Recs   Am–63 AR Gelsthorpe
V'trs   WD–U H WE/BH–M SOC
Fees   £14 D–£17 WE–M
Loc   9 miles E of Leeds between
         Garforth and Barwick-in-Elmet

Gotts Park (1934)

Public
Armley Ridge Road, Armley, Leeds
LS12 2QX
Tel   (0532) 636600
Pro   JK Simpson
Holes   18 L 4960 yds SSS 64
V'trs   U
Fees   £3.75 (£4.10)
Loc   2 miles W of Leeds

Halifax (1895)

Union Lane, Ogden, Halifax HX2 8XR
Tel   (0422) 244171
Mem   450
Sec   JP Clark
Pro   SA Foster (0422) 240047
Holes   18 L 6038 yds SSS 70
Recs   Am–66 J Robinson,
         AMA Bagott, J Rushworth
         Pro–65 PW Good
V'trs   U WE–parties welcome SOC
Fees   £10 (£15)
Loc   4 miles N of Halifax on A629

Halifax Bradley Hall (1907)

Holywell Green, Halifax HX4 9AN
Tel   (0422) 374108
Mem   608
Sec   PM Pitchforth (0422) 376626
Pro   P Wood (0422) 370231
Holes   18 L 6213 yds SSS 70
Recs   Am–65 AR Whitworth
V'trs   U SOC
Fees   £10 (£15)
Loc   S of Halifax on A6112

Halifax West End (1913)

Highroad Well, Halifax HX2 0NT
Tel   (0422) 353608
Mem   266 91(L) 44(J)
Sec   BR Thomas (0422) 367145
Pro   D Rishworth (0422) 363293
Holes   18 L 6003 yds SSS 69
Recs   Am–65 JR Crawshaw, JR
         Smith
         Pro–64 AJ Bickerdike
V'trs   U SOC
Fees   £8 (£10)
Loc   2 miles NW of Halifax

Hanging Heaton (1922)

Whitecross Road, Dewsbury
WF12 7DT
Tel   (0924) 461606
Mem   550
Sec   SM Simpson (0924) 461729
Pro   J Allott (0924) 467077
Holes   9 L 2868 yds SSS 67
Recs   Am–66 P Cockburn
         Pro–AJ Bickerdyke
V'trs   WD–U WE–restricted
Fees   £6 (£8)
Loc   Dewsbury ³/₄ mile (A653)

Headingley (1892)

Back Church Lane, Adel, Leeds
LS16 8DW
Tel   (0532) 673052
Mem   600
Sec   RW Hellawell (0532) 679573
Pro   (0532) 675100
Holes   18 L 6238 yds SSS 70
Recs   Am–67 S Pullan
         Pro–67 GR Tickell
V'trs   U SOC
Fees   £15 D–£20 (£24)
Loc   5 miles NW of Leeds, off A660
         Leeds–Skipton road

Headley (1906)

Headley Lane, Thornton,
nr Bradford BD13 3LX
Tel   (0274) 833481
Mem   200
Sec   JP Clark (0274) 832571
Holes   9 L 2457 yds SSS 64
Recs   Am–61 A Cording (1985)
         Pro–66 M Ingham
V'trs   U (exc Sun)
Fees   £3 (£6)
Loc   5 miles W of Bradford

Horsforth (1907)

Layton Rise, Layton Road, Horsforth,
Leeds LS18 5EX
Tel   (0532) 586819
Mem   365 90(L) 85(J) 80(5)
Sec   CB Carrington
Pro   G Howard (0532) 585200
Holes   18 L 6293 yds SSS 70
Recs   Am–67 S Lax
         Pro–67 HW Muscroft

V'trs	U SOC
Fees	D–£14 (£18)
Loc	6 miles NW of Leeds

Howley Hall (1900)

Scotchman Lane, Morley, Leeds
LS27 0NX
Tel   (0924) 472432
Mem   465
Sec   Mrs A Pepper (0924) 478417
Pro   SA Spinks (0924) 473852
Holes 18 L 6029 yds SSS 69
Recs   Am–66 S Hamer (1984)
V'trs U
Fees   £12 D–£15 (£18 R/D)
Loc   4 miles SW of Leeds on
       B6123

Huddersfield (1891)

Fixby Hall, Lightridge Road, Fixby,
Huddersfield HD2 2EP
Tel   (0484) 420110
Mem   700
Sec   Miss D Rose (0484) 426203
Pro   P Carman (0484) 426463
Holes 18 L 6402 yds SSS 71
Recs   Am–66 JR Crawshaw (1978)
       Pro– 66 G Thornhill(1985)
V'trs U SOC
Fees   £18.50 D–£24 (£20 D–£26)
Loc   2 miles N of Huddersfield, off
       A6170. M62 Junction 24

Ilkley (1890)

Myddleton, Ilkley LS29 0BE
Tel   (0943) 607277
Mem   530
Sec   G Hirst (0943) 600214
Pro   JL Hammond (0943) 607463
Holes 18 L 6249 yds SSS 70
Recs   Am–65 AC Flather (1984)
       Pro–64 B Hutchinson (1972)
V'trs U
Fees   £17 (£25)

Keighley (1904)

Howden Park, Utley, Keighley
Tel   (0535) 603179
Mem   600
Sec   DF Coyle (0535) 604778
Pro   DA Walker (0535) 665370
Holes 18 L 6134 yds SSS 70
Recs   Am–66 RS Mitchell, G Smith
       (1987)
       Pro–65 J Holchaks
V'trs WD–U Sat–NA Sun/BH–NA
       before 2pm –U after 2pm
Fees   £15
Loc   1 mile W of Keighley

Leeds (1896)

Elmete Road, Roundhay, Leeds LS8 2LJ
Tel   (0532) 658775
Mem   480
Sec   GW Backhouse (0532) 659203
Pro   S Thornhill (0532) 658786
Holes 18 L 6097 yds SSS 69
Recs   Am–64 J Whiteley
       Pro–63 P Hall

V'trs	WD–U WE–M
Fees	£12.50 D–£16
Loc	4 miles NE of Leeds off A58

Lightcliffe (1907)

Knowle Top Road, Lightcliffe
Tel   (0422) 202459
Mem   145 92(L) 87(J)
Sec   TH Gooder (0422) 201051
Pro   R Parry
Holes 9 L 5368 metres SSS 68
Recs   Am–66 PH Wolfe, NRA
       Denham
V'trs U–exc comp days Sun am–M
Fees   £10 (£12)
Loc   3 miles E of Halifax

Longley Park (1911)

Maple Street, off Somerset Road,
Huddersfield HD5 9AX
Tel   (0484) 422304
Mem   400
Sec   KLW Ireland (0484) 429826
Pro   J Andrews
Holes 9 L 5324 yds SSS 66
Recs   Am–64 JD Oxley
       Pro–65 PW Booth
V'trs WD–U exc Thurs
       WE–Restricted
Fees   £6.50 (£8)
Loc   Huddersfield ½ mile

Low Laithes (1925)

Parkmill Lane, Flushdyke, Ossett
Tel   (0924) 273275
Mem   450
Sec   D Walker (0924) 376553
Pro   P Browning (0924) 274667
Holes 18 L 6468 yds SSS 71
Recs   Pro–68
V'trs U WE–no parties
Fees   £12 R/D (£18 R/D)
Loc   2 miles N of Wakefield.
       M1 Junction 40

Marsden (1921)

Hemplow, Marsden, nr Huddersfield
Tel   (0484) 844253
Mem   170 42(L) 45(J)
Sec   GC Scott (0484) 537634
Pro   T Morley
Holes 9 L 5702 yds SSS 68
Recs   Am–63 AJ Bickerdike
       Pro–A Bickerdike
V'trs WD–U WE–NA before 4pm
Fees   £5 (£10)
Loc   8 miles S of Huddersfield

Meltham (1908)

Thick Hollins Hall, Meltham,
Huddersfield HD7 3DQ
Tel   (0484) 850227
Mem   450
Sec   BF Precious (0484) 682106
Pro   PF Davies (0484) 851521
Holes 18 L 6145 yds SSS 70
Recs   Am–68 AT Garner
       Pro–69 W Casper

V'trs	U
Fees	£12 (£15)
Loc	5 miles W of Huddersfield

Middleton Park (1934)

Public
Ring Road, Beeston Park, Middleton,
Leeds 10
Tel   (0532) 709506
Pro   D Bulmer
Holes 18 L 5233 yds SSS 66
V'trs U
Fees   £3.70
Loc   3 miles S of Leeds

Moor Allerton (1923)

Coal Road, Leeds LS17 9NH
Tel   (0532) 661154
Mem   1200
Sec   B Jackson
Pro   P Blaze (0532) 665209
       H Clark (Tournament Pro)
Holes 18 L 6542 yds SSS
       9 L 3541 yds SSS
Recs   Am–68
       Pro–65
V'trs WD–U WE–NA SOC
Fees   18 holes–£21 36 holes–£25
Loc   5½ miles N of Leeds

Moortown (1909)

Harrogate Road, Leeds LS17 7DB
Tel   (0532) 686521
Mem   500
Sec   RH Brown
Pro   B Hutchinson (0532) 683636
Holes 18 L 6544 yds SSS 72
Recs   Am–69 C Turner
V'trs WD–U WE/BH–M I
Fees   £20 D–£25 (£25 D–£30)
Loc   5½ miles N of Leeds

Mount Skip (1955)

Wadsworth, Hebden Bridge
Tel   (0422) 842896
Mem   260
Sec   Dr RG Pogson (0422) 843733
Holes 9 L 5114 yds SSS 66
Recs   Am–63 IS Marsland
       Pro–63 M Ingham
V'trs U
Fees   £6
Loc   1 mile N of Hebden Bridge

Normanton (1903)

Snydale Road, Normanton, Wakefield
WF6 1PA
Tel   (0924) 892943
Mem   250
Sec   J McElhinney (0977) 702273
Pro   M Evans (0924) 220134
Holes 9 L 5284 yds SSS 66
Recs   Am–68 S Turner (1988)
       Pro–67 A Dyson (1988)
V'trs U Sun–NA
Fees   £4.50 Sat/BH–£8.50
Loc   1 mile from M62 Junction 31.
       A655 towards Wakefield

Northcliffe (1921)

Highbank Lane, Moorhead, Shipley
BD18 4LJ
Tel (0274) 584085
Mem 660
Sec R Anderson (0532) 567845
Pro S Poot (0274) 587193
Holes 18 L 6065 yds SSS 69
Recs Am–67 R Bell
Pro–67 M James
V'trs U SOC
Fees £12 (£17)
Loc 3 miles NW of Bradford

Otley (1906)

West Busk Lane, Otley LS21 3NG
Tel (0943) 461015
Mem 600
Sec AF Flowers (0943) 465329
Pro S McNally (0943) 463403
Holes 18 L 6235 yds SSS 70
Recs Am–66 J Blears (1989)
Pro–62 GJ Brand (1988)
V'trs U SOC
Fees £17 (£22)
Loc Off Bradford road, Otley

Outlane (1906)

Slack Lane, Outlane, Huddersfield
HD3 3YL
Tel (0422) 374762
Mem 500
Sec P Sykes
Pro D Chapman
Holes 18 L 5735 yds SSS 69
Recs Am–62 G Crosland
Pro–62 W Garside
V'trs U SOC
Fees £8 (£12)
Loc 4 miles W of Huddersfield nr
M62

Painthorpe House (1961)

Painthorpe Lane, Crigglestone,
nr Wakefield
Tel (0924) 255083
Mem 120
Sec H Kershaw (0924) 274527
Holes 9 L 4108 yds SSS 60
Recs Am–64 J Turner, J Whitehouse
V'trs U exc Sun–NA
Fees WD–£2 Sat–£4
Loc 1 mile from M1 Junction 39

Phoenix Park (1922)

Phoenix Park, Thornbury, Bradford 3
Tel (0274) 667573
Mem 180
Sec G Dunn (0274) 662369
Pro B Ferguson
Holes 9 L 4982 yds SSS 64
Recs Am–66 C Lally
V'trs WD/BH–U WE–NA
Fees £5
Loc Thornbury Roundabout

Pontefract & District (1900)

Park Lane, Pontefract WF8 4QS
Tel (0977) 792241
Mem 800
Sec WT Smith (0977) 792115
Pro J Coleman (0977) 706806
Holes 18 L 6227 yds SSS 70
Recs Am–63 DC Rooke
Pro–67 GW Townhill
V'trs I SOC–Tues/Thurs/Fri
Fees £12 (£15)
Loc Pontefract 1 mile on B6134.
M62 Junction 32

Pontefract Park (1973)

Public
Park Road, Pontefract
Tel (0977) 702799
Holes 18 L 4068 yds SSS 62
V'trs U
Fees £2.50 (£3.60)
Loc Between Pontefract and M62
roundabout

Queensbury (1923)

Queensbury, nr Bradford BD13 1QF
Tel (0274) 882155
Mem 220 45(L) 20(J) 25(5)
Sec A Robinson
Pro N Barber
Holes 9 L 5102 yds SSS 65
Recs Am–64 S Rogers, H Wilkerson
Pro–63 P Cowan
V'trs U
Fees £6 (£10)
Loc Bradford 4 miles

Rawdon (1896)

Buckstone Drive, Micklefield Lane,
Rawdon LS19 6BD
Tel (0532) 506040
Mem 200 50(L) 50(J) 100(5)
Sec RA Adams (0532) 506064
Pro (0532) 505017
Holes 9 L 5982 yds SSS 69
Recs Am–67 P White, J Clough
V'trs WD–H WE/BH–M SOC
Fees £8.50
Loc 6 miles NW of Leeds on
A65 Leeds–Skipton road.
A65/A658 Junction

Riddlesden (1927)

Howden Rough, Riddlesden, Keighley
Tel (0535) 602148
Mem 250
Sec Mrs KM Brooksbank
(0535) 607646
Holes 18 L 4185 yds SSS 61
Recs Am–60 M Mitchell (1987)
Pro–59 P Cowan (1983)
V'trs U exc Sun before 10am
Fees £4 (£7)
Loc Keighley 3 miles

Roundhay (1923)

Public
Park Lane, Leeds LS8 2EJ
Tel (0532) 662695
Pro (0532) 661686
Holes 9 L 5166 yds SSS 65
Recs Am–62 AR White
Pro–62 M Bembridge
V'trs U
Fees £3.70 (£4.10)
Loc 4 miles N of Leeds on A58

Ryburn (1910)

Norland, Sowerby Bridge, Halifax
Tel (0422) 831355
Mem 200
Sec J Hoyle (0422) 843070
Holes 9 L 5002 yds SSS 65
Recs Am–64 DS Lumb (1987)
Pro–61 M Pearson (1987)
V'trs U
Fees £3 (£5)
Loc 3 miles S of Halifax

Sand Moor (1926)

Alwoodley Lane, Leeds LS17 7DJ
Tel (0532) 681685
Mem 535
Sec D Warboys (0532) 685180
Pro J Foss (0532) 683925
Holes 18 L 6423 yds SSS 71
Recs Am–65 A Cullodon (1989)
Pro –66 D Jagger, S McNally
(1987)
V'trs WD–U H by arrangement
WE–NA
Fees £24
Loc 5 miles N of Leeds off A61
Harrogate road

Scarcroft (1937)

Syke Lane, Leeds LS14 3BQ
Tel (0532) 892263
Mem 500
Sec RD Barwell (0532) 892311
Pro M Ross (0532) 892780
Holes 18 L 6426 yds SSS 71
Recs Am–67 E Shaw
Pro–65 D Dunk
V'trs WD–U WE/BH–M or by
arrangement SOC–WD exc
Fri
Fees £20 (£27.50)
Loc 7 miles N of Leeds off A58

Shipley (1896)

Beckfoot Lane, Cottingley Bridge,
Bingley BD16 1LX
Tel (0274) 563212
Mem 585
Sec SL Holman (0274) 568652
Pro D Sutcliffe (0274) 563674
Holes 18 L 6218 yds SSS 70
Recs Am–66 GM Shaw
Pro–64 M Ingham (1987)
V'trs U exc Tues before 1.30pm
& Sat before 4pm
Fees £15 (£20)
Loc 6 miles N of Bradford on A650

For explanation of abbreviations, see page 460.

Silsden (1913)

Brunthwaite, Silsden, nr Keighley
Tel   (0535) 52998
Mem 300
Sec   G Davey (0943) 601490
Holes 14 L 4870 yds SSS 64
Recs Am–61
V'trs WE–restricted Sun–U
      after 1pm
Fees £5 (£8)
Loc   5 miles N of Keighley

South Bradford (1906)

Pearson Road, Odsal, Bradford
BD6 1BH
Tel   (0274) 679195
Mem 220
Sec   HH Kellett (0274) 676911
Pro   M Hillas (0274) 673346
Holes 9 L 6004 yds SSS 69
Recs Am–65 GM Yarnold
      Pro–67 S Miguel, A Caygill
V'trs WD–U WE–M
Fees On application
Loc   Bradford 2 miles, nr Odsal
      Stadium

South Leeds (1914)

Gipsy Lane, Ring Road, Beeston,
Leeds LS11 5TV
Tel   (0532) 700479
Mem 560
Sec   J McBride (0532) 771676
Pro   M Lewis (0532) 702598
Holes 18 L 5835 yds SSS 68
Recs Am–66 M Guy
      Pro–68 B Waites
V'trs WD–U WE–M SOC
Fees £10 (£13)
Loc   4 miles S of Leeds.
      2 miles from M62 and M1

Temple Newsam (1923)

Public
Temple Newsam Road, Halton,
Leeds 15
Tel   (0532) 645624
Sec   G Gower
Pro   D Bulmer (0532) 647362
Holes Lord Irwin 18 L 6448 yds
      SSS 71; Lady Dorothy Wood
      18 L 6029 yds SSS 70
V'trs U SOC
Fees £3.50 (£4)
Loc   5 miles NE of Leeds, off Selby
      road

Todmorden (1895)

Rive Rocks, Cross Stone,
Todmorden, Lancs 014 8RD
Tel   (070 681) 2986
Mem 125 40(L) 30(J)
Sec   T Priestley
Holes 9 L 5818 yds SSS 68
Recs Am–67 G Morgan, J May
      Pro–68 B Hunt
V'trs U SOC
Fees £6 (£8)
Loc   2 miles N of Todmorden

Wakefield (1891)

Woodthorpe, Wakefield WF2 6JH
Tel   (0924) 255104
Mem 500
Sec   DT Hall (0924) 250287
Pro   IM Wright (0924) 255380
Holes 18 L 6626 yds SSS 72
Recs Am–67 T Margison (1982)
      Pro–68 HW Muscroft (1982)
V'trs U SOC
Fees £13 (£16)
Loc   3 miles S of Wakefield

West Bowling (1898)

Newall Hall, Rooley Lane,
West Bowling, Bradford BD5 8LB
Tel   (0274) 724449
Mem 400
Sec   MEL Lynn (0274) 393207
Pro   AP Swaine (0274) 728030
Holes 18 L 5570 yds SSS 68
Recs Am–66 TJ Wade
      Pro–66 G Brand
V'trs WD–U H WE–U after 1.30pm
      SOC
Fees £12 (£18)
Loc   Junction of M606 and Bradford
      Ring Road East

West Bradford (1900)

Chellow Grange, Haworth Road,
Bradford BD9 6NP
Tel   (0274) 542767
Mem 450
Pro   SJ Longster (0274) 542102
Holes 18 L 5705 yds SSS 68
Recs Am–63
      Pro–66
V'trs U
Fees £9 (£12)
Loc   3 miles W of Bradford (B6269)

Wetherby (1910)

Linton Lane, Wetherby LS22 4JF
Tel   (0937) 63375
Mem 550
Sec   WF Gibb
Pro   D Padgett
Holes 18 L 6235 yds SSS 70
Recs Am–69 RJ Patterson (1987)
      Pro–66 MB Ingham (1985)
V'trs WE–U after 10am
      SOC–Wed–Fri
Fees £13 (£16)
Loc   Wetherby 3/4 mile. Leave
      A1 at Wetherby roundabout

Whitwood (1987)

Public
Altofts Lane, Whitwood, Castleford
WF10 5PZ
Tel   (0977) 512835
Sec   S Hicks (Hon)
Pro   R Holland
Holes 9 L 6176 yds SSS 69
Recs Am–77 J Knight (1988)
V'trs WD–U WE–booking service
Loc   M62 Junction 31/A655 towards
      Castleford, 1 mile

Woodhall Hills (1906)

Calverley, Pudsey LS28 5QY
Tel   (0532) 564771/554594
Mem 315
Sec   D Harkness
Pro   MD Lord (0532) 562857
Holes 18 L 6102 yds SSS 69
Recs Am–66 PA Crosby
      Pro–66 M Ingham
V'trs WD–U Sat–after 4.30pm
      Sun–after 10.30am
Fees £9 (£12)
Loc   4 miles W of Bradford off A647

Woodsome Hall (1922)

Woodsome Hall, Fenay Bridge,
Huddersfield HD8 0LQ
Tel   (0484) 602971
Mem 394 194(L) 103(J) 65(5)
Sec   EV Hartley (0484) 602739,
      Mrs P Bates
Pro   KB Scarr (0484) 602034
Holes 18 L 6080 yds SSS 69
Recs Am–66 J Hanson
      Pro–65 D Jagger
V'trs U exc Tues–NA before 4 pm
Fees £16 (£20)
Loc   6 miles SE of Huddersfield on
      Sheffield/Penistone road A629

Wortley (1894)

Hermit Hill Lane, Wortley, nr Sheffield
S30 4DF
Tel   (0742) 885294
Mem 300
Sec   JL Dalby
Pro   J Tilson (0742) 886490
Holes 18 L 5983 yds SSS 69
Recs Am–65
      Pro–66
V'trs U SOC
Fees £12 (£18)
Loc   2 miles W of M1 Junction 36,
      off A629

Ireland

Co Antrim

Ballycastle (1890)

Cushendall Road, Ballycastle
BT64 6QP
Tel   (02657) 62536
Mem   703
Sec   TJ Sheehan, ME Page (Hon)
Pro   T Stewart (02657) 62506
Holes 18 L 5882 yds SSS 69
Recs   Am–66 J McAleese, RJ McCoy
         Pro–64 F Daly
V'trs   U H SOC
Fees   £8 (£10) W–£35 M–£85
Loc   N Antrim coast between
         Portrush and Cushendall
         (A2)1477

Ballyclare (1923)

25 Springvale Road, Ballyclare
Tel   (09603) 42352
Mem   400
Sec   H McConnell (09603) 22696
Holes 18 L 5840 yds SSS 71
Recs   Am–69 J Foster
         Pro–69 S Hamill
V'trs   WD–U WE–NA before 4pm
Fees   £10 (£15)
Loc   1¹/₂ miles N of Ballyclare.
         14 miles N of Belfast

Ballymena (1903)

128 Raceview Road, Ballymena
BT42 4HY
Tel   (0266) 861207/861487
Mem   975
Sec   WRG Pogue (Mgr)
Pro   J Gallaher (0266) 861652
Holes 18 L 5168 yds SSS 67
Recs   Am–62 D Cunning
V'trs   WD/Sun–U SOC
Fees   £7 (£9)
Loc   2 miles E of Ballymena on A42

Bushfoot (1890)

Portballintrae, Bushmills
Tel   (02657) 31317
Mem   603
Sec   P Ritchie
Holes 9 L 5572 yds SSS 67
Recs   Am–66 A McIlroy (1989)
V'trs   U Sat–NA after noon SOC
Fees   £6 (£7) W–£20 M–£50
Loc   1 mile N of Bushmills

Cairndhu (1928)

192 Coast Road, Ballygally, Larne
BT40 2QC
Tel   (0574) 83248
Mem   800
Sec   Mrs J Robinson (0574) 83324

Pro   R Walker (0574) 83417
Holes 18 L 6112 yds SSS 69
Recs   Am–64 B McMillen, R Houston
         Pro–64 D Jones, P Townsend
V'trs   U
Fees   £8 (£11)
Loc   4 miles N of Larne

Carrickfergus (1926)

35 North Road, Carrickfergus
BT38 8LP
Tel   (09603) 63713
Mem   800
Sec   ID Jardine
Pro   R Stevenson (09303) 51803
Holes 18 L 5769 yds SSS 68
Recs   Am–64 P Vizard
         Pro–64 N Drew
V'trs   U
Fees   £7 (£10) W–£28
Loc   Carrickfergus ¹/₂ mile via
         Albert Road
Mis   Buggies for hire

Cushendall (1937)

21 Shore Road, Cushendall
Tel   (026 67) 71318
Mem   715
Sec   S McLaughlin (0266) 73366
Holes 9 L 4678 yds SSS 63
Recs   Am–62 S McKillop
V'trs   WE–restricted SOC
Fees   £8 (£10) M–£60
Loc   Cushendall, 25 miles N of
         Larne

Dunmurry (1905)

91 Dunmurry Lane, Dunmurry, Belfast
BT17 9JS
Tel   (0232) 610834
Mem   380 120(L) 75(J)
Sec   Mrs MB Scott
Pro   G Bleakley (0232) 301179
Holes 18 L 5333 metres SSS 68
Recs   Am–68 A Young
         Pro–70 V Bruce
V'trs   Tues & Thurs–NA after 5pm
         Sat–NA before 5pm SOC
Fees   £9 (£12) SOC–£6 (£10)
Loc   Dunmurry ¹/₂ mile.
         Belfast 5 miles

Greenisland (1894)

156 Upper Road, Greenisland,
Carrickfergus BT38 8RW
Tel   (0232) 862236
Mem   480
Sec   J Wyness (0232) 864583
Holes 9 L 5434 metres SSS 68
Recs   Am–67
V'trs   WD–U Sat–NA before 5pm
         SOC–exc Sat
Fees   £7 (£10)
Loc   9 miles NE of Belfast

Larne (1894)

54 Ferris Bay Road, Island Magee,
Larne BT40 3RT
Tel   (0574) 82228
Mem   320
Sec   JB Stewart (09603) 72043
Holes 9 L 6114 yds SSS 69
Recs   Am–66 IA Nesbitt
         Pro–68 N Drew
V'trs   WD–U WE–M after 5pm
         SOC–WD/Sun
Fees   £4 (£8)
Loc   Larne Harbour 1 mile (by sea).
         6 miles N of Whitehead on
         Browns Bay road

Lisburn (1891)

68 Eglantine Road, Lisburn
BT27 5RQ
Tel   (0846) 662186
Mem   977
Sec   TC McCullough
         (0846) 677216
Pro   BR Campbell (0846) 677217
Holes 18 L 5708 metres SSS 72
Recs   Am–68 J Boyd
         Pro–64 D Feherty (1989)
V'trs   WD–U WE–M SOC–Mon &
         Thurs
Fees   £10 (£15)
Loc   3 miles S of Lisburn on A3

Massereene (1895)

51 Lough Road, Antrim BT41 4DQ
Tel   (08494) 63293
Mem   850
Sec   Mrs M Agnew (08494) 62096
Pro   J Smyth (08494) 64074
Holes 18 L 6614 yds SSS 72
V'trs   U SOC
Fees   £10 (£12)
Loc   Antrim ¹/₂ mile

Rathmore (1947)

Bushmills Road, Portrush BT56 8JG
Tel   (0265) 822285
Mem   331
Sec   DR Williamson (0265) 822996
Holes Play over Royal Portrush

Royal Portrush (1888)

Dunluce Road, Portrush BT56 8JQ
Tel   (0265) 822311
Mem   864 255(L)
Sec   Miss W Erskine
Pro   DA Stevenson (0265) 823335
Holes Dunluce 18 L 6772 yds SSS 72
         Valley 18 L 6273 yds SSS 70
         9 holes L 1187 yds
Recs   Dunluce Am–67 G McGimpsey
         Pro–66 J Hargreaves
         Valley Am–65 MJC Hoey

V'trs   WD–U Sat–NA before 2.30pm
        Sun–NA before 10am SOC
Fees   Dunluce £14 (£20)
        Valley £9 (£12)
Loc   Portrush Coastal Rd ¹/₂ mile

Whitehead (1904)

McCrae's Brae, Whitehead,
Carrickfergus BT38 9NZ
Tel   (09603) 53792
Mem   700
Sec   J Niblock, J Sheriff
        (09603) 53631
Holes   18 L 6426 yds SSS 71
Recs   Am–68 A Hope
V'trs   U exc Sat SOC–exc Sat
Fees   £7.50 (£10)
Loc   ¹/₂ mile from Whitehead, off
        road to Island Magee

Co Armagh

County Armagh (1893)

Newry Road, Armagh
Tel   (0861) 522501
Mem   1000
Sec   HD Somerville
Holes   18 L 6184 yds SSS 69
Recs   Am–68
        Pro–65
V'trs   U SOC
Fees   £7 (£10)
Loc   40 miles SW of Belfast

Craigavon

Public
Golf/Ski Centre, Turmoyra Lane,
Silverwood, Lurgan, Craigavon
Tel   (0762) 6606
Sec   MM Shanks (0762) 42413
Holes   18 L 6496 yds SSS 71
Loc   Lurgan 1¹/₂ miles
Mis   12 hole pitch & putt course.
        Floodlit driving range

Lurgan (1893)

The Demesne, Lurgan BT67 9BN
Tel   (0762) 322087
Mem   903
Sec   Mrs G Turkington
Pro   D Paul
Holes   18 L 5836 metres SSS 70
Recs   Am–66 S Magee
        Pro–65 B Todd
V'trs   U SOC
Fees   £10 (£12)
Loc   Lurgan ¹/₄ mile

Portadown (1906)

Carrickblacker, Portadown
Tel   (0762) 355356
Mem   761
Sec   Mrs ME Holloway

Pro   P Stevenson
Holes   18 L 6119 yds SSS 70
Recs   Am–68
        Pro–63
V'trs   WD–U WE–NA
Fees   £6 (£10)
Loc   3 miles S of Portadown towards
        Gilford

Tandragee (1922)

Markethill Road, Tandragee,
Craigavon BT62 2ER
Tel   (0762) 840727
Mem   850
Sec   A Best (0762) 841272
Pro   J Black (0762) 841761
Holes   18 L 6084 yds SSS 69
Recs   Am–62 P Topley
V'trs   U SOC
Fees   £7 (£10)
Loc   Armagh 10 miles.
        Craigavon 8 miles

Belfast

Ballyearl Golf Centre

Public
585 Doagh Road, Newtownabbey
BT36 8RZ
Tel   (02313) 48287
Sec   A Clements (02313) 861211
Holes   9 L 2362 yds Par 3 course
V'trs   U
Fees   £2 (£2.75)
Loc   N of Mossley on B59
Mis   Driving range

Balmoral (1914)

518 Lisburn Road, Belfast
BT9 6EX
Tel   (0232) 381514
Mem   850
Sec   B Jenkins OBE (Mgr)
Pro   J Fisher (0232) 667747
Holes   18 L 5679 metres SSS 70
Recs   Am–66 M Wilson
        Pro–64 D Jones
V'trs   U
Fees   £10 (£15)
Loc   2 miles S of Belfast at
        Balmoral–Kings Hall

Belvoir Park (1927)

Newtownbreda, Belfast BT8 4AN
Tel   (0232) 641159/69281?
Mem   1038
Sec   WI Davidson (0232) 491693/
        646113
Pro   GM Kelly (0232) 646714
Holes   18 L 6476 yds SSS 71
Recs   Am–66 TS Anderson
        Pro–66 P Alliss, EC Brown
V'trs   U Sat–NA
Fees   £12 (£15)
Loc   Belfast 3 miles

Cliftonville (1911)

Westland Road, Belfast
Tel   (0232) 744158
Mem   429
Sec   JM Henderson
Holes   9 L 4678 yds SSS 70
Recs   Am–66 WRA Tennant
        Pro–67 S Hamill
V'trs   U exc Sat
Fees   On application
Loc   Belfast

Fortwilliam (1894)

Downview Avenue, Belfast
Tel   (0232) 370770
Mem   1050
Sec   RJ Campbell
Pro   P Hanna (0232) 770980
Holes   18 L 5642 yds SSS 67
Recs   Am–63 G Glover
        Pro–67 F Daly, J Kinsella
V'trs   U
Fees   £9 (£12)
Loc   2 miles N of Belfast

Gilnahirk (1983)

Public
Upper Bramel Road, Belfast
Tel   (0232) 448477
Mem   200
Sec   K Gray (Mgr)
Pro   K Gray
Holes   18 L 2699 metres SSS
V'trs   U
Fees   £2 (£2.50)
Loc   3 miles SE of Belfast

Knockbracken

Ballymaconaghy Road,
Knockbracken, Belfast BT8 4SB
Tel   (0232) 792108
Mem   300
Sec   P Laverty (Hon)
Pro   D Patterson (0232) 401811
Holes   18 L 5312 yds SSS 68
V'trs   WD–U WE–U after 11am SOC
Fees   £5 (£7)
Loc   2 miles SW of Belfast, near
        Four Winds

Malone (1895)

240 Upper Malone Road, Dunmurry,
Belfast BT17 9LB
Tel   (0232) 612695
Mem   759 379(L) 211(J) 29(S)
Sec   JE Osborough (0232) 612758
Pro   PM O'Hagan (0232) 614917
Holes   18 L 6499 yds SSS 71
        9 L 2895 yds SSS 34
Recs   Pro–68 E Jones
V'trs   Wed–NA after 2pm Sat–NA
        before 5pm SOC–Mon & Thurs
Fees   £10 (£13)
Loc   6 miles S of Belfast

Ormeau (1893)

Ravenhill Road, Belfast BT6 0BN
Tel   (0232) 041000
Mem   250 70(L) 30(J) 28(5)
Sec   R Burnett (0232) 459808
Holes   9 L 5308 yds SSS 65
V'trs   U
Fees   £4 (£5)
Loc   South Belfast

Shandon Park (1926)

73 Shandon Park, Belfast BT5 6NY
Tel   (0232) 793730
Mem   1048
Sec   H Wallace (Mgr)
    (0232) 401856
Pro   B Wilson (0232) 797859
Holes   18 L 6252 yds SSS 70
Recs   Am–64 N Anderson
    Pro–68 CP Posnett
V'trs   WD–U Sat–NA before 5pm
    SOC
Fees   £12 (£16)
Loc   Belfast 3 miles

The Knock Golf Club (1895)

Summerfield, Dundonald, Belfast
BT16 0QX
Tel   (02318) 2249
Mem   870
Sec   SG Managh (02318) 3251
Pro   G Fairweather (02318) 3825
Holes   18 L 5845 metres SSS 71
Recs   Am–67 KH Graham
    Pro–69 PR McGuirk
V'trs   U SOC–Mon & Thurs
Fees   D–£12 (£16)
Loc   4 miles E of Belfast

Co Carlow

Borris (1908)

Deerpark, Borris
Tel   (0503) 73143
Mem   250
Sec   EC Lennon
Holes   9 L 6026 yds SSS 69
Recs   Am–67
V'trs   WD–U Sun–M SOC–WD/Sat
    (Apr–Sept)
Fees   £5 (£6)

Carlow (1899)

Oak Park, Carlow
Tel   (0503) 31695
Mem   820
Sec   Mrs Meaney (0503) 42599
Pro   A Gilbert
Holes   18 L 6347 yds SSS 70
Recs   Am–65 P Mulcare, RD Carr
    Pro–68 C O'Connor
V'trs   U
Fees   £7 (£10)
Loc   Carlow

Co Cavan

Bolturbot (1950)

Erne Hill, Belturbet
Tel   (049) 22287
Mem   150
Sec   JC Enright
Holes   9 L 5180 yds SSS 64
Recs   Am–64 J Costello (1982)
V'trs   U
Fees   £5
Loc   Belturbet 1/2 mile

Blacklion (1962)

Toam, Blacklion, via Sligo
Tel   (072) 53024
Mem   120
Sec   R Thompson
Holes   9 L 5544 metres SSS 69
V'trs   U SOC
Fees   £3 (£4) W–£10
Loc   12 miles SW of Enniskillen
    on A4. 10 miles E of
    Manorhamilton on N16

Cabra Castle (1978)

Kingscourt
Mem   110
Sec   F Leahy (042) 67189
Holes   9 L 5308 metres SSS 68
V'trs   U
Fees   D–£4 (D–£4)
Loc   2 miles E of Kingscourt

County Cavan (1894)

Armmore House, Drumelis
Tel   (049) 31283
Mem   300 150(L) 51(J)
Sec   T O'Reilly (049) 31292
Holes   18 L 5519 metres SSS 69
Recs   Am–66 A Cafferty
    Pro–65 J Purcell (1987)
V'trs   U
Fees   IR£8
Loc   2 miles W of Cavan

Virginia (1946)

Virginia
Mem   280
Sec   S Sheridan (042) 65766
Holes   9 L 4139 metres SSS 62
Recs   Am–64 P Gallagher
V'trs   U
Loc   50 miles NW of Dublin

Co Clare

Drumoland Castle

Public
Newmarket-on-Fergus
Tel   (061) 71144
Mem   150
Sec   M Wright
Holes   18 L 6098 yds SSS 71

Recs   Am–74 Dr C Hackett (1986)
V'trs   U SOC
Fees   D–£10
Loc   19 miles NW of Limerick

Ennis (1907)

Drumbiggle Road, Ennis
Tel   (065) 24074
Mem   497
Sec   J Cooney
Pro   M Ward (065) 20690
Holes   18 L 5358 metres SSS 68
Recs   Am–64 G Roche
    Pro–66 P Skerritt
V'trs   U exc Sun SOC
Fees   £10 SOC–£8 (£9)
Loc   1/2 mile NW of Ennis

Kilkee (1908)

East End, Kilkee
Tel   Kilkee 48
Mem   343 160(L)
Sec   TM Lillis
Holes   9 L 6185 yds SSS 69
Recs   Am–68 D Nagle, N Cotter
V'trs   U SOC (exc July/Aug)
Fees   £5.50 W–£22 M–£45
Loc   E end of Kilkee

Kilrush (1934)

Public
Parknamoney, Kilrush
Tel   (065) 51138
Mem   150
Sec   N O'Regan
Holes   9 L 2739 yds SSS 67
Recs   Am–64 DF Nagle
V'trs   U SOC
Fees   £5
Loc   Kerry–Clare route

Lahinch (1892)

Lahinch
Tel   (065) 81003
Mem   1200
Pro   R McCavery (065) 81408
Holes   Old 18 L 6699 yds SSS 73
    Castle 18 L 5265 yds SSS 67
V'trs   WD–U WE–NA 9–10.30am and
    1–2pm SOC
Fees   £15 (£18) Castle £10
Loc   Ennistymon 2 miles on T69

Shannon (1966)

Shannon Airport
Tel   (061) 61020
Mem   403
Sec   JJ Quigley (061) 61849
Pro   A Pyke (061) 61551
Holes   18 L 6854 yds SSS 73
Recs   Am–63 J Purcell
    Pro–65 D Durnian
V'trs   WD–U SOC
Fees   £12
Loc   Shannon Airport

For explanation of abbreviations, see page 460.

Spanish Point (1915)

Miltown Malbay
Tel   (065) 84198
Mem   100
Sec   G O'Loughlin
Holes   9 L 3820 yds SSS 54
Recs   Am–27 D Twomey
        Pro–23 P Skerritt
V'trs   U
Fees   £5 W–£24
Loc   Miltown Malbay 2 miles

Co Cork

Bandon (1910)

Castlebernard, Bandon
Tel   (023) 41111
Mem   520
Sec   B O'Neill (023) 41998
Pro   T O'Boyle (023) 42224
Holes   18 L 5663 metres SSS 69
Recs   Am–68 J Carroll
V'trs   U
Fees   £8 (£10)
Loc   Bandon 1¹/₂ miles

Bantry Park (1975)

Donemark, Bantry
Tel   (027) 50579
Mem   250
Sec   B Harrington (027) 50665
Holes   9 L 6436 yds SSS 70
Recs   Pro–66 C O'Connor Jr
V'trs   U
Fees   D–£7
Loc   Bantry 1 mile on Glengarriff
        road

Charleville (1909)

Smiths Road, Charleville
Tel   (011) 81257
Mem   250
Sec   T Murphy
Holes   18 L 6380 yds SSS 69
Recs   Am–68 T Murphy
V'trs   U
Fees   £6
Loc   On Cork–Limerick road

Cobh (1986)

Ballywilliam, Cobh
Tel   (021) 812399
Mem   200
Sec   M Hennessy (021) 811372
Holes   9 L 4338 metres SSS 63
Recs   Am–65 G Mellerick
        Pro–64 C O'Connor Sr
V'trs   WD–U WE/BH–NA before
        noon
Fees   £4 (£5)
Loc   16 miles E of Cork.
        1 mile N of Cobh

Cork (1888)

Little Island, Cork
Tel   (021) 353263
Mem   350 160 (L)
Sec   M Sands (021) 353451
Pro   D Higgins (021) 353037
Holes   18 L 6065 metres SSS 72
Recs   Am–66 P Murphy
V'trs   WD–U exc 1–2pm daily &
        Thurs before 4.30pm WE–U
        from 10.30am–12 and after
        2.30pm SOC
Fees   £15 (£17)
Loc   5 miles E of Cork. ¹/₂ mile
        off Cork–Cobh road

Doneraile (1927)

Doneraile
Tel   (022) 24137
Mem   200
Sec   F Carey
Holes   9 L 5528 yds SSS 67
V'trs   U
Fees   £3
Loc   Doneraile ¹/₂ mile

Douglas (1909)

Douglas
Tel   (021) 891086
Mem   839
Sec   B Barrett (021) 895297
Pro   GS Nicholson (021) 362055
Holes   18 L 5664 metres SSS 69
Recs   Am–66 D O'Herlihy
        Pro–64 E Darcy
V'trs   WD–U WE–NA before 11.30am
        SOC–WD
Fees   IR£11 (IR£12)
Loc   Cork 3 miles

Dunmore (1967)

Dunmore, Clonakilty
Tel   (023) 33352
Mem   127
Sec   M Minihan (023) 33858
Holes   9 L 4464 yds SSS 61
Recs   Am–65
        Pro–62
V'trs   U SOC
Fees   £5
Loc   3¹/₂ miles S of Clonakilty

East Cork (1971)

Gortacue, Midleton
Tel   (021) 631687/631273
Mem   250
Sec   M Moloney
Holes   18 L 5207 metres SSS 69
Recs   Am–66 B O'Regan (1983)
V'trs   WD–U WE–NA before noon
        BH–U
Fees   £6
Loc   2 miles N of Midleton on
        L35

Fermoy (1893)

Corin, Fermoy
Tel   Fermoy 31472
Mem   243
Holes   18 L 5825 metres SSS 70
V'trs   U SOC
Loc   Fermoy 2 miles

Glengarriff (1936)

Glengarriff
Tel   (027) 63150
Mem   31
Holes   9 L 4328 yds SSS 61
V'trs   U
Loc   Glengarriff 1 mile

Kanturk (1974)

Fairy Hill, Kanturk
Tel   (029) 50534
Mem   135
Sec   D O'Connell (029) 50696
Holes   9 L 5527 yds SSS 69
Recs   Am–72 D O'Riordan,
        M Arsdeacon (1987)
        J O'Connor (1989)
V'trs   U
Fees   £5
Loc   1¹/₂ miles SW of Kanturk

Kinsale (1912)

Ringenane, Belgooly, Kinsale
Tel   (021) 772197
Mem   310
Sec   JG Fitzsimons
Holes   9 L 5332 metres SSS 68
Recs   Am–66 C Coughlan
V'trs   U WE–NA SOC
Fees   £8
Loc   Kinsale 2 miles.
        Cork 16 miles

Macroom (1924)

Lackaduve, Macroom
Tel   (026) 41072
Mem   273
Sec   J O'Brien
Holes   9 L 5439 metres SSS 68
Recs   Am–66 J Mills
V'trs   U SOC
Fees   D–IR£5
Loc   Macroom ¹/₂ mile

Mallow (1948)

Ballyellis, Mallow
Tel   (022) 21145
Mem   1500
Sec   JP Shannon (022) 22465
Pro   S Conway
Holes   18 L 6559 yds SSS 71
Recs   Am–66 J Murphy (1982)
V'trs   WD–U before 5pm SOC
Fees   D–£10 W–£25
Loc   1¹/₂ miles SE of Mallow
        Bridge

Mitchelstown (1908)

Mitchelstown
Tel (025) 24072
Mem 200
Sec PA Brennan (025) 84115
Holes 9 L 5057 metres SSS 67
Recs Am–64 A Pierce
V'trs U SOC
Fees £6
Loc 30 miles N of Cork

Monkstown (1908)

Parkgarriffe, Monkstown
Tel (021) 841225
Mem 600
Sec JP Curtin (021) 841376
Pro B Murphy (021) 841686
Holes 18 L 5534 metres SSS 68
Recs Am–66
V'trs U
Fees £11 (£12)
Loc 7 miles S of Cork

Muskerry (1897)

Carrigrohane
Tel (021) 385297
Mem 713
Sec JJ Moynihan
Pro WM Lehane (021) 385104
Holes 18 L 5786 metres SSS 70
Recs Am–66 J McHenry, D O'Flynn
Pro–66 J Hegerty
V'trs WD–U exc 4.30–6.30pm
WE–NA before 3.30pm
Fees £10
Loc 6 miles NW of Cork

Skibbereen (1931)

Skibbereen
Tel (028) 21227
Mem 300
Sec J Hamilton (028) 21673
Holes 9 L 5774 yds SSS 68
Recs Am–65 B McDaid
V'trs U
Fees £6 W–£42
Loc 1 mile W of Skibbereen

Youghal (1940)

Knockaverry, Youghal
Tel (024) 92787
Mem 230 140(L) 50(J)
Sec M O'Sullivan
Pro D Higgins
Holes 18 L 6223 yds SSS 69
Recs Am–65 F Wright
V'trs U
Fees IR£8
Loc 30 miles E of Cork

Co Donegal

Ballybofey & Stranorlar (1958)

Ballybofey
Tel (074) 31093
Mem 206 75(L) 30(J)
Sec I Kee (074) 31050
Holes 18 L 5922 yds SSS 69
Recs Am–65 D Cleary
V'trs U SOC
Fees £6
Loc Stranorlar 1/4 mile

Ballyliffin (1947)

Ballyliffin, Clonmany
Tel (077) 76119
Mem 350
Sec KJ O'Doherty (077) 74417
Holes 18 L 6611 yds SSS 72
Recs Am–67 G Doherty
V'trs U SOC–arrange with Sec
Fees IR£6 (IR£8)
Loc 8 miles N of Buncrana.
15 miles N of Londonderry

Buncrana (1951)

Public
Buncrana
Mem 92
Pro NS Doherty
Holes 9 L 2020 yds
V'trs U

Bundoran (1894)

Great Northern Hotel, Bundoran
Tel (072) 41302
Mem 400
Sec JC Roarty (072) 41360
Pro SL Robinson, D Robinson
Holes 18 L 6328 yds
Recs Am–67 J Murray
Pro–66 E Darcy
V'trs WD–U WE–restricted SOC
Fees £9 (£10)
Loc East boundary of Bundoran

Donegal (1960)

Murvagh
Tel (073) 34054
Mem 369
Sec J Nixon (073) 22166
Holes 18 L 7271 yds SSS 73
Recs Am–68 Fr B McBride
V'trs U SOC
Fees £6 (£8)
Loc 7 miles S of Donegal on N18

Dunfanaghy (1903)

Public
Dunfanaghy
Tel (074) 36335
Mem 70
Sec D Arnold (074) 36142
Holes 18 L 5066 metres SSS 66

Recs Am–64 J Brogan
Pro–66 L Wallace
V'trs U SOC
Fees IR£5.50 (IR£6.50)
Loc 1/4 mile from Dunfanaghy on
N56

Greencastle (1892)

Via Lifford, Greencastle
Tel (077) 81013
Mem 300
Sec HM Morris (077) 82042
Holes 9 L 5386 yds SSS 65
Recs Am–62 C McCarroll
Pro–67 D Jones
V'trs WD–U WE–restricted SOC
Fees £5 (£7)
Loc Nr Moville

Gweedore (1923)

Derrybeg, Letterkenny
Tel (075) 31140
Mem 170
Sec C Campbell (075) 31545
Holes 18 L 6230 yds SSS 69
Recs Am–64 S Murphy
V'trs U
Fees £5 (£7) W–£28 M–£95
Loc West Donegal

Letterkenny (1913)

Barnhill, Letterkenny
Tel (074) 21150
Mem 320
Sec T Redden
Holes 18 L 6299 yds SSS 71
Recs Am–67 P Shiels
V'trs U SOC
Fees £6
Loc 1 mile NE of Letterkenny

Narin & Portnoo (1931)

Narin, Portnoo
Tel (075) 45107
Mem 400
Sec S Murray
Holes 18 L 5950 yds SSS 68
Recs Am–64 B McBride
Pro–62 R Browne
V'trs WD–U Sat–restricted 1–2.30pm
Sun–restricted H SOC
Fees £6 Sun–£7 SOC–£3
Loc 6 miles N of Ardara

North West (1891)

Lisfannon, Fahan
Tel (077) 61027
Mem 400
Sec D Coyle (077) 61843
Holes 18 L 6203 yds SSS 69
Recs Am–65 F Friel
Pro–64 M Doherty
V'trs U
Fees IR£5 (IR£10) W–IR£30 M–IR£45
Loc 12 miles N of Londonderry.
Buncrana 2 miles
Mis Links course

For explanation of abbreviations, see page 460.

Otway (1893)

Saltpans, Rathmullen, Letterkenny
Tel   (074) 58319
Mem   110
Sec   H Gallagher (074) 58210
Holes 9 L 4134 yds SSS 60
Recs   Am–29 F Friel
V'trs   U
Fees   D–£3
Loc   By Lough Swilly

Portsalon (1891)

Portsalon, Letterkenny
Tel   Portsalon 59102
Mem   108
Sec   M Kerr
Holes 18 L 5844 yds SSS 68
Recs   Am–68 J Brogan
        Pro–71 J Henderson
V'trs   U
Fees   £4
Loc   20 miles N of Letterkenny

Rosapenna (1898)

Golf Hotel, Rosapenna
Tel   (074) 55301
Mem   89
Sec   JJ McBride
Holes 18 L 6254 yds SSS 70
Recs   Am–M McGinley, D Boyce
        Pro–68 F Daly
V'trs   U
Fees   IR£8 (IR£10)
Loc   Via Letterkenny

Co Down

Ardglass (1896)

Castle Place, Ardglass
Tel   (0396) 841219
Mem   676
Sec   Mrs P Rooney
Holes 18 L 5462 metres SSS 69
Recs   Am–66 J Milligan
        Pro–69 H Jackson
V'trs   U
Fees   £7 (£10)
Loc   Downpatrick 7 miles

Banbridge (1913)

Huntly Road, Banbridge
Tel   (08206) 22342
Mem   425
Sec   TF Fee (08206) 23831
Holes 12 L 5879 yds SSS 68
Recs   Am–65 K Stevenson, R Burns
V'trs   U SOC
Fees   £5 (£6) 1989 prices
Loc   Banbridge 1 mile

Bangor (1903)

Broadway, Bangor BT20 4RH
Tel   (0247) 270922
Mem   1100
Sec   DB Wilson
Pro   N Drew (0247) 462164
Holes 18 L 6372 yds SSS 70

Recs   Am–67 N Anderson
        Pro–66 C O'Connor
V'trs   WD–U before 5pm –M after
        5pm WE–NA before 3pm
        SOC
Fees   £12 (£17)
Loc   1 mile E of Bangor

Bright Castle (1979)

14 Coniamstown Road, Bright,
Downpatrick BT30 8LU
Tel   (0396) 841319
Mem   40
Sec   R Reid
Holes 18 L 6730 yds SSS
Recs   Am–70 A Ennis
V'trs   U SOC
Fees   £4 (£6)
Loc   5 miles from Downpatrick on
        Killough road

Carnalea (1927)

Station Road, Bangor BT19 1EZ
Tel   (0247) 465004
Mem   770
Sec   JH Crozier (0247) 270368
Pro   M McGee (0247) 270122
Holes 18 L 5584 yds SSS 67
Recs   Am–64 P Nelson
V'trs   U SOC–WD
Fees   £7 (£10)
Loc   By Carnalea Station

Clandeboye (1933)

Conlig, Newtownards BT23 3PN
Tel   (0247) 271767/473706
Mem   1077
Sec   TI Marks (0247) 271767
Pro   P Gregory (0247) 271750
Holes 18 L 5915 metres SSS 72
        18 L 5172 metres SSS 67
Recs   Am–68 D Jackson
        Pro–68 J Heggarty, D Jones,
        D Feherty
V'trs   WD–U Sat–M Sun–M before
        10am and 12.30–1.30pm
Fees   Long £10 (£15) Short £9 (£12)
        W–£60
Loc   At Conlig, off A21 Bangor–
        Newtownards road

Donaghadee (1899)

Warren Road, Donaghadee BT21 0PQ
Tel   (0237) 888697
Mem   1250
Sec   CD McCutcheon (0237) 883624
Pro   G Drew (0237) 882392
Holes 18 L 5576 metres Par 71
Recs   Am–65 J Nelson
        Pro–69 E Clarke
V'trs   U Sat–M
Fees   £8 (£10)
Loc   Belfast 18 miles

Downpatrick (1932)

Saul Road, Downpatrick BT30 6PA
Tel   (0396) 2152
Mem   713
Sec   A Cannon

Holes 18 L 5702 metres SSS 69
V'trs   U
Fees   £8 (£10)

Helen's Bay (1896)

Golf Road, Helen's Bay, Bangor
BT19 1TL
Tel   (0247) 852601
Mem   721
Sec   JH Ward (0247) 852815
Pro   T Loughran (0247) 853313
Holes 9 L 5176 metres SSS 67
Recs   Am–67 JR Longmore
        Pro–67 L Esdale
V'trs   WD–U Sat/BH–M Sun–U
Fees   On application
Loc   Belfast 12 miles

Holywood (1904)

Nuns Walk, Demesne Road, Holywood
Tel   (02317) 2138
Mem   800
Sec   GR Magennis (02317) 3135
Pro   M Bannon (02317) 5503
Holes 18 L 5885 yds SSS 68
Recs   Am–61 J Watts
        Pro–64 M Bannon
V'trs   WD–1.30–2.15pm
        Sat–after 5pm
Fees   £10 (£15)

Kilkeel (1948)

Public
Mourne Park, Ballyardle, Kilkeel
Tel   (06937) 62296
Mem   400
Sec   SW Rutherford (06937) 73660
Holes 9 L 5623 metres SSS 69
Recs   Am–65 F Reilly
V'trs   U
Fees   £6.50 (£8)
Loc   3 miles W of Kilkeel on Newry
        road

Kirkistown Castle (1902)

142 Main Road, Cloughey,
Newtownards
Tel   (024 77) 71233/71353
Mem   800
Sec   RC Vine BEM
Pro   J Peden
Holes 18 L 5628 metres SSS 70
Recs   Am–68 Jas Brown
        Pro–71 RJ Polley, C O'Connor
V'trs   WD–U WE/BH–NA 1st tee
        9.30–10.30am and 12–1.30pm
        SOC
Fees   £8 (£13)
Loc   25 miles SE of Belfast

Mahee Island (1930)

Comber, Belfast
Tel   (0238) 541234
Mem   400
Sec   T Reid (Hon)
Holes 9 L 2790 yds SSS 67
Recs   Am–65 C Boyd
        Pro–65 N Drew

V'trs II Sat–NA before 4.30pm
SOC–WD exc Mon
Fees £6 (£10)
Loc Strangford Lough, 14 miles S
of Belfast

Mourne (1946)

36 Golf Links Road, Newcastle
BT33 0AN
Tel (039 67) 23218
Mem 275
Sec S Keenan (Hon)
Holes Play over Royal Co Down

Royal Belfast (1881)

Holywood, Craigavad
Tel (0232) 428165
Mem 1200
Sec IM Piggot
Pro D Carson
Holes 18 L 6184 yds SSS 70
Recs Am–65 RAD McMillan
Pro–67 C O'Connor
V'trs I Sat–NA before 4.30pm
Fees £14 (£16)
Loc E of Belfast on A2

Royal County Down (1889)

Newcastle BT33 0AN
Tel (03967) 23314
Mem 450
Sec PE Rolph
Pro ET Jones (03967) 22419
Holes C'ship 18 L 6968 yds SSS 74
No 2 18 L 4100 yds SSS 60
Recs C'ship Am–66 J Bruen,
JM Jamison
Pro–67 A Compston, B Gadd
V'trs Contact Sec for information
Fees D–£22 (D–£25)
Loc Belfast 30 miles

Scrabo (1907)

233 Scrabo Road, Newtownards
BT23 4SL
Tel (0247) 812355
Mem 750
Pro W Todd
Holes 18 L 5699 metres SSS 71
Recs Am–69 W Caughey (1987)
Pro–67 N Drew (1987)
V'trs WD–U WE–after 5pm SOC
Fees £7 (£9.50)
Loc 2 miles W of Newtownards

The Spa (1907)

20 Grove Road, Ballynahinch BT24 8BR
Tel (0238) 562365
Mem 450
Sec J McC Glass (0232) 812340
Holes 18 L 5938 metres SSS 72
Recs Am–67 R Wallace
V'trs U exc Wed–NA after 3pm
Sat–NA
Fees £5 (£10)

Warrenpoint (1893)

Lr Dromore Rd, Warrenpoint
Tel (069 37) 12215
Mem 1066
Sec J McMahon (069 37) 73695
Pro N Shaw (069 37) 72371
Holes 18 L 5628 metres SSS 70
Recs Am–65 J Carvill
Pro–68 D Feherty
V'trs U SOC
Fees £10 (£12)
Loc 5 miles S of Newry

Dublin City

Carrickmines (1900)

Carrickmines
Tel (0001) 955972
Mem 371
Sec GW McConnell (0001) 863020
Holes 18 L 6044 yds SSS 69
Recs Am–68
Pro–68
V'trs M
Fees £8 Sun–£10 Sat–NA
Loc 6 miles S of Dublin

Castle (1913)

Woodside Drive, Rathfarnham,
Dublin 14
Tel (0001) 904207
Mem 800
Sec LF Blackburne
Pro D Kinsella (0001) 933444
Holes 18 L 6168 metres SSS 69
Recs Am–69 J Bourke
Pro–65 B Browne
V'trs Mon/Thurs/Fri–U Wed–U
before 12.30pm WE/BH–M
SOC
Fees £13
Loc 5 miles S of Dublin

Clontarf (1912)

Donnycarney House, Malahide Road,
Dublin 3
Tel (0001) 311305
Mem 1035
Sec MG O'Brien (0001) 315085
Pro J Craddock (0001) 310016
Holes 18 L 5447 metres SSS 68
Recs Am–65 M O'Shea
Pro–64 H Bradshaw
V'trs WD–U WE–M SOC
Fees £12
Loc Dublin 2 miles

Edmondstown (1944)

Rathfarnham, Dublin 16
Tel (0001) 932461
Mem 420
Sec S Adams (0001) 931082
Pro A Crofton (0001) 934602
Holes 18 L 5663 metres SSS 69
V'trs WD–U WE–NA after noon
Fees £11 (£13)
Loc 7 miles S of Dublin

Elm Park G & SC (1927)

Nutley House, Donnybrook, Dublin 4
Tel (0001) 693438/693014
Mem 1725
Sec H Montag (0001) 693014
Pro S Green (0001) 692650
Holes 18 L 5353 metres SSS 68
Recs Am–63 PF Hogan
Pro–63 P Townsend
V'trs U (phone Pro)
Fees £17 (£22)
Loc 3 miles S of Dublin

Foxrock (1893)

Foxrock, Torquay Road, Dublin 18
Tel (0001) 895668
Mem 550
Sec DJ Garvey (0001) 893992
Pro T O'Connor (0001) 893992
Holes 9 L 5699 metres SSS 69
Recs Am–68 D Campbell
Pro–68 H Jackson
V'trs WD/BH/Sun–M Tues & Sat–NA
Fees £12
Loc 5 miles S of Dublin

Grange (1911)

Whitechurch, Rathfarnham, Dublin 16
Tel (0001) 932832
Mem 1050 235(L) 210(J) 12(5)
Sec JA O'Donoghue (0001) 932889
Pro WD Sullivan (0001) 932299
Holes 18 L 5517 metres SSS 69
Recs Am–64 WB Buckley
Pro–62 C O'Connor Jr
V'trs WD–U exc Tues/Wed pm–NA
WE–M
Fees £20

Howth (1916)

Carrickbrack Road, Sutton, Dublin 13
Tel (0001) 323055
Mem 1200
Sec Ms A MacNiece
Pro JF McGuirk (0001) 393895
Holes 18 L 5573 metres SSS 69
Recs Am–66 M Roe
Pro–71
V'trs WD–U exc Wed WE–M
Fees £10
Loc 9 miles NE of Dublin nr Sutton
Cross

Milltown (1907)

Lower Churchtown Road, Milltown,
Dublin 14
Tel (0001) 977060
Mem 1497
Sec JB Cassidy (0001) 973199/
976090
Pro C Greene (0001) 977072
Holes 18 L 5669 metres SSS 69
Recs Am–64 JB Carr
Pro–64 C Greene
V'trs U
Fees £16 (£24)
Loc 4 miles S of Dublin

Rathfarnham (1896)

Newtown, Dublin 16
Tel   (0001) 931201/931561
Mem   561
Sec   VJ Coyle (0001) 931201
Pro   B O'Hara
Holes   9 L 5787 metres SSS 70
Recs   Am–70 C O'Carrol, N Hynes,
        T O'Donnell
V'trs   WD–U exc Tues WE–NA
Fees   £9
Loc   6 miles S of Dublin

Royal Dublin (1885)

Bull Island, Dollymount, Dublin 3
Tel   (0001) 336346
Mem   825
Sec   JA Lambe
Pro   L Owens (0001) 336477
        (Touring Pro C O'Connor Jr)
Holes   18 L 6858 yds SSS 73
Recs   Am–67 G O'Donovan (1984)
        Pro–63 B Langer, G Cullen
        (1985)
V'trs   U exc Sat
Fees   £25 (£35)
Loc   3¹/₄ miles NE of Dublin, on
        coast road to Howth

St Anne's (1921)

North Bull Island, Dollymount,
Dublin 5
Tel   (0001) 332797
Mem   411
Sec   J Carberry (0001) 336471
Pro   P Skerritt
Holes   18 L 5660 metres SSS 69
Recs   Am–67 S Rodgers
        Pro–64 P Skerritt
V'trs   WE–BH–NA SOC
Fees   £12
Loc   Dublin 5 miles

Stackstown (1975)

Kellystown Road, Rathfarnham,
Dublin 16
Tel   (0001) 942338/941993
Mem   840
Sec   PA Power (0001) 555204
Holes   18 L 5952 metres SSS 72
Recs   Am–72 T O'Donoghue
V'trs   WD–U SOC
Fees   £8 (£10)
Loc   7 miles SE of Dublin

Sutton (1890)

Cush Point, Burrow Road, Sutton,
Dublin 13
Tel   (0001) 323013
Mem   198 162(L) 95(J) 53(5)
Sec   H Quirke
Pro   N Lynch
Holes   9 L 5522 yds SSS 67
Recs   Am–64 M Hanway
        Pro–64 L Owens (1987)
V'trs   Tues–NA Sat–NA before
        5.30pm
Fees   £8 (£10)
Loc   7 miles E of Dublin

Co Dublin

Balbriggan (1945)

Blackhall, Balbriggan
Tel   (0001) 412173
Mem   500
Sec   L Cashell
Holes   18 L 5717 metres SSS 70
Recs   Am–68 R Nugent (1987)
        Pro–71 J Burns, J Kinsella
        (1988)
V'trs   WD–U WE–M SOC
Fees   £9 (£11)
Loc   ¹/₄ mile S of Balbriggan.
        18 miles N of Dublin on N1

Ballinascorney (1971)

Ballinascorney, Tallaght
Tel   (0001) 512516
Mem   320
Holes   9 L 5322 yds SSS 66
V'trs   U
Fees   £6 (£8)

Beaverstown (1985)

Beaverstown, Donabate
Tel   (01) 436439
Mem   600
Sec   E Smyth
Holes   18 L 5662 metres SSS 71
Recs   Am–72 M Perry (1987)
V'trs   WD–U WE/BH–M SOC
Fees   £8 (£10)
Loc   4 miles N of Dublin Airport

Beech Park (1983)

Johnstown, Rathcoole
Tel   (0001) 580522/580100
Mem   500
Sec   M O'Halloran (Sec/Mgr)
Holes   18 5730 metres SSS 70
Recs   Pro–67 B Todd (1989)
V'trs   WD–U exc Tues WE–U after
        3.30pm BH–NA
Fees   £10
Loc   Rathcoole 1 mile on Kilteel
        road

Corballis (1971)

Public
Donabate
Tel   (0001) 436346
Sec   PJ Boylan (0001) 436583
Holes   18 L 4971 yds SSS 64
V'trs   WD–U Sat–NA before 10am
        Sun–NA SOC
Fees   £5 (£6)
Loc   18 miles N of Dublin.
        Donabate 2 miles

Deer Park (1974)

Public
Howth
Tel   (0001) 322624
Mem   250
Sec   J Brady
Holes   18 L 6647 yds SSS 73
        9 hole course

Recs   Am–72 N Hussey
V'trs   U
Fees   £7
Loc   8 miles NE of Dublin
Mis   Par 3 course. Pitch and
        putt

Donabate (1925)

Balcarrick, Donabate
Tel   (0001) 436059
Mem   501
Sec   Mrs C Campion (0001) 436346
Pro   H Jackson
Holes   18 L 6187 yds SSS 69
Recs   Am–67 AJ Coughlan
        Pro–65 M Murphy
V'trs   WE/BH–NA
Loc   Dublin Airport 8 miles

Dublin & County (1972)

Corballis, Donabate
Tel   (0001) 436228
Mem   250
Sec   D Bowes
Holes   Play over Corballis course

Dun Laoghaire (1910)

Dun Laoghaire, Eglinton Park, Dublin
Tel   (0001) 801055
Mem   972
Sec   T Stewart (0001) 803916
Pro   O Mulhall (0001) 801694
Holes   18 L 5463 metres SSS 69
Recs   Am–66 P McCormack Jr
        Pro–65 P Skerritt
V'trs   WD–U exc 1–2pm WE–M after
        5 pm SOC
Fees   IR£16 (£17)
Loc   7 miles S of Dublin

Forrest Little (1972)

Cloghran
Tel   (0001) 401183/401763
Mem   900
Sec   V Maslin
Pro   T Judd Jr
Holes   18 L 5865 metres SSS 70
Recs   Am–66 T Judd (1984)
        Pro–65 C O'Connor Jr (1984)
V'trs   WD–U
Fees   IR£11
Loc   Nr Dublin Airport

Hermitage (1905)

Lucan
Tel   (0001) 265396
Mem   1153
Sec   Miss K Russell
Pro   D Daly (0001) 268491
Holes   18 L 6034 metres SSS 71
Recs   Am–65 T Moraw
        Pro–65 R Davis
V'trs   U SOC
Fees   £16 (£25)
Loc   Dublin 8 miles. Lucan 1
        mile

The Island (1890)

Corballis, Donabate
Tel   (0001) 436104
Mem   600
Sec   LA O'Connor (0001) 436205
Holes   18 L 6320 yds SSS 70
Recs   Am–B Moore, B Byrne
V'trs   U WE–NA before noon
Fees   £15 (£20)
Loc   14 miles N of Dublin

Killiney (1903)

Killiney
Tel   (0001) 851983
Mem   528
Sec   JB Jordan
Pro   P O'Boyle
Holes   9 L 6201 yds SSS 69
Recs   Am–72 N Duke
        Pro–65 H Bradshaw
V'trs   U
Fees   D–£10
Loc   8 miles S of Dublin

Kilternan Hotel (1977)

Public
Kilternan
Tel   (0001) 955559
Mem   255
Sec   T Bradley
Pro   B Malone
Holes   18 L 5413 yds SSS 66
V'trs   M SOC–WD
Fees   £5 (£7)
Loc   5 miles S of Dublin

Lucan (1897)

Celbridge Road, Lucan
Tel   (0001) 280246
Mem   392
Sec   M O'Halloran
Holes   9 L 5747 metres SSS 70
Recs   Am–63 T Rogers
        Pro–67 H Bradshaw
V'trs   WD–U before 3pm WE/BH–M
        SOC–WD exc Thurs
Fees   £8
Loc   14 miles W of Dublin, nr
        Lucan

Malahide (1892)

Coast Road, Malahide
Tel   (0001) 450248
Mem   493
Holes   9 L 5568 yds SSS 67
V'trs   U WE–restricted
Fees   £8
Loc   10 miles N of Dublin.
        Malahide 1/2 mile

Newlands (1926)

Clondalkin, Dublin 22
Tel   (01) 592903
Mem   959
Sec   A O'Neill (01) 593157
Pro   P Heeney (01) 593538

Holes   18 L 6184 yds SSS 69
Recs   Am–66 R Burdon,
        P Hanley Jr
        Pro–68 C O'Connor
V'trs   Tues/Wed pm–NA WD–NA
        1.30–2.30pm WE/BH–NA SOC
Fees   IR£14
Loc   6 miles SW of Dublin

Portmarnock (1894)

Portmarnock
Tel   (01) 323082 (Fax) 01 393738
Mem   971
Sec   W Bornemann
Pro   P Townsend (01) 325157
Holes   27 'A' L 7097 yds SSS 75
        'B' L 7047 yds SSS 75
        'C' L 6596 yds SSS 74
Recs   Am–68 JB Carr
        Pro–64 S Lyle (1989)
V'trs   I WE–XL
Fees   £30 (£40) Ladies–£10 WD only
Loc   8 miles NE of Dublin

Rush (1943)

Rush
Tel   (01) 437548
Mem   322
Sec   BJ Clear
Holes   9 L 5598 metres SSS 69
Recs   Am–68 PJ Dolan
V'trs   WD–U WE–M
Fees   £7
Loc   16 miles N of Dublin

Skerries (1906)

Skerries
Tel   (01) 491204
Mem   748
Sec   AJB Taylor (01) 491567
Pro   J Kinsella (01) 490925
Holes   18 L 5852 metres SSS 70
V'trs   U
Fees   IR£12 (IR£15)
Loc   20 miles N of Dublin

Slade Valley (1970)

Lynch Park, Brittas
Tel   (01) 582207
Mem   500
Sec   P Maguire (01) 582183
Pro   G Egan
Holes   18 L 5337 metres SSS 68
Recs   Pro–64
Fees   D–£7 (£8)
Loc   8 miles W of Dublin off N4

Woodbrook (1921)

nr Bray
Tel   824799
Mem   700
Sec   D Smyth
Pro   W Kinsella
Holes   18 L 6007 metres SSS 71
V'trs   WD–U WE–phone Sec SOC
Fees   £13 (£16)
Loc   Dublin 11 miles

Co Fermanagh

Enniskillen (1896)

Castlecoole, Enniskillen
BT74 6HZ
Tel   (0365) 25250
Mem   600
Sec   CJ Greaves (0365) 24444
Holes   18 L 5574 metres SSS 70
Recs   Am–67 K Prenter
V'trs   U SOC
Fees   D–£7.50
Loc   1 mile SE of Enniskillen, on
        Castlecoole Estate

Co Galway

Athenry (1957)

Derrydonnel, Oranmore
Tel   (091) 94466
Mem   180
Sec   G Doherty (091) 44730
Holes   9 L 5448 yds SSS 67
Recs   Am–69 L Gardner
V'trs   WD–U Sun–M
Fees   £5 Sun–NA
Loc   10 miles E of Galway on
        Athenry road

Ballinasloe (1894)

Ballinasloe
Tel   (0905) 42126
Mem   450
Sec   W O'Rourke (0905) 42435
Holes   18 L 5830 yds SSS 67
Recs   Am–66 D Madden
        Pro–66 C O'Connor
V'trs   U SOC
Fees   £5
Loc   Ballinasloe 2 miles

Connemara (1973)

Aillebrack, Ballyconnelly, nr Clifden
Tel   (095) 23502
Mem   550
Sec   S Birmingham (Hon)
Holes   18 L 6186 metres SSS 73
V'trs   UH SOC–exc Sun & Open
        weeks
Fees   £8–£14
Loc   8 miles SW of Clifden

Galway (1895)

Blackrock, Salthill, Galway
Tel   (091) 23038
Mem   950
Sec   WC Caulfield (091) 22169
Pro   D Wallace
Holes   18 L 5828 metres SSS 70
Recs   Am–65 S Keenan (1987)
        Pro–67 C Greene
V'trs   Restricted Tues & Sun
Fees   £15
Loc   Galway 3 miles

Gort (1924)
Laughtyshaughnessy, Gort
Tel (091) 31336
Mem 120
Sec P Grealish (091) 31375
Pro E O'Connor
Holes 9 L 4976 metres SSS 66
Recs Am–64 G Cooney
  Pro–66 C O'Connor
V'trs U
Fees D–£5
Loc Gort 1 mile on Tubber road

Loughrea (1924)
Graigue, Loughrea
Tel (091) 41049
Mem 185
Holes 9 L 5578 yds SSS 67
Recs Am–67 S Glynn
V'trs U SOC
Fees IR£4 (£5)
Loc 1 mile N of Loughrea, off
  Dublin–Galway road. 20 miles
  E of Galway

Mount Bellew (1929)
Mount Bellew, Ballinasloe
Tel (0905) 9259
Mem 110
Sec T Meehan
Holes 9 L 5564 yds SSS 67
Recs Am–65 I Hayden
V'trs U SOC
Fees £5 W–£25 M–£40

Oughterard (1973)
Oughterard
Tel (091) 82131
Mem 500
Sec J Waters (091) 82381
Pro M Ryan
Holes 18 L 6150 yds SSS 69
Recs Am–71 N Finnegan (1989)
V'trs U
Fees £10 (£15)
Loc 15 miles W of Galway

Portumna (1907)
Portumna
Tel (0509) 41050
Mem 160
Sec G Ryan (0509) 41442
Holes 9 L 5776 yds SSS 68
Recs Am–66 M Harney (1982)
  Pro–63 H Bradshaw
V'trs U
Fees £5
Loc Portumna, on road to Ennis

Tuam (1907)
Barnacurragh, Tuam
Tel (093) 24354
Mem 340
Sec J Hughes
Holes 18 L 6321 yds SSS 70
Recs Am–69 DJ McGrath

Pro–68 R Rafferty (1983)
V'trs Sun–NA SOC–WD
Fees £7
Loc 20 miles N of Galway

Co Kerry

Ballybunion (1896)
Ballybunion
Tel (068) 27146
Mem 800
Sec S Walsh
Pro E Higgins (068) 27209
Holes Old 18 L 6542 yds
  New 18 L 6477 yds
Recs Am–67 P Mulcare
V'trs U SOC
Fees D–£20 W–£70 M–£100

Ceann Sibeal (1924)
Ballyferriter, Tralee
Tel (066) 56255
Mem 122
Sec G Partington (066) 51657
Pro D O'Connor
Holes 18 L 6600 yds SSS 71
V'trs U SOC
Fees D–£10 W–£50 SOC–£7
Loc Dingle Peninsula,
  nr Ballyferriter

Dooks (1889)
Glenbeigh
Tel (066) 68205/68200(members)
Mem 440
Sec M Shanahan (066) 67370
Holes 18 L 5346 metres SSS 68
Recs Am–67 G Sullivan
V'trs WD–UH WE/BH–check first
  SOC–H
Fees £15 (£15)
Loc 3 miles N of Glenbeigh, on
  Ring of Kerry

Kenmare (1903)
Kenmare
Tel (064) 41291
Mem 150
Sec SW Rowe
Holes 9 L 4400 metres SSS 64
Recs Am–64 B Mulcahy
V'trs U
Fees £6

Killarney (1891)
O'Mahoney's Point, Killarney
Tel (064) 31034
Mem 740
Sec T Prendergast
Pro T Coveney (064) 31615
Holes Mahoney's Point 18 L 6152
  metres SSS 72; Killeen 18 L
  6369 metres SSS 73

Recs Mahoney's Point: Am–68
  S Coyne(1968)
  Killeen: Am–73 DF O'Sullivan
V'trs U H SOC
Fees £18
Loc 3 miles W of Killarney

Parknasilla (1974)
Parknasilla
Tel (064) 45122
Mem 30
Sec M Walsh (064) 45233
Pro C McCarthy (064) 45172
Holes 9 L 4834 yds SSS 65
V'trs U
Fees £7
Loc Great Southern Hotel, 2 miles
  E of Sneem village

Tralee (1904)
West Barrow, Ardfert
Tel (066) 36379
Mem 500
Sec JW Kleynhans
Holes 18 L 6210 metres SSS 72
Recs Am–66 G O'Sullivan
V'trs WD–U WE–U after noon
  SOC–WD/Sat
Fees £12 (£14)
Loc 8 miles W of Tralee

Waterville (1889)
Ring of Kerry, Waterville
Tel (0667) 4102
Mem 252
Sec LA Morrissey
Pro L Higgins (0667) 4237
Holes 18 L 7184 yds SSS 74
Recs Pro–65 L Higgins
V'trs U H SOC
Fees £18
Loc Ring of Kerry

Co Kildare

Athy (1906)
Geraldine, Athy
Tel (0507) 31729
Mem 250
Sec M Hannon (0507) 31171
Holes 9 L 6158 yds SSS 69
V'trs WD–U Sat–M SOC–WD
Fees £4 (£6)

Bodenstown (1983)
Bodenstown, Sallins
Tel (045) 97096
Mem 650
Sec P Place
Pro T Halpin
Holes 18 L 7031 yds SSS 72

Cill Dara (1920)

Little Curragh, Kildare Town
Tel   (045) 21433
Mem 200
Sec   P Gill (045) 31946
Holes 9 L 5440 metres SSS 68
Recs   Am–67 NP McAlinden
V'trs   U
Fees   £4 (£6)
Loc   1 mile E of Kildare

Clongowes (1966)

Clongowes Wood College, Naas
Tel   Clongowes Wood 68202
Mem 100
Sec   A Pierce
Holes 9 L 5374 yds SSS 65
Recs   Am–65 V Murray (1987)
V'trs   NA
Loc   Clane 2 miles. Naas 6 miles

Curragh (1883)

Curragh
Tel   (045) 41238/41714
Mem 500 160(L)
Sec   T Byrne (Hon)
Pro   P Lawlor
Holes 18 L 6003 metres SSS 71
Recs   Am–67 S Conlon
       Pro–69 A Whiston
V'trs   WD–check with Sec
Fees   IR£8 (IR£10) 1989 prices
Loc   3 miles S of Newbridge
Mis   Golf played here since 1852.
       Oldest club in the Republic

Knockanally (1985)

Donadea, North Kildare
Tel   (045) 69322
Mem 165
Sec   N Lyons
Pro   P Hickey
Holes 18 L 6484 yds SSS 72
Recs   Pro–66 K O'Donnell,
       D James (1988)
V'trs   U
Fees   £8 (£10)
Loc   Maynooth 7 miles. Kilcock
       5 miles. Enfield 3 miles on
       Dublin–Galway road

Naas (1896)

Kerdiffstown, Naas
Tel   (045) 97509
Mem 514
Holes 9 L 6233 yds SSS 70
V'trs   U SOC
Loc   2 miles N of Naas

Co Kilkenny

Callan (1930)

Geraldine, Callan
Tel   (056) 25136
Mem 150
Sec   M Duggan (052) 54362
Holes 9 L 5844 yds SSS 68

Recs   Am–70 J Madden
       Pro–71 M Kavanagh
V'trs   U SOC
Fees   £4 (£5)
Loc   1 mile SE of Callan.
       Kilkenny 10 miles

Castlecomer (1935)

Castlecomer
Tel   (056) 41139
Mem 150
Sec   S Farrell (056) 41258
Holes 9 L 6985 yds SSS 71
Recs   Am–70 M Curry (1986)
V'trs   U
Fees   £5 (£7)
Loc   11 miles N of Kilkenny

Kilkenny (1896)

Glendine, Kilkenny
Tel   (056) 22125
Mem 900
Sec   S O'Neill
Pro   M Kavanagh (056) 61730
Holes 18 L 6374 yds SSS 70
Recs   Am–68 D White, B Cashell
       Pro–68 B Todd
V'trs   U
Fees   £10 (£12)
Loc   1 mile N of Kilkenny

Co Laois

Abbey Leix (1895)

Abbey Leix, Portlaoise
Tel   (0502) 31450
Mem 207
Holes 9 L 5680 yds SSS 67
V'trs   U
Fees   £4 (£5)
Loc   60 miles SW of Dublin on
       Cork road

Heath (Portlaoise) (1930)

Portlaoise
Tel   (0502) 46533
Mem 375
Sec   J McNamara (0502) 21327
Pro   E Doyle (0502) 46622
Holes 18 L 6247 yds SSS 70
Recs   Am–67 T Tyrrell (1983)
V'trs   U
Fees   £6 (£9)
Loc   4 miles E of Portlaoise
Mis   Floodlit driving range

Mountrath (1929)

Knockanina, Mountrath
Mem 150
Sec   S Reynolds (0502) 32558
Holes 9 L 5300 yds SSS 66
Recs   Am–67 S Carter
V'trs   U
Fees   £4
Loc   Mountrath 2 miles

Portarlington (1909)

Garryhinch, Portarlington
Tel   (0502) 23115
Mem 280
Holes 9 L 5354 metres SSS 68
V'trs   U
Fees   £5 (£6)
Loc   Between Portarlington and
       Mountmellick on L116

Rathdowney (1931)

Rathdowney, Portlaoise
Tel   (0505) 46170
Mem 119
Sec   KF McDermott
Holes 9 L 6086 yds SSS 69
Recs   Am–71 J O'Malley
V'trs   U SOC
Fees   D–£5
Loc   1 mile S of Rathdowney

Co Leitrim

Ballinamore (1941)

Ballinamore
Tel   (078) 44346
Mem 86
Sec   P Reynolds (078) 31410
Holes 9 L 5680 yds SSS 67
Recs   Am–69 P Duigan
V'trs   U SOC
Fees   £3 W–£15
Loc   1¹/₂ miles N of Ballinamore

Carrick-on-Shannon (1910)

Woodbrook, Carrick-on-Shannon
Tel   (078) 67015
Mem 169
Holes 9 L 5584 yds SSS 68
V'trs   U

Co Limerick

Adare Manor (1900)

Adare
Tel   (061) 86204
Mem 350
Sec   T Healy
Holes 9 L 5145 metres SSS 67
V'trs   WD–U WE–M
Fees   D–£10
Loc   10 miles S of Limerick

Castletroy (1937)

Castletroy, Limerick
Tel   (061) 335261
Mem 1066
Sec   L Hayes (061) 335753
Pro   N Cassidy (061) 338283
Holes 18 L 5793 metres SSS 71
V'trs   WD–U Sat am–U Sat pm/Sun–M
       SOC–Mon/Wed/Fri
Fees   £10 (£10)
Loc   2¹/₂ miles N of Limerick on
       Dublin road

Limerick (1891)

Ballyclough, Limerick
Tel   (061) 44083
Mem 1070
Sec   D McDonogh (061) 45146
Pro   J Cassidy (061) 42492
Holes 18 L 5767 yds SSS 70
Recs Am–65 W Rice
      Pro–67 F McGloin, J Kinsella
V'trs WD–U before 5pm exc Tues
      WE–M SOC–WD
Fees £10
Loc   3 miles S of Limerick

Newcastle West (1939)

Newcastle West
Tel   (069) 62015
Mem 167
Holes 9 L 5482 yds SSS 67
V'trs U
Loc   ¹/₂ mile S of Newcastle West

Co Londonderry

Brown Trout

209 Agivey Road, Aghadovey,
Coleraine
Tel   (0265) 868209
Mem 68
Holes 9 L 2500 yds SSS 68
V'trs U SOC
Fees £3 (£5)
Loc   8 miles S of Coleraine

Castlerock (1901)

Circular Road, Castlerock
Tel   (0265) 848314
Mem 920
Sec   RG McBride
Pro   R Kelly
Holes 18 L 6121 metres SSS 72
      9 L 2457 metres SSS 34
Recs Am–68 TBC Hoey
V'trs WD–U SOC Tues & Fri–Ladies
      preference
Fees £10 (£20) 9 hole–£3 (£5)
Loc   5 miles W of Coleraine on A2

City of Derry (1913)

49 Victoria Road, Londonderry
Tel   (0504) 311610/46369
Mem 753
Sec   PJ Doherty
Pro   M Doherty (0504) 311496
Holes Prehen 18 L 6406 yds SSS 71;
      Dunhugh 9 L 4708 yds SSS 63
Recs Am–68 D Ballentine
V'trs WD–U before 4pm –M after
      4pm WE–U H SOC
Fees Prehen £6 (£8) Dunhugh £3
Loc   3 miles from E end of
      Craigavon Bridge towards
      Strabane

Kilrea (1920)

Drumagarner Road, Kilrea
(All correspondence to Sec:
125 Tamlaght Road, Rasharkin)
Tel   (02665) 71397
Mem 240
Sec   WR McIlmoyle
Holes 9 L 4326 yds SSS 62
Recs Am–61 R Rees (1982)
V'trs Tues & Wed–NA after 6pm
      (Apr–Aug) Sat–NA after
      12.30pm
Fees £5 (£5)
Loc   ¹/₂ mile from Kilrea on
      Maghera road

Moyola Park (1976)

Shanemullagh, Castledawson,
Magherafelt BT45 8DG
Tel   (0648) 68468
Mem 600
Sec   M A Steele
Pro   V Teague (0648) 68830
Holes 18 L 6517 yds SSS 71
Recs Am–71 T McNeill
      Pro–70 D Smyth
V'trs U SOC
Fees £8 (£10)
Loc   40 miles N of Belfast by M2

Portstewart (1894)

117 Strand Road, Portstewart BT55 7PG
Tel   (026 583) 2015
Mem 530
Sec   M Moss BA (026 583)
      3839
Pro   A Hunter (026 583) 2601
Holes Strand 18 L 6784 yds
      SSS 72
      Town 18 L 4733 yds SSS 62
Recs Strand Am–69 TBC Hoey,
      D Ballentine
      Pro–66 E Polland
V'trs SOC–by arrangement
Fees Strand £12 (£17) W–£50
      Town £4 (£6) W–£20
Loc   W boundary of Portstewart

Co Longford

Co Longford (1900)

Glack, Dublin Road, Longford
Tel   (043) 46310
Mem 327
Pro   J Frawley
Holes 18 L 5912 yds SSS 68
V'trs U
Loc   Longford ¹/₂ mile

Co Louth

Ardee (1911)

Townparks, Ardee
Tel   (041) 53227
Mem 390
Holes 18 L 5833 yds SSS 69
V'trs U
Fees £8 (£9)
Loc   ¹/₂ mile N of Ardee

County Louth (1892)

Baltray, Drogheda
Tel   (041) 22327
Mem 350
Sec   M Delany (041) 22329
Pro   P McGuirk (041) 22444
Holes 18 L 6978 yds SSS 72
Recs Am–66 F Gannon
      Pro–65 J Heggarty
V'trs By prior arrangement
Fees On request
Loc   3 miles NE of Drogheda

Dundalk (1905)

Blackrock, Dundalk
Tel   (042) 21379
Mem 850
Sec   P Moriarty (042) 21731
Pro   J Cassidy (042) 22102
Holes 18 L 6115 metres SSS 72
V'trs U SOC
Fees £10 (£12)
Loc   3 miles S of Dundalk
Mis   Driving range

Greenore (1896)

Greenore
Tel   (042) 73212
Mem 250
Sec   E McCarten (042) 34711
Holes 18 L 5614 metres SSS 69
Recs Am–67 S McParland
      Pro–67 C O'Connor Sr
V'trs WD–before 5pm SOC
      WE–before noon
Fees £8 (£10)
Loc   15 miles N of Dundalk on
      Greenore road

Co Mayo

Achill Island (1951)

Keel, Achill Island
Tel   (098) 43202
Mem 40
Sec   P Lavelle
Holes 9 L 2723 yds SSS 66
Recs Am–58 P Lavelle (1989)
V'trs U H SOC
Fees £3
Loc   Keel

Ballina (1910)

Mosgrove, Shanaghy, Ballina
Tel   (096) 21050
Mem 128 58(L)
Sec   V Frawley (096) 21795
Holes 9 L 5702 yds SSS 66
Recs Am–64 J Corcoran (1984)
      Pro–66 C O'Connor
V'trs U
Fees £5 (£5) W–£20
Loc   1 mile E of Ballina

Ballinrobe (1895)

Public
Ballinrobe, Claremorris
Tel (092) 41448
Mem 200
Sec P Holian (092) 41659
Holes 9 L 5790 yds SSS 68
Recs Am–67 B Finlay
V'trs U Sun–NA SOC
Fees £5 W–£15 M–£40
Loc 1½ miles NW of Ballinrobe on Castlebar road

Ballyhaunis (1929)

Coolnaha, Ballyhaunis
Tel (0907) 30014
Mem 162
Sec JG Forde (0907) 30013
Holes 9 L 5378 metres SSS 68
Recs Am–68 V Freyne (1986) Pro–70
V'trs U exc Thurs (Ladies Day)–M SOC–WD
Fees £5
Loc 2 miles N of Ballyhaunis. Horan Airport 7 miles

Belmullet (1925)

Belmullet, Ballina
Tel (097) 81093
Mem 50
Sec P McIntyre
Holes 9 L 2829 yds SSS 67
V'trs U
Fees £3
Loc 3 miles W of Belmullet

Castlebar (1910)

Rocklands, Castlebar
Tel (094) 21649
Mem 260
Sec B MacDonald
Holes 18 L 6109 yds SSS 69
Recs Am–67 J Langan
V'trs U
Fees £8
Loc 1 mile from Castlebar towards Galway

Claremorris (1918)

Claremorris
Tel (094) 71527
Mem 140
Sec TJ Farragher (094) 71082
Holes 9 L 6454 yds SSS 69
Recs Am–68 P Killeen Pro–63 C O'Connor
V'trs U
Fees £4 W–£15
Loc 2 miles S of Claremorris

Mulrany (1887)

Public
Mulrany, Westport
Tel (098) 36185
Mem 120
Sec Fr M Kenny (098) 36107

Holes 9 L 6380 yds SSS 70
V'trs U
Fees D–£3 W–£15
Loc Castlebar 20 miles. Westport 18 miles

Swinford (1922)

Brabazon Park, Swinford
Tel (094) 51378
Mem 101
Holes 9 L 5230 yds SSS 65
V'trs U
Fees D–£5 (£12) W–£25
Loc Off Dublin–Castlebar road

Westport (1908)

Carowholly, Westport
Tel (098) 25113
Mem 393
Pro K Mowgaw
Holes 18 L 6355 yds SSS 73
V'trs U
Fees £9 (£10)
Loc Westport 2 miles

Co Meath

Blackbush (1987)

Thomastown, Dunshaughlin
Tel (01) 250021
Mem 650
Holes 18 L 7000 yds SSS 73
      9 L 2800 yds SSS 35
V'trs WD–U WE–NA before 4pm SOC;9 hole course–U
Fees 18 hole–£7 (£10)
      9 hole–£5 (£8)
Loc ½ mile E of Dunshaughlin off N4. Dublin 20 miles
Mis Driving range

Gormanston College (1961)

Franciscan College, Gormanston
Tel (0001) 412203
Mem 160
Sec Br Laurence Brady
Pro B Browne
Holes 9 L 1973 metres SSS
V'trs NA
Loc 22 miles N of Dublin

Headfort (1928)

Kells
Tel (046) 40857
Mem 882
Pro J Purcell (046) 40639
Holes 18 L 6350 yds SSS 70
V'trs U
Fees £8 (£11)
Loc Kells ½ mile

Laytown & Bettystown (1909)

Bettystown
Tel (041) 27170
Mem 777
Pro RJ Browne
Holes 18 L 6254 yds SSS 69
V'trs U SOC–WD
Fees £10 (£15)
Loc 25 miles N of Dublin

Royal Tara (1923)

Bellinter, Navan
Tel (046) 25244/25584
Mem 900
Sec D Foley
Pro A Whiston
Holes 18 L 5757 metres SSS 70
Recs Am–66 M McQuaid
V'trs U
Fees £10 (£12)
Loc 25 miles N of Dublin off N3

Trim (1970)

Newtownmoynagh, Trim
Tel (046) 31463
Mem 350
Sec PJ Darby (046) 31438
Holes 9 L 6266 yds SSS 70
Recs Am–64 P Rayfus
V'trs WD–U exc Ladies day WE–restricted SOC–exc Sun
Fees £8
Loc 2½ miles SW of Trim

Co Monaghan

Castleblayney (1985)

Castleblayney
Mem 140
Sec D McGlynn (042) 40197
Holes 9 L 2678 yds SSS 66
Recs Am–70 J McCarthy (1987)
V'trs U SOC
Fees £3 (£4)
Loc Town centre

Clones (1913)

Scotshouse, Clones
Tel (049) 56017
Mem 217
Holes 9 L 5570 yds SSS 67
V'trs U

Nuremore (1964)

Nuremore, Carrickmacross
Tel (042) 61438
Mem 138
Holes 9 L 6032 yds SSS 69
V'trs U

For explanation of abbreviations, see page 460.

Rossmore (1906)

Rossmore Park, Monaghan
Tel   Monaghan 81316
Mem   310
Sec   B Dawson
Holes 9 L 5859 yds SSS 68
Recs   Am–64 R Berry
V'trs WD–U WE/BH–U exc comp
       days SOC
Fees   £4 (£5)
Loc   3 miles on Monaghan–Cootehill
       road

Co Offaly

Birr (1893)

The Glenns, Birr
Tel   (0509) 20082
Mem   320
Sec   P O'Gorman (0509) 20271
Holes 18 L 6216 yds SSS 70
Recs   Am–66 JB Carr
       Pro–68 RJ Browne
V'trs U SOC–exc Sun
Fees   D–£6
Loc   Birr 2 miles

Edenderry (1910)

Kishavanna, Edenderry
Tel   (0405) 31072
Mem   234
Holes 9 L 5791 yds SSS 69
V'trs U
Fees   £5 (£6)
Loc   1 mile E of Edenderry

Tullamore (1896)

Brookfield, Tullamore
Tel   (0506) 21439
Mem   711
Sec   WM Rossiter (0506) 21310
Pro   JE Kelly
Holes 18 L 6314 yds SSS 71
Recs   Am–64 D White
       Pro–68 H Boyle, J Martin,
       D Jones
V'trs WD–U exc Tues (Ladies Day)
       Sat–M 12.30–3pm Sun–NA SOC
Fees   £8 D–£10
Loc   2¹⁄₂ miles S of Tullamore
Mis   Buggies for hire

Co Roscommon

Athlone (1892)

Hodson Bay, Athlone
Tel   (0902) 92073/92235
Mem   750
Sec   J Reynolds
Pro   M Quinn
Holes 18 L 6500 yds SSS 70
Recs   Am–63 P Egan
       Pro–70 M Quinn
V'trs U SOC–WD
Fees   £10
Loc   Shores of Lough Ree

Ballaghaderreen (1937)

Ballaghaderreen
Mem   112
Sec   Rev L Henry
Holes 9 L 5663 yds SSS 65
Recs   Am–68 F McGovern (1989)
Fees   £5
Loc   Ballaghaderreen 3 miles

Boyle (1911)

Roscommon Road, Boyle
Tel   (079) 62594
Mem   150
Sec   RP Nangle
Holes 9 L 4957 metres SSS 66
Recs   Am–65 A Wynne (1987)
V'trs U SOC
Fees   £4
Loc   Boyle 1¹⁄₂ miles

Castlerea (1905)

Clonalis, Castlerea
Tel   (0907) 20068
Mem   145
Sec   B Stenson (0907) 20279
Holes 9 L 5466 yds SSS 66
Recs   Am–63 R de Lacy Staunton
V'trs U
Fees   £3 (£5)
Loc   Knock Road, Castlerea

Roscommon (1904)

Mote Park, Roscommon
Tel   (0903) 6382
Mem   158
Holes 9 L 5657 yds SSS 69
V'trs U
Fees   £3
Loc   1 mile E of Roscommon

Co Sligo

Ballymote (1940)

Ballymote
Tel   Ballymote 3460
Mem   42
Sec   P Mullen
Holes 9 L 5032 yds SSS 65
Recs   Am–67 P Mullen
V'trs U
Fees   £2
Loc   Carrigans

County Sligo (1894)

Rosses Point
Tel   (071) 77186
Mem   762
Sec   GA Eakins (071) 77134
Pro   J McGonigle (071) 77171
Holes 18 L 6003 metres SSS 72
Recs   Am–65 MD O'Brien
       Pro–67 C O'Connor Sr
V'trs WD–U WE/BH–M 9–10.30am
       and 1.30–2.45pm SOC
Fees   £15 (£15)
Loc   5 miles NW of Sligo

Enniscrone (1931)

Enniscrone
Tel   (096) 36297
Mem   271
Sec   JM Fleming
Holes 18 L 6487 yds SSS 71
Recs   Am–70 J Corcoran, M Canavan
       Pro–71 C O'Connor Sr,
       J O'Leary
V'trs U
Fees   D–£7
Loc   Ballina road, S of Enniscrone

Strandhill (1932)

Strandhill
Tel   (071) 68188
Mem   270
Sec   J Noone (071) 63292
Holes 18 L 5937 yds SSS 68
V'trs WD–U WE/BH–restricted SOC
Fees   IR£7 (IR£8)
Loc   6 miles W of Sligo

Co Tipperary

Cahir Park (1968)

Kilcommon, Cahir
Tel   (052) 41474
Mem   187
Sec   K Murphy
Holes 9 L 6262 yds SSS 69
Recs   Am–68
V'trs U SOC–WD/Sat
Fees   £6 (£6)
Loc   1 mile S of Cahir

Carrick-on-Suir (1939)

Garravone, Carrick-on-Suir
Tel   (051) 40047
Mem   180
Sec   MG Kelly
Holes 9 L 5948 yds SSS 68
Recs   Am–67 C Carleton (1987)
V'trs U SOC–WD/Sat
Fees   £5
Loc   2 miles on Dungarvan road

Clonmel (1911)

Lyreanearle, Mountain Road, Clonmel
Tel   (052) 21138
Mem   538
Sec   Mrs M Lynch (052) 21508
Pro   R Hayes
Holes 18 L 6330 yds SSS 70
Recs   Am–63 M O'Neill
V'trs U
Fees   £6 (£8)
Loc   3 miles SW of Clonmel

Nenagh (1929)

Beechwood, Nenagh
Tel   (067) 31476
Mem   600
Sec   B O'Brien (Hon)

Pro   J Coyle (067) 33242
Holes   18 L 5483 metres SSS 68
Recs   Am–64 P Lyons (1984)
V'trs   U SOC
Fees   £7 Sat–£9 Sun–£12
Loc   3 miles NE of Nenagh on
   Limerick–Dublin road

Rockwell College (1964)

Rockwell College, Cashel
Mem   88
Sec   Rev P Downes (062) 61444
Holes   9 L 4136 yds SSS 60
V'trs   NA
Loc   3 miles S of Cashel on main
   Cork–Dublin road

Roscrea (1893)

Roscrea
Tel   (0505) 21130
Mem   337
Sec   SM Deeley (0505) 21225
Holes   9 L 6059 yds SSS 69
Recs   Am–65 D Corcoran
V'trs   U
Fees   £5
Loc   2 miles on Dublin road

Templemore (1970)

Manna South, Templemore
Tel   Templemore 53
Mem   210
Sec   JK Moloughney
   (0504) 31720
Holes   9 L 5442 yds SSS 66
V'trs   U exc Sun SOC
Fees   £4 (£5)
Loc   1/2 mile S of Templemore

Thurles (1909)

Turtulla, Thurles
Tel   (0504) 21983/22466
Mem   555
Sec   T Ryan (0504) 23787
Pro   S Hunt
Holes   18 L 5904 metres SSS 71
Recs   Am–66 DF O'Sullivan
   Pro–70 H Bradshaw
V'trs   WD–U Sun–NA
Fees   £9 Sat–£10
Loc   1 mile S of Thurles on the
   Horse & Jockey road

Tipperary (1896)

Rathanny, Tipperary
Tel   (062) 51119
Mem   321
Holes   9 L 6074 yds SSS 69
Recs   Am–65 AD Pierse
V'trs   U
Loc   Tipperary 1 mile

Co Tyrone

Dungannon (1890)

Mullaghmore, Dungannon
Tel   (08687) 22098
Mem   425
Sec   J McCausland (08687) 22095
Holes   18 L 5914 yds SSS 68
Recs   Am–62 D Clarke (1989)
V'trs   U
Fees   £7 (£9)
Loc   1 mile W of Dungannon

Fintona (1896)

Ecclesville Demesne, Fintona
Tel   (0662) 841480
Mem   250
Sec   G McNulty (0662) 841514
Holes   9 L 5716 yds SSS 70
Recs   Am–68 E Donnell
   Pro–69 L Higgins, J Kinsilla,
   L Robinson
V'trs   U exc comp days SOC–WD
Fees   D–£5 (£10)
Loc   8 miles S of Omagh

Killymoon (1889)

200 Killymoon Road, Cookstown
BT80 8TW
Tel   (064 87) 63762/62254
Mem   700
Sec   Dr J McBride
Pro   P Leonard
Holes   18 L 5498 metres SSS 69
Recs   Am–64 A O'Neill
   Pro–65 D Smyth
V'trs   U
Fees   £9 (£13)
Loc   1 mile S of Cookstown off
   A29

Newtownstewart (1914)

38 Golf Course Road, Newtownstewart
BT78 4HU
Tel   (06626) 61466
Mem   500
Sec   JE Mackin (06626) 71487
Holes   18 L 5468 metres SSS 69
Recs   Am–67 G Forbes (1987)
   Pro–66 J Fisher
V'trs   U SOC
Fees   £5 (£7) W–£20 M–£40
Loc   2 miles SW of Newtownstewart
   on B84

Omagh (1910)

83A Dublin Road, Omagh
BT78 1HQ
Tel   (0662) 3160/41442
Mem   462
Sec   JA McElholm (0662) 3749
Holes   18 L 5208 metres SSS 67
Recs   Am–63 H Johnston (1985)
V'trs   U
Fees   £5 (£7) M–£25
Loc   Omagh 1/2 mile

Strabane (1908)

Ballycolman, Strabane
Tel   (0504) 382271
Mem   600
Sec   JJ Harron (0504) 883093
Holes   18 L 5458 metres SSS 69
Recs   Am–64 C Patton
   Pro–69
V'trs   U
Fees   £5 (£8)
Loc   1/2 mile from Strabane, nr Fir
   Trees Hotel

Co Waterford

Dungarvan (1924)

Ballinacourty, Dungarvan
Tel   (058) 41605
Mem   340
Sec   N Hayes
Holes   9 L 5721 metres SSS 69
Recs   Am–66 J McHenry (1984)
V'trs   U SOC–WD (Apr–Sept)
   SOC–WE (Oct–Mar)
Fees   D–£7 SOC–£5
Loc   3 miles E of Dungarvan.
   30 miles W of Waterford

Lismore (1965)

Lismore, Ballyin
Tel   (058) 54026
Mem   200
Sec   M O'Shea (058) 54184
Pro   T Maher
Holes   9 L 5127 metres SSS 67
Recs   Am–65 T Murphy (1987)
   Pro–65 L Higgins (1978)
V'trs   U SOC–exc Sun
Fees   £5 W–£20
Loc   1 mile N of Lismore

Tramore (1894)

Tramore
Tel   (051) 86170
Mem   550
Sec   R Brennan
Pro   P McDaid
Holes   18 L 5999 metres SSS 71
Recs   Am–66 E Power
   Pro–66 H Boyle
V'trs   U
Fees   £12 1989 prices
Loc   7 miles S of Waterford

Waterford (1912)

Newrath, Waterford
Tel   (051) 76748
Mem   641
Sec   J Condon
Holes   18 L 6232 metres SSS 70
V'trs   U

For explanation of abbreviations, see page 460.

Co Westmeath

Moate (1940)

Moate
Tel   (0902) 81271
Mem   252
Sec   A Power
Holes 9 L 5348 yds SSS 66
V'trs U
Fees   £4 (£5)
Loc   1 mile N of Moate

Mullingar (1894)

Belvedere, Mullingar
Tel   (044) 48366
Mem   586
Pro   J Burns
Holes 18 L 6370 yds SSS 71
V'trs U
Loc   3 miles S of Mullingar

Co Wexford

Courtown (1936)

Courtown Harbour, Gorey
Tel   (055) 25166
Mem   480
Sec   J Sheehan (055) 21533
Pro   J Coone
Holes 18 L 6398 yds SSS 70
Recs   Am–67 J McGill (1987)
       Pro–68 M Murphy (1976)
V'trs U SOC
Fees   £7 (£10)
Loc   2½ miles SE of Gorey

Enniscorthy (1908)

Knockmarshal, Enniscorthy
Tel   (054) 33191
Mem   300
Sec   J Winters
Holes 18 L 5332 metres SSS 68
V'trs U SOC–exc Sun
Fees   £5 (£7)
Loc   1 mile SW of Enniscorthy

New Ross (1917)

Tinneranny, New Ross
Tel   (051) 21433
Mem   250
Sec   (051) 21451
Holes 9 L 5578 metres SSS 69
Recs   Am–66 M O'Brien
       Pro–65 C O'Connor
V'trs U exc Sun SOC
Fees   £5 (£7)
Loc   1 mile W of New Ross

Rosslare (1908)

Strand, Rosslare
Tel   (053) 32113
Mem   400
Sec   Miss A O'Keefe (053) 32203
Pro   A Skerritt (053) 32238
Holes 18 L 6502 yds SSS 71
Recs   Am–65 D Noonan (1978)

V'trs U SOC
Fees   £8 (£10)
Loc   10 miles S of Wexford

Wexford (1966)

Mulgannon, Wexford
Tel   (053) 42238
Mem   300
Sec   A Doyle (053) 44720
Holes 18 L 6109 yds SSS 69
V'trs U SOC
Fees   £6 (£7)
Loc   Wexford ½ mile

Co Wicklow

Arklow (1927)

Abbeylands, Arklow
Tel   (0402) 32492
Mem   370
Holes 18 L 5770 yds SSS 68
V'trs WD–U Sat–U after 5pm
       Sun–NA SOC–Mon–Sat
Fees   £7 (£8)
Loc   Arklow ½ mile

Baltinglass (1928)

Baltinglass
Tel   (0508) 81530
Mem   350
Sec   D Lord
Pro   M Murphy
Holes 9 L 6070 yds SSS 68
Recs   Am–66 D Kilcoyne,
       Rev McDonnell
       Pro–70 S Hunt
V'trs U SOC
Fees   £4 (£6)
Loc   38 miles S of Dublin

Blainroe (1978)

Blainroe
Tel   (0404) 68168
Mem   600
Sec   W O'Sullivan
Pro   J McDonald
Holes 18 L 6681 yds SSS 72
V'trs U
Fees   £7 (£12) W–£35
Loc   3½ miles S of Wicklow
       on coast

Bray (1897)

Ravenswell Road, Bray
Tel   (0001) 862484
Mem   272
Sec   JM McStravick
Pro   M Walby
Holes 9 L 5230 metres SSS 70
V'trs U before 6pm SOC–WD
Fees   £8
Loc   12 miles S of Dublin

Coollattin (1950)

Coollattin, Shillelagh
Tel   (055) 29125
Mem   350
Sec   R McCrea (055) 26302
Holes 9 L 6070 yds SSS 69
Fees   £4 (£7)
Loc   50 miles S of Dublin

Delgany (1908)

Delgany
Tel   (0404) 874645/874833
Mem   800
Sec   J Deally (0404) 874536
Pro   E Darcy (0404) 874536
Holes 18 L 5249 yds SSS 69
Recs   Am–63
V'trs U exc comp days
       SOC–Mon/Thurs/Fri
Fees   £11 (£14)
Loc   Greystones 2 miles

Greystones (1895)

Greystones
Tel   (0001) 876624
Mem   850
Sec   O Walsh (0001) 874136
Pro   K Daly
Holes 18 L 5387 metres SSS 68
Recs   Am–67
       Pro–66
V'trs Mid–week
Fees   £12 (£15)
Loc   Greystones, 18 miles S of
       Dublin

Old Conna

Ferndale Road, Bray
Tel   (0001) 826055
Mem   550
Pro   N Murphy (0001) 820842
Holes 18 L 6600 yds SSS 72
V'trs WD–U before 4pm SOC
Fees   £12
Loc   2 miles N of Bray

Wicklow (1904)

Dunbur Road, Wicklow
Tel   (0404) 67379
Mem   408
Sec   J Kelly
Holes 9 L 5556 yds SSS 66
Recs   Am–65 W Mitchell, LJ Mooney
       Pro–65 K Daly (1989)
V'trs SOC–WD
Fees   £6 (£10)

Woodenbridge (1884)

Arklow
Tel   (0402) 5202
Mem   210
Sec   TH Crummy
Holes 9 L 6104 yds SSS 68
Recs   Am–67 M Holden, J Kavanagh
V'trs U exc Sat
Fees   £9 (£10)
Loc   45 miles S of Dublin.
       4 miles W of Arklow

Scotland
Border Region

Berwickshire

Duns (1894)

Hardens Road, Duns
Mem	200
Sec	A Campbell (0361) 82717
Holes	9 L 5826 yds SSS 68
Recs	Am–66 WV Paton, G Clark,
	G Wood
V'trs	U SOC
Fees	£6 (£6)
Loc	1 mile W of Duns off A6105

Eyemouth (1880)

Gunsgreen House, Eyemouth
Tel	(08907) 50551
Mem	180
Sec	JW Fleming
Pro	C Maltman
Holes	9 L 2369 metres SSS 65
Recs	Am–63 J Patterson, JD Blackie
V'trs	U
Fees	D–£5

The Hirsel (1948)

Coldstream
Tel	(0890) 2678
Mem	190
Sec	GH Toyne (0890) 2568
Holes	9 L 5680 yds SSS 68
Recs	Am–66 J Martin (1987)
V'trs	U SOC
Fees	£5 (£7)
Loc	1/2 mile W of Coldstream
	(A697)

Lauder (1896)

Public
Lauder
Tel	(05782) 409
Mem	95
Sec	G Bryson
Holes	9 L 6002 yds SSS 70
Recs	Am–70 JFC Jeffries
V'trs	U
Fees	WD–£3.50 Sun–£4
Loc	1/2 mile W of Lauder

Peeblesshire

Innerleithen (1886)

Leithen Water, Leithen Road,
Innerleithen
Tel	(0896) 830951
Mem	175
Sec	S Wyse (0896) 830071
Holes	9 L 5820 yds SSS 68
Recs	Am–66 WN Smith
V'trs	U
Fees	£5 (£5) W–£18
Loc	Innerleithen 1 1/2 miles
	on Heriot Road

Peebles (1892)

Public
Kirkland Street, Peebles
Tel	(0721) 20197
Mem	600
Sec	G Garvie
Holes	18 L 6137 yds SSS 69
Recs	Am–64 D Campbell
	Pro–70 RDBM Shade
V'trs	U
Fees	£6.50 D–£9 (£9 D–£12) W–£40
Loc	23 miles S of Edinburgh

West Linton (1890)

West Linton EH46 7HN
Tel	(0968) 60463
Mem	615
Sec	G Scott (0968) 75843
Pro	D Stewart (0968) 60256
Holes	18 L 6132 yds SSS 69
Recs	Am–67 S MacKenzie (1989)
	Pro–71 B Gallacher
V'trs	U Sun–NA
Fees	£8 D–£10 (£9 D–£12)
Loc	NW Peebles

Roxburghshire

Hawick (1877)

Vertish Hill, Hawick
Tel	(0450) 72293
Mem	510
Sec	GA Rennie (Hon)
Holes	18 L 5929 yds SSS 69
Recs	Am–63 AJ Ballantyne
	Pro–64 N Faldo
V'trs	U
Fees	£5 D–£8 (£8)
Loc	1/2 mile S of Hawick
Mis	Golfing package D–£15

Jedburgh (1892)

Dunion Road, Jedburgh
Tel	(0835) 63587
Mem	200
Sec	K McDonald (0835) 63587
Holes	9 L 5492 yds SSS 67
Recs	Am–64 E Redpath (1987)
V'trs	U
Fees	£5 (£6)
Loc	Jedburgh 1 mile

Kelso (1887)

Berrymoss Racecourse Road, Kelso,
Roxburghshire
Tel	(0573) 23009
Mem	350
Sec	JP Payne (0573) 23259
Holes	18 L 6066 yds SSS 69

Recs	Am–64
V'trs	U SOC
Fees	£5.50 D–£8 (£6.50 D–£10) 1988
	prices
Loc	Inside Kelso racecourse.
	1 mile from Kelso

Melrose (1880)

Dingleton, Melrose
Tel	(089 682) 2855
Mem	300
Sec	W Macrae (089 684) 2391
Holes	9 L 5579 yds SSS 68
Recs	Am–62 G Matthew (1989)
V'trs	U
Fees	£5 (£6)
Loc	S boundary of Melrose

Minto (1926)

Denholm, Hawick
Tel	(0450) 87220
Mem	400
Sec	IR Welch (0450) 72267
Pro	D Dunlop (08356) 2686
Holes	18 L 5460 yds SSS 68
Recs	Am–66 I Oliver
V'trs	U SOC
Fees	£7 (£8)
Loc	6 miles E of Hawick.
	Denholm 1/2 mile

St Boswells (1899)

St Boswells
Tel	(0835) 22359
Mem	260
Sec	GB Ovens
Holes	9 L 5250 yds SSS 65
Recs	Am–62 CI Ovens (1989)
V'trs	U SOC
Fees	£4 (£5)
Loc	1/4 mile off A68 at St Boswells
	Green, by River Tweed

Selkirkshire

Galashiels (1884)

Public
Ladhope Recreation Ground,
Galashiels
Tel	(0896) 3724
Mem	250 60(J)
Sec	WD Millar (0750) 21669
Holes	18 L 5309 yds SSS 67
Recs	Am–62 KW Simpson
	Pro–70 J Braid
V'trs	U SOC
Fees	£4.20 (£4.70)
Loc	1/4 mile NE of Galashiels

Selkirk (1883)

Selkirk
Tel	(0750) 20621
Mem	250
Sec	R Davies (0750) 20427
Holes	9 L 5560 yds SSS 67

For explanation of abbreviations, see page 460.

Recs Am–60 MD Cleghorn
V'trs U SOC
Fees D–£7
Loc   1 mile S of Selkirk on A7

Torwoodlee (1895)

Galashiels
Tel   (0896) 2260
Mem   280
Sec   A Wilson
Holes 9 L 5800 yds SSS 68
Recs Am–64 RV Rutherford
      Pro–64 A Wilson
V'trs U exc Sat–NA SOC
Fees £8 (£10)
Loc   1 mile N of Galashiels on A7

Central Region

Clackmannanshire

Alloa (1891)

Schawpark, Sauchie, Alloa
Tel   (0259) 722745
Mem   535 80(L) 130(J)
Sec   AM Frame
Pro   W Bennett (0259) 724476
Holes 18 L 6240 yds SSS 70
Recs Am–63 AJ Liddle
      Pro–66 R Weir, G Harvey
V'trs U WE–no parties
Fees £7 D–£12 (£12)
Loc   Alloa

Alva

Beauclerc Street, Alva FK12 5LE
Tel   (0259) 60431
Mem   200
Sec   A McGuire (0259) 60455
Holes 9 L 2407 yds SSS 64
Recs Am–63 R Lyon
V'trs U
Fees £3.50 (£4.50)
Loc   Back Road, Alva, on A91
      Stirling–St Andrews road

Braehead (1891)

Cambus, Alloa
Tel   (0259) 722078
Mem   500
Sec   JA Harrison (0259) 215135
Holes 18 L 6013 yds SSS 69 Par 70
Recs Am–64 D Mackison
V'trs U
Fees £8 D–£10 (£10–£15)
Loc   2 miles W of Alloa (A907)

Dollar (1890)

Brewlands House, Dollar
Tel   (02594) 2400
Mem   300
Sec   MB Shea
Holes 18 L 5144 yds SSS 66

V'trs U SOC
Fees £5 D–£6 (£8)
Loc   In Dollar

Muckhart (1908)

Muckhart, by Dollar FK14 7JH
Tel   (025 981) 423
Mem   450 100(L) 100(J)
Sec   RT Glaister
Pro   K Salmoni (025 981) 493
Holes 18 L 6112 yds SSS 70
Recs Am–66 E Carnegie
V'trs U
Fees £6 (£9)
Loc   A91, 3 miles E of Dollar, turn
      right for Rumbling Bridge

Tillicoultry (1899)

Alva Road, Tillicoultry FK13 6BL
Tel   (0259) 50124
Mem   400
Sec   R Whitehead
Holes 9 L 2528 yds SSS 66
Recs Am–63 I McCaig
V'trs WD/WE–U SOC
Fees £3.50 D–£5 (£5.50 D–£7)
Loc   9 miles E of Stirling

Tulliallan (1902)

Kincardine, by Alloa
Tel   (0259) 30396
Mem   525 53(L) 100(J) 19(S)
Sec   JS McDowall (0324) 485420
Pro   S Kelly (0259) 30798
Holes 18 L 5982 yds SSS 69
Recs Am–65 A Pickles, D Johnson
      Pro–70 D Huish, S Walker,
      G Gray
V'trs U exc comp days
Fees £7 (£9)
Loc   5 miles E of Alloa

Perthshire

Callander (1890)

Aveland Road, Callander FK17 8EN
Tel   (0877) 30090
Mem   540
Sec   J McClements (0877) 30866
Pro   W Kelly (0877) 30975
Holes 18 L 5091 yds SSS 66
Recs Am–62 GK MacDonald
      Pro–59 D Matthew
V'trs U SOC
Fees On application
Loc   1/2 mile off A84, E end of town

Dunblane New (1923)

Dunblane
Tel   (0786) 823711
Mem   600
Sec   AG Duncan (Match sec)
Pro   RM Jamieson
Holes 18 L 5878 yds SSS 68

Recs Am–64 GK McDonald
      Pro–64 RM Jamieson
V'trs WD–Mon/Tues/Thurs/Fri am
      WE–M SOC
Fees £16 (£20)
Loc   6 miles N of Stirling

Killin (1913)

Killin
Tel   (05672) 312
Mem   298
Sec   J Blyth (05672) 234
Holes 9 L 2410 yds SSS 65
Recs Am–61 G Smith
V'trs U SOC–Apr/May/Sept
Fees £4.50 (£4.50)
Loc   In Killin

Stirlingshire

Balmore (1906)

Balmore, by Torrance
Tel   (0360) 2120240
Mem   700
Sec   GP Woolard (041) 332 0392
Holes 18 L 5735 yds SSS 67
Recs Am–63 A Brodie
V'trs M SOC
Fees £15 R/D
Loc   2 miles N of Glasgow

Bonnybridge (1924)

Larbert Road, Bonnybridge
Tel   (0324) 812822
Mem   425
Sec   JJ Keilt
Holes 9 L 6058 yds SSS 69
Recs Am–66 D Riddell
      Pro–66 J McTear
V'trs I
Fees By arrangement
Loc   3 miles W of Falkirk

Bridge of Allan (1895)

Sunnylaw, Bridge of Allan
Tel   (0786) 832332
Mem   300
Sec   JC Whaley (0786) 833914
Holes 9 L 4932 yds SSS 65
Recs Am–62 ID McFarlane
V'trs U exc Sat
Fees £5 (£7)

Buchanan Castle (1936)

nr Drymen
Tel   (0360) 60369
Mem   830
Sec   JI Hay (0360) 60307
Pro   C Dernie (0360) 60330
Holes 18 L 6015 yds SSS 69
Recs Am–68 N Macrae
      Pro–66 D Huish, W Milne
V'trs M or by arrangement with
      Sec
Loc   18 miles NW of Glasgow

Campsie (1895)

Crow Road, Lennoxtown
Tel   (0360) 310244
Mem   400
Sec   JM Donaldson (0360) 312249
Holes 18 L 5517 yds SSS 67
Recs   Am-70 J Hope
       Pro-73 K Stevely
V'trs WD-U before 4.30pm
Fees   £6
Loc   B822 Fintry road

Falkirk (1922)

Stirling Road, Camelon, Falkirk
Tel   (0324) 611061
Mem   500
Sec   A Bennie
Holes 18 L 6257 yds SSS 70
Recs   Am-66
V'trs WD-U until 4pm WE-NA
       SOC exc Wed & Sat
Fees   On application
Loc   1½ miles W of Falkirk,
       on A9

Falkirk Tryst (1885)

86 Burnhead Road, Larbert
Tel   (0324) 562415
Mem   450
Sec   JA Stevenson (0324) 562054
Pro   D Slicer (0324) 562091
Holes 18 L 6053 yds SSS 69
Recs   Am-64 J Rankin
       Pro-65 J Chillas
V'trs WD-U exc Wed-NA WE-M
       SOC
Fees   £9 D-£12
Loc   3 miles N of Falkirk

Glenbervie

Stirling Road, Larbert FK5 4SJ
Tel   (0324) 562605
Mem   600
Sec   Mrs M Purves
Pro   G McKay (0324) 562725
Holes 18 L 6469 yds SSS 71
Recs   Am-64 KW Goodwin (1989)
       Pro-63 C Innes
V'trs WD-I WE-M SOC-Tues &
       Thurs
Fees   £15 D-£20
Loc   1 mile N of Larbert on Stirling
       road

Grangemouth (1973)

Public
Polmonthill, Grangemouth FK3 8TF
Tel   (0324) 711500
Mem   700
Sec   G Sligo
Pro   SJ Campbell (0324) 714355
Holes 18 L 6527 yds SSS 71
V'trs U
Fees   £4 (£5)
Loc   3 miles E of Falkirk

Polmont (1901)

Manuelrigg, Maddiston, Falkirk
Tel   (0324) 711277
Mem   200
Sec   P Lees (0324) 713811
Holes 9 L 3044 yds SSS 69
Recs   Am-71 W Shanks
V'trs U Sat NA-before 1pm
Fees   £3 Sat-£4 Sun-£5
Loc   4 miles S of Falkirk

Stirling (1869)

Queen's Road, Stirling FK8 2QY
Tel   (0786) 73801
Mem   1000
Sec   WC McArthur (0786) 64098
Pro   J Chillas (0786) 71490
Holes 18 L 6409 yds SSS 71
Recs   Am-64 R Gregan (1983)
       Pro-64 W Milne (1988)
V'trs WD-U WE-NA SOC
Fees   £12 (£22)
Loc   King's Park, Stirling

Strathendrick (1901)

Drymen
Mem   360
Sec   R Smith (0360) 40582
Holes 9 L 4962 yds SSS 65
Recs   Am-62 P Haggarty
       Pro-64 C Dernie
V'trs M

Dumfries & Galloway

Dumfriesshire

Crichton Royal (1884)

Dumfries
Mem   400
Sec   JP Cairns
Holes 9 L 3084 yds SSS 69
Recs   Am-67 RB Shearman
       Pro-67 D Gemmell
V'trs M
Loc   Dumfries 1 mile on Bankend
       road

Dumfries & County (1912)

Nunfield, Edinburgh Road, Dumfries
DG1 1JX
Tel   (0387) 53585
Mem   600 150(L) 100(J)
Sec   JK Wells (0387) 62045
Pro   GD Gray (0387) 68918
Holes 18 L 5928 yds SSS 68
Recs   Am-64 D James, IR Brotherston
       Pro-63 A Thomson,
       J McAlister, F Mann
V'trs WD-U exc 12.30-2pm-NA
       Sat-NA Sun-NA before 10am

Fees   £10 (£12) W-£35
Loc   1 mile NE of Dumfries,
       on A701

Dumfries & Galloway (1880)

Laurieston Avenue, Maxwelltown,
Dumfries
Tel   (0387) 53582
Mem   450
Sec   J Donnachie (0387) 63848
Pro   J Fergusson (0387) 56902
Holes 18 L 5782 yds SSS 68
Recs   Am-64 R Shearman
       Pro-63 K Baxter
V'trs U
Fees   £8 (£11)
Loc   In Dumfries

Langholm (1892)

Langholm
Tel   (0541) 80559
Mem   150
Sec   T Hutton (0541) 80429
Holes 9 L 2872 yds SSS 68
Recs   Am-65 I Borthwick
V'trs U
Fees   £4 (£4)
Loc   Within Burgh of Langholm

Lochmaben (1926)

Castlehill Gate, Lochmaben DG11 1NT
Tel   (03887) 810552
Mem   350
Sec   JK Purves
Holes 9 L 5304 yds SSS 66
Recs   Am-64 D Hutchison
       Pro-64 G Gray
V'trs WD-U before 5pm WE-U exc
       comp days
Fees   D-£5
Loc   4 miles W of Lockerbie on
       A709. Dumfries 8 miles

Lockerbie (1889)

Corrie Road, Lockerbie
Tel   (057 62) 3363
Mem   360
Sec   JA Carruthers (0387) 810352
Holes 18 L 5418 yds SSS 66
Recs   Am-65 R Nairn (1988)
V'trs U
Fees   £6 W-£25
Loc   ½ mile from Lockerbie
       on Corrie road

Moffat (1884)

Coatshill, Moffat DG10 9SB
Tel   (0683) 20020
Mem   400
Sec   TA Rankin
Holes 18 L 5218 yds SSS 66
Recs   Am-60 GJ Rodaks (1979)
V'trs WD-restricted Wed after 12
       noon
Fees   D-£8 (D-£11)
Loc   1 mile from Beattock on
       A701

Powfoot (1903)

Cummertrees, Annan
Tel   (04617) 227
Mem   820
Sec   RG Anderson (04612) 2866
Pro   G Dick (04617) 327
Holes 18 L 6266 yds SSS 70
Recs   Am–65 C Wright
       Pro–67 J Stevens
V'trs WD–U WE–Limited
Fees   Winter £5 (£6) 5D–£20
       Summer £10 (£12) 5D–£40
Loc   4 miles W of Annan

Sanquhar (1894)

Blackaddie Road, Sanquhar
Tel   (0659) 50577
Mem   180
Sec   DA Hamilton (0659) 67206
Holes 9 L 5630 yds SSS 68
Recs   Am–66 I Brotherston (1982)
       J Copeland
V'trs U SOC
Fees   £6 (£8)
Loc   ¹/₂ mile W of Sanquhar by
       A76. Dumfries 30 miles.
       Prestwick Airport 30 miles

Southerness (1947)

Southerness, Dumfries DG2 8AZ
Tel   (0387) 88677
Mem   680
Sec   WT Train (0387) 53588
Holes 18 L 6554 yds SSS 72
Recs   Am–68 RD Ireland, I Milne
V'trs U SOC
Fees   On application
Loc   16 miles SW of Dumfries

Thornhill (1892)

Black Nest, Thornhill DG3
Tel   (0848) 30546
Mem   570
Sec   RL Kerr (0848) 30218
Holes 18 L 6011 yds SSS 69
Recs   Am–66 BR Kerr
V'trs U
Fees   £8 (£10)
Loc   14 miles N of Dumfries

Colvend (1908)

Sandyhills, nr Dalbeattie DG5 4PY
Tel   (055 663) 398
Mem   400
Sec   JB Henderson
Holes 9 L 2322 yds SSS 63
V'trs U exc Tues after 4.30pm &
       Thurs after 5pm (Apr–Sept)
       SOC
Fees   £5 (£5)
Loc   6 miles S of Dalbeattie on
       A710 Solway Coast road

Dalbeattie (1897)

Dalbeattie
Tel   (0556) 611421
Mem   230
Sec   T Moffat
Holes 9 L 4200 yds SSS 60
V'trs U
Fees   £6 (£6)

Gatehouse (1922)

Gatehouse of Fleet
Mem   200
Sec   I McMillan (055) 74252
Holes 9 L 2398 yds SSS 63
Recs   Am–60 S Martin
V'trs U
Fees   £5.50 W–£28
Loc   ³/₄ mile N of Gatehouse

Kirkcudbright (1895)

Stirling Crescent, Kirkcudbright
Mem   400
Sec   A Gordon (0557) 30542
Holes 18 L 5681 yds SSS 67
Recs   Am–62 S Calladine
V'trs U
Fees   £7 W–£25
Loc   In Kirkcudbright

New Galloway (1902)

New Galloway
Mem   200
Sec   JT Watson (0556) 2794
Holes 9 L 2509 yds SSS 65
Recs   Am–67 N Porteous (1989)
V'trs U
Fees   £5 (£5)
Loc   In New Galloway

Portpatrick Dunskey (1903)

Golf Course Road, Portpatrick
DG9 8TB
Tel   (0776) 81273
Mem   380
Sec   JA Horberry (0776) 81231
Holes 18 L 5644 yds SSS
       9 L 1442 yds
Recs   Am–65 A Cunningham (1986)
       Pro–67 W Guy (1988),8 others
       (1989)
V'trs U SOC
Fees   £8 D–£12 (£10 D–£14) W–£35
       9 hole course D–£4
Loc   8 miles SW of Stranraer

St Medan (1905)

Port William DG8 8NJ
Tel   (098 87) 358
Mem   200
Sec   D O'Neill (098 85) 555
Holes 9 L 2277 yds SSS 62
Recs   Am–61 J Grundy (1989)
V'trs U SOC
Fees   £6 W–£28
Loc   3 miles S of Port William on
       A747

Stranraer (1906)

Creachmore, Leswalt, Stranraer
Tel   (0776) 87245
Mem   450
Sec   WI Wilson CA (0776) 3539
Holes 18 L 6300 yds SSS 71
Recs   Am–66 CG Findlay
       Pro–72 J Panton
V'trs WE–NA before 9.30am and
       12.30–1.30pm
Fees   £8 (£10) W–£37.50
Loc   2 miles from Stranraer on
       A718

Wigtown & Bladnoch (1960)

Wigtown
Tel   (098 84) 3354
Mem   130
Sec   D Heggie (0671) 2556
Holes 9 L 2731 yds SSS 67
Recs   Am–64 R McGinn, DT McRae
V'trs U
Fees   £6 (£8)
Loc   In Wigtown

Kirkcudbrightshire

Castle Douglas (1905)

Abercromby Road, Castle Douglas
Tel   (0556) 2801
Mem   450
Sec   AJ Guy
Holes 9 L 5400 yds SSS 66
Recs   Am–62 W Blayney, J Shepherd
       (1989)
V'trs U
Fees   £5 W–£15 1989 prices
Loc   In Castle Douglas

Wigtownshire

Newton Stewart

Kirroughtree Avenue, Minnigaff,
Newton Stewart
Tel   (0671) 2172
Mem   300
Sec   DF Buchanan
Holes 9 L 5512 yds SSS 67
Recs   Am–66 J Hutchison (1988)
V'trs U
Fees   £5 (£6) W–£22
Loc   Newton Stewart, on A75

Wigtownshire County (1894)

Mains of Park, Glenluce, Newton
Stewart DG8 0NN
Tel   (058 13) 420
Mem   236
Sec   R McCubbin (058 13) 277
Holes 18 L 5715 yds SSS 68
Recs   Am–66 K Hardie
V'trs U exc Wed–NA after 6pm
Fees   £7 (£9)
Loc   8 miles E of Stranraer on
       A75

Fife Region

Fife

Aberdour (1904)

Seaside Place, Aberdour KY3 0TX
Tel   (0383) 860688
Mem   420 160(L)
Sec   BP Drever (0383) 860353
Pro   J Bennett (0383) 860256
Holes   18 L 5469 yds SSS 67
Recs   Am–65 S Meiklejohn, D Miller
V'trs   Sun/comp Sat–NA
Fees   £8 (£11)
Loc   Aberdour
Mis   Visitors may make tee reservations 1 day in advance with Pro

Anstruther (1890)

Marsfield Shore Road, Anstruther
Tel   (0333) 310956
Mem   500
Sec   T Reid (0333) 311966
Holes   9 L 4504 yds SSS 63
Recs   Am–63 R Wallace, T Anderson, A Forrester
V'trs   U SOC
Fees   £4.50 (£6) 1988 prices
Loc   Outskirts of Anstruther

Auchterderran (1904)

Woodend Road, Cardenden
Tel   (0592) 721579
Mem   100
Sec   R Saunderson
Holes   9 L 5400 yds SSS 66
Recs   Am–66 C McRae
V'trs   U
Fees   £2.55 (£3.90)
Loc   1 mile N of town

Balbirnie Park (1983)

Balbirnie Park, Markinch, Glenrothes
Tel   (0592) 752006
Mem   500
Sec   A Grant
Holes   18 L 6210 yds SSS 70
Recs   Am–70 G Birnie
V'trs   U
Fees   £8 D–£10 (£10 D–£15)
Loc   2 miles E of Glenrothes

Balgove (1972)

Public
St Andrews
Holes   9 (Beginners course)
V'trs   U
Fees   £2
Loc   St Andrews Links

Ballingry (1908)

Public
Lochore Meadows Country Park, Crosshill, Lochgelly
Tel   (0592) 860086
Mem   150

Sec   W Glencross (0592) 861316
Holes   9 L 6482 yds SSS 71
Recs   Am–70 II Morris (1987)
V'trs   U
Fees   £3.10 (£4.10)

Burntisland (1797)

Tel   (0592) 873229
Mem   120
Sec   AD McPherson
Holes   Play over Dodhead Course, Burntisland

Burntisland Golf House Club (1898)

Dodhead, Burntisland
Tel   (0592) 873247
Mem   750
Sec   AW Mann (0592) 874093
Pro   S Walker
Holes   18 L 5897 yds SSS 69
V'trs   U
Fees   £10 D–£14 (£13 D–£19)
Loc   1 mile E of Burntisland, on B923

Canmore (1898)

Venturefair, Dunfermline
Tel   (0383) 724969
Mem   480 60(L) 80(J)
Sec   JC Duncan (0383) 726098
Pro   S Craig (0383) 728416
Holes   18 L 5437 yds SSS 66
Recs   Am–61 R Wallace
V'trs   WD–U
Fees   £7 D–£10
Loc   1 mile N of Dunfermline on A823

Crail Golfing Society (1786)

Balcomie Clubhouse, Fifeness, Crail KY10 3XN
Tel   (0333) 50278
Mem   700 200(L)
Sec   G Thomson (0333) 50686
Pro   G Lennie (0333) 50960
Holes   18 L 5720 yds SSS 68
Recs   Am–64 RW Malcolm
        Pro–66 B Gallacher
V'trs   U
Fees   On application
Loc   11 miles SE of St Andrews

Cupar (1855)

Hillarvitt, Cupar
Tel   (0334) 53549
Mem   475
Sec   IR Wilson (0334) 53254
Holes   9 L 5074 yds SSS 65
Recs   Am–62 J Fairfield, C Wilson
V'trs   Sat–NA SOC–WD/Sun
Fees   £4 (£5)
Loc   10 miles W of St Andrews

Dunfermline (1887)

Pitfirrane, Crossford, Dunfermline KY12 8QV
Tel   (0383) 723534
Mem   500
Sec   JA Gillies
Pro   J Montgomery
Holes   18 L 6217 yds SSS 70
Recs   Am–65 AD Martin
        Pro–65 A Brooks
V'trs   WD–I 9.30–4pm SOC–WD
Fees   £10 D–£15
Loc   2 miles W of Dunfermline on A994

Dunnikier Park (1963)

Public
Dunnikier Way, Kirkcaldy KY1 3LP
Tel   (0592) 261599
Mem   600 35(L) 75(J)
Sec   RA Waddell (0592) 200627
Holes   18 L 6601 yds SSS 72
Recs   Am–65 S Duthie (1988)
        Pro–65 A Hunter (1988)
V'trs   U SOC
Fees   £3 (£4.15)
Loc   N boundary of Kirkcaldy
Mis   Dunnikier Park Club plays here

Earlsferry Thistle (1875)

Melon Park, Elie
Tel   (0333) 310053
Mem   60
Sec   J Fyall
Holes   Play over Elie Golf House Club Course

Eden Course (1913)

Public
St Andrews
Tel   (0334) 74296 (Starter)
Holes   18 L 6400 yds SSS 70
V'trs   U SOC
Fees   £9 W–£50 3D–£25 (unlimited play on Eden, Jubilee and New Courses)
Loc   St Andrews Links

Falkland (1976)

Public
The Myre, Falkland KY7 7AA
Tel   (0337) 57404
Mem   210
Sec   Mrs CR Forsythe (0337) 57356
Holes   9 L 2384 metres SSS 66
Recs   Am–67 W Garland (1987)
V'trs   U SOC
Fees   D–£4 (D–£6) W–£15
Loc   On A912 Kirkcaldy–Perth road

Glenrothes (1958)

Public
Golf Course Road, Glenrothes KY6 2LA
Tel   (0592) 758686/758678
Mem   600 35(L) 120(J)

Sec   LD Dalrymple (0592) 754561
Holes   18 L 6444 yds SSS 71
Recs   Am–65 C Birrell
        Pro–69 R Craig, B Lawson
V'trs   U
Fees   £3 (£4.15)
Loc   Glenrothes West

Golf House Club (1875)

Elie, Leven KY9 1AS
Tel   (0333) 330327
Mem   500
Sec   GA Forgie (0333) 330301
Pro   R Wilson (0333) 330955
Holes   18 L 6241 yds SSS 70
        9 L 2277 yds SSS 32
Recs   Am–63 AW Mathers
        Pro–62 K Nagle
V'trs   U July–Sept ballot
        WE–no party bookings
Fees   £12 D–£18 (£16 D–£24)
Loc   St Andrews 12 miles

Jubilee Course (1897)

Public
St Andrews
Tel   (0334) 73938 (Starter)
Holes   18 L 6805 yds SSS 72
V'trs   U SOC
Fees   £10 W–£50 3D–£25 (unlimited
        play over Jubilee, Eden and
        New Courses)
Loc   St Andrews Links

Kinghorn (1887)

Public
Macduff Cres, Kinghorn KY3 9RE
Tel   (0592) 890345
Holes   18 L 5246 SS 67
Recs   Am–62 AJ McIntyre
V'trs   U
Fees   £2.80 (£3.95)
Loc   3 miles W of Kirkcaldy (A921)
Mis   Kinghorn Club plays here

Kinghorn Ladies (1905)

Kinghorn
Tel   (0592) 890345
Mem   47
Sec   Miss E Douglas (0592) 890512
Holes   Play over Kinghorn Municipal

Kinghorn Thistle

Kinghorn KY3 9RE
Tel   (0592) 890345
Mem   180
Holes   Play over Kinghorn Municipal

Kirkcaldy (1904)

Balwearie Road, Kirkcaldy KY2 5LT
Tel   (0592) 260370
Mem   450 80(L)
Sec   C Taylor (0592) 266597
Pro   B Lawson

Holes   18 L 6007 yds SSS 70
Recs   Am–67 B Glaney, R Wallace
V'trs   U
Fees   £5 D–£8 (£6 D–£10)
Loc   SW end of Kirkcaldy

Ladybank (1879)

Annsmuir, Ladybank
Tel   (0337) 30320
Mem   750
Sec   D Downie (0337) 30814
Pro   MJ Gray (0337) 30725
Holes   18 L 6617 yds SSS 72
Recs   Am–65 S Syme (1987)
        Pro–66 W Reilly (1984)
V'trs   WD–U 9.15am–5pm M–after
        5pm WE–NA 10.15am–5pm
        SOC
Fees   £15 (£18) W–£50
Loc   6 miles S of Cupar

Leslie (Fife) (1898)

Balsillie Laws, Leslie, Glenrothes
KY6 3EZ
Mem   300
Sec   M Burns (0592) 741449
Holes   9 L 4940 yds SSS 64
Recs   Am–63 J Spital
        Pro–64 J Chillas
V'trs   U
Fees   £4 (£5)
Loc   M90 Junction 5/7, 11 miles

Leven Golfing Society (1820)

Links Road, Leven KY8 4HS
Tel   (0333) 26096
        (0333) 21390 (Starter)
Mem   350
Sec   J Bennett (0333) 23898
Holes   Play over Leven Links

Leven Links (1846)

Leven
Tel   (0333) 21390 (Starter)
Sec   M Innes (0333) 23509
        (Links Joint Committee)
Pro   G Finlayson
Holes   18 L 6434 yds SSS 71
Recs   Am–64 J Hawkesworth (1984),
        K Goodwin (1986)
        Pro–63 P Hoad (1984)
V'trs   WD–U before 5pm SOC
        Sat–no parties Sun–NA before
        10.30am
Fees   £11 (£14)
Loc $^{1}/_{2}$ mile E of Leven, on
        promenade

Leven Municipal

Public
North Links, Leven KY8 1DH
Tel   (0333) 27057
Pro   J Simpson
Holes   18 L 5600 yds SSS 66
Recs   Am–63 P Lamont

V'trs   WD–U
Fees   £3 (£4)
Loc   Adjoins Leven Links
Mis   Scoonie Club plays here

Leven Thistle (1867)

3 Balfour Street, Leven
Tel   (0333) 26397
Mem   400
Sec   J Scott (0333) 23798
Holes   Play over Leven Links

Lochgelly (1910)

Cartmore Road, Lochgelly
Tel   (0592) 780174
Mem   400
Sec   RF Stuart (0383) 512238
Holes   18 L 5491 yds SSS 67
Recs   Am–64 D Walker (1988)
V'trs   U
Fees   £3.50 (£4.75)
Loc   NW edge of Lochgelly

Lundin (1869)

Golf Road, Lundin Links KY8 6BA
Tel   (0333) 320202
Mem   700
Sec   AC McBride
Pro   DK Webster (0333) 320051
Holes   18 L 6377 yds SSS 71
Recs   Am–65 W Bergin, D Dunk,
        P Brosted
V'trs   WD–U H Sat–NA before
        2.30pm Sun–M H
Fees   £12 D–£18 Sat–£15
Loc   3 miles E of Leven

Lundin Ladies (1891)

Woodielea Road, Lundin Links
KY8 6AR
Tel   (0333) 320022
Mem   220
Sec   Mrs H Melville (0333) 320553
Holes   9 L 4730 yds SSS 67
Recs   Am–68 Miss P Baxter
V'trs   U
Fees   £2.50 D–£3.50 (£3.50 D–£4.50)
Loc   3 miles E of Leven

Methil (1892)

Links House, Links Road, Leven
Tel   (0333) 25535
Mem   50
Sec   ATJ Traill
Holes   Play over Leven Links

New Course (1896)

Public
St Andrews
Tel   (0334) 73938 (Starter)
Holes   18 L 6604 yds SSS 72
Recs   Am–67 GM Mitchell
        Pro–63 F Jowie

V'trs U
Fees £11 W–£50 3D–£25 (unlimited play over Jubilee, Eden and New courses)
Loc St Andrews Links

New Golf Club (1902)
3–6 Gibson Place, St Andrews KY16 9JE
Tel (0334) 73426
Mem 1700
Sec C Jobson (Sec/Mgr)
Holes Play over St Andrews courses

Old Course (15th Century)
Public
St Andrews
Tel (0334) 73393 (Starter)
Holes 18 L 6566 yds SSS 72
Recs Am–66 C McLachlan
Pro–62 C Strange (1987)
V'trs U H I No Sun play SOC
Fees £22.50
Loc St Andrews Links

Pitreavie (1923)
Queensferry Road, Dunfermline KY11 5PR
Tel (0383) 722591
Mem 460
Sec WP Syme
Pro J Forrester (0383) 723151
Holes 18 L 6086 yds SSS 69
V'trs U (phone Pro first) SOC (Parties–max 36–must be booked in advance)
Fees £8 (£16) 1989 prices
Loc 2 miles off M90 between Rosyth and Dunfermline

Royal & Ancient (1754)
St Andrews
Tel (0334) 72112
Mem 1800
Sec MF Bonallack OBE
Pro J Panton (Hon)
Holes Play over St Andrews courses

St Andrews (1843)
Links House, The Links, St Andrews KY16 9JB
Tel (0334) 74637
Mem 1500
Sec WS Simpson (0334) 73017
Holes Play over St Andrews courses
V'trs Rules in accordance with Links Management Committee, Golf Place, St Andrews

St Michael's (1903)
Leuchars
Tel (033483) 365
Mem 455
Sec AJR MacKenzie
Holes 9 L 5578 yds SSS 67

Recs Am–66 N Manzie (1988)
V'trs Sun am–NA (Mar–Oct) SOC
Fees Mon–Sat–£6 Sun–£5 after 1pm
Loc 5 miles N of St Andrews on Dundee road

St Regulus Ladies' (1920)
9 Pilmour Links, St Andrews KY16 9JG
Tel (0334) 74699
Mem 170
Sec Mrs K Ferguson
Holes Play over St Andrews courses

St Rule Ladies' (1898)
12 The Links, St Andrews KY16 9JB
Tel (0334) 72988
Mem 490
Sec Mrs R Hair
Holes Play over St Andrews Courses

Saline (1912)
Kinneddar Hill, Saline
Tel (0383) 852591
Mem 300
Sec R Hutchison (0383) 852344
Holes 9 L 5302 yds SSS 66
Recs Am–A Brown
V'trs U exc medal Sat
Fees £4 (£5)
Loc 5 miles NW of Dunfermline

Scoonie (1951)
North Links, Leven KY8 1DH
Tel (0333) 27057
Mem 300
Sec K Davidson (0592) 714232
Holes Play over Leven Municipal

Scotscraig (1817)
Golf Road, Tayport DD6 9DZ
Tel (0382) 552515
Mem 600
Sec K Gourlay
Holes 18 L 6496 yds SSS 71
Recs Am–65 M Milne Jr
Pro–66 J Berry, M Bembridge, W Lockie
V'trs WD–U WE–by prior arrangement SOC
Fees On application
Loc 10 miles N of St Andrews

Thistle (1817)
St Andrews
Mem 176
Sec Duncan L Joy (0334) 73749
Pro LB Ayton
Holes Play over St Andrews courses

Thornton (1921)
Station Road, Thornton
Tel (0592) 771111
Mem 550
Sec AL Cowan
Holes 18 L 6175 yds SSS 69

Recs Am–65 R Malcolm
V'trs U
Fees £6 (£9) W–£18
Loc Thornton, 1 mile E of A92

Grampian Region

Aberdeenshire

Aboyne (1883)
Formaston Park, Aboyne
Tel (03398) 86328
Mem 725 180(J)
Sec RD Gregson (03398) 86931
Pro I Wright (03398) 86469
Holes 18 L 5304 yds SSS 66
Recs Am–62 G Forbes, C Forbes
Pro–63 S Walker
V'trs U
Fees £8 (£12) W–£35
Loc E end of Aboyne

Auchmill (1975)
Public
Provost Rust Drive, Aberdeen
Tel (0224) 714577
Holes 9 L 2538 metres
V'trs U
Fees Summer £2.30 Winter £1.55
Loc 3 miles NW of Aberdeen

Ballater (1892)
Victoria Road, Ballater AB3 5QX
Tel (03397) 55567
Mem 600
Sec A Ingram
Pro F Mann (03397) 55658
Holes 18 L 6106 yds SSS 69
Recs Am–65 S Henderson
Pro–66 G Collison, F Coutts
V'trs U
Fees £8 (£10) W–£30 F–£50
Loc 42 miles W of Aberdeen on A93

Balnagask
Public
St Fitticks Road, Aberdeen
Tel (0224) 876407
Pro I Smith
Holes 18 L 5468 metres SSS 69
V'trs U
Fees Summer £4.60 Winter £3.10
Loc 1½ miles SE of Aberdeen
Mis Nigg Bay Club plays here

Bon Accord (1872)
Public
19 Golf Road, Aberdeen AB2 1QB
Tel (0224) 633464
Mem 950
Sec JT Burnett
Holes Play over King's Links

For explanation of abbreviations, see page 460.

Braemar (1902)

Cluniebank Road, Braemar AB3 5XX
Tel   (03397) 41618
Mem   287
Sec   LL Curle (03397) 41328
Holes 18 L 4916 yds SSS 64
Recs   Am–64 RA Cheyne (1987),
       H Haas, G Livingstone,
       N Abreau (1988)
       Pro–64 L Vannet (1988)
V'trs U SOC
Fees   £5 D–£6 (£6 D–£8)
Loc   Braemar 1/2 mile

Caledonian (1899)

20 Golf Road, Aberdeen AB2 1QB
Tel   (0224) 632443
Mem   960
Sec   JA Bridgeford
Holes Play over King's Links

Cruden Bay (1791)

Cruden Bay AB4 7NN
Tel   (0779) 812285
Mem   588
Sec   IAD McPherson
Pro   D Symington (0779) 812414
Holes 18 L 6370 yds SSS 71
       9 L 4710 yds SSS 62
       (St Olaf Course)
Recs   Am–66 PJ Macleod (1987),
       D Jamieson (1989)
       Pro–63 D Thomson (1989)
V'trs WD–U WE–H exc comp days
       SOC–WD
Fees   £12 (£15)
Loc   22 1/2 miles NE of Aberdeen

Deeside (1903)

Bieldside, Aberdeen
Tel   (0224) 869457
Mem   500
Sec   NM Scott (0224) 869457
Pro   FJ Coutts (0224) 861041
Holes 18 L 5972 yds SSS 69
       9 L 6632 yds SSS 72
Recs   Am–64 AK Pirie, RH Willox
       Pro–64 S Torrance
V'trs I
Fees   £12 (£15)
Loc   4 miles W of Aberdeen

Dunecht House (1925)

Dunecht, Skene AB3 7AX
Mem   340
Sec   AJ Angus (0224) 743443
Holes 9 L 3135 yds SSS 70
Recs   Am–72 A Angus (1987)
V'trs M
Loc   12 miles W of Aberdeen on
       B944

Fraserburgh (1881)

Philorth, Fraserburgh AB4 5TL
Tel   (0346) 28287
Mem   420 72(L) 130(J)
Sec   JW Love (0346) 27464
Holes 18 L 6217 yds SSS 70

Recs   Am–66 A Ritchie, C McDonald,
       A Ironside
       Pro–67 I Smith
V'trs U SOC
Fees   £7 (£9)
Loc   1 mile E of Fraserburgh

Hazlehead (1927)

Public
Hazlehead, Aberdeen
Tel   (0224) 321830
Sec   J Murchie (0224) 315747
Pro   I Smith
Holes 18 L 5673 metres SSS 70
       18 L 5303 metres SSS 68
       9 hole course
Recs   Am–65 D Jamieson
       Pro–67 P Oosterhuis
V'trs U
Fees   Summer £4.60 Winter £3.10
Loc   3 miles W of Aberdeen
Mis   Hazlehead GC plays here

Huntly (1900)

Huntly
Tel   (0466) 2643
Mem   600
Sec   G Angus
Holes 18 L 5399 yds SSS 66
Recs   Am–61 N Mason
V'trs U
Fees   £6 (£8) W–£20
Loc   38 miles NE of Aberdeen

Insch

Golf Terrace, Insch
Tel   (0464) 20363
Mem   200
Sec   G Miller (0464) 20252/20243
Holes 9 L 5488 yds SSS 67
Recs   Am–67 H McKenzie (1982)
       G Bruce (1988)
V'trs U
Fees   £4 (£5) W–£10
Loc   28 miles NW of Aberdeen off
       A96 Inverness road

Inverallochy

Public
Inverallochy, nr Fraserburgh
Mem   200
Sec   GM Young (034 65) 2324
Holes 18 L 5137 yds SSS 65
Recs   Am–60
V'trs U
Fees   D–£4 (D–£5)
Loc   3 1/2 miles off A92 nr
       Fraserburgh

Inverurie (1923)

Blackhall Road, Inverurie
Tel   (0467) 20207
Mem   450 110(L)
Sec   J Ramage (0467) 24080
Holes 18 L 5096 yds SSS 65

Recs   Am–63 M Percival
V'trs U SOC–WD
Fees   D–£6 (£8)
Loc   16 miles N of Aberdeen.
       1 mile W of Inverurie

Kemnay (1908)

Kemnay
Mem   300
Sec   Dr G Young (0467) 42681
Holes 9 L 2751 yds SSS 67
V'trs WD–U exc after 5.30 Mon
       and Thur Sun–M
Fees   £4 (£5)
Loc   Aberdeen 15 miles

King's Links

Public
Golf Road, Aberdeen AB2 1QB
Tel   (0224) 632269
Pro   B Davidson (0224) 641577
Holes 18 L 5838 metres SSS 71
V'trs U
Fees   Summer £4.60 Winter £3.10
Loc   1 mile E of Aberdeen
Mis   Bon Accord, Caledonian and
       Northern Clubs play here

Kintore (1911)

Kintore
Tel   (0467) 32631
Mem   350 38(L) 60(J)
Sec   Mrs C Lee
Holes 9 L 2688 yds SSS 66
Recs   Am–64
V'trs WD–U before 4.30pm
       Wed–NA 5–8pm
Fees   £4 (£6)

McDonald (1927)

Ellon
Tel   (0358) 20576
Mem   650
Sec   F Chadwick (0358) 21397
Pro   R Urquhart (0358) 22891
Holes 18 L 5986 yds SSS 69
Recs   Am–65
       Pro–67
V'trs U
Fees   On application
Loc   15 miles N of Aberdeen

Murcar (1909)

Bridge of Don, Aberdeen AB2 8BD
Tel   (0224) 704345
Mem   830
Sec   R Matthews (0224) 704354
Pro   A White (0224) 704370
Holes 18 L 6226 yds SSS 70
       9 hole course
Recs   Am–65 R Grant, J Savege,
       E Morrison
       Pro–65 PA Smith
V'trs U before noon
Fees   £10 D–£15 (D–£17)
Loc   5 miles NE of Aberdeen
Mis   9 hole course at Strabathie

Newburgh-on-Ythan (1888)

Newburgh
Mem 200 35(L) 50(J)
Sec AC Stevenson (03586) 89438
Holes 9 L 3202 yds SSS 71
Recs Am–70
 Pro–69 F Coutts
V'trs U exc Tues after 3pm
Fees £6 (£8)
Loc 12 miles N of Aberdeen

Nigg Bay (1955)

Public
St Fitticks Road, Balnagask
Tel (0224) 871286
Mem 850
Sec H Hendry
Holes Play over Balnagask

Northern (1895)

King's Links, Aberdeen
Tel (0224) 21440
Mem 900
Sec F Sutherland
Holes Play over King's Links

Oldmeldrum (1885)

Oldmeldrum
Mem 220
Sec GR Milton (06512) 2212
Holes 9 L 5252 yds
Recs Am–63 GJ Webster
V'trs U
Fees £3 (£4)
Loc 17 miles NW of Aberdeen

Peterhead (1841)

Craigewan, Peterhead
Tel (0779) 72149
Mem 450
Sec A Brandie (0779) 73350
Holes 18 L 6070 yds SSS 69
 9 L 2600 yds SSS 32
Recs Am–64 K Buchan (1988)
 Pro–64 J Farmer (1980)
V'trs U
Fees £5 (£10)
Loc 34 miles N of Aberdeen
 on coast

Royal Aberdeen (1780)

Balgownie, Bridge of Don, Aberdeen
AB2 8AT
Tel (0224) 702571
Mem 350 117(J)
Sec GF Webster
Pro R MacAskill (0224) 702221
Holes 18 L 6372 yds SSS 71
 18 L 4066 yds SSS 60
Recs Am–64 J Fought
 Pro–65 S McAllister
V'trs I H SOC
Fees £18 D–£22 (£22)
Loc 2 miles from Aberdeen, off
 A92 Ellon road

Tarland (1908)

Tarland AB3 4YN
Tel (033 981) 413
Mem 240
Sec JH Honeyman
Holes 9 L 5812 yds SSS 68
Recs Am–67 A Cruickshank
V'trs WD–U WE–Enquiry advisable
 SOC–WD only
Fees £5 (£7)
Loc Aberdeen 30 miles.
 Aboyne 5 miles

Torphins (1894)

Torphins
Tel (033 982) 493
Mem 350
Sec H Shepherd
Holes 9 L 2330 yds SSS 63
Recs Am–64 K Leslie
V'trs U SOC
Fees £4 (£5)
Loc Banchory 6 miles. 1/2 mile W
 of Torphins via Wester Beltie

Turriff (1899)

Rosehall, Turriff
Tel (0888) 62745
Mem 700
Sec JD Stott (0888) 62982
Pro A Hemsley (0888) 63025
Holes 18 L 6105 yds SSS 69
Recs Am–65 J McManus, G Malcolm
 Pro–64 S Aird, P Lawrie (1989)
V'trs H SOC WE–NA befor 10am
Fees £6 D–£9 (£9 D–£12)
Loc Turriff
Mis Buggies for hire

Westhill (1977)

Westhill, Skene
Tel (0224) 740159 (bookings)
 (0224) 743361 (clubhouse)
Mem 500
Sec JL Webster
Pro S Smith
Holes 18 L 5866 yds SSS 69
Recs Am–66 LR Fowler
V'trs WD–U before 4.30pm and after
 7pm –M 4.30–7pm Sat–U after
 3.30pm Sun–U after 10am
Fees £6 D–£8 (£7 D–£10)
Loc Aberdeen 6 miles on A944

Banffshire

Buckpool (1933)

Barhill Road, Buckie AB5 1DU
Tel (0542) 32236
Mem 500
Sec F Macleod (0542) 35368
Holes 18 L 6257 yds SSS 70
V'trs U
Fees D–£6 (D–£8) W–£25
Loc W end of Buckpool, 1/2 mile
 off A98

Cullen (1879)

The Links, Cullen
Tel (0542) 40685
Mem 224
Sec J Douglas
Holes 18 L 4610 yds SSS 62
Recs Am–58 B Main
V'trs U
Fees £4 (£4.50) W–£24

Duff House Royal (1909)

The Barnyards, Banff AB4 3SX
Tel (026 12) 2062
Mem 547 152(L) 132(J)
Sec M Pierog (026 12) 2461
Pro RS Strachan (026 12) 2075
Holes 18 L 6161 yds SSS 69
Recs Am–63 DC Clarke
V'trs WD–U WE–NA 8.30–10am and
 12–2pm; Jul/Aug–NA 5–6.30pm
Fees £6.50 (£9)
Loc Moray Firth coast

Dufftown (1896)

Dufftown
Tel (0340) 20325
Mem 210
Holes 18 L 5308 yds SSS 66
V'trs U
Fees D–£5 (D–£6)
Loc 1 mile from Dufftown on
 Tomintoul road

Keith (1963)

Fife Park, Keith
Tel (054 22) 2649
Mem 250
Sec A Stronach
Holes 18 L 5811 yds SSS 68
Recs Am–65
V'trs U
Fees £4 (£5)

Royal Tarlair (1926)

Buchan Street, Macduff AB4 1TA
Tel (0261) 32548/32897
Mem 556
Sec Mrs E Black
Holes 18 L 5866 yds SSS 68
Recs Am–66 W Sim
V'trs U
Fees £5 D–£6 (£6 D–£8)

Strathlene (1877)

Buckie AB5 2DJ
Tel (0542) 31798
Mem 300
Sec JF Weir
Holes 18 L 5957 yds SSS 69
Recs Am–65 AG Ross
V'trs U SOC
Fees £4 (£6) W–£20
Loc 1/2 mile E of Buckie

Kincardineshire

Auchenblae (1894)

Public
Auchenblae
Mem   60
Sec   AI Robertson (056 12) 407
Holes 9 L 2174 yds SSS 30
Recs   Am–60 AI Robertson
V'trs U exc Wed & Fri 5.30–9pm
Fees   D–£4 (D–£6)
Loc   11 miles S of Stonehaven.
       5 miles N of Laurencekirk

Banchory (1905)

Kinneskie, Banchory
Tel   (033 02) 2365
Mem   700
Sec   E Girvan
Pro   DW Smart (033 02) 2447
Holes 18 L 5284 yds SSS 66
Recs   Am–61 JA Christie, DF Christie
       Pro–61 A Thomson, D Matthew
V'trs U
Fees   £12 (£14)
Loc   18 miles W of Aberdeen

Stonehaven (1888)

Cowie, Stonehaven
Tel   (0569) 62124
Mem   500
Sec   RO Blair
Holes 18 L 5128 yds SSS 65
Recs   Am–61 RG Forbes (1987)
V'trs Sat– NA before 3.45pm
       Sun–NA before 10.45am
Fees   D–£10 W–£32.50 1989 prices
Loc   1 mile N of Stonehaven

Morayshire

Elgin (1906)

Hardhillock, Birnie Road, Elgin
IV30 3SX
Tel   (0343) 2338
Mem   490 150(L) 150(J)
Sec   W McKay
Pro   I Rodger (0343) 2884
Holes 18 L 6401 yds SSS 71
Recs   Am–64 NS Grant
       Pro–66 H Bannerman,
       R Jamieson
V'trs WD–U after 9.30am WE–U
       after 10am SOC
Fees   £7.50 D–£12.50 (£10 D–£15)
Loc   1 mile S of Elgin

Forres (1889)

Muiryshade, Forres IV36 0RD
Tel   (0309) 72949
Mem   716 130(J)
Sec   GA Reaper (0309) 72013
Pro   S Aird (0309) 72250

Holes 18 L 6141 yds SSS 69
Recs   Am–64 A Moir
V'trs U SOC
Fees   £7 (£10)
Loc   1 mile S of Forres

Garmouth & Kingston (1932)

Garmouth, Fochabers
Tel   (034 387) 388
Mem   300
Sec   A Robertson
Holes 18 L 5637 yds SSS 67
Recs   Am–66
       Pro–70
V'trs U SOC
Fees   £4 D £6
Loc   NE of Elgin

Grantown (1890)

Grantown-on-Spey
Tel   (0479) 2079
Mem   420
Sec   D Shepherd (0479) 2667
Holes 18 L 5672 yds SSS 67
Recs   Am–60 G Bain
       Pro–62 D Webster
V'trs U
Fees   £6 (£7)
Loc   E side of Grantown

Hopeman (1923)

Hopeman
Tel   (0343) 830578
Mem   300
Sec   J Blyth (0343) 830336
Holes 18 L 5500 yds SSS 67
V'trs U SOC Sun–U after 9.30am
Fees   £5 (£7) 1989 prices
Loc   7 miles N of Elgin on B9012

Moray (1889)

Stotfield Road, Lossiemouth
IV31 6QS
Tel   (034 381) 2018
Mem   1136
Sec   J Hamilton
Pro   A Thomson (034 381) 3330
Holes Old 18 L 6643 yds SSS 72
       New 18 L 6005 yds SSS 69
Recs   Old Am–68 NS Grant,
       MM Maclnnan
       Pro–66 T Minshall, D Huish
       New Am–67 K Thomson
       Pro–67 AT MacKenzie,
       DW Armor
V'trs U SOC
Fees   Old D–£7 (D–£10) W–£30
       New D–£5 (D–£7) W–£20
       1989 prices
Loc   6 miles N of Elgin

Spey Bay (1907)

c/o Spey Bay Hotel, Spey Bay,
Fochabers IV32 7PJ
Tel   (0343) 820424
Mem   150
Holes 18 L 6059 yds SSS 69
Recs   Am–66 M Cameron
V'trs U
Fees   £4.50 D–£5.50 (£6)
Loc   5 miles off A96 at Fochabers
Mis   Seaside Links

Highland Region

Caithness

Lybster (1926)

Main Street, Lybster
Mem   86
Sec   M Bowman
Holes 9 L 1896 yds SSS 62
Recs   Am–59 E Larnach
V'trs U
Fees   D–£3 W–£10
Loc   13 miles S of Wick on
       A9

Reay (1893)

Reay, by Thurso
Tel   (084 781) 288
Mem   364 42(L) 37(J)
Sec   NH McDonald (084 787)
       222
Holes 18 L 5865 yds SSS 68
Recs   Am–65 RS Taylor
V'trs U exc comp days
Fees   D–£5 W–£18 F–£25
Loc   Thurso 11 miles
Mis   Most northerly sea-side links
       on British mainland

Thurso (1964)

Public
Newlands of Geise, Thurso
Tel   (0847) 63807
Mem   264
Sec   G Bailey (0847) 63425
Holes 18 L 5818 yds SSS 69
Recs   Am–65 E Newman (1983)
V'trs U
Fees   £4 (£5)
Loc   Railway station 2 miles

Wick (1870)

Reiss, Wick KW1 5LJ
Tel   (0955) 2726
Mem   265
Sec   Mrs MSW Abernethy (0955)
       2702
Holes 18 L 5945 yds SSS 69
Recs   Am–63 R Taylor (1988)
       Pro–68 Dai Rees
V'trs U
Fees   £5 (£6) W–£20
Loc   3 miles N of Wick

Inverness-shire

Abernethy (1895)

Nethy Bridge
Tel (047 982) 305
Mem 200
Sec Mrs B Douglas (047 982)
637
Holes 9 L 2484 yds SSS 66
Recs Am–61 I Murray
V'trs U SOC
Fees D–£5
Loc Aviemore 10 miles.
Grantown 5 miles

Boat-of-Garten (1898)

Boat-of-Garten PH24 3BQ
Tel (047 983) 282 (shop)
(047 983) 351 (clubhouse)
Mem 396
Sec JR Ingram
Holes 18 L 5720 yds SSS 68
Recs Am–65 AP Thomson
Pro–70 GW McIntosh
V'trs U
Fees £8 (£10)
Loc 27 miles S of Inverness
Mis Starting Sheet at WE

Carrbridge (1980)

Carrbridge
Tel (047 984) 674
Mem 330
Sec EG Drayson
Holes 9 L 2623 yds SSS 66
Recs Am–63
V'trs U
Fees D–£5 (D–£6)
Loc In Carrbridge

Fort Augustus (1930)

Markethill, Fort Augustus
Mem 110
Sec ID Aitchison (0320) 6460
Holes 9 L 5454 yds SSS 68 (18 tees)
Recs Am–69 F Boyd (1985)
V'trs U
Fees £5 (£5) Mon–Fri £15
Loc W end of Fort Augustus

Fort William (1974)

North Road, Fort William
Tel (0397) 4464
Mem 300
Sec J Allan
Holes 18 L 5686 metres SSS 71
V'trs U
Fees £5
Loc 3 miles N of Fort William, on A82

Inverness (1883)

Culcabock Road, Inverness IV2 3XQ
Tel (0463) 239882
Mem 1100
Sec T Crane
Pro AP Thomson (0463) 231989

Holes 18 L 6226 yds SSS 70
Recs Pro–63 J Farmer
V'trs WE/BH–restricted SOC
Fees £10 D–£14 (£12 D–£16)
Loc 1 mile S of Inverness

Kingussie (1891)

Gynack Road, Kingussie PH21 1LR
Tel (0540) 661374 (clubhouse)
Mem 570
Sec WM Cook (0540) 661600
Holes 18 L 5555 yds SSS 67
Recs Am–64 N Robertson (1989)
Pro–68 AG Havers
V'trs U
Fees £6 1989 price
Loc 1/2 mile from Kingussie, off A9

Newtonmore (1893)

Newtonmore PH20 1AT
Tel (05403) 328
Mem 380
Sec GJ Fraser
Holes 18 L 5880 yds SSS 68
Recs Am–64 I Barclay
V'trs U SOC
Fees D–£7 W–£28
Loc 46 miles S of Inverness

Sconser (1964)

Between Broadford and Sligachan, Isle of Skye
Mem 120
Sec MN Beaton (0478) 2277
Holes 9 L 4796 yds SSS 63
Recs Am–65 JM Rodger
V'trs U
Fees £4 D–£6 W–£12
Loc Between Broadford and Portree

Skeabost (1982)

Public
Skeabost Bridge, Isle of Skye
IV5 19NP
Mem 150
Sec S MacNab Stuart (047 032) 202
(Skeabost House Hotel)
Holes 9 L 3224 yds SSS 62
V'trs U
Fees £3
Loc 6 miles from Portree on Dunvegan road

Torvean (1962)

Public
Glenurquhart Road, Inverness
Tel (0463) 237543/225651
Mem 432
Sec AS Menzies
Holes 18 L 5784 yds SSS 68
Recs Am–67 DC Walker
Pro–70 R Weir
V'trs U
Fees £6 (£7)
Loc W side of Inverness on A82

Traigh

5 Back of Keppoch, Arisaig
Tel (06875) 262
Mem 20
Sec T McEachen
Holes 9 L 2100 yds SSS 68
V'trs U
Fees £2 (£5)
Loc 3 miles W of Arisaig on A830 Fort William–Mallaig road

Nairnshire

Nairn (1887)

Seabank Road, Nairn IV12 4HB
Tel (0667) 52103
Mem 830
Sec D Patrick (0667) 53208
Pro R Fyfe (0667) 52787
Holes 18 L 6556 yds SSS 71
9 L 1918 yds
Recs Am–66 IC Hutcheon
Pro–65 D Small
V'trs U SOC
Fees £15 (£18) W–£50
Loc Nairn West Shore

Nairn Dunbar (1899)

Lochloy Road, Nairn
Tel (0667) 52741
Mem 500
Sec Mrs SJ McLennan
Pro BR Mason (0667) 53964
Holes 18 L 6431 yds SSS 71
Recs Am–67 AP Thomson
V'trs U
Fees £10 (£12) W–£55

Ross & Cromarty

Alness (1904)

Ardross Rd, Alness
Tel (0349) 883877
Mem 300
Sec JG Miller
Holes 9 L 2436 yds SSS 63
Recs Am–62 C MacIver (1983)
C Taylor (1989)
V'trs Mon–NA 5–7pm SOC
Fees £3 (£4)
Loc 1/4 mile N of Alness

Fortrose & Rosemarkie (1888)

Ness Road East, Fortrose
Tel (0381) 20529
Mem 662
Sec Mrs M Collier
Pro GA Hampton (0381) 20733
Holes 18 L 5973 yds SSS 69
Recs Am–64 G Paterson
V'trs U SOC
Fees D–£7.50 (£8) 6D–£30
Loc Black Isle. Inverness 12 miles

Gairloch (1898)

Gairloch IV21 2BQ
Tel   (0445) 2407
Mem   250
Sec   WJ Pinnell
Holes   9 L 1942 yds SSS 63
V'trs   U Sun–NA
Fees   £4 D–£6 W–£20
Loc   60 miles W of Dingwall

Invergordon (1954)

King George Street, Invergordon
Tel   (0349) 852116
Mem   140 50(L) 60(J)
Sec   I Hosie
Holes   9 L 6028 yds SSS 69
Recs   Am–65 D Ross
V'trs   U SOC
Fees   £3 (£4)
Loc   Invergordon

Lochcarron (1911)

Lochcarron, Strathcarron
Mem   124
Sec   GB Jones (05202) 259
Holes   9 L 3470 yds SSS 62
V'trs   U
Fees   £3
Loc   ½ mile E of Lochcarron

Muir of Ord (1875)

Great North Road, Muir of Ord
IV6 7SX
Tel   (0463) 870825
Mem   642
Sec   Mrs C Moir
Pro   JT Hamilton (0463) 870601
Holes   18 L 5202 yds SSS 65
Recs   Am–62 S McIntosh (1989)
V'trs   U SOC
Fees   D–£7 (£8) W–£30
Loc   15 miles N of Inverness on
         A862 or A9/A832

Strathpeffer Spa (1888)

Strathpeffer IV14 9AS
Tel   (0997) 21219
Mem   200 60(L) 80(J)
Sec   N Roxburgh (0997) 21396
Holes   18 L 4792 yds SSS 65
Recs   Am–60 D Krzyzanowski
         Pro–66 A Herd
V'trs   U SOC
Fees   £5 D–£7 5D–£20
Loc   ¼ mile N of Strathpeffer

Tain (1890)

Tain
Tel   (0862) 2314
Mem   400
Sec   WW Russell
Holes   18 L 6207 yds SSS 70
Recs   Am–66 J Miller, S Shaw,
         K Berry
V'trs   U
Fees   £7 D–£10 (£8 D–£12)

Tarbat (1908)

Portmahomack
Tel   (0862 87) 236
Mem   160
Sec   D Wilson
Holes   9 L 2328 yds SSS 63
Recs   Am–63 D Mackay
V'trs   UH Sun–NA SOC
Fees   D–£4 (D–£5)
Loc   6 miles SE of Tain

Sutherland

Bonar–Bridge & Ardgay (1904)

Bonar–Bridge, Ardgay
Mem   100
Sec   A Turner (054 982) 248
         H Sutherland
Holes   9 L 4626 yds SSS 63
Recs   Am–66 D Mackenzie (1989)
V'trs   U
Fees   D–£4
Loc   ½ mile N of Bonar–Bridge on
         A9

Brora (1891)

Golf Road, Brora KW9 6QS
Tel   (0408) 21417
Mem   390
Sec   IG Smith (04083) 3239
Holes   18 L 6110 yds SSS 69
Recs   Am–61 J Miller
         Pro–67 D Huish
V'trs   U exc comp days –H for open
         comps SOC
Fees   £8 W–£35 F–£45 M–£60
Loc   68 miles N of Inverness (A9)

Durness (1988)

Public
Balnakeil, Durness
Mem   80
Sec   Mrs L Mackay (097 181) 364
Holes   9 L 5468 yds SSS 67
Recs   Am–73 J Miller, C Pritchard,
         RR Macdonald (1988)
V'trs   U
Fees   £5 W–£20 F–£30
Loc   57 miles NW of Lairg on
         A838

Golspie (1889)

Ferry Road, Golspie
Tel   (04083) 3266
Mem   420
Sec   JL Catchpole
Holes   18 L 5836 yds SSS 68
Recs   Am–65 J Miller
         Pro–65 D Huish
V'trs   U SOC
Fees   D–£8 W–£40 F–£55
Loc   11 miles N of Dornoch

Helmsdale

Helmsdale
Tel   (043) 12240
Sec   J Mackay, Ivybank,
         Dunrobin Street
Holes   9
V'trs   U
Fees   £3 (£3)

Royal Dornoch (1877)

Golf Road, Dornoch IV25 3LW
Tel   (0862) 810219
Mem   621 180(L) 25(J)
Sec   AS Kinnear (Mgr)
Pro   WE Skinner (0862) 810902
Holes   C'ship 18 L 6577 yds SSS 72
         Struie 18 L 5242 yds SSS 66
Recs   Am–66 DWR Chalmers
         Pro–66 A Webster
V'trs   U
Fees   On application
Loc   51 miles N of Inverness
Mis   Helipad by clubhouse.
         Airstrip nearby

Lothian Region

East Lothian

Aberlady

Aberlady
Mem   32
Sec   K Hope
Holes   Play over Kilspindie course

Bass Rock (1873)

29 Marmion Road, North Berwick
EH39 4NZ
Mem   104
Sec   SH Butterworth (0620) 2038
Holes   Play over North Berwick

Burgh Links (1894)

Public
East Links, North Berwick
Tel   (0620) 2726
Mem   400
Sec   DR Montgomery
         (0620) 2340
Holes   18 L 6079 yds SSS 69
Recs   Am–65 D Drummond
V'trs   U
Fees   On application
Loc   Edinburgh 23 miles
Mis   Glen Club plays here

Dirleton Castle (1854)

Gullane
Tel   (0620) 843496
Mem   100
Sec   RH Atkinson
Holes   Play over Gullane courses

Dunbar (1794)

East Links, Dunbar EH42 1LP
Tel   (0368) 62317
Mem   650
Sec   AJR Poole
Pro   D Small (0368) 62086
Holes 18 L 6426 yds SSS 71
Recs   Am–66 S Easingwood
         Pro–64 R Weir (1989)
V'trs   U SOC
Fees   D–£12 (D–£20) 1989 prices
Loc   ¹/₂ mile E of Dunbar

Gifford (1904)

Gifford
Mem   450
Sec   DA Fantom (062 081) 267
Holes 9 L 6138 yds SSS 69
V'trs   Tues & Wed–NA after 4pm
         WE–NA after noon
Fees   D–£5
Loc   4¹/₂ miles S of Haddington

Glen (1906)

Public
East Links, North Berwick EH39 4LE
Tel   (0620) 2221
Mem   400
Sec   DR Montgomery (0620) 2340
Holes Play over Burgh Links

Gullane (1882)

Gullane EH31 2BB
Tel   (0620) 843115
Mem   711 300(L) 50(J) 125(5)
Sec   To be appointed
Pro   J Hume (0620) 843111
Holes No 1 18 L 6491 yds SSS 71
         No 2 18 L 6127 yds SSS 69
         No 3 18 L 5035 yds SSS 64
         9–hole course available for
         children
Recs   No 1 Am–65 ME Lewis
         Pro–64 RDBM Shade
         No 2 Am–64
         RCH Robertson
         Pro–66 H Bannerman
V'trs   U
Fees   No 1 £26 D–£39 (£35)
         No 2 £12 D–£18 (£15 D–£23)
         No 3 £8 D–£12 (£10 D–£15)
         Children's course free
Loc   18 miles E of Edinburgh

Haddington (1865)

Public
Amisfield Park, Haddington
Tel   (062 082) 3627
Mem   320
Sec   T Shaw (062 082) 2584/3627
Pro   J Muir (062 082) 2727
Holes 18 L 6280 yds SSS 70
Recs   Am–65 S Stephens
V'trs   WD–U WE–U exc 10am–12pm
         and 2–4pm
Fees   £6.25 D–£9 (£8 D–£11.50)
         1989 prices
Loc   17 miles E of Edinburgh on
         A1. ³/₄ mile E of Haddington

The Honourable Company of Edinburgh Golfers (1744)

Muirfield, Gullane EH31 2EG
Tel   (0620) 842123
Mem   695
Sec   Maj JG Vanreenen
Holes 18 L 6601 yds SSS 73
         (Championship 6963 yds)
Recs   Am–71 DED Neave
         Pro–63 R Davis (1987)
V'trs   WD–Tues/Thurs/Fri am only
         WE/BH–NA I H SOC
Fees   £35 D–£50
Loc   NE outskirts of Gullane,
         opposite sign for Greywalls
         Hotel on A198 Edinburgh–
         N Berwick road

Kilspindie (1867)

Aberlady, Longniddry EH32 0QD
Tel   (087 57) 216/358
Mem   430 150(L) 50(J)
Sec   HF Brown (087 57) 358
Holes 18 L 4957 metres SSS 66
Recs   Am–61 G Weir
         Pro–60 L Vannet (1988)
V'trs   U Advisable to phone Sec.
         Play subject to members'
         demands SOC–WD
Fees   On application
Loc   Aberlady

Longniddry (1921)

Links Road, Longniddry EH32 0NL
Tel   (0875) 52141
Mem   980
Sec   GC Dempster CA
Pro   WJ Gray (0875) 52228
Holes 18 L 6219 yds SSS 70
Recs   Am–63 C Hardin (1987)
         Pro–63 P Harrison (1987)
V'trs   U SOC–Mon–Thurs after
         9.18am and 2pm
Fees   £14 D–£20 (£28 R/D)
Loc   13 miles E of Edinburgh off A1

Luffness New (1894)

Aberlady EH32 0QA
Tel   (0620) 843114
Mem   650
Sec   Lt Col JG Tedford
         (0620) 843336
Holes 18 L 6122 yds SSS 69
Recs   Am–63 R Winchester
         Pro–62 C O'Connor
V'trs   M or by arrangement
Fees   On application
Loc   Gullane 1 mile (A198).
         Longniddry 4 miles

Musselburgh (1938)

Monktonhall, Musselburgh
Tel   (031) 665 2005
Mem   500
Sec   JR Brown
Pro   T Stangoe (031) 665 7055

Holes 18 L 6623 yds SSS 72
Recs   Am–65 RS Hall
         Pro–67 EC Brown, B Devlin
         G Cunningham, A Jacklin
V'trs   U
Loc   1 mile S of Musselburgh

Musselburgh Old Course

Silver Ring Clubhouse, Millhill,
Musselburgh
Mem   70
Sec   W Finnigan
Pro   None
Holes 9 L 5380 yds SSS 67
Recs   Am–67 P Hosie
V'trs   WD/BH–U WE–U after 10am
Fees   18 holes–£2.40
Loc   7 miles E of Edinburgh on A1

North Berwick (1832)

West Links, Beach Road,
North Berwick
Tel   (0620) 2135
Mem   300
Sec   R Russell
Pro   D Huish (0620) 3233
Holes 18 L 6315 yds SSS 70
Recs   Am–65 E O'Connell
         Pro–63 G Laing
V'trs   U H
Fees   £12 D–£17.50 (£17.50 D–£25)
Loc   24 miles E of Edinburgh

Rhodes

29 Westgate, North Berwick EH39
Sec   R Walker
Holes Play over North Berwick

Royal Musselburgh (1774)

Prestongrange House, Prestonpans
Tel   (0875) 810276
Mem   700
Sec   RS Gordon
Pro   A Minto (0875) 810139
Holes 18 L 6237 yds SSS 70
V'trs   WD–U WE–M
Fees   £12 D–£20 (£20)
Loc   8 miles SE of Edinburgh on
         A198 North Berwick road
Mis   Electric buggies for hire

Tantallon (1853)

32 Westgate, North Berwick EH39 4AH
Tel   (0620) 2114
Mem   300
Sec   GA Milne
Holes Play over North Berwick
         West Links

Thorntree (1856)

Prestongrange House, Prestonpans
Mem   100
Sec   J Hanratty
Holes Play over Royal
         Musselburgh course

For explanation of abbreviations, see page 460.

Winterfield

Public
Back Road, Dunbar
Tel   (0368) 62280
Mem   300
Sec   M O'Donnell (0368) 62564
Pro   J Sandilands (0368) 63562
Holes 18 L 5053 yds SSS 65
Recs   Am–61 R Walkinshaw,
       J Huggan
       Pro–65 SWT Murray
V'trs U
Fees   On application–phone Pro
Loc   W side of Dunbar

Midlothian

Baberton (1893)

Juniper Green, Edinburgh EH14 5DU
Tel   (031) 453 3361
Mem   800
Sec   DM McBain (031) 453 4911
Pro   K Kelly
Holes 18 L 6098 yds SSS 69
Recs   Am–64 RW Bradley
       Pro–62 B Barnes
V'trs M SOC–WD
Loc   5 miles W of Edinburgh

Braidhills No 1 (1893)

Public
Edinburgh
Tel   (031) 447 6666
       (031) 661 5351 (Ext 209)
       (Bookings)
Pro   J Boath (031) 447 8205
Holes 18 L 5239 yds SSS 68
Recs   Am–65
V'trs U
Loc   3 miles S of Edinburgh

Braidhills No 2 (1894)

Public
Edinburgh
Tel   (031) 447 6666
       (031) 661 5351 (Ext 209)
       (Bookings)
Pro   J Boath (031) 447 8205
Holes 18 L 4832 yds SSS 63
Recs   Am–65
V'trs U
Loc   3 miles S of Edinburgh

Braids United (1897)

Public
Braid Hills Approach, Edinburgh 10
Tel   (031) 447 3327
Mem   100
Sec   G Hind (031) 445 2044
Holes Play over Braids 1 and 2

Broomieknowe (1906)

36 Golf Course Road, Bonnyrigg
EH19 2HZ
Tel   (031) 663 9317
Mem   500
Sec   Dr J Symonds

Pro   M Patchett (031) 660 2035
Holes 18 L 5754 yds SSS 68
Recs   Am–64 P Gallagher
       Pro–64 J Hamilton, A Horne,
       J Hume, WB Murray
V'trs WD–U WE/BH–NA
Fees   £8 (£10)
Loc   7 miles S of Edinburgh

Bruntsfield Links Golfing Society (1761)

32 Barnton Avenue, Davidson's Mains,
Edinburgh EH4 6JH
Tel   (031) 336 2006
Mem   1000
Sec   MW Walton (031) 336 1479
Pro   B Mackenzie (031) 336 4050
Holes 18 L 6407 yds SSS 71
Recs   Am–69 AGG Miller
V'trs I WD–M before 5pm
       H after 5pm SOC
Fees   On application
Loc   3 miles W of Edinburgh

Carrick Knowe (1930)

Public
Glendevon Park, Edinburgh 12
Tel   (031) 337 1096
       (031) 661 5351 (Ext 209)
       (Bookings)
Holes 18 L 6299 yds SSS 70
Recs   Am–64 R Bradley
V'trs U
Fees   £3.50
Loc   5 miles W of Edinburgh
Mis   Carrickvale Club plays here

Carrickvale

Carrick Knowe Municipal,
Glendevon Park, Edinburgh EH12 5VZ
Tel   (031) 337 1932
Mem   450
Sec   W Smart (031) 346 2089
Holes Play over Carrick Knowe

Craigentinny (1891)

Public
Edinburgh
Tel   (031) 554 7501
       (031) 661 5351 (Ext 209)
       (Bookings)
Holes 18 L 5418 yds SSS 66
Recs   Am–64
V'trs U
Fees   £3.50
Loc   2½ miles E of Edinburgh
Mis   Lochend Club plays here

Craigmillar Park (1895)

1 Observatory Road, Edinburgh
EH9 3HG
Tel   (031) 667 2837
Mem   460 100(L) 70(J) 38(5)
Sec   Mrs JH Smith (031) 667
       0047
Pro   B McGhee (031) 667 0047
Holes 18 L 5846 yds SSS 68

Recs   Am–65 J Thomson
       Pro–66 T Stangoe
V'trs WD–I or H before 3.30pm
       WE/BH–NA
Fees   On application
Loc   Blackford, Edinburgh

Dalmahoy

Dalmahoy, Kirknewton, Midlothian
EH27 8EB
Tel   (031) 333 2055
Sec   Mrs I Auld
Pro   B Anderson (031) 333 1436
Holes East 18 L 6639 yds SSS 72
       West 18 L 5212 yds SSS 66
Recs   East Am–69 G Russo
       Pro–62 B Barnes
Fees   On application
Loc   7 miles W of Edinburgh

Duddingston (1895)

Duddingston, Edinburgh EH15 3QD
Tel   (031) 661 1005
Mem   580
Sec   JC Small (031) 661 7688
Pro   A McLean (031) 661 4301
Holes 18 L 6647 yds SSS 72
Recs   Am–64 G Macgregor
       Pro–65 S Torrance
V'trs WD–IH SOC–Tues & Thurs
Fees   £12.50 Soc–£10
Loc   Duddingston Road West

Glencorse (1890)

Milton Bridge, Penicuik, Midlothian
EH26 0RD
Tel   (0968) 77177
Mem   400
Sec   DA McNiven (0968) 77189
Pro   C Jones (0968) 76481
Holes 18 L 5205 yds SSS 66
Recs   Am–62 JH Moore (1985),
       S Middleton (1988)
V'trs WD before 4pm SOC–WD
Fees   £8 (£12) 1989 prices
Loc   8 miles S of Edinburgh

Kingsknowe (1908)

326 Lanark Road, Edinburgh EH14 2JD
Tel   (031) 441 1144
Mem   728
Sec   S McMichael (031) 441 1145
Pro   W Bauld (031) 441 4030
Holes 18 L 5966 yds SSS 69
Recs   Am–63 JJ Little
       Pro–64 WB Murray
V'trs WD–U before 4.30pm WE–M
Fees   £7.50 D–£10 W–£25 M–£65
Loc   SW Edinburgh

Liberton (1920)

297 Gilmerton Road, Edinburgh
EH16 5UJ
Tel   (031) 664 8580
Mem   815
Sec   JM Jackson (031) 664 3009
Pro   PJ Fielding (031) 664 1056
Holes 18 L 5299 yds SSS 66

Recs	Am–61 RMF Jack
	Pro–63 JL Brash
V'trs	Mon/Wed/Fri–NA after 5pm
	WE/BH–No visiting clubs
Fees	£9.50 (£11.50)
Loc	3 miles S of Edinburgh

Lochend

Craigentinny Course, Edinburgh
EH7 6RG

Tel	(031) 554 7960
Mem	320
Sec	DM Drysdale (031) 669 3134
Holes	Play over Craigentinny
	Municipal Course

Lothianburn (1893)

Biggar Road, Edinburgh

Tel	(031) 445 2206
Mem	430 75(L) 75(J) 50(S)
Sec	EW Horberry (031) 445 5067
Pro	P Morton (031) 445 2288
Holes	18 L 5750 yds SSS 69
Recs	Am–63 PW Lamb (1983)
V'trs	WD–U before 5pm –M after
	5pm WE–NA SOC
Fees	£6 D–£8 (£7.50 D–£11) 1989
	prices
Loc	S boundary of Edinburgh

Merchants of Edinburgh (1907)

Craighill Gardens, Morningside,
Edinburgh EH10 5PY

Tel	(031) 447 1219
Mem	686
Sec	JB More (031) 443 1470
Pro	RL Smith (031) 447 8709
Holes	18 L 4889 yds SSS 65
Recs	Am–61 WJ Jeffrey Jr
V'trs	M or I SOC
Fees	£4.50 D–£6
Loc	SW of Edinburgh

Mortonhall (1892)

231 Braid Road, Edinburgh EH10 6PB

Tel	(031) 447 2411
Mem	500
Sec	PT Ricketts (031) 447 6974
Pro	DB Horn (031) 447 5185
Holes	18 L 6557 yds SSS 71
Recs	Am–66 C Cassells
	Pro–68 G Cunningham
V'trs	I
Fees	£13 (£16)
Loc	In Edinburgh

Murrayfield (1896)

43 Murrayfield Road, Edinburgh
EH12 6EU

Tel	(031) 337 1009
Mem	775
Sec	JP Bullen (031) 337 3478
Pro	J Fisher (031) 337 3479

Holes	18 L 5727 yds SSS 68
Recs	Am–64 DED Neave
	Pro–63 WB Murray
V'trs	WD–I WE–M
Fees	£12 D–£18
Loc	2 miles W of Edinburgh

Newbattle (1934)

Abbey Road, Eskbank, Dalkeith
EH22 3AD

Tel	(031) 663 2123
Mem	600
Pro	J Henderson (031) 660 1631
Holes	18 L 6012 yds SSS 69
Recs	Am–65 G Macgregor,
	P Hardwick, J McLean
V'trs	WD–U before 4pm WE–M
Fees	£7.50 D–£12
Loc	6 miles S of Edinburgh on
	A7 and A68

Portobello (1853)

Public

Stanley Street, Portobello, Edinburgh

Tel	(031) 669 4361
	(031) 661 5351 (Ext 209)
	(Bookings)
Mem	60
Sec	B Duffy
Holes	9 L 2419 yds SSS 32
Recs	Am–27
V'trs	U
Fees	WD/WE–£1.75
Loc	3½ miles E of Edinburgh
	on A1

Prestonfield (1920)

6 Priestfield Road North, Edinburgh
EH16 5HS

Tel	(031) 667 1273
Mem	700
Sec	MDAG Dillon
Pro	B Commins (031) 667 8597
Holes	18 L 6216 yds SSS 70
Recs	Am–62 AM Dun
V'trs	Sat–NA 8–10.30am and
	12–1.30pm Sun–NA before
	11.30am SOC
Fees	£11 D–£14 (£15 D–£20)
Loc	2 miles SE of Edinburgh

Ratho Park (1928)

Ratho, Newbridge, Midlothian
EH28 8NX

Tel	(031) 333 1252/1752
Mem	550 98(L) 65(J)
Sec	JC McLafferty (031) 333 1752
Pro	A Pate (031) 333 1406
Holes	18 L 6028 yds SSS 69
Recs	Am–63 C Macphail
	Pro–64 WG Stowe
V'trs	U SOC–Tues/Wed/Thurs
Fees	£15 D–£20 (£25)
Loc	8 miles W of Edinburgh (A71)

Ravelston (1912)

24 Ravelston Dykes Road, Edinburgh
EH4 5NZ

Tel	(031) 315 2486
Mem	610
Sec	F Philip (031) 312 6850
Holes	9 L 5332 yds SSS 66
Recs	Am–67 DE Doig (1987)
	Pro–66 W Murray (1987)
V'trs	WD–I
Loc	Off Queensferry Road (A90),
	Forth Road Bridge road

Royal Burgess Golfing Society of Edinburgh (1735)

181 Whitehouse Road, Barnton,
Edinburgh EH4 6BY

Tel	(031) 339 2012
Mem	620 50(J)
Sec	JP Audis (031) 339 2075
Pro	G Yuille (031) 339 6474
Holes	18 L 6604 yds SSS 72
Recs	Am–64
	Pro–63
V'trs	I
Fees	On request
Loc	Queensferry Road

Silverknowes (1947)

Public

Silverknowes, Parkway, Edinburgh
EH4 5ET

Tel	(031) 336 3843 (Bookings)
Mem	500
Sec	J Munro (031) 336 5359
Holes	18 L 6210 yds SSS 70
Recs	Am–66
V'trs	U
Loc	4 miles W of Edinburgh

Swanston (1927)

111 Swanston Road, Fairmilehead,
Edinburgh 10

Tel	(031) 445 2239
Mem	400
Sec	J Allan
Pro	H Ferguson (031) 445 4002
Holes	18 L 5024 yds SSS 65
Recs	Am–63 G Millar
V'trs	U exc comp days–NA
	WE–NA after 1pm
Fees	£3.45 D–£5.75
Loc	W of Edinburgh, on
	Biggar road (A702)

Torphin Hill (1895)

Torphin Road, Edinburgh EH13 0PG

Tel	(031) 441 1100
Mem	450
Sec	DO Campbell
Holes	18 L 5025 yds SSS 66
Recs	Am–62 G Wilkie, AL Turner

For explanation of abbreviations, see page 460.

V'trs   WD–U WE–U exc comp days
        SOC
Fees   £5 (£8)
Loc   SW boundary of Edinburgh

Turnhouse (1909)

154 Turnhouse Road, Corstorphine,
Edinburgh
Tel   (031) 339 1014
Mem   500
Sec   AB Hay (031) 655 6119
Pro   K Whitson (031) 339 7701
Holes   18 L 6171 yds SSS 69
Recs   Am–65 various
        Pro–64 D Huish
V'trs   M or by arrangement
Loc   Turnhouse Road (A9080)

West Lothian

Bathgate (1892)

Edinburgh Road, Bathgate EH48 1BA
Tel   (0506) 52232
Mem   492
Sec   R Smith (0506) 630505
Pro   S Strachan (0506) 630553
Holes   18 L 6326 yds SSS 70
Recs   Am–64 J McLean
V'trs   U
Fees   £8 (£11)

Deer Park CC (1978)

Carmondean, Livingston EH54 9PG
Tel   (0506) 38843
        (Steward) (0506) 37800
Mem   400
Sec   W Yule
Pro   W Yule
Holes   18 L 6636 yds SSS 72
Recs   Am–72
V'trs   U
Fees   £5 (£8.50)
Loc   Bordering M8, N of Livingston
        New Town (Knightsridge
        District)

Dundas Park (1957)

3 Loch Place, South Queensferry
EH30 9NG
Tel   (031) 331 1601
Mem   450
Sec   RH Crowe
Holes   9 L 5510 metres SSS 69
Recs   Am–66 J McLaren
V'trs   M I SOC
Loc   Dundas Estate (Private),
        S of Queensferry on A8000

Greenburn (1953)

Fauldhouse
Tel   (0501) 70292
Mem   450
Sec   A Morrison (0501) 70865
Holes   18 L 6223 yds SSS 70
Recs   Am–68
V'trs   U
Fees   £3.30 (£4.40)

Harburn (1921)

West Calder, West Lothian EH55 8RS
Tel   (0506) 871256
Mem   488 51(L) 98(J)
Sec   GR Clark (0506) 871131
Pro   R Redpath (0506) 871582
Holes   18 L 5853 yds SSS 68
Recs   Am–62 M Kirk
V'trs   U
Fees   £6.50 (£8.50)
Loc   2 miles S of West Calder

Linlithgow (1913)

Braehead, Linlithgow
Tel   (0506) 842585
Mem   400
Pro   D Smith (0506) 844356
Holes   18 L 5868 yds SSS 68
Recs   Am–64 J Cuddihy (1975)
        Pro–65 J White (1988)
V'trs   U
Fees   £6 D–£7.50 (£8.50 D–£10)
Loc   SW of Linlithgow

Niddry Castle (1983)

Winchburgh
Sec   AM Lamont (0506) 890185
Holes   9 L 5476 yds SSS 67
V'trs   U
Fees   £4 (£6) 1989 prices

Polkemmet (1981)

Public
By Whitburn, West Lothian EH47 0AD
Tel   (0501) 43905
Holes   9 L 2967 metres SSS 37
V'trs   U
Fees   £1.60 (£2)
Loc   Between Whitburn and
        Harthill on B7066
Mis   15–bay driving range

Pumpherston (1895)

Drumshoreland Road, Pumpherston
Tel   (0506) 32869
Mem   265 4(L) 78(J)
Sec   JS Lamond (0506) 32122
Holes   9 L 5154 yds SSS 65
Recs   Am–61 I Loch Jr (1987)
V'trs   M
Loc   14 miles W of Edinburgh

Uphall

Uphall
Tel   (0506) 856404
Mem   500
Sec   A Dobie
Holes   18 L 5567 yds SSS 67
V'trs   U
Fees   £6 (£10)
Loc   Livingston 2 miles

West Lothian (1892)

Airngath Hill, by Linlithgow EH49 7RH
Tel   (0506) 826030
Mem   480
Sec   TB Fraser (0506) 825476
Holes   18 L 6578 yds SSS 71
Recs   Am–66 CK Cox (1987)
        AG O'Neill (1988)
        Pro–68 J Farmer (1980)
V'trs   U
Fees   £7 D–£10 (£9 D–£15)
Loc   1 mile S of town between
        Bo'ness and Linlithgow

Orkney & Shetland Region

Orkney & Shetland

Orkney (1889)

Grainbank, Kirkwall, Orkney
Tel   (0856) 2457
Mem   214
Sec   JR Sim (0856) 2435
Holes   18 L 5406 yds SSS 68
Recs   Am–65 KD Peace
        Pro–71 I Smith
V'trs   U
Fees   £5 W–£20 F–£25 M–£35
Loc   1 mile W of Kirkwall

Shetland (1894)

PO Box 18, Lerwick
Tel   (059 584) 369
Mem   311
Sec   LE Groat (Mgr)
        (059) 3065
Holes   18 L 5776 yds SSS 70
V'trs   U
Fees   £4 (£5)
Loc   3 1/2 miles N of Lerwick

Stromness (1890)

Ness, Orkney
Tel   (0856) 850772
Mem   120
Sec   FJ Groundwater (0856) 850622
Holes   18 L 4665 yds SSS 64
Recs   Am–62 CH Poke
        Pro–66 R Macaskill
V'trs   U
Fees   £4 (£4)
Loc   Stromness, Orkney

Westray

Westray, Orkney
Tel   (085 77) 28
Mem   12
Sec   L Berstan
Holes   9 hole course
Recs   Am–36 Dr W Balfour
V'trs   U Sun–NA

Strathclyde Region

Argyll

Blairmore & Strone (1896)

Strone-by-Dunoon
Tel (036984) 676
Mem 160
Sec AB Horton (036984) 217
Holes 9 L 2122 yds SSS 62
Recs Am–63 JA Kirby (1987)
V'trs Mon–NA after 6pm Sat–NA 12–4pm
Fees £4 (£4) W–£16
Loc High Road at Strone, N of Dunoon

Carradale (1900)

Carradale PA28 6QT
Tel (05833) 387
Mem 172
Sec Dr JA Duncan
Holes 9 L 2387 yds SSS 63
Recs Am–62 S Campbell
V'trs U
Fees D–£3
Loc Carradale, 15 miles N of Campbeltown

Colonsay

Public
Isle of Colonsay PA61 7YP
Tel (09512) 316
Mem 100
Sec K Byrne
Holes 18 L 4775 yds Par 72
V'trs U
Fees Full membership £5 per family per annum
Loc W coast of Colonsay at Machrins

Cowal (1891)

Ardenslate Road, Dunoon
Tel (0369) 2216
Mem 432
Sec J Bruce (0369) 5673
Pro RD Weir (0369) 2395
Holes 18 L 6251 yds SSS 70
Recs Am–64 A Brodie
V'trs U
Fees On application
Loc NE boundary of Dunoon

Craignure (1981)

Isle of Mull Hotel, Isle of Mull
Tel (068 02) 370/351
Mem 57
Sec Mrs S Campbell
Holes 9 L 4436 metres SSS 64
V'trs U
Fees D–£5
Loc Craignure 1 mile

Dunaverty (1889)

Southend
Mem 220
Sec JE Sayers
Pro WM Millan
Holes 18 L 4597 yds SSS 63
Recs Am–61 S Campbell
Pro–65 EC Brown
V'trs U
Fees £1.10 W–£6.50
Loc 10 miles S of Campbeltown

Glencruitten (1905)

Oban
Tel (0631) 62868
Mem 350 105(L) 115(J)
Sec CM Jarvie (0631) 62308
Pro I Auld (0631) 64115
Holes 18 L 4452 yds SSS 63
Recs Am–55 JM Wilson
Pro–60 H Bannerman, G Cunningham
V'trs U
Fees £6.50 (£8)
Loc Oban 1 mile

Innellan (1891)

Innellan
Tel (0369) 3546
Mem 200
Sec JG Arden
Holes 9 L 4878 yds SSS 63
Recs Am–63
V'trs U SOC
Fees £4 (£5)
Loc 4 miles S of Dunoon

Kyles of Bute (1907)

Tighnabruaich
Tel (0700) 811355
Mem 160
Sec DW Gieve
Holes 9 L 2389 yds SSS 32
V'trs U
Fees D–£4 W–£16
Loc 26 miles W of Dunoon

Lochgilphead (1963)

Blarbuie Road, Lochgilphead
Tel (0546) 2340
Mem 210
Sec PW Tait (0546) 2149
Holes 9 L 4484 yds SSS 63
Recs Am–63 T Armour
V'trs U SOC
Fees £4 (£6)
Loc Lochgilphead ¹/₂ mile

Machrie Hotel (1891)

Port Ellen, Isle of Islay
Tel (0496) 2310
Sec M Macpherson
Holes 18 L 6226 yds SSS 70
Recs Am–67 SW Morrison
Pro–67 M Seymour
V'trs U
Fees £15 D–£24
Mis Play over Machrie course

Machrihanish (1876)

Campbeltown, Machrihanish
Tel (0586) 81213
Mem 516 158(L) 125(J)
Sec Mrs A Anderson
Pro K Campbell (0586) 81277
Holes 18 L 6228 yds SSS 70
9 hole course
Recs Am–66 SJ Campbell
Pro–65 R Walker
V'trs U
Fees £10 D–£13 (£15)
Loc 5 miles W of Campbeltown

Tarbert (1910)

Kilberry Road, Tarbert
Tel (08802) 565
Mem 106
Sec JB Sinclair (08802) 676
Holes 9 L 4460 yds SSS 64
Recs Am–63 D Lamont (1989)
Pro–63
V'trs U
Fees £4 D–£5 W–£20
Loc 1 mile W of Tarbert, Lochfyne on B8024

Tobermory (1896)

Tobermory, Isle of Mull
Mem 150
Sec Dr WH Clegg (0688) 2020
Holes 9 L 2460 yds SSS 64
Recs Am–70 D Brown (1988)
V'trs U
Fees D–£5 W–£16
Loc Tobermory, Isle of Mull
Mis Tickets from Western Isles Hotel

Vaul

Scarinish, Isle of Tiree
Mem 100
Sec Mrs P Boyd (087 92) 344
Holes 9 L 3123 yds SSS 70
V'trs U Sun–NA
Fees £3

Ayrshire

Annanhill (1957)

Public
Irvine Road, Kilmarnock
Tel (0563) 21644
Mem 350
Sec RM Davidson (0563) 29502
Holes 18 L 6270 yds SSS 70
Recs Am–65 I McKenzie
Pro–65 J Farmer
V'trs WD/Sun–U Sat–NA SOC–exc Sat
Fees D–£3.75 (D–£8.75)
Loc 1 mile W of Kilmarnock

Ardeer (1880)

Greenhead, Stevenston
Tel (0294) 64542
Mem 500
Sec P Watson (0294) 63630
Holes 18 L 6630 yds SSS 72
Recs Am–67 NG Walker

Pro–68 A Brooks, I Stanley,
R Walker
V'trs U exc Sat–NA
Fees D–£14 (Sun £18)
Loc ¹/₂ mile off A78 N of Stevenston

Auchenharvie (1981)

Public
Moor Park Road, West Brewery Park,
Saltcoats
Mem 100
Sec WJ Thomson
Pro R Rodgers (0292) 603103
Holes 9 L 5300 yds SSS 66
Recs Am–67 R Galloway, J Murphy,
P Rodgers, A Wylie
V'trs U WE–U after 9.30am
Fees £2.40 (£3.60)
Loc Low road between Saltcoats
and Stevenston

Ballochmyle (1937)

Ballochmyle, Mauchline KA5 6RR
Tel (0290) 50469
Mem 860
Sec A Binnie (0292) 79503
Holes 18 L 5952 yds SSS 69
Recs Am–66 NC Brown, I Guthrie,
D Wallace
Pro–65 A Hunter (1987)
V'trs WD/WE–U BH–M
Fees D–£12 (£18)
Loc A70 Kilmarnock–Dumfries
road. 1 mile S of Mauchline
Mis Buggies available

Beith (1896)

Bigholm Road, Beith
Tel (050 55) 3166
Mem 380
Sec M Rattray (050 55) 2011
Holes 9 L 5580 yds SSS 67
Recs Am–64 K Ross
V'trs U exc Sat & Sun pm
Fees D–£5
Loc 1 mile E of Beith

Belleisle (1927)

Public
Ayr
Tel (0292) 41258
Sec H Diamond
Pro JS Easey (0292) 41314
Holes 18 L 6545 yds SSS 71
Recs Am–63 K Gimson
Pro–64 J Farmer
V'trs WD–U WE–H
Fees £5.60 D–£8.80 (£6.70 D–£10.70)
Loc S boundary of Ayr in Belleisle
Park
Mis Belleisle Club plays here

Caprington

Public
Kilmarnock Municipal,
Ayr Road, Kilmarnock
Tel (0563) 21915
Mem 400
Sec F McCulloch

Holes 18 L 5460 yds SSS 69
9 hole course
Recs Am–65 S Fraser
Pro–66 E Brown
V'trs U

Dalmilling (1960)

Public
Westwood Avenue, Whitletts, Ayr
Tel (0292) 63893
Pro D Gemmell
Holes 18 L 5401 yds SSS 66
Recs Am–61 G McKay
V'trs U
Fees £3.50 D–£4.40 (£4.30 D–£6.90)
(1986 prices)
Loc NE boundary of Ayr
Mis Dalmilling Club plays here

Girvan (1900)

Public
Golf Course Road, Girvan
Tel (0465) 4272
Mem 180
Sec WB Tait (0465) 2011
Holes 18 L 5095 SSS 65
Recs Am–61 J Cannon
Pro–61 K Stevely
V'trs U
Fees £4.40 (£5.60)
Loc N side of Girvan

Glasgow Gailes (1787)

Gailes, Irvine
Tel (0294) 311347
Mem 1100
Sec IAD Mann (041) 942 2011
Pro J Steven (041) 942 8507
Holes 18 L 6447 yds SSS 71
Recs Am–62 CW Green
Pro–67 R Brownlie
V'trs WD–I WE–M SOC
Fees £20 (£20)
Loc 1 mile S of Irvine

Irvine (1887)

Bogside, Irvine
Tel (0294) 78139
Mem 450
Sec A MacPherson (0294) 75979
Pro K Erskine (0294) 75626
Holes 18 L 6408 yds SSS 71
Recs Am–65 DA Roxburgh (1981)
Pro–66 R Weir (1987)
V'trs U SOC–WD
Fees £15 D–£20
Loc 1 mile N of Irvine towards
Kilwinning

Irvine Ravenspark (1907)

Public
Irvine
Tel (0294) 79550
Mem 400
Sec RC Palmer (0294) 76983
Pro P Bond (0294) 76467
Holes 18 L 6496 yds SSS 71

Recs Am–66 F Moore
V'trs U
Fees £1.60 (£3.70)

Kilbirnie Place (1922)

Largs Road, Kilbirnie
Tel (0505) 683398
Mem 300
Sec A Rice
Holes 18 L 5411 yds SSS 67
Recs Am–64 G McLean
V'trs U exc Sat
Fees £3.50 Sun–£8
Loc ¹/₂ mile W of Kilbirnie

Kilmarnock (Barassie) (1887)

29 Hillhouse Road, Barassie, Troon
KA10 6SY
Tel (0292) 311077
Mem 430
Sec RL Bryce (0292) 313920
Pro WR Lockie (0292) 311322
Holes 18 L 6473 yds SSS 71
Recs Am–66 JW Milligan (1988)
Pro–63 GP Emmerson,
C Van der Velde (1989)
V'trs WE/Wed–NA SOC–Tues &
Thurs
Fees On application
Loc Opposite Barassie Station

Largs (1891)

Irvine Road, Largs KA30 8EU
Tel (0475) 673594
Mem 800
Sec F Gilmour (0475) 672497
Pro R Stewart (0475) 686192
Holes 18 L 6257 yds SSS 70
Recs Am–C White
V'trs U
Fees £12 D–£18
Loc 1 mile S of Largs

Loudoun Gowf Club (1909)

Galston
Tel (0563) 820551
Mem 475
Sec CA Bruce (0563) 821993
Holes 18 L 5854 metres SSS 68
Recs Am–64 G Davidson
V'trs WD–U WE–M SOC
Fees £8 D–£13
Loc 5 miles E of Kilmarnock

Maybole

Public
Memorial Park, Maybole
Mem 100
Sec H McKay
Holes 9 L 2635 yds SSS 65 (for 18)
Recs Am–64 WW McCulloch
V'trs U
Fees £2 (£2.80) 1989 prices
Loc Off Glasgow–Stranraer road
(A77), S of Maybole

New Cumnock (1901)

New Cumnock
Mem 125
Sec H Smith
Holes 9 L 2365 yds SSS 63
Recs Am–66 D Blackwood
V'trs U
Loc Cumnock Road

Prestwick (1851)

Links Road, Prestwick KA9 1QG
Tel (0292) 77404
Mem 560
Sec JA Reid
Pro FC Rennie (0292) 79483
Holes 18 L 6631 yds SSS 72
Recs Am–68 PM Mayo, P Deeble,
B Andrade (1987)
Pro–67 EC Brown, C O'Connor
V'trs I WD–on application only
Fees On application
Loc Prestwick Airport 1 mile,
nr Railway Station

Prestwick St Cuthbert (1899)

East Road, Prestwick KA9 2SX
Tel (0292) 77101
Mem 698
Sec R Morton
Holes 18 L 6470 yds SSS 71
Recs Am–66 G Hogg (1984)
V'trs WD/BH–U WE–M SOC–WD
Fees £7 D–£12
Loc 1/2 mile E of Prestwick

Prestwick St Nicholas (1851)

Grangemuir Road, Prestwick KA9 1SN
Tel (0292) 77608
Mem 600 125(L) 62(J)
Sec JR Leishman
Pro I Parker (0292) 79755
Holes 18 L 5926 yds SSS 68
Recs Am–63 P Girvan
Pro–63 A Johnstone
V'trs WD–I WE/BH–NA
Fees On application

Routenburn (1914)

Largs
Tel (0475) 673230
Mem 400
Sec JE Smeaton (0475) 674171
Pro R Torrance (0475) 674289
Holes 18 L 5650 yds SSS 67
Recs Am–65 AO Harrington
Pro–65 S Torrance
V'trs U SOC–WD
Fees £2.60 D–£3.70 (£6.30) W–£19

Royal Troon (1878)

Craigend Road, Troon KA10 6EP
Tel (0292) 311555
Mem 800
Sec JD Montgomerie
Pro RB Anderson (0292) 313281

Holes Old (C'ship) 18 L 7097 yds
SSS 74; Old (Medal) 18 L 6641
yds SSS 73; Portland 18 L 6274
yds SSS 71
Recs Old Am–70 CW Green, J Harkis
Pro–64 G Norman (1989)
Portland Am–66 IR Harris,
JH McKay
V'trs WD–I H Mon–Thurs only
(H'cap limit–18) XL WE–NA
Fees D–£40 Old & Portland
D–£25 Portland only
Loc Prestwick Airport 3 miles
Mis Booking required

Seafield (1930)

Public
Ayr
Tel (0292) 41258
Sec H Diamond
Pro JS Easey (0292) 41314
Holes 18 L 5457 yds SSS 67
Recs Am–65 R Gibson
V'trs U
Fees £4 D–£6.25 (£4.65 D–£7.45)
Loc S boundary of Ayr in Belleisle
Park
Mis Belleisle Club plays here

Skelmorlie (1891)

Skelmorlie PA17 5ES
Tel (0475) 520152
Mem 305
Sec P Griffin
Holes 13 L 5056 yds SSS 65
Recs Am–63 J Paton, I Watson, A
Napier, J Christie, P Travers
Pro–69 J Braid, G Duncan
V'trs U exc Sat (Apr–Oct)
Fees D–£7.50 Sun–£12
Loc Wemyss Bay Station 1 1/2 miles

Troon Municipal

Public
Harling Drive, Troon
Tel (0292) 312464
Pro G Cunningham
Holes Lochgreen 18 L 6687 yds
SSS 72; Darley 18 L 6327 yds
SSS 70; Fullarton 18 L 4784 yds
SSS 63
Recs Lochgreen Am–66 R Milligan
Pro–65 J Chillas
Darley Am–66 M Rossi
Pro–66 J White
Fullarton Am–58 A McQueen
V'trs U SOC–exc Sat
Fees Lochgreen/Darley £4.80
D–£7.60 (£5.80 D–£8.60)
Fullarton £3 D–£3.90 (£3.60
D–£6)
Loc 4 miles N of Prestwick at
Station Brae

Troon Portland (1894)

1 Crosbie Road, Troon
Tel (0292) 311555
Mem 120
Sec J Currie (0292) 311863
Holes Play over Troon Portland
of Royal Troon

Troon St Meddans (1907)

Harling Drive, Troon KA10 6NF
Mem 200
Sec DG Baxter (0292) 313291
Holes Play over Troon Municipal
courses Lochgreen SSS 72
and Darley SSS 70

Turnberry Hotel (1906)

Turnberry KA26 9LT
Tel (0655) 31000
Sec CJ Rouse (Gen Mgr)
Pro RS Jamieson
Holes Ailsa 18 L 6950 yds SSS 70
Arran 18 L 6276 yds SSS 69
Recs Ailsa Am–70 GK MacDonald
Pro–63 M Hayes, G Norman
Arran Am–66 AP Parkin
Pro–66 J McTear
V'trs U H after 12 noon (WD/WE)
Fees On application
Loc 5 miles N of Girvan
Mis Turnberry Club plays here

West Kilbride (1893)

West Kilbride KA23 9HT
Tel (0294) 823128
Mem 1000
Sec ED Jefferies (0294) 823911
Pro G Howie (0294) 823042
Holes 18 L 6452 yds SSS 71
Recs Am–67 G Shaw (1987)
Pro–67 J Panton
V'trs WD–U WE–M BH–NA SOC
Fees On application
Loc West Kilbride

Western Gailes (1897)

Gailes, Irvine KA11 5AE
Tel (0294) 311649
Mem 450
Sec JA Clement
Holes 18 L 6614 yds SSS 72
Recs Am–68 ME Lewis
Pro–66 DJ Russell
V'trs WD–I exc Thurs. Booking
necessary
Fees D–£22 (pre–booked)
Loc 3 miles N of Troon

Bute

Brodick (1897)

Brodick, Isle of Arran
Tel (0770) 2349
Mem 525
Sec HM Macrae
Pro PS McCalla (0770) 2513
Holes 18 L 4404 yds SSS 62
Recs Am–61 D Bell, A Neilson
V'trs U
Fees D–£8
Loc Pier 1 mile

Bute (1888)

Kingarth, Isle of Bute
Mem   115
Sec   J Burnside (070083) 648
Holes 9 L 2497 yds SSS 64
Recs   Am–66
V'trs U
Fees   D–£3 W–£9
Loc   Stravanan Bay, off A845
       Rothesay–Kilchattan Bay road

Corrie (1892)

Corrie, Isle of Arran
Tel   (077 081) 223
Mem   220
Sec   J Kerr (077 081) 215
Holes 9 L 1948 yds SSS 61
Recs   Am–62 JC Reid
V'trs U
Fees   D–£3 W–£12 M–£20
Loc   6 miles N of Brodick

Lamlash (1889)

Lamlash, Isle of Arran
Tel   (07706) 296
Mem   435
Sec   J Henderson (07706) 272
Holes 18 L 4681 yds SSS 63
Recs   Am–62 B Morrison
       Pro–64 R Burke
V'trs U
Fees   D–£5 After 4.30pm–£3 W–£25
Loc   3¹/₂ miles S from Brodick Pier
       on A841

Lochranza

Lochranza, Isle of Arran
Tel   (077 083) 273
Mem   20
Sec   EG Riley
Holes 9 L 1700 yds SSS
Recs   Am–26 GM Anderson
V'trs U–novices welcome

Machrie Bay

Machrie Bay, Brodick, Isle of Arran
KA27 8DZ
Tel   (077 084) 267
Mem   160
Sec   M Hood
Holes 9 L 2082 yds SSS 61
Recs   Am–62 A Kelso
       Pro–59 W Hagen
V'trs U
Fees   D–£2.50 W–£8 M–£11
Loc   W coast, 9 miles from Brodick

Millport (1888)

Millport, Isle of Cumbrae KA28
Tel   (0475) 530311
Mem   231 96(L) 98(J)
Sec   WD Patrick (0475) 530308
Holes 18 L 5831 yds SSS 68
Recs   Am–64 AD Harrington
V'trs U

Fees   £6 D–£7 (£7 D–£9.50)
       W–£28 F–£38 M–£66
Loc   Isle of Cumbrae. Car ferry
       from Largs

Port Bannatyne

Port Bannatyne, Isle of Bute
Mem   170
Sec   IL MacLeod (0700) 2009
Holes 13 L 4730 yds SSS 63
Recs   Am–61 J Ewing
       Pro–64 W Watson
V'trs U
Fees   £5 (£5) W–£20
Loc   2 miles N of Rothesay, Isle
       of Bute

Rothesay (1892)

Canada Hill, Rothesay, Isle of
Bute
Tel   (0700) 2244
Mem   300
Sec   A Thom (0700) 2993
Pro   G McKinlay (0700) 3554
Holes 18 L 5358 yds SSS 67
Recs   Am–63 G Murray (1984)
       Pro–72 RDBM Shade (1968)
V'trs U Parties welcome
Fees   £8.50 (£10.50) W–£30
Loc   In Rothesay

Shiskine (1896)

Blackwaterfoot, Isle of Arran
Tel   (077086) 226
Mem   244 76(L) 22(J)
Sec   JR Liddell (Match Sec)
       (077086) 313
Holes 12 L 2990 yds SSS 42
Recs   Am–39 J Melvin, J Brown
       Pro–36 DH McGillivray
V'trs U SOC
Fees   £4 (£4.50) W–£25 1989 prices
Loc   11 miles from Brodick
Mis   Links course

Whiting Bay (1895)

Whiting Bay, Isle of Arran
Tel   (077 07) 407
Mem   290
Sec   WA Jones (077 07) 305
Holes 18 L 4405 yds SSS 63
Recs   Am–63 JD Simpson, D Burn
V'trs U
Fees   D–£4 W–£17 F–£25 M–£40
Loc   Rear of village

Dunbartonshire

Bearsden (1891)

Thorn Road, Bearsden G61 4BE
Tel   (041) 942 2351
Mem   600
Sec   WS Chalmers
Holes 9 L 5977 yds SSS 69
Recs   Am–64 D MacLeod
V'trs M
Loc   7 miles NW of Glasgow

Cardross (1895)

Cardross, Dumbarton
G82 5LB
Tel   (0389) 841213
Mem   800
Sec   R Evans CA (0389) 841754
Pro   R Craig (0389) 841350
Holes 18 L 6466 yds SSS 71
Recs   Am–65 JLS Kinloch
       Pro–67 M Miller, G Weir
V'trs WD–U WE–M SOC
Fees   £10 D–£15
Loc   4 miles W of Dumbarton

Clober (1951)

Craigton Road, Milngavie, Glasgow
G62 7HP
Tel   (041) 956 1685
Mem   676
Sec   G Buchanan (041) 956 5839
Pro   G Lyle
Holes 18 L 5068 yds SSS 65
Recs   Am–61 PW Smith, J Graham
V'trs WD–U before 4.30pm WE–M
       BH–NA SOC
Fees   £7
Loc   7 miles NW of Glasgow

Clydebank & District (1905)

Hardgate, Clydebank
Tel   (0389) 73289
Mem   780
Sec   W Manson (0389) 72832
Pro   C Elliott
Holes 18 L 5815 yds SSS 68
Recs   Am–64 D Galbraith
V'trs WD–I
Fees   D–£12 W–£40 M–£75
Loc   2 miles N of Clydebank

Clydebank Municipal

Public
Overtoun Road, Dalmuir, Clydebank
Tel   (041) 952 6372
Sec   Clydebank District Council
       (041) 941 1331
Pro   R Bowman (041) 952 6372
Holes 18 L 5349 yds SSS 66
Recs   Am–64 FG Jardine, J Semple
       Pro–64 R Bowman
V'trs U exc Sat 11am–2.30pm
Fees   Mon–Sat £2 Sun–£2.40
Loc   8 miles W of Glasgow
Mis   Clydebank Overtoun Club
       plays here

Clydebank Overtoun (1970)

Overtoun Road, Dalmuir, Clydebank
Tel   (041) 952 6372
Mem   160
Sec   JD Byrne (041) 952 6480
Holes Play over Clydebank
       Municipal

Craigmaddie (1977)

Public
Dougalston Golf Course, Milngavie,
Glasgow
Tel   (041) 956 5750
Mem   500
Sec   G More
Holes Play over Dougalston

Cumbernauld (1977)

Public
Palacerigg Country Park,
Cumbernauld G67 3HU
Tel   (0236) 734969
Mem   350
Sec   JH Dunsmore
Holes 18 L 6412 yds SSS 71
Recs   Am–67 G Wilson
       Pro–69 D Mathews
V'trs U SOC–WD only
Fees   £4 (£8)
Mis   Palacerigg GC plays here

Dougalston (1977)

Milngavie, Glasgow
Tel   (041) 956 5750
Sec   W McInnes
Holes 18 L 6269 yds SSS 71
Recs   Am–71 J Carnegie,
       J McLaren (1987)
       Pro–73 B Barnes
V'trs U SOC
Fees   £6 (£7)
Loc   7 miles N of Glasgow on A81
Mis   Craigmaddie Club plays here

Douglas Park (1897)

Hillfoot, Bearsden
Tel   (041) 942 2220
Mem   400 250(L) 100(J)
Sec   To be appointed
Pro   D Scott (041) 942 1482
Holes 18 L 5957 yds SSS 69
Recs   Am–64 F Giovannetti
       Pro–66 A Hunter, S McAllister
V'trs M
Loc   Bearsden, at Hillfoot Station

Dullatur (1896)

Dullatur, Glasgow G68 0AR
Tel   (0236) 723230
Mem   420 60(L)
Sec   W Laing (0236) 27847
Pro   D Sinclair
Holes 18 L 6253 yds SSS 70
Recs   Am–67 JM Moffat (1985)
       Pro–68 J Farmer
V'trs WD–U WE–M
Fees   £10
Loc   3 miles N of Cumbernauld

Dumbarton (1888)

Broadmeadow, Dumbarton
Tel   (0389) 32830
Mem   500
Sec   R Turnbull
Holes 18 L 5981 yds SSS 69

Recs   Am–64 CW Green
V'trs WD–U WE/BH–M
Fees   D–£8
Loc   ³/₄ mile N of Dumbarton

Glasgow (1787)

Killermont, Bearsden, Glasgow
G61 2TW
Tel   (041) 942 2340
Mem   900
Sec   IAD Mann (041) 942 2011
Pro   J Steven (041) 942 8507
Holes 18 L 5968 yds SSS 69
Recs   Am–63 JS Cochran
       Pro–65 H Weetman
V'trs M
Loc   4 miles NW of Glasgow

Hayston (1926)

Campsie Road, Kirkintilloch, Glasgow
G66 1RN
Tel   (041) 776 1244
Mem   445 70(L) 60(J)
Sec   (041) 776 4688
Pro   (041) 775 0882
Holes 18 L 6042 yds SSS 69
Recs   Am–62 LS Mann
       Pro–69 K Stables
V'trs WD–I before 4.30pm
       M after 4.30pm WE–M SOC
Fees   £9
Loc   1 mile N of Kirkintilloch
Mis   Buggies for hire

Helensburgh (1893)

25 East Abercromby Street,
Helensburgh G84 9JD
Tel   (0436) 74173
Mem   825
Sec   Mrs AC McEwan
Pro   J Farrell (0436) 75505
Holes 18 L 6058 yds SSS 69
Recs   Am–64 A Scott
       Pro–65 RT Drummond,
       D Chillas, B Marchbank
V'trs WD–U WE–NA
Fees   £8 D–£12
Loc   25 miles W of Glasgow

Hilton Park (1927)

Auldmarroch Estate, Stockiemuir
Road, Milngavie G62 7HB
Tel   (041) 956 5124/1215
Mem   1200
Sec   Mrs JA Dawson (041) 956
       4657
Pro   W McCondichie (041) 956
       5125
Holes Hilton 18 L 6003 yds SSS 70
       Allander 18 L 5361 yds
       SSS 67
Recs   Hilton Am–65 ND Kelly
       Pro–64 AF Anderson
       Allander Am–66 I Weir
       Pro–63 F Morris, N Wood
V'trs WD–U before 5pm WE–M
Fees   On application
Loc   8 miles N of Glasgow

Kirkintilloch (1894)

Todhill, Campsie Road, Kirkintilloch
C66 1RN
Tel   (041) 776 1256
Mem   420 92(L) 104(J) 35(5)
Sec   H Bannerman (041) 777 7971
Holes 18 L 5269 yds SSS 66
Recs   Am–63 J Hay, R Moir
       Pro–68 R Weir
V'trs M
Loc   7 miles N of Glasgow

Milngavie (1895)

Laighpark, Milngavie G62 8EP
Tel   (041) 956 1619
Mem   390
Sec   WD Robertson
Holes 18 L 5818 yds SSS 68
Recs   Am–64 RGB McCallum,
       R Blair
V'trs M SOC
Fees   On application
Loc   NW of Glasgow

Vale of Leven (1907)

Northfield Road, Bonhill, Alexandria
Tel   (0389) 52351
Mem   450
Sec   W McKinlay (0389) 52508
Holes 18 L 5156 yds SSS 66
Recs   Am–60 G Brown (1988)
       Pro–63 EC Brown (1959)
V'trs U exc Sat (Apr–Sept)
       SOC (max 36 members)
Fees   D–£6 (D–£10)
Loc   Off A82 at Bonhill

Windyhill (1908)

Windyhill, Bearsden
Tel   (041) 942 2349
Mem   650
Sec   AJ Miller
Pro   R Collinson (041) 942 7157
Holes 18 L 6254 yds SSS 70
Recs   Am–66 DJ Shaw
V'trs WD–I Sun–M SOC–WD
Fees   £8
Loc   8 miles NW of Glasgow

Lanarkshire

Airdrie (1877)

Rochsoles, Airdrie
Tel   (0236) 62195
Mem   425
Pro   A McCloskey (0236) 54360
Holes 18 L 6004 yds SSS 69
Recs   Am–64 G Russo, R Marshall
V'trs M I WE/BH–NA SOC
Fees   D–£10.50
Loc   Airdrie 1 mile

Alexandra Park (1880)

Public
Sannox Gardens, Alexandra Parade,
Glasgow
Tel   (041) 556 3711
Mem   250
Sec   G McArthur
Holes 9 L 1968 yds SSS 30

For explanation of abbreviations, see page 460.

V'trs U
Fees £1.10 (£1.40)
Loc ¹/₂ mile E of Glasgow

Bellshill (1905)

Orbiston, Bellshill ML4 2RZ
Tel (0698) 745124
Mem 600
Sec A Currie
Holes 18 L 6607 yds SSS 72
Recs Am–68 J Simpson, A Megan,
M Brown
Pro–70 J McCallum
V'trs U exc WD 5–6.30pm
Fees £9 (£12)
Loc 10 miles S of Glasgow between
Bellshill and Motherwell

Biggar (1895)

Public
Public Park, Broughton Road,
Biggar ML12
Tel (0899) 20618
Mem 400
Sec WS Turnbull (0899) 20566
Holes 18 L 5416 yds SSS 66
Recs Am–62 B Kerr (1987)
Pro–65 W Murray (1981)
V'trs U
Fees £5 (£7.50)

Bishopbriggs (1906)

Brackenbrae Road, Bishopbriggs,
Glasgow G64 2DU
Tel (041) 772 1810
Mem 400
Sec HG Simpson (041) 772 8938
Holes 18 L 6041 yds SSS 69
Recs Am–64 I Gillan, AF Dunsmore,
S Finlayson
Pro–63 M Miller
V'trs M or I
Fees £12
Loc 6 miles N of Glasgow

Blairbeth (1910)

Burnside, Rutherglen
Tel (041) 634 3355
Mem 400
Sec FT Henderson (041) 632 0604
Holes 18 L 5448 yds SSS 67
Recs Am–60 DB Howard
Pro–69 WG Cunningham
V'trs M
Loc 1 mile S of Rutherglen

Bothwell Castle (1922)

Blantyre Road, Bothwell G71
Tel (0698) 853177
Mem 1137
Sec ADC Watson (0698) 852395
Pro WA Walker (0698) 852052
Holes 18 L 6240 yds SSS 70
Recs Am–64 F Jardine (1977)
Pro–65 L Johnson (1986)
V'trs WD–U 8.30am–3.30pm
Fees £8 D–£12
Loc 3 miles N of Hamilton

Calderbraes (1893)

57 Roundknowe Road, Uddingston
Tel (0698) 813425
Mem 300
Sec S McGuigan (041) 773 2287
Holes 9 L 5046 yds SSS 67
Recs Am–65 D Gilchrist (1986)
V'trs M
Loc Start of M74

Cambuslang (1891)

Westburn Drive, Cambuslang G72
7AN
Tel (041) 641 3130
Mem 200 100(L) 75(J)
Sec W Lilly
Holes 9 L 6072 yds SSS 69
Recs Am–65 AM Grant
V'trs I
Loc Cambuslang Station ³/₄ mile

Carluke (1894)

Hallcraig, Carluke
Tel (0555) 71070
Mem 460
Sec J Kyle (0555) 70366
Pro A Brooks (0555) 51053
Holes 18 L 5805 yds SSS 68
Recs Am–64 K Harrison
Pro–64 G Cunningham,
R Davis, W Milne
V'trs WD–U before 4pm WE–NA
Fees £6 D–£9
Loc Glasgow 20 miles

Carnwath (1907)

Main Street, Carnwath
Tel (0555) 840251
Mem 380
Sec GP Pollock (0555) 4359
Holes 18 L 5955 yds SSS 69
Recs Am–65 B Holbrook
V'trs U exc Sat–NA
Fees £10 (£12)
Loc Lanark 7 miles

Cathkin Braes (1888)

Cathkin Road, Rutherglen, Glasgow
G73 4SE
Tel (041) 634 6605
Mem 880
Sec GL Stevenson
Pro S Bree (041) 634 0650
Holes 18 L 6266 yds SSS 71
Recs Am–65 J Graham (1984)
Pro–66 W Milne (1988)
V'trs WD–I
Fees £10
Loc 5 miles S of Glasgow on B759

Cawder (1933)

Cadder Road, Bishopbriggs, Glasgow
Tel (041) 772 7101
Mem 1200
Sec GT Stoddart (041) 772 5167
Pro K Stevely (041) 772 7102
Holes Cawder 18 L 6295 yds SSS 71;
Keir 18 L 5877 yds SSS 68

Recs Cawder Am–68 CW Green
Pro–65 R Weir
Keir Am–63 G Rodaks,
GH Murray
V'trs WD–U WE–NA SOC–WD
Fees £16.50
Loc Bishopbriggs Station 1¹/₄ miles

Coatbridge (1971)

Public
Townhead Road, Coatbridge
Tel (0236) 28975
Mem 300
Sec O Dolan (0236) 26811
Pro G Weir (0236) 21492
Holes 18 L 6020 yds SSS 69
Recs Am–69 A Webster (1989)
V'trs U
Fees £1.75
Loc Townhead

Colville Park (1922)

Jerviston Estate, Motherwell ML1 4UG
Tel (0698) 63017
Mem 540 64(L) 140(J)
Sec E Wood (0698) 66045
Pro Golf Shop (0698) 65779
Holes 18 L 6265 yds SSS 70
Recs Am–65 G King
Pro–66 SD Brown
V'trs M SOC–WD only
Fees £10
Loc 1 mile NE of Motherwell on
A723

Cowglen (1906)

301 Barrhead Road, Glasgow
Tel (041) 632 0556
Mem 450
Sec RJG Jamieson (0292) 266600
Pro J McTear (041) 649 9401
Holes 18 L 6006 yds SSS 69
Recs Am–63 D Barclay Howard
Pro–63 S Torrance
V'trs M
Loc S side of Glasgow

Crow Wood (1925)

Muirhead, Chryston, Glasgow
Tel (041) 799 2011
Mem 558
Sec RD Britton (041) 248 7495
Pro (041) 779 1943
Holes 18 L 6249 yds SSS 70
Recs Am–64 D Chalmers
Pro–66 J McTear
V'trs M
Loc 5 miles NE of Glasgow

Deaconsbank (1922)

Public
Glasgow
Tel (041) 638 7044
Sec C Cosh
Holes 18 L 4800 yds SSS 63
V'trs U
Fees £3.75 (£5.50)
Loc 5 miles S of Glasgow
nr Thornliebank

Douglas Water (1922)

Douglas Water, Lanark
Tel   (055 588) 361
Mem   150
Sec   R McMillan
Holes 9 L 2916 yds SSS 69
Recs   Am–66 H Gold
V'trs U
Fees   £3 (£4)
Loc   7 miles SW of Lanark

Drumpellier (1894)

Drumpellier Ave, Coatbridge
ML5 1RX
Tel   (0236) 24139/28723
Mem   450
Sec   W Brownlie (0236) 23065/
       28538
Pro   I Collins (0236) 32971
Holes 18 L 6227 yds SSS 70
Recs   Am–65 AD Ferguson,
       G Shanks, ISS Russell
       Pro–63 R Weir
V'trs I
Fees   £12.50 D–£18
Loc   8 miles E of Glasgow

East Kilbride (1900)

Chapelside Road, Nerston,
East Kilbride G74 4PF
Tel   (035 52) 20913
Mem   700
Sec   T McCracken (035 52) 47728
Pro   A Taylor (035 52) 22192
Holes 18 L 6419 yds SSS 71
Recs   Am–65 WF Bryce
       Pro–64 D Ingram
V'trs M SOC
Fees   £8 D–£12
Loc   8 miles S of Glasgow

Easter Moffat (1922)

Plains, by Airdrie ML6 8NP
Tel   (0236) 842289/842878
Mem   450
Sec   JG Timmons
Pro   B Dunbar (0236) 843015
Holes 18 L 6221 yds SSS 70
Recs   Am–67
       Pro–66 R Shade
V'trs WD only
Fees   £8 D–£10
Loc   3 miles E of Airdrie

Haggs Castle (1910)

70 Dumbreck Road, Dumbreck,
Glasgow G41 4SN
Tel   (041) 427 0480
Mem   1000
Sec   ARC Alexander (041) 427 1157
Pro   J McAlister (041) 427 3355
Holes 18 L 6464 yds SSS 71
Recs   Am–66 J Semple (1987)
       Pro–62 S Torrance (1984)
V'trs M SOC–Weds only
Fees   SOC–£14 D–£21
Loc   SW Glasgow

Hamilton (1892)

Riccarton, Ferniegair, by Hamilton
Tel   (0698) 282872
Mem   480
Sec   PE Soutter (0698) 286131
Pro   MJ Moir (0698) 282324
Holes 18 L 6255 yds SSS 70
Recs   Am–62 G Hogg
V'trs M or by arrangement
Fees   £10 D–£15
Loc   1½ miles S of Hamilton

Hollandbush (1954)

Public
Acre Tophead, Lesmahagow,
by Coalburn
Tel   (0555) 893484
Mem   500
Sec   J Hamilton
Pro   I Rae (0555) 893646
Holes 18 L 6110 yds SSS 70
Recs   Am–63 G Brown
V'trs U
Fees   £4 (£6)
Loc   Between Coalburn and
       Lesmahagow

King's Park (1934)

Public
150A Croftpark Avenue, Croftfoot,
Glasgow G54
Holes 9 L 2010 yds SSS 30
Recs   Am–27 I Simpson
V'trs U
Fees   D–£1.50 (£1.20)
Loc   Croftfoot Glasgow G54,
       3½ miles S of city centre

Kirkhill (1910)

Greenlees Road, Cambuslang,
Glasgow
Tel   (041) 641 3083 (clubhouse)
       (041) 641 8499 (office)
Mem   570
Sec   CC Stanfield (041) 634 4276
Holes 18 L 5889 yds SSS 69
Recs   Am–63 D Martin
       Pro–68 R Weir
V'trs WD–by prior arrangement
       WE/BH–NA SOC
Fees   £8 D–£12
Loc   Cambuslang

Knightswood (1929)

Public
Lincoln Avenue, Glasgow G13
Tel   (041) 959 2131
Mem   76
Sec   M Kelly (041) 636 1225
Holes 9 L 2736 yds SSS 33
V'trs U
Fees   D–£1.50 (£1.20)
Loc   4 miles W of Glasgow

Lanark (1851)

The Moor, Lanark
Tel   (0555) 3219
Mem   500 130(L) 200(J)
Sec   WW Law
Pro   R Wallace (0555) 61456
Holes 18 L 6426 yds SSS 71
       9 L 1562 yds SSS 28
Recs   Am–64 CV McInally
       Pro–64 AS Oldcorn
V'trs WD–U until 4pm WE–M
       9 hole course–U
Fees   £14 D–£20 9 hole course £2
Loc   30 miles S of Glasgow off A74

Larkhall

Public
Burnhead Road, Larkhall
Tel   (0698) 881113
Mem   400
Sec   I Gilmour
Holes 9 L 6754 yds SSS 72
Recs   Am–69 S Crolla, G Russell
V'trs U exc Tues 5–8pm
       & Sat 7am–5pm
Loc   SW of town on B7109

Leadhills (1935)

Leadhills, Biggar
Tel   (0659) 74222
Mem   100
Sec   H Shaw
Holes 9 L 2031 yds SSS 62
V'trs U
Fees   £3 (£4)
Loc   6 miles off A74 at Abington
Mis   Highest golf course in Great
       Britain; 1500 ft above sea level

Lenzie (1889)

19 Crosshill Road, Lenzie G66 5DA
Tel   (041) 776 1535
Mem   483 125(L) 125(J)
Sec   AW Jones (041) 776 4377
Pro   J McCallum (041) 777 7748
Holes 18 L 5982 yds SSS 69
Recs   Am–64 S Lindsay
       Pro–66 G Weir (1989)
V'trs M SOC
Loc   Glasgow 6 miles

Lethamhill (1933)

Public
Cumbernauld Road, Glasgow G3
Tel   (041) 770 6220
Holes 18 L 5946 yds SSS 68
Recs   Am–70 R Harker
V'trs U
Fees   £2.50 (£3)
Loc   3 miles E of city centre

Linn Park (1924)

Public
Simshill Road, Glasgow
G44
Tel   (041) 637 5871
Mem   90
Sec   R Flanagan

For explanation of abbreviations, see page 460.

Holes   18 L 4592 yds SSS 65
Recs   Am-62 J Cassidy (1989)
V'trs   U
Fees   £2.70 (£3)
Loc   4 miles S of Glasgow

Littlehill (1926)

Public
Auchinairn Road, Bishopbriggs,
Glasgow
Tel   (041) 772 1916
Holes   18 L 6228 yds SSS 70
Recs   Am-69
V'trs   U
Fees   £1.80 D-£3 (£2.40)
Loc   3 miles N of Glasgow

Mount Ellen (1905)

Gartcosh, Glasgow G69 9EY
Tel   (0236) 872277
Mem   480
Sec   WJ Dickson
Pro   I Mathieson
Holes   18 L 5525 yds SSS 68
V'trs   WD-U from 9am-4pm WE-NA
Fees   £6 D-£9
Loc   8 miles NE of Glasgow

Pollok (1892)

90 Barrhead Road, Pollokshaws,
Glasgow G43 1BG
Tel   (041) 632 1080
Mem   500
Sec   A Mathison Boyd (041) 632 4351
Holes   18 L 6257 yds SSS 70
Recs   Am-62 G Shaw
   Pro-62 G Cunningham
V'trs   I XL WE-NA SOC-WD
Fees   £18 D-£22
Loc   3 miles SW of Glasgow on B462

Ruchill (1928)

Public
Brassey Street, Maryhill, Glasgow G20
Mem   60
Sec   DF Campbell (041) 946 7676
Holes   9 L 2240 yds SSS 31
V'trs   U
Fees   D-£1.50 (£1.20)
Loc   2¹/₂ miles NW of Glasgow

Sandyhills (1905)

223 Sandyhills Road, Glasgow G32
9NA
Tel   (041) 778 1179
Mem   460
Sec   G Muir CA (0698) 812203
Holes   18 L 6253 yds SSS 70
Recs   Am-65 J Hay
V'trs   M SOC
Loc   4 miles E of Glasgow

Shotts (1895)

Blairhead, Benhar Road, Shotts
Tel   (0501) 20431
Mem   700
Sec   J McDermott
Pro   G Graham (0501) 22658

Holes   18 L 6290 yds SSS 70
Recs   Am-65 AJ Ferguson
   Pro-65 B Gunson
V'trs   WD-U Sat-NA before 4.30pm
Fees   D-£8 (D-£10)
Loc   Midway between Glasgow &
   Edinburgh. M8, 1¹/₂ miles

Strathaven (1908)

Strathaven ML10 6NL
Tel   (0357) 20539
Mem   650
Sec   AW Wallace (0357) 20421
Pro   M McCrorie (0357) 21812
Holes   18 L 6226 yds SSS 70
Recs   Am-66 RJC Milton, S Kirkland,
   AW Wallace, IA Ferguson
   Pro-63 D Huish
V'trs   WD-I before 4.30pm
   WE/WD after 4.30pm-NA
Fees   On request
Loc   Outskirts of Strathaven,
   off Glasgow road

Strathclyde Park

Public
Mote Hill, Hamilton
Mem   110
Sec   AJ Duncan (0698) 459201
Pro   K Davidson
Holes   9 L 6294 yds SSS 70
Recs   Am-67 A Brown
V'trs   U exc medal days (phone to
   book (0698) 60155)
Fees   £1.20
Loc   Hamilton
Mis   Driving range

Torrance House (1969)

Public
Strathaven Road, East Kilbride
Tel   (035 52) 48638
Mem   650
Sec   Mrs J O'Brien
   (035 52) 49320
Pro   J Dunlop (035 52) 33451
Holes   18 L 6403 yds SSS 71
Recs   Am-67 A Pitt
   Pro-66 I Collins
V'trs   U
Fees   £4.50
Loc   E Kilbride, on Strathaven road

Wishaw (1897)

55 Cleland Road, Wishaw
Tel   (0698) 372869
Mem   475 100(L) 50(J)
Sec   JW Douglas
Pro   JG Campbell (0698) 358247
Holes   18 L 6134 yds SSS 69
Recs   Am-64 W Denholm, A Brown
   Pro-65
V'trs   Sat/WD after 4pm-NA
Fees   £7 D-£9.50 Sun-£14
Loc   In Wishaw

Renfrewshire

Barshaw

Barshaw Park, Paisley
Tel   (041) 889 2908
Mem   68
Sec   W Collins (041) 884 2533
Holes   18 L 5703 yds SSS 67
V'trs   U
Fees   £2.30
Loc   1 mile E of Paisley Cross
   off A737

Bonnyton (1957)

Eaglesham, Glasgow G76 0QA
Tel   (035 53) 2781
Mem   950
Sec   H Beach
Pro   J Poarston (035 53) 2256
Holes   18 L 6252 yds SSS 71
Recs   Am-67 F Black
   Pro-68 J Wilson
V'trs   I SOC-WD
Fees   £14
Loc   SW of Eaglesham

Caldwell (1903)

Caldwell, Uplawmoor
Tel   (050 585) 329
Mem   450
Sec   DP MacLean (041) 333 9770
Pro   K Baxter (050 585) 616
Holes   18 L 6046 yds SSS 69
Recs   Am-64 JM Sharp
   Pro-63 C Innes, G Collinson
V'trs   WD-Contact in advance
   before 4pm-M after 4pm
   WE-M SOC
Fees   £8 D-£11.50
Loc   5 miles SW of Barrhead on
   A736 Glasgow-Irvine road

Cathcart Castle (1895)

Mearns Road, Clarkston
Tel   (041) 638 0082
Mem   700
Sec   WG Buchan (041) 638 9449
Pro   D Naylor (041) 638 3436
Holes   18 L 5832 yds SSS 68
Recs   Am-62 S Black
   Pro-64 A White
V'trs   M
Loc   7 miles SW of Glasgow

Cochrane Castle (1895)

Craigston, Johnstone PA5 0HF
Tel   (0505) 20146
Mem   400
Sec   JC Cowan
Pro   S Campbell (0505) 28465
Holes   18 L 6226 yds SSS 70
Recs   Am-66 D Abercrombie
   Pro-71 S Kelly
V'trs   WD-U WE-M
Fees   £8 D-£12
Loc   ¹/₂ mile S of A737. 1 mile from
   Johnstone

East Renfrewshire (1922)

Pilmuir, Newton Mearns G77 6RT
Tel   (03555) 258
Mem 450
Sec   AL Gillespie CA (041) 226 4311
Pro   GD Clarke (03555) 206
Holes 18 L 6097 yds SSS 70
Recs   Am–64 A Dow
      Pro–65 WR Lockie
V'trs   By arrangement
Loc   2 miles SW of Newton Mearns

Eastwood (1893)

Muirshield, Loganswell,
Newton Mearns, Glasgow G77 6RX
Tel   (03555) 261
Mem 650
Sec   CB Scouler (03555) 280
Pro   K McWade (03555) 285
Holes 18 L 5886 yds SSS 68
Recs   Am–62 IA Carslaw
      Pro–67 P Mills
V'trs   M SOC
Loc   9 miles SW of Glasgow

Elderslie (1908)

Elderslie
Tel   (0505) 23956
Mem 400
Sec   W Muirhead
Holes 18 L 6031 yds SSS 69
Recs   Am–69 J Kyle, B Clarkson
      Pro–R Weir, R Craig
V'trs   M
Loc   Paisley 2 miles

Erskine (1904)

Bishopton PA7 5PH
Tel   (0505) 862302
Mem 400 200(L)
Sec   TA McKillop
Pro   P Thomson (0505) 862108
Holes 18 L 6287 yds SSS 70
Recs   Am–66 IG Riddell
      Pro–64 MC Douglas
V'trs   WD–I WE–M
Fees   £11
Loc   5 miles NW of Paisley

Fereneze (1904)

Barrhead G78 1HJ
Tel   (041) 881 1519
Mem 700
Sec   AD Gourley (041) 221 6394
Pro   A Armstrong (041) 880 7058
Holes 18 L 5821 yds SSS 68
Recs   Am–64 EH McMillan
      Pro–67 R Drummond, D Huish,
      J McTear, R Weir
V'trs   M SOC–WD
Fees   SOC–£10
Loc   9 miles SW of Glasgow

Gleddoch (1974)

Langbank PA14 6YE
Tel   (047 554) 304
Mem 450
Pro   K Campbell (047 554) 704
Holes 18 L 6200 yds SSS 71
Recs   Am–69 DJ McDougall
      Pro–67 J Chillas
V'trs   WD–U WE–M
Fees   £16.50
Loc   16 miles W of Glasgow by
      M8/A8

Gourock (1896)

Cowal View, Gourock PA19 6HD
Tel   (0475) 31001
Mem 660 106(L) 112(J)
Sec   CM Campbell (0475) 38242
Pro   RM Collinson (0475) 36834
Holes 18 L 6492 yds SSS 71
Recs   Am–64 N Skinner
      Pro–69 D Graham
V'trs   WD–I WE–M SOC
Fees   On application
Loc   3 miles SW of Gourock Station

Greenock (1890)

Forsyth Street, Greenock PA16 8RE
Tel   (0475) 20793
Mem 478 149(L) 144(J)
Sec   EJ Black (0475) 26819
Pro   C Ross (0475) 87236
Holes 18 L 5888 yds SSS 68
      9 L 2149 yds SSS 32
Recs   Am–64 MC Mazzoni
      Pro–66 H Thomson, J Panton,
      H Boyle
V'trs   WD–U WE/BH–M
Fees   D–£12 (D–£15)

Kilmacolm (1891)

Kilmacolm
Tel   (050 587) 2139
Mem 623
Sec   RF McDonald
Pro   D Stewart (050 587) 2695
Holes 18 L 5890 yds SSS 68
Recs   Am–64 M Stevenson
      Pro–66 EC Brown
V'trs   WD–U WE–M
Loc   10 miles W of Paisley

Lochwinnoch (1897)

Burnfoot Road, Lochwinnoch
Tel   (0505) 842153
Mem 500
Sec   Mrs E McBride
Pro   G Reilly (0505) 843029
Holes 18 L 6223 yds SSS 70
Recs   Am–67 IJ Gilmour,
      A Hutchieson
      Pro–63 M Miller (1987)
V'trs   WD–U before 4.30pm WE–M
      SOC
Fees   £8 (£10)
Loc   9 miles S of Paisley

Old Ranfurly (1905)

Bridge of Weir
Tel   (0505) 613612
Mem 375
Sec   R MacCallum
Holes 18 L 6089 yds SSS 69
Recs   Am–62 A Hunter (1983)
V'trs   WD–I WE–M SOC
Loc   Bridge of Weir

Paisley (1895)

Braehead, Paisley PA2 8TZ
Tel   (041) 884 2292
Mem 750
Sec   WJ Cunningham (041) 884 3903
Holes 18 L 6424 yds SSS 71
Recs   Am–64 DW Perrie
V'trs   WD–I SOC
Fees   £8 D–£12

Port Glasgow (1895)

Port Glasgow PA14 5XE
Tel   (0475) 704181
Mem 375
Sec   NL Mitchell (0475) 706273
Holes 18 L 5712 yds SSS 68
Recs   Am–63 JW McKechnie
V'trs   WD–U before 5pm –M after
      5pm WE–NA SOC
Fees   £8 D–£12
Loc   1 mile S of Port Glasgow

Ralston (1904)

Ralston, Paisley
Tel   (041) 882 1349
Mem 440 165(L) 100(J)
Sec   JW Horne (041) 883 7045
Pro   D Barbour (041) 810 4925
Holes 18 L 6100 yds SSS 69
Recs   Am–63 J Armstrong
V'trs   M
Loc   2 miles E of Paisley

Ranfurly Castle (1889)

Golf Road, Bridge of Weir
Tel   (0505) 612609
Mem 360 160(L) 100(J)
Sec   Mrs TJ Gemmell
Pro   K Stables (0505) 614795
Holes 18 L 6284 yds SSS 70
Recs   Am–65 WMB Brown
      Pro–65 W Lockie (1989)
V'trs   WD–I WE–M SOC–WD
Loc   7 miles W of Paisley

Renfrew (1894)

Blythswood Estate, Inchinnan Road,
Renfrew PA4 9EG
Tel   (041) 886 6692
Mem 450 110(L) 80(J)
Sec   A Kerr
Pro   J Mulgrew (041) 886 7477
Holes 18 L 6818 yds SSS 73

For explanation of abbreviations, see page 460.

Recs	Am–68 M Smith (1988)
	Pro–70 J Chillas, WB Milne
V'trs	M SOC
Fees	On application
Loc	Glasgow Airport 2 miles

Whinhill (1911)

Beith Road, Greenock
Tel	(0475) 24694
Mem	350
Sec	A Polonis
Holes	18 L 5454 yds SSS 67
Recs	Am–66 W Brewster
V'trs	U
Loc	2 miles S of Greenock

Whitecraigs (1905)

72 Ayr Road, Giffnock, Glasgow
G46 6SW
Tel	(041) 639 1681
Mem	500
Sec	RW Miller (041) 639 4530
Pro	W Watson (041) 639 2140
Holes	18 L 6230 yds SSS 70
V'trs	WD–I WE–M SOC–WD
Fees	£16 D–£20
Loc	Whitecraigs Station 5 mins

Williamwood (1906)

Clarkston Road, Glasgow G44
Tel	(041) 637 1783
Mem	680
Sec	RG Cuthbert (041) 226 4311
Pro	J Gardner (041) 637 2715
Holes	18 L 5878 yds SSS 68
Recs	Am–63 I Carslaw, AA Nicol,
	S Dixon
	Pro–61 BJ Gallacher
V'trs	M
Loc	5 miles S of Glasgow

Stirlingshire

Aberfoyle (1890)

Aberfoyle
Tel	(087 72) 493
Mem	300
Sec	A Macdonald (087 72) 441
Holes	18 L 5204 yds SSS 66
Recs	Am–64 EJ Barnard
V'trs	U
Fees	D–£10
Loc	Braeval, Aberfoyle

Kilsyth Lennox (1900)

Tak–Ma–Doon Road, Kilsyth
Tel	(0236) 822190
Mem	250
Sec	AG Stevenson (0236) 823213
Holes	9 L 5930 yds SSS 69
Recs	Am–66 R Irvine (1986),
	W Erskine (1987)

V'trs	WD–U until 5pm –M after 5pm
	Sat–NA before 4pm Sun–NA
	before 2pm SOC–WD
Fees	£8
Loc	Glasgow 12 miles

Tayside Region

Angus

Arbroath (1877)

Public
Elliot, by Arbroath
Tel	(0241) 72272
Mem	200
Sec	J Thompson (0241) 72069
Pro	L Ewart (0241) 75837
Holes	18 L 6078 yds SSS 69
Recs	Am–65 R Cargill
V'trs	U
Fees	£5 (£7)
Loc	1 mile S of Arbroath

Brechin Golf & Squash Club (1893)

Trinity, Brechin DD9 7PD
Tel	(03562) 2383
Mem	650
Sec	AB May (03562) 2326
Pro	B Mason (03562) 5270
Holes	18 L 5267 yds SSS 66
Recs	Am–61 A Helmsley
V'trs	U ex Wed SOC
Fees	£7 D–£10.50 (£8 D–£11.50)
	Mon–Fri £25
Loc	1 mile N of Brechin on
	Aberdeen road (B966)

Buddon Links (1981)

Public
Carnoustie Golf Links, Links Parade,
Carnoustie DD7 7JE
Tel	(0241) 53249 (Starter's Box)
Sec	EJC Smith (0241) 53789
Holes	18 L 5732 yds SSS 68
V'trs	U
Fees	£5
Loc	12 miles E of Dundee by A92
	or A930

Burnside

Public
Carnoustie Golf Links, Links Parade,
Carnoustie DD7 7JE
Tel	(0241) 53249 (Starter's Box)
Sec	EJC Smith (0241) 53789
Holes	18 L 6020 yds SSS 69
V'trs	WD–U WE–U after 10.30am
Fees	£10
Loc	12 miles E of Dundee by A92
	or A930

Caird Park (1926)

Public
Dundee
Tel	(0382) 453606
Mem	413
Sec	D Farquhar Jr (0382) 457217
Pro	J Black (0382) 459438
Holes	18 L 6303 yds SSS 70
Recs	Am–66 W Thompson (1987)
V'trs	U
Loc	Off Kingsway bypass at
	Mains Loan

Caird Park (1982)

Public
City of Dundee Parks Dept,
353, Clepington Road, Dundee
Tel	(0382) 23141 (Ext 414)
	(Advance bookings Ext 295)
Pro	K Todd
Holes	Yellow 9 L 1692 yds SSS 29
	Red 9 L 1983 yds SSS 29
V'trs	U
Loc	Caird Park Dundee

Caledonia (1887)

Links Parade, Carnoustie
DD7 7JF
Tel	(0241) 52115
Mem	372
Sec	DC Thomson
Holes	Play over Carnoustie courses

Camperdown (1960)

Public
Camperdown Park, Dundee
Tel	(0382) 623398
Mem	600
Sec	R Gordon (0382) 814445
Pro	R Brown
Holes	18 L 6561 yds SSS 72
Recs	Am–68 A Morgan
V'trs	U
Fees	£6.50 (£7.50)
Loc	2 miles NW of Dundee

Carnoustie (1842)

Links Parade, Carnoustie
Tel	(0241) 52480
Mem	900
Sec	DW Curtis
Holes	Play over Carnoustie courses

Carnoustie Championship

Public
Links Parade, Carnoustie DD7 7JE
Tel	(0241) 53249 (Starter's Box)
Sec	EJC Smith (0241) 53789
Holes	18 L 6936 yds SSS 74
Recs	Pro–65 J Newton
V'trs	WD–H Sat–H after 1.30pm
	Sun–H after 11am
Fees	£22 W–£100
Loc	12 miles E of Dundee by A92
	or A930

Carnoustie Ladies (1873)

Links Parade, Carnoustie
Tel (0241) CCQCQ
Mem 106
Sec Mrs S Macdonald (0241) 52073
Holes Play over Carnoustie
Championship, Burnside and
Buddon Links

Carnoustie Mercantile (1896)

Links Parade, Carnoustie
Tel (0241) 52525
Mem 500
Sec R Campbell (0241) 52020
Holes Play over Carnoustie courses

Dalhousie (1868)

Links Parade, Carnoustie
Tel (0241) 53208
Mem 262
Sec GW Ellis
Holes Play over Carnoustie courses

Downfield (1932)

Turnberry Ave, Dundee DD2 3QP
Tel (0382) 825595
Mem 784
Sec RS Imrie
Pro C Waddell (0382) 89246
Holes 18 L 6804 yds SSS 73
Recs Am–67 A Lionella (1967)
     Pro–67 R Weir (1982)
V'trs WD–U 9.30am–12 noon and
     2.18–4pm WE–M
Fees £12 D–£18 1989 prices
Loc North end of Dundee off
     A923 (Timex Circle)

Edzell (1895)

High St, Edzell, by Brechin DD9 7TF
Tel (03564) 235
Mem 650
Sec JM Hutchison (03564) 7283
Pro JB Webster (03564) 462
Holes 18 L 6299 yds SSS 70
Recs Am–65 JKA Bruce (1985)
     Pro–66 AJ Webster (1975)
V'trs WD–NA 5–6.15pm WE–NA
     8–10am & 12.30–2.30pm
     SOC
Fees £9 D–£13.50 (£11 D–£16.50)
     W–£45 M–£90
Loc 6 miles NW of Brechin

Forfar (1871)

Cunninghill, Forfar DD8 2RL
Tel (0307) 62120
Mem 525 175(L) 150(J)
Sec PH Wallace (0307) 63773
Pro P McNiven (0307) 65683
Holes 18 L 5537 metres SSS 69
Recs Am–66 DM Chapman,
     CC Sinclair
     Pro–65 E Brown

V'trs U exc Sat
Fees £11 (£17)
Loc 1½ miles E of Forfar

Kirriemuir (1908)

Kirriemuir
Tel (0575) 72144
Mem 600
Sec Irvine, Adamson & Co (0575)
     72729
Pro A Caira (0575) 73317
Holes 18 L 5541 yds SSS 67
Recs Am–63 JL Adamson, J Murray
V'trs WD–U WE–M SOC
Fees D–£10.50
Loc NE outskirts of Kirriemuir

Letham Grange (1987)

Colliston, Arbroath DD11 4RL
Tel (024) 189373
Mem 450
Sec Ms H MacDougall
Pro D Scott (024) 189377
Holes 18 L 6789 yds SSS 73
Recs Am–73 W Taylor (1987)
     Pro–72 J Farmer (1988)
V'trs WD–U H exc Tues before
     10am WE–M before 10.30am
     & 1–2pm BH–U SOC
Fees £12 D–£18 (£15)
Loc 4 miles N of Arbroath on A993

Monifieth Golf Links

Princes Street, Monifieth, Dundee
Tel (0382) 532767
Mem 1500
Sec JAR Fraser (0382) 78117
Pro I McLeod (0382) 532945
Holes Medal 18 L 6650 yds SSS 72
     Ashludie 18 L 5123 SSS 66
Recs Am–63 JL Adamson
     Pro–64 S Sewgolum
V'trs WD–U Sat–NA Sun–restricted
     SOC
Fees Medal £10 D–£15 (£11 D–£16)
     Ashludie £8 D–£11 (£9 D–£13)
Loc 6 miles E of Dundee
Mis Abertay, Broughty,
     Grange/Dundee and Monifieth
     clubs have playing rights over
     both courses

Montrose

Public
Traill Drive, Montrose DD10 8SW
Tel (0674) 72932
Sec Mrs M Stewart
Pro AJ Webster (0674) 72634
Holes Medal 18 L 6451 yds SSS 71
     Broomfield 18 L 4815 yds
     SSS 63
Recs Pro–Medal 63 G Cunningham,
     D Huish
V'trs WD–U Sat–no 4 ball until 3pm
     (Apr–Sept) WE–NA before
     2pm Sat & 10am Sun

Fees Medal £8.50 (£10)
     Broomfield £6 (£7.50)
Loc 1 mile off A92
Mis Royal Montrose, Caledonia
     and Mercantile clubs play here

Montrose Caledonia (1896)

Dorward Road, Montrose
Tel (0674) 72313
Sec J Adamson (0674) 83438
Holes Play over Montrose and
     Broomfield courses

Montrose Mercantile (1879)

DD10 82W
Tel (0674) 72408
Mem 450
Sec RS West (0674) 75447
Holes Play over Montrose and
     Broomfield courses

New Taymouth

Taymouth St, Carnoustie
Tel (0241) 52425
Mem 450
Sec G Dunton
Holes Play over Carnoustie courses

Panmure (1845)

Barry, by Carnoustie
Tel (0241) 53120
Mem 480
Sec Capt JC Ray
Pro T Shiel
Holes 18 L 6317 yds SSS 70
Recs Am–68 S Macdonald,
     DMA Steel, RDBM Shade
     Pro–65 R de Vicenzo,
     R Cole, D Webster
V'trs WD/Sun–U Sat–NA
Fees £9 D–£14
Loc 2 miles W of Carnoustie

Royal Montrose (1810)

Dorward Road, Montrose DD10 8SW
Tel (0674) 72376
Mem 650
Sec JD Sykes (0674) 73528
Holes Play over Montrose and
     Broomfield courses

Kinross–shire

Bishopshire (1903)

Kinnesswood
Mem 170
Sec AB Moffat (0592) 860379
Holes 9 L 2180 yds SSS 63
Recs Am–63 J Morris
V'trs U
Fees £2 (£3)
Loc 3 miles E of Kinross off M90

For explanation of abbreviations, see page 460.

Green Hotel (1900)

Beeches Park, Kinross
Tel   (0577) 63467
Mem   400
Sec   Mrs M Stewart
Holes   18 L 6111 yds SSS 70
V'trs   U
Fees   £9 (£13.50)
Loc   17 miles S of Perth
Mis   Kinross GC plays here

Kinross

Kinross
Tel   (0577) 62237
Mem   505
Sec   AR Malcolm
Holes   Play over Green Hotel course

Milnathort (1910)

South Street, Milnathort
Tel   (0577) 64069
Mem   400
Holes   9 L 2959 yds SSS 68
Recs   Am–66 D Murphy
V'trs   U SOC
Fees   £5 (£6)
Loc   Between Dunfermline and
        Perth

Perthshire

Aberfeldy (1895)

Taybridge Road, Aberfeldy PH15 2BH
Tel   (0887) 20535
Mem   260
Sec   HE Alexander (0887) 20203
Holes   9 L 2733 yds SSS 67
Recs   Am–66 A McNeill (1987)
        JM Munro (1988)
V'trs   U
Fees   £5 D–£7 W–£25 F–£35
Loc   Aberfeldy, 10 miles off A9

Alyth (1894)

Pitcrocknie, Alyth
Tel   (082 83) 2268
Mem   850
Sec   W Sullivan
Pro   T Melville (082 83) 2411
Holes   18 L 6226 yds SSS 70
Recs   Am–67 E Lindsay, JL Adamson
        Pro–64 I Young
V'trs   U
Fees   £6 D–£9 (£9 D–£13)
Loc   Dundee 16 miles

Auchterarder (1892)

Ochil Road, Auchterarder PH3 1LS
Tel   (0764) 62804
Mem   650
Sec   JI Stewart (0764) 63840
Pro   K Salmoni (0764) 63711

Holes   18 L 5757 yds SSS 68
Recs   Am–66 K Gillon (1989)
        Pro–65 W Guy (1988)
V'trs   U SOC
Fees   £7 D–£10 (£9 D–£14) 1989
        prices
Loc   1 mile SW of Auchterarder

Blair Atholl (1892)

Blair Atholl, Perthshire
Tel   (079 681) 407
Mem   390
Sec   JA McGregor (079 681) 274
Holes   9 L 2855 yds SSS 69
Recs   Am–66
V'trs   U
Fees   D–£6 (D–£7) W–£22
Loc   35 miles N of Perth off
        A9
Mis   Buggies for hire

Blairgowrie (1889)

Rosemount, Blairgowrie PH10 6LG
Tel   (0250) 2594
Mem   1200
Sec   (0250) 2622
Pro   GW Kinnoch (0250) 3116
Holes   Rosemount 18 L 6588 yds
        SSS 72; Lansdowne 18 L 6895
        yds SSS 73; Wee 9 L 4614 yds
        SSS 63
Recs   Rosemount Am–64 B Giraud
        Pro–66 G Norman
        Lansdowne Am–68
        BRN Grieve
        Pro–69 J McAlister
V'trs   Mon/Tues/Thurs–U H
        8.30am–12 & 2–3.30pm Wed/Fri
        WE–restricted
Fees   £18 (£27)
Loc   15 miles NE of Perth off A93.
        16 miles NW of Dundee, off
        A923

Comrie (1891)

Comrie
Mem   170
Sec   DG McGlashan (0764) 70544
Pro   H Donaldson
Holes   9 L 2983 yds SSS 69
Recs   Am–65 A Philp
V'trs   U
Fees   £5 (£6)
Loc   7 miles W of Crieff

Craigie Hill (1982)

Cherrybank, Perth PH2 0NE
Tel   (0738) 24377 (clubhouse)
Mem   700
Sec   WA Miller (0738) 20829
Pro   F Smith (0738) 22644
Holes   18 L 5379 yds SSS 66
Recs   Am–60 G Still (1988)
        Pro–63 W Murray (1986)
V'trs   U exc Sat
Fees   £8 (£10)
Loc   W boundary of Perth

Crieff (1891)

Perth Road, Crieff PH7 3LR
Tel   (0764) 2909 (bookings)
Mem   650
Sec   LJ Rundle (0764) 2397
Pro   DJW Murchie, JM Stark
Holes   Ferntower 18 L 6402 yds
        SSS 71; Dornock 9 L 4772
        yds SSS 63
Recs   Ferntower Am–67
        Pro–66
V'trs   U H NA–12–2pm or after 5pm
        SOC
Fees   Ferntower £12 (£15)
        Dornock £8 (£9) 18 holes
Loc   17 miles W of Perth–A85.
        Crieff 1 mile

Dalmunzic (1048)

Public
Glenshee, Blairgowrie
Tel   (025 085) 226
Mem   52
Sec   S Winton
Holes   9 L 2035 yds SSS 60
V'trs   U
Fees   9 holes £3 D–£5
Loc   22 miles N of Blairgowrie on
        A93 (Dalmunzie Hotel sign)

Dun Ochil (Gleneagles)

Gleneagles
Sec   Dr C Gribble (0786) 822592
Holes   Play over Gleneagles courses

Dun Whinny (Gleneagles) (1936)

12 Anderson Court, Dunblane
FK15 9BE
Tel   (0786) 823174
Mem   70
Sec   RAFG Mackelvie
Holes   Play over Gleneagles courses

Dunkeld & Birnam (1910)

Fungarth, Dunkeld
Tel   (03502) 524
Mem   300
Sec   Mrs W Sinclair (03502) 564
Holes   9 L 5965 yds SSS 66
Recs   Am–64 I Sinclair
V'trs   U
Fees   £6 (£8)
Loc   Dunkeld 1 mile off A923

Dunning (1953)

Rollo Park, Dunning
Sec   JR Stockley
Holes   9 L 4836 yds SSS 64
V'trs   WD–U WE–M (Sat after 4pm)
Fees   £4

Glenalmond

Trinity College, Glenalmond
Sec   J Stewart (073 888) 270
Holes 9 L 5812 yds SSS 68
Recs   Am–70 CMW Robertson
       Pro–72 M Dennis
V'trs M
Loc   10 miles NW of Perth

Gleneagles Hotel

Gleneagles
Tel   (076 46) 3543
Sec   TAK Younger
Pro   I Marchbank (076 46) 2231
Holes King's 18 L 6471 yds SSS 71
       Queen's 18 L 5965 yds SSS 69
       Prince's 18 L 4664 yds SSS 64
       Glendevon 18 L 5719 yds
       SSS 68
Recs   King's Am–65 GM Rutherford
       Pro–62 JM Olazabal
       Queen's Pro–63 C Stadler
V'trs WD–K/Q reserved until
       10.30am and between
       1.30–2.30pm for hotel guests
       and members. WE–K/Q
       reserved for hotel guests and
       members.Visitors must book in
       advance
Fees   On application
Loc   16 miles SW of Perth on A9

Glenearn

c/o Gleneagles Hotel, Auchterarder
Sec   W McIntyre (0786) 71478
Holes Play over Glendevon course,
       Gleneagles

King James VI (1858)

Moncrieffe Island, Perth
Tel   (0738) 25170
       (0738) 32460 (Starter)
Mem   600
Pro   A Coles (0738) 32460
Holes 18 L 6026 yds SSS 69
Recs   Am–63 G Clark
V'trs U exc Sat Sun–by reservation
Fees   D–£7.50 (£15)
Loc   Island in River Tay, Perth

Murrayshall (1981)

Murrayshall, New Scone, Perth
PH2 7PH
Tel   (0738) 52784
Mem   350
Pro   NIM Mackintosh
Holes 18 L 5877 metres SSS 71
Recs   Am–67 G Redford
       Pro–67 J Farmer
V'trs U SOC–WD/WE
Fees   £12 (£18)
Loc   2½ miles E of Perth off A94

Muthill (1935)

Peat Road, Muthill PH5 2AD
Tel   (076 481) 523
Mem   375
Sec   WH Gordon (0764) 3319
Holes 9 L 2371 yds SSS 63
Recs   Am–64 C MacGregor
       Pro–68 RM Jamieson, W Milne
V'trs U
Fees   £4 (£4.50)
Loc   3 miles S of Crieff on A822

North Inch

Public
c/o Perth & Kinross District Council
3 High Street, Perth PH1 5JU
Sec   R Smith (Mgr) (0738) 39911
Holes 18 L 4340 metres SSS 65
V'trs U SOC
Fees   £2.70 (£4.90)
Loc   Nr Perth and A9, by River
       Tay. Follow signs to Bell's
       Sports Centre

Pitlochry (1909)

Golf Course Road, Pitlochry
Tel   (0796) 2792 (Starter)
Mem   350
Sec   DCM McKenzie JP
       (0796) 2114
Pro   J Wilson
Holes 18 L 5811 yds SSS 68
Recs   Am–63 CP Christy, MM Niven
       Pro–64
V'trs U
Fees   D–£10 D–£13 (£9)
Loc   ½ mile from W end of Main
       Street, via Larchwood Road

Royal Perth Golfing Society

1/2 Atholl Crescent, Perth
Tel   (0738) 22265
Mem   250
Sec   R Blake (0738) 33171
Holes 18 L 5141 yds SSS 64
V'trs U No Sunday play
Fees   On application

St Fillans (1903)

South Lochearn Rd, St Fillans
PH6 2NG
Tel   (076 485) 312
Mem   400
Sec   AJN Abercrombie (0764) 3643
Holes 9 L 5268 yds SSS 66
Recs   Am–66 W Gemmell (1989)
V'trs U SOC (max 16)
Fees   D–£5 (D–£6) 5D–£17
Loc   12 miles W of Crieff on A85
       to Crianlarich

Strathtay (1909)

Tighanoisinn, Grandtully PH1 ?QT
Mem   120
Sec   J Armstrong–Payne (08874) 367
Holes 9 L 4082 yds SSS 63
Recs   Am–61 AM Deboys
V'trs U SOC
Fees   D–£4 (£5)
Loc   4 miles W of Ballinluig (A827),
       towards Aberfeldy

Taymouth Castle (1923)

Kenmore PH15 2NT
Tel   (08873) 228
Mem   200
Pro   A Marshall
Holes 18 L 6066 yds SSS 69
Recs   Am–63 MM Niven
V'trs U WE–booking essential SOC
Fees   £11 D–£16 (£14 D–£20)
       Mon–Fri £45
Loc   6 miles W of Aberfeldy
Mis   Buggies available for hire

Western Isles Region

Western Isles

Askernish (1891)

Lochboisdale, South Uist
Mem   30
Holes 9 (18 tees) L 5114 yds SSS 67
Recs   Am–66 K Robertson
V'trs U
Fees   £2 (£2) W–£10
Loc   5 miles NW of Lochboisdale

Stornoway (1890)

Lady Lever Park, Stornoway, Outer
Hebrides
Tel   (0851) 2240
Mem   250
Sec   P Dickie (0851) 3602
Holes 18 L 5119 yds SSS 66
Recs   Am–64 KW Galloway
       Pro–65 JC Farmer
V'trs U Sun–NA
Fees   £5 D–£8 W–£25 F–£35
Loc   In grounds of Lews Castle,
       Isle of Lewis

For explanation of abbreviations, see page 460.

Wales

Clwyd

Abergele & Pensarn (1910)

Tan-y-Goppa Road, Abergele
LL22 8DS
Tel (0745) 824034
Mem 1250
Sec HE Richards
Pro I Runcie (0745) 823813
Holes 18 L 6086 yds SSS 69
Recs Am–J Buckley (1980)
Pro–65 D Vaughan (1987)
V'trs U SOC
Fees £12 (£14)
Loc Abergele

Bryn Morfydd (1982)

The Princess Course, Llanrhaeadr,
nr Denbigh LL16 4NP
Tel (074 578) 280
Mem 20
Sec DJ Willmore
Holes 9 L 1190 yds SSS 27
V'trs U SOC
Fees £2.50 D–£5
Loc 2$\frac{1}{2}$ miles E of Denbigh on A525

Denbigh (1922)

Henllan Road, Denbigh LL16
Tel (074 571) 4159
Mem 450
Sec GC Parry
Pro M Jones
Holes 18 L 5582 yds SSS 67
Recs Am–64 H Parry (1989)
Pro–69 C Defoy (1986)
V'trs U SOC
Fees £8 (£10)
Loc B5382, 2 miles NW of Denbigh

Flint (1966)

Cornist Park, Flint CH6 5HJ
Tel (035 26) 2327
Mem 348
Sec H Griffith (035 26) 2186
Pro M Staton
Holes 9 L 5829 yds SSS 68
Recs Am–67 JP Snead, G Houston
V'trs WD–U before 5pm WE–M
SOC–WD/Sat
Fees D–£5
Loc Station 1$\frac{1}{2}$ miles. Flint 1 mile.
M56 8 miles

Hawarden (1911)

Groomsdale Lane, Hawarden, Deeside
CH5 3EH
Tel (0244) 531447
Mem 320
Sec T Hinks–Edwards (0352) 57955

Pro M Carty
Holes 9 L 5620 yds SSS 67
Recs Am–65 DA Reidford
V'trs M SOC
Loc 6 miles W of Chester off A55

Holywell (1906)

Brynford, Holywell
Tel (0352) 710040
Mem 330
Sec EK Carney (0352) 710539
Pro M Carty
Holes 10 L 3117 yds SSS 71
Recs Am–70 G Houston
Pro–N Jones
V'trs WD–U WE–M
Fees £6 (£8)
Loc 2 miles S of Holywell

Mold (1909)

Pantmywyn, nr Mold
Tel (0352) 740318
Mem 350 55(L) 110(J)
Sec A Newall
Pro M Carty
Holes 18 L 5521 yds SSS 67
Recs Am–65
Pro–64
V'trs U SOC
Fees £7 (£9)
Loc Mold 4 miles

Old Colwyn (1907)

Woodland Avenue, Old Colwyn
LL29 9NL
Tel (0492) 515581
Mem 350
Sec GI Jones
Holes 9 L 5268 yds SSS 66
Recs Am–63 C Oldham,
JD Jones Roberts
Pro–67 DJ Rees
V'trs WD–U WE–by arrangement
SOC
Fees £5 (£6)
Loc Old Colwyn, 2 miles E of
Colwyn Bay

Old Padeswood (1978)

Station Road, Padeswood, nr Mold
Tel (0244) 547401
Mem 500
Sec BV Hellen (0352) 770506
Pro A Davies
Holes 18 L 6728 yds SSS 72
Recs Am–69 L Lockett (1987)
Pro–69 M Redrup
V'trs U exc comp days SOC–WD
Fees £8 D–£12 (£10 D–£14)
Loc 2 miles from Mold on A5118

Padeswood & Buckley (1933)

The Caia, Station Lane, Padeswood,
nr Mold CH7 4JD
Tel (0244) 550537
Mem 592
Sec R McLauchlan
Pro D Ashton (0244) 543636
Holes 18 L 5775 yds SSS 68
Recs Am–66 S Hurstfield
V'trs WD–U 9am–4pm –M after
4pm Sat–U Sun–NA SOC–WD
Ladies Day–Wed
Fees £9 (£11)
Loc 8 miles W of Chester off A5118.
2nd golf club on right

Prestatyn (1905)

Marine Road East, Prestatyn
LL19 7HS
Tel (074 56) 4320/88353
Mem 550
Sec R Woodruff (Mgr)
Pro G Hutchinson
Holes 18 L 6714 yds SSS 73
Recs Am–68 J Bamford
V'trs U
Fees £10 (£12)
Loc 1 mile E of Prestatyn

Rhuddlan (1930)

Rhuddlan, Rhyl LL18 6LB
Tel (0745) 590217
Mem 435 135(L) 100(J)
Sec D Morris
Pro G Cox (0745) 590898
Holes 18 L 6473 yds SSS 71
V'trs H or I Sun–M SOC–WD
Fees £13 (£16)
Loc 3 miles S of Rhyl

Rhyl (1890)

Coast Road, Rhyl
Tel (0745) 353171
Mem 380
Sec GK Watkin (0745) 343377
Holes 9 L 6153 yds SSS 70
Recs Am–67 CH Rees
Pro–67 H Cotton, N von Nida,
C Ward
V'trs U SOC
Fees £7 (£9)
Loc Coast road between Rhyl
and Prestatyn

Ruthin–Pwllglas (1920)

nr Ruthin
Tel (082 42) 2296
Mem 360
Sec RD Roberts (082 42) 4658
Holes 9 L 5313 yds SSS 66

Recs   Am–64 MG Hughes
V'trs   U SOC
Fees   £6 (£8)
Loc   Pwllglas, 2½ miles S of Ruthin

St Melyd (1922)

The Paddock, Meliden Road,
Prestatyn LL19 9NB
Tel   (074 56) 4405
Mem   530
Sec   PA White (074 56) 3147
Pro   NH Lloyd (074 56) 88858
Holes   9 L 5857 yds SSS 68
Recs   Am–67 C Davies
    Pro–68 N Hill
V'trs   U SOC
Fees   £8 (£12)
Loc   On A547 between Prestatyn
    and Meliden

Vale of Llangollen (1908)

Holyhead Road, Llangollen LL20 7PR
Tel   (0978) 860040
Mem   600
Sec   TF Ellis
Pro   DI Vaughan
Holes   18 L 6661 yds SSS 72
Recs   Am–69
    Pro–68
V'trs   U
Fees   £12 (£16)
Loc   1½ miles E of Llangollen
    on A5

Wrexham (1906)

Holt Road, Wrexham
Tel   (0978) 261033
Mem   650
Sec   KB Fisher (0978) 364268
Pro   DA Larvin (0978) 351476
Holes   18 L 6078 yds SSS 69
Recs   Am–67 P Williams, MS Chidley
V'trs   H SOC–WD
Fees   On application
Loc   2 miles NE of Wrexham on
    A534

Dyfed

Aberystwyth (1911)

Bryn-y-Mor, Aberystwyth SY23 2HY
Tel   (0970) 615104
Mem   390
Sec   W Hughes (0970) 623826
Pro   G Brownlie (0970) 625103
Holes   18 L 5868 yds SSS 68
Recs   Am–63 W Pugh, MA Owen
    Pro–64 A Hodson
V'trs   U SOC
Fees   £5 D–£7 (£7 D–£10)
Loc   Aberystwyth ½ mile

Ashburnham (1894)

Cliffe Terrace, Burry Port SA16 0HN
Tel   (05546) 2466
Mem   800
Sec   DE Gravelle (05546) 2269

Pro   RJ Playe (05546) 3846
Holes   18 L 6916 yds SSS 72
Recs   Am–70 CI Morgan
    Pro–67 M Cahill, S Torrance,
    P Townsend
V'trs   H
Fees   £12 D–£16 (£16 D–£20)
Loc   5 miles W of Llanelli

Borth & Ynyslas (1885)

Borth SY24 5JS
Tel   (0970) 871202
Mem   410
Sec   RB Mair
Pro   JG Lewis (0970) 871557
Holes   18 L 6100 yds SSS 70
Recs   Am–65 M Stimson
    Pro–68 JG Lewis
V'trs   U SOC
Fees   £12 (£15)
Loc   Off A487 between
    Aberystwyth and Machynlleth.
    N of Borth

Cardigan (1928)

Gwbert-on-Sea SA43 1PR
Tel   (0239) 612035
Mem   300
Sec   J Rhapps
Pro   C Parsons
Holes   18 L 6207 yds SSS 70
Recs   Am–69 P Daniel
V'trs   U
Fees   D–£8 (£10) W–£28
Loc   2½ miles NW of Cardigan

Carmarthen (1907)

Blaenycoed Road, Carmarthen
Tel   (0267) 87214
Mem   700
Sec   WR Nicholl (0267) 87588
Pro   P Gillis
Holes   18 L 6212 yds SSS 71
Recs   Am–68 M Thomas (1987)
    Pro–69 B Barnes
V'trs   U SOC
Fees   £9 (£10)
Loc   4 miles NW of Carmarthen

Cilgwyn (1977)

Llangybi, Lampeter SA48 8NN
Tel   (0570 45) 286
Mem   150
Sec   JL Jones
Holes   9 L 5318 yds SSS 67
Recs   Am–66 DG Evans
    Pro–69 D Creamer
V'trs   U SOC
Fees   £5 (£6.50) W–£20
Loc   5 miles NE of Lampeter,
    off A485 at Llangybi

Glynhir (1909)

Glynhir Road, Llandybie,
nr Ammanford SA18 2TF
Tel   (0269) 850472
Mem   340
Sec   JT Thomas (0269) 850571
    EP Rees (0269) 2345

Pro   S Rastal (0269) 851010
Holes   18 L 6090 yds SSS 70
Recs   Am–67 P Child
V'trs   U SOC–WD
Fees   Winter £5 (£6) W–£30
    Summer £8 (£10) W–£40
Loc   3½ miles N of Ammanford

Haverfordwest (1904)

Arnolds Down, Haverfordwest
SA61 2XQ
Tel   (0437) 763565
Mem   600
Sec   MA Harding (0437) 764523
Pro   A Pile (0437) 768409
Holes   18 L 5945 yds SSS 70
Recs   Pro–67 AJ Pile
V'trs   U SOC
Fees   £10 (£12) Mon–Fri £30
Loc   1 mile E of Haverfordwest on
    A40 Carmarthen road

Milford Haven (1913)

Hubbertson, Milford Haven
Tel   (06462) 2368
Mem   200 50(L) 40(J)
Sec   TA Elder (06462) 2521
Pro   A Pile
Holes   18 L 6071 yds SSS 71
Recs   Am–76
    Pro–71 B Hugget
V'trs   U SOC
Fees   £7
Loc   W boundary of Milford Haven

Newport (Pembs) (1925)

Newport
Tel   (0239) 820244
Mem   350
Sec   R Dietrich
Holes   9 L 3089 yds SSS 69
Recs   Am–67 A Evans
V'trs   U SOC
Fees   £7 (£7) W–£30
Loc   2½ miles NW of Newport,
    towards Newport Beach

St Davids City (1902)

Whitesands Bay, St Davids
Tel   (03483) 607
Mem   180
Sec   GB Lewis
Holes   9 L 5695 yds SSS 70
V'trs   U SOC–WD
Fees   £8
Loc   2 miles W of St Davids,
    nr Whitesands Bay

South Pembrokeshire (1970)

Defensible Barracks, Pembroke Dock
Tel   (0646) 683817
Mem   250
Sec   GW Thomas (0646) 682035
Holes   9 L 5804 yds SSS 69
Recs   Am–66 S Toy, A Jones
V'trs   U before 4.30pm SOC
Fees   D–£6 Mon–Fri–£15
Loc   Pembroke Dock

For explanation of abbreviations, see page 460.

Tenby (1888)

The Burrows, Tenby
Tel   (0834) 2787
Mem   500
Sec   TR Arnold (0834) 2978
Pro   T Mountford (0834) 4447
Holes   18 L 6450 yds SSS 71
Recs   Am–65 G Clement
V'trs   U SOC
Fees   £11 (£12.50) W–£55

Gwent

Blackwood (1914)

Cwymgelli, Blackwood
Tel   (0495) 223152
Mem   300
Sec   AM Reed–Gibbs
Holes   9 L 5304 yds SSS 66
Recs   Am–65 DL Stevens, NR Phillips,
        R Collett
        Pro–64 F Hill
V'trs   I SOC
Fees   £6 (£8)
Loc   ¹/₄ mile N of Blackwood

Caerleon (1974)

Public
Broadway, Caerleon
Tel   (0633) 420342
Sec   A Campbell
Pro   A Campbell
Holes   9 L 3092 yds SSS
Recs   Am–71 C French (1988)
V'trs   U
Fees   18 holes–£2.90 (£4.20)
        9 holes–£1.90 (£2.50)
Loc   M4 Junction 25, 3 miles
Mis   Driving range

Greenmeadow (1980)

Treherbert Road, Croesyceiliog,
Cwmbran NP44 2BZ
Tel   (06333) 69321
Mem   430
Sec   PJ Richardson
Pro   C Coombs (06333) 62626
Holes   15 L 5593 yds SSS 68
Recs   Am–66 M Challinger (1989)
        Pro–66 C Jenkins (1987)
V'trs   U SOC
Fees   £9 (£11)
Loc   4 miles from Newport on B4042.
        M4 Junction 26

Llanwern (1928)

Golf House, Tennyson Ave,
Llanwern NP6 2DY
Tel   (0633) 412380
Mem   625
Sec   DJ Peak (0633) 412029
Pro   S Price (0633) 415233
Holes   18 L 6139 yds SSS 69
        9 L 5686 yds SSS 69
Recs   Am–65 K Fitzgerald
        Pro–67 G Davies,
        R Richards (1987)

V'trs   WD–U WE–restricted I H SOC
Fees   WD–£14
Loc   1 mile from M4 Junction 24

Monmouth (1921)

Leasebrook Lane, Monmouth
Tel   (0600) 2212
Mem   350
Sec   KA Prichard (0594) 33394
Holes   9 L 5454 yds SSS 66
Recs   Am–65 DJ Wills (1979)
        Pro–68 DR Hemming (1978)
V'trs   U SOC
Fees   £10 (£15) Mon–Fri £35
Loc   Signposted 1 mile along A40
        Monmouth–Ross road

Monmouthshire (1892)

Llanfoist, Abergavenny
Tel   (0873) 3171
Mem   480 106(L) 90(J)
Sec   GJ Swayne (0873) 2606
Pro   P Worthing (0873) 2532
Holes   18 L 6045 yds SSS 69
Recs   Am–66 PS Lewis
        Pro–62 D Thomas
V'trs   U H SOC
Fees   £15 (£20)
Loc   Abergavenny Station 2 miles

Newport (1903)

Great Oak, Rogerstone, Newport
NP1 9FX
Tel   (0633) 892683/894496
        (0633) 892643/896794
Mem   700
Sec   AD Jones
Pro   R Skuse (0633) 893271
Holes   18 L 6370 yds SSS 71
Recs   Am–65 CJ Dinsdale
        Pro–67 M Hughes
V'trs   U SOC–WD exc Tues
        Sat–M 1–4pm
Fees   £15 (£20)
Loc   Newport 3 miles on B4591.
        M4 Junction 27, 1 mile

Pontnewydd (1875)

Maesgwyn Farm, West Pontnewydd,
Cwmbran NP44 1AB
Tel   (06333) 2170
Mem   250
Sec   HR Gabe (06333) 67185
Holes   10 L 5340 yds SSS 67
Recs   Am–63 M Hayward
V'trs   WD–U WE–M SOC
Fees   £8
Loc   W outskirts of Cwmbran

Pontypool (1903)

Lasgarn Lane, Trevethin, Pontypool
Tel   (04955) 763655
Mem   566 65(L) 72(J)
Sec   Mrs E Wilce (04955) 4794
Pro   J Howard (04955) 55544
Holes   18 L 6013 yds SSS 69

Recs   Am–64 M Hayward (1982)
        NR Davies (1985)
        Pro–A Sherborne
V'trs   U
Fees   £10 (£15)
Loc   1 mile N of Pontypool

Rolls of Monmouth (1982)

The Hendre, Monmouth NP5 4HG
Tel   (0600) 5353
Mem   250
Sec   JD Ross
Holes   18 L 6723 yds SSS 72
Recs   Am–71 D Wills
        Pro–68 M Thomas
V'trs   U SOC
Fees   £18 (£21)
Loc   3¹/₂ miles W of Monmouth on
        B4233

St Mellons (1937)

St Mellons, Cardiff CF3 8XS
Tel   (0633) 680401
Mem   500 93(L) 70(J) 27(5)
Sec   Mrs K Newling (0633) 680408
Pro   B Thomas (0633) 680101
Holes   18 L 6225 yds SSS 70
Recs   Am–67 S Hopkins
        Pro–66 E Foster
V'trs   WD–U WE–M
Fees   WD–£14
Loc   4 miles E of Cardiff on A48

St Pierre (1962)

Chepstow NP6 6YA
Tel   (02912) 5261
Sec   T Latty, TJ Cleary
Pro   R Doig
Holes   18 L 6700 yds SSS 73
        18 L 5762 yds SSS 68
Recs   Old Am–69 AM Williams
        Pro–63 H Henning
        New Am–63 M Bearcroft
V'trs   H SOC–WD
Fees   On application
Loc   2 miles W of Chepstow (A48)

Tredegar & Rhymney (1921)

Tredegar, Rhymney
Tel   (0685) 840743
Mem   182
Sec   V Davies
Holes   9 L 5564 yds SSS 67
Recs   Am–64 CL Jones
        Pro–33 WS Phillips
V'trs   U
Fees   £5
Loc   1¹/₂ miles W of Tredegar

Tredegar Park (1923)

Bassaleg Road, Newport NP9 3PX
Tel   (0633) 895219
Mem   800
Sec   AA Skinner DFM (0633) 894433
Pro   ML Morgan (0633) 894517
Holes   18 L 6097 yds SSS 70

Recs   Am–68 SM Vickery
V'trs   I
Fees   £12 (£16)
Loc   Off M4 Junction 27

West Monmouthshire (1906)

Pond Road, Nantyglo NP3 4JX
Tel   (0495) 310233
Mem   300
Sec   CJ Lewis (0495) 312746
Holes   18 L 6118 yds SSS 69
V'trs   U
Fees   On application
Loc   Nr Dunlop Semtex, off Brynmawr Bypass, towards Winchestown
Mis   Highest tee in Wales (14th), 1450 ft above sea level

Gwynedd

Aberdovey (1892)

Aberdovey LL35 0RT
Tel   (065 472) 210
Mem   800
Sec   JM Griffiths (065 472) 493
Pro   J Davies (065 472) 602
Holes   18 L 6445 yds SSS 71
Recs   Am–67 B Macfarlane
    Pro–67 J Smith
V'trs   NA–8.30–9.30am & 1–2pm
Fees   £14 D–£18 (£16 D–£24)
Loc   W end of Aberdovey

Abersoch (1907)

Abersoch
Tel   (075 881) 2622
Mem   600
Sec   P Jones
Holes   9 L 5800 yds SSS 68
V'trs   U SOC
Fees   On application
Loc   ½ mile S of Abersoch

Bala (1973)

Penlan, Bala LL23 7SW
Tel   (0678) 520359
Mem   250
Sec   MJ Wright
Holes   10 L 4934 yds SSS 64
Recs   Am–64 DB Aykroyd
V'trs   WD–U WE–NA pm SOC
Fees   £5 (£7) W–£15
Loc   ½ mile NW of Bala

Bala Lake

Bala LL23 7YF
Tel   (0678) 520344
Mem   50
Sec   D Pickering
Holes   9 hole course
V'trs   U
Fees   £7 (£8)
Loc   1½ miles from Bala on B4403

Betws–y–Coed

Clubhouse, Betws–y–Coed LL24
Tel   (069 02) 556
Mem   300
Sec   GB Archer
Holes   9 L 2515 yds SSS 32
Recs   Am–64 H Greenslade
V'trs   U SOC
Fees   £7 (£8)
Loc   ½ mile off A5 in village

Caernarfon (1907)

Llanfaglan, Caernarfon LL54 5RP
Tel   (0286) 3783
Mem   470
Sec   JI Jones
Holes   18 L 5870 yds SSS 69
Recs   Pro–66
V'trs   U SOC
Fees   £8
Loc   2½ miles W of Caernarfon

Conwy (Caernarvonshire) (1890)

Conway
Tel   (0492) 593400
Mem   700
Sec   EC Roberts (0492) 592423
Pro   JP Lees (0492) 593225
Holes   18 L 6901 yds SSS 73
V'trs   WE–restricted SOC
Fees   £12 (£16)
Loc   ½ mile W of Conway off A55

Criccieth (1905)

Ednyfed Hill, Criccieth
Tel   (0766) 522154
Mem   200
Sec   MG Hamilton (0766) 522697
Holes   18 L 5755 yds SSS 68
V'trs   U
Fees   £5 W–£15
Loc   18 miles S of Caernarfon. 4 miles W of Portmadoc

Dolgellau (1911)

Pencefn Road, Dolgellau
Tel   (0341) 422603
Mem   300
Sec   DW Jones (0341) 422593
Holes   9 L 4671 yds SSS 60
Recs   Am–65 E Owen (1987), EW Owen (1989)
    Pro–61 L James (1937)
V'trs   U SOC
Fees   £6 (£7.50)
Loc   Dolgellau ½ mile

Ffestiniog (1893)

Ffestiniog
Tel   (0766) 831829
Mem   138
Sec   A Roberts
Holes   9 L 5032 metres SSS 66
V'trs   U
Fees   £3 W–£10
Loc   1 mile from Ffestiniog on Bala road

Llandudno (Maesdu) (1915)

Hospital Road, Llandudno LL00 1HU
Tel   (0492) 76450
Mem   950
Sec   J Hallam
Pro   S Boulden (0492) 75195
Holes   18 L 6513 yds SSS 72
Recs   Am–67 G Jones, CT Brown
    Pro–66 PJ Butler
V'trs   U–recognised GC members SOC
Fees   £12 (£16)
Loc   1 mile S of Llandudno Station

Llandudno (North Wales) (1894)

72 Bryniau Road, West Shore, Llandudno LL30 2DZ
Tel   (0492) 75325
Mem   550
Sec   GD Harwood
Pro   JF Waugh (0492) 76878
Holes   18 L 6132 yds SSS 69
Recs   Am–66 JHM Williams, S Goldspink
    Pro–63 WS Collins
V'trs   U SOC–phone Sec
Fees   £12.50 (£16) Mon–Fri £50
Loc   ¾ mile from Llandudno on West Shore

Llanfairfechan (1971)

Llannerch Road, Llanfairfechan LL33 0EB
Tel   (0248) 680144
Mem   330
Sec   MJ Charlesworth (0248) 680524
Holes   9 L 3119 yds SSS 57
Recs   Am–53 MJ Charlesworth (1983)
V'trs   U
Fees   £5 (£6)
Loc   7 miles E of Bangor on A55

Nefyn & District (1907)

Nefyn
Tel   (0758) 720218
Mem   750
Sec   Lt Col RW Parry (0758) 720966
Pro   JR Pilkington
Holes   18 L 6294 yds SSS 71
Recs   Am–68 TG Gruffydd
    Pro–67 I Woosnam
V'trs   H SOC
Fees   £10 (£12) 1989 prices
Loc   1½ miles W of Nefyn

Penmaenmawr (1910)

Conway Old Road, Penmaenmawr LL34 6RD
Tel   (0492) 623330
Mem   500
Sec   Mrs JE Jones (0492) 622085
Holes   9 L 5143 yds SSS 66
Recs   Am–65 M Bellis
V'trs   U
Fees   £6 (£8)
Loc   4 miles W of Conway

For explanation of abbreviations, see page 460.

Portmadoc (1900)

Morfa Bychan, Porthmadog LL49 9UC
Tel	(0766) 512037
Mem	500
Sec	Capt DG Thomas
Pro	P Bright (0766) 513828
Holes	18 L 6309 yds SSS 70
Recs	Am–63 J Morrow
V'trs	U SOC
Fees	D–£10 (D–£12)
Loc	2 miles W of Porthmadog towards Black Rock Sands

Pwllheli (1900)

Pwllheli
Tel	(0758) 612520
Mem	630
Sec	RE Williams
Pro	GD Verity
Holes	18 L 6110 yds SSS 69
Recs	Am–66 MG Hughes (1988) Pro–67 D Screeton
V'trs	U
Fees	On application
Loc	1/2 mile SW of Pwllheli

Rhos-on-Sea Residential (1899)

Pernrhyn Bay, Llandudno
Tel	(0492) 49641
Mem	500
Sec	T Frame
Pro	M Greenough
Holes	18 L 6064 yds SSS 69
Recs	Am–64 JR Jones
V'trs	U
Fees	On application
Loc	On coast at Rhos-on-Sea

Royal St David's (1894)

Harlech LL46 2UB
Tel	(0766) 780203
	(0766) 780857 (bookings)
Mem	700
Sec	RI Jones (0766) 780361
Pro	J Barnett
Holes	18 L 6427 yds SSS 71
Recs	Am–66 JL Morgan (1951), TJ Melia (1976) Pro–64 K Stables (1988)
V'trs	U H SOC
Fees	£16 (£20)
Loc	W of Harlech
Mis	Buggies £10 per round

St Deiniol (1905)

Penbryn, Bangor LL57 1PX
Tel	(0248) 353098
Mem	500
Sec	DL Davies
Pro	P Lovell
Holes	18 L 5048 metres SSS 67
Recs	Am–63 GA Roberts (1979)
V'trs	U
Fees	£6 (£6)
Loc	Off A5/A55 Junction, 1 mile E of Bangor on A5022

Isle of Anglesey

Anglesey (1914)

Rhosneigr
Tel	(0407) 810219
Mem	350
Sec	P Lovell (0407) 811202
Pro	P Roberts (0407) 810703
Holes	18 L 6204 yds SSS 70
V'trs	U
Fees	£6 (£8)
Loc	Holyhead 8 miles

Baron Hill (1895)

Beaumaris LL58 8YW
Tel	(0248) 810231
Mem	360
Sec	ED Thomas
Pro	P Maton
Holes	9 L 5062 metres SSS 67
Recs	Am–65 AW Jones
V'trs	U exc comp days SOC–WD & Sat (apply Sec)
Fees	£6 (£7) W–£25
Loc	1 mile NW of Beaumaris

Bull Bay (1913)

Amlwch LL68 9RY
Tel	(0407) 830960
Mem	650
Sec	JR Tickle
Pro	S Tarrant (0407) 831188
Holes	18 L 6160 yds SSS 70
Recs	Am–66 D McLean, A Llyr Pro–65 M Barton
V'trs	WD–U SOC
Fees	£7.50 (£10.50)
Loc	Amlwch 1/2 mile on A5025

Holyhead (1912)

Trearddur Bay, Holyhead LL65 2YG
Tel	(0407) 3279/2119
Mem	484 225(L) 109(J)
Sec	L Toth
Pro	P Capper (0407) 2022
Recs	Am–64 D McLean Pro–69 H Gould
V'trs	H SOC
Fees	On application
Loc	Holyhead Station 1 mile

Llangefni (1983)

Public
Llangefni
Tel	(0248) 722193
Pro	P Lovell
Holes	9 L 1467 yds
V'trs	U
Fees	£1.25 (£1.85)
Loc	Llangefni 1/2 mile on B511

Mid Glamorgan

Aberdare (1921)

Abernant, Aberdare
Tel	(0685) 871188
Mem	500
Sec	JK Lloyd
Pro	AW Palmer (0685) 878735
Holes	18 L 5875 yds SSS 69
Recs	Am–63 S Dodd (1988) Pro–67 AW Palmer
V'trs	I or H SOC Sat–M
Fees	£9 (£11)

Bargoed (1912)

Heolddu, Bargoed
Tel	(0443) 830143
Mem	400
Soo	J Hoath (0443) 834045
Holes	18 L 6233 yds SSS 69
Recs	Am–67 ID Joseph
V'trs	WD–U WE–M SOC–WD
Fees	£9
Loc	NW boundary of Bargoed

Bryn Meadows Hotel G & CC (1973)

The Bryn, nr Hengoed CF8 7SM
Tel	(0495) 225590/224103
Mem	500
Sec	B Mayo
Pro	P Worthing (0495) 221905
Holes	18 L 6200 yds SSS 69
Recs	Am–66 G Davies Pro–68 S Price
V'trs	U
Fees	£12.50 (£15)
Loc	Newport, Gwent 12 miles

Caerphilly (1905)

Mountain Road, Caerphilly CF8 1HJ
Tel	(0222) 883481
Mem	748
Sec	(0222) 863441
Pro	E McDonald (0222) 869104
Holes	14 L 6063 yds SSS 71
Recs	Am–68 GP Howells Pro–68 B Huggett
V'trs	WD–U WE–M
Fees	£8.50 W–£22.50 M–£55.50
Loc	7 miles N of Cardiff off A469. Rail/bus stations 1/2 mile

Castell Heights (1987)

Blaengwynlais, Caerphilly CF8 1NG
Tel	(0222) 886666 (bookings)
	(0222) 886686 (clubhouse)
Mem	1000
Sec	J Talbot
Pro	R Sandow
Holes	9 L 2688 yds SSS 66
V'trs	U
Fees	9 holes–£3
Loc	4 miles from M4 Junction 32, on Tongwynlais to Caerphilly road. By Mountain Lakes GC

Creigiau (1921)

Creigiau, Cardiff CF4 8NN
Tel   (0222) 890263
Mem   630
Sec   DB Jones
Pro   A Kerr Smith (0222) 891909
Holes   18 L 5800 yds SSS 68
Recs   Am–67 D Samuel
V'trs   WD–U WE/BH–M SOC–WD
Fees   £9
Loc   5 miles NW of Cardiff

Llantrisant & Pontyclun (1927)

Talbot Green, Llantrisant
Tel   (0443) 222148
Mem   500
Sec   JM Williams (0443) 207439
Pro   N Watson (0443) 228169
Holes   12 L 5712 yds SSS 68
Recs   Am–65 TJ Lewis (1974)
        Pro–65 JJ Hastings (1982)
V'trs   WD–U WE/BH–M
Fees   £9
Loc   10 miles N of Cardiff.
        2 miles N of M4 Junction 34

Maesteg (1912)

Mount Pleasant, Maesteg
Tel   (0656) 732037
Mem   500
Sec   WH Harford (0639) 896458
Pro   W Evans
Holes   18 L 5845 yds SSS 69
Recs   Am–69 J James, W Hodgson,
        R Lewis
        Pro–64 G Ryall (1989)
V'trs   U
Fees   £8 (£12)
Loc   1 mile W of Maesteg

Merthyr Tydfil (1908)

Cilsanws Mountain, Cefn Coed,
nr Merthyr Tydfil CF48 2HW
Tel   (0685) 723308
Mem   100
Holes   9 L 5794 yds SSS 68
Recs   Am–70 N Evans
        Pro–70 J Howard
V'trs   U
Fees   £9
Loc   Off A470

Morlais Castle (1900)

Pant, Dowlais, Merthyr Tydfil
Tel   (0685) 722822
Mem   400
Sec   N Powell
Holes   18 L 6320 yds SSS 71
V'trs   U exc Sat 12–4pm Sun 8–12–NA
        SOC–WD (small)
Fees   £10 (£10)
Loc   3 miles N of Merthyr Tydfil,
        nr Mountain Railway

Mountain Ash (1907)

Cefnpennar
Tel   (0443) 472265
Mem   555
Sec   G Matthews (0443) 474022
Pro   J Sim (0443) 478770
Holes   18 L 5535 yds SSS 68
Recs   Am–63 SJ Lewis
        Pro–66 R Evans
V'trs   U
Fees   £10 (£12)
Loc   9 miles NW of Pontypridd

Mountain Lakes (1988)

Blaengwynlais, Caerphilly CF8 1NG
Tel   (0222) 861128
Mem   400
Sec   RS Smith (Hon)
Pro   R Sandow (0222) 886666
Holes   18 L 6851 yds SSS 73
V'trs   H SOC (book with Pro)
Fees   £12 (£15)
Loc   4 miles from M4 Junction 32,
        on Tongwynlais to Caerphilly
        road. By Castell Heights
        GC

Pontypridd (1905)

Ty Gwyn Road, Pontypridd CF37 4DJ
Tel   (0443) 402359
Mem   650
Sec   JG Graham (0443) 400904
Pro   K Gittins (0443) 491210
Holes   18 L 5650 yds SSS 68
Recs   Am–63 J Olding (1979),
        P Price (1985)
V'trs   WD–UH WE/BH–MH
        SOC–WD H
Fees   On application
Loc   E of Pontypridd off A470.
        12 miles NW of Cardiff

Pyle & Kenfig (1922)

Waun–y–Mer, Kenfig CF33 4PU
Tel   (065 671) 3093
Mem   860
Sec   RC Thomas
Pro   R Evans (065 671) 772446
Holes   18 L 6655 yds SSS 73
Recs   Am–70 S Cox, S Curiel,
        N Evans
        Pro–68 D Matthew, C Gray,
        M Steadman
V'trs   WD–U WE–M
Fees   £16
Loc   Porthcawl 2 miles

Rhondda (1910)

Penrhys, Pontygwaith, Rhondda
Tel   (0443) 433204
Mem   400
Sec   K Jones
Holes   18 L 6428 yds SSS 71
V'trs   U H SOC
Fees   £9
Loc   6 miles W of Pontypridd

Royal Porthcawl (1891)

Porthcawl
Tel   (065 671) 2251
Mem   500
Sec   AW Woolcott
Pro   G Poor (065 671) 6984
Holes   18 L 6691 yds SSS 74
Recs   Am–68 S Dodds
        Pro–65 B Barnes
V'trs   I WE/BH–M SOC
Fees   £24 (£35) 1989 prices
Loc   14 miles E of Swansea.
        M4 Junction 37

Southerndown (1905)

Ewenny, Bridgend CF35 5BT
Tel   (0656) 880326
Mem   650
Sec   R Brickell (0656) 880476
Pro   DG McMonagle
Holes   18 L 6705 yds SSS 73
Recs   Am–66 H Stott
        Pro–64 G Hunt
V'trs   WD–U WE/BH–M
        SOC–Tues & Thurs–H
Fees   £18 (£25)
Loc   Ewenny, Ogmore-by-Sea,
        nr Ogmore Castle ruins

Whitehall (1922)

The Pavilion, Nelson, Treharris
Tel   (0443) 740245
Mem   320
Sec   VE Davies
Holes   9 L 5750 yds SSS 68
Recs   Am–66 M Heames
        Pro–62 I Woosnam
V'trs   WD–U WE–M
Fees   £6
Loc   15 miles NW of Cardiff

Powys

Brecon (1902)

Llanfaes, Brecon
Tel   (0874) 2004
Mem   210
Sec   DHE Roderick (0874) 5547
Holes   9 L 5218 yds SSS 66
Recs   Am–61 R Dixon
        Pro–66 WO Moses
V'trs   U
Fees   £5
Loc $\frac{1}{2}$ mile from Brecon on A40

Builth Wells (1923)

Golf Club Road, Builth Wells LD2 3NN
Tel   (0982) 553296
Mem   425
Sec   MA Sanders
Pro   W Evans (0982) 553293
Holes   9 L 5376 yds SSS 67
V'trs   U SOC
Fees   £8 (£10)
Loc   Llandovery road

Cradoc (1967)

Penoyre Park, Cradoc, Brecon
LD3 9LP
Tel   (0874) 3658
Mem   426
Sec   GSW Davies
Pro   D Beattie (0874) 5524
Holes 18 L 6234 yds SSS 71
Recs   Am–65 DK Wood (1982)
V'trs U SOC
Fees   £10 (£14)
Loc   2 miles NW of Brecon off B4520

Knighton (1913)

Little Ffrydd Wood, Knighton
Tel   (0547) 528646
Mem   124
Sec   EJP Bright (Hon)
Holes 9 L 5320 yds SSS 66
Recs   Am–66 M Caine
       Pro–71 H Vardon
V'trs U SOC
Fees   £4 (£6)
Loc   ¹/₂ mile SW of Knighton

Llandrindod (1905)

Llandrindod Wells
Tel   (0597) 2010
Mem   180 30(L) 50(J)
Sec   K Lewis
Holes 18 L 5759 yds SSS 68
Recs   Am–65 CJ Davies (1988)
V'trs U SOC
Fees   £7 (£10)
Loc   1 mile E of Llandrindod Wells

Llanidloes (St Idloes)

Penrhalt, Llanidloes
Tel   (055 12) 2559
Mem   120
Sec   A Wynn Edwards
       (055 12) 2205
Holes 9 L 5210 yds SSS 66
Recs   Am–63 J Davies
V'trs U
Fees   £3 (£4) W–£12
Loc   ¹/₂ mile on Trefeglwys Road

Machynlleth (1905)

Ffordd Drenewydd, Machynlleth
SY20 8UH
Tel   (0654) 2000
Mem   233
Sec   G Holdsworth (0654) 3264
Holes 9 L 5726 yds SSS 67
Recs   Am–65
       Pro–65
V'trs U Sun–NA before 11.30am SOC
Fees   £7
Loc   1 mile E of Machynlleth off
       A489

Old Rectory Hotel (1968)

Llangattock, Crickhowell NP8 1PH
Tel   (0873) 810373
Mem   200
Sec   D Best
Holes 9 L 1409 yds SSS 54

V'trs U
Fees   £6
Loc   8 miles W of Abergavenny

St Giles Newtown (1919)

Pool Road, Newtown
Tel   (0686) 625844
Mem   290
Sec   NO Davies
Pro   DP Owen
Holes 9 L 5864 yds SSS 68
Recs   Am–68 CB Jones
       Pro–64 AP Parkin
V'trs WD/BH–I WE–restricted
Fees   £6 (£7) SOC–£7
Loc   ³/₄ mile E of Newtown

Welshpool (1929)

Golfa Hill, Welshpool
Tel   (093 883) 249
Mem   300
Sec   RGD Jones (0938) 3377
Holes 18 L 5708 yds SSS 69
Recs   Am–65 DH Ryan
       Pro–69 S Bowen
V'trs U
Fees   £6 (£8)
Loc   4¹/₂ miles from Welshpool,
       on Dolgellau road

South Glamorgan

Brynhill (1921)

Port Road, Colcot, Barry
Tel   (0446) 735061
Mem   700
Sec   DP Lloyd (0446) 720277
Pro   P Fountain (0446) 733660
Holes 18 L 6021 yds SSS 69
Recs   Am–68 P Cooper
V'trs WD/Sat–U Sun–M SOC–WD
Fees   £12 Sat–£15 Sun–M SOC–£10
Loc   A4050, 8 miles W of Cardiff

Cardiff (1921)

Sherborne Avenue, Cyncoed, Cardiff
CF2 6SJ
Tel   (0222) 753067
Mem   930
Sec   D Griffiths (0222) 753320
Pro   T Hanson (0222) 754772
Holes 18 L 6015 yds SSS 70
Recs   Am–65 J Lee (1988)
       Pro–63 L Farmer (1987)
V'trs WD–H WE–M
Fees   £20
Loc   3 miles N of Cardiff. 2 miles
       from Pentwyn exit of A48(M).
       M4 Junction 29

Dinas Powis (1914)

Dinas Powis
Tel   (0222) 512727
Mem   650
Sec   JD Hughes
Pro   G Bennett
Holes 18 L 5377 yds SSS 66

Recs   Am–65 P Davidson
       Pro–67 P Fountain
V'trs U
Fees   £7 (£9)
Loc   3 miles W of Cardiff

Glamorganshire (1890)

Lavernock Road, Penarth CF6 2UP
Tel   (0222) 707048
Sec   GC Crimp (0222) 701185
Pro   A Kerr–Smith (0222) 707401
Holes 18 L 6150 yds SSS 70
Recs   Am–65 MG Mouland (1979),
       N Grimmitt (1989)
       Pro–65 A Jacklin (1969)
V'trs WD/WE–H SOC
Fees   £15 (£20)
Loc   5 miles SW of Cardiff

Llanishen (1905)

Cwm Lisvane, nr Cardiff CF4 5UD
Tel   (0222) 752205
Mem   900
Sec   ET Davies (0222) 755078
Pro   RA Jones (0222) 755076
Holes 18 L 5296 yds SSS 66
Recs   Am–64 MJG Strange
       Pro–63 JT Taylor
V'trs WD–U WE–M H SOC
Fees   £15
Loc   5 miles N of Cardiff

RAF St Athan (1977)

Barry CF6 9WA
Tel   (0446) 751043
Mem   415
Sec   DM Llewellyn (0446) 742142
Holes 9 L 5957 yds SSS 69
V'trs U Sun am–NA
Fees   £8 (£10)
Loc   2 miles E of Llantwit Major

Radyr (1902)

Radyr, nr Cardiff CF4 8BS
Tel   (0222) 842442
Mem   880
Sec   Maj MB Richards (0222) 842408
Pro   S Gough (0222) 842476
Holes 18 L 6031 yds SSS 70
Recs   Am–64 P Price
       Pro–63 PW Evans
V'trs WD–H WE–M SOC–Wed &
       Fri
Fees   £10
Loc   5 miles NW of Cardiff

Wenvoe Castle (1936)

Wenvoe, nr Cardiff
Tel   (0222) 591094
Mem   525 100(L) 50(J)
Sec   EJ Dew (0222) 594371
Pro   MA Pycroft (0222) 593649
Holes 18 L 6422 yds SSS 71
Recs   Am–69 P Jones, M Davey
       Pro–68 G Davies
V'trs H SOC
Fees   £12 (£15)
Loc   4 miles W of Cardiff

Whitchurch (Cardiff) (1915)

Pantmawr Road, Whitchurch, Cardiff CF4 6XD
Tel **(0222) 620125**
Mem 438 111(L) 72(J)
Sec (0222) 620985
Pro E Clark (0222) 614660
Holes 18 L 6245 yds SSS 70
Recs Am–62 J Povall
Pro–62 I Woosnam
V'trs WD–U WE/BH–M H SOC–WD
Fees £15 (£17)
Loc 3 miles NW of Cardiff on A470. M4 Junction 32, 2 miles

West Glamorgan

Clyne (1920)

120 Owls Lodge Lane, Mayals, Swansea
Tel **(0792) 401989**
Mem 650
Sec BR Player
Pro M Bevan (0792) 402094
Holes 18 L 6312 yds SSS 71
Recs Am–66 C Dickens
Pro–66 J Bland
V'trs U
Fees £11 (£15)
Loc Swansea

Fairwood Park (1970)

Upper Killay, Swansea
Tel **(0792) 203648**
Mem 725
Sec J Beer
Pro M Evans (0792) 299194
Holes 18 L 6606 yds SSS 72
Recs Am–69 I Roberts, R Maliphant (1989)
Pro–67 J Lomas (1989)
V'trs U SOC
Fees £13 (£15)
Mis Swansea Airport 1/4 mile

Glynneath (1931)

Penycraig, Pontneathvaughan, Glynneath SA11 5UG
Tel **(0639) 720452**
Mem 320
Sec RM Ellis (0639) 720679
Holes 18 L 5425 yds SSS 68
Recs Am–66 JL Davies
Pro–68 D Rees
V'trs U
Fees £6 (£10)
Loc 2 miles N of Glynneath on B4242

Inco (1965)

Clydach, Swansea
Tel **(0792) 844216**
Mem 260
Sec DGS Murdoch (0792) 843336
Holes 13 L 5976 yds SSS 69
Recs Am–68 V Smith, N O'Sullivan
V'trs U
Fees £4 (£5)
Loc Swansea Valley

Langland Bay (1904)

Langland Bay, Swansea SA3 4QR
Tel **(0792) 366023**
Mem 620
Sec TJ Jenkins (0792) 361721
Pro TJ Lynch (0792) 366186
Holes 18 L 5830 yds SSS 69
Recs Am–63 K Jones, S Dodd (1989)
Pro–69 D Ridley
V'trs U SOC
Fees £13 (£14.50)
Loc 6 miles W of Swansea

Morriston (1919)

160 Clasemont Road, Morriston, Swansea A6 6AJ
Tel **(0792) 71079**
Mem 400
Sec LT Lewis (0792) 796528
Pro DA Rees (0792) 772335
Holes 18 L 5773 yds SSS 68
Recs Am–68 MJ Thomas
Pro–64 DA Rees
V'trs U H SOC–WD
Fees £11.50 (£18.50)
Loc 4 miles NW of Swansea on A48. M4 Junction 46, 1 mile

Neath (1934)

Cadoxton, Neath
Tel **(0639) 643615**
Mem 450
Sec JR Evans (0639) 632759
Pro EM Bennett
Holes 18 L 6500 yds SSS 72
Recs Am–69 BOS Vanstone
Pro–66 F Hill
V'trs U
Fees £8 (£12)
Loc Neath 2 miles

Palleg (1930)

Palleg Road, Lower Cwmtwrch, Swansea Valley SA9 1QT
Tel **(0639) 842193**
Mem 200
Sec AW Stanley (0639) 730772
Holes 9 L 3209 yds SSS 72
Recs Am–71 C Williams
V'trs U
Fees £5 (£8)
Loc Upper Swansea Valley. Ystalyfer 1 mile. Ystradgynlais 1 mile

Pennard (1896)

2 Southgate Road, Southgate, nr Swansea SA3 2BT
Tel **(044 128) 3131**
Mem 750
Sec JD Eccles (044 128) 3131/3170
Pro MV Bennett (044 128) 3451
Holes 18 L 6268 yds SSS 71
Recs Am–69 H Guest
Pro–66 G Ryall (1987)
V'trs U H SOC
Fees £10 (£12) W–£30
Loc 8 miles W of Swansea, by A4067 and B4436

Pontardawe (1924)

Cefn Llan, Pontardawe, Swansea
Tel **(0792) 863118**
Mem 320
Sec J Burrington
Pro RA Ryder (0792) 830977
Holes 18 L 6061 yds SSS 70
Recs Am–66 B Fisher
Pro–71 D Thomas, R Brook
V'trs H SOC
Fees £10 (£16.50)
Loc 5 miles N of M4 Junction 45 (A4067)

Swansea Bay (1894)

Jersey Marine, Neath SA10 6JP
Tel **(0792) 812198/814153**
Mem 400
Sec Mrs D Goatcher
Pro M Day
Holes 18 L 6302 yds SSS 70
Recs Am–67 A Evans
V'trs U
Fees £10 (£12)
Loc 1/2 mile from Jersey Marine, off A483 between Swansea and Neath

Driving Ranges in Great Britain and Ireland

Bedfordshire

Mowsbury Driving Range

Kimbolton Road, Bedford. MK41 8DQ.
Tel (0234) 771042
Open 9am–9.30pm. 14 covered floodlit bays.
£1.40 for 60 balls. Tuition available. Loc: 3 miles
N of Bedford on B660.

Tilsworth Golf Centre

Dunstable Road, Tilsworth, Leighton Buzzard,
Beds. *Tel* (0525) 210721/2
Open 10am–9.30pm, 7 days per week. 30 bays.
£1.35 for 50 balls. £2.25 for 100 balls. Floodlit.
9 hole course. Professionals' shop. Professional
tuition - £7 per $^1/_2$ hour. Loc: 2 miles N of
Dunstable, off A5.

Berkshire

Downshire GC

Easthampstead Park, Wokingham, Berks.
Tel Bracknell (0344) 424066
Open 8am-dusk weekdays; 7am-dusk
weekends. Full 18 hole course. 9 hole pitch and
putt. Driving range. Professional. Loc: Off Nine
Mile Ride between Bracknell and Wokingham.

Hawthorn Hill

Drift Road, Hawthorn Hill, Nr Maidenhead,
Berks. SL6 3ST *Tel* (0628) 771030/75588
36 bay covered floodlit driving range. Open
8am-10pm. Full 18 hole public course. £1.80 for
56 balls. Loc: 4 miles S of Maidenhead on A330.

Lavender Park Golf Centre

Swinley Road, Ascot, Berks. *Tel* (0344) 884074
Open 9am-10pm Mon-Fri; 9am-9pm weekends.
£1 for 55 balls. £1.50 for 115 balls. Floodlit.
9 hole course, par 28. Loc: W of Ascot on
B3017.

Sindlesham Driving Range

Mole Road, Wokingham, Berks. RG11 5DB
Tel Wokingham (0734) 788494
Floodlit; 7 days a week, 14 hours a day.
20 bays. £1 machine operated. Professional.

Buckinghamshire

Colnbrook Golf Driving Range

Gallymead Road, Colnbrook, Slough SL3 0EN.
Tel (0753) 682670/685127
Open 7 days, 9.30am–10.30pm. Floodlit.
Professional. Loc: 5 mins from Junction
5 M4 or Junction 14 M25.

Wavendon Golf Centre

Lower End Road, Wavendon, Milton Keynes
MK17 8DA *Tel* (0908) 281811
Open 10am–10pm weekdays; 8am–10pm
weekends. 26 covered floodlit bays. Large
bucket £2.50, small bucket £1.25. PGA tuition.
Club hire. Shop. 9 hole par 3 course. Loc: $1^1/_2$
miles from M1 Junction 13. 10 mins from Milton
Keynes.

Windmill Hill Golf Complex

Tattenhoe Lane, Bletchley, Milton Keynes.
Tel (0908) 78623
23 covered and 5 open bays. Floodlit. Open
9am–9pm Mon–Fri; 9am–8pm Sat/Sun. Full 18
hole golf course. Putting greens. Golf shop.
Tuition. Practice bunker. Loc: 4 miles from
Junction 14 M1 on A421.

Cambridgeshire

Abbotsley Golf Range

Eynesbury Hardwicke, St Neots,
Cambridgeshire PE19 4XN. *Tel* (0480) 217951
Open 8.30am–10.30pm daily. Professional. 14
covered bays. 6 open bays. Floodlit. Putting.
Bunkers. £1.50 for 70 balls. Tuition. Shop. 18 hole

golf course. Loc: 2 miles S of St Neots (B1046). 12 miles W of Cambridge. M11 Junction 13 onto A45.

Channel Islands

Western Golf Range

St Quens Bay, Jersey
Open 10am–dusk. 24 bays. Putting. Crazy golf. 9 hole par 3. Professional. Loc: Five Mile Road.

Cleveland

Middlesbrough Municipal Driving Range

Ladgate Lane, Middlesbrough TS5 7YZ.
Tel (0642) 315533
Open 10am–9pm weekdays. 10am–5pm weekends. 20 covered floodlit bays. Bucket of balls £1.70. Professional tuition (0642) 315361. Loc: 2 miles S of Middlesbrough, nr A174.

Devon

Ilfracombe and Woolacombe Golf Range

Woolacombe Road, Ilfracombe EX34 7HF.
Tel (0271) 66222
Open daily 8am–6pm (Summer). Fri/Sat/Sun only 10am–4pm (Winter). 24 bays - 12 covered. £1.85 for 50 balls. Tuition available. Putting green. Bunkers. Loc: 1 mile from Mullacott Cross on B3343.

Dorset

East Dorset Driving Range

Hyde, Wareham BH20 7NT. *Tel* (0929) 472272
Open 8am–10pm weekdays. 9am–6pm weekends. 22 bays – 12 covered. Basket of balls £1.80. Tuition. Pro shop. Loc: 4 miles from Worgret Heath.

Halstock Driving Range

Common Lane, Halstock, Nr Yeovil. *Tel* (0935) 89689
Open from 10am daily. 12 covered floodlit bays. Bucket of balls £1.70. Tuition available. Practice bunker. Putting green. Loc: 6 miles S of Yeovil off A37.

Iford Bridge Golf Range

Barrack Road, Christchurch
Open 8am–dusk. Putting green. Practice bunker. 14 open bays. Bucket of balls £1.40. Tuition available. Loc: Bournemouth/Christchurch boundary.

Essex

Belhus Park Leisure Complex

South Ockendon, Thurrock. RM15 4PX
Open 9am–10pm weekdays. 9am–6pm (Sat) 9am–8pm (Sun). 11 bays. Bucket of balls £1.40–£2.05. Professional tuition. Loc: 1 mile N of A13/M25 (Dartford Tunnel).

Chingford Golf Range

Waltham Way, Chingford E4 8AQ.
Tel (081) 529 2409
Two-tier golf range. 18 covered floodlit bays. Putting green and practice bunker. 60 or 100 balls. PGA Professional. Open 9.30am–10pm. Club hire. Golf shop. Club repair service. Video lessons. Loc: 1 mile N of North Circular Road at Chingford turn off. 3 miles S of M25 Junction 26.

Colchester Golf Range

Crown Inn, Old Ipswich Road, Ardleigh, Colchester. *Tel* (0206) 230974
Open 10am–9pm Mon-Fri. 10am–5pm Sat/Sun. £1.65 for 50 balls. £1.10 for 30 balls. Floodlit. Club hire. Bunkers. Putting. Professional. Loc: 1 mile NE of Colchester, off A12.

Fairlop Waters

Forest Road, Barkingside, Ilford, Essex.
Tel (081) 500 9911
Open 7.30am–9.30pm. Floodlit. 36 covered bays. 18+9 hole courses. £1 for 40 balls. £1.80 for 70 balls. Golf shop. Full tuition. Loc: 2 miles from S end of M11, by Fairlop Tube Station.

Towerlands

Panfield Road, Braintree, Essex CM7 5BJ.
Tel (0376) 26802
Open 7 days, 8.30am–dusk. 6 bays. £1 for 50 balls. 9 hole course. Loc: 1 mile NW of Braintree

Gloucestershire

Gloucester Hotel & Country Club

Robinswood Hill, Gloucester. *Tel* (0452) 25653
Open 9am–8.30pm, 7 days. 12 bays. Floodlit.
£1 for 50 balls. Full 18 hole course. 9 hole par
3. Loc: 2 miles S of Gloucester.

Hampshire

Portsmouth Golf Centre

Eastern Road, Portsmouth, Hampshire.
Tel (0705) 664549
Open 8am–10pm, 7 days. Floodlit. 30 covered
bays. Professional. Shop. Tuition.

Tadley Driving Range

Bishopswood Lane, Tadley, Basingstoke
RG26 6AT
Open daily 8am–9pm. 12 covered floodlit bays.
Large bucket £2; standard £1.50. Professional
tuition. 9 hole golf course. Pro shop. Loc: 6
miles N of Basingstoke, off A340.

Hertfordshire

Bushey Golf Range

High Street, Bushey WD2 1BJ.
Tel (081) 950 2283/2215
Open daily 9am–10pm. 30 bays – 27 covered
floodlit. Bucket of balls £1. Professional tuition.
9 hole golf course. Loc: 1$\frac{1}{2}$ miles S of Watford.
3 miles W of M1.

Elstree Golf Range

Watling Street, Elstree WD6 3AA
Open 10am–10pm. 45 bays – 40 covered
floodlit. Individual and group tuition available.
Loc: 8 miles N of London. 2 miles from A41
along A5183.

Watford Driving Range

Sheepcot Lane, Garston, Watford, Herts.
Tel (0923) 675560
Open 10am–10.30pm, 7 days. £1 for 55 balls.
Floodlit. Covered tees. Professional. Loc: N
Watford.

Welwyn Hatfield Sports Centre

Gosling Stadium Driving Range, Stanborough
Road, Welwyn Garden City, Herts. *Tel* (0707)
331056
Open 10am daily. 9 bays. Floodlit. Large
basket £1. Cafeteria. Licensed bars. Multi
sports complex. Loc: S of Welwyn Garden
City, nr A1(M).

Whaddon Golf Range

Church Street, Whaddon, Royston, Herts.
Tel (0223) 207325
Open 10am–9pm weekdays. 10am–dusk Sat/Sun.
14 covered bays. £1 for 50 balls. Club hire.
Professional. Loc: 4 miles N of Royston off A14.

Humberside

Hull Golf Centre

National Avenue, Hull, N Humberside.
Tel (0482) 492720
24 covered tees. Open 9am–9pm Mon–Fri.
9am–7.30pm Sat/Sun. Floodlit. £2 jumbo; £1.50
large; £1 small baskets. Pitch and putt.
Professional.

Kent

Chatham Golf Centre

Street-End Road, Chatham, Kent. *Tel* (0634) 48925
Open 7 days, 10am–10pm. Floodlit. Professional
tuition.

Edenbridge G & CC

Crouch House Road, Edenbridge, Kent
TN8 5LQ. *Tel* (0732) 865202
Open 8am–10pm. 16 floodlit bays. Pro shop.
Tuition available. £1.75 per bucket. Putting
green. Par 3 course. Loc: 15 mins from
Sevenoaks and Tonbridge and M25.

Ruxley Golf Centre

Sandy Lane, St Pauls Cray, Orpington, Kent
BR5 3HY. *Tel* (0689) 71490.
Floodlit driving range. 28 covered bays. Tuition.
Club hire. Open 8am–10.30pm. Golf shop. 18 hole
golf course. Loc: off Ruxley roundabout on A20
at Sidcup.

Lancashire

Kearsley Golf Range Ltd

Moss Lane, Kearsley, Bolton, Lancashire
BL4 8SF. *Tel* (0204) 75726
Open 11am–10pm weekdays. 11am–5pm
weekends. Floodlit. Covered tees. Grass tees.
Professional. 9 hole pitch and putt. Loc: 4 miles
S of Bolton on A666.

Phoenix Sporting and Leisure Centre

Fleetwood Road, Norbreck, Blackpool.
Tel (0253) 854846
Open 9am–dusk, 7 days. £1.20 per basket.
Floodlit. 18 bays. Bunkers. Par 3. Professional.
Loc: N of Blackpool.

Leicestershire

Range Inn Golf Range

Melton Road, Leicester. *Tel* (0533) 664400
Open 10am–10pm, 7 days. Floodlit. 20 covered
tees. £1 for 85 balls. 9 hole pitch and putt. 18
hole crazy golf. Loc: N Leicester.

Lincolnshire

Lincoln Golf Range

Washingborough Road, Washingborough,
Lincoln
Open 10.30am–9pm. 20 floodlit bays. PGA
professional. Tuition and club hire. 9 hole
par 3 course. Loc: Washingborough, SW of
Lincoln.

Thonock Driving Range

Thonock, Gainsborough. *Tel* (0427) 613088
Open daily 8am–9pm. 20 covered floodlit
bays. Bucket of balls £1. Tuition.
Loc: N of Gainsborough.

Merseyside

Formby Golf Driving Range

Moss Side, Formby, L37 0AF
Open 9.30am–9.30pm daily. 20 covered floodlit
bays. £1.30 for 45 balls. PGA tuition available.
Putting green. Golf shop. Loc: Formby by-pass
A565. Liverpool 7 miles. Southport 4 miles.

Middlesex

Ealing Golf Range

Rowdell Road, Northolt, Middlesex.
Tel (081) 845 4967
Open 10am–10pm, 7 days. 36 covered floodlit
tees. Putting. £1 per bucket. 4 professionals.
Clubhouse. Loc: A40 Target Roundabout.

Finchley Golf Driving Range

444 High Road, Finchley, London N12.
Tel (081) 445 9697
Open 9am–10pm, 7 days. Bucket from £1.40.
24 floodlit bays. Putting. Professional teaching.
Loc: just off North Circular Road.

Norfolk

Norwich Golf Centre

Long Lane, Bawburgh, Norwich, Norfolk
Open 8am–dusk, 7 days. Bucket of balls £1.50.
9 hole course. Pro shop. Clubhouse. Loc: S of
A47 at rear of Royal Norfolk Showground.

Sprowston Park Driving Range

Wroxham Road, Sprowston, Norwich NR7 8RP.
Tel (0603) 410657
Open 10am–9pm weekdays. 10am–5pm
weekends. 20 covered floodlit bays. Buckets
of balls £1–£1.50–£2. Tuition available. Shop. 18
hole golf course. Loc: A1151, NE of Norwich.

Northamptonshire

Delapre Golf Complex

Eagle Drive, Nene Valley Way, Northampton
36 open and 25 covered bays. Floodlit. Par
3, pitch and putt. Full 18 hole course. Golf
shop. Loc: 3 miles from M1 Junction 15 on A508.

Nottinghamshire

Carlton Forum Golf Target Range

Foxhill Road, Carlton, Nottingham.
Tel (0602) 872333
Open 10am–10pm Mon–Fri. 10am–5pm Sat
& Sun (last buckets of balls sold ½
hour prior to closing). 28 covered tees.
Floodlit. Professional. Loc: N side of
Nottingham

Oxton Driving Range

Oaks Lane, Oxton NG25 0RH.
Tel (0602) 653545
Open 8am–9.30pm daily. 30 covered floodlit
bays. Bucket of balls £1–£1.75. Tuition
available. Loc: 9 miles N of Nottingham on
A614.

Staffordshire

Craythorne Golf Centre

Craythorne Road, Stretton, Burton-on-Trent
DE13 0AZ. *Tel* (0283) 643
Open daily 9am–9pm. 14 covered floodlit
bays. Bucket of balls £1. Tuition. Loc: 1½
miles N of Burton-on-Trent. Signpost to Stretton
at A5121/A3 junction.

Suffolk

Ipswich Golf Centre

Suffolk Show Ground, Bucklesham Road,
Ipswich, Suffolk IP3 8TZ. *Tel* (0473) 726821
Open 8.30am–dusk. 15 bays, 4 covered bays.
Buckets of balls £1–£1.50. Professional. Tuition.
Shop. Loc: 2 miles E of Ipswich.

Surrey

Chessington Golf Centre

Garrison Lane, Chessington, Surrey.
Tel (081) 391 0948
Open 8am–10pm. £1 for 45 balls. 18 covered
bays. Floodlit. Professional tuition. Video lessons.
Repair service. Club hire. 9 hole course.
Loc: Nr Chessington Zoo, off A243.

Crondall Golf Course

Oak Park, Heath Lane, Crondall GU10 5PB
Open daily 9.30am–9pm. 14 covered floodlit
bays. Bucket of balls £1. Professional tuition.
Loc: Off A287 Farnham – Odiham road.

Croydon Golf Centre

175 Long Lane, Addiscombe, Surrey.
Tel (01) 656 1690
Open 10am–10pm Mon–Fri; 10am–9pm Sat/Sun.
£1.30 for 40 balls; £2.60 for 80 balls; £3.20 for 110
balls. Covered tees. Floodlit. Professional. Loc:
3 miles E of Croydon.

Fairmile Hotel

Portsmouth Road, Cobham, Surrey.
Tel (0932) 64419
Open 10am–10pm weekdays; 9am–9pm
weekends. 24 covered tees. Floodlit.
Bunkers. Professional. Putting green.

Hoebridge Golf Centre

Old Woking, Surrey. *Tel* (048 62) 22611/2
25 bays, covered. Floodlit. 18 hole course.
New 9 hole intermediate course. 18 hole par
3 course. Lessons and hire equipment from
Professional. Shop. Loc: 5 mins from A3 on
Woking/West Byfleet Road.

Richmond Driving Range

Twickenham Road, Richmond, Surrey
TW9 2SS. *Tel* (081) 940 5570
Open 9am–8.30pm Mon–Fri; 9am–5.30pm Sat/Sun
(Sept–Apr close at 1pm Sat). 25 covered floodlit
tees. £2 for 75 balls. PGA Professional. Loc: Next
to Royal Mid-Surrey GC, off A316 Chertsey Road
at Richmond.

Sandown Golf Centre

Sandown Park, More Lane, Esher, Surrey.
Tel (0372) 63340
33 floodlit bays. Open 10am–10pm daily. £1.30
for 45 balls; £2.20 for 75 balls; £2.60 for 110 balls.
9 hole public golf course. Range closed during
Race meetings. Loc: Sandown Park racecourse.

Silvermere GC Driving Range

Redhill Road, Cobham, Surrey.
Tel (0932) 67275
Open 10am–10pm daily. 32 floodlit bays. £2
for 70 balls. Contoured landscape. Chipping
targets and baskets. Loc: between Cobham
and Byfleet.

Windlemere Golf Course

Windlesham Road, West End, Woking, Surrey.
Tel (09905) 8727
Open 8am–10pm, 7 days. Floodlit. 12 covered
bays. 9 hole full-length public course. Two
professionals. Large golf shop with repair
services. Clubhouse. Loc: A319 at Lightwater
near Bagshot.

Sussex (East)

Horam Park Driving Range

Chiddingly Road, Horam, East Sussex.
Tel (04353)3477
Open 9am–10pm all year round. Floodlit.
18 covered bays. Professional's shop with
repair service. Tuition with video facilities.
Large bucket of balls £2.00. Club hire. 9
hole course. Loc: $^1/_2$ mile S of Horam on
Chiddingly Road.

Sussex (West)

Fairway Golf Driving Range

Horsham Road, Pease Pottage, Sussex.
Tel (0293) 33000
Open 9am–10.30pm, 7 days. 60p for 60 balls.
Floodlit. Professional. Loc: S of Crawley off A23.

Tyne and Wear

Gosforth Park Golfing Complex

High Gosforth Park, Newcastle-upon-Tyne.
Tel (091) 236 4480
Open 8am–10pm, 7 days. Floodlit. 30 covered
tees. Putting, pitching. Professional. 9 hole
pitch/putt and 18 hole putting green. Loc:
5 miles N of Newcastle.

Washington

Stone Cellar Road, Washington, Tyne and Wear. *Tel* (091) 417 2626
Open 10am–10pm. 21 floodlit bays. Professional. Pitch and putt. 18 hole course. Loc: By A1(M)– north turning to Washington.

Warwickshire

Purley Chase

Ridge Lane, Nuneaton, Warwicks. CV10 0RB. *Tel* (0203) 393118/395348
Open 8am–8pm. 13 covered floodlit bays. £1 per bucket balls. Tuition. Loc: 2 miles S of Mancetter (A5).

Warwick Golf Centre

Racecourse, Warwick CV34 5RX. *Tel* (0926) 494316
Open 10am–9pm weekdays; 9am–4.30pm weekends. Closed race days. Small basket 80p; medium £1.40; large £1.60. 28 covered tees. Floodlit. Target. Putting. Tuition available PGA Professional. Shop. 9 hole course, par 34. Loc: Inside Warwick racecourse.

West Midlands

Four Ashes Golf Centre

Four Ashes Road, Dorridge, Solihull B93 8NQ. *Tel* (0564) 779055
Open 10am–10pm weekdays. 10am–6pm weekends. 26 covered floodlit bays. £1.80 for 90 balls; £1.10 for 45 balls. Tuition available. Club hire. Golf shop. Loc: 3 miles S of Solihull. M42 Junction 4.

Swindon Ridge

Blackhill Wood, Bridgenorth Road, Swindon, Nr Dudley DY3 4PU. *Tel* (0902) 896191
Open 9am–9.30pm weekdays; 9am–6pm weekends. 27 floodlit bays. Professional tuition. £1.70 for 90 balls; £1 for 40 balls. Putting green. Practice bunker. Loc: 5 miles S of Wolverhampton.

Three Hammers Golf Complex

Old Stafford Road, Coven, Nr Wolverhampton WV10 7PP. *Tel* (0902) 790428
Open 9.30am–10pm weekdays; 9am–7pm weekends. Floodlit. 14 covered floodlit bays. 18 hole short course. Loc: 5 miles N of Wolverhampton. 2 miles from M6 Junction 10.

Wiltshire

Broome Manor Driving Range

Broome Manor Golf Complex, Pipers Way, Swindon, Wilts. SN3 1RG. *Tel* (0793) 532403
Open 9.30am–9.30pm, 7 days. (Mondays 12 noon–9.30pm). 25 bays. Floodlit. £1.40 standard; £2 large bucket of balls. Hire of clubs 40p each. Professional. Loc: Swindon 2 miles.

Yorkshire (South)

Austerfield Park Driving Range

Austerfield, Bawtry, Doncaster DN10 6RF
Open daily 8am–9pm. 10 floodlit bays. Bucket of balls £1.20. Tuition. Golf course. Loc: 2 miles from Bawtry on A614.

Yorkshire (West)

Bradley Park Driving Range

Bradley Road, Huddersfield. *Tel* (0484) 539988
Open 9am–10pm. 14 covered floodlit bays. £2 for 80 balls. Tuition available £9–£10.50 for 40 mins. Loc: 1¹⁄₂ miles from M62 Junction 25.

Ireland

Ballyearl Golf Centre

585 Doagh Road, Newtonabbey, BT36 8RZ. *Tel* (023 13) 48287
Open 9am–10pm. Small bucket £1.50, Large £2.50. Professional. 9 hole par 3 course. £2.50 weekdays; £3 weekends. 2-tiered covered floodlit range. 27 bays. Club hire. Loc: 1 mile N of Mossley off B59.

Craigavon Golf Centre

Turmoyra Lane, Silverwood, Lurgan, Craigavon
Open 9am–9.30pm weekdays. 9am–5pm weekends. 20 floodlit covered bays. Professional tuition. Putting green. Pitch and putt. Loc: 1¹⁄₂ miles from Lurgan.

Downpatrick Golf Range

86 Ardglass Road, Downpatrick, Co. Down BT30 7DX. *Tel* (0396) 613558
Open daily 9am–9pm. 24 floodlit bays – 14 covered. Professional tuition. Putting green. Practice bunker. Pro shop. Loc: ¹⁄₂ mile SE of Downpatrick on B1.

Heath Driving Range

The Heath, Portlaoise, Co. Laois. *Tel* (0502) 46533
Open daily until 10pm. 10 covered floodlit
bays. IR£1 for 60 balls. Professional tuition.
18 hole course. Loc: 4 miles NE of Portlaoise.

Knockbracken Golf Centre

Ballymaconaghy Road, Belfast. *Tel* (0232) 643554
Open 9am–11pm. Floodlit. Putting. 18 hole
course. Loc: 2 miles SW of Belfast.

Leopardstown Golf Centre

Foxrock, Dublin 18. *Tel* (0001) 895341/895671
Manager William Hourihane. 9 holes golf course;
18 hole par 3 course 2795 yds. Public course.
Green fees: £4, weekends £4.50 (18 holes); Par
3 - £3. Driving range: 36 indoor bays, 50 outdoor
bays. Floodlit. £1.30-£2. Open WD 10am–10pm,
WE 9am–6pm. Loc: 5 miles S of Dublin.

Lochgeorge Driving Range

Lochgeorge, Claregalway, Co. Galway.
Tel (091) 98202
Open 11am–9pm weekdays and Saturday.
12 noon–7pm Sunday. 15 bays – 8 covered
floodlit. Loc: 7 miles N of Galway on Tuam road.

Scotland

Auchenharvie Driving Range

Moorpark Road West, Stevenston KA20 3HU.
Tel (0294) 603103
Open 9am–9pm weekdays; 9am–4pm weekends.
18 floodlit bays. £2 for 100 balls; £1.10 for 50 balls.
Tuition available. 9 hole golf course. Loc: 1 mile
W of Stevenston.

Clydeway Golf Centre

Blantyre Farm Road, Uddingston, Lanarkshire.
Tel 041-641 8899
Open 10am–9pm weekdays; 10am–6pm
weekends. 25 bays. £2 for 100 balls; £1.20
for 50 balls (1989 prices). Floodlit. Golf shop.
PGA Professional. Tuition. Loc: 1¹/₂ miles from
Glasgow Zoo.

Normandy Golf Range

Inchinnan Road, Renfrew, PA4 9ES.
Tel 041-886 7477
Open 9.30am–8.30pm weekdays; 9.30am–5.30pm
weekends. 20 covered, 5 open bays. Video.
Professional. Floodlit. £1.30 for 50 balls, £2 for
90 balls. Loc: 1 mile W of Glasgow Airport. M8
1 mile.

Polkemmet Driving Range

Polkemmet Country Park, Whitburn, Bathgate,
W. Lothian EH47 0AD
Open daily. 15 covered floodlit bays. £1.60
for 100 balls; £1 for 50 balls. Golf course. Loc:
Between Whitburn and Harthill on B7066.

Port Royal Golf Range

Ingliston, Edinburgh, Lothians. *Tel* 031-333 4377
Open all year. 10am–11pm. 24 bays. Floodlit.
£1.25 per bucket. 9 hole par 3 course.
Professional tuition. Large putting green. Loc:
by Edinburgh Airport.

Strathclyde Park Golf Range

Mote Hill, Hamilton, Lanarkshire
24 bays. Floodlit. Open 9.30am–9.30pm. Large
bucket £2. Small bucket £1.50. 9 hole golf course.
Professional teaching. Loc: A723 just of M74.

Tayside Golf Driving Range

The Downs, Barry, nr Carnoustie DD7 75A.
Tel (0382) 534 226
Tuition. Club hire. £1.40 for 50 balls, £2.50
for 100 balls. Loc: 7 miles from Dundee on
Carnoustie road.

Wales

South Wales Golf Range

Port Road East, Barry. *Tel* (0446) 742434
Open 9am–8pm weekdays. 9am–5pm weekends.
16 covered floodlit bays. Bucket of balls £1.50.
Professional tuition. Putting green. 9 hole par 3
course. Loc: 8 miles from Cardiff on A4050.

Tregroes Driving Range

Fishguard, Dyfed SA65 9QF
Open daily 10am–8pm. 6 covered floodlit bays.
Bucket of balls £1. Tuition available. Loc: 1 mile
S of Fishguard on A40.

France sets the pace for new courses

Michael Gedye

A major influence in recent Continental golf course construction has been the rising interest in the game as a tourist attraction. More courses are being built in resort areas and more golf made available to the travelling player. It is interesting to examine the growth of the game in the three European countries most visited for golf – Spain, Portugal and France – and to review recent and newly opened courses for somewhere fresh to play.

Playing golf on holiday is not a new phenomenon, but it is only over the last 15 years that it has become a substantial factor in the game. This is especially true from autumn to spring and a considerable travelling market has been established. Prime locations have been Spain and Portugal where many newly-built resort courses have combined with winter sunshine to attract a growing number of holiday golfers.

The origins of this activity, however, go back more than a hundred years and, in fact, neither to Spain nor Portugal but to France. France can boast the Continent's first golf course, built near Pau in the south-west in 1856. Around the turn of the century, France also attracted an elegant and sophisticated clientèle to its beaches, spas and casinos during the summer season. The wealthy British came and golf came with them, along three distinct holiday coastlines. In the north, bordering the Channel, Dinard (1887), Dieppe (1897), Fontenay (1902), Le Touquet (1904), Wimereux (1906) and Etretat (1908) all attracted intrepid visitors. Along the Basque coast, early golf was played at Biarritz (1888) and La Nivelle (1907) while on the Côte d'Azur in the south, Cannes Mandelieu (1891), Valescure (1896) and Monte Carlo (1911) provided sport for the rich and fashionable.

Although the game developed at a considerable pace in Great Britain during the twenties and thirties, becoming in the process a touch more cosmopolitan, the concept of playing golf on the Continent changed only marginally for another 50 years.

Then the growth of inexpensive air travel and package holidays opened up the Iberian peninsula; golf followed, laid out in attractive coastal areas to appeal to a winter season market. Growth was rapid and most clubs built in the next 20 years were in or near seaside resorts and aimed at the visitor. Portugal nearly trebled its courses to 23; Spain's increased from 24 to 87, situated mainly along the Costa Brava, Costa del Sol and in the Balearic and Canary Islands.

The pace of development was slower in France. With limited domestic interest and many coastal resort courses in the seasonal north, the number only rose from 99 to 141 by 1984. Then, suddenly, the game took off. Now, five years later, the total is up to 300 with a further 134 courses under construction. No other country in the world is developing facilities for the game at such a rate as France and opportunities for visiting players abound. Golf is still a relatively wealthy pursuit which means that new clubs are well-appointed and equally well-maintained. Since they cater to a young, family market, they also have a comprehensive range of facilities. Two-thirds of French golfers are under 45 years old; one-third are women.

In Portugal, there are currently 28 courses to play, with the possibility of this number doubling within 10 years. There are now 120 golf clubs federated in Spain and its islands, with many more planned or under construction.

To highlight some examples of interesting new developments, I have surveyed the Mediterranean coast from Monaco round to Cape St Vincent at the western tip of Portugal's Algarve. I have also looked at northern France from Dunkerque to Brittany. This is a summary of the new places to play and some assessment of golf to come.

In the stretch of coastline from Monte Carlo to St Tropez, long a haunt of winter sunshine golfers, seven courses have stood the test of time. Three more are under construction, including a Robert Trent Jones 18-hole layout, the Riviera Golf Club, at Mandelieu. A further 11 clubs are scheduled to follow. Newly opened, next door to the refurbished course at Valescure, is Golf du Estérel, a large rolling 18-holes, also by Trent Jones, with umbrella pines and challenging greens.

A little further west is possibly the toughest and most scenic course in France, Golf de Barbaroux. Created around and over a steep hillside in a region of dense forest by Pete and PB Dye, it represents dramatic, at times almost fantasy golf, well worth a visit before it closes to members only. Nearby, between Aix-en-Provence and Marseille, two new courses are in play, Golf de Sainte Baume and Golf du Château l'Arc. The latter winds over an interesting wooded hillside with fine views above an ancient château. Two new courses have also opened north-east of Arles at Les Baux and nearby Mouriès, pleasant golf in a truly scenic setting.

At Montpellier are two superb new golf courses of genuine championship calibre. The first, Golf de Massane at Baillargues, is by American designer Ronald Fream. Laid out in a former vineyard. The location also features a unique teaching centre where up to 250 players can learn and practise all aspects of the game.

Close by is the watersport marina of La Grande Motte, where three Trent Jones courses have been developed over former marshland, notable for the wealth of water hazards. The main 18 holes, 'Les Flamants Roses', hosted a Volvo Tour event in 1989. Further west at Cap d'Agde, another Fream course has opened. Undulating over an old Roman site, it presents an interesting examination in excellent condition with many boulders among other hazards. With 30 courses in play and many more under construction, the southern coast of France has golf for all at a reasonable cost and in an attractive climate.

Golf development has not moved at such a rapid pace in Spain in recent years, although there are indications of many new courses coming in the next 10 years.

On the increasingly golf-minded island of Majorca, eight courses are now in play. Joining the relatively new 9-hole layouts at Bendinat and Pollensa, Canyamel Golf Club has just opened a demanding 18-holes some 60 km from Palma. Vall d'Or, which opened its comfortably undulating nine holes in 1986, should have a further nine ready by late 1990. With some testing short holes, this will be an attractive addition to the choice already offered to the visitor.

The Costa del Sol has long proved an oasis for winter golf. Two new courses have recently been added to the existing 14 and several others, including Seve Ballesteros' Los Arqueros, the Marbella Golf and Country Club and the San Roque Club, designed by Dave Thomas and spearheaded by Tony Jacklin, are due to open soon. La Quinta Golf and Country Club, inland a little west of Marbella, is open now. This still maturing, par 71 course, designed by Manuel

Pinero and Antonio Garcia Garrido, will eventually boast 27 holes. Further along the coast beyond Estepona on the way to Sotogrande and Gibraltar, Golf La Duquesa has a 6756 yards par 72 designed by Robert Trent Jones and built dramatically around a dominant hill. This has highly challenging terrain, whatever your ability, and superb sea views from the higher holes.

On the Portuguese Algarve, new golf development is gaining pace. Front runner is Quinta do Lago, a luxury resort in a pinewood setting by the sea to the west of Faro. The 9-hole D course, designed by American Joe Lee completes 36 holes in four alternate loops. Already in play at the same location are the testing 18 holes of San Lourenço, also designed by Lee. Spacious and demanding, the course skirts a large lagoon and wildlife reserve by the sea. When the Ron Fream-designed Pinheiros Altos course, currently under construction, is complete, Quinta do Lago will be the first resort in Europe with 72 holes on site.

Among other developments nearing completion, Pine Cliffs, a little west of Almancil, has nine holes by Martin Hawtree, while at Vilamoura, the third course, 27 holes by Joe Lee, is due to open in spring 1990 to join the already well-established Old and New courses. At Carvoeiro, a 27-hole golf complex by Ronald Fream should have its first nine ready for play by late 1990. A further 13 sites are either under construction or planned in the Algarve, part of a trend which should see 50 courses throughout Portugal by the end of the century.

Moving to the north of France, the new places to play are, with one exception, in Brittany. The only recently opened course among the many well-established in Normandy is Golf de Saint-Julien at Pont L'Evêque. This is a 27-hole layout with many undulating doglegs, numerous bunkers and strategic water. It is a challenging first effort by designer Alan Prat.

In Brittany, Golf des Ormes, laid out in wooded land by an old château, adds to the excellent La Tronchet in the St Malo area. The well-established and respected course at Brest-Iroise is opening a stiffer third nine by Robin Nelson. Around the corner near Quimper, Golf de l'Odet has a good 18-hole layout in excellent condition and a 9-hole short course. Encircling the Bay of Morbihan, two new courses complement the popular Golf de Saint Laurent. Golf de Baden, by Yves Bureau, is relatively open but well-kept and Golf de Kerver (6813 yards par 72) adds a further good course to the area. Finally, inland at Rennes, Golf de Freslonnière offers a gem of scenic, strategic golf in a forest setting. There are 36 courses around the northern coasts of France, an attractive combination of old and new, with more visitor's golf planned.

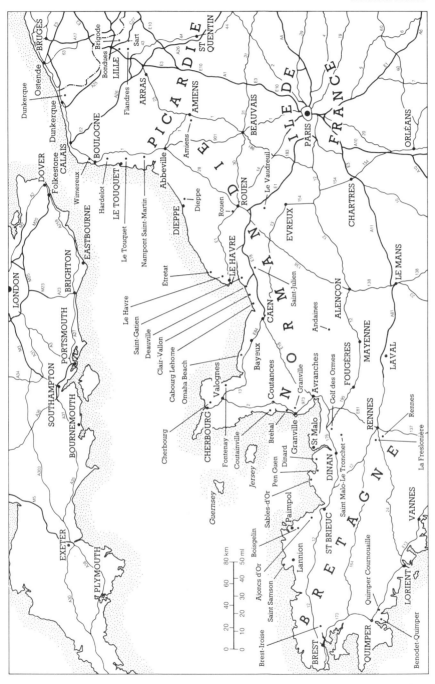

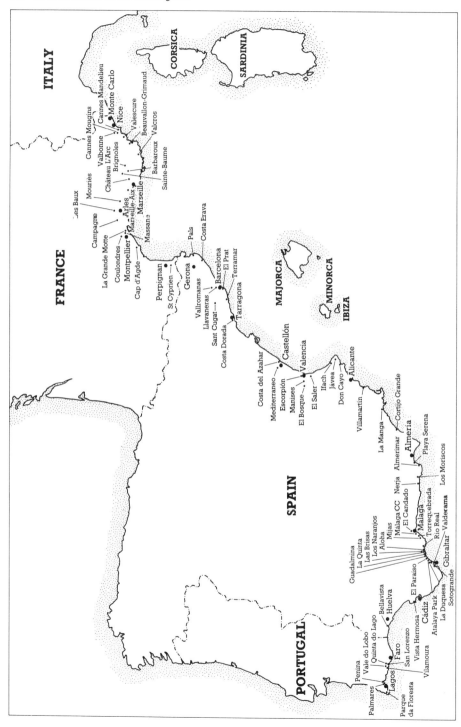

Continental Section

Austria

Achensee (1934)
A-6213 Pertisau/Tyrol
Tel   (05243) 5377
Mem   430
Pro   D Posch, H Egger
Holes   9 L 3920 m SSS 62
Fees   200s (300s)
Loc   Pertisau, 50km NE of Innsbruck

Bad Kleinkircheim–Reichenau (1984)
A-9546 Bad Kleinkircheim
Tel   (04274) 594
Mem   300
Pro   G Manson
Holes   18 L 6127 m SSS 72
Fees   380s
Loc   Kleinkircheim, 50km NW of Klagenfurt via Route 95

Badgastein (1962)
5640 Badgastein, PO Box 15
Tel   (06434) 2775/2516
Mem   330
Pro   S Wildman
Holes   9 L 5804 m SSS 71
Fees   250s (300s) W–1600s
Loc   Badgastein 2km
Mis   Open May–Oct

Ennstal–Weissenbach G & LC (1978)
A-8940 Liezen, Postfach 28
Tel   (03612) 24774
Pro   T Robinson
Holes   9 L 5630 m SSS 70
Fees   300s
Loc   5km SW of Liezen, off Salzburg–Graz road

Enzesfeld (1970)
A-2551 Enzesfeld
Tel   (02256) 81272
Mem   480
Pro   I Gillies, C Davies
Holes   18 L 6176 m SSS 72
Fees   450s (600s)
Loc   32km S of Vienna towards Vienna Neustadt
Mis   WE/Jul/Aug–only with member. Handicap certificate required.

Europa Sport Region (1983)
Golfstr 25, A-5700 Zell am See
Tel   (06542) 6161
Mem   560
Pro   D Shaw

Holes   18 L 6128 m SSS 72
          9 L 5650 m SSS 69
Fees   18 holes 400s (500s)
          9 holes 350s (400s)
Loc   Zell am See, 95km SW of Salzburg
Mis   Driving range D–70s. Open May–Oct

Föhrenwald (1968)
Postfach 105, A-2700 Wiener Neustadt
Tel   (02622) 52171
Mem   400
Pro   A Andrews, S Page, N Hirst
Holes   18 L 6043 m SSS 72
Fees   300s (400s)
Loc   5km S of Wiener Neustadt on Route B54

Golfakademie Seefeld (1987)
A-6100 Seefeld, WM Sportanlagen GmbH
Tel   (05212) 2313/2316
Mem   238
Pro   M Mawdsley
Holes   18 L 6046 m SSS 72
Fees   280s (400s)
Loc   4km W of Seefeld. 24km W of Innsbruck
Mis   Hotel guests 15% reduction. Starting times necessary Jul–Sept

Gut Altentann (1989)
A-5302 Henndorf am Wallersee, Salzburg
Tel   (06214) 60 26
Mem   310
Pro   J Mannie
Holes   18 L 6180 m SSS 72
Fees   800s
Loc   Henndorf, 16km N of Salzburg

Güt Brandlhof (1983)
A-5760 Saalfelden, Sporthotel Güt Brandlhof
Tel   (06582) 2176/555
Mem   195
Pro   N Rayne
Holes   18 L 6300 m SSS 73
Fees   350s (400s)
Loc   Saalfelden, 60km SW of Salzburg towards Zell am See

Hainburg/Donau (1977)
Auf der Heide 762, A-2410 Hainburg
Tel   (02165) 2628
Mem   195
Pro   R Jerman
Holes   9 L 5950 m SSS 71
Fees   250s (350s)
Mis   Open Mar–Nov

Innsbruck–Igls (1956)
A-6074 Rinn, Oberdorf 11
Tel   (05223) 8177
Mem   450
Pro   I Shaw
Holes   18 L 5910 m SSS 71
          9 L 4709 m SSS 66
Fees   380s (500s)
Loc   18 hole course at Rinn, 10km E of Innsbruck.
Mis   Handicap certificate required

Kärntner (1927)
A-9082 Dellach, 16 Maria Wörth
Tel   (04273) 2515
Mem   250
Pro   C Prasthofer, D Marsh
Holes   18 L 5700 m SSS 70
Fees   D–400s
Loc   Dellach, S side of Wörthersee. 15km W of Klagenfurt

Kitzbühel (1955)
A-6370 Kitzbühel
Tel   (05356) 3007
Mem   400
Pro   S Brown, P Wagstaff
Holes   9 L 6085 m SSS 72
Fees   250s (350s)
Loc   Kitzbühel 820 m

Linz–St Florian (1960)
A-4490 St Florian, Tillysburg 28
Tel   (07223) 2873
Mem   640
Pro   S Jackson, R Andrews
Holes   18 L 6091 m SSS 72
Fees   380s (480s)
Loc   St Florian, 15km SE of Linz

Murhof (1963)
A-8130 Frohnleiten, Adriach 53
Tel   (03127) 2101
Mem   380
Pro   GJ Mackintosh
Holes   18 L 6371 m SSS 73
Fees   380s
Loc   Frohnleiten, 25km N of Graz. 150km S of Vienna
Mis   Golf hotel guests–220s

Salzburg Klesheim (1955)
A-5071 Wals, bei Salzburg
Tel   (0662) 850851
Mem   420
Pro   D Howard
Holes   9 L 5700 m SSS 70
Fees   300s (350s)
Loc   5km N of Salzburg

For explanation of abbreviations, see page 460.

Salzkammergut (1932)

A–4820 Bad Ischl, Postfach 145
Tel (06132) 6340
Mem 450
Pro I Hay, F Laimer, Ch Schuster
Holes 9 L 5900 m SSS 71
Fees 350–400s
Loc 6km W of Bad Ischl, nr Strobl. 50km E of Salzburg

Schloss Ernegg (1973)

A–3261 Steinakirchen am Forst NO
Tel (07488) 214 (May–Oct)
Mem 120
Pro P Kreier
Holes 18 L 5670 m SSS 70
  9 L 2076 m SSS 62
Fees 300s (350s)
Loc Steinakirchen, 60km SE of Linz
Mis Driving range, pitch and putt

Schloss Fuschl (1964)

A–5322 Hof/Salzburg
Tel (06229) 390
Mem 200
Pro F Torrano
Holes 9 L 3054 m SSS 61
Fees 150–200s (200s)
Loc Hof, 12km E of Salzburg
Mis Driving range

Schloss Pichlarn (1972)

A–8952 Irdning, Ennstal Steiermark
Tel (03682) 24393
Mem 417
Pro A Mitchell, D Burton, M Caines
Holes 18 L 6123 m SSS 72
Fees D–300s
Loc 5km E of Irdning, off Salzburg–Graz road. 140km SE of Salzburg

Semmering (1926)

Hochstr 108, 2680 Semmering
Pro H Blaschek (02664) 8154
Holes 9 L 3860 m SSS 62
Fees 200s (300s)
Loc 30km SW of Vienna Neustadt
Mis Open May–Oct. Driving range

St Pölten Schloss Goldegg (1989)

3100 St Pölten Schloss Goldegg
Tel (02741) 7360
Mem 100
Pro JC Dockray
Holes 18 L 6249 m SSS 73
Fees 300s (400s)
Loc 8km NW of St Pölten. 60km W of Vienna

Wels (1981)

4512 Weisskirchen/Wels, Weyerbach 37
Tel (07243) 6038
Mem 420
Pro J Wraith
Holes 18 L 6100 m Par 72
Fees 300s (400s)
Loc 5km from Salzburg–Vienna highway. 8km SE of Wels
Mis Driving range, pitch and putt. Handicap certificate required

Wien (1901)

Freudenau 65a, 1020 Wien
Tel (0222) 2189564/2189667
Mem 670
Pro W Walters, T Rogerson
Holes 18 L 5861 m SSS 71
Fees D–600s
Loc 10 mins SE of Vienna
Mis (0222) 2189667 (Caddymaster)

Wienerwald (1981)

Forsthof 211, A–3053 Laaben
Tel (0222) 823111
Mem 50
Holes 9 L 4652 m SSS 65
Fees 300s (500s)
Loc Laaben, 35km W of Vienna

Belgium

Antwerp Region

Bossenstein (1989)

2250 Broechem
Tel (03) 485 64 46
Pro C Renders, T Clarys, A Christiaens
Holes 18 L 6203 m SSS 72
  9 L 1500 m
Fees 1000fr (1500fr)
Loc 15km E of Antwerp. 5km N of Lier
Mis Driving range

Cleydael (1988)

Kasteel Cleydael, 2630 Aartselaar
Tel (03) 887 00 73/887 18 74
Mem 400
Holes 18 L 6059 m SSS 72
Fees 1500fr (2000fr)
Loc 8km S of Antwerp. 40km N of Brussels
Mis Driving range

Inter–Mol (1984)

Begijnhofstraat 11, 2360 Oud–Turnhout
Mem 180
Holes 9 L 1570 m SSS 57
Fees 300fr (400fr)
Loc Turnhout, 50km E of Antwerp

Lilse (1988)

Haarlebeek 3, 2418 Lille
Tel (014) 55 19 30
Mem 350
Pro A Van Damme, F Van Damme
Holes 9 L 4582 m SSS 65
Fees 400fr (600fr)
Loc Lille, 10km SW of Turnhout, nr E7. 25km E of Antwerp

Rinkven G & CC (1980)

St Jobsteenweg 120, 2232 Schilde
Tel (03) 384 0784
Mem 1000
Pro M Waldron, F Dhondt
Holes 27 L 6128 m SSS 73
Fees 1250fr (2500fr)
Loc 17km NE of Antwerp, off E19
Mis Handicap certificate required

Royal Antwerp (1888)

Georges Capiaulei 2, 2080 Kapellen
Tel (03) 666 8456
Mem 950
Pro J Halliwell
Holes 18 L 6140 m SSS 73
  9 L 2264 m SSS 33
Fees 1300fr (1400fr)
Loc Kapellen, 20km N of Antwerp

Steenhoven (1985)

Eerselseweg 40, 2400 Postel–Mol
Tel (014) 37 72 50
Mem 100
Pro J Wilkinson
Holes 18 L 5950 m SSS 71
Fees 1500fr (2500fr)
Loc 30 mins W of Antwerp
Mis Handicap certificate required

Ternesse (1976)

Uilenbaan 15, 2220 Wommelgem
Tel (03) 353 0292
Mem 700
Pro S Bouillon, V Waters
Holes 18 L 5876 m SSS 72
Fees 1250fr (2500fr)
Loc E of Antwerp on E313

Ardennes & South

Château Royal d'Ardenne

5560 Houyet Dinant
Tel (082) 66 62 28
Mem 350
Pro F Masson
Holes 18 L 5363 m SSS 71
Fees 700fr (1000fr)
Loc 9km SE of Dinant on Rochefort road

Falnuée (1987)

55, Rue E Pirson, 5830 Mazy
Tel   (081) 63 30 90
Mem   385
Pro   M Duhamel
Holes 18 L 5700 m SSS 69
Fees   500fr (700fr)
Loc   18km NW of Namur. Mons–
       Liège highway exit 13

Golf d'Andenne (1988)

Ferme du Moulin 52, Stud,
5220 Andenne
Tel   (085) 84 34 04
Mem   150
Pro   F Vercruyce, C Bertier
Holes 9 L 2447 m SSS 66
Fees   500fr (700fr)
Loc   Andenne, 20km E of Namur

Mont Garni (1989)

Rue du Mont Garni 3, 7420 Saint
Ghislain
Tel   (065) 62 27 19
Mem   300
Pro   F Gabias
Holes 18 L 6450 m SSS 74
Fees   800fr (1200fr)
Loc   St Ghislain, 15km W of Mons.
       65km SW of Brussels

Rougemont

Chemin du Beau Vallon 45,
5170 Profondeville
Tel   (081) 41 14 18
Mem   260
Pro   R Braems
Holes 9 L 2356 m SSS 34
Fees   600fr (800fr)
Loc   Profondeville, 10km S of Namur

Royal GC Du Hainaut (1934)

2, Rue de la Verrerie, 7434 Erbisoeul
Tel   (065) 22 96 10/22 94 74(Sec)
Mem   650
Pro   F Lefever
Holes 18 L 6183 m SSS 72
       9 L 3200 m
Fees   D–850fr (1200fr)
Loc   6km NW of Mons towards Ath

East

Flanders–Nippon (1988)

Vissenbroekstraat 15, 3500 Hasselt
Tel   (011) 22 37 93/22 79 55
Mem   300
Pro   J Gulesserian
Holes 18 L 5922 m SSS 72
       9 L 1726 m SSS 32
Fees   1000fr (1500fr)
Loc   Hasselt, 85km E of Brussels

Henri–Chapelle (1988)

Rue du Vivier 3, 4841 Henri–Chapelle
Tel   (087) 88 19 91
Mem   200
Pro   DA Petrie
Holes 18 L 6045 m SSS 72
       9 L 2255 m SSS 34
       9 hole Par 3 course
Fees   1250fr (1500fr)
Loc   Henri–Chapelle, 15km NE of
       Verviers. 40km E of Liège

Limburg G & CC (1966)

Golfstraat No 1, 3530 Houthalen
Tel   (011) 38 35 43
Mem   650
Pro   J Renders
Holes 18 L 6090 m SSS 72
Fees   1000fr (1500fr)
Loc   Houthalen, 15km N of Hasselt

Royal GC des Fagnes (1930)

Balmoral, 4880 Spa
Tel   (087) 77 16 13
Mem   350
Pro   WYS Robertson
Holes 18 L 5948 m SSS 71
Fees   D–800–1000fr
Loc   Spa 5km. 35km SE of Liège

Royal GC du Sart Tilman

541 Route du Condroz, 4200 Ougrée
Tel   (041) 36 20 21
Mem   700
Pro   B Janjic, A Verlegh
Holes 18 L 6002 m SSS 71
Fees   D–1000fr (1500fr)
Loc   10km S of Liège on Route 620
       towards Marche

Spiegelven GC Genk (1988)

Wiemesmeerstraat, 3600 Genk
Tel   (011) 35 36 16
Mem   500
Pro   A Van Pixten
Holes 18 L 6200 m SSS 72
Fees   900fr (1300fr)
Loc   Genk, 18km E of Hasselt

Brussels & Brabant

Brabantse (1982)

Steenwagenstraat 11, 1910 Melsbroek
Tel   (02) 752 82 05
Sec   400
Pro   E Rovzar
Holes 18 L 4618 m SSS 65
Fees   500fr (750fr)
Loc   10km NE of Brussels, nr airport

Château de la Bawette (1988)

Chaussée de la Bawette 5, 1300 Wavre
Tel   (010) 22 33 32
Mem   400
Pro   D Aime, K Murray
Holes 18 L 6145 m SSS 72
       9 L 2200 m SSS 33
Fees   1500fr (2000fr)
Loc   1km N of Wavre. 20km S
       of Brussels

Duisberg Militaire

Hertswegenstraat 39,
1982 Duisburg
Tel   767 9752/3890 (Ext 388)
Holes 9 L 3630 m SSS 60
Fees   D–200fr (300fr)
Loc   Brussels 13km

Golf de Rigenée (1981)

Rue de Châtelet 10a, 6321
Villers–la–Ville
Tel   (071) 87 77 65
Mem   550
Pro   Ch Ditlefsen, H Ladmirant
       F Descampe (Touring)
Holes 18 L 6150 m SSS 72
Fees   700fr (1200fr)
Loc   35km S of Brussels towards
       Charleroi

Keerbergen (1979)

50 Vlieghavenlaan, 2850 Keerbergen
Tel   (015) 23 49 61
Mem   820
Pro   W Vanbegin, D Redvek
       W Mann (015) 23 49 63
Holes 18 L 5530 m SSS 69
Fees   1000fr (1700fr)
Loc   29km NE of Brussels

Royal Amicale Anderlecht (1987)

Dreve Olympique 1, 1070 Bruxelles
Tel   (02) 521 16 87
Mem   320
Pro   P Michielsen, J–P Michielsen
Holes 9 L 2660 m SSS 69
Fees   500fr (800fr)
Loc   Brussels

Royal Golf Club de Belgique (1906)

Château de Ravenstein, 1980
Tervueren
Tel   (02) 767 5801
Mem   1280
Pro   J Williams, C Ledbury
Holes 18 L 6075 m SSS 72
       9 L 1960 m Par 32

For explanation of abbreviations, see page 460.

Fees　1550fr (2550fr)
Loc　Tervueren, 15km E of Brussels
Mis　18 hole course limited to h'cap
　　　(men–20 ladies–24). Phone
　　　before visit. Handicap
　　　certificate required.

Royal Waterloo (1923)

Vieux Chemin de Wavre, 1328 Ohain
Tel　(02) 633 1850/1597
Mem　1300
Pro　G Will, J Blair
Holes　18 L 6260 m SSS 73
　　　18 L 6440 m SSS 72
　　　9 L 2143 m SSS 73
Fees　D–1200fr (D–2000fr)
Loc　22km SE of Brussels
Mis　Handicap certificate required

Sept Fontaines (1987)

1021, Chaussée d'Alsemberg,
1420 Braine l'Alleud
Tel　(02) 353 02 46/353 03 46
Mem　900
Pro　A Watts, T Comens
Holes　18 L 6047 m SSS
　　　18 L 4500m SSS
　　　9 hole short course
Fees　1000fr (1500fr)
Loc　Braine, 15km S of Brussels.
　　　Motorway exit Huizingen

Winge G & CC

Wingerstraat 6, 3210 Sint Joris Winge
Tel　(016) 63 40 53
Mem　300
Pro　F Van Donck, P Townsend,
　　　M Vanmeerbeek
Holes　18 L 6149 m SSS 72
Fees　500–1000fr (1000–1500fr)
Loc　35km E of Brussels via Leuven

West & Oost Vlanderen

Damme G & CC (1987)

Doornstraat 16, 8340 Damme–Sijsele
Tel　(050) 35 35 72
Mem　400
Pro　G Pearce
Holes　18 L 6046 m SSS 72
Fees　1000fr (1300fr)
Loc　10km E of Bruges

Koninklijke GC Ostend (1903)

2 Koninklijke, 8420 De Haan
Tel　(059) 23 32 83
Mem　450
Pro　T Bowden
Holes　18 L 5320 m SSS 68
Fees　950fr (1150fr)
Loc　7km N of Ostend towards
　　　De Haan

Oudenaarde G & CC (1976)

Kasteel Petegem, Kortrykstraat 52
9790 Wortegem–Petegem
Tel　(055) 31 54 81
Mem　650
Pro　C Morton, T Welsh
Holes　18 L 6039 m SSS 73
Fees　D–600fr (1000fr)
Loc　3km SW of Oudenaarde

Royal Latem (1909)

9830 St Martens–Latem
Tel　(091) 82 54 11
Mem　760
Pro　J Verplancke
Holes　18 L 5767 m SSS 70
Fees　1000fr (1500fr)
Loc　10km SW of Ghent on route
　　　N43 Ghent–Deinze

Royal Zoute

Caddiespad 14 8300 Knokke–Heist
Tel　(050) 60 12 27 (Sec)
　　　(050) 60 72 11 (Caddiemaster)
　　　(050) 60 37 81 (Starter)
Mem　1200
Pro　A de Vulder
Holes　18 L 6172 m SSS 72
　　　18 L 3607 m SSS 60
Fees　D–1000–1300fr (1200–1700fr)
Loc　Knokke 1km

Czechoslovakia

Mariánské Lázně (1905)

Mariánské Lázně, Zadub 565
Tel　5195
Mem　160
Pro　N Miroslav
Holes　18 L 6080 m SSS 72
Fees　100kcs (130kcs)
Loc　3km NE of Mariánské Lázně.
　　　160km W of Prague

Oddíl Golfu TJ Semily (1971)

51301 Semily
Mem　68
Holes　8 L 4037 m SSS 64
Fees　D–20kcs
Loc　2km from Semily. 100km NW
　　　of Prague

TJ Golf Praha (1969)

Na Morani 4, 120 00 Praha 2
Tel　292828
Mem　220
Holes　9 L 2978 m SSS 36
Fees　100 kcs (200 kcs)
Loc　Prague Motol, towards Plzeň

TJ Lokomotiva–Ingstav (1967)

Antoninska 5, 60200 Brno
Tel　(05) 75 75 23
Mem　88
Pro　I Koch
Holes　9 L 4758 m SSS 68
Fees　15DM (20DM)
Loc　Brno 80km. Prague 100km
Mis　Open May–Oct

TJ NHKG (1968)

Cingrova 10, 70100 Ostrava 1
Tel　Ostrava 97449 (Clubhouse)
Mem　201
Holes　18 L 5773 m SSS 72
Fees　100kcs
Loc　Silherovice, 15km from Ostrava

TJ Sklo Bohemia Poděbrady (1964)

Tyršova ul 26/111, 29001 Poděbrady
Tel　0324–4383
Mem　55
Holes　9 L 3121 m SSS 72
Fees　40kcs
Loc　E side of Poděbrady

TJ Start VD–Golf (1970)

36069 Karlovy Vary, Manesova 3
Tel　27279
Mem　84
Sec　E Stebel
Holes　18 L 6087 m SSS 72
Fees　100kcs
Loc　Karlovy Vary, 120km W of
　　　Prague

Denmark

Bornholm Island

Bornholm (1971)

Plantegavej 3B, 3700 Rønne
Tel　(53) 95 68 54
Mem　375
Pro　L Karlsen
Holes　18 L 4843 m SSS 68
Fees　100kr (100kr)
Loc　4km E of Rønne

Nordbornholm (1987)

Spellingevej 3, Rø, 3760 Gudhjem
Tel　(03) 98 42 00
Holes　18 L 5472 m SSS 69
Fees　100kr W–500kr
Loc　Rø, 8km W of Gudhjem.
　　　22km NE of Rønne

Funen

Odense (1927)

Hestehaven 201, 5220 Odense
Tel   (09) 95 90 00
Mem   1050
Pro   P Dixon
Holes 18 L 6156 m SSS 71
       9 L 4154 m SSS 60
Fees   80kr (100kr)
Loc   SE outskirts of Odense

SCT Knuds (1954)

Slipshavnsvej 16, DK 5800 Nyborg
Tel   (65) 31 12 12
Mem   621
Pro   H Hansen
Holes 18 L 5788 m SSS 70
Fees   120kr D-140kr (250kr)
Loc   3km SE of Nyborg

Svendborg (1970)

Tordensgårdsvej, Sørup,
5700 Svendborg
Tel   (62) 22 40 77
Mem   520
Pro   S Jensen
Holes 18 L 5692 m SSS 70
Fees   110kr W-600kr
Loc   4km NW of Svendborg

Vestfyns

Rønnemosegård, Krengerupvej 27,
5620 Glamsbjerg
Tel   (09) 72 15 77
Pro   S Tinning
Holes 9 L 5680 m SSS 71
Fees   60kr (75kr)
Loc   Glamsbjerg, 40km SW of
       Odense

Jutland

Aalborg (1908)

Jargersprisvej, Restup Enge 9000,
Aalborg
Tel   (08) 34 14 76
Mem   900
Pro   M Thuen
Holes 16 L 5800 m SSS 70
Fees   D-120kr (150 kr)
Loc   7km SW of Aalborg

Aarhus (1931)

Ny Møsgaardvej 50, 8270 Hojbjerg
Tel   (06) 27 63 22
Mem   1450
Pro   P Greve
Holes 18 L 6043 m SSS 72
       9 L 6093 m SSS 72
Fees   18 hole:100kr (120kr)
       9 hole:60kr (80kr)
Loc   6km S of Aarhus. 18 hole:
       Route 451 South. 9 hole: Route
       E3 North

Brønderslev (1971)

PO Box 94, 9700 Brønderslev
Tel   (98) 82 32 81
Mem   450
Pro   LM Jacobsen
Holes 18 L 5710 m SSS 71
Fees   120kr
Loc   3km W of Brønderslev

Dejbjerg (1968)

Public
Letagervej 1, Dejbjerg, 6900 Skjern
Tel   (97) 35 09 59
Mem   320
Pro   A Thygesen
Holes 9 L 5066 m SSS 67
Fees   D-80kr (D-100kr)
Loc   25km from W coast on
       Skjern–Rinkøbing road
       (route 28). 6km N of Skjern

Ebeltoft (1966)

Strandgårdshøj, 8400 Ebeltoft
Tel   (86) 34 47 87
Mem   400
Holes 18 L 5150 m SSS 67
Fees   D-100kr W-350kr
Loc   1/2 km N of Ebeltoft

Esbjerg (1921)

Sønderhedevej, Marbaek,
6710 Esbjerg
Tel   (05) 26 92 19
Mem   1100
Pro   A Tinning
Holes 18 L 6434 m SSS 74
Fees   100kr
Loc   15km N of Esbjerg

Fanø Island (1900)

6720 Nordby
Tel   (05) 16 32 82
Mem   239
Pro   N Aafeldt
Holes 18 L 4642 m SSS 65
Fees   D-80kr W-400 kr
Loc   Take Fanø Island Ferry
       from Esbjerg

Gyttegård (1978)

Billundvej 43, 7250 Hejnsvig
Tel   (75) 33 56 49
Mem   250
Pro   A Thygesen
Holes 9 L 5442 m SSS 69
Fees   100kr
Loc   2km NE of Hejnsvig. 10km S
       of Grindsted

Haderslev (1971)

Egevej 22, 6100 Haderslev
Tel   (04) 52 83 01
Mem   400
Pro   E Grandison
Holes 18 L 5137 m SSS 67
Fees   D-100kr
Loc   1 1/2 km NW of Haderslev

Herning (1964)

Golfvej 2, 7400 Herning
Tel   (97) 21 18 81
Mem   730
Pro   N Elsfon
Holes 18 L 5571 m SSS 70
Fees   D-100kr
Loc   2km E of Herning on
       Route 15

Himmerlands G & CC

Centervej 1, Gatten, 9670 Løgstør
Tel   (08) 66 16 00
Mem   620
Pro   R Kristensen, S Rolner
Holes 18 L 5277 m SSS 68
       9-hole Par 3 course
Fees   110kr (125kr) W-650kr
Loc   Gatten, 352km NW of Hobro
       towards Løgstør. Course
       signposted W from Gatten

Hjorring (1985)

Vinstrupvej, PO Box 215, 9800 Hjorring
Tel   (98) 90 03 99
Mem   450
Pro   A Routledge
Holes 18 holes SSS 71
Fees   100kr
Loc   N of Hjorring. 35km W of
       Frederikshavn

Holstebro (1970)

Råsted, 7570 Vemb
Tel   (07) 48 51 55
Mem   527
Pro   R Howett
Holes 18 L 5762 m SSS 70
Fees   D-100kr (120kr)
Loc   13km W of Holstebro

Horsens (1972)

Silkeborgvej, 8700 Horsens
Tel   (05) 61 51 51
Mem   400
Pro   G Oakley
Holes 18 + 6 L 5905 m SSS 72
Fees   100kr
Loc   1km W of Horsens towards
       Silkeborg

Hvide Klit

Hvideklitvej 28, 9982 Aalbaek
Tel   (98) 48 90 21/48 84 26
Mem   510
Pro   O Smidt (98) 48 80 08
Holes 18 L 5875 m SSS 72
Fees   160kr
Loc   3km N of Aalbaek.
       24km N of Frederikshavn

For explanation of abbreviations, see page 460.

Juelsminde (1973)

Bobroholtvej 9, 7130 Juelsminde
Tel   (05) 69 34 92
Mem 405
Pro   P Mason
Holes 9 L 6050 m SSS 72
Fees   80kr
Loc   20km S of Horsens on coast.
       2km N of Juelsminde
Mis   6 hole par 3 course

Kolding (1933)

Emerholtvej, 6000 Kolding
Tel   (75) 52 37 93
Mem 610
Pro   F Atkinson (75) 53 37
       93
Holes 18 L 5376 m SSS 69
Fees   120kr (160kr)
Loc   3km N of Kolding

Nordvestjysk (1971)

Nystrupvej 19, 7700 Thisted
Tel   (97) 97 41 41
Mem 340
Pro   M Thuen
Holes 9 L 5713 m SSS 71
Fees   D–100kr (120kr)
Loc   17km NW of Thisted

Randers (1958)

Himmelbovej, Fladbro, 8900 Randers
Tel   (06) 42 88 69
Mem 750
Pro   G Townhill
Holes 18 L 5453 m SSS 69
Fees   120kr (140kr) W–600kr
Loc   5km W of Randers towards
       Silkeborg

Ribe (1981)

Rønnehave, Snepsgårdevej 14,
Postboks 37, 6760 Ribe
Tel   (05) 44 12 30
Mem 265
Pro   P Thomson
Holes 9 L 5222 m SSS 67
Fees   80kr (100kr)
Loc   8km SE of Ribe on Haderslev
       road

Silkeborg (1966)

Sensommervej 15C, 8600 Silkeborg
Tel   (06) 85 33 99
Mem 850
Pro   M Kelly
Holes 18 L 5956 m SSS 72
Fees   120kr
Loc   5km E of Silkeborg

Skive

Resen, 7800 Skive
Tel   (97) 52 44 09
Mem 200
Holes 9 holes SSS 70
Fees   D–60kr
Loc   3km NW of Skive.
       32km NW of Viborg

Sønderjyllands (1970)

Uge Hedegård, 6360 Tinglev
Tel   (04) 68 75 25
Mem 420
Pro   T Mitchell (04) 68 81 98
Holes 18 L 5666 m SSS 69
Fees   D–100kr
Loc   3km NE of Tinglev. 15km S
       of Abenraa

Vejle (1970)

Faellessletgård, Ibaekvej, 7100 Vejle
Tel   (05) 85 81 85
Mem 1040
Pro   D Chad, J Smith
Holes 18 L 6042 yds SSS 71
Fees   130kr (150kr) W–700kr
Loc   5km SE of Vejle
Mis   Driving range. Par 3 course.

Viborg (1977)

Mollevej 26, Overlund, Viborg 8800
Tel   (86) 67 15 69
Mem 500
Pro   A Martin
Holes 18 L 6325 m SSS 73
Fees   180kr
Loc   2km E of Viborg

Zealand

Asserbo (1946)

Bødkergårdsvej,
3300 Frederiksvaerk
Tel   (42) 120329
Mem 450
Pro   J Nielsen
Holes 9 L 5447 m SSS 69
Fees   120kr (160kr) W–700kr
Loc   3km From Frederiksvaerk
       towards Liseleje

Copenhagen (1898)

Dyrehaven 2, 2800 Lyngby
Tel   (01) 63 04 83
Mem 1050
Pro   D Poke, D Hille, H Aafeldt
Holes 18 L 5701 m SSS 70
Fees   150kr (200kr)
Loc   13km N of Copenhagen, in
       deer park

Furesø (1974)

Hestkøbvaenge 4, 3460 Birkerød
Tel   (42) 81 74 44
Mem 1000
Pro   C Smith
Holes 18 L 5679 m SSS 71
Fees   160kr (240kr)
Loc   25km N of Copenhagen
Mis   WE–NA before 10am

Gilleleje (1970)

Ferlevej 52, 3250 Gilleleje
Tel   (49) 71 80 56/71 95 16
Mem 950
Pro   P Dangerfield
Holes 18 L 6641 yds SSS 72
Fees   D–160kr (200kr)
Loc   62km N of Copenhagen
Mis   Free driving range

Hedeland

Staerkendevej 232
2640 Hedehusene
Tel   (42) 13 61 69
Mem 600
Pro   A Palsby–Kristensen
Holes 18 L 6050 m SSS 72
Fees   120kr (150kr)
Loc   7km SE of Roskilde.
       20km SW of Copenhagen

Helsingør

Gl Hellebaekvej, 3000 Helsingør
Tel   (49) 21 29 70
Mem 1081
Pro   R Taylor
Holes 18 L 5705 m SSS 71
Fees   150kr (200kr)
Loc   1¹/₂ km N of Helsingør

Hillerød (1966)

Nysogård, Ny Hammersholt,
3400 Hillerød
Tel   (42) 26 50 46
Mem 950
Pro   M Tulloch (42) 25 40 30
Holes 18 L 5452 m SSS 70
Fees   150kr (220kr)
Loc   3km S of Hillerød
Mis   WE–NA before 12 noon

Holbaek (1964)

Dragerupvej 50, 4300 Holbaek
Tel   (53) 43 45 79
Mem 450
Pro   M Irving, M Davies
Holes 9 L 5960 m SSS 70
Fees   80kr (100kr)
Loc   Kirsebaerholmen, 2km E of
       Holbaek

Kalundborg (1974)

Kildekaergård, Rosnaesvej 225,
4400 Kalundborg
Tel   (03) 50 13 85
Mem 370
Sec   P Jacobsen
Pro   M Irving
Holes 9 L 5064 m SSS 68
Fees   60kr (90kr)
Loc   Rosnaes, 8km W of Kalundborg

Køge (1970)

Gl.Hastrupvej12, 4600 Køge
Tel   (53) 65 10 00
Mem   750
Pro   P Taylor
Holes   18 L 6042 m SSS 72
Fees   120kr (180kr)
Loc   3km S of Køge. Copenhagen
        38km

Kokkedal (1971)

2980 Kokkedal, Kokkedal Alle 9
Tel   (42) 86 99 59
Mem   1130
Pro   N Willett
Holes   18 L 5958 m SSS 72
Fees   140kr (200kr)
Loc   Hørsholm, 30km N of
        Copenhagen
Mis   WE–Visitors pm only.
        Handicap certificate required

Korsør (1964)

Tårnborgparken, Sørnumvej 8,
4220 Korsør
Tel   (53) 57 18 36
Mem   600
Pro   M Irving
Holes   18 L 5998 m SSS 72
Fees   D–120 (D–150kr)
Loc   1km E of Korsør, on Korsør
        Bay
Mis   6 hole Par 3 course

Midtsjaellands

Rødtjørnevej 19, 4180 Sorø
Tel   (53) 63 27 74
Mem   225
Pro   T Card
Holes   9 L 3670 m Par 60
Fees   D–60kr (D–80kr)
Loc   Sorø, 10km W of Ringsted

Mølleåens (1970)

Stenbaekgård, Bastrup,
3450 Lynge
Tel   (42) 18 86 31/18 86 79
Mem   1131
Pro   R Jackson
Holes   18 L 5730 m SSS 70
Fees   130kr (180kr)
Loc   32km NW of Copenhagen
Mis   Driving range

Odsherred (1967)

4573 Hojby, Sjaelland
Tel   (59) 30 20 76
Mem   500
Pro   S Jensen
Holes   18 L 5800 m SSS 71
Fees   110kr (130kr)
Loc   5km SW of Nykøbing

Roskilde (1973)

Kongemarken 34, 4000 Roskilde
Tel   (02) 37 01 80
Mem   562
Pro   T Card
Holes   12 L 4853 m SSS 69
Fees   80kr (120kr)
Loc   5km W of Roskilde

Rungsted (1937)

2960 Rungsted Kyst
Tel   (42) 86 34 44
Mem   1100
Pro   R Beattie
Holes   18 L 5900 m SSS 72
Fees   200kr (250kr)
Loc   Rungsted, 30km N of
        Copenhagen

Søllerød

Søverødvej 239, 2840 Holte
Tel   (42) 80 17 84
Mem   1100
Pro   J Korfitsen (42) 80 18 77
Holes   18 L 5872 m SSS 72
Fees   140kr (200kr)
Loc   19km N of Copenhagen

Storstrømmen (1969)

Virketvej 44, 4863 Eskilstrup, Falster
Tel   (53) 83 80 80
Mem   488
Pro   A Mackay (53) 83 82 02
Holes   18 L 6195 m SSS 73
Fees   D–125kr (D–175kr 3D–310kr)
Loc   15km N of Nykøbing F

Sydsjaellands (1974)

Borupgården, Mogenstrup,
4700 Naestved
Tel   (03) 76 15 03
Mem   550
Pro   K Atkinson
Holes   18 L 5675 m SSS 70
Fees   100kr (140kr)
Loc   10km SE of Naestved towards
        Praestø
Mis   Driving range

Finland

Alands

Haraldsby, 22410 Godby
Holes   13 L 5350 m 5SS 68
Loc   Mariehamn, Aland (off SW
        coast of Finland)

Aulangon (1959)

Hämeenlinna
Tel   Hämeenlinna 21271
Mem   150
Holes   9 L 2450 m SSS 67
Fees   D–25 fmk
Loc   Hämeenlinna 5km

Aura Golf (1958)

Ruissalo 85, 20100 Turku
Tel   (921) 306701/308667
Mem   900
Pro   A Mäki
Holes   18 L 5873 m SSS 71
Fees   120fmk (150fmk) 1989 prices
Loc   Ruissalo Island, 9km SW of
        Turku

Espoon Golfseura (1982)

Box 26, 02781 Espoo
Tel   (90) 811 212
Mem   1100
Pro   D Bird, C Sundman
Holes   18 L 6183 m SSS 74
Fees   120fmk
Loc   Espoo, 24km W of Helsinki

Helsingin Golfklubi (1932)

Talin Kartano, SF–00350 Helsinki 35
Tel   550235/557899
Mem   1170
Pro   S Nyström, J Hämäläinen
Holes   18 L 5900 m SSS 71
Fees   140fmk (160fmk)
Loc   7km W of Helsinki

Kokkolan (1957)

Mantykangas 15, Tallasen 15,
67100 Kokkola
Tel   (968) 18905
Mem   50
Holes   9 L 5890 m SSS 70
Fees   50 fmk (100 fmk)
Loc   Kokkola 2km

Kymen (1964)

Ilmattarenkatu 16, 48700 Kyminlinna
Tel   (952) 14051
Mem   800
Pro   L Hilokoski
Holes   18 L 6120 m Par 72
Fees   100fmk
Loc   Kotka, Mussalo Island.
        120km E of Helsinki

Lahden Golf (1959)

15230 Lahti Takkula
Tel   (918) 841311
Mem   342
Pro   V Kankkoner
Holes   9 L 6102 m SSS 73
Fees   D–60fmk W–300fmk
Loc   Lahti 6km

Mikkelin Golf (1967)

Kalervonkatu 5, 50130 Mikkeli
Tel   (955) 151759
Holes   9 L 2540 m SSS 68
Fees   50fmk (200fmk)
Loc   384km N of Helsinki.
        2km from Mikkeli

Oulu (1964)

Maakotkantie 20, 90250 Oulu
Tel   (981) 571192
Mem   750
Pro   J Alatalo
Holes   9 L 5218 m SSS 68
Fees   70fmk
Loc   Kaukovainio, 3km from Oulu

Porin Golfkerho (1939)

PL 25, 28601 Pori
Tel   (939) 415559
Mem   450
Pro   P Makela
Holes   9 L 5654 m SSS 71
Fees   D–80fmk
Loc   5km NW of Pori, at Kalafornia

Suur-Helsingin (1965)

Franzeninkatu 3B, 81 0050 Helsinki
Tel   855 8687
Mem   800
Pro   M Louhio
Holes   9 L 5970 m SSS 72
Fees   100fmk
Loc   20km N of Helsinki
Mis   Season May–Sept

Tammer Golf (1965)

Box 269, 33101 Tampere 10
Tel   (931) 611316
Mem   1250
Pro   J Pentikäinen
Holes   18 L 5870 m SSS 71
Fees   D–120fmk
Loc   Ruotula, 5km from Tampere
Mis   Open May–Oct

Tuusula (1984)

PL 178,4301 Hyrylä
Tel   (90) 251464/251469
Mem   900
Pro   M Luukkonen
Holes   18 L 5900 SSS 72
Fees   120fmk (150fmk)
Loc   30km N of Helsinki, nr airport

Vaasan-Vaasa (1969)

Sandog 3, 65100 Vaasa 10
Tel   (961) 121742/269989
Mem   206
Holes   9 L 2570 m SSS 70
Fees   50fmk
Loc   Kraklund, 6km SE of Vaasa
      on Route 717
Mis   Driving range

Lappeenranta

Viipurin Golf (1938)

54530 Luumäki
Tel   (953) 16840 (summer)
Mem   510
Pro   P Ahokas
Holes   9 L 2450 m SSS 65
Fees   D–60fmk
Loc   Lappeenranta, behind Etelä-
      Saimaa hospital

France

Bordeaux & Dordogne

Arcachon (1955)

35 Bd d'Arcachon, 33260 La Teste
De Buch
Tel   56 54 44 00
Mem   750
Pro   J Cantagrel, J Artola,
      F du Reau
Holes   18 L 5930 m SSS 71
Fees   D–160–250fr
Loc   Bordeaux 60km

L'Ardilouse (1980)

Domaine de l'Ardilouse,
33680 Lacanau–Océan
Tel   56 03 25 60
Mem   280
Pro   J–L Pega
Holes   18 L 6000 m SSS 72
Fees   140–160fr (160–210fr)
Loc   Bordeaux 45km

Golf Bordelais (1900)

Domaine de Kater, Av d'Eysines
3320 Bordeaux–Caudéran
Tel   56 28 56 04
Mem   492
Pro   M Saubaber, GB Morgan
Holes   18 L 4833 m SSS 67
Fees   160fr (200fr)
Loc   Bordeaux 3km
Mis   Course closed Mon

Golf Municipal de Bordeaux

Avenue de Pernon, 33300 Bordeaux
Tel   56 50 92 72
Mem   1300
Pro   J Delgado, J Purgato,
      V Fructuoso, JM Duhalde
Holes   18 L 6083 m SSS 72
Fees   140fr
Loc   6km from Bordeaux
Mis   Public course. Closed Tues

Golf du Coiroux

19190 Aubazine
Tel   55 27 25 66
Mem   550
Pro   JF Encuentra
Holes   18 L 5420 m SSS 70
Fees   130fr (170fr)
Loc   15km E of Brive
Mis   Public course

Lolivarie (1984)

Sagelat, 24170 Belvès
Tel   53 30 22 69
Mem   60
Pro   F Mayes
Holes   9 L 2200 m SSS 35
Fees   100fr (120fr)
Loc   60km NW of Cahors.
      60km E of Bergerac

Marmande (1989)

Levant de la Carpette, 47200
Marmande
Tel   53 20 87 60
Mem   151
Pro   E Bouquier
Holes   9 L 6106 m SSS 72
Fees   D–100fr
Loc   Marmande, 75km SE of
      Bordeaux
Mis   Pitch and putt

Mas del Teil

46200 Souillac
Tel   65 37 01 48
Mem   120
Pro   P Dugény
Holes   9 L 2040 m SSS 33
Fees   100fr (120fr)
Loc   25km from Brive

Périgueux (1980)

Public
Domaine de Saltgourde,
24430 Marsac
Tel   53 53 02 35
Mem   412
Pro   C Campbell
Holes   18 L 6120 m SSS 71
Fees   90fr W–400fr M–800fr
Loc   Angoulême–Riberac road.
      Périgueux 3km
Mis   Public course

Sporting Club de Cameyrac (1972)

Cameyrac, 33450 Saint–Loubes
Tel   56 72 96 79
Mem   400
Pro   V Bouneau
Holes   18 L 6057 m SSS 72
      9 L 1600 m SSS 28
Fees   120fr (200fr)
Loc   Bordeaux 15km

Brittany

Aioncs d'Or (1976)

Kergrain Lantic, 22410 Saint–Quay
Portrieux
Tel   96 71 90 74
Mem   480
Pro   A Pouette,
       P Rault-Maisonneuve
Holes 18 L 6230 m SSS 72
Fees   130–140fr
Loc   18km N of St Brieuc.
       Étables 6km. Binic 6km
Mis   Public course

Boisgelin

Pléhédel, 22290 Lanvollon
Tel   96 22 31 24
Holes 9 L 2356 m Par 34
Fees   70fr (100fr)
Loc   10km S of Paimpol on D7.
       35km from St–Brieuc

Brest–Iroise

Parc des Loisirs de Lann–Rohou,
29220 Landerneau
Tel   98 85 16 17
Pro   D Jouan, P Le Verche
Holes 18 L 5885 m Par 72
       6 hole short course
Fees   150fr
Loc   15km E of Brest
Mis   Public course

Dinard (1887)

35800 St–Briac–sur–Mer
Tel   99 88 32 07
Mem   360
Pro   A Rosinski
Holes 18 L 5010 m Par 69
Fees   180fr
Loc   Dinard 8km. St Malo 14km

La Freslonière

Le bois Briand, 35650 Le Rheu
Tel   99 60 84 09
Holes 9 hole course
Loc   8km SW of Rennes, off N24

Golf de l'Odet (1986)

Clohars–Fouesnant, 29118 Benodet
Tel   98 54 87 88
Mem   420
Pro   K Strachan, JP Sallat
Holes 18 L 6235 m SSS 73
       9 hole course
Fees   135fr (180fr)
Loc   12km SE of Quimper
Mis   Public course

Golf des Ormes

Château de Ormes, 35120 Dol-de-
Bretagne
Tel   99 48 40 27
Holes 9 hole course
Loc   8km S of Dol, off D795

Pen Guen

22380 Saint–Cast–le–Guildo
Tel   96 41 91 20
Pro   J Bourel, J–M Loustalen
Holes 9 L 2580 m SSS 70
Fees   100–150fr
Loc   Dinard 25km

Quimper–Cornouaille (1959)

Manoir du Mesmeur, 29133
La Forêt–Fouesnant
Tel   98 56 97 09
Mem   250
Pro   L Salgado
Holes 9 L 5641 m SSS 69
Fees   D–120fr W–545fr
Loc   15km SE of Quimper

Rennes (1957)

BP 1117, 35014 Rennes Cedex
Tel   99 64 24 18
Mem   400
Pro   P Le Fur, L Lecoq
Holes 18 L 5845 m SSS 70
Fees   D–120fr (150fr)
Loc   7km S of Rennes via N177
       towards Chavagne

Sables-d'Or-les-Pins (1925)

22240 Fréhel
Tel   96 41 42 57
Mem   140
Pro   G Frangeu
Holes 9 L 5253 m SSS 70
Fees   D–140fr
Loc   Dinard 30km

St Laurent (1975)

Ploemel, 56400 Auray
Tel   97 56 85 18
Mem   450
Pro   J Piron, L Miriel
Holes 18 L 6112 m SSS 72
       9 L 3020 m SSS 35
Fees   110–180fr
Loc   Ploemel, 16km from Carnac
       and Auray
Mis   Public course

St Malo–Le Tronchet (1986)

Le Tronchet, 35540 Miniac Morvan
Tel   99 58 96 69
Mem   250
Pro   C Bourakhowitch
Holes 18 L 6049 m SSS 72
       9 L 2684 m SSS 36
Fees   180fr
Loc   23km S of St Malo off RN 137

Saint–Samson (1964)

Route de Kérénoc,
22660 Ploumour Bodou
Tel   96 23 87 34
Mem   250
Pro   D Fournet
Holes 18 L 5682 m SSS 72
Fees   D–150fr (D–180fr)
Loc   7km N of Lannion on
       Tregastel road

Sauzon (1985)

Sauzon, 56360 Belle–Île
Tel   97 31 64 65
Mem   280
Holes 18 L 6100 m SSS 72
Fees   200fr
Loc   Island off S coast of Brittany,
       near Quiberon
Mis   Public course

Central East

Aix-les-Bains (1936)

Ave du Golf, 73100 Aix–les–Bains
Tel   79 61 23 35
Mem   460
Pro   IS Lambie
Holes 18 L 5597 m SSS 71
Fees   180fr (250fr)
Loc   Aix 2½ km

Les Arcs

Arc 1800, 73700 Bourg–St–Maurice
Tel   79 07 48 00
Mem   396
Pro   A Leclerq, R Gollias
Holes 18 L 4853 m SSS 67
Fees   D–180fr
Loc   Les Arcs, 90km E of Chambery
       on N90
Mis   4 holes pitch and putt

Besançon (1968)

La Chevillote, 25620 Mamirolle
Tel   81 55 73 54
Mem   450
Pro   G Stewart
Holes 18 L 6090 m SSS 72
Fees   150fr (200fr)
Loc   Besançon 12km. Saône 3km

G & CC Bossey

Château de Crevin, 74160 St-Julien-
en-Genevois
Tel   (50) 43 75 25
Pro   JP Charpenel, E Berthet,
       W Reid
Holes 18 L 6145 m Par 71
Fees   WD–250fr
Loc   Geneva 6km
Mis   Driving range

For explanation of abbreviations, see page 460.

656   France

Chamonix (1934)

BP 31 74402 Chamonix Cedex
Tel   50 53 06 28
Mem   292
Pro   R Marro, JC Bonnaz,
       G Ravanel
Holes 18 L 6087 m SSS 72
Fees   150–180fr 5D–850fr
Loc   2km from Chamonix RN 506.
       Geneva 60km

Dijon–Bourgogne (1972)

Bois des Norges, 21490 Norges
La Ville
Tel   80 35 71 10
Mem   450
Pro   B Radcliffe
Holes 18 L 6164 m SSS 72
       9 hole pitch and putt
Fees   140fr (200fr)
Loc   10km N of Dijon towards
       Langres

Divonne (1931)

01220 Divonne–les–Bains
Tel   50 20 07 19
Mem   600
Pro   M Alsurguren, M Suhas
Holes 18 L 6055 m SSS 72
Fees   250fr (450fr)
Loc   Divonne ¹/₂ km. Geneva 18km

Flaine–les–Carroz (1984)

74300 Flaine
Tel   50 90 85 44
Mem   80
Pro   P Lacroix
Holes 18 L 4180 m Par 63
Fees   120–170fr (D–170fr)
Loc   Flaine 4km. Geneva Airport
       60km

Lac d'Annecy (1953)

Echarvines, 74290 Talloires
Tel   50 60 12 89
Mem   400
Pro   J Noailly, D Bonnaz
Holes 18 L 5017 m SSS 68
Fees   175fr (200fr)
Loc   Annecy 13km

Méribel (1973)

BP 24, 73550 Meribel
Tel   79 00 52 67
Mem   230
Pro   G Watine
Holes 18 L 5200 m SSS 70
Fees   200fr (250fr)
Loc   15km S of Moutiers.
       Albertville 35km
Mis   Open June–Oct

Mont–d'Arbois

74120 Megève
Tel   50 21 29 79
Mem   400

Pro   JB Alsuguren, G Parodi,
       P Provençal
Holes 18 L 6100 m SSS 72
Fees   180–260fr
Loc   Megève 2km
Mis   Comps every WE

Royal Golf Évian (1905)

Rive Sud du lac de Genève,
74500 Évian
Tel   50 75 14 00
Mem   240
Pro   Ch Victor, L Burnet, A Pery
Holes 18 L 6048 m SSS 72
Fees   D–110–260fr (D–130–290fr)
Loc   Évian 2km. Geneva Airport
       40km
Mis   All-inclusive stay at Royal Club
       Évian–free access to golf.
       Only 9 holes playable until
       July 1990

Tignes (1968)

Le Val Claret, 73320 Tignes
Tel   79 06 37 42
Pro   B Kvot, D Saadi
Holes 9 L 1820 m
Fees   100fr W–600fr

Central West

Angers (1963)

49320 St Jean des Mauvrets
Tel   41 91 96 56
Mem   350
Pro   J Bourel
Holes 18 L 5460 m Par 70
Fees   140fr (180fr)
Loc   14km SE of Angers.
       Right bank of Loire.

La Baule (1976)

Domaine de Saint–Denac,
44117 Saint–André–des–Eaux
Tel   40 60 46 18
Mem   400
Pro   E Mauger
Holes 18 L 6200 m Par 72
Fees   100–270fr
Loc   La Baule 3km, nr Avrillac
Mis   Driving range

La Bretesche (1968)

Domaine de la Bretesche
44780 Missillac
Tel   40 88 30 03
Mem   300
Pro   T Mathon
Holes 18 L 6040 m SSS 72
Fees   120–250fr
Loc   Pontchâteau 8km. Nantes
       50km. Vannes 50km

Châtellerault (1987)

7 Rue Choisnin, 86100 Châtellerault
Tel   49 86 20 21
Pro   J Ayala
Holes 18 L 5813 m SSS 71
Fees   130fr (150fr)
Loc   La Roche–Posay, 20km E of
       Châtellerault. 40km NE of
       Poitiers

Cognac (1987)

Saint–Brice, 16100 Cognac
Tel   45 32 18 17
Mem   700
Pro   M Vickery
Holes 18 L 6255 m SSS 72
Fees   150fr (200fr)
Loc   5km from Cognac

L'Hirondelle

Chamfleuri 16000 Angoulême
Tel   45 61 16 94
Mem   350
Pro   G Peña
Holes 9 L 2285 m SSS 34
Fees   90fr (120fr)
Loc   Angoulême 1km

Laval (1972)

Le Jariel, 53000 Changé–Les–Laval
Tel   43 53 16 03
Holes 9 L 2839 m SSS 35
Fees   D–90fr (100fr 2D–150fr)
Loc   7km N of Laval

Loudun Saint–Hilaire

Roiffe, 86120 Les Trois–Moutiers
Tel   49 98 78 06
Mem   320
Pro   T Abbas
Holes 18 L 6325 m Par 72
Fees   110fr (160fr)
Loc   Loudun 15km. Saumur 20km
Mis   Public course

Mans Mulsanne (1961)

72230 Arnage
Tel   43 42 00 36
Mem   400
Pro   M Dugue
Holes 18 L 5756 m SSS 71
Fees   150–225fr (220–330fr)
Loc   Mulsanne, 12km from Le Mans
Mis   Handicap certificate required

Mazières

Le Petit Chêne, 79310 Mazières–en–
Gâtine
Tel   49 63 28 33
Mem   150
Pro   V Dufresne–Heniau
Holes 18 L 6060 m SSS 72

Fees 95fr (150fr)
Loc 15km SW of Parthenay.
25km NE of Niort
Mis Public course

Nantes

44360 Vigneux de Bretagne
Tel 40 63 25 82
Mem 430
Pro N Gajan
Holes 18 L 5940 m SSS 72
Fees 130fr (200fr)
Loc Nantes 15km

Poitevin

86000 Terrain des Chalons
Tel 49 61 23 13
Mem 100
Pro P Signeux
Holes 9 L 2660 m SSS 35
Fees 85fr (100fr)
Loc Poitiers 3km

Pornic (1912)

49 bis, Boulevard de l'Océan,
Sainte–Marie/Mer, 44210 Pornic
Tel 40 82 06 69
Mem 280
Pro G Romain
Holes 9 L 5120 m SSS 68
Fees D–100–180fr
Loc Pornic 1km. Nantes 45km.
La Baule 35km.

Royan (1977)

Maine–Gaudin, 17420 Saint–Palais
Tel 46 23 16 24
Mem 415
Pro J–P Prieur
Holes 18 L 6033 m SSS 71
Fees 150fr (180fr)
Loc Saint–Palais, 7km W of Royan
Mis Public course. Closed Tues

Saintonge

Fontcouverte, 17100 Saintes
Tel 46 74 27 61
Mem 350
Pro R Burguet
Holes 9 L 2435 m SSS 68
Fees 80fr (100fr)
Loc Saintes 3km
Mis Public course

Touraine (1971)

Château de la Touche, 37510
Ballan–Miré
Tel 47 53 20 28
Mem 520
Pro M Vol, D Astruc, T Vandooren
Holes 18 L 5671 m SSS 71
Fees 160–200fr (230–250fr)
Loc Villandry, 8km SW of Tours

Central

Albon (1989)

Domaine de Senaud, Albon,
26140 St Rambert d'Albon
Tel 75 03 18 76/75 03 03 90
Mem 350
Pro J Visseaux
Holes 18 L 6211 m Par 72
Fees 160–180fr (220–240fr)
Loc 60km S of Lyon, motorway
exit Chanas

Les Bordes (1987)

La Ferté St Cyr, 41220 Saint-Laurent-
Nouant
Tel 54 87 72 13
Pro C Young
Holes 18 L 6436 m Par 72
Fees 330fr (360fr)
Loc 30km SW of Orléans

Chalon–sur–Saône

Chatenoy–en–Bresse,
71380 Saint–Marcel
Tel 85 48 61 64/85 93 49 65
Mem 750
Pro J Vezin 85 48 62 42
Holes 18 L 5844 m SSS 71
Fees 80fr
Loc 2km SE of Chalon
Mis Public course. Pitch and putt

Champlong (1985)

42300 Villerest
Tel 77 69 70 60
Mem 180
Pro B Le Tanter
Holes 9 L 2008 m Par 31
Fees 70–90fr (90–120fr)
Loc 5km SE of Roanne towards
Clermont–Ferrand
Mis Public course

Charade (1985)

Charade 631, 30 Royat
Tel 73 35 73 09
Mem 250
Pro R Picabea
Holes 9 L 2300 m SSS 32
Fees D–70fr (90fr)
Loc 8km W of Clermont–Ferrand.
Royat 3km

Clairis (1974)

89150 Savigny–sur–Clairis
Tel 86 86 33 90
Mem 180
Pro P Schilling
Holes 9 hole course
Fees 90fr (160fr)
Loc St Valérien, 12km W of Sens

La Commanderie (1964)

L'Aumusse Crottet,
01290 Pont–de–Veyle
Tel 85 33 44 12/85 30 40 24
Mem 250
Pro C Soules, P Wakeford
Holes 18 L 5550 m SSS 69
Fees 150fr (200fr)
Loc 7km from Mâcon on RN 79
to Bourg–en–Bresse

La Dombes (1986)

Mionnay, 01390 St–André–de–Corcy
Tel 78 91 84 84
Mem 220
Pro F Dietsch
Holes 9 L 2484 m SSS 70
Fees 100fr Sat–160fr Sun–200fr
Loc 20km N of Lyon towards Bourg

Golf Municipal de Limoges (1976)

Avenue du Golf, 87000 Limoges
Tel 55 30 21 02
Pro Y Saubaber, R Larretche
Holes 18 L 6218 m SSS 72
Fees 60fr
Loc S of Limoges on N20
Mis Public course

Golf du Nivernais

58470 Magny Cours
Tel 86 58 18 30
Mem 400
Pro P Raguet
Holes 18 L 5665 m Par 71
Fees 80fr (150fr)
Loc 12km from Nevers on N7
towards Moulins
Mis Public course

Golf du Rigolet (1928)

63240 Le Mont–Dore
Tel 73 65 00 79
Pro L Mencagli
Holes 9 L 2115 m SSS 34
Fees D–100fr W–500fr
Loc 2½ km Mont–Dore. 35km SW
of Clermont–Ferrand
Mis Open May–Oct

Golf des Volcans (1984)

La Bruyère des Moines
63870 Orcines
Tel 73 62 15 51
Mem 600
Pro L Roux, G Roux,
O Roux
Holes 18 L 6242 m SSS 72
9 L 1815 m SSS 29
Fees 180fr (250fr)
Loc 12km W of Clermont–Ferrand
on RN 141

Lyon (1964)

38280 Villette–d'Anthon
Tel   78 31 11 33
Mem   750
Pro   L Capoccia
Holes   27 L 6415 m SSS 72
Fees   130fr (250fr)
Loc   Lyon 25km

Lyon–Verger (1977)

69360 Saint–Symphorien D'Ozon
Tel   78 02 84 20
Mem   590
Pro   H Sauzet, P Malartre,
          A Bugnet
Holes   18 L 5800 m SSS 69
Fees   150fr (230fr)
Loc   14km S of Lyon on A7 exit
          Solaizo, or RN7 3km S of Fcyzin
Mis   Closed Fri

Marcilly (1986)

Domaine de la Plaine, 45240
Marcilly–en–Villette
Tel   38 76 11 73
Mem   340
Pro   G Raison, P Guichard
Holes   18 L 6324 m SSS 73
          9 hole course
Fees   100fr (160fr)
Loc   20km SE of Orléans

Mezeyrac (1988)

Soulages Bonneval, 12210 Laguiole
Tel   65 44 41 41
Mem   130
Pro   P Vincent
Holes   9 L 2564 m SSS 68
Fees   100fr (150fr)
Loc   Mezeyrac, NW of Laguiole.
          150km NW of Montpellier

Prunevelle (1930)

Ferme des Petits–Bans, Dampierre-
sur lc-Doubs
Tel   81 98 11 77/33 03 04
Mem   300
Pro   R Lesouder
Holes   18 L 6281 m SSS 73
Fees   130fr (140fr)
Loc   10km S of Montbéliard. A36
          Motorway exit Montbéliard
          Sud via Besançon, on D126
          to Dampierre-sur-le-Doubs
Mis   Open 15 Mar–10 Oct

Sologne (1955)

Country Club des Olleries,
Route de Jouy–le–Potier, Ardon,
45240 La Ferté St Aubin
Tel   38 76 57 33/38 76 50 01
Holes   18 L 7200 yds Par 72
Fees   130fr (220fr)
Loc   25km S of Orléans on RN20

Sporting–Club de Vichy (1907)

Allée Baugnies, 03700 Bellerive/Allier
Tel   70 32 39 11
Mem   450
Pro   Ch Roumaud
Holes   18 L 5427 m SSS 70
Fees   220fr (300fr)
Loc   In Vichy

Sully–sur–Loire

L'Ousseau, 45600 Viglain
Tel   38 36 52 08
Mem   220
Pro   P Antoine
Holes   18 L 5863 m SSS 72
Fees   180fr (350fr)
Loc   Sully–sur–Loire 3km

Val–de–Cher

Nassigny, 03190 Vallon–en–Sully
Tel   70 06 71 15
Mem   200
Pro   JC Gassiat
Holes   18 L 5200 m
Fees   140fr (Sun–200fr 2D–350fr)
Loc   Nassigny, N of Montluçon
          on N144
Mis   Closed Tues

Val de Loire

45450 Donnery
Tel   38 59 20 48/38 59 25 15
Mem   280
Pro   JM Duboc
Holes   18 L 5840 m SSS 71
Fees   D–180fr (250fr 2D–420fr)
Loc   16km E of Orléans

Vaugouard (1987)

Fontenay–sur–Loing,
45210 Ferrières
Tel   38 95 81 52
Mem   350
Pro   P Iturrioz
Holes   18 L 6103 m SSS 72
Fees   180fr (300fr)
Loc   10km N of Montargis.
          Paris 100km

North East

Bâle (1926)

68220 Hagenthal–le–Bas, Ht Rhin
Tel   89 68 50 91
Mem   630
Pro   D Creamer, A Perrone,
          C Bisel
Holes   18 L 6255 m SSS 74
Fees   150fr (220fr)
Loc   St Louis 9km. Basle 15km
Mis   Open Apr–Oct

Bitche (1988)

Rue des Prés, 57230 Bitche
Tel   87 96 15 30
Mem   700
Pro   D Taylor, G Copp
Holes   18 L 6082 m SSS 72
          9 L 2293 m SSS 34
Fees   18 hole:110fr (180fr)
          9 hole:70fr (110fr)
Loc   75km NW of Strasbourg.
          55km SE of Saarbrücken
Mis   Public course

Combles–en–Barrois

55000 Bar–le–Duc
Tel   29 45 16 03
Mem   226
Pro   M Vian
Holes   9 L 2241 m SSS 33
Fees   120fr (150fr)
Loc   Bar–le–Duc, 70km W of Nancy

Golf des Ardennes

Les Poursaudes, 08430 Villers-le-
Tilleul
Tel   24 35 64 65
Mem   180
Pro   B Favre–Victoire
Holes   9 L 2816 m SSS 36
Fees   100fr (150fr)
Loc   20km SE of Charleville

Golf du Rhin (1969)

BP1152, 68053 Mulhouse Cedex
Tel   89 26 07 86
Mem   532
Pro   A Price
Holes   18 L 5991 m SSS 72
Fees   150fr (250fr)
Loc   Île du Rhin–Chalampe.
          20km E of Mulhouse

Images d'Épinal (1985)

Rue du Merle–Blanc, 88001 Épinal
Tel   29 31 45 45
Pro   R Golias, D Mory
Holes   18 L 5700 m SSS 70
Fees   D–60fr
Loc   Épinal, 70km S of Nancy
Mis   Public course

La Largue

Chemin du Largweg, 68580
Mooslargue
Tel   (0033) 89 25 71 11
Mem   150
Pro   K Marriott
Holes   18 L 6150 m SSS 72
Fees   180fr (240fr)
Loc   25km W of Basle

Madine

Nonsard, 55210 Vigneulles
Tel   29 89 56 00/29 89 32 50
Mem   30
Pro   M Brasset

Holes	9 L 2930 m Par 36
Fees	50fr (80fr)
Loc	40km SE of Verdun. 45km SW of Metz
Mis	Public course

Metz–Cherisey (1963)

Château de Cherisey, 57240 Verny

Tel	87 52 70 18
Mem	480
Pro	J Gould, P Schwartzberg
Holes	18 L 6075 m Par 72
Fees	150fr (200fr)
Loc	15km SE of Metz. Nancy 35km

Nancy–Aingeray

Aingeray, 54460 Liverdun

Tel	83 24 53 87/83 24 58 99
Mem	250
Pro	A Gass
Holes	18 L 5525 m SSS 69
Fees	140fr (220fr)
Loc	Nancy 17km

Reims (1928)

Château des Dames de France, 51390 Gueux

Tel	26 03 60 79
Mem	460
Pro	P Harrison
Holes	18 L 6026 m SSS 72
Fees	150fr (250fr)
Loc	Reims 10km

Strasbourg (1934)

Route du Rhin, 67400 Illkirch

Tel	88 66 17 22
Mem	600
Pro	IP Tairraz, N Madeuf
Holes	18 L 6047 m SSS 72
Fees	WD only–200fr
Loc	Strasbourg 10km

Troyes–la Cordelière

10210 Chaource

Tel	25 40 11 05
Mem	380
Pro	M Vian
Holes	18 L 6154 m SSS 72
Fees	180fr (250fr)
Loc	NE of Chaource on N443. Troyes 30km

Vittel

BP 122, 88800 Vittel

Tel	29 08 18 80 (1 May–30 Sept)
Mem	400
Pro	D Mory, M Lachaux
Holes	18 L 6271 m SSS 72 18 L 6100 m SSS 72 9 hole course
Fees	150fr Sat–250fr Sun–200fr
Loc	Vittel, 70km S of Nancy. Épinal 45km

Languedoc & Roussillon

Cap d'Agde

Rue Volvire de Brassac, 34300 Cap d'Agde

Tel	67 26 54 40
Holes	18 L 6395 m SSS
Fees	150–200fr (180–200fr)
Loc	25km E of Béziers

Coulondres (1984)

4, Rue des Erables, 34980 Saint–Gely–du–Fesc

Tel	67 84 13 75
Mem	230
Pro	V Schwechlen
Holes	18 L 6175 m SSS 72
Fees	160fr (180fr)
Loc	10km N of Montpellier towards Ganges

La Grande–Motte

Club–House de Golf, 34280 La Grande–Motte

Tel	67 56 05 00
Mem	300
Pro	P Porquier
Holes	18 L 6200 m SSS 72 18 L 4000 m Par 58 6 hole course
Fees	180fr (230fr 2D–400fr)
Loc	SE of Montpellier. 10km from Airport

Mas de Bombequiols (1986)

34190 St André–de–Buèges

Tel	67 73 72 67
Holes	9 L 2791 m Par 35
Fees	100–160fr
Loc	45km NW of Montpellier towards Ganges

Massane

Domaine de Massane, 34670 Baillargues

Tel	67 87 23 23
Pro	L Landoas, E Thomas, N Outters
Holes	9 L 3403 m SSS 36
Fees	160fr (220fr)
Loc	Baillargues, 9km E of Montpellier

Nîmes Campagne (1968)

Route de Saint Gilles, 30009 Nîmes

Tel	66 70 17 37
Mem	640
Pro	T Lassale, A Brioland
Holes	18 L 6200 m SSS 72
Fees	180fr Sat–250fr Sun–350fr
Loc	8km from Nîmes by Airport

St Cyprien (1974)

Le Mas D'Huston, 66750 St Cyprien Plage

Tel	68 21 01 71
Mem	700
Pro	P Lacroix, J–P Harrismendy, E Bocau, M Malafosse
Holes	18 L 6480 m SSS 73 9 L 2724 m SSS 35
Fees	Hotel guests–160fr (350fr) Others–185fr (395fr)

Lille & Channel Coast

Amiens (1951)

80115 Querrieu

Tel	22 91 02 04
Mem	530
Pro	B Dachicourt
Holes	18 L 6124 m SSS 72
Fees	150fr (250fr)
Loc	7km NE of Amiens on D929

Bondues (1968)

Château de la Vigne, BP 54, 59910 Bondues

Tel	20 23 20 62
Mem	1000
Pro	P Iturrioz, A Vandamme, A White
Holes	18 L 6223 m SSS 73 9 L 3044 m SSS 36
Fees	D–200fr (D–300fr)
Loc	10km NE of Lille
Mis	Handicap certificate required

Brigode (1970)

36 Avenue de Golf, 59650 Villeneuve D'Ascq

Tel	20 91 17 86
Mem	600
Pro	R Pollet
Holes	18 L 6182 m SSS 72
Fees	200fr (300fr)
Loc	8km NE of Lille
Mis	Closed Tues

Dunkerque

Public

Fort Vallières, Coudekerque–Village, 59380 Bergues

Tel	28 61 07 43
Holes	9 L 2785 m SSS 35
Fees	30–45fr (50–70fr)
Loc	SE of Dunkerque
Mis	Public course

Golf des Flandres (1957)

137, Bd Clemenceau, 59700 Marcq (Lille)

Tel	20 72 20 74
Mem	370
Pro	R Loth
Holes	9 L 2317 m SSS 33
Fees	150fr (175fr)
Loc	4km from Lille, on Croise Laroche racecourse

Golf du Sart (1910)

5 Rue Jean Jaures,
59650 Villeneuve D'Ascq
Tel   20 72 02 51
Mem   500
Pro   R Wattinne
Holes   18 L 5721 m SSS 71
Fees   200fr (300fr 2D–480fr)
Loc   Motorway Lille–Ghent,
Exit 9 (Breucq–Le Sart)

Hardelot

Ave du Golf, 62152 Neufchâtel-
Hardelot
Tel   21 83 73 10
Mem   650
Pro   L Maisonnave
Holes   18 L 5870 m SSS 72
Fees   D–230fr (D–290fr)
Loc   Hardelot, 15km S of Boulogne

Nampont-St-Martin (1978)

Maison Forte, 80120 Nampont-St-
Martin
Tel   22 29 92 90
Mem   600
Holes   18 L 5345 m SSS 69
Fees   100fr (120f 3D–250fr)
Loc   12km S of Montreuil sur Mer
on route N1. 30km SE of
Le Touquet
Mis   Driving range

Thumeries (1932)

Bois Lenglart, 59239 Thumeries
Tel   20 86 58 98
Mem   300
Pro   B Tiradon
Holes   9 L 2923 m SSS 35
Fees   140fr (210fr)
Loc   15km S of Lille

Le Touquet (1904)

Ave du Golf, 62520 Lo Touquot
Tel   21 05 20 22
Mem   660
Pro   P Philippon
Holes   18 L 5895 m SSS 71
18 L 6140 m SSS 72
9 hole course
Fees   18 holes 200fr (260fr)
9 holes 100fr (140fr)
Loc   2km S of Le Touquet

Valenciennes

Chemin Vert, 59770 Marly-les-
Valenciennes
Tel   27 46 30 10
Mem   215
Pro   J Roux
Holes   9 L 2380 m SSS 33
Fees   80fr (120fr)
Loc   Valenciennes 2km

Wimereux (1906)

Route d'Ambleteuse, 62930 Wimereux
Tel   21 32 43 20
Mem   600
Pro   H Marconi
Holes   18 L 6361 m Par 62
Fees   150–185fr (160–220fr)
Loc   6km N of Boulogne on D940.
30km S of Calais

Normandy

Bagnoles-de-l'Orne (1925)

Route de Domfront,
61140 Bagnoles–de–l'Orne
Tel   33 37 81 42
Pro   H Dauge
Holes   9 L 2200 m SSS 70
Fees   D–40fr (60fr) W–180fr
Loc   Bagnoles, 80km S of Caen
Mis   Public course

Cabourg–Le Home (1955)

38 Av Président Réné Coty, Le Home
Varaville, 14390 Cabourg
Tel   31 91 25 56
Mem   300
Pro   L Allain
Holes   18 L 5122 m SSS 68
Fees   On application
Loc   Cabourg 4km

Cherbourg (1973)

Domaine des Roches,
50470 La Glacerie
Tel   33 44 45 48
Mem   270
Pro   J–F Lenoir
Holes   9 L 2842 m SSS 36
Fees   90fr (100fr)
Loc   6km S of Cherbourg

Clair Vallon

14510 Houlgate
Tel   31 91 06 97
Pro   A Forrester
Holes   18 L 5830 m SSS 72
Fees   150–180fr (180–200fr)
Loc   On road to Conneville

Coutainville (1925)

Ave du Golf, 50230 Agon–Coutainville
Tel   33 47 03 31
Mem   330
Pro   I Folliot
Holes   9 L 5360 m SSS 69 (18 tees)
Fees   120–180fr
Loc   12km W of Coutances.
75km S of Cherbourg

Dieppe (1897)

76200 Dieppe
Tel   35 84 25 05
Pro   S Ortiz
Holes   18 L 5854 m SSS 71
Fees   140–150fr (170–180fr)
Loc   Dieppe 1¹/₂ km

Fontenay-en-Cotentin (1975)

Fontenay–sur–Mer, 50310 Montebourg
Tel   33 21 44 27
Mem   90
Pro   A Quibeuf (summer)
Holes   9 L 3050 m Par 36
Fees   80fr (100fr)
Loc   32km SE of Cherbourg by
RN13/D42

Golf Municipal de Bréhal (1964)

50290 Bréhal
Tel   33 51 58 88
Mem   320
Holes   9 L 2055 m Par 31
Fees   100–120fr
Loc   10km N of Granville
along St Martin beach
Mis   Public course

Golf du Vaudreuil (1962)

27100 Le Vaudreuil
Tel   32 59 02 60
Mem   350
Pro   J Lecuellet
Holes   18 L 6411 m SSS 73
Fees   130–160fr (200–250fr)
Loc   Louviers 6km. Rouen 25km.
Paris 100km

Granville (1912)

Bréville, 50290 Bréhal
Tel   33 50 23 06
Mem   400
Pro   E Alvarez
Holes   18 L 5854 m Par 72
9 L 2323 m Par 33
Fees   18 hole:110fr (160fr)
9 hole: 80fr (110fr)
Loc   5km from Granville towards
Coutances. MontStMichel30km

Le Havre (1933)

Hameau Saint–Supplix
76930 Octeville–sur–Mer
Tel   35 46 36 50/46 36 11
Mem   450
Pro   R Truman
Holes   18 L 5830 m SSS 70
Fees   150fr (300fr)
Loc   10km N of Le Havre

Marin D'Étretat (1908)

BP No 7, 76790 Étretat
Tel   35 27 04 89/27 04 56
(Clubhouse)
Mem   320
Pro   J Morea
Holes   18 L 5840 m SSS 72
Fees   130–175fr (190–265fr)
Loc   28km N of Le Havre.
Étretat ¹/₂ km

New GC Deauville (1929)

14 Saint Arnoult, 14800 Deauville
Tel   31 88 20 53
Mem   650
Pro   C Hausseguy
Holes   18 L 5933 m SSS 71
        9 L 3033 m SSS 72
Fees   170–220fr (240–330fr)
Loc   3km S of Deauville

Omaha Beach (1986)

Ferme St Sauveur, 14520 Port-en-Bessin
Tel   31 21 72 94
Mem   450
Pro   S Lesné
Holes   18 L 6214 m SSS 72
        9 L 2937m
Fees   180–220fr (220–250fr)
Loc   8km N of Bayeux

Rouen

Rue Boucicaut, Mt St Aignan
Tel   35 76 38 65
Mem   600
Pro   J–P Quibeuf
Holes   18 L 5522 m SSS 70
Fees   D–160fr
Loc   Rouen 3½ km

Saint–Gatien Deauville (1987)

14130 Saint–Gatien–des–Bois
Tel   31 65 19 99
Mem   170
Pro   D Hausseguy, M Ortega
Holes   18 L 6200 m SSS 72
        9 L 3000 m SSS 36
Fees   160–200fr (240–300fr)
Loc   8km E of Deauville.
        Honfleur 8km

Saint–Julien

St Julien–sur–Calonne, 14130 Pont l'Évêque
Tel   31 64 19 15
Holes   18 L 6210 m SSS 72
        9 hole course
Loc   3km SE of Pont l'Évêque

Paris Region

Chantilly (1909)

Vineuil Saint Firmin, 60500 Chantilly
Tel   44 57 04 43
Mem   500
Pro   A Chardonnet, P Léglise,
        G Lamy
Holes   Vineuil 18 L 6597 m SSS 71
        Longères 9 L 2625 m SSS 35
Fees   WD only–300fr
Loc   Paris 45km
Mis   WE–only with member

La Chapelle (1987)

Ferme de Monpichet,
77580 Crécy–la–Chapelle
Tel   (1) 64 04 70 75
Mem   150
Pro   P Merel
Holes   18 L 6211 m SSS 72
Fees   150fr (300fr)
Loc   20km E of Paris by A4

Chaumont-en-Vexin (1963)

60240 Chaumont–en–Vexin
Tel   (1) 44 49 00 81/44 49 14 76
Mem   350
Holes   18 L 6190 m Par 72
Fees   WD–150fr
Loc   Paris 60km

Chevry (1976)

91190 Gif–sur–Yvette
Tel   (1) 60 12 40 33
Pro   D Maxwell, P Maréchal
Holes   9 L 2701 m SSS 36
        9 hole Pitch and putt
Mis   Public course

Compiègne (1895)

Avenue Royale, 60200 Compiègne
Tel   (16) 44 40 15 73
Mem   900
Pro   M Amat
Holes   18 L 5873 m SSS 71
Fees   200fr (350fr)
Loc   Compiègne, 70km NE of Paris

Coudray (1960)

Avenue du Coudray, 91830
Le Coudray–Montceaux
Tel   (1) 64 93 81 76
Mem   850
Pro   JL Schneider, M Lebrun,
        C Langlois
Holes   18 L 5384 m SSS 70
        9 hole course
Fees   200fr (450fr)
Loc   Paris 35km on A6

Domont–Montmorency

Route de Montmorency, 95330 Domont
Tel   (1) 39 91 07 50
Mem   350
Pro   R Changart, Ch Gassiat,
        Ch Chabriel
Holes   18 L 5775 m SSS 71
Fees   240fr (450fr)
Loc   Paris 18km
Mis   Pitch and putt

Fontainebleau (1908)

Route d'Orleans, 77300 Fontainebleau
Tel   64 22 22 95
Mem   450
Pro   JP Hirigoyen, Th Vallin
Holes   18 L 6012 m SSS 72
Fees   330fr (600fr)
Loc   Fontainebleau 2km

Fourqueux (1963)

Rue St Nom 36, 78112 Fourqueux
Tel   (1) 34 51 41 47
Mem   520
Pro   H Gioux
Holes   27 holes–9 L 3135 m Par 37;
        9 L 2890 m Par 36; 9 L 2725
        m Par 37
Fees   290fr (350fr)
Loc   St Germain–en–Laye 4km

Golf d'Isabella (1969)

RN12, Sainte–Appoline, 78370 Plaisir
Tel   (1) 30 54 10 62
Mem   280
Holes   9 L 2454 m SSS 34
Fees   170fr (280fr) 1988 prices
Loc   Paris 28km, RN12 to Dreux

Golf du Prieuré

78440 Gargenville
Tel   (1) 34 76 70 12
Mem   1200
Pro   J Alsuguren, M Lachaux,
        G Bourdy
Holes   18 L 6216 m SSS 72
        18 L 6317 m SSS 72
Fees   225fr (375fr)
Loc   Mantes La Jolie, 10km W of
        Paris. Meulan 9km

La Grenouillère

Île de la Grenouillère,
78290 Croissy–sur–Seine
Tel   (1) 39 18 43 81
Mem   400
Pro   P Lefebvre, A Alsuguren,
        JP Kevorkian, C Paillet
Holes   9 L 2120 m SSS 27
Fees   120fr (240fr)
Loc   Paris 25km

International Club du Lys

Rond–Point du Grand Cerf,
60260 Lamorlaye
Tel   (1) 44 21 26 00
Pro   F Saubaber
Holes   18 L 5986 m SSS 71
        18 L 4798 m SSS 66
Fees   200fr (400fr)
Loc   Chantilly 5km

Meaux–Boutigny (1985)

Le Bordet, Rue de Barrois,
77470 Trilport
Tel   (1) 60 25 63 98
Mem   450
Pro   A Delannoy
Holes   18 L 6100 m SSS 71
        9 hole course
Fees   180fr (300fr)
Loc   45km E of Paris–Highway 4

For explanation of abbreviations, see page 460.

Morfontaine (1926)

Mortefontaine, 60128 Plailly
Tel   (1) 44 54 68 27
Mem   450
Pro   S De Galard, M Philippon
Holes 18 L 6063 m SSS 72
       9 L 2550 m SSS 36
Fees   NA
Loc   Senlis 10km
Mis   Members' guests only

Ormesson (1969)

Chemin du Belvedere,
94490 Ormesson-sur-Marne
Tel   (1) 45 76 20 71
Mem   475
Pro   F Leclercq
Holes 18 L 6129 m SSS 72
Fees   220fr (380fr)
Loc   Paris 21km

Ozoir-la-Ferrière (1926)

Château des Agneaux,
77330 Ozoir-la-Ferrière
Tel   (1) 60 28 20 79
Mem   580
Pro   G Henichard, T Murphy
Holes 18 L 6105 m SSS 72
       9 L 2235 m SSS 33
Fees   18 hole:250fr (400fr)
       9 hole:130fr (250fr)
Loc   From Paris A4 (Sortie
       Val Maubuée)

Racing Club de France

La Boulie, 78000 Versailles
Tel   (1) 39 50 59 41
Mem   1500
Pro   F Castel, M Garaialde,
       JP Quillo, G Watine
Holes 18 L 6055 m SSS 71
       18 L 6206 m SSS 72
       9 hole course
Fees   WD–400fr–by invitation
Loc   Paris 16km

Rochefort

78730 Rochefort-en-Yvelines
Tel   (1) 30 41 31 81
Pro   M Berthouloux
Holes 18 L 5735 m SSS 71
Fees   220fr (420fr)
Loc   Paris 35km

Saint-Aubin (1976)

91190 Saint-Aubin
Tel   (1) 69 41 25 19
Pro   C Chabrier, Q Dubart
Holes 18 L 6200 m SSS 72
Loc   SW of Paris
Mis   Public course

Saint-Cloud (1911)

60 Rue du 19 Janvier, Garches 92380
Tel   (1) 47 01 01 85
Mem   2000
Pro   R Giraud, A Leclerc, JC Bard,
       P Galitzine
Holes 18 L 5980 m SSS 71
       18 L 4857 m SSS 67
Fees   260fr Sat–400fr Sun–500fr
Loc   Porte Dauphine, Paris 9km
Mis   Handicap certificate required

Saint-Germain-en-Laye (1922)

Route de Poissy,
78100 St-Germain-en-Laye
Tel   (1) 34 51 75 90
Mem   800
Pro   M Dallemagne, F Lafitte
       O St-Hilaire, D Hausseguy
Holes 18 L 6024 m SSS 72
       9 L 2030 m SSS 33
Fees   300fr
Loc   20km from Paris
Mis   WE–only with member

Saint-Nom-La-Bretêche (1959)

78860 Saint-Nom-La-Bretêche
Tel   (1) 34 62 54 00
Mem   1600
Sec   P Galitzine
Pro   A Cadet, R Golias, A Ferran,
       P Rouquet, G Leven
Holes 18 L 6685 yds SSS 72
       18 L 6712 yds SSS 72
Fees   WD only–400fr
Loc   Paris 24km on A–13
Mis   Handicap certificate required

St-Pierre-du-Perray (1974)

St-Pierre-du-Perray, 91100 Corbeil
Tel   (1) 60 75 17 47
Pro   E Hemberger
Holes 18 L 6217 m 233472
Loc   SE of Paris off N6
Mis   Public course

Saint-Quentin-en-Yvelines

Base de Loisirs RN12, 78190 Trappes
Tel   (1) 30 50 86 40
Pro   JP Chardonnet
Holes 18 L 5900 m SSS 71
       9 L 3063 m SSS 36
Loc   20km SW of Paris
Mis   Public course

Seraincourt

Gaillonnet, 95450 Vigny
Tel   (1) 34 75 47 28
Mem   380
Pro   J–P Gachet, L Salgado
Holes 18 L 5699 m SSS 70
Fees   200fr (400fr)
Loc   Paris 35km

Vaucouleurs

78910 Civry-la-Forêt
Tel   (1) 34 87 62 29
Mem   400
Pro   D Chaumillon, O Daavet
Holes 18 L 6298 m SSS 72
       18 L 5700 m SSS 68
Fees   200fr (400fr)
Loc   50km W of Paris, between
       Mantes and Houdan

Villarceaux

Chaussy, 95710 Bray-et-Lu
Tel   34 67 73 83
Pro   R Alsuguren
Holes 18 L 6101 m Par 72
Fees   150fr (375fr) 1989 prices
Loc   40km NW of Paris

Villennes (1985)

Public
CV 2 Route d'Orgeval,
78670 Villennes-sur-Seine
Tel   (1) 39 75 30 00
Mem   3000
Pro   P Guy, O Jaret
Holes 9 L 3000 m SSS 36
Fees   88fr (150fr)
Loc   W of Paris of N13
Mis   Driving range. Public course.

Provence & Côte d'Azur

Aix Marseille (1935)

Les Milles 13290
Tel   42 24 40 41/42 24 23 01
Mem   550
Pro   R Cotton, B Cotton, P Cotton
Holes 18L 6291 m SSS 73
Fees   170fr (250fr)
Loc   Aix–en–Provence 7km.
       Marignane airport 15km.
       Marseille 20km

Barbaroux

Route de Cabasse, 83170 Brignoles
Tel   94 59 07 43
Pro   N von Nida
Holes 18 L 6367 m SSS 72
Fees   300fr
Loc   Brignoles, 50km E of Aix.
       35km N of Toulon

La Bastide-du-Roy

06410 Biot
Tel   93 65 08 48
Pro   H Giraud, L Casella,
       R Pettavino
Holes 18 L 5064 m SSS 70
Fees   180fr (200fr)
Loc   Antibes 5km. Nice 15km

Les Baux–De–Provence
Domaine de Manville, 13520 Les
Baux–de–Provence
Tel   90 54 37 02
Mem   250
Pro   W Murray
Holes   9 L 3000 m Par 36
Loc   15km NE of Arles

Beauvallon–Grimaud
Boulevard des Collines, 83120 Sainte
Maxime
Tel   94 96 16 98
Mem   320
Pro   P Delaville
Holes   9 L 2503 m SSS 34
Fees   180–220fr (200–300fr)
Loc   Sainte Maxime 3km.
St Tropez 10km

Cannes (1891)
06210 Mandelieu–La Napoule
Tel   93 49 55 39
Mem   300
Pro   A Monge, R Gorgerino,
R Damiano, C Nunez
Holes   18 L 5871 m SSS 71
9 L 2852 m SSS 34
Fees   240fr (270fr)
Loc   Mandelieu, 7km W of Cannes

Cannes–Mougins (1978)
175 Route d'Antibes, 06250 Mougins
Tel   93 75 79 13
Mem   330 170(L) 50(J)
Pro   M Damiano, L Autiero,
P Lemaire, R Sorrel
Holes   18 L 6300 m SSS 72
Fees   230fr (260fr)
Loc   Cannes 8km. Nice 18km

Château L'Arc (1985)
Domaine de Château L'Arc, 13710
Fuveau
Tel   42 53 28 38
Mem   400
Pro   R Pujol, R Guidetti,
J Pickford
Holes   18 L 6300 m SSS 73
Fees   230fr (330fr) 1989 prices
Loc   15km SE of Aix–en–Provence

Châteaublanc
Les Plans, 84310 Morières-les-Avignon
Tel   90 33 39 08
Mem   250
Pro   J–M Kazmierczack
Holes   18 L 6275 m SSS 73
9 hole Par 3 course
Fees   160fr (250fr) Par 3–100fr
Loc   15km SE of Avignon, nr Airport

Grand Avignon (1988)
BP 121, Les Chênes Verts, 84270
Vedene
Tel   90 31 49 94
Mem   100
Pro   S Lanfranchi, E Rossary
Holes   18 L 6200 m SSS 72
9 hole course
Fees   180fr (250fr)
Loc   Vedene, N of Avignon

Monte Carlo (1910)
06320 La Turbie
Tel   93 41 09 11
Mem   500
Pro   C Houtart, F Ruffier–Meray,
R Halsall
Holes   18 L 5667 m SSS 71
Fees   250fr (350fr)
Loc   Mont Agel, La Turbie, N of
Monte Carlo
Mis   Handicap certificate required

Mouriès
Domaine de Servanes, 13890 Mouriès
Tel   90 47 59 95
Mem   150
Pro   J–M Kazmercziack
Holes   18 L 6025 m SSS 72
Fees   200fr (300fr)
Loc   25km SE of Arles

Opio–Valbonne (1966)
Château de la Begude, 06560 Valbonne
Tel   93 42 00 08
Pro   J Norsworthy
Holes   18 L 6200 m Par 72
Fees   240fr (270fr)
Loc   Cannes 15km. Nice Airport
20km

Pierrevert (1986)
Domaine de la Grande–Gardette,
04860 Pierrevert
Tel   92 72 17 19
Mem   450
Pro   L Dubouexic 92 72 05 69
Holes   18 L 6040 m SSS 72
Fees   180fr (230fr)
Loc   45km NE of Aix–en–Provence.
5km from Manosque

Sainte–Baume (1988)
83860 Nans–les–Pins
Tel   94 78 60 12
Pro   B Diagne, B Lacroix
Holes   18 L 6134 m SSS 72
Fees   150fr (220fr)
Loc   Marseilles 40km. Aix 40km
Mis   Public course

Valcros (1964)
83 La Londe–les Maures
Tel   66 81 02
Pro   P Hurfin
Holes   18 L 5184 m SSS 68
Fees   180fr (250fr)
Loc   Le Lavandou 16km

Valescure (1896)
BP 451, 83704 St–Raphaël Cedex
Tel   98 82 40 46
Mem   520
Pro   E Cougourdan, M Bromet,
M Semo
Holes   18 L 5065 m Par 68
Fees   220fr (250fr)
Loc   St–Raphaël 5km

Vievola (1978)
06430 Tende
Tel   93 04 61 02
Mem   60
Pro   N Giordano
Holes   9 L 2024 m SSS 64
Fees   100fr (160fr)
Loc   4km from Italian border
on RN 204
Mis   Open May–Oct

Pyrenees & South West

Agen Bon–Encontre (1982)
Barre, 47240 Bon–Encontre
Pro   P Navarro
Holes   9 L 2759 m Par 35
Fees   80fr (120fr)
Loc   5km from Agen, on N113
to Toulouse

La Barouge (1956)
81660 Pont de l'Arn
Tel   63 61 08 00
Mem   350
Pro   J–M Roca
Holes   18 L 5623 m SSS 70
Fees   150fr (200fr)
Loc   2km N of Mazamet.
82km E of Toulouse

Biarritz (1888)
Av Edith Cavell, 64200 Biarritz
Tel   59 03 71 80
Mem   650
Pro   R Simpson, O Leglise,
Mlle S Fourment
Holes   18 L 5379 m SSS 69
Fees   150–250fr
Loc   In Biarritz

Casteljaloux (1989)

Route de Mont–de–Marsan, 47700
Casteljaloux
Tel   53 93 51 60
Mem   150
Pro   E Smith
Holes   18 L 5916 m SSS 72
Fees   140–220fr (180–220fr)
Loc   45km NW of Agen

Castelnaud (1987)

"La Menuisière", 47290 Castelnaud de
Gratecambe
Tel   53 01 74 64
Mem   250
Pro   C Arsac
Holes   18 L 6322 m SSS 73
        9 L 2184 m SSS 27
Fees   120–100fr (140–200fr)
Loc   10km N of Villeneuve on N21.
        40km N of Agen
Mis   Driving range

Chantaco (1928)

Route d'Ascain, 64500 St Jean–de–Luz
Tel   (59) 26 14 22/26 19 22
Mem   500
Pro   JC Harismendy
Holes   18 L 5722 m SSS 70
Fees   200fr (250fr)
Loc   2km S of St Jean–de–Luz, on
        Route d'Ascain

Chiberta (1926)

Boulevard des Plages, 64600 Anglet
Tel   59 63 83 20
Mem   800
Pro   P Dufourg, H Brousson
Holes   18 L 5901 m SSS 71
Fees   160–260fr
Loc   Biarritz 3km. Bayonne 5km.
        Airport 5km
Mis   WE/High season–starting
        time necessary

Étangs de Fiac (1989)

Brazis, Fiac, 81500 Lavaur
Tel   63 70 64 70 (Sec)
        63 70 70 85 (Pro)
Mem   350
Pro   M Wallace
Holes   9 L 2837 m SSS 35
Fees   120fr (175fr) W–500fr
Loc   40km NE of Toulouse

Fleurance (1989)

Lassalle, 32500 Fleurance
Tel   62 06 26 26
Mem   100
Pro   G Camlong
Holes   9 L 2878 m Par 35
Fees   100fr (120fr)
Loc   Auch 20km. Agen 50km

Golf d'Albret (1986)

Le Pusocq, 47230 Barbaste
Tel   53 65 53 69
Mem   250
Pro   J Navas
Holes   18 L 5911 m SSS 71
Fees   120fr (150fr)
Loc   Barbaste, 30km W of Agen

Golf de l'Ariège (1986)

09240 La Bastide–de–Serou
Tel   61 64 56 78
Mem   340
Holes   18 L 6000 m SSS 71
Fees   120fr (150fr)
Loc   Unjat, 17km NW of Foix

Golf des Roucous (1907)

82110 Sauveterre
Tel   63 95 83 70
Mem   150
Holes   9 L 2622 m SSS 68
Fees   110fr (150fr)
Loc   38km N of Montauban

Hossegor (1929)

40 150 Hossegor
Tel   58 43 56 99
Mem   470
Pro   Y Hausseguy, M Hausseguy
Holes   18 L 6004 m SSS 71
Fees   230fr
Loc   Bayonne 15km

Lannemezan

La Demi–Lune, 65300 Lannemezan
Tel   62 98 01 01
Mem   280
Pro   R Lasserre
Holes   18 L 5872 m Par 70
Fees   130fr (160fr)
Loc   38km SE of Tarbes

Luchon (1908)

BP 40, 31110 Bagnères de Luchon
Tel   61 79 03 27
Mem   240
Pro   R Picabea
Holes   9 L 2375 m SSS 66
Fees   110fr (140fr)
Loc   Luchon, 90km SE of Tarbes

Mont–de–Marsan

Pessourdat, 40090 Saint–Avit
Tel   58 75 63 05 (Sec)
Mem   150
Pro   O Beaufranc
Holes   9 L 2503 m SSS 34
Fees   100fr
Loc   Mont–de–Marsan 8km.
        80km N of Pau
Mis   Covered practice range

La Nivelle (1907)

Place William–Sharp, 64500 Ciboure
Tel   59 47 18 99/59 47 19 72
Mem   480
Pro   J Palli, R Etchenic
Holes   18 L 5570 m SSS 69
Fees   170–260fr
Loc   1½ km S of St Jean–de–Luz

Pau (1856)

Rue de Golf, 64140 Pau–Billère
Tel   59 32 02 33
Mem   530
Pro   A Harismendy, D Loustalet
Holes   18 L 5389 m SSS 69
Fees   180fr (210fr)
Loc   Pau 2km

Royal GC Artiguelouve

Domaine St Michel, 64230 Lescar
Tel   59 83 09 29
Mem   400
Pro   R Darrieumerlou, A Lopez
Holes   18 L 6063 m Par 71
Fees   150fr (180fr)
Loc   8km from Pau, off Bayonne road

Salies–de–Béarn (1988)

Route d'Orthez, 64270 Salies–de–Béarn
Tel   59 38 37 59
Mem   80
Holes   9 L 2300 m SSS 62
Fees   80–100fr (100–120fr)
Loc   16km W of Orthez.
        Pau 50km. Biarritz 60km

Seignosse (1989)

40510 Seignosse
Tel   58 43 17 32
Holes   18 L 6124 m Par 72
Fees   180–260fr (200–260fr)
Loc   30km N of Biarritz, nr Airport

Tarbes–Laloubère

Public
Hippodrome, 65310 Laloubère
Tel   62 96 11 14
Mem   300
Pro   J Ayala
Holes   9 L 5960 m SSS 72
Fees   120fr
Loc   S of Tarbes
Mis   Public course

Toulouse (1951)

31 Vieille–Toulouse
Tel   61 73 45 48
Mem   380
Pro   R Olalainty
Holes   18 L 5602 m SSS 69
Fees   170fr (220fr)
Loc   Toulouse 8 mins

Toulouse–Palmola (1973)

31680 Buzet-Sur-Tarn
Tel   61 84 20 50
Mem   750
Pro   D Barquez
Holes 18 L 6166 m SSS 72
Fees   200fr (350fr 2D–600fr)
Loc   20km NE of Toulouse

Toulouse–Seilh

Route de Grenade, Seilh, 31840
Aussonne
Tel   (33) 61 42 59 30
Mem   300
Pro   J Garaïalde, J–P Hontas
Holes Red 18 L 6164 m SSS 72
       Yellow 18 L 4146 m SSS 61
Fees   Red 200fr (250fr) Yellow 180fr
       (230fr)
Loc   15km N of Toulouse.
       Airport 5km

Germany

Aachen & Saar

Aachen (1927)

Schürzelter Str 300, 5100 Aachen
Tel   (0241) 12501
Mem   575
Pro   W Van Mook
Holes 18 L 5903 m Par 71
Fees   D–40DM (D–50DM)
Loc   Aachen–Seffent, 5km from
       Aachen

Düren (1975)

Katherinenstr 59, 5160 Düren
Tel   (02421) 800112
Mem   200
Pro   H Gross, R Hamann
Holes 9 L 5706 m SSS 70
Fees   30DM (40DM)
Loc   Trierbachweg

Eifel (1977)

Kölner Str, 5533 Hillesheim
Tel   (06593) 1241
       Fax 06593 9421
Mem   420
Pro   C Gess (06593) 8537
Holes 9 L 6180 m Par 72
Fees   30DM (45DM)
Loc   70km S of Cologne
Mis   Course closed Tues

Nahetal (1970)

Postfach 1518, 6550 Bad Kreusnach
Tel   (06708) 2145/3755
Mem   730
Pro   H Goerke, F Schmaderer,
       G Pietruschka

Holes 18 L 6065 m SSS 72
Fees   40DM (60DM)
Loc   Bad Kreuznach 6km.
       Bad Münster 3km.
       70km SW of Frankfurt

Pfalz (1971)

673 Neustadt, Weinstrasse
Tel   (06327) 2973
Mem   750
Pro   G Hopp, A Suchet
Holes 18 L 6180 m SSS 72
Fees   50DM (60DM)
Loc   Geinsheim, 15km from
       Neustadt towards Speyer

Saar–Pfalz Katharinenhof (1982)

Heinrich–Böckingstr 1,
6600 Saarbrücken
Tel   (0681) 687 9421 (Sec)
       (06843) 8797 (Clubhouse)
Mem   394
Pro   J Morris (06843) 8878
Holes 9 L 6112 m Par 72
Fees   30DM D–50DM (80DM)
Loc   15km S of Saarbrücken towards
       Blieskastel
Mis   WE–only with member

Saarbrücken (1961)

Oberlimbergerweg,
6634 Wallerfangen-Gisingen
Tel   (06837) 401
Mem   800
Pro   W Rappenecker, C Coughlan,
       R Heymanns
Holes 18 L 6231 m SSS 73
Fees   45DM (65DM)
Loc   B406 towards Wallerfangen.
       8km from Saarlouis

Trier–Mosel (1977)

Postfach 1905, 5500 Trier
Tel   (06507) 4374
Mem   370
Pro   H Goerke
Holes 9 L 6100 m SSS 72
Fees   25DM (40DM)
Loc   20km NE of Trier
Mis   Driving range, pitch and putt

Woodlawn

6792 Ramstein Flugplatz
Tel   (06371) 476240
Mem   Military GC–Visitors limited
Pro   E Sudy
Holes 18 L 6225 yds Par 70
Fees $10 ($12)
Loc   Ramstein 3km

Berlin

Berlin G & CC

APO 197442, US Forces Europe
Tel   8196533
Mem   600
Pro   L Beem
Holes 18 L 6350 yds Par 70
Fees $10 ($15)
Loc   Wannsee

Berlin–Wannsee (1895)

Am Stoepchenweg, 1000 Berlin
Tel   8055075
Mem   575
Pro   U Tapperthofen, J Galbraith
Holes 9 L 5690 m SSS 70
Fees   30DM (40DM)
Loc   Berlin 17km

British GC Gatow (1969)

BFPO 45, RAF Gatow
Tel   3092670/3657660
Mem   400
Holes 9 L 5687 m SSS 70
Fees   10DM (20DM)
Loc   16km from Berlin
Mis   British Forces & British
       Passport holders only

Central

Aschaffenburg (1977)

8750 Aschaffenburg, Kirchnerstr 13
Tel   (06021) 91840/(06024) 7222
Mem   560
Pro   M Richardson
Holes 9 L 5000 m SSS 67
Fees   40DM (50DM)
Loc   Hösbach/Feldkahl, 7km E of
       Aschaffenburg

Bad Kissingen (1911)

Euerdorfer Str 11,
8730 Bad Kissingen
Tel   (0971) 3608
Mem   600
Pro   J Dibb, T Pearman
Holes 18 L 5675 m SSS 70
Fees   40DM (50DM)
Loc   Bad Kissingen 2km

Bad Mergentheim (1971)

6990 Bad Mergentheim, Postfach 1304
Tel   (07931) 7579
Pro   H Rosenkranz
Holes 9 L 4230 m Par 64
Fees   25DM (35DM)
Loc   Würzburg 40km

Bad Nauheim

6350 Bad Nauheim, Postfach 1524
Tel   (06032) 2153
Mem   370
Pro   B Raschke (06032) 33797
Holes 9 L 5440 m SSS 68
Fees   35DM (50DM)
Loc   Frankfurt/Main 40km

Bad Wildungen (1930)

3590 Bad Wildungen
Tel   (05621) 4877/2260
Mem   100
Pro   A Stein
Holes 9 L 5670 m Par 70
Fees   D–35DM (45DM)
Loc   Bad Wildungen 1¹/₂ km

Darmstadt–Traisa

Dippelshof, 6109 Mühltal–Traisa
Tel   (06151) 146543
Mem   330
Pro   M Rose
Holes 9 L 5150 m SSS 68
Fees   30DM (40DM)
Loc   Traisa, nr Darmstadt

Frankfurter (1913)

6000 Frankfurt/M 71, Golfstr 41
Tel   (069) 6 66 23 18
Mem   900
Pro   H Strüver, T Gowdy,
       G Winckler
Holes 18 L 6455 yds SSS 71
Fees   D–65DM (85DM)
Loc   Frankfurt 6km. Airport 4km

Hanau–Wilhelmsbad (1959)

Wilhelmsbader Allee 32, 6450 Hanau
Tel   (06181) 82071
       Fax 06181 86967
Mem   860
Pro   M Day
Holes 18 L 6227 m Par 73
Fees   50DM (70DM)
Loc   4km NW of Hanau on
       B8–40/AB66. Frankfurt 16km

Heidelberg (US Army) (1957)

An der Bundestr 291, 6836 Oftersheim
Tel   (06202) 53767
Mem   800
Pro   G Pluckett (Mgr)
Holes 18 L 6650 m SSS 72
Fees $20 ($30)
Loc   Heidelberg 10km

Heidelberg–Lobenfeld (1968)

Biddersbacherhof, 6921 Lobbach–
Lobenfeld
Tel   (06226) 40490/41615
Mem   800
Pro   JP Godefroy (06226) 41955

Holes 18 L 6215 m SSS 72
Fees   30DM (50DM) 1989 prices
Loc   30km E of Heidelberg

Homburg (1899)

Saalburgchaussee 2, 6380 Bad
Homburg
Tel   (06172) 38808
Mem   525
Pro   F Tauber, R Taylor
Holes 10 holes SSS 69
Fees   30DM (50DM)
Loc   On B456 to Usingen

Kronberg G & LC (1954)

Schloss Friedrichshof, Hainstr 25,
6242 Kronberg/Taunus
Tel   (06173) 1426
Mem   506
Pro   A Schilling, J Harder,
       J Thompson, J Harris
Holes 18 L 5365 m SSS 68
Fees   50DM (70DM)
Loc   16km NW of Frankfurt

Main–Taunus (1980)

Lange Seegewann 2, 6200 Wiesbaden–
Delkenheim
Tel   (06122) 52550 (Sec)
Mem   813
Holes 18 L 6044 m SSS 72
Fees   40DM (60DM)
Loc   Next US Air Force Base
       Wiesbaden–Erbenheim
Mis   Driving range–10DM

Mannheim–Viernheim (1930)

Alte Mannheimerstr 3, 6806 Viernheim
Tel   (06204) 71313 (Clubhouse)
       (06204) 71307 (Pro)
Mem   500
Pro   C Jenkins, M Kagel,
       Th Gutmann
Holes 9 L 6060 m SSS 72
Fees   35DM
Loc   Mannheim 10km
Mis   WE–only with member

Mittelrheinischer (1930)

Denzerheide, 5427 Bad Ems
Tel   (02603) 6541
Pro   H Goerke
Holes 18 L 6050 m SSS 72
Fees   35DM (50DM)
Loc   Bad Ems 6km. Koblenz 13km

Oberhessischer Marburg (1973)

Postfach 1828, 3550 Marburg/Lahn
Tel   (06427) 8558
Mem   350
Pro   T Rigby
Holes 9 L 6044 m SSS 72
Fees   30DM (40DM)
Loc   8km N of Marburg off B3
       towards Reddehausen

Paderborner Land (1983)

Wilseder Weg 25, 4790 Paderborn
Tel   (05251) 4377
Pro   A van der Donck
Holes 9 L 5670 m SSS 70
Fees   20DM (30DM)
Loc   Salzkotten/Thule between
       B–1 and B–64

Rhein–Main (1977)

Steubenstrasse 9, 6200 Wiesbaden
Tel   (06121) 373014
Pro   T Cary
Holes 18 L 5966 m SSS 71
Fees $20
Loc   Wiesbaden 6km
Mis   Members and guests only

Rheinblick

6200 Wiesbaden–Marchenland
Tel   Military 3889
Mem   US Forces
Pro   P Greenfield
Holes 18 L 6604 yds SSS 70
Fees $5 ($10)
Loc   Wiesbaden 2km
Mis   Guests limited

Rheintal (1971)

Postfach 1140, 6906 Leimen
Tel   (06224) 7 10 34
Pro   A Winkler
Holes 18 L 5840 m SSS 70
Fees $10 ($15)

Rhoen (1971)

Am Golfplatz, 6417 Hofbieber 1
Tel   (06657) 7077/1334
Mem   600
Pro   N Staples
Holes 18 L 5676 m SSS 70
Fees   30DM (40DM)
Loc   Hofbieber, 11km E of Fulda

Schloss–Braunfels (1970)

Homburger Hof, 6333 Braunfels
Tel   (06442) 4530
Mem   700
Pro   D McLellan, M Lauermann,
       P Smith (06442) 5752
Holes 18 L 6288 m SSS 72
Fees   40DM (70DM)
Loc   70km N of Frankfurt am
       Main

Sennelager (British Army) (1963)

Bad Lippspringe, BFPO 16
Tel   (82) 2515
Sec   AG Bairstow
Holes 18 L 5964 m SSS 72
Fees   (Forces) 20DM (30DM)
       (Civilians) 30DM (40DM)
Loc   Paderborn 9km off Route 1

Spessart (1972)

Eselsweg, 6483 B S S–Alsberg
Tel   (06066) 7601
Mem   700
Pro   L Bolland, S Walker
Holes   18 L 6039 m SSS 72
Fees   45DM (65DM) W–175DM
Loc   70km from Frankfurt via A66
Mis   Handicap certificate required

Taunus G & LC (1979)

Merzhauser Landstr,
6395 Weilrod–Altweilnau
Tel   (06083) 865
Pro   M Bonn, J Wilson
Holes   18 holes SSS 72
Fees   35DM (50DM)
Loc   15km NW of Bad Homburg

Wiesbaden (1893)

Chauseehaus, 6200 Wiesbaden
Tel   (06121) 460238
Mem   470
Pro   M Day, T Robinson
   (06121) 468316
Holes   9 L 5320 m Par 68
Fees   35DM (45DM)
Loc   8km from Wiesbaden, towards
   Schlangenbad

Wiesloch–Hohenhardter Hof G LC (1983)

Hohenhardter Hof, 6908 Wiesloch-
Baiertal
Tel   (06222) 72081
Pro   H Rübmann
Holes   18 L 6080 m SSS 72
Fees   30DM (40DM)
Loc   17km S of Heidelberg

Winterberg (1962)

Postfach 1140, 5788 Winterberg
Tel   (02981) 1770
Mem   220
Pro   D Pugh
Holes   9 L 5680 m SSS 70
Fees   30DM (40DM)
Loc   2km N of Winterberg, nr
   Silbach

Würzburg–Kitzingen (1980)

Augustinerstr 3, 8700 Würzburg
Tel   (0931) 55 77 9
Mem   160
Pro   F Dziwlewski
Holes   9 L 6020 m SSS 72
Fees $8.75 ($15)
Loc   Würzburg 20km

Hamburg & North

Altenhof (1971)

2330 Altenhof, bei Eckernförde
Tel   (04351) 41227
Mem   650
Pro   N Robinson
Holes   18 L 6071 m SSS 72
Fees   40DM (50DM)
Loc   Eckernförde 3km. Kiel 20km

An der Goehrde (1968)

3139 Zernien–Braasche
Tel   (05863) 556
Mem   250
Pro   G Gilligan
Holes   9 L 6107 m SSS 72
Fees   30DM (40DM)
Loc   40km E of Lüneburg.
   30km E of Uelzen

An der Pinnau (1982)

Jebbenberg 32, 2084 Rellingen
Tel   (04106) 8 18 00
Mem   590
Pro   S Arrowsmith, B Griffiths,
   A Arrowsmith
Holes   18 L 6129 m SSS 72
Fees   35DM (45DM)
Loc   Motorway Hamburg–
   Flensburg exit Quickborn.
   Motorway Hamburg–Husum
   exit Pinneberg Nord
Mis   Course address:
   Pinnebergerstr 81, 2085
   Quickborn

Auf der Wendlohe

Oldesloerstr 251, 2000 Hamburg 61
Tel   (040) 550 5014/5
Mem   850
Pro   G Jones, M Bradley, J Gibbons
Holes   18 L 6060 m SSS 72
Fees   40DM
Loc   Hamburg 15km
Mis   WE–only with member

Bad Bramstedt (1975)

2357 Bad Bramstedt, PO Box 1305,
Ochsenweg 38
Tel   (04192) 6376
   Fax 4192 7707
Mem   170
Pro   T Lithgo
Holes   9 5724 m SSS 70
Fees   30DM (40DM)
Loc   S border of Bad Bramstedt, by
   B4. 48km N of Hamburg on A7

Buxtehude (1982)

Zum Lehmfeld 1, 2150 Buxtehude
Tel   (04161) 81333
Mem   500
Pro   M Fitton, S Bates, D Reffin
Holes   18 L 6505 m SSS 74
Fees   40DM (50DM)
Loc   30km SW of Hamburg on
   Route 73 from Harburg

Dithmarschen

Dorfstr 11, 2242 Warwerort
Tel   (04834) 6300
Mem   180
Pro   PH Clark
Holes   9 L 5284 m SSS 68
Fees   25DM (35DM)
Loc   Warwerort, 14km from Heide

Föhr (1966)

2270 Niebum auf Föhr
Tel   (04681) 3277
Mem   301
Pro   A Assmus
Holes   9 L 6100 m SSS 72
Fees   30DM (40DM)
Loc   3km SW of Wyk

Förde Glücksburg

2392 Glücksburg–Bockholm
Tel   (04631) 2547
Mem   290
Pro   D Ohle
Holes   9 holes SSS 72
Fees   30DM (40DM)
Loc   10km NE of Flensburg

Grossensee (1975)

Hamburgerstrasse, 2077 Grossensee
Tel   (04154) 6473
Mem   250
Pro   G Schurr
Holes   9 L 6154 m SSS 72
Fees   30DM (40DM)
Loc   Hamburg 30km

Grossflottbeker (1901)

Otto–Ernst Str 32, 2000 Hamburg
Tel   (040) 827208
Mem   300
Pro   K Storrier
Holes   9 L 4945 m SSS 66
Fees   D–30DM (D–40DM)
Loc   Hamburg 10km

Gut Grambek (1981)

2411 Grambek, Schlosstrasse 21
Tel   (04542) 4627
Mem   460
Pro   HJ Rumpf
Holes   18 L 6029 m SSS 71
Fees   35DM (50DM)
Loc   30km S of Lübeck.
   50km E of Hamburg

Gut Kaden (1984)

Kadenerstrasse 9, 2081 Alveslohe
Tel   (04193) 92021/2/3
Mem   300
Pro   L Kelly
Holes   18 L 6180 m SSS 72
Fees   50DM
Loc   Alveslohe, 30km N of Hamburg
Mis   WE–only with member

Gut Waldhof (1969)

Am Waldhof, 2359 Kisdorferwohld
Tel   (04194) 383
Mem   740
Pro   HJ Jersombeck, T Parker
Holes   18 L 6073 m Par 72
Fees   35DM (45DM)

Loc   34km N of Hamburg via
      Autobahn A7 to Kaltenkirchen,
      or via route B432
Mis   WE-only with member

Hamburg (1906)

In de Bargen 59, 2000 Hamburg
Tel   (040) 812177
Mem   1030
Pro   A Mazza, S Blume
Holes 18 L 5925 m SSS 71
Fees 45DM (60DM)
Loc   Blankenese, Hamburg 14km
Mis   WE-only with member

Hamburg–Ahrensburg (1964)

Am Haidschlag 39–45, 2070
Ahrensburg
Tel   (04102) 513 09
Mem   849
Pro   H Heiser, C Kirchner, P Nitra
Holes 18 L 5782 m SSS 70
Fees 40DM (50DM)
Loc   Hamburg 20km. Motorway exit
      Ahrensburg
Mis   WE-only with member

Hamburg–Waldorfer (1960)

2075 Ammersbek, Schevenbarg
Tel   (040) 6 05 13 37
Mem   850
Pro   K Sallman, G Bennett
Holes 18 L 6154 m SSS 73
Fees 40DM (50DM)
Loc   20km N of Hamburg
Mis   Driving range, pitch and putt

Hamburger GC In der Lüneburger Heide (1957)

2105 Seevetal 1, Am Golfplatz 24
Tel   (04105) 2331
Mem   600
Pro   J Struver, S Wächter
Holes 18 L 5735 m SSS 70
Fees 40DM (50DM)
Loc   Hamburg 25km

Hoisdorf (1977)

Hof Bornbek/Hoisdorf, 2073 Lütjensee
Tel   (04107) 7831
Mem   800
Pro   M Stewart, N Griffith
Holes 18 L 6010 m Par 71
Fees 40DM (50M)
Loc   25km NE of Hamburg

Kitzeberg (1902)

Sophienblatt 46, 2300 Kiel 1
Tel   (0431) 63048/23404
Mem   360
Pro   R Denton
Holes 9 L 5700 m Par 70
Fees 30DM (40DM)
Loc   Kiel 10km

Küsten GC Hohe Klint (1978)

Rosenhof 25, 2190 Cuxhaven
Tel   (04721) 48057
Mem   496
Pro   F O'Conner
Holes 18 L 6150 m SSS 72
Fees 40DM (50DM)
Loc   12km SW of Cuxhaven on
      Route 6, nr Oxstedt

Lohersand (1958)

2371 Lohe–Föhrden, Golfplatz
Tel   (04336) 3333
Mem   284
Holes 9 L 6040 m Par 72
Fees 25DM (30DM)
Loc   Sorgbrück/B77. Rendsburg
      10km

Lübeck–Travemünder (1921)

Kowitzberg 41, 2400
Lübeck–Travemünde
Tel   (04502) 74018
Pro   A Varley
Holes 9 L 6086 m SSS 72
Fees 30DM (50DM)
Loc   Lübeck

Marine Westerland (1980)

2280 Westerland, Marinefliegerhorst
Tel   (04651) 7037
Mem   450
Pro   A Pemöller
Holes 9 L 5234 m SSS 68
Fees 30DM (35DM)
Loc   Sylt Island. 75km W of
      Flensburg by Danish border

Maritim Timmendorfer Strand (1973)

Am Golfplatz, 2408 Timmendorfer
Strand
Tel   (04503) 5152
Mem   785
Pro   R Hinz
Holes 18 L 6095 m SSS 72
      18 L 3755 m SSS 60
Fees D–40DM (D–70DM)
Loc   Lübeck 20km. Hamburg 70km

Mittelholsteinischer Aukrug (1969)

2356 Aukrug–Bargfeld
Tel   (04873) 595
Mem   370
Pro   M Kimberly
Holes 18 L 6140 m SSS 72
Fees 25DM (35DM)
Loc   10km W of Neumunster.
      Mitte exit on Route 430

Norderney (1956)

Box 1233, 2982 Norderney
Tel   (04932) 680
Mem   225
Pro   R Bremer
Holes 9 L 4890 m SSS 66
Fees 25DM (30DM)
Loc   Norderney 7km

Oldenburgischer (1964)

2900 Oldenburg, Postbox 2928
Tel   (04402) 7240
Mem   532
Pro   J Walter
Holes 18 L 6087 m SSS 72
Fees 30DM (40DM) 1989 prices
Loc   Rastede 3km

Ostfriesland (1980)

2964 Wiesmoor, Postbox 1220
Tel   (04944) 3040
Mem   400
Pro   S Parry (04944) 2228
Holes 18 L 6256 m SSS 73
Fees 35DM (50DM)
Loc   25km SW of Wilhelmshaven

St Dionys (1972)

Widukindweg, 2123 St Dionys
Tel   (04133) 6277
Mem   565
Pro   KH Mahl, G Hillson
Holes 18 L 6225 m SSS 73
Fees 40DM (60DM)
Loc   Nr Lüneburg

St Peter–Ording (1971)

Hauke Haien–Weg 1,
2252 St Peter–Ording
Tel   (04863) 1545/746
Mem   150
Pro   T Holroyd
Holes 9 L 5730 m SSS 70
Fees 30DM (35DM)
Loc   St Peter–Bohl

Schloss Lüdersburg (1985)

2127 Lüdersburg bei Lüneburg
Tel   (04153) 6112
Mem   300
Pro   M Rooney, S Griffin
Holes 18 L 6155 m SSS 72
      6 hole Par 3 course
Fees 30DM (45DM) Par 3–15DM
      (25DM)
Loc   16km E of Lüneburg.
      50km SE of Hamburg

Soltau (1982)

Golfplatz Hof Loh,
3040 Soltau–Tetendorf
Tel   (05191) 14077
Mem   420

Holes 18 L 6224 m SSS 73
       9 L 2340 m SSS 54
Fees   30DM (40DM)
Loc   Tetendorf, 3km S of Soltau

Tietlingen (1979)

Tietlingen 6c, 3032 Fallingbostel
Tel   (05162) 38 89
Mem   400
Pro   G MacMillan
Holes 9 L 6042 m SSS 72
Fees   25DM (40DM)
Loc   65km N of Hannover between
       Walsrode and Fallingbostel

Wentorf–Reinbeker (1901)

Golfstrasse 2, 2057 Wentorf
Tel   (040) 7202610/7202141
Mem   380
Pro   W Lloyd
Holes 9 L 5768 m SSS 70
Fees   30DM (45DM)
Loc   Hamburg 25km
Mis   Co-Founder of German
       Golf Union 1907

Wildeshausen (1978)

Glauer Str, 2878 Wildeshausen
Tel   (04431) 1232
Mem   350
Pro   R Foster
Holes 9 L 6080 m SSS 72
Fees   20DM (30DM)
Loc   3km from Wildeshausen,
       on road to Huntlosen

Wilhelmshaven (1979)

Parkstr 19, 2940 Wilhelmshaven
Tel   (04425) 1721
Mem   590
Pro   P Allen
Holes 9 L 6058 m SSS 72
Fees   30DM (40DM)
Loc   8km N of Wilhelmshaven

Worpswede (1974)

Grüner Weg 3, 2822 Schwanewede 1
Tel   (0421) 621425/(04673) 7313
Mem   314
Pro   R Prössel
Holes 9 L 6200 m SSS 72
Fees   40DM (50DM)
Loc   Giehlermuhlen, B74 Osterholz
       –Scharmbeck to Bremen

Wümme (1984)

Hof Emmen, Westerholz,
2723 Scheessel
Tel   (04263) 3352
Pro   K Wright
Holes 9 L 3071 m SSS 36
Fees   25DM (30DM)
Loc   10km N of Rotenberg, between
       Bremen and Hamburg

Zur Vahr (1905)

Bgm–Spitta–Allee 34, 2800 Bremen
Tel   Bremen–(0421) 230041
       Garlstedt–(04795) 417
Mem   1200
Pro   H Weber, M Grantham
Holes Bremen 9 L 5862 m SSS 71
       Garlstedt 18 L 6430 m SSS 75
Fees   Bremen 30DM (40DM)
       Garlstedt 40DM (50DM)
Loc   Bremen–in city. Garlstedt–30
       mins from Bremen

Hanover & Weserbergland

Bad Driburg (1976)

Am Kurpark, 3490 Bad Driburg
Tel   (05253) 842500
Mem   260
Pro   R Issitt
Holes 9 L 6106 m SSS 72
Fees   25DM (30DM) W–130DM
Loc   Paderborn 22km

Bad Salzdetfurth– Hildesheim (1972)

Postfach 1445, 3200 Hildesheim
Tel   (05063) 1516
Pro   W Muller
Holes 9 L 6210 m SSS 72
Fees   25DM (30DM)

Bad Salzuflen G & LC

Clubhaus am Schwaghof, 4902 Bad
Salzuflen
Tel   (05222) 10773
Mem   550
Pro   J Paterson
Holes 18 L 6163 m Par 72
Fees   40DM (50DM)
Loc   Bad Salzuflen 3km

Braunschweig (1926)

Schwarzkopfstr 10, 3300 Braunschweig
Tel   (0531) 691369
Mem   570
Pro   MA Emery
Holes 15 L 5893 m SSS 71
Fees   30DM (40DM)
Loc   Braunschweig 5km

British Army (Hohne) (1962)

Hohne BFPO 30
Tel   (05051) 4549
Mem   260
Holes 9 L 5682 m SSS 71
Fees   20DM (25DM)
Loc   6km S of Bergen Celle

Burgdorf (1970)

Waldstr 27, 3167 Burgdorf–
Ehlershausen
Tel   (05085) 7628/7144
Mem   400
Pro   L Theeuwen
Holes 18 L 6460 m SSS 74
Fees   30DM (40DM)
Loc   B3 Burgdorf-Ehlershausen

Gifhorn (1982)

Postfach 1341, 3170 Gifhorn
Tel   (05371) 16737
Mem   233
Pro   N Coombs
Holes 9 L 6160 m SSS 72
Fees   20DM (30DM)
Loc   Hannover

Göttingen (1969)

Levershausen, 3410 Northeim 1
Tel   (05551) 61915/7952
Mem   580
Pro   W Kreuzer
Holes 18 L 6050 m SSS 72
Fees   30DM (40DM)
Loc   Between Göttingen and
       Northeim

Hannover (1923)

3008 Garbsen 1, Am Blauen See
Tel   (05137) 7 32 35
Mem   600
Pro   H Koch, B Schul
Holes 18 L 5855 m SSS 71
Fees   35DM (50DM)
Loc   Hannover 20km

Harz (1969)

Am Breitenberg 107, 3388 Bad
Harzburg 1
Tel   (05322) 6737/1096
Mem   350
Pro   M Spence
Holes 9 L 5562 m SSS 70
Fees   35DM (40DM)
Loc   Centre of Bad Harzburg.
       50km S of Braunschweig

Herford (1984)

Heideholz 8, 4973 Vlotho–Exter
Tel   (05228) 74 34
Mem   170
Pro   G Pilkington
Holes 9 L 6184 m SSS 72
Fees   20DM (40DM)
Loc   30km NE of Bielefeld.
       80km W of Hanover
Mis   Handicap certificate required

Herzogstadt Celle (1985)

Beukenbusch 1, 3100 Celle
Tel   (05086) 395
Mem   190
Pro   W Knowles

Holes   18 L 5692 m SSS 72
Fees   30DM (40DM)
Loc   6km from Celle towards
        Lüneberg

Isernhagen (1983)

Im Kurzen Felde 24, 3004 Isernhagen
Tel   (05139) 87564
Mem   450
Pro   U Beuns, J Beuns
Holes   18 L 6334 m SSS 72
Fees   25DM (30DM)
Loc   Gut Lohne, 12km NE of
        Hanover

Kassel–Wilhelmshöhe

Wolfsschlucht 27, 3500 Kassel
Tel   (0561) 3 35 09
Pro   P Smith, U Wagener
Holes   18 L 5675 m SSS 70
Fees   40DM (50DM)

Lippischer (1980)

Huxollweg, 4933 Blomberg-Cappel
Tel   (05231) 459
Mem   490
Pro   R Newsome, D Krause
Holes   18 L 6110 m SSS 72
Fees   40DM (50DM)
Loc   12km from Detmold

Pyrmonter (1972)

Postfach 100 828, 3250 Hameln
Tel   (05281) 8196
Mem   300
Pro   S Russell
Holes   9 L 5720 m SSS 70
Fees   30DM (35DM)
Loc   Bad Pyrmont 4km. Hameln
        25km

Salzgitter Liebenburg (1985)

Sportpark Mahner Berg, Postfach
511329, Salzgitter–Bad
Tel   (05341) 37376
Mem   130
Pro   G Dyck
Holes   9 L 6010 m SSS 71
Fees   20DM (30DM)
Loc   Salzgitter Bad, 27km SW of
        Braunschweig

Schloss Schwöbber (1985)

Schloss Schwöbber, 3258 Aerzen 16
Tel   (05154) 2004
Mem   1044
Pro   R Lewington, E Runcie
Holes   18 L 6222 m SSS 73
        18 hole short course
Fees   45DM D–65DM
        (50DM D–75DM)
        Short course–30DM (40DM)
Loc   10km SW of Hameln.
        60km SW of Hanover
Mis   Driving range–20DM

Sieben–Berge (1983)

Schloss Str 1, 3211 Rheden/Gronau
Tel   (05182) 2680
Mem   250
Pro   P Scott
Holes   9 L 6126 m SSS 72
Fees   25DM (35DM)
Loc   Hanover 40km
Mis   Driving range

Weserbergland (1982)

Sparenbergstr 9, 3450 Holzminden
Tel   (15531) 10033
Pro   S Fisher
Holes   18 holes SSS 72
Fees   20DM (30DM)
Loc   35km S of Hameln

Munich & South Bavaria

Altötting–Burghausen (1986)

Piesing 2, 8261 Haiming
Tel   (08678) 7001
Mem   282
Pro   G Schönberg (08678) 7002
Holes   New 9 L 6416 m SSS 74
        Old 9 L 3730 m SSS 60
Fees   30DM (40DM)
Loc   Schloss Piesing, 4km N of
        Burghausen towards Marktl

Augsburg (1959)

Engelshofer Str 2, 8903 Bobingen-
Burgwalden
Tel   (08234) 5621
Mem   675
Pro   P Ries
Holes   18 L 5833 m SSS 71
Fees   40DM (60DM)
Loc   18km SW of Augsburg.
        Munich 50km

Bad Tölz (1973)

Strasse 124, 8170 Wackersberg
Tel   (08041) 9994
Mem   260
Pro   I Lyons, S Allan
Holes   9 L 2942 m SSS 71
Fees   40DM (50DM)
Loc   55km S of Munich.
        W of Bad Tölz

Bad Wörishofen

8951 Rieden, Schlingener Str 27
Tel   (08346) 777
Mem   520
Pro   M Seidel, H Hoerenz,
        A Cawdron

Holes   18 L 6318 m SSS 71
Fees   50DM (70DM)
Loc   10km S of Bad Wörishofen

Berchtesgaden (1955)

Postfach 3460, Berchtesgaden
Tel   (08652) 2100/3787
Mem   230
Holes   9 L 5135 m SSS 67
Fees   20DM (30DM)
Loc   Berchtesgaden 3½ km.
        Motorway 25km

Beuerberg (1982)

Gut Sterz, 8196 Beuerberg
Tel   (08179) 671/728
Mem   570
Pro   A Hahn, JP Koriath, J Bray
Holes   18 L 6518 m SSS 74
Fees   60DM (85DM)
Loc   Beuerberg, 45km SW of
        Munich

Chiemsee

8210 Prien–Bauernberg
Tel   (08051)4820
Mem   365
Pro   R Krause
Holes   9 L 5960 m SSS 71
Fees   40DM (50DM–on request)
Loc   Prien 3km

Dachau (1947)

8060 Dachau, An der Flosslände 1
Tel   (08131) 10879
Mem   250
Pro   C De Castro
Holes   9 L 2960 m SSS 71
Fees   35DM (40DM)
Loc   2km E of Dachau.
        17km NW of Munich

Erding–Grunbach (1973)

8058 Erding, Aribostr 2
Tel   (08122) 6465
Mem   500
Pro   G Warner
Holes   18 L 6140 m SSS 72
Fees   40DM (50DM)
Loc   45 mins from Munich towards
        Vilsbiburg

Eschenried (1983)

Kurfurstenweg 7, 8066 Eschenried
Tel   (08131) 3238/79655
Mem   450
Pro   G Stewart
Holes   9 L 6194 m SSS 72
Fees   35DM (50DM)
Loc   8km NW of Munich

Falkenhof G & LC (1983)

PO Box 1560, D–8263 Burghausen
Tel   (08677) 2394
Mem   160
Pro   S Tasker
Holes 9 L 3030 m SSS 72
Fees   30DM (40DM)
Loc   Falkenhof–Marktl, 48km N of
       Salzburg
Mis   Driving range

Feldafing (1926)

8133 Feldafing, Tutzingerstr 15
Tel   (08157) 7005
Mem   800
Pro   T Flossman, A Steinfurth,
       J Weger
Holes 18 L 5708 m SSS 70
Fees   50DM
Loc   32km S of Munich
Mis   Driving range, pitch and putt.
       WE–only with member

Garmisch–Partenkirchen (1928)

Postfach 1345 Garmisch-
Partenkirchen
Tel   (08824) 8344/1632
Mem   540
Pro   A Hagl
Holes 18 L 6200 m SSS 72
Fees   65DM (80DM)
Loc   Garmisch 6km

Höslwang im Chiemgau (1977)

Chiemseestr 18, 8200 Rosenheim
Tel   (08031) 12198
Pro   F Carli
Holes 9 L 6210 m SSS
Fees   25DM (40DM)

Im Chiemgau (1982)

Kötzing 1, 8224 Chieming
Tel   (08669) 7557
Mem   470
Pro   G Thomson
Holes 18 L 6200 m SSS 73
       9 holes Par 3
Fees   45DM (70DM)
Loc   Salzburg 20km

Leitershofen (1980)

8902 Stadtbergen, Deuringerstr.
Tel   (0821) 434919
Mem   125
Pro   P Garnier–Bradley
Holes 9 L 3090 m SSS 72
Fees   25DM (30DM)
Loc   8901 Stadtbergen-Leitershofen

Margarethenhof am Tegernsee ((1982)

8184 Gmund am Tegernsee
Tel   (08022) 7366
Pro   F Bernardi
Holes 18 L 6056 m SSS 72
Fees   40DM (60DM)
Loc   Munich 50km

München Nord–Eichenried (1989)

Münchenstrasse 55, 8059 Eichenried
Tel   (8123) 1004
Mem   815
Pro   E Dimmit
Holes 18 L 6318 m Par 72
Fees   55DM
Loc   19km NE of Munich

Münchener (1910)

Tölzerstrasse, 8021 Strasslach
Tel   (08170) 450
       Fax 08170 611
Mem   1150
Pro   A Castillo–Fernandez, H Fluss
Holes Strasslach 18 L 6066 m SSS 72
       Thalkirchen 9 L 2528 m SSS 69
Fees   57DM
Loc   Strasslach: 10km from Munich
       Thalkirchen: Munich nr
       Camping Pl.
Mis   WE–only with member

Olching (1981)

8037 Olching, Feurstrasse 89
Tel   (08142) 15963
Mem   550
Pro   C Knauss, D Cabus,
       A Steinfurth
Holes 18 L 6021 m SSS 72
Fees   40DM (60DM)
Loc   Munich M'way A8. 25km to
       Stuttgart. B471 Dachau exit

Reit im Winkl (1985)

Birnbacherstr 34, 8216 Reit im Winkl
Tel   (08640) 8216
Mem   280
Pro   S Mühlbauer
Holes 9 L 5900 m SSS 70
Fees   30DM (40DM)
Loc   100km SE of Munich nr
       Austrian border

St Eurach LGC (1973)

Eurach 8, 8127 Iffeldorf
Tel   (08801) 1332
Mem   489
Pro   W John, D Praun
Holes 18 L 6509 m SSS 74
Fees   WD–80DM
Loc   40km S of Munich
Mis   WE–no guests allowed

Schloss Klingenburg– Günzburg (1979)

Schloss Klingenburg,
8876 Jettingen–Scheppach
Tel   (08225) 3030
Mem   500
Pro   H Bessner, B Herrmann
Holes 18 L 6065 m SSS 72
Fees   50DM (75DM)
Loc   40km W of Augsburg.
       5km from Stuttgart–Munich
       motorway, exit Burgau

Starnberg (1986)

Uneringerstr, 8130 Starnberg/Hadorf
Tel   (08151) 12157
Mem   650
Pro   C Kilian, R Postiglione,
       S Rohrsetzer
Holes 18 L 6344 m SSS 73
Fees   50DM (80DM)
Loc   30km S of Munich
Mis   WE–booking necessary

Tegernseer GC Bad Wiessee (1958)

Robognerhof 1, 8182 Bad Wiessee
Tel   (08022) 8769
Mem   545
Pro   B Pringle, R Buschert
Holes 18 L 5501 m SSS 69
Fees   70DM (90DM)
Loc   Bad Wiessee 1km.
       Munich 55km
Mis   Driving range–10DM

Tutzing (1983)

8132 Tutzing–Deixlfurt
Tel   (08158) 3600
Mem   600
Pro   D Hennings
Holes 18 L 6159 m SSS 72
Fees   60DM (80DM)
Loc   Starnberger See off B2

Werdenfels (1973)

Postfach 1345, 8100 Garmisch-
Partenkirchen
Tel   (08821) 2473
Mem   200
Pro   B Davidson
Holes 9 L 5896 m SSS 71
Fees   35DM (45DM)
Loc   2km S of Garmisch on B23,
       towards Farchant

Wörthsee (1982)

Gut Schluifeld, 8031 Wörthsee
Tel   (08153) 2425
Mem   720
Pro   J Mills, P Pemöller, J Biddle
Holes 18 L 6270 m SSS 73
Fees   50DM (75DM)
Loc   25km from Munich towards
       Lindau on B12
Mis   Pitch and putt

Nuremberg & North Bavaria

Am Reichswald

Postfach 140101, 8500 Nürnberg 14
Tel   (0911) 30 57 30
Pro   J Gornert (0911) 30 59 59
Holes 18 L 6345 m SSS 73
Fees   50DM (75DM)
Loc   Nuremberg 10km

Ansbach

8800 Ansbach, Neustadt 25
Tel   (0981) 5617
Pro   M Woodhouse
Holes 9 L 4200 m Par 66
Fees   30DM
Loc   Colmberg, Ansbach 15km

Bamberg (1973)

Postfach 1525, 8600 Bamberg
Tel   (09547) 7212/7109
Mem   490
Pro   I Donnelly (0951) 43973
Holes 18 L 6175 m SSS 72
Fees   40DM (60DM)
Loc   16km from Bamberg at
       Gut Leimershof

Bayerwald G & LC (1970)

Frauenwaldstr 2, 8392 Waldkirchen
Tel   (08582) 1040
Mem   420
Pro   S Case
Holes 9 L 6080 m SSS 72
Fees   35DM (45DM)
Loc   Waldkirchen, nr Passau

Coburg Schloss Tambach

8636 Weitramsdorf
Tel   (09567) 1212
Mem   265
Pro   P Spencer
Holes 9 L 6150 m SSS 72
Fees   30DM (40DM)
Loc   Tambach, 9km W of Coburg,
       opposite Animal Park

Donau GC Rassbach (1986)

Rassbach 8, 8391 Thyrnau–Passau
Tel   (08501) 1313
Mem   200
Pro   PG Leech
Holes 18 L 6400 m SSS 73
Fees   D–35DM (D–45DM)
Loc   10km E of Passau
Mis   Driving range–5DM

Erlangen (1977)

Postfach 1767, 8520 Erlangen
Tel   (09126) 5040
Mem   180
Pro   W Hachey

Holes 9 holes Par 63
Fees   25DM
Loc   Am Schlienhof, 15km E
       of Erlangen. 15km N of
       Nuremberg
Mis   Members and guests only

Frankische Schweitz (1974)

8553 Ebermannstadt, Postfach 11 10
Tel   (09194) 9228
Mem   230
Pro   K Messingschlager
Holes 9 L 5256 m Par 68
Fees   20DM
Loc   5km E of Ebermannstadt

Furth im Wald (1982)

Voithenberg 1, 8492 Furth im Wald
Tel   (09973) 1240
Mem   180
Pro   J Edgar
Holes 9 L 5903 m SSS 71
Fees   30DM (40DM)
Loc   70km NE of Regensburg

Herzogenaurach (1967)

Altenbergerstr 36, 8500 Nürnberg
Tel   (0911) 616183
Mem   210
Holes 9 L 6090 m SSS 72
Fees   10DM
Loc   Next to Herzo base
Mis   Guests with members only

Hof (1985)

Poststr 2, 8670 Hof
Tel   (09281) 43749
Mem   258
Pro   N Fourie
Holes 9 L 3105 m SSS 72
Fees   35DM (45DM)
Loc   5km NE of Hof

Ingolstadt (1978)

Spitzelmühle, Gerolfingerstr,
8070 Ingolstadt
Tel   (0841) 85778
Mem   320
Pro   J Pugh
Holes 9 L 5500 m SSS 69
Fees   35DM (50DM)
Loc   3km from Ingolstadt towards
       Gerolfing

Lichtenau–Weickershof (1980)

Weickershof 1, 8814 Lichtenau
Tel   (09827) 6907
Mem   438
Pro   F Piater, J Speed (09827) 7288
Holes 18 L 6120 m SSS 72
Fees   40DM (60DM)
Loc   10km E of Ansbach

Oberfranken (1966)

Postfach 1349, 8650 Kulmbach
Tel   (09221) 319
Mem   490
Pro   D Entwhistle, A Parker
       (09221) 1022
Holes 18 L 6152 m SSS 72
Fees   40DM (60DM)
Loc   Thurnau, 18km NW of
       Bayreuth. 14km SW of
       Kulmbach

Oberpfaelzer Wald GLC (1977)

Waldgasse 3B,
8461 Kemnath/Ödengrub
Tel   (09439) 466
Mem   380
Pro   D Holloway
Holes 18 L 5769 m SSS 70
Fees   40DM (50DM)
Loc   Kemnath bei Fuhrn.
       10km E of Schwarzenfeld
       towards Neunburg

Regensburg G & LC (1966)

8411 Altenthann
Tel   (09403) 505
Mem   580
Pro   R Maw, D McGuinness
Holes 18 L 5860 m SSS 72
Fees   50DM (75DM)
Loc   14km from Regensburg,
       near Walhalla

Rottaler (1972)

Bergstr 17, 8333 Linden
Tel   (08561) 2861
Mem   450
Pro   R Porter
Holes 18 L 6100 m SSS 72
Fees   40DM (50DM)
Loc   5km W of Pfarrkirchen on B388.
       120km E of München

Rusel G & LC (1981)

Postfach 1321, Werftstr 17, 8360
Deggendorf
Tel   (09920) 911
Mem   338
Pro   JA Taylor (09920) 1279
Holes 9 L 6070 m SSS 72
Fees   40DM (50DM)
Loc   Deggendorf 10km on Route 11
       towards Regen. Passau 45km
Mis   Driving range, pitch and putt

Sagmühle (1984)

Postfach 1124, 8394 Bad Griesbach
Tel   (08532) 2038
Mem   475
Pro   J O'Flynn, M Knauss, A Kraus,
       G Bundschuh

Holes 18 L 6217 m SSS 72
Fees 10DM (60DM)
Loc 25km SW of Passau

Schlossberg (1985)

Grünbach 4, 8386 Reisbach
Tel (08734) 7035
Mem 470
Pro P Haworth
Holes 18 L 6070 m SSS 72
Fees 35DM (45DM)
Loc Somershausen, 15km from
Dingolfing. 100km NE of
Munich off Route 11

Schmidmühlen G & CC (1970)

8450 Amberg, Lange Gasse 2
Tel (09621) 1846
Mem 105
Pro B Rowe
Holes 9 L 5328 m SSS 68
Fees 20DM (25DM)
Loc Between Regensburg and
Amberg

Stiftland (1982)

Ernestgrün 35, 8591 Neualbenreuth
Tel (09638) 1271/(09632) 1066
Mem 160
Pro P Dunn
Holes 9 L 6122 m SSS 72
Fees 30DM (40DM)
Loc 30km E of Marktredwitz.
50km N of Weiden

Rhineland

Bad Neuenahr G L C (1979)

Remagener Weg, 5483 Bad
Neuenhar–Ahrweiler
Tel (02641) 2325
Mem 590
Pro M Nickel
Holes 18 L 6060 m SSS 72
Fees 50DM (75DM)
Loc From north: M'way A61 to
exit Bad Neuenahr via Sinzig
and Lohrsdorf. From South:
M'way A61 exit Sinzig via
Lohrsdorf

Bergisch–Land

Siebeneickerst 386, 5600 Wuppertal
Tel (02053) 7177
Pro J Bauerdick, W Kothe
Holes 18 L 5920 m SSS 71
Fees 35DM (50DM)
Loc Wuppertal–Elberfeld 8km
Mis WE–only with member.
Driving range

Bielefeld (1977)

Dornbergerstrasse 375,
4800 Bielefeld–Hoberge 1
Tel (0521) 105103
Mem 438
Pro HW Kahre (0521) 104450
Holes 13 holes SSS 72
Fees 30DM
Mis WE–only with member

Bochum (1982)

Im Mailan 127, 4630 Bochum
Tel (0234) 799832
Pro E Newgas
Holes 9 L 5900 m SSS 71
Fees 30DM (40DM)
Loc Bochum–Stiepel

Bonn–Godesberg (1960)

Dechant–Heimbachstr 16,
5300 Bonn 2
Tel (0228) 344003 (Clubhouse)
(0228) 317494 (Sec)
Mem 600
Pro K Riechart, KP Vollrach
Holes 18 L 5900 m Par 71
Fees 35DM (45DM)
Loc Oberbachem, 4km from Bad
Godesberg

Burg Overbach (1984)

Postfach 1213, 5203 Much
Tel (02245) 5550
Mem 700
Pro R Hauser, T Menne,
N Remmel
Holes 18 L 6056 m SSS 72
Fees 40DM (60DM)
Loc 45km from Köln towards Olpe,
off A4

Dortmund (1956)

4600 Dortmund–Reichsmark,
Reichsmarkstr 12
Tel (0231) 774133/774609
Mem 650
Pro V Knörnschild, B Wargel,
F Schneider
Holes 18 L 6240 m SSS 73
Fees 35DM
Loc Dortmund 8km
Mis WE–only with member

Düsseldorf (1961)

Rommerljansweg 12, 4030 Ratingen
Tel Ratingen 81092
Mem 900
Pro J Kupitz, D Hollbach,
A Piater
Holes 18 L 5905 m SSS 71
Fees 50DM (60DM)
Loc Düsseldorf 11km

Düsseldorf/Hösel

Grunerstr 13, 4000 Düsseldorf 1
Tel (0211) 631171/(02102) 68629
Mem 550
Pro F Eckl, M Pyatt
Holes 18 L 6160 m SSS 72
Fees 25DM (35DM)
Loc Hösel, 15km NE of Düsseldorf

Emstal (1977)

Gut Beversundern, Postfach 1431,
4450 Lingen
Tel (0591) 63837
Mem 280
Pro D Bryan
Holes 9 L 5320 m SSS 68
Fees 30DM (40DM)
Loc 3km N of Lingen, Route B70
to Meppen

Essen Haus Oefte (1959)

Laupendahler Landstr, 4300 Essen
Tel (02054) 83911
Mem 650
Pro R Sommer (02054) 84722
Holes 18 L 6100 m SSS 72
Fees 50DM (60DM)
Loc Essen 14km

Essen–Heidhausen (1970)

4300 Essen 16,
Preutenborbeckstrasse 36
Tel (0201) 404111
Mem 780
Pro G Kothe, J McGarva
Holes 18 L 5937 m SSS 71
Fees 35DM (50DM)
Loc Essen 10km on B224, towards
Velbert

Golfriege des Etuf (1962)

Freiherr–vom–Stein Str 92a, 4300
Essen 1
Tel (0201) 441426
Mem 360
Pro U Knappmann
Holes 9 L 4580 m SSS 64
Fees 30DM (40DM)
Loc 6km S of Essen

Hubbelrath (1961)

Bergische Landstrasse 700,
4000 Dusseldorf 12
Tel (02104) 72178/71848
Mem 1417
Pro G Danz, HP Ranft, F
Willemsen,
S Eckrodt, R Noélle, M
Brock
Holes East 18 L 6042 m SSS 72
West 18 L 4325 m SSS 63
Fees 60DM (90DM)
Loc Hubbelrath, 13km E of
Düsseldorf, on Route B7

Issum–Niederrhein (1973)

4174 Issum 1, Pauenweg 68
Tel   (02835) 3626
Mem   645
Pro   S Tomkinson, P Grunwell
Holes   18 L 5862 m SSS 71
Fees   35DM (50DM)
Loc   10km E of Geldern

Juliana (1979)

Frielinghausen 1, 4322 Sprockhövel
Tel   (0202) 647070
        Fax 0202 649891
Mem   500
Pro   G Hillier, M Neumann,
        D Proplesch, F Scheffer
Holes   18 L 6100 m SSS 71
Fees   40DM (50DM)
Loc   30km E of Düsseldorf

Köln G & LC

Golfplatz 2, 5060 Bergisch Gladbach 1
Tel   (02204) 63114/63138
Mem   630
Pro   K Marx, A Stein
Holes   18 L 6045 m Par 72
Fees   50DM (75DM)
Loc   Cologne 15km

Köln–Marienburger (1949)

Schillingsrotter Weg, 5000 Köln 51
Tel   (0221) 384053
Mem   300
Pro   H Becker
Holes   9 L 3075 m SSS 72
Fees   40DM (50DM)
Loc   In Cologne

Krefeld (1930)

Eltweg 2, 4150 Krefeld 12
Tel   (02151) 570071/72
Mem   600
Pro   J Wilkinson, N Brunyard
Holes   18 L 6040 m SSS 72
Fees   70DM (80DM)
Loc   7km SE of Krefeld.
        Düsseldorf 16km

Laarbruch GC (RAF) (1962)

Laarbruch, BFPO 43
Tel   Weeze 895441
Mem   200
Holes   9 L 4471 yds SSS 62
Fees   20DM
Loc   Laarbruch 9 British Forces
Mis   Access to course may be
        restricted

Märkischer Hagen (1964)

5800 Hagen, Tiefendorferstr 48
Tel   (02334) 51778
Mem   400
Pro   D Giese, R Stehmans
Holes   9 L 6114 m SSS 72
Fees   25DM (40DM)
Loc   Hagen–Berchum

Münster–Wilkinghege (1963)

Steinfurterstr 448, 4400 Münster
Tel   (0251) 211201
Mem   700
Pro   CB Westerman, P Phillips
Holes   18 L 5880 m SSS 71
Fees   40DM (50DM)
Loc   Münster 2km

Münsterland (1950)

Bagno, 4430 Steinfurt
Tel   (02551) 5178
Mem   265
Pro   C Leader
Holes   9 L 4834 m Par 66
Fees   30DM (35DM)
Loc   Burgsteinfurt 2km

Niederrheinischer (1956)

4100 Duisburg 28 (Bucholz)
Grossenbaumer Allee 240
Tel   (0203) 721469
Mem   402
Pro   J Dennison
Holes   9 L 6090 m SSS 72
Fees   35DM (45DM)
Loc   Duisburg 8km

Nordkirchen

4717 Nordkirchen, Golfplatz 6
Tel   (02596) 2495
Mem   340
Pro   A Rössler
Holes   9 L 6200 m SSS 72
Fees   30DM (40DM)
Loc   Münster 30km

Osnabrück (1955)

Karmannstrasse 1, 4500 Osnabrück
Tel   (05402) 636
Mem   300
Pro   H Theeuwen
Holes   18 L 5881 m Par 71
Fees   40DM (50DM)
Loc   Osnabrück 13km

RAF Germany (1956)

RAF Brüggen, BFPO 25
Tel   (02163) 88 463/5207
Mem   800
Pro   G Cowley
Holes   18 L 6522 yds SSS 71
Fees   25DM
Loc   On B230, 1km from Dutch/
        German border. 25km W of
        Mönchengladbach

RAF Gütersloh

RAF Gütersloh, BFPO 47
Tel   (05241) 26021 (Ext 426)
Mem   400
Holes   9 L 5761 yds SSS 68
Fees   12DM
Loc   5km W of Gütersloh

RAF Wildenrath

BFPO 42
Tel   (02432) 18 5440
Mem   300 Service personnel
Holes   9 L 4335 yds SSS 61
Fees   10DM
Loc   RAF Wildenrath

Rhein Sieg (1971)

5202 Hennef, Postfach 1216
Tel   (02242) 6501/3047
Mem   280
Pro   H Knopp, D MacLauchlan
Holes   18 L 6070 m Par 72
Fees   30DM (40DM)
Loc   Hennef 3km

Royal Artillery & Dortmund Garrison (1969)

Napier Barracks, BFPO 20
Tel   Dortmund 202551
Mem   420
Holes   18 L 5338 m SSS 70
Fees   15DM (20DM)
Loc   Dortmund Brackel
Mis   Not open to public; visitors
        by prior arrangement only

Sauerland (1958)

Falkenhorst 15, 5760 Arnsberg 1
Tel   (02932) 43 14
Mem   320
Pro   T Croft
Holes   9 L 5874 m SSS 71
Fees   30DM (35DM)
Loc   Nr Herdringen
Mis   Driving range

Schloss Georghausen (1962)

Georghausen 8, 5253 Lindlar–
Hommerich
Tel   (02207) 4938
Mem   730
Pro   G Kessler, G Baum, J Kaynig
Holes   18 L 6045 m SSS 72
Fees   45DM (60DM)
Loc   30km E of Cologne

Schloss Myllendonk (1964)

Myllendonkerstr 113,
4052 Korschenbroich 1
Tel   (02161) 641049
Mem   650
Pro   G Kerkman, I Clegg
Holes   18 L 6120 m SSS 72
Fees   60DM (80DM)
Loc   Korschenbroich, 5km E of
        Mönchengladbach

Schmitzhof (1975)

Arsbeckerstr 160, 5144 Wegberg
Tel   (02436) 479
Mem   650
Pro   E Theeuwen
Holes   18 L 6310 m SSS 73

Fees   30DM (50DM)
Loc   20km SW of Mönchengladbach, in Wegberg–Merbeck

Siegen–Olpe (1966)

5900 Siegen, Bahnhofstr 4
Tel   (0271) 5831/(02762) 7589
Mem   365
Pro   K Hahn
Holes   9 L 5724 m SSS 70
Fees   30DM (35DM)
Loc   Siegen 15km. Cologne 80km
Mis   WE–telephone first

Tecklenburger Land (1971)

Tel   (05455) 1035
Mem   286
Pro   JP Laarman
Holes   9 L 6160 m SSS 72
Fees   30DM (40DM)
Loc   1¹/₂ km W of Autobahn, exit Lengerich/Ibbenbüren. Osnabrück 20km

Varmert (1977)

5883 Kierspe–Varmert
Tel   (02269) 7299
Mem   380
Pro   G Thomas, S Bradbury, T Pitts
Holes   9 L 6048 m SSS 72
Fees   25DM (35DM)
Loc   22km S of Ludenscheid. 50km NE of Cologne

Velper G & CC (1981)

Heinrich–Hensiekstr 1,
4535 Westerkappeln–Velpe
Tel   (05456) 820
Mem   300
Pro   SL Walker (05456) 287
Holes   9 L 5782 m SSS 70
Fees   20DM (30DM)
Loc   8km W of Osnabrück

Vestischer Recklinghausen (1974)

4350 Recklinghausen
Tel   (02361) 26520
Mem   650
Pro   U Lechtermann, E Schilling, W Bollert
Holes   18 L 6111 m SSS 72
Fees   35DM (50DM)
Loc   Nr Loemühle Airport
Mis   Driving range

Waldbrunnen (1983)

Brunnenstr 7, 5461 Windhagen
Tel   (02645) 15621
Mem   312
Pro   M Butzkies
Holes   9 L 4816 m SSS 66
Fees   25DM (35DM)
Loc   Bad Honnef 8km

Warendorf (1987)

Vohren 41, 4410 Warendorf
Tel   (02586) 1792
Holes   9 L 6160 m SSS 72
Fees   30DM (50DM)
Loc   35km from Münster
Mis   Driving range

Wasserburg Anholt (1972)

Am Schloss 3, 4294 Isselburg
Tel   (02874) 3444
Mem   400
Pro   F di Matteo
Holes   18 L 6141 m SSS 72
Fees   35DM D–50DM
        (45DM D–60DM)
Loc   Parkhotel, Wasserburg Anholt. Bocholt 15km

Werl (1973)

Unnaerstr 23, 4760 Werl
Tel   (02377) 6307
Mem   300
Pro   A Stein
Holes   9 L 4640 m SSS 66
Fees   25DM (30DM)
Loc   30km E of Dortmund

Westerwald (1979)

Postfach 1231, 5238 Hachenburg
Pro   H–J Labonte (02620) 2230
Holes   9 holes SSS 72
Fees   30DM (40DM)
Loc   Hachenburg, 60km E of Bonn

Westfälischer Gütersloh

4830 Gütersloh
Tel   (05244) 2340
Mem   600
Pro   M Schwichtenberg
Holes   18 L 6175 m SSS 72
Fees   30DM (60DM)
Loc   Gütersloh 6km

Stuttgart & South West

Algäuer G & LC (1984)

8942 Ottobeuren, Hofgut Boschach
Tel   (08332) 1310
Mem   530
Pro   KH Marx, M Chesters
Holes   18 L 6215 m SSS 72
Fees   40DM (50DM)
Loc   Ottobeuren 2km. Kempten 20km

Bad Herrenalb–Bernbach

7506 Bad Herrenalb
Tel   (07083) 8898
Mem   400
Pro   G Westen, D Randolf
Holes   9 L 5200 m SSS 68
Fees   30DM (35DM)
Loc   Bad Herrenalb 1km

Baden–Baden (1901)

Fremersbergstrasse 127,
Baden–Baden
Tel   (07221) 23579
Mem   400
Pro   E Totzke
Holes   18 L 4575 m Par 64
Fees   40DM (50DM) W–200DM
Loc   Baden–Baden ¹/₂ km

Baden–Hills (1982)

Postfach 1153, 7558 Bischweier
Tel   (07222) 42274
Pro   R Walker
Holes   18 L 5672 m Par 72
Fees   20DM (30DM)
Loc   20km S of Rastatt
Mis   Booking and handicap certificate required

Bodensee Weissensberg (1986)

Lampertsweiler 51,
8995 Weissensberg
Tel   (08389) 89190
        Fax 08389 89191
Pro   A Gauld
Holes   18 L 6112 m SSS 71
Fees   65DM (85DM)
Loc   Lindau 5km
Mis   Handicap certificate required

Freiburg (1970)

7815 Kirchzarten, Krüttweg 1
Tel   (07661) 5569
Mem   510
Pro   P Weggenmann
Holes   18 L 6100 m SSS 72
Fees   45DM (55DM)
Loc   Freiburg–Kappel/Kirchzarten. 7km SE of Freiburg on Route L126b

Freudenstadt (1929)

Postfach 322, 7290 Freudenstadt
Tel   (07441) 3060
Mem   400
Pro   G Fischer
Holes   9 L 5857 m SSS 71
Fees   35DM (55DM)
Loc   Freudenstadt 1km
Mis   Open Apr–Oct

Gütermann Gutach (1924)

7809 Gutach/Breisgau
Tel   (07681) 21243
Mem   300
Pro   I Stewart
Holes   9 L 5280 m SSS 68
Fees   35DM (50DM)
Loc   Freiburg 20km

Haghof G & LC (1983)

Alfdorf 2, 7077 Haghof
Tel   (07182) 3040
Pro   B Reilly
Holes   9 L 2932 m SSS 71
Fees   30DM

For explanation of abbreviations, see page 460.

Loc   Nr Welzheim, 50km NE of
      Stuttgart
Mis   WE–no visitors

Hechingen–Hohenzollern (1955)

Golfplatz Hagelwasen, Hechingen
Tel   (07471) 2600
Mem   380
Pro   K Schieban, P Eisenhut
Holes 9 SSS 70
Fees 35DM
Loc   Hechingen 2km
Mis   WE–only with member

Heilbronn–Hohenlohe (1964)

Postfach 1341, 7107 Neckarsulm
Tel   (07941) 78 86
Mem   380
Pro   B Amara
Holes 9 L 5890 m SSS 71
Fees 40DM (60DM)
Loc   Friedrichsruhe–Öhringen

Hochstatt Härtsfeld–Ries (1981)

7086 Neresheim
Tel   (07326) 79 79?
Pro   P Smith
Holes 9 L 6170 m SSS 72
Fees 25DM (30DM)
Loc   30km E of Heidenheim.
      Munich 100km

Hohenstauffen (1959)

Im Holderbrett 9, 7311 Hochdorf
Tel   (07162) 27171/20050
Mem   160
Pro   R Miller
Holes 9 L 6540 yds SSS 72
Fees 35DM (45DM)
Loc   Donzdorf 15km

Konstanz (1965)

7753 Allensbach 3, Langenrain,
Kargegg
Tel   (07533) 5124
Mem   617
Pro   M Bingger, D Geary
Holes 18 L 6058 m SSS 72
Fees 50DM (70DM)
Loc   15km from Konstanz towards
      Bodmann on route B219
Mis   Members of recognised golf
      clubs only

Lindau–Bad Schachen (1954)

Am Schönbühl 5,
8990 Lindau/Bodensee
Tel   (08382) 78090
Mem   750

Pro   R Richardson, H Kersting,
      B Wargel
Holes 18 L 5690 m SSS 70
Fees 50DM (70DM)
Loc   Lindau 1 1/2 km

Markgräflerland

Marktplatz 12, 7850 Lörrach
Tel   (07621) 403510/660423
Mem   360
Pro   I Martin
Holes 9 L 6100 m SSS 72
Fees 40DM (50DM)
Loc   Kandern, 10km from Lörrach.
      Basle 14km

Oberschwaben–Bad Waldsee ((1968)

7967 Bad Waldsee, Hofgut
Hopfenweiler
Tel   (07524) 5900
Mem   520
Pro   W Jersombeck,
      T Schinnenburg
Holes 18 L 6148 m SSS 72
Fees 45DM (60DM)
Loc   Hofgut Hopfenweiler, nr B30

Oberstdorf

8980 Oberstdorf
Tel   (08322) 2895
Mem   304
Pro   B Rowe
Holes 9 L 2795 m Par 70
Fees 40DM (55DM)
Loc   Oberstdorf 3km. 10km S of
      Sonthofen, nr Austrian border

Oeschberghof L & GC (1976)

Golfplatz 1, 7710 Donaueschingen
Tel   (771) 84525
Mem   500
Pro   T Gerhardt, B Birch,
      S Hilton, D Enters
Holes 18 L 6570 m SSS 74
Fees 60DM (100DM)
Loc   Stuttgart/Zurich airports 1hr
Mis   Handicap certificate required

Ortenau (1981)

7630 Lahr–Reichenbach, Postfach 1469
Tel   (07821) 77217
Mem   320
Pro   PP Jarvis
Holes 9 L 5450 m SSS 70
Fees 20DM (30DM)
Loc   35km SE of Strasbourg.
      50km N of Freiburg

Rhein Badenweiler (1971)

7847 Badenweiler
Tel   (07632) 5031
Mem   450
Pro   JF Halliwell

Holes 18 L 6134 m SSS 72
Fees 40DM (60DM)
Loc   Badenweiler 16km

Rickenbach (1980)

7884 Rickenbach, Postfach 1041
Tel   (07765) 8880
Mem   350
Pro   CR Dew
Holes 9 L 2749 m Par 69
Fees 30DM (50DM)
Loc   Bad Sackingen, 30km E of
      Basle

Schloss Liebenstein G & LC (1982)

Postfach 27, 7129 Neckarwestheim
Tel   (07133) 16019
Mem   800
Pro   W Kretschy, R Hartzheim
Holes 18 L 5847 m SSS 71
Fees 40DM (50DM)
Loc   Stuttgart 35km. Heilbronn
      20km

Schloss Weitenburg (1984)

Sommerhalde 11, 7245 Starzach–Sulzau
Tel   (07472) 8061
Mem   500
Pro   P Ridley, G Pottage, D Kay
Holes 18 L 6069 m SSS 72
      9 hole course
Fees 18 hole:50DM (70DM)
      9 hole:25DM (30DM)
Loc   50km SW of Stuttgart in Neckar
      Valley
Mis   Driving range

Sonnenalp (1976)

Hotel Sonnenalp, 8972 Ofterschwang
Tel   (08321) 7276 (Sec)
      (08321) 720 (Hotel)
Mem   180
Pro   B Kennedy, A MacDonald,
      D Lamplough
Holes 18 L 6040 m SSS 72
Fees 60DM (75DM) Discount for
      hotel guests
Loc   Sonthofen 4km. Fischen 3km

Stuttgarter Neckartal (1974)

Aldingerstr, Gebaudt 975,
7140 Ludwigsburg–Pattonville
Tel   (07141) 871319
Mem   265
Holes 18 L 6084 m SSS 72
Fees 50DM
Loc   Between Stuttgart and
      Ludwigsburg, near
      Kornwestheim
Mis   WE–only with member

Stuttgarter Solitude (1927)

7256 Monsheim
Tel   (07044) 6909
Mem   640
Pro   F Lengsfeld
Holes   18 L 6040 m SSS 72
Fees   50DM (70DM)
Loc   Stuttgart 25km

Ulm (1963)

Postfach 4068, 7900 Ulm
Tel   (0731) 183214
Mem   315
Pro   F Piater
Holes   9 L 6170 m Par 72
Fees   25DM (40DM)
Loc   15km S of Ulm between
        Illerkirchberg and Illerrieden

Waldegg–Wiggensbach (1988)

Hof Waldegg, 8961 Wiggensbach
Tel   (08370) 733
Mem   365
Pro   A Koller, J Taylor
Holes   18 4757 m SSS 65
Fees   40DM (50DM)
Loc   Wiggensbach, 10km W of
        Kempten, nr Swiss/Austrian
        border

Greece

Afantou (1973)

Afantou, Rhodes
Tel   (0241) 51255/51256
Mem   96
Pro   G Sotiropoulous,
        V Anasstassiou
Holes   18 L 6060 m SSS 72
Fees   2000dra (10000dra)
Loc   20km S of Rhodes town

Corfu (1972)

PO Box 71, Corfu
Tel   (0661) 94220/1
Mem   100
Pro   D Crawley
Holes   18 L 6300 m SSS 72
Fees   D–4000dra
Loc   Ermones Bay, 16km W of
        Corfu town

Glyfada (1963)

PO Box 70116 Glyfada, Athens
Tel   (894) 6820/(893) 1721
Mem   1300
Pro   J Sotiropoulos
Holes   18 L 6189 m SSS 72
Fees   3000dra (5000dra)
Loc   12km S of Athens

Porto Carras G & CC (1979)

Porto Carras, Halkidiki
Tel   (0375) 71381/71221
Pro   Mrs P Andrade
Holes   18 L 6086 m SSS 72
Fees   D–2000dra W–10000dra
Loc   Sithonia Peninsula, 100km SE
        of Thessaloniki

Iceland

Akureyri (1935)

PO Box 896, 602 Akureyri
Tel   (9) 622974
Mem   380
Pro   DG Barnwell (9) 623846
Holes   18 L 5851 m SSS 72
Fees   £15
Loc   1km from Akureyri (N coast)
Mis   World's most northern 18–hole
        course. Home of the Arctic
        Open

Borgarness (1973)

PO Box 112, 310 Borgarnes
Tel   (95) 7663
Mem   60
Holes   18 L 5260 m SSS 69
        9 L 2630 m SSS 69
Fees   300 Ikr
Loc   5km from Borgarnes (W coast)

Éskifjardar (1976)

735 Éskifirdi
Mem   50
Holes   9 L 4412 m SSS 66
Fees   D–800 Ikr
Loc   3km W of Éskifjördur (E coast)

Hellu (1974)

Austurveg 1, Huolsvelli
Tel   8166
Mem   74
Holes   9 L 3886 m SSS 61
Fees   100 Ikr
Loc   Huolsvelli (S coast)

Hornafjardar

Hornafirdi
Tel   (97) 8030
Mem   44
Holes   9 L 3610 m SSS 63
Fees   200 Ikr
Loc   Hofn (SE coast)

Húsavíkur

PO Box 23, Kötlum, 640 Húsavík
Tel   (96) 41000
Mem   90
Holes   9 L 2686 m SSS 70

Fees   800 Ikr
Loc   2km from Húsavík (N coast)
Mis   Open June–Sept

Ísafjardar (1978)

PO Box 367, Ísafjördur
Tel   (94) 3035 (Captain)
Mem   75
Holes   9 L 4860 m SSS 67
Fees   D–500 Ikr 1988 prices
Loc   3km W of Ísafjördur (NW coast)
Mis   WE–course often closed for
        comps

Jökull (1973)

Vallholt 15, 355 Ólafsvík
Tel   (354) 93 61198
Mem   48
Holes   9 L 4580 m SSS 65
Fees   D–1000kr
Loc   5km SE of Ólafsvík (W coast)

Keilir (1967)

Hvaleyri, Hafnarfjördur
Tel   53360
Mem   400
Pro   T Asgeirsson.
Holes   18 L 5117 m SSS 68
Fees   1000 Ikr
Loc   Hafnarfjördur, 10km S of
        Reykjavik (SW coast)

Leynir (1965)

PO Box 9, Akranes
Tel   (93) 12711
Mem   160
Holes   9 L 2640 m SSS 70
Fees   800 Ikr
Loc   2km from Akranes (SW coast)

Ness (1964)

PO Box 66, 172 Seltjarnes
Tel   611930
Mem   185
Pro   M Knipe
Holes   9 L 4986 m SSS 68
Fees   1300 Ikr
Loc   3km W of Reykjavík

Ólafsfjardar (1967)

Ólafsfjördur
Mem   25
Holes   9 L 4652 m SSS 65
Loc   Ólafsfjördur (N coast)

Reykjavíkur (1934)

Grafarholti, Box 4071,
124 Reykjavík
Tel   84735
Mem   816
Pro   J Drummond 82815
Holes   18 L 5956 m SSS 70
Fees   1000 Ikr
Loc   8km E of Reykjavík

For explanation of abbreviations, see page 460.

Saudárkróks (1970)

Saudárkrókur
Tel   (95) 35075
Mem   60
Holes   9 L 5708 m SSS 71
Fees   1000 Ikr
Loc   1¹/₂ km W of Saudárkrókur
(N coast)

Selfoss (1971)

Selfoss
Mem   48
Holes   9 L 5070 m SSS 69
Loc   Selfoss (SW coast)

Siglufjardar (1970)

Siglufjördur
Mem   35
Holes   9 L 4950 m SSS 66
Loc   Siglufjördur (N coast)

Sudurnesja (1964)

PO Box 112, 230 Keflavik
Tel   (92) 14100
Mem   165
Holes   18 L 5961 m SSS 73
Loc   N of Keflavik (SW coast).
Airport 5km
Mis   Links course

Vestmannaeyja (1938)

Tel   12363
Mem   221
Pro   P Grünwell
Holes   9 L 2881 m SSS 69
Fees   1000 Ikr
Loc   2km W of town centre.
Large island off S coast.
20 min flight from Reykjavík.

Italy

Como/Milan/ Bergamo

Barlassina CC (1952)

Via Privata Golf 42,
20030 Birago di Camnago (MI)
Tel   (0362) 560621/2/3
Mem   300
Pro   N Rendina, S Betti
Holes   18 L 6073 m SSS 72
Fees   70000L (100.000L)
Loc   22km N of Milan

Bergamo L'Albenza (1960)

Via Longoni 12,
24030 Almenno San Bartolomeo
Tel   (035) 640028/640707
Mem   480
Pro   S Locatelli, M Rendina,
F Ripamonti, C Rocca
Holes   18 L 6198 m SSS 72
9 L 2962 m SSS 36
Fees   40000L (60000L)
Loc   Bergamo 13km. Milan 45km

Carimate (1962)

Via Airoldi, 22060 Carimate
Tel   (031) 790226
Mem   500
Pro   E Songia, M Frigerio, B Molteni
Holes   18 L 5982 m SSS 71
Fees   40000L (60000L)
Loc   15km S of Como.
27km N of Milan

Franciacorta

Loc Castagnola, 25040 Corte Franca
Tel   (030) 984167
Pro   R Napoleoni
Holes   18 L 6060 m SSS 72
9 L 1150 m Par 72
Loc   Nigoline, 25km E of Bergamo

Lanzo Intelvi (1962)

22024 Lanzo Intelvi (CO)
Tel   (031) 840169
Mem   188
Pro   G Frigerio
Holes   9 L 2438 m SSS 66
Fees   25000L (50000L)
Loc   32km NW of Como
Mis   Open May–Oct

Menaggio & Cadenabbia (1907)

Via Golf 12, 22010 Grandola
E Uniti (CO)
Tel   (0344) 32103/31564
Mem   260
Pro   G Delfino
Holes   18 L 5277 m SSS 69
Fees   40000L (60000L)
Loc   5km W of Menaggio.
30km N of Como

Milano (1928)

20052 Parco di Monza (MI)
Tel   (039) 303081/303082
Mem   1050
Pro   G Grappasonni (039) 304561
Holes   18 L 6239 m SSS 73
9 L 2976 m SSS 36
Fees   50000L (60000L)
Loc   6km N of Monza.
18km NE of Milan

Molinetto CC

SS Padana Superiore 11,
20063 Cernusco sul Naviglio (MI)
Tel   (02) 9238500/9249373
Pro   F Perini, M Taricone,
B Giordano
Holes   18 L 6010 m Par 72
Fees   40000L (50000L)
Loc   Cernusco, 10km E of Milan
Mis   Driving range

Monticello (1975)

Via Volta 4, 22070 Cassina Rizzardi
Tel   (031) 928055
Mem   1200
Pro   A Croce, V Damonte,
E Bianchi, A Schiroli,
A Ferlito
Holes   18 L 6413 m SSS 72
18 L 6056 m SSS 72
Fees   40000L (70000L)
Loc   10km SE of Como

La Pinetina (1971)

Via al Golf 4, 22070 Appiano Gentile
Tel   (031) 933202
Mem   420
Pro   M Sabbatino
Holes   18 L 6001 m SSS 71
Fees   35000L (50000L)
Loc   12km SW of Como

La Rossera (1970)

Via Montebello 4, 24060 Chiuduno
Tel   (035) 838600
Mem   230
Pro   R Giglioni, G Watson
Holes   9 L 2510 m SSS 68
Fees   20000L (40000L)
Loc   18km SE of Bergamo

Le Rovedine (1978)

Public
Via C Marx, 20090 Noverasco di
Opera (MI)
Tel   (02) 5242730
Mem   450
Pro   R Benassi, L Marsala,
L Ghirardo, G Veronelli
Holes   9 L 2890 m SSS 71
Fees   17500L (21500L)
Loc   4km S of Milan
Mis   Public course

Royal Sant'Anna (1978)

22040 Annone di Brianza (CO)
Tel   (0341) 577551
Holes   9 L 5370 m SSS 69
Fees   25000L (30000L)
Loc   15km SE of Como. Milano 40km

Vigevano "Santa Martretta" (1974)

Via Chiola 49, 27029 Vigevano (PV)
Tel   (0381) 76872
Mem   208
Pro   A Zito
Holes   9 L 5880 m Par 72
Fees   25000L (40000L)
Loc   25km SE of Novara.
        35km SW of Milan

Villa D'Este (1926)

Via Cantù 13, 22030 Montorfano (CO)
Tel   (031) 200200
Mem   400
Pro   GC Frigerio, P Molteni,
        G Ciprandi
Holes   18 L 5787 m SSS 71
Fees   50000L (70000L)
Loc   Montorfano, 7km SE of Como
Mis   Driving range

Zoate

20067 Zoate di Tribiano (MI)
Tel   (02) 90632183/90631861
Pro   L Grappasoni, S Zerega
Holes   18 L 6116 m Par 72
Loc   Zoate, 17km SE of Milan

Elba

Acquabona

57037 Portoferraio, Isola di Elba (LI)
Tel   (0565) 940066
Mem   220
Pro   G Ciprandi, M Barbi
Holes   9 L 5144 m SSS 67
Fees   20000–40000L
Loc   5km NW of Porto Azzurro

Emilia Romagna
(including Pisa, Bologna & Cremona)

Adriatic GC Cervia (1985)

Via Ielenia Gora, 48016 Milano Marittima
Tel   (0544) 992786
Mem   440
Pro   R Paris
Holes   18 L 6275 m SSS 72
Fees   42000L (55000L)
Loc   20km SE of Ravenna

Bologna (1959)

Via Sabatini 69, 40050 Monte San Pietro
Tel   (051) 969100
Mem   450
Pro   B Ghezzo, C Ferrari

Holes   18 L 6103 m SSS 72
Fees   45000L (55000L)
Loc   20km W of Bologna
Mis   Driving range

Croara (1977)

29010 Croara di Gazzola
Tel   (0523) 977105/977148
Mem   400
Pro   G Turrini, E Vergari,
        P de Ascentiis
Holes   18 L 6065 m SSS 72
Fees   30000L (50000L)
Loc   16km SW of Piacenza.
        84km SE of Milan

Marigola

Via Vallata 5, 19032 Lerici (SP)
Tel   (0187) 970193
Mem   60
Pro   CA Le Chevallier
Holes   9 L 2120 m Par 54
Loc   6km SE of La Spezia

La Rocca (1985)

Via Campi 8, 43038 Sala Baganza
Tel   (0521) 834037
Mem   300
Pro   R Bolognesi
Holes   9 L 2891 m SSS 70
Fees   £10 (£14)
Loc   8km S of Parma

Gulf of Genoa

Degli Ulivi (1932)

Via Campo Golf 59, 18038 San Remo
Tel   (0184) 557093/71945
Mem   450
Pro   M Bianco, G Ammirati,
        G de Andreis, M Bianco
Holes   18 L 5230 m SSS 67
Fees   40000L (60000L)
Loc   5km N of San Remo

Garlenda (1965)

Via Golf 7, 17030 Garlenda
Tel   (0182) 580012. Fax 580561
Mem   600 130(L) 85(J)
Pro   F Zanini, F Picco, G Girardi
Holes   18 L 5973 m SSS 71
Fees   50000L (75000L)
        5D–180000L
Loc   15km N of Alassio

Pineta di Arenzano

Piazza del Golf, 16011 Arenzano (GE)
Tel   (010) 9111817
Mem   550
Pro   S Gori, A Mori, V Mori
Holes   9 L 5527 m SSS 70
Fees   40000L (60000L)
Loc   Arenzano Pineta, 20km W of Genoa

Rapallo (1930)

Via Mameli 377, 16035 Rapallo (GE)
Tel   (0185) 50210/67197
        Fax 0185 50210
Mem   778
Pro   M Canessa, M Erbisti, C Costa,
        A Brizzolari, M Avanzino,
        A Schiaffino
Holes   18 L 5694 m SSS 70
Fees   60000L (Sat–80000L)
Loc   25km SE of Genoa. Nr A12
        motorway exit Rapallo

Lake Garda & Dolomites

Asiago (1967)

Via Meltar 2,36012 Asiago
Tel   (0424) 462721
Mem   492
Pro   B Antonello
Holes   9 L 2948 m SSS 71
Fees   50000L
Loc   3km N of Asiago.
        50km N of Vicenza
Mis   Open Jun–Oct

Bogliaco (1912)

Via Golf 11, 25088 Toscolano Maderno
Tel   (0365) 643006
Mem   300
Pro   L Tavernini
Holes   9 L 2572 m SSS 67
Fees   35000L (50000L)
Loc   Lake Garda, 40km NE of Brescia
Mis   Driving range

Campo Carlo Magno (1922)

c/o Golf Hotel, Madonna di Campiglio
Tel   (0465) 41003
Mem   45
Pro   A Silva
Holes   9 L 4992 m SSS 68
Fees   D–8000L
Loc   Madonna di Campiglio 1km.
        74km NW of Trento
Mis   Open Jul–Sept

Gardagolf (1985)

Via Angelo Omodeo 2, 25080 Soiano Del Lago (BS)
Tel   (0365) 674707 (Sec)
Mem   380
Pro   F Maestroni, F Ghezzo,
        B Maestroni
Holes   18 L 6505 m SSS 74
        9 L 2415 m Par 34
Fees   40000L (50000L)
Loc   Lake Garda, 30km NE of Brescia
Mis   Driving range

For explanation of abbreviations, see page 460.

Verona (1963)

Ca' del Sale 15,
37066 Sommacampagna
Tel   (045) 510060
Mem   480
Pro   E Ridolfi, M Bolognesi
Holes 18 L 6307 m SSS 72
Fees   40000L (50000L)
Loc   7km W of Verona

Naples & South

Napoli

Via Campiglione 11,
80072 Arco Felice (NA)
Tel   (081) 8674296
Holes 9 L 4770 m 333 00
Fees   30000L (35000L)
Loc   Pozzuoli, 10km W of Naples
Mis   Guests with members only.

Porto d'Orra (1977)

PB 102, 88063 Catanzaro Lido
Tel   (0961) 791045
Mem   141
Pro   L de Gori
Holes 9 L 2492 m SSS 70
Fees   25000L
Loc   9km N of Catanzaro Lido

Riva dei Tessali (1971)

74011 Castellaneta
Tel   (099) 6439251
Mem   147
Pro   B Cosenza
Holes 18 L 5960 m SSS 71
Fees   42000L
Loc   34km SW of Taranto

Rome

Castelgandolfo (1987)

Via S Spirito 13, 00040 Castelgandolfo
Tel   9312301/9313084
Mem   390
Pro   A Venier, Z Martinez
Holes 18 L 6025 m SSS 71
Fees   80000L
Loc   22km from Rome

Fioranello

CP 96, 00040 Santa Maria delle Mole
Tel   (06) 608291/608058
Mem   250
Pro   R Croce, A Pelliccioni
Holes 9 L 5276 m SSS 68
Fees   25000L (30000L)
Loc   Santa Maria, 17km SE of Rome
Mis   Driving range

Fiuggi (1928)

Superstrada Anticolana 1,
03015 Fiuggi
Tel   (0775) 55250
Mem   210
Pro   R Terrinoni
Holes 9 L 5697 m SSS 70
Fees   25000L (30000L)
Loc   60km SE of Rome
Mis   Driving range

Marina Velca

01016 Marina Velca/Tarquinia
Tel   (0766) 812109
Mem   150
Pro   R Napoleoni
Holes 9 L 2604 m SSS 50
Fees   D–5000L
Loc   Tarquinia, 80km N of Rome
       on coast

Olgiata (1961)

Largo Olgiata 15, 00123 Roma
Tel   (06) 3789141
Mem   800
Pro   U Grappasonni
Holes 18 L 6396 m SSS 72
       9 L 2968 m SSS 71
Fees   40000L (50000L)
Loc   19km NW of Rome, nr La Storta
Mis   Driving range

Roma (1903)

Via Appia Nuova 716, 00178 Roma
Tel   (06) 78 34 07/78 61 29
Mem   1000
Pro   P Manca, C Croce, M Peri,
       M Sardella, R Bernardini
Holes 18 L 5825 m SSS 71
Fees   6000L
Loc $7^1/_2$ km SE of Rome towards
       Ciampino

Sardinia

Is Molas (1975)

CP 49, 09010 Pula
Tel   (070) 9209062/9208427
       Fax 070 9209996
Mem   310
Pro   A Paolillo
Holes 18 L 6131 m SSS 72
Fees   50000L W–200.000L
Loc   Pula, 32km S of Cagliari.

Pevero (1982)

07020 Porto Cervo
Tel   (0789) 96072/96210/96211
Mem   450
Pro   L Cau
Holes 18 L 6186 m SSS 72
Fees   D–60000–85000L
Loc   Porto Cervo, 30km N of Olbia,
       on Costa Smeralda

Stresa & Lake Maggiore

Alpino Di Stresa (1925)

28040 Vezzo (Novara)
Tel   (0323) 2010$^1/_2$0642
Mem   280
Pro   P Giacono
Holes 9 L 5359 m SSS 67
Fees   30000L (40000L)
Loc   7km W of Stresa

Castelconturbia (1984)

Via Suno, 28010 Agrate Conturbia
Tel   (0322) 832093 (Clubhouse)
Mem   540
Pro   A Angelini, D Murdaca, A Zito
Holes Red 9 L 3330 m Par 36
       Yellow 9 L 3070 m Par 36
       Blue 9 L 3210 m Par 36
Fees   60000L (80000L) 1989 prices
Loc   23km N of Novara. Milan 60km
Mis   Driving range

Piandisole (1964)

Via Pineta 1, 28057 Premeno (NO)
Tel   (0323) 47100
Mem   180
Pro   V Viero
Holes 9 L 2830 m SSS 67
Fees   30000L (40000L)
Loc   Premeno, 30km N of Stresa

Varese (1934)

Via Vittorio Veneto 32, 21020 Luvinate
(VA)
Tel   (0332) 227394/229302
Mem   622
Pro   S Abbiati, M Ballarin
Holes 18 L 5936 m SSS 72
Fees   40000L (60000L)
Loc   5km NW of Varese

Turin & North West

Biella "Le Betulle" (1958)

Valcarozza, 13050 Magnano (VC)
Tel   679151
Mem   300
Pro   M Guersoli, A Reale
Holes 18 L 6100 m SSS 72
Fees   45000L (70000L)
Loc   17km SW of Biella

Cervino (1955)

11021 Cervinia–Breuil (AO)
Tel   (0166) 949131
Mem   350
Holes 9 L 5046 m SSS 67
Fees   40000L–50000L
Loc   53km NE of Aosta

Le Chioccole CC

Loc Frasshetta, Caselina Roma,
12062 Cherasco (CN)
Tel   (0172) 48772
Pro   A Fiammengo, V Pelle
Holes 18 L 5863 m SSS 71
Loc   Cherasco, 45km S of Turin

Claviere (1926)

Strada Nazionale, 10050 Claviere (TO)
Tel   (0122) 878917 (Clubhouse)
           (011) 2398346 (Sec)
Mem   850
Pro   L Merlino, F Giacotto
Holes 9 L 4428 m SSS 63
Fees   30000L (40000L)
Loc   96km W of Turin
Mis   Open Jun–Oct

Courmayeur

11013 Courmayeur
Tel   (0165) 89103
Pro   F Venier
Holes 9 L 2650 m SSS 67
Fees   D–4000L
Loc   5km NE of Courmayeur
Mis   Open Jul–Sept. Driving range

Le Fronde (1975)

Via Sant–Agostino 68,
10051 Avigliana (TO)
Tel   (011) 938053/930540
Mem   350
Pro   M Rolando, A Merletti
Holes 18 L 6081 m SSS 72
Fees   35000L (50000L)
Loc   Avigliana, 20km W ofTurin
Mis   Driving range

Margara (1975)

Via Tenuta Margara 5, 15043 Fubine
(AL)
Tel   (0131) 772377
Mem   170
Pro   G Sità
Holes 18 L 6218 m SSS 72
Fees   10000L (15000L)
Loc   15km NW of Alessandria

I Roveri (1971)

Rotta Cerbiatta 24, 10070 Fiano (TO)
Tel   (011) 923571
Pro   M Vinzi, G Colombatto,
           G Bertaina
Holes 18 L 6218 m SSS 72
           9 L 3107 m SSS 36
Fees   70000L (90000L)
Loc   16km NW of Turin

La Serra

Via Astigliano 42, 15048 Valenza (AL)
Tel   (0131) 954778
Mem   313
Pro   A Caputo

Holes 9 L 2820 m SSS 70
Fees   25000L (35000L)
Loc   4km W of Valenza. 7km N
           of Alessandria
Mis   Open Mar–Nov. Driving range

Sestrieres (1932)

Piazza Agnelli 4, 10058 Sestrieres (TO)
Tel   (0122) 76276/76243
Mem   400
Pro   M Vinzi, S Bertaina
Holes 18 L 4598 m SSS 65
Fees   35000L (45000L)
Loc   Sestrieres, 96km W of Turin
Mis   Highest course in Europe
           Open Jun–Sept

Stupinigi (1972)

Corso Unione Sovietica 506,
10135 Torino
Tel   (011) 343975
Pro   D Canonica, F Luzi
Holes 9 L 1975 m SSS 63
Loc   Mirafiore, Turin
Mis   Closed Aug

Torino (1924)

Via Grange 137, 10070 Fiano
Torinese
Tel   (011) 9235440/9235670
Mem   800
Pro   O Bolognesi, L Merlino,
           S Bertaina
Holes 18 L 6216 m SSS 72
           18 L 6211 m SSS 72
Fees   50000L (70000L)
Loc   23km NW of Turin

Vinovo (1984)

Via Stupinigi 182, 10048 Vinovo
Tel   (011) 9653880
Mem   180
Pro   P Panero, S Fiammengo,
           L Canessa
Holes 9 L 4164 m SSS 62
Fees   25000L (32000L)
Loc   3km SW of Turin

Tuscany & Umbria

Firenze Ugolino

Strada Chiantigiana 3, 50015 Grassina
Tel   (055) 205 1009
Mem   700
Pro   F Rosi, R Campagnoli,
           C Poletti
Holes 18 L 5785 m SSS 70
Fees   40000L (60000L)
Loc   Grassina, 9km S of Florence

Montecatini (1985)

Via Dei Brogi 5, Loc. Pievaccia,
51015 Monsummano Terme
Tel   (0572) 62218
Mem   184
Pro   M Ravinetto

Holes 18 L 6144 m SSS 71
Fees   50000L
Loc   8km N of Montecatini Terme.
           50km NW of Florence (A11)
Mis   Driving range

Perugia (1970)

06074 Santa Sabina–Ellera
Tel   (075) 795204
Mem   380
Pro   A Barlozzi, A Calcari
Holes 9 L 3067 m SSS 70
Fees   25000L (30000L)
Loc   6km NW of Perugia
Mis   Driving range

Punta Ala (1964)

Via del Golf 1, 58040 Punta Ala (GR)
Tel   (0564) 922121
Mem   330
Pro   M Mulas, P Manca,
           F Rosi, GC Poletti
Holes 18 L 6190 m SSS 72
Fees   35000L–50000L
Loc   40km NW of Grosseto.
           Pisa 145km. Florence 150km

Tirrenia (1968)

56018 Tirrenia (PI)
Tel   (050) 37518
Mem   320
Pro   M Ravinetto
Holes 9 L 3065 m SSS 72
Fees   20000L (25000L)
Loc   15km SW of Pisa on coast

Venice & North East

Albarella (1988)

Isola de Albarella,
45010 Rosolino
Tel   (0426) 67124
Pro   L Paolillo
Holes 18 L 6065 m SSS 72
Fees   40000L (50000L)
Loc   64km S of Venice
Mis   Driving range

Ca' della Nave (1986)

Piazza Vittoria 14, 30030 Martellago
Tel   (041) 5401555
Mem   500
Pro   M Napeoleoni
Holes 18 L 6340 m SSS 72
           9 hole Par 3
Fees   60000L
Loc   Martellago, 20km NW of
           Venice

Cansiglio (1956)

CP 152, 31029 Vittorio Veneto
Tel   (0438) 585398
Mem   233
Pro   U Scafa, A della Valentina
Holes 9 L 5666 m SSS 69
Fees   35000L (40000L) 1989 prices
Loc   21km NE of Vittorio Veneto

682 Netherlands

Padova (1966)

35050 Valsanzibio di Galzigano
Tel   (049) 9130078
Mem   600
Pro   A Lionello, P Bernardini
Holes 18 L 6053 m SSS 72
Fees   50000L (60000L)
Loc   Valsanzibio, 20km S of Padua

San Floriano–Gorizia (1987)

Via Oslavia 5, 34070 San Floriano
del Collio
Tel   (0481) 884131/884051
       Fax 0481 884214
Mem   100
Pro   E Pavan
Holes 9 L 2600 m SSS 58
Fees   20000L (25000L)
Loc   6km NW of Gorizia.
       50km SE of Udine, nr Yugoslav
       border
Mis   Open Mar–Dec. Driving range

Trieste (1954)

Via Padriciano 80, 34012 Trieste
Tel   (040) 226159/227062
Mem   200
Pro   E Pavan
Holes 9 L 2725 m SSS 69
Fees   20000L (22000L)
Loc   Padriciano, 7km E of Trieste

Udine (1971)

33034 Fagagna–Villaverde (UD)
Tel   (0432) 800418
Mem   210
Pro   L Tavarini
Holes 9 L 2944 m SSS 71
Fees   30000L
Loc   15km NW of Udine

Venezia (1928)

Via del Forte, 30011 Alberoni
Tel   (041) 731015/731333
       Fax 041 731339
Mem   450
Pro   T Scarso, R Pavan, R Trentin
Holes 18 L 6126 m SSS 72
Fees   50000L (60000L)
Loc   Venice Lido

Villa Condulmer

Via della Croce 3, 31021 Zerman di
Mogliano Veneto
Tel   (041) 457062
Mem   350
Pro   S Ugo
Holes 18 L 5880 m SSS 71
Fees   18000L (Sun–20000L)
Loc   Mogliano Veneto, 17km N of
       Venice

Luxembourg

CC Grand–Ducal de Luxembourg (1936)

1, Route de Treves,
2633 Senningerberg
Tel   Luxembourg 34090
Mem   1200
Pro   E Saquet, S Clough,
       A Bruce
Holes 18 L 5765 m SSS 71
Fees   1200fr (1500fr)
Loc   Luxembourg 7km

Malta

Royal Malta (1888)

Marsa, Malta
Tel   232842/233851
Mem   350
Pro   R Josie
Holes 18 L 5800 yds SSS 67
Fees   £M7 W–£M35
Loc   Marsa, 3 miles from Valetta

Netherlands

Amsterdam & Noord Holland

Amsterdamse (1934)

Zwarte Laantje 4, 1099 CE
Amsterdam
Tel   (020) 943650
Mem   460 80(J)
Pro   Mrs M de Boer,
       J Dale
Holes 9 L 5260 m SSS 68
Fees   30fl (60fl)
Loc   Amsterdam 8km

Kennemer G & CC (1910)

PO Box 85, 2040 AB Zandvoort
Tel   (02507) 12836/18456
Mem   840
Pro   J Buchanan
Holes 27 holes SSS 71:
       Van Hengel 9 L 5860 m
       Pennink 9 L 2874 m
       Colt 9 L 2864 m
Fees   60fl (80fl)
Loc   Zandvoort, 6km from Haarlem

Marine Nieuwediep (1958)

PO Box 932, 1780AX Den Helder
Mem   350
Holes 9 L 4780 m SSS 66
Fees   6fl
Loc   Nieuwe Haven
Mis   Situated on naval base; entry
       by permit or introduction only

De Noordhollandse (1982)

Sluispolderweg 6, 1817 BM Alkmaar
Tel   (072) 156807
Pro   P Horn (072) 156175
Holes 9 L 6171 m SSS 72
Fees   25fl (35fl)
Loc   2km N of Alkmaar
Mis   Public course. Driving range.

Olympus (1973)

Sportpark, Overamstel, Amsterdam
Tel   (020) 651863
Mem   550
Pro   CJ Broekhuysen,
       GW Hutchison
Holes 9 L 2236 m SSS 64
Fees   15fl
Loc   E of Amstel River, nr junction
       with A1

Spaarnwoude (1977)

Het Hoge Land 8,1981 LT Velsen
Tel   (023) 382708
Mem   1500
Pro   AC Wessels
Holes 18 L 5406 m SSS 68
Fees   20fl (22fl)
Loc   Spaarnwoude, Velsen.
       14km W of Amsterdam.
       10km NE of Haarlem

Breda & South West

Domburgsche (1914)

Schelpweg 26, 4357 BP Domburg
Tel   (01188) 1573
Mem   340
Pro   L Verberne
Holes 9 L 5139 m SSS 67
Fees   50fl (60fl)
Loc   15km NW of Middelburg

N–B Toxandria (1928)

Veenstraat 89, 5124 NC Molenschot
Tel   (01611) 1200
Mem   800
Pro   R Leach
Holes 18 L 5925 m SSS 71
Fees   50fl (70fl)
Loc   Breda 8km
Mis   Introduction necessary.
       Please phone in advance

Wouwse Plantage (1981)

Zoomvlietweg 66, 4725 TD
Wouwse Plantage
Tel   (01657) 593
Mem   650

Pro	P Helsby, A McLean
Holes	16 L 5548 m SSS 69
Fees	45fl (55fl)
Loc	Wouwse Plantage (N 13), nr Bergen–op–Zoom
Mis	Handicap certificate required

Eindhoven & South East

Berendonck (1987)

Panhuisweg 39, 6603 KH Wijchen
Tel	(08894) 20039
Mem	300
Pro	W Swart, C Tjerks
Holes	9 L 5788 m SSS 70
Fees	18 holes 25fl (35fl) 9 holes 15fl (25fl)
Loc	Nijmegen 5km
Mis	Public course. WE–comps

De Dommel

Zegenwerp 12, St Michielsgestel
Tel	(04105) 2316
Mem	430
Pro	M Groenendaal
Holes	12 L 5565 m SSS 69
Fees	20fl (30fl)
Loc	's–Hertogenbosch 10km

Eindhovensche (1930)

Eindhovensche Weg 300,
5553 VB Walkenswaard
Tel	(04902) 14816
Mem	500 250(L) 80(J)
Pro	G Jeurissen, J Renders
Holes	18 L 6106 m SSS 71
Fees	50fl (70fl)
Loc	14km S of Eindhoven

Geysteren G & CC (1974)

Het Spekt 2, 5862 AZ Geysteren
Tel	(04784) 1809/2592
Mem	700
Pro	LG van Mook
Holes	18 L 6063 m SSS 72
Fees	60fl (70fl)
Loc	N271 Venlo–Nymegen, via Well and Wanssum

Haviksoord (1976)

Maarheezerweg Nrd 11, 5595 XG
Leende (NB)
Tel	(04906) 1818
Mem	350
Holes	9 L 5856 m SSS 71
Fees	25fl (35fl)
Loc	10km S of Eindhoven
Mis	Handicap certificate required

Het Rijk van Nijmegen (1985)

Postweg 17, 6561 KJ Groesbeek
Tel	(08891) 76644
Mem	550

Pro	B Gee, G Morris, M Kavanagh
Holes	18 L 6114 m SSS 72 9 L 4824 m SSS 66 9 L 4166 m SSS 62
Fees	50fl (75fl)
Loc	5km E of Nijmegen

De Schoot (1973)

Schootsedijk 18, 5491 TD Sint
Oedenrode
Tel	(04138) 73011
Mem	450
Pro	C Brown
Holes	9 L 2392 m SSS 66
Fees	25fl (30fl)
Loc	Eindhoven 20km

Tongelreep G & CC

Velddoornweg 2, 5644 SZ Eindhoven
Tel	(040) 520962
Mem	450
Pro	J Stevens
Holes	9 L 4832 m SSS 68
Fees	30fl (40fl)
Loc	Eindhoven
Mis	WE–by introduction only. Handicap certificate required

Limburg Province

Hoenshuis G & CC (1987)

Hoensweg 17, 6367 GM Voerendaal
Tel	(045) 753300
Mem	600
Pro	R Salmon
Holes	18 L 6118 m SSS 72
Fees	40fl (50fl)
Loc	Limburg, 10km NE of Maastricht
Mis	Driving range

Wittem G & CC

Dalbissenweg, 6281 NC Mechelen
Tel	(04455) 1397
Mem	550
Pro	A Horsman, H Rijnders
Holes	9 L 5880 m SSS 71
Fees	35fl (50fl)
Loc	Wittem 5km. Maastricht 23km

East Central

Edese (1979)

Nationaal Sportcentrum Papendal,
Amsterdamseweg, Arnhem
Tel	(08306) 21985?
Mem	500
Pro	C Borst
Holes	9 L 3050 m SSS 72
Fees	25fl (35fl)
Loc	Between Ede and Arnhem

Hattemse G & CC (1930)

Veenwal 11, 8051 AS Hattem
Tel	(05206) 41909
Mem	400
Pro	E Vaartjes
Holes	9 L 5808 yds SSS 68
Fees	50fl (60fl)
Loc	Off Zwolle–Apeldoorn road

Keppelse (1926)

Oude Zutphenseweg 15, Hoog–Keppel
Tel	(08348) 1416
Mem	200
Pro	C Butti
Holes	9 L 5402 m SSS 67
Fees	25fl (35fl)
Loc	Laag Keppel 1 1/2 km

De Koepel (1983)

Postbox 88, 7640 AB Wierden
Tel	(05496) 76150
Mem	450
Pro	A Young
Holes	9 L 2863 m SSS 70
Fees	40fl (50fl)
Loc	7km W of Almelo

Nunspeetse G & CC (1985)

Plesmanlaan 30, Nunspeet
Tel	(03412) 58034
Mem	575
Pro	W van Mook
Holes	27 holes L 6100 m SSS 72
Fees	60fl (80fl)
Loc	Nunspeet, 25km SW of Zwolle

Rosendaelsche (1895)

Apeldoornsweg 450, 6816 SN Arnhem
Tel	(085) 421438
Mem	800
Pro	JGM Dorrestein, P Coleman (085) 437283
Holes	18 L 6057 m SSS 72
Fees	50fl (70fl)
Loc	5km N of Arnhem on Route N50

Sallandsche "de Hoek" (1934)

PO Box 442, 7400 AK Deventer
Tel	(05709) 1214
Mem	450
Pro	J Balvert (05709) 2774/2705
Holes	9 L 6122 yds SSS 69
Fees	50fl (60fl)
Loc	6km N of Deventer

Twentsche (1930)

Enschedesestraat 381,
7552 CV Hengelo
Tel	(074) 912773
Mem	400
Pro	J Poppe
Holes	9 L 5444 m SSS 69
Fees	25fl (30fl)
Loc	Hengelo 3km

For explanation of abbreviations, see page 460.

Veluwse (1957)

Nr 57, 7436 AC Hoog Soeren
Tel	(05769) 275
Mem	400
Pro	S Gilmour
Holes	9 L 6264 yds SSS 70
Fees	50fl (60fl)
Loc	5km W of Apeldoorn

Zeewolde

Postbus 1461, 1200 BL Hilversum
Tel	(03242) 2103
Mem	900
Pro	P van Wijk, I Flegg
Holes	18 L 5954 m SSS 71
Fees	35–40fl (45–50fl)
Loc	20km N of Hilversum. 60km NE of Amsterdam

North

Gelpenberg (1970)

Gebbeveensweg 1, 7854 TD Aalden
Tel	(05917) 1784
Mem	375
Pro	W Stevens (05917) 1525
Holes	9 L 5867 m SSS 71
Fees	50fl (60fl)
Loc	16km W of Emmen

Lauswolt G & CC (1964)

Harinxmaweg 8A,
9244 CH Beetsterzwaag
Tel	(05126) 2594
Mem	450
Pro	J Too
Holes	9 L 5993 m SSS 71
Fees	50fl (60fl)
Loc	5km S of Drachten

Noord Nederlandse G & CC (1950)

Pollselaan 5, 9756 CJ Glimmen
Tel	(05906) 1275
Mem	700
Pro	KC Visser, K MacDonald
Holes	10 L 5600 m SSS 70
Fees	60fl (90fl)
Loc	A28, Junction Eelde towards Glimmen and Zuidlaren

The Hague & Rotterdam

Broekpolder (1981)

Watersportweg 100, 3138 HD
Vlaardingen
Tel	(010) 4750011/4748140/4748142
Mem	840
Pro	J Stoop, J Hage, M Maddison
Holes	18 L 6048 m SSS 72
Fees	30–45fl (50–70fl)
Loc	Rotterdam 15km by A20 Rotterdam–Hoek van Holland

Haagsche G & CC (1893)

Groot Haesebrokeseweg 22,
2242 EC Wassenaar
Tel	(01751) 79607
Mem	1400
Pro	A Loesberg, S van den Berg
Holes	18 L 5674 m SSS 71
Fees	70fl (90fl)
Loc	Den Haag 6km
Mis	Introduction required–phone

Kleiburg (1974)

c/o Vredenburchlaan 47,
2661 HE Bergenshenhoek
Tel	(01810) 14225
Pro	W Koudijs
Holes	18 L 5534 m SSS 69
Fees	25fl
Loc	25km W of Rotterdam
Mis	Public course

Kralingen (1933)

Kralingseweg 200, 3062 CG Rotterdam
Tel	(010) 4527646
Mem	300
Pro	R Heijkant
Holes	9 L 5277 yds SSS 66
Fees	25fl
Loc	Rotterdam 5km

Noordwijkse (1915)

Randweg 25, PO Box 70,
2200 AB Noordwijk
Tel	(02523) 73761
Mem	900
Pro	T O'Mahoney (02523) 76993
Holes	18 L 6286 m SSS 74
Fees	60fl (80fl)
Loc	5km N of Noordwyk. 15km NW of Leiden
Mis	Links course

Oude Maas (1975)

Veerweg 2, 3161 EX Rhoon
Tel	(01890) 18058
Pro	R Goor
Holes	9 L 5876 m SSS 71 9 hole Par 3
Fees	20fl (32fl)
Loc	10km S of Rotterdam
Mis	Public course

Wassenarse Rozenstein (1984)

Hoge Klei 1, 2242 XZ Wassenaar
Tel	(01751) 17846
Pro	GTG Janmaat
Holes	9 L 6044 m SSS 71
Fees	30fl (60fl)
Loc	14km NE of The Hague
Mis	Driving range, pitch and putt

Zeegersloot (1984)

Kromme Aarweg 5, PO Box 190,
2403 Alphen aan der Rijn
Tel	(01720) 74567
Mem	1000
Pro	J Huurman (01720) 73473
Holes	9 L 2561 m SSS 67 9 hole Par 3 course
Fees	30fl (40fl) Par 3–15fl (25fl)
Loc	By Zegerlake in Alphen. 15km N of Gouda

Utrecht & Hilversum

De Haar (1974)

PO Box 104, Parkweg 5,
3450 AC Vleuten
Tel	(03407) 2860
Mem	450
Pro	B McColl
Holes	9 L 6650 yds SSS 71
Fees	50fl (70fl)
Loc	10km NW of Utrecht

Hilversumsche (1910)

Soestdijkerstraatweg 172,
1213 XJ Hilversum
Tel	(035) 857060
Mem	730
Pro	M Morbey, R Cattell
Holes	18 L 5856 m SSS 71
Fees	60fl (80fl)
Loc	Hilversum 3km on road to Baarn
Mis	Phone booking

Leusdense De Hoge Kleij

Appelweg 4, 3832 Leusden
Tel	(033) 616944
Mem	800
Pro	TJ Giles
Holes	18 L 6053 m SSS 72
Fees	50fl (70fl)
Loc	10km SE of Amersfoort 20km NE of Utrecht via A28
Mis	WE–max handicap 29

Nieuwegeinse (1985)

Postbus 486, 3430 AL Nieuwegein
Tel	(03402) 40769/42192
Mem	430
Pro	R Visser
Holes	9 L 2348 m SSS 66
Fees	25fl (37.50fl)
Loc	Blokhoeve, S of Utrecht
Mis	Driving range

gg

Utrechtse "De Pan" (1894)
Amersfoortseweg 1, 3735 LJ Bosch en Duin
Tel (03404) 55223 (Sec)
(03404) 56225 (Clubhouse)
Mem 800
Pro C Dorrestein (03404) 56427
Holes 18 L 6073 m SSS 72
Fees 50fl (70fl)
Loc Utrecht 10km on A28 Utrecht–Amersfoort
Mis Advisable to ring first

Norway

Bergen
PO Box 470, 5001 Bergen
Tel 182077
Mem 300
Pro S Norris
Holes 9 L 4461 m SSS 66
Fees D–100kr
Loc Bergen 8km

Borregaard (1927)
PO Box 348, 1701 Sarpsborg
Tel (09) 157401
Mem 500
Pro F Mudie
Holes 9 L 4500 m SSS 64
Fees D–100kr
Loc Opsund, 1km N of Sarpsborg

Hedmark
PO Box 1131, 2301 Hamar
Tel (064) 13588
Mem 141
Holes 9 L 3200 m SSS 36
Fees 60kr
Loc Elverum, 35km E of Hamar. 150km N of Oslo

Kjekstad (1976)
PO Box 201, 3440 Royken
Tel (02) 855850/855353
Mem 1125
Pro D Craig
Holes 18 L 5100 m SSS 68
Fees 100kr
Loc 40km SW of Oslo. 12km SE of Drammen on Route 282

Kristiansand (1973)
PO Box 31, N–4601 Kristiansand
Tel (042) 45863
Mem 350
Holes 9 L 2485 m SSS 70
Fees 100kr
Loc 8km E of K'sand off E18

Oslo (1924)
Bogstad, 0757 Oslo 7
Tel (02) 504402
Mem 3025
Pro S Newey
Holes 18 L 6574 yds SSS 72
Fees 200kr (250kr)
Loc 8km NW of Oslo. Follow signs to "Bogstad Camping".
Mis Handicap certificate required (men–24 ladies–32). Restricted WD–9am–1pm WE–3–7pm.

Oustoen (1965)
PO Box 82–Ljan, 1113 Oslo
Tel (472) 535295/486563 (Sec)
Mem 300
Holes 18 L 6200m SSS 71
Fees 200kr
Loc Small island in Oslofjord, 10km W of Oslo
Mis Private club. V'trs must be accompanied by a member.

Skjeberg (1986)
PO Box 149, 1742 Klavestadhaugen
Tel (09) 16 63 10
Mem 400
Pro G Midtvåge
Holes 18 L 5500 m SSS 71
Fees D–100kr
Loc Hevingen, 2km N of Sarpsborg

Stavanger (1956)
Longebakke 45, 4042 Hafrsfjord
Tel 555431
Mem 850
Pro R Lees
Holes 18 L 5090 m SSS 68
Fees 100kr (150kr)
Loc 6km SW of Stavanger

Trondheim (1950)
PO Box 169, 7001 Trondheim
Tel 531885
Mem 330
Pro K Dudmann
Holes 9 L 5632 m SSS 72
Fees 100kr
Loc Trondheim 3km

Vestfold (1958)
PO Box 64, 3101 Tønsberg
Tel (033) 65655 (Sec)
Mem 1050
Pro G Beal
Holes 18 L 5860 m SSS 72
Fees D–120kr (180kr)
Loc Tønsberg 8km

Portugal

Algarve

Alto
Alvor, 8500 Portimão
Tel (082) 20119
Holes 18 L 6659 m SSS
Loc Portimão 5km
Mis Course due to open 1991

Palmares
Palmares, Lagos
Tel 62961/62953
Mem 250
Pro L Espadinha
Holes 18 L 5961 m SSS 72
Fees 4700esc
Loc Meia Praia, 5km E of Lagos

Parque da Floresta (1987)
Budens, 8650 Vila do Bispo
Tel (082) 65333/4/5
Holes 18 L 6476 yds SSS 72
Fees D–4000esc
Loc 16km W of Lagos, nr Salema

Penina (1966)
PO Box 146, Penina, 8502 Portimão
Tel (82) 22051/58
Mem 220
Pro R Liddle, J Lourenço
Holes 18 L 6889 yds SSS 73
9 L 3500 yds SSS 36
9 L 2278 yds SSS 33
Fees 18 hole:D–6000esc
9 hole:D–4000esc
Loc 5km W of Portimão. 12km E of Lagos

Quinta do Lago (1974)
Quinta Do Lago, 8135 Almancil
Tel (089) 94782/94529/96002
Pro D Gomes Silva, P Millhouse
Holes 4 x 9 holes:
A–9 L 3137 m Par 36
B–9 L 3225 m Par 36
C–9 L 3263 m Par 36
D–9 L 3068 m Par 36
Fees 18 holes–10000esc
Loc 15km W of Faro. Airport 20km
Mis Driving range

San Lorenzo
Quinta do Lago, Almancil, 8100 Loulé
Tel (89) 96522
Holes 18 L 6238 m SSS 73
Fees 3750esc (Hotel guests only)
Loc 16km W of Faro

For explanation of abbreviations, see page 460.

Vale do Lobo (1968)

Vale Do Lobo, Almancil
Tel   (089) 94444
Mem   500
Pro   S Walker
Holes   Green 9 L 2813 m SSS 35
         Orange 9 L 2975 m SSS 36
         Yellow 9 L 3036 m SSS 36
Fees   D–6500esc. Hotel Don Filipa–
         4875esc. Villa guests–3250esc
Loc   19km W of Faro. Airport 19km
Mis   27 bay driving range

Vilamoura (1969)

Vilamoura, 8125 Quarteira
Tel   Vilamoura 1 (089) 33652
         Vilamoura 2 (089) 35562
Mem   300
Pro   J Catarino
Holes   Vilamoura 1 10 L 0331 m
         SSS 72; Vilamoura 2 18 L 6192
         m SSS 71
Fees   5500esc (Discounts for
         Vilamoura guests)
Loc   Quarteira, 25km W of Faro
Mis   Vilamoura 3 (27 holes) opening
         1990

Azores

São Miguel

PO Box 55, 9501 Ponta Delgada
Tel   31925/54341
Holes   9 L 5492 m SSS 71
Loc   São Miguel Island
Mis   Driving range

Terceira Island (1954)

9760 Praia da Vitória
Tel   25847
Mem   800
Pro   E Mendes Correia
Holes   18 L 6332 yds SSS 70
Fees   D–US$ 8 (D–US$ 10)
Loc   13km from Angra do Heroismo,
         Praia da Victória and Lajes
         international airport

Lisbon & Central

Aroeira

Fonte da Telha, 2825 Monte da Caparica
Tel   2263244
Pro   A Paulino
Holes   18 L 6171 m SSS 73
Fees   4500esc
Loc   17km S of Lisbon, off Setúbal
         road

Estoril (1945)

Avenida República, 2765 Estoril
Tel   2680176/2681376
Mem   800
Pro   J Rodrigues, H Paulino,
         C Aleixo

Holes   18 L 5210 m SSS 68
         9 L 2350 m SSS 65
Fees   4240esc WD only
Loc   N of Estoril on Sintra road.
         30km W of Lisbon
Mis   WE–members only. Driving
         range

Estoril Sol (1976)

Linhó, 2710 Sintra
Tel   (923) 2461
Mem   65
Pro   D Moita
Holes   9 L 4228 m Par 66
Fees   2500esc
Loc   7km N of Estoril. Lisbon 35km

Lisbon Sports Club (1922)

Casal da Carragueira, Belas,
2475 Queluz
Tel   4310077
Mem   900
Pro   J Baltazar
Holes   14 + 4 L 5866 m SSS 68
Fees   D–3500esc (5000esc)
Loc   Belas–Queluz, 20km NW of
         Lisbon

Marinha G & CC (1984)

Quinta da Marinha, 2750 Cascais
Tel   289881/289901
Mem   500
Pro   A Dantas
Holes   18 L 5606 m SSS 71
Fees   4000esc
Loc   2km W of Cascais.
         32km W of Lisbon
Mis   Driving range

Tróia Golf

Torralta, Tróia, 2900 Setúbal
Tel   (065) 44151/44236
Mem   140
Pro   F Pina
Holes   18 L 6338 m SSS 74
Fees   D–4500esc
Loc   S of Setúbal on Troia peninsula.
         50km S of Lisbon

Vimeiro

Praia do Porto Novo, Vimeiro,
2560 Torres Vedras
Tel   (061) 98157
Holes   9 L 2466 m SSS 35
Fees   2000esc
Loc   Vimeiro, 20km N of Torres
         Vedras. 65km N of Lisbon

Madeira

Santo da Serra (1967)

Sto Antonio da Serra, 9100
Santa Cruz
Tel   55139
Mem   130
Pro   J de Sousa

Holes   9 L 2622 yds SSS 67
Fees   1500esc
Loc   22km E of Funchal. Airport 6km

Northern

Estela (1989)

Rio Alto, Estela, 4490 Povoa de Varzim
Tel   (052) 685567
Mem   400
Pro   CA Agostinho
Holes   18
Recs   L 6107 m SSS 73
Fees   4000esc
Loc   7km N of Povoa de Varzim.
         40km N of Oporto (Route 13)

Miramar (1934)

Praia de Miramar, 4405 Valadares
Tel   (2) 7622067
Mem   500
Pro   M Ribeiro
Holes   9 L 2477 m SSS 66
Fees   3000esc
Loc   Valadares, 12km S of Oporto

Oporto (1890)

Sisto–Paramos, 4500 Espinho
Tel   722008
Mem   600
Pro   E Maganinho
Holes   18 L 5780 m SSS 70
Fees   5000esc
Loc   Espinho, 15km S of Oporto
Mis   Links course

Vidago (1970)

Pavilhão Golf, 5425 Vidago
Tel   97356
Mem   600
Pro   M Carneiro
Holes   9 L 2449 m SSS 63
Fees   D–2000esc
Loc   50km N of Vila Real.
         130km NE of Oporto

Spain

Alicante & Murcia

Don Cayo (1974)

Conde de Altea 49, Altea
Tel   (96) 5840716/5848046
Pro   G Sanz
Holes   9 L 6044 m SSS 72
Fees   D–2800P
Loc   Altea 4km

Ifach (1974)

Crta Moraira–Calpe Km 3,
Urb San Jaime, Benisa
Holes   9 L 3408 m SSS 59
Fees   D–2200P
Loc   Calpe 13km. Moraira 5km

Jávea (1981)

Ctra Benitachell Km4, Jávea
Tel   (96) 579 25 84/579 18 13
Mem   650
Pro   J-A Moyano, J-M Carriles
Holes   9 L 6070 m SSS 72
Fees   D-4000P
Loc   Between Valencia (100km) and Alicante (90km)

La Manga (1971)

30385 Los Belones, Cartagena
Tel   (968) 56 45 11
Mem   2000
Pro   J Weir, J Meliado, V Ballesteros
Holes   North 18 L 5873 m SSS 72
        South 18 L 5838 m SSS 73
        Atamaria 9 L 5118 m SSS 67
Fees   D-4000P (residents)
Loc   Cartagena 20km. Murcia 70km

Villa Martín (1972)

Apartado 35, Torrevieja
Tel   (965) 32 03 50 54 58
Pro   E Pareja
Holes   18 L 5899 m SSS 72
Fees   3500P
Loc   Torrevieja

Almería

Almerimar (1976)

Urb Almerimar, 04700 El Ejido
Tel   (951) 48 02 34
Pro   J Parrón
Holes   18 L 5928 m SSS 72
Fees   4000P W-20000P
Loc   Almeria 36km

Cortijo Grande (1976)

Apdo 2, Cortijo Grande, 04630 Turre
Tel   (51) 479164/479176
Mem   72
Holes   9 holes open 1990
Fees   D-2000P
Loc   20km W of Turre. 85km N of Almería, nr Mojácar

Playa Serena (1979)

Urb Playa Serena, Roquetas de Mar
Tel   (951) 333055
Mem   300
Pro   F Parrón
Holes   18 L 6301 m SSS 72
Fees   D-4800P
Loc   20km S of Almería

Balearic Islands

Canyamel

Urb Canyamel, Crta de Cuevas,
07580 Capdepera, Mallorca
Tel   (971) 56 44 57
Holes   18 L 6115 m SSS 72
Fees   4800P
Loc   70km NE of Palma, nr Cala Ratjada

Pollensa (1984)

Predio Son Porquer, Ctra Palma–
Pollensa Km 49, Apdo No 9, Mallorca
Tel   (971) 53 32 16
Mem   200
Pro   S Luna
Holes   9 L 5624 m SSS 72
Fees   3500P
Loc   Pollensa 3km. Palma 50km

Poniente (1978)

Costa de Calvia, Mallorca
Tel   (971) 68 01 48
Mem   100
Pro   B Salter, P Ruiz, P Rodriguez
Holes   18 L 6430 m SSS 74
Fees   4800P
Loc   12km from Palma towards Andraitx
Mis   Driving range

Real Golf Bendinat (1986)

C. Campoamor, 07184 Calvia, Mallorca
Tel   (971) 40 52 00
Mem   450
Pro   R Galiano
Holes   9 L 2327 m SSS 64
Fees   D-4300P
Loc   7km W of Palma

Real Golf de Menorca (1976)

Apartado 97, Mahón, Menorca
Tel   (971) 36 39 00
Mem   350
Pro   J Tollegrosa
Holes   9 L 5724 m SSS 70
Loc   7km N of Mahón

Roca Llisa (1971)

Apartado 200, Ibiza
Tel   (971) 31 97 18
Mem   500
Pro   G Castillo
Holes   9 L 5902 m SSS 70
Fees   3500P
Loc   8km from Ibiza towards Cala Llonga

Santa Ponsa (1976)

Santa Ponsa, Mallorca
Tel   (71) 69 02 11/69 08 00
Mem   350
Pro   S Bruna
Holes   18 L 6520 m SSS 74
Fees   4800P
Loc   18km from Palma–motorway Andraitx
Mis   Hotel guests 50% discount

Son Parc (1977)

Apdo 634, Mahón, Menorca
Tel   (971) 36 88 06
Mem   300
Holes   9 L 2746 m SSS 69
Fees   D-3800P
Loc   Mercadel, 18km N of Mahón

Son Servera (1967)

07559 Costa de Los Pinos, Son Servera, Mallorca
Tel   (971) 56 78 02
        Fax 56 81 46
Mem   312
Pro   S Sota
Holes   9 L 5956 m SSS 72
Fees   D-3600P
Loc   64km from Palma, via Manacor

Son Vida (1964)

Son Vida, 07013 Palma de Mallorca
Tel   (971) 23 76 20
Mem   500
Pro   F Fuentes
Holes   18 L 5414 m SSS 68
Fees   4000P
Loc   5km NW of Palma

Vall D'Or (1986)

Apdo 23, 07660 Cala D'Or, Mallorca
Tel   (971) 83 70 01/83 70 68
Pro   A Gonzalez
Holes   9 L 5462 m SSS 70
Fees   4100P
Loc   Cala D'Or 6km. Palma 40 mins drive.

Barcelona & Cataluña

Costa Brava (1962)

Santa Cristina d'Aro, Girona
Tel   (972) 83 71 50
Mem   630
Pro   M Gil
Holes   18 L 5558 m SSS 71
Fees   4500–6000P (5500–6000P)
Loc   Playa de Aro 5km. 30km N of Girona

For explanation of abbreviations, see page 460.

688 Spain

Costa Dorada (1983)
Apartado 600, Tarragona
Tel (977) 65 54 16
Pro F Jimenez
Holes 9 L 5944 m SSS 73

Llavaneras (1945)
Camino del Golf, 08392 Sant Andreu
Llavaneres
Tel (93) 792 60 50
Mem 975
Pro F González, J Bertrán,
J Pérez, J González
Holes 9 L 4298 m SSS 63
Fees 3000–4000P (6000P)
Loc Barcelona 32km on N–2

Pals
Pals, Gerona
Tel (972) 63 60 06
Fax 972 637009
Mem 750
Pro J Anglada, M Ramos, J Riera
Holes 18 L 6222 m SSS 72
Fees D–4000–7000P
Loc Bagur 10km. Estartit 15km

Real Golf de Cerdaña (1929)
Apdo 63, Puigcerdá (Gerona)
Tel (972) 88 13 38/88 09 50
Mem 300
Pro S Diaz
Holes 18 L 5735 m SSS 70
Loc Cerdaña, 1km from Puigcerdá.

Real Golf "El Prat" (1956)
8820 El Prat de Llobregat
Tel (93) 379 02 78
Mem 2200
Pro P Marin, M Rodriguez
Holes 3 x 9 holes 5944–6256 m
SSS 72–74
Fees 3640P (6048P)
Loc El Prat, Airport 3km.
Barcelona 15km

Sant Cugat (1914)
08190 Sant Cugat del Valles
Tel (93) 674 39 08/674 39 58
Mem 1500
Pro A Demelo
Holes 18 L 5209 m SSS 68
Fees 3500P (7000P)
Loc Barcelona 20km

Terramar (1922)
Apdo 6, 08870 Sitges
Tel (894) 05 80/894 20 43
Mem 930
Pro A Hernández, S Perez,
J Hernández
Holes 18 L 5578 m SSS 70
Fees 3000–5000P
Loc Sitges, 37km from Barcelona.
Tarragona 60km

Vallromanes (1969)
C/Afveras, 08188 Vallromanes
Tel (93) 568 03 62
Mem 1200
Pro J Gallardo
Holes 18 L 6038 m SSS 72
Fees D–3500P (6700P)
Loc 23km from Barcelona between
Alella and Granollers.
A17 Junction 13/A19 Junction 5

Canary Islands

Costa Teguise (1978)
Lanzarote
Tel (928) 81 35 12
Pro NG Perez
Holes 18 L 6082 m SSS 71
9 L 1455 m SSS 28
Loc 7km N of Arrecife

Golf del Sur (1987)
San Miguel de Abona, Tenerife
Tel (922) 704555
Pro J Golding, M Golding
Holes North 9 L 2510 m SSS 36
Links 9 L 2308 m SSS 35
South course SSS 36
Fees 18 holes 4000P
9 holes 2000P
Loc Tenerife Sur airport 3km

Maspalomas (1968)
Av de Africa, Maspalomas,
35100 Las Palmas de Gran Canaria
Tel (928) 76 25 81/76 73 43
Pro A Gutierrez
Holes 18 L 6216 m SSS 72
Fees D–3000P
Loc S coast of Gran Canaria

Real Golf de Las Palmas (1891)
PO Box 183, 35000 Las Palmas de
Gran Canaria
Tel (928) 35 10 50/35 01 04/35
01 08
Mem 750
Pro F Santana, E Perera, S Sanchez
F Santana
Holes 18 L 5690 m SSS 71
Fees 4500P
Loc Bandama, 14km Las Palmas
Mis Driving range, pitch and putt.
Bandama Hotel guests free.

Tenerife (1932)
El Peñón, Tacoronte, Tenerife
Tel (922) 25 02 40/25 10 48
Mem 626
Pro G Gonzalez
Holes 18 L 5397 m SSS 68
Fees 3500P WD only
Loc N of island, 10 mins from Santa
Cruz

Córdoba

Pozoblanco (1984)
San Gregorio 2, Pozoblanco,
(Córdoba)
Tel (957) 10 02 39/10 00 06
Holes 9 L 3660 m SSS 62
Loc Pozoblanco 3km

Los Villares (1976)
Avda del Generalismo 1–2,
PO Box 463, Córdoba
Tel (957) 35 02 08
Mem 404
Pro JM Carriles
Holes 18 L 6087 m SSS 72
Fees 3000P
Loc Between Córdoba and Obejo

Galicia

Aero Club De Santiago (1976)
General Pardiñas 34, Santiago de
Compostela (La Coruña)
Tel (981) 59 24 00
Pro J Ybarra
Holes 9 L 6151 m SSS 72
Fees 2500P
Loc Santiago Airport

Aero Club de Vigo (1951)
Reconquista 7, Vigo
Tel (986) 22 11 60/24 24
93
Pro DS Roman
Holes 9 L 5734 m SSS 70
Loc Peinador Airport, 8km from
Vigo

La Coruña (1962)
Apartado 737, 15080 La Coruña
Tel (981) 28 52 00
Mem 1500
Pro J Santiago
Holes 18 L 5782 m SSS 72
Fees 2000P
Loc Arteijo, 7km from La Coruña

La Toja (1970)
Isla de La Toja, El Grove,
Pontevedra
Tel (986) 73 07 26/73 08
18
Mem 450
Pro P Medrano
Holes 9 L 6046 m SSS 72
Fees 4000–7000P
Loc La Toja island. Vigo 60km.
Pontevedra 30km

Málaga Region

El Candado (1905)

Urb El Candado, El Palo, Malaga
Tel   (952) 29 46 66
Pro   M Lucas
Holes 9 L 4508 m SSS 65
Loc   Málaga 5km on Route N340

CC Málaga (1925)

Apartado 324, Málaga
Tel   (952) 38 12 55
       Fax 52 38 21 41
Mem   550
Pro   J Sanchez
Holes 18 L 6249 m SSS 72
Fees   4000P
Loc   Torremolinos 3km.
       Málaga 12km. Airport 2km
Mis   Parador guests 50% reduction

Mijas (1976)

Public
Apartado 138, Fuengirola, Málaga
Tel   (957) 47 68 43
Pro   J Rosa
Holes Los Lagos 18 L 6348 m SSS 73
       Los Olivos 18 L 5896 m SSS 71
Fees   D–3500P
Loc   Fuengirola 4km
Mis   Public course. Handicap
       certificate required.

Los Moriscos (1974)

C.Recogidas, 18005 Granada
Tel   (958) 60 04 12
Pro   V Carralero
Holes 9 L 5702 m SSS 71
Fees   D–1800P
Loc   Motril 8km. Málaga 80km.
       Granada 65km

Nerja G & CC

PO Box 154, Nerja, Málaga
Tel   (952) 52 02 08
Pro   A Carsin
Holes 9 L 3000 m SSS 59
Loc   1km E of Nerja on motorway
       Málaga–Almería

Torrequebrada (1977)

Apdo 67, 29630 Benalmadena–Costa
Tel   (52) 44 27 42/56 11 02
Pro   J Jiménez
Holes 18 L 5860 m SSS 72
Fees   5500–6500P W–29000–34000P
Loc   Fuengirola 5km. Airport 14km

Madrid Region

Barberán (1967)

Apartado 150.239, Cuatro Vientos,
Madrid
Tel   (91) 218 85 05
Pro   V Hernandez
Holes 9 L 6127 m SSS 72
Loc   Madrid 10km

Las Encinas de Boadilla (1984)

Crta Boadilla–Pozuelo Km 1400,
Boadilla del Monte, Madrid
Tel   (91) 633 11 00
Mem   400
Pro   A Gomez
Holes 9 L 1464 m SSS 50
Fees   700P (2300P)
Loc   Pozuelo, Madrid 12km

Herreria (1966)

PO Box 28200, San Lorenzo del
Escorial, (Madrid)
Tel   (91) 890 51 11/890 52 44
Mem   3500
Pro   M Aparicio
Holes 18 L 6015 m SSS 72
Fees   3500P (5500P)
Loc   Nr Escorial monastery. Madrid
       50km

Lomas–Bosque (1973)

Urb El Bosque, Villaviciosa de Odón,
(Madrid)
Tel   (91) 616 21 70
Mem   400
Pro   M Alvárez
Holes 27 L 6075 m SSS 72
Fees   3500P (7000P)
Loc   Madrid 20km

La Moraleja (1976)

La Moraleja, Alcobendas (Madrid)
Tel   (91) 650 07 00
Mem   600
Pro   V Barrios, M Montes
Holes 18 L 5617 m SSS 69
Fees   2500P (3000P)
Loc   Madrid–Burgos road

Nuevo de Madrid (1972)

Las Matas (Madrid)
Tel   (91) 630 08 20
Pro   J Marimon
Holes 18 L 6037 m SSS 72
Loc   Madrid 18km

Puerta de Hierro (1904)

28305 Madrid
Tel   (91) 216 1745
Mem   1442
Pro   J Gallardo, J Benito
Holes 18 L 6347 m SSS 73
Fees   2000P (3000P)
Loc   4km N of Madrid on Route VI
Mis   V'trs must be accompanied
       by a member

Real Automovil Club de España (1967)

José Abascal 10, 28003 Madrid
Tel   (91) 657 00 01
Mem   3200
Pro   F Alvarez, J Alvarez, F Valera
Holes 18 L 6505 m SSS 72
       9 hole Par 3 course

Fees   3000P (7000P)
Loc   San Sebastián de los Reyes,
       28km from Madrid on Burgos
       road.

Somosaguas (1971)

Somosaguas, 28011 Madrid
Tel   (91) 212 16 47
Pro   M Cabrera, A Garrido
Holes 9 L 5621 m SSS 69
Fees   2000P (3000P)
Loc   Somosaguas

Valdelaguila (1975)

Apdo 9, Alcalá de Henares,
Madrid
Tel   885 96 59
Pro   A Puebla
Holes 9 L 5714 m SSS 70
Fees   D–1000P (1500P)
Loc   Alcalá de Henares 8km

Villa de Madrid CC (1984)

Crta Castilla, 28040 Madrid
Tel   (91) 207 03 95
Mem   3500
Pro   M Morcillo
Holes 27 L 6118 m SSS 73
Fees   1800P (3600P)
Loc   Madrid 4km
Mis   Municipal club from 1984.
       Course built 1932.

Marbella & Estepona

Aloha (1975)

29660 Nueva Andalucía, Málaga
Tel   (952) 81 08 76/81 37 50/
       81 23 89
Mem   1500
Pro   J Mangas, A Jiménez
Holes 18 L 6261 m SSS 72
       9 hole short course
Fees   10000P
Loc   Marbella 8km

Atalaya Park G & CC (1968)

Crta Benahavis, Estepona, Marbella
Tel   (52) 78 18 94
Mem   500
Pro   D Strachan
Holes 18 L 6212 m SSS 72
Fees   7000P
Loc   Between Marbella/Estepona.
       Puerto Banus 4km. Málaga
       68km. Gibraltar 45 mins
Mis   Hotel guests 50% discount.

Las Brisas (1968)

Apdo 147, Urb Nueva Andalucía,
Marbella
Tel   81 08 75/81 30 21
       Fax 81 55 18
Mem   1250

Pro   3 Miguel
Holes   18 L 6198 m SSS 73
Fees   9000P
Loc   Opposite Puerto Banus.
8km S of Marbella

La Duquesa G & CC (1987)

Urb El Hacho, Manilva, Málaga
Tel   (952) 890425/6
Mem   400
Pro   JM Canizares, S Ruiz
Holes   18 L 6142 m SSS 72
Fees   5000P
Loc   Estepona 15km. Gibraltar
25km

Guadalmina (1959)

Guadalmina Alta, San Pedro de
Alcántara, Marbella
Tel   (952) 78 13 17
Mem   3000
Pro   A Hernandez, F Hernandez
Holes   18 L 6060 m SSS 72
18 L 6200 m SSS 72
9 L 1005 m Par 27
Fees   6000P
Loc   Málaga airport 68km.
Gibraltar 70km
Mis   Driving range

Los Naranjos (1977)

Apdo 64, 29660 Nueva Andalucía,
Marbella
Tel   (952) 81 52 06/81 36 59
Fax 81 14 28
Pro   M Escudero
Holes   18 L 6484 m SSS 75
Fees   D–9000P
Loc   8km S of Marbella.
60km S of Málaga airport

El Paraiso (1974)

Ctra Cádiz–Málaga Km 167, Estepona,
Marbella
Tel   (952) 78 47 12/78 47 16
Mem   750
Pro   J Franco
Holes   18 L 6142 m SSS 73
Fees   5800P
Loc   Marbella 14km

La Quinta (1989)

Crta de Ronda, Marbella
Tel   (952) 78 38 16/78 38 50
Pro   M Pinero, J Pinero
Holes   18 L 5700 m SSS 71
Loc   4km N of San Pedro de
Alcántara

Rio Real (1965)

Apartado 82, Marbella
Tel   (952) 77 17 00 (Ext 3086)
Pro   A Miguel
Holes   18 L 6130 m SSS 72
Fees   D–5200P (Free for Los
Monteros and Inconsol guests)
Loc   Marbella 5km

Sotogrande (1964)

Paseo del Parque, Sotogrande, Cádiz
Tel   (956) 79 20 50/79 20 51
Mem   1000
Pro   T Gonzalez, J Quiros
Holes   18 L 5885 m SSS 72
18 L 6263 m SSS 72
9 L 1299 m SSS 29
Fees   8000P (10000P)
Loc   San Roque, Gibraltar 18km

Valderrama (1985)

Sotogrande, Cádiz
Tel   (56) 79 27 75
Mem   112
Pro   J Zumaquero
Holes   18 L 6326 m SSS 72
Fees   D–7000P
Loc   Gibraltar 30km

North Coast

Barganiza (1982)

Apartado 277, 33080 Oviedo, Asturias
Tel   (985) 74 24 68
Mem   580
Pro   M Bellido
Holes   18 L 5298 m SSS 69
Fees   5000P
Loc   Oviedo–Gijon old road. 12km
from Oviedo via Noreña.

La Bilbaina (1976)

Laucariz, Munguía, Vizcaya
Tel   (94) 674 08 58/674 04 62
Pro   F García, S Larrázabal,
E Garaizar
Holes   18 L 6112 m SSS 72
Fees   D–4000P
Loc   15km N of Bilbao towards
Mungía

Castiello (1958)

Apartado de Correos, 161 Gijón
Tel   (985) 36 63 13
Mem   450
Pro   A Sierra
Holes   18 L 4817 m SSS 67
Fees   2000P
Loc   Oviedo–Gijón old road 4km
Mis   WE–comps during summer

Real Golf de Neguri (1911)

Apdo Correos 9, 49990 Algorta
Tel   (94) 469 02 00/04/08
Mem   2500
Pro   C Celles, L Losada, JM Fuente,
JR Larrazabal
Holes   18 L 6319 m SSS 72
6 hole Par 3 course
Fees   4000P
Loc   La Galea, 20km N of Bilbao

Real Golf de Pedreña (1928)

Apartado 233, Santander
Tel   (942) 50 00 01/50 02 66
Mem   1050
Pro   R Sota
Holes   18 L 5721 m SSS 70

Fees   5000P
Loc   20km from Santander, on Bay
of Santander

Real San Sebastián (1910)

PO Box 6, Fuenterrabia, Guipúzcoa
Tel   (943) 61 68 45/61 68 46
Mem   2500
Pro   Jesús Arruti, José Arruti,
J Gorostegui
Holes   18 L 6020 m SSS 71
Fees   5000P
Loc   Jaizubia Valley. Irún 6km.
San Sebastián 14km.

Real Zarauz (1916)

Apartado 82, Zarauz, Guipúzcoa
Tel   (943) 83 01 45
Mem   1100
Pro   N Belartieta
Holes   9 L 4882 m SSS 67
Fees   D–2000–4000P
Loc   Zarauz 1km. San Sebastián
25km

Pamplona

Ulzama (1965)

Guerendiain (Navarra)
Tel   (948) 30 51 62
Pro   R Echeverría
Holes   9 L 5984 m SSS 71
Loc   21km N of Pamplona

Seville & Gulf of Cádiz

Bellavista (1976)

Crta Huelva–Punta Umbría, Apdo 335,
Huelva
Tel   (955) 31 90 17
Fax 31 90 25
Mem   700
Pro   M Sanchez
Holes   9 L 6252 m SSS 72
Fees   3500–5000P
Loc   6km from Huelva

Pineda de Sevilla (1939)

Apartado 796, Sevilla
Tel   (954) 61 14 00/61 33 99
Pro   P Garrido, L González
Holes   9 L 5684 m SSS 71
Fees   1300P (2000P)
Loc   Seville 3km on Cádiz road

Vista Hermosa (1975)

Apartado 77, Urb Vista Hermosa,
Puerto de Santa María, Cádiz
Tel   (956) 85 00 11/85 66 26
Mem   1300
Pro   M Velasco
Holes   9 L 5492 m SSS 70
Fees   4000–8000P
Loc   25km W of Cádiz. 20km from
Jérez airport

Valencia & Castellón

El Bosque (1989)

46370 Chiva
Tel (96) 251 10 11
Pro A Cortes
Holes 18 L 6224 m SSS 73
Loc Nr Chiva, 30km W of Valencia, off Madrid road

Costa de Azahar (1960)

Ctra Grao–Benicasim, Castellón de la Plana
Tel (964) 22 70 64
Mem 600
Pro A Sanchez
Holes 9 L 2724 m SSS 70
Fees D–2000P W–8000P
Loc Castellón 5km. Benicasim 5km

Escorpión (1975)

Apartado Correos 1, Betera (Valencia)
Tel 1 60 12 11
Mem 1400
Pro A Sanchez, J Rodriguez, P Contreras
Holes 18 L 6345 m SSS 73
Fees 3000P (5000P)
Loc Betera, Valencia 20km

Manises (1964)

Apartado 22.029, Manises (Valencia)
Tel (96) 379 08 50
Mem 110
Pro FE Pinto
Holes 9 L 2607 m Par 72
Loc Manises, Valencia 8km

Mediterraneo CC (1978)

Urb La Coma, Borriol, (Castellón)
Tel (964) 32 12 27
Mem 1300
Pro V Garcia, JR López
Holes 18 L 6038 m SSS 72
Fees 3500–4500P (4500–5000P)
Loc Borriol, 5km NW of Castellón

El Saler (1968)

46012 Parador Luis Vives, El Saler, Valencia
Tel (96) 161 11 86
Mem 700
Pro JA Cabo
Holes 18 L 6485 m SSS 75
Fees D–4500P W–21750P
Loc Nr Oliva, 18km from Valencia towards Cullera

Zaragoza

Aero Club de Zaragoza (1966)

Coso 34, Zaragoza
Tel (976) 21 43 78
Holes 9 L 4953 m SSS 66
Fees 2000P (3000P)
Loc Zaragoza 12km

La Penaza (1973)

Apartado 3039, Zaragoza
Tel (976) 34 28 00/04
Mem 700
Pro F Pino, P García, V Tapia
Holes 18 L 6161 m SSS 72
Fees D–3000P (4000P)
Loc Zaragoza 15km on Madrid road, nr air base

Sweden

Far North

Boden (1946)

Box 107, 961 21 Boden
Tel (0921) 61071
Mem 355
Pro J Gidlund
Holes 9 L 5796 m SSS 73
Fees 50kr
Loc Boden 17km

Gällivare–Malmberget (1973)

Box 52, 972 00 Gällivare
Tel (0970) 23955
Mem 2080
Pro P Mattsson
Holes 9 L 5270 m SSS 70
Fees D–50kr
Loc 4km from Gällivare towards Malmberget

Härjedalsfjällen (1972)

Vintergatan 5, 8290 95 Funäsdalen
Tel (0684) 21240
Mem 520
Pro V Agardh
Holes 18 L 5300 m SSS 72
Fees 100kr

Härnösand (1957)

Box 52, 871 22 Härnösand
Tel (0611) 661 69
Mem 1280
Pro F Guedra
Holes 18 L 5265 m SSS 69
Fees 80kr
Loc Vängnön, 12km N of Härnösand on E4

Luleå (1955)

Box 314, 95125 Luleå
Tel (0920) 56091/56174
Mem 1100
Pro L Stewart
Holes 18 L 5675 m SSS 72
Fees 100kr
Loc Rutvik, 12km E of Luleå

Östersund–Frösö (1947)

Box 40, 83201 Frösön
Tel (063) 43001
Mem 1300
Pro G Knutsson
Holes 18 L 6000 m SSS 73
Fees 100kr
Loc Island of Frösö
Mis Open May–Sept

Öviks GC Puttom (1967)

Box 216, 891 32 Örnsköldsvik
Tel (0660) 64070/64091
Mem 1200
Pro T Mogren (0660) 64080
Holes 18 L 5795 m SSS 72
Fees 100kr
Loc 15km N of Örnsköldsvik on E4
Mis Season Jun–Sept

Piteå (1960)

Nöton, 94190 Piteå
Tel (0911) 14990
Mem 520
Pro A Gillard
Holes 9 L 5905 m SSS 72
Fees 50kr
Loc 2km NE of Piteå
Mis Midnight sun golf Jun/Jul

Skellefteå (1967)

Box 152, 931 22 Skellefteå
Tel (0910) 79333/79866
Mem 1081
Pro N Fosker, S Skinner
Holes 18 L 6135 m SSS 73
Fees 120kr
Loc Skellefteå 5km

Sollefteå–Långsele (1970)

Box 213, 881 01 Sollefteå
Tel (0620) 21477
Mem 712
Holes 18 L 5890 m SSS 72
Fees 80kr
Loc Österforse, 15km SW of Sollefteå (Route 89)

Sundsvall (1952)

Roddvägen 31, 862 00 Kvissleby
Tel (060) 561020
Mem 825
Pro T Bjornsson
Holes 18 L 5885 m SSS 72
Fees 100kr
Loc Skottsund, 15km S of Sundsvall

Umeå (1954)

Vintergatan 18, 902 54 Umeå
Tel (090) 41071/23495
Mem 1167
Pro J Anderson
Holes 18 L 5752 m SSS 72
Fees 120kr
Loc 16km SE of Umeå

Gothenburg

Albatross (1973)

Lillhagsvägen, 422 50 Hisings–Backa
Tel   (031) 551901/550500
       Fax 031 555900
Mem   1000
Pro   P Johansson
Holes 18 L 6020 m SSS 72
Fees   150kr (200kr)
Loc   10km N of Gothenburg on
       Hising Island

Delsjö (1962)

Kallebäck, 412 76 Göteborg
Tel   (031) 406959
Mem   1020
Pro   E Cedervall
Holes 18 L 5785 m SSS 71
Fees   150kr
Loc   5km E of Gothenburg
       (Route 40)
Mis   Driving range

Forsegårdens (1982)

Gamla Forsv 1, 434 47 Kungsbacka
Tel   (0300) 13649
Mem   925
Pro   J Moreau
Holes 18 L 6110 m SSS 72
Fees   100kr (150kr) 1989 prices
Loc   50km S of Gothenburg

Göteborg (1902)

Box 2056, 436 02 Hovås
Tel   (031) 282444
Mem   950
Pro   E Öster
Holes 18 L 5935 yds SSS 69
Fees   150kr (200kr)
Loc   11km S of Gothenburg RD 158

Gullbringa (1967)

442 95 Kungälv
Tel   (0303) 27872/27161
Mem   500
Pro   Peter & Pia Johansson
Holes 18 L 5775 m Par 72
Fees   150kr
Loc   14km W of Kungälv on road
       to Marstrand

Kungsbacka (1971)

Hamra Gaård Pl 515, 43040 Särö
Tel   (031) 936277
Mem   915
Pro   P Nellbeck
Holes 13 L 5855 m SSS 72
Fees   120kr (150kr)
Loc   7km N of Kungsbacka on
       Route 158

Lysegården (1966)

Box 82, 442 21 Kungälv
Tel   (0303) 23426
Mem   1367
Holes 18 L 5670 m SSS 71
       9 L 5444 m SSS 70
Fees   18 hole:120kr. 9 hole:100kr
Loc   Kungälv 10km

Mölndals (1979)

Box 77, 437 21 Mölndal
Tel   (031) 993030
Mem   1200
Pro   D Robinson
Holes 18 L 5625 m SSS 74
Fees   120kr (150kr)
Loc   25km S of Gothenburg

Öijared (1958)

Pl 1082, 448 00 Floda
Tel   (0302) 30604
Mem   1542
Pro   E Dawson
Holes 18 L 5875 m SSS 71
       18 L 5655 m SSS 71
Fees   140kr (180kr)
Loc   Alihgsås 24km. Gothenburg
       35km
Mis   WE–Members & guests only
       before 3pm

Partille (1971)

Box 234, 433 24 Partille
Tel   (031) 987004/987114
Mem   850
Pro   D Olsson
Holes 18 L 5330 m SSS 70
Fees   100kr
Loc   Öjersjö, 1km from Gothenburg

Särö (1899)

Box 74, 43040 Särö
Tel   (031) 936317
Mem   850
Pro   J Rosell, J Hampf
Holes 9 holes Par 27
       9 holes Par 34
Fees   100kr (130kr)
Loc   Gothenburg 18km (Route 158).
       Kungsbacka 10km

Stora Lundby (1983)

Pl 4035, 440 06 Grabo
Tel   (0302) 44200
Mem   1400
Pro   L Svensson, P Houbrandt
Holes 18 L 6040 m Par 72
       9 hole Par 3 course
Fees   18 hole:180kr Par 3–60kr
Loc   On W coast, 20 mins from
       Gothenburg
Mis   Championship course

Skane & South

Ängelholm (1973)

Box 1117, 26222 Ängelholm
Tel   (0431) 30260
Mem   1050
Pro   Y Mahmoud
Holes 18 L 5760 m SSS 72
Fees   90–150kr
Loc   10km E of Ängelholm on route
       114

Barsebäck (1969)

Box 214, 240 22 Löddeköpinge
Tel   (046) 776230
Mem   1795
Pro   I Christersson
Holes Old 18 L 5910 m SSS 72
       New 18 L 5855 m SSS 72
Fees   D–200kr
Loc   35km N of Malmö
Mis   WD–visitors welcome

Båstad (1929)

Box 1037, 26901 Båstad
Tel   (0431) 73136
Mem   1050
Pro   P Hansson
Holes 18 L 5760 m SSS 71
Fees   200kr (250kr)
Loc   4km W of Båstad (Route 115)
Mis   Handicap certificate required

Bedinge (1931)

Box 20, 230 21 Beddingestrand
Tel   (0410) 25514
Mem   700
Pro   I Persson
Holes 18 L 4500 m SSS 66
Fees   D–100kr W–500kr
Loc   Trelleborg 20km

Bokskogen (1963)

Box 30, 230 40 Bara I
Tel   (040) 481004
Mem   1200
Pro   J Larsson
Holes 18 L 6050 m SSS 73
       9 L 5490 m SSS 70
Fees   120kr (160kr)
Loc   Malmö 15km

Bosjökloster (1974)

243 95 Höör
Tel   (0413) 25858
Mem   975
Pro   S Kvillström
Holes 18 L 5890 m SSS 72
Fees   80kr (130kr)
Loc   7km S of Höör. 40km NE
       of Malmö

Eslöv (1966)

Box 150, 241 22 Eslöv
Tel (0413) 18610/13494
Mem 1150
Pro C Wilkström (0413) 16213
Holes 18 L 5670 m SSS 71
Fees 130kr (180kr)
Loc 4km S of Eslöv (Route 113)

F5 (1959)

c/o Byvägen 36, 260 73 Ljungby
Tel (0435) 41467
Mem 600
Holes 9 L 5675 m SSS 72
Fees 60kr
Loc 1km from Ljungbyhed, on the airfield

Falsterbo (1909)

PO Box 71, Fyrvagen 230 11 Falsterbo
Tel (040) 470078
Mem 1000
Pro P Chamberlain
Holes 18 L 6400 yds SSS 72
Fees 170kr (230kr) 1989 prices
Loc 35km S of Malmö
Mis Summer WE–only with member

Flommens (1935)

230 11 Falsterbo
Tel (040) 475016
Mem 1085
Pro B Kristoffersson, G Mueller
Holes 18 L 5610 m SSS 72
Fees 130kr (160kr)
Loc Malmö 35km

Hässleholm (1978)

Skyrup, 282 00 Tyringe
Tel (0451) 53111
Mem 1000
Pro H Damstoft
Holes 18 L 5830 m SSS 72
Fees 100kr (150kr)
Loc Hässleholm 15km. Tyringe 7km

Helsingborg (1924)

26040 Viken
Tel (042) 236147
Mem 450
Holes 9 L 4578 m SSS 65
Fees 60kr (70kr)
Loc 15km N of Helsingborg

Hylliekroken (1983)

Limhamnsvägen 85, 216 18 Malmö
Tel (040) 160262/160900
Mem 1820
Holes 9 L 2080 m Par 54
Fees 55kr (75kr)
Loc 3km SW of Malmö

Kristianstad (1924)

Box 41, 296 00 AN hus
Tel (044) 240656
Mem 1500
Pro D Green
Holes 18 L 5810 m SSS 72
9 L 2945 m SSS 36
Fees D–150kr (D–180kr)
Loc 18km SE of Kristanstad. Airport 20km

Landskrona (1960)

Erikstorp, 261 61 Landskrona
Tel (0418) 19528
Mem 1850
Pro A Olsson, P Hansson
Holes Old 18 L 5700 m SSS 71
New 18 L 4000 m SSS 62
Fees 120kr (150kr) 1989 prices
Loc 4km N of Landskrona towards Borstahusen
Mis Season Mar–Nov

Ljunghusens (1932)

Kinellsvag, Ljunghusen, 236 00 Höllviken
Tel 040 450384
Mem 1231
Pro G Sandegard
Holes 1–18 L 5895 m SSS 73
10–27 L 5670 m SSS 71
19–9 L 5455 m SSS 70
Fees 120–180kr
Loc Falsterbo Peninsula. Malmö 30km

Lunds Akademiska (1936)

Kungsmarken, 225 90 Lund
Tel (046) 99005
Mem 1300
Pro V MacDougall
Holes 18 L 5780 m SSS 72
Fees 100kr (140kr)
Loc 5km E of Lund

Malmö

Box 21068, 20021 Malmö
Tel (040) 292945
Mem 1100
Pro H Bergdahl
Holes 18 L 5720 m SSS 71
Fees 100kr (120kr)
Loc NE of Malmö, by motorway from Gothenburg
Mis Driving range

Mölle (1943)

260 42 Mölle
Tel (042) 47012/47520
Mem 1000
Pro J Pyk
Holes 18 L 5640 m SSS 70
Fees 150kr
Loc Mölle 3km
Mis WE–restrictions in July

Österlen (1945)

Lilla Vik, 272 00 Simrishamn
Tel (0414) 24230
Mem 720
Pro G Mueller (0414) 24005
Holes 18 L 5855 m SSS 72
Fees 100kr
Loc Vik, 8km N of Simrishamn

Östra Göinge (1981)

Box 114, 289 00 Knislinge
Tel (044) 60060
Mem 700
Pro A Lindbergh
Holes 9 L 5236 m Par 68
Fees 60kr
Loc 20km N of Kristianstad

Perstorp (1964)

PO Box 87, 284 00 Perstorp
Tel (0435) 35411
Mem 800
Pro J Kennedy
Holes 18 L 5675 m SSS 71
6 hole short course
Fees 110kr (150kr)
Loc 1km from Perstorp. Helsingborg 48km

Romeleåsen (1969)

Kvarnbrodda, 240 14 Veberöd
Tel (046) 82013/82014
Mem 1150
Pro J Byard
Holes 18 L 5783 m SSS 72
Fees 100kr (150kr)
Loc 6km S of Veberöd. 25km E of Malmö

Rya (1934)

Rya 5500, 225 90 Helsingborg
Tel (042) 221082
Mem 1200
Pro J Grant
Holes 18 L 5761 m SSS 72
Fees 140kr (170kr)
Loc 10km S of Helsingborg

Skepparslov (1984)

Udarpssäteri, 291 69 Kristianstad
Tel (044) 229508
Mem 1040
Pro C Claesson
Holes 18 L 5900 m SSS 72
Fees 100kr (120kr)
Loc 7km W of Kristianstad

Söderåsen (1966)

Box 41, 260 50 Billesholm
Tel (042) 73337
Mem 850
Pro T Lidholm
Holes 18 L 5920 m SSS 73
Fees 100kr (120kr)
Loc Helsingborg 20km

St Ibb (1972)

Ulf Ohrvik Victoriagatan 7c,
261 35 Landskrona
Tel   (0418) 72363
Mem   400
Pro   H Kristensen
Holes 9 L 5180 m SSS 68
Fees   120kr
Loc   Island of Hven
Mis   Ferry from Landskrona

Torekov (1924)

Box 81, 26093 Torekov
Tel   (0431) 63355
Mem   1100
Pro   G Hall
Holes 18 L 5785 m SSS 72
Fees   120–180kr
Loc   3km N of Torekov

Trelleborg (1963)

Pl 3307A, 231 93 Trelleborg
Tel   (0410) 30460
Mem   875
Pro   M Malmstrom
Holes 18 L 5320 m SSS 70
Fees   100kr (120kr)
Loc   5km W of Trelleborg

Vasatorp (1973)

Box 13035, 250 13 Helsingborg
Tel   (042) 235058
Mem   1800
Pro   K Davies (042) 235045
Holes 18 L 5875 m SSS 72
       9 L 2940 m SSS
Fees   150–180kr
Loc   8km E of Helsingborg

Wittsjö (1962)

Ubbaltsgården, 280 22 Vittsjö
Tel   (0451) 22635
Mem   600
Pro   W Falk
Holes 18 L 5366 m SSS 70
Fees   60kr (80kr)
Loc   Vittsjö 2km

Ystad (1930)

Box 162, 27100 Ystad
Tel   (0411) 50350
Mem   800
Pro   B Jones
Holes 18 L 5800 m SSS 72
Fees   100–150kr
Loc   7km E of Ystad towards
       Simrishamn

Stockholm

Ågesta (1958)

Ågesta, 12352 Farsta
Tel   (08) 604 5641
Mem   1367
Pro   R Tomlinson

Holes 18 L 5705 m SSS 72
       9 L 3660 m SSS 59
Fees   D–150kr (D–200kr)
Loc   Farsta

Björkhagen (1973)

Box 430, 121 04 Johanneshov
Tel   (08) 773 0431
Mem   608
Pro   K Johnson
Holes 9 L 4589 m SSS 66
Fees   60kr (90kr)
Loc   10km S of Stockholm

Bro–Balstå (1978)

Box 96, 197 00 Bro
Tel   (758) 41300/41310
Mem   1000
Pro   A Sjöhagen
Holes 18 hole course
Fees   120kr (180kr)
Loc   Thoresta, 30 mins NW of
       Stockholm

Djursholm (1931)

Hagbardsvägen 1, 18263 Djursholm
Tel   (08) 7551477
Mem   1603
Pro   G Deverell
Holes 18 L 5595 m SSS 71
       9 L 4400 m SSS 64
Fees   200kr (250kr)
Loc   12km N of Stockholm

Drottningholm (1956)

PO Box 183, 170 11 Drottningholm
Tel   (08) 759 0085
Mem   850
Pro   Ms C Montgomery
Holes 18 L 5825 m SSS 72
Fees   200kr (250kr)
Loc   Stockholm 10km

Haninge (1983)

Årsta Slott, 136 91 Haninge
Tel   (0750) 32240/32270
Mem   1200
Pro   B Deilert
Holes 18 L 5930 m SSS 73
Fees   160kr (190kr)
Loc   30km SE of Stockholm towards
       Nynäsham

Ingarö (1962)

Fogelvik, 130 35 Ingarö
Tel   (0766) 28244
Mem   740
Pro   RL Morin
Holes 18 L 5603 m SSS 71
Fees   130kr (160kr)
Loc   32km E of Stockholm (Route 74)

Lidingö (1932)

Box 1035, 181 21 Lidingö
Tel   (08) 7657911
Mem   1000

Pro   P Hansson, D Johnston
Holes 18 L 5770 m SSS 71
Fees   200kr
Loc   Stockholm 6km

Lindö (1978)

Box 1043, 186 92 Vallentuna
Tel   (0762) 72260
Mem   500
Holes 18 L 2850 m SSS 71
Loc   Vallentuna, 20km N of
       Stockholm
Mis   Driving range

Nynäshamn (1977)

Box 4,148 00 Ösmo
Tel   (0752) 27190
Mem   1200
Pro   S Ohlsson
Holes 10 L 5730 m 333 72
Fees   180kr
Loc   Nr Nynäshamn, 5 miles from
       Stockholm
Mis   Visitors welcome after 1pm

Saltsjöbaden (1929)

Box 51, 133 21 Saltsjöbaden
Tel   (08) 717 0125
Mem   1200
Pro   M Sheard (08) 717 1035
Holes 18 L 5685 m SSS 72
       9 L 3640 m SSS 60
Fees   18 hole:D–180kr (220kr)
       9 hole:D–130kr (160kr)
Loc   15km E of Stockholm
       (Route 228)

Sollentuna (1967)

Skillingegården, 191 77 Sollentuna
Tel   (08) 754 3625
Mem   1100
Pro   K Ekberg
Holes 18 L 5910 m SSS 72
Fees   180kr (220kr)
Loc   19km N of Stockholm.
       1km W of E4 (Rotebro)
Mis   Handicap certificate required.
       Driving range

Stockholm (1904)

Kevingestrand 20, 182 31 Danderyd
Tel   (08) 755 0031
Mem   993
Pro   K Gow
Holes 18 L 5510 m SSS 71
Fees   200kr
Loc   7km NE of Stockholm
       (Route E3)
Mis   WE–members' guests only

Täby (1968)

Skålhamra Gård, 183 43 Täby
Tel   (0762) 23261
Mem   1240
Pro   T Holmström
Holes 18 L 5776 m SSS 73
Fees   200–250kr
Loc   3km N of Stockholm

Ullna (1981)

Rosenkälla, 18400 Åkersberga
Tel   (0762) 26075
Mem   580
Pro   J Cockin
Holes   18 L 6265 m SSS 72
Fees   300kr
Loc   20km N of Stockholm (E3)
Mis   Open Apr–Oct. Driving range.

Viksjö (1969)

Fjällens Gård, 175 45 Järfälla
Tel   (0758) 16600
Mem   1280
Pro   S Cherif, G Näslund
Holes   18 L 5930 m SSS 73
Fees   160kr (190kr)
Loc   Stockholm 18km

Wermdö G & CC (1966)

Torpa, 139 00 Värmdö
Tel   (0766) 20849
Mem   725
Pro   M Jansson
Holes   18 L 5630 m SSS 72
Fees   210kr (250kr)
Loc   25km E of Stockholm
        (Route 222)

East Central
(Uppland, Vastmanland,
Södermanland, Narke)

Ängsö (1979)

Skultunavägen 7, 722 17 Västerås
Tel   (0171) 41012
Mem   1075
Pro   P Gullberg
Holes   18 holes SSS 72
Fees   100kr (140kr)
Loc   15km E of Västerås

Ärila (1951)

Nicolai, 61192 Nyköping
Tel   (0155) 14967
Mem   1400
Pro   O Jansson
Holes   18 L 5735 m SSS 72
Fees   140kr
Loc   Nyköping 5km

Askersund (1980)

6903 Ammeberg
Tel   (0583) 34440
Mem   950
Pro   L Johansson
Holes   18 L 5800 m SSS 72
Fees   100kr
Loc   10km SE of Askersund towards
        Ammeberg. 1km on road to
        Kärra

Enköping (1970)

Box 206, 19902 Enköping
Tel   (0171) 20830
Mem   630
Pro   A Halim
Holes   18 L 5660 m SSS 72
Fees   80kr (120kr)
Loc   3km E of Enköping, off E18

Eskilstuna (1951)

Strängnäsvägen, 633 49 Eskilstuna
Tel   (016) 142629
Mem   950
Pro   A Robinson
Holes   18 L 5610 m SSS 70
Fees   100kr (120kr)
Loc   Eskilstuna

Fagersta (1970)

Box 2051, 77302 Fagersta
Tel   (0223) 54060
Mem   810
Holes   9 L 5775 m SSS 72
Fees   40kr
Loc   7km W of Fagersta on Route 65

Katrineholm (1959)

Box 74, 641 21 Katrineholm
Tel   (0150) 39011/39012
Mem   950
Pro   S Eriksson
Holes   18 L 5850 m SSS 72
Fees   140kr
Loc   Katrineholm 7km

Korslöt (1963)

Box 278, 731 26 Köping
Tel   (46221) 81090
Mem   950
Pro   B Malmquist
Holes   18 L 5636 m SSS 71
Fees   80kr (110kr)
Loc   5km N of Köping (Route 250)

Linde (1984)

Dalkarlshyttan, 711 31 Lindesberg
Tel   (0581) 13960
Mem   940
Pro   P Karlsson (0581) 15917
Holes   18 L 5631 m SSS 71
Fees   100kr (130kr)
Loc   42km N of Örebro on R60.

Nyby Bruk (1960)

PO Box 587, 63108 Eskilstuna
Tel   (016) 356782
Mem   350
Holes   9 L 6013 m SSS 72
Fees   60kr (100kr)
Loc   Torshälla 2km

Örebro (1939)

Vreta Lannabruk, 710 15 Vintrosa
Tel   (019) 91065
Mem   950
Pro   E Ericson
Holes   18 L 5865 m SSS 72

Fees   110kr (140kr)
Loc   20km W of Örebro on
        Route E18
Mis   6 hole pitch and putt

Roslagen

Box 110, 761 00 Norrtälje
Tel   (0176) 37137
Mem   400
Pro   L Modin
Holes   18 L 5725 m SSS 71
Fees   100kr (150kr)
Loc   Norrtälje 7km

Sala (1970)

Box 16, 733 21 Sala
Tel   (0224) 53077/53055/53064
Mem   920
Pro   T Borgling
Holes   18 L 5570 m SSS 71
Fees   100kr
Loc   Fallet Sala, 8km E of Sala
        towards Uppsala, Route 67/72

Sigtunabygden (1961)

Box 89, 193 00 Sigtuna
Tel   (0760) 54012
Mem   1070
Pro   H Reis
Holes   18 L 5740 m SSS 72
Fees   130kr (200kr)
Loc   Arlanda, 50km N of Stockholm

Södertälje (1952)

Box 91, 151 21 Södertälje
Tel   (0755) 38240
Mem   1100
Pro   B Tomlinson (0755) 47674
Holes   18 L 5875 m SSS 72
Fees   150kr (200kr)
Loc   4km W of Södertälje

Stjernfors (1973)

c/o Hagabacksvej 4, 71700 Storå
Tel   (0580) 41048
Mem   520
Holes   10 L 5548 m SSS 70
Fees   70kr
Loc   Kopparberg 5km

Strängnäs (1968)

Box 21, 645 21 Strängnäs
Tel   (0152) 14731
Mem   1000
Pro   K Jansson (0152) 14702
Holes   18 L 5790 m SSS 72
Fees   100kr (150kr)
Loc   3km S of Strängnäs

Trosa–Vagnhärad (1972)

Box 80, 619 00 Trosa
Tel   (0156) 22211/17617
Mem   788
Pro   C Rose
Holes   9 L 5860 m SSS 72
Fees   90kr
Loc   Trosa 5km toward Uttervik

Upsala (1937)

Box 12015, 750 12 Uppsala
Tel   (018) 461270
Mem   1790
Pro   M Lord (018) 461241
Holes 18 L 6176 m SSS 74
       9 L 1643 m SSS 56
Fees   80kr (120kr)
Loc   Uppsala 10km
Mis   Driving range

Västerås (1931)

Bjärby, 724 81 Västerås
Tel   (021) 357543
Mem   1400
Pro   T Ljungqvist
Holes 18 L 5380 m SSS 69
Fees   100kr (140kr)
Loc   2km N of Västerås

North

Avesta (1963)

Box 168, 77400 Avesta
Tel   (0226) 10363/10866/12766
Mem   950
Pro   G Long
Holes 18 L 5560 m SSS 71
Fees   100kr (120kr)
Loc   Avesta 3km

Bollnäs

Box 72, 82101 Bollnäs
Tel   (0278) 50920/50540
Mem   725
Pro   K Hagström
Holes 14 L 5870 m Par 72
Fees   60kr
Loc   15km S of Bollnäs
       on Route 83

Falun–Borlänge (1956)

Pl 8218, 791 93 Falun
Tel   (023) 31015
Mem   1000
Pro   A Ryberg
Holes 18 L 6085 m SSS 72
Fees   100kr (120kr)
Loc   Aspeboda, between Falun
       13km, and Borlänge 8km.
       Dala Airport 15km

Gävle (1949)

Bönavägen 93, 805 95 Gävle
Tel   (026) 113163
Mem   1350
Pro   W Youngman
Holes 18 L 5735 m SSS 73
       9 L 2910 m SSS 36
Fees   120kr (140kr)
Loc   Gävle 3km

Hagge (1963)

Hagge, 771 00 Ludvika
Tel   (0240) 28087
Mem   610
Pro   U Sandberg
Holes 9 L 5680 m SSS 71

Fees   60kr
Loc   Hagge 2km. Ludvika 6km

Hofors (1965)

Box 117, 813 00 Hofors
Tel   (0290) 85125
Mem   750
Pro   G Sandegård
Holes 18 L 5400 m SSS 70
Fees   60kr (70kr)
Loc   5km SE of Hofors

Högbo (1962)

Daniel Tilas Väg 4, 81192 Sandviken
Tel   (026) 45015
Mem   1400
Pro   G Sandegard
Holes 18 L 5680 m SSS 71
Fees   120kr (150kr)
Loc   6km N of Sandviken
       (Route 272)

Hudiksvall (1964)

Tjuvskär 52 08, 824 00 Hudiksvall
Tel   (0650) 15930
Mem   760
Pro   MB Larsson
Holes 18 L 5750 m SSS 72
Fees   80kr (100kr)
Loc   Hudiksvall 4km

Leksand (1977)

Box 25, 793 01 Leksand
Tel   (0247) 14204
Mem   1061
Pro   P Jönsson (0247) 10749
Holes 18 L 5640 m SSS 71
Fees   110kr (130kr)
Loc   2km N of Leksand

Ljusdal (1973)

Box 151, 827 00 Ljusdal
Tel   (0651) 14366
Mem   520
Holes 9 L 5920 m SSS 72
Fees   40kr
Loc   2km E of Ljusdal

Mora (1980)

Box 264, 792 01 Mora
Tel   (0250) 10182
Mem   585
Pro   P Mickols
Holes 18 L 5600 m Par 72
Fees   100kr (120kr)
Loc   40km NW of Rättvik
Mis   Driving range

Rättvik (1954)

Box 29, 795 00 Rättvik
Tel   (0248) 10773
Mem   950
Pro   S Kvillström
Holes 18 L 5321 m SSS 69
Fees   110kr (130kr)
Loc   Rättvik 2km

Söderhamn (1961)

Oxtorget 1C, 826 00 Söderhamn
Tel   (0270) 51000
Mem   582
Pro   M Andersson
Holes 18 L 5940 m SSS 72
Fees   D–70kr
Loc   Söderhamn 8km

South East

Älmhult (1975)

Box 152, 343 00 Älmhult
Tel   (0476) 14135
Mem   650
Pro   B Mårtensson
Holes 9 L 5350 m SSS 70
Fees   D–70kr
Loc   Askya, Älmhult

Carlskrona (1949)

PO Almo, 370 24 Nättraby
Tel   (0455) 35123
Mem   1000
Pro   A Malmberg
Holes 18 L 5525 m Par 70
Fees   D–120kr
Loc   Karlskrona 15km

Eksjö (1938)

Skedhult, 575 00 Eksjö
Tel   (0381) 13525
Mem   550
Pro   D Nicholson
Holes 18 L 5930 m SSS 72
Fees   100kr (120kr)
Loc   6km from Eksjö on Nässjö road

Emmaboda (1976)

Kyrkogatan, 360 60 Vissefjärda
Tel   (0471) 20505/20540
Mem   612
Holes 9 L 5165 m SSS 68
Fees   60kr
Loc   Emmaboda 12km

Finspång (1965)

Viberga Gård, 612 00 Finspång
Tel   (0122) 13940
Mem   1100
Pro   J Kjellvall
Holes 18 L 5800 m Par 72
Fees   100kr
Loc   3km E of Finspång (Route 51).
       Norrköping 25km.

Hook (1942)

560 13 Hok
Tel   (0393) 21420
Mem   850
Pro   A Steen (0393) 21310
Holes 18 L 5758 m SSS 72
Fees   100kr (130kr)
Loc   Vaggeryd 12km.
       Jönköping 30km

Isaberg (1968)

Box 40, 33200 Gislaved
Tel   (0370) 36330
Mem   1214
Pro   S Carpenter
Holes   18 L 5800 m SSS 72
Fees   150kr W-750kr
Loc   18km N of Anderstorp and
        Gislaved. 10km W of Gnosjö.
        60km S of Jönköping.

Jönköping (1936)

Kettilstorp, 552 67 Jönköping
Tel   (036) 76567
Mem   1241
Pro   A Turnbull
Holes   18 L 6370 m SSS 70
Fees   140kr
Loc   3km S of Jönköping
Mis   WE-NA before 1pm

Kalmar (1947)

Box 278, 391 23 Kalmar 1
Tel   (0480) 72111
Mem   1100
Pro   H Weinhofer
Holes   18 L 5950 m SSS 72
Fees   150kr (180kr)
Loc   9km N of Kalmar

Karlshamn (1962)

Karlshamn 292 00
Tel   (0454) 50085
Mem   720
Pro   B Fredriksson
Holes   18 L 5861 m SSS 72
Fees   D-120kr
Loc   Morrum

Lagan (1966)

Box 63, 34014 Lagan
Tel   (0372) 30450
Mem   950
Pro   F Schröder
Holes   18 L 5600 m SSS 71
Fees   100kr (120kr)
Loc   Lagan, 10km N of Ljungby

Linköping (1945)

Box 10054, 580 10 Linköping
Tel   (013) 120646
Mem   1100
Pro   B Lemke, B Patterson
Holes   18 L 5675 m SSS 71
Fees   130kr
Loc   Linköping 1km

Mjölby (1983)

Box 171, 595 00 Mjölby
Tel   (0142) 12570
Mem   950
Pro   A Starkman
Holes   18 L 5485 m SSS 71
Fees   120kr
Loc   35km WSW of Linköping, on
        E4 between Stockholm and
        Gothenburg.

Motala (1956)

PO Box 204, 59100 Motala
Tel   (0141) 50856/50840 (Sec)
Mem   950
Pro   S Johansson (0141) 50834
Holes   18 L 5855 m SSS 72
Fees   100kr (150kr)
Loc   3km S of Motala (Route 50
        or 32)

Norrköping (1928)

Klinga, Box 2150, 600 02 Norrköping
Tel   (011) 35234
Mem   830
Pro   P Karström (011) 35236
Holes   18 L 5860 m SSS 72
Fees   100kr (120kr)
Loc   Klinga, 2km S of
        Norrköping on E4

Nybro (1971)

Box 235, 382 00 Nybro
Tel   (0480) 55044
Mem   1000
Pro   J Evergren
Holes   18 L 5829 m SSS 72
Fees   80kr (100kr) W-450kr
Loc   Nybro 10km

Öland (1983)

c/o Tullgaten 28, 387 00 Borgholm
Tel   (0485) 11200
Mem   600
Holes   9 hole course
Fees   40kr (50kr)
Loc   Källatorp, 40km N of Borgholm
Mis   Driving range at Ekerum,
        10km S of Borgholm

Oskarshamn (1972)

Box 148, 572 01 Oskarshamn
Tel   (0491) 94033
Mem   900
Pro   I Hult
Holes   18 L 5545 m SSS 72
Fees   100kr (120kr)
Loc   10km from Oskarshamn, on
        Route E66 towards Fliseryd

Ronneby (1964)

Box 26, 372 21 Ronneby
Tel   (0457) 10315
Mem   1050
Pro   F Johnsson
Holes   18 L 5323 m SSS 70
Fees   120kr
Loc   Ronneby 3km

Söderköping (1983)

60590 Norrköping
Tel   (011) 70579
Mem   910
Pro   L Cernold (011) 70039
Holes   18 L 5730 m SSS 72
Fees   100kr (120kr)
Loc   Västra Husby, 9km W of
        Söderköping

Tobo (1971)

Tobo Gård, 598 00 Vimmerby
Tel   (0492) 30028/30346
Pro   L Wiberg
Holes   18 L 5950 m SSS 73
Fees   80kr
Loc   S of Vimmerby off Route 34.
        280km E of Gothenburg

Tranås (1952)

N Storgatan 130, 573 00 Tranås
Tel   (0140) 11661
Mem   900
Pro   S Reese
Holes   18 L 5830 m SSS 72
Fees   100kr
Loc   2km N of Tranås

Vadstena (1956)

Hagalund, 592 00 Vadstena
Tel   (0143) 12743?
Mem   339
Holes   9 L 5486 m SSS 70
Fees   50kr (60kr)
Loc   Vadstena $2^1/_2$ km

Värnamo (1962)

Box 146, 331 01 Värnamo
Tel   (0370) 23123
Mem   625
Pro   A Marshall
Holes   18 L 6253 m SSS 72
Fees   100kr (120kr)
Loc   8km E of Värnamo on
        Route 127
Mis   Driving range

Västervik (1959)

Box 62, 593 22 Västervik
Tel   (0490) 19417
Mem   750
Pro   P Johansson (0490) 31521
Holes   9 L 5720 m SSS 71
Fees   D-80kr
Loc   Västervik 2km

Växjö (1959)

Box 227, 351 05 Växjö
Tel   (0470) 21539
Mem   975
Pro   L Ibsonius (0470) 14004
Holes   18 L 5860 m SSS 72
Fees   100kr (120kr)
Loc   Växjö 3km

Vetlanda (1983)

Box 249, 574 01 Vetlanda
Tel   (0383) 18310
Mem   750
Pro   S Petersson
Holes   18 holes Par 72
Fees   80kr
Loc   Östanå, 3km from Vetlanda.

For explanation of abbreviations, see page 460.

Visby

Box 1038, 621 21 Visby
Tel   (0498) 45058
Mem   965
Pro   F Bergqvist (0498) 45100
Holes 18 L 5855 m SSS 72
Fees   120kr
Loc   Visby 25km

South West

Alingsås (1985)

Hjälmared 4050, 444 95 Alingsås
Tel   (0322) 52421
Mem   1075
Pro   A Liljedahl
Holes 18 L 5650 m SSS 71
Fees   100kr (150kr)
Loc   5km from Alingsås towards
        Borås. Gothenburg 48km

Åtvidaberg (1954)

Box 180, 597 00 Åtvidaberg
Tel   (0120) 11425/12510
Mem   950
Pro   B Nygren (0120) 12510
Holes 18 L 6010 m SSS 72
Fees   120kr
Loc   30km SE of Linköping

Bäckavattnet (1977)

Box 288, 30107 Halmstad
Tel   (035) 44271
Mem   1000
Pro   S Grant
Holes 18 L 5770 m SSS 73
Fees   130kr
Loc   13km E of Halmstad (RD25)

Billingen (1949)

St Kulhult, 540 17 Lerdala
Tel   (0511) 80291
Mem   600
Pro   B Falk (0511) 80298
Holes 18 L 5605 m Par 71
Fees   80kr (100kr)
Loc   Between Skara and Skövde

Borås (1933)

Östra Vik, Kråkered, 50590 Borås
Tel   (033) 50142
Mem   1100
Pro   L Prick
Holes 18 L 5815 m SSS 72
Fees   100kr (120kr)
Loc   6km S of Borås, on new Route
        41 towards Varberg
Mis   Season Apr–Oct

Ekarnas (1970)

Balders Väg 12, 467 00 Grästorp
Tel   (0514) 11450
Mem   3900
Holes 9 L 4480 m SSS 64
Fees   60kr
Loc   25km E of Trollhätten.
        Lidköping 35km

Falkenberg (1949)

Golfvagen, 311 00 Falkenberg
Tel   (0346) 50287
Mem   1350
Pro   S–A Bolten
Holes 27 L 5650–5770 m SSS 72
Fees   100–120kr (190kr)
Loc   5km S of Falkenberg

Falköping

Box 99, 52100 Falköping
Tel   (0515) 31270
Mem   800
Pro   G Johansson
Holes 18 L 5835 m SSS 72
Fees   D–80kr
Loc   7km E of Falköping on
        Route 46 towards Skovde

Halmstad (1930)

302 70 Halmstad
Tel   (035) 30077
Mem   2122
Pro   B Grafton, PO Johansson,
        M Sorling, B Gustafsson
Holes 18 L 5980 m SSS 73
        18 L 5555 m SSS 72
Fees   150–200kr
Loc   Halmstad 9km

Hökensås (1962)

PO Box 116, 544 00 Hjo
Tel   (0503) 16059
Mem   630
Pro   G Nyberg
Holes 18 L 5540 m SSS 71
Fees   100kr (130kr)
Loc   8km S of Hjo on Route 195

Hulta (1972)

Box 54, 517 01 Bollebygd
Tel   (033) 88180
Mem   1200
Pro   W Byard
Holes 18 L 6000 m SSS 73
Fees   150kr
Loc   Nr Gothenburg

Laholm (1964)

Box 101, 312 22 Laholm
Tel   (0430) 30601
Mem   1050
Pro   C Eklund
Holes 18 L 5430 m SSS 70
Fees   130kr (140kr)
Loc   5 miles E of Laholm
        (Route 24)

Lidköping (1967)

Box 2029, 531 02 Lidköping
Tel   (0510) 46122/46144
Mem   900
Pro   T Lundahl
Holes 18 L 5565 m SSS 70
Fees   100kr (120kr)
Loc   5km E of Lidköping

Mariestad (1975)

PO Box 299, 542 23 Mariestad
Tel   (0501) 17383
Mem   1120
Pro   P Billberg
Holes 18 L 5890 m SSS 72
Fees   100kr
Loc   4km W of Mariestad, at
        Lake Vänern

Marks (1962)

Brättingstorpsvägen 28, 51158 Kinna
Tel   (0320) 14220
Mem   1200
Pro   G Nyberg
Holes 18 L 5310 m SSS 69
Fees   120kr (140kr)
Loc   Kinna, 30km S of Borås

Onsjö (1974)

Box 100, 462 00 Vänersborg
Tel   (0521) 64149
Mem   750
Pro   N Goodison (0521) 62575
Holes 18 L 5730 m SSS 72
Fees   80kr (100kr)
Loc   4km S of Vänersborg.
        8km N of Gothenburg.

Töreboda (1965)

Box 18, 545 00 Töreboda
Tel   (0506) 16240
Mem   581
Pro   D McLean
Holes 18 L 5235 m SSS 70
Fees   100kr
Loc   7km E of Töreboda

Trollhättan (1963)

Box 254, 461 26 Trollhättan
Tel   (0520) 41000
Mem   700
Pro   G Clark (0520) 41010
Holes 18 L 6200 m SSS 73
Fees   100kr
Loc   Koberg, 20km SE of Trollhättan

Ulricehamn (1947)

Box 179, 523 01 Ulricehamn
Tel   (0321) 10021
Mem   930
Pro   H Ljung
Holes 18 L 5402 m SSS 70
Fees   D–100kr
Loc   Backasen, 2km E of
        Ulricehamn

Varberg (1950)

Box 39, 432 21 Varberg
Tel   (0340) 37470
Mem   1000
Pro   F Englund
Holes 18 L 5797 m SSS 73
Fees   120kr
Loc   15km E of Varberg

West Central

Arvika

Box 33, 671 01 Arvika 1
Tel (0570) 54133
Pro A Söderqvist
Holes 9 L 5815 m SSS 71
Fees D–70kr
Loc 11km E of Arvika on
     Route 61

Billeruds (1961)

PO Box 192, 661 00 Säffle
Tel (0555) 91313
Mem 925
Pro R Bailey
Holes 18 L 5874 m SSS 72
Fees 120kr
Loc Valnäs, 15km N of Säffle

Fjällbacka (1967)

450 71 Fjällbacka
Tel (0525) 31150
Mem 900
Pro M Ericsson
Holes 18 L 5850 m SSS 72
Fees D–100–150kr
Loc 2km N of Fjällbacka
     (Route 163)

Forsbacka (1969)

Box 136, 662 00 Åmål
Tel (0532) 43055
Mem 550
Pro M El Sayed
Holes 18 L 5860 m SSS 72
Fees 100kr
Loc 6km W of Åmål on
     Route 164

Karlskoga (1975)

Bricketorp 647, 69194 Karlskoga
Tel (0586) 28597
Mem 975
Pro P Glimaker (0586) 28663
Holes 18 L 5705 m Par 72
Fees 120kr
Loc Valåsen, 5km E of Karlskoga
     (Route E18)

Karlstad (1957)

PO Box 294, 651 07 Karlstad
Tel (054) 36353
Mem 1300
Pro T Westberg
Holes 18 L 5900 m SSS 72
       9 L 2900 m SSS
Fees 120kr
Loc 12km E of Karlstad (Route 63)

Kristinehamn (1974)

Box 3037, 681 03 Kristinehamn
Tel (0550) 82310
Mem 650
Holes 18 L 5800 m SSS 71
Fees 100kr
Loc 3km N of Kristinehamn

Lyckorna (1967)

Box 66, 459 00 Ljungskile
Tel (0522) 20 176
Mem 1100
Pro U Ligner
Holes 18 L 5845 m SSS 72
Fees 150kr
Loc 20km S of Uddevalla

Orust (1981)

Pl 8290, 440 80 Ellös
Tel (0304) 053170
Mem 1500
Pro S Eriksson
Holes 18 L 5770 m SSS 72
Fees 110kr (130kr)
Loc Ellös, 10km from Henän.
     80km N of Gothenburg

Saxå (1964)

Asphyttegatan 24, 68200 Filipstad
Tel (0590) 24071
Mem 980
Pro F Speight
Holes 9 L 5860 m SSS 73
Fees 80kr
Loc 15km E of Filipstad (Route 63)

Skaftö (1963)

Röd 4476, 450 34 Fiskebäckskil
Tel (0523) 22544
Mem 700
Pro U Nilsson
Holes 9 L 5305 m SSS 70
Fees 110kr
Loc 4 miles from Uddevalla,
     towards Lysekil and
     Fiskebäckskil

Strömstad (1967)

Box 129, 452 00 Strömstad 1
Tel (0526) 11788
Mem 600
Pro T Hunter (0526) 14244
Holes 18 L 5490 m SSS 71
Fees 100kr W–500kr
Loc 6km N of Strömstad
Mis Driving range

Sunne (1970)

Box 108, 686 00 Sunne
Tel (0565) 60300
Mem 340
Pro A Olsson (0560) 10776
Holes 9 L 2845 m SSS 71
Fees 70kr
Loc 2km from Sunne on Route 234
     to Rottneros

Torreby (1961)

Torreby Slott, 455 00 Munkedal
Tel (0524) 21365/21109
Mem 1200
Pro J Grahn, K Grahn
Holes 18 L 5885 m SSS 72
Fees D–100–150kr
Loc Munkedal 8km. Uddevalla
     30km.

Uddeholm (1965)

683 03 Rada
Tel (0563) 60335/60025
Mem 800
Pro T Palm
Holes 18 L 5833 m SSS 72
Fees D–80kr
Loc 80km N of Karlstad RD62,
     at Lake Rada

Switzerland

Bern

Blumisberg (1959)

3184 Wünnewil
Tel (037) 36 34 38
Mem 670
Pro F Schiroli, W Marx
Holes 18 L 6048 m SSS 73
Fees 60fr (80fr)
Loc Blumisberg, 16km SW of Bern

Neuchâtel (1928)

2072 Saint-Blaise
Tel (038) 33 55 50
Mem 400
Pro J Kressig
Holes 18 L 5840 m SSS 70
Fees 40fr (60fr)
Loc Voens/Saint-Blaise, 5km E of
     Neuchâtel. 30km W of Bern

Bernese Oberland

Crans-sur-Sierre (1906)

3963 Crans-sur-Sierre-Montana
Tel (27) 41 21 68/41 27 03
     Fax 027 41 46 71
Mem 1320
Pro J Bonvin, RJ Barras, J–M Barras,
     B Cordonnier, B Mittaz, A Rey,
     M Bonvin, A Jeanquartier
Holes 18 L 6260 m SSS 72
       9 L 2667 m SSS 35
Fees 18 hole:50fr (60fr)
       9 hole:28fr (32fr)
Loc 20km E of Sion. Geneva 2 hrs

Gstaad-Saanenland (1962)

3780 Gstaad
Tel (030) 426 36
Mem 196
Pro B Herrmann
Holes 9 L 5580 m SSS 69
Fees 25fr (30fr)
Loc Saanenmöser, 15km N of
     Gstaad
Mis Open June–Oct

Interlaken–Unterseen (1964)

Postfach 110, 3800 Interlaken
Tel   (036) 22 60 22
Mem   400
Pro   B Chenaux
Holes   18 L 5980 m SSS 72
Fees   55fr (70fr)
Loc   Interlaken 3km

Riederalp (1986)

3987 Riederalp
Tel   (028) 27 29 32/27 14 63
Mem   250
Pro   M Cole
Holes   9 L 3016 m SSS 54
Fees   25fr (30fr)
Loc   10km NE of Brig
Mis   Season Jun–Oct

Lake Geneva & South West

Bonmont (1983)

Château de Bonmont, 1261 Chéserex
Tel   (022) 69 23 45
Mem   600
Pro   F Boillat, G Kaye, Y Radal
Holes   18 L 6160 m Par 71
Fees   D–60fr
Loc   3km from Nyon. 30km NE of Geneva

Domaine Impérial (1987)

CP 84, 1196 Gland
Tel   (0221) 64 45 45
Mem   1000
Pro   R Guignet, A Jeanquartier, G Martin, M Scopetta
Holes   18 L 6254 m SSS 74
Fees   WD–80fr
Loc   Nyon, 20km N of Geneva
Mis   Visitors–am only (max h'cap 30)

Geneva (1923)

70 Route de la Capite, 1223 Cologny
Tel   (022) 735 75 40
Fax 022 735 7105
Mem   1000
Pro   JM Larretche, H Muscroft, P Bagnoud, J Berthet
Holes   18 L 6250 m Par 72
Fees   60fr
Loc   Geneva 4km
Mis   WE–only with member.

Lausanne (1921)

Le Chalet à Gobet, 1000 Lausanne
Tel   (021) 784 13 15
Mem   850
Pro   A Gallardo, M Gallardo, M More, D Ingram
Holes   18 L 6165 m SSS 74
Fees   60fr (80fr)
Loc   7km N of Lausanne towards Le Mont

Montreux (1900)

Case Post 187, 1820 Montreux
Tel   (025) 26 46 16 (Dir/Sec)
Mem   491
Pro   P Bagnoud, J Bagnoud, J–L Chable
Holes   18 L 6205 m SSS 73
Fees   40fr (50fr)
Loc   Aigle, 15km S of Montreux

Verbier (1969)

1936 Verbier
Tel   (026) 7 49 95
Mem   140
Pro   C Torribio
Holes   18 hole Par 3 course
Fees   D–15fr (20fr)
Loc   Centre of Verbier
Mis   Open Jun–Oct

Villars (1922)

Case Postale 152, 1884 Villars
Tel   (025) 35 42 14
Mem   400
Pro   JL Chable, G Chable
Holes   18 L 4093 m SSS 61
Fees   35fr (50fr)
Loc   7km E of Villars towards Les Diablerets
Mis   Open June–Oct

Lugano & Ticino

Lugano (1923)

6983 Magliaso
Tel   (091) 71 15 57
Mem   900
Pro   D Maina, G Parisi, I Tremolada
Holes   18 L 5740 m SSS 71
Fees   50fr (70fr)
Loc   8km W of Lugano towards Ponte Tresa

Patriziale Ascona (1928)

Via al Lido 81, 6612 Ascona
Tel   (093) 35 21 32
Mem   350 250(L) 50(J)
Pro   V Caccia, F Codiga, F Salmina
Holes   18 L 5893 m SSS 71
Fees   50fr (70fr)
Loc   Ascona, 5km W of Locarno
Mis   Public course

St Moritz & Engadine

Arosa (1947)

7050 Arosa
Tel   (081) 31 22 15
Mem   200
Pro   AM Platz
Holes   9 L 4450 m SSS 64
Fees   D–35fr

Loc   Arosa, 20km S of Chur
Mis   Open June–Sept

Bad Ragaz (1957)

Hans Albrechtstrasse, 7310 Bad Ragaz
Tel   (085) 9 15 56
Mem   700
Pro   C Gaud, M Caligari, T Smith
Holes   18 L 5766 m SSS 70
Fees   60fr (70fr)
Loc   20km N of Chur. 100km SE of Zürich
Mis   Handicap certificate required

Davos (1929)

Postfach, 7270 Davos Dorf
Tel   (083) 5 56 34
Mem   600
Pro   HJ Hörenz
Holes   18 L 5715 yds SSS 67
Fees   50fr (60fr)
Loc   1km outside Davos
Mis   Open May–Oct

Engadin (1892)

7503 Samedan
Tel   (082) 6 52 26
Mem   400
Pro   A Casera, A Chiogna, F Hurtado, I Tremolada, J Wallwork
Holes   18 L 6350 m SSS 72
Fees   60fr
Loc   Samedan, 10km NE of St Moritz

Lenzerheide Valbella (1950)

7078 Lenzerheide
Tel   (081) 34 13 16
Mem   400
Pro   H Schumacher, R Blaesi
Holes   18 L 5269 m Par 69
Fees   50fr
Loc   20km S of Chur towards St Moritz
Mis   Public course

Vulpera (1923)

7552 Vulpera Spa
Tel   (084) 9 96 88
Mem   220
Pro   P Jones
Holes   9 L 2021 m SSS 62
Fees   40fr (50fr) W–230fr
Loc   Tarasp, nr Vulpera. 60km NE of St Moritz

Zürich & North

Breitenloo (1964)

Bassersdorf, 8309 Oberwil
Tel   (01) 836 40 80/836 64 86
Mem   380
Pro   Th Villiger
Holes   18 L 6100 m SSS 72
Fees   50fr (70fr)
Loc   Zürich Airport 8km

Bürgenstock (1928)

6366 Bürgenstock
Tel   (041) 61 24 34
Pro   G Denny
Holes   9 L 1935 m Par 34
Fees   35fr
Loc   15km S of Lucerne
Mis   Open May–Sept

Dolder (1907)

Kuthausstrasse 66, 8032 Zürich
Tel   (01) 47 50 45
Pro   D Dieter, C Brazerol
Holes   9 L 1735 m SSS 58
Fees   WD–50fr
Loc   Zürich
Mis   Open Apr–Nov. WE–only
        members/guests of Hotels
        Waldhaus, Dolder & Grand
        Dolder.

Hittnau–Zürich (1964)

PO Box, 8700 Küsnacht
Tel   (01) 950 24 42
Mem   475
Pro   E Bauer, D Parini
Holes   18 L 5720 m SSS 71
Fees   WD–60fr
Loc   Hittnau, 30km E of Zürich
Mis   WE–closed for non–members

Lucerne (1903)

Dietschiberg CH 6006
Tel   (041) 36 97 87
Mem   350
Pro   L Mudry, B Lagger
Holes   18 L 5700 m SSS 71
Fees   60fr
Loc   Lucerne 2km
Mis   Handicap certificate required.

Ostschweizischer (1948)

9246 Niederbüren
Tel   (071) 81 18 56
Mem   360
Pro   CB Craig
Holes   18 L 5920 m SSS 71
Fees   D–50fr (60fr)
Loc   Niederbüren, 25km NW of
        St Gallen

Schinznach–Bad (1929)

5116 Schinznach-Bad
Tel   (056) 43 12 26
Mem   235
Pro   H Zimmerman, V Krajewski
Holes   9 L 6036 m Par 72
Fees   40fr (50fr)
Loc   6km S of Brugg. 35km W of
        Zürich

Schönenberg

8821 Schönenberg
Tel   (01) 788 16 24
Mem   400
Pro   T Charpié, J Wallwork,
        L Freeman
Holes   18 L 6340 m SSS 73
Fees   D–60fr
Loc   20km S of Zürich

Zürich–Zumikon (1931)

8126 Zumikon ZH
Tel   (01) 918 00 50
Mem   700
Pro   R Lanz, G Denny, B Griss
Holes   18 L 6360 m SSS 74
Fees   WD–90fr
Loc   Zürich 10km
Mis   Visitors must be introduced.
        WE–closed for non–members

Yugoslavia

Bled (1974)

Cesta Svobode 13, 64260 Bled
Tel   (064) 78 282
Mem   350
Pro   D Jurman, M Lamberger
Holes   18 L 6320 m SSS 73
Fees   15Lstg W–91Lstg
Loc   3km W of Bled. Ljubljana
        airport 30km

Part V
The Government of the Game

Introduction

The Editor and Publishers of the Golfer's Handbook are grateful to the General Committee of the Royal & Ancient Club for its agreement to reproduce the Statement of Functions *of the Club. A brief history of how the Royal & Ancient came to be the Governing Body of the Game has been added, followed by a description of the important work of the Championship Committee, especially in its responsibility for The Open.*

The Royal & Ancient Golf Club

In Britain it is not unusual for the Governing Body of a Sport to have its origins in a private club, which later comes to be recognised as the authority through which the game is administered. The Royal & Ancient Golf Club of St Andrews is a prime example and enjoys a similar status to the Marylebone Cricket Club. With the world-wide spread of golf and cricket this century, both have emerged as the international body to which most other countries look for rulings and guidance.

The Royal & Ancient Club's records date back to 1754 when the Society of St Andrews Golfers adopted the rules which had been formulated in 1744 by the Gentlemen Golfers of Leith, later to become the Honourable Company of Edinburgh Golfers; the older club located across the Forth at Muirfield.

When in 1834 King William IV granted the St Andrews Gentlemen Golfers the right and privilege of using the title *Royal & Ancient*, the Honourable Company had temporarily lost cohesion and the R&A gradually acquired the status of the premier club. During the latter half of the Victorian age, in the 1880s and 1890s when, following the spread of the railway system, many new clubs were founded, they looked to the R&A for leadership and advice.

With the appointment of the first Rules of Golf Committee in 1897, the R&A became recognised as the Governing Authority in all countries except the United States and Mexico where the United States Golf Association controls the game. Golf federations of many countries are affiliated to the R&A. This is made clear in the *Statement of Functions* of the R&A, reproduced with the permission of the General Committee. The work of the Championship Committee is expanded in a note below, with particular reference to The Open Championship.

The success of The Open in recent years, both as a spectacle and financially, has meant that the R&A can now support fully the development of the game, while remaining the guardian of its traditions. Its encouragement of young players, especially through the Boys and Youths Championships and the Golf Foundation, has helped produce the higher standards of play and younger champions now so apparent to all followers of the game.

Statement of Functions of the Royal & Ancient Golf Club throughout the world

With the developing interest in golf and the increasing complexity of the administration of the game, the Royal & Ancient Golf Club feels that a statement of its activities in this field would be of interest.

The functions for which the Club is responsible fall into three clearly defined categories. First, functions of an international nature, secondly functions of a national nature, and finally, the running of a Club with wide national and international Membership.

International Functions

In 1897 the Royal & Ancient became the Governing Authority on the Rules of Golf at the suggestion of the leading Golf Clubs in the United Kingdom at the time. Since then an ever increasing number of countries have sought affiliation to it, until today they number over 60, including several other Unions or Associations (eg the Ladies' Golf Union, European Golf Association, South American Golf Federation and Asia-Pacific Golf Confederation).

The Club in its negotiations with the United States Golf Association on matters pertaining to the Rules of Golf is not merely representing Great Britain and Ireland, but these many countries as well.

In 1919, when it took over the running of the Open and Amateur Championships, the Royal & Ancient became responsible for the Rules of Amateur Status and in matters pertaining thereto likewise represents these many countries.

The Royal & Ancient also supplies one of the two Joint Chairmen and Joint Secretaries of the World Amateur Golf Council which is responsible for the organisation of all World Amateur Team Championships.

There is close liaison at all times with the Professional Golfers' Association and the PGA European Tour.

National Functions

Prior to the First World War, a group of Clubs had been responsible for the running of the Open and Amateur Championships. In 1919 a meeting of these Clubs confirmed that the Royal & Ancient should be the Governing Authority for the game and agreed it should assume responsibility for the two Championships.

The decision that the Royal & Ancient should be the Governing Authority was endorsed at a Meeting of the English, Scottish, Irish and Welsh Unions in 1924, at which Meeting what is now the Council of National Golf Unions was formed with the object amongst others of directing the system of Standard Scratch Scores and Handicaps.

In 1948 the Royal & Ancient took over the Boys and in 1963 the Youths Championship from the private interests which had previously run them; this was done at the request of the individuals concerned. In 1969 the Royal & Ancient itself inaugurated the British Seniors Amateur Championship.

In addition to the organisation of five Championships, the Royal & Ancient is also responsible for the selection of Teams to represent Great Britain & Ireland in the Walker Cup, the Eisenhower Trophy, the St Andrews Trophy, and other International Tournaments. It is responsible for the organisation of such events when they are held in Great Britain and Ireland.

Club Functions

The Membership of the Club is limited to a total of 1,800, of which 1,050 may be resident in Great Britain and Ireland and 750 elsewhere: this Overseas Membership is spread over countries throughout the world.

The Membership both at home and abroad is representative and includes many who have given and are giving great services to golf in this country and abroad to many different Unions and Associations. This permits broad and effective representation on all the Club Committees concerned with international and national functions.

Exercise of International Functions

1. Rules of Golf

(a) Committee:
The Rules of Golf Committee exists for the purpose of reviewing the Rules of Golf from

time to time and of making decisions on their interpretation and publishing these decisions where necessary

The Committee consists of twelve Members elected by the Club, of whom three retire each year and are not eligible for re-election for one year, except in the case of the Chairman and Deputy Chairman, and of up to twelve additional persons invited annually to join the Committee from Golf Authorities at home and abroad.

At present the bodies represented are:

Council of National Golf Unions
United States Golf Association
European Golf Association
Australian Golf Union
New Zealand Golf Association
Royal Canadian Golf Association
South African Golf Union
Asia-Pacific Golf Confederation
South American Golf Federation
Japan Golf Association

(b) Revision of the Rules of Golf:
As the only other Governing Authority for the Rules of Golf is the USGA, the R&A works closely with this body when amendments to the Rules are under consideration for the purpose of maintaining uniformity in the Rules and their interpretation. Every four years a Conference takes place with the USGA for the purpose of deciding on the changes to be made. The quadrennial conference held in 1987 made numerous amendments to the 1984 Rules; these were mainly to clarify points of doubt which had emerged since 1984. The changes took effect on January 1st 1988. Although the Conference takes place quadrennially, the Rules are under constant review and investigations as to possible improvements start not long after a revision has taken place, so that ample time can be given to consult with interested parties.

Two years after a revision has taken place an important meeting is held with the USGA in the United States at the time of the Walker Cup to discuss progress and to start clearing the ground for the next Conference.

(c) Decisions:
The Rules of Golf Committee has a Decisions Sub-Committee which answers queries from Clubs and from all the Unions and Associations affiliated to the R&A. Those Decisions which seem to establish important or interesting points of interpretation are available in the form of a loose-leaf Decisions Service published jointly by the R&A and the USGA and issued world-wide. The number of subscribers to this Service is about 3,500 and is increasing steadily as golf expands.

2. Implements and Ball

The Committee consists of four Members elected by the Club, one Member of the Rules of Golf Committee and one Member of the Championship Committee, together with Consultant Members invited by the Committee to advise on technical matters. One of the elected Members retires each year but the Chairman may be re-elected immediately for the sake of continuity.

The Committee works in close co-operation with the USGA I & B Committee in interpreting the Rules and Appendices relating to the control of the form and make of golf clubs and the specifications of the golf ball to ensure that the game and established golf courses are not harmed by technical developments.

3. Rules of Amateur Status

(a) Committee:
The Committee consists of five members, of which four are elected by the Club and one provided by the Council of National Golf Unions. There are also Advisory Members to the Committee, representing the same Golfing Authorities as on the Rules of Golf Committee.

(b) Revision of Rules of Amateur Status:
A procedure, similar to that for the Rules of Golf, is adopted for revision of the Rules of Amateur Status and no policy changes are made without full consultation with all the affiliated Unions, the USGA and the PGA.

(c) Decisions:
The work of the Committee consists of (a) dealing with Applications for reinstatement to Amateur Status, (b) answering inquiries about the nature of prizes, conditions for Tournaments, etc, arising out of the increased impact of commercial sponsors on Amateur golf and the issue of guidelines and Decisions, (c) answering queries from individuals regarding their own position under the Rules and (d) controlling Scholarships and other Grants-in-aid.

Exercise of National Functions

The Championship Committee

The Championship Committee is responsible for the control of the five Championships and of the International Matches and Tournaments mentioned above.

The Committee consists of twelve elected Members elected by the Club, of whom three retire annually and are not eligible for re-election for one year. Two additional Members may also be invited to join the Committee annually together with two Business Members co-opted for four years.

For the organisation of any particular event, others may be co-opted, if required.

The work of this Committee has greatly increased in recent years, as is clearly evident from the staging of the Open Championship, for which prizes in 1984 amounted to £450,000. At the same time, more substantial reserve funds have been built up to ensure the continuance of the Open Championship as a premier world event.

The Committee makes annual donations to a number of golfing bodies, especially those concerned with the training and development of junior golf and for research on greenkeeping matters.

Selection Committee

The Selection Committee consists of a Chairman, who is a Member of the Club, and other Members, who need not be Members of the Club, appointed by the General Committee. These other Members have for some years now been representative of each of the four Home Unions. Normally they hold their appointments for four years.

Exercise of Club Functions

The domestic affairs of the Club are run by Committees which it is not necessary to describe in this statement.

It is appropriate, however, to mention that the Club does not own a Golf Course. It is, nevertheless, much concerned with the maintenance and improvements of all four Golf Courses in St Andrews. These Courses are controlled by the St Andrews Links Trust and are run by the Links Management Committee. Three of the Trustees and four Members of the Management Committee are appointed by the Club and equal numbers are appointed by the North-East Fife District Council. The Chairman of the Trust is appointed by the Secretary of State for Scotland and the current MP is also a Trustee. The Club contributes an annually negotiated sum to the Trust in return for Members' playing privileges.

Finance

International Functions:
After taking into account income derived from subscriptions to the Rules of Golf Decisions Service and the sale of official Rules publications, the net expenses of the Rules of Golf, Rules of Amateur Status and Rules for Implements and Ball are borne by External Activities.

National Functions:
Income and expenditure of all Championships run by the R&A and the expenses of Teams representing Great Britain & Ireland are accounted for in separate divisions of one Account.

Surpluses of all income over expenditure in the External Activities Account are held in reserve to ensure the continuance of the running of the various events at a high standard.

The Royal & Ancient Golf Club as a private Members' Club does not in any way benefit from the External Activities Account.

General Committee

Responsibility for directing and co-ordinating the three functions of the R&A—as a private club, as a governing authority for golf and as the body responsible for organising and running the championships and international matches —rests with the Club's General Committee, which controls all matters of policy. The Committee consists of sixteen R&A Members, eight of whom are elected by the Club; the other eight *ex-officio* members are the Captain and Chairmen of the Finance, Membership, House, Green, Rules of Golf, Championship and Amateur Status Committees.

The execution of the decisions of the Club Committees and of the decisions taken by the Members at Business Meetings is in the hands of the Secretary of the R&A, who is assisted by several senior officers and the appropriate infrastructure of secretaries and clerical staff.

Contacts with Affiliated Golfing Authorities

The R&A endeavours to consult with all those Golfing Authorities concerned whenever an issue of importance arises. This covers, in particular, matters relating to Rules of Golf, Rules of Amateur Status, and the Championships.

Meetings are held when appropriate with representatives of Golfing Authorities in Great Britain & Ireland and the European Golf Association. Consultations with other Golfing Authorities abroad are regularly conducted by correspondence.

In January 1970, a Conference attended by Golfing Unions and Associations in this country and representatives of the European Golf Association was held under the auspices of the R&A to discuss all matters of mutual interest, and in particular to establish the best means of communication in the future between the Unions and Associations concerned. This was followed by a similar Conference at Chantilly, Paris in 1976.

In May 1980 the first ever International Golf

Conference was held in St Andrews at which 33 countries affiliated to the R&A were represented and to which the USGA, PGA and other golfing bodies in this country sent observers. Owing to the great success of this Conference the R&A agreed to organise similar meetings every four years from 1985.

The R&A is represented at Meetings of the World Amateur Golf Council and the Council of National Golf Unions and on the CCPR.

January 1985 (revised)

MF Bonallack OBE
Secretary
Royal And Ancient Golf Club
of St Andrews
Fife KY16 9JD

The Championship Committee

Until 1919 the Open and Amateur Championships of Great Britain were organised by a group of leading Clubs in Scotland and England. The Club where the Championship was to be played was charged with running it for that year. In 1919, the Royal & Ancient, by then the recognised governing authority of the game, was invited to take over the responsibility for both Championships and ever since its Championship Committee has controlled both. Once the course on which a Championship is to be played has been decided, usually several years ahead, the Committee works closely with the Club concerned.

The Amateur, which is nearly as old as The Open, may have lost some of its public appeal with the growth of Professional golf and the defection of so many able young amateurs to its lucrative tour. However, the Amateur Championship is still considered the most prestigious event in the amateur game and is always played on one of the best courses.

The Championship Committee today controls several more events besides the two oldest Championships. The Boys, started privately in 1921, and the Youths, in 1954, both now come under its wing, as does the Seniors which was inaugurated by the R&A in 1969. In addition, the biennial amateur matches against the United States and the Rest of Europe for

the Walker Cup and the St Andrews Trophies respectively, are run by the Committee when played in Great Britain, as also are Boys' and Youths' Internationals against the Rest of Europe. The R&A Selection Committee chooses the team for all these amateur matches, as well as the team which competes for the Eisenhower Trophy, the World Amateur Team Championship. This was first played at St Andrews in 1958 and has since been held every two years in different parts of the world.

The remarkable development of The Open to the great occasion it is today has meant heavily increased responsibilities for the Championship Committee. TV and the media have given it an audience in millions compared with the few thousand interested in the past. The R&A's determination to match the growing interest with a new attitude and astute promotion has given the event the kudos and following it now enjoys. The last 20 years has seen the winner's cheque grow from £1200 to £80,000, the total prize money from £15,000 to £750,000 in 1989, with the attendance regularly in excess of 150,000. The financial success of The Open has provided considerable sums of money for the development of junior golf, and other worthy causes connected to golf.

The R&A works closely with the Club of the course where the Championship is to be played, whose members take on many of the essential duties necessary if it is to run smoothly. These include spectator control where local Clubs take charge of a hole each, usually providing three-hour shifts of up to 16 members at a time. This can involve as many as 800 men daily. Local volunteer stewards also cover such diverse duties as course controllers, supervision of litter collection and spectator stand control. Security, courtesy transport, car park supervision and public catering, to name a few of the mass of services necessary, are provided under contract by companies expert in these fields. Close liaison with the area police authority is vital. Facilities for the Press, Television and the vast tented village, each involving several hundred people, occupy large areas and are a major limiting factor when considering possible venues for future championships.

Important for both competitors and spectators and appreciated by both is the radio network which provides up-to-the-minute scores and positions of the leading players which appear very quickly on the leader boards erected at strategic points round the course. The system developed over many years is as quick, informative and accurate as any in existence.

The Committee consists of thirteen Royal & Ancient members, who devote much time to their tasks. It has a full-time secretary who, together with the Secretary of the Club and some of his staff, is involved in the planning of The Open and other events throughout the year. Members of the Committee work long hours during Open week. From first light at about 5am, when the Head Greenkeeper and a nominated member of the Committee tour the course deciding the pin positions on each green for the day, to dusk when the last competitor comes in, all are occupied, mostly out on the course at selected points, in two-way radio contact with the centre, ready to give a ruling when required. In the final rounds the leading players are accompanied by a member of the committee for the whole round.

The many stands erected around the course, providing seats for sometimes 18,000 spectators, often quite close to greens, make for special problems. A loose shot which ends under a stand will probably mean the ball may be dropped without penalty in an area nearby, which has been pre-designated by the committee; this shot should be of equal difficulty as it would have been if the stand had not been there. In these cases often an official decision is required.

At the end of every round each competitor's card must be immediately checked and recorded following which, in the case of a leader, he will meet the press in the interview room.

It is the Championship Committee too which decides if any round has to be halted, postponed or cancelled due to storm and tempest. Such decisions, so difficult with so many factors, consequent on a postponement, to be considered, have been eased a little with improved weather forecasting and continuous contact with the local weather bureau.

It will be seen that the work of the Committee is never ending with the myriad of tasks necessary to ensure the even flow to a Championship. The success of The Open is due to sound planning, moving with the times and the expertise of the R&A staff which is the executive arm of the Committee. The Open may be the Championship with which all are familiar; however, it must be remembered that the many other events under the R&A's control also require planning and organisation. The work for these events goes on largely unnoticed, but must not be forgotten.

Rules of Golf

As Approved by
The Royal & Ancient Golf Club
of St Andrews, Scotland
and the
United States Golf Association

25th EDITION
EFFECTIVE 1st JANUARY 1988

Rules of Golf Committee

The Rules of Golf Committee shall consist of twelve Members of the Club to be elected by the Club, and additional Members not exceeding ten in number (who need not be Members of the Club) from Golf Authorities at home and abroad invited annually to join the Committee by the twelve Members elected by the Club. Such Invited Members shall, irrespective of the date of their invitation to become Members of the Rules of Golf Committee, remain so only until the date of the first Autumn Business Meeting occurring after their being invited to become Members but may again be invited thereafter. During their term of office such Invited Members (if not Members of the Club) shall be admitted as Temporary Members of the Club.

The Rules of Golf are the subject of quadrennial review by the R&A and the USGA in order to maintain uniformity and keep abreast of changing conditions.

Queries on the Rules may only be referred to the Rules of Golf Committee through the Secretary of the Club or the Association responsible for the competition. Many queries have to be returned unanswered because they have been sent direct to the Committee by individuals.

CONTENTS

FOREWORD   714
CHANGES   715

SECTION
I. Etiquette   716
II. Definitions   716
III. The Rules of Play   720

The Game
1. The Game   720
2. Match Play   720
3. Stroke Play   720

Clubs and the Ball
4. Clubs   721
5. The Ball   722

Player's Responsibilities
6. The Player   723
7. Practice   724
8. Advice; Indicating Line of Play   725
9. Information as to Strokes Taken   725

Order of Play
10. Order of Play   726

Teeing Ground
11. Teeing Ground   726

Playing the Ball
12. Searching for and Identifying Ball   727
13. Ball Played as It Lies; Lie, Area of Intended Swing and Line of Play; Stance   728
14. Striking the Ball   728
15. Playing a Wrong Ball   729

The Putting Green
16. The Putting Green   730
17. The Flagstick   730

Ball Moved, Deflected or Stopped
18. Ball at Rest Moved   731
19. Ball in Motion Deflected or Stopped   732

Relief Situations and Procedure
20. Lifting, Dropping and Placing; Playing from Wrong Place   733
21. Cleaning Ball   735
22. Ball Interfering with or Assisting Play   735
23. Loose Impediments   736
24. Obstructions   736
25. Abnormal Ground Conditions and Wrong Putting Green   737
26. Water Hazards (Including Lateral Water Hazards)   738
27. Ball Lost or Out of Bounds; Provisional Ball   739
28. Ball Unplayable   740

Other Forms of Play
29. Threesomes and Foursomes   740
30. Three-Ball, Best-Ball and Four-Ball
    Match Play   741
31. Four-Ball Stroke Play   741
32. Bogey, Par and Stableford Competitions   742

Administration
33. The Committee   743
34. Disputes and Decisions   744

Appendix 1   746
    Part A Local Rules   746
    Part B Specimen Local Rules   747
    Part C Conditions of the Competition   747

Appendix II Design of Clubs   748

Appendix III The Ball   751
Handicaps   751
Rules of Amateur Status   752
Index   757

Foreword
to the 1988 Edition of the Rules of Golf

The Royal & Ancient Golf Club of St. Andrews and the United States Golf Association have carried out their customary quadrennial review of the Rules of Golf and have agreed upon certain amendments which they believe will improve the Rules.

The extensive changes in the Rules which were introduced in 1984 have received universal approval. Consequently, a minimal number of substantive changes were considered necessary. These are summarised on page 715.

The R.&A. and USGA would like to record their appreciation of the valuable assistance which they have received from a number of golfing bodies throughout the world. The new Rules will become effective on 1st January 1988.

The combining of the Decisions Services of the R.&A. and USGA into a single volume has proved to be an outstanding success and has done much to establish uniformity of interpretation of the Rules worldwide.

We would like to take this opportunity to express our sincere thanks to our respective Committees and all those who have in so many ways helped us in our endeavours.

W.J.F. Bryce
Chairman
Rules of Golf Committee
Royal & Ancient Golf Club of St. Andrews

C. Grant Spaeth
Chairman
Rules of Golf Committee
United States Golf Association

CHANGES
Principal Changes introduced in the 1988 Code

Rule 2. Match Play
Expanded to state that a player may concede the next stroke, a hole or the match, and that a concession may not be declined or withdrawn.

Rule 3-3. Stroke Play. Doubt as to Procedure
If a competitor fails to announce in advance his decision to invoke this Rule, the score with the original ball, rather than the higher score, will count.

Rule 4-4. Maximum of Fourteen Clubs
Amended to state that a player may borrow a club from anyone on the course, but that the person from whom it was borrowed may not thereafter use the club.

Rule 5 and Appendix III
After 1st January 1990 it will no longer be permitted to use the small (1.620″) ball.

Rule 5-3. Ball Unfit for Play
A stricter definition is adopted stating that a ball is unfit for play if it is visibly cut, cracked or out of shape, but a ball is not unfit for play solely because mud or other materials adhere to it, its surface is scratched or scraped or its paint is damaged or discoloured.

Rule 18. Ball at Rest Moved
If a ball at rest moves after address (other than as a result of a stroke) the ball shall be replaced rather than played as it lies. This procedure is now consistent with that prescribed in other sub-sections of this Rule.

Rule 19-5. Ball in Motion Deflected or Stopped by Another Ball
Clarifies that when two balls in motion collide, each player shall play his ball as it lies.

Rule 25-1b (ii) and 1c (ii). Casual Water, Ground Under Repair and Certain Damage to Course. Relief. In a Hazard

Rule 26-1b. Ball in Water Hazard

Rule 28c. Ball Unplayable
Amended to state that the ball must be dropped keeping the point where the ball lay (or where it last crossed the margin of the hazard, as the case may be) between the spot on which the ball is dropped and the hole. It is no longer permitted to stand on that line and drop a ball an arm's length to the side.

The Rules of Golf

Section I   Etiquette

Courtesy on the Course

Safety

Prior to playing a stroke or making a practice swing, the player should ensure that no one is standing close by or in a position to be hit by the club, the ball or any stones, pebbles, twigs or the like which may be moved by the stroke or swing.

Consideration for Other Players

The player who has the honour should be allowed to play before his opponent or fellow-competitor tees his ball.

No one should move, talk or stand close to or directly behind the ball or the hole when a player is addressing the ball or making a stroke.

In the interest of all, players should play without delay.

No player should play until the players in front are out of range.

Players searching for a ball should signal the players behind them to pass as soon as it becomes apparent that the ball will not easily be found. They should not search for five minutes before doing so. They should not continue play until the players following them have passed and are out of range.

When the play of a hole has been completed, players should immediately leave the putting green.

Priority on the Course

In the absence of special rules, two-ball matches should have precedence over and be entitled to pass any three- or four-ball match.

A single player has no standing and should give way to a match of any kind.

Any match playing a whole round is entitled to pass a match playing a shorter round.

If a match fails to keep its place on the course and loses more than one clear hole on the players in front, it should invite the match following to pass.

Care of the Course

Holes in Bunkers

Before leaving a bunker, a player should carefully fill up and smooth over all holes and footprints made by him.

Replace Divots; Repair Ball-Marks and Damage by Spikes

Through the green, a player should ensure that any turf cut or displaced by him is replaced at once and pressed down and that any damage to the putting green made by a ball is carefully repaired. Damage to the putting green caused by golf shoe spikes should be repaired *on completion of the hole.*

Damage to Greens—Flagsticks, Bags, etc.

Players should ensure that, when putting down bags or the flagstick, no damage is done to the putting green and that neither they nor their caddies damage the hole by standing close to it, in handling the flagstick or in removing the ball from the hole. The flagstick should be properly replaced in the hole before the players leave the putting green. Players should not damage the putting green by leaning on their putters, particularly when removing the ball from the hole.

Golf Carts

Local notices regulating the movement of golf carts should be strictly observed.

Damage Through Practice Swings

In taking practice swings, players should avoid causing damage to the course, particularly the tees, by removing divots.

Section II   Definitions

Addressing the Ball

A player has "addressed the ball" when he has taken his stance and has also grounded his club, except that in a hazard a player has addressed the ball when he has taken his stance.

Advice

"Advice" is any counsel or suggestion which could influence a player in determining his play, the choice of a club or the method of making a stroke.

Information on the Rules or on matter of public information, such as the position of hazards or the flagstick on the putting green, is not advice.

Ball Deemed to Move

See "Move or Moved".

Ball Holed
See "Holed".

Ball Lost
See "Lost Ball".

Ball in Play
A ball is "in play" as soon as the player has made a <u>stroke</u> on the <u>teeing ground</u>. It remains in play until holed out, except when it is <u>lost, out of bounds</u> or lifted, or another ball has been substituted under an applicable Rule, whether or not such Rule permits substitution; a ball so substituted becomes the ball in play.

Bunker
A "bunker" is a <u>hazard</u> consisting of a prepared area of ground, often a hollow, from which turf or soil has been removed and replaced with sand or the like. Grass-covered ground bordering or within a bunker is not part of the bunker. The margin of a bunker extends vertically downwards, but not upwards.

Caddie
A "caddie" is one who carries or handles a player's clubs during play and otherwise assists him in accordance with the Rules.

When one caddie is employed by more than one player, he is always deemed to be the caddie of the player whose ball is involved, and <u>equipment</u> carried by him is deemed to be that player's equipment, except when the caddie acts upon specific directions of another player, in which case he is considered to be that other player's caddie.

Casual Water
"Casual water" is any temporary accumulation of water on the <u>course</u> which is visible before or after the player takes his <u>stance</u> and is not in a <u>water hazard</u>. Snow and ice are either casual water or <u>loose impediments</u>, at the option of the player, except that manufactured ice is an <u>obstruction</u>. Dew is not casual water.

Committee
The "Committee" is the committee in charge of the competition or, if the matter does not arise in a competition, the committee in charge of the course.

Competitor
A "competitor" is a player in a stroke competition. A "fellow-competitor" is any person with whom the competitor plays. Neither is <u>partner</u> of the other.

In stroke play foursome and four-ball competitions, where the context so admits, the word "competitor" or "fellow-competitor" includes his partner.

Course
The "course" is the whole area within which play is permitted (see Rule 33-2).

Equipment
"Equipment" is anything used, worn or carried by or for the player except any ball he has played at the hole being played and any small object, such as a coin or a tee, when used to mark the position of a ball or the extent of an area in which a ball is to be dropped. Equipment includes a golf cart, whether or not motorised. If such a cart is shared by more than one player, its status under the Rules is the same as that of a caddie employed by more than one player. See "Caddie".

Fellow Competitor
See "Competitor".

Flagstick
The "flagstick" is a movable straight indicator, with or without bunting or other material attached, centred in the hole to show its position. It shall be circular in cross-section.

Forecaddie
A "forecaddie" is one who is employed by the Committee to indicate to players the position of balls during play. He is an <u>outside agency</u>.

Ground Under Repair
"Ground under repair" is any portion of the <u>course</u> so marked by order of the Committee or so declared by its authorised representative. It includes material piled for removal and a hole made by a greenkeeper, even if not so marked. Stakes and lines defining ground under repair are in such ground. The margin of ground under repair extends vertically downwards, but not upwards.

Note 1: Grass cuttings and other material left on the course which have been abandoned and are not intended to be removed are not ground under repair unless so marked.

Note 2: The Committee may make a Local Rule prohibiting play from ground under repair.

Hazards
A "hazard" is any <u>bunker</u> or <u>water hazard</u>.

Hole
The "hole" shall be $4\frac{1}{4}$ inches (108mm) in diameter and at least 4 inches (100mm) deep. If a lining is used, it shall be sunk at least 1 inch (25mm) below the <u>putting green</u> surface unless

the nature of the soil makes it impracticable to do so; its outer diameter shall not exceed $4^{1}/_{4}$ inches (108mm).

Holed
A ball is "holed" when it is at rest within the circumference of the hole and all of it is below the level of the lip of the hole.

Honour
The side entitled to play first from the teeing ground is said to have the "honour".

Lateral Water Hazard
A "lateral water hazard" is a water hazard or that part of a water hazard so situated that it is not possible or is deemed by the Committee to be impracticable to drop a ball behind the water hazard in accordance with Rule 26-1b

That part of a water hazard to be played as a lateral water hazard should be distinctively marked.

Note: Lateral water hazards should be defined by red stakes or lines.

Loose Impediments
"Loose impediments" are natural objects such as stones, leaves, twigs, branches and the like, dung, worms and insects and casts or heaps made by them, provided they are not fixed or growing, are not solidly embedded and do not adhere to the ball.

Sand and loose soil are loose impediments on the putting green, but not elsewhere.

Snow and ice are either casual water or loose impediments, at the option of the player, except that manufactured ice is an obstruction.

Dew is not a loose impediment.

Lost Ball
A ball is "lost" if:

a. It is not found or identified as his by the player within five minutes after the player's side or his or their caddies have begun to search for it; or

b. The player has put another ball into play under the Rules, even though he may not have searched for the original ball; or

c. The player has played any stroke with a provisional ball from the place where the original ball is likely to be or from a point nearer the hole than that place, whereupon the provisional ball becomes the ball in play.

Time spent in playing a wrong ball is not counted in the five-minute period allowed for search.

Marker
A "marker" is one who is appointed by the Committee to record a competitor's score in stroke play. He may be a fellow-competitor. He is not a referee.

Matches
See "Sides and Matches".

Move or Moved
A ball is deemed to have "moved" if it leaves its position and comes to rest in any other place.

Observer
An "observer" is one who is appointed by the Committee to assist a referee to decide questions of fact and to report to him any breach of a Rule. An observer should not attend the flagstick, stand at or mark the position of the hole, or lift the ball or mark its position.

Obstructions
An "obstruction" is anything artificial, including the artificial surfaces and sides of roads and paths and manufactured ice, except:

a. Objects defining out of bounds, such as walls, fences, stakes and railings;

b. Any part of an immovable artificial object which is out of bounds; and

c. Any construction declared by the Committee to be an integral part of the course.

Out of Bounds
"Out of bounds" is ground on which play is prohibited.

When out of bounds is defined by reference to stakes or a fence or as being beyond stakes or a fence, the out of bounds line is determined by the nearest inside points of the stakes or fence posts at ground level excluding angled supports.

When out of bounds is defined by a line on the ground, the line itself is out of bounds.

The out of bounds line extends vertically upwards and downwards.

A ball is out of bounds when all of it lies out of bounds.

A player may stand out of bounds to play a ball lying within bounds.

Outside Agency
An "outside agency" is any agency not part of the match or, in stroke play, not part of a competitor's side, and includes a referee, a marker, an observer or a forecaddie. Neither wind nor water is an outside agency.

Partner
A "partner" is a player associated with another player on the same side.

In a threesome, foursome, best-ball or four-ball match, where the context so admits, the word "player" includes his partner or partners.

Penalty Stroke

A "penalty stroke" is one added to the score of a player or side under certain Rules. In a threesome or foursome, penalty strokes do not affect the order of play.

Provisional Ball

A "provisional ball" is a ball played under Rule 27-2 for a ball which may be lost outside a water hazard or may be out of bounds.

Putting Green

The "putting green" is all ground of the hole being played which is specially prepared for putting or otherwise defined as such by the Committee. A ball is on the puting green when any part of it touches the putting green.

Referee

A "referee" is one who is appointed by the Committee to accompany players to decide questions of fact and apply the Rules of Golf. He shall act on any breach of a Rule which he observes or is reported to him.

A referee should not attend the flagstick, stand at or mark the position of the hole, or lift the ball or mark its position.

Rub of the Green

A "rub of the green" occurs when a ball in motion is accidentally deflected or stopped by any outside agency (see Rule 19-1).

Rule

The term "Rule" includes Local Rules made by the Committee under Rule 33-8a.

Sides and Matches

Side: A player, or two or more players who are partners.

Single: A match in which one plays against another.

Threesome: A match in which one plays against two, and each side plays one ball.

Foursome: A match in which two play against two, and each side plays one ball.

Three-ball: A match-play competition in which three play against one another, each playing his own ball. Each player is playing two distinct matches.

Best ball: A match in which one plays against the better ball of two or the best ball of three players.

Four-ball: A match in which two play their better ball against the better ball of two other players.

Stance

Taking the "stance" consists in a player placing his feet in position for and preparatory to making a stroke.

Stipulated Round

The "stipulated round" consists of playing the holes of the course in their correct sequence unless otherwise authorised by the Committee. The number of holes in a stipulated round is 18 unless a smaller number is authorised by the Committee. As to extension of stipulated round in match play, see Rule 2-3.

Stroke

A "stroke" is the forward movement of the club made with the intention of fairly striking at and moving the ball, but if a player checks his downswing voluntarily before the clubhead reaches the ball he is not deemed to have made a stroke.

Teeing Ground

The "teeing ground" is the starting place for the hole to be played. It is a rectangular area two club-lengths in depth, the front and the sides of which are defined by the outside limits of two tee-markers. A ball is outside the teeing ground when all of it lies outside the teeing ground.

Through the Green

"Through the green" is the whole area of the course except

a. The teeing ground and putting green of the hole being played; and

b. All hazards on the course.

Water Hazard

A "water hazard" is any sea, lake, pond, river, ditch, surface drainage ditch or other open water course (whether or not containing water) and anything of a similar nature.

All ground or water within the margin of a water hazard is part of the water hazard. The margin of a water hazard extends vertically upwards and downwards. Stakes and lines defining the margins of water hazards are in the hazards.

Note: Water hazards (other than lateral water hazards) should be defined by yellow stakes or lines.

Wrong Ball

A "wrong ball" is any ball other than:

a. The ball in play,

b. A provisional ball or

c. In stroke play, a second ball played under Rule 3-3 or Rule 20-7b.

Note: Ball in play includes a ball substituted for the ball in play when the player is proceeding under an applicable Rule which does not permit substitution.

Section III
The Rules of Play

THE GAME

Rule 1. The Game

1-1. General
The Game of Golf consists in playing a ball from the teeing ground into the hole by a stroke or successive strokes in accordance with the Rules.

1-2. Exerting Influence on Ball
No player or caddie shall take any action to influence the position or the movement of a ball except in accordance with the rules.

PENALTY FOR BREACH OF RULE 1-2:
Match play— Loss of hole; Stroke play— Two strokes.

Note: In the case of a serious breach of Rule 1-2, the Committee may impose a penalty of disqualification.

1-3. Agreement to Waive Rules
Players shall not agree to exclude the operation of any Rule or to waive any penalty incurred.

PENALTY FOR BREACH OF RULE 1-3:
Match play— Disqualification of both sides; Stroke play— Disqualification of competitors concerned.
(Agreeing to play out of turn in stroke play— see Rule 10-2c.)

1-4. Points Not Covered by Rules
If any point in dispute is not covered by the Rules, the decision shall be made in accordance with equity.

Rule 2. Match Play

2-1. Winner of Hole; Reckoning of Holes
In match play the game is played by holes.
Except as otherwise provided in the Rules, a hole is won by the side which holes its ball in the fewer strokes. In a handicap match the lower net score wins the hole.
The reckoning of holes is kept by the terms: so many "holes up" or "all square", and so many "to play".
A side is "dormie" when it is as many holes up as there are holes remaining to be played.

2-2. Halved Hole
A hole is halved if each side holes out in the same number of strokes.
When a player has holed out and his opponent has been left with a stroke for the half,

if the player thereafter incurs a penalty, the hole is halved.

2-3. Winner of Match
A match (which consists of a stipulated round, unless otherwise decreed by the Committee) is won by the side which is leading by a number of holes greater than the number of holes remaining to be played.
The Committee may, for the purpose of settling a tie, extend the stipulated round to as many holes as are required for a match to be won.

2-4. Concession of Next Stroke, Hole or Match
When the opponent's ball is at rest or is deemed to be at rest under Rule 16-2, the player may concede the opponent to have holed out with his next stroke and the ball may be removed by either side with a club or otherwise.
A player may concede a hole or a match at any time prior to the conclusion of the hole or the match.
Concession of a stroke, hole or match may not be declined or withdrawn.

2-5. Claims
In match play, if a doubt or dispute arises between the players and no duly authorised representative of the Committee is available within a reasonable time, the players shall continue the match without delay. Any claim, if it is to be considered by the Committee, must be made before any player in the match plays from the next teeing ground or, in the case of the last hole of the match, before all players in the match leave the putting green.
No later claim shall be considered unless it is based on facts previously unknown to the player making the claim and the player making the claim had been given wrong information (Rules 6-2a and 9) by an opponent. In any case, no later claim shall be considered after the result of the match has been officially announced, unless the Committee is satisfied that the opponent knew he was giving wrong information.

2-6. General Penalty
The penalty for a breach of a Rule in match play is loss of hole except when otherwise provided.

Rule 3. Stroke Play

3-1. Winner
The competitor who plays the stipulated round or rounds in the fewest strokes is the winner.

3-2. Failure to Hole Out

If a competitor fails to hole out at any hole and does not correct his mistake before he plays a <u>stroke</u> from the next <u>teeing ground</u> or, in the case of the last hole of the round, before he leaves the <u>putting green</u>, *he shall be disqualified.*

3-3. Doubt as to Procedure

a. Procedure

In stroke play only, when during play of a hole a competitor is doubtful of his rights or procedure, he may, without penalty, play a second ball. After the situation which has caused the doubt has arisen, the competitor should, before taking further action, announce to his marker or a fellow-competitor his decision to invoke this Rule and the ball with which he will score if the Rules permit.

The competitor shall report the facts to the <u>Committee</u> before returning his score card unless he scores the same with both balls; if he fails to do so, *he shall be disqualified.*

b. Determination of Score for Hole

If the Rules allow the procedure selected in advance by the competitor, the score with the ball selected shall be his score for the hole.

If the competitor fails to announce in advance his decision to invoke this Rule or his selection, the score with the original ball or, if the original ball is not one of the balls being played, the first ball put into play shall count if the Rules allow the procedure adopted for such ball.

Note: A second ball played under Rule 3-3 is not a provisional ball under Rule 27-2.

3-4. Refusal to Comply with a Rule

If a competitor refuses to comply with a Rule affecting the rights of another competitor, *he shall be disqualified.*

3-5. General Penalty

The penalty for a breach of a Rule in stroke play is two strokes except when otherwise provided.

CLUBS AND THE BALL

The Royal & Ancient Golf Club of St. Andrews and the United States Golf Association reserve the right to change the Rules and make and change the interpretations relating to clubs, balls and other implements at any time.

Rule 4. Clubs

If there may be any reasonable basis for doubt as to whether a club which is to be manufactured conforms with Rule 4 and Appendix II, the manufacturer should submit a sample to the Royal & Ancient Golf Club of St Andrews for a ruling, such sample to become its property for reference purposes. If a manufacturer fails to do so, he assumes the risk of a ruling that the club does not conform with the Rules of Golf.

A player in doubt as to the conformity of a club should consult the Royal & Ancient Golf Club of St Andrews.

4-1. Form and Make of Clubs

A club is an implement designed to be used for striking the ball.

A putter is a club designed primarily for use on the putting green.

The player's clubs shall conform with the provisions of this Rule and with the specifications and interpretations set forth in Appendix II.

a. General

The club shall be composed of a shaft and a head. All parts of the club shall be fixed so that the club is one unit. The club shall not be designed to be adjustable except for weight. The club shall not be substantially different from the traditional and customary form and make.

b. Shaft

The shaft shall be generally straight, with the same bending and twisting properties in any direction, and shall be attached to the clubhead at the heel either directly or through a single plain neck or socket. A putter shaft may be attached to any point in the head.

c. Grip

The grip consists of that part of the shaft designed to be held by the player and any material added to it for the purpose of obtaining a firm hold. The grip shall be substantially straight and plain in form and shall not be moulded for any part of the hands.

d. Clubhead

The distance from the heel to the toe of the clubhead shall be greater than the distance from the face to the back. The clubhead shall be generally plain in shape.

The clubhead shall have only one face designed for striking the ball, except that a putter may have two such faces if their characteristics are the same, they are opposite each other and the loft of each is the same and does not exceed ten degrees.

e. Club Face

The face shall not have any degree of concavity and, in relation to the ball, shall be hard and rigid. It shall be generally smooth except for such markings as are permitted by Appendix II. If the basic structural material of the head and face of a club, other than a putter, is metal, no inset or attachment is permitted.

f. Wear

A club which conforms with Rule 4-1 when new is deemed to conform after wear through normal use. Any part of a club which has been purposely altered is regarded as new and must conform, in the altered state, with the Rules.

g. Damage

If a player's club ceases to conform with Rule 4-1 because of damage sustained in the normal course of play, the player may:

    (i) use the club in its damaged state, but only for the remainder of the <u>stipulated round</u> during which such damage was sustained; or

    (ii) without unduly delaying play, repair it.

A club which ceases to conform because of damage sustained other than in the normal course of play shall not subsequently be used during the round.

(Damage changing playing characteristics of club — see Rule 4-2.)

4-2. Playing Characteristics Changed

During a stipulated round, the playing characteristics of a club shall not be purposely changed.

If the playing characteristics of a player's club are changed during a round because of damage sustained in the normal course of play, the player may:

    (i) use the club in its altered state; or

    (ii) without unduly delaying play, repair it.

If the playing characteristics of a player's club are changed because of damage sustained other than in the normal course of play, the club shall not subsequently be used during the round.

Damage to a club which occurred prior to a round may be repaired during the round, provided the playing characteristics are not changed and play is not unduly delayed.

4-3. Foreign Material

No foreign material shall be applied to the club face for the purpose of influencing the movement of the ball.

PENALTY FOR BREACH OF RULE 4-1, -2 or -3:
Disqualification

4-4. Maximum of Fourteen Clubs

a. Selection and Replacement of Clubs

The player shall start a stipulated round with not more than fourteen clubs. He is limited to the clubs thus selected for that round except that, without unduly delaying play, he may:

    (i) if he started with fewer than fourteen, add as many as will bring his total to that number; and

    (ii) replace, with any club, a club which becomes unfit for play in the normal course of play.

b. Borrowing or Sharing Clubs

The addition or replacement of a club or clubs may be made by borrowing from anyone; only the borrower may use such club or clubs for the remainder of the round.

The sharing of a club or clubs is prohibited except that partners may share clubs, provided that the total number of clubs carried by the partners so sharing does not exceed fourteen.

PENALTY FOR BREACH OF RULE 4-4a or b, REGARDLESS OF NUMBER OF EXCESS CLUBS CARRIED:

Match play— At the conclusion of the hole at which the breach is discovered, the state of the match shall be adjusted by deducting one hole for each hole at which a breach occurred. Maximum deduction per round: two holes.

Stroke play— Two strokes for each hole at which any breach occurred; maximum penalty per round: four strokes.

Bogey and par competitions— Penalties as in match play.

Stableford competitions— see Note to Rule 32-1b.

c. Excess Club Declared Out of Play

Any club carried or used in breach of this Rule shall be declared out of play by the player immediately upon discovery that a breach has occurred and thereafter shall not be used by the player during the round.

PENALTY FOR BREACH OF RULE 4-4c:
Disqualification

Rule 5.   The Ball

5-1.   General

The ball the player uses shall conform to specifications set forth in Appendix III on maximum weight, minimum size, spherical symmetry, initial velocity and overall distance when tested under specified conditions.

Note: In laying down the conditions under which a competition is to be played (Rule 33-1), the Committee may stipulate that the ball to be used shall be of certain specifications, provided these specifications are within the limits prescribed by Appendix III, and that it be of a size, brand and marking as detailed on the current List of Conforming Golf Balls issued by the Royal & Ancient Golf Club of St. Andrews.

5-2.   Foreign Material

No foreign material shall be applied to a ball for the purpose of changing its playing characteristics.

PENALTY FOR BREACH OF
RULES 5-1 or 5-2:
Disqualification.

5-3. Ball Unfit for Play

A ball is unfit for play if it is visibly cut, cracked or out of shape. A ball is not unfit for play solely because mud or other materials adhere to it, its surface is scratched or scraped or its paint is damaged or discoloured.

If a player has reason to believe his ball has become unfit for play during play of the hole being played, he may during the play of such hole lift his ball without penalty to determine whether it is unfit, provided he announces his intention in advance to his opponent in match play or his marker or a fellow-competitor in stroke play and gives his opponent, marker or fellow-competitor an opportunity to examine the ball. If he lifts the ball without announcing his intention in advance or giving his opponent, marker or fellow-competitor an opportunity to examine the ball, *he shall incur a penalty of one stroke.*

If it is determined that the ball has become unfit for play during play of the hole being played, the player may substitute another ball, placing it on the spot where the original ball lay. Otherwise, the original ball shall be replaced.

If a ball breaks into pieces as a result of a stroke, the stroke shall be replayed without penalty (see Rule 20-5).

PENALTY FOR BREACH OF RULE 5-3:
Match play— Loss of hole; Stroke play—
Two strokes.

*If a player incurs the general penalty for breach of Rule 5-3, no additional penalty under the Rule shall be applied.

Note 1: The ball may not be cleaned to determine whether it is unfit for play — see Rule 21.

Note 2: If the opponent, marker or fellow-competitor wishes to dispute a claim of unfitness, he must do so before the player plays another ball.

PLAYER'S RESPONSIBILITIES

Rule 6.   The player

Definition

A "marker" is one who is appointed by the Committee to record a competitor's score in stroke play. He may be a fellow-competitor. He is not a referee.

6-1. Conditions of Competition

The player is responsible for knowing the conditions under which the competition is to be played (Rule 33-1).

6-2. Handicap

a. Match Play

Before starting a match in a handicap competition, the players should determine from one another their respective handicaps. If a player begins the match having declared a higher handicap which would affect the number of strokes given or received, *he shall be disqualified;* otherwise, the player shall play off the declared handicap.

b. Stroke Play

In any round of a handicap competition, the competitor shall ensure that his handicap is recorded on his score card before it is returned to the Committee. If no handicap is recorded on his score card before it is returned, or if the recorded handicap is higher than that to which he is entitled and this affects the number of strokes received, *he shall be disqualified* from that round of the handicap competition; otherwise, the score shall stand.

Note: It is the player's responsibility to know the holes at which handicap strokes are to be given or received.

6-3. Time of Starting and Groups

a. Time of Starting

The player shall start at the time laid down by the Committee.

b. Groups

In stroke play, the competitor shall remain throughout the round in the group arranged by the Committee unless the Committee authorises or ratifies a change.

PENALTY FOR BREACH OF RULE 6-3:
Disqualification.
(Best-ball and four-ball play— see Rules 30-3a and 31-2.)

Note: The Committee may provide in the conditions of a competition (Rule 33-1) that, if the player arrives at his starting point, ready to play, within five minutes after his starting time, in the absence of circumstances which warrant waiving the penalty of disqualification as provided in Rule 33-7, the penalty for failure to start on time is *loss of the first hole in match play or two strokes at the first hole in stroke play* instead of disqualification.

6-4. Caddie

The player may have only one caddie at any one time, *under penalty of disqualification.*

For any breach of a Rule by his caddie, the player incurs the applicable penalty.

6-5. Ball

The responsibility for playing the proper ball rests with the player. Each player should put an identification mark on his ball.

6-6. Scoring in Stroke Play

a. Recording Scores
After each hole the marker should check the score with the competitor and record it. On completion of the round the marker shall sign the card and hand it to the competitor. If more than one marker records the scores, each shall sign for the part for which he is responsible.

b. Signing and Returning Card
After completion of the round, the competitor should check his score for each hole and settle any doubtful points with the Committee. He shall ensure that the marker has signed the card, countersign the card himself and return it to the Committee as soon as possible.

PENALTY FOR BREACH OF RULE 6-6b:
Disqualification.

c. Alteration of Card
No alteration may be made on a card after the competitor has returned it to the Committee.

d. Wrong Score for Hole
The competitor is responsible for the correctness of the score recorded for each hole. If he returns a score for any hole lower than actually taken, *he shall be disqualified.* If he returns a score for any hole higher than actually taken, the score as returned shall stand.

Note 1: The Committee is responsible for the addition of scores and application of the handicap recorded on the card—see Rule 33-5.

Note 2: In four-ball stroke play, see also Rule 31-4 and -7a.

6-7. Undue Delay
The player shall play without undue delay. Between completion of a hole and playing from the next teeing ground, the player shall not unduly delay play.

PENALTY FOR BREACH OF RULE 6-7:
Match play—Loss of hole; Stroke play—
Two strokes.
For repeated offence—Disqualification.

If the player unduly delays play between holes, he is delaying the play of the next hole and the penalty applies to that hole.

6-8. Discontinuance of Play

a. When Permitted
The player shall not discontinue play unless:
(i) the Committee has suspended play;
(ii) he believes there is danger from lightning;
(iii) he is seeking a decision from the Committee on a doubtful or disputed point (see Rules 2-5 and 34-3); or
(iv) there is some other good reason such as sudden illness.

Bad weather is not of itself a good reason for discontinuing play.

If the player discontinues play without specific permission from the Committee, he shall report to the Committee as soon as practicable. If he does so and the Committee considers his reason satisfactory, the player incurs no penalty. Otherwise, *the player shall be disqualified.*

Exception in match play: Players discontinuing match play by agreement are not subject to disqualification unless by so doing the competition is delayed.

Note: Leaving the course does not of itself constitute discontinuance of play.

b. Procedure When Play Suspended by Committee
When play is suspended by the Committee, if the players in a match or group are between the play of two holes, they shall not resume play until the Committee has ordered a resumption of play. If they are in the process of playing a hole, they may continue provided they do so without delay. If they choose to continue, they shall discontinue either before or immediately after completing the hole, and shall not thereafter resume play until the Committee has ordered a resumption of play.

PENALTY FOR BREACH OF RULE 6-8b:
Disqualification

c. Lifting Ball When Play Discontinued
When during the play of a hole a player discontinues play under Rule 6-8a, he may lift his ball. A ball may be cleaned when so lifted. If a ball has been so lifted, the player shall, when play is resumed, place a ball on the spot from which the original ball was lifted.

PENALTY FOR BREACH OF RULE 6-8c:
Match Play—Loss of hole; Stroke play—
Two strokes.

Rule 7. Practice

7-1. Before or Between Rounds
a. Match Play
On any day of a match play competition, a player may practise on the competition course before a round.

b. Stroke Play
On any day of a stroke competition or play-off, a competitor shall not practise on the competition course or test the surface of any putting green on the course before a round or play-off. When two or more rounds of a stroke competition are to be played over consecutive days, practice between those rounds on any competition course remaining to be played is prohibited.

Exception: Practice putting or chipping on or near the first teeing ground before starting a round or play-off is permitted.

PENALTY FOR BREACH OF RULE 7-1b: *Disqualification.*

Note: The Committee may in the conditions of a competition (Rule 33-1) prohibit practice on the competition course on any day of a match play competition or permit practice on the competition course or part of the course (Rule 33-2c) on any day of or between rounds of a stroke competition.

7-2. During Round

A player shall not play a practice stroke either during the play of a hole or between the play of two holes except that, between the play of two holes, the player may practise putting or chipping on or near the putting green of the hole last played, any practice putting green or the teeing ground of the next hole to be played in the round, provided such practice stroke is not played from a hazard and does not unduly delay play (Rule 6-7).

Exception: When play has been suspended by the Committee, a player may, prior to re-sumption of play, practise (a) as provided in this Rule, (b) anywhere other than on the competition course and (c) as otherwise permitted by the Committee.

PENALTY FOR BREACH OF RULE 7-2: *Match play—Loss of hole; Stroke play— Two strokes.*

In the event of a breach between the play of two holes, the penalty applies to the next hole.

Note 1: A practice swing is not a practice stroke and may be taken at any place, provided the player does not breach the Rules.

Note 2: The Committee may prohibit practice on or near the putting green of the hole last played.

Rule 8.   Advice; Indicating Line of Play

Definition

"Advice" is any counsel or suggestion which could influence a player in determining his play, the choice of a club or the method of making a stroke.

Information on the Rules or on matters of public information, such as the position of hazards or the flagstick on the putting green, is not advice.

8-1.   Advice

A player shall not give advice to anyone in the competition except his partner. A player may ask for advice from only his partner or either of their caddies.

8-2.   Indicating Line of Play

a. Other Than on Putting Green

Except on the putting green, a player may have the line of play indicated to him by any-one, but no one shall stand on or close to the line while the stroke is being played. Any mark placed during the play of a hole by the player or with his knowledge to indicate the line shall be removed before the stroke is played.

Exception: Flagstick attended or held up — see Rule 17-1.

b. On the Putting Green

When the player's ball is on the putting green, the player, his partner or either of their caddies may, before but not during the stroke, point out a line for putting, but in so doing the putting green shall not be touched. No mark shall be placed anywhere to indicate a line for putting.

PENALTY FOR BREACH OF RULE: *Match play—Loss of hole; Stroke play— Two strokes.*

Note: In a team competition without con-current individual competition, the Committee may in the conditions of the competition (Rule 33-1) permit each team to appoint one person, e.g., team captain or coach, who may give advice (including pointing out a line for putting) to members of that team. Such person shall be identified to the Committee prior to the start of the competition.

Rule 9.   Information as to Strokes Taken

9-1.   General

The number of strokes a player has taken shall include any penalty strokes incurred.

9.2   Match Play

A player who has incurred a penalty shall inform his opponent as soon as practicable. If he fails to do so, he shall be deemed to have given wrong information, even if he was not aware that he had incurred a penalty.

An opponent is entitled to ascertain from the player, during the play of a hole, the number of strokes he has taken and, after play of a hole, the number of strokes taken on the hole just completed.

If during the play of a hole the player gives or is deemed to give wrong information as to the number of strokes taken, he shall in-cur no penalty if he corrects the mistake before his opponent has played his next stroke. If the player fails so to correct the wrong information, *he shall lose the hole.*

If after play of a hole the player gives or is deemed to give wrong information as to the number of strokes taken on the hole just completed and this affects the opponent's understanding of the result of the hole, he shall incur no penalty if he corrects his mistake before any player plays from the next teeing ground or, in the case of the last hole of the match, before all players leave the putting green. If the player fails so to correct the wrong information, *he shall lose the hole.*

9-3.   Stroke Play

A competitor who has incurred a penalty should inform his marker as soon as practicable.

ORDER OF PLAY

Rule 10.   Order of Play

10-1.   Match Play

a. Teeing Ground

The side entitled to play first from the teeing ground is said to have the "honour".

The side which shall have the honour at the first teeing ground shall be determined by the order of the draw. In the absence of a draw, the honour should be decided by lot.

The side which wins a hole shall take the honour at the next teeing ground. If a hole has been halved, the side which had the honour at the previous teeing ground shall retain it.

b. Other Than on Teeing Ground

When the balls are in play, the ball farther from the hole shall be played first. If the balls are equidistant from the hole, the ball to be played first should be decided by lot.

Exception: Rule 30-3c (best-ball and four-ball match play).

c. Playing Out of Turn

If a player plays when his opponent should have played, the opponent may immediately require the player to cancel the stroke so played and play a ball in correct order, without penalty (see Rule 20-5).

10-2.   Stroke Play

a. Teeing Ground

The competitor entitled to play first from the teeing ground is said to have the "honour".

The competitor who shall have the honour at the first teeing ground shall be determined by the order of the draw. In the absence of a draw, the honour should be decided by lot.

The competitor with the lowest score at a hole shall take the honour at the next teeing ground. The competitor with the second lowest score shall play next and so on. If two or more competitors have the same score at a hole, they shall play from the next teeing ground in the same order as at the previous teeing ground.

b. Other Than on Teeing Ground

When the balls are in play, the ball farthest from the hole shall be played first. If two or more balls are equidistant from the hole, the ball to be played first should be decided by lot.

Exceptions: Rules 22 (ball interfering with or assisting play) and 31-5 (four-ball stroke play).

c. Playing Out of Turn

If a competitor plays out of turn, no penalty is incurred and the ball shall be played as it lies. If, however, the Committee determines that competitors have agreed to play in an order other than that set forth in Clauses 2a and 2b of this Rule to give one of them an advantage, *they shall be disqualified.*

(Incorrect order of play in threesomes and foursomes stroke play—see Rule 29-3).

10-3.   Provisional Ball or Second Ball from Teeing Ground

If a player plays a provisional ball or a second ball from a teeing ground, he should do so after his opponent or fellow-competitor has played his first stroke. If a player plays a provisional ball or a second ball out of turn, Clauses 1c and 2c of this Rule shall apply.

10-4.   Ball Moved in Measuring

If a ball is moved in measuring to determine which ball is farther from the hole, no penalty is incurred and the ball shall be replaced.

TEEING GROUND

Rule 11.   Teeing Ground

Definition

The "teeing ground" is the starting place for the hole to be played. It is a rectangular area two club-lengths in depth, the front and the sides of which are defined by the outside limits of two tee-markers. A ball is outside the teeing ground when all of it lies outside the teeing ground.

11-1.   Teeing

In teeing, the ball may be placed on the ground, on an irregularity of surface created by the player on the ground or on a tee, sand or other substance in order to raise it off the ground.

A player may stand outside the teeing ground to play a ball within it.

11-2.   Tee-Markers

Before a player plays his first stroke with any ball from the teeing ground of the hole being played, the tee-markers are deemed to be fixed. In such circumstances, if the player moves or allows to be moved a tee-marker for the purpose of avoiding interference with his stance, the area of his intended swing or his line of play, *he shall incur the penalty for a breach of Rule 13-2.*

11-3. Ball Falling Off Tee

If a ball, when not in play, falls off a tee or is knocked off a tee by the player in addressing it, it may be re-teed without penalty, but if a stroke is made at the ball in these circumstances, whether the ball is moving or not, the stroke counts but no penalty is incurred.

11-4. Playing Outside Teeing Ground

a. Match Play

If a player, when starting a hole, plays a ball from outside the teeing ground, the opponent may immediately require the player to cancel the stroke so played and play a ball from within the teeing ground, without penalty.

b. Stroke Play

If a competitor, when starting a hole, plays a ball from outside the teeing ground, *he shall incur a penalty of two strokes* and shall then play a ball from within the teeing ground.

If the competitor plays a stroke from the next teeing ground without first correcting his mistake or, in the case of the last hole of the round, leaves the putting green, without first declaring his intention to correct his mistake, *he shall be disqualified.*

Strokes played by a competitor from outside the teeing ground do not count in his score.

PLAYING THE BALL

Rule 12.   Searching for and Identifying Ball

Definitions

A "hazard" is any bunker or water hazard.

A "bunker" is a hazard consisting of a prepared area of ground, often a hollow, from which turf or soil has been removed and replaced with sand or the like. Grass-covered ground bordering or within a bunker is not part of the bunker. The margin of a bunker extends vertically downwards, but not upwards.

A "water hazard" is any sea, lake, pond, river, ditch, surface drainage ditch or other open water course (whether or not containing water) and anything of a similar nature.

All ground or water within the margin of a water hazard is part of the water hazard. The margin of a water hazard extends vertically upwards and downwards. Stakes and lines defining the margins of water hazards are in the hazards.

12-1.   Searching for Ball; Seeing Ball

In searching for his ball anywhere on the course, the player may touch or bend long grass, rushes, bushes, whins, heather or the like, but only to the extent necessary to find and identify it, provided that this does not improve the lie of the ball, the area of his intended swing or his line of play.

A player is not necessarily entitled to see his ball when playing a stroke.

In a hazard, if the ball is covered by loose impediments or sand, the player may remove by probing, raking or other means as much thereof as will enable him to see a part of the ball. If an excess is removed, no penalty is incurred and the ball shall be re-covered so that only a part of the ball is visible. If the ball is moved in such removal, no penalty is incurred; the ball shall be replaced and, if necessary, re-covered. As to removal of loose impediments outside a hazard, see Rule 23.

If a ball lying in casual water, ground under repair or a hole, cast or runway made by a burrowing animal, a reptile or a bird is accidentally moved during search, no penalty is incurred; the ball shall be replaced, unless the player elects to proceed under Rule 25-1b.

If a ball is believed to be lying in water in a water hazard, the player may probe for it with a club or otherwise. If the ball is moved in so doing, no penalty is incurred; the ball shall be replaced, unless the player elects to proceed under Rule 26-1.

PENALTY FOR BREACH OF RULE 12-1:
Match play—Loss of hole; Stroke play—
Two strokes.

12-2.   Identifying Ball

The responsibility for playing the proper ball rests with the player. Each player should put an identification mark on his ball.

Except in a hazard, the player may, without penalty, lift a ball he believes to be his own for the purpose of identification and clean it to the extent necessary for identification. If the ball is the player's ball, he shall replace it. Before the player lifts the ball, he shall announce his intention to his opponent in match play or his marker or a fellow-competitor in stroke play and give his opponent, marker or fellow-competitor an opportunity to observe the lifting and replacement. If he lifts his ball without announcing his intention in advance or giving his opponent, marker or fellow-competitor an opportunity to observe, or if he lifts his ball for identification in a hazard, *he shall incur a penalty of one stroke* and the ball shall be replaced.

If a player who is required to replace a ball fails to do so, *he shall incur the penalty* for a breach of Rule 20-3a, but no additional penalty under Rule 12-2 shall be applied.

Rule 13.   Ball Played As It Lies; Lie, Area of Intended Swing and Line of Play; Stance

Definitions

A "hazard" is any bunker or water hazard.

A "bunker" is a hazard consisting of a prepared area of ground, often a hollow, from which turf or soil has been removed and replaced with sand or the like. Grass-covered ground bordering or within a bunker is not part of the bunker. The margin of a bunker extends vertically downwards, but not upwards.

A "water hazard" is any sea, lake, pond, river, ditch, surface drainage ditch or other open water course (whether or not containing water) and anything of a similar nature.

All ground or water within the margin of a water hazard is part of the water hazard. The margin of a water hazard extends vertically upwards and downwards. Stakes and lines defining the margins of water hazards are in the hazards.

13-1.   Ball Played As It Lies

The ball shall be played as it lies, except as otherwise provided in the Rules. (Ball at rest moved – see Rule 18.)

13-2.   Improving Lie, Area of Intended Swing or Line of Play

Except as provided in the Rules, a player shall not improve or allow to be improved:
the position or lie of his ball,
the area of his intended swing,
his line of play or
the area in which he is to drop or place a ball
by any of the following actions:
moving, bending or breaking anything growing or fixed (including immovable obstructions and objects defining out of bounds) or removing or pressing down sand, loose soil, replaced divots, other cut turf placed in position or other irregularities of surface
except as follows:
as may occur in fairly taking his stance,
in making a stroke or the backward movement of his club for a stroke,
on the teeing ground in creating or eliminating irregularities of surface or
on the putting green in removing sand and loose soil as provided in Rule 16-1a or in repairing damage as provided in Rule 16-1c.

The club may be grounded only lightly and shall not be pressed on the ground.

Exception: Ball lying in or touching hazard – see Rule 13-4.

13-3.   Building Stance

A player is entitled to place his feet firmly in taking his stance, but he shall not build a stance.

13-4.   Ball Lying in or Touching Hazard

Except as provided in the Rules, before making a stroke at a ball which lies in or touches a hazard (whether a bunker or a water hazard), the player shall not:
a. Test the condition of the hazard or any similar hazard,
b. Touch the ground in the hazard or water in the water hazard with a club or otherwise, or
c. Touch or move a loose impediment lying in or touching the hazard.

Exceptions:

1. At address or in the backward movement for the stroke, the club may touch any obstruction or any grass, bush, tree or other growing thing.

2. The player may place his clubs in a hazard, provided nothing is done which may constitute testing the soil or improving the lie of the ball.

3. The player after playing the stroke, or his caddie at any time without the authority of the player, may smooth sand or soil in the hazard, provided that, if the ball still lies in the hazard, nothing is done which improves the lie of the ball or assists the player in his subsequent play of the hole.

PENALTY FOR BREACH OF RULE:
Match play—Loss of hole; Stroke play—
Two strokes.
(Searching for ball – see Rule 12-1.)

Rule 14.   Striking the Ball

Definition

A "stroke" is the forward movement of the club made with the intention of fairly striking at and moving the ball, but if a player checks his downswing voluntarily before the clubhead reaches the ball he is deemed not to have made a stroke.

14-1.   Ball to be Fairly Struck At

The ball shall be fairly struck at with the head of the club and must not be pushed, scraped or spooned.

14-2.   Assistance

In making a stroke, a player shall not accept physical assistance or protection from the elements.

PENALTY FOR BREACH OF RULE 14-1 or -2;
Match play—Loss of hole; Stroke play—
Two strokes.

14-3. Artificial Devices and Unusual Equipment

Except as provided in the Rules, during a stipulated round the player shall not use any artificial device or unusual equipment:

a. For the purpose of gauging or measuring distance or conditions which might affect his play; or

b. Which might assist him in gripping the club, in making a stroke or in his play, except that plain gloves may be worn, resin, tape or gauze may be applied to the grip (provided such application does not render the grip non-conforming under Rule 4-1c) and a towel or handkerchief may be wrapped around the grip.

PENALTY FOR BREACH OF RULE 14-3:
Disqualification.

14-4. Striking the Ball More than Once

If a player's club strikes the ball more than once in the course of a stroke, the player shall count the stroke and *add a penalty stroke*, making two strokes in all.

14-5. Playing Moving Ball

A player shall not play while his ball is moving.

Exceptions:

Ball falling off tee—Rule 11-3.
Striking the ball more than once— Rule 14-4.
Ball moving in water—Rule 14-6.

When the ball begins to move only after the player has begun the stroke or the backward movement of his club for the stroke, he shall incur no penalty under this Rule for playing a moving ball, but he is not exempt from any penalty incurred under the following Rules

Ball at rest moved by player—Rule 18-2a.
Ball at rest moving after address— Rule 18-2b.
Ball at rest moving after loose impediment touched—Rule 18-2c.

14-6. Ball Moving in Water

When a ball is moving in water in a water hazard, the player may, without penalty, make a stroke, but he must not delay making his stroke in order to allow the wind or current to improve the position of the ball. A ball moving in water in a water hazard may be lifted if the player elects to invoke Rule 26.

PENALTY FOR BREACH OF RULE 14-5 or -6:
Match play—Loss of hole; Stroke play— Two strokes.

Rule 15. Playing a Wrong Ball

Definition

A "wrong ball" is any ball other than:
a. The ball in play,
b. A provisional ball or
c. In stroke play, a second ball played under Rule 3-3 or Rule 20-7b.

Note: Ball in play includes a ball substituted for the ball in play when the player is proceeding under an applicable Rule which does not permit substitution.

15-1. General

A player must hole out with the ball played from the teeing ground unless a Rule permits him to substitute another ball. If a player substitutes another ball when proceeding under an applicable Rule which does not permit substitution, that ball is not a wrong ball; it becomes the ball in play and, if the error is not corrected as provided in Rule 20-6, *the player shall incur a penalty of loss of hole in match play or two strokes in stroke play.*

15-2. Match Play

If a player plays a stroke with a wrong ball except in a hazard, *he shall lose the hole.*

If a player plays any strokes in a hazard with a wrong ball, there is no penalty. Strokes played in a hazard with a wrong ball do not count in the player's score. If the wrong ball belongs to another player, its owner shall place a ball on the spot from which the wrong ball was first played.

If the player and opponent exchange balls during the play of a hole, the first to play the wrong ball other than from a hazard shall lose the hole; when this cannot be determined, the hole shall be played out with the balls exchanged.

15-3. Stroke Play

If a competitor plays a stroke with a wrong ball, *he shall incur a penalty of two strokes,* unless the only stroke or strokes played with such ball were played when it was lying in a hazard, in which case no penalty is incurred.

The competitor must correct his mistake by playing the correct ball. If he fails to correct his mistake before he plays a stroke from the next teeing ground or, in the case of the last hole of the round, fails to declare his intention to correct his mistake before leaving the putting green, *he shall be disqualified.*

Strokes played by a competitor with a wrong ball do not count in his score.

If the wrong ball belongs to another competitor, its owner shall place a ball on the spot from which the wrong ball was first played.

(Lie of ball to be placed or replaced altered —see Rule 20-3b.)

THE PUTTING GREEN

Rule 16.   The Putting Green

Definitions

The "putting green" is all ground of the hole being played which is specially prepared for putting or otherwise defined as such by the Committee. A ball is on the putting green when any part of it touches the putting green.

A ball is "holed" when it is at rest within the circumference of the hole and all of it is below the level of the lip of the hole.

16-1.   General

a. Touching Line of Putt

The line of putt must not be touched except:

(i)   the player may move sand and loose soil on the putting green and other loose impediments by picking them up or by brushing them aside with his hand or a club without pressing anything down;

(ii)   in addressing the ball, the player may place the club in front of the ball without pressing anything down;

(iii)   in measuring—Rule 10-4;

(iv)   in lifting the ball—Rule 16-1b;

(v)   in pressing down a ball-marker;

(vi)   in repairing old hole plugs or ball marks on the putting green—Rule 16-1c; and

(vii)   in removing movable obstructions—Rule 24-1.

(Indicating line for putting on putting green —see Rule 8-2b.)

b. Lifting Ball

A ball on the putting green may be lifted and, if desired, cleaned. A ball so lifted shall be replaced on the spot from which it was lifted.

c. Repair of Hole Plugs and Ball Marks

The player may repair an old hole plug or damage to the putting green caused by the impact of a ball, whether or not the player's ball lies on the putting green. If the ball is moved in the process of such repair, it shall be replaced, without penalty.

d. Testing Surface

During the play of a hole, a player shall not test the surface of the putting green by rolling a ball or roughening or scraping the surface.

e. Standing Astride or on Line of Putt

The player shall not make a stroke on the putting green from a stance astride, or with either foot touching, the line of the putt or an extension of that line behind the ball. For the purpose of this Clause only, the line of putt does not extend beyond the hole.

f. Position of Caddie or Partner

While making the stroke, the player shall not allow his caddie, his partner or his partner's caddie to position himself on or close to an extension of the line of putt behind the ball.

g. Playing Stroke While Another Ball in Motion

A player shall not play a stroke while another ball is in motion after a stroke on the putting green.

(Lifting ball interfering with or assisting play while another ball in motion—see Rule 22.)

PENALTY FOR BREACH OF RULE 16-1:
Match play—Loss of hole; Stroke play— Two strokes.

16-2.   Ball Overhanging Hole

When any part of the ball overhangs the lip of the hole, the player is allowed enough time to reach the hole without unreasonable delay and an additional ten seconds to determine whether the ball is at rest. If by then the ball has not fallen into the hole, it is deemed to be at rest. If the ball subsequently falls into the hole, the player is deemed to have holed out with his last stroke, and *he shall add a penalty stroke to his score* for the hole; otherwise there is no penalty under this Rule.

(Undue delay—see Rule 6-7.)

Rule 17.   The Flagstick

17-1.   Flagstick Attended, Removed or Held Up

Before and during the stroke, the player may have the flagstick attended, removed or held up to indicate the position of the hole. This may be done only on the authority of the player before he plays his stroke.

If the flagstick is attended, removed or held up by an opponent, a fellow-competitor or the caddie of either with the player's knowledge and no objection is made, the player shall be deemed to have authorised it. If a player or a caddie attends, removes or holds up the flagstick or stands near the hole while a stroke is being played, he shall be deemed to be attending the flagstick until the ball comes to rest.

If the flagstick is not attended before the stroke is played, it shall not be attended or removed while the ball is in motion.

17-2.   Unauthorised Attendance

a. Match Play

In match play, an opponent or his caddie shall not attend, remove or hold up the flagstick without the player's knowledge or authority while the player is making a stroke or his ball is in motion.

b. Stroke Play
In stroke play, if a fellow-competitor or his caddie attends, removes or holds up the flagstick without the competitor's knowledge or authority while the competitor is making a stroke or his ball is in motion, *the fellow-competitor shall incur the penalty* for breach of this Rule. In such circumstances, if the competitor's ball strikes the flagstick or the person attending it, the competitor incurs no penalty and the ball shall be played as it lies, except that, if the stroke was played from the putting green, the stroke shall be replayed.

PENALTY FOR BREACH OF RULE 17-1 or -2:
Match play—Loss of hole; Stroke play—
Two strokes.

17-3. Ball Striking Flagstick or Attendant
The player's ball shall not strike:
a. The flagstick when attended, removed or held up by the player, his partner or either of their caddies, or by another person with the player's knowledge or authority; or
b. The player's caddie, his partner or his partner's caddie when attending the flagstick, or another person attending the flagstick with the player's knowledge or authority, or equipment carried by any such person; or
c. The flagstick in the hole, unattended, when the ball has been played from the putting green.

PENALTY FOR BREACH OF RULE 17-3;
Match play—Loss of hole; Stroke play—
Two strokes, and the ball shall be played as it lies.

17-4. Ball Resting Against Flagstick
If the ball rests against the flagstick when it is in the hole, the player or another person authorised by him may move or remove the flagstick and if the ball falls into the hole, the player shall be deemed to have holed out at his last stroke; otherwise the ball, if moved, shall be placed on the lip of the hole, without penalty.

BALL MOVED, DEFLECTED OR STOPPED

Rule 18. Ball At Rest Moved

Definitions
A ball is deemed to have "moved" if it leaves its position and comes to rest in any other place.
An "outside agency" is any agency not part of the match or, in stroke play, not part of a competitor's side, and includes a referee, a marker,

an observer or a forecaddie. Neither wind nor water is an outside agency.

"Equipment" is anything used, worn or carried by or for the player except any ball he has played at the hole being played and any small object, such as a coin or a tee, when used to mark the position of a ball or the extent of an area in which a ball is to be dropped. Equipment includes a golf cart, whether or not motorised. If such a cart is shared by more than one player, its status under the Rules is the same as that of a caddie employed by more than one player. See "Caddie".

A player has "addressed the ball" when he has taken his stance and has also grounded his club, except that in a hazard a player has addressed the ball when he has taken his stance.

Taking the "stance" consists in a player placing his feet in position for and preparatory to making a stroke.

18-1. By Outside Agency
If a ball at rest is moved by an outside agency, the player shall incur no penalty and the ball shall be replaced before the player plays another stroke.
(Player's ball at rest moved by another ball —see Rule 18-5.)

18-2. By Player, Partner, Caddie or Equipment

a. General
When a player's ball is in play, if:
(i) the player, his partner or either of their caddies lifts or moves it, touches it purposely (except with a club in the act of addressing it) or causes it to move except as permitted by a Rule, or
(ii) equipment of the player or his partner causes the ball to move,
the player shall incur a penalty stroke. The ball shall be replaced unless the movement of the ball occurs after the player has begun his swing and he does not discontinue his swing.
Under the Rules no penalty is incurred if a player accidentally causes his ball to move in the following circumstances:

In measuring to determine which ball farther from hole—Rule 10-4

In searching for covered ball in hazard or for ball in casual water, ground under repair, etc.—Rule 12-1

In the process of repairing hole plug or ball mark—Rule 16-1c

In the process of removing loose impediment on putting green—Rule 18-2c

In the process of lifting ball under a Rule —Rule 20-1

In the process of placing or replacing ball under a Rule—Rule 20-3a

In complying with Rule 22 relating to lifting ball interfering with or assisting play

In removal of movable obstruction—Rule 24-1.

b. Ball Moving After Address

If a player's ball in play moves after he has addressed it (other than as a result of a stroke), the player shall be deemed to have moved the ball and *shall incur a penalty stroke*. The player shall replace the ball unless the movement of the ball occurs after he has begun his swing and he does not discontinue his swing.

c. Ball Moving After Loose Impediment Touched

Through the green, if the ball moves after any loose impediment lying within a club-length of it has been touched by the player, his partner or either of their caddies and before the player has addressed it, the player shall be deemed to have moved the ball and *shall incur a penalty stroke*. The player shall replace the ball unless the movement of the ball occurs after he has begun his swing and he does not discontinue his swing.

On the putting green, if the ball moves in the process of removing any loose impediment, it shall be replaced without penalty.

18-3. By Opponent, Caddie or Equipment in Match Play

a. During Search

If, during search for a player's ball, it is moved by an opponent, his caddie or his equipment, no penalty is incurred and the player shall replace the ball.

b. Other Than During Search

If, other than during search for a ball, the ball is touched or moved by an opponent, his caddie or his equipment, except as otherwise provided in the Rules, *the opponent shall incur a penalty stroke*. The player shall replace the ball.

(Ball moved in measuring to determine which ball farther from the hole—see Rule 10-4.)

(Playing a wrong ball—see Rule 15-2.)

(Ball moved in complying with Rule 22 relating to lifting ball interfering with or assisting play.)

18-4. By Fellow-Competitor, Caddie or Equipment in Stroke Play

If a competitor's ball is moved by a fellow-competitor, his caddie or his equipment, no penalty is incurred. The competitor shall replace his ball.

(Playing a wrong ball—see Rule 15-3.)

18-5. By Another Ball

If a ball in play and at rest is moved by another ball in motion after a stroke, the moved ball shall be replaced.

*PENALTY FOR BREACH OF RULE:
*Match play—Loss of hole. Stroke play—
Two strokes.*

If a player who is required to replace a ball fails to do so, he shall incur the general penalty for breach of Rule 18 but no additional penalty under Rule 18 shall be applied.

Note 1: If a ball to be replaced under this Rule is not immediately recoverable, another ball may be substituted.

Note 2: If it is impossible to determine the spot on which a ball is to be placed, see Rule 20-3c.

Rule 19.   Ball in Motion Deflected or Stopped

Definitions

An "outside agency" is any agency not part of the match or, in stroke play, not part of a competitor's side, and includes a referee, a marker, an observer or a forecaddie. Neither wind nor water is an outside agency.

"Equipment" is anything used, worn or carried by or for the player except any ball he has played at the hole being played and any small object, such as a coin or a tee, when used to mark the position of a ball or the extent of an area in which a ball is to be dropped. Equipment includes a golf cart, whether or not motorised. If such a cart is shared by more than one player, its status under the Rules is the same as that of a caddie employed by more than one player. See "Caddie".

19-1.   By Outside Agency

If a ball in motion is accidentally deflected or stopped by any outside agency, it is a rub of the green, no penalty is incurred and the ball shall be played as it lies except:

a. If a ball in motion after a stroke other than on the putting green comes to rest in or on any moving or animate outside agency, the player shall, through the green or in a hazard, drop the ball, or on the putting green place the ball, as near as possible to the spot where the outside agency was when the ball came to rest in or on it, and

b. If a ball in motion after a stroke on the putting green is deflected or stopped by, or comes to rest in or on any moving or animate outside agency except a worm or an insect, the stroke shall be cancelled and the ball shall be replaced.

If the ball is not immediately recoverable, another ball may be substituted.

(Player's ball deflected or stopped by another ball – see Rule 19-5.)

Note: If the referee or the Committee determines that a competitor's ball has been purposely deflected or stopped by an outside agency, Rule 1-4 applies to the competitor. If the outside agency is a fellow-competitor or his caddie, Rule 1-2 applies to the fellow-competitor.

19-2. By Player, Partner, Caddie or Equipment

a. Match Play

If a player's ball is accidentally deflected or stopped by himself, his partner or either of their caddies or equipment, *he shall lose the hole.*

b. Stroke Play

If a competitor's ball is accidentally deflected or stopped by himself, his partner or either of their caddies or equipment, *the competitor shall incur a penalty of two strokes.* The ball shall be played as it lies, except when it comes to rest in or on the competitor's, his partner's or either of their caddies' clothes or equipment, in which case the competitor shall, through the green or in a hazard, drop the ball, or on the putting green place the ball, as near as possible to where the article was when the ball came to rest in or on it.

Exception: Dropped Ball – see Rule 20-2a. (Ball purposely deflected or stopped by player, partner or caddie – see Rule 1-2.)

19-3. By Opponent, Caddie or Equipment in Match Play

If a player's ball is accidentally deflected or stopped by an opponent, his caddie or his equipment, no penalty is incurred. The player may play the ball as it lies or, before another stroke is played by either side, cancel the stroke and replay it (see Rule 20-5). If the player elects to replay the stroke and the original ball is not immediately recoverable, another ball may be substituted.

If the ball has come to rest in or on the opponent's or his caddie's clothes or equipment, the player may through the green or in a hazard drop the ball, or on the putting green place the ball, as near as possible to where the article was when the ball came to rest in or on it.

Exception: Ball striking person attending flagstick—see Rule 17-3b.

(Ball purposely deflected or stopped by opponent or caddie—see Rule 1-2.)

19-4. By Fellow-Competitor, Caddie or Equipment in Stroke Play

See Rule 19-1 regarding ball deflected by outside agency.

19-5. By Another Ball

If a player's ball in motion after a stroke is deflected or stopped by a ball at rest, the player shall play his ball as it lies. In stroke play, if both balls lay on the putting green prior to the stroke, *the player incurs a penalty of two strokes.* Otherwise, no penalty is incurred.

If a player's ball in motion after a stroke is deflected or stopped by another ball in motion, the player shall play his ball as it lies. There is no penalty unless the player was in breach of Rule 16-1g, in which case *he shall incur the penalty for breach of that Rule.*

Exception: Ball in motion after a stroke on the putting green deflected or stopped by moving or animate outside agency—see Rule 19-1b.

PENALTY FOR BREACH OF RULE:
*Match play—Loss of hole; Stroke play—
Two strokes.*

RELIEF SITUATIONS AND PROCEDURE

Rule 20. Lifting, Dropping and Placing: Playing from Wrong Place

20.1 Lifting

A ball to be lifted under the Rules may be lifted by the player, his partner or another person authorised by the player. In any such case, the player shall be responsible for any breach of the Rules.

The position of the ball shall be marked before it is lifted under a Rule which requires it to be replaced. If it is not marked, the player *shall incur a penalty of one stroke* and the ball shall be replaced. If it is not replaced, *the player shall incur the general penalty* for breach of this Rule but no additional penalty under Rule 20-1 shall be applied.

If a ball or a ball-marker is accidentally moved in the process of lifting the ball under a Rule or marking its position, no penalty is incurred and the ball or the ball-marker shall be replaced.

Note: The position of a ball to be lifted should be marked by placing a ball-marker, a small coin or other similar object immediately behind the ball. If the ball-marker interferes with the play, stance or stroke of another player, it should be placed one or more clubhead-lengths to one side.

20-2. Dropping and Re-dropping

a. By Whom and How

A ball to be dropped under the Rules shall be dropped by the player himself. He shall stand erect, hold the ball at shoulder height and arm's length and drop it. If a ball is dropped by any other person or in any other manner and the error is not corrected as provided in Rule 20-6, *the player shall incur a penalty stroke.*

If the ball touches the player, his partner, either of their caddies or their equipment before or after it strikes the ground, the ball shall be redropped, without penalty. There is no limit to the number of times a ball shall be re-dropped in such circumstances.

(Taking action to influence position or movement of ball—see Rule 1-2.)

b. Where to Drop

When a ball is to be dropped, it shall be dropped as near as possible to the spot where the ball lay, but not nearer the hole, except when a Rule permits or requires it to be dropped elsewhere. If a ball is to be dropped in a hazard, the ball shall be dropped in and come to rest in that hazard.

Note: A ball when dropped must first strike the ground where the applicable Rule requires it to be dropped. If it is not so dropped, Rules 20-6 and -7 apply.

c. When to Re-drop

A dropped ball shall be re-dropped without penalty if it:

(i)   rolls into a hazard;
(ii)   rolls out of a hazard;
(iii) rolls onto a putting green;
(iv) rolls out of bounds;
(v)   rolls back into the condition from which relief was taken under Rule 24-2 (immovable obstruction) or Rule 25 (abnormal ground conditions and wrong putting green);
(vi) rolls and comes to rest more than two club-lengths from where it first struck the ground; or
(vii) rolls and comes to rest nearer the hole than its original position unless otherwise permitted by the Rules.

If the ball again rolls into such position, it shall be placed as near as possible to the spot where it first struck the ground when re-dropped.

If a ball to be re-dropped or placed under this Rule is not immediately recoverable, another ball may be substituted.

20-3. Placing and Replacing

a. By Whom and Where

A ball to be placed under the Rules shall be placed by the player or his partner. A ball to be replaced shall be replaced by the player, his partner or the person who lifted or moved it. In any such case, the player shall be responsible for any breach of the Rules.

If a ball or a ball-marker is accidentally moved in the process of placing or replacing the ball, no penalty is incurred and the ball or the ball-marker shall be re-placed.

b. Lie of Ball to Be Placed or Replaced Altered

If the original lie of a ball to be placed or replaced has been altered:

(i)   except in a hazard, the ball shall be placed in the nearest lie most similar to the original lie which is not more than one club-length from the original lie, not nearer the hole and not in a hazard;
(ii)   in a water hazard, the ball shall be placed in accordance with Clause (i) above, except that the ball must be placed in the water hazard;
(iii) in a bunker, the original lie shall be recreated as nearly as possible and the ball shall be placed in that lie.

c. Spot Not Determinable

If it is impossible to determine the spot where the ball is to be placed:

(i)   through the green, the ball shall be dropped as near as possible to the place where it lay but not nearer the hole or in a hazard;
(ii)   in a hazard, the ball shall be dropped in the hazard as near as possible to the place where it lay but not nearer the hole;
(iii) on the putting green, the ball shall be placed as near as possible to the place where it lay but not nearer the hole or in a hazard.

d. Ball Fails to Remain on Spot

If a ball when placed fails to remain on the spot on which it was placed, it shall be replaced without penalty. If it still fails to remain on that spot:

(i)   except in a hazard, it shall be placed at the nearest spot not nearer the hole or in a hazard where it can be placed at rest;
(ii)   in a hazard, it shall be placed in the hazard at the nearest spot not nearer the hole where it can be placed at rest.

PENALTY FOR BREACH OF RULE 20-
1,-2 or -3;
*Match play—Loss of hole; Stroke play—
Two strokes.*

20-4. When Ball Dropped or Placed is in Play
If the player's ball in play has been lifted, it
is again in play when dropped or placed.
A substituted ball becomes the ball in play
if it is dropped or placed under an applicable
Rule, whether or not such Rule permits substi-
tution. A ball substituted under an inapplicable
Rule is a wrong ball.

**20-5. Playing Next Stroke from Where
Previous Stroke Played**
When, under the Rules, a player elects or is
required to play his next stroke from where a
previous stroke was played, he shall proceed
as follows: if the stroke is to be played from the
teeing ground, the ball to be played shall be
played from anywhere within the teeing ground
and may be teed; if the stroke is to be played
from through the green or a hazard, it shall be
dropped; if the stroke is to be played on the
putting green, it shall be placed.

PENALTY FOR BREACH OF RULE 20-5;
*Match play—Loss of hole; Stroke play—
Two strokes.*

20-6. Lifting Ball Wrongly Dropped or Placed
A ball dropped or placed in a wrong place
or otherwise not in accordance with the Rules
but not played may be lifted, without penalty,
and the player shall then proceed correctly.

20-7. Playing from Wrong Place
For a ball played outside teeing ground, see
Rule 11-4.

a. Match Play
If a player plays a stroke with a ball which
has been dropped or placed in a wrong place,
he shall lose the hole.

b. Stroke Play
If a competitor plays a stroke with (i) his original ball which has been dropped or placed in
a wrong place, (ii) a substituted ball which has
been dropped or placed under an applicable
Rule but in a wrong place or (iii) his ball in
play when it has been moved and not replaced
in a case where the Rules require replacement, *he shall*, provided a serious breach has
not occurred, *incur the penalty prescribed by
the applicable Rule* and play out the hole with
the ball.
If, after playing from a wrong place, a competitor becomes aware of that fact and believes
that a serious breach may be involved, he may,

provided he has not played a stroke from the
next teeing ground or, in the case of the last
hole of the round, left the putting green, declare
that he will play out the hole with a second
ball dropped or placed in accordance with the
Rules. The competitor shall report the facts to
the Committee before returning his score card;
if he fails to do so, *he shall be disqualified.* The
Committee shall determine whether a serious
breach of the Rule occurred. If so, the score with
the second ball shall count and *the competitor
shall add two penalty strokes to his score with
that ball.*
If a serious breach has occurred and the
competitor has failed to correct it as prescribed
above, *he shall be disqualified.*

Note: If a competitor plays a second ball, penalty
strokes incurred by playing the ball ruled not to
count and strokes subsequently taken with that
ball shall be disregarded.

Rule 21. Cleaning Ball

A ball on the putting green may be cleaned
when lifted under Rule 16-1b. Elsewhere, a ball
may be cleaned when lifted except when it has
been lifted:

a. To determine if it is unfit for play (Rule
5-3);
b. For identification (Rule 12-2), in which
case it may be cleaned only to the extent necessary for identification; or
c. Because it is interfering with or assisting play (Rule 22).

If a player cleans his ball during play of a
hole except as provided in this Rule, *he shall
incur a penalty of one stroke* and the ball, if
lifted, shall be replaced.
If a player who is required to replace a ball
fails to do so, *he shall incur the penalty* for
breach of Rule 20-3a, but no additional penalty
under Rule 21 shall be applied.

Exception: If a player incurs a penalty for failing to act in accordance with Rule 5-3, 12-2 or
22, no additional penalty under Rule 21 shall be
applied.

Rule 22. Ball Interfering with or Assisting
Play

Any player may:
a. Lift his ball if he considers that it might
assist any other player or
b. Have any other ball lifted if he considers
that it might interfere with his play or assist the
play of any other player,
but this may not be done while another
ball is in motion. In stroke play, a player

required to lift his ball may play first rather than lift. A ball lifted under this Rule shall be replaced.

If a ball is accidentally moved in complying with this Rule, no penalty is incurred and the ball shall be replaced.

PENALTY FOR BREACH OF RULE:
Match play—Loss of hole; Stroke play—
Two strokes.

Rule 23.   Loose Impediments

Definition

"Loose impediments" are natural objects such as stones, leaves, twigs, branches and the like, dung, worms and insects and casts or heaps made by them, provided they are not fixed or growing, are not solidly embedded and do not adhere to the ball.

Sand and loose soil are loose impediments on the putting green but not elsewhere.

Snow and ice are either casual water or loose impediments, at the option of the player, except that manufactured ice is an obstruction.

Dew is not a loose impediment.

23-1.   Relief

Except when both the loose impediment and the ball lie in or touch a hazard, any loose impediment may be removed without penalty. If the ball moves, see Rule 18-2c.

When a player's ball is in motion, a loose impediment on his line of play shall not be removed.

PENALTY FOR BREACH OF RULE:
Match play—Loss of hole; Stroke play—
Two strokes.

(Searching for ball in hazard—see Rule 12-1.)
(Touching line of putt—see Rule 16-1a.)

Rule 24.   Obstructions

Definition

An "obstruction" is anything artificial, including the artificial surfaces and sides of roads and paths and manufactured ice, except:

a. Objects defining out of bounds, such as walls, fences, stakes and railings;

b. Any part of an immovable artificial object which is out of bounds; and

c. Any construction declared by the Committee to be an integral part of the course.

24-1.   Movable Obstruction

A player may obtain relief from a movable obstruction as follows:

a. If the ball does not lie in or on the obstruction, the obstruction may be removed; if

the ball moves, no penalty is incurred and the ball shall be replaced.

b. If the ball lies in or on the obstruction, the ball may be lifted, without penalty, and the obstruction removed. The ball shall through the green or in a hazard be dropped, or on the putting green be placed, as near as possible to the spot directly under the place where the ball lay in or on the obstruction, but not nearer the hole.

The ball may be cleaned when lifted under Rule 24-1.

When a ball is in motion, an obstruction on the player's line of play other than an attended flagstick and equipment of the players shall not be removed.

24-2.   Immovable Obstruction

a. Interference

Interference by an immovable obstruction occurs when a ball lies in or on the obstruction, or so close to the obstruction that the obstruction interferes with the player's stance or the area of his intended swing. If the player's ball lies on the putting green, interference also occurs if an immovable obstruction on the putting green intervenes on his line of putt. Otherwise, intervention on the line of play is not, of itself, interference under this Rule.

b. Relief

Except when the ball lies in or touches a water hazard or a lateral water hazard, a player may obtain relief from interference by an immovable obstruction, without penalty, as follows:

(i) **Through the Green:** If the ball lies through the green, the point on the course nearest to where the ball lies shall be determined (without crossing over, through or under the obstruction) which (a) is not nearer the hole, (b) avoids interference (as defined) and (c) is not a hazard or on a putting green. The player shall lift the ball and drop it within one club-length of the point thus determined on ground which fulfils (a), (b) and (c) above.

Note: The prohibition against crossing over, through or under the obstruction does not apply to the artificial surfaces and sides of roads and paths or when the ball lies in or on the obstruction.

(ii) **In a Bunker:** If the ball lies in or touches a bunker, the player shall lift and drop the ball in accordance with Clause (i) above, except that the ball must be dropped in the bunker.

(iii) **On the Putting Green:** If the ball lies on the putting green, the player shall lift the ball and place it in the nearest position to where it lay which affords relief from interference, but not nearer the hole nor in a hazard.

The ball may be cleaned when lifted for relief under Rule 24-2b.

(Ball rolling back into condition from which relief taken—see Rule 20-2c(v).)

Exception: A player may not obtain relief under Rule 24-2b if (a) it is clearly unreasonable for him to play a stroke because of interference by anything other than an immovable obstruction or (b) interference by an immovable obstruction would occur only through use of an unnecessarily abnormal stance, swing or direction of play.

Note: If a ball lies in or touches a water hazard (including a lateral water hazard), the player is not entitled to relief without penalty from interference by an immovable obstruction. The player shall play the ball as it lies or proceed under Rule 26-1.

PENALTY FOR BREACH OF RULE:
*Match play—Loss of hole; Stroke play—
Two strokes.*

Rule 25.   Abnormal Ground Conditions and Wrong Putting Green

Definitions

"Casual water" is any temporary accumulation of water on the course which is visible before or after the player takes his stance and is not in a water hazard. Snow and ice are either casual water or loose impediments, at the option of the player, except that manufactured ice is an obstruction. Dew is not casual water.

"Ground under repair" is any portion of the course so marked by order of the Committee or so declared by its authorised representative. It includes material piled for removal and a hole made by a greenkeeper, even if not so marked. Stakes and lines defining ground under repair are in such ground. The margin of ground under repair extends vertically downwards, but not upwards.

Note 1: Grass cuttings and other material left on the course which have been abandoned and are not intended to be removed are not ground under repair unless so marked.

Note 2: The Committee may make a Local Rule prohibiting play from ground under repair.

25-1.   Casual Water, Ground Under Repair and Certain Damage to Course

a. Interference

Interference by casual water, ground under repair or a hole, cast or runway made by a burrowing animal, a reptile or a bird occurs when a ball lies in or touches any of these conditions or when the condition interferes with the player's stance or the area of his intended swing.

If the player's ball lies on the putting green, interference also occurs if such condition on the putting green intervenes on his line of putt.

If interference exists, the player may either play the ball as it lies (unless prohibited by Local Rule) or take relief as provided in Clause b.

b. Relief

If the player elects to take relief, he shall proceed as follows:

(i) **Through the Green:** If the ball lies through the green, the point on the course nearest to where the ball lies shall be determined which (a) is not nearer the hole, (b) avoids interference by the condition, and (c) is not in a hazard or on a putting green. The player shall lift the ball and drop it without penalty within one club-length of the point thus determined on ground which fulfils (a), (b) and (c) above.

(ii) **In a Hazard:** If the ball lies in or touches a hazard, the player shall lift and drop the ball either:

(a) Without penalty, in the hazard, as near as possible to the spot where the ball lay, but not nearer the hole, on ground which affords maximum available relief from the condition;

or

(b) *Under penalty of one stroke,* outside the hazard, keeping the point where the ball lay directly between the hole and the spot on which the ball is dropped.

Exception: If a ball lies in or touches a water hazard (including a lateral water hazard), the player is not entitled to relief without penalty from a hole, cast or runway made by a burrowing animal, a reptile or a bird. The player shall play the ball as it lies or proceed under Rule 26-1.

(iii) **On the Putting Green:** If the ball lies on the putting green, the player shall lift the ball and place it without penalty in the nearest position to where it lay which affords maximum available relief from the condition, but not nearer the hole nor in a hazard.

The ball may be cleaned when lifted under Rule 25-1b.

(Ball rolling back into condition from which relief taken—see Rule 20-2c(v).)

Exception: A player may not obtain relief under Rule 25-1b if (a) it is clearly unreasonable for him to play a stroke because of interference by anything other than a condition covered by Rule 25-1a or (b) interference by such a condition would occur only through use of an unnecessarily abnormal stance, swing or direction of play.

c. Ball Lost Under Condition Covered by Rule 25-1

It is a question of fact whether a ball lost after having been struck toward a condition covered by Rule 25-1 is lost under such condition. In order to treat the ball as lost under such condition, there must be reasonable evidence to that effect. In the absence of such evidence, the ball must be treated as a lost ball and Rule 27 applies.

(i) **Outside a Hazard**—If a ball is lost outside a hazard under a condition covered by Rule 25-1, the player may take relief as follows: the point on the course nearest to where the ball last crossed the margin of the area shall be determined which (a) is not nearer the hole than where the ball last crossed the margin, (b) avoids interference by the condition and (c) is not in a hazard or on a putting green. He shall drop a ball without penalty within one club-length of the point thus determined on ground which fulfils (a), (b) and (c) above.

(ii) **In a Hazard**—If a ball is lost in a hazard under a condition covered by Rule 25-1, the player may drop a ball either;

(a) Without penalty, in the hazard, as near as possible to the point at which the original ball last crossed the margin of the area, but not nearer the hole, on ground, which affords maximum available relief from the condition;

or

(b) *Under penalty of one stroke*, outside the hazard, keeping the point at which the original ball last crossed the margin of the hazard directly between the hole and the spot on which the ball is dropped.

Exception: If a ball lies in a water hazard (including a lateral water hazard), the player is not entitled to relief without penalty for a ball lost in a hole, cast or runway made by a burrowing animal, a reptile or a bird. The player shall proceed under Rule 26-1.

25-2. Embedded Ball

A ball embedded in its own pitch-mark in the ground in any closely mown area through the green may be lifted, cleaned and dropped, without penalty, as near as possible to the spot where it lay but not nearer the hole. "Closely mown area" means any area of the course, including paths through the rough, cut to fairway height or less.

25-3. Wrong Putting Green

If a ball lies on a putting green other than that of the hole being played, the point on the course nearest to where the ball lies shall be determined which (a) is not nearer the hole and (b) is not in a hazard or on a putting green. The player shall lift the ball and drop it without penalty within one club-length of the point thus determined on ground which fulfils (a) and (b) above. The ball may be cleaned when so lifted.

Note: Unless otherwise prescribed by the Committee, the term "a putting green other than that of the hole being played" includes a practice putting green or pitching green on the course.

PENALTY FOR BREACH OF RULE.
Match play—Loss of hole; Stroke play—
Two strokes.

Rule 26.   Water Hazards
(Including Lateral Water Hazards)

Definitions

A "water hazard" is any sea, lake, pond, river, ditch, surface drainage ditch or other open water course (whether or not containing water) and anything of a similar nature.

All ground or water within the margin of a water hazard is part of the water hazard. The margin of a water hazard extends vertically upwards and downwards. Stakes and lines defining the margins of water hazards are in the hazards.

Note: Water hazards (other than lateral water hazards) should be defined by yellow stakes or lines.

A "lateral water hazard" is a water hazard or that part of a water hazard so situated that it is not possible or is deemed by the Committee to be impracticable to drop a ball behind the water hazard in accordance with Rule 26-1b

That part of a water hazard to be played as a lateral water hazard should be distinctly marked.

Note: Lateral water hazards should be defined by red stakes or lines.

26-1. Ball in Water Hazard

It is a question of fact whether a ball lost after having been struck toward a water hazard is lost inside or outside the hazard. In order to treat the ball as lost in the hazard, there must be reasonable evidence that the ball lodged in it. In the absence of such evidence, the ball must be treated as a lost ball and Rule 27 applies.

If a ball lies in, touches or is lost in a water hazard (whether the ball lies in water or not), the player may *under penalty of one stroke:*

a. Play his next stroke as nearly as possible at the spot from which the original ball was last played (see Rule 20-5);
or

b. Drop a ball behind the water hazard, keeping the point at which the original ball last crossed the margin of the water hazard directly between the hole and the spot on which the ball is dropped, with no limit to how far behind the water hazard the ball may be dropped;
or

c. *As additional options available only if the ball lies in, touches or is lost in a lateral water hazard*, drop a ball outside the water hazard within two club-lengths of (i) the point where the original ball last crossed the margin of the water hazard or (ii) a point on the opposite margin of the water hazard equidistant from the hole. The ball must be dropped and come to rest not nearer the hole than the point where the original ball last crossed the margin of the water hazard.

The ball may be cleaned when lifted under this Rule.

(Ball moving in water in a water hazard—see Rule 14-6.)

26-2. Ball Played within Water Hazard

a. Ball comes to rest in Hazard

If a ball played from within a water hazard comes to rest in the hazard after the stroke, the player may:

(i)   proceed under Rule 26-1; or

(ii) *under penalty of one stroke*, play his next stroke as nearly as possible at the spot from which the last stroke from outside the hazard was played (see Rule 20-5).

b. Ball Lost or Unplayable Outside Hazard or Out of Bounds

If a ball played from within a water hazard is lost or declared unplayable outside the hazard or is out of bounds, the player, after taking a *penalty of one stroke* under Rule 27-1 or 28a, may:

(i)   play a ball as nearly as possible at the spot in the hazard from which the original ball was last played (see Rule 20-5); or

(ii) *under an additional penalty of one stroke*, proceed under Rule 26-1b or, if applicable, Rule 26-1c, using as the reference point the point where the original ball last crossed the margin of the hazard before it came to rest in the hazard; or

(iii) *under an additional penalty of one stroke*, play his next stroke as nearly

as possible at the spot from which the last stroke from outside the hazard was played (see Rule 20-5).

Note: If a ball played from within a water hazard is declared unplayable outside the hazard, nothing in Rule 26-2b precludes the player from proceeding under Rule 28b or c.

PENALTY FOR BREACH OF RULE:
Match play—Loss of hole; Stroke play—Two strokes.

Rule 27. Ball Lost or Out of Bounds; Provisional Ball

If the original ball is lost under a condition covered by Rule 25-1 (casual water, ground under repair and certain damage to the course), the player may proceed under that Rule. If the original ball is lost in a water hazard, the player shall proceed under Rule 26.

Such Rules may not be used unless there is reasonable evidence that the ball is lost under a condition covered by Rule 25-1 or in a water hazard.

Definitions

A ball is "lost" if:

a. It is not found or identified as his by the player within five minutes after the player's side or his or their caddies have begun to search for it; or

b. The player has put another ball into play under the Rules, even though he may not have searched for the original ball; or

c. The player has played any stroke with a provisional ball from the place where the original ball is likely to be or from a point nearer the hole than that place, whereupon the provisional ball becomes the ball in play.

Time spent in playing a wrong ball is not counted in the five-minute period allowed for search.

"Out of bounds" is ground on which play is prohibited.

When out of bounds is defined by reference to stakes or a fence, or as being beyond stakes or a fence, the out of bounds line is determined by the nearest inside points of the stakes or fence posts at ground level excluding angled supports.

When out of bounds is defined by a line on the ground, the line itself is out of bounds.

The out of bounds line extends vertically upwards and downwards.

A ball is out of bounds when all of it lies out of bounds.

A player may stand out of bounds to play a ball lying within bounds.

A "provisional ball" is a ball played under Rule 27-2 for a ball which may be lost outside a water hazard or may be out of bounds.

27-1. Ball Lost or Out of Bounds

If a ball is lost outside a water hazard or is out of bounds, the player shall play a ball, *under penalty of one stroke*, as nearly as possible at the spot from which the original ball was last played (see Rule 20-5).

PENALTY FOR BREACH OF RULE 27-1:
*Match play—Loss of hole; Stroke play—
Two strokes*

27-2. Provisional Ball

a. Procedure

If a ball may be lost outside a water hazard or may be out of bounds, to save time the player may play another ball provisionally as nearly as possible at the spot from which the original ball was played (see Rule 20-5). The player shall inform his opponent in match play or his marker or a fellow competitor in stroke play that he intends to play a provisional ball, and he shall play it before he or his partner goes forward to search for the original ball. If he fails to do so and plays another ball, such ball is not a provisional ball and becomes the ball in play *under penalty of stroke and distance* (Rule 27-1); the original ball is deemed to be lost.

b. When Provisional Ball Becomes Ball in Play

The player may play a provisional ball until he reaches the place where the original ball is likely to be. If he plays a stroke with the provisional ball from the place where the original ball is likely to be or from a point nearer the hole than that place, the original ball is deemed to be lost and the provisional ball becomes the ball in play under *penalty of stroke and distance* (Rule 27-1).

If the original ball is lost outside a water hazard or is out of bounds, the provisional ball becomes the ball in play, *under penalty of stroke and distance* (Rule 27-1).

c. When Provisional Ball to Be Abandoned

If the original ball is neither lost outside a water hazard nor out of bounds, the player shall abandon the provisional ball and continue play with the original ball. If he fails to do so, any further strokes played with the provisional ball shall constitute playing a wrong ball and the provisions of Rule 15 shall apply.

Note: If the original ball lies in a water hazard, the player shall play the ball as it lies or proceed under Rule 26. If it is lost in a water hazard or unplayable, the player shall proceed under Rule 26 or 28, whichever is applicable.

Rule 28. Ball Unplayable

The player may declare his ball unplayable at any place on the course except when the ball lies in or touches a water hazard. The player is the sole judge as to whether his ball is unplayable.

If the player deems his ball to be unplayable, he shall, *under penalty of one stroke*:

a. Play his next stroke as nearly as possible at the spot from which the original ball was last played (see Rule 20-5);
or

b. Drop a ball within two club-lengths of the spot where the ball lay, but not nearer the hole;
or

c. Drop a ball behind the point where the ball lay, keeping that point directly between the hole and the spot on which the ball is dropped, with no limit to how far behind that point the ball may be dropped.

If the unplayable ball lies in a bunker and the player elects to proceed under Clause b or c, a ball must be dropped in the bunker.

The ball may be cleaned when lifted under this Rule.

PENALTY FOR BREACH OF RULE:
*Match play—Loss of hole; Stroke play—
Two strokes.*

OTHER FORMS OF PLAY

Rule 29.   Threesomes and Foursomes

Definitions

Threesome: A match in which one plays against two, and each side plays one ball.

Foursome: A match in which two play against two, and each side plays one ball.

29-1. General

In a threesome or a foursome, during any stipulated round the partners shall play alternately from the teeing grounds and alternately during the play of each hole. Penalty strokes do not affect the order of play.

29-2. Match Play

If a player plays when his partner should have played, *his side shall lose the hole.*

29-3. Stroke Play

If the partners play a stroke or strokes in incorrect order, such stroke or strokes shall be cancelled and *the side shall incur a penalty of two strokes.* The side shall correct the error by playing a ball in correct order at the spot from which it first played in incorrect order (see Rule 20-5). If the side plays a stroke from the next teeing ground without first correcting the error or, in the case of the last hole of the round, leaves the putting green without declaring its intention to correct the error, *the side shall be disqualified.*

Rule 30.   Three-Ball, Best-Ball and Four-Ball Match Play

Definitions
Three-Ball: A match play competition in which three play against one another, each playing his own ball. Each player is playing two distinct matches.
Best-Ball: A match in which one plays against the better ball of two or the best ball of three players.
Four-Ball: A match in which two play their better ball against the better ball of two other players.

30-1.   Rules of Golf Apply
The Rules of Golf, so far as they are not at variance with the following special Rules, shall apply to three-ball, best-ball and four-ball matches.

30-2.   Three-Ball Match Play

a. Ball at Rest Moved by an Opponent
Except as otherwise provided in the Rules, if the player's ball is touched or moved by an opponent, his caddie or equipment other than during search, Rule 18-3b applies. *That opponent shall incur a penalty stroke in his match with the player,* but not in his match with the other opponent.

b.   Ball Deflected or Stopped by an Opponent Accidentally
If a player's ball is accidentally deflected or stopped by an opponent, his caddie or equipment, no penalty shall be incurred. In his match with that opponent the player may play the ball as it lies or, before another stroke is played by either side, he may cancel the stroke and replay it (see Rule 20-5). In his match with the other opponent, the ball shall be played as it lies.

Exception: Ball striking person attending flagstick—see Rule 17-3b.

(Ball purposely deflected or stopped by opponent—see Rule 1-2.)

30-3.   Best-Ball and Four-Ball Match Play

a. Representation of Side
A side may be represented by one partner for all or any part of a match; all partners need not be present. An absent partner may join a match between holes, but not during play of a hole.

b. Maximum of Fourteen Clubs
The side shall be penalised for a breach of Rule 4-4 by any partner.

c. Order of Play
Balls belonging to the same side may be played in the order the side considers best.

d. Wrong Ball
If a player plays a stroke with a wrong ball except in a hazard, *he shall be disqualified for that hole,* but his partner incurs no penalty even if the wrong ball belongs to him. The owner of the ball shall replace it on the spot from which it was played, without penalty. If the ball is not immediately recoverable, another ball may be substituted.

e. Disqualification of Side
(i)   *A side shall be disqualified* for a breach of any of the following by any partner:
Rule 1-3 —   Agreement to Waive Rules.
Rule 4-1,
   -2 or -3 – Clubs.
Rule 5-1
   or -2 –   The Ball
Rule 6-2a –   Handicap (playing off higher handicap).
Rule 6-4 –   Caddie.
Rule 6-7 –   Undue Delay (repeated offence).
Rule 14-3 –   Artificial Devices and Unusual Equipment.
(ii)   *A side shall be disqualified* for a breach of any of the following by all partners:
Rule 6-3 –   Time of Starting and Groups.
Rule 6-8 –   Discontinuance of Play.

f. Effect of Other Penalties
If a player's breach of a Rule assists his partner's play or adversely affects an opponent's play, *the partner incurs the applicable penalty in addition to any penalty incurred by the player.*

In all other cases where a player incurs a penalty for breach of a Rule, the penalty shall not apply to his partner. Where the penalty is stated to be loss of hole, the effect shall be to disqualify the player for that hole.

g.   Another Form of Match Played Concurrently
In a best-ball or four-ball match when another form of match is played concurrently, the above special Rules shall apply.

Rule 31.   Four-Ball Stroke Play
In four-ball stroke play two competitors play as partners, each playing his own ball. The lower score of the partners is the score for the hole. If one partner fails to complete the play of a hole, there is no penalty.

31-1. Rules of Golf Apply

The Rules of Golf, so far as they are not at variance with the following special Rules, shall apply to four-ball stroke play.

31-2. Representation of Side

A side may be represented by either partner for all or any part of a stipulated round; both partners need not be present. An absent competitor may join his partner between holes, but not during play of a hole.

31-3. Maximum of Fourteen Clubs

The side shall be penalised for, a breach of Rule 4-4 by either partner.

31-4. Scoring

The marker is required to record for each hole only the gross score of whichever partner's score is to count. The gross scores to count must be individually identifiable; otherwise *the side shall be disqualified*. Only one of the partners need be responsible for complying with Rule 6-6b.

(Wrong score—see Rule 31-7a.)

31-5. Order of Play

Balls belonging to the same side may be played in the order the side considers best.

31-6. Wrong Ball

If a competitor plays a stroke with a wrong ball except in a hazard, *he shall add two penalty strokes to his score for the hole* and shall then play the correct ball. His partner incurs no penalty even if the wrong ball belongs to him.

The owner of the ball shall replace it on the spot from which it was played, without penalty. If the ball is not immediately recoverable, another ball may be substituted.

31-7. Disqualification Penalties

a. Breach by One Partner

A side shall be disqualified from the competition for a breach of any of the following by either partner:

Rule 1-3 –	Agreement to Waive Rules.
Rule 3-4 –	Refusal to Comply with Rule.
Rule 4-1, -2 or -3 –	Clubs.
Rule 5-1 -2 –	The Ball.
Rule 6-2b –	Handicap (playing off higher handicap; failure to record handicap).
Rule 6-4 –	Caddie.
Rule 6-6b –	Signing and Returning Card.
Rule 6-6d –	Wrong Score for Hole, i.e. when the recorded lower score of the partners is lower than actually

taken. If the recorded lower score of the partners is higher than actually taken, it must stand as returned.

Rule 6-7 –	Undue Delay (repeated offence).
Rule 7-1 –	Practice Before or Between Rounds.
Rule 14-3 –	Artificial Devices and Unusual Equipment.
Rule 31-4 –	Gross Scores to count Not Individually Identifiable.

b. Breach by Both Partners

A side shall be disqualified:
(i)   for a breach by both partners of Rule 6-3 (Time of Starting and Groups) or Rule 6-8 (Discontinuance of Play), or
(ii) if, at the same hole, each partner is in breach of a Rule the penalty for which is disqualification from the competition or for a hole.

c. For the Hole Only

In all other cases where a breach of a Rule would entail disqualification, *the competitor shall be disqualified only for the hole at which the breach occurred.*

31-8. Effect of Other Penalties

If a competitor's breach of a Rule assists his partner's play, *the partner incurs the applicable penalty in addition to any penalty incurred by the competitor.*

In all other cases where a competitor incurs a penalty for breach of a Rule, the penalty shall not apply to his partner.

Rule 32. Bogey, Par and Stableford Competitions

32-1. Conditions

Bogey, par and Stableford competitions are forms of stroke competition in which play is against a fixed score at each hole. The Rules for stroke play, so far as they are not at variance with the following special Rules, apply.

a. Bogey and Par Competitions

The reckoning for bogey and par competitions is made as in match play. Any hole for which a competitor makes no return shall be regarded as a loss. The winner is the competitor who is most successful in the aggregate of holes.

The marker is responsible for marking only the gross number of strokes for each hole where the competitor makes a net score equal to or less than the fixed score.

Note: Maximum of 14 Clubs—Penalties as in match play—see Rule 4-4.

b. Stableford Competitions

The reckoning in Stableford competitions is made by points awarded in relation to a fixed score at each hole as follows

Hole Played in	Points
More than one over fixed score or no score returned	0
One over fixed score	1
Fixed score	2
One under fixed score	3
Two under fixed score	4
Three under fixed score	5

The winner is the competitor who scores the highest number of points.

The marker shall be responsible for marking only the gross number of strokes at each hole where the competitor's net score earns one or more points.

Note: Maximum of 14 Clubs (Rule 4-4) — Penalties applied as follows: From total points scored for the round, deduction of two points for each hole at which any breach occurred; maximum deduction per round: four points.

32-3. Disqualification Penalties

a. From the Competition

A competitor shall be disqualified from the competition for a breach of any of the following:

Rule 1-3 –	Agreement to Waive Rules.
Rule 3-4 –	Refusal to Comply with Rule.
Rule 4-1, -2 or -3 –	Clubs.
Rule 5-1 – or -2 –	The Ball.
Rule 6-2b –	Handicap (playing off higher handicap; failure to record handicap).
Rule 6-3 –	Time of Starting and Groups.
Rule 6-4 –	Caddie.
Rule 6-6b –	Signing and Returning Card.
Rule 6-6d –	Wrong Score for Hole, except that no penalty shall be incurred when a breach of this Rule does not affect the result of the hole.
Rule 6-7 –	Undue Delay (repeated offence).
Rule 6-8 –	Discontinuance of Play.
Rule 7-1 –	Practice Before or Between Rounds.
Rule 14-3 –	Artificial Devices and Unusual Equipment.

b. For a Hole

In all other cases where a breach of a Rule would entail disqualification, *the competitor shall be disqualified only for the hole at which the breach occurred.*

ADMINISTRATION

Rule 33. The Committee

33-1. Conditions; Waiving Rule

The Committee shall lay down the conditions under which a competition is to be played.

The Committee has no power to waive a Rule of Golf.

Certain special rules governing stroke play are so substantially different from those governing match play that combining the two forms of play is not practicable and is not permitted. The results of matches played and the scores returned in these circumstances shall not be accepted.

In stroke play the Committee may limit a referee's duties.

33-2. The Course

a. Defining Bounds and Margins

The Committee shall define accurately:

(i)   the course and out of bounds,
(ii) the margins of water hazards and lateral water hazards,
(iii) ground under repair, and
(iv) obstructions and integral parts of the course.

b. New Holes

New holes should be made on the day on which a stroke competition begins and at such other times as the Committee considers necessary, provided all competitors in a single round play with each hole cut in the same position.

Exception: When it is impossible for a damaged hole to be repaired so that it conforms with the Definition, the Committee may make a new hole in a nearby similar position.

c. Practice Ground

Where there is no practice ground available outside the area of a competition course, the Committee should lay down the area on which players may practise on any day of a competition, if it is practicable to do so. On any day of a stroke competition, the Committee should not normally permit practice on or to a putting green or from a hazard of the competition course.

d. Course Unplayable

If the Committee or its authorised representative considers that for any reason the course is not in a playable condition or that there are circumstances which render the proper playing of the game impossible, it may, in match play or stroke play, order a temporary suspension of play or, in stroke play, declare play null and void and cancel all scores for the round in question. When play has been temporarily suspended, it shall be resumed from where it was discontinued, even though resumption occurs on a subsequent day. When a round is cancelled, all penalties incurred in that round are cancelled.

(Procedure in discontinuing play—see Rule 6-8.)

33-3.   Times of Starting and Groups
The Committee shall lay down the times of starting and, in stroke play, arrange the groups in which competitors shall play.

When a match play competition is played over an extended period, the Committee shall lay down the limit of time within which each round shall be completed. When players are allowed to arrange the date of their match within these limits, the Committee should announce that the match must be played at a stated time on the last day of the period unless the players agree to a prior date.

33-4.   Handicap Stroke Table
The Committee shall publish a table indicating the order of holes at which handicap strokes are to be given or received.

33-5.   Score Card
In stroke play, the Committee shall issue for each competitor a score card containing the date and the competitor's name, or in foursome, or four-ball stroke play, the competitors' names.

In stroke play, the Committee is responsible for the addition of scores and application of the handicap recorded on the card.

In four-ball stroke play, the Committee is responsible for recording the better-ball score for each hole and in the process applying the handicaps recorded on the card, and adding the better-ball scores.

In bogey, par and Stableford competitions, the Committee is responsible for applying the handicap recorded on the card and determining the result of each hole and the overall result or points total.

33-6.   Decision of Ties
The Committee shall announce the manner, day and time for the decision of a halved match or of a tie, whether played on level terms or under handicap.

A halved match shall not be decided by stroke play. A tie in stroke play shall not be decided by a match.

33-7.   Disqualification Penalty; Committee Discretion
A penalty of disqualification may in exceptional individual cases be waived, modified or imposed if the Committee considers such action warranted.

33-8.   Local Rules

a. Policy
The Committee may make and publish Local Rules for abnormal conditions if they are consistent with the policy of the Governing Authority for the country concerned as set forth in Appendix I to these Rules.

b. Waiving Penalty
A penalty imposed by a Rule of Golf shall not be waived by a Local Rule.

Rule 34.   Disputes and Decisions

34-1.   Claims and Penalties

a. Match Play
In match play if a claim is lodged with the Committee under Rule 2-5, a decision should be given as soon as possible so that the state of the match may, if necessary, be adjusted.

If a claim is not made within the time limit provided by Rule 2-5, it shall not be considered unless it is based on facts previously unknown to the player making the claim and the player making the claim had been given wrong information (Rules 6-2a and 9) by an opponent. In any case, no later claim shall be considered after the result of the match has been officially announced, unless the Committee is satisfied that the opponent knew he was giving wrong information.

b. Stroke Play
Except as provided below, in stroke play no penalty shall be rescinded, modified or imposed after the competition is closed. A competition is deemed to have closed when the result has been officially announced or, in stroke play qualifying followed by match play, when the player has teed off in his first match.

A penalty of disqualification shall be imposed at any time if a competitor:
(i)   returns a score for any hole lower than actually taken (Rule 6-6d) for any reason other than failure to include a penalty which he did not know he had incurred; or
(ii)   returns a score card on which he has recorded a handicap which he knows is higher than that to which he is entitled, and this affects the number of strokes received (Rule 6-2b).

34-2.   Referee's Decision
If a referee has been appointed by the Committee, his decision shall be final.

34-3.   Committee's Decision

In the absence of a referee, the players shall refer any dispute to the Committee, whose decision shall be final.

If the Committee cannot come to a decision, it shall refer the dispute to the Rules of Golf Committee of the Royal & Ancient Golf Club of St. Andrews, whose decision shall be final.

If the point in doubt or dispute has not been referred to the Rules of Golf Committee, the player or players have the right to refer an agreed statement through the Secretary of the Club to the Rules of Golf Committee for an opinion as to the correctness of the decision given. The reply will be sent to the Secretary of the Club or Clubs concerned.

If play is conducted other than in accordance with the Rules of Golf, the Rules of Golf Committee will not give a decision on any question.

APPENDIX I

LOCAL RULES (RULE 33-8) AND CONDITIONS OF THE COMPETITION (RULE 33-1)

Part A   Local Rules

The Committee may make and publish Local Rules (for Specimen Local Rules see Part B) for such abnormal conditions as:

1.   Obstructions

a. General

Clarifying the status of objects which may be obstructions (Rule 24).

Declaring any construction to be an integral part of the course and, accordingly, not an obstruction, e.g. built-up sides of teeing grounds, putting greens and bunkers (Rules 24 and 33-2a).

b. Stones in Bunkers

Allowing the removal of stones in bunkers by declaring them to be "movable obstructions" (Rule 24).

c. Roads and Paths

(i)   Declaring artificial surfaces and sides of roads and paths to be integral parts of the course, or

(ii)   Providing relief of the type afforded under Rule 24-2b from roads and paths not having artificial surfaces and sides if they could unfairly affect play.

d. Fixed Sprinkler Heads

Providing relief from intervention by fixed sprinkler heads within two club-lengths of the putting green when the ball lies within two club-lengths of the sprinkler head.

e. Temporary Immovable Obstructions

Specimen Local Rules for application in Tournament Play are available from the Royal & Ancient Golf Club of St Andrews.

2.   Areas of the Course Requiring Preservation

Assisting preservation of the course by defining areas, including turf nurseries, young plantations and other parts of the course under cultivation, as "ground under repair" from which play is prohibited.

3.   Unusual Damage to the Course or Accumulation of Leaves (or the like)

Declaring such areas to be "ground under repair" (Rule 25).

Note: For relief from aerification holes see Specimen Local Rule 7 in part B of this Appendix.

4.   Extreme Wetness, Mud, Poor Conditions and Protection of Course

(a.)   **Lifting an Embedded Ball, Cleaning**

Where the ground is unusually soft, the Committee may, by temporary Local Rule, allow the lifting of a ball which is embedded in its own pitch-mark in the ground in an area "through the green" which is not "closely mown" (Rule 25-2) if it is satisfied that the proper playing of the game would otherwise be prevented. The Local Rule shall be for that day only or for a short period, and if practicable shall be confined to specified areas. The Committee shall withdraw the Local Rule as soon as conditions warrant and should not print it on the score card.

In similarly adverse conditions, the Committee may, by temporary Local Rule, permit the cleaning of a ball "through the green".

(b.)   **"Preferred Lies" and "Winter Rules"**

Adverse conditions, including the poor condition of the course or the existence of mud, are sometimes so general, particularly during winter months, that the Committee may decide to grant relief by Local Rule either to protect the course or to promote fair and pleasant play. Such Local Rule shall be withdrawn as soon as conditions warrant.

5.   Other Local Conditions which Interfere with the Proper Playing of the Game

If this necessitates modification of a Rule of Golf the approval of the Governing Authority must be obtained.

Other matters which the Committee could cover by Local Rule include:

6.   Water Hazards

a. Lateral Water Hazards

Clarifying the status of sections of water hazards which may be lateral water hazards (Rule 26).

b. Provisional Ball

Permitting the play of a provisional ball for a ball which may be in a water hazard of such character that it would be impracticable to determine whether the ball is in the hazard or to do so would unduly delay play. In such a case, if a provisional ball is played and the original ball is in a water hazard, the player may play the original ball as it lies or continue the provisional ball in play, but he may not proceed under Rule 26-1.

7.   Defining Bounds and Margins

Specifying means used to define out of bounds, hazards, water hazards, lateral water hazards and ground under repair.

8. Dropping Zones

Establishing special areas in which balls may or shall be dropped when it is not feasible or practicable to proceed exactly in conformity with Rule 24-2b (Immovable Obstruction), Rule 25-1b or Rule 25-1c (Ground Under Repair), Rule 26-1 (Water Hazards and Lateral Water Hazards) or Rule 28 (Ball Unplayable).

9. Priority on the Course

The Committee may make regulations governing Priority on the Course (see Etiquette).

Part B Specimen Local Rules

Within the policy set out in Part A of this Appendix the Committee may adopt a Specimen Local Rule by referring, on a score card or notice board, to the examples given below. However Specimen Local Rules 4, 5 or 6 should not be printed or referred to on a score card as they are all of limited duration.

1. Fixed Sprinkler Heads

All fixed sprinkler heads are immovable obstructions and relief from interference by them may be obtained under Rule 24-2. In addition, if such an obstruction on or within two club-lengths of the putting green of the hole being played intervenes on the line of play between the ball and the hole, the player may obtain relief, without penalty, as follows:

If the ball lies off the putting green but not in a hazard and is within two club-lengths of the intervening obstruction, it may be lifted, cleaned and dropped at the nearest point to where the ball lay which (a) is not nearer the hole, (b) avoids such intervention and (c) is not in a hazard or on a putting green.

PENALTY FOR BREACH OF LOCAL RULE:
Match play—Loss of hole; Stroke play—
Two strokes.

2. Stones in Bunkers

Stones in bunkers are movable obstructions. Rule 24-1 applies.

3. Ground Under Repair: Play Prohibited

If a player's ball lies in an area of "ground under repair" from which play is prohibited, or if such an area of "ground under repair" interferes with the player's stance or the area of his intended swing the player must take relief under Rule 25-1.

PENALTY FOR BREACH OF LOCAL RULE:
Match play—Loss of hole; Stroke play—
Two strokes.

4. Lifting an Embedded Ball

(Specify the area if practical) ... through the green, a ball embedded in its own pitch mark in ground other than sand may be lifted, cleaned and dropped, without penalty, as near as possible to the spot where it lay but not nearer the hole.

PENALTY FOR BREACH OF LOCAL RULE:
Match play—Loss of hole; Stroke play—
Two strokes.

5. Cleaning Ball

(Specify the area if practicable) ... through the green a ball may be lifted, cleaned and replaced without penalty.

Note: The position of the ball shall be marked before it is lifted under this Local Rule—see Rule 20-1.

6. "Preferred Lies" and "Winter Rules"

A ball lying on any "closely mown area" through the green may, without penalty, be moved or may be lifted, cleaned and placed within six inches of where it originally lay, but not nearer the hole. After the ball has been so moved or placed, it is in play.

PENALTY FOR BREACH OF LOCAL RULE:
Match play—Loss of stoke; Stroke play—
Two strokes.

7. Aerification Holes

If a ball comes to rest in an aerification hole, the player may, without penalty, lift the ball and clean it. Through the green, the player shall drop the ball as near as possible to where it lay, but not nearer the hole. On the putting green, the player shall place the ball at the nearest spot not nearer the hole which avoids such situation.

PENALTY FOR BREACH OF LOCAL RULE:
Match play—Loss of hole; Stroke play—
Two strokes

Part C Conditions of the Competition

Rule 33-1 provides, "The Committee shall lay down the conditions under which a competition is to be played". Such conditions should include many matters such as method of entry, eligibility, number of rounds to be played, settling ties, etc. which is not appropriate to deal with in the Rules of Golf or this Appendix.

However there are four matters which might be covered in the Conditions of Competition to which the Commitee's attention is specifically drawn by way of a Note to the appropriate Rule. These are:

1. Specification of the Ball (Note to Rule 5-1)

Arising from the regulations for ball-testing under Rule 5-1, Lists of Conforming Golf Balls will be issued from time to time.

It is recommended that the Lists should be applied to all National and County (or equivalent)

Championships and to all top class events when restricted to low handicap players. In order to apply the Lists to a particular competition the Committee must lay this down in the Conditions of the Competition. This should be referred to in the Entry Form, and also a notice should be displayed on the Club notice board and at the 1st Tee along the following lines:

(Name of Event)

(Date and Club)

The ball the player uses shall be named on the current List of Conforming Golf Balls issued by the Royal & Ancient Golf Club of St. Andrews.

Note 1: A penalty statement will be required and must be either:

(a)"PENALTY FOR BREACH OF CONDITION: Disqualification"

or

(b)"PENALTY FOR BREACH OF CONDITION: *Match play—Loss of each hole at which a breach occurred:Stroke play—Two strokes for each hole at which a breach occurred."*

If option (b) is adopted this only applies to use of a ball which, whilst not on the List of Conforming Golf Balls, does conform to the specifications set forth in Rule 5 and Appendix III. The penalty for use of a ball which does not so conform is disqualification.

Note 2: In Club events it is recommended that no such condition be applied.

2. **Time of Starting (Note to Rule 6-3a)**
    If the Committee wishes to act in accordance with the Note, the following wording is recommended:

    "If, in the absence of circumstances which warrant waiving the penalty of disqualification as provided in Rule 33-7, the player arrives at his starting point, ready to play, within five minutes after his starting time, the penalty for failure to start on time is loss of the first hole in match play or two strokes at the first hole in stroke play."

3. **Practice**
    The Committee may make regulations governing practice in accordance with the Note to Rule 7-1, Exception (c) to Rule 7-2, Note 2 to Rule 7 and Rule 33-2c.

4. **Advice in Team Competitions**
    If the Committee wishes to act in accordance with the Note, the following wording is recommended:

"In accordance with the Note to Rule 8-1 of the Rules of Golf each team may appoint one person (in addition to the persons from whom advice may be asked under that Rule) who may give advice to members of that team. Such person [*if it is desired to insert any restriction on who may be nominated insert such restriction here*] shall be identified to the Committee prior to the start of the competition."

APPENDICES II AND III

Any design in a club or ball which is not covered by Rules 4 and 5 and Appendices II and III, or which might significantly change the nature of the game, will be ruled on by the Royal & Ancient Golf Club of St Andrews and the United States Golf Association.

Note: Equipment approved for use or marketed prior to January 1st, 1984 which conformed to the Rules in effect in 1983 but does not conform to the 1984 Rules may be used until December 31st, 1989; thereafter all equipment must conform to the current Rules.

APPENDIX II

Design of Clubs

Rule 4-1 prescribes general regulations for the design of clubs. The following paragraphs, which provide some detailed specifications and clarify how Rule 4-1 is interpreted, should be read in conjunction with this rule.

4-1b. Shaft
Generally Straight. The shaft shall be at least 18 inches (457mm) in length. It shall be straight from the top of the grip to a point not more than 5 inches (127mm) above the sole, measured along the axis of the shaft and the neck or socket.

Bending and Twisting Properties. The shaft must be so designed and manufactured that at any point along its length;
(i)   it bends in such a way that the deflection is the same regardless of how the shaft is rotated about its longitudinal axis; and
(ii)   it twists the same amount in both directions.

Attachment to Clubhead. The neck or socket must not be more than 5 inches (127mm) in length, measured from the top of the neck or socket to the sole along its axis. The shaft and the neck or socket must remain in line with the heel, or with a point to the right or left of the

CLUBS

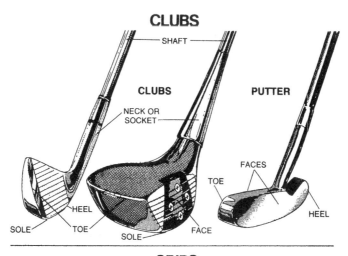

SHAFT

CLUBS **PUTTER**

NECK OR
SOCKET

FACES

TOE

HEEL

SOLE   TOE

SOLE

FACE

HEEL

GRIPS

CLUB GRIP CIRCULAR

PUTTER GRIP FLAT SIDE (Permitted on Putters only)

GROOVES

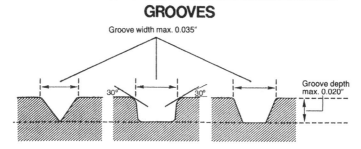

Groove width max. 0.035"

30°   30°

Groove depth
max. 0.020"

EXAMPLES OF PERMISSIBLE GROOVE CROSS-SECTIONS

heel, when the club is viewed in the address position. The distance between the axis of the shaft or the neck or socket and the back of the heel must not exceed 0.625 inches (16mm).

Exception for Putters: The shaft or neck or socket of a putter may be fixed at any point in the head and need not remain in line with the heel. The axis of the shaft from the top to a point not more than 5 inches (127mm) above the sole must diverge from the vertical in the toe-heel plane by at least 10 degrees when the club is in its normal address position.

4-1c.   Grip

(i)   For clubs other than putters, the grip must be generally circular in cross-section, except that a continuous, straight, slightly raised rib may be incorporated along the full length of the grip.

(ii)   A putter grip may have a non-circular cross-section, provided the cross-section has no concavity and remains generally similar throughout the length of the grip.

(iii)   The grip may be tapered but must not have any bulge or waist.

(iv)   For clubs other than putters the axis of the grip must coincide with the axis of the shaft.

4-1d.   Clubhead

Dimensions. The dimensions of a clubhead (see diagram) are measured, with the clubhead in its normal address position, on horizontal lines between vertical projections of the outermost points of (i) the heel and the toe and (ii) the face and the back. If the outermost point of the heel is not clearly defined, it is deemed to be 0.625 inches (16mm) above the horizontal plane on which the club is resting in its normal address position.

Plain in Shape. The clubhead shall be generally plain in shape. All parts shall be rigid, structural in nature and functional.

Features such as holes through the head, windows or transparencies, or appendages to the main body of the head such as plates, rods or fins for the purpose of meeting dimensional specifications, or for aiming or for any other purpose are not permitted. Exceptions may be made for putters.

Any furrows in or runners on the sole shall not extend into the face.

4-1e.   Club Face

Hardness and Rigidity. The club face must not be designed and manufactured to have the effect at impact of a spring which would unduly influence the movement of the ball.

Markings. Except for specified markings, the surface roughness must not exceed that of decorative sandblasting. Markings must not have sharp edges or raised lips, as determined by a finger test. Markings within the area where impact is intended (the 'impact area') are governed by the following:

(i)   **Grooves.** A series of straight grooves with diverging sides and a symmetrical cross-section may be used. (See diagram). The width and cross-section must be generally consistent across the face of the club and along the length of the grooves. Any rounding of groove edges shall be in the form of a radius which does not exceed 0.020 inches (0.5mm). The width of the grooves shall not exceed 0.035 inches (0.9mm), using the 30 degree method of measurement on file with the Royal & Ancient Golf Club of St Andrews. The distance between edges of adjacent grooves must not be less than three times the width of a groove, and not less than 0.075 inches (1.9mm). The depth of a groove must not exceed 0.020 inches (0.5mm).

(ii)   **Punch Marks.** Punch marks may be used. The area of any such mark must not exceed 0.0044 square inches (2.8 sq mm). A mark must not be closer to an adjacent mark than 0.168 inches (4.3mm) measured from centre to centre. The depth of a punch mark must not exceed 0.040 inches (1.0mm). If punch marks are used in combination with grooves, a punch mark may not be closer to a groove than 0.168 inches (4.3mm), measured from centre to centre.

Decorative Markings. The centre of the impact area may be indicated by a design within the boundary of a square whose sides are 0.375 inches (9.5mm) in length. Such a design must not unduly influence the movement of the ball. Markings outside the impact area must not be greater than 0.040 inches (1.00mm) in depth and width.

Non-metallic Club Face Markings. The above specifications for markings do not apply to non-metallic clubs with loft angles less than 24 degrees, but markings which could unduly influence the movement of the ball are prohibited. Non-metallic clubs with a loft or face angle exceeding 24 degrees may have grooves of maximum width 0.040 inches (1.0mm) and maximum depth of $1^{1}/_{2}$ times the groove width, but must otherwise conform to the markings specifications above.

APPENDIX III

The Ball

a. Weight

The weight of the ball shall not be greater than 1.620 ounces avoirdupois (45.93gm).

b. Size

The diameter of the ball shall not be less than 1.680 inches (42.67mm). This specification will be satisfied if, under its own weight, a ball falls through a 1.680 inches diameter ring gauge in fewer than 25 out of 100 randomly selected positions, the test being carried out at a temperature of $23\pm1°C$.

c. Spherical Symmetry

The ball shall be designed and manufactured to perform in general as if it were spherically symmetrical.

As outlined in procedures on file at the Royal & Ancient Golf Club of St. Andrews and the United States Golf Association, differences in peak angle of trajectory, carry and time of flight will be measured when 40 balls of the same types are launched, spinning 20 about one axis and 20 about another axis.

These tests will be performed using apparatus approved by the Royal & Ancient Golf Club of St. Andrews and the United States Golf Association. If in two successive tests differences in the same two or more measurements are statistically significant at the 5% level of significance and exceed the limits set forth below, the ball type will not conform to the symmetry specification.

Measurement	Maximum Absolute Difference of the Means
Peak angle of trajectory	0.9 grid units (approx. 0.4 degrees)
Carry distance	2.5 yards
Flight time	0.16 seconds

Note: Methods of determining whether a ball performs as if it were generally spherically symmetrical may be subject to change as instrumentation becomes available to measure other properties accurately, such as the aerodynamic coefficient of lift, coefficient of drag and moment of inertia.

d. Initial Velocity

The velocity of the ball shall not be greater than 250 feet (76.2m) per second when measured on apparatus approved by the Royal & Ancient Golf Club of St. Andrews. A maximum tolerance of 2% will be allowed. The temperature of the ball when tested shall be $23\pm1°C$.

e. Overall Distance Standard

A brand of golf ball, when tested on apparatus approved by the Royal & Ancient Golf Club of St. Andrews under the conditions set forth in the Overall Distance Standard for golf balls on file with the Royal & Ancient Golf Club of St. Andrews, shall not cover an average distance in carry and roll exceeding 280 yards (256 metres) plus a tolerance of 6%.

Note: The 6% tolerance will be reduced to a minimum of 4% as test techniques are improved.

Notes to Appendix III

1: The size specification in (b) above will take effect from 1st January, 1990. Until that date the previous size specification of a diameter not less than 1.620 inches (41.15mm) will apply.

2: The Overall Distance Standard will apply only to balls which meet the new size specification of a diameter not less than 1.680 inches (42.67mm).

3: In international team competitions, until 31st December, 1989, the previous size specification of a diameter not less than 1.620 inches (41.15mm) will apply.

HANDICAPS

The Rules of Golf do not legislate for the allocation and adjustment of handicaps or their playing differentials. Such matters are within the jurisdiction and control of the National Union concerned and queries should be directed accordingly.

RULES OF AMATEUR STATUS

As approved by the Royal & Ancient Golf Club of St. Andrews

(Effective from 1st January 1987)

Definitions of an Amateur Golfer
An Amateur Golfer is one who plays the game as a non-remunerative or non-profit-making sport.

The Governing Body
The Governing Body of golf for the Rules of Amateur Status in any country is the National Union of the country concerned except in Great Britain and Ireland where the Governing Body is the Royal & Ancient Golf Club of St. Andrews.

Any person who considers any action he is proposing to take might endanger his Amateur Status should submit particulars to the Committee for consideration.

RULE 1

Forfeiture of Amateur Status at any age

The following are examples of acts which are contrary to the Definition of an Amateur Golfer and cause forfeiture of Amateur Status:

1.   Professionalism.
a. Receiving payment or compensation for serving as a Professional golfer or a teaching or playing assistant to a Professional golfer.
b. Taking any action for the purpose of becoming a Professional golfer except applying unsuccessfully for the position of a teaching or playing assistant of a Professional golfer.

Note 1. Such actions including filing application to a school or competition conducted to qualify persons to play as Professionals in tournaments; receiving services from or entering into an agreement, written or oral, with a sponsor or Professional agent; agreement to accept payment or compensation for allowing one's name or likeness as a skilled golfer to be used for any commercial purpose; and holding or retaining membership in any organisation of Professional golfers.

Note 2. Receiving payment or compensation as a shop assistant is not itself a breach of the Rules, provided duties do not include playing or giving instruction.

2.   Playing for Prize Money.
Playing for prize money or its equivalent in a match, tournament or exhibition.

3.   Instruction.
Receiving payment or compensation for giving instruction in playing golf, either orally, in writing, by pictures or by other demonstrations, to either individuals or groups.

Exceptions:

1. Golf instruction may be given by an employee of an educational institution or system to students of the institution or system and by camp counsellors to those in their charge, provided that the total time devoted to golf instruction during a year comprises less than 50 per cent of the time spent during the year in the performance of all duties as such employee or counsellor.

2. Payment or compensation may be accepted for instruction in writing, provided one's ability or reputation as a golfer was not a major factor in his employment or in the commission or sale of his work.

4.   Prizes and Testimonials
(a)   Acceptance of a prize or prize voucher of retail value exceeding as follows:

	In GB & I and rest of Europe	Elsewhere
For an event of more than 2 rounds	£300	$500 US or the equivalent
For an event of 2 rounds or less	£200	$350 US or the equivalent

or such lesser figure, if any, as may be decided by the Governing Body of golf in any country, or

(b)   Acceptance of a testimonial in Great Britain and Ireland and the rest of Europe of retail value exceeding £300, elsewhere of retail value exceeding $500 US or the equivalent, or such lesser figure as may be decided by the Governing Body of golf in any country, or

(c)   For a junior golfer, of such age as may be determined by the Governing Body of golf in any country, taking part in an event limited exclusively to juniors, acceptance of a prize or prize voucher in Great Britain and Ireland and the rest of Europe of retail value exceeding £100; elsewhere of retail value exceeding $200 US or the equivalent, or such lesser figure, if any, as may be decided by the Governing Body of golf in any country, or

(d)   Conversion of a prize or prize voucher into money, or

(e)   Accepting a gratuity in connection with a golfing event.

Exceptions:
1. Prizes of only symbolic value, provided that their symbolic nature is distinguished by distinctive permanent marking.
2. More than one testimonial award may be accepted from different donors even though their total retail value exceeds £300 or $500 US, provided they are not presented so as to evade such value limit for a single award.

Note 1: Events covered. The limits referred to in Clauses (a) or (c) above apply to total prize or prize vouchers received by any one person for any one event or series of events in any one tournament or exhibition, including hole-in-one or other events in which golf skill is a factor.

Note 2: 'Retail value' is the price at which merchandise is available to anyone at a retail source, and the onus of proving the value of a particular prize rests with the donor.

Note 3: Purpose of prize vouchers. A prize voucher may be issued and redeemed only by the Committee in charge of a competition for the purchase of goods from a Professional's shop or other retail source, which may be specified by the Committee. It may not be used for such items as travel or hotel expenses, a bar bill, or a Club Subscription.

Note 4: Maximum Value of Prizes in any event for individuals. It is recommended that the total value of scratch or each division of handicap prizes should not exceed twice the maximum retail value of prize permitted in Rule 1-4(a) and (c) in an 18-hole competition, three times in a 36-hole competition, four times in a 54-hole competition and five times in a 72-hole competition.

Note 5: Testimonial Awards. Such awards relate to notable performances or contributions to golf as distinguished from tournament prizes.

5.   Lending Name or Likeness.
Because of golf skill or golf reputation receiving or contracting to receive payment, compensation or personal benefit, directly or indirectly, for allowing one's name or likeness to be used in any way for the advertisement or sale of anything, whether or not used in or appertaining to golf except as a golf author or broadcaster as permitted by Rule 1-7.

Note: A player may accept equipment from anyone dealing in such equipment provided no advertising is involved.

6.   Personal Appearance.
Because of golf skill or golf reputation, receiving payment or compensation, directly or indirectly, for a personal appearance.

Exception:
Actual expenses in connection with personal appearances may be paid or reimbursed provided no golf competition of exhibition is involved.

7.   Broadcasting or Writing.
Because of golf skill or golf reputation, receiving payment or compensation, directly or indirectly, for broadcasting concerning golf, a golf event or golf events, writing golf articles or books, or allowing one's name to be advertised or published as the author of golf articles or books of which he is not actually the author.

Exceptions:
1.   Broadcasting or writing as part of one's primary occupation or career, provided instruction in playing golf is not included (Rule 1-3).
2.   Part-time broadcasting or writing, provided (a) the player is actually the author of the commentary, articles or books, (b) instruction in playing golf is not included and (c) the payment or compensation does not have the purpose or effect, directly or indirectly, of financing participation in a golf competition or golf competitions.

8.   Expenses.
Accepting expenses, in money or otherwise, from any source to engage in a golf competition or exhibition.

Exceptions:
A player may receive expenses, not exceeding the actual expenses incurred, as follows:
1.From a member of the family or legal guardian;
or
2. As a player in a golf competition or exhibition limited exclusively to players who have not reached their 18th birthday;
or
3. As a representative of his Country, County, Club or similar body in team competitions or team training camps at home or abroad, or as a representative of his Country taking part in a National Championship abroad immediately preceding or following directly upon an international team competition, where such expenses are paid by the body he represents, or by the body controlling golf in the territory he is visiting;
or
4. As an individual nominated by a National or County Union or Club to engage in an event at home or abroad provided that:

(a)   The player nominated has not reached such age as may be determined by the Governing Body of Golf in the country from which the nomination is made.

(b)   The expenses shall be paid only by the National Union or County Union responsible in the area from which the nomination is made and shall be limited to twenty competitive days in any one calendar year. The expenses are deemed in include reasonable travelling time and practice days in connection with the twenty competitive days.

(c)   Where the event is to take place abroad, the approval of the National Union of the country in which the event is to be staged and, if the nominating body is not the National Union of the country from which the nomination is made, the approval of the National Union shall first be obtained by the nominating body.

(d)   Where the event is to take place at home, and where the nomination is made by a County Union or Club, the approval of the National Union or the County Union in the area in which the event is to be staged shall first be obtained.

(*Note:* The Term 'County Union' covers any Province, State or equivalent Union or Association;)

or

5. As a player invited for reasons unrelated to golf skill, e.g. celebrities, business associates, etc., to take part in golfing events;

or

6. As a player in an exhibition in aid of a recognised Charity provided the exhibition is not run in connection with another golfing event.

or

7. As a player in a handicap individual or handicap team sponsored golfing event where expenses are paid by the sponsor on behalf of the player to take part in the event provided the event has been approved as follows:

(a)   where the event is to take place at home the approval of the Governing Body (see Definition) shall first be obtained in advance by the sponsor, and

(b)   where the event is to take place both at home and abroad the approval of the two or more Governing Bodies shall first be obtained in advance by the sponsor. The application for this approval should be sent to the Governing Body of golf in the country where the competition commences.

(c)   where the event is to take place abroad the approval of two or more Governing Bodies shall first be obtained by the sponsor. The application for this approval should be sent to the Governing Body of golf in the country whose players shall be taking part in the event abroad

Note 1: Business Expenses. It is permissible to play in a golf competition while on a business trip with expenses paid provided that the golf part of the expenses is borne personally and is not charged to business. Further, the business involved must be actual and substantial, and not merely a subterfuge for legitimising expenses when the primary purpose is a golf competition.

Note 2: Private Transport. Acceptance of private transport furnished or arranged for by a tournament sponsor, directly or indirectly, as an inducement for a player to engage in a golf competition or exhibition shall be considered accepting expenses under Rule 1-8.

9. Scholarships.
Because of golf skill or golf reputation, accepting the benefits of a scholarship or grant-in-aid other than ones whose terms and conditions have been approved by the Amateur Status Committee of the Royal & Ancient Golf Club of St. Andrews.

10. Membership.
Because of golf skill accepting membership in a Golf Club without full payment for the class of membership for the purpose of playing for that Club.

11. Conduct Detrimental to Golf.
Any conduct, including activities in connection with golf gambling, which is considered detrimental to the best interests of the game.

Rule 2

Procedure for Enforcement and Reinstatement

1. Decision on a Breach. Whenever information of a possible breach of the Definition of an Amateur Golfer by a player claiming to be an Amateur shall come to the attention of the appropriate Committee of the Governing Body, the Committee, after such investigation as it may deem desirable, shall decide whether a breach has occurred. Each case shall be considered on its merits. The decision of the committee shall be final.

2. Enforcement. Upon a decision that a player has acted contrary to the Definition of an Amateur Golfer, the Committee may declare the Amateur Status of the player forfeited or require the player to refrain or desist from specified actions as a condition of retaining his Amateur Status.

The Committee shall use its best endeavours to ensure that the player is notified and may notify any interested Golf Association of any action taken under this paragraph.

3. Reinstatement. The Committee shall have sole power to reinstate a player to Amateur Status or to deny reinstatement. Each application for reinstatement shall be decided on its merits. In considering an application for reinstatement, the Committee shall normally be guided by the following principles:

a. Awaiting Reinstatement.

The professional holds an advantage over the amateur by reason of having devoted himself to the game as his profession; other persons infringing the Rules of Amateur Status also obtain advantages not available to the Amateur. They do not necessarily lose such advantage merely by deciding to cease infringing the Rules. Therefore, an applicant for reinstatement to Amateur Status shall undergo a period awaiting reinstatement as prescribed by the Committee.

The period awaiting reinstatement shall start from the date of the player's last breach of the Definition of an Amateur Golfer unless the Committee decides that it shall start from the date when the player's last breach became known to the Committee.

b. Period Awaiting Reinstatement.

The period awaiting reinstatement shall normally be related to the period the player was in breach. However, no applicant shall normally be eligible for reinstatement until he has conducted himself in accordance with the Definition of an Amateur Golfer for a period of at least two consecutive years. The Committee, however, reserves the right to extend or to shorten such a period. A longer period will normally be required of applicants who have been in breach for more than five years. Players of national prominence who have been in breach for more than five years shall not normally be eligible for reinstatement.

c. One Reinstatement

A player shall not normally be reinstated more than once.

d. Status While Awaiting Reinstatement.

During the period awaiting reinstatement an applicant for reinstatement shall conform with the Definition of an Amateur Golfer.

He shall not be eligible to enter competitions as an Amateur. He may, however, enter competitions, and win a prize, solely among members of a Club of which he is a member, subject to the approval of the Club; but he may not represent such Club against other Clubs.

Forms of Application for Countries under the jurisdiction of the Royal & Ancient Golf Club

(a) Each application for reinstatement shall be submitted on the approved form to the County Union where the applicant wishes to play as an Amateur. Such Union shall, after making all necessary enquiries, forward it through the National Union (and in the case of lady applicants, the Ladies Golf Union) and the appropriate Professional Golfers' Association, with comments endorsed thereon, to the Governing Body of golf in that country. Forms of application for reinstatement may be obtained from the Royal & Ancient Golf Club or from the National or County Unions. The application shall include such information as the Royal & Ancient Golf Club may require from time to time and it shall be signed and certified by the applicant.

(b) Any application made in countries under the jurisdiction of the Royal & Ancient Golf Club of St. Andrews which the Governing Body of golf in that country considers to be doubtful or not to be covered by the above regulations may be submitted to the Royal & Ancient Golf Club of St. Andrews whose decision shall be final.

R. & A. POLICY ON GAMBLING

The Definition of an Amateur Golfer provides that an Amateur golfer is one who plays the game as a non-remunerative or non-profit-making sport. When gambling motives are introduced evils can arise to threaten the integrity of both the game and the individual players.

The R&A does not object to participation in wagering among individual golfers or teams of golfers when participation in the wagering is limited to the players, the players may only wager on themselves or their teams, the sole source of all money won by players is advanced by the players and the primary purpose is the playing of the game for enjoyment.

The distinction between playing for prize money and gambling is essential to the validity of the Rules of Amateur Status. The following constitute golf wagering and not playing for prize money:

1. Participation in wagering among individual golfers.

2. Participation in wagering among teams.

Organised Amateur events open to the general golfing public and designed and promoted to create cash prizes are not approved by the R&A. Golfers participating in such events without irrevocably waiving their right to cash prizes are deemed by the R&A to be playing for prize money.

The R&A is opposed to and urges Unions and Clubs, and all other sponsors of golf competitions to prohibit types of gambling such as: Calcuttas, auction sweepstakes and any other forms of gambling organised for general participation or permitting participants to bet on someone other than themselves or their teams.

Attention is drawn to Rule 1-11 relating to conduct detrimental to the game, under which players can forfeit their Amateur Status. It is the Club which, by permitting competitions where excessive gambling is involved, or illegal prizes are offered, bears the responsibility for which the individual is penalised and Unions have the power to invoke severe sanctions against a Club or individual for consistently ignoring this policy.

INDEX	Rule
Abnormal Ground Conditions	25
Absence of Partner	
Best-ball and four-ball match play	30-3a
Four-ball stroke play	31-2
Addition of Scores and Application of Handicap	
Committee's responsibility	33-5
Addressing the Ball	Def.
Ball falling or knocked off tee	11-3
Ball moving after	18-2b
Administration	
Committee's powers and duties	33
Disputes and decisions	34
Advice	8, Def
Indicating line of play	8-2
Team captain or coach, team competitions	8 note
See also "Information"	
Agreement to Waive Rules Prohibited	1-3
Alteration of Card	6-6c
Animals	
Animate outside agency	19-1
Holes made by burrowing	25-1
Application of Handicap	33-5
Area of Intended Swing: See "Swing'	
Artificial Devices and Unusual Equipment	14-3
Artificial Objects: See "Obstructions"	
Assistance	14-2
Bad Weather, etc.	
Course unplayable	33-2d
Discontinuing play	6-8
Protection from elements	14-2
Ball	
Addressing: see "Addressing"	
Assisting or interfering with lay	22
At rest, moved, touched or lifted	18
Cleaning:	
when allowable	21
on putting green	16-1b
Clothes etc., lying in or on	19-2b
Colliding with ball in motion	19-5
Conforming	5-1, App. III
Covered	12-1
Cut, cracked or out of shape	5-3
Deflected or stopped	19
Dropping and re-dropping	20-2
In play when dropped	20-4
In wrong place	20-7
Wrongly	20-6
Embedded in own pitch-mark	25-2, App. I
Specimen Local Rule	App. I
Exchanged in match play	15-2
Exerting influence on	1-2
Fairly struck at	14-1
Falling off tee	11-3
Holed	Def.
Identifying	12-2
Identification mark	6-5
In long grass etc.	12-1
In motion, deflected or stopped	19

	Rule
Ball – continued	
In play	Def.
Is in play when dropped or placed	20-4
When provisional ball becomes	27-2b
When substituted ball becomes	Def.
Interfering with or assisting play	22
In water, moving	14-6
Lie of	
Altered and ball to be placed or replaced	20-3b
Not to be improved	13-2
Lifting	20-1
Not in play once lifted: see definition of "Ball in Play"	Def.
To determine if unfit for play	5-3
To identify	12-2
When play discontinued	6-8c
See also "Ball: Dropping and re-dropping" and "Ball:Placing and replacing"	
Lost – see "Lost Ball"	
Marking position of	20-1
Moved	18, Def.
Moving	18-2
Playing moving ball	14-5, -6
Mud on	5-3
Out of bounds	27, Def.
Overhanging hole	16-2
Placing and replacing	20-3
In play when placed	20-4
Not replaced	18-5, 20-7
Wrongly	20-6
Played as it lies	13
Played from wrong place	20-7
Teeing ground	11-4
Played out of turn, in wrong order	10
By wrong partner in threesome, foursome – match play	29-2
– stroke play	29-3
Plugged	25-2
Probing for, raking in hazard	12-1
Provisional: See "Provisional Ball"	27
Re-dropping	20-2, -6
Replacing: See "Ball: Placing and replacing"	
Second, when in doubt as to procedure: stroke play	3-3
Specifications	5-1, App. III
Stopped or deflected	19
Striking	
Assistance or protection prohibited	14-2
Fairly	14-1
Flagstick, attendant or attendant's equipment	17-3
More than once	14-4
When in motion	14-5, -6
Substituting for ball unfit for play	5-3
Touched	
By opponent	18-3
By player purposely	18-2a
Unfit for play	5-3

	Rule
Ball – continued	
Unplayable	28
Wrong	15, Def.
In best-ball or four-ball	30-3d
See also "Ball: played from wrong place"	
Ball-Marker	20-1 *note*
See also definition of "Equipment"	Def.
Ball-Marks on Putting Green	16-1c
Best-Ball and Four-Ball Match Play	30-1, -3
	Def.
See "Four-Ball and Best-Ball Match Play"	
Bogey or Par Competitions	32-1
Disqualification penalties – application	32-2
Marker's responsibilities	32-1a
Borrowing Clubs	4-4b
Boundaries: see definitions of	
"Obstructions" and "Out of Bounds"	Def.
Bunker	Def.
Stones in: Specimen Local Rule	App. I
Burrowing Animal: Hole etc. Made by	
Ball in, accidentally moved during search	12-1
Ball lost in	25-1c
Interference by	25-1a
Relief from	25-1b
Relief not available when ball in water hazard	25-1b(ii)
	Exc.
Caddie	Def.
And flagstick	17
Ball moved by fellow competitor's	18-4
Ball moved by opponent's	18-3
Breach of Rule by	6-4
Employed by two players	Def.
Indicating line of putt	8-2b
One only per player	6-4
Position of during putt	16-1f
Smoothing sand or soil in hazard	13-4 Exc. 3
Cart-track: See definition of "Obstructions"	Def.
Casual Water	Def.
Ball in, accidentally moved during search	12-1
Ball lost in	25-1c
Dew is not	Def.
Interference by	25-1a
Relief from	25-1b
In a water hazard: does not exist	Def.
Checking Scores	
Competitor's and marker's duties	6-6
Claims	2-5, 34-1a
About ball's unfitness	5-3 *note* 2
Cleaning Ball	21
Clothes or Equipment, Ball In or On	19-2b, 19-3
Clubs	4, App. II
Assistance in gripping	14-3b
Borrowing	4-4b
Damage	4-1g, 4-2
Foreign material not to be added	4-3
Grounding	
In hazard prohibited	13-4b
Lightly only	13-2

	Rule
Clubs – continued	
Number allowed	4-4
Placed in hazard	13-4 Exc. 2
Playing characteristics not to be changed	4-2
Replacement of	4-4a, b
Sharing, side may share	4-4b
Coin (or Tee) as Ball Marker: not	
Equipment	Def.
Interfering with play: procedure	20-1 note
Committee	Def.
Main duties of	33
Other responsibilities	
Claims: match play	2-5
Competitor in doubt: stroke play: procedure	3-3
Decision: no referee etc.	34-3
Discontinuance/suspension of play	6-8a(1)
Ground under repair:	
marking of etc.	Def.
Local Rule prohibiting play from	Def. note 2
Practice, powers over	7-1 note,
	7-2 Exc.,
	33-2c
Team competitions, advice from team captain etc.	8 note
Competitions	
Combining match and stroke play not allowed	33-1
Committee lays down condition of	33-1
Competitor	Def.
Conceding	
Next stroke, hole or match	2-4
Conditions, Gauging or Measuring	14-3a
Conditions of Competition	33-1
Course	33-2, Def.
Damage	
To ball	5-3
To club	4-1g, 4-2
To course	25-1, 33-2d
To hole	33-2b
Decisions: see "Disputes and Decisions"	
Definitions	Section II
Delay, Undue	6-7
In making stroke from water	14-6
Dew	
is not "Casual Water"	Def.
is not "Loose Impediment"	Def.
Discontinuance of Play	6-8
Disputes and Decisions	34
Points not covered by Rules: Equity	1-4
See also "Claims"	
Disqualification Penalties	
Waiving or modification of by committee	6-3 note
	33-7
Ditch: See definition of "Water Hazard"	Def.
Divots	13-2
Doubt as to Procedure: Stroke Play	3-3
Dropping and Re-Dropping Ball:	
See "Ball: Dropping and re-dropping"	
Embedded Ball	25-2, App. I
Specimen Local Rule	App. I

	Rule
Equipment	Def.
Ball at rest moved by	18
Ball in motion deflected or stopped by	19
Ball striking equipment of flagstick attendant	17-3b
Unusual	14-3
Equity	1-4
Etiquette	Section I
Excess Club	4-4c
Fellow-Competitor	Def.
Fence: See definition of "Obstructions"	Def.
Flagstick	17, Def.
Forecaddie	
An "Outside Agency"	Def.
Foreign Material	
Not to be added to ball	5-2
to club face	4-3
to grip	14-3b
Form and Make of Clubs	4-1, App. II
Four-Ball and Best-Ball Match Play	30-3
Another form of match concurrently	30-3g
Penalties in	30-3e, f
Special Rules for	
Maximum of fourteen clubs	30-3b
Order of play by partners	30-3c
Representation of side, absent partner	30-3a
Wrong ball	30-3d
Four-Ball Stroke Play	31
Penalties in	31-7, -8
Special Rules for	
Maximum of fourteen clubs	31-3
Order of play by partners	31-5
Representation of side, absent partner	31-2
Scoring: recording of scores	31-4
Wrong ball	31-6
Foursome	29
Fourteen Clubs Maximum	4-4
Game of Golf	1-1
General Penalty	
Match play	2-6
Stroke play	3-5
Golf Cart: See "Equipment"	Def.
Grass	
Cuttings: see definition of "Ground Under Repair"	Def.
Bordering or within a bunker: see definition of "Bunker"	Def.
Green: See "Putting Green"	
Grip	4-1c, 14-3b
Ground Under Repair	25, Def.
Ball in, accidentally moved during search	12-1
Ball lost in	25-1c
Interference by	25-1a
Play may be prohibited in	Def. *note 2*
Specimen Local Rule	App. I
Relief from	25-1b
Grounding Club	
In hazard, prohibited	13-4b
Lightly only	13-2

	Rule
Groups	
Players to remain in groups arranged by Committee	6-3b
Halved Hole	2-2
Halved Match	
Not to be decided by stroke play	33-6
Handicap	6-2
Application, Committee's responsibility	33-5
Wrong – match play	6-2a
– stroke play	6-2b
Hazard	Def.
See also "Lateral Water Hazard" and "Water Hazard"	
Hole	Def.
Ball overhanging	16-2
Damaged	33-2b
Failure to complete	3-2
Halved	2-2
Indicating position of	17-1
Made by burrowing animal etc.:	
relief from	25-1a, b
Made by greenkeeper:	
see definition of	
"Ground Under Repair"	Def.
relief from	25-1a, b
New	33-2b
Size of	Def.
See also "Putting Green"	
Hole Plugs and Ball-Marks	16-1c
Holed Ball	Def.
Holing Out	
Penalty incurred after, in match play	2-2
With wrong ball in stroke play	15-3
Honour	Def.
Match play	10-1a
Stroke play	10-2a
Ice and Snow	
See definitions of "Casual Water" and "Loose Impediments"	Def.
Manufactured ice – See definition of "Obstructions"	Def.
Identifying Ball	12-2
In long grass etc.	12-1
Illness	
When play may be discontinued	6-8
Immovable Obstruction	24-2
Improving	
Area in which ball is to be dropped or placed	13-2
Area of intended swing	13-2
Lie or position of ball	13-2
Line of play	13-2
In Play: See "Ball: In Play"	
Indicating Line of Play, Putt:	
See "Line of Play"	
Information	9
On the Rules is not "Advice"	Def.
Interference	
Ball interfering with or assisting play	22

Rule

Interference – continued
By casual water, ground under repair,
    burrowing animal holes etc. 25-1
By immovable obstructions. 24-2
By movable obstructions. 24-1
By ball marker. .... 20-1 *note*
Irregularities of Surface 13-2
Knocking Ball Off Tee 11-3
Late at Start 6-3
In best-ball or four-ball match play 30-3a
In four-ball stroke play 31-2
Lateral Water Hazard .... 26, Def.
Ball in, touching or lost 26-1
Ball in, unplayable – may not be so deemed. 28
Ball moving in. 14-6
Ball played from lost, out of bounds or
    unplayable outside hazard. 26-2b
Ball remaining or coming to rest in
    after stroke. 26-2a
Probing for ball. 12-1
Leaves. 23
See definition of "Loose Impediments". .... Def.
Covering ball in hazard. 12-1
Lie of Ball
Altered prior to placing or replacing 20-3b
Improving, prohibited. 13-2
Lifted or Lifting Ball: See "Ball: Lifting"
Lifting Ball Wrongly Dropped or Placed 20-6
Lightning
Reason for discontinuing play. 6-8
Line of Play
Improving. 13-2
Indicating
    On putting green 8-2b
    Other than on putting green 8-2a, 17-1
Line of Putt: See "Putting Green: Line of Putt"
Lines: See "Stakes or Lines"
Local Rules. .... 33-8, App. I
Loose Impediments .... 23, Def.
Ball covered by in hazard. 12-1
Ball moves after removal or touching of. 18-2c
Lying in or touching hazard 23-1
Lost Ball. .... 27, Def.
In casual water, ground under repair,
    burrowing animal hole etc. 25-1c
In water hazard 26-1
Outside water hazard after stroke within 26-2b
Provisional ball. 27-2
Marker. .... Def.
Duties. 6-6a
    In bogey and par competitions 32-1a
    In four-ball stroke play 31-4
    In stableford. 32-1b
Marking Position of Ball 20-1
Match
May be conceded 2-4
Terms used in reckoning. 2-1
Winner of. 2-3

	Rule
Match Play	
General	2
Ball moved by opponent etc. in	18-3
Combining with stroke play prohibited	33-1
Discontinuing play by agreement	6-8a
Halved hole	2-2
Handicap	6-2a
Wrong Information as to number of strokes taken, penalties incurred	9-2
Match Play Competitions	
Time limit when played over extended period	33-3
Matches	
See definition of "Sides and Matches"	Def.
Material Piled for Removal: See "Ground Under Repair"	
Measuring Distance or Conditions	14-3a
Measuring distance to determine order of play – ball moved	10-4
Modification of Penalty	6-3 *note*, 33-7
Movable Obstruction	24-1
Movable Ball: See "Ball: Moved" and "Ball: moving"	
Mud etc. adhering to Ball	5-3
Observer	Def.
Obstructions	24, Def.
Fixed sprinkler heads: Specimen Local Rule	App. I
Immovable	24-2
Movable	24-1
Order of Play	10
Best-ball and four-ball match play	30-3c
Foursome or threesome	29
Out of Bounds	27, Def.
Provisional ball	27-2
Standing, to play ball in bounds	Def.
Out of Turn: See "Order of Play"	
Outside Agency	Def.
Ball at rest moved by	18-1
Ball in motion accidentally deflected or stopped by	19-1
Ball in motion purposely deflected or stopped by	19-1 *note*
Wind and water are not	Def.
Worms and insects after stroke on putting green	19-1b
Par Competitions	32-1, -1a
Disqualification penalties – application	32-3
Marker's responsibilities	32-1a
Partner	Def.
Absent: best-ball and four-ball match-play	30-3a
four-ball stroke play	31-2
Breach of Rule by: best-ball and four-ball match play	30-3d, e, f
four-ball stroke play	31-6, -7, -8
Path: See definition of "Obstructions"	Def.

Rule

Penalty
Agreement to waive, prohibited 1-3
Best-ball and four-ball match play .... 30-3d, e, f
Four-ball stroke play .... 31-3, -4, -6,
       -7, -8
General: match play 2-6
           stroke play 3-5
Modification or waiving of disqualification 33-7
Power to disqualify 33-7
Time limit for imposition 34-1b
Waiving by Local Rule prohibited 33-8b
Penalty Stroke .... Def.
Order of play in threesome or foursome
    unaffected by 29-1
Pin: See "Flagstick"
Placing and Replacing: See
    "Ball: placing and replacing"
Play: See "Ball: In play", "Order of Play",
    "Suspension of Play", "Discontinuance of Play"
Player's Responsibilities 6
Playing
From wrong place .... 20-7a, b
Moving ball, prohibited 14-5
Out of turn .... 10-1c, -2c
    Wrong partner in threesome or foursome .... 29-2, -3
Outside limits of teeing ground .... 11-4a, b
Second ball when in doubt as to procedure
    (stroke play only) 3-3
Wrong Ball: see "Wrong Ball"
Plugged Ball 25-2
Specimen Local Rule .... App. I
Points not Covered by Rules 1-4
Practice 7
Practice Ground 33-2c
Practice Putting Green .... 25-3 *note*
Practice Swings .... 7-2 *note 1*
Preferred Lies
Specimen Local Rule .... App. I
Protection from Elements 14-2
Provisional Ball .... 27-2, Def.
Played out of turn: teeing ground 10-3
Putting Green 16
Ball in motion: no other ball to be played 16-1g
Ball on .... Def.
Ball overhanging hole 16-2
Cleaning ball 16-1b
Conceding putt 2-4
Lifting ball 16-1b
    When other ball in motion 22
Line of Putt
    Indicating 8-2b
Position of caddie, partner etc. on extension of
    line behind ball prohibited 16-1f
Standing astride or on 16-1e
Touching 16-1a
Repair of hole plugs and ball marks 16-1c
Testing the surface 16-1d
Wrong, includes practice putting green 25-3

	Rule
Rabbit Scrape: See "Burrowing Animal, Hole etc. Made by"	
Re-Dropping Ball	
When required	20-2c
Red Stakes or Lines Define Lateral Water Hazard	Def.
Referee	Def.
Decision final	34-2
Refusal to Comply with Rule:	
Stroke Play	3-4
Replacing	20-3
Ball: see "Ball: Placing and Replacing"	
Substituting ball for ball unfit for play	5-3
Clubs	4-4a, b
Representation of Side	
Best-ball and four-ball match play	30-3a
Four-ball stroke play	31-2
Reptile: See "Burrowing Animal etc.: Hole etc. Made by"	
Road: See definition of "Obstructions"	Def.
Round, Stipulated	Def.
Rub of The Green	19-1, Def.
Rule Includes Local Rule	Def.
Rules and Local Rules	
Agreement to waive prohibited	1-3
Information on, not "Advice"	Def.
Player's infringement, assisting partner	
Best-ball and four-ball match play	30-3f
Four-ball stroke play	31-8
Rules of Golf Committee, Decisions by	34-3
Sand and Loose Soil	
Ball covered by, in hazard	12-1
"Loose Impediment", on putting green only	Def.
Scoring and Score Cards	6-6, 33-5
Bogey, par and stableford competitions	32
Committee's responsibilities	33-5
Checking scores	6-6
Handicap to be correctly recorded on score card	6-2b
Issue of card	33-5
Marker's responsibilities See "Marker"	
No alteration to card once returned	6-6c
Returning wrong score	6-6d, 34-1b
Score card to be returned to Committee as soon	
as possible	6-6b
to be signed by competitor	6-6b
to be signed by marker	6-6a
Searching for Ball	12-1
Ball at rest moved by opponent etc. when	18-3a
Ball lost after five minutes	Def.
In casual water, ground under repair etc.	12-1
Time spent in playing wrong ball: see definition of "Lost Ball"	Def.
Second Ball	
Played when in doubt as to procedure (stroke play only)	3-3
Teeing ground: order of play	10-3
Seeing Ball	12-1
Sharing Clubs	4-4b

	Rule
Sides and Matches	Def.
Slow Play: See "Undue Delay"	
Smoothing Irregularities in a Hazard	13-4, Exc. 3
Snow and Ice	
See definitions of "Casual Water" and	
"Loose Impediments"	Def.
Stableford Competitions	32-1b
Stakes or Lines	
Defining	
"Ground Under Repair"	Def.
"Lateral Water Hazard" – red	Def. *note*
"Out of Bounds"	Def.
"Water Hazard" – yellow	Def. *note*
Stance	Def.
Astride or on line of putt etc.	16-1e
Casual water etc. interfering with	25-1a
In a hazard: see definition of "Addressing	
the Ball"	Def.
Interference with by	
immovable obstruction	24-2a
movable obstruction	24-1a, b
Out of bounds to play ball in bounds	Def.
Outside limits of teeing ground	11-1
Player not to build	13-3
Taking up fairly	13-2
Starting, Time of	6-3
To be arranged by Committee	33-3
Stipulated Round	Def.
Stones	
See definition of "Loose Impediments"	Def.
Striking Ball	
Fairly	14-1
More than once	14-4
Stroke	Def.
Assistance in making	14-2
Ball to be fairly struck at	14-1
Checking downswing voluntarily	Def.
Stroke Play	3
Combining with match play prohibited	33-1
Doubts as to procedure – second ball may be	
played	3-3
Failure to hole out	3-2
Four-ball	31
New holes	33-2b
Order of play	10-2
Playing outside teeing ground	11-4b
Refusal to comply with Rule affecting rights of	
another competitor	3-4
Threesomes and foursomes	29-3
Strokes Taken: Information	9
Suspension of Play	6-8a(i)
Procedure	6-8b
Course unplayable	33-2d
Swing	13
Area of intended – not	
to be altered	13-2
affected by casual water etc.	25-1
affected by immovable obstruction	24-2

	Rule
Swing – continued	
Practice, not a practice stroke	7-2 *note 1*
Tee, Ball Falling or Knocked Off	11-3
Tee, or Coin, as Ball Marker, not Equipment	Def.
Teeing	11-1
Teeing Ground	11, Def.
Playing from tee again	20-5
Playing outside limits of	11-4
Provisional or second ball played from	10-3
Standing outside to play from	11-1
Tee-Markers	11-2
Testing Conditions	
Of hazard	13-4a
Of putting green	16-1d
Three-Ball Match Play	30-1, -2
Threesomes and Foursomes	29
Through The Green	Def.
Ties	
Decision of	33-6
Extending Round to settle	2-3
Time of Starting	6-3, 33-3
Turf, Cut, Placed in Position	13-2
Undue Delay	6-7
In making stroke from water	14-6
Unfit for Play, Ball	5-3
Unplayable Ball	28
Unplayable Course	33-2d
Waiving or Modifying Rule or Penalty	
By Committee	33-1, 33-7
By players, prohibited	1-3
Wall: See definition of "Obstructions"	Def.
Water	
Ball moving in	14-6
Casual: See "Casual Water"	
Not an "Outside Agency"	Def.
Water Hazards	26, Def.
Ball in, touching or lost in	26-1
Ball in, unplayable – may not be so deemed	28
Ball moving in	14-6
Ball played from lost, out of bounds or unplayable outside hazard	26-2b
Ball remaining or coming to rest in after stroke	26-2a
Probing for ball	12-1
Wind	
Not an "Outside Agency"	Def.
Winner of	
Bogey, par or stableford competition	32-1
Hole	2-1
Match	2-3
Stroke competition	3-1
Winter Rules	
Specimen Local Rule	App. I
Wrong Ball	
Balls exchanged in match play	15-2
Best-ball and four-ball match play	30-3d
Four-ball stroke play	31-6
In hazard	15-2, -3

Rule

Wrong Ball – continued
Playing a: match play.. 15-2
             stroke play.. 15-3
Rectification: stroke play 15-3
Substituted ball... 15-1, Def.
Time spent in playing: See definition of
  "Lost Ball".. Def.
Wrong Information About
 Strokes Taken.. 9
Wrong Place, Playing From
Match play.. 20-7a
Stroke play 20-7b
Wrong Score.. 6-6d, 34-1b
Wrongly Dropped or Placed Ball, Lifting........................ 20-6
Yellow Stakes or Lines Define Water Hazard.............. Def. *note*

The Standard Scratch Score and Handicapping Scheme 1983

Revised 1st April 1989

This scheme does not apply to ladies' clubs under the jurisdiction of the Ladies' Golf Union).

Published and administered by the Council of National Golf Unions and adopted by the Unions affiliated to the European Golf Association

Foreword

The Standard Scratch Score and Handicapping Scheme was prepared by the British Golf Unions' Joint Advisory Council in 1925 at the request of the Royal & Ancient Golf Club of St Andrews and has been in operation throughout Great Britain and Ireland since 1st March, 1926.

The Scheme incorporated in this book, known as the Standard Scratch Score and Handicapping Scheme 1983, introduced a new concept in handicapping based on the system presently in use by the Australian Golf Union. The Council of National Golf Unions acknowledges the assistance received from that Union and its officials in formulating the Scheme, which takes account of all scores returned by players under Medal Play conditions.

No change has been made in the present method of fixing the Standard Scratch Score of courses but, on the principle that uniformity and equity in handicapping can be more effectively achieved if there is uniformity and equity in the fixing of Standard Scratch Scores, the Council of National Golf Unions has examined the Course Rating System of the United States Golf Association and has agreed that the Scratch Rating calculated by that procedure may be progressively adopted by National Unions as the Standard Scratch Score pursuant to clause 1.

An amended edition of the Scheme was published on the 1st January 1986 incorporating all amendments from the 1st January 1983 to that date. Further amendments made since the 1st January 1986 are incorporated in this revised edition of the Scheme.

The principal changes are:

(a) The introduction of a Competition Scratch Score (clause 30, Appendices E, F and G).

(b) The discontinuation of the Winter Period following the introduction of the Competition Scratch Score.

(c) For the purpose of calculating the Competition Scratch Score a requirement for players to enter their current Playing Handicaps on score cards when the Qualifying Competition is not a handicap event (clause 13.(9)).

(d) The giving of authority to Unions, at their discretion, to permit Home Clubs to increase handicaps of players in any of the Categories 2, 3 and 4 without reference to the Union or Area Authority (clause 9.(7)).

(e) The giving of authority to Unions, at their discretion, to direct that scores with a nett differential of zero and above returned by a player in Categories 3 and/or 4 at a club where he is not a member shall be disregarded for handicap increase (clause 9.(8)).

(f) Procedure for allotment of handicaps (clause 15.(3)).

(g) The introduction of flexibility into the fixing of Par for individual holes (clause 5).

Copyright 1989 © Council of National Golf Unions.

Part One
Definitions

Definition
A.   UNION.
B.   AREA AUTHORITY.
C.   HOME CLUB.
D.   AFFILIATED CLUB.
E.   HANDICAPPING AUTHORITY.
F.   HANDICAP COMMITTEE.

G. HANDICAPS.
H. CATEGORIES OF HANDICAP.
I. MEASURED COURSE.
J. DISTANCE POINT.
K. MEDAL TEE.
L. MEDAL PLAY CONDITIONS.
M. QUALIFYING COMPETITION.
N. QUALIFYING SCORE.
O. AGGREGATE FOURBALL
    COMPETITION.
P. STANDARD SCRATCH SCORE.
Q. COMPETITION SCRATCH SCORE.
R. NETT DIFFERENTIAL.
S. BUFFER ZONE

Part Two
The Golf Course and the Standard Scratch Score

Clause
1. The STANDARD SCRATCH SCORE.
2. Course measurement.
3. Alterations to courses.
4. Tees.
5. Par.
6. Preferred lies.
7. Permitted adjustments to a MEASURED
    COURSE.

Part Three
Handicapping

8. Introduction.
9. Rights and obligations of the UNION.
10. Rights and obligations of the AREA
    AUTHORITY.
11. Rights and obligations of the AFFILIATED
    CLUB.
12. Rights and obligations of the HANDICAP
    COMMITTEE.
13. Rights and obligations of the player.
14. QUALIFYING SCORES.
15. Allotment of handicaps.
16. Alteration of handicaps.
17. Suspension, lapsing and loss of handicaps.
18. Restoration of handicaps.
19. Powers of the HANDICAP COMMITTEE
    relating to general play.
20. COMPETITION SCRATCH SCORE.
APPENDIX A – Handicap record sheet.
APPENDIX B – Handicap adjustment table.
APPENDIX C – Stableford and par conversion
    table.
APPENDIX D – Decisions.
APPENDIX E – COMPETITION SCRATCH SCORE
    pro forma
APPENDIX F – COMPETITION SCRATCH SCORE
    Table A
APPENDIX G – COMPETITION SCRATCH SCORE
    Table B

Part One
Definitions

Throughout the scheme whenever a word or expression is used which is defined within the following definitions the word or expression is printed in capital letters.

A – Union

A UNION is any national organisation in control of amateur golf in any country.

B – Area Authority

An AREA AUTHORITY is any authority appointed by a UNION to act on behalf of that UNION for the purposes of the Scheme within a specified area.

C – Affiliated Club

An AFFILIATED CLUB is a club affiliated to a UNION or AREA AUTHORITY which pays to the UNION and AREA AUTHORITY a specified annual per capita fee in respect of each eligible member.

D – Home Club

A player's HOME CLUB is an AFFILIATED CLUB of which the player is a member. If the player is a member of more than one AFFILIATED CLUB he shall nominate one as his HOME CLUB.

E – Handicapping Authority

The HANDICAPPING AUTHORITY for a player is his HOME CLUB subject to the overall jurisdiction of the UNION.

F – Handicap Committee

The HANDICAP COMMITTEE is the body appointed by an AFFILIATED CLUB to administer the Scheme within the Club.

G – Handicaps

(1) EXACT HANDICAP – a player's EXACT HANDICAP is his handicap calculated in accordance with the provisions of the Scheme to one decimal place.
(2) PLAYING HANDICAP – a player's PLAYING HANDICAP is his EXACT HANDICAP calculated to the nearest whole number (0.5 is rounded upwards).

H – Categories of Handicap

Handicaps are divided into the following CATEGORIES:
CATEGORY 1: Handicaps of 5 or less.
CATEGORY 2: Handicaps of 6 to 12 inclusive.
CATEGORY 3: Handicaps of 13 to 20 inclusive.
CATEGORY 4: Handicaps of 21 to 28 inclusive.

I – Measured Course

Any course played over by an AFFILIATED CLUB the measured length of which has been certified in accordance with the requirements of clause 2.

J – Distance Point

The DISTANCE POINT is the position of a permanent marker indicating the point from which the length of a hole is measured.

K – Medal Tee

A MEDAL TEE is a rectangular area the front of which shall not be more than 10 yards (9 metres) in front of the relevant DISTANCE POINT and the rear of which shall not be less than 2 yards (2 metres) behind the DISTANCE POINT. NOTE: Special rules apply when the length of a MEASURED COURSE has been temporarily reduced by more than 100 yards (91 metres) – see clause 7(b).

L – Medal Play Conditions

MEDAL PLAY CONDITIONS prevail during stroke, par and Stableford competitions played with full handicap allowance over 18 holes under the Rules of Golf from MEDAL TEES. MEDAL PLAY CONDITIONS shall not prevail when the length of the course played varies by more than 100 yards (91 metres) from the length of the MEASURED COURSE. NOTE: Special rules apply when the length of a MEASURED COURSE has been temporarily reduced by more than 100 yards (91 metres) – see clause 7(b).

M – Qualifying Competition

A QUALIFYING COMPETITION is any competition in which MEDAL PLAY CONDITIONS prevail subject to restrictions and limitations contained in the Scheme or imposed by UNIONS.

N – Qualifying Score

A QUALIFYING SCORE is any score including a "no return" returned in a QUALIFYING COMPETITION.

O – Aggregate Fourball Competition

An AGGREGATE FOURBALL COMPETITION is a QUALIFYING COMPETITION in which the completed scores at each hole of a team of not more than two amateur players are aggregated.

P – Standard Scratch Score

The STANDARD SCRATCH SCORE is the score allotted to an 18 hole golf course after the application of clause 1.

Q – Competition Scratch Score

The COMPETITION SCRATCH SCORE is the score determined by clause 20.

R – Nett Differential

The NETT DIFFERENTIAL is the difference (+ or −) between the nett score returned by a player in a QUALIFYING COMPETITION and the COMPETITION SCRATCH SCORE.

S – Buffer Zone

The BUFFER ZONE is a zone which applies only to scores returned by players in QUALIFYING COMPETITIONS with NETT DIFFERENTIALS of +1 and +2 after application of the COMPETITION SCRATCH SCORE.

Part Two
The Golf Course and the Standard Scratch Score

1. The Standard Scratch Score

1.(1) The STANDARD SCRATCH SCORE is the score which a scratch player is expected to return over a MEASURED COURSE. In the case of a nine-hole course it represents two rounds.
1.(2) The allocation of STANDARD SCRATCH SCORES shall be the responsibility of the UNION.
1.(3) The Table on page 773 will provide a guide to officials in making their assessments.
1.(4) In assessing the STANDARD SCRATCH SCORE of a course, officials will take as the starting point the provisional Standard Scratch Score from the Table. They will then consider the following points:
(a) The terrain and general layout of the course.

Table of Provisional Standard Scratch Scores

Standard length of Course	Lengths included in Standard Length		Provisional Standard Scratch Score
Yards	Yards	Metres	
7100	7001-7002	6402-6584	74
6900	6801-7000	6219-6401	73
6700	6601-6800	6036-6218	72
6500	6401-6600	5853-6035	71
6300	6201-6400	5670-5852	70
6100	5951-6200	5442-5669	69
5800	5701-5950	5213-5441	68
5500	5451-5700	4984-5212	67
5300	5201-5450	4756-4983	66
5100	5001-5200	4573-4755	65
4900	4801-5000	4390-4572	64
4700	4601-4800	4207-4389	63
4500	4401-4600	4024-4206	62
4300	4201-4400	3841-4023	61
4100	4001-4200	3659-3840	60

1 yard = 0.91440 metres
1 metre = 1.09361 yards

(b) Normal ground conditions – Is run average, above average or below average?
(c) Sizes of greens and whether watered or unwatered.
(d) Hazards – Are greens well guarded or open?
(e) Width of fairways, the effect of trees and nature of rough.
(f) Nearness of "out of bounds" to fairways and greens.
(g) Average weather conditions throughout the playing year. Is the course exposed and subject to high winds for most of the year? Is it sheltered from the full effects of adverse weather?
(h) The distance by which the length of the course varies from the standard length shown in column one of the Table.
1.(5) Having considered all these points, officials will fix the STANDARD SCRATCH SCORE of the course by:
(a) Confirming the Provisional Standard Scratch Score as the STANDARD SCRATCH SCORE.
(b) Adding a stroke or strokes to the Provisional Standard Scratch Score.
(c) Deducting a stroke or strokes from the Provisional Standard Scratch Score.
1.(6) At the discretion of the UNION courses of less than 4001 yards may be allocated such STANDARD SCRATCH SCORES as the UNION shall determine.

2. Course Measurement

Measurement shall be by plan or projection along the horizontal plane from the DISTANCE POINT on the MEDAL TEE to the centre of the green of each hole.

In the case of a dog-leg hole, measurement shall be along the centre line of the fairway to the axis and then to the centre of the green. Measurement shall be carried out by a qualified surveyor, or someone competent and experienced in the handling of surveying instruments, who shall grant a certificate showing details of the length of each hole and the total playing length of the course. Subsequent alterations to the length of the course will require a certificate only for the altered hole or holes which shall be measured in the manner prescribed above.

3. Alterations to Courses

When alterations have been carried out to a course increasing or decreasing its length, the club shall submit a "Form of Application" through its AREA AUTHORITY to the UNION. In the case of a new course, a "Form of Application" shall be submitted by the club through its AREA AUTHORITY to the UNION who will fix the STANDARD SCRATCH SCORE. The UNION is responsible for all STANDARD SCRATCH SCORES in the country over which it has jurisdiction.

4. Tees

All clubs with the necessary facilities should have back and forward MEDAL TEES with a yardage measurement from each tee and a separate STANDARD SCRATCH SCORE as measured from back and forward MEDAL TEES permanently marked.

To facilitate the use of the correct tees the Royal & Ancient Golf Club of St Andrews recommends that tee boxes or other objects in use to mark the teeing ground shall be painted as follows:

Ladies' Standard MEDAL TEES	Red
Men's Forward MEDAL TEES	Yellow
Men's Back MEDAL TEES	White

When a National Championship is being played over a course the tee markers may be coloured Blue.

5. Par

The STANDARD SCRATCH SCORE must not be allocated amongst the individual holes, but should be printed as a total on the card. The par figure for each hole should be printed alongside each hole on the card. Par for each hole shall be fixed by the club in relation to the length and playing difficulty of each hole and shall be fixed within the following ranges:

	Yards	Metres
Par 3	0–250	0–229
Par 4	220–500	201–457
Par 5	440+	402+

e.g. if a hole is 460 yards (421 metres) it may be allotted par 4 or 5 depending upon its average playing difficulty.

The total of the Par figures for each hole of a course will not necessarily coincide with the STANDARD SCRATCH SCORE of that course. Par should be used for Stableford and similar competitions.

6. Preferred Lies

When preferred lies are in operation the following points shall be taken into consideration: MEDAL PLAY CONDITIONS will apply notwithstanding the application of a Local Rule for preferred lies as a result of adverse conditions during the period from 1st November to 30th April. Preferred lies may be used during that period but are not mandatory upon clubs during any part thereof. The Local Rule may apply to specified holes only. Outside that period MEDAL PLAY CONDITIONS will not apply if preferred lies are in operation unless the consent of the UNION or AREA AUTHORITY has been first obtained.

It is emphasised that preferred lies shall apply only when a Local Rule has been made and published in accordance with Appendix 1 of the Rules of Golf as follows:

"A ball lying on any "closely mown area" through the green may, without penalty, be moved or may be lifted, cleaned and placed within six inches of where it originally lay, but not nearer the hole. After the ball has been so moved or placed, it is in play."

Penalty for breach of Local Rule: Match Play – Loss of hole; Stroke play – Two strokes.
NOTE: "closely mown area" means any area of the COURSE, including paths through the rough, cut to fair-way height or less. (Rule 25-2).

7. Permitted Adjustment to a Measured Course

Whilst each AFFILIATED CLUB must endeavour to maintain the length of its MEASURED COURSE at all times MEDAL PLAY CONDITIONS nevertheless prevail when the length of a course has been reduced in the following circumstances:

(a) When, to allow movement of the playing position on the MEDAL TEE or the use of a temporary green, the length of the course being played has been reduced by not more than 100 yards (91 metres) from the length of the MEASURED COURSE. The tee positions used must nevertheless be within the area defined by Definition K.
NOTE: The maximum movement forward on any MEDAL TEE must not exceed 10 yards (9 metres) – See Definition K.

(b) When, to allow work to proceed on course alterations or for reasons other than weather conditions, it is necessary to reduce the playing length of the MEASURED COURSE by between 100 and 300 yards (91 and 274 metres). In these circumstances, the club shall reduce the STANDARD SCRATCH SCORE of the MEASURED COURSE temporarily by 1 stroke and report to the UNION, or to such other body nominated by the UNION, the reduction in the STANDARD SCRATCH SCORE, and the reason for it. The club must also notify the UNION or other body when the course has been restored to its measured length and the official STANDARD SCRATCH SCORE reinstated.

Part Three
Handicapping

8. Introduction

8.(1) The Council of National Golf Unions Standard Scratch Score and Handicapping Scheme has been revised to achieve a uniformity and equity in handicapping throughout Great Britain and Ireland and those member countries of the European Golf Association adopting the Scheme. The nature of the game of golf, with its varying playing conditions, makes handicapping a relatively inexact operation. Nevertheless, if the same principles are sensibly and universally applied by HANDICAP COMMITTEES, a high degree of uniformity in handicapping can be achieved. It is therefore of paramount importance that all parties to the Scheme fulfil their obligations to it and these are set out below.
8.(2) Handicapping within the Scheme is delegated to AFFILIATED CLUBS subject to the overall jurisdiction of the UNION.

9. Rights and Obligations of the Union

The UNION:
9.(1) Shall have overall jurisdiction for the administration of the Scheme.

9.(2) May delegate any part of that jurisdiction to an AREA AUTHORITY.

9.(3) Shall ratify all PLAYING HANDICAPS reduced to scratch or below immediately after the reduction.

9.(4) Shall have the right to obtain information upon handicaps from AFFILIATED CLUBS at any time.

9.(5) Shall establish within the UNION conditions, restrictions and limitations to be imposed in respect of competitions deemed to be QUALIFYING COMPETITIONS.

9.(6) Shall settle any dispute referred to it. Its decision shall be final.

9.(7) May at its discretion authorise HOME CLUBS to increase the handicaps of players in any of the CATEGORIES 2, 3, and 4 pursuant to clause 19. When such authority has been given the requirements of clause 19.(2) and (3) that the increase shall be effected by the UNION or AREA AUTHORITY shall not apply. Notwithstanding the foregoing, the Union may, if it considers that handicaps have been unjustifiably increased by a HOME CLUB, require that club to comply with all of the provisions of clause 19.

9.(8) May at its discretion direct that scores returned by a player in CATEGORIES 3 and/or 4 at a club where he is not a member shall be disregarded for handicap increase pursuant to CLAUSE 16.(3).

10. Rights and Obligations of the Area Authority

The AREA AUTHORITY shall:

10.(1) Administer the responsibilities delegated to it by the UNION.

10.(2) Have the right to obtain information upon handicaps from AFFILIATED CLUBS at any time.

11. Rights and Obligations of the Affiliated Club

The AFFILIATED CLUB shall:

11.(1) Act as the HANDICAPPING AUTHORITY for all members for whom it is the HOME CLUB subject to the overall jurisdiction of the UNION.

11.(2) Ensure that the Scheme is properly applied in the club.

11.(3) Ensure that all handicaps are calculated in accordance with the Scheme.

11.(4) Appoint a HANDICAP COMMITTEE to perform the obligations set out in clause 12 below.

12. Rights and Obligations of the Handicap Committee

The HANDICAP COMMITTEE shall:

12.(1) Maintain a list in which the names of competitors must be entered prior to competing in a QUALIFYING COMPETITION at the club.

12.(2) Ensure, so far as possible, that all cards taken out in QUALIFYING COMPETITIONS are returned to the committee including incomplete cards.

12.(3) At the conclusion of each round of a QUALIFYING COMPETITION calculate the COMPETITION SCRATCH SCORE as required by clause 20.

12.(4) Post on the club's notice board all changes of members' PLAYING HANDICAPS immediately they are made.

12.(5) Ensure that a record of members' current PLAYING HANDICAPS is available in a prominent position in the club house.

12.(6) When the club is a player's HOME CLUB:

(a) Maintain on his behalf a handicap record sheet which shall include the information shown in Appendix A.

(b) Ensure his scores are recorded immediately after completion of each QUALIFYING COMPETITION at the HOME CLUB or the reporting of a QUALIFYING SCORE returned elsewhere.

(c) Keep his EXACT HANDICAP up to date at all times.

(d) Notify the UNION and AREA AUTHORITY immediately the committee reduces a member's PLAYING HANDICAPS to scratch or below and obtain ratification from the UNION or, if so delegated, from the AREA AUTHORITY.

NOTE: The reduction is effective before ratification.

(e) Unless some other body has been appointed by the HOME CLUB for this purpose, exercise the power to suspend handicaps contained in clause 17.

(f) When a member changes his HOME CLUB send to the new HOME CLUB a copy of the player's current handicap record sheet.

(g) Specify the conditions which apply when a player wishes to obtain a handicap under the provisions of clause 15.

(h) Exercise the powers to adjust players' handicaps contained in clause 19.

(i) As required by sub clause 19.(5) advise players of changes made to their handicaps under the provisions of clause 19.

13. Rights and Obligations of the Player

The player shall:

13.(1) Have one handicap only which shall be allotted and adjusted by his HOME CLUB. That handicap shall apply elsewhere including other clubs of which the player is a member.

13.(2) If he is a member of more than one AFFILIATED CLUB select one as his HOME CLUB and notify that club and the others of his choice.

13.(3) Not change his HOME CLUB except by giving advance notice of the change which can take effect only at the end of a calendar year unless he has ceased to be a member of his HOME CLUB or both clubs agree to the change taking place at an earlier date.

13.(4) Report to his HOME CLUB the names of all other AFFILIATED CLUBS of which he is, becomes, or ceases to be, a member and report to all other AFFILIATED CLUBS of which he is a member:
(a) The name of his HOME CLUB and any changes of his HOME CLUB and
(b) Alterations to his PLAYING HANDICAP made by his HOME CLUB.

13.(5) Ensure that before competing in a QUALIFYING COMPETITION his entry has been inserted in the competition entry list.

13.(6) Ensure that all competition cards in QUALIFYING COMPETITIONS, whether or not complete, are returned to the organising committee.

13.(7) Subject to the provisions of clause 9.(8) report to his HOME CLUB immediately all QUALIFYING SCORES (including no returns) returned away from his HOME CLUB advising the HOME CLUB of the date of the QUALIFYING COMPETITION, the venue and the COMPETITION SCRATCH SCORE together with the following:
(a) After a stroke play QUALIFYING COMPETITION the gross score returned.
(b) After a Stableford QUALIFYING COMPETITION the par of the course and the number of points scored.
(c) After a par QUALIFYING COMPETITION the par of the course and the score versus par.

NOTE 1: Players are reminded that failure to report scores returned away from their HOME CLUBS (including no returns) is likely to lead to the suspension of offending players' handicaps under the provisions of clause 17.

NOTE 2: In the event of a QUALIFYING COMPETITION being declared abandoned or scores returned being deemed by clause 20 not to be QUALIFYING SCORES the player is required to report the above information only if he has returned a NETT DIFFERENTIAL of less than zero.

13.(8) Prior to playing in any competition at a club other than his HOME CLUB ensure that any appropriate reductions to his PLAYING HANDICAP have been made or alternatively comply with the obligations set out in clause 16.(11).

13.(9) Enter his current PLAYING HANDICAP on all cards returned in a QUALIFYING COMPETITION even though the event may not be a handicap competition.

14. Qualifying Scores

14.(1) The only scores to be recorded on a player's handicap record sheet are:
(a) QUALIFYING SCORES as defined.
(b) NETT DIFFERENTIALS of less than zero returned in any abandoned round of a QUALIFYING COMPETITION or in any round of a QUALIFYING COMPETITION when that round has been deemed under the provisions of clause 20 not to be a QUALIFYING SCORE.
(c) Correct scores in a QUALIFYING COMPETITION which are disqualified for any reason.
(d) Scores returned in a QUALIFYING COMPETITION played over 18 holes on a course reduced in length under the provisions of clause 7.
(e) Scores returned in a QUALIFYING COMPETITION played over a MEASURED COURSE when local rules are in operation for preferred lies (as permitted by clause 6) or for any other purpose provided the rules are authorised by Appendix 1 of the Rules of Golf or have been approved by the Rules of Golf Committee of the Royal & Ancient Golf Club of St Andrews.
(f) The individual scores and no returns returned by players in AGGREGATE FOURBALL COMPETITIONS.
NOTE: The competition must be a QUALIFYING COMPETITION.
NOTE: QUALIFYING SCORES returned in Stableford and par competitions shall be converted into NETT DIFFERENTIALS by using the tables in Appendix C.

14.(2) The following returns shall not be accepted as QUALIFYING SCORES in any circumstances:
(a) Scores returned in any better ball fourball competition.
(b) Scores returned in competitions over less than 18 holes.
(c) Scores returned in any competition which is not played in accordance with the Rules of Golf and authorised Local Rules.
(d) Scores returned in "running medals". A running medal is an extended competition in which the player has the option of selecting the day or days on which he shall compete and/or how many returns he shall make. A competition extended over two or more days solely to accommodate the number of players entered is not a running medal.
(e) Subject to clause 14.(1)(b) scores returned in any round of a QUALIFYING COMPETITION deemed under the provisions of clause 20 not to be QUALIFYING SCORES.
(f) Any competition other than an AGGREGATE FOURBALL COMPETITION in which competitors play in partnership with another competitor.

(g) Stableford and par competitions played with less than full handicap allowance.

(h) Scores returned in events run by organisations which are not HANDICAPPING AUTHORITIES unless such events have been previously approved by a UNION as a QUALIFYING COMPETITION.

15. Allotment of Handicaps

15.(1) The maximum handicap is 28. (Maximum EXACT HANDICAP 28.0.)

15.(2) A handicap can be allotted only to an amateur member of an AFFILIATED CLUB.

15.(3) To obtain a handicap a player shall submit three cards preferably marked over a MEASURED COURSE which shall be adjusted by the HANDICAP COMMITTEE so that any score of more than 2 over par at any hole shall be amended to 2 over par. After these adjustments have been made an EXACT HANDICAP shall be allotted equivalent to the number of strokes by which the best of the three rounds differs from the STANDARD SCRATCH SCORE. The HANDICAP COMMITTEE may allot a player an initial whole number EXACT HANDICAP less than the best score if it has reason to consider that a lower handicap is more appropriate to the player's ability. In exceptional circumstances a higher handicap may be allotted than that indicated by the best score. When a player fails to return cards justifying an EXACT HANDICAP of 28.0 he may, at the discretion of the HANDICAP COMMITTEE, be given an EXACT HANDICAP of 28.0. The player's PLAYING HANDICAP shall equal the EXACT HANDICAP allotted.

15.(4) A player without a handicap shall not be allotted a CATEGORY 1 HANDICAP without the written authority of the UNION, or AREA AUTHORITY if so delegated.

16. Alteration of Handicaps

16.(1) Definition H divides handicaps into the following four CATEGORIES:

CATEGORY 1: Handicaps of 5 or less.
CATEGORY 2: Handicaps of 6 to 12 inclusive.
CATEGORY 3: Handicaps of 13 to 20 inclusive.
CATEGORY 4: Handicaps of 21 to 28 inclusive.

16.(2) If a player returns a NETT DIFFERENTIAL of zero or within the BUFFER ZONE his EXACT HANDICAP is not changed.

16.(3) Subject to the provisions of sub clauses 9.(8), 20.(3) and 20.(4), if a player returns a score with a NETT DIFFERENTIAL of +3 or more or records a "no return" his EXACT HANDICAP is increased by 0.1.

16.(4) If a player returns a NETT DIFFERENTIAL of less than zero his EXACT HANDICAP is reduced by an amount *per stroke that the* NETT DIFFERENTIAL *is below zero*, the amount per stroke being determined by his HANDICAP CATEGORY.

16.(5) The recording of scores shall be kept by NETT DIFFERENTIAL i.e. the difference (+ or −) between the player's nett score and the COMPETITION SCRATCH SCORE. The date, NETT DIFFERENTIAL, EXACT HANDICAP and PLAYING HANDICAP must be recorded on the player's handicap record sheet.

16.(6) EXACT HANDICAPS shall be adjusted as follows, with reference to the handicap adjustment table, Appendix B:

| | | If NETT DIFFERENTIAL is: | |
CATEGORY	PLAYING HANDICAP	Above BUFFER ZONE Add *only*	Below CSS. Subtract for *each* Stroke below
1	Up to 5	0.1	0.1
2	6 to 12	0.1	0.2
3	13 to 20	0.1	0.3
4	21 to 28	0.1	0.4

For example:

If a player on 11.2 returns a score with a NETT DIFFERENTIAL of 4 his EXACT HANDICAP becomes 11.3. If he then returns a score with a NETT DIFFERENTIAL of −7 his EXACT HANDICAP is reduced by 7 times 0.2 = 1.4, i.e. to an EXACT HANDICAP of 9.9 and his PLAYING HANDICAP is 10 which is immediately his new handicap.

16.(7) When a player's handicap is to be reduced so that it goes from a higher CATEGORY to a lower CATEGORY, it shall be reduced at the rate appropriate to the higher CATEGORY only so far as brings his PLAYING HANDICAP into the lower CATEGORY and the balance of the reduction shall be at the rate appropriate to the lower CATEGORY.

For example:

If a player on 21.2 returns a score with a NETT DIFFERENTIAL of −6, i.e. 6 strokes below his PLAYING HANDICAP of 21, his handicap is reduced as follows:

21.2−(2 times 0.4) (i.e. −0.8)=20.4
20.4−(4 times 0.3) (i.e. −1.2)=19.2

16.(8) A player whose EXACT HANDICAP contains 0.5 or over shall be given the next higher handicap, e.g. 12.5 exact would be 13 PLAYING HANDICAP. This applies when handicaps are to be increased or reduced.

NOTE: EXACT HANDICAP −0.5 rounded upwards is PLAYING HANDICAP scratch and not plus one.

16.(9) Reductions shall be made on the day the score becomes known to the HOME CLUB.

16.(10) Increases shall be made at the end of each calendar month or at such shorter intervals as the HOME CLUB may decide.

16.(11) If, for any reason, a player is unable to report to his HOME CLUB a QUALIFYING SCORE or SCORES which may have a NETT DIFFERENTIAL of less than zero or has been unable to ascertain, after reporting such scores, whether or not his PLAYING HANDICAP has been reduced, he shall then, before competing in a further competition at a club other than his HOME CLUB, either:

(a) For that competition only, make such reduction to his PLAYING HANDICAP as shall be appropriate under the Scheme by applying the COMPETITION SCRATCH SCORE if known, otherwise the STANDARD SCRATCH SCORE to his gross score, or

(b) Report to the committee organising the competition any relevant score returned which after deduction of his PLAYING HANDICAP is two above the STANDARD SCRATCH SCORE or less. The committee may, for that competition only, reduce the player's PLAYING HANDICAP.

NOTE: Increases to PLAYING HANDICAPS may not be made under the provisions of this sub clause.

16.(12) The procedure for the restoration of handicaps which have been lost is contained in clause 18.

17. Suspension, Lapsing and Loss of Handicaps

17.(1) The HANDICAP COMMITTEE, or other body appointed by the HOME CLUB for the purposes of this clause, shall suspend the handicap of any player who in its opinion has constantly or blatantly failed to comply with his obligations under the Scheme. The player must be notified of the period of suspension and of any other conditions imposed. No player's handicap shall be suspended without first affording him the opportunity of appearing before the committee or other body.

17.(2) If a player is suspended from membership of his HOME CLUB his handicap shall lapse automatically until his membership is reinstated.

17.(3) A player's handicap is lost immediately he ceases to be a member of an AFFILIATED CLUB or loses his amateur status.

17.(4) Whilst a player's handicap is suspended, lapsed or has been lost he shall not enter or compete in any competition which requires a competitor to be the holder of a handicap for either entering or competing in the competition.

18. Restoration of Handicaps

18.(1) A player who has lost his handicap for any reason other than suspension or lapsing may obtain a new handicap by complying with the requirements of clause 15. When allotting him a handicap the HANDICAP COMMITTEE will give due consideration to the handicap he last held.

A CATEGORY 1 HANDICAP shall not be allotted without the written approval of the UNION, or AREA AUTHORITY if so delegated.

18.(2) The lapsed handicap of a player suspended from membership of his HOME CLUB shall be reinstated when his membership is restored and shall be the same as the handicap he held when his membership was suspended.

19. Powers of the Handicap Committee Relating to General Play

19.(1) Whenever the HANDICAP COMMITTEE of a player's HOME CLUB considers that a player's EXACT HANDICAP is too high and does not reflect his current playing ability the HANDICAP COMMITTEE must, subject to the provisions of sub clause (3) of this clause, reduce his EXACT HANDICAP to the figure it considers appropriate.

19.(2) (a) Whenever the HANDICAP COMMITTEE of a player's HOME CLUB considers that a player's EXACT HANDICAP is too low and does not reflect his current playing ability the HANDICAP COMMITTEE must, subject to the provisions of sub clause (3) of this clause, recommend to the UNION, or AREA AUTHORITY if so delegated, that his EXACT HANDICAP should be increased to the figure it considers appropriate.

(b) In the event of a UNION delegating to HOME CLUBS the unconditional authority to increase the handicaps of players in any of the CATEGORIES 2, 3 and 4 HOME CLUBS need not submit to the UNION or AREA AUTHORITY proposals in respect of any changes of handicaps of players in the nominated CATEGORIES.

19.(3) When the HANDICAP COMMITTEE has decided that the EXACT HANDICAP of a player should be reduced to less than 5.5 or that the EXACT HANDICAP of a player should be increased the HANDICAP COMMITTEE must refer the matter to the UNION, or AREA AUTHORITY if so delegated, with its recommended adjustment. The UNION or AREA AUTHORITY shall then authorise the recommended variation, reject the recommendation or refer the matter back to the HANDICAP COMMITTEE for further consideration. The UNION or AREA AUTHORITY shall be supplied with all the information upon which the recommendation is based and with any further information required.

19.(4) When deciding whether to effect or recommend an adjustment of handicap the HANDICAP COMMITTEE of the player's HOME CLUB shall consider all available information regarding the player's golfing ability.

It shall consider in particular:

(a) The frequency of QUALIFYING SCORES recently returned by the player to and below his PLAYING HANDICAP.

(b) The player's achievements in match play,

fourball better ball competitions and other non-qualifying events.

(c) QUALIFYING SCORES returned by the player in stroke play competitions which are adversely affected by one or more particularly bad holes. It may prove helpful to take into account the number of points the player would have scored if these QUALIFYING SCORES had been in Stableford competitions played with full handicap allowance.

19.(5) The HANDICAP COMMITTEE shall advise a player of any change of handicap under this clause and the change will become effective when the player becomes aware of the adjustment.

19.(6) The HANDICAP COMMITTEE or other body organising a competition at a club which is not the player's HOME CLUB may if it considers his handicap is too high because of scores reported pursuant to sub clause 16.(11)(b) or for any other reason reduce that handicap. Any reduction made under this sub clause shall apply only to the competition for which it is made.

19.(7) Decisions made by a HANDICAP COMMITTEE, UNION or AREA AUTHORITY under this clause shall be final.

NOTES:

1. In the interests of equitable handicapping it is essential that all HANDICAP COMMITTEES keep the handicaps of the members for whom they act as the HOME CLUB under review and that adjustments of handicaps are considered as soon as it comes to the committee's notice that a player's handicap may no longer correctly reflect his current general golfing ability.

2. The HANDICAP COMMITTEE should consider dealing more severely with a player whose general standard of play is known to be improving than it would with a player who it is believed has returned scores below his general ability but whose general playing ability is not considered to be improving.

20. Competition Scratch Score

20.(1) At the conclusion of each round of a QUALIFYING COMPETITION the COMPETITION SCRATCH SCORE shall be calculated by following the procedure set out in Appendix E and applying the relevant Table in either Appendix F or G.

20.(2) In the event of one round of a QUALIFYING COMPETITION extending over more than one day the COMPETITION SCRATCH SCORE shall be calculated for each day.

20.(3) The relevant Table dictates any adjustment to be made to the STANDARD SCRATCH SCORE to provide the COMPETITION SCRATCH SCORE or to direct that the scores returned shall not count as QUALIFYING SCORES (indicated by "N/C" in the Table column heading). When the COMPETITION SCRATCH SCORE has been established all NETT DIFFERENTIALS shall be calculated in relation thereto and handicap adjustments made and entered in the player's Handicap Record Sheets. (See Definition S – BUFFER ZONE.)

20.(4) If the Table indicates that the scores returned shall not count as QUALIFYING SCORES then the COMPETITION SCRATCH SCORE shall be deemed to be three strokes more than the STANDARD SCRATCH SCORE. All players who after the application of the COMPETITION SCRATCH SCORE to their scores have returned a NETT DIFFERENTIAL of less than zero shall have their EXACT HANDICAPS reduced to the extent dictated by the NETT DIFFERENTIAL so calculated. A NETT DIFFERENTIAL of zero or above shall not result in a handicap increase.

20.(5) If a QUALIFYING COMPETITION is abandoned for any reason the COMPETITION SCRATCH SCORE shall be regarded as equal to the STANDARD SCRATCH SCORE and players returning NETT DIFFERENTIALS of less than zero shall have their EXACT HANDICAPS reduced to the extent dictated by the NETT DIFFERENTIAL. A NETT DIFFERENTIAL of zero or above shall not result in a handicap increase.

NOTE: UNIONS, AREA AUTHORITIES and any organisations so authorised by a UNION shall establish the COMPETITION SCRATCH SCORES for any events they organise.

Appendix A

Handicap Record Sheet

NAME _____

HOME CLUB _____

OTHER CLUBS _____

_____

| Date | Nett dif- erential | Handicap | | Date | Nett dif- erential | Handicap | |
		Exact	Playing			Exact	Playing
May 1	D/T	21.0	21	June 30	B/F	19.4	19
6	2	21.0	21	July			
7	4	21.1	21	8	7	19.5	19
20	N/R	21.2	21	9	6	19.6	19
21	−6	19.2	19	29	8	19.7	19 *Note 2*
				30	3	19.8	20
June 4	1	19.2	19	Aug 6	2	19.8	20
5	4	19.3	19	7	−6	18.0	18
25	7	19.4	19	20	0	18.0	18
26	2	19.4	19	21	7	18.1	18

Notes to Appendix A

1. The sheet above shows the PLAYING HANDICAPS when increases are made on the last day of each calendar month.
2. If the increases had been made immediately the PLAYING HANDICAP would have been increased to 20 on the 8th July and the NETT DIFFERENTIALS of 6, 8 and 3 respectively on the 9th, 29th and 30th July would each have been reduced by 1. Thus, with the operation of the BUFFER ZONE, the EXACT HANDICAP would have remained at 19.7 on 31st July and been 0.1 less than those shown thereafter.
3. NETT DIFFERENTIAL is the difference (+ or −) between the Nett Score returned by a player in a QUALIFYING COMPETITION and the COMPETITION SCRATCH SCORE
4. Scores returned on courses other than that of the player's HOME CLUB should be distinguished by marking the NETT DIFFERENTIAL thus: □
5. Reductions of handicaps are effected immediately.
6. Increases of handicaps shall be made at the end of each calendar month or at such shorter intervals as the HOME CLUB may decide.

Appendix B

Table of Handicap Adjustments

Nett Differentials	-1	-2	-3	-4	-5	-6	-7	-8	-9	-10	-11	-12	Over Buffer Zone
Exact Handicaps Up to 5.4	-0.1	-0.2	-0.3	-0.4	-0.5	-0.6	-0.7	-0.8	-0.9	-1.0	-1.1	-1.2	+0.1
5.5– 5.6	-0.2	-0.3	-0.4	-0.5	-0.6	-0.7	-0.8	-0.9	-1.0	-1.1	-1.2	-1.3	+0.1
5.7– 5.8	-0.2	-0.4	-0.5	-0.6	-0.7	-0.8	-0.9	-1.0	-1.1	-1.2	-1.3	-1.4	+0.1
5.9– 6.0	-0.2	-0.4	-0.6	-0.7	-0.8	-0.9	-1.0	-1.1	-1.2	-1.3	-1.4	-1.5	+0.1
6.1– 6.2	-0.2	-0.4	-0.6	-0.8	-0.9	-1.0	-1.1	-1.2	-1.3	-1.4	-1.5	-1.6	+0.1
6.3– 6.4	-0.2	-0.4	-0.6	-0.8	-1.0	-1.1	-1.2	-1.3	-1.4	-1.5	-1.6	-1.7	+0.1
6.5– 6.6	-0.2	-0.4	-0.6	-0.8	-1.0	-1.2	-1.3	-1.4	-1.5	-1.6	-1.7	-1.8	+0.1
6.7– 6.8	-0.2	-0.4	-0.6	-0.8	-1.0	-1.2	-1.4	-1.5	-1.6	-1.7	-1.8	-1.9	+0.1
6.9– 7.0	-0.2	-0.4	-0.6	-0.8	-1.0	-1.2	-1.4	-1.6	-1.7	-1.8	-1.9	-2.0	+0.1
7.1– 7.2	-0.2	-0.4	-0.6	-0.8	-1.0	-1.2	-1.4	-1.6	-1.8	-1.9	-2.0	-2.1	+0.1
7.3– 7.4	-0.2	-0.4	-0.6	-0.8	-1.0	-1.2	-1.4	-1.6	-1.8	-2.0	-2.1	-2.2	+0.1
7.5– 7.6	-0.2	-0.4	-0.6	-0.8	-1.0	-1.2	-1.4	-1.6	-1.8	-2.0	-2.2	-2.3	+0.1
7.7–12.4	-0.2	-0.4	-0.6	-0.8	-1.0	-1.2	-1.4	-1.6	-1.8	-2.0	-2.2	-2.4	+0.1
12.5–12.7	-0.3	-0.5	-0.7	-0.9	-1.1	-1.3	-1.5	-1.7	-1.9	-2.1	-2.3	-2.5	+0.1
12.8–13.0	-0.3	-0.6	-0.8	-1.0	-1.2	-1.4	-1.6	-1.8	-2.0	-2.2	-2.4	-2.6	+0.1
13.1–13.3	-0.3	-0.6	-0.9	-1.1	-1.3	-1.5	-1.7	-1.9	-2.1	-2.3	-2.5	-2.7	+0.1
13.4–13.6	-0.3	-0.6	-0.9	-1.2	-1.4	-1.6	-1.8	-2.0	-2.2	-2.4	-2.6	-2.8	+0.1
13.7–13.9	-0.3	-0.6	-0.9	-1.2	-1.5	-1.7	-1.9	-2.1	-2.3	-2.5	-2.7	-2.9	+0.1
14.0–14.2	-0.3	-0.6	-0.9	-1.2	-1.5	-1.8	-2.0	-2.2	-2.4	-2.6	-2.8	-3.0	+0.1
14.3–14.5	-0.3	-0.6	-0.9	-1.2	-1.5	-1.8	-2.1	-2.3	-2.5	-2.7	-2.9	-3.1	+0.1
14.6–14.8	-0.3	-0.6	-0.9	-1.2	-1.5	-1.8	-2.1	-2.4	-2.6	-2.8	-3.0	-3.2	+0.1
14.9–15.1	-0.3	-0.6	-0.9	-1.2	-1.5	-1.8	-2.1	-2.4	-2.7	-2.9	-3.1	-3.3	+0.1
15.2–15.4	-0.3	-0.6	-0.9	-1.2	-1.5	-1.8	-2.1	-2.4	-2.7	-3.0	-3.2	-3.4	+0.1
15.5–15.7	-0.3	-0.6	-0.9	-1.2	-1.5	-1.8	-2.1	-2.4	-2.7	-3.0	-3.3	-3.5	+0.1
15.8–20.4	-0.3	-0.6	-0.9	-1.2	-1.5	-1.8	-2.1	-2.4	-2.7	-3.0	-3.3	-3.6	+0.1
20.5–20.8	-0.4	-0.7	-1.0	-1.3	-1.6	-1.9	-2.2	-2.5	-2.8	-3.1	-3.4	-3.7	+0.1
20.9–21.2	-0.4	-0.8	-1.1	-1.4	-1.7	-2.0	-2.3	-2.6	-2.9	-3.2	-3.5	-3.8	+0.1
21.3–21.6	-0.4	-0.8	-1.2	-1.5	-1.8	-2.1	-2.4	-2.7	-3.0	-3.3	-3.6	-3.8	+0.1
21.7–22.0	-0.4	-0.8	-1.2	-1.6	-1.9	-2.2	-2.5	-2.8	-3.1	-3.4	-3.7	-4.0	+0.1
22.1–22.4	-0.4	-0.8	-1.2	-1.6	-2.0	-2.3	-2.6	-2.9	-3.2	-3.5	-3.8	-4.1	+0.1
22.5–22.8	-0.4	-0.8	-1.2	-1.6	-2.0	-2.4	-2.7	-3.0	-3.3	-3.6	-3.9	-4.2	+0.1
22.9–23.2	-0.4	-0.8	-1.2	-1.6	-2.0	-2.4	-2.8	-3.1	-3.4	-3.7	-4.0	-4.3	+0.1
23.3–23.6	-0.4	-0.8	-1.2	-1.6	-2.0	-2.4	-2.8	-3.2	-3.5	-3.8	-4.1	-4.4	+0.1
23.7–24.0	-0.4	-0.8	-1.2	-1.6	-2.0	-2.4	-2.8	-3.2	-3.6	-3.9	-4.2	-4.5	+0.1
24.1–24.4	-0.4	-0.8	-1.2	-1.6	-2.0	-2.4	-2.8	-3.2	-3.6	-4.0	-4.3	-4.6	+0.1
24.5–24.8	-0.4	-0.8	-1.2	-1.6	-2.0	-2.4	-2.8	-3.2	-3.6	-4.0	-4.4	-4.7	+0.1
24.9–28.0	-0.4	-0.8	-1.2	-1.6	-2.0	-2.4	-2.8	-3.2	-3.6	-4.0	-4.4	-4.8	+0.1

Appendix C

Table for converting Par and Stableford scores to nett differentials
(Note – the Table is based on full handicap allowance)

Scores versus PAR	7 down	6 down	5 down	4 down	3 down	2 down	1 down	All Square	1 up	2 up	3 up	4 up	5 up	6 up	7 up
STABLEFORD points scored	29	30	31	32	33	34	35	36	37	38	39	40	41	42	43
Par 7 less than CSS	0	-1	-2	-3	-4	-5	-6	-7	-8	-9	-10	-11	-12	-13	-14
Par 6 less than CSS	+1	0	-1	-2	-3	-4	-5	-6	-7	-8	-9	-10	-11	-12	-13
Par 5 less than CSS	+2	+1	0	-1	-2	-3	-4	-5	-6	-7	-8	-9	-10	-11	-12
Par 4 less than CSS	+3	+2	+1	0	-1	-2	-3	-4	-5	-6	-7	-8	-9	-10	-11
Par 3 less than CSS	+4	+3	+2	+1	0	-1	-2	-3	-4	-5	-6	-7	-8	-9	-10
Par 2 less than CSS	+5	+4	+3	+2	+1	0	-1	-2	-3	-4	-5	-6	-7	-8	-9
Par 1 less than CSS	+6	+5	+4	+3	+2	+1	0	-1	-2	-3	-4	-5	-6	-7	-8
Par equal to CSS	+7	+6	+5	+4	+3	+2	+1	0	-1	-2	-3	-4	-5	-6	-7
Par 1 more than CSS	+8	+7	+6	+5	+4	+3	+2	+1	0	-1	-2	-3	-4	-5	-6
Par 2 more than CSS	+9	+8	+7	+6	+5	+4	+3	+2	+1	0	-1	-2	-3	-4	-5
Par 3 more than CSS	+10	+9	+8	+7	+6	+5	+4	+3	+2	+1	0	-1	-2	-3	-4
Par 4 more than CSS	+11	+10	+9	+8	+7	+6	+5	+4	+3	+2	+1	0	-1	-2	-3
Par 5 more than CSS	+12	+11	+10	+9	+8	+7	+6	+5	+4	+3	+2	+1	0	-1	-2
Par 6 more than CSS	+13	+12	+11	+10	+9	+8	+7	+6	+5	+4	+3	+2	+1	0	-1

Example:-
(a) 3 up on a Par 72 course with an CSS of 70. Par is 2 more than CSS so Nett Differential = -1.
(b) 37 Stableford points on a course with Par 68 & CSS 69. Par is 1 less than CSS so Nett Differential = -2.

Appendix D

Decisions

1. Running Medals – Clause 14.(2)(d)

(a) Any competition which can be described as a "Running Medal" is not a QUALIFYING COMPETITION.

(b) The following are defined as "Running Medals":

(i) An 18 hole competition extended over two or more days for any reason other than to accommodate the number of players entered.

(ii) An 18 hole competition played on one day or over several days in which players are allowed to return more than one score.

NOTE: If from a series of any number of scores special prizes are awarded for the best eclectic score or the best nett or gross aggregate of a prescribed number of scores, the individual scores in the series would not be regarded as constituting a "running medal" provided each score is returned under MEDAL PLAY CONDITIONS in a QUALIFYING COMPETITION, as defined in the Scheme, and not returned solely for the purpose of the eclectic, nett or gross aggregate awards.

2. Qualifying Scores

(a) If a club with a large number of QUALIFYING COMPETITIONS in the calendar year wishes to deprive certain of the competitions of their status as QUALIFYING COMPETITIONS it may do so provided competitors are so advised before play commences.

(b) It would be outside the spirit of the Handicapping Scheme to declare that all Club Medal Competitions during a specified period would not be regarded as QUALIFYING COMPETITIONS, although played under full MEDAL PLAY CONDITIONS.

(c) In both (a) and (b) above it would be more appropriate to play unofficial MEDAL COMPETITIONS under conditions which would not give them the status of QUALIFYING COMPETITIONS.

NOTE: A declaration that a competition is not a QUALIFYING COMPETITION disqualifies all scores returned in that competition for handicapping purposes. Thus a player returning a score below his handicap will not have his handicap reduced.

(d) A competition will not lose the status of QUALIFYING COMPETITION when played under conditions when, because of work proceeding or ground conditions in the area, pegging-up has been made obligatory by the club on a restricted area of the course, provided the playing of QUALIFYING COMPETITIONS under such conditions has the prior approval of the UNION or AREA AUTHORITY.

3. Upwards adjustment of Handicaps

(a) Clubs may elect to adjust handicaps upwards at the end of each calendar month or at shorter intervals, including immediate adjustment after completion of each QUALIFYING COMPETITION at the club.

(b) There could be slight differences in EXACT HANDICAPS produced by each method when comparison is made at the end of a calendar month.

(c) The procedure for recording NETT DIFFERENTIALS set out in the Scheme should be adhered to whatever method is used.

(d) There is no objection to clubs electing to adjust handicaps upwards at the end of each calendar month, or at more frequent intervals, taking steps to adjust and record EXACT and PLAYING HANDICAPS so that at the end of each month they correspond with those derived by adjusting handicaps after the playing of each QUALIFYING COMPETITION.

4. Limitation of Handicaps

Clubs have inquired whether they may impose a limit of handicap to some of their competitions e.g. insist that a 24 handicap player competes from a handicap of 18. This is permitted by Rule of Golf 33-1. However, when recording the players' scores for handicapping purposes, adjustments must be made to ensure that the NETT DIFFERENTIAL is recorded from his current PLAYING HANDICAP i.e. in the example quoted 24 instead of 18.

This is comparatively simple for MEDAL COMPETITION, but is impractical for Stableford and Par competitions as it is unlikely for example that a player would record a score at a hole where a stroke allowance of one from an 18 handicap gave him no points, whereas from a handicap of 24 with a stroke allowance of two at that particular hole he might have registered one point.

5. Incomplete Cards and No Returns

(a) All cards must be returned, whether complete or not.

(b) It is expected that every player who enters for an 18-hole QUALIFYING COMPETITION intends to complete the round.

(c) Since an Incomplete Card and a No Return have the effect of increasing a player's handicap, the club would be justified in refusing to accept a card or record a 'N.R.' when the player has walked in after playing only a few holes.

(d) Cards should not be issued to players

when there is obviously insufficient light for them to complete the round.

(e) Sympathetic consideration should be given to players who have had to discontinue play for any cause considered to be reasonable by the organising committee.

(f) Clauses 17 and 19 of the Scheme give clubs the discretion to deal with players who persistently submit Incomplete Cards or make No Returns if they consider they are attempting to 'build a handicap'.

6. Reduction of Handicaps during a Competition

Where the conditions of a competition do not provide otherwise the handicap of a player applying at the beginning of a competition shall apply throughout that competition. This provision shall apply to a competition in which supplementary prizes are awarded for the best scores returned in an individual round or in combinations of individual rounds of the competition. The provisions shall not apply in circumstances where the winner is the player returning the lowest aggregate score in two or more separate competitions.

Where a player's handicap has been reduced during the course of a competition in which the original handicap continues to apply the player shall play from his reduced handicap in all other competitions commencing after the handicap reduction.

7. Overseas Scores

Scores returned in tournaments organised by the European Golf Association are QUALIFYING SCORES for handicapping purposes and must be returned to the HOME CLUB pursuant to clause 13.(7). Other scores returned in overseas tournaments may be returned and used, if considered appropriate, under the terms of clause 19.

8. Clause 19

Applications have been made to CONGU for approval of formulae which reduce handicaps by more than the reductions required by clause 16. Clubs have asked for permission to effect reductions on this basis under the authority given by clause 19. The decision of CONGU is that reductions made in this way are not permitted.

Reductions pursuant to clause 19 can be made only when the HANDICAP COMMITTEE has reason to believe that the handicap of a player may be too high. The Committee must consider all available information regarding the player's ability. A low score in a single event is not sufficient evidence alone to justify a clause 19 reduction.

If the handicap of any player is reduced other than to the extent required by clause 16 or by the correct application of clause 19, the player's handicap will not be a CONGU handicap and cannot be used in any competition for which a CONGU handicap is required.

Stationery

Enquiries regarding storage binders and handicap record sheets suitable for use in connection with the Standard Scratch Score and Handicapping Scheme 1983 to be directed to Hon. Secretary of the Council of National Golf Unions: A. Thirlwell, Formby Golf Club, Formby, Liverpool L37 1LQ.

Forms of application for an alteration to the Basic Standard Scratch Score or an addition for course value to the Provisional Standard Scratch Score may be obtained from the Secretaries of:

(a) County Golf Unions or District Committees.
(b) Area Authorities.
(c) National Golf Unions.
(d) Council of National Golf Unions.

Application of Handicaps

Stroke Index

Each club should draw up a list, called the Stroke Index, giving the order of holes at which any handicap strokes awarded should be taken. This order should be printed on the club's score card. The general principle for fixing the order of the Stroke Index is that the hole at which it is most difficult to achieve par should be Stroke Index 1, the next most difficult, Stroke Index 2 and so on until the easiest which should be Stroke Index 18.

However, certain other factors should be taken into consideration. Stroke Index 1 should not be one of the very early or very late holes on the course. The reason is that if a game were to finish all square and go on to the 19th and subsequent holes to determine the winner, the person in receipt of only one stroke would have an unfair advantage if he were to receive it at the 19th or 20th. Similarly, if Stroke Index 1 were a hole at the very end of the round, then the person in receipt of only one stroke might never be able to use it as the game might well be over by then. In general, therefore, Stroke Index 1 should not be at holes 1, 2, 17 or 18.

The other important factor to be taken into account in fixing the order of Stroke Index is that the strokes should be fairly evenly spread out over the 18 holes. If Stroke Index 1 is in the first 9 holes, Stroke Index 2 should be in the second 9 holes and so on. For example, if a person were to receive, say, four strokes, it would not be fair if he received them all in the early holes or all in the late holes.

Competition Formats and Handicap Allowances

Note 1: *In all calculations of handicap allowances, fractions under $^1/_2$ are ignored and those of $^1/_2$ or over are rounded up to the next higher figure.*

Note 2: *Handicap allowances shown are recommendations only. They are not Rules of Golf. The allowance to be used is at the discretion of the committee who should stipulate that allowance in the conditions of the competition.*

Competitions take two basic forms – match play or stroke play. In match play two players or sides compete against each other on a hole by hole basis. In stroke play a player or side competes against the whole field on his score over the whole round or rounds.

Single

Format
One player competes directly against one other player. It applies only to match play.

Handicap Allowance
The player with the higher handicap of the two receives strokes amounting to $^3/_4$ of the difference between the two players' handicaps. These strokes are taken at the holes indicated by the Stroke Index.

Foursome

Format
Two players form a side and hit alternate shots with one ball. The two players drive alternately from successive tees. Can be used for both match play and stroke play.

Handicap Allowance
Match play: The two players on each side add their handicaps together. The couple with the higher combined handicaps receive strokes amounting to $^3/_8$ of the difference between the combined handicaps of the two sides. These strokes are taken at the holes indicated by the Stroke Index.

Stroke play: The two players forming a side add their handicaps together and divide by 2. This figure is deducted from the side's gross score.

Mixed Foursome

Format
Same as Foursome except that each side must consist of a man and a woman.

Handicap Allowance
Same as Foursome.

Four-Ball Better-Ball

Format
Two players form a side, each playing his own ball throughout. The better score of the partners is the score of the side. Can be used for both match play and stroke play.

Handicap Allowance
Match play: The three players with the highest handicaps of the four each receive strokes amounting to $^3/_4$ of the difference between their own handicaps and that of the lowest handicap of the four. These strokes are taken at the holes indicated by the Stroke Index. *Example:* A–16; B–12; C–20; D–8. Player A would receive $(16–8)\times^3/_4=6$ strokes; B would receive $(12–8)\times^3/_4=3$ strokes; C would receive $(20–8)\times^3/_4=9$ strokes; D would receive 0 strokes.

Stroke play: $^3/_4$ of each player's full handicap

is allocated at the holes according to the Stroke Index and the stroke or strokes deducted at these holes.

Four-Ball Aggregate

Format
Two players form a side, each playing his own ball throughout. The combined score of the two partners is the score for the side. Can be used for both match play and stroke play.

Handicap Allowance
Match play: Same as Four-ball Better-ball.
Stroke play: Same as Four-ball Better-ball.

Greensome

Format
Two players form a side and both drive off each tee. Either ball may be selected to continue the hole and subsequent shots are played alternately until the hole is completed. *Example:* If player A's drive is selected at any hole, B must play the second shot at that hole, A the third shot and so on alternately until the ball is holed and vice versa if player B's drive is selected. Can be used for both match play and stroke play.

Handicap Allowance
Match play: Multiply the lower handicap of the two partners by .6 and the higher handicap by .4 and add the two figures together to give the full greensome handicap of the side. The couple with the higher greensome handicap receive strokes amounting to $^3/_4$ of the difference between the greensome handicaps of the two sides. These strokes are taken at the holes indicated by the Stroke Index. *Example:* A–2; B–10; C–8; D–12. AB *v* CD: Side AB full greensome handicap=(2×.6)+(10×.4)=5.2. Side CD full greensome handicap =(8×.6)+ (12×.4)=9.6. Side CD receives stroke amounting to $^3/_4$ of the difference between the two couples, i.e. (9.6–5.2)×$^3/_4$=3 strokes.
Stroke play: The two players forming a side deduct their full greensome handicap (as calculated above) from their gross score.

Bogey/Par

Format
Each player or side plays against the bogey (or par) for each hole, counting a win if he holes out in less than the bogey (or par) for the hole, a half if he equals it and a loss if he holes out in more. The aggregate of wins, losses and halves is taken to give a final score of so many holes up (or down as the case may be) to bogey (or par). Suitable for stroke play only.

Handicap Allowance
Each player receives strokes amounting to $^3/_4$ of his full handicap. In the case of foursomes, each side receives strokes amounting to $^3/_8$ of the combined handicaps of the partners. In all cases these strokes are allocated at the holes according to the Stroke Index and the stroke or strokes deducted at these holes.

Stableford

Format
The Stableford system of scoring was invented in 1931 by Dr Frank Stableford of the Wallasey and Royal Liverpool Golf Clubs and the first competition was played on 16th May, 1932 at Wallasey GC. Each player or side plays against the par for each hole and receives points according to how he scores in relation to par. The scoring system is as follows: 2 or more over par–0 points; 1 over par–1 point; par–2 points; 1 under par–3 points; 2 under par–4 points; 3 under par–5 points and so on. The number of points gained at each of the 18 holes is added together to give a total points score. Suitable for stroke play only.

Handicap Allowance
$^7/_8$ of full handicap.

Eclectic

Format
Competitors play two or more rounds choosing their better or best score at each hole to make up their eclectic score. Suitable for stroke play only.

Handicap Allowance
If played over two rounds, each competitor deducts five-sixths of his full handicap from his eclectic score for the two rounds. If played over three rounds, deduct four-fifths of his handicap from his eclectic score. If played over four rounds deduct $^3/_4$, five rounds, $^2/_3$, and six or more rounds, $^1/_2$.

Round Robin

Format
This is a form of league where each competitor or side plays every other competitor or side in the league. Suitable for match play only and can be used for singles, foursomes, four-ball better-ball, four-ball aggregate or greensomes, with the appropriate handicap allowance applying according to the type of competition.

Mixed Events

In competitions where men and women compete on an equal footing, the women's handicaps should be increased by the difference between the men's and ladies' Standard Scratch Scores if the women play from the ladies' tees. If the women play from the men's tees, their handicaps should be increased by the difference between the two Standard Scratch Scores plus an equitable figure (somewhere between 2 and 6) to take account of the distance between the men's and ladies' tees, one stroke being added for every 200 yards of difference over the 18 holes.

This adjustment does not apply where each side must consist of a man and woman; it only applies where women are in direct competition with men or where a side may consist of any combination of men and women, i.e. two men, two women or one man and one woman.

Bisques

Instead of receiving strokes to be taken at holes according to the Stroke Index, in match play friendly games, a number of bisques can be agreed upon instead. A bisque is a stroke which may be used at any hole the recipient decides upon after the completion of the hole. Because bisques can be used more advantageously than strokes, which may be of no value at certain holes, a lesser number of bisques than handicap strokes allowance is usually agreed upon. A player may use any number of bisques from his quota at any hole but he must announce whether he is using any of them before any stroke is played from the next tee. The bisque form of handicapping is not used in official competitions. It is suitable only for singles or foursomes, not for four-ball games.

Draws for Match Play Competitions

Cold Draw

When the number of entries is not a whole power of 2, i.e. 4, 8, 16, 32, 64 etc, a number of first round byes are necessary. Subtract the number of entries from the nearest of these numbers above the number of entries to give the number off byes.
Example: (a) 28 entries – subtracting from 32 gives 4 first round byes; (b) 33 entries – subtracting from 64 gives 31 first round byes.

All names (or numbers representing names) are put in a hat and the requisite number of byes drawn out singly and placed in pairs in the second round of the draw, alternately at the top and bottom, i.e. the first two names go at the top of the draw, the next two at the bottom and so on until all the byes have been drawn. If there is an odd number of byes, the last drawn is bracketed

to play against the winner of either the first or last first round match. Having drawn all the byes, the remaining names are then drawn and placed in pairs in the first round in the order drawn in the middle of the draw.

Automatic Draw

When a stroke play qualifying round(s) is used to determine the qualifiers for the ensuing match play, the automatic draw is used, based on the qualifying position of each qualifier, i.e. the leading qualifier is number 1 in the draw, the second qualifier is number 2 and so on.

The following table gives the automatic draw for up to 64 qualifiers. Use the first column for 64 qualifiers, the second column for 32 qualifiers, and so on.

64	32	16	8	4	2
1					
64	1				
33		1			
32	32				
17			1		
48	17				
49		16			
16	16				
9				1	
56	9				
41		9			
24	24				
25			8		
40	25				
57		8			
8	8				
5					1
60	5				
37		5			
28	28				
21			5		
44	21				
53		12			
12	12				
13				4	
52	13				
45		13			
20	20				
29			4		
36	29				
61		4			
4	4				
3					
62	3				
35		3			
30	30				
19			3		
46	19				
51		14			
14	14				
11				3	
54	11				
43		11			
22	22				
27			6		
38	27				
59		6			
6	6				
7					2
58	7				
39		7			
26	26				
23			7		
42	23				
55		10			
10	10				
15				2	
50	15				
47		15			
18	18				
31			2		
34	31				
63		2			
2	2				

The LGU System of Handicapping

Effective from 1 February 1985

CONTENTS

I. Summary of principal changes introduced in the 1989 edition 789
II. Definitions 789

III.   **Introduction**
1. Basis of the system 790
2. Overseas Unions and Clubs 790
3. Queries 790

IV.   **The player's rights and responsibilities**
1. General: Playing off correct handicap 790
   Handicap Reduction 790
   Playing away from Home 790
2. Eligibility to hold an LGU handicap 790
3. How to gain an LGU handicap 790
4. Scores acceptable for LGU handicap 791
5. Calculation of LGU handicap 791
6. Annual Revision and lapsed handicaps 792
7. Special categories of LGU handicap 794
8. Membership of more than one club 795

Index 796

Section 1 Summary of Principal Changes Introduced in the 1989 Edition

1. Category B has been extended to include handicaps 6–9. Handicap categories are now as follows:

A = plus to 3
B = 4 to 9
C = 10 to 18
D = 19 to 29
E = 30 to 36*

2. Scores for handicaps are now acceptable from courses with a SS of 60 or over in all categories.

3. The Extra Day book has been re-introduced and there is a limit of 20 Extra Day cards in any LGU year.
4. Only the first round of an Eclectic competition may count as a competition score for handicapping purposes.
5. All lapsed handicaps may now be increased by 2 strokes at Revision except in categories A and B where the increase may be limited to one if the requisite number of 'competition' or 'away' scores have not been submitted.
NOTE: Suggestions for alterations and additions to the Handicapping System must be received by the Administrator, Ladies Golf Union, before 1st July in order to be considered for adoption in the following year.

Section II Definitions

Throughout the text defined terms are printed as capitals when used for the first time.

Committee

The term **Committee** is deemed to refer to the Committee of the Ladies' Section. The term **Club Committee** refers to the Committee in charge of the course. Where the management of the club and/or course is entirely in the hands of the Ladies' Committee the term **Club Committee** shall be deemed to refer to such.

Completed Scores

A score is deemed completed for handicap purposes when a gross score has been entered on the card for each hole and the card has been checked and signed by both marker and player. The card should also show the player's name and the date.

Differential

The differential is the difference between the gross score and the Scratch Score of the course on which it is returned.
The average differential is the sum of the differentials divided by their number.

Extra Day Scores

An Extra Day Score is one which is not returned in competition.

Handicap Advisers

Handicap Advisers and their Deputies are persons appointed by the National Organisations to assist HANDICAP SECRETARIES in dealing with problems and exceptional cases, and to keep records of all players with handicaps under 4.

Handicap Secretary

A player's Handicap Secretary is the Handicap Secretary of her HOME CLUB. The Handicap Secretary of an INDIVIDUAL MEMBER of the LGU or of a NATIONAL ORGANISATION is respectively, (1) the Administrator of the LGU or (2) the Secretary of the National Organisation. The Handicap Secretary of a visitor from overseas, unless she joins an affiliated club as an annual member, is the Administrator LGU.

Home Club

The Home Club is the club which a member of more than one club has chosen to be that where her handicap records shall be maintained and of which the Handicap Secretary shall be her Handicap Secretary.

Home Course

A Home Course is any course situated at and associated with a player's Home Club.

Individual Members

a. of the LGU: Players temporarily resident overseas are entitled to apply for individual membership of the LGU.
b. of the National Organisations: Players unable to become an annual playing member of an affiliated club may apply to their National Organisation for individual membership.

Lapsed Handicaps

A handicap has lapsed if four scores have not been returned in an LGU year by Category C, D and E players, six scores by Category B players (unless increasing to Category C) and ten scores by Category A players (unless increasing to Category B).

LGU Tees and Teeing Grounds

The LGU tees, indicated by a permanent mark on the right hand side of the tee, are those from which the SCRATCH SCORE has been fixed. The actual teeing ground in play (see Rules of Golf Definition) is indicated by **red** tee markers which, for the convenience of the greenkeeper, may be moved in any direction from the permanent mark provided the hole is not altered in length by more than ten yards.
NOTE: In the event of the teeing ground having been accidentally or otherwise moved beyond the permitted limit the score cannot count for handicap or for LGU Competitions unless a special Scratch Score has been allotted by the National Organisation.

Live score

A live score is one which has been returned (in accordance with Regulation IV.4) in the current LGU year (February 1 to January 31) or in the preceding LGU year.

National Organisation

The National Organisations are: the English Ladies' Golf Association, the Irish Ladies' Golf Union, the Scottish Ladies' Golfing Association and the Welsh Ladies' Golf Union. In the case of overseas affiliated clubs for **National Organisation** read **LGU**.

Scratch Score

The Scratch Score of a course is the score expected of a Scratch player in normal Spring and Autumn conditions of wind and weather.

Section III   Introduction

1. Basis of the System

The chief features of the LGU System of Handicapping are: that all handicaps shall be fixed on the basis of the LGU SCRATCH SCORE; that handicaps shall be assessed on actual scores returned and not on general form; and that the player's handicap shall be the same in every club.

2. Overseas Unions and Clubs

Overseas affiliated Unions and Clubs shall be permitted to make such adjustments to these regulations as may be deemed by their Executive Committee to be necessary on account of climatic or other conditions peculiar to the territory administered by them, so long as these adjustments do not depart from the fundamental principles of the LGU System of Handicapping as stated in the paragraph above or contravene the Rules of Golf as laid down by the Royal & Ancient Golf Club of St Andrews. The LGU must be informed as and when such adjustments are made.

3. Queries

Queries on LGU Regulations or the Rules of Golf should be submitted in accordance with the following procedures:

a. Committees of Affiliated Clubs should submit queries to their NATIONAL ORGANISATION.

b. Members of Affiliated Clubs may submit queries to their National Organisation and must have their statements signed as read on behalf of the Ladies' Committee. If there is any difference of opinion the Committee or opposing party should submit their own statement in writing.

c. Secretaries of Affiliated Clubs should refer queries on handicaps to their HANDICAP SECRETARY.

d. Handicap Secretaries of Affiliated Clubs should refer queries to their HANDICAP ADVISER or National Organisation, in that order.

e. Overseas Unions and Clubs. In the case of clubs affiliated to an affiliated Ladies' Golf Union outside Great Britain and Ireland or directly affiliated to the LGU, queries should be submitted to the LGU. Statements should be signed as read on behalf of such Union or Club Committee.

Correspondence of this nature sent to the LGU and the National Organisations is filed for reference and cannot be returned.

Section IV   The Player's Responsibilities and Rights

1. General

Playing off the Correct Handicap. It is the player's responsibility to know and to apply the Handicapping Regulations and to play off the correct handicap at all times. She should be able to produce a current Handicap Certificate when required to do so. In case of doubt or disagreement between the player and her Handicap Secretary as to what is the player's correct handicap, she should play from the lower until an official decision can be obtained from the Handicap Adviser or the National Organisation.

Handicap Reduction. Any reduction in handicap is automatic and comes into force immediately, **except**

> **i.** in the event of a tie in a competition, where this is resolved by a replay or a play-off; **and**
>
> **ii.** in a 36-, 54- or 72-hole competition played within eight days.

Playing away from Home. A player must notify her Handicap Secretary of any score (which might affect her handicap) returned by her on any course other than at her HOME CLUB.

2. Eligibility to Hold an LGU Handicap

An LGU handicap may be obtained and held by an amateur lady golfer who is **either**

a. an annual playing member, including a country, junior or life member (whether honorary or paying) of a club affiliated to the LGU either directly or through its National Organisation; **or**

b. an individual member of either the LGU or one of the four National Organisations; **or**

c. a temporary member of an affiliated club, provided her membership is to last for a period of not less than twelve months.

NOTE: Should membership cease or expire the player's LGU handicap is no longer valid, but her scores remain LIVE if returned before such cessation or expiry.

3. How to Gain an LGU Handicap

Four scores must be returned on the course or courses of an LGU affiliated club or clubs, the Scratch Score of which must be not less than 60. Play must be in twos (threes and fours are not acceptable), no more than one player per marker, and must be in accordance with Regulations IV.4(a), (b), (c), (d) and (e).

4. Scores Acceptable for LGU Handicap

To be acceptable for handicap:

a. Scores must be returned in accordance with the Rules of Golf as approved by the Royal & Ancient Golf Club of St Andrews and with the Club's Local Rules and By-Laws, which must not contravene any R. & A. Rule or LGU Regulation. The gross score must be entered for every hole.

b. Scores must be returned on the course of an LGU affiliated club with an LGU Scratch Score of not less than 60. Play must be from LGU tees. Scores returned on a course of which the player is not a member must be countersigned by an official of the local ladies' committee, who should certify that the Scratch Score is correctly stated. Completed cards should either be returned in person by the player to her Handicap Secretary without delay or left in the card box of the club visited, together with the name and address of the home club and the cost of postage.

NOTE: Scores returned on non-affiliated courses overseas (see the Lady Golfer's Handbook) may count for handicap at the discretion of the LGU. Such cards, duly countersigned by a local official as showing the correct Scratch Score and accompanied by relevant information about local conditions, type of soil, terrain, course difficulty, etc., should be forwarded to the Administrator, Ladies' Golf Union, The Scores, St Andrews, Fife, with a stamped, addressed envelope to the Handicap Secretary of the player's Home Club.

c. Scores must be marked by an annual playing member of a recognised golf club, who has or has had a handicap. A marker should not mark the card of more than one player.

d. A score must be that of the first round of the day on any one course, except in the case of a competition consisting of 36 holes played on one day, when both scores shall count.

e. Scores may be returned when the following conditions apply:

    i. Winter Conditions. Where, for the preservation of the course, the Club Committee has made a Local Rule that the ball may be teed or placed without penalty through the green.

    ii. Summer Conditions. a. Where, for the preservation of the course, the Club Committee has made a Local Rule that the ball may be placed without penalty through the green; and **b.** where, for the preservation of the course, the Club Committee has made a Local Rule that tee pegs must be used through the green and a deduction from the Scratch Score of two strokes where more than nine holes are affected, and of one stroke where nine or fewer holes are affected, has been made by the Ladies' Committee (and notified to the area Scratch Score Committee member).

    iii. The Green. Where, for the preservation of the green, a temporary hole (see Rules of Golf Definitions) is off but adjacent to the green, provided this does not alter the length of the hole by more than ten yards.

NOTE: LGU TEES. Where, for the preservation of the course, the teeing ground has been moved beyond the permitted ten yards, scores may count for handicap only if a special Scratch Score has been allotted by the National Organisation.

f. All scores returned in Stroke Competitions, even if declared null and void, count for LGU handicap purposes, subject to Regulations IV.4(a) to (e) above and provided competitors play from LGU TEES (see Definition and Note) and the SS of the course is not less than 60. Scores may be returned in twos, threes or fours, as arranged by the Committee.

NOTE: The exception to this is in a competition where the best-ball or better-ball score (see Rules of Golf Definitions) is to count.

g. i EXTRA DAY SCORES must be returned in accordance with Regulations IV.4(a) to (e) and should normally be marked in twos, but at the discretion of the Committee may be marked in threes, in which case a notice to this effect must be posted on the Notice Board (but see Regulation IV.3 for gaining a first handicap). Extra Day Scores marked in fours are not acceptable.

ii Players may take out a maximum of 20 Extra Day cards in any LGU year. Each Club should keep a book for the purpose of a player recording her intention to complete an Extra Day card. A player taking out an Extra Day card on an away course must include this in her 20 and must inform her home club of such a card.

h. Gross scores returned in a competition from which a player has been disqualified under Rule of Golf 6–2b on her nett score shall count for handicap.

i. Eclectic Competitions: The first round only of an eclectic competition may count as a competition score.

5. Calculation of an LGU Handicap

Handicaps are divided into five categories: Silver Division – A, B, C – and Bronze Division – D and E. Handicaps are calculated as follows, on the basis of live scores returned in accordance with Regulation IV.4 above:

NOTE 1: For all handicaps, scores must be returned on courses with a Scratch Score of not less than 60.

NOTE 2: In all calculations above Scratch $^1/_2$, two-thirds and three-quarters count as 1 and one-third, one-quarter count as 0. In all calculations below Scratch fractions of $^1/_2$ and less count as 0, fractions greater than $^1/_2$ count as 1.

a. Bronze Division

(i) **Category E, 36*–30.** The handicap is the difference between the player's best live score and the Scratch Score of the course on which it was played, i.e. the handicap is her best DIFFERENTIAL. If the differential is more than 36 the handicap is 36* (**Example E** [1]) If the differential is 36–30 then that is the handicap (**Example E** [2]). If the best differential is less than 30 the handicap is 30 until the average of the **two** best differentials is less than $29^1/_2$ (**Example E** [3]).

EXAMPLES:

E^1 Best gross score	117	SS 72	Differential	45
				Handicap 36*
E^2 Best gross score	102	SS 69	Differential	33
				Handicap 33
E^3 Best gross scores	101	SS 74	Differential	27
	106	SS 70	Previous best differential	36
			Average differential	31½
				Handicap 30

(ii) **Category D, 29–19.** The handicap is the average of the two best differentials (**Examples D¹, D** [2]), but if the average is less than $18^1/_2$ the handicap is 19 until the average of the **four** best differentials is less than $18^1/_2$ (**Example D** [3]).

EXAMPLES:

D^1 Gross score	99	SS 73	Best differential	26
Gross score	104	SS 73	Previous best differential	31
			Average differential	28½
				Handicap 29
D^2 Gross score	95	SS 71	Best differential	24
Gross score	98	SS 70	Previous best differential	28
			Average differential	26
				Handicap 26

D^3 Gross scores	SS	Best differentials	
87	72	15	
92	72	20	Average 17½ but ... **Handicap 19**
96	73	23	
94	71	23	
Average diff (of four)		20¼	**Handicap 19**

b. Silver Division

(i). **Category C, 18–10.** The handicap is the average of the four best differentials (**Example C** [1]), but if this average is less than $9^1/_2$ the handicap is 10 until the conditions for Category B are fulfilled.

EXAMPLES:

C^1	Best differentials		
	10		
	11		
	13		
	17	Average 12¾	**Handicap 13**

C^2 EDS=Extra Day Scores; CS=Competition Scores, SS not less than 70.

	Best differentials		
	3 (EDS)		
	5 (CS)		
	6 (EDS)		
	7 (CS)	Average 5¼ but ... **Handicap 7**
	8 (CS)		
	9 (CS)		
	10 (CS)		
	9 (CS)		

Average differential of six Comp scores = 8   **Handicap 7**

(ii) **Category B, 9–4.** The handicap is the average of the six best differentials of scores returned in competition. (**Example B** [1]), but if this average is less than $3^1/_2$ the handicap is 4 until the conditions for Category A are fulfilled (**Example B** [2]).

EXAMPLES:

B^1 Best differentials from competition scores on courses with a SS of not less than 70:

7		
5		
5		
6		
4		
4	Average differential 5⅙	**Handicap 5**

B^2 Best differentials from competition scores on courses with a SS of not less than 70: H1, H2=Home Courses, A1, A2 etc.=Away Courses.

3 (H1)		
5 (H2)		
4 (H1)		
2 (H1)		
2 (H1)		
3 (A1)	Average differential 3⅙ but ... **Handicap 4**
6 (A1)		
7 (A2)		
6 (H2)		
8 (A1)	Average differential 4.6	**Handicap 4**

(iii) **Category A, 3 and under.** To obtain a handicap of 3 or under a player must return at least ten scores in competition. Only six of these scores may be from a Home Course, and the remaining four must be from at least two different Away courses. The handicap is the average of the ten best differentials so obtained (**Examples A** [1] **and A** [2]).

EXAMPLES:

A^1 Best differentials from competition scores on courses
with a SS of not less than 70:

    0 (H)
  +1 (H)
  +1 (H)
    0 (H)
    3 (H)
    0 (H)
    1 (A1)
    0 (A1)
    1 (A2)
    3 (A2)   Average differential 0.6

Handicap 1

A^2 Best differentials from competition scores on courses
with a SS of not less than 70:

  +1 (H)
  +1 (H)
  +2 (H)
    1 (A1)
  +2 (H)
  +1 (A2)
    0 (H)
  +1 (H)
    2 (A3)
    0 (A1)   Average differential +0.5

Handicap Scratch (+0.5=0)

6. Annual Revision of Handicaps and Lapsed Handicaps

a. General

On 31 January each year all handicaps shall be recalculated on the basis of scores returned during the preceding twelve months and in accordance with the Regulations in force during that period. Any increase in handicap resulting from such recalculation shall be limited by the Table of Permitted Increases (Table I) for Revised Handicaps set out below. At no other time during the year may a player's handicap be increased (except in accordance with Regulation IV.7(b) or (c)).

TABLE I – TABLE OF PERMITTED INCREASES FOR REVISED HANDICAPS

Handicaps plus to 34 may go up 2 strokes.
Handicap 35 may go up 1 stroke.

A handicap limited by the Table of Permitted Increases for Revised Handicaps should be marked with a * until the calculation of live scores results in a handicap equal to or less than that held.

b. Minimum Number of Scores to be Returned

Handicap Categories E, D, C. To retain a handicap players with handicaps 36*–10 must have returned at least 4 scores.

Handicap Category B. To retain a handicap players with handicaps 9–4 must have returned at least 6 scores. If 6 scores have been returned but not all in competition, the handicap shall be increased by one stroke and shall be marked with a ∅ until the appropriate

scores have been returned and the calculation results in a handicap equal to or less than that held prior to Revision.

Exception: If players with handicap 9 prior to Revision have returned at least 4 scores (not necessarily all in competition) and the average of the best 4 is $9\frac{1}{2}$ or more, the handicap shall be retained and shall be calculated in accordance with Regulations governing handicaps 18–10 and the Table of Permitted Increases (Table I) for Revised Handicaps.

Handicap Category A. To retain a handicap players with handicaps 3 and under must have returned at least 10 scores. If 10 scores have been returned in competition, but the necessary 'away' scores have not been returned, the Revised handicap shall be marked with a ∅ until the necessary 'away' scores have been returned. If 10 scores have been returned but not all in competition, the handicap shall be increased by one stroke and shall be marked with a ∅ until all the necessary conditions have been fulfilled and the calculation results in a handicap equal to or less than that held prior to Revision.

Exception: If players with handicap 3 prior to Revision have returned at least 6 scores in competition and the average of the best 6 is $3\frac{1}{2}$ or more, the handicap shall not lapse and shall be calculated in accordance with 'Regulations Governing Handicaps 9-4' and the 'Table of Permitted Increases (Table I) for Revised Handicaps'.

c. Lapsed Handicaps

A handicap lapses if a player has not returned the minimum number of scores necessary to retain a handicap (see **b.** above). When a player's handicap has lapsed she does not have a valid handicap until the conditions have been fulfilled to regain it (see **d.** below).

d. To Regain a Handicap which has Lapsed

Handicap Categories E, D, C. To regain a handicap which has lapsed players with handicaps 36*–10 must return the number of Extra Day Scores necessary to increase the number of **live** scores to four. The handicap shall then be calculated in accordance with Regulations, but it shall be limited by the Table of Permitted Increases (Table II) for Lapsed Handicaps set out below and must be confirmed, before use, by the player's Handicap Secretary.

Handicap Category B. To regain a handicap which has lapsed players with handicaps 9–4 must return the necessary Extra Day Scores to increase the number of **live** scores to six. The handicap shall then be calculated in accordance with Regulations (except that the scores need not be returned in competition), but it shall be limited by the Table of Permitted Increases

(Table II) for Lapsed Handicaps set out below and must be confirmed, before use, by the player's Handicap Secretary. Until scores returned fulfil all the conditions necessary for this Category of player, the handicap shall be marked with a ∅.

Handicap Category A. To regain a handicap which has lapsed players with handicaps under 4 must return the necessary Extra Day Scores on courses with a Scratch Score of not less than 70 to increase the number of **live** scores to ten.

The handicap shall then be calculated in accordance with Regulations (except that the scores need not be returned in competition), but it shall be limited by the table of Permitted Increases (Table II) for Lapsed Handicaps set out below and must be confirmed, before use, by the player's Handicap Secretary. Until scores returned fulfil all the conditions necessary for this Category of player, the handicap shall be marked with a ∅.

Transition to a Higher Category. The number of scores required to regain a handicap by players in Categories A or B should be determined after taking into account the scores returned and the Table (II) of Permitted Increases for Lapsed Handicaps. For instance, a player previously in Category A, after a lapse of several years may require only six scores, and similarly a player previously in Category B may require only four, if the former handicap category is not maintained or bettered by the scores returned.

TABLE II – TABLE OF PERMITTED INCREASES FOR LAPSED HANDICAPS

(i) If lapsed for less than one year the handicap shall be limited to two strokes higher than that last held.

(ii) For each year in excess of one the handicap may be increased by a further stroke.

EXAMPLES:

	Handicap Lapsed	Necessary EDS Returned	Max Inc over Previous H'cap
(i)	January 31 1981	1981–82 (LGU year)	1 stroke (less than one year)
(ii)		1982–83 (LGU year)	2 strokes (one-two years)
(iii)		1983–84 (LGU year)	3 strokes (two+one year)
		1984–85 (LGU year)	4 strokes (two+two years)
		1985–86 (LGU year)	5 strokes (two+three years) and so on

A handicap limited by the Table of Permitted Increases for Lapsed Handicaps shall be marked with an asterisk.

7. Special Categories of Handicap

a. Juniors. An LGU Junior handicap (limit 45) may be obtained and held by any girl who is a junior, i.e. who has not reached her twelfth birthday on 1 January, by returning two scores over nine specified holes. Any nine holes on the course may be chosen to make up the round, at the discretion of the club, and a special SS for those holes must be obtained from the National Organisation. Each score returned, and the special SS for the nine holes, shall be doubled in order to arrive at the number of strokes above SS. Handicaps will be reduced in accordance with Regulations (one card 45–30, etc.). Juniors may hold a standard LGU handicap but may not hold both.

To retain a Junior LGU handicap two scores over nine holes must be returned annually.

An LGU Junior handicap shall be acceptable for all junior competitions, and these Regulations shall apply to all players with Junior handicaps. Handicap Certificates for LGU Junior handicaps will be issued by the Handicap Secretary and **the date and year when the player will attain her twelfth birthday must be entered on the Handicap Certificate.**

b. Former Professional Golfers. On reinstatement as an amateur a player who has been a professional golfer must apply for a handicap to the Administrator, LGU. The Executive Council shall, at their discretion, allot a handicap of not more than Scratch on the basis of live scores returned during the player's period of probation in accordance with the Regulations for Extra Day Scores and those governing handicaps of 3 and under.

For the first two years after reinstatement the player's Handicap Secretary must submit all scores returned twice yearly on 1 January and 1 July to the Administrator, LGU, The Scores, St. Andrews, Fife, KY16 9AT. Handicaps will be reviewed by the Executive Council and revised at their discretion.

c. After Serious Illness and Disablement. A person wishing to regain a handicap or have her handicap reassessed after serious illness or disablement may apply through her Club Committee to the National Organisation with all relevant details, including a minimum of four live scores returned, so that consideration may be given to the circumstances and the player may obtain a realistic handicap. Handicaps shall be adjusted in accordance with Regulations.

d. Individual Members and Visitors from Overseas. The handicaps of individual members of the LGU or of the National Organisations shall be managed by the Administrator of the LGU or the Secretary of the appropriate National Organisation. All scores returned must be countersigned by the Handicap Secretary of the club at which they were returned and forwarded to the appropriate Secretary, who will act as Handicap Secretary for these players.

Handicaps of visitors from overseas who are

not annual playing members of an affiliated club in Great Britain or Ireland shall be managed by the Administrator of the LGU, to whom scores should be forwarded after countersignature as above.

8. Membership of More than One Club

a. A member belonging to more than one affiliated club must inform the Ladies' Secretary and Handicap Secretary of each club of the names of other affiliated clubs to which she belongs and also of any scores (together with the Scratch Score) which may affect her handicap.

b. Handicap Secretary. If a player is a member of more than one club she must decide which club she wishes to be her Home Club for handicap purposes and notify the Ladies' Secretary of that club accordingly. A player's Handicap Secretary shall be the Handicap Secretary of her Home Club.

c. A member changing her Home Club must take her Handicap Exchange sheet and her Handicap Certificate to the Handicap Secretary of her new Home Club.

d. A member joining an additional club must inform the Ladies' Secretary and the Handicap Secretary of such club of her existing or lapsed handicap, and of the scores, with relative dates, on which it was gained, and also the names of all clubs of which she is or has been a member.

e. A member shall play on the same handicap at all clubs.

For details of the following, please refer to the Lady Golfer's Handbook:

* Scratch Scores
* LGU Tees and Teeing Grounds in Play
* Starting Places
* Handicap Records and Certificates
* LGU Silver and Bronze Medal Competitions
* LGU Gold and Silver Medal Competitions
* LGU Challenge Bowl Competitions
* Coronation Foursomes Competition
* LGU Pendant Competition
* Australian Spoons Competitions

INDEX	Section	No
Acceptable scores for handicap	IV	4.a-h
Additional club		
joining an	IV	8.d
Annual playing member		
eligible to hold LGU handicap	IV	2.a
Average differential		
Definition	II	
Away from home		
scores countersigned by local official	IV	4.b
scores returned to Handicap Secretary	IV	1 and 4.b
Basis of the System	III	1
Both scores count for handicap in 36-hole		
competition	IV	4.d
Bronze Division		
calculation of handicap	IV	5.a
Calculation of handicap	IV	5
Categories of handicap		
special	IV	7.b
Changes to the Handicapping Regulations		
summary of principal	I	
Changing Home Club	IV	8.c
Committee		
Definition	II	
Competition scores		
acceptable for handicap	IV	4.f
handicaps under 7	IV	5.b (ii) and (iii)
Competitions null and void		
scores count for handicap	IV	4.f
Completed scores		
Definition	II	
Deduction from SS in summer conditions	IV	4.e (ii)
Definitions	II	
Differential		
definition	II	
basis of handicap calculations	IV	5
Disablement		
reassessment of handicap after	IV	7.c
Eclectic Competitions	IV	4.i
Eligibility to hold LGU handicap	IV	2
Extra Day Scores		
Acceptable for handicap	IV	4.g
Definition	II	
To increase lives scores to four	IV	6.d
First round of the day	IV	4.d
Former Professional golfers		
handicaps for	IV	7.b
Gaining a handicap	IV	3
Green		
temporary hole for preservation of the course	IV	4.e (iii)
Gross score for every hole	IV	4.a
acceptable for handicap if disqualified on nett score	IV	4.h
Handicap Advisers		
Definition	II	
Queries from Handicap Secretaries	III	3.d

	Section	No
Handicap Certificates		
player should be able to produce.................	IV	1
Handicap Secretaries		
Definition...	II	
Disagreement between player and..............	IV	1
Queries	III	3.d
Home Club		
Definition...	II	
Changing	IV	8.c
Home Course		
Definition...	II	
Illness or Disablement		
reassessment of handicap after....................	IV	7.c
Increases		
Tables of Permitted..	IV	6
Individual members		
Definition...	II	
Eligible for LGU handicap	IV	2.b
Handicaps managed by LGU/National		
Secretary...	IV	7.d
Joining an additional club.............................	IV	8.d
Junior competitions..	IV	7.a
Junior handicaps	IV	7.a
Lapsed handicaps	IV	6.c
Definition...	II	
Regaining...	IV	6.d
LGU Tees and teeing grounds		
Definition...	II	
Moved beyond permitted limit.....................	IV	4.e Note
		4.f
Live score		
Definition...	II	
Calculation of handicap based on................	IV	5
Local Rules for preservation of the course	IV	4.e
Marking of scores		
marker's qualifications.................................	IV	4.c
no more than one per player	IV	3
Members of affiliated clubs		
queries..	III	3.b
Membership		
cessation of expiry of	IV	2 Note
of more than one club....................................	IV	8
National Organisation		
Definition...	II	
Null and void		
see Competitions		
Overseas		
scores returned on non-affiliated courses...	IV	4.b Note
Overseas Unions and clubs		
adjustments to regulations............................	III	2
queries..	III	3.e
Permitted Increases		
Tables of...	IV	6.a, 6.d
	I	4
Permitted limit of ten yards............................	IV	4.e Note
Player's responsibility to know and play off		
correct handicap...	IV	1

INDEX	Section	No
Professional golfers		
handicaps for former	IV	7.b
Queries and disputes		
procedures for submission	III	3
Reduction in handicap		
immediate	IV	1
Regaining a handicap after lapse	IV	6.d
Reinstatement as an Amateur		
handicap after	IV	7.b
Retaining a handicap		
minimum number of scores required	IV	6.b
Revision		
annual	IV	6
Rules of Golf		
scores to be in accordance with	IV	4 a
Scratch Score		
Definition	II	
Deduction in summer conditions	IV	4.e (ii)
Minimum	IV	3, 4.b, 5
Secretaries of affiliated clubs		
queries	III	3.c
Stroke Competitions		
scores count for handicap	IV	4.f
Teeing ground		
moved beyond permitted limit	IV	4.e Note
Teeing/placing through the green	IV	4.e (i) and (ii)
Temporary hole	IV	4.e (iii)
Temporary member		
eligible for LGU handicap	IV	2.c
Visitors from overseas		
handicaps managed by LGU Secretary	IV	7.d

Governing Bodies

Home Unions

Golfing Union of Ireland

The Golfing Union of Ireland, founded in 1891, embraces 263 Clubs. Its objects are:

(1) Securing the federation of the various Clubs.
(2) Arranging Amateur Championships, Inter-Provincial and Inter-Club Competitions, and International Matches.
(3) Securing a uniform standard of handicapping.
(4) Providing for advice and assistance to affiliated Clubs in all matters appertaining to Golf, and generally to promote the game in every way, in which this can be better done by the Union than by individual Clubs.

Its functions include the holding of the *Close* Championship for Amateur Golfers and Tournaments for Team Matches.

Its organisation consists of Provincial Councils in each of the four Provinces elected by the Clubs in the Province – each province electing a limited number of delegates to the Central Council which meets annually.

Welsh Golfing Union

The Welsh Golfing Union was founded in 1895 and is the second oldest of the four National Unions. Unlike the other Unions it is an association of Golf Clubs and Golfing Organisations. The present membership is 121. For the purpose of electing the Executive Council, Wales is divided into ten districts which between them return 22 members.

The objects of the Union are:

(a) To take any steps which may be deemed necessary to further the interests of the game in Wales.
(b) To hold a Championship Meeting or Meetings each year.
(c) To encourage, financially and/or otherwise, Inter-Club, Inter-County, and International Matches, and such other events as may be authorised by the Council.
(d) To assist in setting up and maintaining a uniform system of Handicapping.

(e) To assist in the maintenance of the Sports Turf Research Institute.
(f) To co-operate with the Royal & Ancient Golf Club of St Andrews through the medium of the Council of National Golf Unions.

Note: The union recognises the Royal & Ancient Golf Club of St Andrews as the ruling authority.

The Scottish Golf Union

The Scottish Golf Union was founded in 1920 and embraces 660 clubs. Subject to the stipulation and declaration that the Union recognises the Royal & Ancient Golf Club of St Andrews as the Ruling Authority in the game of golf, the objects of the Union are:

(a) To foster and maintain a high standard of Amateur Golf in Scotland and to administer and organise and generally act as the governing body of amateur golf in Scotland.
(b) To institute and thereafter carry through annually a Scottish Amateur Championship, a Scottish Open Amateur Stroke Play Championship and other such competitions and matches as they consider appropriate.
(c) To administer and apply the rules of the Standard Scratch Score and Handicapping Scheme as approved by the Council of National Golf Unions from time to time.
(d) To deal with other matters of general or local interest to amateur golfers in Scotland.

The Union's organisation consists of Area Committees covering the whole of Scotland. There are 16 Areas, each having its own Association or Committee elected by the Clubs in that particular area and each Area Association or Committee elects one delegate to serve on the Executive of the Union.

The English Golf Union

The English Golf Union was founded in 1924 and embraces 34 County Unions with over 1,350 affiliated clubs, 22 clubs overseas, and over 130 Golfing Societies and Associations. Its objects are:

(1) To further the interests of Amateur Golf in England.
(2) To assist in maintaining a uniform system of handicapping.
(3) To arrange an English Championship; an English Stroke Play Championship; an English County Championship, International and other Matches and Competitions.
(4) To co-operate with the Royal & Ancient Golf Club of St Andrews and the Council of National Golf Unions.
(5) To co-operate with other National Golf Unions and Associations in such manner as may be decided.

The Council of National Golf Unions

At a meeting of Representatives of Golf Unions and Associations in Great Britain and Ireland, called at the special request of the Scottish Golf Union, and held in York, on 14th February, 1924, resolutions were adopted from which the Council of National Golf Unions was constituted.

The Council holds an Annual Meeting in March, and such other meetings as may be necessary. Two representatives are elected from each national Home Union – England, Scotland, Ireland and Wales – and hold office until the next Annual meeting when they are eligible for re-election.

The principal function of the Council, as laid down by the York Conference, was to formulate a system of Standard Scratch Scores and Handicapping, and to co-operate with the Royal & Ancient Championship Committee in matters coming under their jurisdiction. The responsibilities undertaken by the Council at the instance of the Royal & Ancient Golf Club or the National Unions are as follows:

1. The Standard Scratch Score and Handicapping Scheme, formulated in March, 1926, approved by the Royal & Ancient, and last revised in 1983.
2. The nomination of two members on the Board of Management of The Sports Turf Research Institute, with an experimental station at St Ives, Bingley, Yorkshire.
3. The management of the Annual Amateur International Matches between the four countries – England, Scotland, Ireland and Wales.

United States Golf Association

The USGA is the national governing body of golf. Its single most important goal is preserving the integrity and values of the game.

Formed on 22nd December, 1894, a year

when two clubs proclaimed different US Amateur Champions, representatives of five clubs met at a dinner at the Calumet Club in New York City. They created a central governing body to establish uniform rules, to conduct national championships and to nurture the virtues of sportsmanship in golf.

The names of the standing committees give an idea of what the USGA does:

Rules of Golf, Championship, Amateur Status and Conduct, Implements and Ball, Handicap, Women's, Sectional Affairs, Green Section, Public Links, Women's Public Links, Junior Championship, Girls' Junior, Senior Championship, Senior Women's Championship, Bob Jones Award, Museum, Green Section Award, Finance, Public Information, Membership, Regional Association, Associates, Intercollegiate Relations, Mid-Amateur Championship, International Team Selection, Development, Turfgrass Research, Nominating.

The USGA, as the governing body of the game in the United States, makes and interprets the Rules of Golf in co-operation with the Royal & Ancient Golf Club of St Andrews, Scotland; developed and maintains the national system of handicapping; controls the standards of the ball and the implements of the game; works in turfgrass and turf management; and, generally speaking, preserves and promotes the game.

The Professional Golfers' Association

The Professional Golfers' Association was founded in 1901 to promote interest in the game of golf; to protect and advance the mutual and trade interests of its members; to arrange and hold meetings and tournaments periodically for the members; to institute and operate funds for the benefit of the members; to assist the members to obtain employment; and effect any other objects of a like nature as may be determined from time to time by the Association.

Classes of Membership

There shall be nine (9) classes of membership:
(i) Class A   Members engaged as the nominated professional on a full-time basis at a PGA Club, PGA Course or PGA Driving Range in one of the seven Regions; and members engaged as the nominated professional on a full-time basis, at an establishment in one of the seven Regions at which the public can play and/or practise which, in the opinion of the Executive Committee does not qualify as a PGA Club, Course or Driving

Range but does warrant Class A status.

NOTE: Class A(T) – Class A members currently engaged at an establishment which has been inspected and approved as a PGA Training Establishment and currently holds that status will be identified where appropriate by the suffix (T) after their classification.

(ii) Class B   Members engaged by a Class A or D member to assist the nominated professional at any PGA Establishment in one of the seven Regions on a full-time basis.

(iii) Class C   Tournament playing members (men and women).

(iv) Class D   Members engaged as the nominated professional on a full-time basis at a PGA Establishment within the seven Regions which does not qualify as a 'Class A' establishment, or engaged on a full-time basis within the seven Regions by any other Company or any other individual designated by the Executive Committee for this purpose. (Former Class G).

(v) Class E   Honorary Associate Members (HAM). Those who in the opinion of the Executive Committee through their past or continuing membership justify retaining the full privileges of membership as Honorary Associate Members (HAM).

(vi) Class F   Associate Members (AM).
(a) Those who have ceased to be eligible for other categories of membership who in the opinion of the Executive Committee through their past membership justify retaining limited privileges of membership as Associate Members; and
(b) Members of the PGA European Tour or WPGET who do not qualify for Class C membership but who in the opinion of the Executive Committee justify limited privileges of membership as Associate Members.

(vii) Class G Honorary Life Members (HLM) Those recommended by the Board to a Special General Meeting of the Association for election as Honorary Life Members. No form of application is needed nor need reference be made to the Regional Committee concerned.

(viii) Class H Members who are qualified members of the Association, and ineligible for any other class of membership, engaged on a full-time basis at an establishment acceptable to the Association outside the jurisdiction of the seven Regions. (Overseas.)

(ix) Class O   Members who have not qualified at the official training centre of the Association, who are ineligible for any other class of membership, and who are current members of another PGA approved by the Association and have held such membership for not less than two years.

The Management of the Association is under the overall direction and control of a Board. The Association is divided into seven Regions each of which employs a full-time secretary and runs tournaments for the benefit of members within its Region.

The Association is responsible for arranging and obtaining sponsorship of the Ryder Cup, Club Professionals' Championship, PGA Cup matches, Seniors' Championship, PGA Assistants' Championship, Assistants' Match Play Championship and other National Championships.

Anyone who intends to become a club professional must serve a minimum of three years in registration and qualify at the PGA Training School before election as a full Member.

PGA European Tour

To be eligible to become a member of the PGA European Tour a player must possess certain minimum standards which shall be determined by the Tournament Committee. In 1976 a Qualifying School for potential new members was introduced to be held annually. The leading players are awarded cards allowing them to compete in all PGA European Tour tournaments.

In 1985 the PGA European Tour became ALL EXEMPT with no more Monday pre-qualifying. Full details can be obtained from the Wentworth Headquarters.

Women Professional Golfers' European Tour

The Women Professional Golfers' European Tour (WPG European Tour) was founded in 1988 to further the development of women's professional golf throughout Europe and its membership is open to all nationalities. An amateur wishing to join the Tour must be 18 years of age, have a handicap of 1 or less and is on probation for eight rounds in tournaments, during which she must attain certain playing standards as determined by the Tournament Committee.

Government of the Amateur and Open Golf Championship

In December 1919 on the invitation of the clubs who had hitherto controlled the amateur and Open Golf Championships, the Royal & Ancient took over the government of those events. These two championships are controlled by a committee appointed by the Royal & Ancient Golf Club of St Andrews. The Committee shall be called the Royal and Ancient Golf Club Championship Committee and shall consist of twelve members (who shall be members of the Club) to be elected by the Club, and additional members not exceeding two (who shall not necessarily be members of the Club) from Golf Authorities both at home and abroad, who shall be invited annually to join the Committee by the twelve members elected by the Club. Such invited members shall, irrespective of the date of their invitation to become members of the Committee, remain members only until the date of the first Autumn Meeting occurring after the date of their invitation to become members. During their term of office, such invited members (who are not already members of the Club), shall be admitted as honorary temporary members of the Club. Two Business Members, who shall be members of the Club, shall be co-opted on the nomination of the Chairman of the Championship Committee after consultation with the Chairman of the General Committee.

LGU

The Ladies' Golf Union was founded in 1893 with the following objects:
(1) To promote the interests of the game of Golf.
(2) To obtain a uniformity of the rules of the game by establishing a representative legislative authority.
(3) To establish a uniform system of handicapping.
(4) To act as a tribunal and court of reference on points of uncertainty.
(5) To arrange the Annual Championship Competition and obtain the funds necessary for that purpose.
Ninety years on only the language has changed, the present Constitution defining the objects as:
(1) To uphold the rules of the game, to advance and safeguard the interests of women's golf and to decide all doubtful

and disputed points in connection therewith.
(2) To maintain, regulate and enforce the LGU System of Handicapping.
(3) To employ the funds of The Union in such a manner as shall be deemed best for the interests of women's golf, with power to borrow or raise money to use for the same purpose.
(4) To maintain and regulate International events, Championships and Competitions held under the LGU regulations and to promote the interests of Great Britain and Ireland in Ladies International Golf.
(5) To make, maintain and publish such regulations as may be considered necessary for the above purposes.
The constituents of the LGU are:
Home Countries. The English Ladies' Golf Association (founded 1952), the Irish Ladies' Golf Union (founded 1893), the Scottish Ladies' Golfing Association (founded 1904), the Welsh Ladies' Golf Union (founded 1904), plus ladies' societies, girls' schools and ladies' clubs affiliated to these organisations.
Overseas. Affiliated ladies' golf unions and golf clubs in the Commonwealth and any other overseas ladies' golfing organisation affiliated to the LGU.
Individual lady members of clubs within the above categories are regarded as *members of the LGU.*
The Rules of the Game and of Amateur Status, which the LGU is bound to uphold, are those published by the Royal & Ancient Golf Club of St Andrews.
In endeavouring to fulfil its responsibilities towards advancing and safeguarding women's golf, the LGU maintains contact with other golfing organisations – the Royal & Ancient Golf Club of St Andrews, the Council of National Golf Unions, the Golf Foundation, the Central Council of Physical Recreation, the Sports Council, the Women Professional Golfers' European Tour and the Women's Committee of the United States Golf Association. This contact ensures that the LGU is informed of developments and projected developments and has an opportunity to comment upon and to influence the future of the game for women.
Either directly or through its constituent national organisations the LGU advises and is the ultimate authority on doubts or disputes which may arise in connection with the handicapping system and regulations governing competitions played under LGU conditions.
The handicapping system, together with the system for assessment of Scratch Scores, is formulated and published by the LGU. The handicapping system undergoes detailed revision and is republished every four years,

in the year following the revision of the Rules of Golf. Handicap Certificates are provided by the LGU and distributed through the national organisations and appointed club officials to every member of every affiliated club which has fulfilled the requisite conditions for obtaining an LGU handicap. No other form of certificate is recognised as evidence of an LGU handicap.

The funds of the LGU are administered by the Hon. Treasurer on the authority of the Executive Council, and the accounts are submitted annually for adoption in General Meeting.

All ladies' British Open Championships and the Home International matches, at both senior and junior level, are organised annually by the LGU. International events involving a British or a combined British and Irish team are organised and controlled by the LGU when held in this country and the LGU acts as the co-ordinating body for the Commonwealth Tournament in whichever of the four participating countries it is held, four-yearly, by rotation. The LGU selects and trains the teams, provides the uniforms and pays all the expenses of participation, whether held in this country or overseas. The LGU also maintains and regulates certain competitions played under handicap, such as Medal Competitions, Coronation Foursomes, Challenge Bowls, Australian Spoons and the LGU Pendant Competition.

The day-to-day administration of certain of the LGU responsibilities in the home countries is undertaken by the national organisations, such as that concerned with handicapping regulations, Scratch Scores, and the organisation of Challenge Bowls and Australian Spoons Competitions.

Membership subscriptions to the LGU are assessed on a per capita basis of the club membership. To save unnecessary expense and duplication of administrative work in the home countries LGU subscriptions are collected by the national organisations along with their own, and transmitted in bulk to the LGU.

Policy is determined and control over all the LGU's activities is exercised by an Executive Council of eight members – two each elected by the English, Irish, Scottish and Welsh national organisations. The Chairman is elected annually by the Councillors and may hold office for one year only, during which term her place on the Council is taken by her Deputy and she has no vote other than a casting vote. The President and the Hon. Treasurer of the Union also attend and take part in Council meetings but with no vote. The Council meets five times a year.

The Annual General Meeting is held in January. The formal business includes presentation of the Report of the Executive Council for the previous year and of the Accounts for the last completed financial year, the election or re-election of President, Vice-Presidents, Hon. Treasurer and Auditors, and a report of the election of Councillors and their Deputies for the ensuing year and of the European Technical Committee representative. Voting is on the following basis: Executive Council, one each (8); members in the four home countries, one per national organisation (4) and in addition one per 100 affiliated clubs or part thereof (at present 22); one per overseas Commonwealth Union with a membership of 50 or more clubs (at present 3), and one per 100 individually affiliated clubs (1).

The Lady Golfer's Handbook is published annually by the LGU and is distributed free to all affiliated clubs and organisations and to appointed Handicap Advisers. It is also available for sale to anyone interested. It contains the regulations for handicapping and Scratch Score assessment, for British Championships and international matches (with results for the past twenty years) and for LGU competitions, and sets out the Rules of the Union. It also lists every affiliated organisation, with names and addresses of officials, and every affiliated club, with Scratch Score, county of affiliation, number of members, and other useful information.

Miscellaneous Rulings

Limitation of the Golf Ball

At the Autumn Business Meeting, 1920, of the Royal & Ancient Club the following resolution was adopted:

On and after 1st May, 1921, the weight of the ball shall not be greater than 1.62 ounces avoirdupois, and the size not less than 1.62 inches in diameter. The Rules of Golf Committee and the Executive Committee of the United States Golf Association will take whatever steps they think necessary to limit the powers of the ball with regard to distance, should any ball of greater power be introduced.

The United States Golf Association intimated, May, 1929, that they had resolved to adopt *an easier and pleasanter ball for the average golfer*, and from 1st January, 1931, to 31st December, 1932, the standards of specification of the ball in competitions under their jurisdiction was not less than 1.68 inches in diameter, and not greater than 1.55 ounces in weight. In January, 1932, another alteration was made in the specification of the ball, the weight being increased to 1.62 and the size remaining the same, viz, not less than 1.68.

The Royal Canadian Golf Association adopted the USGA specification as from 1st January, 1948. The effect of this difference between the legislation of the Royal & Ancient, the Royal Canadian Golf Association, and the USGA is that golfers competing in the United States and Canada must use a ball that is larger, but no heavier, than the ball which is legal in other parts of the world.

In May, 1951, a special committee was set up by the Royal & Ancient Golf Club and the United States Golf Association to discuss the desirability of uniformity in the Rules of Golf and the form and make of clubs and balls. The committee recommended that both sizes of ball (1.62 inches and 1.68 inches in diameter both having the same weight, 1.62 ounces) be legal in all countries. At their autumn meeting the United States Golfers' Association rejected this proposal but agreed that in international team competition in the United States, the size of the ball be not less than 1.62 inches in diameter.

The matter of a uniform ball world-wide was investigated by a special committee from the R&A and the USGA but was dropped in 1974 when the two bodies could not reach agreement.

In 1987, however, the Royal & Ancient Golf Club of St Andrews proposed and adopted an amendment which decreed that the diameter of the golf ball should be not less than 1.68 inches (42.67 mm) instead of 1.62 inches (41.15 mm). The change of rule was introduced on 1st January 1990. An official statement declared: 'With the steady and, in most countries, rapid decline in the use of the 1.62 inch ("small") ball, the R&A has been considering changing to the 1.68 inch ("large") ball for some time, but has held off from doing so mainly because of the large number of Japanese golfers still using the small ball. With the use of the small ball in Japan now dropping steadily and in most other countries now being at 10% or less, it seems an appropriate time to make this change."

A maximum initial velocity standard of not greater than 250 feet per second on special apparatus was introduced by the R&A in 1976.

The R&A issues lists of conforming golf balls annually.

Limitation of Number of Clubs

At the Business Meeting of the Royal & Ancient Golf Club, May, 1937, the Rules of Golf Committee submitted a recommendation that on and after 1st January, 1938, the preamble to the Rules of Golf shall read: *The game of golf consists of a ball being played from a teeing ground to a hole by successive strokes with clubs (not exceeding fourteen in number) and balls made in conformity with the directions laid down in the clause on 'Form and make of golf clubs and balls'.* The recommendation was not approved by the members.

In September, 1938, at the Business Meeting of the Royal & Ancient, a similar recommendation was approved by the members, and the limitation of the number of clubs to fourteen became operative as from 1st May, 1939. The United States Golf Association decided to limit the number of clubs to fourteen as from 1st January, 1938.

Steel-Shafted Clubs

The Royal & Ancient Golf Club authorised steel shafts, November, 1929, in the following announcement: *The Rules of Golf Committee have decided that steel shafts, as approved by the Rules of Golf Committee are declared to conform with the requirements of the clause in the Rules of Golf on the form and make of golf clubs.*

Laminated Shafts

The Rules of Golf Committee on 5th December, 1932, announced that clubs with laminated shafts built entirely of wood are permissible.

Recognised Golf Clubs

The Rules of Golf Committee, in answering a query, gave the opinion that a recognised Golf Club is one which has regularly appointed office-bearers.

The English Golf Union decided that a recognised Golf Club for the purpose of competitive golf in England is a golf club affiliated to the English Golf Union through its County Union, or where there is no County Union direct to the English Golf Union as an Associate Member.

Championship Conditions

Men

The Amateur Championship

The Championship, until 1982, was decided entirely by match play over 18 holes except for the final which was over 36 holes. Since 1983 the Championship has comprised two stroke-play rounds of 18 holes each from which the top 64 scores over the 36 holes qualify for the match-play stages. Matches are over 18 holes except for the final which is over 36 holes.

Full particulars of conditions of entry and method of play can be obtained from the Championship Entries Department, Royal and Ancient Golf Club, St Andrews, Fife KY16 9JD.

The Seniors' Open Amateur

The Championship consists of 18 holes on each of two days, the lowest 50 scores over the 36 holes and any tying for 50th place then playing a further 18 holes the following day.

Conditions for entry include:

Entrants must have attained the age of 55 years prior to the first day on which the Championship is played.

Entries are limited to 252 competitors.

Full particulars of conditions of entry and method of play can be obtained from Championship Entries Department, Royal and Ancient Golf Club, St Andrews, Fife KY16 9JD.

National Championships

The English, Scottish, Irish and Welsh Amateur Championships are played by holes, each match consisting of one round of 18 holes except the final which is contested over 36 holes.

Full particulars of conditions of entry and method of play can be obtained from the secretaries of the respective national Unions.

English Open Amateur Stroke Play Championship

The Championship consists of one round of 18 holes on each of two days after which the leading 45 and those tying for 45th place play a further two rounds. The remainder are eliminated.

Conditions for entry include:

Entrants must have a handicap not exceeding three.

Where the entries exceed 130, an 18-hole qualifying round is held the day before the Championship. Certain players are exempt from qualifying.

Full particulars of conditions of entry and method of play can be obtained from the Secretary, English Golf Union.

Youths

British Youths' Open Amateur Championship

The Championship consists of 18 holes on each of two days, the lowest 40 scores over the 36 holes and any tying for 40th place then playing a further 36 holes the following day.

Conditions of entry include:

Entrants must be under 21 years of age on the last day on which the Championship is played.

Entries are limited to 150 competitors, the higher handicaps being balloted out if necessary.

Full particulars of conditions of entry and method of play can be obtained from the Championship Entries Department, Royal and Ancient Golf Club, St Andrews, Fife KY16 9JD.

Boys

Boys' Amateur Championship

The Championship is played by match play, each match consisting of one round of 18 holes

except for the final which is over 36 holes.
Conditions of entry include:

Entrants must be under 18 years of age on the last day on which the Championship is played.

Entries are limited to 192 competitors, the higher handicaps being balloted out if necessary.

Full particulars of conditions of entry and method of play can be obtained from the Championship Entries Department, Royal and Ancient Golf Club, St Andrews, Fife KY16 9JD.

Ladies

Ladies' British Open Amateur Championship

The Championship consists of one 18 hole qualifying round on each of two days. If entries exceed 110 there will be 64 qualifiers for matchplay. If entries number 110 or less, 32 will qualify for matchplay. Handicap limit is 4.

Ladies' British Open Amateur Stroke Play Championship

The Championship consists of 72 holes stroke play; 18 holes are played on each of two days after which the first 32 and all ties for 32nd place qualify for a further 36 holes on the third day. Handicap limit is 4.

Ladies' British Open Championship

The Championship consists of 72 holes stroke play. 18 holes are played on each of four days, the field being reduced after the first 36 holes.

Entries accepted from lady amateurs with a handicap not exceeding scratch and from lady professionals.

Full particulars of conditions of entry and method of play for all three Championships can be obtained from the Administrator, LGU, The Scores, St Andrews, Fife KY16 9AT.

National Championships

Conditions of entry and method of play for the English, Scottish, Welsh and Irish Ladies' Close Championships can be obtained from the Secretaries of the respective associations.

Other championships organised by the respective national associations, from whom full particulars can be obtained, include English Ladies', Intermediate, English Ladies' Stroke-Play, Scottish Girls' Open Amateur Stroke Play (under 21) and Welsh Ladies' Open Amateur Stroke Play.

Girls

Girls' British Open Amateur Championship

The Championship consists of two 18-hole qualifying rounds, followed by match-play in two flights each of sixteen players.

Conditions of entry include:

Entrants must be under 18 years of age on the 1st January in the year of the Championship.

Competitors are required to hold a certified LGU international handicap not exceeding 15, or to be members of their National Junior Team for the current year.

Full particulars of conditions of entry and method of play can be obtained from the Administrator, LGU, The Scores, St Andrews, Fife KY16 9AT.

National Championships

The English, Scottish, Irish and Welsh Girls' Close Championships are open to all girls of relevant nationality and appropriate age which may vary from country to country. A handicap limit may be set by some countries.

Full particulars of conditions of entry and method of play can be obtained via the secretaries of the respective associations.

International Match Conditions

Men–Amateur

Walker Cup–Great Britain and Ireland v United States

Deed of Gift to United States Golf Association
International Challenge Trophy

Mr GH Walker of the United States presented a Cup for international competition to be known as *The United States Golf Association International Challenge Trophy*, popularly described as *The Walker Cup*.

The Cup shall be played for by teams of amateur golfers selected from Clubs under the jurisdiction of the United States Golf Association on the one side and from England, Scotland, Wales, Northern Ireland and Eire on the other.

The International Walker Cup Match shall be held every two years in the United States of America and Great Britain and Ireland alternately.

The teams shall consist of not more than ten players and a captain.

The contest consists of 4 foursomes and 8 singles matches over 18 holes on each of two days.

Eisenhower Trophy
(formerly World Cup)

Founded in 1958 in recognition of the need for an official team championship for amateurs. Each country enters a team of four players who play stroke play over 72 holes, the total of the three best individual scores to be counted each day. (One score to be discarded.) The winner to be the team with the lowest aggregate for the 72 holes. The first event was played at St Andrews in 1958 and the trophy has been played for every second year.

European Team Championship

Founded in 1959 by the European Golf Association for competition among member countries of the Association. The Championship is held biennially and played in rotation round the countries which are grouped in four geographical zones.

Each team consists of six players who play two qualifying rounds of 18 holes, the five best scores of each round constituting the team aggregate. Flights for match play are then arranged according to qualifying round rankings. For the match play, teams consist of five players, playing two foursomes in the morning and five singles in the afternoon.

A similar championship is held every year for junior teams.

From 1990, the European Golf Association began organising the International European Championships – formally known as the European Individual Amateur Championships – on an annual basis.

Home Internationals
(Raymond Trophy)

The first official International Match recorded was in 1903 at Muirfield between England and Scotland when singles only were played.

In 1932 International Week was inaugurated under the auspices of the British Golf Unions' Joint Advisory Council with the full approval of the four National Golf Unions. The Council of National Golf Unions is now responsible for running the matches.

Teams of 11 players from England, Scotland, Ireland and Wales engage in matches consisting of 5 foursomes and 10 singles over 18 holes, the foursomes being in the morning and the singles in the afternoon. Each team plays every other team.

The eligibility of players to play for their country shall be their eligibility to play in the Amateur Championship of their country.

Men–Professional

Ryder Cup

This Cup was presented by Mr Samuel Ryder, St Albans, England (who died 2nd January, 1936), for competition between a team of British professionals and a team of American professionals. The trophy was first competed for in 1927. In 1929 the original conditions were varied to confine the British team to British-born professionals resident in Great Britain, and the American team to American-born professionals resident in the United States, in the year of the match. In 1977 the British team was extended to include European players. The matches are played biennially, in alternate continents, in accordance with the conditions as agreed between the respective PGAs.

World Cup
(formerly Canada Cup)

Founded in America in 1953 as an International Team event for professional golfers with the intention of spreading international goodwill.

Each country is represented by two players, the best team score over 72 holes being the winners of the World cup and the best individual score the International Trophy. It is played annually, but not in 1986.

Ladies

Great Britain and Ireland
v United States
(Curtis Cup)

For a trophy presented by the late Misses Margaret and Harriot Curtis of Boston, USA, for biennial competition between teams from the United States of America and Great Britain and Ireland.

The match is sponsored jointly by the United States Golf Association and the Ladies' Golf Union who may select teams of not more than 8 players.

The match consists of 3 foursomes and 6 singles of 18 holes on each of two days, the foursomes being played each morning.

Great Britain and Ireland
v Continent of Europe
(Vagliano Trophy)

For a trophy presented to the Comité des Dames de la Fédération Française de Golf and the Ladies' Golf Union by Monsieur AA Vagliano, originally for annual competition between teams of women amateur golfers from France and Great Britain and Ireland but, since 1959, by mutual agreement, for competition between teams from the Continent of Europe and Great Britain and Ireland.

The match is played biennially, alternately in Great Britain and Ireland and on the Continent of Europe, with teams of not more than 9 players plus a non-playing captain.

The match consists of 4 foursomes and 8 singles, of 18 holes on each of two days. The foursomes are played each morningg.

Women's World Amateur Team Championship
(Espirito Santo Trophy)

For the Espirito Santo Trophy presented by Mrs Ricardo Santo of Portugal for biennial competition between teams of not more than three women amateur golfers who represent a national association affiliated to the World Amateur Golf Council. First competed for in 1964.

The tournament consists of 72 holes stroke play, 18 holes on each of four days, the two best scores in each round each day constituting the team aggregate.

Commonwealth Tournament
(Lady Astor Trophy)

For a trophy presented by the late Viscountess Astor CH, and the Ladies' Golf Union for competition once in every four years between teams of women amateur golfers from Commonwealth countries.

The inaugural Commonwealth Tournament was played at St Andrews in 1959 between teams from Australia, Canada, New Zealand, South Africa and Great Britain and was won by the British team. The tournament is played in rotation in the competing countries, for the present Great Britain, Australia, Canada, and New Zealand, each country being entitled to nominate 6 players including a playing or non-playing captain.

Each team plays every other team and each team match consists of 2 foursomes and 4 singles over 18 holes. The foursomes are played in the morning and the singles in the afternoon.

European Ladies' Amateur Team Championship

The championship is held biennially between teams of amateur women golfers from the European countries. Each team consists of not more than six players who play two qualifying rounds, the five best scores in each round constituting the team aggregate. The match play draw is made in flights according to the position in the qualifying rounds. The match play consists of two foursomes and five singles on each of three days.

A similar championship is held in alternate years for junior ladies' teams, under 22 years of age.

Home Internationals

Teams from England, Scotland, Ireland and Wales compete annually for a trophy presented to the LGU by the late Mr TH Miller. The qualifications for a player being eligible to play for her country are the same as those laid down by each country for its Close Championship.

Each team plays each other team. The matches consist of 6 singles and 3 foursomes, each of 18 holes. Each country may nominate teams of not more than 8 players.

Youths

England v Scotland

The International Match between England and Scotland is played the day before the Youths' Championship begins. This match consists of five foursomes followed by ten singles.

Great Britain and Ireland v Continent of Europe

The International Match between Great Britain and Ireland and the Continent of Europe for the EGA Trophy is played each year over two days. The venue of this match alternates between Great Britain and Ireland and the Continent of Europe. On each day there are four foursomes followed by eight singles.

Boys

England v Scotland; Wales v Ireland

The International Matches between England and Scotland (10 players a side) and Wales and Ireland (10 players a side) are played on the Thursday preceding the Boys' Championship. The following day the winners of these two matches play against each other, as do the losers. To be eligible to play in these matches a boy must qualify by age to be eligible to play in the Boys' Championship.

Great Britain and Ireland v Continent of Europe

The International Match between Great Britain and Ireland and the Continent of Europe for the Jacques Leglise Trophy is played on the Saturday preceding the Boys' Championship. This match consists of four foursomes followed by eight singles.

Girls

Home Internationals

Teams from England, Scotland, Ireland and Wales compete annually for the Stroyan Cup. The qualifications for a player for the Girls' International Matches shall be the same as those laid down by each country for its Girls' Close Championship except that a player shall be under 18 years on the 1st January in the year of the Championship.

Each team, consisting of not more than 8 players, plays each other team, a draw taking place to decide the order of play between the teams. The matches consist of 7 singles, each of 18 holes.

Golf Associations

The Golf Foundation

During the last decade, the growth of golf throughout Britain has scaled new heights with each passing year as more and more people become smitten with its addictive qualities. It was Tony Jacklin who initially sparked this explosion of interest with his victories in the Open Championship and the United States Open nearly 20 years ago and further fuel has been added by the emergence of Spain's Severiano Ballesteros as one of the most exciting players the game has ever seen. The exploits of the world's leading professionals are now regularly beamed into millions of homes via television and so people who would never have dreamed of taking an interest in the game have been fascinated and eventually drawn into finding out for themselves its magnetic qualities.

Many of these people are youngsters – girls and boys who witness the achievements of today's stars and feel that they too would like to experience the allure and charm of golf with dreams, perhaps, of emulating some of the modern day heroes and heroines. In a great many cases, these dreams are frustrated at the outset. If the parents of a child do not play golf then all the questions the child may have about starting golf can go unanswered. He or she may enquire about the game from school teachers but unless one of them is a golfer, it is unlikely that this approach will bear any fruit so the seeds of interest are soon stifled and the child turns to other games which are included in the school curriculum.

It is this gap in the education of young, potential golfers that The Golf Foundation fills. Founded in 1952, The Golf Foundation's original motives of promoting the development of junior golf throughout the country still hold good today and in the space of 37 years, thousands of junior golfers have benefited from its work. From this number have emerged some famous names such as Bernard Gallacher, Brian Barnes, Peter Oosterhuis, Michelle Walker and more recently Paul Way, Michael McLean and Ronan Rafferty all of whom received instruction and assistance under The Golf Foundation Coaching Scheme for Schools and Junior Groups.

This scheme forms the basis of the Foundation's work whereby it subsidises instruction by qualified members of the Professional Golfer's Association (PGA) to students of schools, universities and other places of higher education and to junior members of golf clubs who are in full-time education. This enables schools who do not have golf as part of their sports' programme to take advantage of giving their pupils an introduction to the game and a solid grounding in its techniques.

But the work of the Golf Foundation does not begin and end there; the Foundation realised that young people's initial interest in the game must be sustained. Thus, over the years it has expanded its field of operations to cover the development of a junior golfer right through to the adult ranks. This area includes the awarding of vouchers for individual tuition for promising girls and boys; the sponsoring of Open Coaching Centres during school holidays; the encouragement of school competitive golf and assisting the formation of National and County Schools' Golf Associations; the operation of a film and visual aids service; the organisation of the Team Championship for Schools and the Age Group Championships; the promotion of an Eclectic Competition for club juniors; the operation of a Merit Award Scheme whereby juniors can have their progress measured and rewarded. The Foundation has recently initiated the Coaching Award for Teachers in School whereby teachers who play golf themselves receive basic instruction from PGA professionals which they can then impart to pupils so that the pupils have some grounding when they receive further instruction under the Golf Foundation Coaching Scheme for Schools and Junior Groups.

The Foundation also makes an annual award to the boy or girl showing the most improvement as a result of Golf Foundation tuition and in 1983 this award was won by a 17-year-old boy who is deaf and has limited speech – proof, if any were needed, of the therapeutic powers of the game and evidence of the particular interest the Golf Foundation takes in handicapped young people.

The implementation of these activities and

the running of the coaching scheme costs a great deal of money and the Golf Foundation relies heavily on club golfers for a large part of its income. Organisations within the game and companies also assist in providing funds so that its work can continue and expand.

At present, the future of British golf looks bright but in order to maintain that progress, more and more youngsters must be given the opportunity to learn about and play golf. As one old scribe once wrote, *it is a game at which you may exhaust yourself but never your subject,* and it is a game that teaches self-discipline, good manners, sportsmanship and an appreciation of other people's qualities. It is *the game of a lifetime* for it can be played by people of all ages. The Golf Foundation hopes that you too, once you have experienced the pleasures of golf, will find it a lasting source of enjoyment.

The National Association of Public Golf Courses

(Affiliated to English Golf Union)

1927 saw the foundation of the Association by the late FG Hawtree (Golf Course Architect) and the late JH Taylor (five times Open Champion). They were both farsighted enough to see the need for cohesion between *Private* golf, *Public* golf and the Local Councils. Up to the outbreak of World War II the Association struggled on, sustained by a small amount of very welcome financial support from the News of the World. This enabled the *unofficial* Championship to be staged.

After the War, the Association was revitalised and the Championship was recognised by the National Union – and so from a shaky start of 240 qualifiers – there are now some 3500 Public Course golfers trying to qualify, from a total estimated membership of 50,000. The success and importance of the *Public Courses Championship of England* prompted the commencement of the Championship for Ladies and then the Championship for Juniors – which share equal importance. Soon after the establishment of Individual Championships there came the introduction of various Club Team events, and these have now progressed to National Level with a vast following from Club members. Thus the Association now organises some 14 national events annually for the membership.

Some years ago it was realised that the Local Councils (Course Management Authorities) could not enjoy official recognition and membership of the County Unions or National Unions except through the Association, this has now been remedied and many CMA are full subscribing members of the Association, and many others permit the *Courtesy of the Course* for all our National & Zonal Tournaments. Advice is offered to CMA – when requested – on such matters as Course Construction, Club formation and Integration, establishment of Standard Scratch Score and Par Values, and many other topics concerned with the management of the game of golf.

Some overseas organisations and Councils have already sought our advice and help in recent years, when forming their own Courses, Clubs and Associations.

The Constitutional aims have not changed over the years, and the Association is proud to have maintained these Aims through the activities provided by the National Executive of the Association. The aims are:
1. To unite the Clubs formed on Public Courses in England and Wales, and their Course Managements in the furtherance of the interests of Amateur Golf.
2. To promote Annual Public Courses Championships and such other matches, competitions and Tournaments as shall be authorised by the executive of the Association.
3. To afford direct representation of Public Course Interests in the National Union.

The total organisation of the Association is wholly voluntary and honorary, from the President down through Vice-Presidents, Chairmen, Secretary, Treasurer and Zone Secretaries. It is quite fantastic for an unpaid Organisation to cover such an exacting *field* of work, but most gratifying to the National Executive who have secured the progress of recent years.

Association of Golf Club Secretaries

Membership is 1500, consisting of Secretaries and retired Secretaries of Clubs largely situated in Great Britain but also from 200 Clubs in other parts of the World. The Association offers from the Headquarters at Bakewell, Derbyshire advice on all aspects of Golf Club Management, and a training course for new and intending Secretaries. Apart from national events, including a Conference, the Association organises golfing and business meetings for its members at regional level. There are 12 regions within the British Isles.

Association of Golf Writers

Secretary: Renton Laidlaw, Evening Standard, 2 Derry Street, London W8 5EE.

The Sports Turf Research Institute
(Bingley, West Yorkshire)

The Institute is officially recognised as the national centre for sports and amenity turf. Non-commercial and non-profit making, its affairs are administered by a Board, whose members are nominated by the sport controlling bodies in membership of the Institute. Golf is represented by nominees of the Royal & Ancient Golf Club of St Andrews, four individual National Golf Unions, and the Councils of National Golf Unions.

The institute's aim is to raise the standard of turf used for all sports. Valuable data is accumulated from research activities and is disseminated to subscribing clubs and organisations.

The British Association of Golf Course Architects

Objects of the Association: to encourage the highest standards of Golf Course Design and Construction; to have the fullest regard to the best interests of Members' Clients; to maintain a Register of Members fully qualified by training and experience in the design and construction of Golf Courses; to promote the interests of its members and the game of golf; to support research and development in golf course Design, Construction and Maintenance; to enable members to meet together, share knowledge and experience, and discuss matters affecting their work; to follow the best accepted principles of golf course architecture with the object of providing the maximum enjoyment of the game for all players.

The British Association of Golf Course Constructors

Objects: To promote the development of the golf course construction industry, to promote the adoption of policies to ensure a high quality of workmanship and working practices, to collect and disseminate information of value regarding the construction of golf courses to other members of the association, to members of the allied industries and to the public to promote the training and education of personnel within the industry and to maintain agreed standards of golf course construction by adherence to contractual procedures and codes of practice.

British and International Golf Greenkeepers' Association

The Association was formed in 1987 resulting from an amalgamation of the British, English and Scottish Associations. The Association has an official magazine, *Greenkeeping Management* which is issued free to all members.

The objects are to promote and advance all aspects of greenkeeping; to assist and encourage the proficiency of members; to arrange an International Annual Conference, educational seminars, functions and competitions; to maintain a Benevolent Fund; to act as an employment agency; to provide a magazine; to

collaborate with any body or organisation which may benefit the Association or its members or with which there may be a common interest; to carry out and perform any other duties which shall be in the general interests of the Association or its members.

National Golf Clubs' Advisory Association

The National Golf Clubs' Advisory Association was founded in 1922. The objects are to protect the interests of Golf Clubs in general and to give legal advice and direction, under the opinion of Counsel, on the administrative and legal responsibilities of Golf Clubs. In cases taken to the Courts for decisions on any points which in the opinion of the Executive Committee involve principles affecting the general interests of affiliated clubs financial assistance may sometimes be given.

European Golf Association
Association Européenne de Golf

Formed at a meeting held at Luxembourg, 20th November, 1937, membership shall be restricted to European National Amateur Golf Associations or Unions. The Association shall concern itself solely with matters of an international character. The Association shall have as its prime objects:

(a) To encourage international development of golf and strengthen bonds of friendship between the national organisations and to encourage the formation of new ones.

(b) To co-ordinate dates of the Open and Amateur Championships of its members.

(c) To arrange when such have been decided upon, European Team Championships and Matches of international character.

(d) To decide and publish the Calendar dates of the Open and Amateur Championships and Matches.

Golf Club Stewards' Association

The Golf Club Stewards' Association was founded as early as 1912. Its members are Stewards in Golf Clubs throughout the UK and Eire. It has a National Committee and Regional Branches in the South, North-West, Midlands, East Anglia, Yorkshire, Wales and the West, North-East Scotland and Ireland. The objects of the Association are to promote the interests of members; to administer a Benevolent Fund for members in need and to arrange golf competitions and matches. It also serves as an Agency for the employment of Stewards in Golf Clubs.

Addresses of British and Overseas Golfing Organisations

United Kingdom

National

Amateur Golf Championship
Sec, MF Bonallack, OBE, Royal and Ancient Golf Club, St Andrews. *Fax* (0334) 77580.

Artisan Golfers' Association
Hon Sec, A Everett, 51 Rose Hill, Park West, Sutton, Surrey. *Tel* 01-644 7037.

Association of Golf Club Secretaries
Sec, J Crowther, Victoria Mill, Buxton Road, Bakewell, Derbyshire DE4 1DA.
Tel (062 981) 4314.

Boys' Amateur Golf Championship
Sec, MF Bonallack, OBE, Royal & Ancient Golf Club, St Andrews.

British Association of Golf Course Architects
Hon Sec & Treas, MG Hawtree, 5 Oxford Street, Woodstock, Oxford OX7 1TQ.
Tel (0993) 811976.

British Association of Golf Course Constructors
Howard Swan, Telford Farm, Willingale, Ongar, Essex CM5 OQF. *Tel* (0277) 896229, *Fax* (0245) 491620.

British & International Golf Greenkeepers' Association
Exec Dir, Neil Thomas BA
Educ Officer, David Golding, Aldwark Manor, Aldwark, Alne, York Y06 2NF. *Tel* (03473) 581/2 *Fax* (03473) 8864.

Regional Administrators

Scottish Region Mr C Kennedy, 82 Dumbreck Road, Glasgow, G41 9DW. *Tel* 041-427 4701 (*home*), 041-427 4242 (*office*).

Northern Region Mr D Hannam, 12 Moorfield Avenue, Menston, Nr Ilkley, W Yorks LS29 6HB. *Tel* (0943) 72008.

Midland & North Wales Mr A Phipps-Jones, 1 Devonshire Place, Priors Park, Tewkesbury, Glos GL20 5ES. *Tel* (0684) 295405 (*club*), (0684) 850129 (*home*).

South East Region Mr N Exley, 1 The Farmhouse, Hills Lane, Northwood, Middx HA6 2QL. *Tel* (09274) 25329 (*club*), (09274) 24737 (*home*).

South West & South Wales Region Mr G Child, Archways, Churston Road, Churston Ferrers, South Devon. *Tel* (0803) 845274, (0803) 844056 (*home*).

British Left-Handed Golfers' Society
Hon Sec, AC Kirkland, Squirrel Cottage, Mereheath Lane, Knutsford, Cheshire.
Tel (0565) 4671.

Council of National Golf Unions
Hon Sec, Alan Thirlwell, Formby GC, Golf Road, Formby, Liverpool L37 1LQ.
Tel (070 48) 72164.

Golf Club Stewards' Association
Sec, G Shaw, 50 The Park, St Albans, Herts. *Tel* (0727) 57334.

Chairman, Roger Gregory, Southwick Park Golf Club, Southwick Park, Fareham, Hants. *Tel* (0705) 380131.

Special Events, DJ Lithgow, Great Barr Golf Club, Chapel Lane, Great Barr, Birmingham B43 7BA. *Tel* 021-357 1232.

Regional Secretaries

South Roy Martin, Edward Court Hotel, Wokingham, Berks *Tel* (0734) 775886.

Midlands Carol Reay, Robin Hood Golf Club. *Tel* 021-706 0159.

North East B Duncan, Whitburn Golf Club, Lizard Lane, Tyne & Wear, *Tel* (0783) 292144.

Yorkshire K Millington, Whitby Golf Club. *Tel* (0947) 601632/2602768.

Wales & West C Hursey, Hockley Golf Club, Winchester, Hants. *Tel* (0962) 714572.

Golf Foundation
Dir Miss Lesley Attwood, 57 London Road, Enfield, Middx EN2 6DU. *Tel* 01-367 4404.

Golf Society of Great Britain
Mrs EJ Drummond, Southview, Warren Road, Thurlestone, Devon TQ7 3NT. *Tel* (0548) 560630.

Hill Samuel School Foursomes
Competition Hon Sec, GR Scott, Yew Tree Cottage, 93 Wells Road, Malvern, Worcs WR14 4PB. *Tel* (0684) 565605.

Hole in One Golf Society
Sec, EW Parker, 1 Vigilant Way, Gravesend, Kent. *Tel* (0474) 534200.

Ladies' Golf Union
Administrator, Mrs Alma Robertson, The Scores, St Andrews, Fife KY16 9AT. *Tel* (0334) 75811.

The Society of One-Armed Golfers
Hon Sec, Don Reid, 11 Coldwell Lane, Felling, Tyne and Wear NE10 9EX. *Tel* 091-469 4742.

The Professional Golfers' Association
Exec Dir, J Lindsey, National Headquarters, Apollo House, The Belfry, Sutton Coldfield, West Midlands, B76 9PT. *Tel* (0675) 70333 *Telex* 338481 (PGA G) *Fax* (0675) 70674.

Scottish Region *Sec,* Sandy Jones, Glenbervie Golf Club, Stirling Road, Larbert FK5 4SJ. *Tel* (0324) 562451.

Irish Region *Sec,* Michael McCumiskey, Dundalk Golf Club, Blackrock, Dundalk, Co Louth, Eire. *Tel* (010 353) 4221193/7 *Fax* (010 353) 4221899.

North Region Headquarters, *Sec* Norman Fletcher, No 2 Cottage, Bolton Golf Club, Lostock Park, Chorley New Road, Bolton, Lancs BL6 4AJ *Tel* (0204) 496137/8 *Fax* (0204) 47959.

West Region *Sec,* Bill Morton, Exeter Golf and Country Club, Topsham Road, Countess Wear, Exeter, Devon EX2 7AE. *Tel* (0392) 877657 *Fax* (0392) 876382.

Midland Region *Sec,* Ronald Smith, PGA National Headquarters, Apollo House, The Belfry, Sutton Coldfield, West Midlands B76 9PT. *Tel* (0675) 70841 *Fax* (0675) 70674.

South Region *Sec,* Gordon Robert, Tyrrells Wood Golf Club, Leatherhead, Surrey KT22 8QP. *Tel* (0372) 370111.

East Region *Sec,* David Wright, John O'Gaunt Golf Club, Sutton Park, Sandy, Biggleswade, Beds SG19 2LY. *Tel* (0767) 261888.

PGA European Tour
Executive Director, KD Schofield, PGA European Tour, The Wentworth Club, Wentworth Drive, Virginia Water, Surrey GU25 4LS. *Tel* Wentworth (099 04) 2881.

Women Professional Golfers' European Tour
Exec Dir, Joe Flanagan, The Tytherington Club, Macclesfield, Cheshire SK10 2JP. *Tel* (0625) 611444.

Public Schools' Old Boys' Golf Association
Jt Secs, P de Pinna, Bruins, Wythwood, Haywards Heath, West Sussex. *Tel* (*home*) (0444) 454883 (*office*) 01-929 0811 and JBM Urry, Dormers, 232 Dickens Heath Road, Shirley, Solihull, West Midlands. *Tel* (*home*) (0564) 823114, (*office*) 021-328 5665.

Public Schools' Golfing Society
Hon Sec, JNS Lowe, Flushing House, Church Road, Great Bookham, Surrey KT23 3JT. *Tel* (0372) 58651.

Seniors' Championship
Sec, MF Bonallack, OBE, Royal and Ancient Golf Club, St Andrews.

Senior Golfers' Society
Sec, Brigadier D Ross CBE, Milland Farmhouse, Liphook, Hants GU30 7JP. *Tel* (042 876) 200.

Sports Turf Research Institute
Bingley, West Yorks BD16 1AU. *Tel* (0274) 565131, *Fax* (0274) 561 891.

Youths' Amateur Golf Championship
Sec, MF Bonallack, OBE, Royal and Ancient Golf Club, St Andrews.

England

Bedfordshire County Golf Union
Hon Sec, CLE Spurr, 8, Gainsborough Avenue, St Albans, Herts AL1 4NL. *Tel* (0727) 57834.

Bedfordshire Ladies' County Golf Association
Hon Sec, Mrs M Clark, 3 Sherbourne Avenue, Luton, Beds LU2 7BB. *Tel* (0582) 575883.

Berks, Bucks and Oxon Union of Golf Clubs
Sec, R Stewart, Leyacre, Lodersfield, Lechlade, Glos GL7 3DJ. *Tel* (0637) 52926.

Berks, Bucks and Oxon Golfers Alliance
Hon Sec, Monica Green, Wayside, Aylesbury Road, Monks Risborough, Aylesbury, Bucks.

Berkshire Ladies' County Golf Association
Hon Sec, Mrs BE Baird, 11 Lynton Green, College Road, Maidenhead, Berks SL6 6AN. *Tel* (0628) 21462.

Buckinghamshire Ladies' County Golf Association
Hon Sec, Mrs S Tunstall, Springfield Bungalow, Butlers Cross, Aylesbury, Bucks. *Tel* (0296) 624375.

Cambridgeshire Area Golf Union
Sec, RAC Blows, 2a Dukes Meadow, Stapleford, Cambs CB2 5BH. *Tel* (0223) 842062.

Cambs and Hunts Ladies' County Golf Association
Hon Sec, Mrs A Guy, 19 Greenfield Close, Stapleford, Cambs. CB2 5BF. *Tel* (0223) 843267.

Channel Islands Ladies' GA
Sec, Mrs JMT Willis, Oakebirch, Park Estate, St Brelade, Jersey.

Cheshire County Ladies' Golf Association
Hon Sec, Mrs R Btesh, 48 Melrose Crescent, Hale, Altrincham, Cheshire. *Tel* 061-980 6140.

Cheshire PGA
Tournament Director, Keith Brain, The Virgate, Abbey Way Hartford, Northwich, Cheshire CW8 1LY.

Cheshire Union of Golf Clubs
Hon Sec, BC Jones, 4 Curzon Mews, Wilmslow, Cheshire SK9 5JN. *Tel* (0625) 532866.

Cornwall Golf Union
Hon Sec, JG Rowe, 8 Lydcott Crescent, Widegates, Looe, Cornwall PL13 1QG. *Tel* (05034) 492.

Cornwall Ladies' County Golf Association
Hon Sec, Mrs A Eddy, Penmester, Hain Walk, St Ives, Cornwall. *Tel* (0736) 795392.

Cumbria Ladies' County Golf Association
Hon Sec, Mrs T Turner, Cawdor, Garth Heads Road, Appleby, Cumbria CA16 6UD. *Tel* (07683) 51672.

Cumbria Union of Golf Clubs
Hon Sec, T Edmondson, Thorn Lea, Lazonby, Penrith, Cumbria. *Tel* (0768) 83231.

Derbyshire Alliance
Hon Sec, R Reid, c/o Buxton & High Peak GC, Fairfield, Buxton, Derbyshire. *Tel* (0298) 3112.

Derbyshire Ladies' County Golf Association
Hon Sec, Mrs D Cartledge, 11 Pine Close, Smalley, Derbyshire DE7 6EH. *Tel* (0332) 880929.

Derbyshire PGA
Sec, Mr M Ronan, Erewash Valley Golf Club, Stanton-by-Dale, Nr. Ilkeston, Derby. *Tel* (0602) 324667.

Derbyshire Union of Golf Clubs
Hon Sec, CF Ibbotson, 67 Portland Close, Mickleover, Derby DE3 5BR. *Tel* (0332) 512465.

Devon County Golf Union
Hon Sec, J Marshall, *Appledowne,* Keyberry Park, Newton Abbot, Devon TQ12 1DF. *Tel* (0626) 52999.

Devon County Ladies' Golf Association
Hon Sec, Miss M Saint, 16 Gower Ridge Road, Plymstock, Plymouth PL9 9DR. *Tel* (0752) 404691.

Devon Professional Golfers' Alliance
Hon Sec, Michael J Dunk, Sunhaven, 2 Landscore Close, Crediton, Devon. *Tel* (036 32) 3145.

Dorset County Golf Union
Hon Sec, Lt Col MD Hutchins, 38 Carlton Road, Bournemouth BH1 3TG. *Tel* (0202) 290821.

Dorset Ladies' County Golf Association
Miss JM Rhodes, 4 Egdon Glen Crossways, Dorchester, Dorset DT2 8BQ. *Tel* (0305) 852547.

Durham County Golf Union
Hon Sec, WP Murray, Highnam Lodge, Park Mews, Hartlepool, Cleveland TS26 0DX. *Tel* (0429) 273185.

Durham County Ladies' Golf Association
Sec, Mrs CF Anderson, 107 Harlsey Road, Hartburn, Stockton-on-Tees.

English Golf Union
Sec, K Wright, 1–3 Upper King Street, Leicester LE1 6XF. *Tel* (0533) 553042 *Fax* (0533) 471322.

Midland Group Sec, RJW Baldwin, Chantry Cottage, Friar Street, Droitwich, Worcs. WR9 8EQ. *Tel* (0905) 778560.

Northern Group Hon Sec, EG Bunting, 7 Northbrook Court, Hartlepool, Cleveland TS26 0DJ. *Tel* (0429) 274828.

South Eastern Group *Hon Sec,* MA Hobson, 22 Wye Court, Malvern Way, Ealing, London W13 8EA. *Tel* 01-997 7466.

South Western Group *Sec,* JT Lumley, Hartland, Potterne, Devizes, Wilts SN10 5PA. *Tel* (0380) 3935.

English Ladies' Golf Association
Sec, Mrs MJ Carr, Edgbaston Golf Club, Church Road, Birmingham B15 3TB. *Tel* 021-456 2088.

Northern Division *Hon Sec,* Mrs L Young, 10 Cleehill Drive, North Shields, Tyne and Weir NE29 9EW. *Tel* 091-257 6925.

Midlands Division *Hon Sec,* Mrs C Stevenson, 3 Leaholme Gardens, Pedmore, Stourbridge, West Midlands DY9 0XX. *Tel* (0562) 884582.

South-Eastern Division *Hon Sec,* Mrs E Block, 71 Parkanaur Avenue, Thorpe Bay, Essex SS1 3JA. *Tel* (0702) 588336.

South-Western Division *Hon Sec,* Mrs VJ Wilde, 19 Ferndown Close, Kingsweston, Bristol. *Tel* (0272) 683543.

English Schools' Golf Association
Hon Sec, R Snell, 20 Dykenook Close, Whickham, Newcastle-upon-Tyne. *Tel* 091-488 3538.

Essex County Amateur Golf Union
Hon Sec, EV Sadler, 9 Willow Walk, Hadleigh, Benfleet, Essex SS7 2RW. *Tel* (0702) 559871.

Essex Ladies' County Golf Association
Hon Sec, Mrs J Bourne, 1 The Paddocks, Stock, Essex. *Tel* (0277) 810466.

Essex Professional Golfers' Association
Sec, John E Douglas, 7 Theydon Grove, Epping, Essex.

Gloucestershire and Somerset Professional Golfers' Association
Sec, Noel Boland, Cotswold Hills GC. *Tel* (0242) 515263.

Gloucestershire Golf Union
Hon Sec, RF Crisp, 2 Hartley Close, Sandy Lane, Charlton Kings, Cheltenham GL53 9DN. *Tel* (0242) 514024.

Gloucester Ladies' County Golf Association
Hon Sec, Mrs L Williams, 1 Avon Crescent, Cumberland Road, Bristol BS1 6XQ. *Tel* (0272) 264606.

Hampshire Ladies' County Golf Association
Hon Sec, Mrs E Buckley, 182 Bassett Green Road, Southampton, Hants SO2 3LW. *Tel* (0703) 789273.

Hampshire, Isle of Wight and Channel Islands Golf Union
Hon Sec/Treas, JLS McCracken, *Glyngarth,* Tower Road, Hindhead, Surrey GU26 6SL. *Tel* (042 873) 4090.

Hampshire Professional Golfers' Association
Hon Sec, Chris Maltby, 3 Lilly Close, Kempshott Down, Basingstoke, Hants RG22 5NT. *Tel* (0256) 466070.

Herts County Professional Golfers' Alliance
Hon Sec, RA Gurney, 1 Field Lane, Letchworth, Herts SG6 3LF *Tel* (0462) 682256.

Hertfordshire County Ladies' Golf Association
Hon Sec, Mrs EM Copley, 22 The Avenue, Radlett, Herts WD7 7DW. *Tel* (0923) 857184.

Hertfordshire Golf Union
Hon Sec, WA de Podesta, 2 The Heath, Radlett, Herts WD7 7DF. *Tel* (0923) 857184.

Isle of Man Golf Union
Hon Sec, GR Hotchkiss, 22 Mount View Road, Onchan, Isle of Man. *Tel* (0624) 22991.

Isle of Wight Ladies' Golf Association
Hon Sec, Mrs F Harrison, 47 Palmers Road, Wootton, Isle of Wight. *Tel* (0983) 883864.

Kent County Golf Union
Hon Sec, BM Evans, 52 Queens Road, Littlestone, New Romney, Kent TN28 8LY. *Tel* (0679) 63613.

Kent County Ladies' Golf Association
Hon Sec, Mrs D Hall-Thompson, Colleton House, North Road, Hythe, Kent CT21 4AS. *Tel* (0303) 66285.

Kent Professional Golfers' Union
Sec, E Impett, 20 The Grove, Barnham, Kent. Tel (0227) 831655.

Lancashire Ladies' County Golf Association
Hon Sec, Miss P Hurst, 25 Park Road, Golborne, Warrington, Cheshire WA3 3PU.

Lancashire PGA
Sec, George Hill, 32 Pembridge Road, Blackley, Manchester M9 2LE. *Tel* 061-795 8547.

Lancashire Union of Golf Clubs
Sec, N Hardman, 4 Cedarwood Close, Lytham Hall Park, Lytham, Lancs FY8 4PD. *Tel* (0253) 733323.

Leicestershire and Rutland Ladies' County Golf Association
Hon Sec, Mrs DL Sabey, 4 Bailey's Lane, Burton Overy, Leics LE8 ODD. *Tel* (053759) 2697.

Leicestershire and Rutland Golf Union
Hon Sec, GH Upward, 187 Leicester Road, Groby, Leicester. *Tel* (0533) 873675.

Leicestershire Professional Golfers' Association
Sec, Mr D Freeman, 218 Hamilton Lane, Scraptoft, Leics. *Tel* (0533) 414735.

Lincolnshire Ladies' County Association
Hon Sec, Mrs G Newcombe, 7 Chapman Street, Market Rasen, Lincs LN8 3JU. *Tel* (0673) 842287.

Lincolnshire Professional Golfers' Association
Sec, Robin Lawie, Seacroft GC, Skegness, Lincs. *Tel* (0754) 3020.

Lincolnshire Union of Golf Clubs
Hon Sec, TJ Hale *Dapselah,* Allenby Cres., Fotherby, Nr Louth LN11 0UJ. *Tel* (0507) 604298.

Middlesex County Golf Union
Hon Sec, PSV Cooke, 36 Grants Close, Mill Hill, London NW7 1DD. *Tel* 01-349 0414.

Middlesex Ladies' County Golf Association
Hon Sec, Mrs C Hume, 62 Church Crescent, London N3 1BJ.

Middlesex Professional Golfers' Association
Sec, Mrs FS Brown, Hampstead Golf Club, Winnington Road, London N2 OTU. *Tel* 01-455 7089.

Midland Golf Union
Hon Sec, RJW Baldwin, Chantry Cottage, Friar Street, Droitwich, Worcs WR9 8EQ. *Tel* (0905) 778560.

Norfolk County Golf Union
Hon Sec/Treas, RJ Trower, 12a Stanley Avenue, Thorpe, Norwich, Norfolk. *Tel* (0603) 31026.

Norfolk Ladies' County Association
Hon Sec, Mrs VM Munro, 17 Taylor Avenue, Cringleford, Norfolk NR4 6XY. *Tel* (0603) 56049.

Norfolk PGA
Hon Sec, M Garrett, Sheringham GC, Sheringham, Norfolk. *Tel* (0263) 823488.

North East and North West PGA
Sec Ray Sentance, 7 Larch Lea, Ponteland, Newcastle upon Tyne NE20 9LG. *Tel* (0661) 25151.

Northamptonshire Golf Union
Joint Hon Secs, RG Halliday and TCA Knight, c/o 12 Edge Hill Road, Duston, Northampton NN5 6BY. *Tel* (0604) 51031.

Northamptonshire Ladies' County Golf Association
Hon Sec, Mrs MML Coker, 534 Wellingborough Road, Northampton NN3 3HZ. *Tel* (0604) 409298.

Northamptonshire PGA
Hon Sec, G Mobbs, Ivycroft, Back Lane, Chapel Brampton, Northants. *Tel* (0605) 843305.

Northumberland Ladies' County Golf Association
Hon Sec, Mrs M Canning, 23 Mast Lane, Cullercoats, North Shields NE30 3DF. *Tel* 091-252 5382.

Northumberland Union of Golf Clubs
Hon Sec, WE Procter, 5 Oakhurst Drive, Kenton Park, Gosforth, Newcastle-upon-Tyne NE3 4JS. *Tel* 091-285 4981 *(home),* 091-274 5310 *(office).*

Nottinghamshire County Ladies' Golf Association
Hon Sec, Mrs B Jackson, Cranmer Lodge, Main Street, Kinoulton, Notts, NA12 3EL. *Tel* (0949) 81201.

Nottinghamshire PGA
Sec, RW Futer, 52 Barden Road, Mapperley, Nottingham NG3 5QD. *Tel* (0602) 269635.

Nottinghamshire Union of Golf Clubs
Hon Sec, E Peters, 48 Weaverthorpe Road, Woodthorp, Notts NG5 4NB. *Tel* (0602) 266560.

Oxfordshire Ladies' County Golf Association
Hon Sec, Miss BM Nicklin, 532 Banbury Road, Oxford OX2 8EG. *Tel* (0865) 58300.

Sheffield PGA
Sec, Graham Walker, Hillsborough GC, Worrall Road, Sheffield S6 4BE. *Tel* (0742) 332666.

Sheffield Union of Golf Clubs
Sec, JHV Wheeler, 8 Newfield Court, 586 Fulwood Road, Sheffield S10 3QE.

Shropshire and Herefordshire Union of Golf Clubs
Hon Sec, JR Davies, 23 Poplar Crescent, Bayston Hill, Shrewsbury SY3 OQB. *Tel* (0743) 722655.

Shropshire and Herefordshire PGA
Sec, Mr P Hinton, Bridgnorth Golf Club, Stanley Lane, Bridgnorth, Shropshire. *Tel* (07462) 2045.

Shropshire Ladies' County Golf Association
Hon Sec, Mrs O Higgs, 122 Fieldhouse Drive, Muxton, Telford, Salop TF8 8BB. *Tel* (0952) 604522.

Somerset Golf Union
Hon Sec, GC Bacon, Longwood, Grange Road, Saltford, Bristol BS18 3AG. *Tel* (0225) 872166.

Somerset Ladies' County Golf Association
Hon Sec, Mrs P Harker, 83 Milford Avenue, Wick, Nr Bristol, Avon BS15 5PP. *Tel* (027 582) 3087.

South-Western Counties Golf Association
Hon Sec/Treas, JT Lumley, Hartland, Potterne, Devizes, Wilts. SN10 5PA. *Tel* (0380) 3935.

Staffordshire Ladies' County Golf Association
Hon Sec, Mrs DB Banks, 11 Westhill, Finchfield Hill, Wolverhampton WV3 9HL. *Tel* (0902) 753370.

Staffordshire and Shropshire Union of Professional Golfers
Sec, E Griffiths, 22 Wynn Road, Penn, Wolverhampton. *Tel* (0902) 332180 *(home).*

Staffordshire Union of Golf Clubs
Hon Sec, A Smith, 19 Broadway, Walsall, W Midlands WS1 3EX. *Tel* (0922) 24988.

Suffolk County Golf Union
Hon Sec, JJ Kerrison, Heath View, Purdis Avenue, Ipswich, Suffolk IP3 8UE. *Tel* (0473) 724753.

Suffolk Ladies' County Golf Association
Hon Sec, Miss A Seward, 20 Meadowside, Snowdon Hill, Wickham Market, Woodbridge, Suffolk. *Tel* (0728) 747609.

Suffolk PGA
Sec, Mark Jillings, Bury St Edmunds GC, Fornham All Saints, Bury St Edmunds, Suffolk IP28 2LG. *Tel* (0284) 755978.

Surrey County Golf Union
Hon Sec, MW Ashton, Rushmoor Cottage, Rushmoor Close, Fleet, Hants GU13 9LD. *Tel* (0252) 614078.

Surrey Ladies' County Golf Association
Hon Sec, Mrs A Fox, 19 Lackford Road, Chipstead, Surrey CR3 3TB. *Tel* (07375) 52112.

Surrey PGA
Sec, P Bowles, 27 Lower Wood Road, Claygate, Surrey KT10 0EU. *Tel* (0372) 63882.

Sussex County Golf Union
DG Pulford, 12 Rodmell Avenue, Saltdean, Brighton, E Sussex BN2 8LT. *Tel* (0273) 304415.

Sussex County Ladies' Golf Association
Hon Sec, Mrs FR Milton, Flat 1, 22 Granville Road, Eastbourne, East Sussex BN20 7HA. *Tel* (0323) 28452.

Sussex Professional Golfers' Union
Sec, C Pluck, 96 Cranston Avenue, Bexhill-on-Sea, Sussex. *Tel* (0424) 221298.

Warwickshire Ladies' County Golf Association
Hon Sec, Mrs J Plant, 57 White House Green, Solihull, W Midlands B91 1SP. *Tel* 021-705 8062.

Warwickshire Professional Golfers' Association
Sec, J Tunnicliffe, 5 Church Lane, Stoneleigh, Warwickshire. *Tel* (0203) 418113.

Warwickshire Union of Golf Clubs
Hon Sec, JBM Urry, Dormers, 232 Dickens Heath Road, Shirley, Solihull B90 1QQ. *Tel (home)* (0564) 823114; *(office)* 021-328 5665.

Wiltshire County Golf Union
Hon Sec/Treas, RF Eu'hlay, 10 Priory Park, Bradford-on-Avon, Wilts. BA15 1QU. *Tel* (022 16) 6401.

Wiltshire Ladies' County Golf Association
Hon Sec, Mrs P Board, South Lodge, Northleigh, Bradford-on Avon, Wilts. *Tel* (02216) 3387.

Wiltshire PGA
L Ross, *Professional,* Marlborough GC, The Common, Marlborough, Wilts. *Tel* (0672) 52493.

Worcestershire Association of Professional Golfers
Sec, Chris Thompson, Droitwich GC, Ford Lane, Droitwich WR9 0BH, Worcs. *Tel* (0905) 770207.

Worcestershire County Ladies' Golf Association
Hon Sec, Mrs B Ward, Silverdale, Hunters Ride, Lawnswood, Stourbridge, Worcs DY7 5QN.

Worcestershire Union of Golf Clubs
Hon Sec, WR Painter, 70 Cardinal Drive, Kidderminster, Worcs DY10 4RY. *Tel* (0562) 823109.

Yorkshire Ladies' County Golf Association
Hon Sec, Mrs M Elliott, Ingle Court, Lepton, Huddersfield, Yorks. *Tel* (0484) 602011.

Yorkshire Professional Golfers' Association
Hon Sec, David Bulmer, Temple Newsam GC, Halton, Leeds 15, N Yorks. *Tel* (0532) 647362/641464.

Yorkshire Union of Golf Clubs
Hon Sec, Alan Cowman, 50 Bingley Road, Bradford, West Yorks BD9 6HH. *Tel* (0274) 542661.

Ireland

Irish Golf Union
Sec, Ivan ER Dickson, Glencar House, 81 Eglington Road, Donnybrook, Dublin 4. Tel (0001) 694111.

Ulster Branch Sec, Alfred Collis MBE, 58a High Street, Holywood, Co Down, BT18 9AE. Tel Holywood 7427 (home), Holywood 3708 (office).

Leinster Branch Sec, Ken Haughton, 1 Clonskeagh Square, Clonskeagh Road, Dublin 14. Tel Dublin (0001) 696977/696727.

Munster Branch Hon Sec, Richard Barry, Sunville, Dromsligo, Mallow, Co Cork. Tel (office) (22) 21117/221123; (home) (22) 22760.

Connacht Branch Hon Sec, Tom Greally, Abbey Hotel, Roscommon. Tel (home) Roscommon 26240.

Irish Ladies' Golf Union
Sec, Miss MP Turvey, 1 Clonskeagh Square, Clonskeagh Road, Dublin 14. Tel Dublin (0001) 696244.

Northern District Hon Sec, Mrs L Watson, 14D Adelaide Park, Belfast BT9 6FX. Tel (0232) 682152.

Southern District Hon Sec, Mrs N Flynn, 11 Barnstead Drive, Church Road, Blackrock, Cork. Tel Cork (21) 291698.

Eastern District Hon Sec, Mrs D O'Sullivan, 4 Castletown Court, Celbridge, Co. Kildare.

Western District Hon Sec, Mrs A Bradshaw, Dooney Rock, Cleveragh Drive, Sligo. Tel Sligo (71) 62351.

Midland District Hon Sec, Mrs B Jordan, 6 Glena Terrace, Spawell Road, Wexford. Tel Wexford (53) 22865.

Scotland

Aberdeen Ladies' County Golf Association
Hon Sec, Mrs SAH Bain, 9 Earlswell Place, Cults, Aberdeen AB1 9LG. Tel (0224) 861502.

Angus Ladies' County Golf Association
Hon Sec, Mrs DJ Gordon, The Hawthorns, 7 Grange Avenue, Monifieth, Dundee Tel (0382) 532799.

Ayrshire Ladies' County Golf Association
Hon Sec, Mrs A McMillan, 8 Station Road, Prestwick KA9 1AQ. Tel (0292) 77330.

Border Counties' Golf Association
Sec, Mr Sproule, 22 Woodlands Park, Coldstream, Berwickshire Tel (0890) 2251.

Dumfriesshire Ladies' County Golf Association
Hon Sec, Miss MJ Greig, Strathdon, 10 Nelson Street, Dumfries. Tel (0387) 54429.

Dunbartonshire and Argyll Ladies' County Association
Hon Sec, Mrs M Gibson, 49 Ledi Drive, Bearsden, Glasgow G61 4JN. Tel 041-942 4328.

East Lothian Ladies' County Association
Hon Sec, Mrs IG Campbell, Glenlair, Main Street, Gullane. Tel (0620) 842534.

Fife County Ladies' Golf Association
Hon Sec, Mrs CH Matheson, Greyfriars, Greyfriars Garden, St Andrews. Tel (0334) 72639.

Galloway Ladies' County Golf Association
Hon Sec, Mrs Y Gordon, 3 Seggies, Kirkcudbright. Tel (0557) 30542.

Lanarkshire Ladies' County Golf Association
Hon Sec, Mrs GE Duncanson, 75 Kenmure Gardens, Bishopbriggs, Glasgow G64 2BZ. Tel 041-772 1720.

Midlothian County Ladies' Golf Association
Hon Sec, Mrs K MacKay, 37 Thomson Drive, Currie, Midlothian EH14 5EY. Tel 031-449 3441.

Northern Counties' Ladies Golf Association
Hon Sec, Mrs A Cranston, 15 Boarstone Avenue, Inverness. Tel (0463) 221317.

Perth and Kinross Ladies' County Golf Association
Hon Sec, J Jones, Broom, Caledonian Crescent, Auchterarder, Perthshire. Tel (0764) 62254.

Renfrewshire Ladies' County Golf Association
Hon Sec, Miss MA Stewart, 21 Holmwood Road, Glasgow G44 3AS. Tel 041-637 1307.

Stirling and Clackmannan Ladies' Golf Association
Sec, Mrs JC Williamson, 7 Craighorn Drive, Falkirk FK1 5NX. Tel (0324) 29672.

Scottish Golf Union
Sec, JW Hume, The Cottage, 181a Whitehouse Road, Barnton, Edinburgh EH4 6BY. Tel 031-339 7546.

Area Associations:
Angus G Hardie, Conachan, 4 Cliffburn Road, Arbroath, Angus DD11 5BB. Tel (0241) 73018 (home).

Argyll and Bute J Forgreive, 6 Dalintart Drive, Oban. *Tel* (0631) 65298 *(home)*, (0631) 63626 *(office)*.

Ayrshire RL Crawford, 14 Maxwell Gardens, Hurlford, Kilmarnock, Ayrshire KA1 5BY. *Tel* (0563) 31932 *(home)*, (0563) 21190 *(office)*.

Borders IF Sproule, 22 Woodlands Park, Coldstream. *Tel* (0890) 2251 *(home)*.

Clackmannanshire H Hunter, 13 Airlie Court, Gleneagles Village, Auchterarder, Perthshire PH3 1SA. *Tel* (0764) 63832 *(home)*.

Dunbartonshire RW Jenkins, Dunedin, 14 Hawthorn Avenue, Lenzie G66 4RA. *Tel* 041-776 1148.

Fife BR Wright, 2 West Fergus Place, Kirkcaldy, Fife KY1 1UR. *Tel* (0592) 263304 *(home)*, (0592) 206605 *(office)*.

Glasgow GO McInnes, 4 Dalziel Court, 56 Dalziel Drive, Glasgow G41. *Tel* 041-427 3156 *(home)*, 041-226 4471 *(office)*.

Lanarkshire JT Durrant, 30 Woodlands Crescent, Bothwell, Glasgow G71 8PP. *Tel* (0698) 852331.

Lothians IR Graham, 29 Morningside Grove, Edinburgh EH10 5PX. *Tel* 031-447 3281.

North JP Ford, Timbertop, Croy, Inverness IV1 2PH. *Tel* (066 78) 363.

North-East IAD McPherson, Cruden Bay Golf Club, Cruden Bay, Peterhead, AB4 7NN. *Tel* (0779) 812395 *(home)*, (0779) 812285 *(office)*.

Perth and Kinross DY Rae, 18 Carlownie Place, Auchterarder PH3 1BT *Tel* (0764) 62837.

Renfrewshire JI McCosh, *Muirfield*, 20 Williamson Place, Johnstone, Renfrewshire PA5 9DU. *Tel* (0505) 27974 *(home)*.

South JH Somerville, Cherry Cottage, Kirkcudbright. *Tel* (0557) 30445.

Stirlingshire RM McLaren, 2 Ochil Crescent, Auchterarder PH3 1NA. *Tel* (0764) 62167.

Scottish Golfer's Alliance
Sec/Treas, Mrs MA Caldwell, 5 Deveron Avenue, Giffnock, Glasgow G48 6NH.

Scottish Ladies' Golfing Association
Sec, Mrs LH Park, Chacewood, 49 Fullarton Drive, Troon KA10 6LF. *Tel* (0292) 313047.

Scottish Ladies' Golfing Association— County Golf
Hon Sec, Miss MJ Greig, Strathdon, Nelson Street, Dumfries. *Tel* (0387) 54429.

Scottish Schools' Golf Association
Hon Sec, Mr Edward Dixon, History Dept, Grangemouth High School, Grangemouth, Central Region.

West of Scotland Girls' Golfing Association
Hon Sec, Mrs PI McKay, 7 Gardenside Avenue, Uddingston, Glasgow G71 7BU.

Wales

Anglesey Golf Union
Hon Sec, GP Jones, 20 Gwelfor Estate, Cemaes Bay, Anglesey. *Tel* (0407) 710755.

Brecon and Radnor Golf Union
Hon Sec GL Williams, 10 Penpentre, Llanfaes, Brecon.

Caernarvonshire and Anglesey Ladies' County Golf Association
Hon Sec, Mrs BR Williams, Deunant, Llangefni, Anglesey LL7 7YP. *Tel* (0248) 722338.

Caernarvonshire and District Golfing Union
Hon Sec, R Eric Jones, 23 Bryn Rhos, Rhosbodrual, Caernarfon, Gwynedd LL55 2BT. *Tel* (0286) 3486.

Denbighshire Golfing Union
Hon Sec, J. Johnson, 15 Ffordd Elfed, Wrexham, Clwyd.

Denbighshire and Flintshire Ladies' County Golf Association
Hon Sec, Mrs M Jackson, Cilgwyn, Bryn Glas, Ruthin, Clwyd. *Tel* (08242) 2249.

Dyfed Golfing Union
Hon Sec, JR Jones, 55 Clover Park, Haverfordwest, Dyfed.

Flintshire Golfing Union
Hon Sec, H Griffith, Cornist Lodge, Cornist Park, Flint, Clwyd. *Tel* (03526) 2186.

Glamorgan County Golf Union
Hon Sec, John Banfill, 332 North Road, Cardiff. *Tel* (0222) 628493.

Glamorgan Ladies' County Golf Association
Mrs S Williams, 19 Trem-y-Don, Barry, South Glamorgan. *Tel* (0446) 734865.

Gwent Golf Union
Sec, CM Buckley, 3 Oak Court, Woodfield Park, Blackwood, Gwent. *Tel* (0495) 223520.

Mid Wales Ladies County Golf Association
Sec, Miss A James, Ael-y-Bryn, Pontfaen Road, Lampeter, Dyfed. *Tel* (0570) 422463.

Monmouthshire Ladies' County Golf Association
Hon Sec, Mrs Ruth Morris, Flat 2, 405 Chepstow Road, Newport, Gwent. *Tel* (0633) 279638.

North Wales PGA
Sec, Peter Bright, Porthmadog Golf Club, Morfa Bycham, Porthmadog, Gwynedd. *Tel* (0766) 3828.

South Wales Professional Golfers' Association
Hon Sec, B Thomas, St Mellons Golf Club, Mid-Glam. *Tel* (0633) 680101.

Welsh Golfing Union
Sec, DG Lee, 5 Park Place, Cardiff, South Glamorgan. *Tel* (0222) 238467.

Welsh Ladies' Golf Union
Hon Sec, Miss P Roberts, Ysgoldy Gynt, Llanhennock, Newport, Gwent NP6 1LT. *Tel* (0633) 420642.

Overseas

America: USA & Canada

American Ladies' Professional Golf Association
Commissioner, William A Blue, 2570 Volusia Avenue, Suite B, Daytona Beach, Florida 32114. *Tel* (904) 254 8800 *Fax* (904) 254 4755.

American Professional Golfers' Association
Chief Executive Officer, John J Rossi, Box 12458, 100 Avenue of the Champions, Palm Beach Gardens, Florida 33418. *Tel* (407) 624 8400.

Canadian Ladies' Golf Association
Executive Director, Leonard Murphy, 1600 James Naismith Drive, Gloucester, Ontario, K1B 5N4. *Tel* (613) 748 5642.

Canadian Professional Golfers' Association
General Manager, Robert H Noble, 59 Berkeley Street, Toronto M5A 2W5. *Tel* Toronto (416) 368 6104.

Canadian (Royal) Golf Association
Golf House, RR no 2, Oakville, Ontario L6J 4Z3, Canada.

Provincial Golf Associations
British Columbia *Sec/Treas,* RE Maze, Room 322, 1675 West 8th Ave, Vancouver, BC V6J 1V2.

Alberta *Manager,* ER Wood, 200-H Haddon Road, Calgary, Alberta T2V 2Y6.

Saskatchewan *Exec Dir,* WF Macrae, 2205 Victoria Avenue, Regina, Saskatchewan S4P 0S4.

Manitoba *Exec Dir,* DI Macdonald, 1700 Ellice Ave, Winnipeg, Manitoba R3H 0B1.

Ontario *Exec Dir,* WJ Williams, 400 Esna Park Drive, Unit 11, Markham, Ontario L3R 1H5.

Quebec *Exec Director,* CH Gribbin, 3300 Cavendish Blvd, Suite 250, Montreal, Quebec H4B 2M8.

New Brunswick *Sec/Treas,* EA Trites, 3 Sunset Lane, St John, New Brunswick E2H 1C8.

Nova Scotia *Sec/Treas,* W MacDonald, 14 Limardo Drive, Dartmouth, Nova Scotia B3A 3X4.

Newfoundland–Labrador *Sec,* CR Cook, PO Box 5361, St Johns, Newfoundland.

Prince Edward Island *Sec/Treas,* David Kassner, PO Box 51, Charlottetown, PEI C1A 7K2.

Golf Course Association
111 East Wacker Drive, Chicago, Illinois 60601, USA. *Tel* Chicago (312) 644 6610.

International Golf Association
Executive Director, Burch Riber, PO Box 176, Glenville Station, Greenwich, CT 06831-0876. *Tel* (203) 531 1113 *Fax* (203) 531 4373.

TPA Tour
(USA), *Commissioner,* Deane R Beman, Sawgrass, Ponte Vedra, Florida 32082.

United States Golf Association
Executive Director, David B Fay, USGA Golf House, Liberty Corner Road, Far Hills, New Jersey 07931. *Tel* Jersey City (201) 234 2300.

Central America

Bahamas Golf Federation
Sec, Calvin Cooper, PO Box F.3854, Free Port, Grand Bahama, Bahamas.

Barbados Golf Association
Sec, TM Hanton, c/o Sandy Lane GC, St James, Barbados.

Bermuda Golf Association
Sec-Treas, Mrs Eric N Parker, PO Box 433, Hamilton 5, Bermuda. *Tel* 809 298 1367.

Jamaica Golf Association
Constant Spring Golf Club, Constant Spring, Kingston 8, Jamaica.

Mexican Golf Association
Cincinnati, No. 40-104, Mexico 18, DF.

Trinidad and Tobago Golf Association

Texaco Trinidad Inc, Point-a-Pierre, Trinidad, West Indies.

South America

Asociación Argentina de Golf

Gen Manager, JT Salorio; *Hon Sec,* Ignacio JR Soba Rojo, Corrientes 538, Piso 11, 1043 Buenos Aires, Argentina.

Argentine Professional Golfers' Association

Av. Corrientes 538, Piso 11 (1043) Buenos Aires, Argentina.

Asunción Golf Union

Casilla de Correo 302, Asunción, Paraguay.

Bolivian Golf Federation (Federación Boliviana de Golf)

Sec, Raul Zabalaga, Casilla de Correo 6130, La Paz, Bolivia.

Brazilian Golf Confederation

(Confederacão Brasileira de Golf), *Exec Sec,* AE Nardy, Rua 7 de Abril, 282-8°, and -S/83-01044, São Paulo, Brazil.

Chilean Golf Federation

Casilla 13307, Correo 21, Santiago, Chile.

Colombian Golf Union (Federación Colombiana de Golf)

Sec, Louis Restrepo, Carrer 7A, 72-64 of Int 26 Apartado 90985, Bogotá, Colombia.

Ecuador Golf Federation (Asociación Equatoriana de Golf)

Casilia 521, Guayaquil, Ecuador.

Guyana Golf Union

c/o Demerara Bauxite Co Limited, Mackenzie, Guyana.

Paraguay Golf Association

Asunción GC, Casilla de Correo 302, Asunción, Paraguay.

Peru Golf Federation (Federación Peruana de Golf)

Sec, HB Sanchez, Casilla 5637, Lima, Peru.

South American Golf Federation

Hon Sec, E Anchordoqui, Guipuzcoa 486-P7, Montevideo, Uruguay.

Uruguay Golf Association (Asociación Uruguaya de Golf)

Sec, Jorge Brignoni, Casilla de Correo 1484, Montevideo.

Venezuela Golf Federation

Unidad Comercial, *La Florida,* Local 5, Avenida Avila, La Florida, Caracas 1050, Venezuela.

Asia and Far East

Asia-Pacific Golf Confederation

Sec Gen, EJH Yong, 52, 1st Floor, Jalan Hang, Lekiu 50100, Kuala Lumpur.

Asia Professional Golf Circuit

Co-ordinator, John Benda, Asia Golf Circuit Agency, 230 East Foothill Drive, Phoenix, Arizona 85020. *Tel* (602) 395 9384 *Fax* (602) 395 9370

Ceylon Golf Union

2 Gower Street, Colombo 5, Sri Lanka.

Professional Golfers' Association of the Republic of China

2nd Floor, No: 100 Pei-Ling 5th Road, Taipei, Taiwan, R.O.C. *Tel* (02) 8220318/8229684.

Hong Kong Golf Association

Sec, Michael J Steele, Room 110, Yuto Sang Bldg 37, Queens Road, Central, Hong Kong.

Hong Kong Professional Golfers' Association

Hon Sec, AR Hamilton, PO Box 690, Hong Kong. *Tel* Hong Kong (5) 222111. *Telex* HX73751.

Indian Golf Union

Hon Sec, Raj Bir Singh, Tata Centre (3rd Floor), 43 Chowringhee Road, Calcutta 700071.

Indonesian Golf Association

Hon Sec, MST Aziz, Jalan Rawamangun Muka Raya, Jakarta 13220. *Tel* 4891208 *Telex* 61396 DJACOM IA.

Japan Golf Association

Sec Gen, Miss A Kato, 606-6th Floor, Palace Building, Marunouchi, Chiyoda-ku, Tokyo, Japan. *Tel* Tokyo (3) 215 0003.

Japan Ladies' Professional Golfers' Association

Kuranae Kogyo Kaikan 7F, Shinbasi 2-19-10, Minato-ku, Tokyo. *Tel* Tokyo (3) 571 0928.

Japan Professional Golf Association

Sec Gen, Kikuo Minakata, Tomin-Ueno Building, 4F, 1-7-15, Higashi-Ueno, Taito-Ku, Tokyo 110, Japan.

Korean Golf Association

Sec General, Room 1B, 13th Floor, Manhattan Bldg, 36-2, Yeo-Eui-Do-Dowg, Yeong Deung Po-Ku, Seoul, Korea. *Tel* Seoul (2) 783 4748/2783 4749.

Malaysian Golf Association

Hon Sec, TK Kee, 12A Persiaran Ampang, 55000 Kuala Lumpur, Malaysia.

New Guinea Papua Territory Amateur Golf Association

Sec, Jack Page, PO Box 382, Lae, TPNG.

Pakistan Golf Federation
Hon Sec, Zafar Ahmed, PO Box No 1295,
Rawalpindi, Pakistan. *Telex* PGF/13-A-1V

Papua New Guinea Ladies' Golf Association
Mrs Mavis Harvey, PO Box 1256, Port Moresby,
TPNG. *Tel* 675 214745.

Republic of the Philippines Golf Association
Sec, Vince Villafuerte, 209 Administration
Building, Rizal Memorial Sports Complex,
Vito Cruz, Manila, Philippines. *Tel* 632-8164766
Fax 632-819-149.

Singapore Golf Association
Hon Sec, Gerald Loong, Singapore Golf
Association, 4 Battery Rd, No 12-00 Bank of
China Building, Singapore 0104. *Telegraphic
address* Golfing Singapore; *Telex* RS 42354
Acapas.

Sri Lanka Ladies' Golf Union
c/o Royal Colombo Golf Club, PO Box 309,
Colombo, Sri Lanka.

Sri Lanka Golf Union
2 Gower Street, Colombo 5, Sri Lanka.

Thailand Golf Association
Hon Sec, Likhit Sudarat, Railway Training,
Vibhavadee Centre Rangsit Road,
Bangkok 10900, Thailand. *Tel* 51 34988/9
Telex 20806 SCCFOOD TH.

Australasia

Australian Golf Union
Sec, CA Phillips, Golf Australia House, 155
Cecil Street, South Melbourne, Victoria 3205.

Members of the Union:
Victoria *Sec,* TS Duguid, Victorian Golf
Association, PO Box 187, Elsternwick, Victoria
3185.

New South Wales *Sec,* B Scott, New South
Wales Golf Association, 17-19 Brisbane Street,
Darlinghurst, NSW 2010.

Tasmanian Golf Council, *Sec,* A Rollins, GPO
Box 940K, Hobart 7001. *Tel* Hobart (02) 348315.

Queensland *Sec,* W Kennedy, Queensland Golf
Union, PO Box 260, Mt Gravatt, Queensland 4122,
Australia.

Western Australia *Sec,* G Fitzhardinge, Western
Australian Golf Association Inc, PO Box 455 South
Perth, W Aust. 6151.

South Australia *Sec,* MH Hall, South
Australia Golf Association, 249 Henley Beach
Road, Torvensville, South Australia 5031.

Australian Ladies' Golf Union
Executive Director, Mrs KD Brown,
22 McKay Road, Rowville 3178, Victoria.
Tel Melbourne (3) 763 6919.

Members of the Union:
Victoria *Sec,* Miss K Mahlook, 589 Malvern
Road, Toorak, 3142, Victoria.

New South Wales *Sec,* Miss Wendy V Weil,
17 Brisbane Street, Darlinghurst, NSW 2010.
Tel 264 7327.

Queensland *Sec,* Mrs M Barnett, PO Box 83,
Chermside, 4032, Queensland. *Tel* 221 6677.

Western Australia *Sec,* Mrs M Cutter, Suite
1-4, Stratham House, 49 Melville Parade,
South Perth. *Tel* 368 2618.

South Australia *Sec,* Mrs GA Small, 13 Pitcairn
Ave, Urrbrae, 5064. *Tel* 79 3200.
Tasmania *Sec,* Mrs IP Allen, 45 Balmoral Road,
Kingston Beach, 7151. *Tel* 29 5120.

Australian Professional Golfers' Association
Sec, Barbara Molesworth, 4/140 George Street,
Hornsby, New South Wales, 2077.
Tel (02) 476 3333 *Fax* (02) 477 7625.

New Zealand Golf Association (Inc)
Dominion Sports House, Mercer Street,
Wellington, PO Box 11842.
Tel Wellington (4) 845 408. *Telegrams* Enzedgolf.

New Zealand Professional Golfers' Association
Sec, Sqn Ldr AR Bleakley, PO Box 21-482,
Auckland 8. *Tel* Auckland (9) 836 4703.

New Zealand Ladies' Golf Union
Sec, Mrs PE Jessup, PO Box 13-029, Wellington
4, New Zealand. *Tel/Fax* 793 868.

Africa (south of Sahara)

Botswana Golf Union
Hon Sec, Robert Stewart, PO Box 1033,
Gaborone, Botswana. *Tel* Gaborone (31) 53989
(home).

Ghana Golf Association
Sec, MM Ezan, PO Box 8, Achimola, Ghana.

Kenya Golf Union
PO Box 49609, Nairobi. *Tel* Nairobi (2) 720074.

Kenya Ladies' Golf Union
PO Box 45615, Nairobi, Kenya.

Malawi Golf Union
PO Box 1198, Blantyre, Malawi.

Malawi Ladies' Golf Union
PO Box 5319, Limbe, Malawi.

Nigerian Golf Association
Sec Ms N Chinakw, c/o National Sports Commission, Surulere, PO Box 145, Lagos.

Sierra Leone Golf Federation
Pres, JS Baird, PO Box 575, Freetown, Sierra Leone.

South African Golf Union
Exec Dir, JM Kellie, PO Box 1537, Cape Town 8000. *Cablegram address:* Sagolfunion, Cape Town. *Tel* Cape Town (21) 467585 *(office)*, (21) 653617 *(home)*.

Provincial Unions:
Border Golf Union *Hon Sec,* Mrs J Davenport, Box 1773, East London 5200, CP. *Tel* (0431) 403899.

Eastern Province Golf Union *Hon Sec,* CAL Fowles, PO Box 146, Port Elizabeth 6000, CP. *Tel* (041) 21919.

Karoo Golf Association *Hon Sec,* Mrs CL Hobson, PO Box 71, Middleburg 5900, CP.

OFS & Northern Cape Golf Union *Hon Sec,* RF Davidson, PO Box 517, Bloemfontein 9300, OFS. *Tel* (051) 470511.

Natal Golf Union *Sec,* RT Runge, PO Box 1939, Durban 4000, Natal. *Tel* (031) 223877.

South-West Africa Golf Union *Hon Sec,* H Hanstein, PO Box 2989, Windhoek 9000. (061) 222786.

Transkei Golf Union *Sec,* Philip Geldehuys, PO Box 210, Umtata, Transkei.

Transvaal Golf Union *Sec,* RC Witte, PO Box 391661, Bramley 2018, Transvaal. *Tel* (011) 6403714/5.

Western Province Golf Union *Sec* BW Myles, Box 153, Howard Place, 7450, CP. *Tel* (021) 536728.

South African Ladies' Golf Union
Sec, Mrs E Cutler, PO Box 135, Vereeniging, Transvaal, South Africa.

South African Professional Golfers' Association
Sec, Lee Wiltshire, PO Box 55253, Posbus Northlands, 2116 Johannesburg. *Tel* (011) 884 3404; *Fax* (011) 884 3436.

Swaziland Golf Union
A Rutt, PO Box 1739, Mbabane, Swaziland.

Tanzania Golf Union
Hon Sec, Bashir Tejani, Tanzania Golf Union, PO Box 4879, Dar es Salaam, Tanzania.

Uganda Golf Union
Sec, PO Box 2574, Kampala, Uganda.

Zaire Golf Federation
Pres, Tshilombo Mwin Tshitol, BP 1648, Lubumbashi, Zaire. *Tel* 2269.

Zambian Golf Union
Hon Sec, Amon T Chibiya, PO Box 37445, Lusaka, Zambia. *Telex* ZA 40098.

Zambia Ladies' Golf Union
Sec, Mrs C Howell, PO Box 32150, Lusaka, Zambia. *Tel* Lusaka (1) 251668, *Telex* ZA 40098.

Zimbabwe Golf Association
Sec, B de Kock, PO Box 3327, Harare, Zimbabwe.

Zimbabwe Ladies' Golf Union
PO Box 3814, Harare, Zimbabwe.

Europe

Austrian Golf Federation
Sec, Mrs Waltraud Neuwirth, Haus des Sports, Prinz-Eugen-Strasse 12, A-1040 Vienna, Austria. *Tel* Vienna (222) 505 32 45; *Fax* (222) 505 49 62.

Belgian Royal Federation of Golf
Sec, Roger Duys, Siège Administratif et Secretariat, Chemin de Baudemont 23, 1400 Nivelles. *Tel* (067) 220440 *Fax* (067) 220444.

Czechoslovak Golf Federation
Sec, H Goldscheider, Na Porici, 12, 11530 Prague 1.
Tel Prague (2) 2350065-84 *Telex* 122650.

Danish Golf Union (Dansk Golf Union)
Gen Sec, JF Larsen, Toftevj 26, 2625 Vallensbaek, Denmark. *Tel* Copenhagen (2) 64 06 66.

European Golf Association
Gen Sec, C Storjohann, En Ballègue, Case Postale CH-1066, Epalinges, Lausanne, Switzerland. *Tel* 010-41-21-7843532 *Telex* 450804 Golf; *Fax* 41-21-7843536.

Amateur Technical Committee: *Hon Sec,* JL Dupont, 51 Av Victor Hugo, 93300 Aubervilliers. *Tel* Paris (1) 833 4949.

Finnish Golf Union (Finlands Golfforbund)
Hon Sec, J Huhtanen, Radiokatu 12, SF-00240 Helsinki. *Tel* Helsinki (90) 1581; *Telex* 121797.

French Golf Federation (Fédération Française de Golf)
Hon Sec, J Labatut, 69 Avenue Victor Hugo, 75783 Paris, Cedex 16. *Tel* Paris (1) 45021355; *Telex* 614 406 FF Golf, *Fax* 33 (1) 45003068.

French Professional Golfers' Association
69 Avenue Victor Hugo, 75116 Paris 16, France. *Tel* Paris (1) 500 43 72.

German Golf Association (Deutscher Golf Verband)
Sec, Heinz Biemer, Postfach 2106, 6200 Wiesbaden, W Germany. *Tel* 010 49 (6121) 526041; *Telex* 4 186 459, *Fax* 49 (6121) 599493.

German PGA (Deutscher Golflehror Verband)
Sec, Mrs Suzanne Mühlbauer, Eberlestrasse 13, 89 Augsberg, W Germany. *Tel* 010 49 (821) 528900.

Hellenic Golf Federation
Hon Sec, George Th Lusi, PO Box 70003, GR 16610, Glyfada, Athens, Greece. *Tel* Athens (1)894 6820 or Athens (1)894 1933, *Telex* 212493 MYLG GR or 224524 DIOR GR.

Hungarian Golf Association
President, Dr F Gati, c/o Hungerian Blue Danube Golf Club, 111 Milkos-ug 11, 12, H-1035 Budapest.

Iceland Golf Union (Golfsanband Islands)
Gen Sec, Frimann Gunlaugsson, Reykjavik 121, PO Box 1076, Iceland. *Tel* Reykjavik (1) 686686; *Telex* 2314 1S1 1S.

International Greenkeepers' Assoc
Hon Sec, Mrs B Harradine, Via Golf, CH6987, Caslano, Switzerland.

Italian Golf Federation (Federazione Italiana Golf)
Sec, Luigi Orlandini, 388 Via Flaminia I-00196 Rome. *Tel* Rome (6) 394 641. *Telex* 613192 Golfed I.

Luxembourg Golf Club Grand Ducal
Sec, Miss J Schwartz, 1 Route de Treve 2633, Senningerberg, Luxembourg. *Tel* (352) 34090.

Netherlands Golf Federation
Man Dir, Henk J Heyster, Soestdijkerstraatweg 172, 1213XJ, Hilversum, Netherlands. *Tel* 010 3135-830565, *Fax* 31 (35) 834897.

Netherlands Professional Golfers' Assoc
Sec, A Wessels, Karel De Grotelaan 190, Deventer, Netherlands.

Norwegian Golf Union (Norges Golfforbund)
Gen Sec, Anna Donnestad, Hauger Skolevei 1, 1351 Rud, Norway. *Tel* Oslo (2) 51 88 00; *Telex* 18586 NIFN.

Portuguese Golf Federation (Federación Portuguesa de Golfe)
Sec, Senhora Manuela Abreu, Rua Almeida Brandao 39, 1200 Lisbon, Portugal. *Tel* Lisbon (1) 661126; *Telex* 43447 FISPOR P.

Slovenian Golf Association
Sec, M Bozio, Golf Association of Slovenia, c/o Golf Club Bled, C. Svobode 13, 64260 Bled, Yugoslavia.

Spanish Golf Association (Real Federación Espanola de Golf)
Gen Sec L Alvarez De Bohorquez, Capitan Haya 9-5 Dcha, Madrid 28020, Spain. *Tel* 010 34 455 26 82 / 455 27 57; *Fax* 91-456-3290.

Swedish Golf Federation (Svenska Golf Forbundot)
Sec Gen, Lars Granberg, PO Dox 84, S-182 11 Danderyd, Sweden. *Tel* Stockholm (8) 753 04 55; *Telex* 16608, *Fax* 08-7558439.

Swedish PGA
Executive Director, Christer Lindberg, *Chairman,* John Cockin. PO Box 35, S-181 21 Lidingö, Sweden. *Tel* Stockholm (8) 767 83 23.

Swiss Golf Association (Association Suisse de Golf)
Sec, JC Storjohann, En Ballègue, Case Postale CH-1066, Epalinges, Lausanne. *Tel* Lausanne (21) 32 7701. *Telex* 45450804.

Swiss Professional Golfers' Association
Hon Sec, Jakob Kressig, Perrelet 9, 2074 Marin, Switzerland. *Tel* (038) 33 23 79.

Yugoslavia Golf Federation
Golf association of Slovenia, Kublarjeva 34, Yu-61000 Ljubljana.

Middle East

Egyptian Golf Federation
c/o Gezira Sporting Club, Gezira, Cairo, Egypt. *Tel* Cairo (2) 80 6000.

Israel Golf Union
Sec, Alon Ben-David, PO Box 1010, Caesarea 30660, Israel.

Libyan Golf Union
PO Box 879, Tripoli, Libya.

United Arab Emirates Golf Union
c/o Gazira Sporting Club, Gazira, Cairo, Egypt. *Tel* Cairo (2) 80 6000.

Part VI
Golf History

The Origin of Golf

David Hamilton

Beginnings

The game of golf was not a sudden invention; it evolved and matured out of many other stick-and-ball games played in medieval Europe. France had its game of *chole* and England had a stick-and-ball game called 'cambuca'. Only two games, however, are serious contenders as the forerunner of the modern game of golf. The first was *colf* (or *koffe*), popular in the Low Countries, and the second was the game already known as 'golf' (or 'gouff' or 'gollfe' in the random, phonetic spelling of the day), which is persistently mentioned in Scottish records from medieval times onwards.

Dutch *colf*

The Dutch *colf* was popular and appears frequently in early Dutch records – of which many more have survived than the few scrappy Scottish documents of the same period – from 1300 onwards. A major study by Steven van Hengel, *Early Golf* (privately published in 1982), has at last described the game from original documents. A single iron-headed club, which had considerable loft, was used. It seems to have been mostly a town game, played towards a target such as a door, and may have been popular with children. The game became a nuisance in the towns, but only occasionally did regulations successfully move it out into the open fields nearby, where it may have been played into a hole in the ground. The Dutch towns where *colf* was popular were inland and, without adjacent coastal links, it could not be played very successfully outside the towns. When the canals were frozen, a form might be played using a post, or even a hole, in the ice as the target.

In Scotland, early records are less well preserved, and portrait and landscape painting did not exist. Nevertheless, sufficient is known about the early game of 'golf' to suggest that until about 1650 it may have resembled *colf*, as many records show that it was played in the churchyard or street. Scotland and the Low Countries were closely linked by trade, and hence there are good reasons why the games should have been similar.

Move to links

But by 1650 another version of the Scottish golf can be seen emerging as the dominant form, changing it to resemble the modern game. At this time it moved out of the towns on to the hard links – land beside the east-coast towns and ports, where in winter (and early golf was a winter game) a game of skill developed, combining lengthy shots with accuracy as the hole was neared. Wooden-headed clubs, which could be expensive, were now the kind most in use and even in the Low Countries were known as 'Scotch cleeks'. In Scotland an iron club was reserved for bunkers or ruts. The target in this long game was a hole in the ground.

The earliest description of the Scottish game of golf, taken from a Latin grammar for schools, Aberdeen 1632. It mentions bunkers, iron clubs, holes and sand used for teeing up. (Courtesy of Aberdeen University Library.)

Why should the game have been different in Scotland from that played elsewhere in Europe and why should it have changed in this way? Perhaps the interest of the aristocracy and the Stuart monarchs was important, since they took up golf seriously; they could afford to buy the expensive equipment. For this reason golf appeared in London after the Union of the Crowns, when James VI of Scotland ascended the throne of Great Britain as James I. In Scotland too, the east-coast ports, notably Leith near Edinburgh, had links, whereas the Low Countries' *colf*-playing towns were inland, with wet, heavy land in winter.

There is no evidence that the Dutch game evolved along the same lines as its Scottish counterpart, and indeed *colf* disappeared about 1700, probably eliminated by the growth of the towns and the congestion of their streets. Ball-and-stick games in Holland developed in a different way to give *kolf*, an indoor game played over a short, formal court. It seems reasonable to conclude that, in the absence of other evidence, golf as we now know it evolved in Scotland, but perhaps later than was once supposed.

The first Clubs

In the late 1600s, golf was popular in Scotland along the east coast and two centres in particular were of interest. St Andrews had keen aristocratic student golfers, whose fathers were among those who played at Leith. Numerous diaries and local records show the popularity of Leith, and it was not surprising that here the world's first Golf Club was founded – the Honourable Company of Edinburgh Golfers. There were many golfing cliques in Leith and the club's foundation was probably a response to the fading fortunes of the town, in decline after the Union of the Parliaments. Already the Leith races were popular and a trophy had been given by the Town Council. The new Company of Golfers was also provided with a trophy – a silver club – and though this did not herald any sudden change in the game, it did mean that rules had to be drawn up for the new competition – the first rules of golf.

Other Clubs were founded in the seventeenth century, imitating the Leith golfers, and, as Scottish attitudes relaxed in an increasingly sociable century, these Clubs became known for their heavy drinking and hearty eating. They seem to have had little turnover of members, who were often bound together for reasons other than golf – often military or masonic. The Clubs played a valuable role in supporting the early club- and ballmakers, and were vigilant in protecting the rights of the townspeople to use the links for recreation. Many records show that golf was still popular with the tradespeople of the towns, who were not members of the Golf Clubs. Whether these poorer golfers played with the expensive equipment used by the rich or with a cheaper club and ball is not certain.

Temporary cessation

The early 1800s saw a crisis in the Scottish game. Industrialization brought rapid expansion to the towns without regard for amenities, and public links such as those

The Trophy for the Gentlemen Golfers of Edinburgh (later the Honourable Company) on display.

at Leith, Aberdeen, Glasgow and Leven were throttled. Some Clubs, like the Honourable Company of Edinburgh Golfers and the Glasgow Club, ceased to exist for a spell and others dispersed to new, quieter areas, such as Musselburgh. The game itself appeared to be less popular.

The game takes off

But in the year 1848 a revolution in the game occurred. The appearance of the new gutty ball, made out of malleable gutta-percha, produced a cheap, durable alternative to the short-lived featherie or the wooden ball of the common game. Less dramatic but of similar significance was the change from the brittle woods to tough hickory for club shafts. To the older men who earned their living by club- and ball-making, like Allan Robertson, it seemed that their trade was in danger, but others, like 'old' Tom Morris, realized that the new equipment might help spread the game. In this belief they were correct beyond any reasonable expectation. The new well-off middle class produced by the growth of industry flocked to Scotland for their holidays using the expanding rail network. St Andrews and North Berwick were favourite places and there the visitors imitated the games of the old leisured class. Their wives and families also learned the game on these Scottish holidays, and women's golf was born at St Andrews. Celebrities such as AJ Balfour, then Secretary of

State for Ireland, were keen players and helped its popularity further.

Back home, in England and elsewhere, they drew up plans for courses for which they hired Scottish help. From Scotland poured a stream of designers and professionals, like Willie Dunn and, later, Donald Ross. The Carnoustie Club (drawn from the artisans of the town) produced a remarkable number of young emigrés who could be found playing golf and tending the courses all over North America.

English and US expansion
Blackheath claimed great antiquity, dating back to the Stuart kings. The first English Club of the modern era, however, was perhaps the Old Manchester Club (1818), though the first of the continuous modern era was the Royal North Devon (1864) at Westward Ho!, a Club which had the distinction of raising JH Taylor who became the first professional to beat the Scots at their own game. In Ireland, Royal Belfast (1881) was the first golf club to be formed, and in Europe, Pau (1856) led the way. Britain's expanding Empire spread golf around the world. In Britain, a new burst of Club foundation occurred, reaching its peak in the 1890s. The number of clubs rose from less than 100 in 1875 to 1300 in 1900. Golf had been played in a small way in America before the foundation of the St Andrews Golf Club of Yonkers in 1888, but the Club's pioneers had met with ridicule. This Club's course was primitive, but by 1895 came America's first open championship links, at Newport, Rhode Island – although

'Old' and 'young' Tom Morris.

as late as 1899 leading British professionals like Harry Vardon met little opposition on tours in America.

Early competitive play
Competitive golf dates from the inter-Club matches of the early nineteenth century, the first of which was recorded in 1818 when two of the Edinburgh Clubs playing over Bruntsfield Links, the Burgess Golfing Society and the Bruntsfield Links Club, competed against each other. In 1857 the Prestwick Club organized a successful inter-club tournament, and in 1860 they arranged an event for professional golfers, which later became known as the Open Championship. They may have wished to show the skills of the invited professionals, particularly their own man, Tom Morris, whom they had hired as a ball- and club-maker, and who looked after the Prestwick links – the first such salaried post for a golfer. Sadly, Allan Robertson did not live to play in the competition, though the year previously he was the first to have broken 80 in a round over the Old Course. The Open was unusual in being a stroke-play competition, as the early inter-Club tournaments were match play.

New horizons
Golf prospered and by the time of Willie Park's success the small number of professional golfers could hope for larger stakes in challenge matches and the rewards of occasional tournaments. Park was perhaps the first to capitalize on his fame in the modern way as a golf consultant and by publicizing his own branded clubs, notably an infallible putter, and by using mass production, advertising and postal sales he was highly successful. At St Andrews the first golf club manufacturing firm that had not been set up by a professional golfer appeared – the Forgan's firm, which survived for almost a century.

Scottish professional dominance ended in 1894 when an English-born professional, JH Taylor, won the Open. The rise of American golf was signalled when WJ Travis won the British Amateur Championship in 1904.

Though a home-bred player, JJ McDermott, had won the US Open in 1911, it was Francis Ouimet's win in 1913 that caught the popular imagination. Another feature of the growing dominance of America was the appearance of the Haskell ball in 1902, quickly capturing the market. Club design changed to suit the new ball: heads became deeper and the scarehead design changed to the socket joint.

Improved status
Professionals' status remained low until the end of the century and they were usually called by their second names only. Even Open Champions had to tee the ball up for their amateur

From George M Colville Five Open Champions and the Musselburgh Golf Story, *Musselburgh 1980.*

From George M Colville Five Open Champions and the Musselburgh Golf Story, *Musselburgh 1980.*

partners in exhibition matches, and even James Braid never entered Walton Heath clubhouse by the front door. JH Taylor organized the professionals in Britain, promoting their image until they became national figures even outside the narrow world of sport. Their new-found popularity was marked by an increasing number of tournaments, notably the sponsorship by the *News of the World* of the first tournament of the modern era. The changing status of professionals in Britain was pioneered and continued by Henry Cotton, who, on being appointed to Ashridge GC in 1937, made the bold stipulation that he be made an honorary member of the Club. The modern professional had arrived.

Today golf is played world-wide, and is perhaps the most popular participant outdoor sport in the world. The government of the game still bears out its Scottish origins – the Royal and Ancient Golf Club of St Andrews shares with the United States Golf Association the regulation of all golf. And only in Scotland is it still universally the game of the ordinary people.

Evolution of the Rules of Golf

J Stewart Lawson

Authors note: Revised Rules of Golf came into force on 1 January 1988, but 1984 was a significant date in the evolution of the Rules.

The late Henry Longhurst always maintained that perfectly adequate rules for the game of golf could be written on the back of a score card. When challenged to show how this could be done, Henry produced a set of ten Rules, the key one reading: *The game shall be played in the traditional manner* . . . Sadly, Henry was never pressed to say to which of the many different traditions he was referring. Should we, for example, be following the Leith system (*At Holling, you are to play your Ball honestly for the Hole, and not to play upon your Adversary's Ball, not lying in your way to the Hole* – The Gentlemen Golfers, 1744) or the Brunonian system (*It shall be deemed fair to play a ball against the adversary's ball, provided the player does not touch the adversary's ball with his club* – Edinburgh Burgess Golfing Society 1814)?

No doubt there are many traditionalists who will shake their heads mournfully over the 1984 version of the Rules of Golf. Not only are the playing rules presented in an entirely new and, it is hoped, more logical order, but several important changes of principle and procedure have also been made. What many people forget, however, is that from the very outset the rules of the game have been organic: they have grown and proliferated; they have changed their form and shape many times; and, by discarding provisions as they became outmoded, they have supported Darwin's theory of the survival of the fittest. Nevertheless, through all phases of this evolution, the organism's backbone has remained unaffected: the game of golf still *consists in playing a ball from the* teeing ground *into the hole by a* stroke *or successive strokes in accordance with the Rules* – Rule 1-1.

Early rules

Golf in Scotland had managed to survive three centuries without any apparent need for written rules when, in 1744, the Gentlemen Golfers at Leith drew up thirteen Articles & Laws in

Playing at Golf, the occasion being the first competition for the City of Edinburgh's Silver Club and the Gentlemen Golfers apprehending that entrants from other parts of the country might not be familiar with the Leith tradition. As other golfing societies were formed in the ensuing years, each drew up its own rules of play, but the leadership of the Gentlemen Golfers, later to become The Honourable Company of Edinburgh Golfers, was generally acknowledged. From the 1830s onwards, however, due to a temporary eclipse of the Honourable Company, this leadership gradually passed to the Society of St Andrews Golfers, which in 1834 had been granted the title of Royal and Ancient Golf Club of St Andrews. This shift of influence to the Royal and Ancient is illustrated by the fact that, whereas in 1810 the first 15 Rules of the Glasgow Golf Club were, with one minor difference, word for word the same as those of the Honourable Company, in 1851 the newly formed Prestwick Golf Club decided to adopt the St Andrews Rules of Play.

The last quarter of the nineteenth century saw a tremendous expansion of golf both at home and overseas, and there was a growing demand for a uniform code of rules. Widespread interest was shown when the Royal and Ancient announced the publication of a new set of Rules in 1891, and great importance was attached to the revisions these contained. It was natural, in these circumstances, that the leading clubs should invite the Royal and Ancient to assume responsibility for producing a uniform code, and the first Rules of Golf Committee was appointed in 1897. The United States Golf Association had been organized in 1894, and these two bodies, the Royal and Ancient and the USGA, now became the game's two governing authorities, responsible for the formulation of rules and for their interpretation. During the first half of the present century, the Royal and Ancient and the USGA shared the same basic code of rules, but each body issued its own interpretative Decisions, and many differences arose, particularly in the area of the game's equipment: the Royal and Ancient's banning of the centre-shafted putter after WJ Travis had won the

British Amateur with a Schenectady; the eventual disagreement (now at last resolved) over the minimum size of the golf ball; and the legalization of steel shafts by the USGA some years before the Royal and Ancient followed suit. Interpretation of the playing rules also differed, and the USGA, without the same long tradition of match play, had no qualms about abolishing the stymie.

Royal and Ancient–USGA co-operation

By 1950 there was a grave danger of the Royal and Ancient and the USGA drifting farther apart, but conferences held in 1951, which representatives from Canada and Australia also attended, resulted in the formulation of a uniform code, the only initial difference being over the size of the ball; a couple of minor divergencies in the playing rules which arose later did not last long and uniformity has been maintained ever since. Arrangements were also made in 1951 for the Royal and Ancient and the USGA to meet periodically to review the Rules, and these meetings now take place every four years; on the Royal and Ancient's part, only after detailed consultation with the 65 Golfing Unions and Associations affiliated to it. It would have been anomalous, however, to have uniform rules if they were not being interpreted in the same way. A comprehensive analysis of Royal and Ancient and USGA Decisions carried out a few years ago revealed several important differences of interpretation, and a Joint Decisions Committee was therefore appointed to establish uniformity in this area as well as in the Rules themselves. So successful has this new venture been that in 1984 the Royal and Ancient and the USGA jointly published a book of uniform Decisions on the Rules of Golf, now revised annually and the two bodies have co-operated in the production of films about the Rules.

One alteration in the 1984 Rules may have startled more than traditionalists: the change in the manner in which a ball is to be dropped. In future, the player *shall stand erect, hold the ball at shoulder height and arm's length and drop it* (Rule 20-2a) and there is no requirement that he must face the hole when doing so. The chief reason for this change was that the spot where the ball first strikes the ground when dropped is important (see Rule 20-2c), but under the old Rule how was the player – standing erect, facing the hole and dropping the ball over his shoulder

– to identify that spot with any certainty? The change is certainly a major one, and the traditionalists might claim that the old Rule embodied a procedure hallowed by nearly two and a half centuries of usage. But would they be right?

Ways of dropping the ball

Article 8 of the 1744 code at Leith required a player whose ball was lost to *drop another Ball*, but it did not say in what manner this should be done. In 1754 at St Andrews the player was at liberty to take his ball out of *water, or any watery filth, and throw it behind the hazard six yards at least*. The Edinburgh Burgess Golfing Society varied not only the manner of dropping but even the identity of the dropper: in 1773 the ball was to be dropped by *the opposite party*, i.e. the opponent; in 1776 it was to be thrown over his head by the player; in 1807 the player was to drop it over his shoulder; and in 1839 the *right* shoulder was specified. Facing the hole when dropping was first introduced by the Honourable Company of Golfers at Leith in 1809, but the method of dropping varied again: *the player shall . . . fronting the hole to which he is playing, drop the ball over the back of his head.* Finally, in 1829 and 1834 the Musselburgh Golf Club required that the ball be dropped by *a cady*. Which of these several variations on the dropping theme would the traditionalists accept as Henry Longhurst's *traditional manner*?

The first written Rules of Golf were no more than 14 years old when it was thought necessary to amend them, but it was clear that the Gentlemen Golfers in 1758 believed that they had now got the wording absolutely right and that no further change would be required. Did not their Captain, Thomas Boswall, preface the amendment with these bold words, *That in all time Coming the Law shall be . . .*? Successive generations of legislators have been equally sanguine in believing that they have produced a perfect set of rules, and the Royal and Ancient and the USGA doubtless hope that the 1984 code has closed all loopholes and provided for all eventualities. Is evolution now complete? Has the definitive tradition at last been established? Only time will tell.

Editor's note: J Stewart Lawson was Chairman of The Rules of Golf Committee 1973-77, Trustee of the Royal and Ancient Golf Club, St Andrews, from 1979 and Captain of the Club 1979-80.

The Championships of Great Britain

History of the Open Championship

The Open Championship was initiated by Prestwick Golf Club in 1860 and was played there until 1870. The Club presented the Championship Belt which was to be held for a year by the winner and which would become the absolute property of any player who won three years in succession. The competition consisted of three rounds of the 12 holes Prestwick then had, to be played on one day. The Open did not become a four round contest until 1892. There were few entrants in the early years and nearly all were professionals, who were sometimes also greenkeepers and clubmakers, with a few amateurs.

Young Tom Morris won the Belt outright in 1870. There was no contest the following year, but in 1872 Prestwick, the Royal and Ancient and the Honourable Company, who were still playing at Musselburgh, subscribed to provide the present trophy, which was not to be won outright. Since then only three winners would have so earned it: Jamie Anderson and Bob Ferguson during the following ten years and Peter Thomson since in 1954-56. The Championship was to be held on the courses of the three subscribing Clubs in turn. Young Tom won the first for the new cup in 1872 at St Andrews, but died tragically young in 1875.

The three courses continued to be used until 1892 when it was first played at Muirfield to where the Honourable Company had moved. That year was also the first in which the Championship became a 72-hole contest over two days. In 1890, at Prestwick, John Ball had become the first amateur to win. Only two others have followed his success, Harold Hilton in 1892 and 1897, and Bobby Jones in 1926, 1927 and 1930. Roger Wethered tied with Jock Hutchison at St Andrews in 1920, but lost the play-off; if he had not incurred a penalty stroke through treading on his ball in the third round, he may well have won.

The Triumvirate

The year 1894 saw the first occasion the Open was played in England at Sandwich and the first English professional to win, JH Taylor. He won again the next year and for the fifth time in 1913. Harry Vardon and James Braid were the two others of the *great triumvirate* who together won sixteen Opens between 1894 and 1914. Taylor's five wins were spread over twenty years and Vardon's six over nineteen. Braid's wins were concentrated into ten years from 1901 to 1910, all of them in Scotland. Vardon won three times at Prestwick but never at St Andrews where Taylor and Braid both won twice. Only Taylor managed a win at Hoylake. No other player won more than once during their supremacy. The winning scores at the time were very high by today's standards, for although the courses were marginally shorter, the equipment and clothing were primitive compared with those in use today. At Sandwich Taylor's score was 326, or 38 over an average of 4s. His 304 at Hoylake in 1913 was played in appalling weather, wearing a tweed jacket, cap and boots, and using wooden shafts and leather grips. He had no protective clothing or umbrella and won by 8 strokes from Ted Ray. The last winning total over 300 was Hagen's 301 at Hoylake in 1924.

Better Standards

That improved equipment has defeated the greater length and heavier rough of today's Championship courses is suggested by comparing the average winning scores for decades of this century.

Decade	Average winning score	Decade	Average winning score
1905-14	302	1956-65	280
1920-29	295	1966-75	280
1930-39	289	1976-85	277
1946-55	284		

Of the 118 Opens held so far, twenty Scots have won, eighteen Americans, fifteen English, three Australians, two South Africans and one each from France, Ireland, New Zealand, Argentina and Spain. The Scots have won thirty-nine times but only twice since Braid in 1910 (Duncan in 1920 and Lyle in 1985), the USA thirty-one times, England twenty-seven, Australia and South Africa seven times each, Spain three times and each of the others once. Since the triumvirate's day ended, the only Englishman to win more than once has been Sir Henry Cotton with three victories. The Americans have won thirty out of the last sixty-three Opens played.

It will be seen that certain nationalities tend to dominate for a decade or so; the Scots until 1893, then the English until 1914, the USA in the 1920s and until 1933 when the English had a short resuscitation. The Commonwealth were to the fore from 1949 to 1965 (Locke, Thomson, Nagle and Charles) with the Americans coming back again to win in 13 out of 18 years between 1966 and 1983. Equally dominating in their periods were Hagen and Jones in the twenties, Cotton in the thirties, Locke and Thomson the fifties, and thereafter Palmer, Nicklaus, Player, Trevino, Watson and Ballesteros.

Open Courses
Only fourteen courses have accommodated the Open. Prestwick, discarded after 1925 as unsuitable for large crowds, still leads with twenty-four occasions, twenty of them before 1900. St Andrews follows with twenty-three. The second group comprises Muirfield with thirteen, Sandwich eleven and Hoylake with ten. Hoylake's last Open was in 1967; that it is not used now is due not to any lack of quality of the course but to lack of space. Deal appeared in 1909 and 1920, and was due again in 1948 but the sea broke across the course, and Sandwich came in for the last time until 1981. Troon and Lytham St Annes each held an Open between the wars, Carnoustie two and Princes, Sandwich, when Sarazen won in 1932, one; this course, which was used as a tank training ground during the second war, has not been asked again. In 1951, Portrush, the only Irish course to stage an Open, also provided the only English winner between Cotton and Jacklin in Max Faulkner. Birkdale and Turnberry are firmly established in the rota which appears to have settled at four Scottish courses, St Andrews, Muirfield, Troon and Turnberry (this will be five if, hopefully, Carnoustie reappears), and three in England, Lytham St Annes, Birkdale and Sandwich.

Traditionally the Open is only played on Links courses. While there may yet be new venues by the sea capable of being stretched and groomed to be worthy of holding an Open, the many other considerations to be weighed, such as an adequate road system to carry vast crowds and nearly as many acres as the course covers to accommodate the tented village and services, it is not easy to see where the Championship Committee will turn. It is possible, even likely, in this present age that a links course of repute with the necessary acreage round it, will be developed by a consortium that will bid for an Open and succeed.

Qualifying
How does one qualify to play in an Open? Since qualifying was first introduced in 1914, there have been numerous changes. Regional qualifying was tried for a year in 1926. At one of the courses used, Sunningdale, Bobby Jones (and even he had to qualify!) played what many consider the classic round of golf: a 66, all 4s and 3s, never over par, 8 birdies, 33 putts and 33 other shots.

Until 1963 all competitors, even the holder, had to play two qualifying rounds on the Open course on the Monday and Tuesday of the Open week. The qualifiers then had one round on Wednesday, one on Thursday and the leading group of between 40 and 60 players finished with two rounds on Friday. In 1963 certain exemptions from qualifying were introduced. The two rounds on the Friday were dropped in 1966 in favour of one round each on Friday and Saturday; not until 1980 was the first round played on Thursday and the last on Sunday. As the entry continued to increase, in 1970 nearby courses were used for qualifying and in 1977 regional qualifying was reintroduced in up to four areas in the previous week with final qualifying on nearby courses later.

There have been surprisingly few ties involving a play-off, only eleven in 116 Championships. The first should have been in 1876 involving David Strath and Bob Martin. However, Strath took umbrage over a complaint against him and refused to play again, Martin being declared the winner. Until 1963 ties were decided over 36 holes; the last two, between Nicklaus and Sanders at St Andrews in 1971 and Watson and Newton at Carnoustie in 1975, were played over 18. Two years ago it was decided that in the event of a tie, the winner would be found immediately by a play-off over specified holes, followed by 'sudden death' if necessary. This happened in 1989 when Calcavecchia beat Norman and Grady over 4 holes after finishing level on 275.

Prize Money
In 1863 the total prize money was £10, its distribution among the fourteen entrants, six of whom were amateurs, is unknown. A year later it had risen by over 50% to £16, with the winner taking £6. By 1989 the total prize fund had risen to £750,000 of which Mark Calcavecchia received £80,000. All 80 qualifiers for the last day received £2400 or more (except Russell Claydon, the only amateur to play the last two rounds). Additionally winners of the qualifying rounds won smaller amounts. Until about 1955, the winner's and leaders' rewards were very modest; even in 1939 the cheque for the first man was £100 out of a total of £500. With some justification the prestige of winning the Open then was adjudged to be of much more value than any monetary award. The growth since the 1950s has been astonishing and is evidence that, while it is still a tremendous asset for any man to have won the Open, the authorities have recognised that it will not maintain its leading place without substantial reward.

The rapid advance of the Open to the major spectacle it has become is due to a combination of factors. Not least of these is the TV presentation of the BBC, acknowledged as the world's best in golf, the interest and enthusiasm of thousands of spectators keen to watch on the spot rather than on the box, and the Royal and Ancient's promotion of this world fair of golf that it has become. Behind it all has been the foresight of successive Championship Committees and, in the late 1960s and 1970s, the masterly spreading of the gospel by Keith Mackenzie, Secretary of the R&A in 1966-82, that is so ably continued by his successor, Michael Bonallack.

The detailed list of Open Winners can be found on pages 156-158.

Laurence Viney

The Amateur Championship

Early History

Golf has always been a competitive game and club medals have been keenly contested since the nineteenth century. Many of the leading amateurs were members of several clubs and, aided by an excellent railway system, they competed against each other at such venues as St Andrews, Prestwick, Hoylake and Musselburgh. An embryonic *open amateur competition* was held in the late 1850s (the first being won by Robert Chambers, the publisher, in 1858, but there seems to have been little enthusiasm for such an event and it died around the time of the first Open Championship (1860). The best amateurs began to enter the Open from 1861. By the 1870s, there was renewed interest in organising a tournament for amateurs only but nothing happened, probably because no one club took a strong enough lead. A proposal in 1877 to the membership of the R&A that it sponsor a sort of Amateur Championship (involving club members and others nominated by members) was defeated.

It fell to the Hoylake golfers to set in motion the championship we now know as *The Amateur*. In 1884 the Secretary of Royal Liverpool, Thomas Potter, proposed that an event – open to all amateurs – should be organised. This original intention was not carried out until 1886 and so the winner of 1885 (AF Macfie) triumphed over a strong but limited, field drawn from certain clubs. The clubs which were responsible for the running of the championship until the R&A took over in 1920 – and who made contributions for the purchase of the trophy – were:

Royal and Ancient
Royal Burgess Golfing Society of Edinburgh
Royal Liverpool
Royal St George's
Royal Albert, Montrose
Royal North Devon

Royal Aberdeen
Royal Blackheath
Royal Wimbledon
Royal Dublin
Alnmouth
North Berwick, New Club
Panmure, Dundee
Prestwick
Bruntsfield Links Golfing Society, Edinburgh
Dalhousie
Gullane
Formby
Honourable Company of Edinburgh Golfers
Innerleven
King James VI, Perth
Kilspindie
Luffness
Tantallon
Troon
West Lancashire

The first championship was not without its teething troubles. The format which was adopted allowed both golfers to proceed to the next round if their match was halved, so the first championship had three semi-finalists – and Macfie got a bye into the final. From 1886, the usual format was adopted.

More serious than the problem of an idiosyncratic draw, however, was the question of amateur status, raised for the first time in 1886.

The committee had to decide if it should accept the entries of John Ball III and Douglas Rolland. As a 15-year-old, Ball had finished fourth in the 1878 Open at Prestwick and on the advice of Jack Morris he accepted the prize money of 10s (50p). Rolland, a stonemason, had accepted second prize in the 1884 Open. Rolland's entry to the Amateur was refused while Ball's was accepted. Ball went on to win the championship a record eight times and the Open Championship of 1890.

The Format

After such a difficult start, the format of 18-hole matches with a 36-hole final remained until 1956. This arrangement made for many closely fought matches, as shown in 1930, the year of RT Jones' Grand Slam triumph. Jones' only victory in the event came in the right year and it is worth pointing out that, in making his way to the final, he won in the fourth round at the 19th (by laying a stymie) against Cyril Tolley, the holder, and his victories in the sixth round and in the semi-final were by the narrowest of margins. In addition, the fact that the draw was not seeded sometimes meant early meetings between top golfers; for example, in 1926 the visiting American Walker Cup Team members, von Elm and Ouimet, met in the second round and von Elm went on to meet Jesse Sweetser in the third. As a result of such events, there was some pressure for the introduction of seeding the draw but it was not until 1958 that the practice was officially adopted. In the fifties and sixties there were other changes in format in an attempt to satisfy large numbers of golfers who wished to play and to ensure a worthy winner.

The popularity of the championship has posed difficulties for the R&A. The mathematically ideal number of entrants to be fitted into a convenient format is 256. In 1950, 324 entered the championship causing golf to be played on the Old Course for 14 hours a day. In order to restrict the numbers turning up to the championship proper, an experiment in regional qualifying was held in 1958 (again a St Andrews year) and 488 players with handicaps of 5 and under played 36 holes of stroke play on 14 courses. This system was quickly replaced and in 1961 the handicap limit was lowered (to 3) and a balloting-out of higher handicaps was introduced so that 256 were left to play for the trophy. This method was followed until 1983 with the introduction of 36 holes of stroke play to find 64 players for match play, from which to find the eventual winner.

There was also pressure for the introduction of 36-hole matches. As early as 1922 the R&A's championship committee canvassed the opinion of the 252 men who played that year. Nineteen of these voted in favour of 36-hole matches, seven for district qualification, fifty-two voted for a stroke play qualification followed by 18-hole matches and the others who replied wanted no change to the system. In 1956 and 1957 the last 3 rounds were played over 36 holes, in 1958 and 1959 the semi-final and final were over 36 holes and then the old format returned.

There is constant pressure on the organisers to find a format to satisfy the needs of large numbers of home and foreign players, to take into account differences in national handicapping systems, to preserve the atmosphere of the championship, to maintain match play as a central feature of top-level amateur golf and even to take into account the vagaries of the weather. The task is almost impossible and it is unlikely that the championship will continue in its present form for all time.

The Winners

Any man who wins the Amateur is a considerable golfer but attention should be paid to certain outstanding champions. John Hall of Royal Liverpool won the title eight times between 1888 and 1912. It is interesting to note that he never successfully defended his title Michael Bonallack triumphed five times between 1961 and 1970, including an incredible hat-trick of final victories in which he successively beat Joe Carr and Bill Hyndman twice.

Several golfers have successfully defended their title: Horace Hutchinson, Harold Hilton, Lawson Little, Peter McEvoy and Philip Parkin, while others have won twice or more – Johnny Laidlay, Freddie Tait, Bob Maxwell, Cyril Tolley, Edward Holderness, Frank Stranahan, Joe Carr and Trevor Homer.

The oldest man to win was the Hon Michael Scott, at the age of 54 in 1933. The youngest winners – John Beharrell and Bobby Cole – were both 18 years and 1 month old. Cole's victory over Ronnie Shade was achieved over 18 holes – play being affected by poor visibility. The first overseas winner was Walter Travis who won in 1904 – one consequence of his victory was the banning of the use of centre-shafted putters. The first continental winner was the Frenchman, Philippe Ploujoux, who won in 1981. A visiting Walker Cup team always makes for an exciting championship and from fifteen visits to Great Britain the title has crossed the Atlantic twelve times. Indeed, on six occasions the final was an all-American affair.

No doubt there have been hundreds of thrilling matches played in the championship but few can have been as pulsating as the 1899 final at Prestwick where Johnny Ball beat Freddie Tait at the 37th hole. The victory must have been a sweet one for Ball, since Tait, the hero of Scotland, had won the previous year over Ball's home links of Hoylake. Tait was killed the following year in the Boer War. *The great battle* as Jones described his 4th round tie against Tolley in 1930 rivals the Ball-Tait final for tense excitement and for sheer brilliance of scoring Michael Bonallack's 1st round in the final of 1968 must take pride of place.

The Amateur Championship was 100 years old in 1985 and in essence it has changed remarkably little. How will the Championship react to changes such as the increasing popularity of the game at home and abroad, the lure of the professional ranks with its dependence on stroke play and the increasing commercialism of all sport? There is every reason to believe that it will continue to stand for all that is great in golf.

David Christie

Royal Golf Clubs

David Stirk

When one considers the number of names preceded, or followed by, the word 'Royal', it must, in general, appear as if the term can be tacked on to a name at will by anyone who fancies the idea. It is hard to believe that the Royal Oak public houses, the Theatre Royals and the Royal Insurance were all given the title by the reigning Monarch personally, any more than titles such as the Kings Arms and the Queen's Head were bestowed by the Monarch to honour those royal appendages.

Equally, there are certain titles of 'Royal' which, even to the uninitiated, appear to have real significance and to have been specially bestowed with royal approval.

In Queen Victoria's reign the term 'Royal' was granted only by the Queen, through the Home Secretary, to whom most of the requests were channelled. In 1881, the then Home Secretary suggested that the granting of the title should be given up, because so many bodies and institutions assumed it without permission. The Queen, however, wished to continue the custom, and her Private Secretary was instructed to deal with all applications, referring them to the Home Office.

Applications from the Empire would first be referred to the Governor of the Province, or the Governor General of the Dominion. If he approved, the matter would then be referred to the Colonial or Dominions Office and they, in turn, would pass the matter on to the Queen's Private Secretary. No doubt the Home Office would investigate the matter and make its recommendations to the Queen, submitting the necessary documents for her signature.

The designation 'Royal' was only valid during the reign of the Monarch who had bestowed it. Thus, on the Accession of a new Monarch, further application would have to be made.

King George V agreed on his accession that there was no need for institutions, societies etc, holding the title 'Royal' to re-apply for permission to continue the title at the beginning of each new reign. He also took the view that the title should only be bestowed on bodies and institutions that were pre-eminent. The policies concerning overseas requests remained the same. As far as

Royal Golf Clubs are concerned, they are not entitled to the title 'Royal' unless that honour has been bestowed upon them by the reigning Monarch; such honours cannot be bestowed by the Prince of Wales nor by any other relative or member of the Royal Family. It appears, however, that in the 1880s and 1890s several members of the Royal Family 'granted' unofficially 'Royal' status to a few clubs and sought confirmation by the Queen and Home Office subsequently.

It is the intention of this article to stir the interest of the reader in Royal Golf Clubs; space does not allow of a complete detailed account of every Royal Club throughout the world. By the same token there is also no intention to make invidious comparisons between one Royal Golf Club and another, but to place before the reader some facts and statistics which may encourage him or her to investigate in more detail those aspects which are of particular interest.

An attempt to investigate the 'Royals' produces a very mixed reaction but, in general, the author acknowledges, with gratitude, the great interest shown by many clubs contacted and the information provided by many Secretaries and Club Captains, despite the fact that such requests often meant a tedious and time-consuming search of Club archives—yet more work for those who were already under considerable pressure of work.

It does seem that a letter from the reigning Monarch to a Golf Club, conferring on it the permission to call itself 'Royal', is of such interest and importance to that Golf Club that, except perhaps in the case of golf clubs that are 100 years old or more (in which case the records may have been lost) or in which a fire or some other disaster has resulted in the complete disappearance of records, any Club that has such a document will preserve it with great care—or at least have the date of conferral noted in the Minutes of the Club. It seems reasonable then to assume that a Club which can find no evidence, and which still has its Minute Books intact, has canonised itself and uses the title 'Royal' by its own tradition rather than by Royal consent.

The rules that apply to Royal Clubs in the

United Kingdom and in the Commonwealth do not, of course, apply in other countries. As an example, the Secretary to the Fédération Royale Belge de Golf, tells me that there are nine Royal Clubs in Belgium and that the title 'Royal' can be granted to any club that has been in existence more than 50 years. He goes on to say that the nine Royal Clubs listed were all made 'Royal' after only 25 years because the rules 20 years ago were different.

There are 38 'Royal' golf clubs in Great Britain, perhaps 20 in Belgium and Spain, the only other European countries to have them, and over 20 more in the Commonwealth.

In the Republic of Ireland there is the Royal Tara Golf Club. Until 1966, it was known as the Bellinter Golf Club, but then awarded itself the Royal purple, based on the premise that in the eleventh and twelfth centuries Tara was reputed to be the home of the ancient kings of Ireland, who, on the distaff side were Spanish. The whole sounds a charming piece of Irish history and, in the words of my kind informant, 'we do benefit, to a great extent, from the title, and we get invited to all Royal functions'. In the Republic also is the very authentic Royal Dublin Golf Club, though I must confess that I do not know how or when it acquired its title. Also there is the Royal Curragh which does not use the 'Royal' to which it is still entitled.

There are three Royal Clubs in Northern Ireland, Royal Belfast, Royal Portrush and Royal County Down. Whereas in England, Scotland and Northern Ireland Royal Clubs take their status pretty calmly and with such little outward evidence of pride that they appear almost complacent, in the Commonwealth, or at least in those parts of the Commonwealth which do not scorn the title 'Royal', it is regarded with every evidence of active pride. Virtually all the Commonwealth 'Royals' were readily able to give the date on which the honour was conferred and often the details of the special circumstances relating to it.

Yet in parts of what used to be the Empire, some of the Royals have also been allowed to lapse; but it is not only in the Commonwealth that this has happened. In 1931 there was a Royal Bodmin Golf Club in Cornwall, but this title has now been dropped. It is possible that they conferred the purple on themselves because the County is the Royal Duchy of Cornwall.

Of the Clubs in the United Kingdom that are Royal by tradition rather than by Royal consent, Royal Tarlair and Duff House Royal are examples. Neither can find evidence of Royal Patronage. Duff House Royal was played on by Princess Louise Duchess of Fyfe, eldest daughter of King Edward VII, who is said to have expressed a wish that the Club should be called 'Royal', but it would seem that the reigning Monarch declined to oblige.

Another Club that has awarded itself the affix 'Royal' is the Royal Forest of Dean Golf Club, situated in the Forest of that name. No doubt the title is good for business but it is not authentic. On the other hand the Royal Epping Forest is fully authorised to its Royal status and has always had a Royal Duke as its patron in its 100 years' existence.

One must not assume that only those Clubs with the title 'Royal' are important, the Honourable Company of Edinburgh Golfers, a pre-eminently important Golf Club, has no Royal title.

Golf Clubs attained Royal status at varying times in their history and some of the older Clubs were not made Royal until after Clubs junior to them had achieved it. An example of this occurs in England where Blackheath, by far the oldest Club in England, was given Royal status in 1901, whereas the North Devon and West of England Golf Club (founded 1864) became the Royal North Devon Golf Club in 1868.

In conclusion, there is no evidence of a Royal Ladies Golf Club, but there is evidence, kindly supplied to me by Mr Laurence Viney, of a Royal Ladies Golf Club in the past. On 29 April 1932, the Secretary of State informed the Ashdown Forest Ladies Club that they had been granted Royal status. At that time the Ladies Club had its own 9 hole golf course and its own Clubhouse. In 1956, owing to financial difficulties, the Club ceased to exist as a separate entity and was merged with the Royal Ashdown Forest Men's Club, thus depriving the golf world of an unique Royal Ladies Club.

'Royal' Facts
The first Golf Club to be made 'Royal' was the Royal Perth Golfing Society in 1833. The first 'Royal' Golf Club in England was the Royal North Devon Golf Club in 1868. The youngest 'Royal' Golf Club is Royal Troon, which became Royal in 1978. The list of Royal Clubs: Great Britain and the Channel Islands, 38; rest of the world, 40.

Acknowledgements
While thanks are due from the Author to those many Secretaries and Captains of Golf Clubs too numerous to mention individually who were kind enough to supply information from their Club archives, the Author wishes, particularly to thank the following:
Mr Laurence Viney, Editor of The Golfer's Handbook, *for his encouragement and for supplying much information. Elizabeth H Cuthbert, Deputy Registrar, The Royal Archives, Round Tower, Windsor Castle, for explanations concerning the use of the term 'Royal' and for historical background. The Secretary, Canadian Golf Association. Mr JM Kellie, Executive Director, South African Golf Union. Mr HE Touzel, Chairman of the History and Archives Committee of the Royal Melbourne Golf Club, who kindly supplied me with much information on the Royal Clubs of Australia.*

Famous Players of the Past

In making the difficult choice of the names to be included, effort has been made to acknowledge the outstanding players and personalities of each successive era from the early pioneers to the stars of recent times.

Anderson, Jamie

Born 1842, died 1912. Winner of three consecutive Open Championships (1877-78-79). Born at St Andrews, he was the son of *Old Daw*, a St Andrews caddie and character. Jamie began golf when 10 years old, and rapidly developed into a fine player, noted for straight hitting and good putting. Anderson's method was to play steadily and on one occasion at St Andrews he remarked that he had played 90 consecutive holes without a bad shot or one stroke made otherwise than he had intended. He was for a period professional to Ardeer Club, but returned to St Andrews to follow his vocation of playing professional.

Anderson, Willie

Born in Scotland, 1878, died 1910. One of the Scottish emigrants to America, his flat swing won him the US Open in 1901, 1903, 1904 and 1905. He shares the record of four Open titles with Jones, Hogan and Nicklaus, and remains the only man to win three in a row.

Armour, Thomas D

Born Edinburgh, 1896. Died 1968. Open Champion, 1931. US Open Champion, 1927. USPGA 1930. He had a distinguished amateur career – including the French Open Amateur and tied first place in the Canadian Open. He had the unique distinction of playing in 1921 for Britain against the US as an amateur and in 1925 as a professional for the US against Britain in the unofficial international matches that preceded the inception of the Walker Cup and Ryder Cup events. When he came to the end of his tournament career he quickly gained an outstanding reputation as a coach, and books he wrote on the technique of the game were best-sellers.

Auchterlonie, William

Born St Andrews in 1872, died 1963. Won the Open title at Prestwick at the age of 21 with a set of seven clubs which he had made himself and shortly afterwards founded the famous club-making firm in St Andrews. He never played with more than his seven clubs and was a great believer that a golfer had to be master of the half, three-quarter and full shots with each club. As professional to the Royal and Ancient Golf Club from 1935 to his death he saw one of his ambitions fulfilled – the Centenary Open at St Andrews in 1960.

Ball, John

One of the greatest amateur golfers of all time. Born at Hoylake, 24th December, 1862, his father owned the Royal Hotel, Hoylake, prior to the formation of the golf links and when there was a small racecourse on the land later formed into the Royal Liverpool Links. The links became John Ball's playground. In 1878, when fifteen years old, he competed in the Open Championship, finished fourth, eight strokes behind the winner and ahead of many famous Scottish professionals of that time. Between 1888 and 1912 he won the Amateur Championship eight times. In 1890 he was the first amateur to win the Open Championship. He played for England against Scotland continuously from 1902 to 1911, captaining the side each year. He was Amateur Champion in 1899 when war with South Africa broke out and Ball served in that campaign with the Cheshire Yeomanry and did not compete in the Championships of 1900-01-02. In the First World War he served in the Home Forces. He played in his last Amateur Championship in 1921, the year of the first American invasion, and he reached the fifth round although in his fifty-eighth year. Modest and retiring, he rarely spoke about his golf. On the morning of his last round in the Championship he remarked to a friend in the clubhouse, *If only a storm of wind and rain would sweep across the links from the Welsh hills I feel I could beat all of them once again*. But it was a week of torrid heat and he failed. He retired to his farm in North Wales, where he died in December 1940.

Barton, Miss Pamela

Born London, 4th March, 1917. Died 13th November, 1943. At the age of twenty-two when the Second World War broke out, Miss Pamela Barton had already achieved great fame in the golfing world. She won the Ladies' Championship, 1936-39, runner-up, 1934-35, the American Ladies' Championship, 1936 and the French Ladies' Championship, 1934. In 1936, at the age of nineteen, she held both the British and American Ladies' Championships, the first person to do so since 1909. Miss Barton played for England in the home internationals in 1935-36-37-38-39; for Great Britain v United States in 1934-36; v France, 1934-36-37-38-39. She was a member of the Ladies' Golf Union teams which toured Canada and America, 1934, and Australia and New Zealand in 1935. Of a charming and cheerful disposition, Miss Barton, who became a Flight-Officer in the WAAF, was killed in a plane crash at an RAF airfield in Kent.

Braid, James

Born Elie, Fife, 6th February, 1870. Died London, 27th November, 1950. One of the greatest figures in golf of all times, James Braid, with Harry Vardon and JH Taylor, made up the Triumvirate which dominated British professional golf for twenty years before the First World War. He was the first person to win the Open Championship five times. This record was later equalled by Taylor and beaten by Vardon. Braid's achievements were remarkable for the short time in which they were accomplished. In ten years he won five times and was second on three occasions. His victories were in 1901, 1905, 1906, 1908, 1910. He won the Match Play Tournament four times, 1903-5-7-11, a record which was unequalled till 1950, and the French Open Championship in 1910. He played for Scotland v England in 1903-4-5-6-7-9-10-12 and for Great Britain against America, 1921. A joiner by trade, Braid played as an amateur in Fife and Edinburgh and in 1893 went to London and worked as a club-maker. Taylor and Vardon were well established in the golfing world before Braid turned professional in 1896 and he quickly came into prominence by finishing level with Taylor, who by that time had been Champion twice, in a challenge match. In a historic international foursomes, Braid partnered by Alex Herd lost to Vardon and Taylor in a match for £400 over four courses. A tall powerful player who lashed the ball with *divine* fury, he was famous for his imperturbability; no matter how the game was progressing he always appeared outwardly calm and it was this serenity of temperament which assisted him to his Championship victories on two occasions. A man of few words, it was once said that *Nobody could be as wise as James Braid looked.* One of the founder members of the Professional Golfers' Association, Braid did much to elevate the status of the professional golfer. Braid made a major contribution to golf architecture; Gleneagles, Rosemount, Carnoustie and Dalmahoy all bear his stamp. He was admired and respected by all who knew him, as much for his modest and kindly nature as for his prowess as a golfer. He was professional at Romford for eight years and at Walton Heath for forty-five, and was for twenty-five years an honorary member of the latter club, becoming one of its directors. He was made an honorary member of the Royal and Ancient Golf Club in the last years of his life and had the distinction of being the only honorary member of the Parliamentary Golfing Society.

Campbell, Miss Dorothy Iona

Born Edinburgh, 1883. Died in America, 1946. Won British Ladies' Championship, 1909-11; Scottish Ladies' Championship, 1905-6-8; American Ladies' Championship, 1909-10; Canadian Ladies' Championship 1910-11-12. One of only two women golfers to win the British, American and Canadian Championships, the other being Marlene Stewart (Mrs M Stewart Streit). Played for Scotland in international matches and for British Ladies v American Ladies.

Campbell, Willie

A native of Musselburgh, Willie Campbell never shirked a match anywhere or with anybody, and it was only on rare occasions that he did not win. He was a tall, strapping fellow, and was regarded as one of the finest match players of the time, fearless and courageous. In 1887 Campbell was professional at Prestwick, and in the Open Championship of that year he seemed destined to win but took eight strokes with three holes left. He joined the outflow of Scots professionals to the USA in 1891 where he died at the age of 33.

Compston, Archie Edward Wones

Born Penn, Wolverhampton, 14th January, 1893, died September, 1962. One of the outstanding personalities of British golf in the years between the two World Wars who fought hard to resist the developing dominance of the American invasion. He played in three Ryder Cup matches – in 1927, 1929 and 1931. In a 72 hole Challenge match he beat Hagen by 18 and 17 in 1928 at Moor Park and in the Open which followed he finished third to Hagen. He tied for second place in the Open of 1925.

Cotton, Sir Henry

Henry Cotton, born in Cheshire in 1907, bestrode the British professional scene as player, teacher, writer, course architect and encourager of youth from 1930 until his death in December 1987, a few days before his well-deserved knighthood was announced. The only Briton to win the Open more than once since 1914, his three victories at Sandwich in 1934, Carnoustie in 1937 and Muirfield in 1948 were pinnacles in a dedicated, sometimes controversial, but highly successful career. All three victories contained at least one memorable round. His 65 at Sandwich, after which a golf ball was named, his last round 71 at Carnoustie in a downpour and his record 66 at Muirfield, with King George VI among the spectators, showed a style of play and life admired by all. No man did more to raise the status of the professional golfer. His insistence of Honorary Membership of clubs to which he was attached – Waterloo Brussels, Ashridge, Royal Mid-Surrey and Temple near Maidenhead – began a practice now followed by many clubs with their professionals. As Ryder Cup player and Captain, founder-member of the Golf Foundation, and his Rookie of the Year award, he led by example. His reward, which many would say came too late, was the first knighthood given for service to golf. His many playing successes included winning 11 Continental Opens, five finals in the News of the World Match-play Tournament, which at the time was second only in prestige to the Open. He won this twice, was four times selected for the Ryder Cup team, being Captain in 1937 and non-playing Captain in 1953. Captain of the PGA in 1934 and 1954, he had many other lesser tournament wins. During the war, in which he served in the RAF, he played exhibition matches in aid of the Red Cross and encouraged his fellow professionals to do likewise. After he retired from Championship play, he devoted his time to writing articles for the golf press, several books, support for the Golf Foundation and the development of his beloved Penina in Portugal where he spent much of his last years. He was elected to Honorary Membership of the Royal and Ancient Club in 1968 and was aware of his coming knighthood when he died a few days before it was announced.

Darwin, Bernard

One of the most respected and widely known personalities in the game died soon after his 85th birthday in 1961. As a graceful and authoritative writer on golf and golfers he had no equal. He knew intimately every player and every course of note throughout the world, and his phenomenal memory, fluent pen and gentle humour established him as the top historian of the game over many years. In 1937 he was awarded the CBE for his services to literature, which included journalism, books of children's stories and other sports besides golf. He was captain of the Royal and Ancient Club in 1934-35, and played internationally for England from 1902 until 1924 and in the first Walker Cup match

(1922). He had travelled to the US to report the match for *The Times* and had been called in to play and captain the side when Robert Harris fell ill. During his playing career he won many amateur titles and trophies. He was a grandson of Charles Darwin.

The Dolemans

Four brothers, natives of Musselburgh, who were associated with golf for seventy years. John, born 1826, died at Musselburgh 1918; AH, born 1836, died at Blackpool 1914; William born 1838, died at Glasgow 1918, and Frank born Musselburgh 1848, died Edinburgh, 1929. William was the best player. He was first amateur in the Open Championship in 1865-68, 1870 and 1872. He played in nearly every Amateur Championship up to 1911, and at Hoylake in 1910, when 73 years of age, he won his tie in the first round. AH was one of the pioneers of golf in England, and founder of golf at Lytham and St Annes. John,, the eldest, introduced golf to Nottingham. In 1908 he took part in an octogenarian foursome, which was continued annually until 1914. Frank was a club-maker and for many years he carried on a golf club-making business at the ancient Wright's Houses, Bruntsfield Links, Edinburgh.

Duncan, George

Died on 15th January, 1964, aged 80. He was the last Scottish-born winner of the Open title domiciled in Britain. He won the title in 1920 and his victory was achieved after two opening rounds of 80 which left him 13 strokes behind the leader. Two years later, at Sandwich, he finished second to Hagen after one of the most exciting finishes up to that time. Hagen had finished and was already being hailed as the winner when Duncan, a very late starter, reached the 18th hole needing a 4 to tie. He failed but his round was notable as the only one under 70 in that Open and the first to break 70 in the Open since 1904. Prior to the first war, Duncan was a prominent challenger to the established Triumvirate and would probably have achieved greater fame but for the war years during which he would have been at his prime. One of the fastest players of all time, he wasted no time especially on the greens and his book *Golf at a Gallop* was appropriately titled.

The Dunns

The twin brothers Dunn, born at Musselburgh in 1821, were prominent in golf between 1840 and 1860. In 1849, old Willie Dunn and Jamie Dunn played their great match against Allan Robertson and old Tom Morris. Willie Dunn became custodian in the Blackheath Links until 1864, and he then returned to Leith, and later to North Berwick, where he died at the age of 59. Willie Dunn was celebrated for the peculiar grace of his style and, as the longest driver of his day, he was a doughty match fighter, and one of his famous games was with Allan Robertson in 1843, when he played the St Andrews champion 20 rounds, and lost by 2 rounds and 1 to play. Another famous match was in 1852, when, partnered by Sir Robert Hay, he played Allan Robertson and Old Tom. Jamie Dunn, his twin brother, was also a fine player. Willie's son went to America, and won the first Championship of America in 1894. He was among the first to experiment with the idea of steel shafts. About 1900 he inserted thin steel rods in split cane and lancewood shafts. He invented a coneshaped paper tee, the forerunner of the wooden tee, and was a pioneer of indoor golf schools. He died in London in 1952.

Ferguson, Bob

Born Musselburgh, 1848. Died 1915. Started to caddie on Musselburgh when aged 8. In 1866, when 18, he won the first prize in the Leith Tournament, in which all the great professionals of the day took part. The late Sir Charles Tennant put up the money for young Ferguson, who, in 1868 and 1869, beat Tom Morris six times. In 1875, at Hoylake, with young Tom Morris representing Scotland in a foursome, he beat Bob Kirk, Blackheath, and John Allan, Westward Ho! representing England. He won the Open Championship in 1880, 1881, and 1882. In 1883 he tied with Willie Fernie, losing the 36-hole play-off by one stroke. After this Championship he became ill with typhoid, and was never able to reproduce his great form. He became the custodian of the Musselburgh links, taught the young and was widely respected in the community.

Fernie, Willie

Born St Andrews 1851; died Troon, June 1924. In 1880 he went to Dumfries as greenkeeper. In 1882 he was second to Bob Ferguson in the Open Championship and after a tie with the same player he won the Open Championship in 1883 at Musselburgh after a 36-hole play-off. He became professional to Felixstowe and Ardeer and in 1887 to Troon, and was there as professional until February, 1924. He was a very stylish player and in great demand as a teacher. He played in many important stake matches, the two biggest being against Andrew Kirkaldy over Troon, Prestwick and St Andrews which he won by 4 and 3, and against Willie Park over Musselburgh and Troon which he lost by 13 and 12. He played for Scotland against England in 1904.

Hagen, Walter C

Born Rochester, New York, 21st December, 1892. Died October, 1969. The first of the great golfers with star quality. People flocked to see him as much because he was a *character* as for his outstanding skill and many achievements. He did not want to be a millionaire, but merely to

live like one, and this he did in dramatic style as when he used a hired Rolls-Royce as a changing room at the Open because professionals were not admitted to the clubhouse, and when he gave the whole of his first prize in the Open to his caddie. He also pioneered stylish dressing on the course. As a player he had great mastery of the recovery shot, nerves of steel beneath his debonair exterior and a fine putting touch. His best achievement was probably his four consecutive wins in the USPGA championship when the event was decided by matchplay over 36 holes. He won the US Open in 1914 and 1919 and the Open in 1922-24-28-29 and represented the US against Britain on seven occasions. His world tours with Kirkwood, his extrovert approach and the entertainment he provided on and off the course were the forerunners of the spectacular development of golf as a spectator sport. In spite of his being a contemporary of the immortal Bobby Jones, his personality was such that he was never overshadowed.

Herd, Alexander (Sandy)

Born at St Andrews in 1868, died London, 18th February, 1944. His life in the forefront of the game was more prolonged than his contemporaries of the Victorian era, and when he took part in his last Open at St Andrews in 1939 he was 71 and his appearances in the Championship covered a span of 54 years. A brilliant shot player, success often eluded him as he was prone to leave his putts short and to indecision. On his first appearance in the Open, at the age of 17, he possessed only four clubs and although he was frequently in contention it was not until 1902 that he won the Championship. He was the first player to win the Open using a rubber-cored ball. In 1920 at Deal and again the following year at St Andrews he was joint leader in the Open after three rounds. In 1926, aged 58, he won the PGA match-play tournament at Royal Mid-Surrey in a 36-hole final, having played five rounds in the previous three days to reach it. Those three achievements when he was in his fifties are convincing proof of the longevity of his game. His life in golf brought him into competition with all the great Victorians – Taylor, Vardon, Kirkaldy, Braid and Park – and continued through the Jones and Hagen era up to the days of Locke, Cotton, Rees and Sarazen and others who, over 100 years after Herd's birth, were still playing Open Championship golf.

Hilton, Harold Horsfall

Born at West Kirby, a few miles from Hoylake, 12th January, 1869. Died 5th March, 1942. He was one of the most scientific of golfers. He learned his game at Royal Liverpool, where he won success in Boys' Competitions. In 1892, the year the Open Championship was extended to

72 holes, he won, and again in 1897. He won the Amateur Championship and the Irish Open Championship four times each, the St George's Cup twice, the American Amateur Championship once and became the first player, and the only Britisher, to hold both the US and British Amateur titles at the same time. He was small, 5 feet 7 inches, but immensely powerful in build. Hilton made a major contribution to golf literature as the first editor of *Golf Monthly*.

Hunter, Charles
Born Prestwick, 1836; died Prestwick, 24th January, 1921. A caddie and club-maker under old Tom Morris at Prestwick, he was for three years professional at the Blackheath Club, London, and succeeded old Tom as the Prestwick Club professional in 1864. He played in the first Open Championship at Prestwick in 1860, and he was a conspicuous figure at every championship and tournament held at Prestwick, acting as starter and in charge of the house flag up till the time of his death. He did not take much part in professional competitions, preferring to attend to his club-making and his members. In fact, during one championship round, while playing a niblick shot, he received word that the Lord Ailsa wished him to come at once and pick him out a set of clubs. He put his niblick back in his bag, pocketed his ball and returned to his workshop. In 1919 he was presented with his portrait in oils by the Prestwick Club, and a replica hangs in the Club. At the Open Championship of 1914 at Prestwick, he was the recipient of a presentation from his brother professionals. As a man of fine integrity, his friendship was valued by all golfers of his time.

Hutchinson, Horatio Gordon
Born London, 16th May, 1859, died in London, 28th July, 1932; an eminent golfer from the early eighties until 1907. He was a stylish and attractive player. Won the Amateur Championship in 1886 and 1887, runner-up 1885 (the first year of the Championship), and he was in the final in 1903. He was a semi-finalist in 1896, 1901, and 1904. He represented England v Scotland 1902-3-4-6-7, and was chosen in 1905 but illness prevented him taking his place. His career in the front rank of the game extended over twenty years. He was a voluminous and pleasant writer on golf and out-door life. He was the first Englishman to captain the Royal and Ancient. In other years he was also Captain of Royal Liverpool, Royal St George's and President of Royal North Devon.

Jones, Robert Tyre
Born Atlanta, Georgia, USA, 17th March 1902. Died 18th December, 1971 after many years of a crippling spinal disease. By the time he retired from competitive golf in 1930 at the age of 28, Jones had established himself as one of the greatest golfers of all time, if not the greatest. He represented America in the Walker Cup from its inauguration in 1922 until 1930 and played in the match against Great Britain in 1921. His victories included the US Open in 1923-26-29-30 (tied in 1925 and 1928 but lost the play-off; second in 1922 and 1924); US Amateur 1924-25-27-28-30 (runner-up in 1919 and 1926); Open Championship 1926-27-30; Amateur Championship 1930. In 1930, Jones reached a pinnacle which will probably never be equalled when he achieved the Grand Slam – winning in one year the Open and Amateur Championships of America and Britain. He then retired from championship golf. His stylish swing was the subject of admiration wherever he went – full, flowing, smooth, graceful and rhythmical. Yet he was of such a nervous disposition that he was frequently physically sick and unable to eat during a championship. During his championship winning years, Jones was also a keen scholar and gained first-class honours degrees in law, English literature and mechanical engineering at three different universities. He finally settled on a legal career with his own practice in Atlanta. It was there that he and his friend Clifford Roberts conceived and developed the idea of the great Augusta National course and the Masters tournament, now a fitting memorial to the *Master Golfer* himself. In recognition of his great skill and courage, and the esteem in which he was held in Britain and St Andrews, he was made an honorary member of the Royal and Ancient in 1956 and two years later, when in St Andrews as captain of the US team in the inaugural competition for the Eisenhower Trophy, he was given the Freedom of the Burgh of St Andrews. As a final tribute, a memorial service was held for him in St Andrews. The 10th hole of the Old Course, St Andrews (previously nameless) is now called after him.

Kirkaldy, Andrew
Born Denhead, near St Andrews, 18th March, 1860. Died St Andrews, 16th April, 1934. A rugged type of the old school of Scottish professionals, he was the last survivor of that race. After army service in Egypt and India he was appointed professional at Winchester. He had no liking for the steady sedate life of an English professional and after six weeks returned to his native St Andrews, where he lived the rest of his days acting as a playing professional until he was appointed professional to the Royal and Ancient Golf Club. He was a man of powerful physique. He was a beautiful golfer to watch, particularly his iron shots. In the Open Championship, 1889, he tied with Willie Park at Musselburgh, but lost on the replay. He played in many money matches and the most notable was in 1895. JH Taylor had

won the Open Championship in 1894, the first English professional to do so, and prior to the Open Championship, at St Andrews in 1895, the young English champion challenged the world for £50 a-side. Kirkaldy accepted and won by a hole. Candid, outspoken, sometimes uncouth, Kirkaldy in his old age was respected by princes and peers.

Laidlay, John Ernest

Born in East Lothian in 1860, Johnny Laidlay played high-quality golf for fifty years – a testimony to his technique and temperament. In all, he won more than 130 medals. At a time when golf was booming and the opposition tough, he won the Amateur Championship twice (1889, 1891) was runner-up three times and beaten semi-finalist three times. He was second in the 1893 Open Championship when his characteristically good putting failed. He played for Scotland every year from 1902 until 1911, when he was fifty-one. The longevity of his very individual swing was perhaps due to his early golfing experiences at Musselburgh where he saw Young Tom Morris, knew Willie Park well and played a lot with Bob Ferguson (including a famous round by moonlight). His contribution to the game was the overlapping grip – known erroneously as the Vardon grip. Laidlay played cricket for Scotland (vs Yorkshire – taking 6 wickets for 18 runs); he was a pioneer of wildlife photography and carved beautiful furniture. He died at Sunningdale in 1940.

Leitch, Miss Charlotte Cecilia Pitcairn (Cecil)

Born Silloth, Cumbria, 13th April, 1891. Died London, 16th September, 1977. Although Cecil Leitch had reached the semi-final of the British Ladies' Championship in 1908 at the age of 17 and had won the French Ladies' Championship in 1912, it was in 1914 that she really established herself as Britain's dominant woman golfer when she won the English Ladies', the French Ladies' and the British Ladies'. She retained each of these titles when they were next held after World War I (the English in 1919 and the British and French in 1920) and who can say how many times she might have won them in the intervening years. In all she won the French Ladies' in 1912-14-20-21-24, the English Ladies' in 1914-19, the British Ladies' in 1914-20-21-26 and the Canadian Ladies' in 1921. Her total of four victories in the British Ladies' has never been bettered and has been equalled only by her great rival Joyce Wethered, against whom in the 1920s she had many memorable matches. Miss Leitch was an outspoken person who occasionally battled with the golfing authorities. Her strong attacking play mirrored her personality. Aged 19, in 1910 she accepted the challenge from Harold Hilton, at his peak, to take on any woman golfer over 72 holes

giving half a stroke (a stroke at every second hole). Miss Leitch won this famous challenge match by 2 and 1 and later also beat John Ball, eight times Amateur Champion. Right to the end of her life, Cecil Leitch took an active interest in golf, attending major events whenever possible.

Little, W Lawson, Jun

Born Newport, RI, 23rd June, 1910, died February, 1968. As an amateur he established two records in that he won both the Amateur and American Amateur Championships in 1934 and again in 1935. In the final of the 1934 Amateur he won by the margin of 14 and 13 and for the 23 holes played he was ten under 4's. He turned professional in 1936 and won the Canadian Open in the same year and in 1940, won the US Open after a play-off.

Locke, Arthur D'Arcy

Bobby Locke, the son of Northern Irish emigrants, was born near Johannesburg on 20th November 1917 and died on 9th March 1987. He turned professional in 1938 after a very successful amateur career, in which he won the South African Boys' Championship, the South African Amateur (twice) and Open Championship (twice) as well as finishing leading amateur in the Open Championships of 1936 and 1937. As a result of his visits to Britain, he developed a characteristic hook to increase his length and although never a long hitter, his deadly short game made him a formidable competitor. In his first year as a professional he won the Irish, Transvaal, South African and New Zealand Open Championships as well as the South African Professional title. During the war, Locke flew Liberator bombers for nearly 2000 hours. He left the South African Air Force weighing four stones heavier and immediately resumed his winning way. Second to Snead at St Andrews in the 1946 Open, he was encouraged to visit America where he was greatly successful. He beat Snead 12–2 in a series of matches and won five tournaments in 1947, two in 1948, three in 1949 and one in 1950. Locke had bad relations with the USPGA who disliked his success and they banned him from their tournaments. Locke concentrated his efforts on Europe. He won the Open Championship four times—1949-50-52-59—as well as the Open Championships of Canada (1947), France (1952-53), Germany (1954), Switzerland (1954), Egypt (1954) and South Africa (six times as a professional). He also won a number of British titles including the Dunlop Masters, Spalding, the Lotus, Daks and Bowmaker Tournaments. The 1957 Open Championship was the first to be shown on television and the first in which the leaders went out last. Locke won by 3 strokes and his score of 279 was the first time 280 had been beaten at St Andrews. Locke had to mark his ball on the 72nd hole and in front of the cameras replaced it on the wrong spot. The R and A decided to let his score stand as he had derived no advantage from his technical error and disqualification would have been inequitable and against the spirit of the game. Bobby Locke will be remembered as a beautifully dressed golfer — plus fours, white shirt and tie — with a superb temperament, especially after a disastrous hole, great self discipline, the highest standards of behaviour and a wonderful short game. He was virtually in retirement when he had a serious car crash. On recovery he continued to play golf but his competitive career was at an end. He was made an honorary member of the R and A in 1976.

Longhurst, Henry
Died 22nd July, 1978, aged 69. After leaving Cambridge University, he acquired a job as a golf writer in which he could indulge his love of the game and be paid for it. He never ceased to be amazed at his own good fortune. His regular weekly article in the *Sunday Times* became compulsory reading for the golfing cognoscenti. From writing he became involved in radio and, later, television, through which he became world famous as a commentator. Television was the perfect medium for his talents. His humour, easy manner, gifted observation and perception, mellow voice, calm delivery and economy of word were all perfectly suited to a slow-moving sport, and from his vast knowledge and understanding of the game, he was always able to fill in any gaps in the action with an apt story or two. Longhurst also wrote several amusing books about different periods of his life, including a brief spell as an MP. He was awarded the CBE for his services to golf and was one of only a handful of people to be made an honorary member of the Royal and Ancient Golf Club. His own golf was good enough to have won the German Open Amateur in 1936 and to be runner-up in the French Open Amateur in 1937.

Massy, Arnaud
Born Biarritz in 1877, died 1958. Was the first overseas player to win the Open in 1907 from Taylor, Vardon and Braid; tied with Vardon in 1911 and lost play-off, conceding on the 35th hole.

Micklem, Gerald
Gerald Micklem, born in 1911, devoted so much of his life to the benefit of golf, both as player and administrator, that he will always be remembered for his dedication to the cause of amateurs and professionals alike. He was one of the last true Corinthians, an almost forgotten appellation, who gave his time unsparingly to the game's development, whether locally at his favourite Sunningdale, at the Royal and Ancient or on the international scene. After a pre-war Oxford Blue, he was English Champion in 1947 and 1953, four times in the Walker Cup side between 1947 and 1955 and non-playing Captain in 1957 and 1959, and 12 years a Home International from 1947. He was second in the Brabazon and also won the St George's Challenge Cup, the Berkshire Trophy, the President's Putter and several Royal and Ancient Members' medals. When he ceased to play in tournaments, his administrative responsibilities were legion. Captain of many English and British teams in European and International events, he took a leading part in the development of the Open, being Chairman of the Championship Committee of the Royal and Ancient during a key period. It was in this appointment that he made his greatest contribution to the future of the game. It was his vision and enterprise which led to the spectacle that the Open is today, as the most prestigious and best organised Championship anywhere in the world. He was Captain of the Royal and Ancient Club in 1968. To the end of his life he lent his support to most golf ventures and many were the amateurs and professionals whom he helped and who were made welcome at his home, close to Sunningdale, and who remember his generosity and advice given, based on his wide knowledge of the game.

Mitchell, Abe
Born East Grinstead, 1887, died 1947. *The finest player who never won an Open Championship* was the tribute paid by JH Taylor. He finished in the first 6 five times in the Open and was 3 times winner of the Match Play Championship. Along with Duncan and later Compston, he was one of the few British hopes against the American invasion of the twenties.

The Morrisses
Old Tom Morris and his son, young Tom Morris, played a prominent part in golf in the period from 1850 to 1875. The father was born at St Andrews on 16th June, 1821. At the age of eighteen, he was apprenticed to Allan Robertson in the ball-making trade. When Morris was thirty years of age, Colonel Fairlie of Coodham took him to Prestwick, and he remained there until 1865, when he returned to St Andrews and became greenkeeper to the Royal and Ancient Golf Club, a position he held until 1904. Young Tom was born at St Andrews in 1851, and exhibited early remarkable powers as a golfer. At the age of sixteen he won the Open Professional Tournament at Montrose against the best players in the country, and he won the Championship Belt outright by scoring three successive victories in 1868-9-70. The Championship lapsed for a year,

but when it was resumed in 1872, young Tom scored his fourth successive victory. There is no doubt that young Tom was the finest golfer of his time, but the tragic death of his wife, while he was engaged playing with his father in a great golf match at North Berwick against the brothers Willie and Mungo Park, had a most depressing effect on him, and he only survived his wife by a few months. Near the finish of this match, a telegram reached North Berwick intimating that, following her confinement, young Tom's wife was dangerously ill. The telegram was held over by Provost Brodie and not handed to young Tom until the end of the match. The yacht of John Lewis, an Edinburgh golfer, was put at the service of the Morrises but before the party embarked, a second telegram brought the sad news to young Tom that his wife had died. It was a mournful party that made the voyage across the Forth to St Andrews. The brilliant young golfer never recovered from the shock, and he died on Christmas Day of the same year, 1875, at the age of twenty-four. There was a second son, JOF Morris, who played in professional tournaments, but, although a fine golfer, he never approached the brilliant execution of his elder brother. Old Tom competed in every Open Golf Championship up to and including 1896, which, curiously, was the year Harry Vardon scored his first victory in the Open Championship. Old Tom died at St Andrews in 1908. He was respected throughout the golfing world for his honest, sturdy qualities. His portrait hangs in the Royal and Ancient Clubhouse, and the home green at St Andrews is named in his memory. A monument, with a sculpted figure of Young Tom, in golfing pose, was erected by public subscription in St Andrews Cathedral Churchyard and a smaller memorial stone was placed on the grave when Old Tom died.

Ouimet, Francis D

Born Brookline, Mass, 1893, died 1967. Described as the player who started the golf boom in the US when as a young amateur he tied with Vardon and Ray for the 1913 US Open and then won the play-off. In an illustrious career he won the US Amateur twice and was a member of every Walker Cup team from 1922 to 1934 and was non-playing Captain from then until 1949. The first non-British national, to be elected Captain of the Royal and Ancient Golf Club in 1951. He was prominent in golf legislation and administration in America and a committee member of the USGA for many years.

The Parks

Brothers Willie and Mungo Park of Musselburgh are famous in the annals of golf for the numerous money matches they played. Willie had the distinction of winning the very first Open Championship in 1860 and repeated his victory in 1863, 1866 and 1875. For twenty years Willie had a standing challenge in *Bell's Life*, London, to play any man in the world for £100 a side. Willie took part in numerous matches against Tom Morris for very large stakes and in the last of these at Musselburgh in 1882, the match came to an abrupt end when Park was 2 up with 6 to play. The referee stopped play because spectators were interfering with the balls. Morris and the referee retired to Foreman's public house. Park sent a message saying if Morris did not come out and finish the match he would play the remaining holes alone and claim the stakes. This he did. Mungo followed in his brother's footsteps by winning the Open Championship in 1874. He was for many years greenkeeper and professional at Alnmouth. Willie's son, Willie Jun, kept up the golfing tradition of the family by winning the Open in 1887 and 1889. He designed many golf courses in Europe and America, sometimes in conjunction with property development as at Sunningdale, and was the pioneer of the modern ideas of golf course construction. Like his forebears he took part in many private challenge matches, the one against Harry Vardon at North Berwick in 1899 being watched by the greatest crowd ever for that time and for many years afterwards. Willie Jun died in 1925 aged 61. The third generation of this golfing family sustained a prominent golf association through Miss Doris Park (Mrs Aylmer Porter), daughter of Willie Jun, who had a distinguished record in ladies' international and championship golf.

Philp, Hugh

The master craftsman among the half-dozen club-makers located in St Andrews in the early days of the nineteenth century. He was especially skilled in making a wooden putter with a long head of pear shaped design. He is believed to have made not many more than one hundred putters. The wooden putter was for centuries a favoured club at St Andrews for long approach putting. The creations of Hugh Philp are highly prized by golf club collectors. After his death in 1856 his business was carried on by Robert Forgan.

Ray, Edward

Born Jersey in 1877, died 1943. His early days coincided with the famous Triumvirate and it was not until 1912 that he won the Open and was runner-up the following year to Taylor. He was again runner-up in 1925 at the age of 48. In 1913 he tied for the US Open with Ouimet and Vardon, but lost the play-off. After the war he returned to America and won the US Open title in 1920 and was the last British player to hold the title until Tony Jacklin, in 1970. He and Vardon were the only British players to win both the US

Open and the Open until they were joined by
Jacklin. Noted for his long driving and powers of
recovery, he was invariably to be seen playing
with a pipe clenched between his teeth.

Rees, David James
One of Britain's outstanding golfers from the
1930s to the 1960s. He played in nine Ryder
Cup matches between 1937 and 1961, and was
also non-playing captain in 1967. In 1957, he captained the only British PGA team to win the Ryder
Cup since 1933. He was three times a runner-up
in the Open Championship and once third, and
won the PGA Match-Play Championship four
times, and the Dunlop Masters twice, in addition to numerous other tournament successes
in Britain, on the Continent of Europe, and in
Australasia. At the age of 60, in 1973, he finished
third in the Martini Tournament. He was made an
honorary member of the Royal and Ancient GC in
1976. Born in March, 1913, he died in November,
1983.

Robertson, Allan
Born St Andrews, 1815, died 1858. According to
tradition, he was never beaten in an individual
stake match on level terms. A short, thick-set
man, he had a beautiful well-timed swing, and
several golfers who could recall Robertson, and
who saw Harry Vardon at his best, were of the
opinion that there was considerable similarity
in the elegance and grace of the two players.
Tom Morris, senior, worked in Allan Robertson's
shop, where the principal trade was making
feather balls. A disagreement occurred between
Robertson and Morris on the advent of the gutta
ball, because Old Tom decided to play with the
invention, and Allan considered the gutta might
damage his trade in featheries. Allan, through
agents, endeavoured to buy up all gutta balls
in order to protect his industry of feather balls.
Allan Robertson and Tom Morris never seem
to have come together in any single match for
large stakes, but it is recorded that they never
lost a foursome in which they were partners.

Sayers, Bernard
Born Leith, 1857, died at North Berwick, 9th
March, 1924. Of very small stature, one of the
smallest professionals, and light of build, he
nevertheless took a leading position in the game
for over forty years with his outstanding skill and
rigid physical training. He engaged in numerous
stake matches and played for Scotland against
England in every match form 1903 to 1913, except
1911. He played in every Open Championship
from 1880 to 1923. Of a bright and sunny disposition, he contributed much to the merriment of
championship and professional gatherings. He
taught princes and nobles to play the game,
was presented to King Edward, and received

a presentation from King George, when Duke
of York.

Smith, Mrs Frances (née Bunty Stephens)
Died July 1978, aged 53. Dominated post war
women's golf by winning the British Ladies'
Championship in 1949 and 1954 (runner-up
1951-52), the English Ladies' in 1948-54-55
(runner-up 1959) and the French Ladies' in 1949.
She represented Great Britain in the Curtis Cup
on six consecutive occasions form 1950 to 1960. A
pronounced pause at the top of her swing made
her style most distinctive. She was awarded the
OBE for her services to golf and was president of
the English Ladies' Golf Association at the time of
her death.

Smith, Horton
Died October, 1963, aged 55. Came to notice
first from Joplin, Missouri, when 20 years old, and
brilliantly embarked on the professional circuit
in the winter of 1929 when he won all but one
of the open tournaments in which he played. He
was promoted to that year's Ryder Cup team and
also played in 1933 and 1935. He won the first US
Masters Tournament in 1934 and again in 1936
as well as more than thirty other major events.
On his 21st birthday he won the French Open.
He was President of the American PGA, 1952-54
and received two national distinctions; the Ben
Hogan Award for overcoming illness or injury,
and the Bobby Jones Award for distinguished
sportsmanship in golf. The day after the Ryder
Cup match which he attended in Atlanta in 1963
he collapsed and died in a Detroit hospital.

Smith, Macdonald
Born at Carnoustie in 1890, died at Los Angeles
in 1949. Was one of the great golfers who
never won the Open Championship, in which
he consistently finished in a high place, coming
second in 1930 and 1932, third in 1923 and 1924,
fourth in 1925 and 1934 and fifth in 1931. He went
to America before he was twenty. In the Open
Championship at Prestwick in 1925 he entered
the last round with a lead of five strokes over
the field, but a wildly enthusiastic Scottish crowd
of 20,000 engulfed and overwhelmed him. The
sequel to these unruly scenes was the introduction of gate money the following year and
Prestwick was dropped from the rota for the
Open.

Tait, Frederick Guthrie
Freddie Tait was born at 17 Drummond Place,
Edinburgh (his father PG Tait was a Professor
in Edinburgh University), on 11th January, 1870.
He was killed in the South African War at
Koodoosberg Drift, 7th February, 1900. He joined
the Royal and Ancient in 1890, and on 5th August
that year he beat all previous amateur records

for St Andrews by holing the course in 77, and in 1894 he reduced the record to 72. He was first amateur in the Open Championship in 1894 (Sandwich), 1896 (Muirfield), 1899 (Sandwich). He was third in 1896 and 1897. He won the Amateur Championship in 1896 at Sandwich, beating in successive rounds GC Broadwood, Charles Hutchings, JE Laidlay, John Ball, Horace Hutchinson, and HH Hilton, the strongest amateurs of the day. He repeated his victory in 1898 at Hoylake, and in 1899 he fought and lost at the 37th the historic final with John Ball at Prestwick. There is a Freddie Tait Cup given annually to the best amateur in the South African Open Championship. This cup was purchased from the surplus of the fund collected during the visit of the British amateur golfers to South Africa in 1928.

Taylor, John Henry
Last survivor of the famous Triumvirate – Taylor, Braid and Vardon – died at his Devonshire home in February, 1963, within a month of his 92nd birthday. He was born at Northam, North Devon, 19th March, 1871, and had been professional at Burnham, Winchester and Royal Mid-Surrey. JH won the Open Championship five times – in 1894-95-1900-09-13 – and also tied with Harry Vardon in 1896, but lost the replay. He was runner-up also in 1904-05-06-14. His brilliant career included the French and German Open Championships and he was second in the US Open in 1900. Among the many honours he received were honorary membership of the Royal and Ancient Golf Club in 1949. He was regarded as the pioneer of British professionalism and helped to start the Professional Golfers' Association. He did much to raise the whole status of the professional and, in the words of Bernard Darwin, *turned a feckless company into a self-respecting and respected body of men.* On his retirement in 1957 the Royal North Devon Golf Club paid him their greatest compliment by electing him President.

Tolley, Cyril James Hastings
Born in 1896, Tolley was a dominant figure in amateur golf in the inter-war period. He won the first of two Amateur Championships in 1920 while still a student at Oxford and continued to win championships and represent England and Britain until 1938. Among other titles he won the Welsh Open (1921 and 1923) and remains the only amateur to have won the French Open (1924 and 1929). A powerful hitter with a delicate touch, Tolley was a crowd pleaser. He is remembered as much for a match he lost as much as for some of his victories. Having won the Amateur Championship in 1929, Tolley was a favourite to win at St Andrews in 1930. The draw was unseeded and he met Bobby Jones in the fourth round. A huge crowd turned out to watch an extremely

exciting match which Jones won on the 19th with a stymie. The rest is history. Tolley was elected Captain of the R and A in 1948. He died in 1978.

Travis, Walter J
Born in Australia in 1862, died in New York 1925. Travis was the first overseas golfer to win the British Amateur, at Sandwich in 1904. He won the title using a centre-shafted putter, which was subsequently banned for many years. He won the US Amateur Championship in 1900, having taken up the game four years previously at the age of 35. He repeated his victory in 1901 and 1903 and was a semi-finalist five times between 1898 and 1914, winning also the stroke competition six times between 1900 and 1908. The *Old Man* as he was known is reckoned to have been one of the finest judges of distance who ever played golf.

Vardon, Harry
Born Grouville, Jersey, died at South Herts on 20th March, 1937. Created a record by winning the Open Championship six times, his wins being in 1896, 1898, 1899, 1903, 1911 and 1914. He also won the American Open in 1900 and tied in 1913, subsequently losing the play-off. He had a serious illness in 1903 and it was said that he never quite regained his former dominance, particularly on the putting green. That he was the foremost golfer of his time cannot be disputed and he innovated the modern upright swing and popularised the over lapping grip invented by JE Laidlay. Had it not been for ill-health and the intervention of World War I, his outstanding records both in the UK and America would almost certainly have been added to in later years. But in any event his profound influence on the game lives on. More than 100 years after his birth his achievements are still the standard of comparison with the latter day giants of the game.

Wethered, Roger H
Born 3rd January, 1899, in Malden, Surrey and died in 1983, aged 84. He was one of the outstanding amateurs of the period between the two World Wars, winning the Amateur Championship in 1923, and being runner-up in 1928 and 1930. He won the President's Putter of the Oxford and Cambridge GS five times (once a tie) between 1926 and 1936, played against the United States six times between 1921 and 1934, and for England against Scotland every year from 1922 to 1930. He was captain of the Royal and Ancient in 1946. But he will probably be best remembered for the fact that he tied with Jock Hutchison, a Scot who had settled in the United States, for first place in the 1921 Open Championship at St Andrews, having incurred a penalty stroke in the course of the event by

inadvertently stepping backwards and treading on his ball, while Hutchison, in the first round, had had a hole in one. Wethered was reluctant to stay on for the 36-hole play-off the following day because of a cricket engagement in England, but was persuaded to do so, only to be beaten by nine strokes, 150 to 159. No British amateur has come so close to winning the Open Championship since.

Wood, Craig Ralph
Born Lake Placid, New York, 18th November, 1901. Died 1968. Visited Great Britain for first time in 1933, and tied for Open Championship with Denny Shute, but lost on replay. Won American Open Championship, 1941; US Masters' Tournament, 1941; Canadian Open Championship, 1942; runner-up American PGA Championship, 1934. In 1936 second in USPGA Championship. A member of the American Ryder Cup team, 1931-33-35, and US Australian team, 1937. In 1939 tied for US Open, but lost on replay.

Zaharias, Mrs George (Mildred *Babe* Didrikson)
Born at Port Arthur, Texas, USA, in June 1915, and died of cancer at Galveston in September 1956. In the 1932 Olympic Games she established three world records for women: 80 metres hurdles, javelin, and high jump. On giving up athletics she took up golf and won the Texas Women's Open in 1940-45-46; Western Open, 1946. In 1947 won the Ladies' Championship, being the first American to do so. In August 1947 she turned professional and went on to win the US National Women's Open, 1948-50. In winning the Tampa Open, 1951, she set up a then women's world record aggregate of 288 for 72 holes. She was voted Woman Athlete of the year 1932-45-46-47-50, and in 1949 was voted Greatest Female Athlete of the Half-Century. First woman to hold the post of head professional to a golf club. The *Babe* was a courageous and fighting character who left her mark in the world of sport.

Part VII
Interesting Facts and Record Scoring

Interesting Facts and Unusual Incidents

Royal Golf Clubs

● The right to the designation *Royal* is bestowed by the favour of the Sovereign or a member of the Royal House. In most cases the title is granted along with the bestowal of royal patronage on the club. The Perth Golfing Society was the first to receive the designation *Royal*. That was accorded in June 1833. King William IV bestowed the honour on the Royal and Ancient Club in 1834. The most recent Club to be so designated is the Royal Troon in 1978.

Royal and Presidential Golfers

● In the long history of the Royal and Ancient game no reigning British monarch has played in an open competition. The Duke of Windsor, when Prince of Wales in 1922, competed in the Royal and Ancient Autumn Medal at St Andrews. He also took part in competitions at Mid-Surrey, Sunningdale, Royal St George's and in the Parliamentary Handicap. He also occasionally competed in American events, sometimes partnered by a professional, and on a private visit to London in 1952 he competed in the Autumn competition of Royal St George's at Sandwich scoring 97. As Prince of Wales he had played on courses all over the world and, after his abdication, as Duke of Windsor he continued to enjoy the game for many years.
● King George VI (when Duke of York) in 1930 and the Duke of Kent in 1937 also competed in the Autumn Meeting of the Royal and Ancient, these occasions being after they had formally played themselves into the Captaincy of the Club and each returned his card in the medal round.
● King Leopold of Belgium played in the Belgian Amateur Championship at Le Zoute, the only reigning monarch ever to have played in a national championship. The Belgian King played in many competitions subsequent to his abdication. In 1949 he reached the quarter-finals of the French Amateur Championship at St Cloud, playing as Count de Rethy.
● King Baudouin of Belgium in 1958 played in the triangular match Belgium-France-Holland

and won his match against a Dutch player. He also took part in the Gleneagles Hotel tournament (playing as Mr B de Rethy), partnered by Dai Rees in 1959.
● HRH Prince Claus of the Netherlands played in the American-Express Pro-Am preceding the 1971 Dutch Open. His handicap was 18. Partnered by Peter Oosterhuis, he won the same event in 1974 with a score of 62.
● US President Gerald Ford played in the pro-am before the 1975 Jackie Gleason Classic in a group which included Jack Nicklaus. Following his defeat in the 1977 presidential election, he became a fairly frequent competitor at pro-am tournaments and succeeded in holing in one (his first ever) during the 1977 Memphis Classic.
● The King of Morocco is an enthusiastic golfer and plays frequently with top professionals, in particular Billy Casper.
● Exiled King Constantine of Greece is also a keen golfer. Since 1973 he has played in several pro-am tournaments.
● President Kaunda of Zambia is a keen supporter and player of the game. There is a 9-hole course in the grounds of the Presidential Palace at Lusaka where he plays regularly.

First Lady Golfer

● Mary Queen of Scots, who was beheaded on 8th February, 1587, was probably the first lady golfer so mentioned by name. As evidence of her indifference to the fate of Darnley, her husband who was murdered at Kirk o' Field, Edinburgh, she was charged at her trial with having played at golf in the fields beside Seton a few days after his death.

Record Championship Victories

● In the Amateur Championship at Muirfield, 1920, Captain Carter, an Irish golfer, defeated an American entrant by 10 and 8. This is the only known instance where a player has won every hole in an Amateur Championship tie.
● In the final of the Canadian Ladies Championship at Rivermead, Ottawa, 1921, Cecil Leitch

defeated Mollie McBride by 17 and 15. Miss Leitch only lost 1 hole in the match, the ninth. She was 14 up at the end of the first round, and only 3 holes were necessary in the second round, Miss Leitch winning them all. She won 18 holes out of 21 played, lost 1, and halved 2.

● In the final of the French Ladies' Open Championship at Le Touquet in 1927, Mlle de la Chaume (St Cloud) defeated Mrs Alex Johnston (Moor Park) by 15 and 14, the largest victory in a European golf championship.

● At Prestwick in 1934, W Lawson Little, Presidio, San Francisco, defeated James Wallace, Troon Portland, by 14 and 13 in the final of the Amateur Championship, the record victory in the Amateur Championship. Wallace failed to win a single hole.

● The largest victory in the Walker Cup in 18-hole matches was in 1979 when American Scott Hoch beat Jim Buckley by 9 and 7. Buckley had a back injury.

Outstanding Records in Championships, International Matches and on the Professional Circuit

● The record number of victories in the Open Championship is six, held by Harry Vardon who won in 1896-98-99-1903-11-14.

● Five-time winners of the Championship are JH Taylor in 1894-95-1900-09-13; James Braid in 1901-05-06-08-10; Peter Thomson in 1954-55-56-58-65 and Tom Watson in 1975-77-80-82-83. Thomson's 1965 win was achieved when the Championship had become a truly international event. In 1957 he finished second behind Bobby Locke. By winning again in 1958 Thomson was prevented only by Bobby Locke from winning five consecutive Open Championships.

● Four successive victories in the Open by *Young* Tom Morris is a record so far never equalled. He won in 1868-69-70-72. (The Championship was not played in 1871.) Other four-time winners are Bobby Locke in 1949-50-52-57, Walter Hagen in 1922-24-28-29, Willie Park 1860-63-66-75, and *Old* Tom Morris 1861-62-64-67.

● Since the Championship began in 1860, players who have won three times in succession are Jamie Anderson, Bob Ferguson, and Peter Thomson.

● Robert Tyre Jones won the Open three times in 1926-27-30; the Amateur in 1930; the American Open in 1923-26-29-30; and the American Amateur in 1924-25-27-28-30. In winning the four major golf titles of the world in one year (1930) he achieved a feat unlikely ever to be equalled. Jones retired from competitive golf after winning the 1930 American Open, the last of these Championships, at the age of 28.

● Jack Nicklaus has had the most wins (six) in the US Masters Tournament, followed by Arnold Palmer with four.

● In modern times there are four championships generally regarded as standing above all others – the Open, US Open, US Masters, and USPGA. Four players have held all these titles, Gene Sarazen, Ben Hogan, Gary Player, and Jack Nicklaus, who in 1978 became the first player to have held each of them at least three times. His record in these events is – Open 1966-70-78; US Open 1962-67-72-80; US Masters 1963-65-66-72-75-86; USPGA 1963-71-73-75-80. His total of major championships is now 18.

The nearest approach to achieving the Grand Slam of the Open, US Open, US Masters and USPGA in one year was by Ben Hogan in 1953 when he won the first three and could not compete in the USPGA as it then overlapped with the Open Championship.

● In 1975 Jack Nicklaus came very near to winning the Grand Slam, winning the Masters and the USPGA and finishing only two shots and one shot behind the winning scores in the US Open and the Open Championship respectively.

● The record number of victories in the US Open is four, held by W Anderson, Bobby Jones, Ben Hogan and Jack Nicklaus.

● Bobby Jones (amateur), Gene Sarazen, Ben Hogan, Lee Trevino and Tom Watson are the only players to have won the Open and US Open Championships in the same year. Tony Jacklin won the Open in 1969 and the US Open in 1970 and for a few weeks was the holder of both.

● John Ball holds the record number of victories in the Amateur Championship, which he won eight times. Next comes Michael Bonallack with five wins.

● In winning the Amateur Championship in 1970 Michael Bonallack became the first player to win in three consecutive years.

● Cecil Leitch and Joyce Wethered each won the British Ladies' title four times.

● The English Amateur record number of victories is held by Michael Bonallack, who won the title five times.

● The Scottish Amateur record is held by Ronnie Shade, who won five titles in successive years – 1963-64-65-66-67. His long reign as Champion ended when he was beaten in the fourth round of the 1968 Championship after winning 44 consecutive matches.

● Joyce Wethered established an unbeaten record by winning the English Ladies' in five successive years from 1920 to 1924 inclusive.

● In winning the Amateur Championships of Britain and America in 1934 and 1935 Lawson Little won 31 consecutive matches. Other dual winners of these championships in the same year are RT Jones (1930) and Bob Dickson (1967).

● Gary Player won the South African Open for the 13th time in 1981. He has also won the Australian Open seven times.

● Peter Thomson's victory in the 1971 New Zealand Open Championship was his ninth in that championship.

● In a four week spell in 1971, Lee Trevino won in succession the US Open, the Canadian Open and the Open Championships.

● The finalists in the 1970 Amateur Championship, MF Bonallack and W Hyndman, were the same as in 1969. This was the first time the same two players reached the final in successive years.

● Seve Ballesteros holds the record for most wins in one year on the European Tour, six in 1986; this followed his record equalling number in 1985. The best British players have been Bernard Hunt in 1963, Nick Faldo in 1983, and Ian Woosnam in 1987, each with five victories.

● On the US professional circuit the greatest number of consecutive victories is 11, achieved by Byron Nelson in 1945. Nelson also holds the record for most victories in one calendar year, again in 1945 when he won a total of 18 tournaments.

● Jack Nicklaus and the late Walter Hagen have had five wins each in the USPGA Championship. All Hagen's wins were in successive years and at match play; all Nicklaus's at stroke play.

● In 1953 Flori van Donck of Belgium had seven major victories in Europe, including the Open Championships of Switzerland, Italy, Holland, Germany and Belgium.

● In 1947 Norman von Nida (Australia) had seven major tournament victories in England.

● Mrs Anne Sander won four major amateur titles each under a different name. She won the US Ladies' in 1958 as Miss Quast, in 1961 as Mrs Decker, in 1963 as Mrs Welts and the British Ladies' in 1980 as Mrs Sander.

● The highest number of appearances in the Ryder Cup matches is held by Christy O'Connor who made his tenth appearance in 1973.

● The greatest number of appearances in the Walker Cup matches is held by Irishman Joe Carr who made his tenth appearance in 1967.

● In the Curtis Cup Mary McKenna made her ninth consecutive appearance in 1986.

● Players who have represented their country in both Walker and Ryder Cup matches are Fred Haas, Ken Venturi, Gene Littler, Jack Nicklaus, Tommy Aaron, Mason Rudolph, Bob Murphy, Lanny Wadkins, Tom Kite, Jerry Pate, Craig Stadler, Jay Haas and Bill Rodgers (US), and Norman Drew, Peter Townsend, Clive Clark, Peter Oosterhuis, Howard Clark, Mark James, Michael King, Paul Way and Sandy Lyle (British Isles).

Remarkable Recoveries in Match Play

● There have been two remarkable recoveries in the Walker Cup Matches. In 1930 at Sandwich, JA Stout, Great Britain, round in 68, was 4 up at the end of the first round against Donald Moe. Stout started in the second round, 3, 3, 3, and was 7 up. He was still 7 up with 13 to play. Moe, who went round in 67, won back the 7 holes to draw level at the 17th green. At the 18th or 36th of the match, Moe, after a long drive placed his iron shot within three feet of the hole and won the match by 1 hole.

● In 1936 at Pine Valley, George Voigt and Harry Girvan for America were 7 up with 11 to play against Alec Hill and Cecil Ewing. The British pair drew equal at the 17th hole, or the 35th of the match, and the last hole was halved.

● In the 1965 Piccadilly Match-Play Championship Gary Player beat Tony Lema after being 7 down with 17 to play.

● Bobby Cruickshank, the old Edinburgh player, had an extraordinary recovery in a 36-hole match in a USPGA Championship for he defeated Al Watrous after being 11 down with 12 to play.

● In a match at the Army GC, Aldershot, on 5th July, 1974, for the Gradoville Bowl, MC Smart was eight down with eight to play against Mike Cook. Smart succeeded in winning all the remaining holes and the 19th for victory.

Oldest Champions

Open Championship

Belt: 46 years. Tom Morrissen in 1867.
Cup: 44 years 93 days. Roberto De Vicenzo in 1967.
44 years 42 days. Harry Vardon in 1914.
42 years 97 days. JH Taylor in 1913.
Amateur Championship: Hon Michael Scott, 54 years, Hoylake 1933.
British Ladies Amateur: Mrs Jessie Valentine, 43 years, Hunstanton 1958.
Scottish Amateur: JM Cannon, 53 years, Troon 1969.
English Amateur: Terry Shingler, 41 years 11 months, Walton Heath 1977. Gerald Micklem, 41 years 8 months, Royal Birkdale 1947.
UK Professional: Dai Rees, 60 years, equal second Martini International, Barnton 1973.
US Open: Ted Ray (GB), 43 years, Inverness Ohio 1920.
US Amateur: Jack Westland, 47 years, Seattle 1952. Westland was defeated in the 1931 final, 21 years previously, by Francis Ouimet at Beverley, Chicago, Illinois.
US Masters: Jack Nicklaus, 46 years, in 1986.
USPGA: Julius Boros, 48 years, in 1968. Lee Trevino, 43 years, in 1984.

USPGA Tour: Sam Snead, 52 years, Greensborough Open in 1965. Julius Boros lost play-off in Westchester Classic 1975. Sam Snead, 61 years, equal second in Glen Campbell Open 1974.

Youngest Champions

Open Championship
Belt: 17 years 5 months. Tom Morris, jun in 1868.
Cup: 21 years 25 days. Willie Auchterlonie in 1893.
21 years 5 months. Tom Morris, jun in 1872.
22 years 103 days. Severiano Ballesteros in 1979.
Amateur Championship: JC Beharrell, 18 years 1 month, Troon 1956. R Cole (S Africa) 18 years 1 month, Carnoustie 1966.
British Ladies Amateur: May Hezlett, 17 years, Newcastle Co Down 1899. Michelle Walker, 18 years, Alwoodley 1971.
English Amateur: Nick Faldo, 18 years, Lytham St Annes 1975. Paul Downes, 18 years, Birkdale 1978.
English Amateur Stroke Play: Ronan Rafferty, 16 years, Hunstanton 1980.
British Ladies Open Stroke Play: Janet Melville, 20 years, Foxhills 1978.

Disqualifications

Disqualifications are now numerous, usually for some irregularity over signing a scorecard or for late arrival at the first tee. We therefore show here only incidents in major events involving famous players or players who were in a winning position or, alternatively, incidents which were in themselves unusual.

● JJ McDermott, the American Open Champion 1911-12, arrived for the Open Championship at Prestwick in 1914 to discover that he had made a mistake of a week in the date the championship began. The American could not play as the qualifying rounds were completed on the day he arrived.
● An amusing case was that of a competitor in the Amateur Championship at Prestwick in 1922. He boarded the train at Ayr thinking it stopped at Prestwick, but it did not halt until Troon some miles further on. The railway runs alongside the first hole at Prestwick and the player frantically yelled from the train that he would be back as soon as he could, but that was of no avail.
● The Hon Michael Scott was disqualified in the third round of the 1910 Amateur Championship for not being on the tee in time. He was also disqualified in the 1924 championship when the starting times owing to slowness on the course were nearly 40 minutes late. Scott calculated

that his starting time would be at least half an hour late, but he failed to observe that there was an interval of forty-five minutes in the times for starting, and consequently starting had resumed at times given on the programme.
● In the Amateur Championship at Sandwich in 1937, Brigadier-General Critchley, arriving from New York at Southampton on the *Queen Mary*, which had been delayed by fog, flew by specially chartered aeroplane to Sandwich. He circled over the clubhouse, so that the officials knew he was nearly there, but he arrived six minutes late, and his name had been struck out. At the same championship a player, entered from Burma, who had travelled across the Pacific and the American Continent, and also was on the *Queen Mary*, travelled from Southampton by motor car and arrived four hours after his starting time to find after journeying more than halfway round the world he was *struck out*.
● An unprecedented disqualification was that of A Murray in the New Zealand Open Championship, 1937. Murray, who was New Zealand Champion in 1935, was playing with JP Hornabrook, New Zealand Amateur Champion, and at the 8th hole in the last round, while waiting for his partner to putt, Murray dropped a ball on the edge of the green and made a practice putt along the edge. Murray returned the lowest score in the championship, but he was disqualified for taking the practice putt.
● At the Open Championship at St Andrews in 1946, John Panton, Glenbervie, in the evening practised putting on a green on the New Course, which was one of the qualifying courses. He himself reported his inadvertence to the Royal and Ancient and he was disqualified.
● At the Open Championship, Sandwich, 1949, C Rotar, an American, qualified by four strokes to compete in the championship but he was disqualified because he had used a putter which did not conform to the accepted form and make of a golf club, the socket being bent over the centre of the club head. This is the only case where a player has been disqualified in the Open Championship for using an illegal club.
● In the 1957 American Women's Open Championship, Mrs Jackie Pung had the lowest score, 298 over four rounds, but lost the championship. The card she signed for the final round read *five* at the 4th hole instead of the correct *six*. Her total of 72 was correct but the error, under rigid rules, resulted in her disqualification. Betty Jameson, who partnered Mrs Pung and also returned a wrong score, was also disqualified.

Longest Match

● WR Chamberlain, a retired farmer, and George New, a postmaster at Chilton Foliat, on 1st August, 1922, met at Littlecote, the 9-hole course of Sir Ernest Wills, and they agreed to play every Thursday afternoon over the course. This they did until New's sudden death on 13th January, 1938. An accurate record of the matches was kept giving details of each round including wind direction and playing conditions. In the elaborate system nearly two million facts were recorded. They played 814 rounds, and aggregated 86,397 strokes, of which Chamberlain took 44,008 and New 42,371. New, therefore, was 1,637 strokes up. The last round of all was halved, a suitable end to such an unusual contest.

Longest Ties

● The longest known ties in 18-hole match play rounds in major events were in an early round of the News of the World Match Play Championship at Turnberry in 1960, when WS Collins beat WJ Branch at the 31st hole and in the third round of the same tournament at Walton Heath in 1961 when Harold Henning beat Peter Alliss also at the 31st hole.

● In the 1970 Scottish Amateur Championship at Balgownie, Aberdeen, E Hammond beat J McIvor at the 29th hole in their second round tie.

● CA Palmer beat Lionel Munn at the 28th hole at Sandwich in 1908. This is the record tie of the British Amateur Championship. Munn has also been engaged in two other extended ties in the Amateur Championship. At Muirfield, in 1932, in the semi-final, he was defeated by John de Forest, the ultimate winner, at the 26th hole, and at St Andrews, in 1936, in the second round he was defeated by JL Mitchell, again at the 26th hole.

The following examples of long ties are in a different category for they occurred in competitions, either stroke play or match play, where the conditions stipulated that in the event of a tie, a further stated number of holes had to be played – in some cases 36 holes, but mostly 18. With this method a vast number of extra holes was sometimes necessary to settle ties.

● The longest known was between two American women in a tournament at Peterson (New Jersey) when 88 extra holes were required before Mrs Edwin Labaugh emerged as winner.

● In a match on the Queensland course, Australia, in October, 1933, HB Bonney and Col HCH Robertson versus BJ Canniffe and Dr Wallis Hoare required to play a further four 18-hole matches after being level at the end of the original 18 holes. In the fourth replay Hoare and Caniffe won by 3 and 2 which meant that 70 extra holes had been necessary to decide the tie.

● After finishing all square in the final of the Dudley GC's foursomes competition in 1950, FW

Mannell and AG Walker played a further three 18-hole replays against T Poole and E Jones, each time finishing all square. A further 9 holes were then arranged when Mannell and Walker won by 3 and 2 making a total of 61 extra holes to decide the tie.

● RA Whitcombe and Mark Seymour tied for first prize in the Penfold £750 Tournament at St Annes-on-Sea, in 1934. They had to play off over 36 holes and tied again. They were then required to play another 9 holes when Whitcombe won with 34 against 36. The tournament was over 72 holes. The first tie added 36 holes and the extra 9 holes made an aggregate of 117 holes to decide the winner. This is a record in first-class British golf but in no way compares with other long ties as it involved only two replays – one of 36 holes and one of 9.

● In the American Open Championship at Toledo, Ohio, in 1931, G Von Elm and Billy Burke tied for the title. Each returned aggregates of 292. On the first replay both finished in 149 for 36 holes but on the second replay Burke won with a score of 148 against 149. This is a record tie in a national open championship.

● Paul Downes was beaten by Robin Davenport at the 9th extra hole in the 4th round of the 1981 English Amateur Championship. A record marathon match for the championship.

● Severiano Ballesteros was beaten by Johnny Miller at the 9th extra hole of a sudden-death play-off at the 1982 million dollar Sun City Challenge, a record for any 72 hole professional event.

● In the semi-finals of the Wentworth Mixed Foursomes at Aldeburgh GC on 28th August, 1983, John Raison and Jackie Sheffield beat Andrew Mangeot and June Mangeot (the holders) at the 9th extra hole (the 27th).

Long Drives

It is impossible to state with any certainty what is the longest ever drive. Many long drives have never been measured and many others have most likely never been brought to our attention. Then there are several outside factors which can produce freakishly long drives, such as a strong following wind, downhill terrain or bonehard ground. Where all three of these favourable conditions prevail outstandingly long drives can be achieved. Another consideration is that a long drive made during a tournament is a different proposition from one made for length alone, either on the practice ground, a long driving competition or in a game of no consequence. All this should be borne in mind when considering the long drives shown here.

● Tommie Campbell of Portmarnock is regarded as having hit the longest drive without any favourable conditions prevailing with a drive of 392 yards at Dun Laoghaire GC in July 1964.

● Playing in Australia, American George Bayer is reported to have driven to within chipping distance of a 589 yards hole. *It was certainly a drive of over 500 yards,* said Bayer acknowledging the strong following wind, sharp downslope where his ball landed and the bonehard ground.

● American senior professional Mike Austin, playing in the US National Seniors' Open at Las Vegas in 1974, amazingly drove his ball many yards through the 5th green at Winterwood GC, a hole measuring 450 yards. The total length of his downwind drive, which struck hard ground, was given at 515 yards.

● In September, 1934, over the East Devon course, THV Haydon, Wimbledon, drove to the edge of the 9th green which was a hole of 465 yards, giving a drive of not less than 450 yards. The hole was downhill and presumably other favourable conditions were also present. Haydon is also reported to have nearly driven the 15th hole (420 yards) at Royal Wimbledon in October, 1929. The ball finished just short of the green on a hole which was slightly uphill all the way and when the following wind was described as only a breeze.

● EC Bliss drove 445 yards at Herne Bay in August, 1913. The drive was measured by a Government Surveyor who also measured the drop in height from tee to resting place of the ball at 57 feet.

● Craig Wood of America in the play-off for the 1933 Open Championship at St Andrews drove into the bunkers in the face of the hill short of the 5th green. This was estimated at 430 yards. There was a considerable following wind and the ground was parched dry.

● George Johnson in 1972, with the assistance of a following wind, drove a ball 413 yards at the 8th hole at Delamere Forest.

Long Carries

● At Sitwell Park, Rotherham, in 1935, W Smithson, the home professional, drove a ball which carried a dyke at 380 yards from the 2nd tee.

● George Bell, of Penrith GC, New South Wales, Australia, using a number 2 wood drove across the Nepean River, a certified carry of 309 yards in a driving contest in 1964.

● After the 1986 Irish Professional Championship at Waterville, Co. Kerry, four long-hitting professionals tried for the longest-carry record over water, across a lake in the Waterville Hotel grounds. Liam Higgins, the local professional, carried 310 yards and Paul Leonard 311, beating the previous record by 2 yards.

● In the 1972 Algarve Open at Penina, Henry Cotton vouched for a carry of 305 yards over a ditch at the 18th hole by long-hitting Spanish professional Francisco Abreu. There was virtually no wind assistance.

● At the Home International matches at Portmarnock in 1949 a driving competition was held in which all the players in the English, Scottish, Welsh and Irish teams competed. The actual carry was measured. The longest was 280 yards by Jimmy Bruen.

● When Walter Hagen was in Britain for the Open Championship in 1928, he drove a ball from the roof of the Savoy Hotel to the other side of the Thames.

● On 6th April, 1976, Tony Jacklin hit a number of balls into Vancouver harbour, Canada, from the 495-foot high roof of a new building complex. The longest carry was measured at 389 yards.

Long Hitting

There have been numerous long hits, not on golf courses, where an outside agency has assisted the length of the shot. Such an example was a 'drive' by Liam Higgins in 1986, on the Airport runway at Baldonal, near Dublin, of 632 yards.

Longest Albatrosses

● The longest-known albatrosses (three under par) recorded at par 5 holes are:

● 609 yards–15th hole at Mahaka Inn West Course, Hawaii, by John Eakin of California on 12th November, 1972.

● 602 yards–16th hole at Whiting Field Golf Course, Milton, Florida, by 27-year-old Bill Graham with a drive and a 3-wood, aided by a 25 mph tail wind.

● The longest-known albatrosses in Open Championships are:

580 yards–14th hole at Crans-sur-Sierre, by American Billy Casper in the 1971 Swiss Open.

558 yards–5th hole at Muirfield by American Johnny Miller in the 1972 Open Championship.

Eagles (Multiple and Consecutive)

● Wilf Jones scored three consecutive eagles at the first three holes at Moor Hall GC when playing in a competition there on August Bank Holiday Monday 1968. He scored 3, 1, 2 at holes measuring 529 yards, 176 yards and 302 yards.

● In a round of the 1980 Jubilee Cup, a mixed foursomes match play event of Colchester GC, Mrs Nora Booth and her son Brendan scored three consecutive gross eagles of 1, 3, 2 at the 8th, 9th and 10th holes.

● In the Wisconsin (USA) Oil Dealers' annual 18-hole tournament, Bernard Antisdel scored an eagle 2 at the same 285-yards hole in four consecutive years, from 1960 to 1963.

● Three players in a four-ball match at Kington GC, Herefordshire, on 22nd July, 1948, all had eagle 2s at the 18th hole (272 yards). They were RN Bird, R Morgan and V Timson.

● Four Americans from Wisconsin on holiday at Gleneagles in 1977 scored three eagles and a birdie at the 300-yard par-4 14th hole on the King's course. The birdie was by Dr Kim Lulloff and the eagles by Dr Gordon Meiklejohn, Richard Johnson and Jack Kubitz.

● In an open competition at Glen Innes GC, Australia on 13th November, 1977, three players in a four-ball scored eagle 3s at the 9th hole (442 metres). They were Terry Marshall, Roy McHarg and Jack Rohleder.

Speed of Golf Ball and Club Head and Effect of Wind and Temperature

● In *The Search for the Perfect Swing*, a scientific study of the golf swing, a first class golfer is said to have the club head travelling at 100 mph at impact. This will cause the ball to leave the club at 135 mph. An outstandingly long hitter might manage to have the club head travelling at 130 mph which would produce a ball send-off speed of 175 mph. The resultant shot would carry 280 yards.

● According to Thomas Hardman, Wilson's director of research and development, wind will reduce or increase the flight of a golf ball by approximately $1\frac{1}{2}$ yards for every mile per hour of wind. Every two degrees of temperature will make a yard difference in a ball's flight.

Highest Golf Courses

● The highest golf course in the world is thought to be the Tuctu GC in Peru which is 14,335 feet above sea-level. High courses are also found in Bolivia with the La Paz GC being about 13,500 feet. In the Himalayas, near the border with Tibet, a 9-hole course at 12,800 feet has been laid out by keen golfers in the Indian Army.

● The highest known course in Europe is at Sestriere in the Italian Alps, 6,500 feet above sea-level.

● The highest courses in Great Britain are Leadhills in Scotland at 1,500 feet, Tredegar in Wales rising to 1,300 feet and Church Stretton in England at 1,250 feet.

● Although no course exists at the place, Captain FES Adair tells of playing shots on a suitable piece of grassy ground over 16,000 feet when crossing a pass into Tibet.

Lowest Courses

● The lowest known course in the world was at Kallia, south of Jericho. No longer in existence, this 9-hole course, running along the shore of the Dead Sea, lay 1,250 feet below normal sea-level.

Most Northerly Course

● The most northerly course is the Akureyri Golf Club in Iceland which is situated 65°40' North of the equator. Not far south is the Luleå course in Sweden, at 65°35' North.

Coldest Courses

● Golf courses are to be found in every climate. A Scot founded the Polar Bear Club in the Arctic. Eskimos became members.

● A group of golfers at Thule air base held a competition in 1975 at the top of Mount Dundas in Greenland, some 800 miles from the North Pole. The golfers carried their own piece of carpet which served as teeing grounds and greens.

● Missionary Dave Freeman in 1975 founded the High Country Club, a 9-hole course with sand greens off the shores of the Beaufort Sea in Northern Canada, 400 miles inside the Arctic Circle. Membership is over 700. Another keen golfer in this area, Bill Josh, the base manager of the local airline at Victoria Island, each winter stakes out 9 holes on the Beaufort Sea when it freezes over. The temperature is said to fall to below minus 40 degrees.

● Although shut in for three years amid the eternal snow and ice of the Antarctic, Arbroath golfer Munro Sievwright did not neglect his practice with club and ball. His luggage included three clubs and a dozen red painted golf balls. In the light of the midnight sun he hit adventurous shots along the white wasteland on *fairways* of hard-packed snow. Munro, a physicist at the Antarctic Survey Base at Halley Bay, won the Carnoustie Craw's Nest Tassie in 1962, and was in the Edinburgh team which won the Scottish Universities' Championship in 1963.

● In September, 1956, Major Gus Watson, chief scientific officer of the British Antarctic Expedition's advance party, radioed the following account of life at the explorer's base camp: *Summer has come to the Antarctic – and with it the golfing season. Our two carpenters brought their clubs with them and now they spend much of their spare time driving, chipping and putting in the area around the hut.*

Longest Courses

● The longest course in the world is Dub's Dread GC, Piper, Kansas, USA measuring 8,101 yards (par 78).

● The longest course for the Open Championship was 7,252 yards at Carnoustie in 1968.

Longest Holes

● The longest hole in the world, as far as is known, is the 6th hole measuring 782 metres (860 yards) at Koolan Island GC, Western Australia. The par of the hole is 7. There are several holes over 700 yards throughout the world. At Teyateyaneng, South Africa, one hole measures 619 yards and another 37 yards.
● The longest hole for the Open Championship was 577 yards (6th hole) at Troon in 1973.

Longest Tournaments

● The longest tournament held was over 144 holes in the World Open at Pinehurst, N Carolina, USA, first held in 1973. Play was over two weeks with a cut imposed at the halfway mark.
● An annual tournament is played in Germany on the longest day of the year, comprising 100 holes' medal play. We are told that the players usually lose several pounds in weight during the tournament. The best return, in 1968, was 417 strokes.

Largest Entries

The Open—1413, St Andrews, 1984.
The Amateur—488, St Andrews, 1958.
British Youths'—244, Woodhall Spa, 1979.
The Boys'—247, Formby, 1980.
Ladies' British Open Amateur—157, St Andrews, 1975.
British Ladies Stroke Play—120, Formby, 1985.
British Girls'—94, Hesketh, 1985.
English Amateur—370, Moortown, 1980, also Woodhall Spa, 1984.
English Open Amateur Stroke Play—313, Royal Cinque Ports, Deal 1984.
Irish Amateur—302, Portmarnock, 1974.
Scottish Amateur—244, Gullane, 1983.
Scottish Open Amateur Stroke Play—249, Dunbar, North Berwick, 1985.
Scottish Boys'—354, North Berwick, 1973.
Welsh Amateur—108, Prestatyn, 1980.
Welsh Boys'—112, Glamorganshire, 1975.
● US Open—The US Open of 1988 received a record 5880 entries. 5775 were accepted. At 12 courses around the country 504 players, who had been successful at local qualifying venues, joined 96 players who were exempt from local qualifying. The 600 playing in sectional tournaments included 94 Amateurs. The 98 leaders joined 58 players exempt from Local Sectional qualifying to complete the 156 players in the US Open.
● The largest entry for a PGA ETPD event was 398 for the 1978 Colgate PGA Championship. Since 1985, when the all-exempt ruling was introduced, all PGA tournaments have had 144 competitors, slightly more or less.

● In 1952, Bobby Locke, the Open Champion, played a round at Wentworth, against any golfer in Britain. Cards costing 2s. 6d. each ($12^{1}/_{2}$p), were taken out by 24,000 golfers. The challenge was to beat the local par by more than Locke beat the par at Wentworth; 1,641 competitors, including women, succeeded in *beating* the Champion and each received a certificate signed by him. As a result of this challenge the British Golf Foundation benefited to the extent of £3,026, the proceeds from the sale of cards. A similar tournament was held in the United States and Canada when 87,094 golfers participated; 14,667 players bettered Ben Hogan's score under handicap. The fund benefited by $80,024.

Largest Prize Money

● The largest prize money for an event in Britain was £839,000 in the Dunhill Nations Cup at St Andrews in October 1988.
● In 1988 the total prize money at the Open at Royal Lytham and St Annes was £750,000, with a first prize of £80,000.
● The Machrie Tournament of 1901 was the first tournament with a first prize of £100. It was won by JH Taylor, then Open Champion, who beat James Braid in the final.
● The world's richest tournament is the annual Million Dollar Sun City Challenge, held at the Gary Player Country Club in Bophuthatswana, first played in 1982 with a first prize of $500,000.
● (For prize money in the Open Championship see under Conditions and History of Open Championship.)

Attendance at Open Championship

Year	Attendance	Year	Attendance
1962	37,098	1976	92,021
1963	24,585	1977	87,615
1964	35,954	1978	125,271
1965	32,927	1979	134,501
1966	40,182	1980	131,610
1967	29,880	1981	114,522
1968	51,819	1982	133,299
1969	46,001	1983	142,894
1970	81,593	1984	193,126
1971	70,076	1985	141,619
1972	84,746	1986	134,261
1973	78,810	1987	131,142
1974	92,796	1988	205,285
1975	85,258	1989	160,369

Holing-in-One

Holing-in-One – Odds Against

● At the Wanderers Club, Johannesburg in January, 1951, forty-nine amateurs and professionals each played three balls at a hole 146 yards long. Of the 147 balls hit, the nearest was by Koos de Beer, professional at Reading Country Club, which finished $10^1/_2$ inches from the hole. Harry Bradshaw, the Irish professional who was touring with the British team in South Africa, touched the pin with his second shot, but the ball rolled on and stopped 3 feet 2 inches from the cup.

● A competition on similar lines was held in 1951 in New York when 1,409 players who had done a hole-in-one held a competition over several days at short holes on three New York golf courses. Each player was allowed a total of five shots, giving an aggregate of 7,045 shots. No player holed-in-one, and the nearest ball finished $3^1/_2$ inches from the hole.

● A further illustration of the element of luck in holing-in-one is derived from an effort by Harry Gonder, an American professional, who in 1940 stood for 16 hours 25 minutes and hit 1,817 balls trying to do a 160 yard hole-in-one. He had two official witnesses and caddies to tee and retrieve the balls and count the strokes. His 1,756th shot struck the hole but stopped an inch from the hole. This was his nearest effort.

● Cyril Wagner, another American professional, got a hole-in-one in 805 shots.

● From this and other similar information an estimate of the odds against holing-in-one at any particular hole within the range of one shot was made at somewhere between 1,500 and 2,000 to 1 by a proficient player. Subsequently, however, statistical analysis in America has come up with the following odds: a male professional or top amateur 3,708 to 1; a female professional or top amateur 4,648 to 1; an average golfer 42,952 to 1.

Hole-in-One First Recorded

● Earliest recorded hole-in-one was in 1868 at the Open Championship when Tommy Morris (Young Tom) did the 8th hole 145 yards Prestwick in one stroke. This was the first of four Open Championships won successively by Young Tom.

● The first hole-in-one recorded with the 1.66 in ball was in 1972 by John G Salvesen, a member of the R & A Championship Committee. At the time this size of ball was only experimental. Salvesen used a 7-iron for his historical feat at the 11th hole on the Old Course, St Andrews.

Holing-in-One in Important Events

Since the day of the first known hole-in-one by Tom Morris jun, at the 8th hole (145 yards) at Prestwick in the 1868 Open Championship, holes-in-one, even in championships, have become too numerous for each to be recorded. Only where other unusual or interesting circumstances prevailed are the instances shown here.

● 1878–Jamie Anderson, competing in the Open Championship at Prestwick, holed the 17th hole in one. Anderson was playing the next to last hole, and though it seemed then that he was winning easily, it turned out afterwards that if he had not taken this hole in one stroke he would very likely have lost. Anderson was just about to make his tee shot when Andy Stuart (winner of the first Irish Open Championship in 1892), who was acting as marker to Anderson, remarked he was standing outside the teeing ground, and that if he played the stroke from there he would be disqualified. Anderson picked up his ball and teed it in a proper place. Then he holed-in-one. He won the Championship by one stroke.

● 1885–AF Macfie in the fourth round of the initial competition at Hoylake for the Amateur Championship, holed the 14th or *Rushes* hole in one. Since then this particular hole at Hoylake has strangely enough been the scene of several holes-in-one in major championships; in 1898 by S Winkley Smith, West Middlesex, in the Amateur Championship; in 1902 by Daniel Brown, Musselburgh, in the Open Championship; and in 1925 by GNP Humphries, Stourbridge, in the English Amateur Championship.

● 1889–In the Open Championship at Musselburgh an amateur, who partnered Andrew Kirkaldy, holed the last hole in one. It was almost dark when the championship finished and when the player hit his cleek shot the green could scarcely be made out from the tee.

● 1906–R Johnston, North Berwick, competing in the Open Championship, did the 14th hole at Muirfield in one. Johnston played with only one club throughout – an adjustable head club.

● 1925–JH Taylor, in his second round in the Open Championship at Prestwick, did the 2nd hole in one stroke. In contrast, Murdoch (Troon Municipal), who played with Taylor, took 14 at the 1st hole.

● 1930–Maurice McCarthy, jun, in the qualifying stroke competition of the United States Amateur Championship at Merion did a hole-in-one. McCarthy tied for the last place and qualified for the Championship on the *play off*.

● 1933–In the final round of the Irish Open Championship over 36 holes at Newcastle, Co Down, on 23rd September, 1933, Eric Fiddian, Stourbridge, who was boy champion in 1927 and English champion in 1932, was opposed to Jack McLean. In the first round Fiddian did the 7th hole, 128 yards, in one stroke, and in the second round he did the 14th hole, 205 yards, also in one stroke. These remarkable strokes did not carry Fiddian to victory for he was defeated by 3 and 2.

● 1959–The first hole-in-one in the US Women's Open Championship was recorded. It was by Patty Berg on the 7th hole (170 yards) at Churchill Valley CC, Pittsburgh.

● 1962–On 6th April, playing in the second

round of the Schweppes Close Championship at Little Aston, H Middleton of Shandon Park, Belfast, holed his tee shot at the 159 yards 5th hole, winning a prize of £1,000. Ten minutes later, playing two matches ahead of Middleton, RA Jowle, son of the professional, Frank Jowle, holed his tee shot at the 179 yards 9th hole. As an amateur he was rewarded by the sponsors with a £30 voucher.

● 1962–Dick Mayer, US professional, won £17,857 for scoring a hole-in-one in the Palm Springs tournament. This was the third successive year the feat had been performed in this tournament. The sponsors insured against *aces* with Lloyds of London.

● 1963–By holing out in one stroke at the 18th hole (156 yards) at Moor Park on the first day of the Esso Golden round-robin tournament, HR Henning, South Africa, won the £10,000 prize offered for this feat.

● 1967–Tony Jacklin in winning the Masters tournament at St George's, Sandwich, did the 16th hole in one. His ace has an exceptional place in the records for it was seen by millions on TV, the ball in view in its flight till it went into the hole in his final round of 64.

● 1971–John Hudson, 25-year-old professional at Hendon, achieved a near miracle when he holed two consecutive holes-in-one in the Martini Tournament at Norwich. They were at the 11th and 12th holes (195 yards and 311 yards respectively) in the second round. (See also section entitled *Holing Successive Holes-in-One*.)

● 1971–In the Open Championship at Birkdale, Lionel Platts holed-in-one at the 212-yard 4th hole in the second round. This was the first instance of an Open Championship hole-in-one being recorded by television. It was incidentally Platts' seventh ace of his career.

● 1972–Two holes-in-one were recorded at the 180-yard 5th hole at Pebble Beach in the US Open. They were achieved by Jerry McGee in the third round and Bobby Mitchell in the final round.

● 1973–Peter Butler achieved what is thought to be the first hole-in-one in the Ryder Cup when he holed out at the 16th hole at Muirfield in the 1973 match.

● 1973–In the 1973 Open Championship at Troon, two holes-in-one were recorded, both at the 8th hole, known as the Postage Stamp, in the first round. They were achieved by Gene Sarazen and amateur David Russell, who were by coincidence respectively the oldest and youngest competitors.

● Mrs Argea Tissies, whose husband Hermann took 15 at Royal Troon's Postage Stamp 8th hole in the 1950 Open, scored a hole-in-one at the 2nd hole at Punta Ala in the second round of the Italian Ladies Senior Open of 1978. Exactly 5 years later on the same date, at the same time of day, in the same round of the same tournament

at the same hole, she did it again with the same club.

● In less than two hours play in the second round of the 1989 US Open at Oak Hill Country Club, Rochester, New York, four competitors – Doug Weaver, Mark Wiebe, Jerry Pate and Nick Price – each holed the 167 yards 6th hole in one. The odds against four professionals achieving such a record in a field of 156 are reckoned at 332,000 to 1. A spectator watching golf for the first time commented that of the first 32 players to play the hole, only four played it well.

Holing-in-One – Longest Holes

● Bob Mitera, when a 21-year-old American student, standing 5 feet 6 inches and weighing under 12 stones, claimed the world record for the longest hole-in-one. Playing over the appropriately named Miracle Hill course at Omaha, on 7th October, 1965, Bob holed his drive at the 10th hole, 447 yards long. The ground sloped sharply downhill. He was further aided by a strong following wind and (he admits) a lot of luck.

● Two longer holes-in-one have been achieved, but because they were at dog-leg holes they are not generally accepted as being the longest holes-in-one. They were 480 yards (5th hole, Hope CC, Arkansas) by L Bruce on 15th November, 1962 and 477 yards (14th hole, Martin County CC, Stuart, Florida) by Billy Newman on 13th August, 1972. The estimated length by cutting the corner was around 360 yards.

● In March, 1961, Lou Kretlow holed his tee shot at the 427 yards 16th hole at Lake Hefner course, Oklahoma City, USA.

● Another very long hole accomplished in one was the 9th hole at Hillcrest Golf Club, Winston-Salem, North Carolina, USA, by Mr Cardwell. The hole (425 yards) is a par four. The authenticity of this feat was vouched for by Ken C Abels, the Manager of the Hillcrest Golf Club.

● A ball driven by a driving machine holed out in one at the 435-yard 1st hole at Hermitage Country Club, Richmond, Virginia, USA.

● The longest known hole-in-one in Great Britain was the 393-yard 7th hole at West Lancashire GC, where in 1972 the assistant professional Peter Parkinson holed his tee shot.

● Other long holes-in-one recorded in Great Britain have been 380 yards (5th hole at Tankersley Park) by David Hulley in 1961; 380 yards (12th hole at White Webbs) by Danny Dunne on 30th July, 1976; 370 yards (17th hole at Chilwell Manor, distance from the forward tee) by Ray Newton in 1977; 365 yards (10th hole at Harewood Downs) by K Saunders in 1965; 365 yards (7th hole at

Catterick Garrison CC) by Leslie Bruckner on 18th July, 1980.

● The longest-recorded hole-in-one by a woman was that accomplished in September, 1949 by Marie Robie – the 393-yard hole at Furnace Brook course, Wollaston, Mass, USA.

● In April 1988, Mary Anderson, a bio-chemistry student at Trinity College, Dublin, holed-in-one at the 290-yard 6th hole at the Island GC, Co Dublin, the longest known hole-in-one by a woman in Great Britain.

Holing-in-One – Greatest Number by One Person

47–Amateur Norman Manley of Long Beach, California.

42–US professional Art Wall between 1936 and April 1979.

35–Mancil Davis, professional at the Trophy Club, Forth Worth, Texas. Davis achieved his last in 1979 at the age of 25.

31–British professional CT le Chevalier who died in 1973.

20–British amateur, Jim Hay of Kirkintilloch GC.

10–Mrs Olga Penman, formerly of Harewood Downs GC.

At One Hole

10-Joe Vitullo at 16th hole of Hubbard GC, Ohio.

5–Left-hander, the late Fred Francis at 7th (now 16th) hole of Cardigan GC.

Holing-in-One – Greatest Frequency

● The greatest number of holes-in-one in a calendar year is 11, by JO Boydstone of California in 1962.

● John Putt of Frilford Heath GC had six holes-in-one in 1970, followed by three in 1971.

● Douglas Porteous, of Ruchill GC, Glasgow, achieved seven holes-in-one in the space of eight months. Four of them were scored in a five-day period from 26th to 30th September, 1974, in three consecutive rounds of golf. The first two were achieved at Ruchill GC in one round, the third there two days later, and the fourth at Clydebank and District GC after another two days. The following May, Porteous had three holes-in-one, the first at Linn Park GC incredibly followed by two more in the one round at Clober GC. (See also *Holing-in-One Twice in One Round.*)

● Mrs Kathleen Hetherington of West Essex has holed-in-one five times, four being at the 15th hole at West Essex. Four of her five aces were within seven months in 1966.

● Mrs Dorothy Hill of Dumfries and Galloway GC holed-in-one three times in 11 days in 1977.

●James C Reid of Brodick, aged 59 and 8

handicap in 1987, has achieved 14 holes-in-one, all but one on Isle of Arran courses. His success, in spite of severe physical handicaps of a stiff left knee, a damaged right ankle, two discs removed from his back and a hip replacement is remarkable. He plays regularly, walks the course, but uses a walking stick for balance.

Holing Successive Holes-in-One

● Successive holes-in-one are rare; successive par 4 holes-in-one may be classed as near miracles. NL Manley performed the most incredible feat in September, 1964, at Del Valle Country Club, Saugus, California, USA. The par 4 7th (330 yards) and 8th (290 yards) are both slightly downhill, dog-leg holes. Manley had *aces* at both, en route to a course record of 61 (par 71).

● The first recorded example in Britain of a player holing-in-one stroke at each of two successive holes was achieved on 6th February, 1964, at the Walmer and Kingsdown course, Kent. The young assistant professional at that club, Roger Game (aged 17) holed out with a No. 4 wood at the 244-yard 7th hole, and repeated the feat at the 256-yard 8th hole, using a No. 5 iron.

● The first occasion of holing-in-one at consecutive holes in a major professional event occurred when John Hudson, 25-year-old professional at Hendon, holed-in-one at the 11th and 12th holes at Norwich during the second round of the 1971 Martini tournament. Hudson used a 4-iron at the 195-yard 11th and a driver at the 311-yard downhill 12th hole.

● Assistant professional Tom Doty (23 years), playing in a friendly match on a course near Chicago in October, 1971 had a remarkable four hole score which included two consecutive holes-in-one, sandwiched either side by an albatross and an eagle: 4th hole (500 yards)–2; 5th hole (360 yards dog-leg)–1; 6th hole (175 yards) 1; 7th hole (375 yards)–2. Thus he was 10 under par for four consecutive holes.

Holing-in-One Twice (or more) in Same Round by Same Person
(See also Successive Holes-in-One)

What might be thought to be a very rare feat indeed – that of holing-in-one twice in the same round – has in fact happened on many occasions as the following instances show. It is, nevertheless, compared to the number of golfers in the world, still something of an outstanding achievement. The first occasion known to us was in 1907 when J Ireland playing in a three-ball match at Worlington holed the 5th and 18th holes in one stroke and two years later in 1909 HC Josecelyne holed the 3rd (175 yards) and the 14th (115 yards) at Acton on 24th November.

● The Rev Harold Snider, aged 75, scored his first hole-in-one on 9th June, 1976 at the 8th hole of the Ironwood course, near Pheonix. By the end of his round he had scored three holes-in-one, the other two being at the 13th (110 yards) and 14th (135 yards). Ironwood is a par-3 course, giving more opportunity of scoring holes-in-one, but, nevertheless, three holes-in-one in one round on any type of course is an outstanding achievement.

● The first mention of two holes-in-one in a round by a woman is of special note in that it was followed later by a similar feat by another lady at the same club. On 19th May, 1942, Mrs W Driver, of Balgowlah Golf Club, New South Wales, holed out in one at the 3rd and 8th holes in the same round, while on 29th July, 1948, Mrs F Burke at the same club holed out in one at the 2nd and 8th holes.

● The youngest-known person to have had two holes-in-one in one round was a 14-year-old American, Peter Townsend.

● The youngest British player was Ian Robertson in June, 1972, at Torphin Hill GC, Edinburgh, when 15 years old. The holes were the 252-yard 9th and 210-yard 14th.

● The youngest woman to have performed the feat was a 17-year-old, Marjorie Merchant, playing at the Lomas Athletic GC, Argentina, at the 4th (170 yards) and 8th (130 yards) holes.

Holes-in-One on the Same Day

●In July 1987, at the Skerries Club, Co Dublin, Rank Xerox sponsored two tournaments, a men's 18-hole four-ball with 134 pairs competing and a 9-hole mixed foursomes with 33. During the day each of the four par-3 holes on the course were holed-in-one, the 2nd by Noel Bollard, 5th by Bart Reynolds, 12th by Jackie Carr and 15th by Gerry Ellis.

Two Holes-in-One at Same Hole in Same Game

First in World
● George Stewart and Fred Spellmeyer at the 18th hole, Forest Hills, New Jersey, USA in October 1919.

First in Great Britain
● Miss G Clutterbuck and Mrs HM Robinson at the 15th hole (120 yards), St Augustine GC, Ramsgate, on 8th May, 1925.

First in Denmark
●In a Club match in August 1987 at Himmerland, Steffan Jacobsen of Aalborg and Peter Forsberg

of Himmerland halved the 15th hole in one shot, the first known occasion in Denmark.

First in Australia
●Dr & Mrs B Rankine, playing in a mixed 'Canadian foursome' event at the Osmond Club near Adelaide, South Australia in April 1987, holed-in-one in consecutive shots at the 2nd hole (162 metres), he from the men's tee with a 3-iron and his wife from the Ladies' tee with a $1\frac{1}{2}$ wood.

Holing-in-One and Holing a Full Shot to Win a Championship or Match

Ending a match by holing-in-one or with a full shot is infrequent enough to be worthy of placing on record individually here.

● The most lucrative holing of a full shot to win occurred in the *Tam O'Shanter* World Championship at Chicago in 1953. Chandler Harper appeared to have victory and the first prize of $25,000 in the bag when Lew Worsham holed a full wedge shot of some 135 yards for a 2 at the 410-yard last hole of the tournament to win by one stroke.

● In the first round of the Oxford and Cambridge Society's President's Putter at Rye, January, 1937, between PHF White, the West of England Champion, 1936, and Leonard Crawley, Crawley was two up and six to play. White won the next three to take the lead and then holed the 17th – 230 yards – with his tee shot to win by 2 and 1.

● Willie Park, in 1898, at Troon in the second half of his match for £200 against Willie Fernie, holed a full brassie shot at the 7th hole – the 61st of the match – to win, the most dramatic ending to a first class professional match.

● When FE McCarroll (Queen's University), Belfast, won the Boyd Quaich at St Andrews in 1966, his 291st and last shot, played with a sand wedge, finished in the hole for an eagle 2.

● MG Milton completed a match in the Moray and Nairn league on 22nd May, 1972, at Nairn Dunbar GC by holing-in-one at the 174-yard 15th to win by 5 and 3.

●In the 1973 Welsh Amateur at Ashburnham, Ted Davies, defending champion, ended one of his matches by holing-in-one at the 13th hole.

● In the 1974 Home International matches at the Royal St David's GC, against Ireland in the top foursomes match, Sandy Pirie of Scotland holed-in-one at the last hole giving Scotland a one-hole victory.

● Two Australian golfers, John Wise and Glen Hutton, influenced by the fact that two tennis players had signed a contract for a 100 match series, agreed to play a similar golf series limited to ten matches per year. In 1967 Hutton won the 99th match to lead in the series by one match.

In the 100th match Wise holed-in-one at the last hole to win the hole, the game and end the series all square.

● In the Assistants' Championship at Worsley, 1950, Harry Weetman (Hartsbourne Golf Club), who won the Championship for the second year in succession, holed his tee shot at the 172-yard 18th hole in the final round – the 72nd hole of the championship. Weetman, however, had had several strokes in hand for victory.

Holing-in-One — Miscellaneous Incidents
(See also Holing-in-One in the Championships)

● The late Harry Vardon, who scored the greatest number of victories in the Open Championship, only once did a hole-in-one. That was in 1903 at Mundesley, Norfolk, where Vardon was convalescing from a long illness.
● Walter Hagen, one of the greatest and most colourful golfers of all time, in his long career also did only one hole-in-one – at the 6th hole at Worcester, Mass, in 1925. It was the first shot played with a new ball, he used a No 1 iron and it was the first of July.
● In April 1984 Joseph McCaffrey and his son, Gordon, each holed-in-one in the Spring Medal at the 164 yard 12th hole at Vale of Leven Club, Dunbartonshire.
● Having watched Paul Hahn play a trick shot from a kneeling position, 16-year-old Jim Hadderer, of Elgin, Illinois, USA, tried the same gag at a 190-yard hole at the Wing Park course in 1965. He improved on Hahn's performance by popping the ball into the hole in one.
● Identical twins, John and Desmond Rosser scored holes-in-one in consecutive rounds at Auckland GC, New Zealand. Playing in a medal competition on Saturday 15th March, 1975 with his twin and two other members, John, the elder twin, holed-in-one at the 10th hole with his wedge. In their next game, the following Wednesday, the twins were again playing in a four-ball with two other members when Desmond holed-in-one at the 13th hole using his driver.
● In 1977, 14-year-old Gillian Field after a series of lessons holed-in-one at the 10th hole at Moor Place GC in her first round of golf.
● Having taken some golf lessons in Britain, Mrs Joan Birtley of Flamstead, Herts., accompanied her husband on a business trip to America in 1977. At Doral CC, Miami, Mrs Birtley hired some clubs and played her first-ever round of golf. At the 4th hole (116 yards) she holed-in-one.
● By holing-in-one at the 2nd hole in a match against D Graham in the 1979 Suntory World Match Play at Wentworth, Japanese professional Isao Aoki won himself a Bovis home at Gleneagles worth, inclusive of furnishings, £55,000.
● In the 1979 French Open, Willie Milne appeared to have won a Mercedes car when he holed-in-one. However the organisers later declared the prize had been withdrawn. Threatening to sue, Milne was subsequently presented with a Mercedes.
● When he holed-in-one at the 105-yard 14th hole at Tahoe Paradise course, USA, in the Harrah Invitational Tournament in 1965, Dick Kolbus, from Oakland, California, won an $18,500 Rolls-Royce car.
● JoAnn Washam twice holed-in-one in the 1979 Kemper Open, a USLPGA Tournament.
● R Buckell, a member of Pinner Hill GC and W Dunbar, playing together in a society outing over Pinner Hill on 30th August, 1969, each holed-in-one at the 17th hole (225 yards).
● Veteran American, Earl Hooke, of Paris, Texas, holed-in-one in the month of July in four consecutive years, 1968 to 1971.
● Golfers in three consecutive groups at Blowing Rock CC, North Carolina, one day in 1979 each holed-in-one at the 156-yard 7th hole. They were Charles Wood, Harold Beal and Wallace Brawley.
● Russell Dewald, Ray Newman and Hal Martin, players in three consecutive games, holed-in-one on 23rd January, 1980 at the 14th hole (120 yards) at Lakewood CC, Florida.
● On the morning after being elected captain for 1973 of the Norwich GC, JS Murray hit his first shot as captain straight into the hole at the 169 yards first hole.
● Bob Dellow and John Watt, of Millicent Golf Club in South Australia, playing with another two members in a competition on 24th July, 1970, each holed-in-one at the 153-yard 13th hole. The following day, one of the other members of the four, Greg Nitschke, holed-in-one at the same hole.
● Using the same club and ball, 11-handicap left-hander Christopher Smyth holed-in-one at the 2nd hole (170 yards) in two consecutive medal competitions at Headfort GC, Co Meath, in January, 1976.
● In a knock-out competition at Ely, Cambridgeshire, on 13th October, 1962, Mr Challis drove to within four feet of the 1st hole (170 yards). His opponent, Mr Delwage, pitched his second shot; his ball struck that of Mr Challis, knocking it into the hole and giving him the hole-in-one.
● Dr Tucker, New Orleans, Louisiana, 1936, put his name down for a hole-in-one golf tournament. After doing so he walked out to the contest hole – 160 yards – and hit the ball with an iron. The ball trickled into the hole. Elated, Dr Tucker rushed back to the clubhouse, only to find that the competition was not due to begin until two weeks later.

● The late Miss Gertrude Lawrence, a distinguished actress, when playing golf for the first time, holed-in-one with her first tee shot.
● In an RAF outing in 1973 at Peterborough Milton GC two holes-in-one were made with the same ball but not by the same person. The first was in the morning singles by Des Tuson at the 142-yard 11th hole. Then in the afternoon, playing in a greensome competition, his partner, Keith Schofield, holed-in-one at the 174-yard 2nd hole. The ball was then carefully put away.
● Joe Kirkwood holed-in-one on 11 occasions including one when doing a Newsreel Movie at the 5th (168 yards), Sea Island, Georgia, and another when he was performing trick shots off the face of a watch at the 1st (268 yards), Cedar Rapids, Iowa.
● A woman who has only her right arm, Mrs Frank Andreucci, of Florida, holed-in-one at the 136-yard 13th hole at Crystal Lake CC in 1971.
● At Royal Hong Kong Golf Club, Susan Tonroe, aged 16, and her brother, aged 11, each did the 7th hole in one in junior competitions in the same week.
● Playing over Rickmansworth course at Easter, 1960, Mrs AE (Paddy) Martin achieved a remarkable sequence of *aces*. On Good Friday she sank her tee shot at the third hole (125 yards). The next day, using the same ball and the same No. 8 iron, at the same hole, she scored another *one*. And on the Monday (same ball, same club, same hole) she again holed out from the tee. (See also *Holing-in-One in Successive Rounds*).
● Playing in the Eastern Inter-County Foursomes in May 1974, RJ Taylor holed-in-one at the 188-yards 16th hole at Hunstanton on three consecutive days. Leading Bookmakers reckoned the odds against such a feat at 5 million to one.
● Joan Jankins, aged 12, achieved a hole-in-one at the 240-yard 3rd hole at Abersoch, Gwynedd, in October 1984.
● In January 1985 Otto Bucher of Switzerland, aged 99, holed-in-one at the 130-yard 12th hole at the La Manga Championship South course in Spain.
● At Barton-on-Sea in February 1989 Mrs Dorothy Huntley-Flindt, aged 91, who plays 18 holes regularly, holed in one at the par 3 13th. The following day Mr John Chape, a fellow member in his 80s, not to be outdone, holed the par 3 5th in one.
● In 1988 senior citizen Mrs Joan Hall twice holed in one in 19 days at the 12th at Immingham and the 5th at Market Rasen. Three months later she achieved a third ace at Immingham's 17th.
● When taking part in the Yorex National Long Driving Championship, Mark Law, 6 handicap, holed the 1st hole at Goring and Streatley in one. By doing so he lost the Club's competition

as his ball was running to finish well beyond the green when it struck the flag-stick and dropped into the hole, another competitor having finished past the hole.

Bookmakers and Golf
(See also Wagers, Curious and Large)

● Wagering on a heavy scale has been associated with golf from its earliest days, but the first time a bookmaker appeared at a golf tournament and shouted the odds was in 1898 in a professional tournament at Carnoustie. In 1927, at the Open Championship at St Andrews, a Glasgow bookmaker and two assistants mixed among the crowds following the players and shouting the odds. In the Open Championship at Portrush, 1951, a bookmaker set up his stand during the qualifying rounds and shouted the odds. In 1934 various bookmakers' lists were promiscuously issued and publicly advertised, giving odds for the Amateur and Open Championships, and representatives of different commission agents attended the two championships and touted for bets, but this was carried out individually and odds were not publicly shouted. Since 1934 reputable bookmakers in London and the Provinces annually bet to any sum on the Amateur and Open Championships.
● At the John Player Classic Tournament at Turnberry in 1971 a firm of bookmakers had a stand in the tented village. A lot of bets were placed including several by competitors. There was much talk of the possibilities of malpractice this could lead to, and as a result, the authorities decided to ban on-course betting in British tournaments. Then in 1980 the PGA gave permission to the Coral Leisure Group for a mobile betting office to be situated on the course at several major tournaments but no head to head bets were allowed to be offered.

Challenge Matches

One of the first recorded professional challenge matches was in 1843 when Allan Robertson beat Willie Dunn in a 20-round match at St Andrews over 360 holes by 2 rounds and 1 to play. Thereafter until about 1905 many matches are recorded, some for up to £200 a side – a considerable sum for the time. The Morrises, the Dunns and the Parks were the main protagonists until Vardon, Braid and Taylor took over in the 1890s. Often matches were on a home-and-away basis over 72 holes or more, with many spectators; Vardon and Willie Park Jr attracted over 10,000 at North Berwick in 1899.

Between the wars Walter Hagen, Archie Compston, Henry Cotton and Bobby Locke all played several such matches. Compston surprisingly beat Hagen by 18 up and 17 to play at Moor Park in 1928; yet typically Hagen went on to win the Open the following week at Sandwich. Cotton played classic golf at Walton Heath in 1937 when he beat Densmore Shute for £500 a side at Walton Heath by 6 and 5 over 72 holes.

After 1945 the appeal of Challenge matches waned, mainly due to the increasing number of professional tournaments available.

Curious and Large Wagers

(See also bets recorded under Cross-Country Matches, *and in* Challenge Matches)

● In the Royal and Ancient Club minutes an entry on 3rd November, 1870 was made in the following terms: *Sir David Moncreiffe, Bart, of Moncrieffe, backs his life against the life of John Whyte-Melville, Esq, of Strathkinnes, for a new silver club as a present to the St Andrews Golf Club, the price of the club to be paid by the survivor and the arms of the parties to be engraved on the club, and the present bet inscribed on it. No balls to be attached to it. In testimony of which this bet is subscribed by the parties thereto.* Thirteen years later, Mr Whyte-Melville, in a feeling and appropriate speech, expressed his deep regret at the lamented death of Sir Robert Moncrieffe, one of the most distinguished and zealous supporters of the club. Whyte-Melville, while lamenting the cause that led to it, had pleasure in fulfilling the duty imposed upon him by the bet, and accordingly delivered to the captain the silver putter. Whyte-Melville in 1883 was elected captain of the club a second time; he died in his eighty-sixth year in July, 1883, before he could take office and the captaincy remained vacant for a year. His portrait hangs in the Royal and Ancient clubhouse and is one of the finest and most distinguished pictures in the smoking room.

● Bobby Jones won the four major championships in 1930 (the Amateur, the Open, the American Amateur and the American Open). Long odds had been laid against such a result by bookmakers, and extensive sums were paid out.

● In 1914 Francis Ouimet, who in the previous autumn had won the American Open Championship after a triangular tie with Harry Vardon and Ted Ray, came to Great Britain with Jerome D Travers, the holder of the American amateur title, to compete in the British Amateur Championship at Sandwich. An American syndicate took a bet of £30,000 to £10,000 that one or other of the two United States champions would be the winner. It only took two rounds to decide the bet against the Americans. Ouimet was beaten by a then quite unknown player, HS Tubbs, while Travers was defeated by Charles Palmer, who was fifty-six years of age at the time.

● 1907 John Ball for a wager undertook to go round Hoylake during a dense fog in under 90, in not more than two and a quarter hours and without losing a ball. Ball played with a black ball, went round in 81, and also beat the time.

● The late Ben Sayers, for a wager, played the eighteen holes of the Burgess Society course scoring a four at every hole. Sayers was about to start against an American, when his opponent asked him what he could do the course in. *Fours* replied Sayers, meaning 72, or an average of 4s for the round. A bet was made and the American then added, *Remember a three or a five is not a four.* There were eight bogey 5s and two 3s on the Burgess course at the time Old Ben achieved his feat.

● After a hole had been halved in one at Forest Hills, New Jersey, one of the players offered to bet $10,000 to $1 that the occurrence would not be repeated at the hole during his lifetime.

● Cross-country and freak matches, embraced on another page, have been fruitful of many wagers, and matches have been played between distinguished golfers using only a putting cleek against players carrying all their clubs. At Hoylake a match was fixed between a scratch golfer and a handicap 6 player. They played level, the handicap player having the right to say *Boo* three times on the round. He said *Boo* at the 13th hole and won the match easily with two *Boos* in hand, the scratch player, of course, being affected by always anticipating the *Boo.*

● A match was arranged on a south of England course for a considerable bet between a scratch player and a long-handicap man, playing level, the scratch man to drink a whisky-and-soda on each tee. On the 16th tee the scratch man, who had a hole lead, collapsed, and was not very well for some time afterwards.

● In June, 1950, Bryan Field, vice-president of the Delaware Park racecourse, USA, who had not played golf for several years, accepted a wager that, without practice, he would not go round Pine Valley, rated one of the hardest courses in the world, in less than 300 shots. With borrowed clubs, he set off at 8am planning to finish in time for lunch. He started 7, 9, 4, 11, and when he got a 10 at the 5th, one of the most testing on the course, after putting three tee shots into the lake, it was obvious that he was well on the way to winning the bet. With an 11 at the 8th, another difficult hole he reached the turn in 73. Coming home in 75, Mr Field holed the course in 148 and won his wager with 152 strokes in hand. He took two hours, fifty minutes to complete the round.

Feats of Endurance

Although golf is not a game where endurance, in the ordinary sense in which the term is employed in sport, is required, there are several instances of feats on the links which demanded great physical exertion.

● In 1971 during a 24-hour period from 6 pm on 27th November until 5.15 pm on 28th November, Ian Colston completed 401 holes over the 6,061 yards Bendigo course, Victoria, Australia. Colston was a top marathon athlete but was not a golfer. However prior to his golfing marathon he took some lessons and became adept with a 6-iron, the only club he used throughout the 401 holes. The only assistance Colston had was a team of harriers to carry his 6-iron and look for his ball, and a band of motor cyclists who provided light during the night. This is, as far as is known, the greatest number of holes played in 24 hours on foot on a full-size course.

● In 1934 Col Bill Farnham played 376 holes in 24 hours 10 minutes at the Guildford Lake Course, Guildford, Connecticut, using only a mashie and a putter.

● To raise funds for extending the Skipton GC course from 12 to 18 holes, the club professional, 24-year-old Graham Webster, played 277 holes in the hours of daylight on Monday 20th June, 1977. Playing with nothing longer than a 5-iron he averaged 81 per 18-hole round. Included in his marathon was a hole-in-one.

● Michael Moore, a 7 handicap 26-year-old member of Okehampton GC, completed on foot 15 rounds 6 holes (276 holes) there on Sunday, 25th June, 1972, in the hours of daylight. He started at 4.15 am and stopped at 9.15 pm. The distance covered was estimated at 56 miles. Nine brief stoppages for salty soup were made. His time for 6 rounds was 6 hours 2 minutes; for 12 rounds, 12 hours 58 minutes.

● On 21st June, 1976, 5-handicapper Sandy Small played 15 rounds (270 holes) over his home course Cosby GC, length 6,128 yards, to raise money for the Society of Physically Handicapped Children. Using only a 5-iron, 9-iron and putter, Small started at 4.10 am and completed his 270th hole at 10.39 pm with the aid of car headlights. His fastest round was his first (40 minutes) and slowest his last (82 minutes). His best round of 76 was achieved in the second round.

● In 1957, Bert L Scoggins, a US serviceman, played 260 holes in one day on the American golf course at Berlin. He started out at 2.30 am, and played continuously for 18 hours, walking 56 miles in the course of his marathon feat. His lowest single round score was 84.

● Bill Falkingham, jun, of Amstel GC, Victoria, Australia, played 257 holes between 12.30 am and 6.15 pm on 14th December, 1968. The first three holes were played in darkness. He was accompanied by his brother and a friend who held a torch to assist direction. Ten balls were lost but the first ball lasted eight rounds. His best round was 90 over a course measuring 6,673 yards, par 73, over which a gale force wind blew all day, in a temperature of 90 degrees. During the morning he trod on a snake but did not stop to kill it. He was sustained by only sandwiches and soft drinks and although completely exhausted when he finished he had completely recovered next morning and went out for another round.

● During the weekend of 20th-21st June, 1970, Peter Chambers of Yorkshire completed over 14 rounds of golf over the Scarborough South Cliff course. In a non-stop marathon lasting just under 24 hours, Chambers played 257 holes in 1,168 strokes, an average of 84.4 strokes per round.

● Stan Gard, a member of North Brighton Golf Club, New South Wales, in 1938 completed fourteen rounds and four holes on his home course. Gard started his marathon performance at 12.55 am, and finished with the aid of car lights at 9.30 pm. He played consistent golf, his best being 78 in the tenth round, and his worst 92 in the second round.

● Bruce Sutherland, on the Craiglockhart Links, Edinburgh, started at 8.15 pm on 21st June, 1927, and played almost continuously until 7.30 pm on 22nd June, 1927. During the night four caddies with acetylene lamps lit the way, and lost balls were reduced to a minimum. He completed fourteen rounds. Mr Sutherland, who was a physical culture teacher, never recovered from the physical strain and died a few years later.

● Sidney Gleave, motor cycle racer, and Ernest Smith, golf professional, Davyhulme Club, Manchester, on 12th June, 1939, played five rounds of golf in five different countries – Scotland, Ireland, Isle of Man, England and Wales. Smith had to play the five rounds under 80 in one day to win the £100 wager. They travelled by plane, and the following was their programme with time taken and Smith's score:

Start—Prestwick St Nicholas (Scotland), 3.40 am. Score 70. Time taken, 1 hour 35 minutes. 2nd Course—Bangor (Ireland), 7.15 am. Score 76. Time taken, 1 hour 30 minutes. 3rd Course—Castletown (Isle of Man), 10.15 am. Score 76. Time taken, 1 hour 40 minutes. 4th

Course –Blackpool, Stanley Park (England), 1.30 pm. Score 72. Time taken, 1 hour 55 minutes. 5th Course—Hawarden (Wales), 6 pm. Score 68 (record). Time taken, 2 hours 15 minutes.

● On Wednesday, 3rd July, 1974, ES Wilson, Whitehead, Co Antrim and Dr GW Donaldson, Newry, Co Down, played a nine-hole match in each of seven countries in the one day. The first 9 holes was at La Moye (Channel Islands) followed by Hawarden (Wales), Chester (England), Turnberry (Scotland), Castletown (Isle of Man), Dundalk (Eire) and Warrenpoint (N Ireland). They started their first round at 4.25 am and their last round at 9.25 pm. Wilson piloted his own plane throughout.

● Rick Garcia and Don Tanner from Gallup, New Mexico, played 18 holes, selected from seven States, in one day in 1976 to raise money for muscular dystrophy. The States concerned were Texas, New Mexico, Colorado, Utah, Arizona, California and Nevada. A distance of over 2,000 miles was covered by private plane.

● In June 1986 to raise money for the upkeep of his medieval church, the Rector of Mark with Allerton, Somerset, the Rev Michael Pavey, played a sponsored 18 holes on 18 different courses in the Bath & Wells Diocese. With his partner, the well-known broadcaster on music, Antony Hopkins, they played the 1st at Minehead at 5.55 am and finished playing the 18th at Burnham and Berrow at 6.05 pm. They covered 240 miles in the 'round' including the distances to reach the correct tee for the 'next' hole on each course. Par for the 'round' was 70. Together the pair raised £10,500 for the church.

●To raise funds for the Marlborough Club's centenary year (1988), Laurence Ross, the Club professional, in June 1987, played 8 rounds in 12 hours. Against a par of 72, he completed the 576 holes in 3 under par, playing from back tees and walking all the way.

Fastest Rounds

● Dick Kimbrough, 41, completed a round on foot on 8th August, 1972, at North Platte CC, Nebraska (6,068 yards) in 30 minutes 10 seconds. He carried only a 3-iron. Earlier the same year Kimbrough played 364 holes in 24 hours.

● At Mowbray Course, Cape Town, November 1931, Len Richardson, who had represented South Africa in the Olympic Games, played a round which measured 6,248 yards in 31 minutes 22 seconds.

● The women's all-time record for a round played on a course of at least 5,250 yards is held by Dianne Taylor, 37, Jacksonville, Florida. She played the 5,692 yards University GC at Jacksonville in 55 minutes 54 seconds on 7th April, 1980.

● Faster rounds have been recorded, but they have not been done on foot. The fastest of these was achieved by 3 handicap Ken Wildey at Calcot Park GC on 20th July, 1980. Wildey, riding in a motorised cart, completed the 6,010 yards course in 24 minutes 3 seconds.

The sole purpose in each of the above instances was speed. The following are examples of fast rounds in a match or competition.

● On 14th June, 1922, Jock Hutchison and Joe Kirkwood (Australia) played round the Old Course at St Andrews in 1 hour 20 minutes. Hutchison, out in 37, led by three holes at the ninth and won by 4 and 3.

● In April, 1934, after attending a wedding in Bournemouth, Hants, Captain Gerald Moxom hurried to his club, West Hill in Surrey, to play in the captain's prize competition. With daylight fading and still dressed in his morning suit, he went round in 65 minutes and won the competition with a net 71 into the bargain.

● Fastest rounds can also take another form – the time taken for a ball to be propelled round 18 holes. The fastest known round of this type is 8 minutes 53.8 seconds on 25th August, 1979 by 42 members at Ridgemount CC Rochester, New York, a course measuring 6,161 yards. The Rules of Golf were observed but a ball was available on the following tee to be driven off the instant the ball had been holed at the preceding hole.

Slow Play

Standards have changed dramatically over the years as to what constitutes slow play as the following statement, which first appeared in the 1949 Golfer's Handbook, shows: *Slow motion golf has marred many championships, and notorious tortoises have been known to take three-and-a-half hours in a championship tie.*

Nowadays a round taking three-and-a-half hours is commonplace, but for the sake of history we record here examples of what was considered very slow play up to 1950.

● When Henry Cotton and RA Whitcombe played Bobby Locke and Sid Brews at Walton Heath, 1938, for a stake of £500 a side, the match made headlines with the slowness of play. Locke, who was engaging in his first important professional match in Great Britain, was ultra-careful, and the marshalling of the crowd — there were 5,000 spectators present during the second round – caused many delays, sometimes as much as 10 minutes being required for the players to leave one green and play off the next tee. The first round took three hours 40 minutes and the second round four hours 15 minutes. Cotton and Whitcombe won by 2 and 1. Locke, although on the defeated side, played phenomenal golf. He went round in 63. Walton Heath tees were far extended and it was a cruel test.

● In the Scottish Amateur Championship, 1922, at St Andrews, a competitor was deplorably slow and in one tie his opponent, in the hope of shaming the sloth into quickening his play brought to the links a camp bed, which was carried round by others who had been playing in the championship. The camp bed was placed at the side of each green, and while the tortoise crawled about studying the line of the putt, his opponent reclined on the bed and nonchalantly observed the antics of his rival. The attempt to secure a speed-up in the play was unsuccessful and the tortoise was even more deliberate in his play.

● The Amateur Championship, St Andrews, 1950, was remarkable for slowness of play and the inordinate time taken by some players to play their shots. The main cause of the slowness was the time taken to study putts. In some cases five minutes were spent over a stroke on the greens, although the record entry of 324 and the huge double greens of the Championship Course were also contributory to the sluggish pace. Many matches took four hours to complete and five couples waited at some tees. A record for the championship was made on the third day when play in the third and fourth rounds occupied 14 hours. The first ball was struck at 8 am and the last match finished on the 17th green in the lamplit dusk shortly before 10 pm. In the final between FR Stranahan and RD Chapman the first nine holes of the morning round took an hour and 50 minutes to play. A field telephone message was sent to the referee, Colonel CO Hezlet, Portrush, to warn the players that the second round would start at the scheduled time. This increased the pace slightly and the round was finished in three hours 40 minutes, the slowest round in the final of the championship at that time.

Curious Scoring

● Three threes, four fours, five fives and six sixes is one of only two progressive combinations that can work out for 18 holes. A player in a South African competition had this sequence and noticed the curiosity in scoring. The other combination is five fives, six sixes and seven sevens.

● RH Corbett, playing in the semi-final of the Tangye Cup at Mullim in 1916, did a score of 27. The remarkable part of Corbett's score was that it was made up of nine successive 3s, bogey being 5, 3, 4, 4, 5, 3, 4, 4, 3.

● At Little Chalfont in June 1985 Adrian Donkersley played six successive holes in 6, 5, 4, 3, 2, 1 from the 9th to the 14th holes against a par of 4, 4, 3, 4, 3, 3.

● On 2nd September, 1920, playing over Torphin, near Edinburgh, William Ingle did the first five holes in 1, 2, 3, 4, 5.

● In the summer of 1970, Keith McMillan, on holiday at Cullen, had a remarkable series of 1, 2, 3, 4, 5 at the 11th to 15th holes.

● Playing at Addington Palace, July, 1934, Ronald Jones, a member of Hendon Club, holed five consecutive holes in 5, 4, 3, 2, 1.

● Harry Dunderdale of Lincoln GC scored 5, 4, 3, 2, 1 in five consecutive holes during the first round of his club championship in 1978. The hole-in-one was the 7th, measuring 294 yards.

● At Westerhope near Newcastle in January

1986 Alan Crosby, the Club professional, played the first four holes in 4, 3, 2, 1 against the par of 4, 4, 3, 4.

● In 1965 at Kenya's Karen Country Club four members in a 4-ball holed the par 5 15th hole in 2, 3, 4 and 5, a total of 6 under par.

● In a club competition Mr A Mitchell had every digit from 1 to 8 on his card.

● At Nairn in August 1985 Brian Crowther of Swinton Park and Andrew Watson of Kelso, each 12 handicap, completed 18 holes without halving a hole. Crowther won at the 19th.

● PC Chase and John North finished all square in their regular weekly match at Woking GC on 30th October, 1972, without having halved a single hole. An actuarial calculation put the odds against this at 1,413,398-1.

● Another instance of this occurred in a first round foursomes match in the Halford-Hewitt Cup at Deal in 1979 when a Hurstpierpoint pair beat St Bee's at the 19th hole, without any hole being halved. The first ten holes were exchanged, St Bee's winning the next four and Hurstpierpoint the following five.

● At the Open Amateur Tournament of the Royal Ashdown Forest in 1936 Bobby Locke in his morning round had a score of 72, accomplishing every hole in 4.

● Severiano Ballesteros in winning the 1978 Swiss Open scored four rounds of 68.

● In a four-ball match in 1936, Richard Chapman partnered by Joe Ezar, the *Clown* prince of golf, against the Hon Michael Scott and Bobby Locke, then 18 years old, were four down and five to play. Ezar asked Scott if he had ever seen five birdies in a row. Scott replied that he could not recall that happening and so Ezar made a bet on the same and pulled the match out 1 up by shooting five birdies to win the match.

● Henry Cotton told of one of the most extraordinary scoring feats ever. With some other professionals he was at Sestrieres in the thirties for the Italian Open Championship and Joe Ezar, a colourful character in those days on both sides of the Atlantic, accepted a wager from a club official – 1,000 lira for a 66 to break the course record; 2,000 for a 65; and 4,000 for a 64. *I'll do 64*, said Ezar, and proceeded to jot down the hole-by-hole score figures he would do next day for that total. With the exception of the ninth and tenth holes where his predicted score was 3, 4 and the actual score was 4, 3, he accomplished this amazing feat exactly as nominated.

High Scores

● In the qualifying competition at Formby for the 1976 Open Championship, Maurice Flitcroft, a 46-year-old crane driver from Barrow-in-Furness, took 121 strokes for the first round and then withdrew saying, *I have no chance of qualifying.* Flitcroft entered as a professional but had never before played 18 holes. He had taken the game up 18 months previously but, as he was not a member of a club, had been limited to practising on a local beach. His round was made up thus: 7, 5, 6, 6, 6, 6, 12, 6, 7–61; 11, 5, 6, 8, 4, 9, 5, 7, 5–60, total 121. After his round Flitcroft said, *I've made a lot of progress in the last few months and I'm sorry I did not do better. I was trying too hard at the beginning but began to put things together at the end of the round.* R and A officials who were not amused by the bogus professional's efforts, refunded the £30 entry money to Flitcroft's two fellow-competitors.

● Playing in the qualifying rounds of the 1965 Open Championship at Southport, an American self-styled professional entrant from Milwaukee, Walter Danecki, achieved the inglorious feat of scoring a total of 221 strokes for 36 holes, 81 over par. His first round over the Hillside course was 108, followed by a second round of 113. Walter, who afterwards admitted he felt *a little discouraged and sad*, declared that he entered because he was *after the money*.

● The highest individual scoring ever known in the rounds connected with the Open Championship occurred at Muirfield, 1935, when a Scottish professional started 7, 10, 5, 10, and took 65 to reach the 9th hole. Another 10 came at the 11th and the player decided to retire at the 12th hole. There he was in a bunker, and after playing four shots he had not regained the fairway.

● In 1883 in the Open Championship at Musselburgh, Willie Fernie, the winner, had a 10, the only time double figures appeared on the card of the Open Champion of the year. Fernie won after a tie with Bob Ferguson, and his score for the last hole in the tie was 2. He holed from just off the green to win by one stroke.

● In the first Open Championship at Prestwick in 1860 a competitor took 21, the highest score for one hole ever recorded in this event. The record is preserved in the archives of the Prestwick Golf Club, where the championship was founded.

● In the first round of the 1980 US Masters, Tom Weiskopf hit his ball into the water hazard in front of the par-3 12th hole five times and scored 13 for the hole.

● American Ben Crenshaw took 11 shots at the 16th hole at Firestone CC in the third round of the 1976 World Series. He hit three consecutive wedge shots into the lake in front of the green.

● In the French Open at St Cloud, in 1968, Brian Barnes took 15 for the short 8th hole in the second round. After missing putts at which he hurriedly snatched while the ball was moving he penalised himself further by standing astride the line of a putt. The amazing result was that he actually took 12 strokes from about three feet from the hole.

● In 1938, in the final two rounds of the Open Championship, the players who had qualified for this stage had to contend with a hurricane during the greater part of the day. So fierce was the wind that the players had difficulty in keeping their stance during their swing. Scores of nine for individual holes were numerous; there were many 10's and one player had 14, the equal third highest score ever recorded for a single hole in the Open Championship.

● US professional Dave Hill 6-putted the fifth green at Oakmont in the 1962 US Open Championship.

● In the 1973 Transvaal Open at Germiston GC, Canadian professional Ken Trowbridge took 16 putts on the last green in a deliberate move to protest over the condition of the greens.

● Many high scores have been made at the Road Hole at St Andrews. Davie Ayton, on one occasion, was coming in a certain winner of the Open Championship when he got on the road and took 11. In 1921, at the Open Championship, one professional took 13. In 1923, competing for the Autumn Medal of the Royal and Ancient, JB Anderson required a five and a four to win the second award, but he took 13 at the Road Hole. Anderson was close to the green in two, was twice in the bunkers in the face of the green, and once on the road. In 1935, RH Oppenheimer tied for the Royal Medal (the first award) in the Autumn Meeting of the Royal and Ancient. On the play-off he was one stroke behind Captain Aitken when they stood on the 17th tee. Oppenheimer drove three balls out of bounds and eventually took 11 to the Road Hole.

● In the English Amateur at Hunstanton in 1931, a competitor pitched five times into a ditch before giving up the hole.

● In the 1974 Tallahassee Open, Mike Reasor, a regular PGA tour competitor, qualified for the final 36 holes in which he then scored 123 and 114. After making the halfway cut, Reasor injured his left shoulder in a riding accident, but because of the automatic entry into the next tournament given to all who completed the current one, he decided to play on using only his right arm for the last two rounds.

● British professional Mark James scored 111 in the second round of the 1978 Italian Open. He played the closing holes with only his right hand due to an injury to his left hand.

● In the 1927 Shawnee Open, Tommy Armour took 23 strokes to the 17th hole. Armour had won the American Open Championship a week earlier. In an effort to play the hole in a particular way, Armour hooked ball after ball out of bounds and finished with a 21 on the card. There was some doubt about the accuracy of this figure and on reaching the clubhouse Armour stated that it should be 23. This is the highest score by a professional in a tournament.

Freak Matches

● In 1912, the late Harry Dearth, an eminent vocalist, attired in a complete suit of heavy armour, played a match at Bushey Hall. He was beaten 2 and 1.

● In 1914, at the start of the First World War, JN Farrar, a native of Hoylake, was stationed at Royston, Herts. A bet was made of 10-1 that he would not go round Royston under 100 strokes, equipped in full infantry marching order, water bottle, full field kit and haversack. Farrar went round in 94. At the camp were several golfers, including professionals, who tried the same feat but failed.

● Captain Pennington, who was killed in an air crash in 1933, took part in a match *from the air* against AJ Young, the professional at Sonning. Captain Pennington, with 80 golf balls in the locker of his machine, had to find the Sonning greens by dropping the balls as he circled over the course. The balls were covered in white cloth to ensure that they did not bounce once they struck the ground. The airman completed the course in 40 minutes, taking

29 *strokes*, while Young occupied two hours for his round of 68.

● In April 1924, at Littlehampton, Harry Rowntree, an amateur golfer, played the better ball of Edward Ray and George Duncan, receiving an allowance of 150 yards to use as he required during the round. Rowntree won by 6 and 5 and had used only 50 yards 2 feet of his handicap. At one hole Duncan had a two – Rowntree, who was 25 yards from the hole, took this distance from his handicap and won the hole in one. Ray (died 1945) afterwards declared that, conceded a handicap of one yard per round, he could win every championship in the world. And he might, when reckoning is taken of the number of times a putt just stops an inch or two or how much difference to a shot three inches will make for the lie of the ball, either in a bunker or on the fairway. Many single matches on the same system have been played. An 18 handicap player opposed to a scratch player should make a close match with an allowance of 50 yards.

● The first known instance of a golf match by telephone occurred in 1957, when the Cotswold Hills Golf Club, Cheltenham, England, won a golf tournament against the Cheltenham Golf Club, Melbourne, Australia, by six strokes. A large crowd assembled at the English club to wait for the 12,000 miles telephone call from Australia. The match had been played at the suggestion of a former member of the Cotswold Hills Club, Harry Davies, and was open to every member of the two clubs. The result of the match was decided on the aggregate of the eight best scores on each side and the English club won by 564 strokes to 570.

Golf Matches Against Other Sports

● HH Hilton and Percy Ashworth, many times racket champion, contested a driving match, the former driving a golf ball with a driver, and the latter a racket ball with a racket. Best distances: Against breeze – Golfer 182 yards; Racket player 125 yards. Down wind – Golfer 230 yards; Racket player 140 yards. Afterwards Ashworth hit a golf ball with the racket and got a greater distance than with the racket ball, but was still a long way behind the ball driven by Hilton.

● In 1913, at Wellington, Shropshire, a match between a golfer and a fisherman casting a $2^{1}/_{2}$ oz weight was played. The golfer, Rupert May, took 87; the fisherman JJD Mackinlay, required 102. The fisherman's difficulty was in his short casts. His longest cast, 105 yards, was within 12 yards of the world record at the time, held by a French angler, Decautelle. When within a rod's length of a hole he ran the weight to the rod end and dropped into the hole. Five times he broke his line, and was allowed another shot without penalty.

● In December, 1913, FMA Webster, of the London Athletic Club, and Dora Roberts, with javelins, played a match with the late Harry Vardon and Mrs Gordon Robertson, who used the regulation clubs and golf balls. The golfers conceded two-thirds in the matter of distance, and they won by 5 up and 4 to play in a contest of 18 holes. The javelin throwers had a mark of two feet square in which to *hole out* while the golfers had to get their ball into the ordinary golf hole. Mr Webster's best throw was one of 160 feet.

● Several matches have taken place between a golfer on the one side and an archer on the other. The wielder of the bow and arrow has nearly always proved the victor. In 1953 at Kirkhill Golf Course, Lanarkshire, five archers beat six golfers by two games to one. There were two special rules for the match; when an archer's arrow landed six feet from the hole or the golfer's ball three feet from the hole, they were counted as holed. When the arrows landed in bunkers or in the rough, archers lifted their arrow and added a stroke. The sixth archer in this match called off and one archer shot two arrows from each of the 18 tees.

● In 1954, at the Southbroom Club, South Africa, a match over 9 holes was played between an archer and a fisherman against two golfers. The participants were all champions of their own sphere and consisted of Vernon Adams (archer), Dennis Burd (fisherman), Jeanette Wahl (champion of Southbroom and Port Shepstone), and Ron Burd (professional at Southbroom). The conditions were that the archer had holed out when his arrows struck a small leather bag placed on the green beside the hole and in the event of his placing his approach shot within a bow's length of the pin he was deemed to have 1-putted. The fisherman, to achieve a 1-putt, had to land his sinker within a rod's length of the pin. The two golfers were ahead for brief spells, but it was the opposition who led at the deciding 9th hole where *Robin Hood* played a perfect approach for a birdie.

● An *Across England* combined match was begun on 11th October, 1965, by four golfers and two archers from Crowborough Beacon Golf Club, Sussex, accompanied by *Penny*, a white Alsatian dog, whose duty it was to find lost balls. They teed *off* from Carlisle Castle via Hadrian's Wall, the Pennine Way, finally holing out in the 18th hole at Newcastle United Golf Club in 612 teed shots. Casualties included 110 lost golf balls and 19 lost or broken arrows. The match took five-and-a-half days, and the distance travelled was about 60 miles. The golfers were Miss P Ward, K Meaney, K Ashdown and CA Macey; the archers were WH Hulme and T Scott. The first arrow was fired from the battlements of Carlisle Castle, a distance of nearly 300 yards, by Cumberland Champion R Willis, who also fired the second arrow right across the River Eden. R Clough, president of Newcastle United GC, holed the last two putts. The match was in aid of *Guide Dogs for the Blind* and *Friends of Crowborough Hospital.*

Cross-country Matches

● Taking 1 year, 114 days, Floyd Rood golfed his way from coast to coast across the United States. He took 114,737 shots including 3,511 penalty shots for the 3,397 mile *course.*
● Two Californian teenagers, Bob Aube (17) and Phil Marrone (18) went on a golfing safari in 1974 from San Francisco to Los Angeles, a trip of over 500 miles lasting 16 days. The first six days they played alongside motorways. Over 1,000 balls were used.
● In 1830, the Gold Medal winner of the Royal and Ancient backed himself for 10 sovereigns to drive from the 1st hole at St Andrews to the toll bar at Cupar, distance nine miles, in 200 teed shots. He won easily.
● In 1848, two Edinburgh golfers played a match from Bruntsfield Links to the top of Arthur's Seat – an eminence overlooking the Scottish capital, 822 feet above sea level.
● On a winter's day in 1898, Freddie Tait backed himself to play a gutta ball in 40 teed shots from Royal St George's Clubhouse, Sandwich, to the Cinque Ports Club, Deal. He was to hole out by hitting any part of the Deal Clubhouse. The distance as the crow flies was three miles. The redoubtable Tait holed out with his 32nd shot, so effectively that the ball went through a window.
● On 3rd December, 1920, P Rupert Phillips and W Raymond Thomas teed up on the first tee of the Radyr Golf Club and played to the last hole at Southerndown. The distance as the crow flies was 15½ miles, but circumventing swamps, woods, and plough, they covered, approximately, 20 miles. The wager was that they would not do the *hole* in 1,000 strokes, but they holed out at their 608th stroke two days later. They carried large ordnance maps.
● In 1900 three members of the Hackensack (NJ) Club played a game of four-and-a-half hours over an extemporised course six miles long, which stretched from Hackensack to Paterson. Despite rain, cornfields, and wide streams, the three golfers – JW Hauleebeek, Dr ER Pfaare, and Eugene Crassons – completed the round, the first and the last named taking 305 strokes each, and Dr Pfaare 327 strokes. The players used only two clubs, the mashie and the cleek.
● On 12th March, 1921, A Stanley Turner, Macclesfield, played from his house to the Cat and Fiddle Inn, five miles distance, in 64 strokes. The route was broken and hilly with a

rise of nearly 1,000 feet. Turner was allowed to tee up within two club lengths after each shot and the wagering was 6-4 against his doing the distance in 170 strokes.
● In 1919, a golfer drove a ball from Piccadilly Circus and, proceeding via the Strand, Fleet Street and Ludgate Hill, *holed out* at the Royal Exchange, London. The player drove off at 8 am on a Sunday, a time when the usually thronged thoroughfares were deserted.
● On 23rd April, 1939, Richard Sutton, a London stockbroker, played from Tower Bridge, London, to White's Club, St James's Street, in 142 strokes. The bet was he would not do *the course* in under 200 shots. Sutton used a putter, crossed the Thames at Southwark Bridge, and hit the ball short distances to keep out of trouble.
● Golfers produced the most original event in Ireland's three-week national festival of An Tostal, 1953 – a cross-country competition with an advertised £1,000,000 for the man who could hole out in one. The 150 golfers drove off from the first tee at Kildare Club to hole out eventually on the 18th green, five miles away, on the nearby Curragh course, a distance of 8,800 yards. The unusual hazards to be negotiated included the main Dublin-Cork railway line and highway, the Curragh Racecourse, hoofprints left by Irish thoroughbred racehorses out exercising on the plains from nearby stables, army tank tracks and about 150 telephone lines. The Golden Ball Trophy, which is played for annually – a standard size golf ball in gold, mounted on a black marble pillar beside the silver figure of a golfer on a green marble base, designed by Captain Maurice Cogan, Army GHQ, Dublin — was for the best gross. And it went to one of the longest hitters in international golf – Amateur Champion, Irish internationalist and British Walker Cup player Joe Carr, with the remarkable score of 52.
● Four Aberdeen University students (as a 1961 Charities Week stunt) set out to golf their way up Ben Nevis (4,406 feet). After losing 63 balls and expending 659 strokes, the quartet, about halfway up, conceded victory to Britain's highest mountain.

Long-lived Golfers

● The oldest golfer who ever lived we believe was Arthur Thompson of British Columbia, Canada. He equalled his age when 103 at Uplands GC, a course of over 6,000 yards. He died two years later aged 105 but it is not known whether he played after the age of 103. Mr Thompson also features in the section *Low Scoring Veterans.*.
● Nathaniel Vickers celebrated his 103rd birthday on Sunday, 9th October, 1949, and died the following day. He was the oldest member of the

United States Senior Golf Association and until 1942 he competed regularly in their events and won many trophies in the various age divisions. When 100 years old, he apologised for being able to play only 9 holes a day. Vickers predicted he would live until 103 and he died a few hours after he had celebrated his birthday.

● American George Miller, who died in 1979 aged 102, played regularly when 100 years old.

● In his 93rd year, the Rev Harcourt Just had a daily round of six to 10 holes at St Andrews. In 1950, the Town Council gave him the *Courtesy of the Course*, which excused the venerable minister paying the yearly charge.

● George Swanwick, a member of Wallasey, celebrated his 90th birthday with a luncheon at the club on 1st April, 1971. He played golf several times a week, carrying his own clubs and had holed-in-one at the ages of 75 and 85. His ambition was to complete the sequence aged 95 . . . but he died in 1973 aged 92.

● The 10th Earl of Wemyss played a round on his 92nd birthday, in 1910, at Craigielaw. When 87 the Earl was partnered by Harry Vardon in a match at Kilspindie, the golf course on his East Lothian estate at Gosford. The venerable earl, after playing his ball, mounted a pony and rode to the next shot. He died on 30th June, 1914, in his 96th year.

● FL Callender, aged 78, in September 1932, played nine consecutive rounds in the Jubilee Vase, St Andrews. He was defeated in the ninth, the final round, by 4 and 2. Callender's handicap was 12. This is the best known achievement of a septuagenarian in golf.

● Mr Bernard Matthews, aged 82, of Banstead Downs Club, handicap 6, holed the course in 72 gross in August 1988. A week later he holed it in 70, twelve shots below his age. He came back in 31, finishing 4, 3, 3, 2, 3, against a par of 5, 4, 3, 3, 4. Mr Matthews's eclectic score at his Club is 37, or one over 2's.

Playing in the Dark

On numerous occasions it has been necessary to hold lamps, lighted candles, or torches at holes in order that players might finish a competition. Large entries, slow play, early darkness and an eclipse of the sun have all been causes of playing in darkness.

● At the Open Championship in Musselburgh in November 1889 many players finished when the light had so far gone that the adjacent street lamps were lit. The cards were checked by candlelight. Several players who had no chance of the championship were paid small sums to withdraw in order to permit others who had a chance to finish in daylight. This was the last championship at Musselburgh.

● At the Southern Section of the PGA tour-

nament on 25th September, 1907, at Burnham Beeches, several players concluded the round by the aid of torch lights placed near the holes.

● In the Irish Open Championship at Portmarnock in September, 1907, a tie in the third round between WC Pickeman and A Jeffcott was postponed owing to darkness, at the 22nd hole. Pickeman on the following morning won at the 24th.

● The qualifying round of the American Amateur Championship in 1910 could not be finished in one day, and several competitors had to stop their round on account of darkness, and complete it early in the morning of the following day.

● On 10th January, 1926, in the final of the President's Putter, at Rye, EF Storey and RH Wethered were all square at the 24th hole. It was then 5 pm and so dark that, although a fair crowd was present, the balls could not be followed, and the tie was abandoned and the Putter held jointly for the year. The winner of the Putter each year affixes the ball he played; for 1926 there are two balls, respectively engraved with the names of the finalists.

● In the 1932 Walker Cup contest at Brooklyn, a total eclipse of the sun occurred.

● At Perth, on 14th September, 1932, a competition was in progress under good clear evening light, and a full bright moon. The moon rose at 7.10 and an hour later came under eclipse to the earth's surface. The light then became so bad that on the last three greens competitors holed out by the aid of the light from matches.

● At Carnoustie, 1932, in the competition for the *Craw's Nest* the large entry necessitated competitors being sent off in 3-ball matches. The late players had to be assisted by electric torches flashed on the greens.

● In February, 1950, Max Faulkner and his partner, R Dolman, in a Guildford Alliance event finished their round in complete darkness. A photographer's flash bulbs were used at the last hole to direct Faulkner's approach. Several

others of more than 100 competitors also finished in the darkness. At the last hole they had only the light from the clubhouse to aim at and one played his approach so boldly that he put his ball through the hall doorway and almost into the dressing room.

● On the second day of the 1969 Ryder Cup contest, the last 4-ball match ended in near total darkness on the 18th green at Birkdale. With the help of the clubhouse lights the two American players, Lee Trevino and Miller Barber, and Tony Jacklin for Britain each faced putts of around five feet to win their match. All missed and their game was halved.

● The occasions mentioned above all occurred in competitions where it was not intended to play in the dark. There are, however, numerous instances where players set out to play in the dark either for bets or for novelty.

● On 29th November, 1878, RW Brown backed himself to go round the Hoylake links in 150 strokes, starting at 11 pm. The conditions of the match were that Mr Brown was only to be penalised *loss of distance* for a lost ball, and that no one was to help him to find it. He went round in 147 strokes, and won his bet by the narrow margin of three strokes.

● In 1876 David Strath backed himself to go round St Andrews under 100, in moonlight. He took 95, and did not lose a ball.

● In September 1928, at St Andrews, the first and last holes were illuminated by lanterns, and at 11 pm four members of the Royal and Ancient set out to play a foursome over the 2 holes. Electric lights, lanterns, and rockets were used to brighten the fairway, and the headlights of motor cars parked on Links Place formed a helpful battery. The 1st hole was won in four, and each side got a five at the 18th. About 1,000 spectators followed the freak match, which was played to celebrate the appointment of Angus Hambro to the captaincy of the club.

● In 1931, Rufus Stewart, professional, Kooyonga Club, South Australia, and former Australian Open Champion, played 18 holes of exhibition golf at night without losing a single ball over the Kooyonga course, and completed the round in 77.

● At Ashley Wood Golf Club, Blandford, Dorset, a night-time golf tournament is arranged annually with up to 180 golfers taking part over four nights. Over £6000 has been raised in four years for the Muscular Dystrophy Charity.

● At Pannal, 3rd July, 1937, RH Locke, playing in bright moonlight, holed his tee shot at the 15th hole, distance 220 yards, the only known case of holing-in-one under such conditions.

● In August, 1970, a group of Canadians held a stroke competition at the Summit Golf and Country Club, Ontario, in total darkness. Organised by Peter Kennedy, seven competitors took part, starting at midnight. Special rules drawn up included only a 1-stroke penalty for a lost ball, but if 12 balls were lost the competitor had to retire. The best score was 84 by Lief Pettersen.

Fatal and Other Accidents on the Links

The history of golf is, unfortunately, marred by a great number of fatal accidents on or near the course. In the vast majority of such cases they have been caused either by careless swinging of the club or by an uncontrolled shot when the ball has struck a spectator or bystander. In addition to the fatal accidents there is an even larger number on record which have resulted in serious injury or blindness. We do not propose to list these accidents, which have hitherto been recorded in the Golfer's Handbook, except where they have some unusual feature. We would remind all golfers of the tragic consequences which have so often been caused by momentary carelessness. The fatal accidents which follow have an unusual cause and other accidents given may have their humorous aspect.

● In July, 1971, 43-year-old Rudolph Roy was killed at a Montreal course when, in playing out of woods, the shaft of his club snapped, rebounded off a tree and the jagged edge plunged into his body.

● Harold Wallace, aged 75, playing at Lundin Links with two friends in 1950, was crossing the railway line which separates the fifth green and sixth tee, when a light engine knocked him down and he was killed instantly.

● Edward M Harrison, November, 1951, while playing alone on the Inglewood Country Club, Seattle, apparently broke the shaft of his driver and the split shaft pierced his groin. He tried to reach the clubhouse, but collapsed and bled to death 100 yards from the ninth tee where the accident happened.

● In the summer of 1963, Harold Kalles, of Toronto, Canada, died six days after his throat had been cut by a golf club shaft, which broke against a tree as he was trying to play out of a bunker.

● At Jacksonville, Florida, on 18th March, 1952, two women golfers were instantly killed when hit simultaneously by the whirling propellor of a navy fighter plane. They were playing together when the plane with a dead engine and coming in against the wind, out of control, hit them from behind. The pilot, who had been making a test flight from the Navy Air Station which adjoins the golf course, stepped out of the burning plane and did not know for some seconds that the plane had killed the women.

● In September, 1956, Myrl G Hanmore, aged 50, died from an accident at the Riviera Country Club, Los Angeles, apparently caused when he lost control of a golf car on a steep incline and was crushed between the vehicle he was driving and one he was towing from the first tee to a storage barn.

● On a Welsh course a player had played a shot out of a bunker and jumped up to see the result, when he was hit on the head by a ball driven from behind. He felt no ill effects at the moment, except a slight smarting of the eyes, but within a week he was totally blind.

● At Knott End Golf Club, on 20th June, 1953, Charles Langley, playing in a competition for the Captain's Prize, hit his tee shot from the 10th and struck the cone-shaped wood marker at the ladies' tee, which was approximately nine feet from where Mr Langley had teed his ball. The ball rebounded at lightning speed striking and destroying Mr Langley's left eye.

● Gary Player was accidentally pushed into a lake beside the 18th hole at Congressional CC by young spectators seeking his autograph as he came off the green after a practice round for the 1976 Championship.

● The ambulance crew responded in minutes to a call from the Point Grey Golf and CC in Vancouver, British Columbia, reporting a golfer had suffered a heart attack. But the supposed *victim* definitely was not suffering. Justice JM Coody, 95, a retired member of British Columbia's supreme court had been spotted resting in a golf car. A passing golfer asked what the problem was and he thought the judge replied, *Heart failure*. He didn't. Justice Coody's car was stalled. He'd actually said *Cart failure*.

Lightning on the Links

There have been a considerable number of fatal and serious accidents through players and caddies having been struck by lightning on the course. The Royal and Ancient and the USGA have, since 1952, provided for discontinuance of play during lightning storms under the Rules of Golf (Rule 37, 6) and the United States Golf Association have given the following guide for personal safety during thunderstorms:

(a) Do not go out of doors or remain out during thunderstorms unless it is necessary. Stay inside of a building where it is dry, preferably away from fireplaces, stoves, and other metal objects.

(b) If there is any choice of shelter, choose in the following order:
  1. Large metal or metal-frame buildings.
  2. Dwellings or other buildings which are protected against lightning.
  3. Large unprotected buildings.
  4. Small unprotected buildings.

(c) If remaining out of doors is unavoidable, keep away from:

  1. Small sheds and shelters if in an exposed location.
  2. Isolated trees.
  3. Wire fences.
  4. Hilltops and wide open spaces.

(d) Seek shelter in:
  1. A cave.
  2. A depression in the ground.
  3. A deep valley or canyon.
  4. The foot of a steep or overhanging cliff.
  5. Dense woods.
  6. A grove of trees.

Note – Raising golf clubs or umbrellas above the head is dangerous.

● A serious incident with lightning involving well-known golfers was at the 1975 Western Open in Chicago when Lee Trevino, Jerry Heard and Bobby Nichols were all struck and had to be taken to hospital. At the same time Tony Jacklin had a club thrown 15 feet out of his hands.

● Two well-known competitors were struck by lightning in European events in 1977. They were Mark James of Britain in the Swiss Open and Severiano Ballesteros of Spain in the Scandinavian Open. Fortunately neither appeared to be badly injured.

Spectators Interfering with Balls

● Deliberate interference by spectators with balls in play during important money matches was not unknown in the old days when there was intense rivalry between the *schools* of Musselburgh, St Andrews, and North Berwick, and disputes arose in stake matches caused by the action of spectators in kicking the ball into either a favourable or an unfavourable position.

● Tom Morris, in his last match with Willie Park at Musselburgh, refused to go on because of interference by the spectators, and in the match on the same course about 40 years later, in 1895, between Willie Park junior and JH Taylor, the barracking of the crowd and interference with play was so bad that when the Park-Vardon match came to be arranged in 1899, Vardon refused to accept Musselburgh as a venue.

● Even in modern times spectators have been known to interfere deliberately with players' balls, though it is usually by children. In the 1972 Penfold Tournament at Queen's Park, Bournemouth, Christy O'Connor jun had his ball stolen by a young boy, but not being told of this at the time had to take the penalty for a lost ball. O'Connor finished in a tie for first place, but lost the play-off.

● In 1912 in the last round of the final of the Amateur Championship at Westward Ho! between Abe Mitchell and John Ball, the drive of the former to the short 14th hit an open umbrella held by a lady protecting herself from the heavy rain, and instead of landing on the green the ball was diverted into a bunker. Mitchell, who was leading at the time by 2 holes, lost the hole and Ball won the Championship at the 38th hole.

● In the match between the professionals of Great Britain and America at Southport in 1937 a dense crowd collected round the 15th green waiting for the Sarazen-Alliss match. The American's ball landed in the lap of a woman, who picked it up and threw it so close to the hole that Sarazen got a two against Alliss' three.

● In a memorable tie between Bobby Jones and Cyril Tolley in the 1930 Amateur Championship at St Andrews, Jones' approach to the 17th green struck spectators massed at the left end of the green and led to controversy as to whether it would otherwise have gone on to the famous road. Jones himself had deliberately played for that part of the green and had requested stewards to get the crowd back. Had the ball gone on to the road, the historic Jones Quadrilateral of the year – the Open and Amateur Championships of Britain and the United States – might not have gone into the records.

● Now that golf has become such a widely enjoyed spectator sport with vast crowds lining the fairways, instances of a ball being deflected by spectators are no longer unusual, but are accepted as an almost normal occurrence in major events. In general it is thought that this is usually in favour of the player, as the ball is often destined for bad or even unplayable positions when it is stopped by impact with an onlooker. It is also to the advantage of a player that a ball is seldom lost, as its position is nearly always pin-pointed by a spectator in the area.

● In the 1983 Suntory World Match-play Championship at Wentworth Nick Faldo hit his second shot over the green at the 16th hole into a group of spectators. To everyone's astonishment and discomfiture the ball reappeared on the green about 30 ft from the hole, propelled there by a thoroughly misguided and anonymous spectator. The referee ruled that Faldo play the ball where it lay on the green. Faldo's opponent, Graham Marsh, understandably upset by the incident, took three putts against Faldo's two, thus losing a hole he might well otherwise have won. Faldo won the match 2 and 1, but lost in the final to Marsh's fellow Australian Greg Norman by 3 and 2.

Golf Balls Killing Animals and Fish, and Incidents with Animals

● An astounding fatality to an animal through being hit by a golf ball occurred at St Margaret's-at-Cliffe Golf Club, Kent on 13th June, 1934, when WJ Robinson, the professional, killed a cow with his tee shot to the 18th hole. The cow was standing in the fairway about 100 yards from the tee, and the ball struck her on the back

of the head. She fell like a log, but staggered to her feet and walked about 50 yards before dropping again. When the players reached her she was dead.

● JW Perret, of Ystrad Mynach, playing with Chas R Halliday, of Ralston, in the qualifying rounds of the Society of One Armed Golfers' Championship over the Darley course, Troon, on 27th August, 1935, killed two gulls at successive holes with his second shots. The *deadly* shots were at the 1st and 2nd holes.

● On the first day of grouse shooting of the 1975 season (12th August), 11-year-old school-boy, Willie Fraser, of Kingussie, beat all the guns when he killed a grouse with his tee shot on the local course.

● On 10th June, 1904, while playing in the Edinburgh High Constables' Competition at Kilspindie, Captain Ferguson sent a long ball into the rough at the Target hole, and on searching for it found that it had struck and killed a young hare.

● Playing in a mixed open tournament at the Waimairi Beach Golf Club in Christchurch, New Zealand, in the summer of 1961, Mrs RT Challis found her ball in fairly long spongy grass where a placing rule applied. She picked up, placed the ball and played her stroke. A young hare leaped into the air and fell dead at her feet. She had placed the ball on the leveret without seeing it and without disturbing it.

● In 1906 in the Border Championship at Hawick, a gull and a weasel were killed by balls during the afternoon's play.

● A golfer at Newark, in May, 1907, drove his ball into the river. The ball struck a trout 2lb in weight and killed it.

● On 24th April, 1975, at Scunthorpe GC, Jim Tollan's drive at the 14th hole, called *The*

Mallard, struck and killed a female mallard duck in flight. The duck was stuffed and is displayed in the Scunthorpe Clubhouse.

● Playing over the Killarney Course, June, 1957, a golfer sliced his ball into one of the lakes and knocked out a trout rising to catch a fly. His friend waded into the water to get the ball – and the trout.

● A Samuel, Melbourne Club, at Sandringham, was driving with an iron club from the 17th tee, when a kitten, which had been playing in the long grass, sprang suddenly at the ball. Kitten and club arrived at the objective simultaneously, with the result that the kitten took an unexpected flight through the air, landing some 20 yards away.

● As Susan Rowlands was lining up a vital putt in the closing stages of the final of the 1978 Welsh Girls' Championship at Abergele, a tiny mouse scampered up her trouser leg. After holing the putt, the mouse ran down again. Susan, who won the final admitted that she fortunately had not known it was there.

● While on tour with British professionals 1936-37, in South Africa, Abe Mitchell, at the first hole on the Hill course at Port Elizabeth, noticed that his club struck something hard when he played his second shot from the edge of the rough. Taking another swing he *unearthed* a tortoise upon which his ball had perched from the tee shot.

Interference by Birds and Animals

● Crows, ravens, hawks and seagulls frequently carry off golf balls, sometimes dropping the ball actually on the green, and it is a common incident for a cow to swallow a golf ball. A plague of crows on the Liverpool course at Hoylake are addicted to golf balls – they stole 26 in one day – selecting only new balls. It was suggested that members should carry shotguns as a 15th club!

● A match was approaching a hole in a rather low-lying course, when one of the players made a crisp chip from about 30 yards from the hole. The ball trickled slowly across the green and eventually disappeared into the hole. After a momentary pause, the ball was suddenly ejected on to the green, and out jumped a large frog.

● In Massachusetts a goose, having been hit rather hard by a golf ball which then came to rest by the side of a water hazard, took revenge by waddling over to the ball and kicking it into the water.

● A large black crow named Jasper which frequented the Lithgow GC in New South Wales, Australia, stole 30 golf balls in the club's 1972 Easter Tournament.

● As Mrs Molly Whitaker was playing from a bunker at Beachwood course, Natal, South Africa, a large monkey leaped from a bush and clutched her round the neck. A caddie drove it off by clipping it with an iron club.

● Jimmy Stewart playing in the 1982 Singapore Open at the Bukit course approached his ball for his second shot at the 3rd hole and found a 10 foot cobra also making for his ball. He killed the snake only to see another emerge from the dead snake's mouth. This too was killed.

● In 1921, on the course at Kirkfield, Ontario, P McGregor and H Dowie were all square going to the home hole in the final, and when they reached the green McGregor needed to hole a long putt to win the match. It seemed to have stopped on the lip of the hole when a large grasshopper landed squarely on the ball and caused it to drop into the hole and decide the match in favour of McGregor.

● In the summer of 1963, SC King had a good

drive to the 10th hole at the Guernsey Club. His partner, RW Clark, was in the rough, and King helped him to search. Returning to his ball, he found a cow eating it. Next day, at the same hole, the positions were reversed, and King was in the rough. Clark placed his woollen hat over his ball, remarking, *I'll make sure the cow doesn't eat mine.* On his return he found the cow thoroughly enjoying his hat; nothing was left but the pom-pom.

Armless, One-armed, Legless and Ambidextrous Players

● In September, 1933, at Burgess Golfing Society of Edinburgh, the first championship for one-armed golfers was held. There were 43 entries and 37 of the competitors had lost an arm in the 1914-18 war. Play was over two rounds and the championship was won by WE Thomson, Eastwood, Glasgow, with a score of 169 (82 and 87) for two rounds. The Burgess course was 6,300 yards long. Thomson drove the last green, 260 yards. The championship and an international match are played annually.
● In the Boys' Amateur Championship 1923, at Dunbar and 1949 at St Andrews, there were competitors each with one arm. The competitor in 1949, RP Reid, Cupar, Fife, who lost his arm working a machine in a butcher's shop, got through to the third round.
● There have been cases of persons with no arms playing golf. One, Thomas McAuliffe, who held the club between his right shoulder and cheek, once went round Buffalo CC, USA, in 108.
● Group Captain Bader, who lost both legs in a flying accident prior to the World War 1939-45, took part in golf competitions and reached a single-figure handicap in spite of his disability.
● In 1909, Scott of Silloth, and John Haskins of Hoylake, both one-armed golfers, played a home and away match for £20 a side. Scott finished five up at Silloth. He was seven up and 14 to play at Hoylake but Haskins played so well that Scott eventually only won by 3 and 1. This was the first match between one-armed golfers. Haskins in 1919 was challenged by Mr Mycock, of Buxton, another one-armed player. The match was 36 holes, home and away. The first half was played over the Buxton and High Peak Links, and the latter half over the Liverpool Links, and resulted in a win for Haskins by 11 and 10. Later in the same year Haskins received another challenge to play against Alexander Smart of Aberdeen. The match was 18 holes over the Balgownie Course, and ended in favour of Haskins.
● In a match, November, 1926, between the Geduld and Sub Nigel Clubs – two golf clubs connected with the South African gold mines of

the same names – each club had two players minus an arm. The natural consequence was that the quartet were matched. The players were – AWP Charteris and E Mitchell, Sub Nigel; and EP Coles and J Kirby, Geduld. This is the first record of four one-armed players in a foursome.
● At Joliet Country Club, USA, a one-armed golfer named DR Anderson drove a ball 300 yards.
● Left-handedness, but playing golf right-handed, is prevalent and for a man to throw with his left hand and play golf right-handed is considered an advantage, for Bobby Jones, Jesse Sweetser, Walter Hagen, Jim Barnes, Joe Kirkwood and more recently Johnny Miller were eminent golfers who were left-handed and ambidextrous.
● In a practice round for the Open Championship in July, 1927, at St Andrews, Len Nettlefold and Joe Kirkwood changed sets of clubs at the 9th hole. Nettlefold was a left-handed golfer and Kirkwood right-handed. They played the last nine, Kirkwood with the left-handed clubs and Nettlefold with the right-handed clubs.
● The late Harry Vardon, when he was at Ganton, got tired of giving impossible odds to his members and beating them, so he collected a set of left-handed clubs, and rating himself at scratch, conceded the handicap odds to them. Vardon won with the same monotonous regularity.
● Ernest Jones, who was professional at the Chislehurst Club, was badly wounded in the war in France in 1916 and his right leg had to be amputated below the knee. He persevered with the game, and before the end of the year he went round the Clacton course balanced on his one leg in 72. Jones later settled in the United States where he built fame and fortune as a golf teacher.
● Major Alexander McDonald Fraser of Edinburgh had the distinction of holding two handicaps simultaneously in the same club – one when he played left-handed and the other for his right-handed play. In medal competitions he had to state before teeing up which method he would use.
● Former England test cricketer Brian Close once held a handicap of 2 playing right-handed, but after retiring from cricket in 1977 decided to apply himself as a left-handed player. His left-handed handicap at the time of his retirement was 7. Close had the distinction of once beating Ted Dexter, another distinguished test cricketer and noted golfer twice in the one day, playing right-handed in the morning and left-handed in the afternoon.

Blind and Blindfolded Golf

● Major Towse, VC, whose eyes were shot out during the South African War, 1899, was probably the first blind man to play golf. His only stipulations when playing the game were that he should be allowed to touch the ball with his hands to ascertain its position, and that his caddie could ring a small bell to indicate the position of the hole. Major Towse, who played with considerable skill, was also an expert oarsman and bridge player. He died in 1945, aged 81.

● The United States Blind Golfers' Association in 1946 promoted an Invitational Golf Tournament for the blind at Country Club, Inglewood, California. This competition is held annually and in 1953 there were 24 competitors and 11 players completed the two rounds of 36 holes. The winner was Charley Boswell who lost his eyesight leading a tank unit in Germany in 1944.

● In July, 1954, at Lambton Golf and Country Club, Toronto, the first international championship for the blind was held. It resulted in a win for Joe Lazaro, of Waltham, Mass, with a score of 220 for the two rounds. He drove the 215-yard 16th hole and just missed an ace, his ball stopping 18 inches from the hole. Charley Boswell, who won the United States Blind Golfers' Association Tournament in 1953, was second. The same Charles Boswell, of Birmingham, Alabama holed the 141-yard 14th hole at the Vestavia CC in one in October, 1970.

● Another blind person to have holed-in-one was American Ben Thomas while on holiday in South Carolina in 1978.

● Rick Sorenson undertook a bet in which, playing 18 holes blindfolded at Meadowbrook Course, Minneapolis, on 25th May, 1973, he was to pay $10 for every hole over par and receive $100 for every hole in par or better. He went round in 86 losing $70 on the deal.

● Alfred Toogood played in a match at Sunningdale in 1912 blindfolded. His opponent was Tindal Atkinson, and Toogood was beaten 8 and 7. I Millar, Newcastle-upon-Tyne, played a match, blindfolded, against AT Broughton, Birkdale, at Newcastle, County Down, in 1908. Putting matches while blindfolded have been frequently played.

● Wing-Commander *Laddie* Lucas, DSO, DFC, MP, played over Sandy Lodge golf course in Hertfordshire on 7th August, 1954, completely blindfolded and had a score of 87.

Trick Shots

● Joe Kirkwood, Australia, specialised in public exhibitions of trick and fancy shots. He played all kinds of strokes after nominating them, and among his ordinary strokes nothing was more impressive than those hit for low flight. He played a full drive from the face of a wristlet watch, and the toe of a spectator's shoe, full strokes at a suspended ball, and played for slice and pull at will, and exhibited his ambidexterity by playing left-handed strokes with right-handed clubs. Holing six balls, stymieing, a full shot at a ball catching it as it descended, and hitting 12 full shots in rapid succession, with his face turned away from the ball, were shots among his repertoire. In playing the last named Kirkwood placed the balls in a row, about six inches apart, and moved quickly along the line. Kirkwood, who was born in Australia lived for many years in America. He died in November, 1970 aged 73.

● Joe Ezar, an American professional, who specialised in trick shots, included in his show a number of clowning acts with balls.

● On 2nd April, 1894, a 3-ball match was played over Musselburgh course between Messrs Grant, Bowden, and Waggot, the clubmaker, the latter teeing on the face of a watch at each tee. He finished the round in 41 the watch being undamaged in any way.

● At Westbrook, USA, in 1901, ET Knapp drove a ball off the top of a hen's egg. The egg was slightly dented on one end to afford a hold for the ball.

● At Esher, 23rd November, 1931, George Ashdown, the club professional, in a match played his tee shot for each of the 18 holes from a rubber tee strapped to the forehead of Miss Ena Shaw.

● EA Forrest, a South African professional in a music hall turn of trick golf shots, played blindfolded shots, one being from the ball teed on the chin of his recumbent partner.

● The late Paul Hahn, an American trick specialist could hit four balls with two clubs. Holding a club in each hand he hit two balls, hooking one and slicing the other with the same swing. Hahn had a repertoire of 30 trick shots. In 1955 he flew completely round the world, exhibiting in 14 countries and on all five continents.

Balls Colliding and Touching

● Competing in the 1980 Corfu International Championship, Sharon Peachey drove from one tee and her ball collided in mid-air with one from a competitor playing another hole. Her ball ended in a pond.

● Playing in the Cornish team championship in 1973 at West Cornwall GC Tom Scott-Brown, of West Cornwall GC, and Paddy Bradley, of Tehidy GC, saw their drives from the fourth and eighth tees collide in mid-air.

● Playing in a 4-ball match at Guernsey Club in June, 1966, all four players were near the 13th green from the tee. Two of them – DG Hare and

S Machin – chipped up simultaneously; the balls collided in mid-air; Machin's ball hit the green, then the flagstick, and dropped into the hole for a birdie 2.

● Playing to the 13th hole on Carnoustie course on 6th October, 1911, the Rev AR Taylor's ball met in the air the ball of another player, who had struck off from the 14th tee. The balls met so square – if one can use such an expression – that they rebounded a long distance straight back towards the players who hit them.

● In May, 1926, during the meeting of the Army Golfing Society at St Andrews, Colonel Howard and Lieutenant-Colonel Buchanan Dunlop, while playing in the foursomes against J Rodger and J Mackie, hit full iron shots for the seconds to the 16th green. Each thought he had to play his ball first, and hidden by a bunker the players struck their balls simultaneously. The balls, going towards the hole about 20 yards from the pin and five feet in the air, met with great force and dropped either side of the hole five yards apart.

● In 1972, before a luncheon celebrating the centenary of the Ladies' Section of Royal Wimbledon GC, a 12-hole competition was held during which two competitors, Mrs L Champion and Mrs A McKendrick, driving from the eighth and ninth tees respectively, saw their balls collide in mid-air.

● In 1928, at Wentworth Falls, Australia, Dr Alcorn and EA Avery, of the Leura Club, were playing with the professional, E Barnes. The tee shots of Avery and Barnes at the 9th hole finished on opposite sides of the fairway. Unknown to each other, both players hit their seconds (chip shots) at the same time. Dr Alcorn, standing at the pin, suddenly saw two balls approaching the hole from different angles. They met in the air and then dropped into the hole.

● At Rugby, 1931, playing in a 4-ball match, H Fraser pulled his drive from the 10th tee in the direction of the ninth tee. Simultaneously a club member, driving from the ninth tee, pulled his drive. The tees were about 350 yards apart. The two balls collided in mid-air.

● Two golf balls, being played in opposite directions, collided in flight over Longniddry Golf Course on 27th June, 1953. Immediately after Stewart Elder, of Longniddry, had driven from the third tee, another ball, which had been pulled off line from the second fairway, which runs alongside the third, struck his ball about 20 feet above the ground. SJ Fleming, of Tranent, who was playing with Elder, heard a loud crack and thought Elder's ball had exploded. The balls were found undamaged about 70 yards apart.

Three and Two Balls Dislodged by One Shot

● In 1934 on the short 3rd hole (now the 13th) of Olton Course, Warwickshire, JR Horden, a scratch golfer of the club, sent his tee shot into long wet grass a few feet over the back of the green. When he played an *explosion* shot three balls dropped on to the putting green, his own and two others.

● AM Chevalier, playing at Hale, Cheshire, March, 1935, drove his ball into a grass bunker, and when he reached it there was only part of it showing. He played the shot with a niblick and to his amazement not one but three balls shot into the air. They all dropped back into the bunker and came to rest within a foot of each other. Then came another surprise. One of the *finds* was of the same manufacture and bore the same number as the ball he was playing with.

● Playing to the 9th hole, at Osborne House Club, Isle of Wight, George A Sherman lost his ball which had sunk out of sight on the sodden fairway. A few weeks later, playing from the same tee, his ball again was plugged, only the top showing. Under a local rule he lifted his ball to place it, and exactly under it lay the ball he had lost previously.

Balls in Strange Places

● Playing at the John O' Gaunt Club, Sutton, near Biggleswade (Bedfordshire), a member drove a ball which did not touch the ground until it reached London – over 40 miles away. The ball landed in a vegetable lorry which was passing the golf course and fell out of a package of cabbages when they were unloaded at Covent Garden, London.

● In the English Open Amateur Stroke Play at Moortown in 1974, Nigel Denham, a Yorkshire County player, in the first round saw his overhit second shot to the 18th green bounce up some steps into the clubhouse. His ball went through an open door, ricochetted off a wall and came to rest in the men's bar, 20 feet from the windows. As the clubhouse was not out of bounds Denham decided to play the shot back to the green and opened a window 4 feet by 2 feet through which he pitched his ball to 12 feet from the flag. (Several weeks later the R & A declared that Denham should have been penalised two shots for opening the window. The clubhouse was an immovable obstruction and no part of it should have been moved.)

● In the Open Championship at Sandwich, 1949, Harry Bradshaw, Kilcroney, Dublin, at the 5th hole in his second round, drove into the rough and found his ball inside a beer bottle with the neck and shoulder broken off and four sharp points sticking up. Bradshaw, if he had treated the ball as in an unplayable lie might have been involved in a disqualification, so he decided to play it where it lay. With his blaster he smashed the bottle and sent the ball about 30 yards. The hole, a par 4, cost him 6.

● Kevin Sharman of Woodbridge GC hit a low, very straight drive at the club's 8th hole in 1979. After some minutes' searching, his ball was found embedded in a plastic sphere on top of the direction post.

● On the Dublin Course, 16th July, 1936, in the Irish Open Championship, AD Locke, the South African, played his tee shot at the 100-yard 12th hole, but the ball could not be found on arrival on the green. The marker removed the pin and it was discovered that the ball had been entangled in the flag. It dropped near the edge of the hole and Locke holed the short putt for a *birdie* two.

● On a London course a player found his ball inside a derelict boot.

● While playing a round on the Geelong Golf Club Course, Australia, Easter, 1923, Captain Charteris topped his tee shot to the short 2nd hole, which lies over a creek with deep and steep clay banks. His ball came to rest on the near slope of the creek bank. He elected to play the ball as it lay, and took his niblick. After the shot, the ball was nowhere to be seen. It was afterwards found embedded in a mass of gluey clay stuck fast to the face of the niblick. It could not be shaken off. Charteris did what was afterwards approved by the R&A, cleaned the ball and dropped it behind without penalty.

● In October, 1929, at Blackmoor Golf Club, Bordon, Hants, a player driving from the first tee holed out his ball in the chimney of a house some 120 yards distant and some 40 yards out of bounds on the right. The owner and his wife were sitting in front of the fire when they heard a rattle in the chimney and were astonished to see a golf ball drop into the fire.

● A similar incident occurred in an inter-club match between Musselburgh and Lothianburn at Prestongrange in 1938 when a member of the former team hooked his ball at the 2nd hole and gave it up for lost. To his amazement a woman emerged from one of the houses adjacent to this part of the course and handed back the ball which she said had come down the chimney and landed on a pot which was on the fire.

● In July, 1955, J Lowrie, starter at the Eden Course, St Andrews, witnessed a freak shot. A visitor drove from the first tee just as a north-bound train was passing. He sliced the shot and the ball disappeared through an open window of a passenger compartment. Almost immediately the ball emerged again, having been thrown back on to the fairway by a man in the compartment, who waved a greeting which presumably indicated that no one was hurt.

● Many balls have been hit into the pockets of spectators, stewards, other competitors and even the players' own pockets. They have also been found in trouser turn-ups and in the folds of sweaters and waterproofs.

● At Coombe Wood Golf Club a player hit a ball towards the 16th green where it landed in the vertical exhaust of a tractor which was mowing the fairway. The greenkeeper was somewhat surprised to find a temporary loss of power in the tractor. When sufficient compression had built up in the exhaust system, the ball was forced out with tremendous velocity, hit the roof of a house nearby, bounced off and landed some three feet from the pin on the green.

● There have been many occasions when misdirected shots have finished in strange places after an unusual line of flight and bounce. At Ashford, Middlesex, John Miller, aged 69, hit his tee shot out of bounds at the 12th hole (237 yards). It struck a parked car, passed through a copse, hit more cars, jumped a canopy, flew through the clubhouse kitchen window, finishing in a cooking stock-pot, without once touching the ground. Mr Miller had previously done the hole-in-one on four occasions.

Balls Hit to and from Great Heights

● In 1798 two Edinburgh golfers undertook to drive a ball over the spire of St Giles' Cathedral, Edinburgh, for a wager. Mr Sceales, of Leith, and Mr Smellie, a printer, were each allowed six shots and succeeded in sending the balls well over the weather-cock, a height of more than 160 feet from the ground.

● Some years later Donald McLean, an Edinburgh lawyer, won a substantial bet by driving a ball over the Melville Monument in St Andrew Square, Edinburgh – height, 154 feet.

● Tom Morris in 1860, at the famous bridge of Ballochmyle, stood in the quarry beneath and, from a stick elevated horizontally, attempted to send golf balls over the bridge. He could raise them only to the pathway, 400 feet high, which was in itself a great feat with the gutta ball.

● Captain Ernest Carter, on 28th September, 1922, drove a ball from the roadway at the 1st tee on Harlech Links against the wall of Harlech Castle. The embattlements are 200 feet over the level of the roadway, and the point where the ball struck the embattlements was 180 yards from the point where the ball was teed. Captain Carter, who was laid odds of £100 to £1, used a baffy.

● In 1896 Freddie Tait, then a subaltern in the Black Watch, drove a ball from the Rookery, the highest building on Edinburgh Castle, in a match against a brother officer to hole out in the fountain in Princes Street Gardens 350 feet below and about 300 yards distant.

● Prior to the 1977 Lâncome Tournament in Paris, Arnold Palmer hit three balls from the second stage of the Eiffel Tower, over 300 feet above ground. The longest was measured at 403 yards. One ball was hooked and hit a bus but no serious damage was done as all traffic had been stopped for safety reasons.

● Long drives have been made from mountain peaks, across the gorge at Victoria Falls, from the Pyramids, high buildings in New York, and from many other similar places. As an illustration of such freakish *drives* a member of the New York Rangers' Hockey Team from the top of Mount Edith Cavell, 11,033 feet high, drove a ball which struck the Ghost Glacier 5,000 feet below and bounced off the rocky ledge another 1,000 feet – a total drop of 2,000 yards. Later, in June, 1968, from Pikes Peak, Colorado (14,110 feet), Arthur Lynskey hit a ball which travelled 200 yards horizontally but 2 miles vertically.

Remarkable Shots

● Remarkable shots are to be numbered as the grains of sand; around every 19th hole, legends are recalled of astounding shots. One shot is commemorated by a memorial tablet at the 17th hole at the Lytham and St Annes Club. It was made by Bobby Jones in the final round of the Open Championship in 1926. He was partnered by Al Watrous, another American player. They had been running neck and neck and at the end of the third round, Watrous was just leading Jones with 215 against 217. At the 16th Jones drew level then on the 17th he drove into a sandy lie in broken ground. Watrous reached the green with his second. Jones took a mashie-iron (the equivalent to a No. 4 iron today) and hit a magnificent shot to the green to get his 4. This remarkable recovery unnerved Watrous, who 3-putted, and Jones, getting another 4 at the last hole against 5, won his first Open Championship with 291 against Watrous' 293. The tablet is near the spot where Jones played his second shot.

● Arnold Palmer (USA), playing in the second round of the Australian Wills Masters tournament at Melbourne, in October, 1964, hooked his second shot at the 9th hole high into the fork of a gum tree. Climbing 20 feet up the tree, Palmer, with the head of his No. 1 iron reversed, played a *hammer* stroke and knocked the ball some 30 yards forward, followed by a brilliant chip to the green and a putt.

● In the foursome during the Ryder Cup at Moortown in 1929, Joe Turnesa hooked the American side's second shot at the last hole behind the marquee adjoining the clubhouse, Johnny Farrel then pitched the ball over the marquee on to the green only feet away from the pin and Turnesa holed out for a 4.

● In 1922, Peter Robertson, Braid Hills, Edinburgh, holed the Road Hole, St Andrews (17th, Old Course) in two shots, a drive and a brassie.

● Lew Worsham, in the *World's Championship* at Tam O'Shanter, 9th August, 1953, at the last hole from a distance of 135 yards, holed a wedge shot for a two at the 410-yard hole. This incredible shot made him the winner by one stroke and gave him the greatest jackpot in golf at that time, $25,000. The difference between the first and third prizes was equivalent to £5,000.

Miscellaneous Incidents and Strange Golfing Facts

● Gary Player of South Africa was honoured by his country by having his portrait on new postage stamps which were issued on 12th December, 1976. It was the first time a specific golfer had ever been depicted on any country's postage stamps. In 1981 the US Postal Service introduced stamps featuring Bobby Jones and Babe Zaharias. They are the first golfers to be thus honoured by the United States.

● Jack McMillan, Head Greenkeeper at Sunningdale, has five sons, each of whom is following his father. All are Head Greenkeepers: Stewart McMillan at Leatherhead, Bobby at Hindhead, Billy at Effingham, Ian at Hankley Common and Cameron at Liphook.

● Prior to the 1976 Curtis Cup Match, members of the British Isles and United States teams were presented to the Queen at Buckingham Palace, the first occasion this has occurred.

● In February, 1971, the first ever golf shots on the moon's surface were played by Captain Alan Shepard, commander of the Apollo 14 spacecraft. Captain Shepard hit two balls with an iron head attached to a makeshift shaft. With a one-handed swing he claimed he hit the first ball 200 yards aided by the reduced force of gravity on the moon. Subsequent findings put this distance in doubt. The second was a shank. Acknowledging the occasion the R&A sent Captain Shepard the following telegram: *Warmest congratulations to all of you on your great achievement and safe return. Please refer to Rules of Golf section on etiquette, paragraph 6, quote – before leaving a bunker a player should carefully fill up all holes made by him therein, unquote.* Shepard presented the club to the USGA Museum in 1974.

● Charles (Chick) Evans competed in every US Amateur Championship held between 1907 and 1962 by which time he was 72 years old. This amounted to 50 consecutive occasions discounting the six years of the two World Wars when the championship was not held.

● In winning the 1977 US Open at Southern Hills CC, Tulsa, Oklahoma, Hubert Green had to contend with a death threat. Coming off the 14th green in the final round, he was advised by USGA officials that a phone call had been received saying that he would be killed. Green decided that play should continue and happily he went on to win, unharmed.

● It was discovered at the 1977 USPGA Championship that the clubs with which Tom Watson had won the Open Championship and the US Masters earlier in the year were illegal, having grooves which exceeded the permitted specifications. The set he used in winning the 1975 Open Championship were then flown out to him and they too were found to be illegal. No retrospective action was taken.

● Mrs Fred Daly, wife of the former Open champion, saved the clubhouse of Balmoral GC, Belfast, from destruction when three men entered the professionals' shop on 5th August, 1976 and left a bag containing a bomb outside the shop beside the clubhouse when refused money. Mrs Daly carried the bag over to a hedge some distance away where the bomb exploded 15 minutes later. The only damage was broken windows. On the same day several hours afterwards, Dungannon GC in Co Tyrone suffered extensive damage to the clubhouse from terrorist bombs. Co Down GC, proposed venue of the 1979 home international matches suffered bomb damage in May that year and through fear for the safety of team members the 1979 matches were cancelled.

● A small plane crash-landed on the 18th fairway during the pro-am preceding the 1978 Hawaiian Open, coming to rest about 50 yards short of the 18th green where American professional Jim Simons and his amateur partners were putting.

● The Army Golfing Society and St Andrews on 21st April, 1934, played a match 200-a-side, the largest golf match ever played. Play was by foursomes. The Army won 58, St Andrews 31 and 11 were halved.

● In an issue of the PGA Official Journal in 1976, it was stated *Ladies will now be permitted full privileges of membership including sectional and national voting at Annual Meetings; be eligible for election to committees and be permitted to play in section events off the back tees with the men.*

● The government of Fiji, where the 1978 men's and women's world amateur team championships were held in 1978, refused to allow teams from South Africa to compete because of South Africa's apartheid policy.

● On the eve of the 1979 World Cup in Greece, Dale Hayes and Hugh Baiocchi, representing South Africa, were compelled to withdraw when the Greek government, on a demand from the anti-apartheid committee of the United Nations, refused permission for them to compete.

● In November, 1983, as John Gallacher (39), a 9-handicap player, was driving off at the 9th hole at Machrihanish in a winter league 4-ball

tie, a Hercules transport plane from Germany coming in to land at the adjoining RAF airfield passed overhead, and was struck by Gallacher's ball. A mark that could have been caused by a golf ball was subsequently found on the aircraft's fuselage, but Gallacher's ball was never found.

● In 1986 Alistair Risk and three colleagues on the 17th green at Brora, Sutherland, watched a cow giving birth to twin calves between the markers on the 18th tee, causing them to play their next tee shots from in front of the tee. Their application for a ruling from the R and A brought a Rules Committee reply that while technically a rule had been broken, their action was considered within the spirit of the game and there should be no penalty. The Secretary added that the Rules Committee hoped that mother and twins were doing well.

● In view of the increasing number of people crossing the road (known as Granny Clark's Wynd) which runs across the first and 18th fairways of the Old Course, St Andrews, as a right of way, the St Andrews Links committee decided in 1969 to control the flow by erecting traffic lights, with appropriate green for go, yellow for caution and red for stop. The lights are controlled from the starter's box on the first tee. Golfers on the first tee must wait until the lights turn to green before driving off and a notice has been erected at the Wynd warning pedestrians not to cross at yellow or stop.

● A traffic light for golfers was also installed in 1971 on one of Japan's most congested courses. After putting on the uphill 9th hole of the Fukuoka course in Southern Japan, players have to switch on a go-ahead signal for following golfers waiting to play their shots to the green.

● A 22-year-old professional at Brett Essex GC, Brentwood, David Moore, who was playing in the Mufulira Open in Zambia in 1976, was shot dead it is alleged by the man with whom he was staying for the duration of the tournament. It appeared his host then shot himself.

● The first round of the Amateur Championship in 1887 and again in 1953, both strangely enough at Hoylake, consisted of only one tie, all the other competitors receiving byes. The first round of the English Ladies' in 1924 and the Scottish Amateur in 1932 also consisted of only one tie.

● Patricia Shepherd has won the ladies' club championship at Turriff GC Aberdeenshire 30 consecutive times from 1959 to 1988.

● Mrs Jackie Mercer won the South African Ladies' Championship in 1979, 31 years after her first victory in the event as Miss Jacqueline Smith.

● At Geelong course, near Melbourne, Australia, while FD Walter was driving off, the strap of his wrist watch broke. The watch fell on top of the ball at the exact moment of impact. The player picked up the watch unbroken 40 yards down the fairway.

● Lee Trevino, a few days after winning the 1972 Open Championship, thereby thwarting Jack Nicklaus' attempt to win all four major championships in the one year, was knocked down and kicked during an exhibition match at Scioto CC, Ohio. Ohio is the state in which Nicklaus was born.

● After playing a tee shot at Heworth, County Durham, in 1968, Mrs Helen Paterson found her ball impaled on the peg tee.

● During the Royal and Ancient medal meeting on 25th September, 1907, a member of the Royal and Ancient drove a ball which struck the sharp point of a hatpin in the hat of a lady who was crossing the course. The ball was so firmly impaled that it remained in position. The lady was not hurt.

● At the Northwest Park course, Washington, USA in 1975, fighting broke out between the members of two 4-ball games. One group claimed the other was holding them back and the other group claimed the group behind had driven into them. Clubs were used as weapons resulting in serious injuries including a fractured skull. Police had to be called.

● John Cook, professional at Brickendon Grange, and former English Amateur champion, narrowly escaped death during an attempted coup against King Hassan of Morocco in July 1971. Cook had been playing in a tournament arranged by King Hassan, a keen golfer, and was at the King's birthday party in Rabat when rebels broke into the party demanding that the king give up his throne. Cook and many others present were taken hostage. Over 200 people were killed before King Hassan surrendered minutes before the group which included Cook was due for the firing squad.

● When playing from the 9th tee at Lossiemouth golf course in June, 1971, Martin Robertson struck a Royal Navy jet aircraft which was coming in to land at the nearby airfield. The plane was not damaged.

● At a court in Inglewood, California, in 1978, Jim Brown was convicted of beating and choking an opponent during a dispute over where a ball should have been placed on the green.

● FG Tait, at St Andrews, drove a ball through a man's hat and had to pay the owner 5/- (25p) to purchase a new one. At the end of the round he was grumbling to old Tom Morris about the cost of this particular shot, when the sage of St Andrews interrupted him: *Eh, Mr Tait, you ought to be glad it was only a new hat you had to buy, and not an oak coffin.*

● During the Northern Ireland troubles a home-made hand grenade was found in a bunker at Dungannon GC, Co Tyrone, on Sunday, 12th September, 1976.

● At Rhymney and Tredegar, South Wales, on 10th September, 1934, the hard felt hat of a pedestrian who was crossing the fairway was hit by the drive of a golfer. The man fell, but his head was only slightly grazed. The ball had gone right through the hat and was found 20 yards farther on.

● To mark the centenary of the Jersey Golf Club in 1978, the Jersey Post Office issued a set of four special stamps featuring Jersey's most famous golfer, Harry Vardon. The background of the 13p stamp was a brief biography of Vardon's career reproduced from the Golfer's Handbook.

● In 1977, William Collings tried to hit his ball over a grapefruit tree at Eldorado CC, Palm Desert, California. He hit the shot thin and the ball became embedded in a grapefruit.

● Three boys who searched a pond at Buchanan Castle GC, near Glasgow, one day in 1975, found 604 old balls which were valued at £8. However, they were charged and found guilty of stealing the balls and fined £10, £20 and £30 in court.

● Driving from the 11th tee at the Belfairs Golf Course, Leigh, on 4th September, 1935, the player heard a startled exclamation. Hurrying to investigate, he discovered that his shot, at 160 yards distance, had smashed the pipe of a man taking a stroll over the course. The ball had cut the pipe clean out of the man's mouth without hurting him.

● At the international between British and American women golfers for the Curtis Cup at Chevy Chase, Washington, USA, on 27th September, 1934, a number of State policemen stood around the first tee. They were in their shirt-sleeves, with revolvers and cartridges in their ammunition belts and handcuffs dangling from their hips.

● Forty-one-year-old John Mosley went for a round of golf at Delaware Park GC, Buffalo, New York, in July, 1972. He stepped on to the first tee and was challenged over a green fee by an official guard. A scuffle developed, a shot was fired and Mosley, a bullet in his chest, died on the way to hospital. His wife was awarded $131,250 in an action against the City of Buffalo and the guard. The guard was sentenced to $7^{1}/_{2}$ years for second-degree manslaughter.

● When three competitors in a pro-am event in 1968 in Pennsylvania were about to drive from the 16th tee, two bandits (one with pistol) suddenly emerged from the bushes, struck one of the players and robbed them of wrist watches and $300.

● A 5-hole miniature course has been built on top of a seven-storey garage at Pompano Beach, Florida.

● In the 1932 Walker Cup match at Brooklyn, Leonard Crawley succeeded in denting the cup. An errant iron shot to the 18th green hit the cup, which was on display outside the clubhouse.

● A mayor in an English Midland town at the opening ceremony of a new course had to putt on the 18th green. The unfortunate man missed the ball completely.

● There has rarely been a man who played better golf than the late Harry Vardon played in 1898 and 1899. All the same, at Wheaton, Illinois, in the American Open Championship, in 1900, which he won, he made the humiliating mistake of regarding a six-inch putt with such indifference that, in trying to knock it gaily into the hole, he missed the ball entirely, and struck his club into the ground, thus counting a stroke.

● Three golf officials appeared in court in Johannesburg, South Africa, accused of violating a 75-year-old Sunday Observance Law by staging the final round of the South African PGA championship on Sunday, 28th February, 1971. The championship should have been completed on the Saturday but heavy rain prevented any play.

● At the 11th hole at Troon in the 1962 Open Championship, Max Faulkner carelessly tapped the ball against his foot, and the hole ultimately cost him 11 strokes.

● In the Open Championship of 1876, at St Andrews, Bob Martin and David Strath tied at 176. A protest was lodged against Strath alleging he played his approach to the 17th green and struck a spectator. The Royal and Ancient ordered the replay, but Strath refused to play off the tie until a decision had been given on the protest. No decision was given and Bob Martin was declared the Champion.

● At Rose Bay, New South Wales, on 11th July, 1931, DJ Bayly MacArthur, on stepping into a bunker, began to sink. MacArthur, who weighed 14 stone, shouted for help. He was rescued when up to the armpits. He had stepped on a patch of quicksand, aggravated by excess of moisture.

● The late Bobby Cruickshank was the victim of his own jubilation in the 1934 US Open at Merion. In the 4th round while in with a chance of winning

he half-topped his second shot at the 11th hole. The ball was heading for a pond in front of the green but instead of ending up in the water it hit a rock and bounced on to the green. In his delight Cruickshank threw his club into the air only to receive a resounding blow on the head as it returned to earth.

● A dog with an infallible nose for finding lost golf balls was, in 1971, given honorary membership of the Waihi GC, Hamilton, New Zealand. The dog, called Chico, was trained to search for lost balls, to be sold back to the members, the money being put into the club funds.

● By 1980 Waddy, an 11-year-old beagle belonging to Bob Inglis, the secretary of Brokenhurst Manor GC, had found over 35,000 golf balls.

● On 6th July, 1938, N Bathie, playing on Down-field, Dundee, was about to hit an iron shot when the ball was suddenly whisked away. Then the player was spun completely round. He had been caught in the fringe of a whirlwind. The whirlwind lifted a wooden shelter 60 feet into the air and burst it into smithereens over the 11th green. A haystack was uprooted and a tree razed.

● In a match over Queen's Park, Bournemouth, Archie Compston, finding that his ball had finished in the branches of a tree, played a shot with his club at the full stretch of his arms, above his head. The result was a wonderful shot which almost reached the green.

● Donald Grant, a competitor in the Dornoch Open Amateur Tournament in 1939, cycled from London and tied for second place in the first round of the competition with 74.

● Herbert M Hepworth, Headingley, Leeds, Lord Mayor of Leeds in 1906, scored one thousand holes in 2, a feat which took him 30 years to accomplish. It was celebrated by a dinner in 1931 at the Leeds club. The first 2 of all was scored on 12th June, 1901, at Cobble Hall Course, Leeds, and the 1,000th in 1931 at Alwoodley, Leeds. Hepworth died in November, 1942.

● Fiona MacDonald was the first female to play in the Oxford and Cambridge University match at Ganton in 1986.

●Mrs Sara Gibbon won the Farnham (Surrey) Club's Grandmother's competition 48 hours after her first grand-child was born.

● Mrs Joy Traill of Kloof CC, South Africa, holed from off the green six times in a round there on 20th October, 1977 at the age of 70.

● Nineteen-year-old Ron Stutesman holed chips at five consecutive holes in a round at Orchard Hills CC, Washougal, USA in January, 1978.

● On Saturday, 12th July, 1975, 16-year-old, 3-handicap Colin Smith, of Cowal GC broke his handicap on three different courses. Playing in the Glasgow Youths' Championship at Cawder he scored 73 over the Cawder Course (SSS 71) and 70 over the Keir Course (SSS 68). Then in the evening in the Poseidon Trophy at his home club he scored 70 (SSS 70).

● At Carnoustie in the first qualifying round for the 1952 Scottish Amateur Championship a competitor drove three balls in succession out of bounds at the 1st hole and thereupon withdrew.

Strange Local Rules

● The Duke of Windsor, who played on an extraordinary variety of the world's courses, once took advantage of a local rule at Jinja in Uganda and lifted his ball from a hippo's footprint without penalty.

● Another local rule in Uganda read: *If a ball comes to rest in dangerous proximity to a crocodile, another ball may be dropped.*

● At the Glen Canyon course in Arizona a local rule provides that *If your ball lands within a club length of a rattlesnake you are allowed to move the ball.* It would be no surprise if players under these circumstances just gladly opted for the *unplayable ball* rule.

● Signs that have been seen in Africa intimate that *Elephants have right of way* and warn *You are in wild animal country.*

● The 6th hole at Koolan Island GC, Western Australia also serves as a local air strip and a local rule reads *Aircraft and vehicular traffic have right of way at all times.*

● A local rule at the RAF Waddington GC reads *When teeing off from the 2nd, right of way must be given to taxi-ing aircraft.*

Record Scoring

Open Championship

Lowest 72 Hole Aggregate
268 by Tom Watson at Turnberry in 1977.

Lowest 72 Holes
Birkdale	275	Tom Watson in 1983
Carnoustie	279	Tom Watson and Jack Newton in 1975
Hoylake	278	Roberto De Vicenzo in 1967
Lytham	277	Bob Charles and Phil Rodgers in 1963
Muirfield	271	Tom Watson in 1980
Prince's	283	Gene Sarazen in 1932
St Andrews	276	Severiano Ballesteros in 1984
Sandwich	276	B Rogers in 1981
Troon	276	Arnold Palmer in 1962 and Tom Weiskopf in 1973
Turnberry	268	Tom Watson in 1977

Lowest 18 Holes
63 by Mark Hayes at Turnberry in 1977, by Isao Aoki at Muirfield in 1980 and Greg Norman at Turnberry in 1986.

Scores of 64
Horacio Carbonetti, Muirfield	1980
Hubert Green, Muirfield	1980
Tom Watson, Muirfield	1980
Craig Stadler, Birkdale	1983
Graham Marsh, Birkdale	1983
Christy O'Connor Jr, Sandwich	1985
Severiano Ballesteros, Turnberry	1986
Rodger Davis, Muirfield	1987

Scores of 65
Henry Cotton, Sandwich	1934
Eric Brown, Lytham	1958
Leopoldo Ruiz, Lytham	1958
Peter Butler, Muirfield	1966
Christy O'Connor, Lytham	1969
Neil Coles, St Andrews	1970
Jack Nicklaus, Troon	1973
Jack Newton, Carnoustie	1975

Angel Gallardo, Turnberry	1977
Tom Watson, Turnberry (twice)	1977
Jack Nicklaus, Turnberry	1977
Tommy Horton, Turnberry	1977
Bill Longmuir, Lytham	1979
Severiano Ballesteros, Lytham	1979
Gordon Brand, Sandwich	1981
Severiano Ballesteros, Lytham	1988

Lowest 18 Holes
Birkdale	64	Craig Stadler and Graham Marsh in 1983
Carnoustie	65	Jack Newton in 1975
Hoylake	67	Roberto De Vicenzo and Gary Player in 1967
Lytham	65	Eric Brown and Leopoldo Ruiz in 1958; Christy O'Connor in 1969; Bill Longmuir and Severiano Ballesteros in 1979 and 1988
Muirfield	63	Isao Aoki in 1980
Prince's	68	Arthur Havers in 1932
St Andrews	65	Neil Coles in 1970
Sandwich	64	Christy O'Connor Jr in 1985
Troon	65	Jack Nicklaus in 1973
Turnberry	63	Mark Hayes in 1977 Greg Norman in 1986

Lowest 9 Holes
28 by Denis Durnian at Birkdale (outward half of second round in 1983.

29 by Tom Haliburton and Peter Thomson at Lytham (outward half) in 1963; by Tony Jacklin at St Andrews (outward half) in 1970; by Bill Longmuir at Lytham (outward half) in 1979; by David J Russell at Lytham (outward half) in 1988

Scores of 30
Eric Brown, St Andrews (outward half)	1957
Eric Brown, Lytham (inward half)	1958
Leopoldo Ruiz, Lytham (outward half)	1958
Phil Rodgers, Muirfield (inward half)	1966
Jimmy Kinsella, Birkdale (outward half)	1971

Lee Trevino, Muirfield (inward half) 1972
Harry Bannerman, Muirfield
(outward half) 1972
Bert Yancey, Troon (outward half) 1973
Christy O'Connor, Jr. Birkdale
(outward half) 1976
Arnold Palmer, Turnberry (inward
half) 1977
Jack Nicklaus, Lytham (outward half) 1979
Denis Watson, Muirfield (inward half) 1980
Tom Watson, Muirfield (inward half) 1980
Lee Trevino, Birkdale (outward half) 1983
Sam Torrance, St Andrews
(outward half) 1984
Christy O'Connor, Sandwich
(outward half) 1985
Tsuneyuki Nakajima, Turnberry
(inward half) 1986
Ross Drummond, Muirfield (inward half) 1987

Lowest First 36 Holes
132 by Henry Cotton at St George's in 1934.

Lowest Final 36 Holes
130 by Tom Watson at Turnberry in 1977.

Lowest 18 Holes by an Amateur
66 by Frank Stranahan at Troon in 1950.

Lowest Score in Qualifying Rounds
63 by Frank Jowle at St Andrews in 1955; by Peter Thomson at Lytham in 1958; by Maurice Bembridge at Delamere Forest in 1967; and by Malcolm Gunn at Gullane No 2 in 1972.

Lowest Qualifying Round by an Amateur
65 by Ronnie Shade at St Andrews in 1964.

Other Outstanding Scoring
In the Southern Section Qualifying competition for the Open Championship in 1926 played at Sunningdale, Bobby Jones had rounds of 68 and 66. His round of 66 (six under par) was regarded as an almost perfect round. Never over par, he missed only one green in regulation or better figures – the short 13th where he was a few yards short but achieved par with a single putt. His round consisted of 33 out, 33 in. He had 33 putts and 33 other shots, which shows the high quality of his golf through the green.

Dale Hayes of South Africa had rounds of 68 and 64 over Hesketh in the qualifying rounds for the 1971 Open Championship. Hayes at the time was aged 19 years and one week and had been a professional for only eight months.

European PGA Tour

Lowest 72 Hole Aggregate
258 (14 under par) by David Llewellyn (Wales) in 1988 AGF Biarritz Open; 259 (25 under par) by Mark McNulty (Zimbabwe) in 1987 German Open at Frankfurt.

Lowest 9 Holes
27 (9 under par) by José-María Canizares (Spain) in 1978 Swiss Open at Crans-sur-Sierre; 27 (7 under par) by Robert Lee (England) in 1985 Johnnie Walker Monte Carlo Open at Mont Agel; 27 (6 under par) by Robert Lee in 1987 Portuguese Open at Estoril.

Lowest 18 Holes
60 (11 under par) by Baldovino Dassu (Italy) in 1971 Swiss Open at Crans-sur-Sierre; 60 by David Llewellyn (Wales) in 1988 AGF Biarritz Open.

Lowest 36 Holes
125 (13 under par) by Sam Torrance (Scotland) in 1985 Johnnie Walker Monte Carlo Open at Mont Agel; 125 (13 under par) by Lu Liang Huan (Taiwan) in 1971 French Open at Biarritz; 125 (11 under par) by David Llewellyn in 1988 AGF Biarritz Open.

Lowest 54 Holes
192 (24 under par) by Anders Forbrand (Sweden) in 1987 Ebel European Masters Swiss Open at Crans-sur-Sierre.

Largest Winning Margin
17 strokes by Bernhard Langer in the 1979 Cacharel Under-25s' Championship in Nîmes.

Highest Winning Score
306 by Peter Butler (England) in 1963 Schweppes PGA Close Championship at Royal Birkdale.

Miscellaneous British

Andrew Brooks recorded a 72-hole aggregate of 259 in winning the Skol (Scotland) tournament at Williamwood in 1974.

Playing on the ladies' course (4,020 yards) at Sunningdale on 26th September, 1961, Arthur Lees, the professional there, went round in 52, 10 under par. He went out in 26 (2, 3, 3, 4, 3, 3, 3, 3, 2) and came back in 26 (2, 3, 3, 3, 2, 3, 4, 3, 3).

AE Smith, the Woolacombe Bay professional, recorded a score of 55 in a game there with a club member on 1st January, 1936. The course measured 4,248 yards. Smith went out in 29 and came back in 26 finishing with a hole-in-one at the 18th hole.

Other low scores recorded in Britain are by CC Aylmer, an English International who went round Ranelagh in 56; George Duncan, Axenfels in 56; Harry Bannerman, Banchory in 56 in 1971; Ian Connelly, Welwyn Garden City in 56 in 1972; James Braid, Hedderwick near Dunbar in 57; H Hardman, Wirral in 58; Norman Quigley, Windermere in 58 in 1937; Robert Webster, Eaglescliffe in 58, in 1970.

Harry Weetman scored 58 in a round at Croham Hurst on 30th January, 1956. The course measured 6,171 yards.

D Sewell had a round of 60 in an Alliance Meeting at Ferndown, Bournemouth, a full-size course. He scored 30 for each half and had a total of 26 putts.

In September 1986, Jeffrey Burn, handicap 1 of Shrewsbury GC scored 60 in a club competition, made up of 8 birdies, an eagle and 9 pars. He was 30 out and 30 home and no 5 on his card.

Andrew Sherborne, a 20-year-old amateur, went round Cirencester in 60 strokes.

Dennis Gray completed a round at Broome Manor, Swindon (6,906 yards, SSS 73) in the summer of 1976 in 60 (28 out, 32 in).

Playing over Aberdour on 13th June, 1936, Hector Thomson, British Amateur champion, 1936, and Jack McLean, former Scottish Amateur champion, each did 61 in the second round of an exhibition. McLean in his first round had a 63, which gave him an aggregate 124 for 36 holes.

Steve Tredinnick in a friendly match against business tycoon Joe Hyman scored a 61 over West Sussex (6,211 yards) in 1970. It included a hole-in-one at the 12th (198 yards) and a 2 at the 17th (445 yards).

Another round of 61 on a full-size course was achieved by 18-year-old Michael Jones on his home course, Worthing GC (6,274 yards) in the first round of the President's Cup in May, 1974.

In the Second City Pro-Am tournament in 1970, at Handsworth, Simon Fogarty did the second 9 holes in 27 against the par of 36.

In the second round of a 36-hole open amateur competition at Sandyhills GC on 10th September, 1978, Barclay Howard completed the last 9 holes in 27.

RH Corbett, in 1916, in the semi-final of the Tangye Cup at Mullim did 9 holes in 27 as did Dr James Stothers of Ralston over the 2,056 yards 9-hole course at Carradale, Argyll, during the summer of 1971. In each case the total was made up of nine 3s.

US Open

Lowest 72 Hole Aggregate
272 by Jack Nicklaus at Baltusrol in 1980.

Lowest 18 Holes
63 by Johnny Miller at Oakmont in 1973 in the final round and by Jack Nicklaus and Tom Weiskopf at Baltusrol in 1980, both in the first round.

Lowest 9 Holes
30 by Jimmy McHale in 1947, Arnold Palmer in 1960, Ken Venturi in 1964, Bob Charles and Tom Shaw in 1971, and Raymond Floyd in 1980.

Lowest 36 Holes
134 by Jack Nicklaus at Baltusrol in 1980.

Lowest 54 Holes
204 by Jack Nicklaus and Isao Aoki at Baltusrol in 1980.

US Professional events

Lowest 72 Hole Aggregate
257 (60, 68, 64, 65) by Mike Souchak in the 1955 Texas Open.

Lowest 18 Holes
59 by Sam Snead in the third round of the Greenbrier Open (Sam Snead Festival) at White Sulphur Springs, West Virginia in 1959 and by Al Geiberger in the second round of the 1977 Danny Thomas Memphis Classic at Colonial CC when preferred lies were in operation.

Lowest 9 Holes
27 by Mike Souchak in the 1955 Texas Open and by Andy North in the 1975 BC Open.

Lowest First 36 Holes
126 by Tommy Bolt in 1954. (On the US mini-tour a 36-hole score of 123 was achieved by Bob Risch in the 1978 Mesa Centennial Open.)

Lowest Final 36 Holes
122 by Sam Snead in the Greenbrier Open (Sam Snead Festival) in 1959. On the USPGA Tour it is 125 by Ron Streck in the 1978 Texas Open.

Lowest 54 Holes
189 by Chandler Harper in the 1954 Texas Open (last three rounds).

192 by Bob Gilder in the 1982 Westchester Classic (first three rounds).

Largest Winning Margin
16 strokes by J Douglas Edgar in the 1919 Canadian Open Championship and by Bobby Locke in the 1948 Chicago Victory National Championship.

Miscellaneous USA

The lowest scores recorded for 18 holes in America are 55 by EF Staugaard in 1935 over the 6,419 yards Montebello Park, California, and 55 by Homero Blancas in 1962 over the 5,002 yards Premier course in Longview, Texas. Staugaard in his round had 2 eagles, 13 birdies and 3 pars.

Equally outstanding is a round of 58 (13 under par) achieved by a 10 year old boy, Douglas Beecher, on 6th July, 1976 at Pitman CC, New Jersey. The course measured 6,180 yards from the back tees, and the middle tees, off which Douglas played, were estimated by the club professional to reduce the yardage by under 180 yards.

In 1941 at a course in Portsmouth, Virginia, measuring 6,100 yards, Chandler Harper scored 58.

Jack Nicklaus in an exhibition match at Breakers Club, Palm Beach, California, in 1973 scored 59 over the 6,200 yards course.

Ben Hogan, practising on a 7,006-yard course at Palm Beach, Florida, went round in 61 – 11 under par.

The lowest 9-hole score in America is 25, held jointly by Bill Burke over the second half of the 6,384 yards Normandie CC, St Louis in May, 1970 at the age of 29; by Daniel Cavin who had seven 3s and two 2s on the par 36 Bill Brewer Course, Texas in September, 1959; and by Douglas Beecher over the second half of Pitman CC, New Jersey on 6th July, 1976 at the amazingly young age of 13. The back 9 holes of the Pitman course measured 3,150 yards (par 35) from the back tees, but even though Douglas played off the middle tees, the yardage was still over 3,000 yards for the 9 holes. He scored 8 birdies and 1 eagle.

Horton Smith scored 119 for two consecutive rounds in winning the Catalina Open in California in December, 1928. The course, however, measured only 4,700 yards.

National Opens – excluding Europe and USA

Lowest 72 Hole Aggregate
255 by Peter Tupling in the Nigerian Open at Lagos, 1981.

Lowest 36 Hole Aggregate
124 (18 under par) by Sandy Lyle in the 1978 Nigerian Open at Ikoyi GC, Lagos. (Lyle was in his first year as a professional.)

Lowest 18 Holes
59 by Gary Player in the second round of the 1974 Brazilian Open at Gavea GC (6,185 yards), Rio de Janeiro.

Professional Events – excluding GB and USA

Lowest 72 Hole Aggregate
260 (66, 62, 69, 63) by Bob Charles in the Spalding Masters at Tauranga, New Zealand, in 1969.

Lowest 18 Hole Aggregate
60 by Australian Billy Dunk at Merewether, NSW in November, 1970.

Lowest 9 Hole Aggregate
27 by American Bill Brask at Tauranga in the New Zealand PGA in 1976.

Miscellaneous – excluding GB and USA

Tony Jacklin won the 1973 Los Lagartos Open with an aggregate of 261, 27 under par.

Henry Cotton in 1950 had a round of 56 at Monte Carlo (29 out, 27 in).

In a Pro-Am tournament prior to the 1973 Nigerian Open, British professional David Jagger went round in 59.

Max Banbury recorded a 9-hole score of 26 at Woodstock, Ontario, playing in a competition in 1952.

Women

The lowest score recorded on a full-size course by a woman is 62 by Mary (Mickey) Wright of Dallas, Texas. This was achieved on the Hogan Park course (6,286 yards) at Midland, Texas, in November, 1964. It was equalled by 16-year-old Rae Rothfelder on 9th July, 1978 at Diamond Oak G&CC, Fort Worth, Texas, a course measuring 6,124 yards.

The lowest 72-hole score on the US Ladies' PGA circuit is 271 by Hollis Stacy in the 1977 Rail Muscular Dystrophy.

The lowest 9-hole score on the US Ladies' PGA circuit is 29, first achieved by Marlene Bauer Hagge in 1971 and equalled by Carol Mann (1975), Pat Bradley (1978 and again in 1979), Alexandra Reinhardt (1978), and Silvia Bertolaccini (1979).

The lowest score for 36 holes on the USLPGA circuit is 131 achieved by Kathy Martin in the 1976 Birmingham Classic and by Silvia Bertolaccini in the 1977 Lady Keystone Open.

The lowest 9-hole score on the WPGA circuit is 30 by Susan Moon at Valbonne in 1979.

In the Women's World Team Championship in Mexico in 1966, Mrs Belle Robertson, playing for the British team, was the only player to break 70. She scored 69 in the third round.

At Westgate-on-Sea GC (measuring 5,002 yards), Wanda Morgan scored 60 in an open tournament in 1929.

Since scores cannot properly be taken in match play no stroke records can be made in match play events. Nevertheless we record here two outstanding examples of low scoring in the finals of national championships. Mrs

Catherine Lacoste de Prado is credited with a score of 62 in the first round of the 36-hole final of the 1972 French Ladies' Open Championship at Morfontaine. She went out in 29 and came back in 33 on a course measuring 5,933 yards.

In the final of the English Ladies' Championship at Woodhall Spa in 1954, Frances Stephens (later Mrs Smith) did the first nine holes against Elizabeth Price (later Mrs Fisher) in 30. It included a hole-in-one at the 5th. The nine holes measured 3,280 yards.

Amateur National Championships

The following examples of low scoring cannot be regarded as genuine stroke play records since they took place in match play. Nevertheless they are recorded here as being worthy of note.

Michael Bonallack in beating D Kelley in the final of the English championship in 1968 at Ganton did the first 18 holes in 61 with only one putt under two feet conceded. He was out in 32 and home in 29. The par of the course was 71.

Charles McFarlane, playing in the fourth round of the Amateur Championship at Sandwich in 1914 against Charles Evans did the first nine holes in 31, winning by 6 and 5.

This score of 31 at Sandwich was equalled on several occasions in later years there. Then, in 1948, Richard Chapman of America went out in 29 in the fourth round eventually beating Hamilton McInally, Scottish Champion in 1937, 1939 and 1947, by 9 and 7.

In the fourth round of the Amateur Championship at Hoylake in 1953, Harvie Ward, the holder, did the first nine holes against Frank Stranahan in 32. The total yardage for the holes was 3,474 yards and included one hole of 527 yards and five holes over 400 yards. Ward won by one hole.

Francis Ouimet in the first round of the American Amateur Championship in 1932 against George Voigt did the first nine holes in 30. Ouimet won by 6 and 5.

Low scores by Amateurs in Open competitions

The 1970 South African Dunlop Masters Tournament was won by an amateur, John Fourie, with a score of 266, 14 under par. He led from start to finish with rounds of 65, 68, 65, 68, finally winning by six shots from Gary Player.

Jim Ferrier, Manly, won the New South Wales championship at Sydney in 1935 with 266. His rounds were: 67, 65, 70, 64, giving an aggregate 16 strokes better than that of the runner-up. At the time he did this amazing score Ferrier was 20 years old and an amateur.

Most holes below par

EF Staugaard in a round of 55 over the 6,419 yards Montbello Park, California, in 1935, had 2 eagles, 13 birdies and 3 pars.

American Jim Clouette scored 14 birdies in a round at Longhills GC, Arkansas, in 1974. The course measured 6,257 yards.

Jimmy Martin in his round of 63 in the Swallow-Penfold at Stoneham in 1961 had 1 eagle and 11 birdies.

In the Ricarton Rose Bowl at Hamilton, Scotland, in August, 1981, Wilma Aitken, a women's amateur internationalist, had 11 birdies in a round of 64, including 9 consecutive birdies from the 3rd to the 11th.

Mrs Donna Young scored 9 birdies and 1 eagle in one round in the 1975 Colgate European Women's Open.

Consecutive holes below par

Lionel Platts had 10 consecutive birdies from the 8th to 17th holes at Blairgowrie GC during a practice round for the 1973 Sumrie Better-Ball tournament.

Roberto De Vicenzo in the Argentine Centre of the Republic Championship in April, 1974 at the Cordoba GC, Villa Allende, broke par at each of the first 9 holes. (By starting his round at the 10th hole they were in fact the second 9 holes played by Vicenzo.) He had 1 eagle (at the 7th hole) and 8 birdies. The par for the 3,602 yards half was 37, completed by Vicenzo in 27.

Nine consecutive holes under par have been recorded by Claude Harmon in a friendly match over Winged Foot GC, Mamaroneck, NY, in 1931; by Les Hardie at Eastern GC, Melbourne, in April, 1934; by Jimmy Smith at McCabe GC, Nashville, Tenn, in 1969; by Jim DeForest on a 9-hole sand-green course at New Salem, North Dakota, in August, 1974; by 13-year-old Douglas Beecher, in 1976, at Pitman CC, New Jersey; and by Rick Sigda at Greenfield CC, Mass, in 1979.

TW Egan in winning the East of Ireland Championship in 1962 at Baltray had 8 consecutive birdies (2nd to 9th) in the third round.

On the USPGA circuit 8 consecutive holes below par have been achieved twice – by Bob Goalby in the 1961 St Petersburg Open, and by Fuzzy Zoeller in the 1976 Quad Cities Open.

Seven successive birdies have been recorded by Peter Thomson at Wentworth in the 1958 Dunlop; by Bernard Hunt at Wentworth in the

1958 Daks; by Angel Miguel at Wentworth (East) in the 1960 Daks; by Peter Butler at Fulford in the 1971 Benson and Hedges; by Peter Townsend at Wentworth in 1974 Viyella PGA; and by Brian Waites at the RAC in the 1980 Bob Hope Classic.

The United States Ladies' PGA record is 7 consecutive holes below par achieved by Carol Mann in the Borden Classic at Columbus, Ohio in 1975.

Miss Wilma Aitken recorded 9 successive birdies (from the 3rd to the 11th) in the 1981 Ricarton Rose Bowl.

Low scoring rarities

In the qualifying rounds of the 1956 Dunlop Tournament at Sunningdale, Arthur Lees, the resident professional, played 27 consecutive holes without taking more than a 4 at any hole. His first round was 65 and his second 69.

At Standerton GC, South Africa, in May, 1937, FF Bennett, playing for Standerton against Witwatersrand University, did the 2nd hole, 110 yards, in three 2s and a 1. Standerton is a 9-hole course, and in the match Bennett had to play four rounds.

In 1973 in the 36-hole Club Championship at Mufulira GC, Zambia, Amateur HG McQuillan, completed two rounds in 65 and 66 for a winning score of 131.

In 1957 a four-ball comprising HJ Marr, E Stevenson, C Bennett and WS May completed the 2nd hole (160 yards) in the grand total of 6 strokes. Marr and Stevenson both holed in 1 while Bennett and May both made 2.

The old Meadow Brook Club of Long Island, USA, had five par 3 holes and George Low in a round there in the 1950s scored 2 at each of them.

In a friendly match on a course near Chicago in 1971, assistant professional Tom Doty (23 years) had a remarkable low run over four consecutive holes: 4th (500 yards) 2; 5th (360 yards, dogleg) 1; 6th (175 yards) 1; 7th (375 yards) 2.

RW Bishop, playing in the Oxley Park, July medal competition in 1966, scored three consecutive 2s. They occurred at the 12th, 13th and 14th holes which measured 151, 500 and 136 yards respectively.

In the 1959 PGA Close Championship at Ashburnham, Bob Boobyer scored five 2s in one of the rounds.

American Art Wall scored three consecutive 2s in the first round of the US Masters in 1974. They were at the 4th, 5th and 6th holes, the par of which was 3, 4 and 3.

Nine consecutive 3s have been recorded by RH Corbett in 1916 in the semi-final of the Tangye Cup; by Dr James Stothers of Ralston GC over the 2,056 yards 9-hole course at Carradale,

Argyll during the summer of 1971; by Irish internationalist Brian Kissock in the Homebright Open at Carnalea GC, Bangor in June, 1975; and by American club professional Ben Toski.

The most consecutive 3s in a British PGA event is seven by Eric Brown in the Dunlop at Gleneagles (Queen's Course) in 1960.

Hubert Green scored eight consecutive 3s in a round in the 1980 US Open.

The greatest number of 3s in one round in a British PGA event is 11 by Brian Barnes in the 1977 Skol Lager tournament at Gleneagles.

Fewest putts

The lowest known number of putts in one round is 14, achieved by Colin Collen-Smith in a round at Betchworth Park, Dorking in June, 1947. He single-putted 14 greens and chipped into the hole on four occasions. Professional Richard Stanwood in a round at Riverside GC, Pocatello, Idaho on 17th May, 1976 took 15 putts, chipping into the hole on five occasions. Several instances of 16 putts in one round have been recorded in friendly games.

For 9 holes, the fewest putts is 5 by Ron Stutesman for the first 99 holes at Orchard Hills G&CC, Washington, USA in 1978.

Walter Hagen in nine consecutive holes on one occasion took only seven putts. He holed long putts on seven greens and chips at the other two holes.

In competitive stroke rounds in Britain and Ireland, the lowest known number of putts in one round is 18, in a medal round at Portpatrick Dunskey GC, Wilmslow GC professional Fred Taggart is reported to have taken 20 putts in one round of the 1934 Open Championship. Padraigh Hogan (Elm Park), when competing in the Junior Scratch Cup at Carlow in 1976, took only 20 putts in a round of 67.

The fewest putts in a British PGA event is believed to be 22 by Bill Large in a qualifying round over Moor Park High Course for the 1972 Benson and Hedges Match Play.

Overseas, outside the United States of America, the fewest putts is 19 achieved by Robert Wynn (GB) in a round in the 1973 Nigerian Open and by Mary Bohen (US) in the final round of the 1977 South Australian Open at Adelaide.

The USPGA record for fewest putts in one round is 18, held by Sam Trahan in the 4th round of the 1979 Philadelphia Classic. For 9 holes the USPGA record is 8, by Jim Colbert in the 1967 Greater Jacksonville Open.

The fewest putts recorded for a 72-hole USPGA tournament is 94 by George Archer in the 1980 Heritage Classic.

The fewest putts recorded by a woman is 17, by Joan Joyce in the Lady Michelob tournament, Georgia in May, 1982.

Index

Aachen, 665
Aalborg, 651
Aarhus, 651
Abbey Hill, 496
Abbey Leix, 593
Abbey Park G & CC, 519
Abbeydale, 576
Abbotsley, 497
Abbotsley Golf Range, 636
Aberdare, 632
Aberdour, 603
Aberdovey, 631
Aberfeldy, 626
Aberfoyle, 455, 624
Abergele and Pensarn, 628
Aberlady, 610
Abernethy, 609
Abersoch, 631
Aberystwyth, 629
Aboyne, 605
Abridge G & CC, 511
Accrington & District, 530
Achensee, 647
Achill Island, 594
Acquabona, 679
Adare Manor, 593
The Addington, 558
Addington Court, 558
Addington Palace, 558
Adriatic GC Cervia, 679
Aero Club de Santiago, 688
Aero Club de Vigo, 688
Aero Club de Zaragoza, 691
Afantou, 677
Agen Bon-Encontre, 663
Ågesta, 694
Airdrie, 619
Airlinks, 544
Aix-les-Bains, 655
Aix Marseille, 662
Ajoncs d'Or, 655
Akureyri, 677
Alands, 653
Albarella, 681
Albatross, 692
Albon, 657
Aldeburgh, 556
Aldenham G & CC, 520
Alderley Edge, 499
Alderney, 498
Aldwark Manor, 574
Alexandra Park, 619
Alfreton, 505

Algäuer G & LC, 675
Alingasås, 698
Allendale, 549
Allerton Park, 541
Allestree Park, 505
Alloa, 600
Almerimar, 687
Almhult, 696
Alness, 609
Alnmouth, 549
Alnmouth Village, 549
Alnwick, 549
Aloha, 689
Alpino di Stresa, 680
Alresford, 444, 515
Alsager G & CC, 554
Alston Moor, 503
Alt, 530
Altenhof, 667
Alto, 685
Alton, 516
Altötting-Burghausen, 670
Altrincham Municipal, 536
Alva, 600
Alwoodley, 578
Alyth, 626
Am Reichswald, 672
Amateur Review, 16–18
Amiens, 659
Ampfield Par Three, 516
Ampleforth College, 574
Amsterdamse, 682
L'Ancresse, 498
An der Goehrde, 667
An der Pinnau, 667
Andover, 516
Ängelholm, 692
Angers, 656
Anglesey, 632
Ångsö, 695
Annanhill, 615
Ansbach, 672
Anstruther, 455, 603
Antrim clubs and courses, 583–4
Appleby, 503
Apsley Guise & Woburn Sands, 493
Aquarius, 525
Arbroath, 624
Arcachon, 654
architects and constructors, golf course, 812
Arcot Hall, 549
Les Arcs, 655

Ardee, 594
Ardeer, 615
Ardglass, 588
L'Ardilouse, 654
Ärila, 695
Arkley, 520
Arklow, 598
Army Golf Club, 516
Aroeira, 686
Arosa, 700
Arrowe Park, 541
Arvika, 699
Aschaffenburg, 665
Ashbourne, 505
Ashburnham, 629
Ashdown Forest Hotel, 563
Ashford, 525
Ashford Manor, 544
Ashley Wood, 508
Ashridge, 520
Ashton & Lea, 530
Ashton-in-Makerfield, 541
Ashton-on-Mersey, 536
Ashton-under-Lyne, 536
Asiago, 679
Askernish, 627
Askersund, 695
Asserbo, 652
Association Européenne de Golf, 812
Association of Golf Club Secretaries, 810
Association of Golf Writers, 391, 811
Astbury, 499
Atalaya Park G & CC, 689
Athenry, 591
Atherstone, 568
Athlone, 596
Athy, 592
Åtvidaberg, 698
Auchenblae, 608
Auchenharvie, 616
Auchenharvie Driving Centre, 642
Auchmill, 605
Auchterarder, 626
Auchterderran, 603
Auf der Wendlohe, 667
Augsburg, 670
Aulangon, 653
Aura Golf, 653
Australia/New Zealand Tour results, 94–6
Austerfield Park, 576

Austerfield Park Driving Range, 641
Austrian clubs and courses, 647–8
Avesta, 696
Avon clubs and courses, 466, 492–3
Avro, 499
awards, annual, 145–7
Axe Cliff, 506
Aycliffe, 510
Baberton, 612
Bäckavattnet, 698
Backworth, 567
Bacup, 530
Bad Bramstedt, 667
Bad Driburg, 669
Bad Herrenalb-Bernbach, 675
Bad Kissingen, 665
Bad Kleinkirchheim-Reichenau, 647
Bad Mergentheim, 665
Bad Nauheim, 666
Bad Neuenahr GLC, 673
Bad Ragaz, 700
Bad Salzdetfurth-Hildesheim, 669
Bad Salzuflen G & LC, 669
Bad Tölz, 670
Bad Wildungen, 666
Bad Wörishofen, 670
Baden-Baden, 675
Baden-Hills, 675
Badgastein, 647
Badgemore Park, 552
Bagnoles-de-l'Orne, 660
Baildon, 578
Bakewell, 505
Bala, 631
Bala Lake, 631
Balbirnie Park, 603
Balbriggan, 590
Bâle, 658
Balgove, 603
Ballaghaderreen, 596
Ballards Gore, 511
Ballater, 605
Ballina, 594
Ballinamore, 593
Ballinascorney, 590
Ballinasloe, 591
Ballingry, 603
Ballinrobe, 595
Ballochmyle, 616
Ballybofey & Stranorlar, 587

Ballybunion, 592
Ballycastle, 454, 583
Ballyclare, 583
Ballyearl Golf Centre, 584, 641
Ballyhaunis, 595
Ballyliffin, 587
Ballymena, 583
Ballymote, 596
Balmoral (Belfast), 584
Balmore, 600
Balnagask, 605
Baltinglass, 598
Bamberg, 672
Bamburgh Castle, 549
Banbridge, 588
Banchory, 608
Bandon, 586
Bangor (Co Down), 588
Banstead Downs, 444, 558
Bantry Park, 586
Barbaroux, 662
Barberán, 689
Barganiza, 690
Bargoed, 632
Barlassina CC, 678
Barlaston, 554
Barnard Castle, 510
Barnehurst, 525
Barnham Broom Hotel, 546
Barnsley, 576
Baron Hill, 632
La Barouge, 663
Barrow, 503
Barrow Hills, 558
Barseback, 692
Barshaw, 622
Barton-on-Sea, 516
Basildon, 511
Basingstoke, 516
Basingstoke Hospitals, 516
Bass Rock, 610
Båstad, 692
La Bastide-du-Roy, 662
Batchwood Hall, 520
Bath, 492
Bathgate, 614
La Baule, 656
Les Baux-de-Provence, 663
Bawburgh, 546
Baxenden & District, 530
Bayerwald G & LC, 672
Beacon Park, 536
Beaconsfield, 496
Beadlow Manor Hotel G & CC, 493
Beamish Park, 510
Bearsden, 618
Bearsted, 525
Bearwood, 494
Beau Desert, 554
Beauchief Municipal, 576
Beauport Park, 564
Beauvallon-Grimaud, 663
Beaverstown, 590
Beccles, 556

Beckenham Place Park, 525
Bedale, 574
Bedford & County, 493
Bedfordshire clubs and courses, 468, 493–4
Bedfordshire GC, 493
Bedinge, 692
Bedlingtonshire, 549
Beech Park, 590
Beeston Fields, 550
Beith, 616
Belfairs, 511
Belfast clubs and courses, 584–5
The Belfry, 569
Belgian clubs and courses, 648–50
Belhus Park Leisure Complex, 637
Belhus Park Municipal, 511
Bellavista, 690
Belleisle, 616
Bellingham, 549
Bellshill, 620
Belmont House, 519
Belmullet, 595
Belton Park, 444, 535
Belturbet, 585
Belvoir Park, 584
Ben Rhydding, 578
Bentham, 574
Bentley G & CC, 511
Berchtesgaden, 670
Berendonck, 683
Bergamo L'Albenza, 678
Bergen, 685
Bergisch-Land, 673
Berkhamsted, 445, 520
Berkshire clubs and courses, 464, 494–6
Berkshire GC, 494
Berlin G & CC, 665
Berlin-Wannsee, 665
Berwick-upon-Tweed, 445, 549
Besançon, 655
Betchworth Park, 558
Betws-y-Coed, 631
Beuerberg, 670
Beverley & East Riding, 523
Bexley Heath, 526
Biarritz, 663
Bidston, 541
Bielefeld, 673
Biella 'Le Betulle', 680
Bigbury, 506
Biggar, 620
La Bilbaina, 690
Billeruds, 699
Billingen, 698
Billingham, 501
Bingley (St Ives), 578
Birch Grove, 511
Birchwood, 499
Birley Wood, 576
Birr, 596

Birstall, 533
Birtley (Portobello), 567
Bishop Auckland, 510
Bishopbriggs, 620
Bishopshire, 625
Bishopswood, 516
Bishop's Stortford, 520
Bitche, 658
Björkhagen, 694
Blackburn, 530
Blackbush, 595
Blackley, 536
Blacklion, 585
Blackmoor, 516
Blackpool North Shore, 530
Blackpool Park, 530
Blackwell, 519
Blackwell Grange, 510
Blackwood, 630
Blainroe, 598
Blair Atholl, 626
Blairbeth, 620
Blairgowrie, 626
Blairmore & Strone, 615
Blankney, 535
Bled, 701
Bloxwich, 569
Blue Circle, 505
Blumisberg, 699
Blyth, 549
Boat-of-Garten, 609
Bochum, 673
Boden, 691
Bodensee Weissensberg, 675
Bodenstown, 592
Bogliaco, 679
Bognor Regis, 565
Bohunt Manor, 516
Boisgelin, 655
Bokskogens, 692
Boldmere, 569
Boldon, 567
Bollnäs, 696
Bologna, 679
Bolton, 536
Bolton Municipal, 536
Bolton Old Links, 537
Bon Accord, 605
Bonar-Bridge & Ardgay, 610
Bondues, 659
Bonmont, 700
Bonn-Godesberg, 673
Bonnybridge, 600
Bonnyton, 622
Boothferry, 523
Bootle, 541
Borås, 698
Border Region clubs and courses, 482, 599–600
Les Bordes, 657
Borgarness, 677
Bornholm, 650
Borregaard, 685
Borris, 585
Borth & Ynyslas, 629
Boscombe, 508

Boscombe Ladies, 508
Bosjökloster, 692
El Bosque, 691
Bossenstein, 648
G & CC Bossey, 655
Boston, 535
Bothwell Castle, 620
Bournemouth & Meyrick Park, 445, 508
Bowring, 541
Boxmoor, 446, 520
Boyce Hill, 512
Boyle, 596
Boys' tournament results, 135–8, 258–62
Brabantse, 649
Brackenwood, 541
Brackley Municipal, 537
Bradford, 578
Bradford Moor, 578
Bradley Park, 578
Bradley Park Driving Range, 641
Braehead, 600
Braemar, 606
Braeside, 526
Braidhills No. 1, 612
Braidhills No. 2, 612
Braids United, 612
Braintree, 512
Bramall Park, 537
Bramhall, 499
Bramley, 558
Brampton (Talkin Tarn), 503
Bramshaw, 516
Brancepeth Castle, 510
Brand Hall, 569
Branshaw, 578
Branston, 554
Braunschweig, 669
Bray, 598
Breadsall Priory Hotel G & CC, 505
Brean, 553
Brechin Golf & Squash Club, 624
Brecon, 633
Breightmet, 537
Breitenloo, 700
Bremhill Park, 573
Brent Valley, 544
Brest-Iroise, 655
La Bretesche, 656
Brickendon Grange, 520
Bridge of Allan, 600
Bridgnorth, 446, 552
Bridlington, 523
Bridport & West Dorset, 508
Bright Castle, 588
Brighton & Hove, 564
Brigode, 659
Brinkworth, 573
Las Brisas, 689
Bristol & Clifton, 492
British and International Golf Greenkeepers' Association, 812
British and Irish national

championships, past results, 170–85
British Army (Hohne), 669
British Association of Golf Course Architects, 794, 812
British Association of Golf Course Constructors, 812
British GC Gatow, 665
British Isles Players, 310
Bro-Balstå, 694
Broadstone, 508
Broadway, 514
Brocton Hall, 555
Brodick, 617
Broekpolder, 684
Brokenhurst Manor, 516
Bromborough, 542
Bromley, 526
Brønderslev, 651
Brookdale, 537
Brookman's Park, 520
Broome Manor, 573
Broome Manor Driving Range, 641
Broome Park, 526
Broomieknowe, 612
Brora, 610
Brough, 523
Brown Trout, 594
Bruntsfield Links Golfing Society, 612
Bryn Meadows Hotel G & CC, 632
Bryn Morfydd, 628
Brynhill, 634
Buchanan Castle, 600
Buckingham, 496
Buckinghamshire clubs and courses, 464, 496–7
Buckpool, 607
Buddon Links, 624
Bude & North Cornwall, 502
Budock Vean Hotel, 502
Builth Wells, 633
Bull Bay, 632
Bulwell Forest, 550
Buncrana, 587
Bundoran, 587
Bungay & Waveney Valley, 556
Bunsay Downs, 512
Burford, 552
Burg Overbach, 673
Burgdorf, 669
Bürgenstock, 701
Burgh Links, 610
Burghley Park, 446, 535
Burhill, 558
Burley, 516
Burnham & Berrow, 447, 554
Burnham Beeches, 496
Burnham-on-Crouch, 512
Burnley, 530
Burnside, 624
Burntisland, 603

Burntisland Golf House Club, 603
Burslem, 555
Burton on Trent, 555
Bury, 447, 537
Bury St Edmunds, 556
Bush Hill Park, 544
Bushey G & CC, 521
Bushey Golf Range, 638
Bushey Hall, 521
Bushfoot, 454, 583
Bute, 618
Buxtehude, 667
Buxton & High Peak, 505
Ca' della Nave, 681
Cabourg-Le Home, 660
Cabra Castle, 585
Caerleon, 630
Caernarfon, 631
Caerphilly, 632
Cahir Park, 596
Caird Park (1926), 624
Caird Park (1982), 624
Cairndhu, 583
Calcot Park, 494
Calderbraes, 620
Calderfields, 570
Caldwell, 622
Caledonia, 624
Caledonian, 606
Callan, 593
Callander, 455, 600
Calverley, 578
Camberley Heath, 558
Cambridgeshire clubs and courses, 468, 497–8
Cambridgeshire Moat House Hotel, 497
Cambuslang, 620
Came Down, 509
Camperdown, 624
Campo Carlo Magno, 679
Campsie, 601
El Candado, 689
Canford School, 509
Canmore, 603
Cannes, 663
Cannes-Mougins, 663
Canons Brook, 512
Cansiglio, 681
Canterbury, 526
Canwick Park, 535
Canyamel, 687
Cap d'Agde, 659
Caprington, 616
Cardiff, 634
Cardigan, 629
Cardross, 618
Carholme, 535
Carimate, 678
Carlisle, 503
Carlow, 585
Carlow clubs and courses, 585
Carlskrona, 696
Carlton Forum Golf Target Range, 639
Carluke, 620

Carlyon Bay, 502
Carmarthen, 629
Carnalea, 588
Carnoustie, 624
Carnoustie Championship, 624
Carnoustie Ladies, 625
Carnoustie Mercantile, 625
Carnwath, 620
Carradale, 615
Carrbridge, 609
Carrick Knowe, 612
Carrick-on-Shannon, 593
Carrick-on-Suir, 596
Carrickfergus, 583
Carrickmines, 589
Carrickvale, 612
Castelconturbia, 680
Castelgandolfo, 680
Castell Heights, 632
Casteljaloux, 664
Castelnaud, 664
Castiello, 690
Castle, 589
Castle Douglas, 602
Castle Eden & Peterlee, 501
Castle Fields, 578
Castle Hawk, 537
Castle Point, 512
Castlebar, 595
Castleblayney, 595
Castlecomer, 593
Castlerea, 596
Castlerock, 594
Castletown, 524
Castletroy, 593
Cathcart Castle, 622
Cathkin Braes, 620
Catterick Garrison, 574
Cavan clubs and courses, 585
Cave Castle Hotel, 523
Cavendish, 505
Cawder, 620
Ceann Sibéal, 592
centenary clubs, 444–59
Central Region clubs and courses, 486, 600–601
Cervino, 680
Chadwell Springs, 521
Chalon-sur-Saône, 657
Chamonix, 655, 656
championship conditions, 805
Champlong, 657
Channel Islands clubs and courses, 498–9
Channels, 512
Chantaco, 664
Chantilly, 661
Chapel-en-le-Frith, 505
La Chapelle, 661
Charade, 657
Charleville, 586
Charnwood Forest, 447, 533
Chartridge Park, 496
Château L'Arc, 663

Château de la Bawette, 649
Château Royal d'Ardenne, 648
Châteaublanc, 663
Châtellerault, 656
Chatham Golf Centre, 638
Chaumont-en-Vexin, 661
Cheadle, 537
Chelmsford, 512
Cherbourg, 660
Cherry Lodge, 526
Cherwell Edge, 552
Chesham & Ley Hill, 496
Cheshire clubs and courses, 476, 499–501
Cheshunt Park, 521
Chessington Golf Centre, 558, 640
Chester, 499
Chester-Le-Street, 510
Chesterfield, 505
Chesterfield Municipal, 505
Chesterton, 552
Chestfield (Whitstable), 526
Chevin, 505
Chevry, 661
Chiberta, 664
Chiemsee, 670
Chigwell, 512
Childwall, 542
Chiltern Forest, 496
Chilwell Manor, 550
Chingford, 512
Chingford Golf Range, 637
Le Chioccole CC, 681
Chippenham, 573
Chipping Norton, 448, 552
Chipping Sodbury, 492
Chipstead, 558
Chislehurst, 526
Chorley, 530
Chorleywood, 448, 521
Chorlton-cum-Hardy, 537
Christchurch, 509
Chulmleigh, 506
Church Stretton, 553
Churchill & Blakedown, 519
Churston, 448, 507
Cilgwyn, 629
Cill Dara, 593
Cirencester, 515
City of Coventry (Brandon Wood), 568
City of Newcastle, 567
City of Wakefield, 578
Clacton, 512
Clair Vallon, 660
Clairis, 657
Clandeboye, 588
Clare clubs and courses, 585–6
Claremorris, 595
Claviere, 681
Clayton, 578

Cleckheaton & District, 578
Cleethorpes, 523
Cleeve Hill, 515
Clevedon, 492
Cleveland clubs and courses, 478, 501–2
Cleveland GC, 501
Cleydael, 648
Cliftonville, 584
Clitheroe, 530
Clober, 618
Clones, 595
Clongowes, 593
Clonmel, 596
Clontarf, 589
Close House, 567
Club Secretaries, Association of, 811
Clwyd clubs and courses, 490, 628–9
Clydebank & District, 618
Clydebank Municipal, 618
Clydebank Overtoun, 618
Clydeway Golf Centre, 642
Clyne, 634, 635
Coatbridge, 620
Cobh, 586
Cobtree Manor Park, 526
Coburg Schloss Tambach, 672
Cochrane Castle, 622
Cockermouth, 503
Cocks Moor Woods, 570
Cognac, 656
Colchester, 512
Colchester Golf Range, 637
Cold Ashby, 548
Colnbrook Golf Driving Range, 636
Colne, 530
Colonsay, 615
Colvend, 602
Colville Park, 620
Colworth, 493
Combles-en-Barrois, 658
La Commanderie, 657
Compiègne, 661
Comrie, 626
Concord Park, 576
Congleton, 499
Connacht clubs and courses, 480
Connemara, 591
Consett & District, 510
Conwy (Caernarvonshire), 458, 631
Cooden Beach, 564
Coollattin, 598
Coombe Hill, 559
Coombe Wood, 559
Copenhagen, 652
Copt Heath, 570
Copthorne, 565
Corballis, 590
Corfu, 677

Corhampton, 516
Corinthian, 526
Cork, 586
Cork clubs and courses, 586–7
Cornwall clubs and courses, 466, 502–3
Corrie, 618
Cortijo Grande, 687
La Coruña, 688
Cosby, 533
Costa de Azahar, 691
Costa Brava, 687
Costa Dorada, 688
Costa Teguise, 688
Costessey Park, 546
Cotswold Edge, 515
Cotswold Hills, 515
Cottesmore, 565
Coudray, 661
Coulondres, 659
Coulsdon Court, 559
County and District championships, past results, 270–306
County Armagh GC, 584
County Cavan GC, 585
County Longford GC, 594
County Louth GC, 594
County Sligo GC, 596
Courmayeur, 681
Courtown, 598
Coutainville, 660
Coventry, 570
Coventry Hearsall, 570
Cowal, 615
Cowdray Park, 565
Cowes, 525
Cowglen, 620
Coxmoor, 550
Cradoc, 634
Craigavon, 584
Craigavon Golf Centre, 641
Craigentinny, 612
Craigie Hill, 626
Craigmaddie, 619
Craigmillar Park, 612
Craignure, 615
Crail Golfing Society, 603
Cranbrook, 526
Crans-sur-Sierre, 699
Cray Valley, 526
Craythorne Golf Centre, 555, 639
Creigiau, 633
Cretingham, 556
Crewe, 499
Crews Hill, 544
Criccieth, 631
Crichton Royal, 601
Crieff, 626
Crimple Valley, 574
Croara, 679
Croham Hurst, 559
Crompton & Royton, 537
Crondall, 559
Crondall Golf Course, 640
Crook, 510
Crookhill Park, 576

Crosland Heath, 579
Crow Wood, 620
Crowborough Beacon, 564
Croydon Golf Centre, 640
Cruden Bay, 606
Cuddington, 559
Culdrose, 502
Cullen, 607
Cumbernauld, 619
Cumbria clubs and courses, 478, 503–5
Cupar, 603
Curragh, 593
Cushendall, 583
Czechoslovakian clubs and courses, 650
Dachau, 670
Dalbeattie, 602
Dale Hill, 564
Dalhousie, 625
Dalmahoy, 612
Dalmilling, 616
Dalmunzie, 626
Damme G & CC, 650
Danish clubs and courses, 650–53
Darenth Valley, 526
Darlington, 510
Darmstadt-Traisa, 666
Dartford, 526
Dartmouth (W Midlands), 570
Darwen, 530
Datchet, 449, 494
Davenport, 537
Daventry & District, 548
Davos, 700
Davyhulme Park, 537
Deaconsbank, 620
Dean Wood, 530
Deane, 537
Deangate Ridge, 526
Deer Park (Dublin), 590
Deer Park CC, 614
Deeside, 606
Degli Ulivi, 679
Dejbjerg, 651
Delamere Forest, 499
Delapre, 548
Delapre Golf Complex, 639
Delgany, 598
Delsjö, 692
Denbigh, 628
Denham, 496
Denton, 537
Derby, 505
Derbyshire clubs and courses, 472, 505–6
Dereham, 546
Derry, City of, 594
Devon clubs and courses, 466, 506–8
Dewsbury District, 579
Dibden, 517
Didsbury, 537
Dieppe, 660
Dijon-Bourgogne, 656
Dinard, 655

Dinas Powis, 634
Dinsdale Spa, 510
Dirleton Castle, 610
Disley, 538
Diss, 556
Dithmarschen, 667
Divonne, 656
Djursholm, 694
Dolder, 701
Dolgellau, 631
Dollar, 456, 600
Domaine Impérial, 700
La Dombes, 657
Domburgsche, 682
De Dommel, 683
Domont-Montmorency, 661
Don Cayo, 686
Donabate, 590
Donaghadee, 588
Donau GC Rassbach, 672
Doncaster, 576
Doncaster Town Moor, 576
Donegal, 587
Donegal clubs and courses, 587–8
Doneraile, 586
Donnington Valley, 494
Dooks, 592
Dore & Totley, 576
Dorking, 559
Dorset clubs and courses, 466, 508–10
Dortmund, 673
Dougalston, 619
Douglas (Co Cork), 586
Douglas Municipal (Isle of Man), 524
Douglas Park, 619
Douglas Water, 621
Down clubs and courses, 588–9
Downes Crediton, 507
Downfield, 625
Downpatrick, 588
Downpatrick Golf Range, 641
Downshire, 494
Downshire GC Driving Range, 636
Drayton Park, 555
Driffield, 523
Drift, 559
driving ranges, 636
Droitwich, 519
Drottningholm, 694
Druids Heath, 570
Drumoland Castle, 585
Drumpellier, 621
Dublin & County, 590
Dublin City clubs and courses, 589–90
Dublin clubs and courses, 590–91
Duddingston, 612
Dudley, 570
Duff House Royal, 607
Dufftown, 607
Duisberg Militaire, 649

Dukinfield, 538
Dullatur, 619
Dulwich & Sydenham Hill, 559
Dumbarton, 619
Dumfries & County, 601
Dumfries & Galloway clubs and courses, 484, 601–2
Dumfries & Galloway GC, 601
Dun Laoghaire, 590
Dun Ochil (Gleneagles), 626
Dun Whinny (Gleneagles), 626
Dunaverty, 615
Dunbar, 611
Dunblane New, 600
Dundalk, 594
Dundas Park, 614
Dunecht House, 606
Dunfanaghy, 587
Dunfermline, 603
Dungannon, 454, 597
Dungarvan, 597
Dunham Forest G & CC, 538
Dunkeld & Birnam, 626
Dunkerque, 659
Dunmore, 586
Dunmurry, 583
The Dunnerholme, 504
Dunnikier Park, 603
Dunning, 626
Duns, 599
Dunscar, 538
Dunstable Downs, 493
Dunstanburgh Castle, 549
Dunwood Manor, 517
La Duquesa G & CC, 690
Düren, 665
Durham City, 511
Durham clubs and courses, 478, 510–11
Durness, 610
Düsseldorf, 673
Düsseldorf/Hösel, 673
Dutch clubs and courses, 682–5
Duxbury Park, 531
Dyfed clubs and courses, 490, 629–30
The Dyke, 564
Dyrham Park CC, 521
Eaglescliffe, 501
Ealing, 544
Ealing Golf Range, 639
Earlsferry Thistle, 603
Easingwold, 574
East Berkshire, 494
East Bierley, 579
East Brighton, 564
East Cork, 586
East Devon, 507
East Dorset Driving Range, 637
East Dorset (Lakey Hill), 509
East Herts, 521

East Kilbride, 621
East Renfrewshire, 623
East Sussex National, 564
Eastbourne Downs, 564
Easter Moffat, 621
Eastham Lodge, 542
Eastwood, 623
Eaton (Chester), 499
Eaton (Norfolk), 546
Ebeltoft, 651
Eden Course (St Andrews), 603
Edenbridge G & CC, 527
Edenbridge G & CC Driving Range, 638
Edenderry, 596
Edese, 683
Edgbaston, 570
Edmondstown, 589
Edwalton, 550
Edzell, 625
Effingham, 559
Effingham Park, 566
Eifel, 665
Eindhovensche, 683
Ekarnas, 698
Eksjö, 696
Elderslie, 623
Elfordleigh Hotel G & CC, 507
Elgin, 608
Elland, 579
Ellesborough, 496
Ellesmere, 538
Ellesmere Port, 499
Elm Park G & SC, 589
Elsham, 535
Elstree, 521
Elstree Golf Range, 638
Eltham Warren, 449, 527
Ely City, 497
Emmaboda, 696
Emstal, 673
Las Encinas de Boadilla, 689
Enderby, 533
Enfield, 544
Engadin, 700
English Golfing Union, 799
Enköping, 695
Enmore Park, 554
Ennis, 585
Enniscorthy, 598
Enniscrone, 596
Enniskillen, 591
Ennstal-Weissenbach G & CC, 647
Entry Hill, 492
Enville, 570
Enzesfeld, 647
Epsom, 559
Erding-Grunbach, 670
Erewash Valley, 506
Erlangen, 672
Erskine, 623
Esbjerg, 651
Eschenried, 670
Escorpión, 691
Éskifjardar, 677

Eskilstuna, 695
Eslöv, 693
Espoon Golfseura, 653
Essen Haus Oefte, 673
Essen-Heidhausen, 673
Essex clubs and courses, 468, 511–14
Estela, 686
Estoril, 686
Estoril Sol, 686
Étangs de Fiac, 664
Eton College, 495
Europa Sport Region, 647
European Golf Association, 812
Evesham, 519
Exeter G & CC, 507
Eyemouth, 599
F5, 693
Fagersta, 695
Fairfield Golf & Sailing Club, 538
Fairhaven, 531
Fairlop Waters, 512
Fairlop Waters Driving Range, 637
Fairmile Hotel Driving Range, 640
Fairway Golf Driving Range, 640
Fairwood Park, 635
Fakenham, 546
Falkenberg, 698
Falkenhof G & LC, 671
Falkirk, 601
Falkirk Tryst, 601
Falkland, 603
Falköping, 698
Falmouth, 502
Falnuée, 649
Falsterbo, 693
Falun-Borlänge, 696
Fanø Island, 651
Farnham, 559
Farnham Park, 496, 559
Faversham, 527
Feldafing, 671
Felixstowe Ferry, 556
Feltwell, 547
Fereneze, 623
Fermanagh clubs and courses, 591
Fermoy, 586
Ferndown, 509
Fernfell G & CC, 559
Ferrybridge "C", 579
Ffestiniog, 631
Fife Region clubs and courses, 486, 603–5
Filey, 574
Filton, 492
Finchley, 544
Finchley Golf Driving Range, 639
Finnish clubs and courses, 653–4
Finspång, 696
Fintona, 597
Fioranello, 680
Firenze Ugolino, 681

Fishwick Hall, 531
Fiuggi, 680
Fjällbacka, 699
Flackwell Heath, 496
Flaine-les-Carroz, 656
Flamborough Head, 523
Flanders-Nippon, 649
Fleetlands, 517
Fleetwood, 531
Fleming Park, 517
Flempton, 557
Fleurance, 664
Flint, 628
Flixton, 538
Flommens, 693
Föhr, 667
Föhrenwald, 647
Fontainebleau, 661
Fontenay-en-Cotentin, 660
Förde Glücksburg, 667
Forest of Arden Hotel G & CC, 570
Forest of Dean, 515
Forfar, 625
Formby, 542
Formby Golf Driving Range, 639
Formby Ladies', 542
Fornham Park, 557
Forres, 608
Forrest Little, 590
Forrester Park, 512
Forsbacka, 699
Forsegårdens, 692
Fort Augustus, 609
Fort William, 609
Fortrose & Rosemarkie, 609
Fortwilliam (Belfast), 584
Fosseway CC, 492
Four Ashes Golf Centre, 641
Fourqueux, 661
Foxhills, 560
Foxrock, 589
Franciacorta, 678
Frankfurter, 666
Frankische Schweitz, 672
Fraserburgh, 606
Freiburg, 675
French clubs and courses, 654–65
Freshwater Bay, 525
La Freslonière, 655
Freudenstadt, 675
Frilford Heath, 552
Frinton, 512
Le Fronde, 681
Fulford (York), 574
Fulford Heath, 570
Fulneck, 579
Fulwell, 544
Furesø, 652
Furness, 504
Furth im Wald, 672
Gainsborough, 535
Gairloch, 610
Galashiels, 599
Gällivare-Malmberget,

691
Galway, 591
Galway clubs and
courses, 591–2
Ganstead Park, 523
Ganton, 574
Gardagolf, 679
Garesfield, 567
Garforth, 579
Garlenda, 679
Garmisch-Partenkirchen,
671
Garmouth & Kingston, 608
Gatehouse, 602
Gathurst, 538
Gatley, 538
Gatton Manor Hotel, 560
Gatwick Manor, 566
Gävle, 696
Gay Hill, 570
Gelpenberg, 684
Geneva, 700
German clubs and
courses, 665–77
Gerrards Cross, 496
Geysteren G & CC, 683
Ghyll, 574
Gifford, 611
Gifhorn, 669
Gilleleje, 652
Gillingham, 527
Gilnahirk, 584
Girls' tournament results,
136–9, 263–6
Girton, 498
Girvan, 616
Glamorganshire, 459, 634
Glasgow, 619
Glasgow Gailes, 616
Gleddoch, 623
Glen, 611
Glen Gorse, 533
Glenalmond, 627
Glenbervie, 601
Glencorse, 456, 612
Glencruitten, 615
Gleneagles Hotel, 627
Glenearn, 627
Glengarriff, 586
Glenrothes, 603
Glossop & District, 506
Gloucester Hotel &
Country Club
Driving Range, 638
Gloucestershire clubs
and courses, 466,
514–15
Gloucestershire Hotel,
515
Glyfada, 677
Glynhir, 629
Glynneath, 635
Goal Farm, 560
Gog Magog, 498
Goldenhill, 555
golf, origins of, 828
Golf d'Albret, 664
Golf d'Andenne, 649
Golf des Ardennes, 658
Golf de l'Ariège, 664

Golf Bordelais, 654
Golf Club Stewards'
Association, 812
golf clubs, in England,
492–582
in Europe, 647–701
in Ireland, 583–98
in Scotland, 599–627
in Wales, 628–35
Golf du Coiroux, 654
Golf des Flandres, 659
Golf Foundation, 140–4,
810
Golf House Club, 604
Golf d'Isabella, 661
Golf Municipal de Bréhal,
660
Golf Municipal de
Bordeaux, 654
Golf Municipal de
Limoges, 657
Golf du Nivernais, 657
Golf de l'Ordet, 655
Golf des Ormes, 655
Golf du Prieuré, 661
Golf du Rhin, 658
Golf de Rigenée, 649
Golf du Rigolet, 657
Golf des Roucous, 664
Golf du Sart, 660
Golf del Sur, 688
Golf de Vaudreuil, 660
Golf des Volcans, 657
Golfakademie Seefeld,
647
golfing organisations
(addresses), British,
813
overseas, 821
golfing unions, 799
Golfriege des Etuf, 673
Golspie, 610
Goodwood, 566
Goring & Streatley, 495
Gorleston, 547
Gormanston College, 595
Gort, 592
Gosforth, 567
Gosforth Park Golfing
Complex, 567, 640
Gosport & Stokes Bay,
517
Göteborg, 692
Göttingen, 669
Gotts Park, 579
Gourock, 623
governing bodies, 799
Grampian Region clubs
and courses, 488,
605–8
Granary Hotel G & CC,
547
CC Grand-Ducal de
Luxembourg, 682
La Grande-Motte, 659
Grand Avignon, 663
Grange, 570, 589
Grange Fell, 504
Grange-over-Sands, 504
Grange Park

(Lancashire), 542
Grange Park (Yorkshire),
576
Grangemouth, 601
Grantown-on-Spey, 457,
608
Granville, 660
Great Barr, 570
Great Harwood, 531
Great Lever & Farnworth,
538
Great Salterns, 517
Great Yarmouth &
Caister, 547
Greek clubs and courses,
677
Green Haworth, 531
Green Hotel, 626
Greenburn, 614
Greencastle, 587
Greenisland, 583
Greenkeepers'
Association, 812
Greenmeadow, 630
Greenmount, 538
Greenock, 457, 623
Greenore, 594
Greenway Hall, 555
La Grenouillère, 661
Greystones, 598
Griffin, 493
Grim's Dyke, 544
Grimsby, 523
Grossensee, 667
Grossflottbeker, 667
Gstaad-Saanenland, 699
Guadalmina, 690
Guildford, 560
Gullane, 611
Gullbringa, 692
Gut Altentann, 647
Güt Brandlhof, 647
Gut Grambek, 667
Gut Kaden, 667
Gut Waldhof, 667
Gütermann Gutach, 675
Gweedore, 587
Gwent clubs and courses,
490, 630–31
Gwynedd clubs and
courses, 490, 631–2
Gyttegård, 651
Haagsche G & CC, 684
De Haar, 684
Habberley, 519
Haddington, 611
Haderslev, 651
Hadley Wood, 521
Hagge, 696
Haggs Castle, 621
Haghof G & LC, 675
Hagley, 571
Haigh Hall, 538
Hainault Forest, 513
Hainburg/Donau, 647
Hainsworth Park, 523
Hale, 538
Halesowen, 571
Halifax, 579
Halifax Bradley Hall, 579

Halifax West End, 579
Hallamshire, 576
Hallowes, 506
Halmstad, 698
Halstock, 509
Halstock Driving Range,
637
Haltwhistle, 549
Ham Manor, 566
Hamburg, 668
Hamburg-Ahrensburg,
668
Hamburg-Waldorfer, 668
Hamburger GC in der
Luneburger Heide,
668
Hamilton, 621
Hampshire clubs and
courses, 464, 515–19
Hampstead, 544
Hanau-Wilhelmsbad, 666
handicapping, 770
ladies, 789
Handsworth, 571
Hanging Heaton, 579
Haninge, 694
Hankley Common, 560
Hannover, 669
Harborne, 571
Harborne Church Farm,
571
Harburn, 614
Hardelot, 660
Harefield Place, 544
Harewood Downs, 496
Härjedalsfjällen, 691
Härnösand, 691
Harpenden, 521
Harpenden Common, 521
Harrogate, 574
Harrow School, 544
Hartlepool, 501
Hartley Wintney, 517
Hartsbourne CC, 521
Hartswood, 513
Harwich & Dovercourt,
513
Harwood, 530
Harz, 669
Hässleholm, 693
Haste Hill, 544
Hastings, 564
Hatchford Brook, 571
Hatfield London, 521
Hattemse G & CC, 683
Haverfordwest, 629
Haverhill, 557
Havering, 513
Haviksoord, 683
Le Havre, 660
Hawarden, 628
Hawick, 599
Hawkhurst, 527
Hawkstone Park, 553
Hawthorn Hill, 495
Hawthorn Hill Driving
Range, 636
Haydock Park, 542
Hayling, 517
Hayston, 619

Haywards Heath, 566
Hazel Grove, 539
Hazlehead, 606
Hazlemere G & CC, 496
Headfort, 595
Headingley, 579
Headley, 579
Heath Driving Range, 642
Heaton Moor, 539
Heaton Park, 539
Heath (Portlaoise), 593
Hechingen-Hohenzollern, 676
Hedeland, 652
Hedmark, 685
Heidelberg-Lobenfeld, 666
Heidelberg (US Army), 666
Heilbronn-Hohenlohe, 676
Helen's Bay, 588
Helensburgh, 619
Hellu, 677
Helmsdale, 610
Helsby, 499
Helsingborg, 693
Helsingin Golfklubi, 653
Helsingør, 652
Henbury, 492
Hendon, 545
Henley, 552
Henri-Chapelle, 649
Herefordshire GC, 519
Herefordshire &
    Worcester clubs and
    courses, 472, 519–20
Herford, 669
Hermitage, 590
Herne Bay, 527
Herning, 651
Herreria, 689
Hertfordshire clubs and
    courses, 468, 520–23
Herzogenaurach, 672
Herzogstadt Celle, 669
Hesketh, 542
Hessle, 524
Heswall, 542
Heworth (N Yorks), 574
Heworth (Tyne & Wear),
    567
Hexham, 549
Heysham, 531
Hickleton, 576
High Elms, 527
High Post, 573
Highcliffe Castle, 509
Highgate, 545
Highland Region clubs
    and courses, 488,
    608–10
Highwoods (Bexhill), 564
Hill Barn, 566
Hill Valley G & CC, 553
Hillerød, 652
Hillingdon, 545
Hillsborough, 577
Hillside, 542
Hilltop, 571

Hilton Park, 619
Hilvorqumsche, 684
Himley Hall, 571
Himmerlands G & CC,
    651
Hinckley, 533
Hindhead, 560
Hindley Hall, 531
L'Hirondelle, 656
The Hirsel, 599
Hittnau-Zürich, 701
Hjorring, 651
Hobson Municipal, 511
Hochstatt Härtsfeld-Ries,
    676
Hockley, 517
Hoebridge Golf Centre,
    560, 640
Hoenshuis G & CC, 683
Hof, 672
Hofors, 696
Högbo, 696
Hohenstauffen, 676
Hoisdorf, 668
Hökensås, 698
Holbaek, 652
Holiday Inn, 545
Hollandbush, 621
Hollingbury Park, 564
Holme Hall, 524
Holstebro, 651
Holsworthy, 507
Holtye, 527
Holyhead, 632
Holywell, 628
Holywood, 588
Homburg, 666
Home Park, 560
Honiton, 507
The Honourable
    Company of
    Edinburgh Golfers
    (Muirfield), 611
Hook, 696
Hopeman, 608
Horam Park, 564
Horam Park Driving
    Range, 640
Hornafjardar, 677
Hornsea, 524
Horsenden Hill, 545
Horsens, 651
Horsforth, 579
Horwich, 539
Höslwang im Chiemgau,
    671
Hossegor, 664
Houghton-le-Spring, 567
Houldsworth
    (Levenshulme), 539
Hounslow Heath, 545
Howley Hall, 580
Howstrake, 524
Howth, 589
Hoylake Municipal, 542
Hubbelrath, 673
Huddersfield, 580
Hudiksvall, 696
Hull, 524
Hull Golf Centre, 638

Hulta, 698
Humberside clubs and
    courses, 474, 523–4
Humberstone Heights,
    533
Hunstanton, 547
Huntercombe, 552
Huntly, 606
Hurst, 495
Húsavikur, 677
Huyton & Prescot, 542
Hvide Klit, 651
Hylliekroken, 693
Hythe Imperial, 527
Icelandic clubs and
    courses, 677–8
Ifach, 686
Ifield, 566
Iford Bridge Golf Range,
    637
Ilford, 513
Ilfracombe, 507
Ifracombe &
    Woolacombe Golf Range,
    637
Ilkeston, 506
Ilkley, 449, 580
Im Chiemgau, 671
Images d'Épinal, 658
Immingham, 524
Inco, 635
Ingarö, 694
Ingestre Park, 555
Ingol Golf & Squash Club,
    531
Ingolstadt, 672
Innellan, 615
Innerleithen, 599
Innsbruck-Igls, 647
Insch, 606
Interlaken-Unterseen,
    700
Inter-Mol, 648
International Club du
    Lys, 661
international match
    conditions, 807
International team
    results, 1989, 39–40
    past, 213–23, 233–45,
    247–57
Inverallochy, 606
Invergordon, 610
Inverness, 609
Inverurie, 606
Ipswich (Purdis Heath),
    557
Ipswich Golf Centre, 640
Ireland, 583–98
Ireland, Golfing Union of,
    799
Irvine, 616
Irvine Ravenspark, 616
Is Molas, 680
Isaberg, 697
Ísafjardar, 677
Isernhagen, 670
The Island, 591
Isle of Anglesey clubs
    and courses, 490, 632

Isle of Man clubs and
    courses, 476, 524–5
Isle of Purbeck, 509
Isle of Wight clubs and
    courses, 464, 525
Isles of Scilly, 502
Issum-Neiderrhein, 674
Italian clubs and courses,
    678–82
Iver, 497
Ivinghoe, 497
Jávea, 687
Jedburgh, 599
John O'Gaunt, 493
Jökull, 677
Jönköping, 697
Jubilee Course (St
    Andrews), 604
Juelsminde, 652
Juliana, 674
Juniors' tournaments
    results, 135–9, 258–66
Kalmar, 697
Kalundborg, 652
Kanturk, 586
Karlshamn, 697
Karlskoga, 699
Karlstad, 699
Kärntner, 647
Kassel-Wilhelmshohe,
    670
Katrineholm, 695
Kearsley Golf Range Ltd,
    638
Kedleston Park, 506
Keerbergen, 649
Keighley, 580
Keilir, 677
Keith, 607
Kelso, 599
Kemnay, 606
Kendal, 504
Kenilworth, 568
Kenmare, 592
Kennemer G & CC, 682
Kent clubs and courses,
    462, 525–30
Keppelse, 683
Kerry clubs and courses,
    592
Keswick, 504
Kettering, 548
Kibworth, 533
Kidderminster, 519
Kilbirnie Place, 616
Kildare clubs and
    courses, 592–3
Kilkee, 585
Kilkeel, 588
Kilkenny, 593
Kilkenny clubs and
    courses, 593
Killarney, 592
Killin, 600
Killiney, 591
Killymoon, 597
Kilmacolm, 623
Kilmarnock (Barassie),
    616
Kilrea, 594

Kilrush, 586
Kilspindie, 611
Kilsyth Lennox, 624
Kilternan Hotel, 591
Kilton Forest, 551
King James VI, 627
Kinghorn, 604
Kinghorn Ladies, 604
Kinghorn Thistle, 604
King's Links, 606
King's Lynn, 547
King's Norton, 519
King's Park, 621
Kingsdown, 573
Kingsknowe, 612
Kingsthorpe, 548
Kingsway, 524
Kingswood, 560
Kington, 519
Kingussie, 609
Kingweston, 554
Kinross, 626
Kinsale, 586
Kintore, 606
Kirkby Lonsdale, 504
Kirkby Muxloe, 533
Kirkbymoorside, 574
Kirkcaldy, 604
Kirkcudbright, 602
Kirkhill, 621
Kirkintilloch, 619
Kirkistown Castle, 588
Kirriemuir, 625
Kitzbühel, 647
Kitzeberg, 668
Kjekstad, 685
Kleiburg, 684
Knaresborough, 575
Knebworth, 521
Knighton, 634
Knighton Heath, 509
Knights Grange, 499
Knightswood, 621
The Knock Golf Club, 585
Knockanally, 593
Knockbracken, 584
Knockbracken Golf
    Centre, 642
Knole Park, 527
Knott End, 531
Knowle, 492
Knutsford, 499
De Koepel, 683
Køge, 653
Kokkedal, 653
Kokkolan, 653
Kolding, 652
Köln G & LC, 674
Köln-Marienburger, 674
Koninklijke GC Ostend,
    650
Konstanz, 676
Korslöt, 695
Korsør, 653
Kralingen, 684
Krefeld, 674
Kristiansand, 685
Kristianstad, 693
Kristinehamn, 699
Kronberg G & LC, 666

Kungsbacka, 692
Küsten GC Hohe Klint,
    668
Kyles of Bute, 615
Kymen, 653
Laarbruch GC (RAF), 674
Lac d'Annecy, 656
Ladbrook Park, 569
Ladies' Amateur
    tournament results,
    246–57
Ladies' British Open
    Championship, 115,
    168
Ladies' Golf Union (LGU),
    802
Ladybank, 604
Lagan, 697
Lahden Golf, 653
Lahinch, 585
Laholm, 698
Lakeside (Rugeley), 555
Laleham, 560
Lamberhurst, 450, 527
Lamlash, 618
Lanark, 621
Lancashire clubs and
    courses, 476, 530–33
Lancaster G & CC, 531
Landskrona, 693
Langholm, 601
Langland Bay, 635
Langley Park, 527
Lannemezan, 664
Lansdown, 492
Lansil, 531
Lanzo Intelvi, 678
Laois clubs and courses,
    593
Largs, 616
La Largue, 658
Larkhall, 621
Larne, 583
Lauder, 599
Launceston, 502
Lausanne, 700
Lauswolt G & CC, 684
Laval, 656
Lavender Park, 495
Lavender Park Golf
    Centre, 636
Laytown & Bettystown,
    595
Leadhills, 621
Leamington & County,
    569
Leasowe, 542
Leatherhead, 560
Leckford & Longstock,
    517
Lee-on-the-Solent, 517
Lee Park, 542
Leeds, 580
Leeds Castle, 527
Leek, 555
Lees Hall, 577
Leicestershire clubs and
    courses, 470, 533–5
Leicestershire GC, 450,
    534

Leigh, 539
Leighton Buzzard, 494
Leinster clubs and
    courses, 480
Leitershofen, 671
Leitrim clubs and
    courses, 593
Leksand, 696
Lenzerheide Valbella,
    700
Lenzie, 621
Leominster, 519
Leopardstown Golf
    Centre, 642
Leslie (Fife), 604
Letchworth, 521
Letham Grange, 625
Lethamhill, 621
Letterkenny, 587
Leusdense De Hoge
    Kleij, 684
Leven Golfing Society,
    604
Leven Links, 604
Leven Municipal, 604
Leven Thistle, 604
Lewes, 564
Leyland, 531
Leynir, 677
LGU, 802
LGU system of
    handicapping, 789
Liberton, 612
Lichtenau-Weickershof,
    672
Lickey Hills, 571
Lidingö, 694
Lidköping, 698
Lightcliffe, 580
Lilleshall Hall, 553
Lilley Brook, 515
Lilse, 648
Limburg G & CC, 649
Lime Trees Park, 545
Limerick, 594
Limerick clubs and
    courses, 593–4
Limpsfield Chart, 560
Lincoln, 535
Lincoln Golf range, 639
Lincolnshire clubs and
    courses, 470, 535–6
Lindau-Bad Schachen,
    676
Linde, 695
Lindö, 694
Lindrick, 577
Lingdale, 534
Lingfield Park, 560
Linköping, 697
Links (Newmarket), 557
Links Country Park Hotel,
    547
Linlithgow, 614
Linn Park, 621
Linz-St Florian, 647
Liphook, 517
Lippischer, 670
Lisbon Sports Club, 686
Lisburn, 583

Lismore, 597
Little Aston, 571
Little Chalfont, 497
Little Hay Golf Complex,
    522
Little Lakes, 519
Littlehampton, 566
Littlehill, 622
Littlestone, 527
Liverpool Municipal, 543
Ljunghusens, 693
Ljusdal, 696
Llandrindod, 634
Llandudno (Maesdu), 631
Llandudno (North
    Wales), 631
Llanfairfechan, 631
Llangefni, 632
Llanidloes (St Idloes), 634
Llanishen, 634
Llantrisant & Pontyclun,
    633
Llanwern, 630
Llanymynech, 553
Llavaneras, 688
Lobden, 531
Lochcarron, 610
Lochend, 613
Lochgelly, 604
Lochgeorge Driving
    Range, 642
Lochgilphead, 615
Lochmaben, 601
Lochranza, 618
Lochwinnoch, 623
Lockerbie, 601
Loftus Hill, 575
Lohersand, 668
Lolivarie, 654
Lomas-Bosque, 689
London Scottish, 560
Londonderry clubs and
    courses, 594
Long Ashton, 492
Longcliffe, 534
Longford clubs and
    courses, 594
Longley Park, 580
Longniddry, 611
Longridge, 531
Looe, 502
Lothian Region clubs and
    courses, 482, 610–14
Lothianburn, 613
Loudoun Gowf Club, 616
Loudun Saint-Hilaire, 656
Loughrea, 592
Louth, 535
Louth clubs and courses,
    594
Low Laithes, 580
Lowes Park, 539
Lübeck-Travemünder,
    668
Lucan, 591
Lucerne, 701
Luchon, 664
Ludlow, 553
Luffenham Heath, 534
Luffness New, 611

Lugano, 700
Luleå, 681
Lullingstone Park, 528
Lundin, 604
Lundin Ladies, 604
Lunds Akademiska, 693
Lurgan, 584
Lutterworth, 534
Luxembourg, 682
Lybster, 608
Lyckorna, 699
Lydney, 515
Lyme Regis, 509
Lymm, 500
Lyon, 658
Lyon-Verger, 658
Lysegården, 692
Lytham (Green Drive),
    532
Macclesfield, 500
McDonald, 606
Machrie Bay, 618
Machrie Hotel, 615
Machrihanish, 615
Machynlleth, 634
Macroom, 586
Madine, 658
Maesteg, 633
Magdalene Fields, 549
Mahee Island, 588
Maidenhead, 495
Main-Taunus, 666
CC Málaga, 689
Malahide, 591
Malden, 561
Maldon, 513
Malkins Bank, 500
Mallow, 586
Malmö, 693
Malone, 584
Malta, 682
Malton & Norton, 575
Manchester GC Ltd, 539
Manchester (Greater)
    clubs and courses,
    476, 536–41
La Manga, 687
Mangotsfield, 493
Manises, 691
Mannheim-Viernheim,
    666
Mannings Heath, 566
Manor House Hotel, 507
Mans Mulsanne, 656
Mansfield Woodhouse,
    551
Mapperley, 551
maps, British and Irish,
    463–91
    Mediterranean and
        Algarve, 646
    Northern France, 645
March, 498
Marcilly, 658
Margara, 681
Margarethenhof am
    Tegernsee, 671
Mariánské Lázně, 650
Mariestad, 698
Marigola, 679

Marin d'Étretat, 660
Marina Velça, 680
Marine Nieuwediep, 682
Marine Westerland, 668
Marinha G & CC, 686
Maritim Timmendorfer
    Strand, 668
Market Drayton, 553
Market Harborough, 534
Market Rasen, 535
Markgräflerland, 676
Märkischer Hagen, 674
Marks, 698
Marlborough, 573
Marmande, 654
Marple, 539
Marsden, 580
Marsden Park, 532
Maryport, 504
Mas de Bombequiois, 659
Mas del Tell, 654
Masham, 575
Maspalomas, 688
Massane, 659
Massereene, 583
Matlock, 506
Maxstoke Park, 569
Maybole, 616
Maylands, 513
Mayo clubs and courses,
    594–5
Mazières, 656
Meath clubs and courses,
    595
Meaux-Boutigny, 661
Mediterraneo CC, 691
Mellor & Townscliffe, 539
Melrose, 599
Meltham, 580
Melton Mowbray, 534
Menaggio &
    Cadenabbia, 678
Mendip, 554
Men's Amateur
    tournament results,
    101–13, 224–45
Meole Brace, 553
Meon Valley Hotel G &
    CC, 517
Mercantile (Carnoustie),
    625
Mercantile (Montrose),
    625
Merchants of Edinburgh,
    613
Mere G & CC, 500
Méribel, 656
Merseyside clubs and
    courses, 476, 541–4
Merthyr Tydfil, 633
Methil, 604
Metz-Cherisey, 659
Meyrick Park, 509
Mezeyrac, 658
Mickleover, 506
Mid Glamorgan clubs
    and courses, 490,
    632–3
Mid Herts, 522
Mid Kent, 528

Middlesbrough, 501
Middlesbrough
    Municipal, 501
Middlesbrough
    Municipal Driving
    Range, 637
Middlesex clubs and
    courses, 462, 544–6
Middlesex GC, 544
Middleton Park, 580
Midtsjaellands, 653
Mijas, 689
Mikkelin Golf, 653
Milano, 678
Millfield, 535
Milford Haven, 629
Mill Hill, 545
Mill Ride, 495
Millbrook, 494
Millport, 618
Milltown, 589
Milnathort, 626
Milngavie, 619
Minchinhampton, 515
Minehead & West
    Somerset, 554
Minto, 599
Miramar, 686
Mitcham, 561
Mitcham Village, 561
Mitchelstown, 587
Mittelholsteinscher
    Aukrug, 668
Mittelrheinischer, 666
Mjölby, 697
Moate, 598
Moffat, 601
Mold, 628
Molinetto CC, 678
Mölle, 693
Mølleåens, 653
Mölndals, 692
Monaghan clubs and
    courses, 595–6
money lists, 64, 92, 122
Monifieth Golf Links, 625
Monkstown, 587
Monmouth, 630
Monmouthshire, 630
Mont-d'Arbois, 656
Mont Garni, 649
Mont-de-Marsan, 664
Monte Carlo, 663
Montecatini, 681
Monticello, 678
Montreux, 700
Montrose, 625
Montrose Caledonia, 625
Montrose Mercantile, 625
Moor Allerton, 580
Moor Hall, 571
Moor Park, 522
Moore Place, 561
Moortown, 580
Mora, 698
La Moraleja, 689
Moray, 608
Morecambe, 532
Morfontaine, 662
Los Moriscos, 689

Morlais Castle, 633
Morpeth, 549
Morriston, 635
Mortonhall, 613
Moseley, 571
Motala, 697
Mount Bellew, 592
Mount Ellen, 622
Mount Oswald, 511
Mount Skip, 580
Mountain Ash, 633
Mountain Lakes, 633
Mountrath, 593
Mouriés, 663
Mourne, 589
Mowsbury, 494
Mowsbury Driving
    Range, 636
La Moye, 498
Moyola Park, 594
Muckhart, 600
Muir of Ord, 610
Muirfield (The
    Honourable Company
    of Edinburgh
    Golfers), 611
Mullingar, 598
Mullion, 502
Mulrany, 595
München Nord-
    Eichenried, 671
Münchener, 671
Mundesley, 547
Munster clubs and
    courses, 480
Münster-Wilkinghege,
    674
Münsterland, 674
Murcar, 606
Murhof, 647
Murrayfield, 613
Murrayshall, 627
Muskerry, 587
Musselburgh, 611
Musselburgh Old
    Course, 611
Muswell Hill, 545
Muthill, 627
N–B Toxandria, 682
Naas, 593
Nahetal, 665
Nairn, 609
Nairn & Portnoo, 587
Nairn Dunbar, 609
Nampont-St-Martin, 660
Nancy-Aingeray, 659
Nantes, 657
Napoli, 678
Los Naranjos, 690
National Association of
    Public Golf Courses,
    811
National Golf Clubs'
    Advisory
    Association, 812
Neath, 635
Nefyn & District, 631
Nelson, 532
Nenagh, 596
Nerja G & CC, 689

Ness, 677
Neuchâtel, 699
Nevill, 528
New Course (St
    Andrews), 604
New Cumnock, 617
New Forest, 517
New Galloway, 602
New GC Deauville, 661
New Golf Club (St
    Andrews), 605
New Mills, 500
New Ross, 598
New Taymouth, 625
New Zealand (Surrey),
    561
Newark, 551
Newbattle, 613
Newbiggin-by-the-Sea,
    550
Newbold Comyn, 569
Newburgh-on-Ythan, 607
Newbury & Crookham,
    495
Newcastle Municipal, 555
Newcastle-under-Lyme,
    555
Newcastle United, 567
Newcastle West, 594
Newlands, 591
Newport (Gwent), 630
Newport (IoW), 525
Newport (Pembs), 629
Newquay, 502
Newton Abbot (Stover),
    507
Newton Green, 557
Newton Stewart, 602
Newtonmore, 609
Newtownstewart (Co
    Tyrone), 597
Niddry Castle, 614
Niederrheinischer, 674
Nieuwegeinse, 684
Nigg Bay, 607
Nîmes Campagne, 659
La Nivelle, 664
Noord Nederlandse G &
    CC, 684
De Noordhollandse, 682
Noordwijkse, 684
Nordbornholms, 650
Norderney, 668
Nordkirchen, 674
Nordvestjysk, 652
Norfolk clubs and
    courses, 468, 546-8
Normanby Hall, 524
Normandy Golf Range,
    642
Normanton, 580
Norrköping, 697
North Berwick, 611
North Downs, 561
North Foreland, 528
North Hants, 518
North Inch, 627
North Manchester, 539
North Middlesex, 545
North Oxford, 552

North Shore, 535
North Warwickshire, 571
North West, 587
North Wilts, 450, 573
North Worcestershire,
    571
Northampton, 548
Northamptonshire clubs
    and courses, 470,
    548-9
Northamptonshire
    County, 548
Northcliffe, 581
Northenden, 539
Northern, 607
Northumberland clubs
    and courses, 478,
    549-50
Northumberland GC, 567
Northwood, 545
Norwegian clubs and
    courses, 685
Norwich Golf Centre, 639
Nottingham City, 551
Nottinghamshire clubs
    and courses, 470,
    550-52
Notts, 551
Nuevo de Madrid, 689
Nuneaton, 569
Nunspeetse G & CC, 683
Nuremore, 595
Nybro, 697
Nyby Bruk, 695
Nynäshamn, 694
Oadby, 534
Oakdale, 575
Oaks Sports Centre, 561
Oberfranken, 672
Oberhessischer
    Marburg, 666
Oberpfaelzer Wald GLC,
    672
Oberschwaben-Bad
    Waldsee, 676
Oberstdorf, 676
Oddil Golfu TJ Semily,
    650
Odense, 651
Odsherred, 653
Oeschberghof L & GC,
    676
Offaly clubs and courses,
    596
Öijared, 692
Okehampton, 507
Ólafsfjardar, 677
Öland, 697
Olching, 671
Old Colwyn, 628
Old Conna, 598
Old Course (St Andrews),
    605
Old Fold Manor, 522
Old Manchester, 539
Old Padeswood, 628
Old Ranfurly, 623
Old Rectory Hotel, 634
Old Thorns Hotel, 518
Oldenburgischer, 668

Oldham, 539
Oldmeldrum, 607
Olgiata, 680
Olton, 572
Olympus, 682
Omagh, 597
Omaha Beach, 661
Onneley, 555
Onsjö, 698
Open Championship,
    29-31, 156-64
Opio-Valbonne, 663
Oporto, 686
orders of merit, 41, 94,
    97, 99-100, 101, 114
Ordnance Survey, 518
Örebro, 695
Orkney, 614
Orkney & Shetland
    Region clubs and
    courses, 488, 614
Ormeau, 585
Ormesson, 662
Ormonde Fields, 506
Ormskirk, 532
Orsett, 513
Ortenau, 676
Orton Meadows, 498
Orust, 699
Osborne, 525
Oskarshamn, 697
Oslo, 685
Osnabrück, 674
Österlen, 693
Östersund-Froso, 691
Ostfriesland, 668
Ostra Göinge, 693
Ostschweizischer, 701
Oswestry, 553
Otley, 581
Otway, 588
Oude Maas, 684
Oudenaarde G & CC, 650
Oughterard, 592
Oulu, 654
Oundle, 548
Oustoen, 685
Outlane, 581
Overseas national
    championships, past
    results, 186-203
Overseas players, 343
Öviks GC Puttom, 691
Oxfordshire clubs and
    courses, 464, 552
Oxley Park, 572
Oxton, 551
Oxton Driving Range, 639
Ozoir-la-Ferrière, 662
Paderborner Land, 666
Padeswood & Buckley,
    628
Padova, 682
Painswick, 515
Painthorpe House, 581
Paisley, 623
Palleg, 635
Palmares, 685
Pals, 688
Panmure, 625

Pannal, 575
Panshanger, 522
El Paraiso, 690
Park Hall, 555
Parknasilla, 592
Parkstone, 509
Parque da Floresta, 685
Partille, 692
Pastures, 506
Patriziale Ascona, 700
Patshull Park, 572
Pau, 664
Peacehaven, 564
Pease Pottage, 566
Peebles, 599
Peel, 524
Pen Guen, 655
La Penaza, 691
Penina, 685
Penmaenmawr, 631
Penn, 572
Pennard, 635
Penrith, 451, 504
Penwortham, 532
Périgueux, 654
Perivale Park, 545
Perranporth, 502
Perstorp, 693
Perugia, 681
Peterborough Milton, 498
Peterhead, 607
Petersfield, 518
Pevero, 680
Pfalz, 665
PGA European Tour, 801
    1989 results, 42-57
    past results, 204-10
    satellite tours, 59-63
Phoenix, 577
Phoenix Park, 581
Phoenix Sporting and
    Leisure Centre, 638
Piandisole, 680
Picketts Lock, 545
Pierrevert, 663
Pike Fold, 539
Pike Hills, 575
Piltdown, 565
Pincda de Sevilla, 690
Pineta di Arenzano, 679
La Pinetina, 678
Pinner Hill, 545
Pipps Hill CC, 513
Pitcheroak, 520
Piteå, 691
Pitlochry, 627
Pitreavie, 605
Playa Serena, 687
Pleasington, 532
Poitevin, 657
Polkemmet, 614
Polkemmet Driving
    Range, 642
Pollensa, 687
Pollok, 622
Polmont, 601
Poniente, 687
Pontardawe, 635
Pontefract&District,581
Pontefract Park, 581

Ponteland, 550
Pontnewydd, 630
Pontypool, 630
Pontypridd, 633
Porin Golfkerho, 654
Pornic, 657
Port Bannatyne, 618
Port Glasgow, 623
Port Royal Golf Range, 642
Port St Mary, 525
Portadown, 584
Portarlington, 593
Porters Park, 522
Portmadoc, 632
Portmarnock, 591
Porto Carras G & CC, 677
Porto d'Orra, 680
Portobello, 613
Portpatrick Dunskey, 602
Portsalon, 588
Portsmouth, 518
Portsmouth Golf Centre, 638
Portstewart, 594
Portuguese clubs and courses, 685–6
Portumna, 592
Potters Bar, 522
Poult Wood, 528
Poulton-le-Fylde, 532
Poulton Park, 500
Powfoot, 602
Powys clubs and courses, 490, 633–4
Pozoblanco, 688
Praa Sands, 502
Prenton, 543
Prestatyn, 628
Prestbury, 500
Preston, 532
Prestonfield, 613
Prestwich, 540
Prestwick, 617
Prestwick St Cuthbert, 617
Prestwick St Nicholas, 617
Prince's, 528
Priors Hall, 548
Professional Golfers' Association (PGA), 800
Professional Review, 12–14
Programme of Events, 1990, 148–54
Prudhoe, 550
Prunevelle, 658
Puerta de Hierro, 689
Pumpherston, 614
Punta Ala, 681
Purley Chase, 569
Purley Chase Driving Range, 641
Purley Downs, 561
Puttenham, 561
Pwllheli, 632
Pyecombe, 566
Pyle & Kenfig, 633

Pype Hayes, 572
Pymmenter, 670
Queen's Park (Bournemouth), 509
Queens's Park (Cheshire), 500
Queensbury, 581
Quietwaters, 513
Quimper-Cornouaille, 655
La Quinta, 690
Quinta Do Lago, 685
RAC Country Club, 561
Racing Club de France, 662
Radcliffe-on-Trent, 551
Radyr, 634
RAF Benson, 552
RAF Germany, 674
RAF Gütersloh, 674
RAF Henlow, 494
RAF Marham, 547
RAF North Luffenham, 534
RAF St Athan, 634
RAF Upavon, 573
RAF Waddington, 535
RAF Wildenrath, 674
Ralston, 623
Ramsey, 498
Ramsey (I of M), 525
Randers, 652
Ranfurly Castle, 623
Range Inn Golf Range, 639
Rapallo, 679
Rathdowney, 593
Rathfarnham, 590
Rathmore, 583
Ratho Park, 613
Rättvik, 696
Ravelston, 613
Ravensworth, 568
Rawdon, 581
Reading, 495
Real Automovil Club de España, 689
Real Golf Bendinat, 687
Real Golf de Cerdaña, 688
Real Golf "El Prat', 688
Real Golf de Las Palmas, 688
Real Golf de Menorca, 687
Real Golf de Neguri, 690
Real Golf de Pedreña, 690
Real San Sebastián, 690
Real Zarauz, 690
Reay, 608
Redbourn, 522
Reddish Vale, 540
Redditch, 520
Redhill & Reigate, 561
Regensburg, 672
Reigate Heath, 561
Reims, 659
Reit im Winkl, 671
Renfrew, 623

Renishaw Park, 577
Rennes, 655
Retford, 551
Reykjavikur, 677
Rhein Badenweiler, 676
Rhein-Main, 666
Rhein Sieg, 674
Rheinblick, 666
Rheintal, 666
Rhodes, 611
Rhoen, 666
Rhondda, 633
Rhos-on-Sea Residential, 632
Rhuddlan, 628
Rhyl, 459, 628
Ribe, 652
Richmond (Surrey), 561
Richmond (N Yorks), 575
Richmond Driving Range, 640
Richmond Park, 561
Rickenbach, 676
Rickmansworth, 522
Riddlesden, 581
Riederalp, 700
Het Rijk van Nijmegen, 683
Ringway, 540
Rinkven G & CC, 648
Rio Real, 690
Ripon City, 575
Rishton, 532
Riva dei Tessali, 680
RLGC Village Play, 543
RMCS Shrivenham, 573
Robin Hood, 572
Roca Llisa, 687
La Rocca, 679
Rochdale, 540
Rochefort, 662
Rochester & Cobham Park, 528
Rochford Hundred, 513
Rockwell College, 597
Roehampton, 561
The Rolls of Monmouth, 630
Roma, 680
Romeleåsens, 693
Romford, 513
Romiley, 500
Romsey, 518
Ronneby, 697
Rookery Park, 557
Rosapenna, 588
Roscommon clubs and courses, 596
Roscommon GC, 596
Roscrea, 597
Roseberry Grange, 511
Rosendaelsche, 683
Roskilde, 653
Roslagen, 695
Ross-on-Wye, 520
Rossendale, 532
La Rossera, 678
Rosslare, 598
Rossmore, 596
Rothbury, 550

Rotherham, 577
Rothesay, 618
Rothley Park, 574
Rottaler, 672
Rouen, 661
Rougement, 649
Roundhay, 581
Roundwood, 577
Routenburn, 617
Le Rovedine, 678
I Roveri, 681
Rowany, 525
Rowlands Castle, 518
Royal Aberdeen, 607
Royal Amicale Anderlecht, 649
Royal & Ancient Golf Club of St Andrews, 6–7, 10, 307, 605, 706
Royal Antwerp, 648
Royal Artillery & Dortmund Garrison, 674
Royal Ascot, 495
Royal Ashdown Forest, 565
Royal Belfast, 589
Royal Birkdale, 543
Royal Blackheath, 528
Royal Burgess Golfing Society of Edinburgh, 613
Royal Cinque Ports, 528
Royal County Down, 589
Royal Cromer, 547
Royal Dornoch, 610
Royal Dublin, 590
Royal Eastbourne, 565
Royal Epping Forest, 513
royal golf clubs, 838
Royal GC Artiguelouve, 664
Royal Golf Club de Belgique, 649
Royal GC des Fagnes, 649
Royal GC du Hainaut, 649
Royal GC du Sart Tilman, 649
Royal Golf Évian, 656
Royal Guernsey, 451, 498
The Royal Household GC, 495
Royal Jersey, 498
Royal Latem, 650
Royal Liverpool, 543
Royal Lytham & St Annes, 532
Royal Malta, 682
Royal Mid-Surrey, 562
Royal Montrose, 625
Royal Musselburgh, 611
Royal North Devon, 507
Royal Norwich, 547
Royal Perth Golfing Society, 627
Royal Porthcawl, 633
Royal Portrush, 583
Royal St David's, 632
Royal St George's, 528

Royal Sant'Anna, 078
Royal Tara, 595
Royal Tarlair, 607
Royal Troon, 617
Royal Waterloo, 650
Royal West Norfolk, 547
Royal Wimbledon, 562
Royal Winchester, 518
Royal Worlington &
    Newmarket, 557
Royal Zoute, 650
Royan, 657
Royston, 522
Ruchill, 622
Ruddington Grange, 551
Rugby, 569
Ruislip, 545
rules of golf, amateur
    status, 752
    ball, 722
    club designs, 721
    definitions, 716
    evolution of, 828
    gambling, 755
    local rules, 746
Runcorn, 500
Rungsted, 653
Rusel G & LC, 672
Rush, 591
Rushcliffe, 551
Rushden, 548
Rushmere, 557
Ruthin-Pwllglas, 628
Ruxley, 528
Ruxley Golf Centre, 638
Rya, 693
Ryburn, 581
Ryde, 525
Rye, 565
Ryston Park, 547
Ryton, 568
Saar-Pfalz Katharinenhof,
    665
Saarbrücken, 665
Sables-d'Or-les-Pins, 655
Saddleworth, 540
Safari Tour, 1989 results,
    92–3
Saffron Walden, 513
Saqmühle, 672
St Andrews, 605
St Anne's, 590
St Annes Old Links, 532
Saint-Aubin, 662
St Augustines, 528
St Austell, 502
Sainte-Baume, 663
St Bees, 504
St Boswells, 599
St Clements, 498
Saint-Cloud, 662
St Cyprien, 659
St Davids City, 629
St Deiniol, 632
St Dionys, 668
St Enodoc, 451, 503
St Eurach LGC, 671
St Fillans, 627
St-Gatien Deauville, 661
St George's Hill, 562

Saint-Germain-en-Laye,
    662
St Giles Newtown, 634
St Helens, 543
St Ibb, 694
St Idloes (Llanidloes), 634
St Ives (Hunts), 498
Saint-Julien, 661
St Laurent, 655
St Malo-Le Tronchet, 655
St Medan, 602
St Mellion, 503
St Mellons, 630
St Melyd, 629
St Michael Jubilee, 500
St Michael's, 605
St Neot's, 452, 498
Saint-Nom-la-Bretêche,
    662
St Peter-Ording, 668
St Pierre, 630
St-Pierre-du-Perray, 662
St Polten Schloss
    Goldegg, 648
Saint-Quentin-en-
    Yvelines, 662
St Regulus Ladies', 605
St Rule Ladies', 605
Saint-Samson, 655
Saintonge, 657
Sala, 695
Sale, 540
El Saler, 691
Salies-de-Béarn, 664
Saline, 605
Salisbury & South Wilts,
    573
Sallandsche "de Hoek',
    683
Saltburn, 501
Saltford, 493
Saltsjöbaden, 694
Salzburg Kleshiem, 647
Salzgitter Liebenburg,
    670
Salzkammergut, 648
San Floriano-Gorizia, 682
San Lorenzo, 685
Sand Moor, 581
Sandbach, 500
Sandford Springs, 518
Sandilands, 535
Sandiway, 500
Sandown Golf Centre,
    640
Sandown Park, 562
Sandwell Park, 572
Sandy Lodge, 522
Sandyhills, 622
Sanquhar, 602
Sant Cugat, 688
Santa Ponsa, 687
Santo da Serra, 686
São Miguel, 686
Särö, 692
Saudárkroks, 678
Sauerland, 674
Saunton, 507
Sauzon, 655
Saxå, 699

Scarborough North Cliff,
    575
Scarborough South Cliff,
    575
Scarcroft, 581
Schinzbach-Bad, 701
Schloss-Braunfels, 666
Schloss Ernegg, 648
Schloss Fuschl, 648
Schloss Georghausen,
    674
Schloss Klingenburg-
    Günzburg, 671
Schloss Liebenstein G &
    LC, 676
Schloss Lüdersburg, 668
Schloss Myllendonk, 674
Schloss Pichlarn, 648
Schloss Schwöbber, 670
Schloss Weitenberg, 676
Schlossberg, 673
Schmidmühlen G & CC,
    673
Schmitzhof, 674
Schönenberg, 701
De Schoot, 683
Sconser, 609
Scoonie, 605
Scotscraig, 605
Scottish Golfing Union,
    799
Scrabo, 589
Scraptoft, 534
SCT Knuds, 651
Scunthorpe, 524
Seacroft, 536
Seafield, 617
Seaford, 565
Seaford Head, 565
Seaham, 511
Seahouses, 550
Seascale, 504
Seaton Carew, 501
Sedbergh, 504
Seignosse, 664
Selby, 575
Selfoss, 678
Selkirk, 599
Selsdon Park Hotel, 562
Selsey, 566
Semmering, 648
Sene Valley Folkestone
    & Hythe, 528
Sennelager (British
    Army), 666
Sept Fontaines, 650
Seraincourt, 662
Serlby Park, 551
La Serra, 681
Sestrieres, 681
Settle, 575
Shandon Park, 585
Shanklin & Sandown, 525
Shannon, 585
Shaw Hill G & CC, 533
Sheerness, 528
Sheffield Transport Dept,
    577
Sherborne, 510
Sheringham, 547

Sherwood Forest, 551
Shetland, 614
Shifnal, 553
Shillinglee Park, 562
Shipley, 581
Shirehampton Park, 493
Shirland, 506
Shirley, 572
Shirley Park, 562
Shiskine, 618
Shooter's Hill, 528
Shortlands, 529
Shotts, 622
Shrewsbury, 553
Shropshire clubs and
    courses, 472, 552–3
Sickleholme, 506
Sidcup, 529
Sidmouth, 507
Sieben-Berge, 670
Siegen-Olpe, 675
Siglufjardhar, 678
Sigtunabygden, 695
Silecroft, 504
Silkeborg, 652
Silkstone, 577
Silloth-on-Solway, 504
Silsden, 582
Silverdale, 533
Silverknowes, 613
Silvermere, 562
Silvermere GC Driving
    Range, 640
Sindlesham Driving
    Range, 636
Sittingbourne & Milton
    Regis, 529
Sitwell Park, 577
Skaftö, 699
Skeabost, 609
Skellefteå, 691
Skelmorlie, 617
Skepparslov, 693
Skerries, 591
Skibbereen, 587
Skips, 514
Skipton, 575
Skive, 652
Skjcbcrg, 000
Slade Valley, 591
Slaley Hall G & CC, 550
Sleaford, 536
Sligo clubs and courses,
    596
Söderäsen, 693
Söderhamn, 696
Söderköping, 697
Södertälje, 695
Sollefteå-Långsele, 691
Sollentuna, 694
Søllerød, 653
Sologne, 658
Soltau, 668
Somerset clubs and
    courses, 466, 553–4
Somosaguas, 689
Son Parc, 687
Son Servera, 687
Son Vida, 687
Sønderjyllands, 652

Sonnenaln, 676
Sonning, 495
Sony Ranking, 99
Sotogrande, 690
South African Sunshine
    Circuit results, 97–8
South Beds, 494
South Bradford, 582
South Glamorgan clubs
    and courses, 490,
    634–5
South Herts, 522
South Leeds, 582
South Moor, 511
South Pembrokeshire,
    629
South Shields, 568
South Staffordshire, 572
South Wales Golf Range,
    642
Southampton, 518
Southerndown, 633
Southerness, 602
Southfield, 552
Southport & Ainsdale, 543
Southport Municipal, 543
Southport Old Links, 543
Southsea, 518
Southwick Park, 518
Southwold, 557
Southwood, 518
The Spa (Co Down), 589
Spaarnwoude, 682
Spalding, 536
Spanish clubs and
    courses, 686–91
Spanish Point, 586
Spessart, 667
Spey Bay, 608
Sphinx, 572
Spiegelven GC Genk, 649
Sporting Club de
    Cameyrac, 654
Sporting-Club de Vichy,
    658
Sports Turf Research
    Institute, 811
Springfield Park, 540
Springhead Park, 524
Sprowston Park, 547
Sprowston Park Driving
    Range, 639
Stackstown, 590
Staddon Heights, 507
Stafford Castle, 555
Staffordshire clubs and
    courses, 472, 554–6
Stamford, 540
Stand, 540
Standard Scratch Score
    and handicapping
    scheme, 770
Stanedge, 506
Stanmore, 546
Stanton-on-the-Wolds,
    551
Starnberg, 671
Stavanger, 685
Staverton Park, 548
Steenhoven, 648

Stevenage, 522
Stillland, 670
Stinchcombe Hill, 515
Stirling, 601
Stjernfors, 695
Stockholm, 694
Stockport, 500
Stocksbridge & District,
    577
Stocksfield, 550
Stockwood Park, 494
Stoke by Nayland, 514
Stoke Poges, 497
Stoke Rochford, 536
Stone, 556
Stoneham, 518
Stonehaven, 608
Stoneyholme, 504
Stora Lundby, 692
Stornoway, 457, 627
Størstrommen, 653
Stourbridge, 572
Stowe, 497
Stowmarket, 557
Strabane, 597
Strandhill, 596
Strängnäs, 695
Stranraer, 602
Strasbourg, 659
Stratford-on-Avon, 569
Strathaven, 622
Strathclyde Park, 622
Strathclyde Park Golf
    Range, 642
Strathclyde Region clubs
    and courses, 484,
    615–24
Strathendrick, 601
Strathlene, 607
Strathpeffer Spa, 610
Strathtay, 627
Strawberry Hill, 546
Stressholme, 511
Stromness, 457, 614
Strömstad, 699
Stupinigi, 681
Stuttgarter Neckartal, 676
Stuttgarter Solitude, 677
Sudbury, 546
Sudurnesja, 678
Suffolk clubs and courses,
    468, 556–8
Sully-sur-Loire, 658
Sundridge Park, 529
Sundsvall, 691
Sunne, 699
Sunningdale, 562
Sunningdale Ladies, 562
Surbiton, 562
Surrey clubs and
    courses, 462, 558–63
Sussex (East) clubs and
    courses, 462, 563–5
Sussex (West) clubs
    and courses, 462,
    565–7
Sutton (Dublin), 455, 590
Sutton Bridge, 536
Sutton Coldfield, 572
Sutton Park, 524

Suur-Helsingin, 654
Svendborg, 651
Swaffham, 548
Swansea Bay, 635
Swanston, 613
Swedish clubs and
    courses, 691–9
Swindon Range, 641
Swindon (W Midlands),
    572
Swindon (Wilts), 573
Swinford, 595
Swinley Forest, 495
Swinton Park, 540
Swiss clubs and courses,
    699–701
Sydsjaellands, 653
Täby, 694
Tadley Driving Range,
    638
Tadmarton Heath, 552
Tain, 458, 610
Tammer Golf, 654
Tamworth, 556
Tandragee, 584
Tandridge, 562
Tankersley Park, 577
Tantallon (North
    Berwick), 611
Tapton Park, 506
Tarbat, 610
Tarbert, 615
Tarbes-Laloubère, 664
Tarland, 607
Taunton & Pickeridge,
    554
Taunus G & LC, 667
Tavistock, 508
Taymouth Castle, 627
Tayside Golf Driving
    Range, 642
Tayside Region clubs
    and courses, 486,
    624–7
Tecklenburger Land, 675
Tees-side, 502
Tegernseer GC Bad
    Wiessee, 671
Tehidy Park, 503
Teignmouth, 508
Telford Hotel G & CC,
    553
Temple, 495
Temple Newsam, 582
Templemore, 597
Tenby, 630
Tenerife, 688
Tenterden, 529
Terceira Island, 686
Ternesee, 648
Terramar, 688
Tewkesbury Park Hotel,
    515
Thames Ditton & Esher,
    562
Thetford, 548
Theydon Bois, 514
Thirsk and Northallerton,
    575
Thistle, 605

Thonock Driving Range,
    639
Thornbon Park, 511
Thorne, 577
Thornhill, 602
Thornton, 605
Thorntree, 611
Thorpe Hall, 514
Thorpe Wood, 498
Thorpeness Hotel, 557
Three Hammers Golf
    Complex, 641
Three Rivers, 514
Thumeries, 660
Thurles, 597
Thurlestone, 508
Thurso, 608
Tidworth Garrison, 518
Tietlingen, 669
Tignes, 656
Tilgate, 566
Tillicoultry, 600
Tilsworth, 494
Tilsworth Golf Centre,
    636
Tinsley Park, 577
Tipperary, 597
Tipperary clubs and
    courses, 596–7
Tirrenia, 681
Tiverton, 508
TJ Golf Praha, 650
TJ Lokomotiva-Ingstav,
    650
TJ NHKG, 650
TJ Sklo Bohemia
    Poděbrady, 650
TJ Start VD-Golf, 650
Tobermory, 615
Tobo, 697
Todmorden, 582
La Toja, 688
Tolladine, 520
Tongelreep G & CC, 683
Töreboda, 698
Torekov, 694
Torino, 681
Torphin Hill, 613
Torphins, 607
Torquay, 508
Torrance House, 622
Torreby, 699
Torrequebrada, 689
Torrington, 508
Torvean, 609
Torwoodlee, 600
Toulouse, 664
Toulouse-Palmola, 665
Toulouse-Seilh, 665
Le Touquet, 660
tour statistics, 58, 79–80,
    91
Touraine, 657
Towerlands, 514
Towerlands Driving
    Range, 637
Towneley, 533
Tracy Park, 493
Traigh, 609
Tralee, 592

Tramore, 997
Tranås, 697
Tredegar & Rhymney, 630
Tredegar Park, 630
Tregenna Castle Hotel, 503
Tregroes Driving Range, 642
Trelleborg, 694
Trent Park, 546
Trentham, 556
Trentham Park, 556
Trevose, 503
Trier-Mosel, 665
Trieste, 682
Trim, 595
Tróia Golf, 686
Trollhättan, 698
Trondheim, 685
Troon Municipal, 617
Troon Portland, 617
Troon St Meddans, 617
Trosa-Vagnhärad, 695
Troyes-la Cordelière, 659
Truro, 503
Tuam, 592
Tudor Park, 529
Tullamore, 596
Tulliallan, 600
Tunbridge Wells, 529
Tunshill, 540
Turnberry Hotel, 617
Turnhouse, 614
Turriff, 607
Turton, 533
Tutzing, 671
Tuusula, 654
Twentsche, 683
Twickenham, 546
Tylney Park, 519
Tyne & Wear clubs and courses, 478, 567–8
Tynedale, 550
Tynemouth, 568
Tyneside, 568
Tyrone clubs and courses, 597
Tyrrells Wood, 562
The Tytherington, 500
Uddeholm, 699
Udine, 682
Ullesthorpe Court, 534
Ullna, 695
Ulm, 677
Ulricehamn, 698
Ulster clubs and courses, 480
Ulverston, 504
Ulzama, 690
Umeå, 691
United States Golfing Union, 800
Uphall, 614
Upminster, 514
Uppsala, 696
Upton-by-Chester, 500
US Ladies' Open Championship, 123, 168–9

US Ladies' PGA Tour results, 123–30
US Masters Championship, 35–6, 166
US Open Championship, 33–4, 164–6
USPGA Championship, 37–8, 166–7
USPGA Senior Tour, 1989 results, 81–90
USPGA Tour, 1989 results, 65–78
Utrechtse "De Pan', 685
Uttoxeter, 556
Vaasan-Vaasa, 654
Vadstena, 697
Val-de-Cher, 658
Val de Loire, 658
Valcros, 663
Valdelaguila, 689
Valderrama, 690
Vale do Lobo, 686
Vale of Leven, 619
Vale of Llangollen, 629
Valenciennes, 660
Valescure, 663
Vall d'Or, 687
Vallromanas, 688
Varberg, 698
Varese, 680
Varmert, 675
Värnamo, 697
Vasatorp, 694
Västerås, 696
Vastervik, 697
Vaucouleurs, 662
Vaugouard, 658
Vaul, 615
Växjö, 697
Vejle, 652
Velper G & CC, 675
Veluwse, 684
Venezia, 682
Ventnor, 525
Verbier, 700
Verona, 680
Verulam, 522
Vestfold, 685
Vestfyns, 651
Vestischer Recklinghausen, 675
Vestmannaeyja, 678
Vetlanda, 697
Viborg, 652
Vicars Cross, 501
Vidago, 686
Vievola, 663
Vigevano "Santa Martretta', 679
Viipurin Golf, 654
Viksjö, 695
Vilamoura, 686
Villa Condulmer, 682
Villa d'Este, 679
Villa de Madrid CC, 689
Villa Martín, 687
Villarceaux, 662
Los Villares, 688
Villars, 700
Villennes, 662

Vimeiro, 686
Vinovo, 681
Virginia, 585
Visby, 698
Vista Hermosa, 690
Vittel, 659
Vivary Park, 554
Vulpera, 700
Wakefield, 582
Waldbrunnen, 675
Waldegg-Wiggensbach, 677
Waldringfield Heath, 557
Wallasey, 543
Wallsend, 568
Walmer & Kingsdown, 529
Walmersley, 540
Walmley (Wylde Green), 572
Walsall, 573
Walton Hall, 501
Walton Heath, 563
Wanstead, 514
Wareham, 510
Warendorf, 675
Warkworth, 550
Warley, 573
Warley Park, 514
Warren (Devon), 508
Warren (Essex), 514
Warren (Merseyside), 543
Warren Heath, 558
Warrenpoint, 589
Warrington, 501
Warwick, 569
Warwick Golf Centre, 641
Warwickshire clubs and courses, 472, 568–9
Washington (Tyne and Wear), 568
Washington Driving Range, 641
Wassenarse Rozenstein, 684
Wasserburg Anholt, 675
Waterford, 597
Waterford clubs and courses, 597
Waterhall, 565
Waterlooville, 519
Waterville, 592
Watford Driving Range, 638
Wath-upon-Dearne, 577
Wavendon Golf Centre, 636
Wearside, 568
Weinerwald, 648
Welcombe Hotel, 569
Wellingborough, 548
Wells, 554
Wels, 648
Welsh Golfing Union, 799
Welshpool, 634
Welwyn Garden City, 523
Welwyn Hatfield Sports Centre, 638

Wentorf-Reinbeker, 669
Wentworth, 563
Wenvoe Castle, 634
Werdenfels, 671
Werl, 675
Wermdö G & CC, 695
Werneth, 540
Werneth Low, 540
Weserbergland, 670
West Berkshire, 495
West Bowling, 582
West Bradford, 582
West Byfleet, 563
West Chiltington, 566
West Cornwall, 503
West Derby, 543
West Essex, 514
West Glamorgan clubs and courses, 490, 635
West Herts, 452, 523
West Hill, 563
West Hove, 565
West Kent, 529
West Kilbride, 617
West Lancashire, 543
West Linton, 458, 599
West Lothian, 614
West Malling, 529
West Middlesex, 546
West Midlands clubs and courses, 472, 569–73
West Monmouthshire, 631
West Surrey, 563
West Sussex, 567
West Wilts, 574
Westerhope, 568
Western Gailes, 617
Western Golf Range, 499, 637
Western Isles Region clubs and courses, 488, 627
Western Park, 534
Westerwald, 675
Westfälischer Gütersloh, 675
Westgate & Birchington, 529
Westhill, 607
Westhoughton, 541
Westmeath clubs and courses, 598
Weston-super-Mare, 493
Weston Turville, 497
Westonbirt, 515
Westport, 595
Westray, 614
Westwood, 556
Wetherby, 582
Wexford, 598
Wexford clubs and courses, 598
Wexham Park, 497
Weymouth, 510
WGPET, 801
Whaddon Golf Range, 638
Whalley, 533
Wheatley, 578

Whetstone, 534
Whickham, 568
Whinhill, 624
Whipsnade Park, 523
Whitburn, 568
Whitby, 576
Whitchurch (Cardiff), 635
White Lodge, 563
Whitecraigs, 624
Whitefield, 541
Whitehall, 633
Whitehead, 584
Whiteleaf, 497
Whitewebbs, 546
Whiting Bay, 618
Whitley Bay, 452, 568
Whitsand Bay Hotel, 503
Whitstable and Seasalter, 529
Whittaker, 541
Whittington Barracks, 556
Whitwood, 582
Wick, 608
Wicklow, 598
Wicklow clubs and courses, 598
Widnes, 501
Widnes Municipal, 501
Wien, 648
Wiesbaden, 667
Wiesloch-Hohenhardter Hof G LC, 667
Wigan, 541
Wigtown & Bladnoch, 602
Wigtownshire County, 602
Wildernesse, 453, 529

Wildeshausen, 669
Wilhelmshaven, 669
Willesley Park, 534
William Wroe, 541
Williamwood, 624
Willingdon, 565
Wilmslow, 501
Wilpshire, 453, 533
Wilton, 502
Wiltshire clubs and courses, 466, 573–4
Wimbledon Common, 563
Wimbledon Park, 563
Wimereux, 660
Windermere, 505
Windlemere, 563
Windlemere Golf Course, 640
Windmill Hill, 497
Windmill Hill Golf Complex, 636
Windwhistle G & CC, 554
Windyhill, 619
Winge G & CC, 650
Winter Hill, 495
Winterberg, 667
Winterfield, 612
Wirral Ladies, 543
Wishaw, 622
Withernsea, 524
Withington, 541
Wittem G & CC, 683
Wittsjö, 694
Woburn, 497
Woking, 563
Wollaton Park, 552

Wolstanton, 556
Wombwell Hills, 578
Women's Amateur tournament results, 131–4, 246–57
Women's Golf (review), 20–1
Women's Open Championship, 115, 123, 168–9
Women's PGET results, 115–21
Woodbridge, 558
Woodbrook, 591
Woodcote Park, 563
Woodenbridge, 598
Woodford, 453, 514
Woodhall Hills, 582
Woodhall Spa, 536
Woodham G & CC, 511
Woodlands Manor, 529
Woodlands Vale, 548
Woodlawn, 665
Woodsome Hall, 582
Woodthorpe Hall, 536
Wooler, 550
Woolton, 544
Worcester G & CC, 520
Worcestershire, 520
Workington, 505
Worksop, 552
Worlebury, 493
Worplesdon, 563
Worpswede, 669
Worsley, 541
Worthing, 567

Wörthsee, 671
Wortley, 582
Wouwse Plantage, 682
Wrangaton (South Devon), 508
Wrekin, 553
Wrexham, 629
writers, golf, 811
Wrotham Heath, 530
Wümme, 669
Würzburg-Kitzingen, 667
Wyboston Lakes, 494
Wyke Green, 546
Yelverton, 508
Yeovil, 554
York, 453, 576
Yorkshire (North) clubs and courses, 474, 574–6
Yorkshire (South) clubs and courses, 474, 576–8
Yorkshire (West) clubs and courses, 474, 578–82
Youghal, 587
Youths' tournament results, 136, 267–9
Ystad, 694
Yugoslavian clubs and courses, 701
Zeegersloot, 684
Zeewolde, 684
Zoate, 679
Zur Vahr, 669
Zürich-Zumikon, 701